FUNDAMENTALS OF
FINANCIAL ACCOUNTING

PC 3-7

PC 3-11

FUNDAMENTALS OF
FINANCIAL ACCOUNTING

Glenn A. Welsch

College of Business Administration
The University of Texas at Austin

Daniel G. Short

College of Business Administration
The University of Texas at Austin

George Richard Chesley

School of Business Administration
Dalhousie University

1987   First Canadian Edition

IRWIN

Homewood, Illinois   60430

ISBN   0-256-05542-4

Library of Congress Catalog Card No. 86–81840

Printed in the United States of America

1 2 3 4 5 6 7 8 9 0 MP 4 3 2 1 0 9 8 7

To Dianna, Christy, and Allison

Preface

This First Canadian Edition retains the integrity and experience of four previous United States editions while at the same time presenting the rules, practices, materials, and problems that reflect the unique environment of Canadian accounting.

Chapters are divided into sections. The objectives of each section are delineated and questions, exercises, problems, and cases are grouped so they follow the sequence of the sections as much as possible. Key terms and definitions are highlighted in the text and reviewed at the end of the chapter. Demonstration problems, with solutions, are provided at the end of each chapter to assist in the review of procedural matters.

The text is designed so that it is suitable for a one-semester course in financial accounting (outlines for which are provided in the Instructor's Manual), but it contains sufficient material for two semesters if this is the objective. Conceptual, analytical, practical, and procedural approaches to teaching can all be accommodated depending on the time available and the objectives of the course.

This book presents an introduction to financial accounting, which has as its primary subject matter the communication of relevant financial information to external parties. The scope and style of this book reflect the belief that a certain level of knowledge of the accounting model, the measuring process involved, the data classifications, and the terminology are essential to the interpretation and effective use of financial statements. A conceptual philosophy, however, is integrated throughout the presentation.

This volume represents a significant departure from the traditional financial accounting textbook in several respects. First, it makes possible a high level of flexibility for the instructor by presenting separately designated comprehensive discussions of a broad range of subject areas. This approach allows more materials to be presented than usually can be covered in an undergraduate financial accounting course (however, because of its design this text is completely adequate for a graduate course). The coverage gives the instructor the flexibility to select those topics appropriate to individual course objectives. The available material avoids forcing the instructor to choose between (a) presenting a minimum course or (b) devoting considerable time to developing supplementary textual and homework assignments. Secondly, this text provides additional flexibility by discussing a number of topics not normally included in an elementary textbook. In our judgment, much of the traditional material is essential; however, the recent thrusts and changes in financial accounting make it imperative that significant topics such as cash flows, inflation accounting, and consolidated reporting be accorded comprehensive treatment. This volume gives special emphasis to the concepts, rationale, measurement, and reporting of these new directions.

The primary features of this book and its accompanying instructional materials are as follows:

- The characteristics of the environment in which the accounting process operates are emphasized in the first chapter and are integrated throughout the other chapters.
- In the first chapter, the student is presented with a comprehensive description of the end products of the financial accounting process—the external financial statements and related disclosures. These financial disclosures are continually used throughout the other chapters.
- This volume presents more than the maximum amount of material that can ordinarily be covered in a one-semester undergraduate course. This additional material provides flexibility for the instructor in the use of the text and alternative material for its repeated use.
- Accounting is presented as an information processing model designed to enhance communication from the entity to the users of its financial reports. This emphasis permits accommodation of an information system's philosophy with the current utilitarian approach to accounting.
- The discussions emphasize concepts, standards, and generally accepted accounting principles as the rationale for the way things are done in accounting.
- Throughout the chapters, the measuring approaches used in accounting and reporting to decision makers are emphasized.
- Throughout, the primary focus is on the corporation rather than on the sole proprietorship or the partnership. Case examples are utilized. As a consequence, income taxes, dividends, earnings per share, and capital stock are discussed.
- One or more supplements follow some of the chapters. These supplements focus on special topics including such clerical and mechanical aspects of the accounting process as special journals, subsidiary ledgers, payrolls, and petty cash. Separation of topics in supplements facilitates their exclusion, or order of selection without affecting the continuity of the course.
- A special supplement at the end of the text presents an overview of income taxes for the individual taxpayer and for corporations.

- A special supplement presents the 1984 annual report of Consolidated-Bathurst, Inc. Reference to this award winning report is integrated throughout the discussions and problems/cases in the various chapters.

These features are of particular importance to nonaccounting majors because the first semester usually is their only exposure to the fundamentals of financial accounting. Topics included in this text such as consolidated statements, tax accounting, and the effects of general and specific inflation can be used to expose these students to real life financial problems that will be of concern to them later in their careers.

Answers to questions such as how much time should be spent on each chapter, how much homework should be required, and what materials should be omitted depend on the objectives of the particular course, the time constraints, and the backgrounds of the students. The Instructor's Manual presents a number of possible options.

Acknowledgments

A book cannot be written without the assistance of many persons. My colleague Ray Carroll, Steve Alisharon of the University of British Columbia, David Hope of St Mary's University, John Hughes of Memorial University, and Dick Marshall of McGill University all provided valuable comments and suggestions for presenting the material. Of course, I accept responsibility for what might have been overlooked.

My colleagues Chuck Dirksen and Edgar Scott spent long hours with the computer assignments and the income taxation material in the text. Their assistance with this material was invaluable to me. The secretarial and editorial assistance provided by Susan DeYoung, Lorele Cormier, my wife Dianna, and my daughter Christy was exceptional. Discussions with my colleagues Tony Atkinson, John Parker, and Peter Secord assisted and enriched the development of this text.

The U.S. authors of this volume, Glenn Welsch, and Daniel Short deserve mention for the latitude they provided to me. While I have retained the major thrust of their work, they permitted me the freedom to present my view of the Canadian environment.

My appreciation is extended for the cooperation provided by the Canadian Institute of Chartered Accountants and the Society of Management Accountants of Canada. Both groups permitted me to adapt and use their material in this book. They, of course, are not responsible for the editorial and content changes I made to their material. Tom Boudreau of Merrill Lynch Canada, Inc., of Halifax kindly provided me with share and bond exhibits.

Suggestions and comments on this text and the related materials by faculty and students are invited.

G. R. (Dick) Chesley

Contents

comparative amounts for the previous year.
Overview of CC/CD effects. Reporting the
effects of changing prices.

1

Perspectives—Accounting Objectives and Communication

OBJECTIVE OF THIS BOOK

The objective of this book is to develop your knowledge of, and your ability to use, financial accounting information. Accounting often is subdivided into financial accounting and management accounting. This volume on financial accounting focuses on the use of accounting information in the decision-making processes of individuals and groups external to the business; that is, owners, investors, potential investors, creditors, and the public at large. Management accounting focuses on the role of accounting information in the decision-making processes of managers with responsibilities inside the organization. Whether you ultimately become an owner, a manager, an investor, or a creditor, or even if your only interest in a business entity is that of a concerned citizen, an understanding of accounting will enhance significantly your effectiveness as a decision maker. Also, as you study this volume you will develop an understanding of how accounting information is used in resource-allocation decisions in all types of organizations such as profit-making enterprises, nonprofit endeavours, governmental entities, and social programs. In practically all organizations, long-term success depends in large part on the quality of the resource-allocation decisions that are made. In the broad sense, accounting information is used to aid in the decision-making process and as a measure of the financial results after the decisions are made and implemented.

This book is designed for students who have had no prior academic study of accounting. The chapters usually are divided into parts to facilitate study and to provide flexibility in the selection of materials for emphasis consistent with the time available. Supplements to the chapters are provided to permit additional flexibility; they include (1) more advanced discussion of selected topics and (2) strictly procedural aspects of selected topics.

PURPOSE OF THIS CHAPTER

The purpose of this chapter is to present a broad perspective of the objectives of accounting and of the environment in which accounting usually operates. To accomplish this purpose, the chapter is divided into two parts:

Part A—The objectives and environment of accounting

Part B—Communication of accounting information

Part A—The Objectives and Environment of Accounting

ACCOUNTING DEFINED

Accounting can be defined as the collection of financial data about an organization and the analysis, measurement, recording, and reporting of that information to decision makers. An accounting system processes the *(a)* flows of resources into (inflows) and out of (outflows) the organization; *(b)* resources controlled (i.e., assets) by the organization; and *(c)* claims against those resources (i.e., debts). In addition, accounting requires judgment and interpretation in analyzing, reporting, and using the reported financial results. The accounting flow of economic information of an entity can be summarized as in Exhibit 1–1.

EXHIBIT 1–1
Flow of economic information in accounting

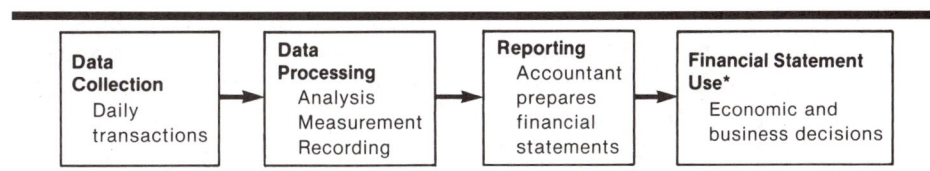

Data Collection	Data Processing	Reporting	Financial Statement Use*
Daily transactions	Analysis Measurement Recording	Accountant prepares financial statements	Economic and business decisions

*Financial statements, as discussed in financial accounting, are prepared primarily for investors and creditors and those that advise investors and creditors. Financial statements are commonly prepared under the assumption of reasonably sophisticated and diligent users.

If you have studied economics, you will perceive that it has a relationship with accounting. Economics has been defined as the study of how people and society choose to employ scarce productive resources that could have alternative uses to produce various commodities and distribute them for consumption, now or in the future, among various persons and groups in society[1]. This definition suggests a relationship to the definition of accounting. Like economics, accounting has a conceptual foundation that provides guidelines for the collection, measurement, and communication of financial information about the organization. Management accounting often is viewed as encompassing the financial planning and controlling process that focus on the future allocations of the scarce resources of the organization. Thus, accounting collects, measures, interprets, and reports information on the same human activities that are the focus of economics. Economics attempts to explain economic relationships primarily on a conceptual level, whereas accounting attempts to report the economic relationships primarily on the practical level. However, accounting measurements must be made as consistent as is possible with economic concepts. Accounting must deal with the very real and complex problems of measuring in monetary terms the economic effects of **exchange transactions** (i.e., resource inflows and outflows), the resources held, and the claims against those resources for each entity. Throughout this volume many of the theoreti-

---

[1]Paul A. Samuelson, *Economics*, 9th ed. (New York: McGraw-Hill, 1975).

3

cal and practical issues that arise in the measurement process will be discussed from the accounting viewpoint.

ACCOUNTING OPERATES IN A COMPLEX ENVIRONMENT

The environment in which accounting operates is affected by such broad pervasive forces as the type of *(a)* government (e.g., democracy versus communism), *(b)* economic system (e.g., free enterprise versus socialism), *(c)* industry (e.g., technological versus agrarian), *(d)* organizations within that society (labor unions), and *(e)* regulatory controls (i.e., private sector versus governmental). Also, accounting is influenced significantly by the educational level and economic development reflected in the society.

In various ways each of us is associated with social, political, and economic organizations such as businesses, churches, fraternal organizations, political parties, governments, schools, environmental groups, chambers of commerce, and professional associations. Many of these organizations deal with important resource allocation and societal problems for which decisions must be made. These organizations are essential to the workings of a society; indeed, they constitute much of what we call society. Thus, the future quality of our society depends in large measure upon the collective decisions of the managers of such organizations.

Fundamental to a dynamic and successful society is the ability of each organization to measure and report its accomplishments, to undergo critical self-analysis, and, by means of sound decisions, to renew itself and grow so that individual and societal objectives are served best. Essentially, society, and the various organizations that comprise it, thrives in direct proportion to the efficiency with which it allocates scarce resources of human talent, materials, services, and capital. To accomplish this broad goal, organizations and persons interested in those organizations need information about how the resources that the organization controls are obtained and used. Broadly, accounting information is designed to meet this need.

Therefore, accounting is a system designed by members of the society and continuously is undergoing change to meet the evolving needs of society. The environmental characteristics of a society are diverse and complex; therefore, accounting always is facing new challenges. For example, an inflationary spiral necessitates the development of accounting concepts and procedures that will report changes in "real" values separately from purely inflationary effects (see Chapter 17).

Throughout this textbook you will study how accounting is responding to the environment in North America. In the next few paragraphs we will discuss two environmental characteristics—**measurement in dollars** and the **types of business entities**—because they have pervasive effects on accounting concepts and procedures.

Measurement in dollars

A monetary system provides the primary way to measure and communicate information about the flow of resources in and out of an organization. In a monetary system, the unit of exchange (Canadian dollars in our case) is the common denominator used to measure value. Thus, the monetary unit provides a means for expressing the available resources and the resource flows of both the society as a whole and the various organizations which comprise that society. Accounting provides monetary measurement of inputs (resources received) and outputs (goods produced and services rendered), and as a consequence, it provides benchmarks for evaluating the efficiency of organizations.

Accounting measures the resources, claims against those resources, and resource flows of organizations within a society in terms of the monetary unit of that society. Accounting uses the monetary system of each country within which it operates. One of the critical problems in accounting is the conversion of financial amounts from one monetary system to another monetary system in measuring resources and resource flows for multinational activities. To deal with this problem, accounting has adopted a **unit-of-measure assumption** (see Exhibit 2–6) which holds that the common denominator or "measuring stick" used for accounting measurements in Canada is the dollar and that the dollar is a useful measuring unit.[2]

Types of business entities

This book will focus primarily on accounting for profit-making entities. In our environment there are three main types of business entities. They will be referred to often throughout this volume; therefore, their primary characteristics are explained below.

A **sole proprietorship** is an unincorporated business that is owned by one person. This type of business entity is common in the fields of services, retailing, and farming. Usually, the owner also is the manager. Legally, the business and the owner are not separate entities—they are one and the same. However, accounting views the business as a **separate entity** to be accounted for separately from its owner.

A **partnership** is an unincorporated business that is owned by two or more persons known as partners. The agreements between the owners are set forth in a partnership contract. This contract specifies such matters as division of profits each period and distribution of resources of the business upon termination of its operations. As in the case of a sole proprietorship, a partnership is not legally separate from its owners. Legally, in a general partnership, each partner is responsible for the debts of the business (i.e., each general partner has what is called unlimited liability). However, accounting views the partnership as a separate business entity to be accounted for separately from its several owners.

A **corporation** is a business that is incorporated under the laws of a particular province or the Government of Canada; the owners are known as share-

---

[2]The exchange unit (dollars) changes in purchasing power due to the effects of inflation and deflation; simply put, the dollar does not always command the same amount of **real** goods. Thus, money does not have the most basic element of any measurement unit (i.e., a metre always is the same length); that is, uniformity in magnitude. During inflation and deflation, the monetary unit is not uniform in magnitude because one unit will command fewer, or more, real goods respectively than before.

holders. Ownership is represented by shares of capital stock that can usually be bought and sold freely. When an approved application is filed by the organizers, the government issues a charter that gives the corporation the right to operate legally as a separate legal entity; that is, separate and apart from its owners. The owners enjoy ''limited liability,'' which means that they are liable for the debts of the corporation only to the extent of their investments therein. The charter specifies the types and amounts of capital stock that can be issued. The shareholders **elect** a governing board of directors, which in turn **employs** managers and exercises general supervision of the corporation.[3] Accounting for the business entity focuses on the corporation, not on the directors and managers as individuals.

In terms of economic importance, the corporation is the dominant form of business organization in Canada. The advantages of the corporate form include (a) limited liability for the shareholders, (b) continuity of life, (c) ease in transferring ownership (shares), and (d) opportunities to raise large amounts of money by selling shares to a large number of people. Because of these advantages, most large and medium-sized businesses (and many small ones) are organized as corporations. Therefore, we shall emphasize this form of business. Nevertheless, the accounting concepts, standards, and measurement procedures that we will discuss also generally apply to the other types of businesses.

One of the essentials of any measurement process is a precise definition of specifically what is to be measured. Examples of specific things to be measured are the population of Manitoba, the rainfall in Halifax, the voter registrations in British Columbia, and the bank deposits in Alberta (each for a stipulated time). Similarly, in the measurement of resources and resource flows, accounting requires precise definition of the specific entity for which monetary or financial data are to be collected, measured, and reported. When a specific entity is defined carefully, it is often referred to as an **accounting entity.** The whole nation can be thought of as a specific entity, so can each business unit, and so can each individual person. In any measurement scheme, the definition of that which is to be measured often involves difficult problems. For example, in measuring the population of Manitoba should the amount include service personnel? university students? jail inmates? long-term visitors? hotel guests? Similarly, in defining an accounting entity, there are important problems to be resolved. For example, if we are to account for, say, Adams Company, it is defined as a separate and specific accounting entity. Thus, the accounting entity has a specialized definition that is known as the **separate-entity assumption.**[4] **The separate-entity assumption holds that for accounting measurement purposes, the particular entity being accounted for is distinguished carefully from all similar and related entities and persons.** Under this assumption, an

---

[3]There are a number of specialized types of entities that we do not discuss, such as joint ventures, mutual funds, cooperatives, investment trusts, and syndicates. Consideration of these is beyond the scope of this book.

[4]A list of the fundamental assumptions and principles underlying accounting is summarized in Exhibit 2–6.

accounting entity is held to be separate and distinct from its owner(s). An entity is viewed as **owning the resources** (i.e., **assets**) used by it and as **owing the claims** (i.e., **debts**) against those assets. For measurement purposes, the assets, debts, and activities of the entity are kept completely separate from those of the owners and other entities. For example, in the case of Adams Company, the personal assets, debts, and activities of the owners are not included in the accounting measurements of the business itself.

THE USE OF ACCOUNTING INFORMATION BY DECISION MAKERS

Your role as a future decision maker is significant, whether you become a manager, investor, professional person, owner of a business, or simply an interested citizen. Decision makers use various approaches for selecting one alternative solution to a given problem from among a set of several alternative solutions to that problem. Selection of the preferred alternative constitutes the basic decision. In the process of reaching decisions, the decision maker is concerned about the **future** because a decision cannot change the past; however, an effective decision maker does not neglect the past. Knowledge and interpretation of what has happened in the past can aid in making decisions because history may shed considerable light on what the future is likely to hold. Thus, one of the fundamental inputs to decision making is dependable and relevant historical data. A large portion of historical data that are relevant to business decisions are expressed in monetary terms. They include costs (i.e., resources expended), revenues (i.e., resources earned), assets (i.e., things owned), liabilities (i.e., amounts owed), and owners' equity (i.e., total assets less total liabilities of the entity). Thus, accounting provides an important information base for decision making. The information provided by accounting must be understandable and relevant to the decision maker to preclude unwarranted interpretations in the decision-making process. This is a primary reason why measurements in accounting must adhere to certain standards and concepts.

Accounting reports (i.e., financial statements) serve those who use the reported information in three related ways:

1. Accounting provides information that is helpful in making decisions. Most important decisions, regardless of the type of endeavour involved, are based, in part, upon complex financial considerations. Accounting provides an important information base and a particular analytical orientation that help the decision maker assess the potential financial implications and potential outcomes of various alternatives that are being considered. The primary role of accounting is to facilitate decision making by investors, creditors, and others.

2. Accounting reports the economic effects of past decisions on the entity. Once a decision is made and implementation starts, there are important and often subtle economic effects on the entity. These economic effects often are critical to the success

of the endeavour. Thus, the evolving effects of past decisions must be measured continuously and periodically reported so that the decision maker can be informed of continuing and new problems, and of successes, over time. Thus, accounting provides a continuing **feedback** of the economic effects of a series of decisions already made, the results of which are communicated to the decision maker by means of periodic financial statements.

3. Accounting keeps track of a wide range of items to meet the financial score-keeping and safeguarding responsibilities imposed on all organizations. These include how much cash is available for use; how much customers owe the company; what debts are owed by the organization; what items are owned by the company, such as machinery and office equipment; and inventory levels on hand.

Most entities, such as a business or a hospital, engage in activities over an extended period of time during which resources are committed and used with the expectation that there will be desirable results in the form of goods and/or services. During the period of continuing activities, those involved in the organization, be they owners, sponsors, or managers, need information about the continuing amounts of resources committed, resources used, resources on hand, and outputs (goods and services); and this information should be reported, interpreted, and evaluated periodically. The accounting process is designed to provide a continuing flow of such information to all interested parties. A typical flow of accounting information in an entity is diagrammed in

EXHIBIT 1–2
Accounting information flows in a decision and implementation cycle

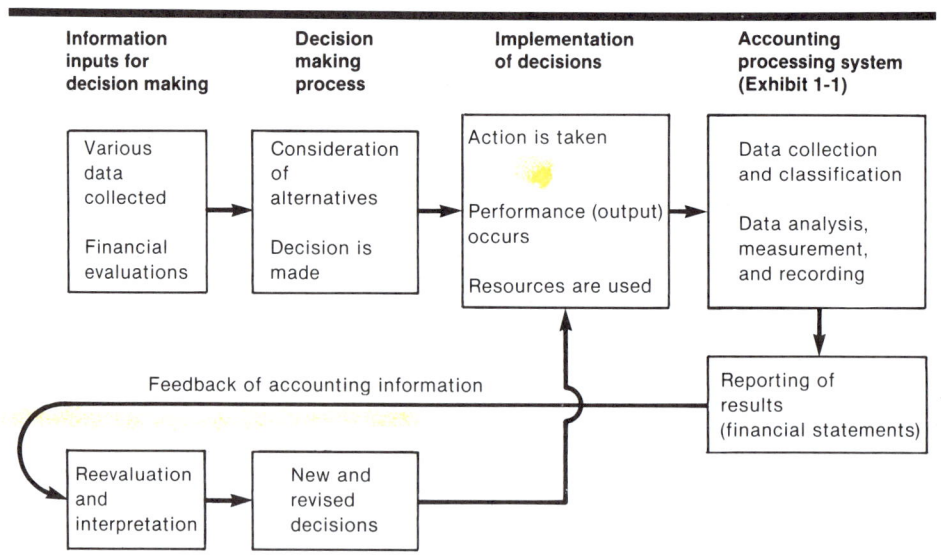

Information inputs for decision making	Decision making process	Implementation of decisions	Accounting processing system (Exhibit 1-1)
Various data collected / Financial evaluations	Consideration of alternatives / Decision is made	Action is taken / Performance (output) occurs / Resources are used	Data collection and classification / Data analysis, measurement, and recording

Feedback of accounting information

| Reevaluation and interpretation | New and revised decisions | | Reporting of results (financial statements) |

Exhibit 1–2. The financial statements constitute the primary source of relevant information on a continuing basis (feedback). This information is important **feedback** concerning the outcome of a particular decision.

A business

First, the objectives of a business are formulated by the organizers. Initially, the owners provide the funds, which often are supplemented by funds provided by creditors. These funds then are used by the managers of the business to acquire machinery, inventory, services, and other resources. Assume you are the manager of the entity and that you develop a "business plan" for operating the business. As the business operates, additional resources flow in from the sale of goods and services. Many other activities occur, many of which involve either the inflow or outflow of resources. As the manager of the business, you need information, on a continuing basis, that tells about the status of the resources. You need to know such things as sources and amounts of funds, revenues (goods and services sold), expenses, the amounts invested in such things as equipment and inventory, the cash situation, the amount spent for research and development, and the amount of money used in the sales efforts.

As the manager, you need information about resources and flows of resources for two fundamental reasons. First, accounting information in response to these and similar questions may aid you in making sound decisions about the entity that can improve its effectiveness and efficiency. Second, accounting information tells you (and other interested parties) what the **score** was during the immediate past periods. This scorekeeping is important to the evaluation and control of performance. In Exhibit 1–2, financial evaluations and interpretations are shown as one of the information inputs to the decision-making process. The exhibit also depicts the accounting processing system which involves **data collection, measurement, evaluation, and reporting of the results.** In the reporting phase, the accounting information is communicated as an aid in making new decisions and in revising prior decisions.

Now, assume instead that you are a shareholder (an owner) who has a substantial amount of money invested in the business but you have little opportunity to directly influence the management. As a shareholder, you must select from among three alternatives: (1) retain your ownership interest, (2) expand or contract it, or (3) dispose of it completely. As a shareholder, you also are interested in decisions that will lead to expansion of the business and raise its level of efficiency. As a consequence of these concerns, you need to have financial information such as the trend of sales, the level of expenses, the amount of earnings, the amount invested by the entity in various assets (such as inventory and machinery), the debts of the business, and the cash balance. In other words, as an investor you need to know how the management is allocating the scarce resources provided by you and the other owners and the creditors. Such information would be necessary to you in selecting one of the three alternatives listed above. The primary objective of the periodic financial statements is to provide, on a continuing basis, information bearing on these alternatives. The accounting information provided should be an important part of the decision-making process of the shareholders in ways similar to those depicted in Exhibit 1–2.

A hospital   Now, assume you are on the board of governors of a local hospital and, as a consequence, share the responsibility for the basic decisions and guidelines for its continued operation at an efficient level. Similar to the owner of a business, you have a wide variety of questions concerning its revenues, expenses, funds tied up in buildings and equipment, cost of charity services, and so on, that are in the scorekeeping category. Also, you are concerned with whether enough resources are being allocated to such activities as emergency care, sanitation, and nursing services. Before any sound decisions in these areas can be made for the future, you must have information about the past and current allocation of resources to them and about the quality and quantity of output or benefits. Thus, as a governor, you have many information needs that are important to your decisions for the future.

Now, consider the manager of the hospital. The manager needs accounting information about the operations of the hospital similar to that discussed above for the manager of a business, and for the same reasons. Typically, the manager will need more **detailed** accounting information than the governor. In any event, whether one is a governor or manager of the hospital, financial measurement and the reporting results should be continuing inputs to the decision-making process. This situation suggests the importance of accounting information which was emphasized in an interesting way in *Forbes* magazine (August 17, 1981) as follows:

> In all of mainland China there are about 30 CPAs. Some might call this a sign of how advanced the Chinese civilization really is, but for the Chinese—who are making an effort to bring their economy into the 20th century—it's a major obstacle. Now the leaders in the Chinese government want modern accounting systems—translation: Western accounting systems—and they want them fast. After all, this is a nation with some 400,000 manufacturing concerns and one accounting firm.

HISTORICAL PERSPECTIVES

Accounting is as old as the exchange processes (whether barter or monetary) that gradually developed with civilization. The earliest written records, including the Scriptures, contain references to what now is called accounting.

Accounting evolved in response to the economic needs of society. Prior to the 15th century it apparently followed no well-defined pattern except that it developed in answer to specific governing and trading needs of the era. The first known treatment of the subject of accounting was written in 1494, two years after the discovery of America. An Italian monk and mathematician, Fr. Luca Pacioli, described an approach that had been developed by the Italian merchants of the time to account for their activities as owner-managers of business ventures. Pacioli laid the foundations of the basic "accounting model" that is used to this day. As economic activity moved from the feudal system to agriculture and then to the Industrial Revolution, accounting adapted to the evolving needs. As business units became more complex and broader in scope, accounting evolved in response to the increased planning and control responsibilities of management. As governments increased in size and became more centralized, accounting was developed to meet the increased accountabilities.

In the 17th and 18th centuries, the Industrial Revolution in England provided the impetus for the development of new approaches in accounting. That impetus was particularly in the direction of management accounting and the accumulation of data concerning the cost of manufacturing each product. In the latter half of the 19th century, English accountants, small in numbers but large in competence, appeared on the North American scene. By 1900, the lead in accounting developments, provided earlier by the English, began to shift to North America. Since the turn of the century, accounting has experienced dynamic, and sometimes controversial, growth.

In the period since 1900, accountancy has attained the stature of a profession similar to law, medicine, engineering, and architecture. As with all recognized professions, it is subject to licensing, observes a code of professional ethics, requires a high level of professional competence, is dedicated to service to the public, requires a high level of academic study, and rests on a "common body of knowledge." The accountant, in addition to meeting specified academic requirements, may have to obtain a licence from the province in order to become a public accountant in that province. The primary objective of this licencing was the attainment of high standards of professional competence by accountants engaged in serving the public.

As is common with physicians, engineers, lawyers, and architects, accountants commonly are engaged in professional practice or are employed by businesses, government entities, nonprofit organizations, and so on. Accountants employed in these activities often take and pass professional examinations.

Practice of public accounting

A public accountant (PA) can offer professional services to the public for a fee, as does the lawyer and physician. In this posture, the accountant is known appropriately as an independent PA because certain responsibilities also extend to the general public (third parties) rather than being limited to the specific business or other entity that pays for the services. Independent PAs, although paid by their clients, are not employees of their clients. This concept of independence from the client is a unique characteristic of the accounting profession. The consequences of this uniqueness are not as widely understood as perhaps they should be. For example, the lawyer and the physician, in case of malpractice or incompetence, generally are subject to potential liability (lawsuits) that may extend only to the client or patient involved (and the family). In contrast, the independent PA, in case of malpractice or negligence in the audit function, is subject to potential liability that may extend to all parties (whether known to the PA or not) who have suffered loss or failed to make a profit through reliance on financial statements "approved" by PA.

While a single individual may practice public accounting, usually two or more individuals organize an accounting firm in the form of a partnership.

Firms vary in size from a one-person office, to regional firms, to the national firms, some of which have hundreds of offices located around the world. Nearly all accounting firms render three types of services: auditing, management advisory services, and tax services.

Auditing.   One important function performed by the PA in public practice is the audit or attest function. Its purpose is to lend reliability to the financial reports; that is, to assure that they are believable (i.e., relevant, accurate, and not biased). Primarily, this function involves an examination of the financial reports prepared by the management of the entity in order to assure that they are in conformance with **generally accepted accounting concepts and standards** (discussed in Part B). In carrying out this function, the independent PA examines the underlying transactions, including the collection, classification, and assembly of the financial data incorporated in the financial reports. In performing these tasks, established professional standards must be maintained and the information reported must conform to **generally accepted accounting principles** (often referred to as **GAAP**) appropriate for the entity involved. Additionally, the PA is responsible for verifying that the financial reports "fairly present" the resource inflows and outflows and the financial position of the entity. The magnitude of these responsibilities may be appreciated when it is realized that the number of transactions involved in a major enterprise runs into the billions each year. The PA does not examine each one of these transactions; rather, professional approaches are used to ascertain beyond reasonable doubt that they were measured and reported properly.

Occasionally, the auditor may encounter attempts to manipulate accounting reports, for example, to increase reported profit by omitting certain expenses or to overstate financial position by omitting certain debts. There are many intentional and unintentional opportunities for preparing misleading financial reports. The audit function performed by an independent PA is the best protection available to the public in this respect. Many investors have learned the pitfalls of making investments in enterprises that do not have their financial reports examined by an independent PA.

At the conclusion of an audit, the independent PA is required to provide an **auditor's opinion** that indicates whether the financial statements are appropriate and not misleading. For example, a recent auditor's opinion was described in *The Wall Street Journal* (July 27, 1982) as follows: "Price Waterhouse & Co. (an accounting firm) qualified its opinion of Newberry Energy Corp.'s 1982 annual report, noting that the company's Canadian subsidiary may default on its debt and be placed in receivership. The company had a net loss of $4.8 million in fiscal 1982, compared with earnings of $537,000 a year earlier."

Management advisory services.   Many independent PA firms also offer advisory or consulting services. These services usually are accounting based and encompass such activities as the design and installation of accounting, data processing, profit-planning (i.e., budget) and control systems; financial advice;

forecasting; inventory controls; cost-effectiveness studies; and operational analyses. This facet of public practice is experiencing rapid growth.

Tax services. PAs in public practice usually are involved in rendering income tax services to their clients. These services include both tax planning as a part of the decision-making process, tax compliance, and also determination of the income tax liability (reported on the annual tax return). Because of the increasing complexity of provincial and federal tax laws, particularly income tax laws, a high level of competence in this area is required. PAs specializing in taxation can provide this competence. The PA's involvement in tax planning often is quite significant. Virtually every major business decision carries with it significant tax impacts; so much so, in fact, that tax-planning considerations frequently govern the decision.

Employment by organizations

Many accountants are employed by profit-making and nonprofit organizations. A company or other organization, depending upon its size and complexity, may employ from one up to hundreds of accountants. In a business enterprise, the chief financial officer (usually a vice president or controller—sometimes comptroller) is a member of the management team. This responsibility usually entails a wide range of management, financial, and accounting duties. Exhibit 1–3 shows a typical organizational arrangement of the financial function in a business enterprise. In the business entity, accountants typically are engaged in a wide variety of activities, such as general management, general accounting, cost accounting, profit planning (i.e., budgeting) and control, internal auditing, and electronic data processing. A common pattern in recent

**EXHIBIT 1–3
Typical organization of the financial function**

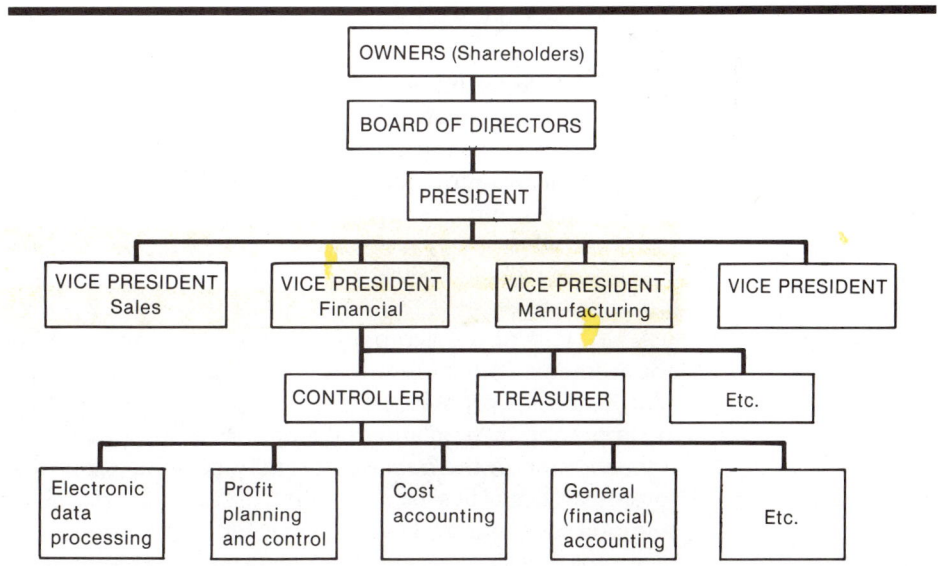

years has been the selection of a "financial expert" as the chief executive or president of the company. One primary function of the accountants in organizations is **management accounting;** that is, to provide data that are useful for internal managerial decision making and for controlling operations. In addition, the functions of external reporting, tax planning, control of assets, and a host of related responsibilities normally are performed by accountants in industry. The role of accountants within organizations is emphasized in management accounting texts.

Employment in the public sector

The vast and complex operations of governmental units, from the local to the international level, create a great need for accountants. Accountants employed in the public sector perform functions similar to those performed by their counterparts in private organizations. Additionally, various provincial and federal regulatory agencies and their auditing departments utilize the services of accountants in carrying out their regulatory duties.

Finally, accountants are involved in varying capacities in the evolving programs of pollution control, health care, minority enterprises, and other socially oriented programs, whether sponsored by private industry or by government.

GROUPS INVOLVED IN ACCOUNTING INNOVATION

The designation PA used in the previous section is a generic designation that will be used in this text to denote all accountants (particularly professionally designated ones) engaged in public accounting practice. In Canada, three professional groups dominate the practice of public accounting and thus the development of accounting thought. The role of each is described briefly.

The Canadian Institute of Chartered Accountants (CICA)

Of the three professional groups in Canada, the predominant group is the CICA through their Accounting Standards Committee. In addition to CAs from across Canada, membership of this committee is made up from members of the Canadian Council of Financial Analysts, Financial Executives Institute of Canada, and the Society of Management Accountants. This committee is charged with the responsibility of issuing pronouncements which are incorporated in the *CICA Handbook*. This *Handbook* constitutes the official source of generally accepted accounting principles for most profit-oriented enterprises in Canada. Part of the acceptance of this predominance for the committee's pronouncements comes from the legal sanction given to the *Handbook* in the Canada Business Corporations Act and various provincial statutes involved with incorporation or regulation of profit-oriented enterprises.

In addition to the *Handbook* pronouncements, other CICA Committees sponsor research studies of accounting issues and publish the Public Sector Accounting Statements. The Public Sector Statements represent an attempt to improve the financial accounting practice of governments in Canada.

The Certified General Accountants of Canada (CGAC)

The CGAs have recently begun a loose-leaf book entitled the *GAAP Guide*. This book provides a summary of *CICA Handbook* pronouncements and highlights differences between Canadian standards and the various ones in the United States and those of the International Accounting Standards Committee (IASC). In addition, the CGA Research Foundation publishes research monographs on various topics of interest to practitioners and academics.

The Society of Management Accountants of Canada (SMAC)

Members of the Society of Management Accountants (designated Certified Management Accountants, CMAs)[5] serve as members of the Accounting Standards Committee who issue *Handbook* pronouncements. The society sponsors on its own a number of research studies that concentrate on management accounting issues but a few provide background research for financial accounting problems.

The Canadian Academic Accounting Association (CAAA)

The CAAA is an association of academic and professional accountants. While it does not certify professional competence like the other three groups, it does provide a forum for the discussion of issues in financial accounting through their annual meeting, their research monographs, and their journal, *Contemporary Accounting Research*. CAAA committees and individual members also provide analyses of various recommendations and publications of the other associations.

Because of the close ties of Canadian business to the United States, research and pronouncements in that country are important to Canadian accountants.

At the present time, four important groups in the United States predominate in the development of financial accounting concepts and practice. The groups are the American Institute of Certified Public Accountants, the Financial Accounting Standards Board, the U.S. Securities and Exchange Commission, and the American Accounting Association. The past and present roles of each group are reviewed briefly below.

American Institute of Certified Public Accountants (AICPA)

This institute was organized a few years prior to the turn of the century by a group of accountants engaged in public and industrial accounting. Membership currently is limited to certified public accountants (CPAs). It carries on a wide-ranging program encompassing professional development, publications, and the development and communication of accounting standards and procedures. During the approximate period 1930–50, the AICPA's Committee on Accounting Procedure issued a number of *Accounting Research Bulletins (ARBs)* that enunciated certain **recommended** financial accounting principles and procedures. Realizing the need for a more concentrated effort to develop accounting standards, in 1959 the AICPA organized the Accounting Principles Board (APB) to replace the former committee. The APB issued 31 numbered *Opinions* during its existence from 1959 through mid-1973. The *Opinions* dealt with many

---

[5]The CMA designation replaced the RIA (Registered Industrial Accountant) designation on July 1, 1985.

of the difficult issues of financial accounting; as a consequence, many of them were highly controversial. Throughout this volume you will encounter a few references to the *ARBs* and numerous references to APB *Opinions.*

Financial Accounting Standards Board (FASB)

The FASB began operating June 1, 1973, and continues the development of accounting standards designed to enhance the usefulness and reliability of financial reports. Accounting is a complex and frequently controversial professional activity. In the light of these controversies, the AICPA in 1972 decided to reassess the approaches to establishing financial accounting concepts and standards. As a consequence of this reassessment, the APB was discontinued, and in its place the Financial Accounting Standards Board was established and continues to function. The seven FASB members are appointed by an independent board of trustees and serve on a full-time basis (in contrast to the previous groups, each member receives full-time compensation). The FASB was organized to be independent. It has as its sole function the establishment and improvement of accounting concepts and standards. The accounting profession, through the FASB, intends to keep the standards-setting function in the private sector rather than to have the standards imposed by laws and governmental agencies.

Securities and Exchange Commission (SEC)

This government regulatory agency operates under authority granted by the Securities Acts of 1933 and 1934. These acts were in response to the manipulations, irrational speculation, and lack of credible financial information that existed when the stock market crash occurred in 1929–30. The acts gave the SEC authority to prescribe accounting guidelines for the financial reports required to be submitted by corporations that sell their securities in interstate commerce (i.e., registered companies, which primarily are those listed on the stock exchanges). This list includes most of the large, and some medium-sized, corporations. The SEC requires these corporations to submit periodic financial reports, which are maintained in the files of the Commission as a matter of public record. Also, a prospectus, which is a preliminary statement presented to prospective buyers or investors, is required before the sale of securities. From the beginning, the SEC, as a matter of policy, usually has followed the accounting concepts, standards, and procedures established by the accounting profession. The SEC publishes *Regulation S-X* and issues *Accounting Series Releases (ASR)*, which prescribe the special guidelines to be followed by registered companies in preparing the financial reports submitted in conformance with the Securities Acts. Throughout its existence, the SEC has exerted a significant impact on accounting. Its staff has worked closely with the accounting profession on the evolution and improvement of accounting standards.

American Accounting Association (AAA)

This association was organized during the World War I period by a group of university accounting professors. The Association sponsors and encourages the improvement of accounting teaching and accounting research (primarily on a theoretical plane), and publishes a magazine, *The Accounting Review.* Its committees issue reports that, coupled with the research activities of individual academicians, exert a pervasive influence on the development of accounting theory and standards.

In summary, the prior discussions of the environment in which accounting operates suggest the importance of competitive and successful businesses (from the smallest to the largest) to a free enterprise economy. Economic success in a competitive business economy means earning reasonable profits and providing funds (cash) to meet broad **reinvestment needs.** Adequate reinvestment in businesses means more jobs, better wages, continuing technological advances, expansion of efficient productive capacity, adequate dividends for investors, and more tax revenue to the government (to support socially desirable programs and other governmental activities). The economic dimensions of this success by individual businesses are communicated in accounting reports.

Part B—Communication of Accounting Information

This part of the chapter introduces the end product of the accounting processing system—the periodic financial statements. These statements are viewed as an important means of communicating financial information about the entity. Additionally, this part emphasizes the purpose and nature of financial statements. Various approaches are used to derive the dollar amounts; discussion of these approaches will be included in subsequent chapters. In Chapters 1 and 2 we introduce the **basic financial statements** prior to discussion of how they are derived in order to provide an initial overview of how the end product appears. The remaining chapters concentrate on the economic analyses, measurements, and recording of the transactions that necessarily precede financial statement preparation.

COMMUNICATION CONCEPTS AND APPROACHES

Communication consists of a flow of information from one party to one or more other parties. For communication to be effective, the recipient must understand what the sender intends to convey. The process of communication involves numerous problems in understanding precisely the words, symbols, and sounds used by the parties involved. Accounting seeks to communicate by words and symbols financial information that is relevant to the decisions typically made by investors, creditors, and other interested parties. As you make decisions of varying sorts, reliance is placed upon certain information that often is unique to each type of decision. Often, each of us must make decisions without adequate information. Either the needed information is not available in time or the cost and time entailed in developing it is prohibitive when compared to its potential benefits.[6] The nature and form in which information is "packaged" and the avenues used to communicate it sometimes af-

---

[6]This sentence suggests the concept of **benefit-cost analysis;** that is, a comparison of the cost of pursuing a particular course of action, compared with the economic benefits or advantages derived from that course of action.

fect the decision. For example, some individuals are more influenced by graphic than by quantitative presentations, others find narrative preferable to tabular expression, some prefer summaries rather than details, and still others are not interested in technical presentations of any sort.

Financial information and the means used to communicate it frequently have strong and pervasive behavioral impacts[7] upon decision makers. The behavioral impacts of accounting extend to both positive and negative motivations of people. The frequency, form, and quality of one's communications with others are often important to motivations.

The terminology and symbols of accounting were developed over a long period of time in the search for ways to communicate financial information effectively. As is common with other professions, such as law and medicine, the terminology and symbols of accounting are somewhat technical. Accounting has developed in direct response to the needs of people. As a consequence, it is continuously evolving new concepts, terminology, procedures, and means of communication. In the chapters to follow, you should pay special attention to the terminology of accounting.

OVERVIEW OF EXTERNAL FINANCIAL STATEMENTS

Financial statements often are classified as (1) internal (i.e., management accounting) statements and (2) external (i.e., financial accounting) statements. Internal financial statements are not distributed to parties outside the entity. They are used exclusively by, and are prepared under the direction of, the **managers** of the entity; therefore, they are prepared to meet specific internal policies and guidelines established by those managers.

In contrast, **external** financial statements are distributed to parties (i.e., external decision makers) outside the entity (which include shareholders and creditors). External parties are unable to specify guidelines for preparation of the statements. The information presented on financial statements is intended to help investors and others make better economic decisions. Thus, financial statements must present information that is relevant to economic decisions; it must be useful for predicting the future successes (and failures) of the business. **Relevance** is an important **qualitative characteristic** of financial statements. To ensure that external parties may understand the information reported in financial statements, the entity is required to conform to specific and well-known **generally accepted accounting principles (GAAP)** that are developed by the accounting profession.

---

[7] A behavioral impact is an individual's response to external forces. An individual may be motivated toward or away from certain courses of action by information or observations that come to his or her attention. For example, one may be motivated to purchase a large automobile rather than a small one for reasons of prestige. However, a financial report showing the relative costs of operating the two automobiles may motivate the individual to purchase the small automobile. Thus, the financial report exerted a significant behavioral impact on the decision maker.

This textbook discusses the development of external financial reports. The next several pages present an **overview** of the external financial statements required by GAAP.

A primary objective of the accounting processing system is the development of financial statements that communicate relevant information to decision makers. An understanding of financial statements at the outset places you in an excellent position to interpret them and to understand how the accounting process operates. The three primary financial statements for a profit-making entity for **external reporting** to owners, potential investors, creditors, and other decision makers are the—

1. Income statement (more descriptively, statement of revenues, expenses, and income).
2. Balance sheet (more descriptively, statement of assets, liabilities, and owners' equity).
3. Statement of changes in financial position (more descriptively, statement of cash inflows and outflows, or of working capital; abbreviated SCFP).

These three required statements summarize the financial activities of the business entity for each specific period of time. They can be produced at any time (such as end of the year, quarter, or month) and can apply to any time span (such as 10 years, 1 year, 1 quarter, or 1 month). The heading of each statement contains a very specific statement of the **time dimension** of the report. Although these three statements directly relate to each other, for convenience, at this point in your study, they will be considered separately. First, we will illustrate them for a simple business situation; the next chapter discusses and illustrates them in a more complex situation.

The income statement

The income statement is designed to report the profit performance of a business entity for a specific period of time, such as a year, quarter, or month. Profit is a word that is used widely in our language, but accountants prefer to use the technical term **net income** which is defined as the difference between revenues and expenses for the specified period. An income statement presents the **results of operations;** that is, it reports, for a **specific period of time** in accordance with the time-period assumption (e.g., "For the Year Ended December 31, 19A"), the items that comprise the total **revenues,** the total **expenses,** and the resulting **net income** (see Exhibit 1–4).

Exhibit 1–4 presents the income statement for the first year of operations of Business Aids, Inc., an enterprise that renders professional secretarial, reproduction, and mailing services for a fee. Business Aids was organized by three individuals as a **corporation.** Each owner (called a shareholder) received 1,000 shares of capital stock as evidence of ownership. The **heading** of the statement specifically identifies the name of the entity, the title of the report, and the period of time over which the reported net income was earned. Note that the date encompasses a period of time—in this case, one year. There are three

EXHIBIT 1–4
Income statement
(simplified)

BUSINESS AIDS, INC. —Name of entity		
Income Statement —Title of report }HEADING		
For the Year Ended December 31, 19A —Period of time		

Revenues:

Stenographic revenue	$30,000	
Printing revenue	20,000	
Mailing revenue	13,000	
Total revenues		$63,000

Expenses:

Salary expense	30,750	
Employee benefits expense	1,100	
Rent expense for office space	2,400	
Rental payments for copiers	6,600	
Utilities expense	400	
Advertising expense	960	
Supplies expense	90	
Interest expense	100	
Depreciation expense on office equipment	600	
Total expenses (excluding income tax)		43,000
Pretax income		20,000
Income tax expense ($20,000 × 17%)		3,400
Net income		$16,600
Earnings per share (EPS) ($16,600 ÷ 3,000 shares)		$5.53

major captions: **revenues, expenses,** and **net income.** The detail presented under each caption is intended to be sufficient to meet the needs of decision makers interested in Business Aids, Inc. This latter point is significant because the composition and the detail of a financial statement vary, depending on the characteristics of the business entity and the needs of the users.

Revenues. Revenues represent the sales amount of goods sold or services rendered by the entity to others for which the entity will receive (or has received) cash or something else of value. When a business sells goods or renders services, if not on credit, it receives cash immediately. If on credit, it receives an **account receivable** which is collected in cash later. In either case, the business recognizes revenue for the period as the sum of the cash and credit sales for goods sold and for services rendered. Sometimes the cash for a revenue is collected **before** the revenue is earned as in the case of revenue collected in advance of occupancy. Thus, revenue may be thought of as an inflow of resources that results from a profit-making activity. Revenue is measured in dollars as the bargained **cash-equivalent** price agreed on by the two parties to the transaction.[8] Various terms are used in financial statements to describe revenue, such as sales revenue, service revenue, rental revenue, and interest revenue. Revenues are discussed in more detail in Chapter 4.

---

[8]Revenue sometimes is called income, such as rent income, interest income, and royalty income, but this practice tends to cause confusion. Ideally, **income should be used to refer only to the differences between revenues and expenses.**

Expenses. Expenses represent the dollar amount of resources expended or used up by the entity during a period of time to earn revenues. Expenses may require the immediate payment of cash or some other resource, or the payment of cash or some other resource may occur some time after the expense is incurred. In some cases, cash is paid **before** the expense is incurred, as in the case of the payment of office rent in **advance of occupancy.** For accounting purposes, an expense is reported on the income statement in the period in which it is incurred (i.e., used), which is not necessarily the same as the period in which the cash is paid. **The period in which an expense is deemed to be incurred**[9] **is the period in which the goods are used or the services are received.**

An expense may represent the cost of **using** equipment or buildings that were purchased for continuing use in operating the business rather than for sale. Such items often have a high initial cost at the date of acquisition, and through use, each one is worn out (or becomes obsolete) over an extended period of time known as **useful life.** As such items are used in operating the business, a portion of their cost becomes an expense. This kind of expense is known as **depreciation expense.** For example, on January 1, 19A, Business Aids purchased office equipment for its own use at a cost of $6,000. It was estimated that the office equipment would have a useful life of 10 years. Therefore, the **depreciation expense** each year for using the equipment is measured as $6,000 ÷ 10 years = $600. The income statement for 19A (Exhibit 1–4) reports this amount as an expense.[10] It also reports interest expense for one year on the $1,000, 10 percent note payable (i.e., $1,000 × 0.10 = $100). Because a corporation is subject to income tax on its income, Business Aids incurred income tax expense of $3,400 (i.e., $20,000 × 0.17 = $3,400). Observe that Business Aids reported both **pretax** and **aftertax** income amounts.[11]

Net income. Net income (often called profit by nonaccountants) is the excess of total revenues over total expenses. If the total expenses exceed the total revenues, a **net loss** is reported. When revenues and expenses are exactly equal for the period, the business is said to have operated at **breakeven.**

Earnings per share (EPS). The amount of earnings per share (EPS) is reported immediately below net income if the business is organized as a corporation. EPS is derived by dividing net income by the number of shares of **common** stock outstanding. Because Business Aids had 3,000 shares of common

---

[9]Incurred, as used in this context, means that the amount involved should be accounted for (i.e., recorded in the accounting system) during the specific period.

[10]Accounting for depreciation is discussed in detail in Chapter 9.

[11]Most corporations are subject to income taxes at rates that vary provincially and by nature of the business conducted. Some of these specifics will be discussed in "Special Supplement A" at end of this book. Sole proprietorships and partnerships, as business entities, are not subject to income taxes. In each of these situations, the owner, or owners, must report the income of the entity on their own individual income tax returns. For illustration purposes, an average tax rate is used herein to ease the arithmetic.

stock outstanding (i.e., 1,000 shares were owned by each of the three share-holders) and a net income of $16,600, EPS was computed as $16,600 ÷ 3,000 shares = $5.53 per share for the year. Especially in recent years, EPS has been accorded an extensive amount of attention by security analysts and others. As a consequence, the accounting profession has come to accept it as an important information input for investors. Specific accounting guidelines were prescribed by the *CICA Handbook*, Section 3500, for computing and reporting EPS.

Some people view the income statement as the most important of the three required financial statements because it is designed to report the amount of net income and the details of how that amount was earned. They view the earning of income as the most important factor in a business. The **accounting model** for the income statement is:

$$\text{Revenues} - \text{Expenses} = \text{Net income (i.e., R} - \text{E} = \text{NI)}$$

The amount of net income for the period represents a net increase in resources (or a net decrease if a loss) that flowed into the business entity during that period as a result of operational activities (i.e., profit-making activities).

The balance sheet

The purpose of the balance sheet is to report the **financial position** of a business at a **particular point** in time. Financial position refers to the amount of resources (i.e., assets) and the liabilities (i.e., debts) of the business on a specific date. As a consequence, this statement frequently is called the statement of financial position. A more descriptive title would be the statement of assets, liabilities, and owners' equity. These are the three major captions on the statement.[12]

Exhibit 1–5 presents the balance sheet at the end of the first year of operations for Business Aids, Inc. Observe that the heading specifically identifies the name of the entity, the title of the report, and the specific date of the statement. Note the specific point in time—in this case, December 31, 19A—is stated clearly on the balance sheet. This contrasts with the dating on the income statement, which indicates a period of time (such as one year). After the statement heading, the **assets** are listed on the left and the **liabilities** and **owners' equity** on the right. The result is that the two sides "balance." The accounting model for the balance sheet specifies this relationship as follows:[13]

$$\text{Assets} = \text{Liabilities} + \text{Owners' equity (i.e., A} = \text{L} + \text{OE)}$$

As is the case with any equation, its elements may be rearranged. For example, the model frequently is expressed to reflect the fact that owners' equity

---

[12]The designation "balance sheet" is unfortunate because it is not descriptive in any sense. It implies that the central fact is that it balances arithmetically, although this actually is an incidental feature. Because of the widespread use of the term, it will be used in this book.

[13]Owners' equity for a corporation usually is called shareholders' equity. Alternative formats for the balance sheet are discussed later.

EXHIBIT 1–5   **Balance sheet (simplified)**

BUSINESS AIDS, INC.
Balance Sheet
At December 31, 19A

Assets			Liabilities		
Cash		$13,600	Accounts payable	$ 900	
Accounts receivable		13,000	Income taxes payable	500	
Land		20,000	Note payable, short term, 10%	1,000	
Office equipment	$6,000				
Less: Accumulated			Total liabilities		$ 2,400
depreciation	600	5,400	**Shareholders' Equity**		
			Contributed capital:		
			Capital stock (3,000 shares, par		
			value $10 per share)	30,000	
			Contributed surplus	3,000	
				33,000	
			Retained earnings	16,600	
			Total shareholders' equity		49,600
			Total liabilities and shareholders'		
Total assets		$52,000	equity		$52,000

is a residual (i.e., the difference between the assets and liabilities of the entity), viz:

Assets − Liabilities = Owners' equity (i.e., A − L = OE)

The accounting model is a basic building block in the total accounting process.[14] Next, we will define and discuss each of the three items in this model.

Assets. Fundamentally, assets are the resources owned by the entity. They may be tangible (physical in character) such as land, buildings, and machinery, or intangible (characterized by legal claims or rights) such as amounts due from customers (legal claims called accounts receivable) and patents (protected rights). In short, assets have present and **future** value, whether physical or not, and are owned by the entity.[15] The FASB, in its **Statement of Financial Accounting Concepts No. 3,** defined assets as "probable future economic benefits obtained or controlled by a particular entity as a result of past transactions or events."

Observe in the balance sheet, given in Exhibit 1–5, that each **asset** listed has an assigned dollar amount. The **cost principle** states that assets generally should be **measured** on the basis of the total cost incurred to acquire them (see Exhibit 2–6). To illustrate, the balance sheet for Business Aids reports "Land,

---

[14]The model also may be expressed as Assets = Equities. In this formulation, **equities** is used to denote (1) liabilities, or creditors' equity, which represent claims of creditors; and (2) owners' equity, which represents claims of the owners.

[15]Assets also include prepaid expenses and deferred charges because these present valid rights or claims in the future for goods and services paid for in advance. These kinds of assets are discussed in later chapters.

$20,000''; this is the amount of resources that was paid for the land when it was acquired. It may well be that because of market changes, the market value of the land at December 31, 19A (date of the balance sheet), actually was more or less than $20,000. Nevertheless, the balance sheet would report the land at its original acquisition cost. It follows that the balance sheet does not necessarily show the current **market value** of the assets listed.

It is appropriate to inquire why accountants do not change the measurement of each asset for each subsequent balance sheet to reflect the then market values. This revaluation is not done because the acquisition cost is factually objective (i.e., not an estimate), whereas current market value of the assets owned by the entity would have to be estimated at the end of each year. The estimate would be very subjective because the assets are not sold each year-end. Such subjectivity potentially could reduce the reliability of the financial statements.

Liabilities.   Liabilities are debts or obligations owed by the entity to the creditors. They arise primarily as a result of the purchase of goods or services from others on credit and through cash borrowings to finance the business. The FASB, in **Statement of Financial Accounting Concepts No. 3,** defined liabilities as "future sacrifices arising from present obligations of a particular entity to transfer assets or provide services to other entities in the future as a result of past transactions or events."

If a business fails to pay its creditors, the law may accord the creditors the right to force the sale of assets sufficient to meet their claims.[16]

Business entities frequently borrow money on a **note payable.** In this case, a liability known as notes payable is created. A note payable, which may be short term or long term, specifies a definite maturity or payment date and the rate or amount of interest charged by the lender. Also, many businesses purchase goods and services on open account that does not involve notes, thus creating a liability known as **accounts payable.** Another type of liability arises from the fact that income taxes frequently are paid, at least in part, several months after the end of the year. As a consequence, a liability to the government, **income taxes payable,** must be reported until the taxes are paid fully. You may observe in Exhibit 1–5 that Business Aids listed three liabilities and the amount of each. In respect to amounts, liabilities present few measurement problems because most liabilities are reported at the amount (i.e., the principal) of the debt established by the parties to the transaction.

Owners' equity.   The accounting model (A − L = OE) shows owners' equity to be equal to the total assets minus the total liabilities of the business. Because creditors' claims legally come first, the owners' equity represents a **residual interest** or claim of the owners to the assets. Owners' equity sometimes is called net worth, capital, or proprietorship. However, the preferable designations are (*a*) owner's equity for a sole proprietorship; (*b*) partners' eq-

---

[16]In case of dissolution or sale of all the assets of a business, legally the creditors must be paid first and any remainder goes to the owners.

uity for a partnership; and (c) shareholders' equity for a corporation. Owners' equity in a business is derived from two sources: (1) **contributed capital,** which is the investment of cash or other assets in the business by the owner or owners; and (2) **retained earnings** (or income), which is the amount of accumulated earnings of the business less losses and withdrawals.[17] When the owners receive cash or other assets from the business through withdrawals (defined later), the total amount of owners' equity is reduced. When the business incurs a loss, owners' equity also is reduced.

In Exhibit 1–5, the shareholders' equity section reports the following:

1. **Contributed capital**—The three shareholders invested a total of $33,000 in the business and received 3,000 shares of capital stock having a par value of $10 per share (par value will be discussed in Chapter 12). They invested $11 per share, or $1 per share above par value. The 3,000 shares issued are reported at their par value (3,000 × $10) as "Capital stock"; and the remainder, often called a premium (3,000 shares × $1 = $3,000), is reported as "Contributed surplus."

2. **Retained earnings**—The accumulated amount of earnings **less** all losses and dividends paid to the shareholders since formation of the corporation is reported as "Retained earnings." During the first year, the business earned $16,600, as shown on the income statement (Exhibit 1–4). This amount is reported as retained earnings on the balance sheet for Business Aids at this date because no dividends were declared or paid to the shareholders during the first year (since organization).

3. **Total shareholders' equity**—The sum of the investment ($33,000) plus the retained earnings ($16,600) = $49,600. This amount may be verified in terms of the basic accounting model: Assets ($52,000) − Liabilities ($2,400) = shareholders' equity ($49,600).

If, by contrast, a cash dividend of $6,000 had been declared and paid to the three shareholders during the year, the balance sheet would have reflected cash of $7,600 ($13,600 − $6,000) and retained earnings of $10,600 ($16,600 − $6,000).

Statement of changes in financial position (SCFP)

In recent years, the **financing activities** (i.e., sources of funds) of businesses have become increasingly complex. The business entity of today requires substantial funds for operations and expansion. These funds come from four sources: (1) owner investment, (2) borrowings, and (3) earning a profit and (4) selling noncash assets. In recognition of the need by users of financial statements for information concerning the sources and uses of funds by the busi-

---

[17]The term *retained earnings* usually is used by businesses organized as corporations. In contrast, sole proprietorships and partnerships usually do not employ this term because it is included in the owners' capital account(s). These distinctions are discussed later.

EXHIBIT 1–6
Statement of
changes in financial
position (SCFP)
(simplified)

BUSINESS AIDS, INC.
Statement of Changes in Financial Position, Cash Basis
For the Year Ended December 31, 19A

Sources of cash (inflows):
From operations:
From cash revenues $50,000
Less: Cash used for expenses 44,400
Cash inflow from operations . . . . $ 5,600
Financing:
Investment by owners (shares issued for cash) 33,000
Loan—note payable 1,000
Cash inflow from financing 34,000
Total cash inflow during the year 39,600
Uses of cash (outflows):
Investing:
To purchase office equipment 6,000
To purchase land 20,000
Total cash used for investing purposes 26,000
Change—increase in cash during the year $13,600

ness, *CICA Handbook*, Section 1540, was issued. This standard requires a **Statement of Changes in Financial Position (SCFP)**[18] to accompany the income statement and the balance sheet.

The objective of the SCFP is to communicate to the statement users information about the sources (inflows) and uses (outflows) of cash (or, alternatively, working capital, defined later). Exhibit 1–6 presents a SCFP for Business Aids for a specific period of time (i.e., "For the Year Ended December 31, 19A"). At this point you need not be concerned about the derivation of the amounts illustrated. Rather, your attention is called to the two basic classifications: cash sources (inflows of cash) and cash uses (outflows of cash). The difference between them represents the increase, or decrease, in cash during the period. Because investors and creditors often are interested in future cash flows, this statement provides past information on cash flows that is useful in projecting the future cash flows of the business. The accounting model for the SCFP is:

Cash inflows − Cash outflows = Net change in cash (i.e., CI − CO = NC)

The SCFP is derived from an analysis of the balance sheet and the income statement. For example, total revenue reported on Exhibit 1–4 (the income statement) of $63,000, less $13,000 of the revenue (mailing) extended on credit, equals $50,000, which represents the cash inflow from revenue in Exhibit 1–6. Similarly, total expenses of $46,400 (including income tax expense), shown on

[18]The SCFP is an outgrowth of an earlier "statement of sources and applications of funds". While new titles for the statement have been proposed such as statement of operating, financing, and investing activities, the traditional title will be retained for simplicity. See Chapter 15 for a more extensive discussion of this statement.

Exhibit 1–4, less the **noncash expenses** of $600 for depreciation, $900 for accounts payable, and $500 for income taxes payable, equals the $44,400 reported in Exhibit 1–6 as the cash used for expenses. Thus, the net income earned of $16,600 caused a cash inflow of $5,600. Shares of capital stock were sold causing a cash inflow of $33,000, and a loan was obtained to secure another $1,000, giving a total cash inflow during the year of $39,600. During the year, $26,000 cash was expended for office equipment and land. Consequently, the statement reports that $13,600 more cash was received than was spent during the year.

A detailed discussion of the SCFP is deferred to Chapter 15 because its preparation requires special procedures that are best understood after your knowledge of accounting is substantial.

DEMONSTRATION CASE

At the end of most chapters, one or more demonstration cases will be presented that provide an overview of the primary issues discussed in the chapter. Each demonstration case is followed by a recommended solution. The case should be read carefully; then you should try to prepare your solution prior to studying the recommended solution. This form of self-study is highly recommended.

The introductory case presented below is to start you thinking, in monetary terms, of some of the resource inflows and outflows of a business. It deals with reporting certain accounting information for the first year of a business entity that was organized by three individuals. See what you can do with the case before studying the recommended solution. (Note: It will test your comprehension of Part B of the chapter and also your analytical skills.)

ABC Service Corporation was organized by three investors (Able, Baker, and Cain) on January 1, 19A. On that date, as start-up cash, each investor bought 1,000 shares of the corporation's capital stock (par value $10 per share) and paid $12 per share. On the same day, the corporation borrowed $10,000 from a local bank and signed a three-year note payable at 15 percent interest payable each December 31. On January 1, 19A, the corporation purchased two specially designed service trucks for $20,000 cash. Operations were started immediately.

At the end of 19A, the corporation had completed the following business transactions (summarized):

   a. Performed services and billed customers for $100,500, of which $94,500 was collected in cash by year-end.
   b. Paid $55,500 cash for expenses (including the annual interest on the note owed to the local bank).
   c. Paid $7,000 cash to the Revenue Canada Taxaton (technically the Receiver General) for income taxes, and at the end of the year still owed the government $1,000 (the average tax rate was 20 percent).

EXHIBIT 1–7
Format of financial
statements—ABC
Service Corporation

ABC SERVICE CORPORATION
Income Statement

Date _____

Revenues: Computations
  Service revenues . . . . $_____   _____
Expenses:
  Various expenses . . . . $_____   _____
  Interest expense . . . .   _____   _____
  Depreciation expense . . . .   _____   _____
    Total expenses . . . . $_____
Pretax income . . . .
  Income tax expense . . . .   _____   _____
Net income . . . . $_____
  Earnings per share . . . . $_____   _____

ABC SERVICE CORPORATION
Balance Sheet

Date _____

Assets:
  Cash . . . . $_____   _____
  Accounts receivable . . . .   _____   _____
  Service trucks . . . . $_____   _____
    Less: Accumulated
      depreciation   _____   _____
Total assets . . . . $_____
Liabilities:
  Note payable . . . . $_____   _____
  Income taxes payable . . . .   _____   _____
    Total liabilities . . . . $_____
Shareholders' Equity:
  Capital stock, par $_____

    shares_____ . . .   _____   _____
  Contributed surplus . . . .   _____   _____
  Retained earnings . . . .   _____   _____
    Total shareholders' equity . . .   _____
    Total liabilities and
      shareholders' equity . . . . . . $_____

    d. Depreciated the two service trucks on the basis of a four-year
    useful life (disregard any residual value at the end of the four-
    year life).

Required:

    Complete the two financial statements for 19A by entering the correct
amounts (show computations in the space provided) in Exhibit 1–7. The suggested solution is given in Exhibit 1–8.

EXHIBIT 1–8
Suggested
solution—ABC
Service Corporation

ABC Service Corporation
Income Statement

Date ___For the Year Ended December 31, 19A___

		Computations
Revenues:		
Service revenues...................	$100,500	Given
Expenses:		
Various expenses.................. $54,000		Given
Interest expense................... 1,500		$10,000 × 15%
Depreciation expense 5,000		$20,000 ÷ 4 years
Total expenses	$ 60,500	
Pretax income......................	40,000	
Income tax expense...............	8,000	$40,000 × 20%
Net income	$ 32,000	
Earnings per share..............	$ 10.67	$32,000 ÷ 3,000 shares

ABC Service Corporation
Balance Sheet

Date _____At December 31, 19A_____

Assets:		$36,000 + $10,000 + $94,500
Cash	$ 58,000	−$55,500 − $7,000 − $20,000
Accounts receivable...............	6,000	$100,500 − $94,500
Service trucks $20,000		Given, cost of trucks
Less: Accumulated depreciation 5,000	15,000	$20,000 ÷ 4 years = $5,000
Total assets	$ 79,000	
Liabilities:		
Note payable..................... $10,000		Given, bank loan
Income taxes payable 1,000		Given, amount unpaid
Total liabilities...................	$ 11,000	
Shareholders' Equity:		
Capital stock, par ___$10___;		
shares ___3,000___.............. 30,000		3,000 × $10
Contributed surplus 6,000		3,000 × ($12 − $10)
Retained earnings 32,000		From income statement*
Total shareholders' equity	68,000	
Total liabilities and		
shareholders' equity	$ 79,000	

*Beginning RE ($–0–) + Net income ($32,000) − Dividends ($–0–) = Ending RE ($32,000).

SUMMARY OF CHAPTER

Accounting interacts with practically all aspects of the environment: social, economic, and political. Any open society is a complex one that is characterized by organizations—businesses, political parties, governmental entities, churches, social institutions, and private groups and associations. Each organization, whether local or international in scope, is an accounting entity. The essence of accounting is the measurement and reporting of financial information for an accounting entity. The measurement and reporting of the inflows and outflows of scarce resources and the financial position of each accounting entity is essential to (1) effective management of each such organization and (2) the understanding and evaluation of it by interested outside parties. Measurement of the financial characteristics of each such organization is essential because each one of you is an important decision maker, both in respect to each of your economic interests and as a concerned citizen in the broader sense. Your decision-making potential is enhanced if you understand the financial impacts of alternative solutions to particular problems.

Part B of the chapter explained and illustrated the basic features of the three required **external** financial reports—the income statement, the balance sheet, and the statement of changes in financial position.

The **income statement,** as the statement of operations, reports revenues, expenses, and the net income for a stated **period of time.** Earnings per share (EPS), which expresses the relationship between net income and the number of shares of common stock outstanding, was illustrated.

The **balance sheet,** as the statement of financial position, reports dollar amounts for the assets, liabilities, and owners' equity at a specific **point in time.**

The **statement of changes in financial position (SCFP),** as the statement of the inflows and outflows of funds, reports those flows for a specific **period of time.**

The fundamental accounting model, **Assets = Liabilities + Owners' Equity,** was introduced as the foundation for the balance sheet and the accounting process in general. The financial statements for a small company were illustrated. In the next chapter you will move one step forward and look at a more complex situation and, at the same time, add more concepts to your knowledge about the characteristics of the external financial statements of a business entity.

IMPORTANT TERMS DEFINED IN THIS CHAPTER

Terms (alphabetically)	Key words in definitions of important terms used in chapter	Page reference
AAA	American Accounting Association.	16
Accounting entity	A business or other organization; (a unit) for accounting.	6
AICPA	American Institute of Certified Public Accountants.	15
Assets	Items owned; have value.	23
Auditing	Attest function; reliability; auditors' opinion.	12
Balance sheet	Position statement; Assets = Liabilities + Owners' Equity.	22
CAAA	Canadian Academic Accounting Association.	15
Canada Business Corporations Act	Act of Government of Canada regulating the incorporation and operation of corporations.	14
Cash inflows	Cash received; increase Cash account.	26
Cash outflows	Cash paid; decrease Cash account.	26
CGAC	Certified General Accountants of Canada.	15
CICA	Canadian Institute of Chartered Accountants.	14
CICA Handbook	Source of GAAP published by the Accounting Standards Committee of CICA.	15

Terms (alphabetically)	Key words in definitions of important terms used in chapter	Page reference
CMA	Certified Management Accountant; designation used by members of the Society of Management Accountants.	15
Contributed capital	Total amount invested by shareholders.	25
Corporation	A separate legal entity; shares of stock represent ownership.	5
Depreciation	Allocation of cost of operational asset; based on use	21
EPS	Earnings per share; common stock.	21
Exchange transaction	An enforceable agreement; resources involved.	3
Expenses	Outflow of assets; for goods and services used.	21
FASB	Financial Accounting Standards Board.	16
GAAP	Generally accepted accounting principles.	12
Income statement	Required report; operations; income; EPS.	19
ISAC	International Accounting Standards Committee.	15
Liabilities	Obligations; debts; promise to pay.	24
Management advisory services	Service rendered by PA firms; consulting; complements audit and tax services.	12
Net income	Revenues − Expenses.	19
Owners' equity	Assets − Liabilities.	24
Partnership	Nonstock; two or more owners.	5
Retained earnings	Accumulated earnings; reduced by dividends.	25
Revenues	Inflow of resources from sale of goods and services.	20
RIA	Traditional designation for members of the Society of Management Accountants.	15
SCFP	Statement of changes in financial position.	25
SEC	Securities and Exchange Commission; government.	16
Separate-entity assumption	Business unit; separate from owners for accounting and reporting purposes.	6
SMAC	Society of Management Accountants of Canada.	15
Sole proprietorship	Nonstock; one owner.	5
Unit-of-measure assumption	Monetary unit used to account for an entity; the dollar; affected by inflation. The assumption is that the value of the monetary unit is stable.	5

QUESTIONS FOR DISCUSSION

Part A

1. Define accounting briefly and summarize the accounting flow of economic information about an entity.

2. Explain the unit-of-measure assumption including its relationship to accounting.

3. Briefly distinguish among a sole proprietorship, partnership, and corporation.

4. What is meant by an accounting entity? Why is a business treated as a separate entity for accounting purposes? Explain the separate-entity assumption.

5. Briefly explain the three ways that financial statements serve statement users.

6. List and briefly explain the three primary services provided by PAs.

7. Briefly explain the role of the:
    a. FASB.
    b. CICA.
    c. CAAA.

Part B

8. Financial statements are the end products of the accounting process. Explain.

9. Generally, how would you define communication?

10. The accounting process generates financial reports for both "internal" and "external" audiences. Identify some of the groups in each audience.

11. Complete the following:

Name of statement	*A more descriptive name*
a. Income statement	a. _____
b. Balance sheet	b. _____
c. Statement of changes in financial position (SCFP)	c. _____

12. What information should be included in the heading of each of the three required financial statements?

13. Explain why the income statement and the SCFP are dated "For the Year Ended December 31, 19X," whereas the balance sheet is dated "At December 31, 19X."

14. Define revenue.

15. Define expense.

16. Briefly define the following: income, loss, and breakeven.

17. What are the purposes of (a) the income statement, (b) the balance sheet, and (c) the SCFP?

18. Explain the accounting model for the income statement. What are the major items reported on the income statement?

19. Explain the accounting model for the balance sheet. Define the three major components reported on the balance sheet.

20. Explain the accounting model for the SCFP. Explain the three major components reported on the statement.

21. Why is owners' equity frequently referred to as a residual interest?

22. What are the two primary sources of owners' equity in a business?

23. What are the appropriate titles for owners' equity for (a) a sole proprietorship, (b) a partnership, and (c) a corporation?

EXERCISES

Part A

E1–1. Given below is a list of important abbreviations used in Part A of the chapter. These abbreviations also are used widely in business. For each abbreviation give the full designation. The first one is used as an example.

Abbreviation	*Full designation*
1. PA	Public Accountant
2. APB	
3. CICA	
4. AAA	
5. CMA	
6. AICPA	
7. IASC	
8. FASB	
9. CGA	

Part B

E1–2. Review the chapter explanations of the income statement and the balance sheet models. Apply these models in each independent case below to compute the two missing amounts for each case. Assume it is the end of 19A, the first full year of operations for the company.

Independent Cases	Total Revenues	Total Assets	Total Expenses	Total Liabilities	Net Income (Loss)	Shareholders' Equity
A	$95,000	$150,000	$88,000	$92,000	$	$
B		112,000	61,000		10,000	70,000
C	80,000	92,000	86,000	26,000		
D	65,000			40,000	9,000	77,000
E			81,000	73,000	(6,000)	88,000

E1–3. Rose Corporation was organized by three individuals on January 1, 19A, to render electronic repair services. At the end of 19A, the following income statement was prepared:

Rose Corporation
Income Statement
For the Year Ended December 31, 19A

Revenues:
Service sales (cash)	$178,000	
Service sales (credit)	12,000	
Total revenues		$190,000

Expenses:
Salaries	71,000	
Rent	12,000	
Utilities	10,000	
Advertising	11,000	
Supplies	18,000	
Interest	3,000	
Depreciation	5,000	
Total expenses		130,000
Pretax income		60,000
Income tax expense		13,200
Net income		$ 46,800
EPS		$2.34

Required:

a. What was the average monthly revenue amount?
b. What was the monthly rent amount?
c. Explain why "Supplies, $18,000" is an expense.
d. Explain why "Interest, $3,000" is reported as an expense.
e. Explain what is meant by "Depreciation, $5,000."
f. What was the average income tax rate for Rose Corporation?
g. How many shares of capital stock were outstanding?
h. Can you determine how much cash the company had on December 31, 19A?

E1–4. Assume you are the owner of "The College Shop," which specializes in items of special interest to college students. At the end of January 19A you find that (for January only):

a. Sales, per the cash register tapes, totaled $70,000, plus one sale on credit (a special situation) of $300.
b. With the help of a friend (who had majored in accounting), you determined that all of the goods sold during January had cost you $33,000 when they were purchased.
c. During the month, according to the cheque book, you paid $32,000 for salaries, utilities, supplies, advertising, and other expenses; however, you have not yet paid the $500 monthly rent for January on the store and fixtures.

On the basis of the data given, what was the amount of income for January (disregard income taxes)? Show computations. (Hint: A convenient form to use would have the following major side captions: revenue from sales, expenses, and the difference—income.)

E1–5. Small Company, Incorporated, a small service organization, prepared the following report for the month of January 19A:

Service Revenue, Expenses, and Income

Service revenues:
Cash services (per cash register tape)	$75,000	
Credit services (per charge bills; <u>not yet collected</u> ⨯ by end of January)	25,000	$100,000

Expenses:
Salaries and wages (paid by cheque).......................	40,000	
Salary for January not yet paid .. ⨯........................	1,000	
Supplies used (taken from on hand, purchased for cash during December)..... ⨯................................	2,000	
Estimated cost of wear and tear on used delivery ⨯ truck for the month (depreciation).......................	400	
Other expenses (paid by cheque)...........................	16,600	60,000
Pretax income		40,000
Income tax expense (not yet paid)		8,000
Income for January.......................................		$ 32,000

Required:

a. You have been asked by the owner (who knows very little about the financial side of business) to compute the "amount that cash increased in January 19A from the operations of the company."   You decided to prepare a detailed report for the owner with the following major side captions: cash inflows (collections), cash outflows (payments), and the difference—net increase (or decrease) in cash.

b. What was the average income tax rate?

c. See if you can reconcile the "difference—net increase (decrease) in cash" you computed in *(a)* with the income for January 19A.

E1–6. Libby Corporation was organized by five individuals on January 1, 19A. At the end of January 19A, the following monthly financial data are available:

Total revenues	$90,000
Total expenses (excluding income taxes)...................	70,000
Cash balance, January 31, 19A............................	15,000
Receivables from customers (all considered collectible)	10,000
Merchandise inventory (by inventory count at cost)	30,000
Payables to suppliers for merchandise purchased from them (will be paid during February 19A)	9,000
Total shareholders' equity on January 1, 19A..............	26,000

Assume a 20 percent tax rate on the income of this corporation; the income taxes will be paid during the first quarter of 19B.

Required:

Complete the following two statements for Libby Corporation:

LIBBY CORPORATION
Income Statement
For the Month of Janaury 19A

Total revenues	$_____
Less: Total expenses (excluding income tax)......	_____
Pretax income	_____
Less: Income tax expense.......................	_____
Net income	$_____

LIBBY CORPORATION
Balance Sheet
At January 31, 19A

Assets:
Cash..	$_____
Receivables from customers....................	_____
Merchandise inventory	_____
Total assets..................................	$_____

Liabilities
Payables to suppliers.........................	$_____
Income taxes payable.........................	_____
Total liabilities	_____
Total shareholders' equity......................	_____
Total liabilities and shareholders' equity..........	$_____

E1–7. Kyle Realty, Incorporated, has been operating for five years and is owned by three investors. S. T. Kyle owns 60 percent of the total outstanding stock of 9,000 shares and is the managing executive in charge. On December 31, 19C, the following financial items for the entire year were determined: commissions earned and collected in cash, $150,000, plus $20,000 uncollected; rental service fees earned and collected, $20,000; salaries expense paid, $60,000; commissions expense paid, $45,000; employee benefits paid, $4,000; rent paid, $2,200 (not including December rent yet to be paid); utilities expense paid, $700; promotion and advertising paid, $6,400; and miscellaneous expenses paid, $300. There were no other unpaid expenses at December 31. Kyle Realty rents its office space but owns the furniture therein. The furniture cost $5,000 when acquired and has an estimated life of 10 years (depreciate an equal amount each year). The average corporate income tax rate is 30 percent. Also during the year, the company paid the owners "out of profit" cash dividends amounting to $10,000. You have been requested to complete the following income statement:

_____		
_____		
_____		
Revenues:		
Commissions earned..........................	$_____	
Rental service fees	_____	
Total revenues		$_____
Expenses:		
Salaries expense................................		_____
Commission expense..........................		_____
Employee benefits		_____
Rent expense..................................		_____
Utilities expense................................		_____
Promotion and advertising		_____
Miscellaneous expenses		_____
Depreciation expense		_____
Total expenses (excluding income taxes)		_____
Pretax income		_____
Income tax expense..............................		_____
Net income	$	49,490
Earnings per share (EPS)	$	_____

E1–8. University Bookstore was organized as a corporation by Jane Nash and Roy Opel; each contributed $35,000 cash to start the business and each received 3,000 shares of common stock, par $10 per share. The store completed its first year of operations on December 31, 19A. On that date, the following financial items for the year were determined: December 31, 19A, cash on hand and in the bank, $42,000; December 31, 19A, amounts due from customers from sales of books, $6,100; store and office equipment, purchased January 1, 19A, for $40,000 (estimated useful life 10 years; depreciate an equal amount each year); December 31, 19A, amounts owed to publishers for books purchased, $6,000; and a note payable, 10 percent, one year, dated July 1, 19A, to a local bank for $2,000. No dividends were declared or paid to the shareholders during the year.

Required:

a. You have been asked to complete the balance sheet at the end of 19A shown below.
b. What was the amount of net income for the year?
c. Show how the $100 liability for interest payable was computed. Why is it shown as a liability on this date?

Assets		**Liabilities**	
Cash	$____	Accounts payable..............	$____
Accounts receivable............	____	Notes payable.................	
Store and office equipment	$____	Interest payable	100
Less: Accumulated		Total liabilities.................	$____
depreciation to date.........	____ ____		
		Shareholders' Equity	
		Common stock	____
		Contributed surplus	
		Retained earnings	6,000
		Total shareholders' equity	____
		Total liabilities and	
Total assets	$____	shareholders' equity	$____

E1–9. Rice Manufacturing Corporation is preparing the annual financial statements for the shareholders. A SCFP, cash basis, must be prepared. The following data on cash flows were developed for the entire year ended December 31, 19D; cash inflow from operating revenues, $270,000; cash expended for operating expenses, $190,000; sale of unissued Rice shares for cash, $30,000; cash dividends declared and paid to shareholders during the year, $20,000; and payments on long-term notes payable, $40,000. During the year, a small tract of land was sold for $10,000 cash (which was the same price that Rice had paid for the land in 19C) and $41,000 cash was expended for two new machines. The machines were used in the factory.

Required:

Prepare a SCFP, cash basis, for 19D. Follow the format illustrated in the chapter.

E1–10. On June 1, 19F, Rand Corporation prepared a balance sheet just prior to going out of business. The balance sheet totals reflected the following:

Assets (no cash) $100,000
Liabilities   60,000
Shareholders' equity   40,000

Shortly thereafter, all of the assets were sold for cash.

Required:

a.   How would the balance sheet appear immediately after the sale of the assets for cash for each separate case? Use the format given below.

		Balances immediately after sale		
	Cash received for the assets	Assets	− Liabilities =	Shareholders' Equity
Case A	$110,000	$_____	$_____	$_____
Case B	100,000	_____	_____	_____
Case C	90,000	_____	_____	_____

b.   How should the cash be distributed in each separate case? (Hint: Creditors have a priority claim over owners upon dissolution.) Use the format given below.

	To creditors	To Shareholders	Total
Case A	$_____	$_____	$_____
Case B	_____	_____	_____
Case C	_____	_____	_____

PROBLEMS/CASES

Part A

PC1–1.   D. X. Jones owns and operates the DXJ Sporting Goods Company (a sole proprietorship). An employee prepares a financial report for the business at each year-end. This report lists all of the resources (assets) owned by Jones (including such personal items as the home owned and occupied by Jones). It also lists all of the debts of the business (but not the "personal" debts of Jones).

Required:

a.   From the accounting point of view, in what ways do you disagree with what is being included and excluded from the report of business assets and liabilities?

b.   Upon questioning, Jones responded, "Don't worry about it, we use it only to support a loan from the bank." How would you respond to this comment?

PC1–2.   You are one of three partners who own and operate the Triple X Refreshments Company. The company has been operating for seven years, and one of the other partners has prepared the company's annual financial statements. Recently you proposed that "the statements should be audited each year because it would benefit each of us and preclude possible disagreements about the division of profits." The partner that prepared the statements proposed that his "Uncle Ray, who has a lot of financial experience can do the job and at little cost." Your other partner remained silent.

Required:

a. What position would you take on the proposal? Justify your response.
b. Explain what you would strongly recommend and give the basis for your recommendation.

PC1–3. Below are listed five transactions completed by Ace Company during the year 19A:

a. Sold services for cash, $9,000.
b. Purchased a microcomputer for use in performing the accounting function of the company: cost, $12,000; paid cash. *investment*
c. Paid salaries, $20,000 cash.
d. Borrowed cash, $10,000 on a 12 percent interest-bearing note.
e. The owner of Ace Company purchased a special pickup for his personal use; cost, $15,000; paid cash from his personal funds.

Required:

Complete the tabulation given below to indicate the effects (in dollars) of each of the above transactions on the balance sheet, income statement, and SCFP of Ace Company. Consider only the effects on the date the transactions were completed. Provide explanatory comments to support your response for each transaction. Use "+" for increase and "−" for decrease on the income statement and balance sheet.

Financial statements	Transaction				
	(a)	(b)	(c)	(d)	(e)
Income statement:					
Revenues	$	$	$	$	$
Expenses					
Balance sheet:					
Assets					
Liabilities					
Owners' equity					
SCFP:					
Cash inflow					
Cash outflow					

Explanations:

PC1–4. On January 1, 19A, three individuals organized TRI Service Company. Each individual invested $5,000 cash in the business. On December 31, 19A, they prepared a list of resources (assets) owned and a list of the debts (liabilities) to support a company loan request of $50,000 to a local bank. None of the three investors had studied accounting. The two lists prepared were as follows:

Company resources:

Cash	$ 3,000
Service supplies inventory (on hand)	5,000
Service trucks (four practically new)	60,000
Personal residences of organizers (three houses)..................	190,000
Service equipment used in the business (practically new)..........	24,000
Bills due from customers (for services already completed)	18,000
Total	$300,000

Obligations of the company:

Unpaid wages to employees	$ 17,000
Unpaid taxes	6,000
Owed to suppliers	7,000
Owed on service trucks and equipment (to a finance company)	41,000
Loan from Organizer T	12,000
Total	$ 83,000

Required:

a. If you were advising the local bank with respect to the two lists, what issues would you raise for consideration? Explain the basis for each question and include any recommendations that you have (consider the separate-entity assumption).

b. In view of your response to *(a)*, what do you think the amount of **net resources** (i.e., assets minus liabilities) of the company would be? Show your computations.

PC1–5. Simple Service Company was organized on January 1, 19A. At the end of the first quarter (three months) of operations, the owner prepared a summary of its operations as shown in the first column of the following tabulation:

Summary of Transactions	Computation of Profit	Computation of Cash
1. Services performed for customers, $60,000, of which one sixth remained uncollected at the end of the quarter.	$ + 60,000	$ + 50,000
2. Cash borrowed from the local bank, $10,000 (one-year note).		
3. Purchased a small service truck for use in the business; cost, $8,000; paid 20 percent down, balance on credit.		
4. Expenses, $40,000, of which one fifth remained unpaid at the end of the quarter.		
5. Purchased service supplies for use in the business, $2,000, of which one fourth remained unpaid (on credit) at the end of the quarter. Also, one fifth of these supplies were unused (still on hand) at the end of the quarter.		
6. Wages earned by employees, $12,000, of which one sixth remained unpaid at the end of the quarter.		
7. Purchased land for future use for $20,000 cash.		
Based only on the above transactions, compute the following for the quarter:		
Profit (or loss)	$	
Cash inflow (or outflow)		$

Required:

a. For each of the seven transactions given in the tabulation above, enter what you consider the correct amounts. Enter a zero when appropriate. The first transaction is answered by way of illustration.

b. For each transaction, briefly explain the basis for your dollar response. (Hint: Profit and cash flow totals are not the same.)

Part B

PC1–6. DC Corporation was organized by Donald Dunn and Cynthia Cummings; they had previously operated the company as a partnership. Each owner has 10,000 shares of capital stock of DC Corporation. At the end of the accounting year, 19H, the company bookkeeper prepared the following incomplete balance sheets (amounts simplified for problem purposes):

DC CORPORATION
Balance Sheet

1.	Assets:		
2.	Cash		$28,000
3.	Accounts receivable		15,000
4.	Equipment*	$ _____	
5.	Less: Accumulated depreciation	10,000	40,000
6.	Total_____		$83,000
7.	_____		
8.	Accounts payable	$ 8,000	
9.	Income tax payable	1,000	
10.	Note payable, short term, 15%†	4,000	
11.	_____		_____
12.	_____		
13.	Capital stock, $_____ par value	20,000	
14.	Contributed surplus	10,000	
15.	Retained earnings	40,000	
16.	_____		70,000
17.	Total liabilities and shareholders' equity		$_____

*Equipment has a 10-year estimated life; equal amounts expensed each year.
†Note dated July 1, 19H, time to maturity, 12 months.

Required (the lines are numbered above for problem reference purposes):

1. Define the term *assets* as used on the balance sheet.
2. What would be DC's cash balance in the bank assuming the company has $500 cash on hand on December 31, 19H?
3. Explain why "Accounts receivable" represents an asset.
4. Compute the amount that the equipment cost when it was acquired by DC Corporation.
5. Explain "Accumulated depreciation." What does the $10,000 indicate?
6. Enter the correct caption here.
7. Enter the correct caption here.
8. Explain why "Accounts payable" is a liability.
9. Explain what this liability represents.
10. What amount of interest expense applies to the year 19H? Note, the amount computed will be shown on the income statement as "Interest expense."
11. Enter the appropriate caption and amount here.
12. Enter the appropriate caption here.
13. Enter the amount of the par value per share of capital stock.
14. What was the total issue price per share of capital stock?
15. Explain what the $40,000 amount means.
16. Enter appropriate caption here.
17. Enter correct amount here.
18. Do you have any suggestions with respect to the heading of the statement?

PC1-7. Davis Corporation was organized on January 1, 19A. At the end of 19A, the company had not yet employed an accountant. However, an employee who was "good with numbers" prepared the following statements at that date:

DAVIS CORPORATION
December 31, 19A

Income from sales of merchandise.............................	$180,000
Total amount paid for goods sold during 19A	(95,000)
Selling costs..	(30,000)
Depreciation (on service vehicles used)	(15,000)
Income from services rendered.................................	50,000
Salaries and wages paid	(60,000)
Income taxes (at tax rate of 17%)	(5,100)
Profit for the year 19A..	$ 24,900

DAVIS CORPORATION
December 31, 19A

Resources:

Cash...		$ 31,000
Merchandise inventory (held for resale)		44,000
Service vehicles.....................................		45,000
Retained earnings (profit earned in 19A)		24,900
Grand total...................................		$144,900
Debts:		
Payables to suppliers		$ 15,000
Note owed to bank..................................		20,000
Due from customers................................		12,900
Total...		47,900
Supplies on hand (to be used in rendering services)....	$12,000	
Depreciation (on service vehicles)....................	15,000	
Capital stock.......................................	70,000	
Total..		97,000
Grand total...................................		$144,900

Required:

The above statements have some incorrect captions, some items that are under the wrong caption, and the statement headings are incomplete. Prepare a correct income statement and balance sheet. (Hint: All figures [except totals] are correct; the balance sheet total should be $129,900.)

PC1–8. Upon graduation from high school, Jack Kane immediately accepted a job as a plumber's helper for a large local plumbing company. After three years of hard work, Jack received a plumber's license, whereupon he decided to go into business for himself. He had saved $5,000 which he decided to invest in the business. His first step was to transfer this amount from his savings account to a business bank account for "Kane Plumbing Company, Incorporated." His lawyer had advised him to start as a corporation. He then purchased, with cash, a used panel truck for $3,000 and secondhand tools for $800; rented space in a small building; inserted an ad in the local paper; and opened the doors on October 1, 19A. Immediately, Jack found himself very busy and, after one month, employed a helper. Although he knew practically nothing about the financial side of the business, Jack realized from his experience that a number of reports were required and that costs and collections had to be controlled carefully. Accordingly, at the end of the year, prompted in part by concern about his income tax situation (previously he only had to report salary), he recognized the need for financial statements. His wife, Jane, undertook "to develop some financial statements for the business." With the help of a friend, on December 31, 19A, she gathered the following data for the three months just ended: Deposits in the bank account of collections for plumbing services totaled $30,000. The following cheques were written: plumber's helper, $7,550; payroll taxes paid, $150; supplies purchased and used on jobs, $9,000; oil, gas, and maintenance on truck, $1,100; insurance, $300; rent, $500; utilities and telephone, $650; and miscellaneous expenses, $400 (including advertising). In addition, there were uncollected bills to customers for plumbing services amounting to $2,000, and the rent for December amounting to $100 had not been paid. The income tax rate on this corporation may be assumed to be 17 percent. Also assume that the "wear and tear on the truck and tools due to use during the three months" was estimated by Jack to be $250.

Required:

a.   Prepare an income statement for Kane Plumbing for the three months October–December 19A. Use the following main captions: revenues from services, expenses, pretax income, and net income. (Hint: Expenses, excluding income taxes, totaled $20,000.)

b.   Do you visualize that Jack may have a need for one or more additional financial reports for 19A and thereafter? Explain.

PC1–9.   During the summer, between her junior and senior years, Mandy Walker was faced with the need to earn sufficient funds for the coming academic year. Unable to obtain a job with reasonable remuneration, she decided to try the lawn-care business for three months. After a survey of the market potential, Mandy acquired a used pickup truck on June 1 for $1,200. On each door she painted "Mandy's Lawn Service, PH. XX." Additionally, she spent $600 for mowers, trimmers, and tools. To acquire these items she borrowed $2,000 cash on a note (endorsed by a friend) at 15 percent interest per annum, payable at the end of the three months (ending August 31).

At the end of the summer, Mandy realized that she had "done a lot of work and her bank account looked good," which prompted her to become concerned about how much profit the business had earned.

A review of the cheques stubs showed the following: Deposits in the bank of collections from customers totaled $11,400. The following cheques were written: gas, oil, and lubrication, $880; pickup repairs, $150; repair of mowers, $80; miscellaneous supplies used, $100; helpers, $4,725; employee benefits, $175; payment for assistance in preparing employees' forms, $75; insurance, $150; telephone, $90; and $2,075 to pay off the note including interest (on August 31). A notebook kept in the pickup, plus some unpaid bills, reflected that customers still owed her $600 for lawn services rendered and that she owed $100 for gas and oil (credit card charges). She estimated that the "wear and tear" for use of the truck and the other equipment for three months amounted to $400.

Required:

a.   Prepare an income statement for Mandy's Lawn Service covering the three months, June, July, and August 19A. Use the following main captions: revenues from services, expenses, and net income. Because this is a sole proprietorship, the company will not be subject to income tax. (Hint: Total revenues amounted to $12,000.)

b.   Do you visualize a need for one or more additional financial reports for this company for 19A and thereafter? Explain.

PC1–10.   Western Realty Company was organized early in 19A as a corporation by four investors, each of whom invested $5,000 cash. The company has been moderately successful, despite the fact that internal financial controls are inadequate. Although financial reports have been prepared each year (primarily in response to income tax requirements), sound accounting practice has not been followed. As a consequence, the financial performance of the company was known only vaguely by the four shareholders. Recently, one of the shareholders, with the agreement of the others, sold his shares to a local accountant. The new shareholder was amazed when handed the report below, which was prepared by an employee for the last meeting of the board of directors. The accountant could tell at a glance that the reported profit was wrong and quickly observed that no interest expense was shown on a $10,000, 14 percent note payable that had been outstanding throughout the year. Also, no recognition had been given to office equipment that was purchased on January 1, 19D, at a cost of $14,000 with an estimated five-year useful life.

WESTERN REALTY
Profit Statement
December 31, 19D

Commissions earned (all collected)	$130,000
Property management revenue (exclusive of $1,200 not collected)	8,000
Total	138,000
Salaries paid	31,000
Commissions paid	38,000
Employee benefits paid	3,300
Office supplies expense	120
Rent paid	2,400
Utilities paid	500
Advertising (excluding the December bill for advertising of $4,000 not yet paid)	28,000
Miscellaneous expenses	400
Total	103,720
Profit for the year	$ 34,280

EPS: $34,280 ÷ 10,000 shares = $3.43.

Required:

You have been asked to redraft the income statement, including corrections. Assume an average income tax rate of 20 percent. (Hint: The correct EPS is $2.18.)

PC1–11. Assume you are president of Joy Retailers, Incorporated. At the end of the first year (December 31, 19A) of operations, the following financial data are available for the company:

Cash	$ 16,300
Receivables from customers (all considered collectible)	15,000
Inventory of merchandise (based on physical count and priced at cost)	78,000
Equipment owned, at cost (at year-end, the estimated value to the business for future use was 90% of cost)	20,000
Note payable, one year, 12% annual interest, owed to the bank (dated July 1, 19A)	20,000
Interest on the note through December 31, 19A (due to be paid to the bank on June 30, 19B; $20,000 × 12% × 6/12)	1,200
Salary payable for 19A (on December 31, 19A, this was owed to an employee who was away because of an emergency; will return around January 10, 19B, at which time the payment will be made)	1,100
Total sales revenue	100,000

Expenses paid, including the cost of the merchandise sold
   (excluding income taxes at a 17% rate; the taxes will be paid
   during the first quarter of 19B)................................ 70,700
Capital stock, 10,000 shares outstanding 80,000

Required (show computations):

a.   Prepare a summarized income statement for the year 19A. (Hint: EPS is $2.075.)
b.   Prepare a balance sheet at December 31, 19A.

PC1–12.   At December 31, 19A, Big J Corporation had been in operation for one year. At the date of organization, each of the 10 investors paid in $10,000 cash and each received 100 shares of capital stock. Due to a need for more cash, on January 1, 19A, the corporation also borrowed $90,000, at 12 percent interest per year, on a note from a local bank. Interest on the note is payable each December 31, and the loan matures December 31, 19D. On December 31, 19A, the income statement and the balance sheet (summarized) were as follows:

Income Statement
For the Year Ended December 31, 19A

Total revenue	$70,000
Total expenses	44,360
Pretax income.........................	25,640
Income tax expense ($25,640 × 20%)	5,128
Net income	$20,512

Balance Sheet
At December 31, 19A

Assets		Liabilities	
Cash..........................	$ 24,154	Income taxes payable............	$ 1,282*
Remaining assets...............	187,640	Notes payable, long term	90,000
		Shareholders' Equity	
		Capital stock (1,000 shares).......	100,000
		Retained earnings	20,512
		Total liabilities and	
Total assets....................	$211,794	Shareholders' equity...........	$211,794

*Three fourths of the income taxes were paid during the year on a quarterly basis (i.e., $5,128 × 0.25 = $1,282).

An independent PA audited the above amounts. The PA found that the bookkeeper had neglected to include two transactions that occurred on December 31, 19A:

1.   Payment of a cash dividend of $7.50 per share to each shareholder.
2.   Cash payment of interest for one year on the long-term note payable owed to the bank.

Required:

Other than for these two transactions, the amounts were correct. Recast the income statement and the balance sheet to include the effects of these two transactions. Assume a 20 percent tax rate. (Hint: The corrected balance sheet total is $193,494.)

PC1–13.   At the end of 19A, Foster Corporation prepared the following annual income statement and balance sheet:

FOSTER CORPORATION
Income Statement
For the Year Ended December 31, 19A

Revenues	$280,000
Expenses...........................	248,000
Income before taxes..................	32,000
Income taxes (average rate, 30%)......	9,600
Net income.........................	$ 22,400

FOSTER CORPORATION
Balance Sheet
At December 31, 19A

Assets			Liabilities		
Cash.............................		$ 18,000	Accounts payable		$ 8,000
Accounts receivable		22,000	Income taxes payable		
Inventory (by count)		76,800	(one half unpaid)		4,800
Fixtures..........................	$25,000		Notes payable, 12%		
Less: Accumulated deprecia-			(due June 30, 19B)		20,000
tion.........................	7,000	18,000	Total liabilities...............		32,800
			Shareholders' Equity		
			Common stock, par		
			$10, 5,000 shares................	$50,000	
			Contributed surplus...............	10,000	
			Retained earnings.................	42,000	
			Total shareholders' equity		102,000
Total assets......................		$134,800	Total liabilities and shareholders' equity		$134,800

An independent audit of the above statements and underlying records revealed the following:

1. Depreciation expense included in total expense was $2,000 for 19A; it should have been $2,500.
2. A tentative order was received from a customer on December 31, 19A, for goods having a sales price of $10,000 and was included in sales revenue and accounts receivable. The goods were on hand (and included in the ending inventory), and it is quite likely a sale may not materialize; the customer will decide by January 20, 19B. This tentative order should not have been recognized as a sale in 19A.

Required:

Other than these two items, the amounts on the financial statements were correct. Recast the two statements to take into account the depreciation error and the incorrect recognition of the tentative order. Show computations and assume an average income tax rate of 30 percent. (Hint: Revised EPS is $3.01.)

PC1–14. As an individual who is reading this book, you are an accounting entity. You are not a sole proprietorship, a partnership, or a corporation but you are an entity. As such you can represent yourself by financial statements and you may have to for purposes of obtaining a bank loan or to provide financial information for one purpose or another. You have assets, liabilities, and owner's equity. The question is what are they, how can they be valued, and should they be included in your statement of financial position?

Required:

a. List all your attributes that you believe to be assets. Determine how you might value these assets. Use costs, benefits, or resale value of these assets. You may disguise your personal fortune if you feel better about it.

b. List your liabilities. Consider those for which you will have to use assets to extinguish. Value those you can and consider how you determined the value.

c. What is your owner's equity? Where did it come from? List the total amount and as many sources as possible including what you were born with.

2

Financial Reporting and the Fundamental Accounting Concepts

PURPOSE OF THIS CHAPTER

Chapter 1 introduced the primary elements of the income statement, balance sheet, and statement of changes in financial position. This chapter expands that discussion of external financial statements to include the classifications used on the statements. Also, it introduces some additional fundamental accounting concepts. Thus, the purpose of this chapter is to expand your background knowledge of financial statements. This knowledge will facilitate your study and understanding of the subsequent chapters. To accomplish this purpose, the chapter is divided into two parts.

Part A—Content of financial statements for external decision makers:

Discusses and illustrates the subclassifications of the financial information presented on external financial statements.

Part B—Uses of financial information in decision making and the fundamental concepts of accounting:

Expands the discussion in Chapter 1 of the use of financial information in decision making.

Presents the fundamental concepts that underlie the accounting for, and reporting of, information in the financial statements.

Part A—Content of Financial Statements for External Decision Makers

CLASSIFICATION OF ITEMS ON THE FINANCIAL STATEMENTS

External decision makers (that use financial statements) are varied as to background, education, experience, financial interests, and problems because they include investors, creditors, employees, governmental agencies, unions, customers, and other interested parties. Financial statements often are referred to as **general-purpose financial statements** because they are prepared to serve the diverse needs of these groups.

To enhance the clarity and usefulness of financial statements to the wide range of decision makers, **subclassifications** of the economic information presented are included on the financial statements.

In this part of the chapter, the discussions will include a comprehensive illustration of the financial statements of a medium-sized company. We then will briefly discuss a more complicated set of actual financial statements as they were presented by a large, well-known company—Consolidated-Bathurst Inc. (see Special Supplement B immediately preceding the Index).

This part of the chapter continues our introduction to financial statements so you should concentrate on understanding the nature of the classifications and the presentation of accounting information in the financial statements rather than on how the amounts shown were derived. At the conclusion of this chapter, we do not anticipate that you will absorb all aspects of the financial statements that are presented; however, the primary features of each statement should be understood. You also should appreciate the importance of the end product of the accounting process—the financial statements. You will be able to maintain perspective in the chapters that follow when studying the details of information processing, measuring, and reporting in terms of the accounting model. As you study the subsequent chapters, you should return frequently to this one for reference points and further study. Also, the exhibits presented in this chapter will be helpful as a guide in solving some of the assigned problems in subsequent chapters.

To assist the users of financial statements, some standardization of classifications has evolved. When classifications are included on the statements, they sometimes are referred to as **classified financial statements.** Classified financial statements vary in terminology and arrangement from those for Business Aids given in Chapter 1. These differences reflect the fact that financial statements are tailored to the **needs of a wide range of decision makers,** depending upon the type of company and the characteristics of the industry. As a basis for discussion of these classifications, this section presents the financial statements for Diamond, Inc., a large department store that has been in business for more than 40 years.

The income statement

Exhibit 2–1 presents an income statement for Diamond.[1] It follows this basic model: **Revenues − Expenses = Net income.** Therefore, Exhibit 2–1, stripped of the detailed items, shows the following subclassifications:

(1) **Revenues**

(2) **Expenses:**
　　　Cost of goods sold (which is an expense)
　　　Operating expenses
　　　Financial expenses
　　　Income tax expense

(3) **Income:**
　　　Income before extraordinary items
　　　　Extraordinary gains and losses
　　　Net income

(4) **Earnings per share (EPS)**

We will discuss the meaning of each of these classifications.

Revenues. Revenues were defined in Chapter 1. The revenue of a business that sells services is called **service revenue.** The revenue of a business that sells products or merchandise is called **sales revenue.** Merchandise sold and later returned by the customer represents **returned sales** and reduces revenue. Similarly, allowances granted to customers, say, for a defect in the goods purchased from the store, reduce revenue. Such returns and allowances are **contra revenues** rather than expenses.[2] Therefore, **gross sales** for the period must be reduced by these two amounts to derive the correct net revenue amount, or **net sales revenue,** for the period. Observe the manner of reporting sales revenue in Exhibit 2–1.

Expenses. Expenses were defined in Chapter 1. An income statement may be designed to reflect several classifications of expenses. These classifications tend to vary, depending upon the type of business. For a merchandising business, which is one that sells goods manufactured by others, the usual classifications of expenses are as follows:

1. Cost of goods sold. This expense reflects the amount of expense that was incurred for the merchandise (or goods) sold during the period. For example, Diamond sold goods during the period, at selling price, amounting to $3,615,000 net revenue. This merchandise, when purchased by Diamond, cost $2,416,000 as reflected in Exhibit 2–1. The difference between these two

---

[1]The income statement discussed and illustrated in this section is sometimes referred to as a **multiple-step** income statement because it shows several groupings of data and after each group (or step) shows a step difference. Each such difference is appropriately labeled, such as gross margin on sales. In contrast, a single-step income statement would be similar to that illustrated in Exhibit 1–4 because only two major categories (revenues and expenses) were shown and there were no intermediate "step" differences. Many published income statements follow the single-step format. The classifications illustrated for Diamond are used frequently; however, they are not mandatory.

[2]Contra as used in accounting means an offset to, or a reduction of, a basic amount.

**EXHIBIT 2–1
Income statement
classifications
illustrated**

DIAMOND, INC.
Income Statement
For the Year Ended December 31, 19D

(1) Rev.	Gross sales revenue........................		$3,620,000
	Less: Sales returns and allowances..........		5,000
	Net sales revenue...........................		$3,615,000
(2) Exp.	Less: Cost of goods sold....................		2,416,000
	Gross margin on sales......................		1,199,000
	Operating expenses:		
	Selling (distribution) expenses:		
	Sales salaries...........................	$399,000	
	Advertising and promotion..............	200,000	
	Depreciation, store equipment...........	15,000	
	Insurance...............................	18,000	
	Taxes (excluding income tax expense).....	13,200	
	Warranty expense......................	3,000	
	Amortization of trademarks...............	2,000	
	Miscellaneous..........................	9,800	
	Total selling expenses...............	660,000	
	General and administrative expenses:		
	Administrative salaries..................	170,000	
	Rent expense...........................	9,000	
	Office supplies used.....................	8,100	
	Estimated losses on doubtful accounts.....	3,600	
	Depreciation, office equipment...........	1,000	
	Insurance...............................	2,000	
	Taxes (excluding income tax expense).....	400	
	Miscellaneous..........................	1,900	
	Total general and administrative expenses......................	196,000	
	Total operating expenses.........		856,000
	Pretax income from operations...............		343,000
	Financial expenses and financial revenues:		
	Interest expense.........................	56,000	
	Revenue from investments and funds.......	13,000	
	Net financial expense..................		43,000
	Pretax income..............................		300,000
	Income tax on normal operations...........		138,000
(3) Inc.	Income before extraordinary items............		162,000
	Extraordinary items:		
	Gain on sale of land held for appreciation*......................	51,000	
	Less: Income tax on the gain.............	13,000	38,000
	Net income.................................		$ 200,000
(4) EPS	Earnings per share (EPS) of common stock:		
	Income before extraordinary items..........		$ 9.13
	Extraordinary items.......................		2.54
	Net income.................................		$11.67

*We have assumed that this transaction met the criteria for an extraordinary item. The land was sold for $56,000 less its very low cost of $5,000, resulting in a pretax gain of $51,000.

amounts, $1,199,000, is known as the **gross margin on sales** (formerly called gross profit on sales). The gross margin indicates the markup on all of the goods sold during the period.[3] To illustrate, the average markup based **on cost** for Diamond was $1,199,000 ÷ $2,416,000 = 49.6 percent; and based **on selling price,** it was $1,199,000 ÷ $3,615,000 = 33.2 percent.

2. *Operating expenses.* These are the usual expenses that were incurred in operating the business during the period. Often they are subclassified further, as reflected in Exhibit 2–1, between **selling expenses** and **general and administrative expenses. Selling expenses** (often called distribution expenses) comprise all amounts incurred during the period in performing the sales activities. **General and administrative expenses** include the overall business expenses that are not directly related to selling activities, such as the president's salary and the expenses of the accounting department.

3. *Financial expenses.* These are the expenses incurred as a result of borrowing money or for credit extended to the company. The cost of credit usually is referred to as **interest expense.** Interest on debt is a **financing expense** rather than an operating expense; therefore, it is set out in a separate category from cost of goods sold and operating expenses.

Some businesses also **collect** interest for credit they have extended to others which is called **interest revenue** (discussed in a later chapter). When the amount of interest revenue is not substantial, instead of reporting it under the revenue caption along with sales and service revenue, sometimes it is offset against interest expense as shown on Exhibit 2–1. When interest revenue is reported under the revenue classification, "gross margin on sales" cannot be reported because gross margin would include revenues not related to sales. For this reason, and the desire to report both financial expenses and financial revenue under one caption, companies often report these two items as shown in Exhibit 2–1.

Extraordinary items. This is a special classification used to report nonoperating gains and losses. These items are defined in accounting as having the following three characteristics:

1. They should not be typical of normal business activities.
2. They should not be expected to occur regularly.
3. They should not have to be considered as recurring factors in any evaluations of normal operations.

Therefore, they are set out separately to aid the user in evaluating the profit performance of the business. To include them in the usual, regular, ongoing revenue or expense categories would lead the user to believe extraordinary items are normal and will occur again in the forseeable future. Observe in

---

[3]Markup is the amount added to the cost of an item to determine its sale price. Markup can be expressed as an amount or as a percent.

Exhibit 2–1 that **extraordinary items** are reported **after** the caption "Income before extraordinary items" and immediately **before** net income.[4]

Income tax expense. This is the amount of income tax expense incurred for the period encompassed by the income statement. Income tax expense will appear only on the income statements of corporations because other forms of business organization discussed in Chapter 1 are not subject to income tax. The amount of income subject to tax is defined by the Income Tax Act and often does not agree with the "accounting" income amount shown on the income statement. Detailed consideration of income taxes is beyond the scope of this book (however, see the overview in Special Supplement A that follows the last chapter). We will use simplified tax rates and computations of income taxes to demonstrate appropriate reporting of the income tax expense and income taxes payable.

Observe in Exhibit 2–1 that total income tax expense is $138,000 + $13,000 = $151,000. When there are extraordinary items, income tax expense must be reported in two parts:

1. Income tax based on normal operations is reported above the caption "Income before extraordinary items" ($138,000 in Exhibit 2–1).
2. Income tax based on the extraordinary items is reported with those items ($13,000 in Exhibit 2–1).

Income Amounts Observe on the income statement (Exhibit 2–1) that three separate "income" amounts are reported; pretax income (an optional step amount), income before extraordinary items (required when there are extraordinary items), and net income. Income before extraordinary items is the difference between "ordinary" revenues and expenses. Net income always is the last item in the body of the income statement; as a result, it often is called the bottom-line figure. It is after extraordinary items and has no qualifications. **Net income is the difference between total revenues and total expenses** (including extraordinary items).

Earnings per share (EPS). A corporation (but not a sole proprietorship or a partnership) is required to report EPS amounts on the income statement or in a note referenced from the income statement. An EPS amount must be reported for income before extraordinary items and for net income.[5] The com-

---

[4]CICA Handbook, Section 3480 mandates that the following format be used at the bottom of the income statement when there are extraordinary items:
Income before extraordinary items.
Extraordinary items (net of any related income tax).
Net income.

[5]CICA Handbook, Section 3500, requires that the two EPS amounts as shown on Exhibit 2–1 be reported; viz, (1) on income before extraordinary items and (2) on net income. However, many companies also report an EPS amount for the extraordinary category, as shown on Exhibit 2–1. Companies with few shareholders are exempted from disclosing EPS unless they wish to do it. Thus, EPS disclosure is required for most of the larger corporations.

putation of EPS was illustrated and discussed briefly in Chapter 1. In that chapter, Business Aids, Inc., reported only one EPS amount because there were no extraordinary items. In contrast, Diamond reported three EPS amounts because there was an extraordinary item.[6]

The balance sheet

The balance sheet for Diamond, presented in Exhibit 2–2, is based on the accounting model: **Assets − Liabilities = Owners' equity** (see Chapter 1). To assist decision makers, each of the three major categories of items—assets, liabilities, and owners' equity—is subclassified on the basis of one of its primary characteristics. The following subclassifications usually are used:[7]

Balance Sheet

Assets **(by order of liquidity)**	**Liabilities** **(by order of time to maturity)**
Current assets	Current liabilities
Long-term investments and funds	Long-term liabilities
Operational (i.e., fixed) assets	
Intangible assets	**Owners' Equity** **(by order of permanency)**
Deferred charges	Contributed capital
Other assets	Retained earnings
	Unrealized capital

Exhibit 2–2 (Diamond's balance sheet) presents the three major categories—assets, liabilities, and owners' equity—in a **vertical** arrangement that is called the **report format.** In contrast, the balance sheet for Business Aids (Exhibit 1–5). presented the major categories in a **horizontal** arrangement with the assets to the left and the liabilities and owners' equity to the right which is called the **account format.** Both formats are used.

We will discuss each of the subclassifications on the balance sheet.

Current assets. Current assets are resources (i.e., assets) owned by the entity that are reasonably expected to be realized in cash or used up within one year from the balance sheet date or during the **normal operating cycle** of the business, whichever is the longer. The normal operating cycle tends to vary

---

[6]EPS amounts are computed **only for common stock outstanding** (preferred stock is discussed in a later chapter). At this point in your study you need not be concerned about the computation of EPS amounts when both common and preferred stock are outstanding. This topic will be discussed later. However, for those interested, the amounts on Exhibit 2–1 were computed as follows:

Income before extraordinary items:
($162,000 − $25,000, the dividend claim
    of the preferred stock) ÷ 15,000 shares = $ 9.13
Extraordinary gain:
$38,000 ÷ 15,000 shares =   2.54
Net income:
($200,000 − $25,000) ÷ 15,000 shares = $11.67

[7]The subclassification titles vary somewhat in actual practice. For example, operational assets often are called property, plant, and equipment.

**EXHIBIT 2–2
Balance sheet
classifications
illustrated**

DIAMOND, INC.
Balance Sheet
At December 31, 19D

Assets

Current assets:

Cash.		$ 150,000
Short-term investments.		40,000
Accounts receivable	$425,000	
Less: Allowance for doubtful accounts	15,000	410,000
Notes receivable, short term		20,000
Merchandise inventory		1,510,000
Office supplies inventory		1,000
Prepaid insurance.		4,000
Total current assets		$2,135,000

Long-term investments and funds:

Shares of X Corporation	10,000	
Sinking fund to pay bonds.	150,000	
Total long-term investments and funds		160,000

Operational assets: *Used within Comp to generate revenue.*

Store equipment	150,000	
Less: Accumulated depreciation	60,000	90,000
Office equipment	16,000	
Less: Accumulated depreciation	4,000	12,000
Total operational assets.		102,000

Intangible assets: *cannot touch, usually a right.*

Trademarks . . . . *Goodwill*	60,000

Other assets:

Land acquired for future store site.		68,000
Total assets.		$2,525,000

Liabilities

Current liabilities:

Accounts payable	$ 180,000	
Notes payable, short term	100,000	
Wages payable	16,000	
Income tax payable	30,000	
Estimated warranty obligations.	24,000	
Total current liabilities.		$ 350,000

Long-term liabilities:

Bank notes payable (maturity 19F).	100,000	
Bonds payable (7%, maturity 19N).	500,000	
Total long-term liabilities		600,000
Total liabilities.		950,000

Shareholders' Equity

Contributed capital:

Preferred stock, 5%, cumulative nonconvertible, 5,000 shares outstanding, par $100	500,000	
Common stock, 15,000 shares outstanding, no par	750,000	
Contributed surplus from the issue of preferred stock	50,000	
Total contributed capital.	1,300,000	

Retained earnings (see statement of retained

earnings below).	275,000	
Total shareholders' equity		1,575,000
Total liabilities and shareholders' equity.		$2,525,000

(handwritten margin notes: "Know This", "Normally not into 2 categories", "If goes under share 550,000")

for each business because it is the average time required for the normal operating cycle—cash investment in inventory to cash collection from customers. For a merchandising company it may be represented graphically as in Exhibit 2–3.

Observe the Diamond's balance sheet (Exhibit 2–2) reported seven different current assets starting with cash and ending with prepaid insurance. Current assets are listed on the balance sheet essentially in order of decreasing liquidity. **Liquidity** refers to the average period of time required to convert a noncash resource to cash. In addition to cash, current assets include short-term or temporary investments, accounts receivable, notes receivable, inventories, and prepaid expenses.

Short-term investments are current assets because it is expected that they will be sold for cash within the next year or the next operating cycle, whichever is longer. **Accounts receivable** are amounts due the company on "open account" from customers and are current assets because they are expected to be collected in the near future. Observe the **contra amount** (contra because it is an offset), allowance for doubtful accounts. This contra amount will be discussed in Chapter 6. It represents an estimate of the amount of accounts receivable that will be uncollectible (i.e., bad debts). **Notes receivable, short term,** is a current asset for essentially the same reason as accounts receivable. **Merchandise inventory** is a current asset because it represents merchandise on hand that will be sold for cash or on short-term credit in the near future. **Office supplies inventory** represents items on hand that will be consumed (i.e., used) in the short term. **Prepaid expenses** are goods or services paid for in advance of their use, such as a two-year insurance premium paid at the beginning of the term of the coverage. As each year of the coverage passes, a portion of the premium paid becomes expense. To illustrate, assume a two-year insurance premium of $600 was paid on January 1, 19D. At the end of 19D, half of the insurance period would have expired. Therefore, **Insurance expense** for 19D would be $300 and the remaining $300 would be reported on the 19D balance

EXHIBIT 2–3
Operating cycle for a retail business

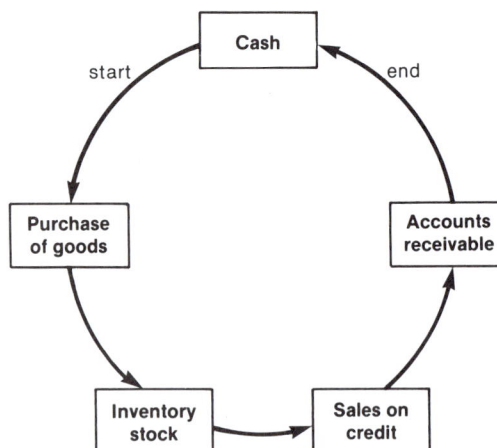

sheet as a current asset because the company still has insurance coverage due for one more year. Similarly, in 19E, Insurance expense would be $300 and there would be no prepaid insurance on this policy at December 31, 19E.

Financial institutions and others who lend funds to a company are interested in the current assets of the borrower because such assets provide one indication of the **short-term ability of the business to meet early maturing debts.** For example, a banker making a decision to grant short-term credit to Diamond would consider the amount of each current asset at the date of the loan and throughout its term as important to the lending decision. Such amounts also would be useful in making cash and income projections about the future.

Long-term investments and funds. This noncurrent asset classification reports the investments the company intends to hold for the long run (more than one year, or the operating cycle, whichever is longer). **Long-term investments include such items as the shares and bonds of other companies that have been purchased as investments, real estate investments, and so on.** This classification also includes cash set aside in **special funds** (such as a savings account) for use in the future for a specified long-term purpose. The "Sinking fund to pay bonds" reported in Exhibit 2–2 represents cash set aside for a special purpose. This fund will be expended at maturity date to retire (i.e., pay off) the bonds payable reported under "Long-term liabilities."[8] While the fund is in existence, it will earn interest revenue that will be reflected on the income statement as revenue from investments and funds (see "Revenue from investments and funds" on Exhibit 2–1).

Operational assets. This classification sometimes is called **property, plant, and equipment** or **fixed assets.** It includes those assets having physical substance (i.e., they are tangible) that were acquired for use in **operating the business** rather than for resale as inventory items or simply held as investments. Typically, they include buildings owned; land on which the buildings reside; and equipment, tools, furniture, and fixtures used in operating the business. They are long-lived and are used in the production and/or sale of other assets or services. Operational assets, with the exception of land, are depreciated over time as they are used (i.e., worn out). Because their productive usefulness decreases as they are used, their initial cost is apportioned to expense over their estimated useful lives. This apportionment of cost over useful life is known as **depreciation.** Land is not depreciated because it does not wear out as do machinery, buildings, and equipment. The amount of depreciation computed for **each period** is reported on the income statement as depreciation **expense,** and the **cumulative,** or accumulated, amount of depreciation expense for all past periods from acquisition date is **deducted** (as a contra amount) on the balance sheet from the cost of the asset to derive **"book or**

---

[8]The term *sinking fund,* although widely used in accounting, is not descriptive. It simply refers to a cash fund set aside to pay a long-term debt at the maturity or due date, or for other future needs.

carrying value.'' To illustrate, for Diamond, the depreciation for office equipment was determined and reported as follows:

1. **Income statement (Exhibit 2–1)**—Depreciation expense on office equipment for 19D, $1,000, computed as follows:

$$\frac{\text{Cost of the equipment}}{\text{Estimated useful life}} = \frac{\$16,000}{16 \text{ years}}$$
$$= \$1,000 \text{ depreciation expense (each year)}$$

2. **Balance sheet (Exhibit 2–2)**—The amounts shown for office equipment represent the following:

Office equipment, cost when acquired on January 1, 19A	$16,000
Accumulated depreciation expense from January 1, 19A, to December 31, 19D ($1,000 × 4 years)	4,000
Difference—book value on December 31, 19D, the amount of equipment cost not yet allocated to depreciation expense	$12,000

The difference, $12,000, usually is called the **book value** or **carrying value** of the office equipment. At the end of the 16th year, the book value of the office equipment will be zero because the equipment has no **residual** value at the end of its useful life to the entity. Depreciation expense on store equipment was computed on the basis of a 10-year life (i.e., $150,000 ÷ 10 years = $15,000). Depreciation is discussed in detail in Chapter 9.

Intangible assets. This classification includes those long-lived assets that have no **physical existence** (i.e., they are intangible) and have a long life. Their value is derived from the **rights and privileges** that accompany ownership. Examples are patents, trademarks, copyrights, franchises, and goodwill. Intangible assets usually are not acquired for resale but rather are used in the continuing operations of the business. Thus, in this respect, they are similar to operational assets. Diamond reported one intangible asset—trademarks (see Exhibit 2–2). Intangible assets are discussed in detail in Chapter 9.

Deferred charges. This classification represents long-term prepayments for goods and services that are expected to contribute to the earning of revenues in the future. They are the same as the current asset prepaid expenses (defined above), except that the prepayment extends **beyond** one year or the operating cycle, whichever is longer. For example, the prepayment of a five-year insurance premium of $500 on January 1, 19A, theoretically would be reported as follows at December 31, 19A:

Income statement:	
Insurance expense for 19A	$100
Balance sheet:	
Current assets:	
Prepaid insurance	100
Deferred charges:	
Prepaid insurance	300

When the prepaid amounts are relatively small (i.e., not material), the total amount of the long-term prepayment often is reported as a prepaid expense. Observe in Exhibit 2–2 that Diamond did not report any deferred charges.

Other assets. A business may own assets that do not fit reasonably into one of the preceding classifications. Thus, a miscellaneous category called other assets may be needed. For example, operational assets retired from service and held for disposal would be reported under this category in a manner similar to the land acquired for future store site in Exhibit 2–2.

Current liabilities. Current liabilities are those short-term debts at the balance sheet date that are expected to be paid out of the current assets listed on the same balance sheet. Short-term liabilities are expected to be paid during the coming year or the operating cycle of the business, whichever is longer. Diamond's balance sheet (Exhibit 2–2) reports five different current liabilities that sum to $350,000. Accounts payable represent amounts owed on open account to suppliers of merchandise purchased for resale. Short-term notes payable evidence interest-bearing debt that will mature within the coming year (or operating cycle if it is longer), and wages payable represent amounts due employees not yet paid at balance sheet date. Income tax payable reflects the amount of income tax that must be paid to the government in the near future. Estimated warranty obligations represent future amounts that will have to be expended to fulfill guarantees on merchandise already sold or services already rendered.

Working capital is not a separate classification on the balance sheet; however, it is a widely used concept that is based on current assets and current liabilities. It can be expressed as a dollar amount or as a ratio as follows:

As a dollar amount:

Computation:	Total current assets	−	Total current liabilities	=	Working capital dollars
Example based on Diamond:	$2,135,000	−	$350,000	=	$1,785,000

As a ratio:

Computation:	Total current assets	÷	Total current liabilities	=	Working capital ratio
Example:	$2,135,000	÷	$350,000	=	6.10

Thus, the working capital of Diamond for 19D was $1,785,000, and the amount of current assets was 6.10 times the amount of current liabilities. Working capital (in dollars or as a ratio) is a measure of the liquidity of the business, that is, its ability to pay its short-term debts and early maturities of its long-term debts. For example, a banker considering a short-term loan may not be impressed by a large amount of current assets; the working capital ratio may be, say, .80, which indicates that current assets are only 80 percent of current liabilities.

Long-term liabilities.   Long-term liabilities represent all of the liabilities that do not qualify as current liabilities. Thus, long-term liabilities are those that will not be paid within one year of the balance sheet date (or within one operating cycle if it is longer). They are different from current liabilities only because of the extended period before maturity. Exhibit 2–2 reports two long-term liabilities for Diamond: "Bank notes payable" (due 2 years hence) which represents amounts borrowed from a bank; and "Bonds payable," (due 10 years from the date of the balance sheet) which represents amounts borrowed from long-term investors.

Owners' equity.   Owners' equity (called shareholders' equity for a corporation) represents the residual claim of the owners (i.e., A − L = OE). This claim results from the initial contributions of the shareholders (usually called **contributed capital**) plus the accumulated earnings of the company less the accumulated dividends declared (usually called **retained earnings**). Exhibit 2–2 reports these two categories of shareholders' equity in order to disclose the two **sources** of owners' equity. Often there is more than one class of capital stock, and each is reported separately. Diamond's balance sheet reports two classes of capital stock: (1) preferred stock, 5,000 shares outstanding; and (2) common stock, 15,000 shares outstanding.[9]

The amount labeled "Contributed surplus from the issue of preferred stock," indicates that the preferred stock initially was sold at an average price of $110 per share. This was $10 per share above its par value of $100 per share because the "excess" was $10 × 5,000 shares = $50,000. The par value is reported as one amount, and the excess is reported separately. The sum of the two amounts represents the amount contributed by the shareholders when the shares were sold initially. The amount of owners' equity ($1,575,000) can be verified as total assets ($2,525,000) minus total liabilities ($950,000). The amount of owners' equity does not represent the amount that the shareholders would receive if the business were sold; simply it is the **"book value"** of their residual claim.

THE STATEMENT OF RETAINED EARNINGS

The balance sheet for Diamond (Exhibit 2–2) is supplemented by the **statement of retained earnings** (Exhibit 2–4). The information in this statement is

---

[9]Preferred stock is designated so because it has certain specified preferences over the common stock. In this particular case, the preferred stock is reported as having two preferences: (1) a dividend preference of 5 percent—this means that dividends on the preferred stock must be paid each year equivalent to 5 percent of the par value per share of the preferred before any dividends can be paid on the common stock; and (2) a cumulative preference—this means that should dividends equivalent to 5 percent not be paid on the preferred stock for any year, the amount not paid will cumulate and must be paid in subsequent years before any dividends can be paid on the common stock. Capital stock is discussed in detail in Chapter 12.

EXHIBIT 2–4
Statement of retained earnings illustrated

DIAMOND, INC.	
Statement of Retained Earnings	
For the Year Ended December 31, 19D	
Beginning balance, retained earnings, January 1, 19D	$220,000
Add net income for 19D	200,000
Total	420,000
Less dividends declared and paid during 19D	145,000
Ending balance, retained earnings, December 31, 19D	$275,000

necessary to attain "full disclosure." Some companies report the information on the balance sheet. The statement of retained earnings explains the increases and decreases in retained earnings during the period. The statement starts with the balance of retained earnings at the beginning of the period. To that balance, net income for the year is added and dividends declared during the year are deducted. Dividends reduce retained earnings on the date they are **declared,** even if they have not yet been paid in cash, because a **legally enforceable obligation** to pay arises on the declaration date. A dividend is **not an expense** on the income statement; rather it is a **distribution** of accumulated earnings. Note that net income for the period ($200,000 for Diamond) is carried from the income statement to the statement of retained earnings, and in that manner it is then carried to shareholders' equity on the balance sheet. Thus, each period net income increases shareholders' equity. After a number of years of operations, retained earnings becomes the primary **source** of shareholders' equity in most corporations.

THE STATEMENT OF CHANGES IN FINANCIAL POSITION (SCFP)

The statement of changes in financial position (SCFP)[10] was discussed briefly in Chapter 1, and a very simple situation was illustrated in Exhibit 1–6. In contrast, a more complex situation (Diamond's) is illustrated in Exhibit 2–5. The SCFP has as its primary purpose the reporting of all inflows (i.e., sources) of cash (or working capital if prepared on that basis) and all outflows (i.e., uses) of cash (or working capital). This information is particularly useful to decision makers (such as shareholders, other potential investors, and creditors of the business) in assessing the probable **future** amounts, timing, and uncertainty of net cash inflows to the business.

The SCFP for Diamond is typical of many retail businesses. For example, the following analytical points may be observed:

1. Total cash inflows amounted to $371,700, and total cash outflows amounted to $263,000, which caused a net increase in cash of $108,700.

---

[10]Proposals have been made in Section 1540 of the *CICA Handbook* to entitle this statement Cash Flow Information. The title, SCFP, may still be retained if required by law. Discussions of refinements to this statement are provided in Chapter 15.

EXHIBIT 2–5
Statement of changes in financial position (SCFP), classifications illustrated

DIAMOND, INC.
Statement of Changes in Financial Position, Cash Basis
For the Year Ended December 31, 19D

Sources of cash:

From operations:			
Sales revenue		$3,615,000	
Revenue from investments		13,000	
		3,628,000	
Adjustments for **noncash** revenue for this period (deduction)		(5,000)*(a)	
Cash inflow from sale and investment revenues		3,623,000	
Expenses, including cost of goods sold	$3,466,000*(b)		
Adjustments for **noncash** expenses (deduction)	(71,700)*(c)		
Cash outflow for expenses		3,394,300	
Net cash inflow from continuing operations and investments			$228,700
From extraordinary items (net of income taxes):			
Disposal of land ($56,000–$13,000)			43,000*(d)
From bank note, long term			100,000
Total cash generated (inflows) during the year			371,700

Uses of cash:

To pay dividends during the period:			
On preferred stock		25,000	
On common stock		120,000	
To increase bond sinking fund		50,000	
To purchase land for future store site		68,000	
Total cash used (outflows) during the year			263,000
Increase in cash during the year			$108,700

Explanations:
*At this point in your study, there is no need to be concerned with the derivation of these amounts; however, they may be calculated as follows:

(a)The adjustment of $5,000 to revenue was due to an increase in accounts receivable of that amount during the period, which means that this amount of cash will be collected later.

(b)Expenses from the income statement (Exhibit 2–1):

Cost of goods sold	$2,416,000
Operating expenses	856,000
Interest expense	56,000
Income tax expense	138,000
Total expenses (for this period)	$3,466,000

(c)Noncash expenses from the income statement (Exhibit 2–1):

Depreciation expense, store equipment	$15,000
Amortization of trademarks	2,000
Estimated losses on doubtful accounts	3,600
Depreciation expense, office equipment	1,000
Subtotal	21,600
Net change in accruals, deferrals, and accounts payable (data not given herein)	50,100
Total	$71,700

(The cash outflow related to the noncash expenses occurred before, or will occur after, this period.)

(d)The land was sold for $56,000 cash, of which $13,000 was paid for income taxes on the gain, leaving a net cash inflow of $43,000 from this source (also see Exhibit 2–1).

2. Of the total cash inflows of $371,700, 62 percent (i.e., $228,700 ÷ $371,700) came from **operations** of the business. This statistic is especially important because it represents the normal operations that are likely to continue into the future. In contrast, the $43,000 cash inflow from **extraordinary items,** because they are by definition unusual and infrequent, cannot be expected to continue into the future.

3. Of the total cash outflows of $263,000, 55 percent was for dividends paid to the shareholders. This outflow will vary depending upon the decision by the board of directors of the corporation each year as to dividends.

Part B—Uses of Financial Information in Decision Making and the Fundamental Concepts of Accounting

FINANCIAL STATEMENTS RELATED TO THE DECISION PROCESSES OF EXTERNAL DECISION MAKERS

Individual external decision makers (see Chapter 1) do not participate directly in the preparation of the financial statements they use or directly in the development of the accounting guidelines (i.e., GAAP) used in the preparation of such statements. Rather, decision makers seek to elicit (select) information from the financial reports that will help them make better decisions than otherwise on specific problems they encounter.

In this part of the chapter, the selection and analysis by decision makers of relevant information from the financial statements is introduced. This part also presents an outline of the **fundamental concepts** that underlie financial accounting and reporting. This outline is presented in this chapter as a point of reference that will be used throughout the chapters to follow.

The broad objective of financial reporting is to provide information that is useful in making decisions. This objective responds to the fact that the investors (i.e., the owners), potential investors, and creditors are concerned primarily with the probable **future cash** returns they can reasonably expect to receive on their investments. The future returns are related to the profits (and losses) of the business and to the resources (assets) it owns and its liabilities. In a similar manner, the creditors of the business are concerned about their future cash returns in the form of interest to be received and collection of the principals of the liabilities at maturity dates.[11] Decision makers are concerned directly with the future rather than with the past; therefore, decision makers must

---

[11]*FASB Statement of Financial Accounting Concepts No. 1,* "Objectives of Financial Reporting by Business Enterprises" (Stamford, Conn., November 1978), states: "Since investors' and creditors' cash flows are related to enterprise cash flows, financial reporting should provide information to help investors, creditors, and others assess the amounts, timing, and uncertainty of prospective net cash inflows to the related enterprise.

make projections regarding the future. This fact means that the financial information reported in financial statements should have **qualitative characteristics** that focus on their decision-making needs. The information must be **relevant** to their needs, and it must be **reliable.**

Recent past events and trends, if measured and reported appropriately, provide an important basis on which decision makers develop reasonable estimates concerning the future. Financial statements report periodically on the revenues, expenses, incomes, assets, and liabilities of a business; therefore, they provide valuable data for most financial projections made by investors.

In addition to considering the data reported on the financial statements, decision makers must bring to bear in their projections knowledge of such factors as technological changes, environmental influences, competitive forces, behavioral considerations, general economic conditions, and industry characteristics.

Throughout the chapters that follow you will learn more about how financial statements may help decision makers assess the **future prospects** of a business. At this time, only an introduction is possible. For this introduction we will refer to the financial statements of Diamond presented in Part A of this chapter (Exhibits 2–1 through 2–5).

In assessing the probable future cash returns of Diamond, a decision maker probably would want to carefully examine and analyze the company's recent financial statements, say, for the past three to five years. For example, the SCFP (Exhibit 2–5) would reveal trends as to the primary **sources** and **uses** of cash, such as the amount of cash generated by operations (62 percent) or from loans (27 percent), and the primary cash-demanding activities such as the payment of dividends (55 percent) and the purchase of long-lived assets (26 percent). A knowledge of each source and each use over several consecutive years would be helpful in projecting future sources and uses of cash.

In a similar manner, a decision maker would make other analyses of the income statement and the balance sheet because they report past financial performance of the company. The income statement reports the normal operational activities that, if continued, would be expected to generate future cash inflows. The performance levels (i.e., efficiency) of the business that can be projected will indicate future cash flows that may reasonably be expected from this primary source. In a similar manner, certain assets reported on the balance sheet provide a basis for projecting other probable cash inflows (such as from the sale of an investment or a tract of land), and the reported liabilities indicate significant future cash demands. These brief comments suggest the importance of understanding **what financial statements say** and what they **do not say** and, just as importantly, how to analyze them to maximize their usefulness in the decision-making process.

The analysis of financial statements is emphasized in the various chapters that follow with an overall view presented in Chapter 16. By way of introduction, the concept of **proportional relationships** is presented as one phase of such an analysis. Proportional analysis involves the selection of two important amounts from the financial statements that are related in a meaningful way.

One, known as the **base amount,** is divided into the other to express the proportional relationship between them. The result may be expressed as a ratio, a percent, or sometimes as a dollar amount. Two examples already have been presented: (1) earnings per share and (2) working capital. Two additional examples based on the financial statements of Diamond, Inc., which focus on **profitability,** as presented below:

1. $$\text{Profit margin} = \frac{\text{Net income}}{\text{Net sales}} = \frac{\$162,000}{\$3,615,000} = 0.045$$

   Thus, for the year, Diamond earned 4.5 percent on each dollar sales.[12]

2. Along with EPS the concept of **return on investment** (ROI) is widely used to measure profitability.

The concept of ROI is especially useful to decision makers. It is particularly significant because it expresses the relationship between **income** and **investment.** The income statement provides the income amount, and the balance sheet provides the investment amount.

The concept of ROI is applied frequently by almost everyone in one way or another. To illustrate, suppose you invested $1,000 on January 1, 19A, and at the end of 19A you received back $1,200. Disregarding income taxes, you may say that you earned $200 during the year on your investment. Based on these amounts, what would be your ROI (i.e., the return on your investment)? You may calculate that your return for the year was $200 ÷ $1,000 = 20 percent on the investment. Similarly, the ROI for a **business** for a specific period of time may be computed as follows:

$$\frac{\text{Net income}}{\text{Investment (owners' equity)}} = \text{Return on investment (ROI)}$$

The ROI earned by Diamond for 19D would be computed as follows:[13]

$$\frac{\$162,000 \text{ (from Exhibit 2–1)}}{\$1,575,000 \text{ (from Exhibit 2–2)}} = 10.29\%$$

FUNDAMENTAL CONCEPTS UNDERLYING FINANCIAL ACCOUNTING AND REPORTING

This section presents an overview of the theoretical or conceptual foundation of financial accounting and reporting. This conceptual foundation is pre-

---

[12]To compute profit margin when there are extraordinary items, income before extraordinary items rather than net income usually should be used to avoid the distortion caused by the unusual and infrequently recurring items.

[13]Depending upon the nature of the problem and the preference of the decision maker, the income amount may be either (1) income before extraordinary items or (2) net income. Similarly, the investment amount used may be either (1) owners' equity or (2) total equity (i.e., liabilities plus owners' equity). When total equity is used, interest expense (net of tax) should be added back to income (see Chapter 16).

sented (in Exhibit 2–6), in overall perspective, to facilitate your study and understanding of the "why" as you study the "how" of accounting in the chapters that follow. Upon completion of this chapter you are not expected to fully understand this conceptual structure, nor to appreciate its full significance (and certainly not to memorize it). Rather, the conceptual foundation is presented here to help you answer questions as they arise during your study of subsequent chapters. By studying both the *how* of accounting and *why* it is done in specific ways, you will develop a much better understanding of the process of accounting and be able to **interpret** its results in more meaningful and useful ways.

The fundamental concepts underlying financial accounting and reporting that have been specified by the accounting profession may be broadly characterized as follows.[14]

1. **Users** of financial statements identified.
2. **Objectives** of financial statements.
3. **Qualitative characteristics** of financial statements.
4. **Implementation assumptions** of financial statements.
5. **Elements** of financial statements.
6. **Implementation principles** of accounting.
7. **Detailed** accounting practices and procedures.

In later chapters, it will be important when considering specific procedures and practices to remember that the concepts discussed here are proposals only. Practice may differ in both conceptual terms and in the results achieved. However, the concepts listed here can and do serve as a useful basis from which to judge existing practices.

Each of the above seven characterizations is summarized and illustrated in Exhibit 2–6.

Financial accounting and reporting to **external** parties must conform to specific **concepts** and guidelines formulated primarily by the accounting profession to protect the interests of the external decision makers by assuring, to the extent it is practical, that the external financial statements are reasonably complete, relevant, reliable, and not misleading. These fundamental concepts are in a process of continuing evolution to meet the changing needs of society and to keep the financial accounting measurements and reporting relevant to the current problems of external decision makers. Changes are initiated primarily because of financial reporting problems related to new developments in business, improved ways to measure economic effects, and expansion of international businesses. The evolving problems of financial reporting are the subject of much research by accountants (in academia, practice, and industry) and the groups involved in accounting innovations discussed in Chapter 1.

---

[14]Financial Accounting Standards Board, *Statement of Financial Accounting Concepts No. 1*, "Objectives of Financial Reporting by Business Enterprises" (November 1978); *No. 2*, "Qualitative Characteristics of Accounting Information" (May 1980); and *No. 3*, "Elements of Financial Statements of Business Enterprises," (December 1980), Stamford, Conn.

EXHIBIT 2–6   **Summary of the fundamental concepts underlying financial accounting and reporting (based on *FASB Statements of Concepts Nos. 1, 2, and 3****

Fundamentals	*Brief Explanation*	*Example*
USERS of financial statements (persons to whom they are directed—the audience)	Primarily **decision makers** who are "average prudent investors" and are willing to study the information with diligence.	Investors, creditors, including those who advise or represent investors and creditors.
OBJECTIVES of financial statements (decision usefulness)	To provide economic information about a business that is useful in projecting the **future cash flows** of that business.	The operations of a business are summarized in **net income** which is the primary long-term source of **cash** generated by a business.
QUALITATIVE characteristics of financial statements (necessary to make the reported information useful to decision makers)	Characteristics that make financial statements useful, viz: 1. Relevance—affects decisions; timely presentation has predictive and feedback value. 2. Reliability (believable)—unbiased, accurate, and verifiable.	1. The financial statements are available soon after their dates have been audited and present complete information. 2. Audited financial statements.
IMPLEMENTATION ASSUMPTIONS of financial statements (imposed by the business environment)	1. Separate-entity assumption—each business is accounted for separately from its owners and other entities. 2. Continuity (going-concern) assumption—assumes the entity will not liquidate, will continue to pursue its objectives. 3. Unit-of-measure assumption—accounting measurements will be in the monetary unit. 4. Time-period assumption—accounting reports are for short time periods.	1. XYZ Company is a separate entity; its owners and creditors are other entities. 2. Accounting for XYZ Company will assume it will carry on its normal operations. 3. Assets, liabilities, owners' equity, revenues, expenses, etc., are measured in dollars. 4. Financial statements of XYZ Company are prepared each year.
ELEMENTS of financial statements (basic items reported on the financial statements)	**Income statement:** 1. Revenues—Inflows of net assets, or settlements of liabilities from sale of goods and services that constitute the entity's **ongoing or major operations.** 2. Expenses—Outflows or using up of assets, or incurrence of liabilities for delivery of goods or services, and other activities that constitute the entity's **ongoing or major operations.** 3. Gains—Increases in net assets from **peripheral or incidental transactions,** and all other activities except those from revenues or investments by owners.	1. Sale of merchandise for cash or on credit. 2. Wages earned by employees paid in cash or owed. 3. Sale of a tract of land for a price **more** than its cost when acquired.

*These concepts are not mandated definitions in Canada but they do serve as a convenient summary of the concepts needed to understand Canadian accounting.

EXHIBIT 2–6   *(continued)*

Fundamentals	*Brief Explanation*	*Example*
ELEMENTS *(continued)*	4. Losses—Decreases in net assets from **peripheral or incidental transactions** and other events except those from expenses or distributions to owners.	4. Sale of a tract of land for a price **less** than its cost when acquired.
ELEMENTS *(continued)*	**Balance sheet:** 5. Assets—Probable future economic benefits, owned by the entity as a result of past transactions. 6. Liabilities—Probable future sacrifices of economic benefits as a result of past transactions; involves transfer of assets or services. 7. Owners' equity—Residual interest of owners after all debts are paid (i.e., Assets − Liabilities = Owners' Equity).	5. Land, buildings, equipment, patent. 6. Note owed to the bank, taxes owed but not yet paid, unpaid wages. 7. Capital stock outstanding, retained earnings.
IMPLEMENTATION PRINCIPLES of accounting (how to apply the concepts)	1. Cost principle—Cost (cash equivalent cost given up) is the appropriate basis for initial recording of assets, liabilities, owners' equity, revenues, expenses, gains, and losses. 2. Revenue principle—The cash equivalent amount received for the sale of goods or services is recognized as earned revenue when ownership transfers or as the services are rendered. 3. Matching principle—Revenues are recognized in conformity with the revenue principle; then all expenses incurred in earning that revenue must be identified and recorded in the period in which those revenues are recognized. 4. Reporting principle—The financial statements of an entity should **disclose** (present) all of the **relevant** economic information about that entity. 5. Reliability principle—The financial statements of an entity should report economic data that are unbiased (neutral), verifiable, and faithfully present what they purport to represent. 6. Comparability principle—Accounting information reported should be comparable among similar entities, and the accounting principles should be applied in a consistent manner across periods.	1. XYZ Company purchased a machine; record the cash equivalent given up, $10,000, as the cost of the machine. 2. Sale of merchandise for $2,000, half cash and half on credit—record sale revenue of $2,000 on date of sale. 3. Sales of merchandise during the period of $100,000 is recorded as earned; the cost of those goods, $60,000, is recorded as expense of that period. 4. Report inventory on the balance sheet and explain in a note the inventory accounting policies. 5. Report the cash balance on the balance sheet excluding noncash items such as postage stamps and IOUs. 6. In accounting for inventories; do not use FIFO one period and average the next period, then back to FIFO.

EXHIBIT 2–6   *(concluded)*

Fundamentals	Brief Explanation	Example
Exceptions to the above principles (based on practical reasons)	1. Materiality—Amounts of relatively small significance must be recorded; however, they need not be accorded strict theoretical treatment (for cost-benefit reasons).	1. Purchase of a pencil sharpener for $4.98 (an asset) may be recorded as expense when purchased.
	2. Rational conservatism—Exercise care not to overstate assets and revenue and not to understate liabilities and expenses.	2. A loss that is a probable, but not known for sure, should be recorded.
	3. Industry peculiarities—Unique characteristics of an industry may require special accounting approaches.	3. Financial institutions do not use the classification, current assets.
ACCRUAL BASIS	Revenues, expenses, assets, liabilities, and owners' equity are accounted for and reported on the basis of when the economic effect occurred rather than when the related cash is received or paid.	XYZ Company sold merchandise for $1,000 on December 20, 19A, on a 30-day credit basis. The cash was collected in full on January 20, 19B. The sale should be recorded and reported in 19A (not 19B).
DETAILED accounting practices and procedures (detailed measurement and recording guidelines)	1. Those related to asset and income measurement.	1. Straight-line versus accelerated depreciation.
	2. Those related to reporting accounting information.	2. Separate reporting of extraordinary items (net of income tax); terminology.
	3. Other accounting procedures.	3. Control and subsidiary ledgers; special journals; bank reconciliations, worksheets.

ACCRUAL BASIS ACCOUNTING

The definition of revenues given in Chapter 1 states that revenue is considered **earned** (i.e., realized) in the period when the revenue **transaction takes place** rather than when the cash is collected. Therefore, the total amount of revenues reported on the income statement for the period should include sales and services of that period collected in cash plus all sales and services of the period on credit, even though the cash may be collected the next period. Similarly, when rent (for example) is collected in advance, rent revenue should be reported on the income statement for the period in which occupancy occurred, rather in the period of cash collection. Assume rent revenue of $1,200 is collected on December 1, 19A, for 12 months' future occupancy ending November 30, 19B. Rent revenue **earned** in 19A would be $100 and 19B, $1,100.

In a similar manner, the definition of expenses in Chapter 1 states that expenses are considered **incurred** (i.e., used) in the period when the goods or services are **used** or **consumed**. Therefore, the total amount of expense **incurred** should be reported on the income statement of the period. In some cases, the expense-incurring services and goods are obtained on credit whereby the cash is paid in a later period; and in other cases, the cash is paid in advance of use of the goods or services (as in the case of prepayment of a three-year insurance premium on a building). In each of these cases, the date of the cash flow is disregarded in determining the period in which the expense should be reported on the income statement.

The approach described above for determining when to report revenues and expenses is necessary to measure revenues properly for the period and to **match** expenses correctly with those revenues. This process is known as the **matching principle** (see Exhibit 2–6). This method of determining when revenues and expenses are to be reported is known as **accrual accounting.** It is required by generally accepted accounting principles (GAAP). In contrast, individuals and very small businesses sometimes use the **cash basis** for their records, which means that all revenues are considered earned only when the cash is collected, and all expenses are considered incurred only when the cash is paid. This method does not conform to GAAP because it incorrectly measures such revenues and expenses due to the fact that the related activities precede or lag the cash-flow dates.

SOME MISCONCEPTIONS

Some people naively confuse a bookkeeper with an accountant and bookkeeping with accounting. In effect, they confuse one of the minor parts with the whole of accounting. Bookkeeping involves the routine and clerical part of accounting and requires only minimal knowledge of the accounting model and its application. A bookkeeper may record the repetitive and uncomplicated transactions in most businesses and may maintain the simple records of a small business. In contrast, the accountant is a highly trained professional competent in the design of information systems, analysis of complex transactions and economic events, interpretation and analysis of financial data, financial reporting, financial advising, auditing, taxation, and management consulting.

A prevalent misconception is that all of the financial affairs of an entity are subject to precise and objective measurement each period and that the accounting results reported in the financial statements are exactly what happened that period. In contrast, accounting numbers are influenced by estimates in many respects as illustrated in subsequent chapters. Many people believe that accounting should measure and report the market value of the entity (including its assets), but accounting does not attempt to do this. In order to understand financial statements and to interpret them wisely for use in decision making, the user must be aware of their limitations as well as their usefulness. One should understand what the financial statements do and do not attempt to accomplish.

Another misconception related to financial statements is that because of their quantitative nature, they are inflexible in use. As you study accounting you will appreciate that it requires considerable **professional judgment in application** on the part of the accountant in order to capture the economic essence of complex transactions. Thus, accounting is stimulating intellectually; it is not a cut-and-dried subject. Rather, it is one that calls upon your intelligence, analytical ability, creativity, and judgment. Accounting is a communication process involving an audience (users) with a wide diversity of knowledge, interest, and capabilities; therefore, it will call upon your ability as a communicator. The language of accounting encompasses concisely written phrases and symbols used to convey information about the resource flows measured for specific organizations.

As you study accounting and later as a decision maker, you must be wary of these misconceptions. To adequately understand financial statements and to be able to interpret the "figures" wisely, you must have a certain level of knowledge of the concepts and the measurement procedures used in the accounting process. You must learn what accounting "is really like" and appreciate the reasons why certain things are done the way they are. This level of knowledge cannot be gained simply by reading a list of the "concepts" and a list of the misconceptions. Neither can a generalized discussion of the subject matter suffice. A certain amount of involvement, primarily problem solving (similar to the requirement in mathematics courses), is essential in the study of accounting. Therefore, we provide problems aimed at the desirable knowledge level for the user (as well as the preparer) of financial statements.

ACCOUNTING—AN INFORMATION PROCESSING SYSTEM

Accounting is the process of recording the detailed financial history of the entity and, from that information, deriving the financial statements. Thus, the **accounting process** involves the accumulation, analysis, measurement, recording, interpretation, classification, and summarization of the results of each of the many business transactions that affected the entity during a time period. After this processing, accounting then transmits messages to decision makers. The messages are in the form of financial statements, and the decision makers are the users. Accounting does not create the basic information (raw financial data); rather, the raw financial data result from the day-to-day transactions initiated, participated in, and completed by the enterprise. The accounting system includes procedures for collecting these data; and as an **information system,** the accounting process is designed to record these data and capture the **economic essence** of each transaction.[15]

An accounting system should be designed to classify financial information on a basis suitable for decision-making purposes and to process the tremendous quantities of data efficiently and accurately. The information system must be designed to report the results periodically, in a realistic and concise format that is understandable to users who often have only a limited technical knowledge of accounting. The information system must be designed to accommodate the special and complex needs of the **internal** management of the entity. These

---

[15]The accounting information system should be viewed as a part of the overall information system that necessarily operates in any entity.

internal needs extend primarily to the planning and control responsibilities of the managers of the enterprise; they are discussed in management accounting.

The accountant has the primary responsibility for developing an accounting information system that is essential for most entities, whether operating on a profit or nonprofit basis. In designing an information system, the accountant must consider the factors of (1) cost; (2) benefit; (3) timeliness (i.e., reports must be rendered shortly after the end of the accounting period); and (4) requirements of various outside influences, such as governmental regulatory agencies.

The accounting information processing system will be discussed in Chapters 4–6.

OVERVIEW OF AN ACTUAL ANNUAL REPORT

The preceding discussions illustrated two sets of simplified financial statements that were stripped of many of the surrounding features. To complete our overview of the financial statements of a business, we present the complete **1984 Annual Report** of Consolidated-Bathurst Inc. This **published** report is presented as **Special Supplement B** at the end of this textbook, just preceding the Index, because it will be referred to throughout the remaining chapters.

A corporation such as Consolidated-Bathurst Inc. is said to "publish" its annual financial report because it is printed and distributed to each shareholder and to others upon request. Companies whose shares are traded on the stock exchanges (and some others) distribute such annual reports. A published annual report typically includes a number of features in addition to the financial statements, such as the president's letter to the shareholders, a list of the principal officers of the company, promotional data on the company's products (including pictures), and other information deemed by the management to be of interest.

The primary components of the annual report presented in Special Supplement B were labeled by Consolidated-Bathurst Inc. as follows.[16]

1. Consolidated Balance Sheet.
2. Statement of Consolidated Earnings.
3. Statement of Consolidated Retained Earnings.
4. Statement of Consolidated Changes in Financial Position.
5. Notes to Consolidated Financial Statements.
6. Auditors' Report.
7. Comparative Data.
8. Financial Review.

---

[16]The statements are labeled "Consolidated." This word indicates that the parent company owns more than 50 percent of the outstanding voting shares of one or more other companies. This ownership gives the parent company a **controlling interest,** and the other companies are designated as subsidiaries. To prepare the statements on a **consolidated basis,** the financial statements of the subsidiaries are added on a line-by-line basis to those of the parent company. This subject is discussed further in Chapter 14.

As recommended by *CICA Handbook,* Section 1500, **comparative** amounts are presented. That is most of the items reported show the amount for the current year (e.g., 1984) and the preceding year (e.g., 1983).

On the next few pages we will briefly discuss the eight primary components (listed above) of the Consolidated-Bathurst Inc. Annual Report and relate them to the preceding discussions. A number of items are included in this report that you will not understand at this point of your study; however, you may be surprised to learn how many of those items you understand already. Most of the items that you do not understand will be discussed in subsequent chapters.

We ask you to refer to Special Supplement B at the end of this book (preceding the Index) as you read the brief discussion of the primary components of the 1984 financial statements for Consolidated-Bathurst that follows.

Consolidated balance sheet

The title "Consolidated Statement of Financial Position" is often used. This statement is dated "December 31, 1984" because it is "as of" that specific date, which is referred to as the end of the **accounting period.** You can observe in this balance sheet that Consolidated-Bathurst follows closely the classifications of assets, liabilities, and owners' equity discussed in the chapter. Although most companies use an accounting period that ends December 31, others use periods ending in any particular month they so define. March seems to be the most popular month after December.

Statement of consolidated earnings

This statement usually is called the "Income Statement" or "Statement of Income." The Consolidated-Bathurst income statement is for the **year ended** December 31, 1984 because it covers a period of time, rather than at a specific date. Businesses often use an accounting period that is different from the calendar year because they want to conform to their particular "natural operating year," which ends when the operating activities are the lowest for that business.

Look at the Consolidated-Bathurst Annual Report and observe that the Consolidated Statement of Earnings starts with **Revenues** (not Sales) and ends with **Net earnings.** Immediately following this caption are the earnings per share (EPS) amounts.

Statement of consolidated retained earnings

This statement like the Statement of Consolidated Earnings is for the year ended December 31, 1984. It begins with the balance of retained earnings reported in the previous annual report. Next an adjustment is made to the balance for the beginning of the period. This amount represents a prior period adjustment resulting from a change in accounting procedures in the current year from those used in the previous year. A full discussion of prior period adjustments is presented in Chapter 12. Notice, however, that the Auditors' Report also references this change in accounting procedures because it represents a violation of the comparability principle (also referred to as the consistency principle) discussed in Exhibit 2–6.

Once the restated beginning balance is calculated on the statement, net earnings is added and dividends are subtracted to arrive at the retained earnings at the end of the year. The excess cost of purchasing common shares over stated value is a loss on the purchasing of the company's own shares. This topic is discussed in Chapter 12 in the section "Treasury Stock."

Dividends per share for each class of shares outstanding is not formally part of the retained earnings statement. These amounts are calculated by dividing the dividend amounts by the number of shares to which the dividends were paid. They are disclosed for informational purposes only.

Statement of consolidated changes in financial position

This statement is dated the same as the income statement because it covers the full accounting period of one year (as opposed to a specific date similar to the balance sheet).

Observe that the SCFP (a short abbreviation for the statement of changes in financial position) tells you where Consolidated-Bathurst obtained its cash during the year and what it did with the cash (much more about the SCFP later).

Notes to consolidated financial statements

One of the broad fundamentals underlying accounting, listed under **implementation principles** in Exhibit 2–6, is the **reporting principle.** This principle relates directly to the financial statements. It specifies that there should be complete and understandable reporting on the financial statements of all relevant economic **information** relating to the economic activities of the entity. To meet the requirements of this principle, the quantitative expressions in the financial statements frequently must be supported by narrative and detailed elaboration. As a consequence, practically all published financial statements will include a section called "Notes to Financial Statements." The notes are considered to be an **integral part** of the financial statements and are important to understanding and interpreting the amounts reported. Take a quick look at the 16 notes presented by Consolidated-Bathurst; you may find some of them very interesting (e.g., Note 5 about $35 million loss).

Also, we suggest that you look at **Note 1.** Because of the importance of the **accounting policies** used by a company, *CICA Handbook,* Section 1505, requires that they be set out separately in the financial report. As you study this book you will learn that there are often two or more acceptable ways to record a particular transaction. Given this fact, financial statement users, may encounter difficulties in interpreting the financial results reported without knowing which alternative was used by the company. The **summary of significant accounting policies** must be included with the financial statements to meet this need of statement users. Observe that Consolidated-Bathurst explained its accounting policies in respect to nine different items reported on its financial statements.

Auditors' report

The independent CA firm, as the outside auditor, is required to express an **independent opinion** on the financial statements or to state that an opinion cannot be expressed. The standard auditor's report contains at least two paragraphs. The first paragraph, known as the **scope** paragraph, describes the general nature of the audit that was performed. The second paragraph, known as the **opinion** paragraph, reports the opinion of the auditors in respect to the financial statements after the audit was completed. The opinion paragraph in the auditor's report for Consolidated-Bathurst states:

> These consolidated financial statements present fairly the financial position of the Corporation as at December 31, 1984, and the results of its operations and changes in its financial position for the year then ended in accordance with generally accepted accounting principles applied, except for the change in accounting for foreign currency translation and after giving effect to the retroactive change in accounting for preoperating expenses as explained in Notes 1 and 2, respectively, to the consolidated financial statements, on a basis consistent with that of the preceeding year.

The key words in the above opinion are "present fairly" and "generally accepted accounting principles." If the statements do not meet these two standards, the independent CA must **qualify** the opinion. When an auditor qualifies an opinion in the auditors' report, a separate paragraph can be included between the scope and opinion paragraphs to explain the nature of the qualification. If, however, a short qualification can be written it can be included within the body of the opinion paragraph as the auditors did for Consolidated-Bathurst. Note the words "except for." These words signify that the auditors have qualified their opinion for the specific points mentioned. A comparability violation is a violation of an accounting principle (consistency) and will bring fourth a qualified report by the auditors.

The auditor's opinion relates to the "fair presentation" of the financial report in its entirety; therefore, the opinion is viewed as a necessary and critically important part of the financial report.

Comparative data

This back section of the annual report presents a 10-year summarized listing of key income and balance sheet information. This information is useful in attempting to study the financial history of the company so predictions about its future can be made.

Financial review

The Financial Review section of the annual report is located prior to the Statement of Consolidated Earnings. Numerous discussions and tables are contained in this section including reports about the effects of changing prices on earnings and certain balance sheet accounts. Chapter 17 contains a detailed examination of the nature of this supplementary information. Notice as well the information about sales for various product lines and geographical regions. This information, termed segment data, provides an indication of the relative importance of various aspects of the operations of Consolidated-Bathurst and an indication of their relative profitability.

DEMONSTRATION CASE

On January 1, 19A, Baker Retail Corporation was organized by five promoters; each one paid in $10,000 cash and each one received 10,000 shares of Baker stock, par $0.20 per share. At the end of 19A, the following account balances (in alphabetical order) were reported:

Account	Amount	Account	Amount
Accounts payable...............	$ 45,000	Income taxes payable (none paid)	$?
Accounts receivable..............	40,000	Interest expense................	3,600
Accumulated depreciation, store		Investment in shares of Able	
equipment	?	Corporation...................	25,000
Administrative expenses*.........	104,800	Long-term notes payable	30,000
Allowance for doubtful accounts ..	1,000	Merchandise inventory...........	101,500
Cash	17,500	Retained earnings	?
Common stock	10,000	Revenue from investments and ...	
Contributed surplus	?	funds........................	5,600
Cost of goods sold...............	554,400	Sales revenue	997,000
Extraordinary gain, pretax........	8,000	Sales returns	7,000
Income tax expense, on operations	?	Selling expenses................	265,800
Income tax, on extraordinary gain		Store equipment (acquired January	
	?	1, 19A)	20,000
....		Used equipment held for disposal	1,000

*Includes depreciation expense of $4,000 on store equipment. Excludes income tax expense.

Required (show computations of the six missing amounts):

    a. Prepare 19A income statement for Baker, assuming an income tax rate of 20 percent on all items.

    b. Prepare a classified balance sheet for Baker at December 31, 19A, assuming no dividends were declared or paid during 19A.

Suggested solution

Requirement a:

BAKER CORPORATION
Income Statement
For the Year Ended December 31, 19A

Gross sales revenue................................	$997,000	
Less: Sales returns	7,000	
Net sales revenue..................................		$990,000
Less: Cost of goods sold...........................		554,400
Gross margin on sales..............................		435,600
Operating expenses:		
Selling expenses	265,800	
Administrative expenses..........................	104,800	
Total operating expenses		370,600
Income from operations		65,000
Financial expenses and financial revenues:		
Revenue from investments........................	5,600	
Interest expense	3,600	
Net financial revenue		2,000
Pretax income		67,000
Income tax on operations ($67,000 × 20%)		13,400
Income before extraordinary items..................		53,600
Extraordinary gain, pretax	8,000	
Less: Income tax on the gain ($8,000 × 20%)......	1,600	6,400
Net income.......................................		$ 60,000

Earnings per share of common stock:

Income before extraordinary items	$53,600 ÷ 50,000 shares =	$1.07
Extraordinary gain.	6,400 ÷ 50,000 shares =	0.13
Net income	$60,000 ÷ 50,000 shares =	$1.20

Requirement b:

BAKER CORPORATION
Balance Sheet
At December 31, 19A

Assets

Current assets:		
Cash		$ 17,500
Accounts receivable	$40,000	
Less: Allowance for doubtful accounts.	1,000	39,000
Merchandise inventory		101,500
Total current assets		158,000
Long-term investments and funds:		
Shares of Able Corporation.		25,000
Operational assets:		
Store equipment	20,000	
Less: Accumulated depreciation (Same as depreciation		
expense in year 19A only).	4,000	16,000
Other assets:		
Used equipment held for disposal		1,000
Total assets		$200,000

Liabilities

Current liabilities:		
Accounts payable	$45,000	
Income taxes payable ($13,400 + $1,600)	15,000	
Total current liabilities		$ 60,000
Long-term liabilities:		
Notes payable.		30,000
Total liabilities		$ 90,000

Shareholders' Equity

Contributed capital:		
Common stock, par $0.20, 50,000 shares outstanding	10,000	
Contributed surplus (50,000 × $0.80)	40,000	
Total contributed capital	50,000	
Retained earnings (no dividends, same as net income).	60,000	
Total shareholders' equity.		110,000
Total liabilities and shareholders' equity		$200,000

SUMMARY OF CHAPTER

This chapter presented the commonly used subclassifications of financial information on the income statement, balance sheet, and statement of changes in financial position. You learned some of the analytical approaches used by the decision makers who rely on financial reports. You also learned to expect variations in the terminology and format of financial reports.

Financial reports of an existing company were presented to reinforce your understanding and for reference as you study the accounting process in the chapters to follow. The knowledge of financial statements, gained in Chapter 1 and in this chapter, should assure that in studying the details and complexities of accounting, you can maintain a broad view of accounting and keep in mind the nature of the end product—the periodic financial statements. We reemphasize this point because, not infrequently, students soon become immersed in details and lose the broad perspective of the end results—the financial statements and their use.

In Part B of the chapter, a summarization of the fundamentals underlying financial accounting and reporting (i.e., for external decision makers) was presented. In essence, this is a summarization of the major considerations of the chapters that follow. It is presented at this time as a basic foundation to which your attention will be directed in the remaining chapters. It will serve as a basis for understanding much of the "why and how" of financial accounting and reporting. You should return to it often to maintain overall perspective.

IMPORTANT TERMS DEFINED IN THIS CHAPTER

Terms alphabetically	Key words in definitions of important terms used in chapter	Page reference
Accrual accounting	Record revenues and expenses when transaction occurs.	69
Book value	Cost minus any contra amount; carrying value.	58
Classified statements	Subcaptions on financial statements; aids users.	49
Contra amount	An offset to a major related account.	50
Cost of goods sold	Cost; inventory sold; deduct as an expense.	50
Current assets	Short-term; convert to cash; year or operating cycle.	54
Current liabilities	Short-term; debt; payable from current assets.	59
Deferred charges	Long-term; prepayments of expense.	58
Depreciation	Operational asset cost; expense based on usage.	57
Extraordinary items	Gains or losses; unusual and infrequent.	52
Financial expenses	Interest on debt.	52
Fixed assets	Operational assets; property, plant, and equipment.	57
Gross margin on sales	Sales revenue minus cost of goods sold.	52
Gross sales	Total sales; prior to returned sales.	50
Income tax expense	Expense; based on income; payable to government.	53
Intangible assets	Has value; no physical substance.	58
Liquidity	Nearness of noncash item to cash.	56
Long-term investments	Shares, bonds, other investments; hold beyond current year or operating cycle, if longer.	57
Long-term liabilities	Debt; due beyond current year or operating cycle, if longer.	60
Matching principle	First measure revenue; then determine expenses incurred to earn it.	70
Net sales	Gross sales minus sales returns.	50
Normal operating cycle	Period of time from cash payment back to cash receipt.	54
Operating expenses	Normal expenses of the business; related to normal operations.	52
Operational assets	Property, plant, and equipment; used in normal operations.	57

Terms alphabetically	Key words in definitions of important terms used in chapter	Page reference
Other assets	Miscellaneous classification on balance sheet.	59
Prepaid expenses	Expenses paid in advance of usage, short-term.	56
Prior period adjustment	An adjustment to beginning retained earnings.	73
Profit margin	Net income ÷ net sales.	65
ROI	Return on investment; Income ÷ Investment.	65
Returned sales	Goods sold; later returned.	50
Statement of retained earnings	Reports accumulated earnings minus accumulated dividends.	60
Working capital	Current assets minus current liabilities.	59

QUESTIONS FOR DISCUSSION

Part A

1. What is the primary purpose of subclassification of the information presented on financial statements?

2. What are the four major classifications on the income statement?

3. Distinguish between gross sales revenue and net sales revenue.

4. Explain the subclassification "Financial expenses and financial revenues" on a multiple-step income statement.

5. Define extraordinary items. Why should they be reported separately on the income statement?

6. Explain EPS. What EPS amounts should be reported on the income statement?

7. Briefly explain how income tax expense is reported on the income statement when there are extraordinary items.

8. List the six subclassifications of assets reported on a balance sheet.

9. Briefly define (a) current assets, (b) current liabilities, and (c) working capital.

10. What is a prepaid expense?

11. Distinguish between a prepaid expense and a deferred charge.

12. On a balance sheet, investments may be reported under either (a) current assets or (b) long-term investments and funds. Explain.

13. In respect to operational assets, as reported on the balance sheet, briefly explain (a) cost, (b) accumulated depreciation, (c) book value, and (d) carrying value.

14. What are the subclassifications of liabilities on a balance sheet?

15. Briefly explain two major subclassifications of owners' equity for a corporation.

16. What is the purpose of a statement of retained earnings?

17. What are the three major subclassifications on a SCFP?

18. What is meant by a comparative financial statement? Why are comparative financial statements desirable?

19. Briefly, what does the independent auditors' report encompass?

Part B

20. What is proportional analysis? Why is it often useful in interpreting financial statements?

21. Explain *(a)* profit margin and *(b)* ROI.

22. What is the basic objective of financial accounting and reporting?

23. What are the two primary qualitative characteristics of financial accounting and reporting?

24. Match the following:

Fundamentals		*Statement*
_____ Users	A.	Special journals
_____ Objective	B.	Cost, revenue, matching, reporting, reliability, comparability.
_____ Qualitative characteristics	C.	Investors, creditors, and other external groups.
_____ Implementation assumptions	D.	Relevance and reliability.
_____ Elements of financial statements	E.	Materiality, conservatism, industry peculiarities.
	F.	Useful in projecting future cash flows.
_____ Implementation principles	G.	Separate entity, continuity, unit of measure, time period.
_____ Exceptions	H.	Assets, liabilities, owners' equity, revenues, expenses, gains, and losses.
_____ Detailed practices and procedures		

25. Explain the basic difference between cash basis accounting and accrual basis accounting.

26. Distinguish between accounting and bookkeeping.

27. Explain why a major part of accounting may be viewed as an information system.

28. Speculate as to the type of situation(s) that would lead to a prior period adjustment.

29. The comparability principle states that accounting principles should be applied in a consistent manner across periods. Consolidated-Bathurst violated this principle twice in 1984. What was done about it and how does this action change the wording of the principle from that provided in this chapter?

30. The opinion paragraph of the auditors' report for Consolidated-Bathurst contains two key sets of words among others: "present fairly" and "in accordance with "generally accepted accounting principles." Is the amount for store equipment in Exhibit 2–2 presented fairly when it is valued at historical cost less accumulated depreciation? Would selling price be fairer? How can the two quotations from the auditors' report be connected to make historical cost "fair"?

EXERCISES

Part A

E2–1. Bill and Marcie Wilson organized the BMW Hardware Company on January 1, 19A, as a corporation. The primary activities involved a hardware store that they bought from the retiring owner. On that date, 20,000 shares of common stock were issued to three shareholders (Bill, Marcie, and the former owner of the store); $100,000 cash was received from the shareholders.

At the end of the first year, December 31, 19A, the records maintained by Marcie showed the following:

   a. Merchandise sold: for cash, $180,000; on credit, $20,000.
   b. Interest on debt: paid in cash, $2,000; owed but not yet paid, $500.
   c. Salaries and wages: paid in cash, $40,500, owed but not yet paid, $1,000.
   d. Other operating expenses, $5,000.
   e. Cost of the merchandise sold, $101,000.
   f. Services sold (all for cash), $10,000.
   g. Extraordinary (EO) loss, $5,000 (subject to income tax).
   h. Average corporate income tax rate on all items, 20 percent.

Required:

   a. Complete the following income statement for the year, 19A:

     Revenues
     Expenses:
       Cost of goods sold
       Operating expenses
       Financial expenses
     Pretax income from operations
       Income tax expense
     Income before EO item
       EO loss
     Net income
     EPS

   b. What was the total amount of income tax expense for 19A? Explain.
   c. Explain why the $100,000 cash paid by the organizers is not considered to be revenue.

E2–2. The accounting records of Doyle Corporation reflected the following summarized data for the year ended December 31, 19B: sales revenue, $100,000; gross margin rate (markup on selling price), 52 percent; financial (interest) expense, $2,000; extraordinary gain, $5,000; average income tax rate (on all items), 20 percent; operating expenses, $30,000; common stock outstanding, 10,000 shares; and dividends declared and paid, $3,000.

Required:

   a. You have been asked to prepare a detailed income statement for 19B. Show your computations. (Hint: EPS on net income is $2 per share.)
   b. You also have been asked to compute the amount of retained earnings at the end of 19B (the January 1, 19B, balance was $11,000). Show your computations.

c. What was the total amount of income tax expense for 19B? Explain what the EPS amount on "Income before extraordinary items" means. What is its significance compared to EPS on net income?

E2–3. Below is listed terminology related to the income statement. Match the terms with the brief definitions by entering the appropriate letter to the left for each term.

Terminology

_____ Cost of goods sold
_____ Gross sales
_____ Financial expense
_____ Interest revenue
_____ Extraordinary items
_____ Service revenue
_____ Sales returns and allowances
_____ Income tax expense on operations
_____ Income before extraordinary items
_____ Net sales
_____ Net income
_____ Gross margin on sales
_____ EPS
_____ Distribution expenses
_____ Operating expenses
_____ Pretax income from operations
_____ Income Tax Act
_____ General and administrative expenses

Brief definition

A. Defines the amount of income subject to income tax.
B. Items that are unusual and infrequent.
C. Sales of services for cash or on credit.
D. Revenues + Gains − Expenses − Losses (including EO items).
E. Expenses incurred to sell goods.
F. Total sales prior to returns and allowances.
G. Amount of income tax excluding EO items.
H. Time cost of money (borrowing); interest expense.
I. Expenses of managing the company.
J. Sales minus returns and allowances.
K. Distribution plus general administrative expenses.
L. Return earned by lending money or selling on credit (time cost of money).
M. Net sales revenue minus cost of goods sold.
N. After-tax income from operations (excluding EO items).
O. Income divided by common shares outstanding.
P. Income from operations before income tax and before EO items.
Q. None of the above.

E2–4. Following is a list of major classifications and subclassifications on the balance sheet. Number them in the order in which they normally appear on a balance sheet.

_____ Current liabilities
_____ Liabilities
_____ Owners' equity
_____ Long-term liabilities
_____ Long-term investments and funds
_____ Intangible assets
_____ Operational assets
_____ Current assets
_____ Retained earnings
_____ Contributed capital
_____ Assets
_____ Other assets
_____ Deferred charges

E2–5. EPS Corporation has just completed the 19C income statement (there were no extraordinary items), except for the EPS computations. Net income has been determined to be $150,000. Common stock outstanding during the year was 30,000 shares, and preferred stock, 6 percent ($10 par value), outstanding was 10,000 shares. Compute the EPS amount for the income statement. (Hint: First subtract the preferred dividends claim of $100,000 × 6% = $6,000.) Explain why the $6,000 should be subtracted.

E2–6. Fowler Corporation (common stock, 6,000 shares outstanding) is preparing the income statement for the year ended December 31, 19D. The pretax operating income has been determined to be $100,000, and there was a $30,000 pretax loss on earthquake damages to one of the plants properly classified as an extraordinary item. Total income tax expense has been determined correctly to be $28,000 on the basis of a 40 percent tax rate on operations and on the earthquake loss. You have been requested to complete the income statement starting with "pretax operating income." Explain why the income tax amount is separated into two parts in this situation.

E2–7. Candy Corporation was organized in 1970 by 10 investors. Each investor paid in $12 cash per share and received 1,500 shares of $10 par value common stock. In 1980, to raise more capital, Candy Corporation issued 5,000 shares of 7 percent preferred, non-participating, cumulative stock, par $20 per share, and received total cash of $125,000. On December 31, 1984, retained earnings amounted to $75,000.

  a. Prepare the shareholders' equity section of the balance sheet at December 31, 1984.
  b. Explain what the $75,000 balance in retained earnings on December 31, 1984, represents.

E2–8. Below is listed terminology related to the balance sheet. Match the terms with the brief definitions by entering the appropriate letter to the left for each term.

Terminology		*Brief definition*
_____ Retained earnings	A.	A miscellaneous category of assets.
_____ Current liabilities	B.	Current assets minus current liabilities.
_____ Liquidity	C.	Total assets minus total liabilities.
_____ Contra asset account	D.	Balance sheet arranged with assets, liabilities, and owners' equity in descending order (vertical).
_____ Prepaid expense	E.	Nearness of assets to cash (in time).
_____ Accumulated depreciation	F.	Assets expected to be realized within one year or operating cycle, if longer
_____ Intangible assets	G.	Same as carrying value; cost less annual depreciation to date.
_____ Other assets		
_____ Report format	H.	Prior period adjustment.
_____ Deferred charges	I.	Accumulated earnings minus accumulated dividends.
_____ Normal operating cycle	J.	Current assets divided by current liabilities.
_____ Book value	K.	Asset offset account (subtracted from asset).
_____ Tangible assets	L.	Short-term prepayment of an expense prior to its use or consumption.
_____ Working capital	M.	Assets that do not have physical substance.
_____ Liabilities	N.	Items owned by the business that have future economic values.
_____ Operational assets		
_____ Owners' equity	O.	Liabilities expected to be paid out of current assets within the next year or operating cycle, if longer.
_____ Working capital ratio	P.	Liability offset account (deducted from liability).
_____ Current assets	Q.	The average cash-to-cash time involved in the operations of the business.
_____ Assets		
_____ Long-term liabilities	R.	Sum of the annual depreciation expense on an asset from its acquisition to date.
_____ Contra liability account	S.	A long-term prepaid expense.
_____ None of the above	T.	All liabilities not classified as current liabilities.
	U.	Assets that have physical substance.
	V.	Obligation to give up (pay) economic benefits in the future.

E2–9. On July 1, 19A, Risky Company paid $4,800 cash for a two-year insurance premium. The premium was for a new insurance policy covering all of the assets owned. It is now

December 31, 19A, and you are asked to respond to the following questions (show your computations):

a. How much should be reported for **insurance expense** on the income statement for the year ended December 31, 19A?

b. What amount of **prepaid insurance** should be reported on the December 31, 19A, balance sheet? How should it be classified?

E2–10. Investor Manufacturing Corporation is preparing its annual financial statements at December 31, 19B. The company has two investments in shares of other corporations:

a. Common stock of Me Corporation: 1,000 shares purchased for $80,000 during 19A. Me Corporation is a supplier of parts to Investor Corporation; therefore, the latter "intends to hold the shares indefinitely." The shares acquired represented 2 percent of the total shares outstanding. Me stock was selling at $95 at the end of 19B.

b. Common stock of No Corporation: purchased 500 shares at a cost of $60 per share on August 15, 19B. Investor made this investment to "temporarily use some idle cash that probably will be needed next year." No shares were selling at $70 at the end of 19B.

You have been requested to illustrate and explain the basis for the classification and amount that should be reported for each investment on the 19B balance sheet of Investor Corporation.

E2–11. Tabor Company is preparing the balance sheet at December 31, 19X. The following assets are to be reported:

1. Building, purchased 15 years ago (counting 19X); original cost, $330,000; estimated useful life, 20 years from date of purchase; and no residual value.
2. Land, purchased 15 years ago (counting 19X); original cost, $25,000.

Required:

a. You are requested to show how the two assets should be reported on the balance sheet. What is the amount of the book value of these assets?

b. What amount of depreciation expense should be reported on the 19X income statement? Show computations.

E2–12. The amounts listed below were selected from the annual financial statements for Lazar Corporation at December 31, 19C (end of the third year of operations):

From the 10C income statement:
Sales revenue	$300,000
Cost of goods sold	(180,000)
All other expenses (including income tax)	(90,000)
Net income	$ 30,000

From the December 31, 19C, balance sheet:
Current assets	$ 90,000
All other assets	275,000
Total assets	$365,000
Current liabilities	$ 50,000
Long-term liabilities	89,000
Capital stock, par $10	150,000
Contributed surplus	15,000
Retained earnings	61,000
Total liabilities and shareholders' equity	$365,000

Required:

You have been asked to analyze the data on the 19C financial statements of Lazar by responding to the following questions. Show computations.

a. How much was the gross margin on sales?
b. What was the amount of EPS?
c. What was the amount of working capital?
d. What was the working capital ratio?
e. What was the average sales price per share of the capital stock?
f. Assuming no dividends were declared or paid during 19C, what was the beginning balance (January 1, 19C) of retained earnings?

Part B

E2–13.   At the end of the accounting year, December 31, 19B, the records of Wilson Corporation reflected the following summarized data:

Revenues for the year (net)	$ 150,000
Expenses for the year (including $3,000 income taxes)	(138,000)
Net income......................................	$ 12,000
Total assets (including current assets of $48,000)	$ 200,000
Liabilities (including current liabilities of $20,000)	$ 90,000
Shareholders' equity (including capital stock, par $10, sold for $80,000, and retained earnings)...........	110,000
Total liabilities and shareholders' equity............	$ 200,000

Required:

For analytical and interpretative purposes you have been asked to complete the following tabulation:

Item	Computation	Briefly, What Does It Mean?
a. Average income tax rate		
b. Profit margin		
c. EPS		
d. Working capital amount		
e. Working capital ratio		
f. ROI		
g. Amount of long-term liabilities		
h. Amount of retained earnings		

E2–14. The accounting records of Ready Service Company reflected the amounts shown below:

	For the year		
	19A	19B	19C
Service revenue:			
Cash....................................	$40,000	$50,000	
On credit...............................	15,000	11,000	
19C revenue collected in advance of 19C (not included in the $50,000)		3,000	
Additional cash collections for:			
19A service revenue......................	6,000	5,000	
19B service revenue	2,000	7,000	$3,000
Expenses:			
Paid in cash	25,000	30,000	
On credit..............................	5,000	7,000	
19C expenses paid in advance of 19C (not included in the $30,000)		1,000	
Additional cash payments for:			
19A expenses...........................	3,000	2,000	
19B expenses	1,000	3,000	3,000

Required:

Complete the following tabulation (show computations):

	For the year	
	19A	19B
a. Service revenue that would be reported:		
Accrual basis............................	$_____	$_____
Cash basis	$_____	$_____
b. Expenses that would be reported:		
Accrual basis............................	$_____	$_____
Cash basis	$_____	$_____

E2–15. Listed below are the fundamental concepts of accounting. You are to match these concepts with the corresponding brief definition. Enter the appropriate letter to the left for each concept.

Fundamental concepts	Brief description
_____ Primary users of financial statements	A. To prepare the income tax return of the business.
_____ Broad objective of financial reporting	B. Separate entity, going concern, time periods, and unit of measure.
_____ Qualitative characteristics of financial statements	C. Examples: straight-line versus accelerated depreciation and special journals.
_____ Implementation assumptions	D. To provide financial information that is useful in projecting future cash flows.
_____ Elements of financial statements	E. Relevance and reliability.
_____ Implementation principles	F. Investors, creditors, and those who advise and represent them (decision markers).
_____ Exceptions to implementation principles	G. Materiality, industry peculiarities, and rational conservatism.
_____ Detailed accounting practices and procedures	H. Assets, liabilities, owners' equity, revenues, expenses, gains, and losses.
_____ None of the above	I. Revenue, cost, matching, reporting, reliability, and comparability.

E2–16.   This exercise is designed to aid in understanding of the contents of actual published financial statements and to observe differences in format and terminology. You are to base your response upon the 1984 Annual Report of Consolidated-Bathurst (C-B). Refer to **Special Supplement B** at the end of this textbook, immediately preceding the Index. Base your response on the 1984 data.

a.   Balance sheet:
    (1)   What title was used by C-B?
    (2)   Give the following amounts: Assets = Liabilities + Owners' Equity.
    (3)   How many shares of common stock had been issued by the end of 1984?
    (4)   How much was invested in inventories at the end of 1984?

b.   Income statement:
    (5)   What title was used by C-B?
    (6)   How can you tell that the C-B statements are comparative?
    (7)   How much revenue was from sales to customers in 1984? How much did the merchandise cost that was sold in 1984?
    (8)   Were any extraordinary items reported in 1984?
    (9)   How many EPS amounts were reported in 1984?

c.   Statement of retained earnings:
    (10)   What title was used by C-B?
    (11)   What was the amount of dividends paid?
    (12)   What amount was carried to the balance sheet?

d.   Statement of changes in financial position:
    (13)   What was the net cash provided from operations?
    (14)   How much cash was spent for property, plant, and equipment?

e.   Notes to the financial statements:
    (15)   What caused the extraordinary loss of $35 million on the income statement? What was the effect on EPS?
    (16)   What was the 1984 effective tax rate (percent)?

f.   Supplementary information:
    (17)   What line of business (segment) earned the greatest operating profit?
    (18)   How much did inflation change the 1984 earnings before extraordinary items?
    (19)   How much did general inflation increase the 1984 inventory, property, and plant?
    (20)   How many people were employed by Consolidated-Bathurst in Canada?

PROBLEMS/CASES

Part A

PC2–1.   Flat Tire Company is developing its annual financial statements for 19D. The following amounts have been determined to be correct: sales, $300,000; distribution expenses, $37,000; interest expense, $3,000; general and administrative expenses, $20,000; extraordinary loss, $15,000; sales returns and allowances, $3,000; cost of goods sold, $160,000; and interest revenue, $1,000.

Required:

a.   Prepare a classified income statement for 19D. Assume 20,000 shares of common stock outstanding during the year and an average income tax rate on all items of 20 percent. (Hint: EPS on net income is $2.52 per share.)

b. Subsequent to preparation of the above income statement you were asked to explain some aspects of it, specifically:
    (1) What is the difference between sales returns and sales allowances?
    (2) Is gross margin on sales a reliable measure of profitability? Explain.
    (3) What was the total amount of income tax expense? Explain.
    (4) What would be the effect on EPS had the company issued a stock split that would have increased the outstanding shares to 40,000?

PC2–2. (Analytical)
        Below is a partially completed income statement of WRY Corporation for the year ended December 31, 19B.

Item	Other data	Amounts	
Gross sales revenue		$	$
Sales returns and allowances	5% of gross sales		
Net sales revenue			200,000
Cost of goods sold			
Gross margin on sales	Average markup on sales, 40%		
Operating expenses:			
Selling expenses			
General and administrative expenses		20,000	
Total operating expenses			
Pretax income from operations			
Financial revenue and expense:			
Interest revenue		3,000	
Interest expense		1,000	
Net financial revenue			
Pretax income			
Income tax on operations			
Income before EO items:			
EO gain		10,000	
Income tax effect			
Net EO gain			
Net income			
EPS (on common stock):			
Income before EO gain			1.00
EO gain			
Net income			

Required:

Based upon the data given above, and assuming (1) a 20 percent income tax rate on all items and (2) 20,000 common shares outstanding, complete the above income statement. Show all computations.

PC2–3. Ace Jewelers is developing the annual financial statements for 19C. The following amounts have been determined to be correct at December 31, 19C: cash, $41,200; accounts receivable, $49,000; merchandise inventory, $110,000; prepaid insurance, $600; investment in shares of Z Corporation (long term), $31,000; store equipment, $50,000; used store equipment held for disposal, $9,000; allowance for doubtful accounts, $800; accumulated depreciation, store equipment, $10,000; accounts payable, $43,000; long-term notes payable, $40,000; income taxes payable, $7,000; retained earnings, $80,000; and common stock, 100,000 shares outstanding, par $1 per share (originally sold and issued at $1.10 per share).

Required:

a. You have been requested to prepare a classified balance sheet at December 31, 19C. (Hint: The balance sheet total is $280,000.)

b. What is the book or carrying value of the:
   (1) Inventory?
   (2) Accounts receivable?
   (3) Store equipment?
   (4) Notes payable (long term)?
   Explain briefly what these values mean.

c. What is the (1) amount of working capital and (2) the working capital ratio? Explain briefly what each of these amounts mean.

d. List any **contra** accounts. What does **contra account** mean?

PC2–4. Acme Trading Corporation is developing the annual financial statements for 19C. The information given below has been verified as correct. The company sells merchandise to retail outlets only. Note that in some instances only totals are provided to shorten the solution.

Financial Data, 19C

Income Statement			**Balance Sheet**	
Sales revenue		$273,000	Cash.	$ 31,000
Selling expenses		44,700	Accounts receivable	30,000
Interest expense		2,200	Allowance for doubtful accounts	1,000
Administrative expense*		23,300	Accounts payable	61,000
Sales returns		3,000	Retained earnings	72,000
Cost of goods sold		130,000	Merchandise inventory	138,000
Extraordinary loss (earth-			Investment in shares of K Corp.	
quake)		10,000	(long term)	4,000
Income tax expense on			Income taxes payable	5,000
operations (30%)	$21,000		Accumulated depreciation, store equipment	30,000
Tax savings on extraor-			Store equipment (acquired January 1, 19A)	90,000
dinary loss (30%)	3,000	18,000	Used equipment held for disposal	38,000
Revenue from divi-			Common stock, par $10 per share	100,000
dends on invest-			Long-term notes payable	46,000
ment in K Corp.			Contributed surplus	16,000
shares		200		

*Includes depreciation expense of $10,000.

Required:

a. On the basis of the listed data, you have been asked to prepare a classified income statement and a balance sheet for the year ended December 31, 19C. (Hint: EPS on net income is $4.20.)

b. Compute the average markup earned on cost, the amount of working capital, and the working capital ratio. Briefly interpret each.

c. What estimated life is being used to depreciate the store equipment assuming no residual or scrap values? Also, reconcile the balance in the accumulated depreciation account with the related expense on the income statement.

PC2–5. Tasty Bakery is developing its annual financial statements for 19X. The following cash-flow data have been determined to be correct for the year 19X: sales revenue (including $12,000 not collected), $300,000; expenses, $270,000 (including $21,000 of noncash items); cash received from sales of used machine, $1,000; cash received for extraordinary item, $900; cash borrowed on a five-year note payable, $20,000; cash disbursement for dividends, $12,000; cash expenditure to purchase two new delivery trucks, $9,900; and cash paid on mortgage payable, $5,000.

Required:

a. Prepare a SCFP, cash basis for 19X. (Hint: The cash balance increased by $34,000 during the year.)

b. As a basis for making future cash flow projections, what information on the SCFP for Tasty Bakery would you focus on especially? Explain.

PC2–6. Although Baker's Retail Store has been operating for only four years, the sales volume increase each year has been excellent; apparently it was occasioned by the location, a friendly atmosphere in the store, and a large stock of goods for customer selection. Despite this appearance of success, the company continually has experienced a severe cash shortage, and a recent analysis by a consultant revealed significant inventory overstocking in numerous lines. Baker's Retail Store was organized as a corporation by Samuel Baker (now president) and four additional investors. Each owner invested $41,000 cash and received 4,000 shares of common stock (par value $10 per share). Although Sam Baker is recognized as an excellent retailer, he exhibits very little interest in the financial reports. At a recent meeting of the board of directors, the inadequacy of the financial reports of the company was discussed. The board voted to engage an independent CA "to examine the accounting system, submit audited financial statements, analyze the financial situation, and make appropriate recommendations to the Board." The independent CA has just been handed the following financial statements for 19D which were prepared for the last board meeting by the "store bookkeeper" (to simplify this case, assume that all of the amounts are correct; also, only representative amounts have been included):

BAKER'S RETAIL STORE, INC.
Profit Statement
December 31, 19D

Incomes

Sales for the year	$572,000	
Interest collected on charge accounts	1,000	
Dividends received on shares of Y Corporation	200	$573,200

Costs

Salaries, sales	66,500	
Salaries, administrative	36,000	
Depreciation, office equipment	1,200	
Depreciation, store equipment	6,000	
Store rent	18,000	
Office supplies used	800	
Store supplies used	1,900	
Cost of goods sold for the year	340,000	
Bad debt losses (estimated)	300	
Promotion costs	60,000	
Interest on debts	5,000	
Loss on earthquake damage (extraordinary loss)	1,200	
Insurance and taxes (two-thirds selling and one-third administrative)	6,000	
Miscellaneous expenses, sales	2,000	
Miscellaneous expenses, administrative	700	
Sales returns	8,000	
Income taxes on operations $8,000, less tax saving on earthquake loss $400; net taxes	7,600	561,200
Profit		$ 12,000

Balance Sheet
December 31, 19D

Resources		Debts	
Cash	$ 3,500	Accounts payable............................	$ 20,000
Accounts receivable (offset for allowance for		Notes payable, short term....................	10,000
bad debts $500	33,500	Notes payable, long term	80,000
Merchandise inventory (at cost)..............	269,200	Rent due (for December 19D)................	1,500
Office supplies inventory....................	300	Income taxes owed	4,600
Store supplies inventory	1,600		
Prepaid insurance	1,200	**Capital**	
Investment in shares of Y Corporation, long		Stock, par $10.............................	200,000
term	5,000	Excess paid over par.......................	5,000
Store equipment (offset for accumulated		Retained earnings	36,000
depreciation, $25,600).....................	36,800		
Office equipment (offset for accumulated			
depreciation, $6,000)......................	6,000		
	$357,100		$357,100

Required:

a. Recast the income statement and balance sheet using preferred subclassifications and terminology. (Hint: EPS on income before extraordinary items is $0.64.)

b. Compute the amount of working capital and the working capital ratio. Show computations. Explain the meaning of the results. Do they appear to you to be favourable? Explain.

PC2–7. Ready Repair Company, a successful local automobile repair shop, is preparing its 19E financial statements. On January 1, 19E, the company acquired a substantial quantity of new shop equipment (and the related tools) for use in its testing and repair operations. The equipment involved a cash expenditure of $18,000. On the basis of experience, the owner estimated that the useful life of the new equipment would be five years for the company, at which time the equipment would sell for approximately 20 percent of the original cost.

Your advice is requested on two questions:

a. How much depreciation expense should be reported on the 19E income statement?

b. How should the new equipment be reported on the December 31, 19E, balance sheet? Show your computations and explanations. (Hint: Residual value is 20 percent and should not be depreciated because it will be recovered at the time of disposal. Analyze this situation and try to derive a logical approach for the computation of depreciation expense assuming the equipment will be used approximately the same amount each year.)

Part B

PC2–8. On December 31, 19D, Friendly Department Store (a corporation) prepared its annual financial statements. The income statement and balance sheet amounts are summarized below:

Income Statement
For the Year Ended December 31, 19D

Sales revenue	$ 200,000
Cost of goods sold.........................	(120,000)
All other operating expenses................	(60,000)
Income tax expense........................	(3,400)
Net income	$ 16,600

Balance Sheet
At December 31, 19D

Current assets.............................		$ 66,000
Operational assets (cost $210,000)		180,000
All other assets...........................		34,000
Total assets		$ 280,000
Current liabilities		$ 30,000
Long-term liabilities.......................		80,000
Total liabilities......................		110,000
Capital stock, par $10	$100,000	
Contributed surplus	30,000	
Retained earnings	40,000*	170,000
Total liabilities plus shareholders' equity......		$ 280,000

*During 19D, a $5,000 dividend was declared and paid which has been subtracted from this amount.

Required:

For analytical and interpretative purposes you have been asked to compute each of the following amounts. Show computations and briefly explain what each amount communicates to users of this statement.

a.   Profit margin.
b.   Gross margin.
c.   Average income tax rate.
d.   EPS.
e.   Working capital amount.
f.   Working capital ratio.
g.   ROI.
h.   Average sales price of the capital stock.
i.   January 1, 19D, balance (beginning) of retained earnings.
j.   Accumulated depreciation at December 31, 19D.

PC2–9.   You are considering making a $20,000 investment in the common shares of either X Corporation or Y Corporation. The companies operate in different industries, and their managements have followed different financing policies. In reviewing the latest financial statements you observe the following data:

	X Corporation		Y Corporation	
From the balance sheets:				
Total assets		$240,000		$240,000
Total liabilities..............		100,000		10,000
Shares outstanding		5,000		10,000
From the income statements:				
Revenues		107,000		107,000
Expenses:				
Interest expense (rate 15%)	$15,000		$ 1,500	
Income tax expense.......	29,280*		29,280†	
Remaining expenses	18,800	63,080	32,300	63,080
Net income		$ 43,920		$ 43,920

*($107,000 − $15,000 − $18,800) × 0.40 = $29,280.
†($107,000 − $1,500 − $32,300) × 0.40 = $29,280.

From these amounts you observe that the two companies have (1) the same total amount of assets ($240,000), (2) the same amount of revenues ($107,000), and (3) the same net income ($43,920). In respect to these three factors, the two companies appear to be equally attractive. However, as part of your analysis, you decide to investigate further by comparing the following: profit margin, return on shareholders' investment (owners' equity), EPS, and the aftertax, or net, interest rate.

Required:

a. Compute the above amounts for each company. Show computations. (Hint: The pretax interest rate is 15 percent. Interest expense is deductible on the income tax return; therefore, the after-tax rate would be less. Try to determine this lower rate by logical analysis.)

b. Based upon the data given and your analysis, which company would you select for the investment? Explain the basis for your choice.

PC2–10. You are considering investing $50,000 in either A Corporation or B Corporation. Both companies have been operating in the same industry for a number of years. Your decision model calls for an evaluation and interpretation of the financial statements for the last five years; however, you have obtained the statements for last year only. Those statements provided the following data:

	A Corporation	B Corporation
Sales.....................................	$500,000	$700,000
Gross margin on sales......................	210,000	301,000
Income before extraordinary items............	60,000	55,000
Net income...............................	20,000	64,000
Total assets..............................	300,000	400,000
Total liabilities (average interest rate 14%)......	100,000	100,000
Owners' equity (total)	200,000	300,000
Shares outstanding.........................	10,000	30,000
Income tax rate (average)	40%	40%

Required:

a. Based upon the above data (aside from other factors), what analytical steps would you suggest? Provide computations for each suggestion.

b. On the basis of your analytical results only, which company appears preferable as the investment choice? Explain why.

PC2–11. The financial statements at the end of the fiscal year for Watts Corporation are summarized below at June 30, 19F:

Income Statement

Sales revenue	$800,000
Cost of goods sold.........................	460,000
Gross margin on sales......................	340,000
Operating expenses and income taxes	292,000
Income before extraordinary items	48,000
Extraordinary gain (net of income taxes)	60,000
Net income	$108,000

Balance Sheet

Current assets............................	$ 98,000
Investments.............................	90,000
Operational assets (net)	330,000
Other assets.............................	70,000
Total assets	$588,000
Current liabilities	$ 98,000
Long-term liabilities......................	40,000
Total liabilities......................	138,000
Capital stock, 8,000 shares.................	400,000
Contributed surplus	3,000
Retained earnings	47,000
Total shareholders' equity	450,000
Total liabilities and shareholders' equity	$588,000

Required:

Several important investment decisions are under consideration by a large shareholder. Among the analytical data desired by the investor are certain financial ratios. Accordingly, you have been engaged to provide advice, including the following ratios:

Profit margin:
  1. Profit margin based on net income.
  2. Profit margin based on income before extraordinary items.

Return on investment (ROI):
  3. ROI based on net income and total shareholders' equity.
  4. ROI based on income before extraordinary items and total shareholders' equity.

Earnings per share (EPS):
  5. EPS based on net income.
  6. EPS based on income before extraordinary items.

For each of the three ratio categories given above, select the one that you would deem most relevant and explain the basis for your selection.

PC2–12. Below are listed the fundamental concepts of accounting. You are to match a "brief description of the transaction or event "given to the right with a concept by entering the appropriate letter to the left which *best* matches the description with the concept applied.

Fundamental concept applied

__E__ Users of financial statements
__I__ Objective of financial statements
Qualitative characteristics:
__D__ Relevance
__I__ Reliability
Implementation assumptions:
__M__ Separate entity
__X__ Continuity
__B__ Unit of measure
__R__ Time period
Elements of financial statements:
__A__ Revenues
__E__ Expenses
__V__ Gains
__N__ Losses
__C__ Assets
__G__ Liabilities

Brief description of transaction or event

A. Recorded a $1,000 sales of merchandise.
B. Counted (inventoried) the unsold items at the end of the period and valued them in dollars.
C. Acquired a vehicle for use in operating the business.
D. Reported the amount of depreciation expense because it likely will affect decisions of statement users.
E. Identified as the investors, creditors, and others interested in the business.
F. Used special accounting approaches because of the uniqueness of the industry.
G. Sold and issued bonds payable of $1 million.
H. Paid a contractor for an addition to the building with $10,000 cash and $20,000 market value of the shares of the company ($30,000 was deemed to be the cash equivalent price).
I. Engaged an outside independent PA to audit the financial statements.
J. Sold merchandise and services for cash and on credit during the

_W_ Owner's equity
Implementation principles:
_H_ Cost
_K_ Revenue
_J_ Matching
_U_ Reporting
_Q_ Reliability
_O_ Comparability
Exceptions to principles:
_T_ Materiality
_P_ Conservatism
_E_ Industry peculiarities

year then determined the cost of those goods sold and the cost of rendering those services.

K. Established an accounting policy that revenue shall be recognized only when ownership to the goods sold passes to the customer.

L. Designs and prepares the financial statements to assist the users to project the future cash flows of the business.

M. Established a policy not to include in the financial statements the personal financial affairs of the owners of the business.

N. Sold an asset at a loss that was a peripheral or incidental transaction.

O. Prepared financial statements for 19C that also repeats the statements for 19B.

P. Valued an asset, such as inventory, at less than its purchase cost because the replacement cost is less.

Q. Prepared reliable financial statements; unbiased and verifiable.

R. Dated the income statement "For the Year Ended December 31, 19B."

S. Used services from outsiders—paid cash for some and obtained the remainder on credit.

T. Acquired an asset (a pencil sharpener which will have a useful life of five years) and recorded it as an expense when purchased for $1.99.

U. Disclosed on the financial statements all relevant financial information about the business; necessitated the use of notes to the financial statements.

V. Sold an asset at a gain that was a peripheral or incidental transaction.

W. Assets, $500,000 − Liabilities, $300,000 = $200,000.

X. The accounting and reporting assumes a "going concern."

Y. None of the above.

PC2–13. Art Little Company (not a corporation) prepared the income statement given below including the two footnotes:

ART LITTLE COMPANY
Income Statement, Cash Basis
For the Year Ended December 31, 19B

Sales revenue (does not include $20,000 of sales on credit
   because collection will be in 19C) $100,000
Expenses (does not include $10,000 of expenses on credit
   because payment will be made in 19C) 75,200
Profit .... $ 24,800

Additional data:
a. Depreciation on operational assets (a company truck) for the year amounted to $15,000. Not included in expenses above.
b. On January 1, 19B, paid a two-year insurance premium on the truck amounting to $400. This amount is included in the expenses above.

Required:

a. Recast the above income statement on the *accrual basis* in conformity with GAAP. Show computations and explain each change.

b. Explain why the cash basis does not measure income as well as the accrual basis.

PC2–14. *Forbes* magazine (December 8, 1980, p. 57) reported the following: "One firm sold shares for a new coal mining company. The prospectus stated that the firm had acquired 15,000 acres of land with proven coal deposits. What the 'entrepreneurs' who raked in some $20 million didn't mention in the prospectus was that they had only leased surface rights to the land. So the only way they could possibly get any coal out of it was if the black stuff came popping out of its own volition."

Required:
a. What is a prospectus (see Chapter 1)?
b. In your opinion should the firm referred to above be required to disclose all of the facts cited above (say, in a prospectus)? Why?
c. If the firm referred to above were to prepare a financial statement for external parties, should they be required to disclose the facts cited above, or should disclosure be optional for this situation? Explain.

PC2–15.   Under the caption "Missing Footnotes," *Forbes* magazine (April 26, 1982, page 70), reported the following:

> Here's a footnote U.S. Steel Corp. neglected to include in its recently mailed 1981 annual report: As a result of its $6 billion-plus acquisition of Marathon Oil, U.S. Steel also got as part of the bargain a contingent liability of more than $369 million. That's more than one third of the profits U.S. Steel reported last year.
>
> Here's a footnote Du Pont should be including in its latest annual report. As a result of its $7.8 billion purchase last year of Conoco, Du Pont inherited a contingent liability of about $315 million. That's more than one fifth of the combined corporations' reported earnings in 1981.
>
> The reason for both potential liabilities is the Department of Energy's long-standing dispute with the major oil companies over alleged pricing violations and overcharges. Marathon's $369 million liability was calculated from a continuous audit of the company's records by federal energy officials from 1974 to 1980. Conoco's contingent liability is derived from Department of Energy notices alleging probable violation in 1979 and 1980. The $315 million contingent liability appeared in Conoco's last quarterly report issued for the second quarter of last year, just before its accounts were consolidated with Du Pont's. Marathon reported its $369 million potential liability in its last annual report.

Required:
a. In your opinion, how would a contingent liability differ from a full-blown liability? Hint: Consider what the word *contingent* means in the general sense.
b. In your opinion should the two companies (U.S. Steel Corporation and Du Pont be required to disclose (i.e., include a footnote to the financial statements) the facts about the respective contingent liabilities? Why?
c. If your answer to (b) is yes, who should be the "police person"? Explain.

PC2–16.   This case is designed to help you understand the contents of actual published financial statements and to observe differences in format and terminology. It is based upon the 1984 Annual Report of Consolidated-Bathurst (C-B) which is presented in Special Supplement B immediately preceding the Index. Respond to the questions based upon the data for the year labeled 1984:

a. Balance sheet:
    (1) What title did C-B use?

(2) How can you determine that the financial statements are comparative, aside from the title?

(3) What was the amount of working capital?

(4) What was the book, or carrying, value of the property, plant, and equipment?

(5) How much did customers owe the company?

(6) How much did C-B owe for unpaid income taxes on a current basis?

(7) How many shares were outstanding of (a) common stock and (b) preferred stock?

b. Income statement:

(8) What title did C-B use?

(9) What was the primary source of revenues?

(10) What was the amount of income tax expense?

(11) How much was research expense?

(12) How much did the goods cost that were sold to customers?

(13) How much did C-B earn on each share of common stock after the extraordinary loss?

c. Statement of retained earnings:

(14) What title did C-B use?

(15) Complete the following:

Beginning balance as previously reported.........	$_____
Prior period adjustment........................	
As restated	
Net earnings..................................	$_____
Excess of cost of purchasing common shares over stated value............................	
Dividends—preferred...........................	
—common	
Ending balance................................	$_____

(16) What amount was carried (a) from the income statement and (b) to the balance sheet?

d. Statement of changes in financial position:

(17) How was "funds" measured in this statement?

(18) What was the amount of the net funds from operations?

(19) How much was the cash from borrowing (on loans, notes, and long-term debt)?

(20) Was the total amount of dividends all paid in case?

(21) How much did funds change?

e. Notes to the financial statements:

(22) How many notes did C-B present?

(23) What is the title of Note 1?

(24) Are the majority of domestic inventories valued on the basis of LIFO, FIFO, or average?

(25) Did C-B have any legal proceedings pending?

(26) Which quarter of the year had the highest amount of net earnings, worldwide?

f. Auditors' report:

(27) What title was used for this report?

(28) Did the auditors give a "good" or "bad" opinion about the financial statements?

g. Supplementary information:
    (29) What line of business (i.e., segment) had the lowest operating profit? What geographical area had the lowest operating profit?
    (30) What was the adjustment to the historical cost of inventories to increase the value to current cost? To property, plant, and equipment?
    (31) How many people were (a) employees and (b) shareholders?

3

Transaction Analysis

PURPOSE OF THIS CHAPTER

In Chapters 1 and 2 you studied the fundamentals of financial accounting and the financial statements. Your attention now is turned to the accounting process—the way in which the ongoing transactions within a business are recorded, analyzed, and classified in a form from which the periodic financial statements can be developed. In this chapter you will learn the fundamentals of the accounting model and how to analyze business transactions to determine and record quantitatively their economic impacts on that model.

To accomplish these purposes, this chapter is divided into two parts as follows:

Part A—The accounting model and transaction analysis

Part B—The accounting information processing cycle

Part A—The Accounting Model and Transaction Analysis

NATURE OF TRANSACTIONS

Accounting focuses on certain events that have an economic impact on the entity. Those particular events are recorded as a part of the accounting process and generally are referred to as **transactions.** A broad definition of transactions includes (1) those events that involve an exchange of resources (assets) and/or obligations (liabilities) between the business (i.e., the accounting entity) and one or more parties other than the entity; and (2) certain events (or economic occurrences) that are not between the entity and one or more parties but yet have a direct and measurable effect on the accounting entity. Examples of the first category of transactions include the purchase of a machine, the sale of merchandise, the borrowing of cash, and the investment in the business by the owners. Examples of the second category of transactions include (1) **economic events,** such as a drop in the replacement cost of an item held in inventory and a flood loss; and (2) **time adjustments,** such as depreciation of an operational asset (as a result of use) and the "using up" of prepaid insurance. Throughout this textbook, the word *transaction* will be used in the broad sense to include both types of events.[1]

Most transactions are evidenced by a **business document** of some sort; in the case of a sale on credit, a charge ticket or invoice is prepared, and in the case of a purchase of goods, an invoice is received. In certain other transactions, such as a cash sale, there may be no document other than the cash register tape. The documents that underlie, or support, transactions usually are called **source documents.** The important requirement, from the accounting point of view, is that procedures be established to capture the data on **each transaction as it occurs.** Once this has been done, the data processing characteristics of the accounting system advance the economic impact of each transaction on the entity from initial recording to its final resting place—the periodic financial statements.

The fundamental feature of most transactions with **external parties** is an exchange where the business entity both gives up something and receives something in return. For example, in the case of a sale of merchandise for cash, the entity gives up resources (the goods sold) and receives in return another resource (cash). In the case of a credit sale of merchandise, the resource received at the time of sale is an account receivable (an asset). Later, another transaction occurs when the account receivable is collected; here, the resource relinquished is the receivable and the resource received is cash. As another example, in the purchase of an asset (either merchandise for resale or a truck purchased for use in the business), the entity acquires the asset and gives up

---

[1] A narrow definition of a transaction limits it to the first category, that is, events between the entity and one or more parties other than the entity. This definition is useful in certain circumstances and is conceptually correct. However, accounting recognizes a number of events that are not transactions in the strict sense, therefore, we have defined the term in the broader sense to generalize our terminology.

cash, or in the case of a credit purchase incurs a liability. Another transaction occurs later when the debt is paid. At that time, the entity gives up a resource (cash) and "receives" satisfaction of the debt. The sale or purchase of services can be analyzed in the same way. Thus, transactions have a **dual economic effect** on the accounting entity. We will return to this dual effect when we consider the accounting model in Part B of this chapter.

THE FUNDAMENTAL ACCOUNTING MODEL

The fundamental accounting model expresses in an algebraic format the status of the assets, debts, and owners' claims of an accounting entity at any specific point in time. In Chapters 1 and 2 you learned the **fundamental accounting model** when you studied the balance sheet (the position statement), viz:

$$\textbf{Assets = Liabilities + Owners' equity}$$

You also learned that owners' equity is (1) increased by investments (i.e., contributions) by the owners, (2) decreased by withdrawals by owners (such as dividends), (3) increased by revenues, and (4) decreased by expenses.[2] Thus, we can expand the fundamental accounting model as follows:

$$\textbf{Assets = Liabilities + Owners' equity}$$

	Decreased by:	Increased by:
	Withdrawals	Investments
	Expenses	Revenues

The fundamental accounting model is a broad economic description of an accounting entity that accommodates the **recording** of each transaction that directly affects the enterprise. The **dual economic effect** of each transaction (discussed below) is recorded in terms of this expanded accounting model. The dual effect is captured by the same accounting process, whether that processing system is handwritten, mechanized, or computerized.

To illustrate how specific transactions are analyzed and how the dual economic effect is recorded in terms of the fundamental accounting model, let's consider a simple but realistic situation. Throughout the example you should note particularly that (1) each transaction is recorded separately; (2) in recording each transaction, the equality of the fundamental accounting model is maintained (that is, assets will always equal liabilities plus owners' equity); and (3) the **dual effect,** as discussed in the preceding section, is recorded for each transaction.

---

[2]Owners' equity sometimes is referred to as equity capital and occasionally as net worth. The latter term is not recommended because it implies that owners' equity on the balance sheet states what the owners' claim is actually worth, which is not the case.

The fundamental accounting model illustrated

B. Bass and three friends started a dry cleaning business on January 1, 19A, by investing a total of $20,000 cash from their personal savings accounts. In return for their contribution, each investor was issued 200 shares of the capital stock of the newly organized **corporation**—Bass Cleaners, Inc. Remember that the accounting entity, Bass Cleaners, Inc., is to be distinguished from the four investors in accordance with the separate-entity assumption (Exhibit 2–6). Exhibit 3–1 lists a series of transactions for the year 19A and illustrates the dual effect of each transaction in terms of the accounting model for the business. Also, it provides the information for developing the **income statement** and **balance sheet** shown in Exhibit 3–2. This illustration should be studied carefully as you read the next few paragraphs.

On the balance sheet, because Bass is a corporation, shareholders' equity is represented by the two **sources**: contributed capital and retained earnings.[3] **Retained earnings** represents the accumulated earnings of the corporation to date, less all dividends declared to date. This aspect of the balance sheet was explained and illustrated in Chapters 1 and 2.

From this simple example you can view the broad perspective of the **accounting process**. As transactions occur, they create **raw economic data**. The data from each transaction are subjected to **transaction analysis** to determine the **dual economic effect** of the transaction on the business in terms of the fundamental accounting model. The dual effect then is recorded in the accounting system. Finally, at the end of the accounting period, the financial statements are constructed from the data accumulated in the accounting system.

Bass Cleaners, as reflected in Exhibits 3–1 and 3–2, illustrates two primary data processing problems:

1. An efficient method is needed for **keeping track of (i.e., recording) the amounts** of each kind of asset (cash, accounts receivable, equipment, inventory, etc.); each kind of liability (accounts payable, notes payable, bonds payable, etc.); and each category of owners' equity (capital stock, revenues, and expenses).

2. An efficient and systematic method of continuous **checking** is needed to assure accuracy during the recording process.

The account.   The need to record transactions efficiently and to check the accuracy of the recording led early accountants to develop a series of **accounts.** A separate account is used for each kind of asset, liability, and owners' equity. **An account is a standardized arrangement for recording data by categories.** In

---

[3]Owners' equity usually is designated to indicate the kind of ownership arrangement used as follows:

Corporation.............	Shareholders' equity
Sole proprietorship......	Owner's capital
Partnership.............	Partners' capital

EXHIBIT 3–1 Transaction analysis illustrated

BASS CLEANERS INC.
Transaction Analysis—19A

Transactions	Dual effect of each transaction on the entity				
	Assets	=	Liabilities	+	Shareholders' Equity
a. Bass Cleaners received $20,000 cash invested by owners; 800 shares ($25 par value) issued to the four owners........	Cash + $20,000				Capital stock (800 shares) + $20,000
b. Borrowed $5,000 cash on 12% note payable........	Cash + 5,000		Note payable + $5,000		
c. Purchased delivery truck for cash at cost of $8,000........	Cash − 8,000 Delivery truck + 8,000				
d. Cleaning revenue collected in cash, $40,000........	Cash + 40,000				Cleaning revenue + 40,000
e. Cleaning revenue earned in 19A, but the bill is not collected, $4,000........	Accounts receivable + 4,000				Cleaning revenue + 4,000
f. Operating expenses paid in cash, $25,800........	Cash − 25,800				Operating expenses − 25,800
g. Operating expenses incurred in 19A but not paid, $2,000......			Accounts payable + 2,000		Operating expenses − 2,000
h. Paid 12% interest on the $5,000 note payable, (b) above, with cash ($5,000 × 12% = $600).......	Cash − 600				Interest expense − 600
i. Depreciation expense for one year on truck ($8,000 ÷ 5 years = $1,600)........	Truck − 1,600				Operating expenses, depreciation − 1,600
j. Cash dividend of $1,800 declared and paid to shareholders*........	Cash − 1,800				Retained earnings (or dividends paid) − 1,800
k. Collected $1,000 cash on accounts receivable in (e)........	Cash + 1,000 Accounts receivable − 1,000				
l. Paid $500 cash on accounts payable in (g)........	Cash − 500		Accounts payable − 500		
Totals (end of accounting period)........	Total assets $38,700	=	Total liabilities $6,500	+	Total shareholders' equity $32,200

Observe how these items and their respective **ending balances** flow into the **financial statements,** Exhibit 3–2.

*A cash dividend is not an expense; it is a withdrawal of resources by the owners.

EXHIBIT 3–2
Income statement
and balance sheet
illustrated

Observe that these items and their respective amounts were developed in the transaction analysis illustrated in Exhibit 3–1.

BASS CLEANERS, INC.
Income Statement
For the Year Ended December 31, 19A

Cleaning revenue ($40,000 + $4,000).		$44,000
Operating expenses ($25,800 + $2,000 + $1,600	$29,400	
Interest expense	600	30,000
Net income.		$14,000
EPS (14,000 ÷ 800 shares)		$17.50

Note: To simplify the illustration, income taxes are disregarded.

BASS CLEANERS, INC.
Balance Sheet
At December 31, 19A

Assets

Cash ($20,000 + $5,000 − $8,000 + $40,000 −		
$25,800 − $600 − $1,800 + $1,000 − $500		$29,300
Accounts receivable ($4,000 − $1,000).		3,000
Delivery truck	$ 8,000	
Less: Accumulated depreciation	1,600	6,400
Total assets.		$38,700

Liabilities

Notes payable	5,000	
Accounts payable (2,000 − $500)	1,500	
Total liabilities		$ 6,500

Shareholders' Equity

Contributed capital:		
Capital stock (800 shares)	20,000	
Retained earnings (beginning retained earnings, $–0–, plus net income,		
$14,000, minus dividends declared and paid, $1,800)	12,200	
Total shareholders' equity		32,200
Total liabilities and shareholders' equity.		$38,700

most accounting systems, you will find **separate** accounts, individually labeled, for each asset, such as cash, inventory, accounts receivable, equipment, land; for each liability, such as accounts payable, notes payable, taxes payable; and for each element of owners' equity, such as capital stock, sales revenue, service revenue, and various kinds of expenses. For example, the **Cash account** for Bass Cleaners may appear as shown in Exhibit 3–3.

Now we will discuss and illustrate how accounts are used to help resolve the two data processing problems listed above.

1. **Keeping track of the amounts for each item**—To do this, a separate **account** is set up for each item that will be reported on the financial statements. Each account is designed so that

EXHIBIT 3–3
Ledger account (T-account format), illustrated

		CASH		
Left or Debit Side			Right or Credit Side	Acct. No. 101
(Increases)			(Decreases)	
Investment by owners	20,000		To purchase truck	8,000
Loan from bank	5,000		Operating expenses	25,800
Cleaning revenue	40,000		Interest expense	600
Collections on accounts			Dividends declared and paid	1,800
receivable	1,000		Payment on accounts payable	500
	66,000			36,700
Balance (difference				
66,000 − 36,700)	29,300			

all increases are entered on one side (e.g., on the left side of the Cash account in Exhibit 3–3) and all decreases are entered on the other side (e.g., on the right side of the Cash account in Exhibit 3–3). To illustrate the increased efficiency possible, compare the list of plus and minus amounts on the cash lines of Exhibit 3–2 with the location arrangement in Exhibit 3–3. Also, imagine thousands or millions of such increases and decreases during the year in a typical business. In contrast, the Cash account shown in Exhibit 3–3 reflects a left side total of $66,000 and a right side total of $36,700; the difference, $29,300, is the ending cash balance (as reported on the balance sheet in Exhibit 3–2). When the total amount on the decrease side of the Cash account is larger than the total amount on the increase side, a cash deficit (bank overdraft) is indicated. The account system is very flexible; for example, instead of being set up in T-account form (as in Exhibit 3–3), it can be set up in other formats such as the columnar form as in Exhibit 3–7. The account system can be used with either (or a combination of) handwritten, mechanical, or computerized approaches.

2. **Providing a systematic method of checking for accuracy during the recording process**—To resolve this problem, the account was designed to provide **dual equalities or balances** that may be summarized as follows:

Equalities	Basis
a. Assets = Liabilities + Owners' equity	Algebraic relationship in the fundamental accounting model
b. Debits = Credits	Algebraic relationship between account increases and decreases

These two basic equalities may be explained as follows:

    a. The fundamental accounting model, **Assets = Liabilities + Owners' equity,** is an algebraic representation of the economic position of an entity at any point in time. By definition, it always balances and can be rearranged mathematically (e.g., Assets − Liabilities = Owners' equity). Observe in Exhibit 3–1 that the analysis of each transaction, and the cumulative effects of all transactions, were always in balance in terms of this algebraic model (as shown in the balance sheet in Exhibit 3–2). Thus, the first check for accuracy listed above is applied continuously throughout the accounting process.

    b. Now we will consider the second accuracy test listed above, **Debits = Credits.** In this context, it is useful to think of an account as having two sides (i.e., parts), the **left side,** which in accounting is called the **Debit** side, and the **right side,** which in accounting is called the **Credit** side. These designations are shown in Exhibit 3–3.[4]

The Debits = Credits feature in accounting. To be useful as an accuracy check, the relationships described above, must be systematic, complementary, and flexible. Recall from Chapter 1 that in 1494 a mathematician (Pacioli) first described the fundamental accounting model used today. Perceiving the importance of accuracy, and after designing the T-account (similar to that illustrated in Exhibit 3–3), Pacioli applied an algebraic concept that has proven to be of great significance in minimizing errors in the accounting process. The fundamental accounting model, **Assets = Liabilities + Owners' equity,** is an algebraic model that has mathematical equality. Pacioli added another algebraic balance feature to the basic model to minimize errors in recording increases and decreases in each account. Let's see how it was done.

Pacioli perceived that having designed the T-account with two sides to reflect increases and decreases, he could add another algebraic **balancing feature** by simply **reversing** the position in the account of the "increases" and "decreases" on the **opposite sides** of the basic accounting model. This second algebraic balance feature is still used to this day; it has the "+" and "−" **in reverse order** on the opposite sides of the accounting model in this way:

	Assets		=	Liabilities		+	Owners' equity	
	Debit	*Credit*		*Debit*	*Credit*		*Debit*	*Credit*
	+	−		−	+		−	+

Observe that **debit** always refers to the left side of an account and **credit** always refers to the right side of an account. **Thus, debit and credit positions**

---

[4]Handwritten or manually maintained accounts in the formats shown here are used primarily in small businesses. Highly mechanized and computerized systems retain the concept of the account but not this format. T-accounts are useful primarily for instructional purposes.

do not change; only the plus and minus signs change positions. The addition of this algebraic concept resulted in the second "balancing" feature; that is, **debits always should equal credits.** Thus, the system used for recording increases and decreases in the accounts may be tabulated as follows:[5]

	Increases	Decreases
Assets	Debit	Credit
Liabilities	Credit	Debit
Owners' equity	Credit	Debit

Debits and credits for revenues and expenses. After some practice you will become comfortable using the words *debit* and *credit* to signify changes in assets, liabilities, and owners' equity accounts. However, some persons are confused about the proper terms to reflect changes in revenue and expense accounts. Remember that owners' equity is increased by credits and decreased by debits. Revenues increase owners' equity; therefore, **revenues are recorded as credits.** Expenses decrease owners' equity; therefore, **expenses are recorded as debits.** In other words, the debit/credit relationship for owners' equity accounts is applied to revenues and expenses.[6]

In summary, the balancing features of the fundamental accounting model are:

1. **Assets = Liabilities + Owners' equity**
2. **Debits = Credits**

The next section of this chapter illustrates the use of accounts and emphasizes application of the fundamental accounting model and its dual balancing feature.

TRANSACTION ANALYSIS

Information processing in an accounting system involves collecting raw economic data on each transaction, analyzing the data in terms of the fundamental accounting model (often called **transaction analysis**), **recording** (entering) the results of the analysis in the accounting system (i.e., in the accounts discussed above), and finally, **preparing** the periodic financial statements. This section introduces transaction analysis.

Transaction analysis is a term used frequently to describe the process of studying each transaction to determine its **dual effect** on the entity in terms of the accounting model. In transaction analysis, a careful distinction is made

---

[5]Historically, and continuing to the present, accountants refer to the left side as the debit side and to the right side as the credit side. For accounting purposes, the terms **debit** and **credit** have no other meanings. The words **to debit** and **to credit** should not be confused with "increase" or "decrease" as will become clear in the next few paragraphs. Contrary to what some people think, there is no implication of "goodness" attached to credits or "badness" attached to debits (or vice versa).

[6]To "charge an account" is a frequently used expression meaning to **debit** an account. Thus, the word *debit* is used as both a verb and a noun.

between the cash basis and the accrual basis methods. In Chapter 2, the distinction between **cash basis accounting** and **accrual basis accounting** was discussed briefly. Recall that the accrual basis is required by GAAP. The concept of **accrual accounting requires that revenues and expenses be measured and reported in the accounting period in which the transactions occur rather than when the related cash is received or paid.**

Now, let's see how **each transaction** is subjected to transaction analysis to determine (1) its dual economic effect on the entity and (2) how that dual effect is recorded in the accounts (i.e., in terms of the fundamental accounting model).

Recall that for each transaction recorded, **two separate balances** must be maintained, viz: (1) Assets = Liabilities + Owners' equity and (2) Debits = Credits. Bass Cleaners, Inc., will be used to demonstrate transaction analysis and the basic recording process. You should analyze each transaction (listed in Exhibit 3–1) and trace the manner in which the dual effect is recorded in the accounting model by using T-accounts (rather than simple plus and minus as in Exhibit 3–1). The transactions are entered in Exhibit 3–4 in T-accounts and are keyed with letters for ready reference. You should study Exhibit 3–4 intensively (and even restudy it in tandem with the next several chapters) in order to understand clearly *(a)* the fundamental accounting model, *(b)* transaction analysis, *(c)* recording the dual effects of each transaction, and *(d)* the dual-

EXHIBIT 3–4
Transaction analysis, journal entries, and T-accounts illustrated

Bass Cleaners, Inc.

a. **Received $20,000 cash invested by the four owners and in turn issued 800 shares of capital stock (par value $25 per share).**

Transaction analysis—This transaction increased the company's cash by $20,000, which is recorded in the **Cash** account as a debit (increase); liabilities were unaffected; and owners' equity was increased by $20,000, which is recorded in the **Capital Stock** account as a credit (increase). The entry (recording) in the accounting system may be summarized conveniently as follows (credits are listed last and also are indented for easy identification):

	Debit	*Credit*
Cash (asset)...	20,000	
Capital stock (owners' equity)		20,000

The two **accounts** would appear as follows:

Cash (asset)				**Capital Stock (owners' equity)**		
Debit		*Credit*		*Debit*		*Credit*
(*a*)	20,000			(*a*)		20,000

Dual check for accuracy—The entry meets both tests: Assets (+$20,000) = Liabilities (–0–) + Owners' equity (+$20,000), and Debits ($20,000) = Credits ($20,000).

EXHIBIT 3–4
(continued)

b. **Borrowed $5,000 cash from the bank on a 12 percent note payable.**

Transaction analysis—This transaction increased cash by $5,000, which is recorded in the **Cash** account as a debit (increase); liabilities were increased by $5,000, which is recorded in the **Notes Payable** account as a credit (increase); and owners' equity was unchanged. The entry in the accounting system may be summarized as follows:

Cash (asset).	5,000	
Notes payable (liability)		5,000

The **accounts** affected would appear as follows:

Cash (asset)				**Notes Payable (liability)**		
Debit		*Credit*		*Debit*		*Credit*
(a)	20,000			(b)		5,000
(b)	5,000					

Dual check for accuracy—The entry meets both tests: Assets (+$5,000) = Liabilities (+$5,000) + Owners' Equity (–0–), and Debits ($5,000) = Credits ($5,000).
The 12 percent refers to the interest charge for a year. If the loan is not paid for a year, 12 percent interest will be required. Proportionately smaller amounts are required for periods less than a year.

c. **Purchased a delivery truck for cash at a cost of $8,000.**

Transaction analysis—This transaction increased the asset, **Delivery Truck,** by $8,000, which is recorded in that asset account as a debit (increase); and the cash was decreased by $8,000, which is recorded in the asset account **Cash** as a credit (decrease). Liabilities and owners' equity were not affected. The entry in the accounting system may be summarized conveniently as follows:

Delivery truck (asset)	8,000	
Cash (asset).		8,000

The two accounts affected would appear as follows:

Delivery Truck (asset)				**Cash (asset)**		
Debit		*Credit*		*Debit*		*Credit*
(c)	8,000		(a)	20,000	(c)	8,000
			(b)	5,000		

Dual check for accuracy—The entry meets both tests: Assets (delivery truck, +$8,000 and cash, –$8,000) = Liabilities (–0–) + Owners' Equity (–0–), and Debits ($8,000) = Credits ($8,000).

d. **Cleaning revenue earned and collected in cash, $40,000.**

Transaction analysis—This transaction increased cash by $40,000, which is recorded in the asset account **Cash** as a debit (increase); liabilities were unaffected; and owners' equity

EXHIBIT 3–4
(continued)

was increased by $40,000 as a result of earning revenue. Owners' equity is credited (increased) for $40,000. A separate owners' equity account, **Cleaning Revenue,** is used to keep track of this particular revenue. The entry may be summarized as follows:

Cash (asset)...	40,000	
Cleaning revenue (owners' equity)..................		40,000

The two accounts affected would appear as follows:

Cash (asset)				**Cleaning Revenue (owners' equity)**			
Debit		*Credit*		*Debit*		*Credit*	
(a)	20,000	(c)	8,000			(d)	40,000
(b)	5,000						
(d)	40,000						

Dual check for accuracy—The entry meets both tests: Assets (+ $40,000) = Liabilities (–0–) + Owners' equity (+ $40,000), and Debits ($40,000) = Credits ($40,000).

e. **Cleaning revenue earned, but the cash was not yet collected, $4,000.**

Transaction analysis—This transaction increased the company's asset, **Accounts Receivable,** by $4,000, which is recorded as a debit (increase) to that account; liabilities were unaffected; and owners' equity was increased by $4,000. Owners' equity is credited (increased) by $4,000 using a separate account, **Cleaning Revenue,** which is used to keep track of this particular revenue. The entry in the accounting system may be summarized as follows:

Accounts receivable (asset)..............................	4,000	
Cleaning revenue (owners' equity)...................		4,000

The effect on the two **accounts** would appear as follows:

Accounts Receivable (asset)				**Cleaning Revenue (owners' equity)**			
Debit		*Credit*		*Debit*		*Credit*	
(e)	4,000					(d)	40,000
						(e)	4,000

Dual check for accuracy—The entry meets both tests: Assets (+ $4,000) = Liabilities (–0–) + Owners' Equity (+ $4,000), and Debits ($4,000) = Credits ($4,000).

f. **Expenses incurred and paid in cash, $25,800.**

Transaction analysis—This transaction decreased cash by $25,800, which is recorded in the **Cash** account as a credit (decrease); liabilities were unaffected; and owners' equity was decreased by $25,800 as a result of paying expenses. Owners' equity is decreased by debiting a separate account, **Operating Expenses,** which is used to keep track of this particular expense. The accounting entry may be summarized as follows:

EXHIBIT 3-4
(continued)

| Operating expense (owners' equity)..................... | 25,800 | |
| Cash (asset)....................................... | | 25,800 |

The effect on the two **accounts** would appear as follows:

| **Operating Expenses (owners' equity)** | | | | **Cash (asset)** | | |
Debit		Credit		Debit		Credit
(f) 25,800			(a)	20,000	(c)	8,000
			(b)	5,000	(f)	25,800
			(d)	40,000		

Dual check for accuracy—The entry meets both tests.

g. **Expenses incurred, but the cash not yet paid, $2,000.**

Transaction analysis—This transaction did not affect the company's assets; liabilities were increased by $2,000, which is recorded as a credit (increase) to **Accounts Payable;** and owners' equity was decreased $2,000 by debiting a separate account, **Operating Expenses,** which is used to keep track of this particular type of expense. The entry summarized is:

| Operating expenses (owners' equity)...................... | 2,000 | |
| Accounts payable (liability)........................... | | 2,000 |

The two **accounts** affected would appear as follows:

| **Operating Expenses (owners' equity)** | | | **Accounts Payable (liability)** | | |
Debit		Credit	Debit		Credit
(f) 25,800				(g)	2,000
(g) 2,000					

Dual check for accuracy—The entry meets both tests.

h. **Paid cash for interest incurred on note payable in** (b) **($5,000 × 12% = $600).**

Transaction analysis—This transaction decreased cash by $600, which is recorded as a credit (decrease) in the **Cash** account; the principal amount of the related liability ($5,000) was unchanged; however, owners' equity was decreased by the amount of the interest ($600) because the payment of interest (but not principal of the note) represents an expense. Owners' equity is decreased by debiting a separate account, **Interest Expense,** which is used to keep track of this particular type of expense. The entry summarized is:

| Interest expense (owners' equity)........................... | 600 | |
| Cash (asset) .... | | 600 |

EXHIBIT 3–4
(continued)

The two **accounts** affected would appear as follows:

Interest Expense (owners' equity)				Cash (asset)		
Debit		*Credit*		*Debit*		*Credit*
(h)	600		(a)	20,000	(c)	8,000
			(b)	5,000	(f)	25,800
			(d)	40,000	(h)	600

Dual check for accuracy—The entry meets both tests.

i. **Depreciation expense on the truck for one year ($8,000 ÷ 5 years = $1,600).**

Transaction analysis—This transaction is caused by the **internal** use (wear and tear) of an asset owned for operating purposes. This use is quantified and recorded as depreciation expense. Owners' equity was decreased by this expense, which is recorded as a debit to a separate account for this type of expense, **Operating Expenses** (alternatively, a separate expense account, called depreciation expense, could have been used). Assets (i.e., the delivery truck) was decreased because a part of the cost of the asset was "used up" in operations. Instead of directly crediting (decreasing) the asset account, Delivery Truck, a related **contra account, Accumulated Depreciation, Delivery Truck,** is credited so that the total amount of depreciation can be kept separate from the cost of the asset. This procedure will be explained and illustrated in detail in Chapter 9. The entry summarized is:

> Operating expenses (owners' equity)...................... 1,600
>   Accumulated depreciation, delivery
>   truck (contra account).................................. 1,600

The two **accounts** affected would appear as follows:

Operating Expenses (owners' equity)				Accumulated Depreciation, Delivery Truck (contra account)		
Debit		*Credit*		*Debit*		*Credit*
(f)	25,800				(i)	1,600
(g)	2,000					
(i)	1,600					

Dual check for accuracy—The entry meets both tests: Assets (−$1,600) = Liabilities (–0–) + Owners' Equity (−$1,600), and Debits ($1,600) = Credits ($1,600).

j. **Declared and paid cash dividends to shareholders, $1,800.**

Transaction analysis—This transaction decreased the company's cash by $1,800, which is recorded in the **Cash** account as a credit (decrease); liabilities were unaffected; owners' equity was decreased by $1,800 as a result of the resources (cash) paid out of the business to the shareholders. Owners' equity is debited (decreased) by using a separate account, **Retained Earnings,** which is used to keep track of this kind of decrease in owners' equity (and certain increases explained later). Dividends declared and paid decreases owners' equity but it does not represent an expense (which also decreases owners' equity), rather it represents a cash distribution of "earnings" to the owners. The entry summarized is:

EXHIBIT 3–4
(continued)

```
Retained earnings (or dividends paid) . . . . . . . . . . . . . . . . . . . . .    1,800
     Cash (asset). . . . . . . . . . . . . . . . . . . . . . . . . . . . . . . . . . . . . . . .            1,800
```

The two **accounts** would appear as follows:

Retained Earnings (owners' equity)			Cash (asset)			
Debit		*Credit*		*Debit*		*Credit*
(j)	1,800		(a)	20,000	(c)	8,000
			(b)	5,000	(f)	25,800
			(d)	40,000	(h)	600
					(j)	1,800

Dual check for accuracy—The entry meets both tests.

k. **Collected $1,000 cash on accounts receivable in** *(e).*

Transaction analysis—This transaction increased the asset cash by $1,000, which is recorded as a debit (increase) in the **Cash** account; another asset, **Accounts Receivable,** was decreased, which is recorded as a credit (decrease) of $1,000. Liabilities and owners' equity were unaffected because there was a change in two assets with no change in total assets. The entry summarized is:

```
Cash (asset). . . . . . . . . . . . . . . . . . . . . . . . . . . . . . . . . . . . . . . . . .    1,000
     Accounts receivable (asset) . . . . . . . . . . . . . . . . . . . . . . . . . . .            1,000
```

The two **accounts** would appear as follows:

Cash (asset)				Accounts Receivable (asset)			
Debit		*Credit*		*Debit*		*Credit*	
(a)	20,000	(c)	8,000	(e)	4,000	(k)	1,000
(b)	5,000	(f)	25,800				
(d)	40,000	(h)	600				
(k)	1,000	(j)	1,800				

Dual check for accuracy—The entry meets both tests.

l. **Paid $500 cash on accounts payable in** *(g).*

Transaction analysis—This transaction decreased cash by $500, which is recorded as a credit (decrease) in the **Cash** account; the $500 decrease in liabilities is recorded as a debit (decrease) to the **Accounts Payable** account. Owners' equity was unaffected because there was no revenue or expense involved in this transaction, merely the payment of a debt. The entry summarized is:

EXHIBIT 3–4
(concluded)

Accounts payable (liability)	500
Cash (asset)	500

The two **accounts** would appear as follows:

Accounts Payable (liability)				**Cash (asset)**			
Debit		*Credit*		*Debit*		*Credit*	
(*l*)	500	(*g*)	2,000	(*a*)	20,000	(*c*)	8,000
				(*b*)	5,000	(*f*)	25,800
				(*d*)	40,000	(*h*)	600
				(*k*)	1,000	(*j*)	1,800
						(*l*)	500

Dual check for accuracy—The entry meets both tests.

For further illustration purposes, each one of the above accounts is repeated in Exhibit 3–6 and their balances (i.e., the total increases minus the total decreases in each account) are shown in Exhibit 3–8.

balancing system. Exhibit 3–4 was designed to emphasize these important aspects of the accounting processing system.

Observe in Exhibit 3–4 that each transaction affected at least two different accounts because the economic position of the entity, in terms of the fundamental accounting model—Assets = Liabilities + Owners' equity—always is affected in at least two ways. This dual-effect characteristic of the model is the reason its application often is referred to as a **double-entry** system.

The fundamental accounting model and the mechanics of the debit-credit concept in T-account format can be summarized as follows, where + means increase and − means decrease:

Assets		=	**Liabilities**		+	**Owners' equity**	
Debit	*Credit*		*Debit*	*Credit*		*Debit*	*Credit*
+	−		−	+		−	+

Revenue (increase in owners' equity)

Debit	*Credit*
	(To record)

Expenses (decrease in owners' equity)

Debit	*Credit*
(To record)	

Note particularly that an increase in **revenue** (a credit) represents an increase in owners' equity and an increase in **expense** (a debit) represents a **decrease** in owners' equity. When a revenue is earned, the resources (i.e., assets) of the business are increased (or liabilities may be decreased) and, because of the dual effect, owners' equity is increased by the same amount. In contrast, when an expense is incurred, the net resources of the business are decreased (i.e., assets are decreased and/or liabilities increased), and because of the dual effect, the owners' equity is decreased by the same amount.

Part B—The Accounting Information Processing Cycle

The accounting information processing cycle is **repeated each period.** It involves a series of **sequential** phases (steps), starting with the transactions and extending through the accounting period in the accounting system and finally to the preparation of the required financial statements: income statement, balance sheet, and statement of changes in financial position. In this part, we will consider the primary sequential phases in the information processing cycle in the order in which they usually are accomplished, viz: (1) collecting raw data, (2) analyzing transactions, (3) recording transactions in the **journal,** (4) transferring data from the journal to the **ledger,** (5) preparing a **trial balance,** and (6) preparing the required **financial statements.**

PHASE 1—COLLECTING RAW DATA

The initial phase in the accounting information processing cycle is the collection of raw economic data on each transaction affecting the entity.[7] Such economic data are collected continuously throughout the accounting period as transactions occur. Transactions involving **external** parties usually generate **source documents** that provide essential data. Examples are sales invoices, cash register tapes, purchase invoices, and signed receipts. Documentation must be generated **internally** for certain economic effects such as depreciation and the using up of office supplies already on hand. It is important to realize that most of the raw data (and the supporting documents) entered into an accounting system are not generated by the accounting function but through the various **operating** functions of the business. The quality of the **outputs** of an information processing system is determined primarily by the quality (and timeliness) of the inputs of raw data based on transactions; therefore, a carefully designed and controlled data collection system is essential. Thus, the ini-

---

[7]Recall that transactions include (*a*) events that involve an exchange between two or more separate entities (or persons) and (*b*) events that are not between entities but nevertheless have a particular economic impact on the entity being accounted for.

tial data collection procedure constitutes an integral and important subsystem of an accounting information processing system.

PHASE 2—ANALYZING TRANSACTIONS

This phase in the accounting information processing system was explained and illustrated in Exhibit 3–4. Recall that the objective of this mental process is the determination of the **economic effects** on the entity of each transaction in terms of the basic accounting model: Assets = Liabilities + Owners' equity. When transaction analysis is completed, the economic effects of the transactions analyzed are then entered **formally** into the accounting system.

PHASE 3—RECORDING TRANSACTIONS IN THE JOURNAL

After transaction analysis, the economic effect of each transaction is **formally** entered into the accounting system in a record known as a **journal.**

In a simple situation, the transactions of a business entity could be recorded directly in the separate accounts. However, in more complex situations, it is essential that the economic effects of each transaction on the accounting model be recorded in one place in **chronological order** (i.e., in order of date of occurrence). The accounting record designed for this particular purpose is known as the **journal.** Typically, the dual effects are recorded first in the journal and later are transferred, or posted, to the appropriate accounts (refer to the various "entry summaries" and T-accounts used for Bass Cleaners in Exhibit 3–4).

The journal contains a chronological listing of each entry for all of the transactions. The **format** of the entry in the journal for each transaction is designed to facilitate posting and to link the dual effects of the accounting model and the debit and credit features. For example, in Exhibit 3–4, transaction (a) for Bass Cleaners would appear in the journal in the following format in which the **debit always is listed first and the credit is listed last and indented** for each identification.

	Debit	Credit
(Date) Cash	20,000	
Capital stock		20,000
To record investment of cash by owners.		

Observe that for instructional purposes, in Exhibit 3–4, this same format was used to summarize the required entry for each transaction. The physical linking of the dual effects of each transaction in the journal is in contrast to the separate accounts, where each transaction is separated physically between two or more accounts. For example, you will recall (Exhibit 3–4) that the dual effect of the above entry for Bass Cleaners would appear in separate accounts as follows:

Cash			Capital Stock		
(Date)	20,000			(Date)	20,000

The **journal** is the place of original (or first) entry of the dual economic effects of each transaction and, as a result, it is known as **the book of original entry.** The journal serves three useful purposes:

1. It provides for the initial and orderly listing (by date) of each transaction immediately after the transaction is subjected to transaction analysis.
2. It provides a single place to record the dual economic effects of each transaction without any further subclassifications of the data.
3. It facilitates later tracing; checking for possible errors; and reconstruction of a transaction, its analysis, and its recording.

The journal is the only place in the accounting system where the dual economic effects of each entry are linked physically and recorded chronologically.

To increase your understanding, let's see how the journal is used in a manually maintained system. The first three transactions for Bass Cleaners have been entered in a typical journal shown in Exhibit 3–5. Recording the transactions in the journal in this manner is known as **journalizing,** and the entries made are called **journal entries.** In summary, you should observe in particular that (1) each transaction and event is first recorded in the journal as a separate

EXHIBIT 3–5
Journal illustrated

	JOURNAL				Page 1
Date	Account Titles and Explanation	Folio	Debit	Credit

Jan. 1	Cash
	    Capital stock
	      Investment of cash by owners
		101
		301
			20,000	
				20,000

Jan. 3	Cash
	    Note-payable
	      Borrowed cash on 12% note
		101
		202
			5,000	
				5,000

Jan. 6	Delivery truck
	    Cash
	      Purchased delivery truck for use in
	      the business
		111
		101
			8,000	
				8,000

entry; (2) each entry in the journal is dated, and entries are recorded in chronological order; (3) for each transaction, the debits (accounts and amounts) are entered first, the credits follow and are indented; and (4) as a consequence, for each transaction, the effects on the accounting model and the debits and credits are linked in one entry. These features provide an "audit or tracing trail" that facilitates subsequent examination of past transactions and assists in the location of errors. The journal also is designed to simplify subsequent accounting (as will be demonstrated later).

PHASE 4—POSTING TO THE LEDGER

In the preceding illustration for Bass Cleaners, a **separate account** was set up for each kind of asset, liability, and owners' equity. An accounting system typically will contain a large number of such accounts. Collectively, the accounts are contained in a record known as a **ledger.** The ledger may be organized in numerous ways. Handwritten accounting systems may use a looseleaf ledger—one page for each account. In the case of a "machine" accounting system, a separate machine card is maintained for each account. In the case of a computerized accounting system, the ledger is maintained on magnetic tape or similar electronic storage devices, but there are still separate accounts as in the other systems. Each account also is identified by name as well as by an assigned number.

Exhibit 3–6 shows the ledger for Bass Cleaners in T-account format. The ledger (i.e., the accounts contained in it) contains information that first was recorded in the journal and then transferred, or **posted,** to the appropriate accounts in the ledger. This transfer from the chronological arrangement in the journal to the account format in the ledger is a very important reclassification of the data because the ledger reflects the data classified (by separate accounts) as assets, liabilities, and owners' equity rather than chronologically.

A business using a manual handwritten system typically will record the transactions in the journal each day and **post** to the ledger less frequently, say, every few days. Of course, the timing of these **information processing activities** varies with the size and complexity of the entity.

The T-account format as illustrated in Exhibit 3–6 is useful for instructional purposes. However, the typical account format used is **columnar** as illustrated in Exhibit 3–7. It maintains the debit-credit concept but is arranged to provide columns for date, explanation, folio (F), and running balances.

To post, the debits and credits reflected in the journal entries are transferred directly as debits and credits to the indicated accounts in the ledger. In both the journal (Exhibit 3–5) and ledger (as in the Cash account, in Exhibit 3–6 or as in Exhibit 3–7), you can observe that there is a "folio" column, which is included to provide a numerical **cross-reference** between the journal and the ledger (this cross-reference often is said "to provide an audit trail"). For example, the journal shown in Exhibit 3–5 shows a folio number of 101 for Cash, which indicates the account in the ledger to which that amount was posted.

EXHIBIT 3–6
Ledger illustrated
(T-accounts)

BASS CLEANERS, INC.
LEDGER at December 31, 19A

ASSETS	=	LIABILITIES	+	OWNERS' EQUITY

Cash

(a)	20,000	(c)	8,000
(b)	5,000	(f)	25,800
(d)	40,000	(h)	600
(k)	1,000	(j)	1,800
		(l)	500

(Net debit balance, $29,300)

Notes Payable

		(b)	5,000

Capital Stock

		(a)	20,000

Retained Earnings*

(j)	1,800		

Accounts Receivable

(e)	4,000	(k)	1,000

(Net debit balance, $3,000)

Accounts Payable

(l)	500	(g)	2,000

(Net credit balance, $1,500)

Cleaning Revenue

		(d)	40,000
		(e)	4,000

(Net credit balance, $44,000)

Delivery Truck

(c)	8,000		

Operating Expenses

(f)	25,800		
(g)	2,000		
(i)	1,600		

(Net debit balance, $29,400)

Accumulated
Depreciation
Delivery Truck†

		(i)	1,600

Interest Expense

(h)	600		

Totals	$38,700	=	$6,500	+	$32,200

Note: The accounting model, Assets = Liabilities + Owner's equity, given at the top of this exhibit and the totals at the bottom are shown only for your convenience in study; they would not appear in an actual ledger.

*Retained Earnings is an owner's equity account that reports accumulated earnings minus dividends paid to date. Dividends paid reduce cash and owners' equity (see Chapter 12). Dividends paid is a distribution to owners—not an expense because it does not contribute to earning revenue.

†The delivery truck is depreciated over a five-year period because that is its estimated useful life to Bass Cleaners. Depreciation refers to the "wearing out" of the truck due to use. The truck is assumed to wear out at a steady rate each year throughout its life; therefore, the annual depreciation is $8,000 ÷ 5 years = $1,600. This amount is recorded in an account called Accumulated depreciation; it is a negative, or contra, account to the Delivery Truck account. The $1,600 also is an expense for the year. For further explanation of depreciation, see Chapter 9.

EXHIBIT 3–7
Ledger account in
columnar format
illustrated

	Account Title Cash				Account Number 101
Date	Explanation	F	Debit	Credit	Balance
Jan. 1	Investments	1	20,000		20,000
3	Borrowing	3	5,000		25,000
6	Truck purchased	3		8,000	17,000
7	Cleaning revenue	4	40,000		57,000
8	Operating expenses	4		25,800	31,200
10	Interest expense..................................	5		600	30,600
15	Payments to owners..............................	7		1,800	28,800
16	Collections on receivables	8	1,000		29,800
17	Payments on accounts payable	8		500	29,300

You will recall that this is the account number assigned to cash in Exhibit 3–3. Similarly, if you look at the ledger account for Cash, as shown in Exhibit 3–7, you will observe on the first line of the account the folio number 1, which indicates that the particular amount posted came from page 1 of the journal. Folio numbers are entered during the **posting** process; therefore, the folio numbers indicate whether posting has been accomplished. Transferring amounts from the journal to the ledger is called **posting.** The data ends up in the ledger; therefore, it sometimes is referred to as the **book of final entry.**

PHASE 5—THE TRIAL BALANCE

At the end of the accounting period, in order to verify recording accuracy, and for subsequent processing uses, a **trial balance** is prepared directly from the ledger. A trial balance is simply a listing, in ledger account order, of the ledger **accounts** and their respective net **ending** debit or credit **balances.** The ending balance shown for each account is the difference between the total of the debits and the total of the credits in the account. Exhibit 3–8 shows the trial balance of Bass Cleaners at December 31, 19A. It was prepared directly from the ledger accounts given in Exhibit 3–6.

A trial balance serves two purposes in the accounting information processing cycle:

1. It provides a check on the equality of the debits and credits as reflected in the ledger accounts at the end of the period (or whenever taken).
2. It provides financial data in a convenient form for preparation of the financial statements.

PHASE 6—FINANCIAL STATEMENTS

At the end of the accounting period, several phases of the accounting process will be complete, viz: (1) all transactions for the period will have been analyzed and entered in the journal in chronological order, (2) all amounts in

EXHIBIT 3–8
Trial balance
illustrated

BASS CLEANERS, INC.
Trial Balance
December 31, 19A

	Balance	
Account titles	*Debit*	*Credit*
Cash	$29,300	
Accounts receivable......................	3,000	
Delivery truck...........................	8,000	
Accumulated depreciation, delivery truck ...		$1,600
Notes payable...........................		5,000
Accounts payable........................		1,500
Capital stock (800 shares).................		20,000
Retained earnings (explained later).........	1,800	
Cleaning revenues........................		44,000
Operating expenses.......................	29,400	
Interest expense	600	
Totals	$72,100	$72,100

the journal will have been posted (transferred) to the ledger accounts, and (3) a trial balance will have been prepared from the ledger.

The next phase is preparation of the required financial statements that were discussed and illustrated in Chapters 1 and 2. The trial balance provides the basic data needed to prepare the financial statements at the end of the accounting period. The income statement and balance sheet for Bass Cleaners, prepared from the trial balance shown in Exhibit 3–8, were illustrated in Exhibit 3–2.

The demonstration case that follows should be studied carefully because it provides a summary of the six phases of the accounting processes discussed in this chapter. A good understanding of the accounting process is necessary before you study the subsequent chapters.

DEMONSTRATION CASE—THE ACCOUNTING INFORMATION PROCESSING SYSTEM

We have selected this case of a small business to demonstrate the complete **accounting information processing cycle** from the initial capture of the raw economic data to the financial statements developed at the end of the accounting year. Only representative and summary transactions have been selected to keep the length of the case within reason. Small amounts are used to simplify the illustration. You should study each step in the accompanying solution carefully because it reviews the concepts, principles, and procedures introduced in Chapters 1–3.

On January 3, 19A, M. Hall and P. Garza organized a corporation to build and operate an apartment complex called La Paloma. At the start, each one invested $40,000 cash and in turn received 3,000 shares of $10 par value stock. Therefore, on that date the following entry was recorded in the journal:

January 3, 19A:

Cash..	80,000	
Capital stock, par $10 (6,000 shares)		60,000
Contributed surplus...		20,000

Shortly thereafter, land was acquired for $30,000 and a construction contract was signed with a builder. The first apartments were rented on July 1, 19B. The owners decided to use a **fiscal year** of July 1 through June 30 for business purposes (instead of a fiscal year which agrees with the calendar year).

It now is July 1, 19C, the beginning of the second year of rental operations; therefore, certain accounts in the ledger will have balances carried over from the prior fiscal year ended June 30, 19C. A complete list of the accounts in the ledger that will be needed for this case, with the balances carried over from the previous fiscal year, is given in Exhibit 3–9. Ledger account (folio) numbers are provided at the left.

Typical transactions (most of them summarized) for the 12-month fiscal year—July 1, 19C, through June 30, 19D—are listed below. To facilitate tracing, instead of using dates, we will use the letter notation to the left of each transaction.

a. On November 1, 19C, paid $3,000 cash for a two-year casualty insurance policy covering the building, its contents, and liability coverage.

b. Rental revenue earned: collected in cash, $105,500; and uncollected by June 30, 19D, $2,000.

c. Paid accounts payable (amount owed from the prior year for expenses), $6,000.

d. Purchased a tract of land, at a cost of $35,000, as a planned site for another apartment complex to be constructed in "about three years." Cash of $5,000 was paid, and a long-term note payable (12 percent interest per annum, interest payable each six months) was signed for the balance of $30,000.

e. Operating expenses incurred and paid in cash were:

Utilities and telephone expense	$23,360
Apartment maintenance expense	1,200
Salary and wage expense	6,000

f. At the end of the fiscal year (June 30, 19D), the following bills for expenses incurred had not been recorded or paid: June telephone bill, $40; and miscellaneous expense, $100.

g. Paid interest for six months on the long-term note at 12 percent per annum. (Refer to item [d].) (Hint: Interest = Principal × Rate × Time.)

EXHIBIT 3–9
Trial balance for
demonstration case

LA PALOMA APARTMENTS
Ledger Balances
July 1, 19C (start of Year 2 of rental operations)

Account No.	Account titles	Debit	Credit
101	Cash	$ 18,000	
103	Accounts receivable (or rent receivable).....................		
105	Supplies inventory..	2,000	
112	Prepaid insurance		
121	Land (apartment site)	30,000	
122	La Paloma apartment building	200,000	
123	Accumulated depreciation, apartment building		$ 10,000
125	Furniture and fixtures....................................	60,000	
126	Accumulated depreciation, furniture and fixtures		12,000
131	Land for future apartment site		
201	Accounts payable..		6,000
202	Property taxes payable		
203	Income taxes payable		
204	Mortgage payable, 10% (apartment building).................		180,000
205	Note payable, long term, 12%		
301	Capital stock (par $10, 6,000 shares)......................		60,000
302	Contributed surplus		20,000
303	Retained earnings (accumulated earnings to June 30, 19C).....		22,000
401	Rent revenue..		
521	Utilities and telephone expense		
522	Apartment maintenance expense...........................		
523	Salary and wage expense.................................		
524	Insurance expense		
525	Property tax expense.....................................		
526	Depreciation expense		
527	Miscellaneous expenses		
531	Interest expense		
532	Income tax expense......................................		
	Totals	$310,000	$310,000

h. An inventory count at the end of the fiscal period, June 30, 19D, showed remaining supplies on hand amounting to $400. Supplies used are considered a miscellaneous expense.

i. By the end of the fiscal period, June 30, 19D, one third (8 months out of 24 months) of the prepaid insurance premium of $3,000 paid in transaction (a) had expired because of passage of time.

j. Depreciation expense for the year was based on an estimated useful life of 20 years for the apartment and 5 years for the furniture and fixtures (assume no residual or salvage value).

k. The property taxes for the year ending June 30, 19D, in the amount of $2,700 have not been recorded or paid.

l. Cash payment at year-end on the mortgage on the apartment was:

On principal....................	$20,000
Interest ($180,000 × 10%)	18,000
Total paid	$38,000

 m. Income tax expense for the year ending June 30, 19D, was computed to be $5,940 (i.e., a 20 percent average rate). Assume that this obligation will be paid in the next period.

Required:

Complete the accounting information processing cycle by solving each of the following:

 1. Set up a ledger with T-accounts that includes all of the accounts listed on the trial balance given in Exhibit 3–9; include the account numbers as given. Enter the July 1, 19C, balances in each account in this manner:

Cash	101
Balance 18,000	

 2. Analyze, then **journalize** (i.e., enter in the journal), each transaction listed above for the period July 1, 19C, through June 30, 19D. Number the journal pages consecutively starting with 1.

 3. **Post** all entries from the journal to the ledger; use the folio columns for account numbers.

 4. **Prepare** a trial balance at June 30, 19D.

 5. **Prepare** an income statement for the fiscal year ending June 30, 19D.

 6. **Prepare** a balance sheet at June 30, 19D.

Suggested solution

Requirement 1—Ledger (see subsequent pages):

Requirement 2—Journal:

JOURNAL   Page 1

Date	Account Titles and Explanation	Folio	Debit	Credit
a.	Prepaid insurance	112	3,000	
	Cash	101		3,000
	Paid insurance premium for two years in advance.			
	(Explanatory note: An asset acccunt, Prepaid Insurance, is debited because a future service, insurance coverage, is being paid for in advance.)			
b.	Cash	101	105,500	
	Accounts receivable (or rent receivable)	103	2,000	
	Rent revenue	401		107,500
	To record rent revenues earned for the year, of which $2,000 has not yet been collected.			
c.	Accounts payable	201	6,000	
	Cash	101		6,000
	Paid a debt carried over from previous year.			
d.	Land for future apartment site	131	35,000	
	Cash	101		5,000
	Note payable, long term (12%)	205		30,000
	Purchased land as a site for future apartment complex. (This is a second tract of land acquired; the present apartment building was constructed on the first tract.)			
e.	Utilities and telephone expense	521	23,360	
	Apartment maintenance expense	522	1,200	
	Salary and wage expense	523	6,000	
	Cash	101		30,560
	Paid current expenses.			
f.	Utilities and telephone expense	521	40	
	Miscellaneous expenses	527	100	
	Accounts payable	201		140
	Expenses incurred, not yet paid.			

Requirement 2 (continued):

JOURNAL   Page 2

Date	Account Titles and Explanation	Folio	Debit	Credit
g.	Interest expense	531	1,800	
	Cash	101		1,800
	Paid six months' interest on a long-term note ($30,000 × 12% × 6/12 = $1,800).			
h.	Miscellaneous expenses	527	1,600	
	Supplies inventory	105		1,600
	To record as expense supplies used from inventory during the year.			
	(Explanatory note: Supplies are bought in advance of use; hence, at that time they are recorded as an asset, Supplies Inventory. As the supplies are used from inventory, the asset thus used becomes an expense. Refer to Supplies Inventory account [$2,000 − $400 = $1,600].)			
i.	Insurance expense	524	1,000	
	Prepaid insurance	112		1,000
	To record as an expense the cost of the insurance that expired ($3,000 × 8/24 = $1,000).			
j.	Depreciation expense	526	22,000	
	Accumulated depreciation, apartment building	123		10,000
	Accumulated depreciation, furniture and fixtures	126		12,000
	Depreciation expense for one year.			
	Computation:			
	Apartment:			
	$200,000 ÷ 20 years = $10,000.			
	Furniture and fixtures:			
	$60,000 ÷ 5 years = $12,000.			
k.	Property tax expense	525	2,700	
	Property taxes payable	202		2,700
	Property taxes for the current year, not yet paid			
l.	Mortgage payable (10%)	204	20,000	
	Interest expense	531	18,000	
	Cash	101		38,000
	Payments on principal of mortgage payable plus interest expense.			
m.	Income tax expense	532	5,940	
	Income tax payable	203		5,940
	Income tax for the year; payable later.			

Requirements 1 and 3—Ledger:

LEDGER

Cash					101
Date	F	Amount	Date	F	Amount
Balance		18,000	(a)	1	3,000
(b)	1	105,500	(c)	1	6,000
			(d)	1	5,000
			(e)	1	30,560
			(g)	2	1,800
			(l)	2	38,000

(Net debit balance, $39,140)

Accounts Receivable					103
(b)	1	2,000			

Supplies Inventory					105
Balance		2,000	(h)	2	1,600

Prepaid Insurance					112
(a)	1	3,000	(i)	2	1,000

Land (Apartment Site)					121
Balance		30,000			

La Paloma Apartment Building					122
Balance		200,000			

Accumulated Depreciation, Apartment Building					123
			Balance		10,000
			(j)	2	10,000

Furniture and Fixtures					125
Date	F	Amount	Date	F	Amount
Balance		60,000			

Accumulated Depreciation, Furniture and Fixtures					126
			Balance		12,000
			(j)	2	12,000

Land for Future Apartment Site					131
(d)	1	35,000			

Accounts Payable					201
(c)	1	6,000	Balance		6,000
			(f)	1	140

Property Taxes Payable					202
			(k)	2	2,700

Income Taxes Payable					203
			(m)	2	5,940

Mortgage Payable (10%) (apartment building)					204
(l)	2	20,000	Balance		180,000

Requirements 1 and 3 (continued):

Notes Payable, Long Term (12%)					205
Date	F	Amount	Date	F	Amount
			(d)	1	30,000

Capital Stock					301
			Balance		60,000

Contributed Surplus					302
			Balance		20,000

Retained Earnings					303
			Balance		22,000

Rent Revenue					401
			(b)	1	107,500

Utilities and Telephone Expense					521
(e)	1	23,360			
(f)	1	40			

Apartment Maintenance Expense					522
(e)	1	1,200			

Salary and Wage Expense					523
(e)	1	6,000			

Insurance Expense					524
Date	F	Amount	Date	F	Amount
(i)	2	1,000			

Property Tax Expense					525
(k)	2	2,700			

Depreciation Expense					526
(j)	2	22,000			

Miscellaneous Expenses					527
(f)	1	100			
(h)	2	1,600			

Interest Expense					531
(g)	2	1,800			
(l)	2	18,000			

Income Tax Expense					532
(m)	2	5,940			

Requirement 4:

LA PALOMA APARTMENTS
Trial Balance
June 30, 19D

Account No.	Account titles	Debit	Credit
		Balance	
101	Cash	$ 39,140	
103	Accounts receivable (or Rent receivable)	2,000	
105	Supplies inventory..	400	
112	Prepaid insurance (16 months)..............................	2,000	
121	Land (apartment site)	30,000	
122	La Paloma apartment building	200,000	
123	Accumulated depreciation, apartment building		$ 20,000
125	Furniture and fixtures......................................	60,000	
126	Accumulated depreciation, furniture and fixtures		24,000
131	Land for future apartment site	35,000	
201	Accounts payable..		140
202	Property taxes payable		2,700
203	Income taxes payable		5,940
204	Mortgage payable (10%) (apartment building)		160,000
205	Note payable, long term (12%)..............................		30,000
301	Capital stock (par $10, 6,000 shares)		60,000
302	Contributed surplus		20,000
303	Retained earnings (accumulated earnings to June 30, 19C)..		22,000
401	Rent revenue..		107,500
521	Utilities and telephone expense	23,400	
522	Apartment maintenance expense.............................	1,200	
523	Salary and wage expense....................................	6,000	
524	Insurance expense..	1,000	
525	Property tax expense..	2,700	
526	Depreciation expense	22,000	
527	Miscellaneous expenses	1,700	
531	Interest expense	19,800	
532	Income tax expense..	5,940	
	Totals	$452,280	$452,280

Requirement 5:

LA PALOMA APARTMENTS
Income Statement
For the Year Ended June 30, 19D

Revenue:		
Rent revenue........................		$107,500*
Operating expenses:		
Utilities and telephone expense	$23,400	
Apartment maintenance expense......	1,200	
Salary and wage expense.............	6,000	
Insurance expense	1,000	
Property tax expense.................	2,700	
Depreciation expense	22,000	
Miscellaneous expenses	1,700	
Total operating expenses		58,000
Income from apartment operations		49,500
Financial expense:		
Interest expense		19,800
Pretax income		29,700
Income tax expense..................		5,940
Net income		$ 23,760
EPS ($23,760 ÷ 6,000 shares)		$3.96

*Notes:
a. These amounts were taken directly from Requirement 4, the trial balance.
b. No products are sold by this business; therefore, gross margin cannot be reported.

Requirement 6:

LA PALOMA APARTMENTS
Balance Sheet
At June 30, 19D

Assets

Current assets:			
Cash		$ 39,140*	
Accounts receivable...................................		2,000	
Supplies inventory......................................		400	
Prepaid insurance		2,000	
Total current assets			$ 43,540
Operational assets:			
Land (apartment site).................................		30,000	
La Paloma apartment building	$200,000		
Less: Accumulated depreciation, building..............	20,000	180,000	
Furniture and fixtures.................................	60,000		
Less: Accumulated depreciation, furniture and			
fixtures	24,000	36,000	
Total operational assets			246,000
Other assets:			
Land acquired for future apartment site†.................			35,000
Total assets			$324,540

Liabilities

Current liabilities:

Accounts payable......................................	140	
Property taxes payable	2,700	
Income taxes payable	5,940	
Total current liabilities		$ 8,780

Long-term liabilities:

Mortgage payable......................................	160,000	
Note payable, long term...............................	30,000	
Total long-term liabilities		190,000
Total liabilities.......................................		198,780

Shareholders' Equity

Contributed capital:

Capital stock, par $10 (6,000 shares)	60,000	
Contributed surplus	20,000	
Total contributed capital.............................	80,000	
Retained earnings (beginning balance $22,000 +		
net income $23,760)...................................	45,760	
Total shareholders' equity		125,760
Total liabilities and shareholders' equity		$324,540

*These amounts were taken directly from Requirement 4, the trial balance.

†Classified as "other" rather than "operational" because this land is not being used currently for operating purposes.

SUMMARY OF CHAPTER

This chapter discussed the **fundamental accounting model** and the six phases of the accounting process. You studied the nature of transactions that provide the raw economic data that are entered into the accounting information system. You learned that the fundamental accounting model—Assets = Liabilities + Owners' Equity—provides the basic framework for transaction analysis and the recording of the dual effect of each transaction. The accounting model encompasses two balancing features that must be met with respect to each transaction and event recorded, viz: (1) assets must equal liabilities plus owners' equity and (2) debits must equal credits. After transaction analysis, the dual effects of each transaction are recorded first in the journal and then are posted to the ledger. The journal provides a chronological record of the transactions, and the ledger reflects a **separate** account for each kind of asset, liability, and owners' equity. Normally, asset accounts will have debit balances, whereas liability accounts will have credit balances. Owners' equity accounts normally will show credits for the capital stock and retained earnings accounts—expenses will show debit balances, and revenues will show credit balances. The accounting information processing system accumulates the financial data needed to develop the periodic financial statements: the income statement, balance sheet, and statement of changes in financial position (SCFP).

This chapter also discussed and illustrated the **accounting information processing cycle** for a business entity. It represents a cycle because it is **repeated** each accounting period (usually one year). The sequential phases in the information processing cycle may be outlined as follows:

Phase 1: **Collecting raw data**—Economic data are collected for each transaction at the time of occurrence. Sales invoices, charge tickets, freight bills, notes, signed receipts, and so on, are source documents collected in this step.

Phase 2: **Analyzing transactions**—Each transaction undergoes transaction analysis to determine how it affects the fundamental accounting model: Assets = Liabilities + Owners' equity.

Phase 3: **Journalizing**—Each transaction is recorded **chronologically** in the

EXHIBIT 3–10
Sequential phases of an accounting information system

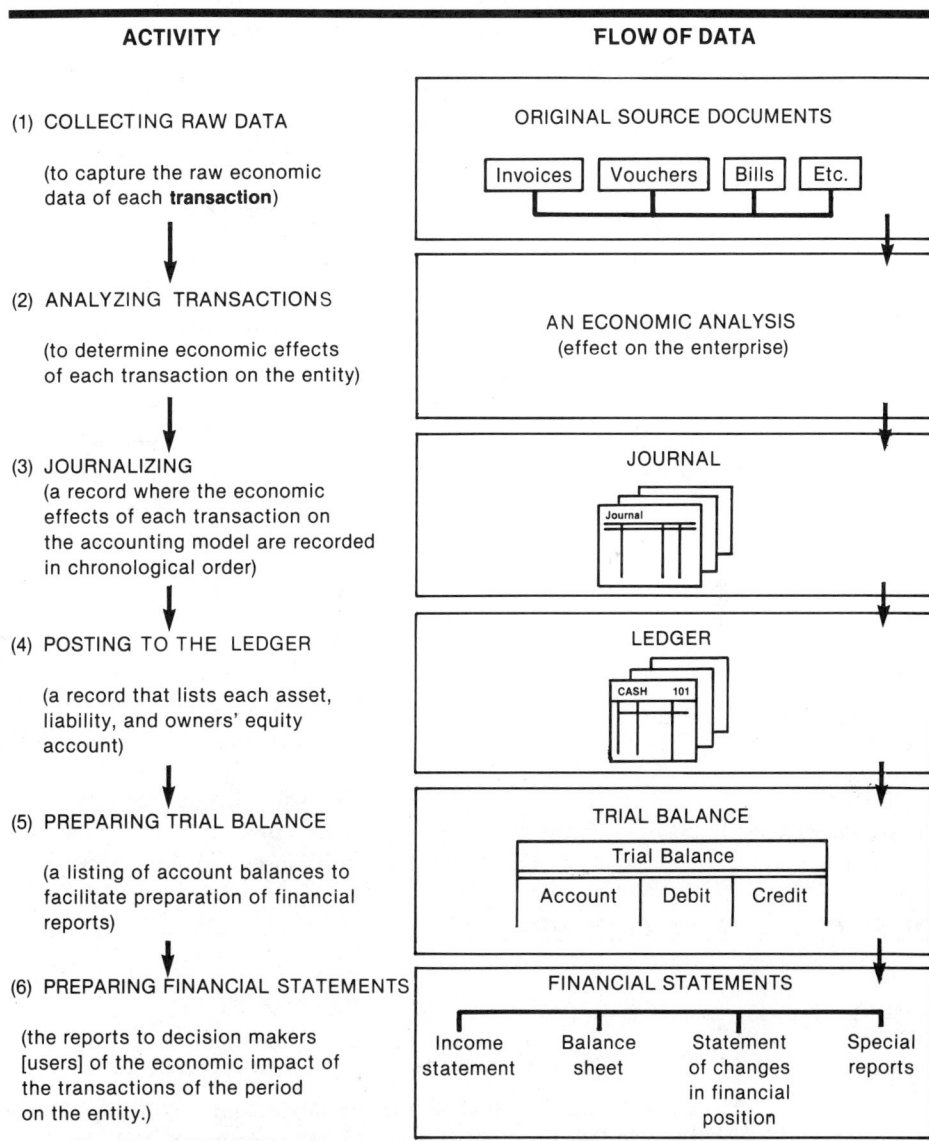

ACTIVITY	FLOW OF DATA
(1) COLLECTING RAW DATA (to capture the raw economic data of each **transaction**)	ORIGINAL SOURCE DOCUMENTS Invoices Vouchers Bills Etc.
(2) ANALYZING TRANSACTIONS (to determine economic effects of each transaction on the entity)	AN ECONOMIC ANALYSIS (effect on the enterprise)
(3) JOURNALIZING (a record where the economic effects of each transaction on the accounting model are recorded in chronological order)	JOURNAL Journal
(4) POSTING TO THE LEDGER (a record that lists each asset, liability, and owners' equity account)	LEDGER CASH 101
(5) PREPARING TRIAL BALANCE (a listing of account balances to facilitate preparation of financial reports)	TRIAL BALANCE Trial Balance Account | Debit | Credit
(6) PREPARING FINANCIAL STATEMENTS (the reports to decision makers [users] of the economic impact of the transactions of the period on the entity.)	FINANCIAL STATEMENTS Income statement | Balance sheet | Statement of changes in financial position | Special reports

journal, which indicates the date, account titles to be debited and credited, the related amounts, and an explanation.

Phase 4: **Posting**—Each amount entered in the journal is transferred, or posted, to the appropriate account in the ledger.

Phase 5: **Preparing trial balance**—At the end of the accounting period, the balance in each account (i.e., the net debit or credit balance) in the ledger is determined. The balance of each ledger account then is listed on a trial balance. The equality of debits and credits is also checked.

Phase 6: **Preparing financial statements**—The information on the trial balance is used to develop the periodic financial statements composed of the income statement, balance sheet, and statement of changes in financial position.

The above cycle also is presented in graphic format for study purposes in Exhibit 3–10. As we progress in our study, additions to and elaborations of this information processing cycle will be introduced.

IMPORTANT TERMS DEFINED IN THIS CHAPTER

Terms (alphabetically)	Key words in definitions of important terms used in chapter	Page reference
Accounting information processing cycle	Accounting information; sequential phases (steps); transactions to financial statements.	116
Accrual accounting	Revenues and expenses; measured and reported; on transaction date; not cash basis.	103
Analyzing transactions	Assessment of economic effects of each transaction on the entity.	108
Credit	Algebraic balancing feature; "right side" of T-account; decreases assets; increases liabilities and owners' equity.	107
Debit	"Left side" of T-account; increases assets; decreases liabilities and owners' equity.	107
Fundamental accounting model	Asset = Liabilities + Owners' Equity.	102
Journal	Record transactions chronological order; journalizing chronological order.	117
Journalizing	Recording in the journal; original entry.	118
Ledger	Separate accounts for each revenue, expense, asset, liability, and owners' equity.	119
Posting	Transferring data from journal to ledger.	121
Source documents	Transaction documents; sales invoices.	116
Trial balance	List of accounts; account balances; equality check.	121

QUESTIONS FOR DISCUSSION

Part A

1. Define a business transaction. Why does accounting focus on each business transaction?

2. Give the fundamental accounting model and briefly explain each variable included in it, including revenues, expenses, and investments and withdrawals by owners.

3. Explain why revenues increase and expenses decrease owners' equity.

4. What is the meaning of "to debit" and "to credit"?

5. Complete the following matrix by entering either debit or credit in each cell.

Item	Increases	Decreases
Assets		
Liabilities		
Owners' equity		
Revenues		
Expenses		

6. Complete the following matrix by entering either increase or decrease in each cell.

Item	Debit	Credit
Assets		
Liabilities		
Owners' equity		
Revenues		
Expenses		

Part B

7. Briefly explain what is meant by transaction analysis.

8. Define journal. What purposes does it serve?

9. Define ledger. What purpose does it serve?

10. Distinguish between journalizing and posting.

11. What is the purpose of the folio notations in the journal and in the ledger accounts?

12. What is a trial balance? What purposes does it serve?

13. What does the term audit trail imply?

14. Define what is meant by fiscal period as used in accounting.

15. Briefly outline the accounting information processing system for a business.

16. Name two general characteristics of an accounting system that a designer of such a system should consider to help ensure that the data from any given transaction are actually captured by the system rather than being omitted by the system. For example, cash could be collected by not recorded.

17. Transactions and the happenings surrounding them contain a lot of data that could potentially be captured by the system. When designing a form to capture transaction data one must know what should be captured by the accounting system. What fundamental concept listed in Exhibit 2–6 in the preceding chapter helps to determine what data about a transaction should be captured?

18. The idea of dual economic effect that each transaction and its entry has implies the potential for two possible values: first, the value of what the entity gives up and second, the value of what the entity receives. If they should be different, which value should be used so that the records can remain in balance? (Hint, Exhibit 2–6 in the last chapter may help.)

EXERCISES

Part A

E3–1. Friday Corporation has been operating for one year, 19A. At the end of 19A, the financial statements have been prepared. Below are a series of separate and independent cases based on the 19A financial statements. For each independent case, and the financial relationship it addresses, you are to supply the missing item and its amount.

Case	Data	Missing	
		Item	Amount
Example	Assets, $70,000; owners' equity, $30,000	Liabilities	$40,000
A	Revenues, $100,000; expenses, $62,000		
B	Liabilities, $30,000; owners' equity, $50,000		
C	Cash inflows, $80,000; increase in cash, $20,000		
D	Liabilities, $42,000; assets, $81,000		
E	Net income, $35,000; expenses, $63,000		
F	Net income, $20,000; revenues, $93,000		
G	Expenses, $80,000; revenues, $80,000		
H	Revenues, $80,000; expenses, $90,000		
I	Increase in cash, $18,000; cash outflows, $60,000		
J	Cash outflows, $60,000; cash inflows, $40,000		

E3–2. During its first week of operations, January 1–7, Small Retail Company completed eight transactions, the effects of which are indicated in the dollar amounts given below.

Required:

a. You are to give a brief explanation of each transaction. Assume each transaction stands alone, but may be related to prior transactions unless specifically stated otherwise. Also, if alternate explanations are possible, explain each. Decreases are in parentheses.

Item	Transaction Effect								Ending Balance
	1	2	3	4	5	6	7	8	
Cash	$10,000	$15,000	$(4,000)	$80,000	$(9,000)	$(50,000)	$(11,000)	$ 7,000	$38,000
Accounts receivable				10,000				(7,000)	3,000
Store fixtures					9,000				9,000
Land			12,000						12,000
Accounts payable						20,000	(11,000)		9,000
Notes payable		15,000	8,000						23,000
Capital stock	10,000								10,000
Revenues				90,000					90,000
Expenses						70,000			70,000

b. Based only upon the above tabulation of the effects of each of the eight transactions, provide the following amounts at the end of the week (show computations):

```
Total assets _____  $ _____
Total liabilities _____  $ _____
Total owners' equity _____  $ _____
Income _____  $ _____
Proof of owners' equity _____  $ _____
```

E3–3. For each transaction below indicate the effect upon assets, liabilities, and owners' equity by entering a plus for increase and a minus for decrease.

Transaction	Effect Upon		
	Assets	Liabilities	Owners' Equity
a. Issued shares to organizers for cash.			
b. Borrowed cash from local bank.			
c. Purchased equipment on credit.			
d. Earned revenue, collected cash.			
e. Incurred expenses, on credit.			
f. Earned revenue, on credit.			
g. Paid cash for (e).			
h. Incurred expenses, paid cash.			
i. Earned revenue, collected three fourths cash, balance on credit.			
j. Theft of $100 cash.			
k. Declared and paid cash dividends.			
l. Collected cash for (f).			
m. Depreciated equipment for the period.			
n. Incurred expenses, paid four fifths cash, balance on credit.			
o. Paid income tax expense for the period.			

E3–4. Jiffy Service Company, Inc., was organized by four investors. The following transactions were completed:

a. The investors paid in $40,000 cash to start the business. Each one was issued 1,000 shares of capital stock, par value $10 per share.

b. Equipment for use in the business was purchased at a cost of $8,000, one half was paid in cash and the balance is due in six months.

c. Service fees were earned amounting to $54,000, of which $6,000 was on credit.

d. Operating expenses incurred amounted to $33,000, of which $3,000 was on credit.
e. Cash was collected for $4,000 of the service fees performed on credit in (c) above.
f. Paid cash, $2,000, on the operating expenses that were on credit in (d) above.
g. Investor A borrowed $10,000 from a local bank and signed a one-year, 10 percent note for that amount.

Required:

Set up a format similar to the following and enter thereon each of the above transactions that should be recorded by Jiffy. Transaction (a) is entered as an example.

Transactions	*Assets*	*= Liabilities + Owners' Equity*
a. Investment of cash in the business	Cash + $40,000	Capital stock + $40,000

Also determine the total amounts for assets, liabilities, and owners' equity after completing the recording.

E3–5. The following transactions were completed by Duster Service Company during the year 19X:
1. The organizers paid in cash and in turn received 10,000 shares of capital stock.
2. Duster borrowed cash from the local bank.
3. Duster purchased a delivery truck, paid three fourths cash, and the balance is due in six months.
4. Earned revenues, collected cash in full.
5. Expenses incurred, paid cash in full.
6. Earned revenues, on credit (cash not collected in 19X).
7. Expenses incurred, on credit (cash not paid in 19X).
8. Declared and paid cash dividend to shareholders.
9. Collected half of the amount on credit in 6.
10. Paid all of the credit amount in 7.
11. A spare tire was stolen from the delivery truck (not insured).
12. During the period the delivery truck depreciated ($ amount).

Required:

Below is given a tabulation. For each transaction given above enter in the tabulation a D for debit and a C for credit to reflect the effects on the assets, liabilities, and owners' equity (separate groups are given for owners' equity).

Accounting Model	Transactions											
	1	2	3	4	5	6	7	8	9	10	11	12
a. Assets												
b. Liabilities												
Owners' equity: c. Investments												
d. Revenues												
e. Withdrawals												
f. Expenses												

(Note: In some cases there may be both a D and C in the same box.)

E3–6. Snappy Service Company, Inc., was organized and issued 10,000 shares of its capital stock for $30,000 cash. The following transactions occurred during the current accounting period:

a. Received the cash from the organizers.
b. Service fees earned amounted to $35,000, of which $25,000 was collected in cash.
c. Operating expenses incurred amounted to $23,000, of which $17,000 was paid in cash.
d. Bought two machines for operating purposes at the start of the year at a cost of $9,000 each; paid cash.
e. One of the machines was destroyed by fire one week after purchase; it was uninsured. The event to be considered is the fire. (Hint: Set up a fire loss expense account.)
f. The other machine has an estimated useful life to Snappy of 10 years (and no residual value). The event to be considered is the depreciation of the equipment because it was used for one year in rendering services.
g. Shareholder Able bought a vacant lot (land) for $5,000 cash.

Required:

a. Set up appropriate T-accounts and record in them the dual effects on the accounting model of each of the above transactions that should be recorded by Snappy. Key the amounts to the letters starting with (a). Number the following accounts consecutively starting with 101 for cash: Cash, Accounts Receivable, Machines, Accumulated Depreciation, Accounts Payable, Service Fees Earned, Operating Expenses, Fire Loss Expense, Depreciation Expense, and Capital Stock.
b. Complete the following by entering the correct totals:

Assets................	$_____
Liabilities.............	$_____
Owners' equity	$_____
Debits................	$_____
Credits...............	$_____
Net income	$_____

Part B

E3–7. Match the following phases with the brief descriptions of the accounting processing cycle by entering the appropriate letters in the blanks to the left.

Phases of the accounting processing information cycle (sequential order)	*Brief description of phases*
_____ Raw data collection	A. Income statement, balance sheet, SCFP.
_____ Transaction analysis	B. Transfer of amount for each account, affected by the transaction; results in a reclassification of the data.
_____ Journalizing	C. A listing of each account and its debit or credit ending balance; checks debits = credits.
_____ Posting	D. Source documents that underlie each transaction.
_____ Trial balance	E. A chronological record is prepared that reflects the economic effects of each transaction.
_____ Financial statements	F. A careful study of each transaction and determination of its economic effects on the entity.

E3–8. The following T-accounts for Community Service Company, Inc., reflect five different transactions (entries). You are requested to prepare a journal entry for each transaction and write a complete description of each transaction.

Cash				
(a)	70,000	(c)	9,000	
(b)	20,000	(e)	1,500	
(d)	2,000	(f)	5,000	

Accounts Payable			
(e)	1,500	(c)	2,000

Capital Stock, Par $10	
(a)	70,000

Accounts Receivable			
(b)	4,000	(d)	2,000

Note Payable	
(f)	15,000

Service Revenue	
(b)	24,000

Equipment	
(f)	20,000

Operating Expenses	
(c)	11,000

E3–9. On January 1, 19A, Ellen Wood and Hyeok Yi organized the WY Service Inc. The transactions of the company for the first 45 days are summarized below.

Required:

a. You are requested to analyze each transaction and enter it in a journal similar to the one illustrated in Exhibit 3–5.

19A

Jan. 1 Cash invested by the organizers was Wood, $40,000 (for 4,000 shares); and Yi, $30,000 (for 3,000 shares).

3 Paid monthly rent, $1,000.

15 Purchased equipment for use in the business that cost $18,000; paid one third down and signed a 12 percent note payable for the balance. Monthly payments (24) comprised of part principal and part interest are to be paid on the note.

30 Paid cash for operating expenses amounting to $18,000; in addition, operating expenses of $2,000 were incurred on credit.

30 Service fees earned amounted to $40,000, of which $35,000 was collected and the balance was on credit.

Feb. 10 Collected $2,000 on account for service fees previously performed and originally recorded as an account receivable.

12 Paid $1,000 on the operating expenses previously incurred and originally recorded as an account payable.

15 Paid $565 on the equipment note, including $120 interest expense.

b. Compute the amount of income based solely on the above transactions. Also, compute the ending cash balance.

E3-10. Kool Air Conditioning Service Incorporated, has been operating for three years. I. M. Kool, the majority shareholder, built it up from a one-person organization to an operation requiring 10 employees. In the past, few records were maintained; however, Kool now realizes the need for a complete accounting system. The size and complexity of the business is partially indicated by the following selected transactions completed during the first five months of 19E:

Jan. 15 Purchased three new service trucks at $12,000 each; paid a third down and signed a 12 percent one-year, interest-bearing note for the balance. Twelve monthly payments, each including principal and interest, are to be made on the note.

31 Service revenue earned in January amounted to $85,000, which included $5,000 on credit (due in 90 days).

31 Operating expenses incurred in January amounted to $60,000, which included $4,000 on credit (payable in 60 days).

Feb. 5 Dividends declared and paid of $2,000 in cash to the shareholders.

15 Paid $2,132 on the truck note, which included $240 interest.

Apr. 15 Paid 19D taxes on business property, $150; this amount was recorded in 19D as a liability (property taxes payable).

May 1 Collected $4,400 on the services extended on credit in January.

Required:

a. Journalize the above transactions in a form similar to that illustrated in Exhibit 3–5. Number the journal pages consecutively, starting with 51.

b. Post to T-accounts in the ledger; use the folio columns and enter dates. Number the ledger accounts as follows: Cash, 101; Accounts Receivable, 102; Trucks, 103; Accounts Payable, 104; Note Payable, 105; Property Taxes Payable, 106; Retained Earnings, 107; Service Revenue, 108; Operating Expenses, 109; and Interest Expense, 110. As you post, keep in mind that there would be prior amounts carried over from 19D in some of the ledger accounts.

c. Compute the ending balance of cash and the net income, based only on the above transactions.

E3–11. The bookkeeper of Careless Company prepared the following trial balance at December 31, 19B:

Account titles	Debit	Credit
Notes receivable	$ 4,000	
Supplies inventory		$ 200
Accounts payable	800	
Land	16,000	
Capital.................		20,000
Cash...................	7,045	
Interest revenue	200	
Notes payable		5,000
Operating expenses	19,000	
Interest expense		800
Other assets............	9,583	
Service revenues.........		30,583
Total.............	$56,583	$56,583

An independent PA (auditor) casually inspected the trial balance and concluded that it contains several errors. You have been requested to draft a correct trial balance and to explain any errors that you discover. All of the amounts are correct except "other assets."

E3–12. Dunn Service Company competes in an industry where the extension of credit to customers is common. For some time after the business was organized by A. D. Dunn and two friends, the only records maintained were for cash receipts and cash payments. Dunn (the company president) stated, "I watched my cash balance to see how I was doing; if cash went up I assumed a profit of that amount, and, to the contrary, if cash went down, I assumed a loss." As the company expanded and became involved in more credit, Dunn realized that "I must look at the revenue earned and the expenses incurred on an accrual basis, as well as looking at the cash situation." The following information illustrates the current situation of Dunn Company for the month of January 19B:

Service revenues:
    Cash collected for services performed in January 19B $36,000
    Services performed in January 19B on credit   4,000

Operating expenses:
    Cash paid for expenses incurred in January 19B.   17,000
    Expenses incurred in January 19B on credit   25,000

(Disregard income taxes.)

Required:

a. Prepare a special statement to reflect cash inflows, cash outflows, and the change in cash that was caused by the above summarized transactions.

b. Prepare an income statement (accrual basis) to show computation of revenues earned, expenses incurred, and the net income or loss for January 19B.

c. Explain why the cash and accrual results were different.

d. Basically, what does this case suggest as to the inappropriateness of the cash basis to reflect profit performance? Explain and relate to the revenue and matching principles.

PROBLEMS/CASES

Part A

PC3–1. Listed below are the ledger accounts of the AAA Rental Incorporated.

a. Cash.
b. Accounts receivable.
c. Common shares.
d. Bonds payable.
e. Rent revenue.
f. Prepaid insurance premiums.
g. Interest revenue.
h. Investments, long term.
i. Interest expense.
j. Machinery and equipment.
k. Patents.
n. Income tax expense.
m. Property taxes payable.
n. Loss on sale of operational assets.
o. Land, plant site (in use).

p. Contributed surplus
q. Supplies inventory.
r. Notes payable, short term.
s. Retained earnings.
t. Short-term investments.
u. Other assets.
v. Operating expenses.
w. Income taxes payable.
x. Gain on sale of operational assets.
y. Land held for future plant site.
z. Revenue from investments.
aa. Wages payable.
bb. Accumulated depreciation.
cc. Merchandise inventory.

Complete a tabulation similar to the following (enter two check marks for each item above):

			Type of Account	Usual balance	
Item	Asset	Liability	Owners' equity (including revenues and expenses)	Debit	Credit
a.	✓	....		✓	
Etc.					

PC3–2. Ready Service Company has been operating for three years. At the end of 19C, the accounting records reflected assets of $320,000 and liabilities of $110,000. During the year 19D, the following summarized transactions were completed:

a. Revenues of $150,000, of which $10,000 was on credit.

b. Issues an additional 1,000 shares of capital stock, par $10 per share, for $10,000 cash.

c. Purchased equipment that cost $15,000, paid cash $10,000, and the balance is due next year.

d. Expenses incurred were $110,500, of which $15,000 was on credit.

e. Collected $8,000 of the credit amount in (a).

f. Declared and paid cash dividends to shareholders of $15,000.

g. Paid $11,000 of the credit amount in (d).

h. Borrowed $10,000 cash, on a 12 percent interest-bearing note, from a local bank (on December 31, 19D), payable June 30, 19E.

i. Cash amounting to $500 was stolen (not covered by insurance).

j. Depreciation on equipment was $1,000 for 19D.

Required:

a. Compute the amounts for assets, liabilities, and owners' equity as of the end of 19D. Use the following format for your response:

	Assets		Liabilities		Owners' Equity	
	Debit	Credit	Debit	Credit	Debit	Credit
Balances, January 1, 19D						
Transactions:						
a. Revenues						
b. Etc.						
Balances, December 31, 19D						

b. What was the amount of net income for 19D? Show computations.

c. What two accounts did you debit for transaction (a)? Explain why.

d. Explain why the dividend declared and paid is not an expense.

PC3–3. Toni Company was organized on January 1, 19A, by J. B. Troy; S. T. Olen; R. R. Neans, and B. T. Irwin. Each organizer invested $8,000 in the company and, in turn, each was issued 8,000 shares of capital stock. To date they are the only shareholders.

During the first quarter (January–March 19A) the company completed the following transactions (summarized and simplified for instructional purposes):

1. Collected a total of $32,000 from the organizers and in turn issued the shares of capital stock.

2. Purchased equipment for use in the business; paid $8,000 cash in full.
3. Purchased land for use in the business; paid $4,000 cash and gave a $6,000, one-year, 12 percent interest-bearing note for the balance.
4. Earned service revenues of $40,000 of which $36,000 was collected in cash, the balance was an open account credit.
5. Incurred $28,000 operating expenses of which $25,000 was paid in cash, the balance was owed on open account credit.
6. In addition, shareholder Tory reported to the company that 500 shares of his Toni stock had been sold and transferred to shareholder Irwin for a cash consideration of $6,000.

Required:

a. Was Toni Company organized as a sole-proprietorship, a partnership, or a corporation? Explain the basis for your answer.
b. What was the issue price per share of the capital stock?
c. The records of the company, during the first quarter, were inadequate. You have been able to prepare the summary of transactions given above. To develop a quick assessment of their economic effects on Toni Company you have decided to complete the tabulation which follows and to use plus ($+$) for increases and minus ($-$) for decreases for each transaction.

Item	Transactions—Effects						Ending Amounts
	1	2	3	4	5	6	
Cash	$	$	$	$	$	$	$
Accounts receivable							
Land							
Equipment							
Accounts payable							
Notes payable							
Capital stock							
Service revenues							
Operating expenses							

d. Did you include the Tory-Irwin transaction in the above tabulation? Why?
e. Based only upon the completed tabulation above, provide the following amounts (show computations):
   (1) Income for the quarter.
   (2) Total assets at the end of the quarter.
   (3) Total liabilities at the end of the quarter.
   (4) Total owners' equity at the end of the quarter.
   (5) Cash balance at the end of the quarter.
   (6) Net amount of cash inflow from operations, that is, from revenues and expenses combined.
   (7) How much interest must be paid on the note at its maturity date?

PC3–4. SEC Company was organized during January 19A by T. E. Scott, W. D. Evans, and R. L. Cates. On January 20, 19A, the company issued 5,000 shares to each of its organizers. Below is a schedule of the **cumulative** account balances immediately after each of the first 10 transactions.

Accounts	Transactions—Cumulative Balances									
	1	2	3	4	5	6	7	8	9	10
Cash	$75,000	$70,000	$87,000	$77,000	$66,000	$66,000	$70,000	$58,000	$55,000	$54,000
Accounts receivable			8,000	8,000	8,000	11,000	11,000	11,000	11,000	11,000
Office fixtures		20,000	20,000	20,000	20,000	20,000	20,000	20,000	20,000	20,000
Land				14,000	14,000	14,000	14,000	14,000	14,000	14,000
Accounts payable					2,000	2,000	2,000	7,000	4,000	4,000
Notes payable		15,000	15,000	19,000	19,000	19,000	19,000	19,000	19,000	19,000
Capital stock	75,000	75,000	75,000	75,000	75,000	75,000	79,000	79,000	79,000	79,000
Revenues			25,000	25,000	25,000	28,000	28,000	28,000	28,000	28,000
Expenses					13,000	13,000	13,000	30,000	30,000	31,000

Required:

a. Write a brief explanation of each of the 10 transactions indicated in the above schedule. Assume each transaction stands alone, although some transactions are indirectly related to prior transactions. If alternate transactions are possible explain each.

b. Based only on the above schedule, provide the following amounts after transaction 10 (show computations):

Income (loss) _____ $_____
Total assets _____ $_____
Total liabilities _____ $_____
Total owners' equity _____ $_____
Proof of owners' equity _____ $_____
Net cash inflow (outflow) from operations _____ $_____

PC3–5. Listed below is a series of accounts for Acme Service Company, Incorporated, which has been operated for three years. These accounts are listed and numbered for identification. Below the accounts is a series of transactions. For each transaction indicate the account(s) to be debited and credited by entering the appropriate account number(s) to the right of each transaction.

1. Cash.
2. Accounts receivable.
3. Supplies inventory.
4. Prepaid insurance.
5. Equipment.
6. Accumulated depreciation, equipment.
7. Patents.
8. Accounts payable.
10. Wages payable.

11. Income tax payable.
12. Capital stock, par $10.
13. Contributed surplus
14. Service revenues.
15. Operating expenses.
16. Income tax expense.
17. Interest expense.
18. None of the above (explain).

Transactions	*Debit*	*Credit*
a. Example—Investment by shareholders to start the business; cash was received for shares in excess of the par value.	1	12,13
b. Purchased equipment for use in business; paid half cash and gave note payable for the balance.	____	____
c. Paid cash for salaries and wages.	____	____
d. Collected cash for services performed this period.	____	____

    e. Collected cash for services performed last period.   _____ _____

    f. Performed services this period on credit.   _____ _____

    g. Paid operating expenses incurred this period.   _____ _____

    h. Paid cash for operating expenses incurred last period.   _____ _____

    i. Incurred operating expenses this period, to be paid next period.   _____ _____

    j. Purchased supplies for inventory (to be used later); paid cash.   _____ _____

    k. Used some of the supplies from inventory for operations.   _____ _____

    l. Purchased a patent; paid cash.   _____ _____

    m. Made a payment on the equipment note (*b*) above; the payment was part principal and part interest expense.   _____ _____

    n. Collected cash on accounts receivable for services previously performed.   _____ _____

    o. Paid cash on accounts payable for expenses previously incurred.   _____ _____

    p. Paid three fourths of the income tax expense for the year; the balance to be paid next period.   _____ _____

    q. On last day of current period, paid in cash for an insurance policy covering the next two years.   _____ _____

PC3–6. Listed below is a series of accounts for Speedo Service Inc. The accounts are numbered for identification.

1. Cash	20. Capital stock, par $10 per share.
2. Accounts receivable.	21. Contributed surplus.
3. Service supplies inventory.	25. Service revenues.
4. Trucks and equipment.	26. Operating expenses.
5. Accumulated depreciation.	27. Depreciation expense.
10. Accounts payable.	28. Interest expense.
11. Notes payable	29. Income tax expense.
12. Income tax payable.	30. None of the above (explain).

During 19X, the company completed the selected transactions given in the tabulation that follows.

Required:

    To the right indicate the accounts (by identification number) that should be debited and credited and the respective amounts. The first transaction is used as an example.

Transaction	Debit		Credit	
	Acct. No.	Amount	Acct. No.	Amount
Example: Investment by organizers to start the business, $80,000 cash for 5,000 shares, par $10 per share.	1	80,000	20 21	50,000 30,000
a. Purchased panel truck for use in the business for $12,000; paid one-fourth cash and signed a 10 percent interest-bearing note for the balance.				
b. Service revenues earned, $120,000 of which $10,000 was on credit.				
c. Operating expenses incurred, $80,000, of which $20,000 was on credit.				
d. Purchased service supplies, $500, paid cash (placed in supplies inventory).				
e. Collected 9,000 of the credit amount in (b).				
f. Paid $13,000 of the credit amount in (c).				
g. Used $300 of the service supplies (taken from inventory) for service operations.				
h. Depreciation on the truck for the year, $2,000.				
i. Paid six months' interest on the note in (a).				
j. Income tax expense for the year, $4,000, paid three-fourths cash, balance payable by April 1 of next year.				

Part B

PC3–7. The ledger accounts for Mission Real Estate Company, a corporation (organized two years previously), provided the trial balance shown below for the year ended at March 31, 19C (the end of the annual fiscal period).

Trial Balance
At March 31, 19C

Account titles	Debit	Credit
Cash	$ 41,000	
Accounts receivable	53,800	
Office supplies inventory	200	
Automobiles (company cars)	26,000	
Accumulated depreciation, automobiles		$ 12,000
Office equipment	2,000	
Accumulated depreciation, office equipment		1,000
Accounts payable		12,150
Income tax payable		
Salaries and commissions payable		1,000
Notes payable, long term		20,000
Capital stock (par $1; 30,000 shares)		30,000
Contributed surplus		5,000
Retained earnings (on April 1, 19B)		7,350
Dividends declared and paid during the fiscal year	10,000	
Sales commissions earned		90,000
Management fees earned		8,000
Operating expenses (detail omitted to conserve time)	46,000	
Depreciation expense (on autos and including $333 on office equipment)	6,000	
Interest expense	1,500	
Income tax expense		
Totals	$186,500	$186,500

Required:

a. Prepare an income statement for the year ended March 31, 19C. The above trial balance does not include income taxes. Assume an average tax rate of 30 percent and that the income tax will be paid later. (Hint: EPS is $1.04.)

b. Prepare a balance sheet at March 31, 19C. For both requirements refer to Exhibits 2–1 and 2–2 for examples of the statement formats. (Hint: Total assets, $110,000.)

c. Examine the income statement and develop journal entries that were made for the following:

   1. Depreciation expense for the year (automobiles).
   2. Income tax expense for the year.
   3. Dividends declared and paid during the year.

PC3–8. Box Home Repair Service was organized two years ago by M. E. Box and three friends. By the end of the second year, three crews were operating and Box (the company president) felt that the business was a success. Although prices charged were high, the customers appeared pleased in view of the quality of the work done and the efficiency with which repairs were completed. The following account balances were reflected by the ledger on January 1, 19B:

Account No.	Account titles	Debit	Credit
101	Cash	$ 6,550	
105	Accounts receivable............................	3,700	
110	Building supplies inventory (for use on repair jobs)...	1,500	
120	Trucks...	15,000	
121	Accumulated depreciation on trucks................		$ 6,000
200	Accounts payable................................		3,000
201	Income tax payable		
205	Notes payable, short term........................		5,000
210	Wages payable		250
220	Note payable, long term..........................		10,000
300	Capital stock, par $1 per share....................		2,500
400	Service revenue		
501	Operating expenses..............................		
502	Depreciation expense		
503	Interest expense................................		
504	Income tax expense.............................		
	Totals	$26,750	$26,750

During 19B the following transactions occurred:

a. Paid the $250 wages payable carried over from 19A.

b. Purchased, for cash, additional building supplies for future use, $1,100 (debit the Building Supplies Inventory account).

c. The shareholders' invested an additional $10,000 cash in the business and were issued 10,000 shares of Box capital stock.

d. Purchased an additional truck for $9,500 cash.

e. Collected $2,800 cash on the accounts receivable.

f. Paid the $5,000 short-term note, plus six months' interest at 12 percent per annum.

g. Repair fees earned in 19B, $97,000, which included $7,000 earned in 19B but uncollected (i.e., on credit).

h. Paid operating expenses of $60,000 cash. Additional operating expenses of $4,000 were incurred; the cash will be paid for these in 19C.

i. According to an inventory count of the building supplies at December 31, 19B, unused supplies amounted to $800. (Hint: Supplies used should be debited to Operating Expenses: Supplies used = Amount on hand at start + Additional purchased − Ending inventory.)

j. Depreciation on the three trucks was computed on the basis of an estimated useful life of five years. The new truck will not be depreciated in 19B because it was acquired near the end of the year.

k. Paid $6,000 on the long-term note, plus 12 percent interest on the $10,000 for one year.

l. Paid $5,000 on accounts payable.

m. Income tax expense $5,340 (20 percent rate), all paid in cash.

Required:

1. Set up the ledger accounts listed above and enter the beginning balances; label these as "Balance."

2. Analyze each transaction, then enter it directly in the ledger accounts (you will not need additional accounts). Key your entries with the letter designation (in place of a date). No journal is required; however, it may be helpful to prepare each journal entry on scratch paper before entering it in the ledger.

3. Prepare a trial balance at December 31, 19B. (Hint: Trial balance total, $124,500.)
4. Prepare an income statement (Hint: EPS, $1.71.)

PC3–9. Fast Stenographic and Mailing Service, Incorporated, was organized by three individuals during January 19A. Each investor paid in $11,000 cash, and each received 1,000 shares of $10 par value. During 19A, the transactions listed below occurred. The letters at the left of each item will serve as the date notation.

a. Received the $33,000 investment of cash by the organizers and issued the shares.
b. Purchased office equipment which cost $6,000; paid cash.
c. Paid $400 cash for a two-year insurance policy on the office equipment (debit the asset account, Prepaid Insurance).
d. Purchased a delivery truck at a cost of $12,000; paid $7,000 down and signed a $5,000, 90-day, 12 percent, interest-bearing note payable for the balance.
e. Purchased office supplies for cash to be used in the stenographic and mailing operations, $2,000. The supplies are for future use (therefore, debit the asset account, Office Supplies Inventory).
f. Revenues earned during the year were:

	Cash	On credit
Stenographic fees	$55,000	$6,000
Mailing fees	8,000	2,000

g. Operating expenses incurred during the year were (excluding transactions [h] through [l]):

Cash	$26,000
On credit	$14,000

h. Paid the $5,000 note on the panel truck. Cash paid out was for the principal plus the interest for three months.
i. Purchased land for a future building site at a cost of $20,000; paid cash.
j. Depreciation on the truck for 19A, was computed on the basis of a five-year useful life; on the office equipment, a useful life of 10 years was assumed (compute full-year depreciation on each and assume no residual value).
k. By December 31, 19A, insurance for one year had expired. Prepaid Insurance should be decreased, and an expense recorded.
l. An inventory of the office supplies reflected $300 on hand at December 31, 19A. Supplies Inventory should be reduced, and an expense recognized.
m. Income tax expense, based on a 20 percent rate, was $5,190 (to be paid in 19B).

Required:

1. Analyze and prepare a journal entry for each transaction listed. Use a form similar to Exhibit 3–5 and include a brief explanation after each transaction.
2. Prepare an income statement that reports total revenues, total expenses, pretax income, income taxes, net income, and EPS. No ledger is required; therefore, you can complete this requirement by either (a) selecting and aggregating amounts from the entries made in Requirement 1, or (b) setting up the needed T-accounts on scratch paper. (Hint: Net income, $20,760.)
3. What is the ending balance of cash? Show computations. In general, why is the ending balance of cash different than net income?

PC3–10.   (Covers the complete information processing cycle) Able, Baker, and Cain organized ABC Realty as a corporation to conduct a real estate and rental management business. Each contributed $20,000 cash and received 1,500 shares (par value $10 per share). They commenced business on January 1, 19A. The transactions listed below, representative of those during the first year, were selected from the actual transactions for case purposes.

Assume for case purposes that these transactions comprise all of the transactions for the year. This case demonstrates the complete information processing cycle from the capture of raw economic data to the final output—the financial statements. Use the numbers at the left as the date notation.

1. Received $60,000 cash invested by shareholders and issued 4,500 shares. See the list of accounts given below.
2. On January 1, 19A, purchased office equipment that cost $6,000; paid one-third cash and charged the balance (one third due in 6 months, and the remaining third is due in 12 months). Credit Accounts Payable for the amount not paid in cash.
3. Purchased land for future office site: cost, $20,000; paid cash.
4. Paid office rent in cash, 11 months at $200 per month (debit Rent Expense). Beginning with this transaction, set up separate accounts for each type of expense.
5. Sold nine properties and collected sales commissions of $56,000. Set up an account, "Realty Commissions Revenue."
6. Paid salaries and commissions expense to salespersons amounting to $52,000 and miscellaneous expenses amounting to $1,000.
7. Collected rental management fees, $20,000. Set up an account, "Rental Management Revenue."
8. Paid utilities, $1,400.
9. Paid auto rental fees (auto rented for use in business), $3,600.
10. Paid for advertising, $7,500.
11. At year-end, the December rent had not been paid (credit Rent Payable).
12. The estimated life of the office equipment was 10 years; assume use for the full year in 19A and no residual value.
13. Additional commissions earned during 19A on sale of real estate amounted to $64,000 of which $14,000 was uncollected at year-end.
14. Paid the installment of $2,000 on the office equipment (see 2 above). Assume no interest.
15. Assume an average income tax rate of 30 percent; 19A tax expense of $21,450 will be paid in 19B.

Required:

a.   Analyze, then journalize, each of the above transactions in chronological order. Number the journal pages consecutively, starting with 1.

b.   Post each transaction from the journal to the ledger; use T-accounts as follows:

Account No.	Account titles	Account No.	Account titles
101	Cash	401	Realty commission revenue
102	Accounts receivable	402	Rental management revenue
103	Office equipment	501	Rent expense
104	Accumulated depreciation, office equipment	502	Salary and commission expense
105	Land for future office site	503	Miscellaneous expense
201	Accounts payable	504	Utilities expense
202	Rent payable	505	Auto rental expense
203	Income tax payable	506	Advertising expense
301	Capital stock, par $10	507	Depreciation expense
302	Contributed surplus	508	Income tax expense

Use folio cross-references when posting.

c.   Prepare a trial balance from the ledger; check the equality of debits and credits. (Hint: Trial balance total is $224,250, including cash of $94,300.)

d.   Use the data on the trial balance to prepare an income statement and balance sheet. Refer to Exhibits 2–1 and 2–2 for the format of these statements. Because of its complexity, preparation of a statement of changes in financial position is deferred to a later chapter. (Hint: EPS, $11.12.)

PC3–11.   SD Moving and Storage Company, Inc., was organized four years ago (January 19A) by O. Snow and R. P. Dean. Each contributed $20,000 cash initially and was issued 2,000 shares of capital stock, par value $10 per share. Since that time, a good portion of the earnings has been left in the business for growth. SD owns a large warehouse and 11 hauling vans. At the beginning, few financial records were maintained; however, it now has one person who devotes full time to records and reports. Disagreements with Revenue Canada prompted the company to approach an independent PA for advice. As a consequence, the first audit was performed for 19C. For purposes of this case, we will utilize only representative accounts and transactions to minimize the time requirements. Assume that the accounts for SD showed the following balance on January 1, 19D (the fiscal and calendar years agree):

Account No.	Account titles	Debit	Credit
101	Cash	$ 21,500	
103	Accounts receivable........................	15,000	
110	Supplies inventory.........................	2,500	
112	Prepaid insurance		
131	Land (on which warehouse is located).......	10,000	
133	Warehouse.................................	80,000	
134	Accumulated depreciation, warehouse........		$ 16,000
135	Moving vans	75,000	
136	Accumulated depreciation, moving vans......		30,000
151	Land for future office building		
201	Accounts payable..........................		10,000
202	Income tax payable		
210	Notes payable, long term (10%).............		30,000
301	Capital stock, par $10 (4,000 shares)		40,000
302	Retained earnings		78,000
303	Dividends declared and paid		
401	Trucking revenues.........................		
402	Storage revenues		
501	Operating expenses........................		
502	Depreciation expense		
505	Interest expense		
506	Income tax expense........................		
	Totals	$204,000	$204,000

Representative transactions for 19D follow (use the letter notation at the left for dating purposes):

a. Purchased land for future office building at a cost of $13,000; paid cash.
b. Revenues earned:

	Cash	Credit
Trucking	$220,000	$40,000
Storage	30,000	2,000

c. Paid $1,600 cash for a two-year insurance policy covering the trucks and warehouse. This payment was made on January 2, 19D (debit Prepaid Insurance).
d. Purchased additional supplies for use in operations for cash, $1,600; these supplies are to be used as needed. Debit Account No. 110.
e. At end of 19D paid $10,000 on the principal of the long-term note payable, plus 10 percent interest on the $30,000 for 12 months.
f. Operating expenses incurred:

Cash	$195,000
On credit	23,000

g. Collections on part of accounts receivable (for trucking and storage services on credit), $38,000 (see [b] above).
h. Payments on part of accounts payable (expenses and services previously incurred on credit), $20,000 cash.
i. Declared and paid cash dividend of $33,000 in December 19D (debit Account No. 303).
j. A full year's depreciation expense for 19D was computed on the basis of the following useful lives: warehouse, 20 years; and moving vans, 5 years (assume no residual values). Debit Account No. 502.
k. On December 31, 19D, an inventory showed supplies remaining on hand (unused) amounting to $1,800. Reduce Supplies Inventory and recognize an expense (Account No. 501).
l. On December 31, 19D, one year of insurance had expired.
m. Income tax expense (30 percent rate), $14,670; paid in cash except for one fourth which will be paid during April 19E.

Required:

1. Set up T-accounts for each account listed above (the above list includes all of the accounts needed) and enter therein the beginning balances given in the following manner.

Cash		101
Balance	21,500	

2. Set up a journal similar to Exhibit 3–5 and enter each of the transactions. Use the letter designation for dating and include a short explanation after each entry. Number the journal pages consecutively starting with 1.
3. Post each transaction entered in the journal to the ledger accounts; complete the folio columns in both the journal and ledger.
4. Prepare a trial balance from the ledger accounts at December 31, 19D. (Hint: The trial balance total is $511,667, including cash of $21,297).
5. Prepare a classified income statement and balance sheet. See Exhibits 2–1 and 2–2 for the formats for these statements. To support the balance sheet, prepare a statement of retained earnings as follows:

Appropriate Heading

Balance, January 1, 19D.................................... $_____
Add: Net income for 19D .... _____
    Total... _____
Deduct: Dividends declared and paid in 19D................ _____
Balance, December 31, 19D (reported on balance sheet)...... $_____
(Hint: EPS is $8.56.)

PC3–12. (Note: This is a special case to test your analytical skills.) Simon Lavoie, a local attorney, decided to sell his practice and retire. He has had discussions with an attorney from another city who desires to relocate. The discussions have entered the complex stage of agreeing on a price. Among the important factors have been the financial statements on Lavoie's practice. Lavoie's secretary, under his direction, maintained the records. Each year they developed a "Statement of Profits" on a cash basis from the incomplete records maintained, and no balance sheet was prepared. Upon request, Lavoie provided the other attorney with the following statement for 1984 prepared by his secretary:

S. LAVOIE
Statement of Profits
1984

Legal fees collected		$92,000
Expenses paid:		
Rent for office space	$10,400	
Utilities.....................	360	
Telephone	2,900	
Office salaries...............	19,000	
Office supplies	900	
Miscellaneous expenses	1,600	
Total expenses		35,160
Profit for the year		$56,840

Upon agreement of the parties, you have been asked to "look into the financial figures for 1984." The other attorney told you that "I question the figures because, among other things, they appear to be on a 100 percent cash basis." Your investigations revealed the following additional data at December 31, 1984:

a. Of the $62,000 legal fees collected in 1984, $28,000 was for services performed prior to 1984.
b. At the end of 1984, legal fees of $7,000 for services performed during the year were uncollected.
c. Office equipment owned and used by Lavoie cost $3,000 and had an estimated remaining useful life of 10 years.
d. An inventory of office supplies at December 31, 1984, reflected $200 worth of items purchased during the year that were still on hand. Also, the records for 1983 indicate that the supplies on hand at the end of that year were approximately $125.
e. At the end of 1984 a secretary, whose salary is $12,000 per year, had not been paid for December because of a long trip that extended to January 15, 1985.
f. The phone bill for December 1984, amounting to $1,500, was not paid until January 11, 1985.
g. The office rent paid of $10,400 was for 13 months (it included the rent for January 1985).

Required:

a. On the basis of the above information, prepare an income statement for 1984 on an accrual basis. Show your computations for any amounts changed from those in the statement prepared by Lavoie's secretary. (Suggested solution format with four column headings: Items; Cash Basis Per Lavoie Statement, $; Explanation of Changes; and Corrected to Accrual Basis Per GAAP, $.)
b. Write a comment to support your schedule prepared in (a). The purpose should be to briefly explain the reasons for your changes and to suggest some other important items that should be considered in the pricing decision.

PC3–13. Refer to the financial statements of Consolidated-Bathurst given in Special Supplement B immediately preceding the Index. Respond to the following questions for the 1984 annual accounting period.

1. On what date did the 1984 accounting period end?
2. Complete the following fundamental accounting model by providing the amounts
   Assets, $_____ = Liabilities, $_____ + Owners' Equity, $_____.
3. How much was the revenue from sales to customers? $_____.
4. What was the dual economic effect on the company of the sales to customers?
   (a) _____ $_____
   (b) _____ $_____
5. What was the dual economic effect on the company of the cost of the products sold?
   (a) _____ $_____
   (b) _____ $_____
6. What was the dual economic effect on the company of the cash dividends declared and paid on preferred shares?
   (a) _____ $_____
   (b) _____ $_____

7. Prepare the journal entry to record other income assuming it all was received in cash.

8. Prepare a journal entry to record corporate administrative expense assuming it was all paid in cash.

9. What amount was shown in the trial balance at the end of the 1984 annual accounting period for (a) long-term debt and (b) cash and short-term deposits?

10. What was the amount of "depreciation and amortization?" Prepare a journal entry to record this amount.

PC3–14. (Note: This problem uses a spreadsheet computer program.)

1. Use the structure of E3–5 and the accounts of PC3–10 to record the transactions listed in PC3–10.

2. Sum each account across, then sum the totals down to see if the accounts balance. (Hint: The sum down should be $0 if the accounts are in balance because a credit should be entered as a minus.)

3. Below the transactions section, prepare an income statement and a balance sheet. References in the statements can be used to transfer amounts. Sum to achieve totals. Calculate EPS (Hint: EPS, $11.12).

C·H·A·P·T·E·R

4

Matching of Expenses with Revenue Each Period

PURPOSE OF THIS CHAPTER

Net income is one of the more significant single amounts developed through the accounting process. In this chapter we will focus on several critical issues involved in the measurement of net income. We will examine some of the complications posed when the lifespan of a business is divided into a series of equal time periods, such as one year. We will consider the problem of realistically identifying revenues within the selected time period and then identifying the expenses that were incurred in order to earn the revenues for that period.

To accomplish these purposes, this chapter is divided into two parts as follows:

Part A—Recognition of revenues and expenses

Part B—Adjusting entries illustrated

Part A—Recognition of Revenues and Expenses

RELATIONSHIPS AMONG FINANCIAL STATEMENTS

The required financial statements—the balance sheet, income statement, and statement of changes in financial position—were discussed in the preceding chapters. In this section we will continue our discussion by emphasizing the relationships among the financial statements. These three financial statements plus the accompanying notes, supporting schedules, and the auditors' opinion should be viewed as the entire financial report for the selected time period. This entire reporting package is necessary to meet the varied needs of a diverse population of financial statement users.

EXHIBIT 4–1
Relationships among financial statements

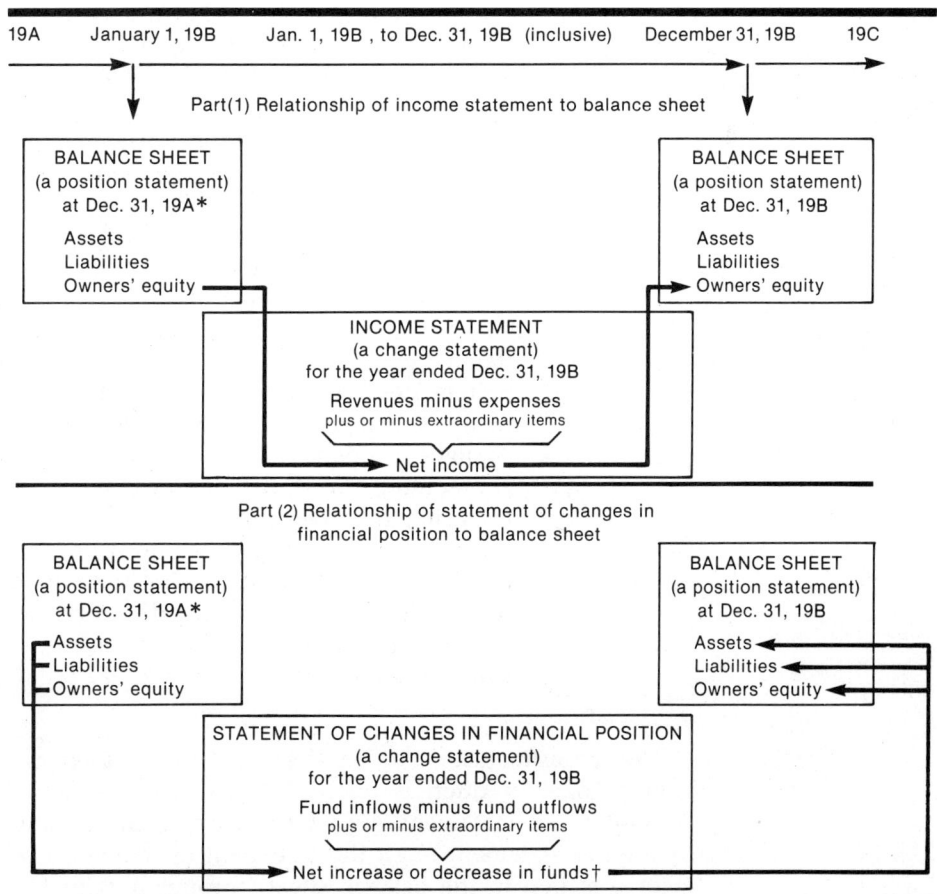

| 19A | January 1, 19B | Jan. 1, 19B , to Dec. 31, 19B (inclusive) | December 31, 19B | 19C |

Part(1) Relationship of income statement to balance sheet

BALANCE SHEET
(a position statement)
at Dec. 31, 19A*

Assets
Liabilities
Owners' equity

BALANCE SHEET
(a position statement)
at Dec. 31, 19B

Assets
Liabilities
Owners' equity

INCOME STATEMENT
(a change statement)
for the year ended Dec. 31, 19B

Revenues minus expenses
plus or minus extraordinary items

Net income

Part (2) Relationship of statement of changes in financial position to balance sheet

BALANCE SHEET
(a position statement)
at Dec. 31, 19A*

Assets
Liabilities
Owners' equity

BALANCE SHEET
(a position statement)
at Dec. 31, 19B

Assets
Liabilities
Owners' equity

STATEMENT OF CHANGES IN FINANCIAL POSITION
(a change statement)
for the year ended Dec. 31, 19B

Fund inflows minus fund outflows
plus or minus extraordinary items

Net increase or decrease in funds†

*This balance sheet also is at the beginning of 19B.

†Funds are measured as either cash or working capital in the SCFP

Exhibit 4–1 presents the basic relationships among the three financial statements for a fiscal year, such as January 1 through December 31, 19B. This exhibit emphasizes that the **beginning financial position** of the entity is reported in the balance sheet at the end of the **prior** period and its **ending** financial position is reported in the balance sheet at the end of the **current** year. In addition to information concerning financial position as of specific dates, decision makers (users of the financial report) need information about what happened **during** the current year that **caused** the financial position of the entity to change. The **changes** in financial position between the beginning and ending of the current accounting period are communicated to users in two different "change" statements as follows:

1. **Income statement**—The income statement explains **changes** in owners' equity during the period as a result of **operations.** Net income increases owners' equity, which is shown graphically in Exhibit 4–1, Part 1. The detailed amounts of revenue, expense, and extraordinary items that **caused** this particular change in financial position during the period are reported on the income statement for the period. Therefore, the income statement reports detailed information to explain **one major category of changes** in financial position during the selected time period; this category of changes resulted from **operations** and **extraordinary items.** The accompanying notes and supporting schedules add qualitative elaboration of the income statement.

2. **Statement of changes in financial position (SCFP)**—This statement is designed to report, or explain, all the **causes of changes** in financial position (i.e., assets, liabilities, and owners' equity) during the period that result from the operating, financing and investing activities. Thus, the SCFP reports all of the entity's **sources** (i.e., inflows) of funds and all of its **uses** (i.e., outflows) of funds during the period. The financial position of the entity was changed as a result of these inflows and outflows of funds. The SCFP may be prepared to measure **funds** as either cash or as working capital (explained later).

The three financial statements are linked together in important ways. This linking together often is referred to as **articulation,** which means that an amount in one statement (e.g., net income on the income statement) is carried to another statement (e.g., the statement of retained earnings). Similarly, net income is tied to the balance sheet (through retained earnings)—and to the SCFP (discussed later). Decision makers can better interpret the financial statements when they clearly understand these relationships. Your understanding of these relationships will be important as you study Part B of this chapter and all of the remaining chapters.

TIME-PERIOD ASSUMPTION

Our discussion above of the relationships among the three required financial statements emphasized the timing of financial statements. Each financial statement should specifically identify its **time dimension** (see Chapter 1). Exhibit 4–1 reemphasizes that the time dimension of the balance sheet is at a **specific date** (such as "At December 31, 19X"). In contrast, the two "change" statements cover a **specified period of time** (such as, "For the Year Ended December 31, 19X").

The lifespan of most business entities is indefinite, but decision makers need current information about the entity. Therefore, the lifespan of an entity is divided into a series of short time periods, such as one year, for many measurement or financial reporting purposes. This division of the activities of a business into a series of equal time periods is known as the **time-period assumption** (see Exhibit 2–6), which is fundamental to the accounting process and financial reporting.

Because annual periods tend to be dominant throughout our society, the accounting period usually is viewed as being 12 consecutive months. As a consequence, the emphasis in accounting is on **annual** financial statements. Many companies use a year that corresponds to the natural cycle of their business, such as July 1 through June 30, rather than to the calendar year. An accounting year that does not necessarily correspond to the calendar year is known as a **fiscal year.** In addition to the annual financial statements, many businesses prepare and publish quarterly financial reports for external distribution. These usually are called **interim reports.** Also, in addition to annual reports, monthly financial statements frequently are prepared exclusively for **internal management** purposes.

Dividing the lifespan of a business into short time periods, such as a year, for measurement purposes often poses complex accounting problems because some **transactions start in one accounting period and are,** in effect, **concluded in a subsequent period.** This continuity of the effects of a transaction may occur for all classifications; for example:

a. **Assets**—A machine that is purchased in one year may be depreciated over the next 10 years.

b. **Liabilities**—A note payable is signed that requires interest payments each of three years and payment of the principal at the end of the third year.

c. **Owners' equity**—Shares are sold in one year with a cash down payment plus two equal annual installment payments and issuance of the shares at the date of the last installment.

d. **Revenues**—Rent is collected in one year for six months in advance, and two of the occupancy periods (months) extend into the next year.

e. **Expenses**—An insurance premium on property is paid in advance for two years of future coverage.

The time-period assumption has a significant impact on the recognition of periodic revenues and expenses.

PERIODIC RECOGNITION OF REVENUES AND EXPENSES

The process of earning **revenues** through the sale of goods and services and the incurring of **expenses** necessary to earn those revenues is **continuous.** Some revenue and expense transactions cover an extended period of time between their initiation and completion. This causes a problem because financial reports must be made for a specific time period, such as a month, quarter, or year. Therefore, a careful **cutoff** must be made among the selected time periods so that the revenues and expenses for each separate period can be measured reliably.

Frequently, it is difficult to identify a specific revenue and/or expense with a particular accounting period. In response to this problem, the **revenue principle** and the **matching principle** have evolved as two of the broad fundamentals underlying accounting (see Exhibit 2–6). These two principles focus on the measurement of **net income** for each time period. **The revenue principle takes a timing precedence over the matching principle in the measurement process.** First, the revenues earned for the period from the sale of goods and services are measured; next, the matching principle is applied to measure the expenses incurred in earning those particular revenues. To reemphasize, for accounting measurement purposes, the revenue and matching principles require a careful **cutoff** of revenues and expenses at the end of each accounting period and a proper matching of expenses with revenues.

The revenue principle

The revenue principle was defined briefly in Chapter 2, Exhibit 2–6. The revenue principle holds that revenue should be recognized in the period in which it is **earned** (often referred to as realized).[1] Revenue is identified with a specific accounting period by considering **when** the revenue transaction occurred rather than considering when the related cash is collected. The income statement for each accounting period must report all of the revenues **earned** during the period covered, but must not report any revenues earned in prior or following periods.

To apply the revenue principle, the general guideline is that revenue is considered earned (realized) when the **earning process** is substantially completed. In the case of the sale of **goods,** the earning process is substantially completed when **ownership** of the goods passes from the seller to the buyer. In the case of the sale of **services,** the earning process is substantially completed as the services are performed (rather when the services finally are completed in all

---

[1]The revenue principle is a complex principle that has a significant impact on net income. The full details of this principle are beyond the scope of a first course. A recent CICA proposed pronouncement (*Accounting Exposure Draft,* October 1985) presents the more common general rules and exceptions that are presented in this chapter. The additional technicalities of the principle will have to be left for future study.

respects). This general guideline is applied to most revenue transactions; however, there are few **exceptions** as follows:

1. **Long-term credit sales coupled with a relatively small down payment**—Such sales often pose the question of **risk** that full collection will not be made ultimately (i.e., a default and repossession may occur). For example, in the case of land development companies, one common practice has been to sell undeveloped land for a down payment of approximately 5 percent coupled with a 10- to 30-year debt payment period. Because of the number of defaults that this industry experienced, the current accounting guideline in the United States is that sales revenue should not be recorded as **earned** until the period in which the total cash collected is at least 10 percent of the sale price.

2. **Installment sales**—Often there is a high risk of default when a company sells high-cost items of merchandise with a relatively low cash down payment and liberal credit terms (such as the sale of an expensive TV set). Such situations may require application of **installment-sales accounting.** This method of recognition of revenue is applied when the characteristics of the sale transaction are: (1) a relatively small down payment is required; (2) the payment period is long and calls for monthly payments of principal plus interest; (3) the seller retains conditional ownership of the goods until full payment is made; and (4) bad debt losses cannot be estimated reliably. When all of these characteristics exist in combination, there is a relatively high risk that the merchandise will be repossessed because of nonpayment (default). The installment method of accounting is used in this situation. Under this method, the revenue is considered to be earned as the **cash is collected.** As a consequence, this method is close to cash basis accounting.

3. **Long-term construction contracts**—Revenue and expense recognition problems arise for the **construction contractor** when a construction contract extends across two or more accounting periods. For example, assume a building contractor signs a contract to build a large plant at a cost of $3,500,000 and the construction period is three years, starting January 1, 19A. The contractor estimates a construction cost of $3,200,000; that is, an estimated profit of $300,000. The question is: should the profit be reported as (1) earned in 19C when the project is completed or (2) allocated on an estimated basis to each of the three years? One accounting method used is called the **completed contract method.** Under this method, all of the profit is recognized as earned in the year of **completion.** This method is conservative because recognition of profit is deferred until

completion when the actual profit is known. Another accounting method used for long-term construction contracts is called the **percentage-of-completion method.** It permits **allocation** of profit to each of the three construction periods based on estimates (usually based on the ratio of actual costs incurred during the period to total costs of the project) covering the three-year period. Specifically, one common form of the calculation involves the following:

$$\begin{array}{c} \text{Total accrued} \\ \text{profit} \end{array} = \frac{\text{Costs incurred to date}}{\begin{array}{c} \text{Costs incurred to date} \\ + \\ \text{Estimated costs to} \\ \text{complete} \end{array}} \times \begin{array}{c} \text{Expected profit} \\ \text{on contract} \end{array} \qquad (1)$$

$$\begin{array}{l} \text{Profit recognized} = \text{Total accrued profit from (1)} - \qquad (2) \\ \text{in current year} \qquad \text{Profit accrued in prior years.} \end{array}$$

A portion of the estimated $300,000 would be recognized as profit each year during the construction period.

At the present time, a contractor is permitted to select either method of accounting for long-term construction contracts; however, the percentage-of-completion method can be used only if reliable estimates can be made. Many accountants believe that this choice between two **accounting alternatives** for the same set of facts is not sound, but these accountants do not agree on which method is preferable in all cases. Lack of agreement among accountants as to the best measurement approach is primarily the reason for the approval of accounting alternatives. Similarly, there are a number of other areas of accounting where measurement and recognition alternatives are permitted for the same set of facts. The accounting profession is striving to eliminate such alternative accounting choices.

The reliability principle

The discussions above of revenue recognition illustrate the **qualitative characteristic of reliability** (see Exhibit 2–6) which holds that all economic data reported on the financial statements must be unbiased, accurate, and verifiable. Thus, the discussion of the percentage-of-completion method of revenue recognition can be used **only if the estimates used in it are reliable,** otherwise the completed contract method must be used. Similarly, the installment-sales method can be used to recognize revenue on credit sales **only if reliable estimates of bad debt losses cannot be made.** The qualitative characteristic of reliability does not permit the reporting of biased or unrealistic estimates of assets, liabilities, revenues, gains, expenses, or losses. Thus, the **reliability** characteristic exerts a significant impact on accounting and reporting.

The matching principle

Expenses are defined in Exhibit 2–6. The matching principle focuses on the measurement of expenses and the matching of them with the periodic revenues **earned** during the period. The matching principle holds that all of the expenses incurred in earning revenues should be identified, or matched, with the revenues earned, period by period.

When applying the matching principle, it is necessary to consider the purposes for which the expenses were incurred. If the expenses are associated with a specific revenue, as is the usual case, the expenses should be identified with the period in which that revenue was earned. In this way, the expenses are matched with the revenues of each period so that income for each period is measured correctly. Expenses incurred in earning the revenues of the period should be reported in that period. Resources expended in one period to earn revenues in other periods should be apportioned to those other periods.

Application of the revenue and matching principles is to identify revenues and expenses among consecutive accounting periods. This identification, or cutoff, by periods often requires that a special type of end-of-period accounting entries be made. Collectively, such entries usually are referred to as **adjusting entries.**

ADJUSTING ENTRIES

Adjusting entries are required by the revenue and matching principles to effect a precise identification, or **cutoff,** of revenues and expenses among consecutive accounting periods because some completed transactions recorded in one accounting period have economic consequences that extend over one or more other accounting periods. As a result, **adjusting entries** may be necessary to change certain account balances at the end of the accounting period, not to correct errors but to reflect these interperiod economic consequences. To illustrate, assume a company purchased a machine for use in the business on January 1, 19A, that cost $50,000 with an estimated useful life of five years (no residual value). On January 1, 19A (the date the transaction was completed), an asset account—machinery—was debited (increased) for $50,000. However, by December 31, 19A (end of the accounting period), the machine has depreciated to $40,000. Therefore, due to a subsequent economic event (use of the machine), an **adjusting entry** must be made to (a) decrease the book value of the asset by $10,000 and (b) record depreciation expense of $10,000.

Adjusting entries possess four fundamental characteristics as follows:

1. An **income statement** account balance (revenue or expense) is changed.
2. A **balance sheet** account balance (asset or liability) is changed.
3. They usually are recorded at the end of the accounting period.
4. They never directly affect the Cash account.

When considering what adjusting entries are needed it is important to remember that the adjusting entries should never affect the cash account. The cash account contains only transactions that should have been recorded as part of the regular entries. Adjustments are not considered to be the regular entries that are necessary to record transactions; therefore, the cash account should always be correct before adjustments are made. Bank reconciliations (discussed in Chapter 8) and cash counts will be used to make sure all regular entries have been recorded before the adjustments are made.

Adjusting entries are required by four types of transactions as follows:

Revenues (revenue principle applied):

1. **Revenue collected in advance but not yet earned**—Revenue collected in advance of being **earned** must be apportioned (deferred) to the period or periods in which it will be earned. In this situation, cash collection **leads** (precedes) revenue recognition.

   Example: On December 1, 19A, Alpha Company collected $1,000 cash for December 19A and January 19B rent (i.e., $500 per month). On the transaction date, the company debited Cash and credited Rent Revenue for $1,000

   Analysis on December 31, 19A: Rent revenue was earned in 19A for only one month, December; the other monthly rent will be earned in 19B; however, cash was collected in 19A for both months. Therefore, on December 31, 19A, an **adjusting** entry for $500 must be made to (a) decrease (debit) rent revenue and (b) increase (credit) rent revenue collected in advance. The $500 credit balance in this account must be reported on the 19A balance sheet as a **liability** because the company owes the renter occupancy for one month (January 19B).

2. **Revenue earned but not yet collected or recorded**—Revenue not collected nor recorded but earned in the current accounting period should be recorded as **earned** in the current period, even though the related cash will be collected in a subsequent period. In this case, cash collection **lags** revenue recognition.

   Example: On December 31, 19A, Alpha Company completed two phases of a service job for a customer; the third phase will be done in January 19B. The total contract price was $1,200 (i.e., $400 per phase) cash payable upon completion of all phases.

   Analysis on December 31, 19A: Service revenue of $800 (i.e., $1,200 × 2/3) was earned in 19A, although not yet recorded or collected. Therefore, an **adjusting** entry for $800 must be made on December 31, 19A, to (a) increase (debit) accounts receivable and (b) increase (credit) service revenue because revenue for the first two phases has been earned in 19A; a receivable must be recorded because the collection of cash will be made in 19B

Expenses (matching principle applied):

3. **Expense paid in advance**—Expense paid in advance of use of the services or goods must be apportioned (deferred) to the period, or periods, in which such services or goods will be used. In this situation, cash payment **leads** expense recognition.

   Example: On January 1, 19A, Alpha Company paid a two-year premium of $800 for property insurance; the coverage is for 19A and 19B (i.e., $400 per year). The company recorded this transaction on January 1, 19A, as a debit (increase) of $800 to Prepaid Insurance (an asset), and a decrease (credit) to Cash.

   Analysis on December 31, 19A: On this date half of the benefit of the insurance coverage has been received. Half of the related insurance premium has expired (i.e., $800 ÷ 2 = $400); the other half remains prepaid. Therefore, on December 31, 19A, an **adjusting** entry for $400 must be made to (a) increase (debit) insurance expense and (b) decrease (credit) prepaid insurance. This entry records the $400 expense for 19A and leaves $400 in the asset account, Prepaid Insurance. Prepaid insurance is an asset because Alpha Company has an obligation from the insurance company to provide insurance coverage for 19B (the premium already has been paid).

4. **Expense incurred but not recorded**—Expense incurred (the services or goods have been used) in the current accounting period but not yet recorded or paid (the related cash payment will be in a subsequent period) should be recorded as expense in the current period. In this situation, cash payment lags expense recognition.

   Example: On December 31, 19A, Alpha Company employees have earned $1,000 in wages that will be paid in cash on the next payroll date January 6, 19B.

   Analysis on December 31, 19A: The company has incurred wage expense in 19A of $1,000 (the employees were helping to earn 19A revenues), and because the employees have not been paid, the company has a $1,000 liability on December 31, 19A. Therefore, an **adjusting** entry for $1,000 must be made on December 31, 19A, to (a) debit (increase) Wage Expense and (b) credit (increase) Wages Payable. This liability will be reported on the 19A balance sheet and will be paid on the next payroll date, January 6, 19B.

In summary, adjusting entries are made at the **end** of each accounting period, after the regular entries are completed. At this time, the accountant must make a careful check of the records and supporting documents to determine whether there are any situations such as those listed above for which **adjusting entries** should be made. In practically all situations, one or more such entries invariably will be required at the end of each accounting period. If any required adjusting entries are not made, revenue for the period may be measured incorrectly and/or expenses may not be matched with the revenues earned during the period. In either instance, the result would be incorrect measurement of amounts on both the income statement and the balance sheet for **both** the current and subsequent period or periods.

Adjusting entries are not unusual. They require no additional competence, only a knowledge and analysis of the actual facts in respect to each item. In Chapter 3, the illustrations, exercises, and problems/cases included several adjusting entries (depreciation expense, prepaid insurance, supplies used, and accrued or unpaid wages) routinely made without special identification or concern.

Terminology

Accountants frequently use two technical terms both in respect to adjusting entries and in a more general sense. Throughout this textbook and in many of your subsequent courses (and in the outside environment) you will encounter the terms **accrued** (or to accrue) and **deferred** (or to defer). Basic and practical definitions for our purposes are: **Accrued,** in the case of expenses, means not yet paid; and in the case of revenues, not yet collected. **Deferred,** in the case of revenues, means collected in advance and, in the case of expenses, paid in advance. To summarize:

Term	Definition	Example
1. Accrued expense	An expense incurred, not yet paid	Wages earned by employee but not yet paid
2. Accrued revenue	A revenue earned, not yet collected	Services performed in advance of collection
3. Deferred revenue	A revenue not yet earned, collected in advance	Rent collected in advance of occupancy
4. Deferred expense	An expense not yet incurred, paid in advance	Insurance premium paid in advance

A CASE STUDY

The discussions in this chapter focus on the allocation of revenues and expenses among two or more consecutive accounting periods. Such allocations often have a major impact on the **income statement** and **balance sheet** amounts for the current period. For example, an article in *Forbes* ("A Question of Judgment," February 16, 1981) discussed some interesting allocation issues. The article stated, "Tucked away in the middle of an ordinary-looking press release mailed out by ABC (the TV network) in December was a line noting that the method of assigning expenses to each showing of prime-time series and movies was being changed." Trivial? Not to an experienced broadcast accountant. That little change could make quite a difference on the bottom line." The "expenses" referred to in this citation often amount to approximately $500 million for "a prime-time series or movie."

The accounting issue discussed in the article was how much of the $500 million should be (a) allocated to expense to be matched with the **first** showing and (b) how much of the $500 million should be **deferred** as an asset on the balance sheet (and later allocated as expense to subsequent showings). The article continues, "What ABC seems to have done is reduce the first-time charge from 80% to around 75% of the show's cost. That doesn't sound like much until you consider the numbers involved." To illustrate the cited amounts:

	Millons of dollars	
	Expense (80 percent)	Asset (20 percent)
Former Method:		
$500 million allocated, 80%/20%	$400	$100
New Method:		
$500 million allocated, 75%/25%	375	125
Difference: Increase in reported income and assets	$ 25	$ 25

The article explained: "For ABC, that little switch could well turn a loss into a profit in the first quarter of this year and could also boost earnings thereafter. Of course, from the auditors' point of view, there is nothing wrong with doing a little shifting like this—as long as it's within reason. Management is supposed to know better than their CPA firm how much revenue can be expected on these later broadcasts."

The past has shown that "deferring writeoffs of bombs was a common route to high profits in the movie industry until 1973 when practices there were tightened considerably. But the networks may still have a few skeletons in their closets. The point is, networks can change their minds conveniently about the prospects of shows anytime they need an earnings boost—and few shareholders would be the wiser for it."

This case example demonstrates that revenue and expense allocations often (a) involve substantial amounts and (b) significantly affect reported income. As a result, the users of financial statements (and the business press) pay close attention to the allocation decisions made by the managements of the reporting companies.

Part B—Adjusting Entries Illustrated

This part of the chapter continues the discussion of adjusting entries. It provides detailed illustrations and explanations of numerous adjusting entries. Our emphasis will be on the **analysis** of specific examples to determine the appropriate adjusting entry and the related entries that are made in subsequent periods. These illustrations will increase your understanding of the application of the accounting model, measurement of periodic revenues and expenses, and determination of income. Throughout the examples to follow, we will refer to **High-Rise Apartments** (organized as a corporation on January 1, 19A) and will assume that the **current annual accounting period ends December 31, 19B.**

REVENUE COLLECTED IN ADVANCE (DEFERRED REVENUE)

Businesses may collect cash and record it in advance of earning the related revenue from the sale of services or goods. The amount collected in advance is called unearned or deferred revenue. Unearned revenue must be apportioned to the period in which the services are performed or the sale is completed in accordance with the **revenue principle** (see Exhibit 2–6 and earlier in this chapter). When unearned revenue has been received, an **adjusting entry** usually is required at the end of the period to recognize (1) the correct amount of revenue **earned** during the current period and (2) the remaining obligation in the future to provide the related goods or services. We will analyze one such situation for High-Rise Apartments that occurs because some tenants pay their rent in the middle of each month. (Note: Each **adjusting** entry is letter coded for reference in the illustrations to follow.)

Example: On December 11, 19B, two tenants paid rent for one month from December 11, 19B, through January 10, 19C, in the amount of $1,500. The sequence of entries recorded by High-Rise would be:

December 11, 19B—date of the transaction:

Cash	1,500	
Rent revenue		1,500
To record one month's rent for the period December 11, 19B, through January 10, 19C.		

December 31, 19B—end of the accounting period:

Analysis: The $1,500 cash collected included rent revenue for December 19B of $1,500 × $20/30$ = $1,000, and rent revenue collected in advance for January 19C of $1,500 × $10/30$ = $500. Therefore, an **adjusting entry** is required on December 31, 19B, to (a) reduce the balance in rent revenue by $500 and (b) record the obligation to furnish occupancy in 19C for one third of a month which was paid in advance of that year. This $500 is a current liability that will be paid in January 19C by providing occupancy rights:

a. December 31, 19B (end of the accounting period)—**adjusting entry:**[2]

Rent revenue...	500	
Rent collected in advance..		500
To adjust the accounts for revenue collected in advance as of the end of the current period.		

The $1,000 (i.e., $1,500 − $500) rent revenue would be reported on the 19B income statement and the rent revenue collected in advance of $500 would be reported on the 19B balance sheet as a current liability.

January 19C:

Rent revenue collected in advance....................................	500	
Rent revenue..		500
To record the rent revenue from the liability account to the 19C revenue account because it now has been earned.		

In overall perspective, the three entries above (*a*) recorded the cash transaction and (*b*) allocated the total rent collected between the two periods (19B and 19C) as rent revenue in each period as earned.

REVENUE EARNED PRIOR TO COLLECTION (ACCRUED REVENUE)

At the end of the current accounting period, analysis may reveal that some revenue has been **earned** (in accordance with the revenue principle) but has

---

[2]Observe that the entry at collection date, December 11, 19B, could have been recorded in a way that would preclude the need for an adjusting entry later, viz:

Cash..	1,500	
Rent revenue		1,000
Rent collected in advance		500

Alternatively, it could be accounted for as follows with the same end result:

December 11, 19B:

Cash..	1,500	
Rent collected in advance		1,500

December 31, 19B—adjusting entry:

Rent collected in advance	1,000	
Rent revenue		1,000

not yet been recorded or collected. Such unrecorded revenue usually is referred to as unrecorded revenue or accrued revenue.

The revenue principle states that if revenue was earned in the current accounting period, it must be recorded and reported in that period along with the asset that has been created (an account receivable). This recording is accomplished by making an **adjusting** entry at the end of the current period to recognize *(a)* a receivable for the amount earned but not yet collected and *(b)* the amount of revenue earned. We will analyze a typical situation for High-Rise Apartments and give the sequence of entries.

Example: On December 31, 19B, the manager of High-Rise Apartments analyzed the rental records and found that one tenant had not paid the December rent amounting to $600. The sequence of entries recorded by High-Rise would be:

b. December 31, 19B (end of the accounting period)—**adjusting entry:**

Rent revenue receivable	600	
Rent revenue.		600
To record rent revenue earned in 19B but not collected by year end.		

January 19C—date of collection:

Cash	600	
Rent revenue receivable		600
To record 19C collection of receivable for 19B rent revenue.		

The adjusting entry at the end of 19B served two measurement purposes: (1) to record rent revenue earned in 19B of $600 and (2) to record a receivable (an asset) for occupancy provided in 19B for which $600 cash will be collected in January 19C. Rent revenue receivable is reported on the December 31, 19B, balance sheet as a current asset.

EXPENSES PAID IN ADVANCE (PREPAID OR DEFERRED EXPENSE)

Frequently a company either pays cash or incurs a liability in one accounting period for assets purchased or services obtained that will be used in one or more future accounting periods to help earn revenues during those future periods. Such transactions create an asset because of the future benefits; that asset usually is called a **prepaid expense** (or a deferred expense). As the future periods pass, the related revenues are earned (in accordance with the revenue principle). Then, as the revenues are earned, period by period, the **prepaid** expense amount must be apportioned to the appropriate periods in accordance with the **matching principle.** For example, if the related revenues are earned over three accounting periods, the prepaid expense must be apportioned to each of those three periods in order to measure net income for each period.

For High-Rise Apartments we will analyze **three** such transactions that occurred in 19B.

Prepaid insurance

On January 1, 19B, High-Rise paid cash of $2,400 in advance for a two-year insurance policy on the apartment building. The sequence of entries by High-Rise for this **prepaid expense** would be:

January 1, 19B—date of the transaction:

Prepaid insurance (an asset account)................................	2,400	
Cash...		2,400
To record prepayment of a two-year premium on building.		

December 31, 19B—end of the accounting period:

> **Analysis:** The $2,400 cash paid on January 1, 19B, was for insurance coverage for two full years; therefore, insurance **expense** for each of the two years will be $1,200. At the end of 19B, an adjusting entry must be made to (a) reduce prepaid insurance by $1,200 and (b) record insurance expense of $1,200 for 19B.

c. December 31, 19B (end of the accounting period)—**adjusting entry:**

Insurance expense	1,200	
Prepaid insurance.............		1,200
To record 19B insurance expense for 12 months ($2,400 × $^{12}\!/_{24}$ = $1,200).		

The adjusting entry serves two measurement purposes: (1) it apportions insurance expense to the current period for **matching** purposes and (2) it adjusts (reduces) the Prepaid Insurance account to the correct asset amount ($1,200) for the **unexpired** insurance remaining at the end of 19B. That is, at the end of 19B, the company was entitled to one more year of insurance protection (with a cost of $1,200) and hence had a current **asset.**

December 31, 19C (end of next accounting period)—**adjusting entry:**

Insurance expense	1,200	
Prepaid insurance		1,200
To record 19C insurance expense.		

This entry apportions insurance expense to 19C and reduces the prepaid insurance balance to zero because the policy term ends on December 31, 19C.

Depreciation

On January 1, 19A, a contractor completed an apartment building for High-Rise. The contract price of $360,000 was paid in cash. The building has an estimated **useful life** of 30 years and an estimated $60,000 **residual value** at the end of the 30 years. This transaction involved the acquisition of an asset (building) that may affect the financial statements for the next 30 years (including 19A). At this point, we will consider one continuing effect—depreciation. The sequence of entries by High-Rise is discussed below.

January 1, 19A—date of acquisition of building:

Apartment building	360,000	
Cash		360,000
To record full payment for construction cost of the building.		

d.   December 31, 19B (end of the accounting period)—**adjusting entry:**

Depreciation expense	10,000	
Accumulated depreciation, building		10,000
To record straight-line depreciation expense for one year ($360,000 − $60,000) ÷ 30 years = $10,000.		

The adjusting entry for depreciation expense would be repeated at the end of **each year** over the 30-year life of the building. The **estimated** amount expected to be recovered when the asset finally is sold or disposed of is known as the **residual value** (sometimes it is called scrap or salvage value). For computing depreciation, the cost of the asset must be **reduced** by the residual value. The difference ($360,000 − $60,000 = $300,000) is the net amount of cost to be depreciated over the estimated useful life. Thus, the annual depreciation expense on the apartment building would be ($360,000 − $60,000) ÷ 30 years = $10,000.[3] The residual value of $60,000 is deducted because it is the amount of cost that is expected to be recovered at the end of the useful life (of the building) to the company.

In overall perspective, the adjusting entry serves two measurement purposes: (1) it allocates a part of the cost of the building to expense for the current period for matching purposes and (2) it adjusts (reduces) the amount of the asset to represent the undepreciated cost of the asset. The credit to Accumulated Depreciation, Building could have been made directly to the building account with the same effect; however, it is desirable, for reporting purposes, to keep the balance of the asset account Apartment Building at original cost. This is accomplished by setting up an asset **contra,** or **offset,** account titled Accumulated Depreciation, Building. You will recall from Chapters 2 and 3 that on the balance sheet the building would be shown on one line at its acquisition cost and a deduction on the next line for accumulated depreciation (see Exhibit 2–2). The difference between the acquisition cost and accumulated depreciation amounts often is referred to as the **book value,** or **carrying value,** of the asset. The book or carrying value does not represent the current **market** value of the asset. The book or carrying value does not represent the current **market** value of the asset because accounting for depreciation is a cost allocation process rather than a market valuation process.

Supplies inventory and expense

On January 1, 19B, the inventory of maintenance supplies was $100; these were **unused** supplies on hand carried over from the previous year. High-Rise purchases maintenance supplies, not for resale but for use as needed, and they are kept in a small storeroom from which supplies are withdrawn as needed. On March 18, 19B, additional supplies were purchased at a cost of $500 and were placed in the storeroom. No accounting entry is made when the supplies are withdrawn for use. To determine the amount of supplies **used** during the period, an inventory of the supplies remaining on hand is taken at the end of the period. At December 31, 19B, the inventory of the supplies in the storeroom showed $200 in supplies on hand. The sequence of entries by High-Rise would be:

---

[3]This example assumes straight-line depreciation, that is, an equal amount of depreciation expense is apportioned to each period. Other methods of depreciation will be discussed in Chapter 9.

March 18, 19B—date of purchase of supplies:

Inventory of maintenance supplies (an asset)........................... 500
    Cash 500
To record purchase of maintenance supplies for addition to inventory.
Note: This entry increases the inventory account balance from $100 to
$600.

---

e. December 31, 19B (end of the accounting period)—**adjusting entry:**

Maintenance expense 400
    Inventory of maintenance supplies 400
To record the amount of supplies used from inventory ($100 + $500 −
$200 = $400).

Analysis: Before the adjusting entry is made, the balance in the Inventory of Maintenance Supplies account is $600 (i.e., beginning inventory, $100, plus the purchase, $500); however, the actual inventory count at this date reflected $200, which means that usage of supplies was $400 (i.e., $100 + $500 − $200 = $400). The above adjusting entry is required to *(a)* reduce the inventory account by $400 (so that the asset, inventory, will be reflected as $200 per the inventory count) and *(b)* to record an expense for the amount of supplies used, $400. Therefore, the 19B income statement will report supplies expense of $400, and the 19B balance sheet will report a current asset—inventory of maintenance supplies—of $200.

EXPENSES INCURRED PRIOR TO PAYMENT (ACCRUED EXPENSES)

Most expenses are incurred and paid for during the same period; however, at the end of the accounting period there usually are some expenses that have been **incurred** (i.e., the goods and/or services that already have been used) but are **not yet recorded,** usually because payment has not been made. Such unpaid expenses are referred to as **accrued expenses.** Such expenses must be recorded in the current period because they must be **matched** with the revenues of the current period in accordance with the **matching principle.** Also, the liability for those unpaid expenses must be recorded and reported on the balance sheet of the current period. These effects are recorded by using an adjusting entry. We will analyze and illustrate **three** such transactions each of which required an adjusting entry by High-Rise Apartments.

Salary and wage expense

On December 31, 19B, the manager of High-Rise was on vacation and due to return January 10, 19C. As a consequence, the manager's December salary of $900 was not paid or recorded by December 31, 19B. The sequence of entries by High-Rise for the accrued salary expense (disregard payroll taxes at this time) would be:

f. December 31, 19B (end of the accounting period)—**adjusting entry:**

Salary expense	900	
Salaries payable (or accrued salaries payable)......................		900
To record salary expense and the liability for December salary not yet paid.		

January 10, 19C—date of payment of the December 19B salary:

Salaries payable	900	
Cash		900
To record payment of a December 19B salary.		

The adjusting entry served two measurement purposes: (1) to record an expense incurred in 19B for matching with revenues and (2) to record the liability for the salary owed at the end of 19B for balance sheet purposes. The second entry (in 19C) recorded the payment of that liability.

Property tax expense and liability

On December 28, 19B, a tax bill amounting to $5,700 was received from the city for 19B property taxes. The taxes are due on February 15, 19C; therefore, they were unpaid and unrecorded at the end of 19B. The sequence of entries for High-Rise would be:

g. December 31, 19B (end of the accounting period)—**adjusting entry:**[4]

Property tax expense	5,700	
Property tax payable		5,700
To record 19B property taxes incurred and the related liability.		

---

[4]This is an example of a situation where there may or may not be an adjusting entry. For example, assume the tax bill was received on December 5, 19B. At that date, a **current entry** probably would have been made identical to the adjusting entry given above. Under these circumstances, an adjusting entry at December 31, 19B, would not be needed.

This adjusting entry records the incurred, but unpaid, tax expense for 19B, in accordance with the matching principle, and also the tax liability that must be reported on the 19B balance sheet.

February 15, 19C—payment of the 19B liability for property tax:

Property tax payable	5,700	
Cash..		5,700
To record payment of property tax liability.		

Interest expense   On November 1, 19B, High-Rise borrowed $30,000 cash from a local bank on a 90-day note with an annual interest rate of 12 percent. The principal plus interest is due in three months. The sequence of entries by High-Rise is:

November 1, 19B—date of transaction:

Cash..	30,000	
Note payable, short term		30,000
To record a three-month, 12 percent loan from a bank.		

Analysis: At December 31, 19B, the end of the accounting period, two months have passed since the note was signed; therefore, interest expense for two months has **accrued** on the note because interest legally accrues with the passage of time, notwithstanding the fact that the interest is payable in cash at the maturity date. At year-end, there is a **liability** for interest for the two months at the end of 19B. This expense and the related liability have not yet been recorded; therefore, an **adjusting entry** is necessary to (a) debit interest expense for $600 (i.e., $30,000 \times 12\% \times {}^2\!/_{12} = \$600$) and (b) credit interest payable for the same amount. The adjusting and payment entries would be:

h.   December 31, 19B (end of the accounting period)—**adjusting entry:**

Interest expense	600	
Interest payable (or accrued interest payable).......................		600
To record accrued interest expense for two months on note payable		
($30,000 \times 12\% \times {}^2\!/_{12} = \$600$).		

January 31, 19C—maturity date; payment of the principal of the note and interest:

Note payable, short term	30,000	
Interest payable (per adjusting entry)	600	
Interest expense (19C—$30,000 \times 12\% \times \frac{1}{12}$)....................	300	
Cash...		30,900
To record payment of principal plus interest on note payable at maturity date.		

RECORDING ADJUSTING ENTRIES

The preceding examples demonstrated the application of the revenue and matching principles at the **end** of the accounting period by using adjusting entries. In situations when certain economic effects have not been recorded, appropriate adjusting entries are necessary to ensure that both the income statement and balance sheet will be correct. Adjusting entries are made to **allocate** revenue and expense among the current and one or more future periods so that expenses are matched properly with revenues each accounting period.

Basically, adjusting entries relate to transactions that start in one period and, in effect, continue into one or more subsequent periods. Therefore, an analysis to determine whether an adjusting entry is needed, and if so, how it should be made, must be based on the **sequence** of related events covering the periods affected. The demonstration cases at the end of this chapter illustrate how adjusting entries are influenced by particular situations.

Adjusting entries are entered first in the journal (dated the last day of the accounting period) immediately after all of the regular transactions are recorded. The adjusting entries then are **posted** from the journal to the ledger accounts in the usual way. Recording in the journal and posting to the ledger are necessary because adjusting entries reflect economic events, and their effects must be processed through the accounting information system and into the financial statements in the same manner as the regular transactions. These procedures are illustrated in the next chapter within the context of a complete information processing cycle.

In some instances, it is difficult to draw a distinct line between regular and adjusting entries, and there are no real reasons to make the distinction, other than the fact that adjusting entries (a) usually must be made at the **end** of the accounting period and (b) **update** certain income statement and balance sheet accounts. The important point is that adjusting entries (as well as many other entries) are necessary to appropriately measure periodic revenues and to match expenses with those revenues that were earned during the period.

DEMONSTRATION CASE A

(Try to resolve the requirements before proceeding to the suggested solution that follows.)

New Service Corporation is owned by three shareholders and has been in operation for one year, 19A. Cash flow and expenses are critical control problems. Minimal record keeping has been performed to save money. One secretary performs both the secretarial and recordkeeping functions. Because of a loan application made by the corporation, the bank has requested an income statement and balance sheet. Accordingly, the secretary prepared the following (summarized for case purposes):

Profit Statement
Annual—December 31, 19A

Revenues:	
Service	$ 78,500
Expenses:	
Salaries and wages..............	(43,200)
Utilities.......................	(1,800)
Miscellaneous	(4,000)
Net profit......................	$ 29,500

Balance Sheet
December 31, 19A

Assets

Cash	$ 4,000
Accounts receivable..............	35,500
Supplies inventory...............	8,000
Equipment......................	40,000
Other assets....................	16,000
Total assets	$103,500

Liabilities

Accounts payable.................	$ 9,000
Income taxes payable	
Note payable, one year, 12%	10,000

Net Worth

Capital stock, par $10	50,000
Premium........................	5,000
Retained profits	29,500
Total liabilities and net worth......	$103,500

After reading the two statements, the bank requested that an independent PA examine them. The PA found that the secretary used some obsolete captions and terminology and did not include the effects of the following data (i.e., the adjusting entries):

   a. Supplies inventory on hand at December 31 amounted to $3,000.

   b. Depreciation for 19A. The equipment was acquired during January 19A; estimated useful life, 10 years, and no residual value.

    c. The note payable was dated August 1, 19A, and the principal plus interest are payable at the end of one year.

    d. Rent expense of $3,600 was included in miscellaneous expense.

    e. Income taxes; assume an average tax rate of 17 percent.

Required:

1. Recast the above statements to incorporate the additional data, appropriate captions, preferred terminology, and improved format. Show computations.
2. Prepare the adjusting entries (in journal form) for the additional data at December 31, 19A.
3. Comment on any aspects of this situation that the bank loan officer should note in particular if they appear to be unusual.

Suggested solution

Requirement 1:

NEW SERVICE CORPORATION
Income Statement
For the Year Ended December 31, 19A

	Amounts reported	Effects of adjusting entries*	Corrected amounts
Revenue:			
Service revenue	$ 78,500		$ 78,500
Expenses:			
Salaries and wages	43,200		43,200
Utilities.................................	1,800		1,800
Supplies expense.........................		(a) + 5,000	5,000
Depreciation expense		(b) + 4,000	4,000
Interest expense..........................		(c) + 500	500
Rent expense		(d) + 3,600	3,600
Miscellaneous expense....................	4,000	(d) − 3,600	400
Total expenses	49,000		58,500
Pretax income............................	$ 29,500		20,000
Income tax expense ($20,000 × 17%).......		(e) + 3,400	3,400
Net income			$16,600
ESP ($16,600 ÷ 5,000 shares)...............			$3.32

NEW SERVICE CORPORATION
Balance Sheet
At December 31, 19A

Assets

Cash	$ 4,000		$ 4,000
Accounts receivable	35,500		35,500
Supplies inventory	8,000	(a) − 5,000	3,000
Equipment.................................	40,000		40,000
Accumulated depreciation..................		(b) − 4,000	(4,000)
Other assets	16,000		16,000
Total assets	$103,500		$94,500

Liabilities

Accounts payable	$ 9,000		$ 9,000
Income taxes payable		(e) + 3,400	3,400
Interest payable		(c) + 500	500
Note payable, one year, 12%	10,000		10,000
Total liabilities	19,000		22,900

Shareholders' Equity

Capital stock, par $10 (5,000 shares)..........	50,000		50,000
Contributed surplus	5,000		5,000
Retained earnings	29,500	− 29,500 + 16,600	16,600
Total liabilities and shareholders' equity	$103,500		$94,500

Note: Observe changes in captions, terminology, and format.
*The letters identify the adjustments shown under Requirement 2.

Requirement 2:

Adjusting entries at December 31, 19A;

a.	Supplies expense...	5,000	
	Supplies inventory		5,000
	To reduce supplies inventory to the amount on hand December 31, 19A, $3,000, and to record supplies expense, $8,000 − $3,000 = $5,000.		
b.	Depreciation expense	4,000	
	Accumulated depreciation.....................................		4,000
	Depreciation for one year, $40,000 ÷ 10 years = $4,000.		
c.	Interest expense...	500	
	Interest payable		500
	To record interest expense and the interest accrued (a liability) from August 1 to December 31, 19A ($10,000 × 12% × 5/12 = $500).		
d.	Rent expense	3,600	
	Miscellaneous expense..		3,600
	To record rent expense in the proper account.		
e.	Income tax expense..	3,400	
	Income tax payable		3,400
	To record income tax expense and the liability for unpaid tax as computed on the income statement.		

Requirement 3:

The loan officer should note particularly the following:

a. The overstatement of net income (by 78 percent; i.e., $29,500 ÷ $16,600) and total assets (by 10 percent; i.e., $103,500 ÷ $94,500), which suggests either (1) an attempt to mislead or (2) the need for better accounting.

b. The very high amount in accounts receivable compared to cash and total assets. This fact suggests inadequate evaluation of credit and/or inefficiency in collections.

c. The small amount of cash compared with accounts payable (a current liability).

d. Inclusion of rent expense in miscellaneous expense.

e. Inappropriate captions, terminology, and format.

DEMONSTRATION CASE B

(Try to resolve the requirements before proceeding to the suggested solution that follows.)

This case is presented to illustrate **why** and **how** adjusting entries are influenced directly by the manner in which an **initial entry** is made. Determination of whether an **adjusting entry** is needed, and if so, how it should be made, requires a careful **analysis of this situation.**

Situation: On July 1, 19A, Company K paid a two-year insurance premium of $1,200. The annual accounting period ends on December 31.

Required:

1. How much of the premium should be reported as expense in the 19A, 19B, and 19C income statements?

2. What is the amount of prepaid insurance on December 31, 19A? How should this amount be reported on the 19A financial statements?

3. Company K could have recorded the $1,200 payment on July 1, 19A, in one of three ways as follows:

Case A:

Prepaid insurance	1,200	
Cash		1,200

Case B:

```
Insurance expense ..............................................    1,200
     Cash.......................................................              1,200
```

Case C:

```
Prepaid insurance................................................      900
Insurance expense ..............................................      300
     Cash.......................................................              1,200
```

For each case, give the appropriate adjusting entry (at December 31, 19A) in journal form and then post to ledger T-accounts. If no adjusting entry is required, explain why.

Suggested solution

Requirement 1:

Insurance expense: 19A—$1,200 \times$ 6/24 = \$300 (½ year)
                    19B—$1,200 \times$ 12/24 = 600 (1 year)
                    19C—$1,200 \times$ 6/24 = 300 (½ year)

Requirement 2:

Prepaid insurance on December 31, 19A—$1,200 \times 18/24 = \$900$. This account should be reported on the balance sheet at December 31, 19A, as a current asset. Theoretical strictness suggests that $300 of the $900 should be reported as a deferred charge (a noncurrent asset) because this asset will not be liquidated within the next year; however, this distinction usually is not made in practice when the effect is not material as in this case.

Requirement 3:

Adjusting entry at December 31, 19A:

JOURNAL				**LEDGER**

CASE A

JOURNAL		LEDGER
Adjusting entry:		**Prepaid Insurance**
Insurance expense 300		Initial entry 1,200 | Adj. entry 300
Prepaid insurance.......... 300		
To reduce prepaid insurance to $900, and to record insurance expense for 19A, $300.		**Insurance Expense**
		Adj. entry 300 |

CASE B

Adjusting entry:		Insurance Expense			
Prepaid insurance.............. 900		Initial entry	1,200	Adj. entry	900
Insurance expense	900				
To record prepaid insurance at the end of 19A, $900, and to reduce insurance expense to $300 for 19A.		Prepaid Insurance			
		Adj. entry	900		

CASE C

Adjusting entry:	Prepaid Insurance			
No adjusting entry is needed at December 31, 19A, because the correct amounts for both prepaid insurance at December 31, 19A, $900, and insurance expense for 19A, $300 were recorded on the transaction date, July 1, 19A. An adjusting entry would be needed at the end of 19B and also at the end of 19C.	Initial entry	900		
	Insurance Expense			
	Initial entry	300		

SUMMARY OF CHAPTER

This chapter focused on the **revenue** and **matching** principles, and the adjusting entries that are necessary to apply those principles. Matching expenses with revenue for the period is critical because the lifespan of an enterprise, although indefinite in length, must be divided into a series of short time periods (usually one year) for periodic performance measurements. Primary among those performance measurements are the economic effects reported in the periodic financial statements.

In the measurement of net income, the **revenue principle** holds that revenues earned in the period through sale of goods or performance of services must be identified, measured, and reported for that period. The **matching principle** holds that the expenses incurred in earning those revenues must be identified, measured, and matched with revenues earned in the period in order to determine periodic net income. To implement the matching principle, certain transactions and events whose economic effects extend from the current period to one or more future accounting periods must be analyzed at the end of the accounting period. This analysis is the basis for allocating their expense effects to the future periods during which they will aid in the generation of revenues. The allocation of some revenues and expenses to two or more accounting periods requires the use of **adjusting entries.** Adjusting entries follow the same concepts and procedures as entries for the usual transactions except that they are made at the end of the accounting period. At the end of the accounting period they are entered first in the journal and then are posted to the ledger in the same manner as are other entries.

IMPORTANT TERMS DEFINED IN THIS CHAPTER

Terms (alphabetically)	Key words in definitions of terms used in chapter	Page reference
Accrue (accrued)	An expense incurred but not yet paid; a revenue earned but not yet collected.	168
Adjusting entries	End-of-period entries required by the revenue and matching principles to attain a cutoff between periods.	165
Contra account	An account, related to a primary account, that is an offset (or reduction) to the primary account.	175
Defer (deferred)	An expense paid in advance of use; a revenue collected in advance of earning.	168
Depreciation	Expense of using (wearing out) a building, machinery, fixtures, etc., each period of useful life.	174
Expenses incurred but not recorded	Expenses actually incurred but not yet paid or recorded.	167
Expenses paid in advance	Cash paid for goods, or services, before those goods or services are used; prepaid expenses.	167
Fiscal year	An accounting period of 12 months that does not necessarily end on December 31.	161
Interest expense	Time value of money; the cost of borrowing money (or other assets acquired).	178
Matching principle	All costs incurred to earn the revenues of the period must be identified then matched with revenue by recording as expense.	165
Reliability principle	Financial statements must be unbiased, accurate, and verifiable.	164
Residual value	Value (estimated) of an operational asset at the end of its useful life to the business (scrap or salvage value).	174
Revenue collected in advance	Revenue collected in cash before that revenue is earned. Precollected revenue.	166
Revenue earned but not yet collected or recorded	Revenue not yet collected, or recorded, but already earned. Accrued revenue.	166
Revenue principle	Recognize revenue in the period **earned** rather when the cash is received; earning process completed.	162
Supplies inventory	Supplies purchased and still on hand; unused supplies at the end of period.	175
Time-period assumption	Division of the operating activities of a business into a series of equal time periods (usually one year) for accounting purposes.	161

QUESTIONS FOR DISCUSSION

Part A

1. Identify the two **change** statements and briefly explain why they are referred to as change statements.

2. Explain the time-period assumption.

3. What is an interim report?

4. Briefly define natural business year, calendar year, and fiscal year as used in accounting.

5. Identify the *(a)* revenue and *(b)* expense recognition problem related to the time-period assumption.

6. Explain the revenue principle and the matching principle.

7. Contrast the completed contract method with the percentage-of-completion method of recognizing revenues for long-term construction contracts.

8. What is an adjusting entry? Explain why such entries are necessary.

9. What are the three fundamental characteristics of adjusting entries?

10. Briefly define each of the following: accrued expense, accrued revenue, deferred expense, and deferred revenue.

Part B

11. AB Company collected $600 rent for the period December 15, 19A, to January 15, 19B. The $600 was credited to Rent Revenue Collected in Advance on December 15, 19A. Give the adjusting entry required on December 31, 19A (end of the accounting period).

12. On December 31, 19B, Company T recorded the following adjusting entry:

    Rent revenue receivable   500
        Rent revenue   500

    Explain the situation that caused this entry and given the subsequent related entry.

13. On July 1, 19A, M Company paid a two-year insurance premium of $400 and debited prepaid insurance for that amount. Assuming the accounting period ends in December, give the adjusting entries that should be made at the end of 19A, 19B, and 19C.

14. Explain "estimated residual value." Why is it important in measuring depreciation expense?

15. Explain why adjusting entries are entered in the journal on the last day of the accounting period and then are posted to the ledger.

16. The revenue principle takes precedence over the matching principle in determining when recognition is to occur on the income statement. Yet the inability to reliably estimate bad debt losses may be a reason for deferring the recognition of revenue to later periods. Why? (Hint: Consider the specifics of the revenue principle and also the definition of the value for revenue in Exhibit 2–6.)

17. Two guidelines are provided to help determine when revenue can be recognized. First, recognize revenue in the period in which the earnings process is substantially completed. Second, recognize revenue when reliable estimates are available. Relate these two guidelines to each other and state which is more general in its application. (Hint: Consider the revenue recognition examples in this chapter.)

18. The section of this chapter entitled "A Case Study" quotes an article in Forbes about ABC and how expenses were assigned. It states, "of course, from the auditors' point of view, there is nothing wrong with doing a little shifting like this—as long as it's within reason." What would the auditors consider to be wrong if it is not "within reason"?

19. Financial statements communicate information to users. Why do accountants present accumulated depreciation on the balance sheet when they could disclose simply the book value, that is, the net of the cost less accumulated depreciation?

20. Prepaid insurance is charged to expense in the period corresponding to the expiry of the policy. One reason for making such a charge is to match insurance expense with the revenue for the period. How can matching be used for such a justification when it would seem to be difficult to know what revenue is earned by the insurance policy? Would inventory be easier to match?

EXERCISES

Part A

E4–1. Match the following (each letter may be used more than once and each reporting item may be associated with several letters):

Reporting Item		*Description*
_____ Income statement	A.	Reports sources of funds.
_____ Balance sheet	B.	Reports EPS.
_____ Statement of	C.	Reports retained earnings.
changes in financial	D.	Reports on operations.
position	E.	Reports financial position.
_____ Notes to the	F.	Reports uses of funds.
financial statement	G.	Reports extraordinary items.
	H.	Reports inflows and outflows of cash or working capital.
	I.	Provides qualitative explanations.
	J.	Dated: At December 31, 19X.
	K.	Dated: For the year ended December 31, 19X.

E4–2. Match the following:

Term		*Analysis of the records revealed that—*
__D__ Deferred revenue	A.	At the end of the year wages payable of $2,500 had not been recorded or paid.
_____ Accrued revenue	B.	Supplies for office use were purchased during the year at a cost of $600 and $100 of the office supplies remained on hand (unused) at year-end.
_____ Deferred expense		
_____ Accrued expense	C.	Interest of $300 on a note receivable was earned at year-end, although collection of the interest is not due until the following year.
	D.	At the end of the year service revenue of $1,000 was collected in cash but was not yet earned.

E4–3. Tiger Construction Company, Incorporated, specializes in major commercial construction. In 19A, the company signed a contract to build a large warehouse. The contract price was $2,000,000, and the estimated construction cost was $1,400,000. Construction was started on June 1, 19A, and completed March 31, 19B. Actual construction costs were higher than originally estimated; the actual 19A costs were $420,000; and 19B, $1,080,000.

Required:

a. Complete the following tabulation for each separate case. Assume income recognition under percentage of completion is allocated on the basis of actual costs incurred to total estimated costs.

		Pretax income to be recognized	
Case	Method	19A	19B
A.....	Completed contract	$ _____	$ _____
B.....	Percentage of completion	_____	_____

b. Which method would you recommend for Tiger? Explain the basis for your choice.

E4–4. It is December 31, 19B, end of the annual accounting period for TT Service Company. Below are listed six independent transactions (summarized) that affected the company during 19B. The transactions are to be analyzed in terms of their effects on the balance sheet and income statement for 19B.

   a. On January 1, 19A, the company purchased a machine that cost $10,000 cash (estimated useful life five years and no residual value).
      (1) Show how the machine should be reported on the 19B balance sheet.
      (2) Show how the 19B income statement should report the effects of the machine usage.
   b. On September 1, 19B, the company signed a $10,000, 12 percent, one-year note payable. The principal plus interest is payable on the maturity date.
      (1) Show how the liability should be reported on the 19B balance sheet.
      (2) Show how the effects of the note should be reported on the 19B income statement.
   c. During 19B, service revenues of $90,000 were collected of which $10,000 was collected in advance.
      (1) Show how the $10,000 should be reported on the 19B balance sheet.
      (2) Show how the 19B income statement should report the effects of the transaction.
   d. In 19B, expenses paid in cash amounted to $60,000 of which $5,000 was paid for expenses yet to be incurred (prepaid).
      (1) Show how the 19B balance sheet should report the $5,000.
      (2) Show how the income statement should report this situation.
   e. In 19B, $85,000 cash revenues were collected and in addition revenues of $5,000 were on credit.
      (1) Show how the $5,000 should be reported on the 19B balance sheet.
      (2) Show how the 19B income statement should report the revenues.
   f. In 19B, expenses amounting to $56,000 were paid in cash and in addition expenses of $3,000 were on credit.
      (1) Show how the $3,000 should be reported on the 19B balance sheet.
      (2) Show how the expenses should be reported on the 19B income statement.

E4–5. XT Company started operations on January 1, 19A. It is now December 31, 19A (end of the annual accounting period) and the part-time bookkeeper needs your assistance in analyzing the following three transactions:

   a. On January 1, 19A, the company purchased a special machine for a cash cost of $15,000. The machine has an estimated useful life of five years and no residual value.

b. During 19A, the company purchased office supplies that cost $400. At the end of 19A, office supplies of $100 remained on hand.

c. On July 1, 19A, the company paid cash of $300 for a two-year insurance policy on the machine.

Required:

Complete the following schedule as of the end of 19A:

Selected Balance Sheet Amounts

	Amount to be reported
Assets:	
Machine..	$ _____
Accumulated depreciation	_____
Carrying value...	_____
Office supplies inventory	_____
Prepaid insurance..	_____

Selected Income Statement Amounts

Depreciation expense......................................	$ _____
Office supplies expense....................................	_____
Insurance expense	_____

Part B

E4–6. Rich Department Store is completing the accounting process for the year just ended, December 31, 19B. The transactions during 19B have been journalized and posted. The following data in respect to adjusting entries are available:

a. Office supplies inventory at January 1, 19B, was $120. Office supplies purchased and debited to Office Supplies Inventory during the year amounted to $360. The year-end inventory showed $80 of supplies on hand.

b. Wages earned during December 19B but unpaid and unrecorded at December 31, 19B, amounted to $1,400. The last payroll was December 28, and the next payroll will be January 6, 19C.

c. Three fourths of the basement of the store is rented for $800 per month to another merchant, J. B. Smith, who sells compatible, but not competitive, merchandise. On November 1, 19B, the store collected six months' rent in advance from Smith amounting to $4,800, which was credited in full to Rent Revenue when collected.

d. The rest of the basement is rented to Spears Specialty; at $360 per month, payable monthly. On December 31, 19B, the rent for November and December 19B was neither collected nor recorded. Collection is expected January 10, 19C.

e. Delivery equipment that cost $21,000 was being used by the store. Estimates in respect to equipment were (1) useful life five years and (2) residual value at the end of five years, $1,000. Assume depreciation for a full year for 19B and that the asset will be depreciated evenly over its useful life.

f. On July 1, 19B, a two-year insurance premium amounting to $1,000 was paid in cash and debited in full to Prepaid Insurance.

g. Rich operates an alteration shop to meet its own needs. In addition, the shop does alterations for J. B. Smith. At the end of December 31, 19B, J. B. Smith had not paid for alterations completed amounting to $450, and this amount has not been recorded as Alteration Shop Revenue.

Required:

Give the adjusting entry for each situation that should be entered in the records of Rich Department Store at December 31, 19B.

E4–7. On April 1, 19B, Davis Corporation received a $4,000, 15 percent note from a customer in settlement of a $4,000 open account receivable. According to the terms, the principal of the note, plus the interest, are payable at the end of 12 months. The annual accounting period for Davis ends on December 31, 19B.

Required:

a. Give the journal entry for Davis for receipt of the note on April 1, 19B.
b. Give the adjusting entry required on December 31, 19B.
c. Give the journal entry on date of collection, March 31, 19C.

On August 1, 19B, to meet a cash shortage, Davis Corporation obtained a $20,000, 12 percent loan from a local bank. The principal of the note, plus interest expense, are payable at the end of 12 months.

Required:

d. Give the journal entry for Davis on the date of the loan, August 1, 19B.
e. Give the adjusting entry required on December 31, 19B.
f. Give the journal entry on date of payment, July 31, 19C.

E4–8. Kay Company is in the process of making adjusting entries for the year ended December 31, 19B. In developing information for the adjusting entries for the year ended December 31, 19B, the accountant learned that on September 1, 19B, a two-year insurance premium of $2,400 was paid.

Required:

a. What amount should be reported on the 19B income statement for insurance expense?
b. What amount should be reported on the December 31, 19B, balance sheet for prepaid insurance?
c. Give the adjusting entry at December 31, 19B, under each of two cases:

Case 1—Assume that when the premium was paid on September 1, 19B, the bookkeeper debited the full amount to Prepaid Insurance.

Case 2—Assume that when the premium was paid September 1, 19B, the bookkeeper debited Insurance Expense for the full amount.

(Hint: In Case 2 be sure that after the adjusting entry, you end with the same amount in the Prepaid Insurance account as in Case 1.)

E4–9. Wise Manufacturing Company uses a large amount of shipping supplies that are purchased in large volume, stored, and used as needed. At December 31, 19B, the following data relating to shipping supplies were obtained from the records and supporting documents:

Shipping supplies on hand, January 1, 19B	$ 2,000
Purchases of shipping supplies during 19B	13,000
Shipping supplies on hand, per inventory December 31, 19B	4,000

Required:

a. What amount should be reported on the 19B income statement for shipping supplies expense?

b. What amount should be reported on the December 31, 19B, balance sheet for shipping supplies inventory?

c. Give the adjusting entry at December 31, 19B, assuming the purchases of shipping supplies were debited in full to Shipping Supplies Inventory ($13,000).

d. What adjusting entry would you make assuming the bookkeeper debited Shipping Supplies Expense for the $13,000 supplies? (Hint: In solving (c) and (d), be sure that each solution ends up with the same amount remaining in the Shipping Supplies Inventory account.)

E4–10. On December 31, 19B, Moncton Company prepared an income statement and balance sheet and failed to take into account three adjusting entries. The income statement, prepared on this incorrect basis, reflected a pretax income of $20,000. The balance sheet reflected total assets, $90,000; total liabilities, $30,000; and owners' equity, $60,000. The data for the three adjusting entries were:

1. Depreciation was not recorded for the year on equipment that cost $55,000; estimated useful life, 10 years, and residual value, $5,000.

2. Wages amounting to $8,000 for the last three days of December 19B were not paid and not recorded (the next payroll will be on January 10, 19C).

3. Rent revenue of $3,000 was collected on December 1, 19B, for office space for the period December 1, 19B, to February 28, 19C. The $3,000 was credited in full to Rent Revenue when collected.

Required:

Complete the following tabulation (indicate deductions with parentheses):

Item	Pretax income	Total assets	Total liabilities	Owners' equity
Balances reported	$20,000	$90,000	$30,000	$60,000
1. Effects of depreciation	_____	_____	_____	_____
2. Effects of wages............	_____	_____	_____	_____
3. Effects of rent revenue......	_____	_____	_____	_____
Correct balances	======	======	======	======

E4–11. Supreme Auto Rentals, Inc. completed its first year of operations on December 31, 19A. Because this is the end of the annual accounting period, the company bookkeeper prepared the following tentative income statement:

Income Statement, 19A

Rental revenue	$102,000
Expenses:	
Salaries and wages.....................................	$26,400
Maintenance expense	10,000
Rent expense (on location).............................	8,000
Utilities expense.......................................	3,000
Gas and oil expense	2,000
Miscellaneous expense (items not listed above)...........	400
Total expenses	49,800
Income	$52,200

An independent PA reviewed the income statement and developed additional data as follows:

accrued expense

1. Wages for the last three days of December amounting to $600 were not recorded or paid (disregard payroll taxes).
2. The telephone bill for December 19A amounting to $200 has not been recorded or paid.
3. Depreciation on rental autos, amounting to $20,000 for 19A, was not recorded.
4. Interest on a $20,000, one-year, 12 percent note payable dated November 1, 19A, was not recorded. The 12 percent interest is payable on maturity date of the note.
5. Rental revenue includes $2,000 rental revenue for the month of January 19B.

defer til next period

6. Maintenance expense includes $1,000, which is the cost of maintenance supplies still on hand (per inventory) at December 31, 19A.
7. Assume the income tax is 20 percent. Assume payment of income tax will be made in 19B.

Required:

a. Prepare a correct income statement for 19A assuming 10,000 shares are outstanding. Show computations.
b. Give the adjusting entry at December 31, 19A, for each of the additional data items. If none is required explain why.

E4–12. On December 15, 19C, the bookkeeper for Kingston Company prepared the income statement and balance sheet given below (summarized) but neglected to consider three of the adjusting entries.

	As prepared	Effects of adjusting entries	Corrected amounts
Income statement:			
Revenues	$95,000	———	———
Expenses	(83,000)	———	———
Income tax expense............		———	———
Income	$12,000	———	———
Balance sheet:			
Assets			
Cash	$18,000	———	———
Accounts receivable...........	26,000	———	———
Rent receivable		———	———
Equipment*	40,000	———	———
Accumulated depreciation	(8,000)	———	———
	$76,000		
Liabilities			
Accounts payable..............	$10,000	———	———
Income taxes payable		———	———
Owners' Equity			
Capital stock	50,000	———	———
Retained earnings	16,000	———	———
	$76,000		

*Acquired January 1, 10-year life, no residual value; straight-line depreciation.

Data on the three adjusting entries:

1. Depreciation on the equipment was not recorded for 19C.
2. Rent revenue earned of $1,000 for December 19C was neither collected or recorded.
3. Income taxes for 19C were not paid or recorded; assume an average rate of 20 percent.

Required:

a. Prepare the three adjusting entries (in journal form) that were omitted.
b. Complete the two columns to the right in the above tabulation to reflect the correct amounts on the income statement and balance sheet.

E4–13. (Analytical) TK Company's comparative balance sheets for 19A and 19B reported the following selected amounts:

	19A	19B
Assets:		
Prepaid insurance premium............	$500	$700
Liabilities:		
Rent revenue collected in advance......	900	500

The 19B income statement reported the following amounts:

	19B
Expenses:	
Insurance expense......	$ 750
Revenues:	
Rent revenue...........	7,200

Required:

a. Compute the total amount of insurance premium that was paid in cash during 19B. Show computations.
b. Compute the total amount of rent revenue that was collected in cash during 19B. Show computations.

PROBLEMS/CASES

Part A

PC4–1. Rust Company, a locally owned corporation, invests in commercial rental properties. Rust's annual accounting period ends on December 31. At the end of each year, numerous adjusting entries must be made because many transactions completed during current and prior years have economic effects on the financial statements of the current and future years. This case is concerned with several such transactions that have been selected for your analysis. Assume the current year is 19D.

Transaction A:

On July 1, 19A, the company purchased office equipment for use in the business at a cash cost of $9,000. The company estimates that the equipment will have a useful life of 10 years and no residual value.

a. Over how many accounting periods will this transaction affect the financial statements of Rust? Explain.

b. Assuming straight-line depreciation, how much depreciation expense should be reported in year 19A and in 19D?

c. What would be the amount of accumulated depreciation immediately after the adjusting entries are made on December 31, 19D?

d. Would an adjusting entry be made at the end of each year during the life of the equipment? Explain why or why not.

Transaction B:

On October 1, 19D, the company collected $12,000 rent on some office space. This amount represented the monthly rent in advance for the six-month period, October 1, 19D, through March 31, 19E. Rent revenue was increased (credited) by $12,000.

a. Over how many accounting periods will this transaction affect the financial statements of Rust? Explain.

b. How much rent revenue on this office space should Rust report in 19D? Explain.

c. Did this transaction create a **liability** as of the end of 19D? Explain.

d. Should an adjusting entry be made on December 31, 19D? Explain why. If your answer is yes, give the adjusting entry.

Transaction C:

On December 31, 19D, the company owed employees unpaid and unrecorded wages of $5,000 because the payroll was paid on December 27 and between this day and year-end employees worked three more days in December 19D.

a. Over how may accounting periods would this transaction affect the financial statements of Rust? Explain.

b. How would this $5,000 affect the 19D income statement and balance sheet of Rust?

c. Should an adjusting entry be made on December 31, 19D? Explain why. If your answer is yes, give the adjusting entry.

Transaction D:

On January 1, 19D, Rust agreed to supervise the planning and subdivision of a large tract of land for a customer—J. Dolan. This service job, to be performed by Rust, involved four separate phases. By December 31, 19D, three phases had been fully completed to the satisfaction of Dolan. The remaining phase will be done during 19E. The total price for the four phases (agreed upon in advance by both parties) was $40,000. Each phase involves approximately the same amount of services. On December 31, 19D, no cash had been collected by Rust for the services already performed.

a. Should Rust record any service revenue on this job for 19D? Explain why. If yes, how much?

b. If your answer to (a) is yes, should Rust make an adjusting entry on December 31, 19D; if yes, give the entry. Explain.

PC4–2. The following information was provided by the records and related documents of Mic Mac Garden Apartments (a corporation) at the end of the annual fiscal period, December 31, 19B:

Revenue:

1. Rental revenue collected in cash during 19B for occupancy in 19B (credited
   to Rent Revenue) $497,000
2. Rental revenue earned for occupancy in December 19B but not collected
   until 19C. 8,000
3. In December 19B, collected rent revenue in advance for January 19C. 6,000

Salary expense:

4. Cash payment made in January 19B for salaries incurred (earned) in
   December 19A. 3,000
5. Salaries incurred and paid during 19B (debited to Salary Expense) 58,000
6. Salaries earned by employees during December 19B but not to be paid until
   January 19C. 2,000
7. Cash advance to employees in December 19B for salaries to be earned in
   January 19C. 4,000

Supplies used:

8. Maintenance supplies on hand (Inventory) on January 1, 19B 2,000
9. Maintenance supplies purchased for cash during 19B (debited to
   Maintenance Supplies Inventory when purchased) 8,000
10. Maintenance supplies on hand (Inventory) on December 31, 19B 1,500

Required:

Under the revenue and matching principles, what amounts should be shown on the 19B, income statement for *(a)* rent revenue, *(b)* salary expense, and *(c)* maintenance supplies expense? Show computations with explanations for each numbered item.

PC4–3.   On January 1, 19A, four individuals organized WAS Company. The company has been operating for two years, 19A and 19B. Given below are data relating to six selected transactions that affect both years. The annual accounting period ends December 31.

a.   On January 1, 19A, the company purchased a computer for use in the business at a cash cost of $14,000. The computer has an estimated useful life of seven years and no residual value. It will be depreciated on a straight-line basis.

b.   On September 1, 19A, the company borrowed $10,000 cash from Montreal Bank and signed a one-year, 12 percent, interest-bearing note. The interest and principal are payable on August 31, 19B.

c.   The company owns its office building. On October 1, 19A, the company leased some of its office space to A. B. Smith for $6,000 per year. Smith paid this amount in full on October 1, 19A, and expects to use the space for one year only. The company increased (debited) Cash for $6,000 and increased (credited) Rent Revenue for $6,000 on October 1, 19A.

d.   Office supplies were purchased for use in the business. Cash was decreased (credited) and Office Supplies Inventory was increased (debited). The unused supplies at each year-end are determined by inventory count. The amounts were:

Year	Purchased	Inventory
19A	$700	$200
19B	500	300

e.   Wages are paid by the company at the end of each two weeks. The last payroll date in December usually is four days before December 31. Consequently, at each year-end, unpaid wages exist that are paid in cash on the first payroll date in the next year. The wages paid in cash and the wages incurred but not yet paid or recorded at each year-end were:

Year	Wages paid in cash during the year	Wages unpaid and unrecorded Dec. 31
19A......	$30,000	$2,000
19B	36,000	3,000

f.   On July 1, 19A, the company paid a two-year insurance premium (on the computer) of $240. At that date, the company increased (debited) an asset account—Prepaid Insurance—and decreased (credited) Cash, $240.

Required:

Complete the following schedule for 19A and 19B by entering the amounts that should be reported on the financial statements of WAS Company. Show computations.

Balance sheet:

	19A	19B
Assets		
Computer...........................	$_____	$_____
Less: Accumulated depreciation	_____	_____
Carrying value......................	_____	_____
Office supplies inventory	_____	_____
Prepaid insurance...................	_____	_____
Liabilities		
Note payable, Montreal Bank	_____	_____
Interest payable....................	_____	_____
Rent revenue collected in advance....	_____	_____
Wages payable	_____	_____

Income statement:

	19A	19B
Rent revenue.......................	$_____	$_____
Depreciation expense................	_____	_____
Interest expense	_____	_____
Office supplies expense	_____	_____
Wage expense......................	_____	_____
Insurance expense	_____	_____

Part B

PC4–4.   Jackson Service Company is preparing the adjusting entries for the year ended December 31, 19B. On that date, the bookkeeper for the company assembled the following data:

1.   On December 31, 19B, salaries earned by employees but not yet paid or recorded amounted to $6,000.
2.   Depreciation must be recognized on a service truck that cost $9,000 on July 1, 19B (estimated useful life six years and no residual value).
3.   Cash of $1,000 was collected on December 28, 19B, for services to be rendered during 19C (Service Revenue was credited).
4.   On December 27, 19B, Jackson received a tax bill of $200 from the city for 19B property taxes (on service equipment) which is payable (and will be paid) during January 19C.
5.   On July 1, 19B, the company paid $840 cash for a two-year insurance policy on the service truck (2 above).

6. On October 1, 19B, the company borrowed $10,000 from a local bank and signed a 12 percent note for that amount. The principal and interest are payable on maturity date, September 30, 19C.

Required:

a. The bookkeeper has asked you to assist in preparing the appropriate adjusting entries at December 31, 19B. For each situation above, give the appropriate adjusting entry with a brief explanation. If none is required, explain why.

b. Based on your entries given in Requirement (a), complete the following schedule to reflect the amounts and balance sheet classifications:

			Balance sheet classification (one check on each line)		
Item No.	Accounts	19B Amount	Assets	Liabilities	Owners' Equity
1	Salaries payable	$_____	_____	_____	_____
2	Accumulated depreciation	_____	_____	_____	_____
3	Revenue collected in advance......	_____	_____	_____	_____
4	Property tax payable	_____	_____	_____	_____
5	Prepaid insurance	_____	_____	_____	_____
6	Interest payable	_____	_____	_____	_____

PC4–5. Slow Transportation Company is at the end of its accounting year December 31, 19B. The following data that must be considered to answer the requirements was developed from the company's records and related documents:

1. On July 1, 19B, a three-year insurance premium on equipment was paid. The amount of $900 was debited in full to Prepaid Insurance on that date.

2. During 19B, office supplies amounting to $1,000 were purchased for cash and debited in full to Supplies Inventory. At the end of 19A, the inventory count of supplies remaining on hand (unused) showed $200. The inventory of supplies on hand (unused) at December 31, 19B, showed $300.

3. On December 31, 19B, B&R Garage completed repairs on one of Slow's trucks at a cost of $650; the amount is not yet recorded and, by agreement, will be paid during January 19C.

4. In December 19B, a tax bill, on trucks owned during 19B, amounting to $1,400 was received from the city. The taxes, which have not been recorded, are due and will be paid on February 15, 19C.

5. On December 31, 19B, Slow completed a hauling contract for an out-of-province company. The bill was for $7,500 payable within 30 days. No cash has been collected, and no journal entry has been made for this transaction.

6. On July 1, 19B, Slow purchased a new hauling van at a cash cost of $21,600. The estimated useful life of the van was 10 years, with an estimated residual value of $1,600. No depreciation has been recorded for 19B (compute depreciation for six months in 19B).

7. On October 1, 19B, Slow borrowed $6,000 from the local bank on a one-year, 15 percent note payable. The principal plus interest is payable at the end of 12 months.

Required:

a. Give the adjusting entry required on December 31, 19B, related to each of the above transactions. Give a brief explanation with each entry.

b. Assume Slow Transportation Company had prepared a tentative income statement for 19B that did not include the effect of any of the above items and that the tentative pretax income computed was $30,000. Considering the above items, compute the corrected pretax income for 19B. Show computations.

PC4–6. This case, taken from the experiences of Frindly Department Store, has been selected to give you an opportunity to test your analytical ability in transaction analysis and in developing the adjusting entries where there are both notes receivable and notes payable. The annual fiscal period ends on December 31, 19B. Each of the two situations otherwise is independent.

Situation A—Frindly arranged a line of credit whereby a local bank will loan Frindly cash for short-term working capital needs. Repayment will vary from 60 to 90 days. Occasionally, the company also borrows a substantial amount on a long-term basis. On October 1, 19B, Frindly borrowed $40,000 on a one-year, 12 percent note. The principal plus interest is payable at the end of 12 months.

Situation B—Frindly sells approximately 40 percent of its goods on credit; accounts are due at the end of the month in which the sale is made. From time to time, special efforts must be made to collect an account. J. Doe was such a case. Doe owed $1,000 on an account and was unable to pay. After lengthy negotiations, on November 1, 19B, Doe gave Frindly a 15 percent note for the $1,000 coupled with a mortgage on two personal automobiles. The note matures at the end of two years. At the end of the first full year, Doe agreed to pay half of the principal ($500) plus interest on the amount of principal outstanding during the year. The remaining principal plus interest is payable at the end of the second year.

Required:

a. What amount should be shown on income statement for 19B for each situation?
b. What items and amount(s) should be shown on Frindly's balance sheet at December 31, 19B, for each situation?
c. Give the adjusting journal entry required for each situation at December 31, 19B. Show computations.
d. What would be the amount of error in 19B pretax income if the adjusting entries given in (c) were omitted? Explain.

PC4–7. Rapid Service Company has completed its annual financial statements for the year ended December 31, 19C. The income statement (summarized) reflected the following:

Revenues:	
Service	$95,600
Rental (office space)	2,400
Total revenues	98,000
Expenses:	
Salaries and wages	44,000
Service supplies used	2,600
Depreciation expense	2,000
Maintenance of equipment	2,000
Rent expense (service building)	8,400
Oil and gas for equipment	1,800
Insurance expense........................	200
Utilities expense.........................	800
Other expenses	6,200
Total expenses	68,000
Pretax income...........................	$30,000

An audit of the records and financial statements by a PA revealed that the following items were not considered:

1. Service revenue of $700 earned yet not collected on December 31, 19C, was not included in the $95,600 on the income statement.
2. The $2,600 of service supplies used included $600 of service supplies still on hand in the supplies storeroom on December 31, 19C.
3. Rent revenue of $100 that was collected in advance and not yet earned by December 31, 19C, was included in the $2,400 on the income statement.
4. Property tax for 19C of $400 was billed during December 19C, but will be due and paid during January 19D (not included in the above amounts on the income statement).
5. A two-year insurance premium of $400 was paid on July 1, 19B; no premiums were paid in 19C.

Required:

a. Recast the above income statement to include, exclude, or omit each of the items identified by the PA. Use a format similar to the following:

	Amounts		*Amounts that*
Items	*as reported*	*Corrections*	*should be reported*

b. The owner of the company asked you to explain the following:
(1) The insurance premium was paid in 19B; therefore, why was insurance expense reported in 19C?
(2) Although the company paid no cash for depreciation expense, $2,000 was included in 19C as expense. Why was this so?

PC4–8. (Analytical) Sims Service Company has completed its financial statements for the year ended December 31, 19A. The balance sheet correctly reported the following selected items and amounts:

Assets
1. Prepaid insurance (one-year policy was purchased and paid for on May 1, 19A; debited Prepaid Insurance) .... $ 480
2. Service truck (purchased on January 1, 19A) $7,700
   Accumulated depreciation (no residual value) 1,100   6,600

Liabilities:
3. Rent collected in advance (cash collected for annual rent on October 1, 19A; credited Rent Revenue) 600
4. Salaries payable (monthly salary for J. Doe was not yet paid) 1,500

Required:

a. What amount of insurance premium was paid on May 1, 19A? Assuming the premium paid originally was recorded as a debit to Prepaid Insurance and a credit to Cash, give the adjusting entry that was made on December 31, 19A.
b. What was used as the estimated useful life of the service truck? Give the adjusting entry that was made on December 31, 19A.
c. What was the amount of cash collected for rent on October 1, 19A? Give the adjusting entry that was made on December 31, 19A.

d. What was J. Doe's total annual salary? How much of it was paid in cash during 19A? Give the adjusting entry that was made on December 31, 19A.

PC4–9. Modern Service Company is completing the information processing cycle at the end of its fiscal year, December 31, 19B. Below is listed the correct balance for each account at December 31, 19B (a) before the adjusting entries for 19B and (b) after the adjusting entries for 19B.

		Account balance, December 31, 19B			
		Before adjusting entries		After adjusting entries	
		Debit	Credit	Debit	Credit
a.	Cash.....................................	$ 8,000		$ 8,000	
b.	Service revenue receivable			400	
c.	Prepaid insurance	300		200	
d.	Operational aasets.........................	120,200		120,200	
e.	Accumulated depreciation, equipment........		$ 21,500		$ 25,000
f.	Income taxes payable				5,500
g.	Capital stock..............................		70,000		70,000
h.	Retained earnings, January 1, 19B...........		14,000		14,000
i.	Service revenue		60,000		60,400
j.	Salary expense............................	37,000		37,000	
k.	Depreciation expense			3,500	
l.	Insurance expense.........................			100	
m.	Income tax expense........................			5,500	
		$165,500	$165,500	$174,900	$174,900

Required:

a. Compare the amounts in the columns before and after the adjusting entries in order to reconstruct the four adjusting entries that were made in 19B. Provide a brief explanation of each.

b. Compute the amount of income assuming (1) it is based on the amounts, "before adjusting entries" and (2) it is based on the amounts, "after adjusting entries." Which income amount is correct? Explain why.

PC4–10. This is a case to test your ability to analyze a specific situation and to determine whether an adjusting entry is required and, if so, what the entry should be.

General situation: On December 1, 19A, Voss collected cash, $4,000, which was for office space rented to an outsider. The rent collected was for the period December 1, 19A, through March 31, 19B. The annual accounting period ends on December 31.

Required:

a. How much of the $4,000 should Voss report as revenue on the 19A annual income statement? How much of it should be reported as revenue on the 19B income statement?

b. What is the amount of rent revenue collected in advance as of December 31, 19A? How should Voss report this amount on the 19A financial statements?

c. On December 1, 19A, Voss could have recorded the $4,000 collection in one of three different ways as follows:

Case A:

Cash..	4,000	
Rent revenue		4,000

Case B:

Cash..	4,000	
Rent revenue collected in advance		4,000

Case C:

Cash	4,000	
Rent revenue......................................		1,000
Rent revenue collected in advance.................................		3,000

For each case, give the appropriate adjusting entry (in journal form) at December 31, 19A. If no adjusting entry is required, explain why.

    d. Do you believe one of the approaches shown above is better than the other two? Which one? Explain.

PC4–11.   (Comprehensive)   Morris Transportation Corporation has been in operation since January 1, 19A. It is now December 31, 19A, the end of the annual accounting period. The company has not done well financially during the first year, although transportation revenue has been fairly good. The three shareholders manage the company but they have not given much attention to recordkeeping. In view of a serious cash shortage, they asked a local bank for a $10,000 loan. The bank requested a complete set of financial statements. The 19D annual financial statements given below were prepared by a clerk and then were given to the bank.

MORRIS TRANSPORTATION CORPORATION
December 31, 19A

Income Statement

Transportation revenue	$90,000
Expenses:	
Salaries.............................	20,000
Maintenance	15,000
Other expenses......................	25,000
Total expenses	60,000
Net income	$30,000

Balance Sheet

Assets

Cash	$ 1,000
Receivables	4,000
Inventory of maintenance supplies	5,000
Equipment...........................	30,000
Remaining assets	37,000
Total assets	$77,000

Liabilities

Accounts payable.....................	$ 7,000

Capital

Capital stock	40,000
Retained earnings	30,000
Total liabilities and capital	$77,000

After briefly reviewing the statements and "looking into the situation," the bank requested that the statements be redone (with some expert help) to "incorporate depreciation, accruals, inventory counts, income taxes, and so on." As a consequence of a review of the records and supporting document by CGA, the following additional information was developed:

1. The inventory of maintenance supplies of $5,000 shown on the balance sheet has not been adjusted for supplies used during 19A. An inventory count of the maintenance supplies on hand (unused) on December 31, 19A, showed $2,000. Supplies used are debited to Maintenance Expense.
2. The insurance premium paid in 19A was for years 19A and 19B; therefore, the prepaid insurance at December 31, 19A, amounted to $1,000. The total insurance premium was debited in full to Other Expenses when paid in 19A.
3. The equipment cost $30,000 when purchased January 1, 19A, and has an estimated useful life of five years (no residual value). No depreciation has been recorded for 19A.
4. Unpaid (and unrecorded) salaries at December 31, 19A, amounted to $1,500.
5. At December 31, 19A, hauling revenue collected in advance amounted to $3,000. This amount was credited in full to Transportation Revenue when the cash was collected earlier during 19A.
6. Assume an income tax rate of 20 percent.

Required:

a. Give the six adjusting entries (in journal form) required by the above additional information for December 31, 19A.
b. Recast the above statements after taking into account the adjusting entries. You do not need to use subclassifications on the statements. Suggested form for the solution:

		Changes		
	Amounts			*Correct*
Items	*reported*	*Plus*	*Minus*	*amounts*
(List here each item from the two statements)				

(Hint: the correct balance sheet total is $69,000.)
c. Compute the amount of the error in (1) net income and (2) total assets due to the omission of the adjusting entries. Draft a brief nontechnical report for the bank explaining causes of the differences.

PC4–12. (Comprehensive) Small Company is completing the information processing cycle for its annual accounting period that ended on December 31, 19D. All of the current entries for 19D were entered correctly in the accounting system. A list of all of the ledger accounts and their respective balances (i.e., an unadjusted trial balance) was prepared immediately after the last current entry was journalized and posted.

The accountant was away from work for a few days. During this time, a new assistant to the president requested that the bookkeeper prepare an income statement and balance sheet immediately "for our use" despite a suggestion by the bookkeeper that "the adjustments have to be determined by the CMA." Consequently, the following statements (summarized for case purposes) were prepared by the bookkeeper and given to the assistant.

Income Statement
For the Year Ended
December 31, 19D

Revenues:

Sales	$240,000
Services	50,000
Total revenues	290,000

Expenses:

Cost of goods sold	150,000
Salaries and wages	65,000
Utilities	18,000
Other expenses	7,000
Total expenses	240,000
Net income	$ 50,000

Balance Sheet
At December 31, 19D

Assets

Cash	$ 23,000
Accounts receivable	61,000
Inventory	130,000
Prepaid insurance	6,000
Equipment*	100,000
Accumulated depreciation, equipment	(30,000)
Remaining assets	10,000
Total assets	$300,000

Liabilities

Accounts payable	$ 41,000
Income taxes payble	
Notes payable, one year, 15%	20,000

Shareholders' Equity

Capital stock, par $10	150,000
Contributed surplus	15,000
Retained earnings	74,000
Total liabilities and shareholders' equity	$300,000

*Acquired January 1, 19A; estimated life, 10 years, and no residual value.

After returning, the CMA immediately prepared another set of statements which included the following additional data:

a. The inventory at the end of December 19D should have been $120,000 instead of $130,000.

b. The prepaid insurance amount of $6,000 was the total premium paid on July 1, 19D, which covered a two-year period from payment date. (The $6,000 was debited to Prepaid Insurance.)

c. Depreciation for 19D was not recorded. (Hint: Refer to the balance sheet.)

    d. Interest on the note payable was not recorded. The note was dated November 1, 19D, and the principal plus interest is payable at the end of one year.

    e. Assume an average income tax rate of 20 percent.

Required:

    a. Prepare the appropriate adjusting entry, in journal form, for each item of additional data.

    b. Recast the income statement and balance sheet to incorporate the additional data. Suggested format:

Items	Amounts reported	Changes Plus	Minus	Correct amounts
Income statement:				
Balance sheet:				

    c. Draft a brief nontechnical explanation for the management to adequately explain why the second set of financial statements should replace the first set. (Hint: Correct EPS is $1.49.)

PC4–13. Refer to the Consoliated-Bathurst financial statements given at the end of this textbook immediately preceding the Index. Respond to the following questions for the 1984 annual accounting period.

    1. On what date did the 1984 accounting year end?

    2. What was the name of the firm of independent CAs?

    3. Reconcile the beginning and ending balances of retained earnings.

    4. Explain how (use amounts as well as words) the revenue item "income from investments and short-term deposits" affects the 1984 balance sheet; assume all cash transactions.

    5. Explain how C-B applied the time-period assumption.

    6. Explain how C-B applies the revenue and matching principles. Use "Net sales" and "Cost of goods sold" as examples.

    7. What is the primary indicator in the financial statements that the company applied the reliability principle?

    8. What amount was recorded in the adjusting entry for "depreciation"? Give the journal entry to record that amount.

    9. How much was the accrued expenses related to salaries, wages, and commissions? Prepare the journal entry to record that amount if you can find it.

    10. How much did owners' equity increase (decrease) due to the sale and issuance or redemption of preferred shares during 1984?

PC4–14. Carbonated Beverage Ltd. (CB), was federally incorporated in 1970. In the initial years, the company produced an orange drink for sale at sporting and entertainment events in Western Canada. In 1974, operations were expanded to include sales to bars, restaurants, and fast-food outlets. To penetrate additional markets, CB started manufacturing a wide variety of soft drinks and acquired the distributorship of another company's cola syrup. Sold under the brand name "Sun Brite," the soft drink sales were only moderately successful.

    In 1976, a management review indicated, that, while sales of the new soft drink line had increased, CB's cost to manufacture was also greater than that of its competitors. Much of the net income was being made on the distribution of cola syrup.

    In an attempt to improve profitability, the company entered the retail market in 1977.

To finance this expansion, CB obtained funds from two sources: bank loans and the issue of shares to the public. The funds were used to purchase a bottling plant in Vancouver and to provide working capital during the first year of operation. In the first year, the retail operation incurred a loss that in subsequent years became a profit.

CB continued to expand until it had a nationwide bottling and distribution network. Some bottlers it owned; some in smaller cities were independents who bottled other products as well. CB sold its own syrup to these independents.

In 1980, CB acquired a vending company's operations. By expanding these operations, CB was able to manufacture and sell vending machines as well as soft drinks through the vending machines.

The contract between CB and local operators of vending machines (CB does not operate its own machines) stipulates that local operators must sell only CB products.

The major portion of all matching sales was done using what is termed a conditional sales contract. This contract specifies an initial down payment of $350 and monthly payments of $75 per month for the next 48 months. Maintenance of machines is the responsibility of the operator.

The syrup and cups for the machines are purchased directly from CB or from local independent bottlers who in turn buy the supplies from CB. The independents receive a discount from CB sufficient to permit them to make a 20 percent markup on their cost.

During 1982, CB expects to sell 7,000 machines. Each machine costs $1,500 to manufacture. The cash sales price for those few who have the cash is $3,400.

Required:

In August 1982, you were engaged as an independent adviser. Prepare a report to the president of CB which:

a. Outlines the major accounting issues faced by the company.
b. Identifies alternative policies to deal with the issues outlined.
c. Provides recommendations on the preferred policies.

(CICA Adapted)

5

Information Processing in an Accounting System

PURPOSE OF THIS CHAPTER

In Chapter 3, Part B, we discussed the accounting information processing cycle and in Chapter 4 we discussed one important phase of that cycle—adjusting entries. The purpose of this chapter is to expand those discussions to include all of the phases and procedures in the accounting information processing cycle. This cycle is a systematic approach to periodic recording, measuring and classifying of financial data, and preparing periodic financial statements, and as such is repeated each accounting period.

Students who plan to major in accounting need a solid understanding of accounting information processing from the professional and technical points of view. Other students, particularly those interested in careers in management, need a general understanding of the information processing cycle because, as managers, they will have to assess such things as (1) the capabilities and limitations of such a system, (2) the basic adaptations that should be expected for different types and sizes of entities, (3) cost-benefit relationships (i.e., the benefit of financial information versus the cost of providing the information), (4) the internal control implications of the system, and (5) the relationship of the accounting information processing system to the overall information system of the entity.

In addition to the discussions of information processing in this chapter, the following supplement is provided:

Supplement 5A—Reversing entries

MANUAL, MECHANICAL, AND ELECTRONIC DATA PROCESSING

Information processing refers to the sequence and approaches used in accounting to accomplish the following: (1) collecting economic data about the activities of the company (by means of business documents), (2) recording the effects of the activities of the company in the accounting system in terms of the accounting model, (3) classifying and recording the data collected, and (4) preparing the periodic financial statements. In most entities, an extremely large amount of accounting data must be handled. Although information processing can be time consuming and costly to the enterprise, a well-designed processing system provides a smooth, uninterrupted, and efficient flow of data from the points of occurrence of the day to day transactions to the financial statements at the end of the accounting period. The processing of accounting data may be performed in one of three ways, or, as is the usual case, by a combination of them. The three approaches may be described briefly as follows:

1. **Manual data processing**—With this approach, the accounting work is performed by hand (i.e., manually). Manual processing of accounting data has been employed in our discussions in the previous chapters. The manual approach is used extensively in small entities. Also, in large- and medium-sized businesses, certain parts of the information process often are performed manually. The manual approach is useful for discussing and illustrating the application of accounting concepts, principles, and measurement procedures. Also, it is convenient for explaining and illustrating the accounting process because you can readily see what is being done. You cannot see what is going on inside a computer.

2. **Mechanical data processing**—Mechanical data processing often is used in accounting to record repetitive transactions that occur in large numbers. Mechanical processing of accounting data employs accounting machines that vary widely in type and application. They encompass mechanical devices, some of which display a combination typewriter-adding machine keyboard. Mechanical processing encompasses not only the strictly mechanical devices, such as posting machines, but also punched-card equipment. The latter consists of (1) keypunch machines, on which cards are punched to record the transactions; (2) sorting machines, which sort the cards in a predetermined order; and (3) tabulating machines, which print the output, such as a listing of the expenses for the period. Although mechanical data processing is used today, it is being superseded rapidly by electronic data processing.

3. **Electronic data processing**—Electronic processing of accounting data uses electronic computers of varying size and sophistication. When electronic data processing is employed, the use of manual and mechanical activities in an accounting system is

reduced to a minimum. Because of the large capability to store data and the speed with which such data can be manipulated and recalled, electronic data processing is widely used in accounting. Electronic data processing involves the use of "hardware" and "software." The computer and equipment related to it (usually called peripheral equipment) constitute the **hardware. Software** includes (a) the computer programs that must be designed as instructions to the computer and (b) other items related to the operation of the system. Other items include materials used in operating the system, training materials, and studies of various sorts. Electronic data processing is applied widely to such accounting problems as payrolls, billings for goods and services, accounts receivable, accounts payable, inventories, and even to the preparation of detailed financial statements. The rapid development of microcomputers and software "packages" for them has made it technically and economically feasible for even the smallest businesses (and individuals) to maintain their accounting system electronically.

EXPANDING THE ACCOUNTING INFORMATION PROCESSING CYCLE

The discussions in this chapter expand the accounting information processing cycle introduced in Chapter 3, Part B. You should review that introductory material (particularly Exhibit 3–10) before proceeding further. Our discussion of the accounting information processing cycle is expanded in this chapter to encompass **four additional phases** indicated by an **asterisk** in Exhibit 5–1. Each phase in a complete accounting information processing cycle is outlined in that exhibit in the chronological (timing) order in which each phase is usually implemented.

The four phases added (6, 8, 9, and 10) are information processing phases only and involve no new accounting concepts or principles beyond those that you have already learned in the first four chapters These four added phases are designed to provide an orderly flow of the data processing work **at the end of the accounting period** and usually are helpful in completion of the financial statements with minimum effort. Also, they tend to decrease errors and omissions. The phases discussed in Chapter 3 will be reviewed, and the four added phases will be discussed and illustrated in detail in the remainder of this chapter. These illustrations use a manual system for instructional purposes.

Phase 1— Collecting raw economic data from completed transactions

This phase is a necessary continuing activity that collects **source documents** (such as sales invoices) from all of the transactions as they occur. The collection process involves all operations of the entity and a large number of employees (including nonaccountants). Source documents provide data to be analyzed and recorded in the accounting system. The source documents must be collected in a timely manner and must provide complete and accurate data about each transaction.

EXHIBIT 5–1
Outline of all phases of the accounting information processing cycle

Phases Completed during the Accounting Period

1. Collection of raw economic data generated by the transactions of the entity; supported with business documents.
2. Transaction analysis of all current transactions (as they occur) to determine the economic effects on the entity in terms of the accounting model.
3. Journalizing the results of the analysis of the current transactions. This phase encompasses recording the entries in chronological order in the journal.
4. Posting the current entries from the journal to the respective accounts in the ledger.

Phases Completed Only at the End of the Accounting Period

5. Preparation of an unadjusted trial balance from the ledger.
*6. Preparation of an accounting worksheet:
  a. Collection of data for adjusting entries and analysis of the data in the context of the accounting model.
  b. Separation of the adjusted data among the income statement, balance sheet, and statement of changes in financial position.
7. Preparation of financial statements:
  a. Income statement.
  b. Balance sheet.
  c. Statement of changes in financial position (SCFP; discussed in Chapter 15).
*8. Adjusting entries (at the end of the period):
  a. Recorded in the journal.
  b. Posted to the ledger.
*9. Closing the revenue and expense accounts in the ledger:
  a. Recorded in the journal.
  b. Posted to the ledger.
*10. Preparation of a post-closing trial balance.

Phase Completed Only at the Start of the Next Accounting Period

11. Optional *reversing entries* (see Supplement 5A).

*Phases added in this chapter to complete the entire cycle.

Phase 2— Analyzing transactions

Primarily this is a mental activity performed by accountants in order to identify and measure the economic impact of each transaction on the entity in terms of the basic accounting model: Assets = Liabilities + Owners' equity. The analysis of each transaction involves determination of the specific asset, liability, and owners' equity accounts that should be increased and/or decreased to properly reflect the economic consequences of each transaction. Analysis of transactions requires, for each transaction, the supporting source document(s) and often other related information.

Phase 3— Journalizing

Journalizing is the process of recording the results of the **transaction analysis** of each completed transaction in the **journal** in the debit-credit format. Thus, the economic impacts of each transaction on the entity are recorded first in the journal in chronological order.

Phase 4— Posting

Accounting data first are recorded in the journal (Phase 3), next these data are transferred or **posted** to the **ledger** to reclassify and aggregate the information in terms of the fundamental accounting model: Assets = Liabilities + Owners' equity. The ledger is composed of a number of separate accounts; one for each kind of asset, liability, and owners' equity. Thus, posting to the ledger reorders the data from the chronological order in the journal to the classifications explicit within the fundamental accounting model. The ledger is viewed as the basic accounting record because it provides appropriately classified economic data about the entity that will be used to complete the remaining phases of the accounting information processing cycle (including preparation of the periodic financial statements).

Chapter 3 illustrated the use of a **trial balance** to prepare the periodic financial statements. However, the **remaining phases** of the accounting information processing cycle were not discussed or illustrated. Phases 5 through 10 are known as **end-of-period** phases. We will now discuss the specific procedures associated with the remaining phases.

Phase 5—Preparation of an unadjusted trial balance

At the **end of the accounting period,** after all current transactions have been recorded in the journal (journalized) and then posted to the ledger, a listing of all **ledger** accounts and their balances is prepared. This listing is called an **unadjusted trial balance** because it serves to check the equalities of the accounting model (A = L + OE and Debits = Credits) but does **not** include the effects of the particular group of end-of-period entries called **adjusting entries** which were discussed and illustrated in Chapter 4, Part B.

Phase 6—The worksheet

The outline presented in Exhibit 5–1 lists six different phases that are completed at the end of the accounting period, including a **worksheet.** The end-of-period phases involve numerous related details and the possibility of errors. Preparation of the worksheet that precedes the journalizing and posting of the adjusting and closing entries (Phases 8 and 9) is designed to minimize the possibility of errors. Once completed, the worksheet provides all of the data needed to complete the remaining end-of-period phases in the accounting information processing cycle. It accomplishes this broad purpose by bringing together in one place, in an orderly way, the (1) unadjusted trial balance, (2) adjusting entries, (3) income statement, (4) statement of retained earnings, (5) balance sheet, and (6) the closing entries (explained later).[1]

Preparation of a worksheet. The simplified case used in Chapter 4 for High-Rise Apartments will be used to illustrate the preparation of a typical worksheet at the end of the accounting year, December 31, 19B. To facilitate explanation, two exhibits are presented:

Exhibit 5–2—Worksheet format with **unadjusted** trial balance and adjusting entries.

---

[1]This entire section on the worksheet can be omitted without affecting the remaining chapters.

Exhibit 5–3—Worksheet completed; reflects the **income statement, statement of retained earnings,** and **balance sheet.**

The sequential steps involved in developing the worksheet are:

Step 1—Set up the worksheet **format** by entering the appropriate column headings. This step is illustrated in Exhibit 5–2, which includes in the left column the account titles (taken directly from the ledger) and six separate pairs of debit/credit money columns. Each pair of the six money columns represents one of the end-of-period phases of the accounting information processing cycle.

Step 2—Enter the **unadjusted** trial balance as of the end of the accounting period directly from the ledger into the first pair of debit/credit columns. When all of the current entries for the period, **excluding** the adjusting entries, have been recorded in the journal and posted to the ledger, the amounts for the **unadjusted** trial balance are the balances of the respective ledger accounts. Before proceeding to the next step, the equality of the debits and credits in the unadjusted trial balance should be assured by totaling each column (totals $481,460). When a worksheet is used, there is no real need to develop a **separate** adjusted trial balance (Phase 5).

Step 3—The second pair of debit/credit columns, headed "Adjusting Entries," is completed by developing and then entering the adjusting entries **directly** on the worksheet. The adjusting entries for High-Rise Apartments shown in Exhibit 5–2 were illustrated (with the same letter codes) and discussed in detail in Chapter 4, Part B. To facilitate examination (for potential errors), future reference, and study, the adjusting entries usually are coded on the worksheet as illustrated in Exhibit 5–2. Some of the adjusting entries may require the addition of one or more account titles in addition to those of the original trial balance listing (see last four account titles in Exhibit 5–2). After the adjusting entries are completed on the worksheet, the equality of debits and credits for those entries is checked (totals $19,900).

The remaining steps to complete the worksheet are reflected by the last eight columns in Exhibit 5–3. These steps are:

Step 4—The pair of debit/credit columns headed "Adjusted Trial Balance" is completed. Although not essential, this pair of columns helps to assure accuracy. Simply, the adjusted trial balance is the line-by-line combined amounts of the unadjusted trial balance, plus or minus the amounts entered as adjusting entries in the second pair of columns. For example, the Rent Revenue account reflects a $128,463 credit balance under Unadjusted Trial Balance. To this amount is **added** the **credit** amount, $600, and **minus** the **debit** amount, $500, giving a combined amount of $128,563, which is entered as a **credit** under Adjusted Trial Balance. For those accounts that were unaffected by the adjusting entries, the unadjusted trial balance amount is carried directly across to the Adjusted Trial Balance column.

EXHIBIT 5–2   Worksheet format with unadjusted trial balance and adjusting entries

HIGH-RISE APARTMENTS, INC.
Worksheet for the Year Ended December 31, 19B

Account Titles	Unadjusted Trial Balance		Adjusting Entries		Adjusted Trial Balance		Income Statement		Retained Earnings		Balance Sheet	
	Debit	Credit	Debit	Credit	Debit	Credit	Debit	Credit	Debit	Credit	Debit	Credit
Cash	2,297											
Prepaid insurance	2,400			(c) 1,200								
Inventory of maintenance supplies	600			(e) 400								
Land	25,000											
Apartment building	360,000											
Accumulated depreciation, building		10,000		(d) 10,000								
Notes payable		30,000										
Rent collected in advance				(a) 500								
Mortgage payable		238,037										
Capital stock, 500 shares		50,000										
Retained earnings, Jan. 1, 19B		24,960										
Dividends declared and paid	12,000											
Rent revenue		128,463	(a) 500	(b) 600								
Advertising expense	500											
Maintenance expense	3,000		(e) 400									
Salary expense	17,400		(f) 900									
Interest expense	19,563		(h) 600									
Utilities expense	34,500											
Miscellaneous expenses	4,200											
Insurance expense			(c) 1,200									
Depreciation expense			(d) 10,000									
Salaries payable				(f) 900								
Property tax expense			(g) 5,700									
Property tax payable				(g) 5,700								
Interest payable				(h) 600								
Rent revenue receivable			(b) 600									
	481,460	481,460	19,900	19,900								

EXHIBIT 5–3   Worksheet completed

HIGH-RISE APARTMENTS, INC.
Worksheet for the Year Ended December 31, 19B

Account Titles	Unadjusted Trial Balance		Adjusting Entries*		Adjusted Trial Balance		Income Statement		Retained Earnings		Balance Sheet	
	Debit	Credit	Debit	Credit	Debit	Credit	Debit	Credit	Debit	Credit	Debit	Credit
Cash	2,297				2,297						2,297	
Prepaid insurance	2,400			(c) 1,200	1,200						1,200	
Inventory of maintenance supplies	600			(e) 400	200						200	
Land	25,000				25,000						25,000	
Apartment building	360,000				360,000						360,000	
Accumulated depreciation, building		10,000		(d) 10,000		20,000						20,000
Notes payable		30,000				30,000						30,000
Rent collected in advance				(a) 500		500						500
Mortgage payable		238,037				238,037						238,037
Capital stock, 500 shares		50,000				50,000						50,000
Retained earnings, Jan. 1, 19B		24,960				24,960				24,960		
Dividends declared and paid	12,000				12,000				12,000			
Rent revenue		128,463	(a) 500	(b) 600		128,563		128,563				
Advertising expense	500				500		500					
Maintenance expense	3,000		(e) 400		3,400		3,400					
Salary expense	17,400		(f) 900		18,300		18,300					
Interest expense	19,563		(h) 600		20,163		20,163					
Utilities expense	34,500				34,500		34,500					
Miscellaneous expenses	4,200				4,200		4,200					
Insurance expense			(c) 1,200		1,200		1,200					
Depreciation expense			(d) 10,000		10,000		10,000					
Salaries payable				(f) 900		900						900
Property tax expense			(g) 5,700		5,700		5,700					
Property tax payable				(g) 5,700		5,700						5,700
Interest payable				(h) 600		600						600
Rent revenue receivable			(b) 600		600						600	
	481,460	481,460	19,900	19,900	499,260	499,260	97,963	128,563				
Income tax expense†			(i) 6,120		6,120		6,120					
Income tax payable				(i) 6,120		6,120						6,120
Net income‡			6,120	6,120			24,480			24,480		
							128,563	128,563	12,000	49,440		
Retained earnings, Dec. 31, 19B§									37,440			37,440
									49,440	49,440	389,297	389,297

*Explanation of adjusting entries is provided in Exhibit 5–4.

†Revenues, $128,563 − Pretax expenses, $97,963 = $30,600; $30,600 × tax rate, 20% = $6,120.

‡Pretax income, $30,600 − Income tax, $6,120 = $24,480.

§$49,440 − $12,000 = $37,440.

After each line has been completed, the equality of the debits and credits under Adjusted Trial Balance is checked (total $499,260).

Step 5—The amount of each line, under Adjusted Trial Balance, is extended horizontally across the worksheet and entered (a) as a debit, if it is a debit under Adjusted Trial Balance, or as a credit, if it is a credit under Adjusted Trial Balance; and (b) under the financial statement heading (income statement, retained earnings, or balance sheet) on which it must be reported. You can see that each amount in the adjusted trial balance columns (1) was entered under **only one** of the six remaining columns, and (2) that debits remain debits and credits remain credits in the extending process.

Step 6—At this point, the two Income Statement columns are summed (subtotals). The difference between these two subtotals represents the **pretax income (or loss).** Income tax expense then is computed by multiplying this difference by the tax rate. In Exhibit 5–3, the computation was (pretax revenues, $128,563—pretax expenses, $97,963) × tax rate, 20% = $6,120. The **adjusting entry** for income tax then was entered at the bottom of the worksheet (a "loopback"). Income tax expense and income tax payable now can be extended horizontally to the Income Statement and Balance Sheet columns. Net income is entered as a **balancing debit** amount in the Income Statement column and as a credit (i.e., increase) in Retained Earnings.

Step 7—The two Retained Earnings columns are summed, and the difference is the ending balance of retained earnings. This balance amount is entered as a balancing debit amount (under Retained Earnings) and also as a balancing credit amount (i.e., an addition to owners' equity) under Balance Sheet. At this point, the two Balance Sheet columns should sum to equal amounts. The continuous checking of equality of debits and credits in each pair of debit/credit columns helps to assure the correctness of the worksheet. However, the balancing feature alone does not assure that the worksheet contains no errors. For example, if an expense amount (a debit) were extended to either the Retained Earnings debit column or to the Balance Sheet debit column, the worksheet would balance in all respects; however, at least two money columns would be in error. Therefore, special care must be exercised in selecting the appropriate debit/credit columns during the horizontal extension process.[2]

The completed worksheet, Exhibit 5–3, provides the data needed to complete the remaining phases of the accounting information processing cycle as follows (summarized from Exhibit 5–1):

---

[2]The number of paired columns on a worksheet can be reduced by omitting both, or either, the Adjusted Trial Balance columns and the Retained Earnings columns. Also, the number of columns can be reduced further by using only one money column for each set instead of separate debit and credit columns (for example, the credits can be indicated by parentheses).

Phase	Phase description	Source on worksheet
7	Prepare income statement	Income Statement columns
	Prepare balance sheet	Balance Sheet columns
	Prepare statement of retained earnings	Retained Earnings columns
8	Record adjusting entries in journal and post to ledger	Adjusting Entries columns
9	Record closing entries in journal and post to ledger	Income Statement and Retained Earnings columns
10	Post-closing trial balance	Prepare from ledger and check with Balance Sheet columns.

**Phase 7—
Preparing
financial
statements from
the worksheet**

The completed worksheet provides in one place the amounts needed to prepare the income statement, balance sheet, and statement of retained earnings. The statement of retained earnings usually is prepared by corporations (see Exhibit 2–4 for example). This statement ties together the income statement and the shareholders' equity section of the balance sheet. For example, the statement of retained earnings for High-Rise Apartments would be as follows:

HIGH-RISE APARTMENTS, INC.
Statement of Retained Earnings
For the Year Ended December 31, 19B

Retained earnings balance January 1, 19B..........	$24,960
Add net income of 19B	24,480
Total....................................	49,440
Less dividends declared and paid in 19B	12,000
Retained earnings balance, December 31, 19B	$37,440

The task of preparing the income statement and balance sheet is simply one of properly **classifying** the data provided by the worksheet. Classified financial statements were illustrated in Exhibit 3–2; therefore, they will not be repeated here.

The worksheet described above does not provide data for the statement of changes in financial position (SCFP). This statement requires special analytical procedures; as a consequence, a special worksheet must be used to develop it. The special worksheet will be discussed and illustrated in Chapter 15.

**Phase 8—
Recording
adjusting
entries in the
accounts**

Immediately after completion of the worksheet, the financial statements are prepared and distributed to the interested users. Observe that by using the worksheet, preparation and distribution of the financial statements are not delayed by the remaining phases of the accounting cycle. After the financial statements have been prepared, the **adjusting entries** reflected on the completed worksheet are entered in the journal and then posted to the ledger. These entries are "dated" as of the last day of the accounting period. This task is a clerical one because the entries merely are copied from the worksheet into the journal. The adjusting entries for High-Rise Apartments, with a **folio** notation to indicate that posting is completed, are illustrated in Exhibit 5–4. The ledger,

EXHIBIT 5–4
Adjusting entries
illustrated

JOURNAL

Date 19B	Account Titles and Explanation	Folio	Debit	Credit
Dec. 31	*a.* Rent revenue	340	500	
	Rent collected in advance	204		500
	To adjust the accounts for revenue collected in advance.			
31	*b.* Rent revenue receivable	102	600	
	Rent revenue	340		600
	To adjust for rent revenue earned in 19B, but not yet collected.			
31	*c.* Insurance expense	356	1,200	
	Prepaid insurance	103		1,200
	To adjust for insurance expired during 19B.			
31	*d.* Depreciation expense	360	10,000	
	Accumulated depreciation, building	113		10,000
	To adjust for depreciation expense for 19B.			
31	*e.* Maintenance expense	351	400	
	Inventory of maintenance supplies	104		400
	To adjust for supplies used from inventory during 19B.			
31	*f.* Salary expense	352	900	
	Salaries payable	206		900
	To adjust for salaries earned but not yet recorded or paid.			
31	*g.* Property tax expense	361	5,700	
	Property tax payable	207		5,700
	To adjust for 19B property tax incurred, but not yet recorded or paid.			
31	*h.* Interest expense	353	600	
	Interest payable	209		600
	To adjust for accrued interest expense for two months on note payable ($30,000 \times 12\% \times 2/12 = 600).			
31	*i.* An adjusting entry for income tax expense will be computed on the worksheet when the pretax income is computed thereon. The entry will be:			
	Income tax expense	370	6,120	
	Income tax payable	208		6,120

with the adjusting entries posted, is shown in Exhibit 5–6. This phase is required to enter the economic effects of the adjusting entries into the accounting system.

**Phase 9—
Closing the
revenue and
expense
accounts**

In our study of the fundamental accounting model, we have emphasized that the **revenue** and **expense** accounts are subdivisions of retained earnings which itself is a part of **owners' equity.** The revenue, gain, expense, and loss accounts can be thought of as "income statement accounts," whereas the remainder of the accounts can be viewed as "balance sheet accounts." The revenue, gain, expense, and loss accounts are often called **temporary** (or nominal) accounts because data are temporarily collected in them for the **current accounting period only.** At the end of each period, their balances are transferred, or **closed,** to the Retained Earnings account. This periodic clearing out or closing of the balances of the income statement accounts into Retained Earnings serves two purposes: (1) it transfers net income (or loss) to retained earnings (i.e., owners' equity), and (2) it establishes a zero balance in the revenue and expense accounts to start the next accounting period. In this way, the **income statement accounts** again are ready to serve their **temporary** periodic collection function for the next period. The journal entries that clear out the temporary accounts are called **closing entries.**

In contrast, the **balance sheet accounts** (assets, liabilities, and owners' equity) are not closed periodically; therefore, they are often called **permanent** (or real) accounts. To illustrate, the ending cash balance of one accounting period must be in the Cash account at the start of the next accounting period. The only time a permanent account has a zero balance is when the item represented (such as machinery or notes payable) is no longer owned (or is fully depreciated) or owed. The balance at the end of the period in each balance sheet account is carried forward in the ledger as the **beginning** balance for the next period.

In summary, the **closing entries,** made at the end of the accounting period to transfer the balances of all revenue and expense accounts, simply represent a mechanical phase. To close an account means to transfer its balance to another designated account by means of an entry. For example, an account that has a credit balance (such as a revenue account) would be closed by **debiting** that account for an amount equal to its balance and crediting the account to which the balance is to be transferred. In the closing process, a credit balance is always transferred to another account as a credit, and similarly a debit is always transferred as a debit for the same amount. The closing entries are **dated** the last day of the accounting period and are entered in the journal in the usual debit-credit format and are immediately posted to the ledger.

Another temporary account, called Income Summary, sometimes is used to facilitate the closing procedure. It is a clearance account used to "clear" the revenues and expenses to retained earnings. To illustrate the closing procedure, assume the following summarized data from the accounts of Alpha Corporation at December 31, 19E, the end of the accounting period:

Shareholders' Equity Accounts

Capital stock, 5,000 shares, par $10	$ 50,000
Retained earnings beginning balance January 1, 19E	15,000
Total revenues earned during 19E......................	100,000
Total expenses incurred during 19E	80,000
Total dividends declared and paid during 19E............	10,000

The four required closing entries, assuming an **income summary account** is used, would be dated December 31, 19E, and would appear in the journal as follows:

a.	Revenue..	100,000	
	Income summary		100,000
	To close the revenue amount into Income Summary.		
b.	Income summary......................................	80,000	
	Expenses..		80,000
	To close the expense amount into Income Summary.		
c.	Income summary......................................	20,000	
	Retained earnings		20,000
	To close the Income Summary amount (i.e., net income) into Retained Earnings.		
d.	Retained earnings	10,000	
	Dividends declared and paid...........................		10,000
	To close the dividends paid amount into Retained Earnings.		

After the above closing entries are posted to the ledger accounts, the temporary accounts—revenue, expenses, and income summary—will reflect zero balances. Similarly, the dividends account will reflect a zero balance. The Retained Earnings account (a permanent account) will reflect an ending balance calculated as follows: $15,000 + $20,000 − $10,000 = \underline{$25,000}$.

Posting each of the above closing entries is diagrammed, and their effects on the **temporary and permanent ledger** accounts are shown in the following T-accounts for instructional purposes only:

ALPHA CORPORATION

Revenue				Capital Stock, Par $10	
	Balance	100,000		Balance	50,000
(a) Closing 100,000			(a)		

Expenses				Income Summary	
Balance 80,000	(b) Closing 80,000		(b)	(a) Revenues 100,000	
				(b) Expenses 80,000	
				(c) Closing 20,000	

Dividends Declared and Paid			(c)	Retained Earnings	
Balance 10,000	(d) Closing 10,000		(d)	Balance 15,000	
			(d) Dividends 10,000	(c) Income 20,000	

Ending balance, $25,000

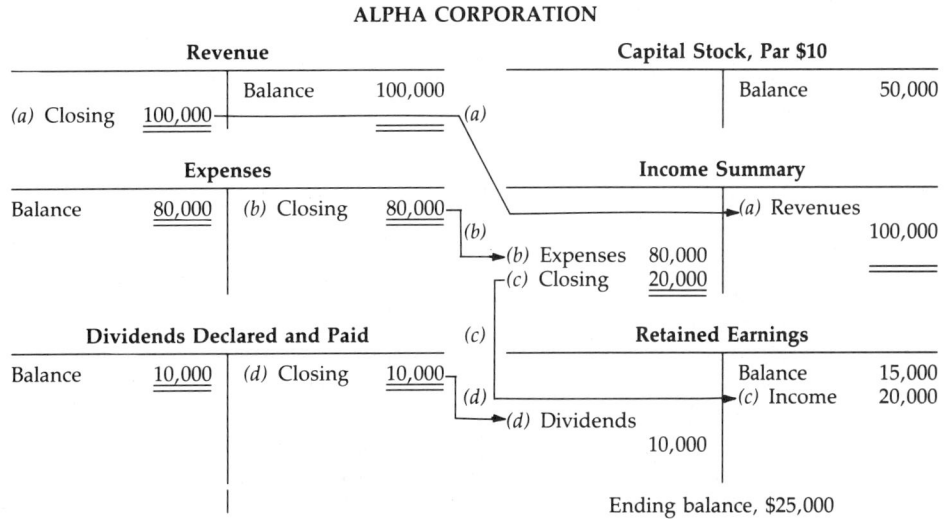

In the above example of Alpha Corporation, only one revenue and one expense account were used for illustrative purposes. However, **all** income statement accounts must be closed at the end of the accounting period using the closing procedure illustrated above. In the above example, we assumed that dividends declared and paid were recorded previously as a debit to a **temporary** account, Dividends Declared and Paid, rather than as a direct debit to Retained Earnings. Therefore, the temporary account, Dividends Declared and Paid, was closed into Retained Earnings. When this temporary account is not used, a closing entry for it obviously is not needed.

Closing entries illustrated, High-Rise Apartments, Inc. Now, let's return to High-Rise Apartments and apply the closing procedure. The closing entries in the journal are shown in Exhibit 5–5; the posting notation (folio) to the ledger also is indicated. Observe that **all** of the revenue and expense accounts are closed, and in the process their balances are transferred into Retained Earnings. Also, the Dividends Declared and Paid account is closed into Retained Earnings.

For instructional purposes, the ledger accounts with (1) the trial balance totals, (2) the adjusting entries posted, and (3) the closing entries posted (in black boxes) are shown in Exhibit 5–6 in T-account format. The boxes are used to facilitate your study of the mechanics of each step. You should observe that **all** of the adjusting and closing amounts are verifiable or traceable directly to the completed worksheet (Exhibit 5–3).

One additional point should be emphasized. The closing entry in the journal for expenses (and for revenues when there is more than one) is a **compound** entry, which saves closing time and space (of course, a separate closing entry could be made for each separate expense account). Notice that the total debit to Income Summary in each entry can be taken from the worksheet.

EXHIBIT 5–5
Closing entries
illustrated (High-
Rise Apartments,
Inc.)

JOURNAL

Date 19B	Account Titles and Explanation	Folio	Debit	Credit
Dec. 31	Rent revenue	340	128,563	
	Income summary	330		128,563
	To transfer revenues into Income Summary.			
31	Income summary ($97,963 + $6,120)	330	104,083	
	Advertising expense	350		500
	Maintenance expense	351		3,400
	Salary expense	352		18,300
	Interest expense	353		20,163
	Utilities expense	354		34,500
	Miscellaneous expenses	355		4,200
	Insurance expense	356		1,200
	Depreciation expense	360		10,000
	Property tax expense	361		5,700
	Income tax expense	370		6,120
	To transfer expense amounts into Income Summary.			
31	Income summary	330	24,480	
	Retained earnings	305		24,480
	To transfer Net Income into Retained Earnings.			
31	Retained earnings	305	12,000	
	Dividends declared and paid	306		12,000
	To transfer Dividends Declared and Paid into Retained Earnings.			

EXHIBIT 5–6
Ledger accounts
illustrated (High-
Rise Apartments,
Inc.)

LEDGER—19B

Cash	101		Property Tax Payable	207		Maintenance Expense	351
2,297			(g) 5,700		(e)	3,000 400	(7) 3,400

Rent Revenue Receivable	102		Income Tax Payable	208		Salary Expense	352
(b) 600			(i) 6,120		(f)	17,400 900	(7) 18,300

Prepaid Insurance	103		Interest Payable	209		Interest Expense	353
2,400	(c) 1,200		(h) 600		(h)	19,563 600	(7) 20,163

EXHIBIT 5–6
(continued)

Inventory of Maintenance Supplies		104
600	(e)	400

Mortgage Payable	251
	238,037

Utilities Expense		354
34,500	(7)	34,500

Land		110
25,000		

Capital Stock	301
	50,000

Miscellaneous Expenses		355
4,200	(7)	4,200

Apartment Building		111
360,000		

Retained Earnings		305
(7) 12,000		24,960
	(7)	24,480

Insurance Expense		356
(c) 1,200	(7)	1,200

Accumulated Depreciation, Building		113
		10,000
	(d)	10,000

Dividends Declared and Paid		306
12,000	(7)	12,000

Depreciation Expense		360
(d) 10,000	(7)	10,000

Notes Payable	201
	30,000

Income Summary		330
(7) 104,083	(7)	128,563
(7) 24,480		

Property Tax Expense		361
(g) 5,700	(7)	5,700

Rent Collected in Advance		204
(a)		500

Rent Revenue		340
(a) 500		128,463
(7) 128,563	(b)	600

Income Tax Expense		370
(i) 6,120	(7)	6,120

Salaries Payable		206
(f)		900

Advertising Expense		350
500	(7)	500

For illustrative purposes:
· Unadjusted balances are in black.
· Adjusting entries are lettered.
· Closing entries are enclosed in boxes.

After the closing process is completed, observe that all of the temporary (i.e., the income statement) accounts are closed to a zero balance and are ready for reuse during the next accounting period for accumulating the revenues and expenses of that period. The Retained Earnings account now has an ending balance of $37,440, which will be reported on the December 31, 19B, balance sheet as a part of shareholders' equity.[3]

**Phase 10—
Post-closing
trial balance**

Despite guidance provided by the worksheet, occasional errors may be made in the adjusting and closing mechanics. After the completion of those two phases, it is desirable to verify the equality of the ledger account balances. This verification in computerized accounting systems can be practically automatic. In other systems it may be done by using a printing calculator or an adding machine. Instead, some accountants prefer to prepare another formal trial balance, called a **post-closing trial balance,** before starting a new period. All of the income statement accounts have been closed to retained earnings; therefore, the post-closing trial balance will reflect balances **only** for the permanent accounts classified as assets, liabilities, and owners' equity. These balances should be identical with those shown in the last two columns of the worksheet (Exhibit 5–3). The ending balances reflected in the ledger accounts, after the closing process, will be the beginning balances for the next period.

REVERSING ENTRIES

Some accountants add an **optional phase** to the accounting information processing cycle, which is known as **reversing entries.** This phase is dated as of the **first day of the next accounting period** and is used for the sole purpose of **facilitating** certain subsequent entries in the accounts. Reversing entries are related specifically to certain adjusting entries that already have been journalized and posted to the accounts. When appropriate, such adjusting entries are reversed on the first day of the next period (i.e., the debits and credits simply are reversed). This reversal process requires what are called reversing entries. Reversing entries are **strictly optional** and involve only bookkeeping mechanics rather than accounting concepts and principles. Supplement 5A, at the end of this chapter, discusses and illustrates reversing entries for those who desire to become familiar with this optional facilitating technique.

----

[3]A common bookkeeping approach to "ruling a permanent T-account" with a carry-forward balance is as follows:

Retained Earnings			305
Dividends (19B)	12,000	Jan. 1, 19B, balance	24,960
Balance carried forward		Net income (19B)	24,480
to 19C	37,440		
	49,440		49,440
		Jan. 1, 19C, balance	37,440

INTERIM FINANCIAL STATEMENTS

Many companies prepare interim financial statements **during** the accounting year for each month or each quarter. **Monthly** financial statements, when prepared, almost always are for **internal** management uses only. In contrast, many larger companies prepare **quarterly** financial statements for internal management use and also present a summarized version of them to their shareholders and other external parties.

When monthly or quarterly interim financial statements are prepared, the company usually does not go through the phases of **interim adjusting and closing entries.** The formal phases of journalizing and posting adjusting entries typically are performed **only** at the end of the annual accounting period. Instead, the company prepares a worksheet to facilitate preparation of the interim financial statements. Therefore, the worksheet serves another very useful purpose when interim monthly or quarterly financial statements are prepared. At the end of each interim period, an **unadjusted** trial balance is taken from the ledger accounts and entered directly on an interim (say, monthly) worksheet. The interim worksheet then is completed by entering the interim adjusting entries thereon and extending the adjusted amounts to the Retained Earnings, Income Statement, and Balance Sheet columns. The interim statements (say, monthly) are prepared on the basis of the worksheet. In such situations, the remaining phases of the accounting information processing cycle (adjusting entries recorded, closing entries recorded, and post-closing trial balance) need not be completed at the end of each interim period.

SUMMARY OF CHAPTER

This chapter focused on the **accounting information processing cycle** that must be completed in situations where periodic financial statements are developed for both external and internal users. The cycle captures raw economic data on transactions as they occur, then records and processes their economic effects on the entity and communicates these effects by means of the periodic financial statements. The information system must be designed to measure net income, financial position, and funds flow accurately and effectively. Such an information system also must be designed to fit the specific characteristics of the entity.

We cannot overemphasize that the worksheet, the closing entries, and the post-closing trial balance phases are mechanical data processing procedures and do not involve any new accounting principles or measurement approaches.

The 10 phases discussed in this chapter constitute the accounting information processing cycle that is repeated each accounting period in all accounting systems. The information processing system captures the economic essence of all transactions at their points of incurrence and carries those effects to the end result—the periodic financial statements. Numerous adaptations of the procedures used to implement the cycle are observed in actual situations because entities have different characteristics such as size, type of industry, complexity, accounting expertise, and sophistication of the management.

The information processing activities in a particular entity can be efficient, effective, and timely in terms of the outputs (the financial statements), but unfortunately, the opposite may be true. The quality of the system depends on the competence of those performing the data processing tasks and the importance attached by the management and owners to the financial measurement of operating results and financial position. In this context, the information processing system of an entity is significant to all parties interested in the entity because the end results—the financial statements—are important in their decision-making models.

SUPPLEMENT 5A—REVERSING ENTRIES

After completion of Phase 10 of the accounting information processing cycle (i.e., the post-closing trial balance), an **optional facilitating phase** may be added as Phase 11 (see Exhibit 5–1). This optional phase involves **reversing entries.** Reversing entries are **dated at the beginning of the next period** and relate **only to certain adjusting entries** made at the end of the immediate prior period. Certain adjusting entries may be reversed on the first day of the next period **solely to facilitate recording subsequent related entries.** Unlike most of the prior phases in the accounting information processing cycle, reversing entries are strictly optional and involve only bookkeeping mechanics rather than accounting principles or concepts.

The reversing entry phase is presented because (1) it introduces a common data processing technique used in most companies, whether the system is manual, mechanical, or computerized; and (2) a knowledge of the circumstances under which this phase may be used gives some additional insight into certain relationships in the efficient processing of accounting information.[4]

Reversing entries are given this name because they reverse, at the start of the next accounting period, the effects of certain adjusting entries made at the end of the previous period. **Reversing entries are always the opposite of the related adjusting entry.** It may be desirable to "reverse" certain adjusting entries; other adjusting entries should not be reversed.

To illustrate reversing entries and the type of situation where a reversing entry will simplify the subsequent accounting entry, assume that Day Company is in the process of completing the information processing cycle at the end of its accounting period, December 31, 19B. To place the reversing entry in context, Exhibit 5–7 presents a situation that shows (1) an adjusting entry on December 31, 19B; (2) the reversing entry that could be made on January 1, 19C; and (3) the subsequent entry on January 13, 19C, that was facilitated or simplified. To demonstrate the facilitating effect of a reversing entry, we also

---

[4]Knowledge of reversing entries is important primarily to students who plan to study accounting at the advanced level. This knowledge is not significant for study of the remaining chapters in this book.

EXHIBIT 5–7
Purpose of reversing entries illustrated

DAY COMPANY

Situation: The payroll was paid on December 28, 19B; the next payroll will be on January 13, 19C. At December 31, 19B, wages of $3,000 were earned for the last three days of the year but had not been paid or recorded.

With reversing entry	Without reversing entry

a. **The preceding adjusting entry:**

December 31, 19B, adjusting entry to record the $3,000 accrued (unpaid) wages:

Wage expense	3,000		Wage expense	3,000	
Wages payable			Wages payable		
(a liability)		3,000	(a liability)		3,000

b. **The closing entry:** The revenue and expense accounts are closed to Income Summary after the adjusting entries are completed and posted to the ledger.

December 31, 19B. closing entry:

Income summary	3,000		Income summary	3,000	
Wage expense . . .		3,000	Wage expense . . .		3,000

c. **The reversing entry:** The information processing cycle in 19B is complete. All closing entries have been posted, and the post-closing trial balance has been verified. At this point in time, January 1, 19C, the accountant should decide whether it is desirable to reverse any of the 19B adjusting entries (i.e., any reversing entries) to simplify the **subsequent related entries.** Question: Would a reversing entry on January 1, 19C, simplify the entry to be made on January 13, 19C, when the wages are paid?

January 1,19C, reversing entry.

Wages payable			No reversing entry assumed.
(a liability)	3,000		
Wage expense . . .		3,000	

d. **The subsequent entry that was facilitated:** The payroll of $25,000 was completed and paid on January 13, 19C. This subsequent payment entry is to be recorded. Question: Did the reversing entry facilitate or simplify this entry?

January 13, 19C, payroll entry:

Wage expense	25,000		Wages payable	3,000	
Cash		25,000	Wage expense	22,000	
			Cash		25,000

*Explanation: Observe that when the reversing entry was used, this last entry required only one debit, contrasted with two debits when no reversing entry was made. This difference was due to the fact that the reversing entry served to (1) clear out the liability account, Wages Payable, and (2) set up a temporary **credit** in the Wage Expense account. After the last entry, to record the payment of the payroll, both accounts affected—Wage Expense and Wages Payable—are identical in balance under both approaches. If the reversing entry is not made, the company must go to the trouble of identifying how much of the $25,000 paid on January 13, 19C, was expense and how much of it was to pay the liability set up in the adjusting entry at the end of the prior period ([a] above).

EXHIBIT 5–8   Reversing entries illustrated journal and ledger

Situation: On September 1, 19A, Company X loaned $1,200 on a one-year, 10 percent, interest-bearing note. On August 31, 19B, the company will collect the $1,200 principal plus $120 interest revenue. The annual accounting period ends December 31.

JOURNAL	LEDGER

a. September 1, 19A—To record the loan:

```
Note receivable . . . . . . . . . . . .   1,200
    Cash . . . . . . . . . . . . . . . . . . .           1,200
```

Cash

		x,xxx	(a) 9/1/19A	1,200
(e) 8/31/19B	1,320			

b. December 31, 19A (end of the accounting period)— Adjusting entry for four months' interest revenue earned but not collected ($1,200 × 10% × 4/12 = $40):

```
Interest receivable . . . . . . . . . . .    40
    Interest revenue . . . . . . . . .              40
```

Note Receivable

(a) 9/1/19A	1,200	(e) 8/31/19B	1,200

Interest Receivable

(b) 12/31/19A	40	(d) 1/1/19B	40

c. December 31, 19A—To close interest revenue:

```
Interest revenue . . . . . . . . . . . .    40
    Income summary . . . . . . . .              40
```

Interest Revenue

(c) 12/31/19A	40	(b) 12/31/19A	40
(d) 1/1/19B	40	(e) 8/31/19B	120

Income Summary

		(c) 12/31/19A	40

d. January 1, 19B—To reverse adjusting entry of December 31, 19A:

```
Interest revenue . . . . . . . . . . . .    40
    Interest receivable . . . . . . . .              40
```

Note: To demonstrate the facilitating feature, assume the reversing entry *(d)* was not made. The August 31, 19B, entry would be more complex, viz:

```
Cash . . . . . . . . . . . . . . . . . . . . . . . . . . . . . . . .   1,320
    Note receivable . . . . . . . . . . . . . . . . . . . .           1,200
    Interest receivable . . . . . . . . . . . . . . . . .               40
    Interest revenue . . . . . . . . . . . . . . . . . . .               80
```

Observe that after this entry, the Interest Receivable account reflects a zero balance and Interest Revenue reflects a **debit** balance of $40 (four months' interest).

e. August 31, 19B—Subsequent entry; to record collection of note plus interest for one year:*

```
Cash . . . . . . . . . . . . . . . . . . . . . . .   1,320
    Note receivable . . . . . . . . . .           1,200
    Interest revenue . . . . . . . .               120
```

*Observe that after this entry the Note Receivable account has a zero balance and the Interest Revenue an $80 balance which represents eight months' interest revenue earned in 19B.

have presented entries in the tabulation reflecting the same situation assuming no reversing entry. You should study carefully the two sets of entries and the explanatory comments in Exhibit 5–7.

Exhibit 5–8 presents another illustration of the effects of reversing entries. It is presented to emphasize the facilitating feature of reversing entries as reflected in both the journal and ledger. The **reversing entry** is lettered to facilitate your study.

In the above discussion we explained that certain adjusting entries could be reversed to facilitate or simplify subsequent related entries and that certain adjusting entries would **not** be reversed. How does one decide which entries may be reversed to advantage? There is no inflexible rule that can be provided. The accountant must analyze each situation and make a rational choice. In general, it can be said that short-term accruals and deferrals are candidates for reversal.

The adjusting entry to record depreciation and other entries of this type should never be reversed. In these situations, the adjusting entry is not followed by a subsequent "collection or payment" entry; therefore, it would be not only pointless to reverse the adjusting entry for depreciation but would introduce an error into the accounts because the accumulated depreciation account would reflect a zero balance throughout the period. Thus, many adjusting entries are not candidates for reversal, and those that are candidates are easily identified if one considers the nature of the subsequent related entry (i.e., whether there is a subsequent collection or payment).

Perhaps the most compelling reason for reversing entries is to increase the likelihood that the effects of certain adjusting entries will not be overlooked when recording the next related transaction in the following period.

IMPORTANT TERMS DEFINED IN THIS CHAPTER

Terms (alphabetically)	Key words in definitions of important terms used in chapter	Page reference
Accounting information processing cycle	Accounting phases (steps) from the time a transaction is completed to the financial statements.	210
Closing entries	End-of-period entries to close all revenue and expense accounts to retained earnings (through income summary).	219
Computer hardware	Computer and other equipment used with it.	210
Computer software	Computer programs and instructions for using an electronic computer.	210
Electronic data processing	Accounting process performed (in whole or in part) using electronic computers.	209
Manual data processing	Accounting process performed (in whole or in part) in handwriting; manually.	209
Mechanical data processing	Accounting process performed (in whole or in part) using machines.	209
Permanent (real) accounts	Permanent (or real) accounts are the balance sheet accounts; no closing entries.	219

Terms (alphabetically)	Key words in definitions of important terms used in chapter	Page reference
Post-closing trial balance	Trial balance prepared after all of the closing entries have been posted.	224
Reversing entries	Recorded at beginning of next accounting period; backs out certain adjusting entries; facilitates subsequent entries.	224
Temporary (nominal) accounts	Income statement accounts; closed at the end of the accounting period.	219
Worksheet	A "spreadsheet" designed to minimize errors and to provide data for the financial statements.	212

QUESTIONS FOR DISCUSSION

1. Briefly explain the nature of an accounting information processing system.

2. Distinguish among manual, mechanical, and electronic data processing. How does each relate to accounting information processing?

3. Briefly identify, in sequence, the 11 phases of the accounting information processing cycle.

4. Contrast transaction analysis with journalizing.

5. Compare journalizing with posting.

6. Explain in what way posting reflects a change in classification of the data.

7. Contrast an unadjusted trial balance with an adjusted trial balance. What is the basic purpose of each?

8. What is the basic purpose of the worksheet?

9. Why are adjusting entries entered on the worksheet?

10. Why are adjusting entries recorded in the journal and posted to the ledger even though they are entered on the worksheet?

11. What are the purposes of closing entries? Why are they recorded in the journal and posted to the ledger?

12. Distinguish among (a) permanent, (b) temporary, (c) real, and (d) nominal accounts.

13. Explain why the income statement accounts are closed but the balance sheet accounts are not.

14. What is a post-closing trial balance? Is it a useful part of the accounting information processing cycle? Explain.

15. What are reversing entries? When are reversing entries useful? Give one example of an adjusting entry that (a) should be reversed and (b) another one that should not be reversed (based on Supplement 5A).

16. Businesses in many industries have significant fluctuations in the amount of sales that are made during the months or quarters that make up their fiscal year. If prepaid insurance is assigned to expense in the period representing the expiry of the insurance

policy because of the need to match expenses with revenue, how can this practice be justified when revenue is fluctuating significantly for each interim period? If prepaid insurance is felt to be insignificant, what about straight-line depreciation?

17. How should a business decide on whether to use manual, mechanical, or electronic data processing?

EXERCISES

E5–1. Small Company prepared the unadjusted trial balance given below at the end of the accounting year, December 31, 19B. To simplify the case, the amounts given are in thousands of dollars.

Account title	Debit	Credit
Cash	$ 19	
Accounts receivable.........................	22	
Prepaid insurance	3	
Machinery (10-year life, no residual value)	30	
Accumulated depreciation, machinery		$ 3
Accounts payable...........................		2
Wages payable		
Income tax payable		
Capital stock, nopar (1,000 shares)		40
Retained earnings		5
Dividends declared and paid during 19B........	2	
Revenues (not detailed)		56
Expenses (not detailed).......................	30	
Totals	$106	$106

Other data not yet recorded at December 31, 19B:
1. Insurance expired during 19B, $1.
2. Depreciation expense for 19B, $3.
3. Wages payable, $2.
4. Income tax rate, 30 percent.

Required:

(Note: A worksheet may be used but is not required.)
a. Complete the income statement and balance sheet given below for 19B.
b. Give the adjusting entries for 19B.
c. Give the closing entries for 19B.

Income Statement, 19B

Revenues (not detailed)......	$_____
Expenses (not detailed)	_____
Pretax income..............	_____
Income tax expense..........	_____
Net income	$_____
EPS	$_____

Balance Sheet, 19B

Assets		Liabilities	
Cash	$ _____	Accounts payable	$ _____
Accounts receivable	_____	Wages payable	_____
Prepaid insurance	_____	Income tax payable	_____
Machinery	_____	**Owners' Equity**	
Accumulated depreciation	_____	Capital stock	_____
		Retained earnings	_____
Total	$ _____	Total	$ _____

E5–2. Assume that the worksheet at December 31, 19B, for Boise Realty Corporation has been completed through "Adjusted Trial Balance" and you are ready to extend each amount to the several columns to the right. The columns that will be used are listed below with code letters:

Code	Columns
A	Income Statement, debit
B	Income Statement, credit
C	Retained Earnings, debit
D	Retained Earnings, credit
E	Balance Sheet, debit
F	Balance Sheet, credit

Below are listed representative accounts to be extended on the worksheet. You are to give, for each account, the code letter that indicates the proper worksheet column to the right of "Adjusted Trial Balance" to which the amount in each account should be extended. Assume normal debit and credit balances.

Account titles	Code
1. Cash	
2. Inventory of office supplies	
3. Interest payable	
4. Capital stock	
5. Commissions earned	
6. Rent revenue collected in advance	
7. Salary expense	
8. Sales return	
9. Retained earnings, beginning balance (a credit)	
10. Building	
11. Mortgage payable	
12. Income tax payable	
13. Sales commissions receivable	
14. Accumulated depreciation on building	
15. Contributed surplus	
16. Dividends declared and paid	
17. Income tax expense	
18. Prepaid insurance	
19. Net income amount (indicate both the debit and credit on the worksheet)	
20. Net loss amount (indicate both the debit and credit on the worksheet)	
21. Retained earnings, ending balance amount (indicate both the debit and credit on the worksheet)	

E5–3.   Miller Company is completing the annual accounting information processing cycle at December 31, 19B. The worksheet, as shown below, has been started (to simplify, amounts given are in thousands of dollars).

Account No.	Account	Unadjusted trial balance	
		Debit	Credit
101	Cash...................................	$ 20	$
102	Accounts receivable	38	
103	Inventory	22	
104	Prepaid insurance......................	3	
110	Equipment (10-year life, no residual value)	70	
111	Accumulated depreciation, equipment		7
119	Accounts payable		11
120	Wages payable		
121	Income tax payable		
122	Revenue collected in advance		
123	Note payable, long term (10% each December 31)........................		20
130	Capital stock, par $10		60
131	Contributed surplus.....................		10
140	Retained earnings.......................		15
141	Dividends declared and paid.............	8	
145	Revenues		99
146	Expenses..............................	61	
147	Income tax expense		
	Totals.........................	$222	$222

Data not yet recorded for 19B:

a.   Insurance expense, $1.
b.   Depreciation expense, $7.
c.   Wages earned by employees not yet paid, $2.
d.   Revenue collected by Miller not yet earned, $3.
e.   Income tax rate, 20 percent. (Note: No accrued interest is recorded because interest is paid on each December 31.)

Required:

Complete the worksheet in every respect (you may use account numbers instead of account titles). Set up additional column headings for Adjusting Entries, Adjusted Trial Balance, Income Statement, Retained Earnings, and Balance Sheet. Record all revenues and expenses (except income tax) in the two accounts given (145 and 146).

E5–4. West Corporation, a small company, is completing the annual accounting information processing cycle at December 31, 19B. The worksheet has been started as reflected below.

Account Titles	Unadjusted Trial Balance	
	Debit	Credit
Cash	$ 17,000	
Accounts receivable	15,000	
Equipment	20,000	
Accumulated depreciation		$ 6,000
Other assets	54,500	
Accounts payable		9,000
Long-term note payable		15,000
Capital stock, par $10		30,000
Contributed surplus		1,500
Retained earnings		15,000
Revenues		80,000
Expenses	50,000	
	$156,500	$156,500
Income tax expense		
Income tax payable		
Net income		

Data not yet recorded for 19B:

a. Depreciation expense, $2,000.
b. Income tax rate, 30 percent.

Required:

Complete the worksheet in all respects. Set up additional column headings, for Adjusting Entries, Adjusted Trial Balance, Income Statement, Retained Earnings, and Balance Sheet.

E5–5. Moline Service Company is in the process of completing the information processing cycle at the end of the fiscal year, December 31, 19B. The worksheet and financial statements have been prepared, and the next step is to journalize the adjusting entries. The two trial balances given below were taken directly from the completed worksheet.

		December 31, 19B			
Account Titles		Unadjusted Trial Balance		Adjusted Trial Balance	
		Debit	Credit	Debit	Credit
a.	Cash	$ 8,000		$ 8,000	
b.	Accounts receivable			700	
c.	Prepaid insurance	300		250	
d.	Equipment	120,200		120,200	
e.	Accumulated depreciation, equipment		$ 21,500		$ 25,500
f.	Income tax payable				4,000
g.	Capital stock, par $10		50,000		50,000
h.	Retained earnings, January 1, 19B		14,000		14,000
i.	Service revenues		60,000		60,700
j.	Salary expense	17,000		17,000	
k.	Depreciation expense			4,000	
l.	Insurance expense			50	
m.	Income tax expense			4,000	
		$145,500	$145,500	$154,200	$154,200

Required:

By examining the amounts in each trial balance, reconstruct the four adjusting entries that were made between the unadjusted trial balance and the adjusted trial balance. Give a brief explanation of each adjusting entry.

E5–6. The accountant for Rocky Corporation has just completed the following worksheet for the year ended December 31, 19D (note the shortcuts used by the accountant to reduce the number of vertical columns on the worksheet):

Account Titles	Unadjusted Trial Balance (credits)	Adjusting Entries Debit	Adjusting Entries Credit	Income Statement (credits)	Balance Sheet (credits)
Cash	15,000				15,000
Prepaid insurance	300		100		200
Accounts receivable	20,000				20,000
Machinery	80,000				80,000
Accumulated depreciation	(24,000)		8,000		(32,000)
Other assets	13,700				13,700
Accounts payable	(7,000)				(7,000)
Rent collected in advance			200		(200)
Interest payable			450		(450)
Income tax payable			3,375		(3.375)
Notes payable, long term	(10,000)				(10,000)
Capital stock, par $10	(50,000)				(50,000)
Retained earnings	(18,000)				(18,000)
Revenues	(80,000)	200		(79,800)	
Expenses (not detailed)	60,000	100		60,100	
Depreciation expense		8,000		8,000	
Interest expense		450		450	
Income tax expense		3,375		3,375	
Net income				7,875	(7,875)
Totals	–0–	12,125	12,125	–0–	–0–

Required:

a. Prepare the adjusting entries in journal form required on December 31, 19D. Write a brief explanation with each entry.
b. Prepare the closing entries at December 31, 19D.

E5–7. For each of the 10 independent situations, give the journal entry by entering the appropriate code(s) and amounts.

Code	Account	Code	Account
A	Cash	K	Interest revenue
B	Office supplies inventory	L	Wage expense
C	Revenue receivable	M	Depreciation expense
D	Office equipment	N	Interest expense
E	Accumulated depreciation	O	Supplies expense
F	Note payable	P	Capital stock
G	Wages payable	Q	Retained earnings
H	Interest payable	R	Dividends declared and paid
I	Rent revenue collected in advance	S	Income summary
J	Service revenues	X	None of the above

Independent Situations	Debit		Credit	
	Code	Amount	Code	Amount
a. Accrued wages, unrecorded and unpaid at year-end, $400.				
b. Service revenue collected and recorded as revenue, but not yet earned, $700.				
c. Dividends declared and paid during year and debited to Dividends account, $900. Give entry at year-end.				
d. Depreciation expense for year not yet recorded, $650.				
e. Balance at year-end in Service Revenue account, $59,000. Give entry at year-end.				
f. Service revenue earned but not yet collected at year-end, $300.				
g. Balance at year-end in Interest Revenue account, $360. Give entry at year-end.				
h. Office Supplies Inventory account at year-end, $550; inventory of supplies on hand at year-end, $100.				
i. At year-end interest on note payable not yet recorded or paid, $180.				
j. Balance at year-end in Income Summary account after all revenue and expense accounts have been closed, $9,900 (credit).				

E5–8. (Based on the Supplement 5A) Dover Company has completed the accounting information processing cycle for the year ended December 31, 19A. Reversing entries are under consideration (for January 1, 19B) for two different adjusting entries (of December 31, 19A). For case purposes, the relevant data are given in T-accounts, viz:

Prepaid Insurance

1/1/19A Balance	600	(a) 12/31/19A Adj. entry	400

Insurance Expense

(a) 12/31/19A Adj. entry	400	(c) 12/31/19A Closing entry	400

Accrued Wages Payable

		(b) 12/31/19A Adj. entry	1,000

Wage Expense

| Paid during 19A | 18,000 | (d) 12/31/19A Closing entry 19,000 |
| (b) 12/31/19A Adj. entry | 1,000 | |

Income Summary

12/31/19A Closing entries		12/31/19A	
(c)	400	Closed to Retained	
(d)	19,000	Earnings	19,400

Required:

Would a reversing entry on January 1, 19B, facilitate the next related entry for (a) Prepaid Insurance and (b) Accrued Wages Payable? Explain why.

PROBLEMS/CASES

PC5–1. Rye Company was very careless about its financial records during its first year of operations, 19A. It is December 31, 19A, end of the accounting period. An outside CGA examined the records and discovered numerous errors. Five of those errors are described in the tabulation below. Assume each error is independent of the others. Analyze each error and indicate its effect on 19A and 19B income, assets, and liabilities *if not corrected*. Use these codes to indicate the effect of each dollar amount: O = overstated; U = understated, and N = no effect. Write an explanation of your analysis of each transaction to support your response. The first error is used as an example.

| Independent Errors | Effect on | | | | | |
| | Pretax Income | | Assets | | Liabilities | |
	19A	19B	19A	19B	19A	19B
a. Depreciation expense for 19A, not recorded in 19A, $800.	O−800	N	O−800	O−800	N	N
b. Wages earned by employees during 19A, not recorded or paid in 19A, but will be paid in 19B, $600.						
c. Revenue earned during 19A, but not collected or recorded until 19B, $400.						
d. Amount paid in 19A and recorded as expense in 19A, but not an expense until 19B, $700.						
e. Revenue collected in 19A and recorded as revenue in 19A, but not earned until 19B, $500.						
f. Sale of services and cash collected in 19A. Recorded as a debit to Cash and as a credit to Accounts Receivable, $900.						

Explanation of analysis of errors if not corrected:

a. Failure to record depreciation in 19A caused depreciation expense to be too low; hence, income was overstated by $800. Also, accumulated depreciation is too low by $800, which causes assets to be overstated by $800 until the error is corrected.

PC5–2. General Services Company, Inc., a small service company, maintains its records without the help of an accountant. After considerable effort, an outside accountant prepared the following trial balance as of the end of the annual accounting period, December 31, 19C:

Account titles	Debit	Credit
Cash	$ 24,900	
Accounts receivable.............................	33,000	
Service supplies inventory.......................	500	
Prepaid insurance	600	
Service trucks (5-year life, no residual value)	20,000	
Accumulated depreciation, service trucks		$ 8,000
Other assets....................................	10,000	
Accounts payable...............................		1,000
Wages payable		
Income tax payable		
Note payable (3 years, 10% each December 31)......		10,000
Capital stock, par $10...........................		30,000
Contributed surplus		3,000
Retained earnings		8,000
Dividends declared and paid	1,000	
Service revenues................................		70,000
Expenses (not detailed)*........................	40,000	
Income tax expense.............................		
	$130,000	$130,000

*Excludes income tax expense.

Data not yet recorded at December 31, 19C:
1. The supplies inventory count on December 31, 19C, reflected $200.
2. Insurance expired during 19C, $200.
3. Depreciation expense for 19C, $4,000.
4. Wages earned by employees not yet paid on December 31, 19C, $500.
5. Income tax rate, 20 percent.

Required:

Note: A worksheet may be used but is not required.

a. You have been asked to complete the statements given below (show computations) for 19C.
b. Give the 19C adjusting entries.
c. Give the 19C closing entries.

Income Statement, 19C

Service revenues		$_____
Expenses (not detailed)	$_____	
Supplies expense.	_____	
Insurance expense	_____	
Depreciation expense.	_____	
Wage expense	_____	
Total expenses		_____
Pretax income		_____
Income tax expense		_____
Net income.		$_____
EPS.		$_____

Balance Sheet, 19C

Assets		Liabilities	
Cash	$_____	Accounts payable.	$_____
Accounts receivable.	_____	Wages payable	_____
Service supplies inventory.	_____	Income tax payable	_____
Prepaid insurance	_____	Note payable, long term.	_____
Service trucks	_____	Total liabilities.	_____
Accumulated depreciation, trucks	_____		
Other assets.	_____	**Shareholders' Equity**	
		Capital stock, par $10	_____
		Contributed surplus	_____
		Retained earnings	_____
		Total shareholders' equity	_____
		Total liabilities and shareholders'	
Total assets	$_____	equity	$_____

PC5–3. Delta Company was organized on January 1, 19A. At the end of the first year of operations, December 31, 19A, the bookkeeper prepared the following two trial balances (amounts in thousands of dollars):

Account titles	Unadjusted trial balance Debit	Unadjusted trial balance Credit	Adjusted trial balance Debit	Adjusted trial balance Credit
Cash.	$ 30	$	$ 30	$
Accounts receivable	25		25	
Prepaid insurance	3		2	
Rent receivable			1	
Operational assets.	48		48	
Accumulated depreciation, operational assets				6
Other assets	4		4	
Accounts payable		11		11
Wages payable.				2
Income tax payable.				2
Rent revenue collected in advance				3
Note payable, 10% (dated January 1, 19A).		30		30
Capital stock, par $10 per share		50		50
Retained earnings				
Dividends declared and paid	2		2	
Revenues (total).		92		90
Expenses (total including interest)	71		80	
Income tax expense			2	
Totals.	$183	$183	$194	$194

Required:

Note: A worksheet may be completed, but is not required.

a. Based upon inspection of the two trial balances, give the 19A adjusting entries developed by the bookkeeper (provide brief explanations).
b. Based upon the above data, give the 19A closing entries with brief explanations.
c. Respond to the following questions (show computations):
   (1) How many shares were outstanding at year-end?
   (2) What was the estimated useful life of the operational assets assuming no residual value?
   (3) What was the amount of interest expense that was included in the total expenses?
   (4) What was the balance of Retained Earnings on December 31, 19A?
   (5) What was the average income tax rate?
   (6) How would the two accounts (a) Rent Receivable and (b) Rent Revenue Collected in Advance be reported on the balance sheet?
   (7) In general, explain why cash increased by $30,000 during the year despite the fact that net income was very low comparatively.
   (8) What was the amount of EPS for 19A?
   (9) What was the selling price of the shares?
   (10) When was the insurance premium paid and over what period of time did the coverage extend?

PC5–4. The ledger accounts of Home Service Company at the end of the second year of operations, December 31, 19B (prior to the closing entries), were as shown below. The 19B adjusting entries are identified by letters, and account numbers are given to the right of the account name.

Cash   101
Bal. 20,000

Inventory, Maintenance Supplies   102
Bal. 500 | (a) 400

Service Equipment   103
Jan. 1, 19A 90,000

Accumulated Depreciation, Service Equipment   104
Bal. 18,000 / (d) 18,000

Note payable, 10 Percent   201
Jan. 3, 19B 10,000

Wages Payable   202
(e) 600

Interest Payable   203
(b) 1,000

Revenue Collected in Advance   204
(c) 7,000

Capital Stock, Par $10   301
Bal. 50,000

Cont. Surplus   302
Bal. 6,000

Retained Earnings   303
Bal. 9,000

Service Revenues   304
(c) 7,000 | Bal. 220,000

Remaining Assets	105		Income Tax Payable	205		Expenses	305
Bal	42,500		(f)	6,600	Bal	160,000	
					(a)	400	
					(b)	1,000	
					(d)	18,000	
					(e)	600	
					(f)	6,600	

Required:

a. Develop three 19B trial balances of Home Service Company using the following format:

Account No.	Unadjusted Trial Balance		Adjusted Trial Balance		Post-Closing Trial Balance	
	Debit	Credit	Debit	Credit	Debit	Credit
101						

b. Write an explanation of each adjusting entry for 19B.

c. Give the closing journal entries (do not use Income Summary).

d. What was the apparent useful life of the service equipment? What assumptions must you make to answer this question?

e. What was the average income tax rate for 19B?

f. What was the issue (sale) price per share of the capital stock?

PC5–5. Stimson Corporation has partially completed the following worksheet for the year ended December 31, 19E:

Account Titles	Unadjusted Trial Balance		Adjusting Entries	
	Debit	Credit	Debit	Credit
Cash	18,770			
Accounts receivable	25,680			
Supplies inventory	180			(a) 110
Interest receivable			(b) 300	
Long-term note receivable, 10%	6,000			
Equipment	75,000			
Accumulated depreciation		30,000		(c) 7,500
Accounts payable		11,000		
Short-term notes payable, 12%		8,000		
Interest payable				(d) 320
Income tax payable				(e) 4,000
Capital stock, par $10		40,000		
Contributed surplus		2,000		
Retained earnings		7,000		
Service revenue		67,680		
Interest revenue				(b) 300
Expenses (not detailed)	40,050		(a) 110	
Depreciation expense			(c) 7,500	
Interest expense			(d) 320	
Income tax expense			(e) 4,000	
Totals	165,680	165,680	12,230	12,230

Required:

a. Add additional columns for Adjusted Trial Balance, Income Statement, Retained Earnings, and Balance Sheet; and complete the worksheet.

b. Give the 19E closing entries.

c. Explain why the adjusting and closing entries must be journalized and posted.

PC5–6. Ontario Corporation is completing the accounting information processing cycle for the year ended December 31, 19C. The unadjusted trial balance, taken from the ledger, was as follows:

Account No.	Account titles	Unadjusted trial balance Debit	Credit
101	Cash.......................................	$ 43,550	
103	Accounts receivable (net)	17,000	
105	Prepaid insurance	450	
107	Interest receivable..........................		
120	Long-term note receivable, 12%	6,000	
150	Equipment	90,000	
151	Accumulated depreciation		$ 20,000
170	Other assets	30,000	
201	Accounts payable		14,000
203	Wages payable..............................		
205	Interest payable.............................		
210	Long-term note payable, 15%		10,000
300	Capital stock, par $10.......................		80,000
301	Contributed surplus.........................		12,000
310	Retained earnings...........................		24,000
311	Dividends declared and paid during 19C......	8,000	
320	Service revenue.............................		150,000
322	Interest revenue		
350	Expenses (not detailed)*	115,000	
351	Depreciation expense........................		
360	Interest expense		
207	Income tax payable.........................		
		$310,000	$310,000

*Includes wage expense and insurance expense.

Additional data for adjusting entries:

a. Expired insurance during 19C was $150.

b. Interest on the long-term note receivable (dated September 1, 19C) is collected annually each August 31.

c. The equipment was acquired on January 1, 19A (assume no estimated residual value).

d. At December 31, 19C, wages earned but not yet paid or recorded, amounted to $3,000.

e. Interest on the long-term note payable (dated May 1, 19C) is paid annually each April 30.

f. Assume a 20 percent average income tax rate.

Required:

a. Complete a worksheet for the year ended December 31, 19C. Key the adjusting entries with letters. (Hint: Net income is $16,872.)

b. Prepare a single-step income statement, a statement of retained earnings, and an unclassified balance sheet.

c. Write a brief explanation of each adjusting entry reflected on the worksheet.

d. Give the closing entries in journal form. Explain why they must be journalized and posted to the ledger.

PC5–7. (Note: This is an extended case selected to review Chapters 2, 3, 4, and 5.) W&P Moving and Storage Service, Incorporated, has been in operation for several years. Revenues have increased gradually from both the moving and storage services. The **annual** financial statements prepared in the past have not conformed to GAAP. The newly employed president decided that starting at the end of 1984, accurate and complete balance sheet, income and cash-flow statements would be prepared. The first step was to employ a full-time bookkeeper and engage a local public accounting firm for assistance. It is now December 31, 1984, the end of the current fiscal year. The bookkeeper has developed a trial balance. A member of the staff of the public accounting firm will advise and assist the bookkeeper in completing the accounting information processing cycle for the first time. The unadjusted trial balance at December 31, 1984, is shown below.

Unadjusted Trial Balance, December 31, 1984

Debits		Credits	
Cash	$ 25,880	Accumulated depreciation	$ 18,000
Accounts receivable..............	2,030	Accounts payable................	6,000
Office supplies inventory.........	150	Wages payable	
Prepaid insurance	600	Interest payable	
Land for future building		Revenue collected in	
site.........................	6,000	advance	
Equipment.....................	68,000	Income tax payable	
Remaining assets (not		Note payable (12%)..............	30,000
detailed)......................	27,000	Capital stock, par $10	20,000
Salary expense	74,000	Retained earnings,	
Advertising expense	1,000	January 1, 1984..............	21,600
Utilities expense.................	1,270	Hauling revenue.................	106,400
Maintenance expense	6,500	Storage revenue	14,000
Miscellaneous	570		
Insurance expense...............			
Wage expense...................			
Depreciation expense			
Interest expense.................			
Income tax expense.............			
Dividends declared and			
paid.........................	3,000		
	$216,000		$216,000

Examination of the records and related documents provided the following additional information that should be considered for adjusting entries:

a. A physical count of office supplies inventory at December 31, 1984, reflected $40 on hand. Office supplies used are considered to be a miscellaneous expense. No office supplies were purchased during the year.

b. On July 1, 1984, a two-year insurance premium was paid amounting to $600.

c. The equipment cost $68,000 when acquired. It is estimated to have a 10-year useful life to the company and an $8,000 residual value.

d. Unpaid and unrecorded wages earned by employees at December 31, 1984, amounted to $1,200.

e. The $30,000 note payable was signed on October 1, 1984, for a 12 percent bank loan, principal and interest are due at the end of 12 months from that date.

f. Storage revenue collected and recorded as earned before December 31, 1984, included $400 collected in advance from one customer for storage time in 1985. (Hint: Reduce storage revenue.)

g. Gasoline, oil, and fuel purchased for the vehicles and used during the last two weeks of December 1984 amounting to $300 have not been paid for nor recorded (this is considered maintenance expense).

h. The average income tax rate is 20 percent which produces income tax expense of $5,600.

Required:

a. Enter the unadjusted trial balance on a ~~worksheet~~; then, based on the above data, enter the adjusting entries. Complete the worksheet. (Hint: The adjusted trial balance total is $230,000.)

b. Using the worksheet, prepare a single-step income statement, statement of retained earnings, and balance sheet. (Hint: The balance sheet total is $105,400.)

c. Using the worksheet, prepare the 1984 adjusting entries in journal form.

d. Using the worksheet, prepare 1984 closing entries in journal form.

PC5–8. (Note: This is an extended case selected to review Chapters 2, 3, 4, and 5.) Charter Air Service, Incorporated, was organized to operate a charter service in a city of approximately 350,000 population. The 10 organizers were issued 7,500 shares of $10 par-value stock for a total of $75,000 cash. To obtain facilities to operate the charter services, the company rents from the city hangar and office space at the city airport for a flat monthly rental. The business has prospered because of the excellent service and the high level of maintenance on the planes. It is now December 31, 1984, end of the annual accounting period, and the accounting information processing cycle is in the final phase. Following are representative accounts and unadjusted amounts selected from the ledger at December 31, 1984, for case purposes:

Unadjusted Trial Balance, December 31, 1984

Debits		*Credits*	
Cash	$ 24,600	Accumulated depreciation,	
Prepaid insurance	6,000	aircraft	$ 60,000
Maintenance parts inventory	18,000	Notes payable, 12%	100,000
Aircraft	260,000	Capital stock, par $10	75,000
Salary expense	90,000	Retained earnings, January	
Maintenance expense	24,000	1, 1984	20,600
Fuel expense	63,000	Charter revenue	262,400
Advertising expense	2,000		
Utilities expense	1,400		
Rent expense	14,000		
Dividends declared and			
paid	15,000		
	$518,000		$518,000

For the adjusting entries, the following additional data were developed from the records and supporting documents:

a. On January 1, 1984, the company paid a three-year insurance premium amounting to $6,000.

b. The aircraft, when purchased on January 1, 1981, cost $260,000; and the estimated useful life to the company is approximately 10 years. The equipment has an estimated residual value of $60,000.

c. On July 1, 1984, the company borrowed $100,000 from the bank on a five-year, 12 percent loan. Interest is payable annually starting on June 30, 1985.

d. Charter revenue, on occasion, is collected in advance. On December 31, 1984, collections in advance amounted to $1,000; when collected, this amount was recorded as Charter Revenue.

e. Rent amounting to $14,000 on hangar and office space was paid during the year and recorded as Rent Expense. This included rent paid in advance amounting to $2,000 for January and February 1985. The total amount was recorded as Rent Expense in 1984.

f.   The inventory of maintenance parts at December 31, 1984, showed $7,000. All parts purchased are debited to Maintenance Parts Inventory when purchased.

g.   For case purposes, assume an average income tax rate of 20 percent which results in income tax expense of $6,000.

Required:

a.   Enter the above accounts and unadjusted balances from the ledger on a worksheet. (The following accounts should be added at the bottom of the worksheet because they will be needed for the adjusting entries: Insurance Expense, Depreciation Expense, Interest Expense, Interest Payable, Revenue Collected in Advance, Prepaid Rent Expense, Income Tax Expense, and Income Tax Payable.)

b.   Based on the additional data given above, enter the 1984 adjusting entries on the worksheet.

c.   Complete the worksheet. (Hint: The adjusted trial balance total is $550,000.)

d.   Based on the worksheet, prepare a single-step income statement, a statement of retained earnings, and a classified balance sheet. (Hint: The total on the balance sheet is $217,600.)

e.   Journalize the 1984 adjusting entries.

f.   Journalize the 1984 closing entries.

PC5–9.   (Based on the Supplement 5A) Alvin Corporation has completed all information processing including the annual financial statements at December 31, 19D. The adjusting entries recorded at that date were as follows:

a.	Insurance expense	150	
	Prepaid insurance		150
b.	Interest receivable..	200	
	Interest revenue		200
c.	Supplies expense..	80	
	Supplies inventory		80
d.	Depreciation expense...	2,000	
	Accumulated depreciation		2,000
e.	Wage expense	500	
	Wages payable...		500
f.	Interest expense	300	
	Interest payable...		300
g.	Income tax expense	4,000	
	Income tax payable..		4,000

Required:

For each of the above adjusting entries indicate whether it usually would be reversed. Give the reversing entry in each instance (if none, so state) and explain the basis for your response.

PC5–10. Refer to the financial statements of Consolidated-Bathurst given immediately preceding the Index. Respond to the following for the 1984 annual accounting year, which ended on December 31, 1984.

1. Below are ten T-accounts; each account has the abbreviation "Bal." for balance. You are to (a) enter the correct balance, and (b) diagram all of the closing entries (and show the transferred amounts).

Total Expenses (total costs and expenses)		Net Sales	
Bal.			Bal.

Minority Interest		Other Income and Equity Earnings	
Bal.			Bal.

Income Tax Expense (provision for taxes on income)		Income Summary	
Bal.			Bal.

Extraordinary Charge		Retained Earnings	
Bal.			Bal.

Dividends		Excess Cost of Purchasing Common Shares over Stated Values	
Bal.		Bal.	

2. Journalize each of the closing entries and provide an explanation of the purpose of each one.
3. From among the above accounts, list the accounts and their balances that would appear on a post-closing trial balance.
4. From among the above accounts, list the accounts and their balances that would be reported on the 1984 balance sheet.
5. Were there any income tax effects not included in the income tax expense amount that you entered above? Explain.

PC5–11. Ace Taxi Ltd. owns and operates a fleet of 50 automobiles. All expenses are charged to the company. After every shift, each driver records the expenses incurred for gas and oil, tires or repairs and the unit number of the automobile. Not all of the 50 autos in the fleet need necessarily be used during one shift. This expense report is turned in by the driver together with an account of the kilometers travelled.

Management wants a daily report in unit sequence that will provide the following information:

Unit number	Gas oil	Tires	Repairs	Kilometers	Cost per 100 km.
xxx	xxx.xx	xx.xx	xx.xx	xxxx	xx.xx

It is suggested that the unit number be used as a subscript for the array of data. The following is a flowchart for the report where 999 is used as a unit number to signify the end of the array of data.

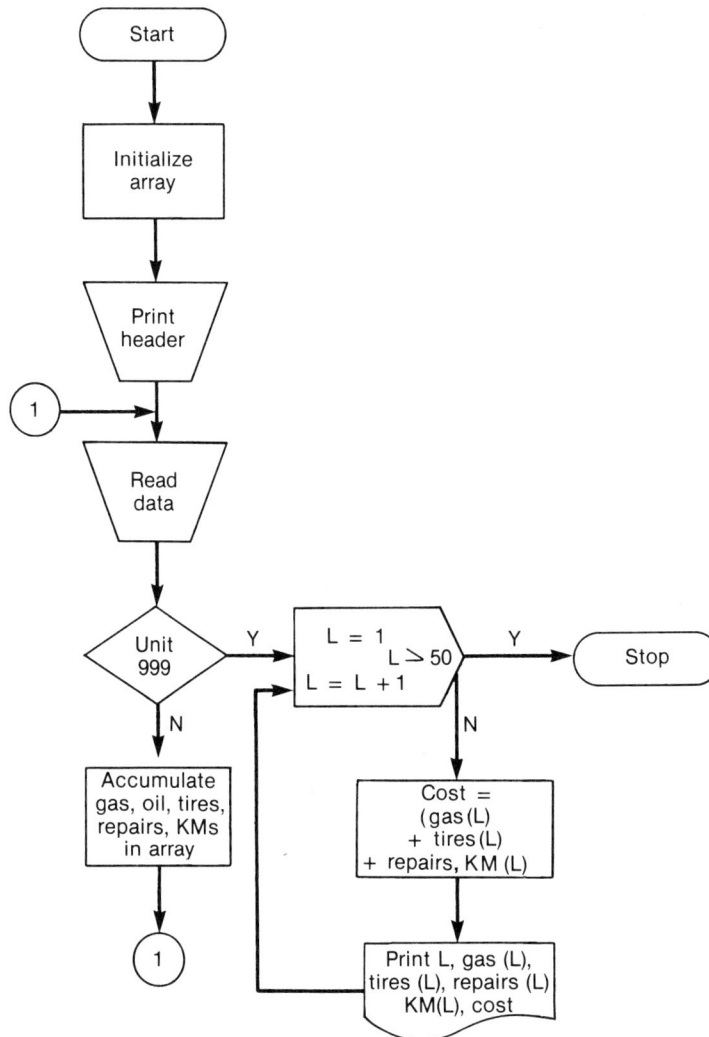

Required:

Write a computer program to produce the report.

(SMAC Adapted)

PC5–12.   The Lemon Company operates a used car lot in a medium-sized city. They have up to 200 cars at any time, and the published selling price is 20 percent greater than the price Lemon paid for the car.

It costs the company $5 per day to keep a car on the lot.

Salesmen are authorized to sell any car on the lot at the minimum selling price which is the original cost, plus one half of the markup, plus storage costs.

The owner wishes to know the minimum amount of profit on each car and therefore wants a daily report in unit number sequence that will provide the following information:

Unit number.
Original cost of the car.
Number of days the car has been on the lot.
Published selling price.
Minimum selling price.
Profit on each car if it were sold for the minimum selling price.

For each car on the lot, an input record is prepared daily and contains the following:

Unit number	3 digits
Original cost	5 digits (dollars only)
Number of days the car has been on the lot	3 digits

This input is not in any sequence, and a unit number of 999 signals end of data.

Required:

Write a program to produce the report. Headings are required. Variable names are to be identified through the use of REM statements.

(SMAC Adapted)

PC5–13.   Using any standard computer spreadsheet program prepare Parts A and B of PC5–7. (Hint: use only the columns after the account titles with numbers in them from Exhibit 5–2 and construct the statements on the bottom of the spreadsheet.)

6

Accounting for Sales Revenue and Cost of Goods Sold

PURPOSE OF THIS CHAPTER

The purchasing and selling functions are important activities for most businesses involved in retail, wholesale, or manufacturing operations. Retail and wholesale merchandising businesses devote much of their energies to buying and selling goods. Practically all manufacturing businesses also devote significant efforts and resources to purchasing and selling activities. Usually, a manufacturing business purchases raw materials for conversion into finished products, which then are sold. It is not uncommon for a service business also to be involved in purchasing and selling activities. Because of the importance of the purchasing and selling functions, decision makers who use financial statements devote considerable attention to analysis of the marketing successes and failures of a business.

Our discussions in the preceding chapters relating to the measurement of assets, liabilities, income, and cash flows usually were limited to service businesses, but those discussions are as appropriate for merchandising and manufacturing companies as for service businesses. Recall that Business Aids, Inc., was a service business (Exhibit 1–4). However, Diamond, Inc. (Exhibit 2–1) was a merchandising business.

Two distinguishing features on the income statements of retail, wholesale, and manufacturing businesses (as opposed to service businesses) are (1) sales revenue and (2) cost of goods sold.[1] For example, Diamond's income statement (Exhibit 2–1) reported cost of goods sold of $2,416,000 (which was 67 percent of net sales revenue).

This chapter will discuss and illustrate the measuring, recording, and reporting of sales revenue and cost of goods sold for retail, wholesale, and manufacturing businesses as follows:

Part A—Accounting for sales revenue (including credit sales and bad debts)

Part B—Accounting for cost of goods sold (including accounting for inventories)

---

[1]Similar titles sometimes used are "cost of sales" and "cost of products sold." Regardless of the title, it is an expense.

This chapter also includes the following supplements:

Supplement 6A—Data processing; control accounts and subsidiary ledgers

Supplement 6B—Aging accounts receivable

Aside from these two directly related problems, this chapter will not consider other manufacturing activities. That topic is discussed in management accounting.

Part A—Accounting for Sales Revenue

Accounting for sales revenue requires careful measurement of the economic effects of each sale of goods in accordance with the revenue principle (Exhibit 2–6). Sales may be for cash or on credit and also may involve the trade-in of noncash assets. Determination of the correct amount of sales revenue to be recorded and the appropriate period in which sales revenue should be recognized sometimes poses special problems. The **revenue principle** holds that sales revenue is (a) measured as the **market value** of the considerations received, or the market value of the item sold, whichever is the more clearly determinable; and (b) usually revenue is recognized in the accounting period when ownership of the goods passes from the seller to the buyer. Problems in implementing this principle will be discussed and illustrated in this part of the chapter.

For illustrative purposes, the income statement for Campus Corner, Inc. (Exhibit 6–1) will be used to emphasize the selling and purchasing activities of a small business.[2]

In Exhibit 6–1 observe that cost of goods sold (an expense) is set out separately from the remaining expenses which makes it possible to report a step difference called **gross margin on sales**.[3] This difference between net sales revenue and cost of goods sold reflects the total amount of **markup** on all goods sold during the period. It is expressed in dollars on the income statement ($40,000) and often is reported as the gross margin ratio (Gross margin on sales, $40,000 ÷ Net sales revenue, $100,000 = .40, or 40 percent). For Campus Corner, it can be said that (a) for each $1 of net sales the average gross margin was $0.40, or (b) the average markup maintained on sales was 40 percent of sales.[4]

---

[2] In this chapter, to simplify the illustrations, we ordinarily shall not show the detailed operating expenses. In the single step format for the income statement, revenues would be reported under a major caption "Revenues." However, all expenses, including cost of goods sold, would be reported under a major caption "Expenses." Therefore, in the single step format, gross margin on sales is not reported.

[3] This often is called gross profit on sales or simply gross margin or gross profit. The term *profit*, whether net or gross, has fallen into disfavour.

[4] This percent is based on sales revenue rather than cost. The markup percent on cost would be $40,000 ÷ $60,000 = 66⅔ percent.

EXHIBIT 6–1
Income statement

		Amount	Percentage analysis
CAMPUS CORNER, INC			
Income Statement (multiple-step format)			
For the Year Ended December 31, 19F			
Gross sales		$108,333	
Less: Sales returns and allowances		8,333	
Net sales revenue		100,000	100
Cost of goods sold		60,000	60
Gross margin on sales		40,000	40
Operating expenses:			
Selling expenses (detailed)	$15,000		
Administrative expenses (detailed)	10,000	25,000	25
Pretax income		15,000	15
Income tax expense		3,000	3
Net income		$ 12,000	12
EPS ($12,000 ÷ 10,000 shares)		$1.20	

RECORDING SALES REVENUE

When ownership of goods passes from the seller to the buyer, the seller must record revenue for the sale transaction. Under the revenue principle, the sales price (net of any discounts) is the measure of the amount of revenue realized. If the sale is for cash, the amount of revenue to be recorded simply is the amount of cash that was received. If the sale is on credit, the revenue is the **cash equivalent** of the assets to be received **excluding** any financing charges (i.e., interest). If the sale is for noncash items (such as the sale of goods for other goods), the amount of revenue to recognize is the cash equivalent of the goods received or given up, whichever is the more clearly determinable. Thus, under the revenue principle, Campus Corner would recognize a sale in 19F (i.e., when ownership passes) as follows:

a. Cash sales for the day per the cash register tapes:

Jan. 2	Cash	2,000	
	Sales revenue		2,000

b. Credit sales for the day per all charge tickets:

Jan. 2	Accounts receivable	1,000	
	Sales revenue		1,000

Alternatively, if it is desired to maintain a **separate sales revenue** account in the ledger for the sales of each department, the two entries above could be as follows:[5]

Jan. 2	Cash....................................	2,000	
	Accounts receivable	1,000	
	Sales, Department 1..................		1,000
	Sales, Department 2..................		1,500
	Sales, Department 3..................		500

Credit sales and sales discounts

A substantial portion of the sales made by many businesses is on credit. When merchandise is sold on credit, the terms of payment should be definite so there will be no misunderstanding as to the amounts and due dates. In fact, credit terms usually are printed on each credit document. Frequently, credit terms are abbreviated by symbols such as, "n/10, EOM," which means the net amount (i.e., the sales amount less any sales returns) is due not later than 10 days after the end of the month (EOM) in which the sale was made. In other cases, the terms may be "n/30," which means that the net amount is due 30 days after the date of the invoice (i.e., after date of sale). In still other cases, **sales discounts** (often called cash discounts) are granted to the purchaser to encourage early payment. For example, the credit terms may be "2/10, n/30," which means that if cash payment is made within 10 days from the date of sale, the customer may deduct 2 percent from the invoice price; however, if not paid within the 10-day discount period, the full sales price (less any returns) is due in 30 days from date of sale.

When a cash discount is granted, a customer is motivated to pay within the discount period because by doing so the savings are substantial. For example, with terms 2/10, n/30, 2 percent is saved by paying 20 days early, which equates to approximately 37 percent annual interest. As a consequence, credit customers usually will take advantage of the sales discount. Credit customers conceivably may borrow cash from a bank (at a lower interest rate) in order to take advantage of cash discounts, and thus avoid paying a high interest rate that would result from not taking cash discounts. Because the cash discount on sales almost always will be taken, the Sales Revenue account should be credited (i.e., increased) for the cash that probably will be received rather than for the gross sales amount. To do otherwise would be inconsistent with the **revenue principle** which holds that sales revenue should be measured as the cash or cash equivalent received for the goods sold. To illustrate the proper

---

[5]See Supplement 6A for an applicable data processing procedure.

procedure, assume a sale by Campus Corner of $1,000 with terms 2/10, n/30. The sequence of entries would be as follows:

a.   January 18, date of sale on credit:

net method

```
Accounts receivable..............................    980
    Sales revenue ................................           980
    Terms: 2/10, n/30 ($1,000 × 0.98 = $980).
```

b.   January 27, date of collection if payment is made **within** the discount period (the usual case):

```
Cash ...........................................    980
    Accounts receivable............................           980
```

January 31, date of collection if payment is made **after** the discount period (the unusual case):

```
Cash...........................................   1,000
    Sales discount revenue* .......................            20
    Accounts receivable ...........................           980
    *Interest revenue sometimes is used because
    conceptually it is in the nature of interest revenue earned.
```

The preferred method for recording sales revenues, which was illustrated, is known as the **net method.** As an alternative, some companies use the **gross method of recording sales revenues.** Under the gross method, sales revenue is recorded without deducting the amount of the cash discount. Thus, the following entries would be made by Campus Corner if the gross method were used instead of the net method (as was the case in the previous illustration):

a.   January 18, date of sale on credit:

gross method

```
Accounts receivable ...........................   1,000
    Sales revenue..................................          1,000
```

b. January 27, date of collection if payment is made **within** the discount period (the usual case):

```
Cash.......................................  980
Sales discounts ...............................   20
       Accounts receivable..........................        1,000
       Terms 2/10, n/30 ($1,000 × 0.98 = $980).
```

c. January 31, date of collection if payment is made **after** the discount period (the unusual case):

```
Cash........................................  1,000
       Accounts receivable .......................        1,000
```

The Sales Discounts account (used with the gross method) can be reported as *(a)* a contra revenue account, *(b)* an addition to selling expense, or *(c)* an interest expense. The gross method overstates both accounts receivable and sales revenue. While the net method is theoretically preferable, most companies will select the method that they believe involves the most bookkeeping convenience because the differences are not significant.

Cash discounts should be distinguished from **trade discounts.** A cash discount is a price concession given to encourage early payment of an account. A trade discount is a device sometimes used by vendors for quoting sales prices; the amount **after** the trade discount is the sales price. For example, an item may be quoted at $10 per unit subject to a 20 percent trade discount on orders of 100 units or more; thus, the price for the larger order would be $8 per unit.

In recent years there has been a trend toward more credit sales, particularly at the retail level. However, the use of cash discounts appears to be declining. They are also somewhat unfair because the effect is to charge the cash customers more than the credit customers who pay within the discount period.

Extending credit usually entails a significant increase in the amount of record-keeping required because detailed records must be maintained for each credit customer. Some businesses have their credit sales handled by a credit card company (such as MasterCard or Visa) that charges a fee for this service. The fee paid to the credit card company is recorded as a collection expense (and not a sales discount). Supplement 6A discusses some aspects of the detailed records maintained for credit customers.

MEASURING BAD DEBT EXPENSE

Despite careful credit investigation, there will be a few credit customers who do not pay their obligations. ==When an account receivable proves uncollectible, the business incurs a **bad debt loss.**== Businesses that extend credit do so with the expectation that there will be a certain amount of bad debt losses on credit sales. As a matter of fact, an extremely low rate of bad debt losses may be evidence of too tight a credit policy. If the credit policy is too restrictive, many credit customers who would pay their bills on a timely basis may be turned away. Thus, bad debt losses can be thought of as a necessary expense associated with generating credit sales.

To account for bad debt losses, the matching principle requires that bad debt expense be matched with the period's sale revenues that gave rise to those losses. This requirement is difficult to implement because it may be one or more years after the particular sale was made before the business will be aware of the fact that the customer will be unable to pay.

To satisfy the matching principle in credit situations, the **bad debt allowance method** was developed to measure bad debt expense. ==The allowance method recognizes that bad debt losses are incurred in the year in which the sales that generated those losses were made rather than in the year that the customer is unable to pay.== There is no way of telling in advance which individual accounts ultimately will prove worthless; therefore, the allowance method is based upon the concept of **estimating** in each accounting period what the probable amount of bad debt losses due to uncollectible accounts will be during the collection period. The estimate is made on the basis of total credit sales for the period because the individual accounts that will be bad are not known in the period of sale.

Estimating the probable amount of expense due to uncollectible accounts is neither complex nor fraught with major uncertainties. For a company that has been operating for some years, experience provides a sound basis for projecting probable future bad debt losses related to credit sales, and new companies often rely on the experience of similar companies that have been operating for a number of years, if such information is available. To illustrate, an analysis of accounting data on total credit sales and total uncollectible accounts for the past five years by Campus Corner indicated an average bad debt loss of .9 percent of total credit sales, viz:

Year	Bad-debt losses	Credit sales
19A.........	$ 440	$ 54,000
19B	480	57,000
19C	620	53,000
19D........	500	66,000
19E	660	70,000
	$2,700	$300,000

Aggregate: $2,700 ÷ $300,000 = .9 percent average loss rate for the five-year period 19A–E

Usually a company will adjust the average loss rate of the past to reflect future expectations. Campus Corner expects a small increase in uncollectible accounts from 19F sales; therefore, it increased the expected loss rate to 1.0 percent.

Now let's see how the allowance method would be applied to the above example. Assuming net credit sales in 19F of $40,000, we would record bad debt expense of $40,000 × 1% = $400 in 19F. This estimate would require the following **adjusting entry** at the end of the accounting period, December 31, 19F:

Bad debt expense..	400	
Allowance for doubtful accounts (or bad debts)....................		400
To adjust for the estimated bad debt loss based on credit sales with an average expected loss rate of 1 percent ($40,000 × 1% = $400).		

Bad debt expense of $400 would be reported on the 19F income statement, and it would be matched with the related sales revenue for 19F, the year in which the credit was granted. The Bad Debt Expense account is closed at the end of each accounting period along with the other expense accounts. Rather than crediting the Accounts Receivable account, the credit in the above entry was made to a **contra account** descriptively titled "Allowance for Doubtful Accounts" because there is no way of knowing which account receivable is involved. Other acceptable titles for this contra account are "Allowance for Bad Debts" and "Allowance for Uncollectible Accounts." The balance in Allowance for Doubtful Accounts **always** is considered as a subtraction from the balance of Accounts Receivable. Thus, the two accounts would be reported in the current asset section of the balance sheet as follows:

CAMPUS CORNER, INC.
Balance Sheet (partial)
At December 31, 19F

Current assets:		
Cash		$34,000
Accounts receivable........................	$100,000	
Less: Allowance for doubtful accounts......	2,400*	97,600

    *This amount assumes a balance of $2,000 carried forward prior to the above entry.

Allowance for Doubtful Accounts carries a cumulative credit balance; it is not closed because it is a balance sheet account. It sometimes is described as a contra account, an asset reduction account, or an offset account, but more frequently as a **valuation account.** These descriptions derive from the fact that the balance of the allowance account is the total amount of the accounts receivable that is estimated to be uncollectible. Thus, the difference between the balances of Accounts Receivable and the allowance account measures the estimated net realizable value of accounts receivable. In the above example, the difference between the two accounts—$97,600—represents the **estimated net realizable value** of accounts receivable (also called the book value of accounts receivable).

In the above illustration, the bad debt estimate was based only on credit sales. Occasionally, a company bases the estimate on total sales (i.e., cash plus credit sales). This practice is illogical because (1) it is impossible to have a bad debt loss on a cash sale (except in the case of a "hot" (NSF) cheque which is uncollectible), and (2) a shift in the relative proportion between cash and credit sales would affect the accuracy of the estimate. The total amount of credit sales for each period can be determined (because these transactions are recorded in Accounts Receivable as debits); therefore, there is no reason for not using credit sales as the base for the estimate. Another method of estimating bad debt losses (known as aging accounts receivable) is explained and illustrated in Supplement 6B.

Writing off a bad debt

When an individual customer's account receivable ultimately is determined to be uncollectible (i.e., bad), the amount should be removed from the Accounts Receivable account with an offsetting debit to the allowance account. This entry does not record a bad debt loss (expense) because the estimated expense was recorded with an adjusting entry in the period of sale (one or more years earlier), and the related allowance account was established to absorb the later write-off. To illustrate, assume Campus Corner sold J. Doe merchandise on credit in 19D amounting to $100 (which was properly credited to 19D Sales Revenue and debited to Accounts Receivable). At the end of 19F, Campus Corner decided that it would never collect the $100; accordingly, they made the following entry:

December 31, 19F;

```
Allowance for doubtful accounts .....................................    100
    Accounts receivable (J. Doe) .....................................             100
    To write off a receivable from J. Doe determined to be uncollectible.
```

Observe that the above entry did not affect the income statement because the expense already has been recorded (when the adjusting entry was made at the end of 19D). Also, the entry did not change the **net realizable value** (i.e., the book value) of Accounts receivable. The difference between Accounts Receivable and the allowance account remains the same as before the entry, viz:

	Before write-off	*After write-off*
Accounts receivable	$100,000	$99,900
Less: Allowance for doubtful accounts	2,400	2,300
Difference—estimated net realizable value	$ 97,600	$97,600

Actual write-offs compared with estimates. The uncollectible accounts actually written off seldom will equal the estimated amounts previously recorded. If the accounts actually written off are less than the estimated amount, the Allowance for Doubtful Accounts will continue with a credit balance.[6] If an account is written off as bad and the customer subsequently pays it, the write-off entry should be reversed and the collection should be recorded in the usual way. For example, if $80 were collected on J. Doe's account that was previously written off then the entries would be:

Accounts receivable (J. Doe)	80	
Allowance for doubtful accounts		80
To restore the account of J. Doe and adjust the allowance.		
Cash	80	
Accounts receivable (J. Doe)		80
To record the collection.		

The reason for this apparently cumbersome approach is to provide a record of the collection in the accounts receivable account of J. Doe.

Terminology. The caption "Accounts receivable" often appears on the balance sheet under current assets without additional descriptive terms; however, a more descriptive designation such as "Receivables from trade customers" is preferable. Receivables from other than the regular trade customers, such as loans to officers or employees, should not be included in the accounts receivable category. Rather, such nontrade receivables should be reported as separate items.

SALES RETURNS AND ALLOWANCES

Many businesses permit customers to return unsatisfactory or damaged merchandise and receive a cash or credit refund. In some cases, rather than taking back such merchandise, a cash or credit adjustment may be given to the customer. To measure correctly sales revenue, such transactions must be recorded by, in effect, reversing the sales entry. Although the Sales account could be debited (i.e., reduced) to record these reductions in sales, a separate account entitled "Sales Returns and Allowances" often is used. This account serves an important control objective by informing management of the volume of returns and allowances. If cash is refunded, the Cash account is credited. Alternatively, if a credit adjustment is given, accounts receivable of the cus-

---

[6]On the other hand, if the amount written off is more than the allowance balance, there will be a temporary debit balance in the allowance account. This situation will be resolved when the next adjusting entry is made. It indicates that the estimated loss rate used may be too low.

tomer must be credited. The Sales Returns and Allowances account is a contra revenue account; therefore, it is a deduction from gross sales revenue (as shown in Exhibit 6–1). To illustrate, assume a customer, F. Fox, bought five new lamps from Campus Corner for $500. Fifteen days after payment, Fox returned one lamp that was damaged. The sequence of entries by Campus Corner would be:

Date of sale:

```
Accounts receivable (F. Fox) .........................................    500
    Sales revenue ....................................................            500
  To record sale.
```

Date of sale return:

```
Sales returns and allowances ........................................    100
    Cash*.............................................................            100
  To record sale return, 1 unit.
    *If payment had not been made this credit would be to Accounts Receivable.
```

Part B—Accounting for Cost of Goods Sold

NATURE OF COST OF GOODS SOLD

The income statement shown in Exhibit 6–1 (Campus Corner) reported an expense called cost of goods sold, which is unique to nonservice types of businesses. Cost of goods sold (CGS) is a relatively simple concept. Sales revenue represents the merchandise sold during the accounting period valued at **sales price,** whereas cost of goods sold is the same merchandise valued at **cost.** Thus, revenue and expense are matched on the income statement in conformity with the **matching principle** (see Exhibit 2–6). Cost of goods sold includes the cost of all merchandise sold during the period, but it excludes the cost of all merchandise remaining on hand at the end of the accounting period (i.e., the ending merchandise inventory).

Typically, a business will start each accounting period with a stock of merchandise on hand for resale which is called the **beginning** (or initial) **inventory (BI).** The merchandise on hand at the end of an accounting period is called the **ending** (or final) **inventory (EI)** for that period, which automatically becomes the beginning inventory for the next period.

During the accounting period, the beginning inventory usually is increased by the purchase or manufacture of additional merchandise. The sum of the beginning inventory and the **purchases (P)** during the period represents the **goods available for sale** during that period. If all of the goods available for sale were sold during the period, there would be no ending inventory. Typically, not all of the goods available for sale are sold; therefore, a quantity of goods remains on hand which is the ending inventory for the period. From these facts we can state the cost of goods sold (CGS) model as follows:

$$BI + P - EI = CGS$$

To illustrate, Campus Corner reported cost of goods sold of $60,000 (Exhibit 6–1), which was determined as follows:

Beginning inventory (January 1, 19F)	$40,000
Add purchases of merchandise during 19F	55,000
Goods available for sale	95,000
Deduct ending inventory (December 31, 19F)	35,000
Cost of goods sold	$60,000

INVENTORY SYSTEMS

To compute cost of goods sold, three amounts must be known: (1) beginning inventory, (2) purchases of merchandise during the period, and (3) ending inventory. The ending inventory of one accounting period is the beginning inventory of the succeeding period. Therefore, the beginning inventory amount always will be available from the preceding period. The amount of purchases for the period will be accumulated in the accounting system. The amount of the **ending** inventory can be determined by using one of two distinctly different inventory systems:

1. **Periodic inventory system**—Under this system, no up-to-date record of inventory is maintained during the year. An actual physical count (i.e., an inventory count) of the goods remaining on hand is required at the **end of each period.** The number of units of each type of merchandise on hand then is multiplied by the purchase cost per unit to compute the dollar amount of the ending inventory. Thus, the amount of goods on hand at any point during the year is not known until the last day of the period when the inventory count is completed. Also, the amount of cost of goods sold cannot be determined until the inventory count is completed.

2. **Perpetual inventory system**—This system involves the maintenance of up-to-date inventory records in the accounting system throughout the period. For each type of goods stocked, a detailed record is maintained that shows (a) units and cost of the beginning inventory, (b) units and cost of each purchase, (c) units and cost of the goods for each sale, and (d) the units

and amount on hand at any point in time. This up-to-date record is maintained on a transaction-by-transaction basis throughout the period. **Thus, the inventory record provides both the amount of ending inventory and the cost of goods sold amount at any point in time.**

Periodic inventory system

The periodic inventory system requires an actual count of the goods on hand at the end of the period and valuation of the units at their purchase cost. The primary reasons for using the periodic inventory system are low cost and convenience. Consider the cost and difficulty associated with a grocery store attempting to keep track of the number of units sold and the cost of each purchase and sales of the thousands of low-priced items that usually are stocked. When small items are sold for cash (as in a grocery store), usually no record is made at the cash register of the cost and quantity of each item (rather the total sales price is entered into the cash register). The primary disadvantage of a periodic inventory system is the lack of inventory control (for purchasing purposes and detection of theft).[7] Nevertheless, many companies use the periodic system either for all items offered for sale or for only the small, low-cost items.

A periodic inventory system applies the cost of goods sold model given on the previous page as follows:

Model:	Beginning inventory	+	Purchases of the period	−	Ending inventory	=	Cost of goods sold
	↓		↓		↓		↓
Source:	Carried over from prior period		Accumulated in the Purchases account		Measured at end of period by physical inventory count		Computed as a residual amount

A periodic inventory system may be outlined sequentially as follows:

1. **Record all purchases**—During the period, the purchase cost of all goods bought is recorded in an account called Purchases (or Merchandise Purchases). Thus, a credit or cash purchase would be recorded as follows:

January 14, 19F:

Purchase......................................	9,000	
Accounts payable (or Cash)................		9,000

---

[7]Because of this important disadvantage, large chain stores now have computerized perpetual inventory systems tied in directly to the cash registers.

2. **Record all sales**—During the period, the sales price received for all goods sold is recorded in a Sales Revenue account. Thus, a credit or cash sale would be recorded as follows:

January 30, 19F:

Accounts receivable (or Cash)...................	8,000	
Sales revenue...............................		8,000

3. **Count the number of units on hand**—At the end of the current period, the Inventory account balance still reflects the inventory amount carried over from the prior period because **no entries** are made to the Inventory account during the current period. Thus, to measure the ending inventory for the current period, a physical inventory count must be made of all goods on hand. A physical count is necessary because, under the periodic inventory system, a transaction-by-transaction unit and cost record is not maintained. This count must be made at the end of each period for which financial statements are to be prepared. Taking a physical inventory count is discussed later.

4. **Compute the dollar valuation of the ending inventory**—The dollar amount of the ending inventory quantities is computed by multiplying the number of units on hand (determined in 3 above) by their unit purchase cost. The dollar amounts of all of the types of goods stocked are summed to measure the total ending inventory valuation for the company.

5. **Compute cost of goods sold**—After the ending inventory valuation is measured (as in 4 above), cost of goods sold for the period was computed as follows for Campus Corner:

CAMPUS CORNER, Inc.
Schedule of Cost of Goods Sold
For the Year Ended December 31, 19F

Beginning inventory (carried over from the last period in the Inventory account)	$40,000
Add purchases for the period (accumulated balance in the Purchases account)	55,000
Goods available for sale	95,000
Less ending inventory (determined by physical count, per above)......	35,000
Cost of goods sold (as shown in Exhibit 6–1)................	$60,000

*Based on the data given earlier.

Perpetual inventory system

A perpetual inventory system typically involves a considerable amount of clerical effort; however, it is effective in measuring inventory and cost of goods sold and in maintaining inventory control. The maintenance of a separate inventory record for each type of goods stocked on a transaction-by-transaction basis usually is desirable, particularly for control purposes. To minimize bookkeeping difficulties, most perpetual inventory systems are computerized. Whether the accounting system is manual, mechanical, or computerized, the data that are recorded and reported are the same. For instructional purposes, let's look at a manual approach. Assume, for this illustration only, that Campus Corner stocks and sells only one item, called Super X. The following events apply to 19F:

Jan.   1   Beginning inventory—8 units, at unit cost of $5,000.
July   14   Purchased—11 additional units, at unit cost of $5,000.
Nov. 30   Sold—13 units, at unit sales price of $8,333.
Dec. 31   Return sale—1 unit (returned to stock and refunded sales price).

The perpetual inventory record for this single item stocked is shown in Exhibit 6–2.[8]

The beginning inventory, purchases, cost of goods sold, and ending inventory amounts on the above perpetual inventory record agree with the amounts computed earlier using the periodic inventory system. In this situation, the two systems will produce the same end results unless an error has been made. However, each of the two systems will serve the company in different ways because the periodic system provides no details regarding the inventory

EXHIBIT 6–2
Perpetual inventory record

PERPETUAL INVENTORY RECORD

Item____Super X____   Code____No. 33____   Minimum stock____10____
Location_Storage No. 4_   Valuation basis__Cost__   Maximum stock____20____

Date	Explanation	Goods Purchased			Goods Sold			Balance on Hand		
		Units Rec'd	Unit Cost	Total Cost	Units Sold	Unit Cost	Total Cost	Units	Unit Cost	Total Cost
Jan. 1	Beginning inventory							8	5,000	40,000
July 14	Purchase	11	5,000	55,000				19	5,000	95,000
Nov. 30	Sale				13	5,000	65,000	6	5,000	30,000
Dec. 31	Return sale				(1)	5,000	(5,000)	7	5,000	35,000
Recap: Total purchases		11		55,000						
Total cost of goods sold					12		60,000			
Ending inventory								7		35,000

---

[8]Measuring inventories and cost of goods sold when there are different unit purchase costs in deferred to Chapter 7.

changes whereas the perpetual system provides all of the details on a day-to-day basis.

When the perpetual inventory system is computerized, the computer does exactly what was done manually in Exhibit 6–2; however, a computerized system does it with tremendous speed and accuracy. Computerization effectively overcomes many of the difficulties associated with the perpetual system, which permits large, medium, and even small companies to use the perpetual system.

A perpetual inventory system may be outlined sequentially as follows:

1. **Record all purchases**—During the period, the purchase cost of each type of goods bought is entered in the **Inventory** ledger account as an increase and in a detailed perpetual inventory record (Exhibit 6–2). Thus, a cash or credit purchase of goods for resale would be recorded as follows (refer to Exhibit 6–2):

July 14, 19F:

Inventory* (Super X, code 33)	55,000	
Accounts payable (or Cash)		55,000

*Also entered in the perpetual inventory record as shown in Exhibit 6–2.

2. **Record all sales**—During the period, each sale is recorded by means of **two companion entries.** One entry is to record the sales revenue at **sales price,** and the other entry is to record the **cost of goods sold at purchase cost.** The sales revenue is recorded in the Sales Revenue account, and the cost of goods sold is recorded in the Cost of Goods Sold account. Thus, a credit or cash sale would be recorded as follows (refer to data presented in Exhibit 6–2):

November 30, 19F:

a. To record the sales revenue at the sales price of $8,333 per unit:

Accounts receivable (or Cash)	108,329	
Sales revenue (13 units @ $8,333)....		108,329

b. To record the cost of goods sold (at cost per the perpetual inventory record—Exhibit 6–2):

Cost of goods sold*......................	65,000	
Inventory (13 units @ $5,000)		65,000

*Also entered in the perpetual inventory record as shown in Exhibit 6–2.

3. **Record all returns**—During the period, both **purchase returns and sales returns** are recorded in the Inventory account and on the perpetual inventory record at cost. For example, the return by a customer of one unit of Super X on December 30 requires companion entries to reverse the two entries made on the date of sale, shown above (only for the number of units returned). The return would be recorded as follows (refer to Exhibit 6–2):

a. To record the sales return at sale price (one unit):

Sales returns and allowances (1 unit @ $8,333)	8,333	
Accounts receivable (or Cash)		8,333

b. To record the return of the unit to inventory:

Inventory (1 unit @ $5,000)................	5,000*	
Cost of goods sold....................		5,000

*This amount was provided by the perpetual Inventory record; also it is restored to the perpetual inventory record as shown in Exhibit 6–2.

4. **Use cost of goods sold and inventory amounts**—At the end of the accounting period, the balance in the Cost of Goods Sold account provides the total amount of that expense that is reported on the income statement. It is not necessary to use the cost of goods sold model to compute the expense because under the perpetual inventory system the Cost of Goods Sold account in the ledger always is up to date. Similarly, the Inven-

tory account would reflect the ending inventory amount that would be reported on the balance sheet. The sum of all the inventory balances in the various perpetual inventory records should equal the balance in the Inventory account in the ledger at any point in time.

This illustration demonstrates that when a perpetual inventory system is used, it is not necessary to take a physical inventory count of the merchandise remaining on hand at the end of the accounting period in order to measure the inventory amount and cost of goods sold. However, because clerical errors, theft, and spoilage may occur, a physical inventory should be taken from time to time to check upon the accuracy of the perpetual inventory records. If an error is found, the perpetual inventory records and the Inventory account must be changed to agree with the physical count.

To summarize, there are two basic accounting differences between periodic and perpetual systems:

1. Inventory account:
   a. Periodic—During the period, the balance in the Inventory account is not changed; thus, it reflects the beginning inventory amount. During the period, each purchase is recorded in the Purchases account. As a consequence, the ending inventory for each accounting period must be measured by physical count, then valued (or "costed") at unit purchase cost.
   b. Perpetual—During the period, the Inventory account is increased for each purchase and decreased (at cost) for each sale. Thus, at the end of the period, it measures the correct amount of ending inventory.
2. Cost of Goods Sold account:
   a. Periodic—During the period, no entry is made for cost of goods sold. At the end of the period, after the physical inventory count, cost of goods sold is measured as:

$$\text{Beginning inventory} + \text{Purchases} - \text{Ending inventory} = \text{Cost of goods sold}$$

   b. Perpetual—During the period, cost of goods sold is recorded at the time of each sale and the Inventory account is reduced (at cost). Thus, the system measures the amount of cost of goods sold for the period.

The perpetual inventory system is used widely because of the following advantages over the periodic inventory system:

1. It provides up-to-date inventory amounts (units and dollar cost for each item).
2. It provides the cost of goods sold amount without the necessity of taking a periodic inventory count.

3. It provides continuing information necessary to maintain minimum and maximum inventory levels by appropriate timing of purchases.
4. It provides continuing information about the quantity of goods on hand at various locations.
5. It provides a basis for measuring the amount of theft.
6. It provides cost of goods sold information needed to record sales at both selling price and cost.
7. It is readily adaptable for use by computers that quickly process large quantities of inventory data.

For these reasons there has been an increase in the use of the perpetual inventory system and a decrease in use of the periodic inventory system.

ADDITIONAL ISSUES IN MEASURING PURCHASES

In accordance with generally accepted accounting principles (GAAP), goods purchased for resale are recorded as a purchase at the date that **ownership** passes from the seller to the buyer. Normally, ownership is considered to pass when the goods are received and not when the purchase order is placed. Goods purchased should be recorded at their **cash equivalent cost** in accordance with the cost principle. Cost includes the cash equivalent price paid to the vendor (seller) plus other amounts paid for transportation and handling in order to get the goods into location and condition for intended use. Cost does not include expenditures such as interest paid on cash borrowed to make the purchase. In accounting for purchases, several measurement problems frequently are encountered. Many of these problems are similar to those discussed in Part A of this chapter from the perspective of the seller.

Purchase returns and allowances

Goods purchased may be returned to the vendor (seller) because they do not meet specifications, arrive in unsatisfactory condition, or otherwise are unsatisfactory. When the goods are returned or when the vendor makes an allowance because of the circumstances, the effect on the cost of purchases must be measured. The purchaser will receive a cash refund or a reduction in the liability to the vendor for the purchase. To illustrate, assume Campus Corner returned to Company B, for credit, unsatisfactory goods that cost $1,000. The return would be recorded by Campus Corner (which uses the periodic system) as follows:

Accounts payable (or cash)...	1,000	
Purchase returns and allowances*		1,000
*Inventory is credited when the perpetual inventory system is used.		

Purchase returns and allowances are accounted for as a deduction from the cost of purchases.

Transportation-in

Under the cost principle, assets should be measured and recorded at their **cash equivalent cost.** Thus, the **purchase cost** of goods acquired for resale should include all freight and other transportation-in costs incurred by the purchaser. When a perpetual inventory system is used, transportation costs paid on goods purchased should be apportioned to each inventory item and included in the inventory cost amount entered in the perpetual inventory. When a periodic inventory system is used, such costs should be entered as a debit (i.e., increase) to the Purchases account. However, because of the problems associated with apportioning a freight bill to the several items it may cover, often it is more practical to use a separate ledger account entitled "Transportation-in," or "Freight-in." Also, for control purposes it is often useful to separately classify this significant cost. Thus, in this situation the journal entry to record a payment for transportation charges upon delivery of merchandise acquired for resale would be:

```
Jan. 17   Transportation-in .........................................   3,000
              Cash...............................................            3,000
```

At the end of the period, the balance in the Transportation-in account would be reported as an addition to the cost of purchases.

Assuming freight-in and purchase returns, cost of goods sold may be reflected as follows on the income statement when periodic inventory procedures are used (refer to Campus Corner):

Cost of goods sold:		
Beginning inventory		$40,000
Purchases....................................	$53,000	
Add: Freight-in.............................	3,000	
Deduct: Purchase returns and allowances	(1,000)	
Net purchases.............................		55,000
Goods available for sale		95,000
Less: Ending inventory........................		35,000
Cost of goods sold........................		$60,000

Purchase discounts

A situation that corresponds to cash discounts on sales occurs when merchandise is purchased for resale—except that the cash discount is received rather than given. When merchandise is purchased on credit, terms such as 2/10, n/30 sometimes are specified. This means that if payment of the purchase invoice cost is made within 10 days from date of purchase, a 2 percent purchase discount is granted. If payment is not made within the discount period, then the full purchase invoice cost is due 30 days after purchase. To illustrate, assume Campus Corner purchases goods from a number of suppliers. On January 17, the company purchased goods from Vendor B that had a $1,000 invoice price with terms, 2/10, n/30. On January 26, Campus Corner will pay $980 for the goods. Therefore, the purchase should be recorded on the net basis by Campus Corner as follows:[9]

January 17—date of purchase:

Purchases*	980	
Accounts payable.		980
*Inventory is debited when a perpetual inventory system is used.		

January 26—date of payment, within the discount period:

Accounts payable.	980	
Cash		980

If for any reason Campus Corner did not pay within the 10-day discount period, the following entry would result:

Feb. 1 Accounts payable	980	
Purchase discounts lost (or Interest expense).	20	
Cash		1,000

Purchase discounts lost should be reported on the income statement as a financial expense along with interest expense on debts.

---

[9]Some persons prefer to record the transaction at the date of purchase at the gross amount; that is, at $1,000. In this instance, payment within the discount period would result in credit to an account called Purchase Discounts, $20. The purchase discount credit would then be reported as a revenue, or as a deduction from purchases. This credit is not revenue and if deducted in full from purchases on the income statement would tend to misstate both inventory and purchases. In contrast, the net basis has the distinct advantage in that recording the **purchase discount lost** calls direct attention to inefficiency—failure to take the discount. The gross approach conceptually and practically is deficient for reasons similar to those cited with respect to sales discounts.

TAKING A PHYSICAL INVENTORY

We explained earlier in the chapter that whether a periodic or perpetual inventory system is used, a physical inventory count must be taken from time to time. When a **periodic** inventory system is used, the inventory must be counted (and costed) at the **end of each period** because the financial statements cannot be prepared without this key amount. When a perpetual inventory system is used, the inventory count may be scheduled at various times to verify the perpetual inventory records. The two steps in taking a **physical inventory count** are:

1. **Quantity count**—The **count** of merchandise is made after the close of business on the inventory date. Normally, it would be difficult to count the goods accurately during business hours when sales activities are taking place. A physical count is made of all items of merchandise on hand and entered on an appropriate form. An inventory form, such as the one shown in Exhibit 6–3, may be used. Special care must be exercised in the quantity count to be sure that all of the merchandise owned by the business is included, wherever located, and that all items for which the entity does not have legal ownership are excluded. Occasionally, a business will have possession of goods it does not own (see discussion of consignments in Chapter 7).

EXHIBIT 6–3
Physical inventory form

Campus Corner
PHYSICAL INVENTORY SHEET

Date of Inventory __12/31/F__ Department __4 (and last)__ Taken by __M.R.__

Location	Identification of Merchandise	Quantity on Hand	Date Purchased	Unit Cost	Unit Market Price*	Unit Cost (LCM)	Inventory Amount
1	Headsets #8-16	20	12/2/F	$ 20	$ 21	$ 20	$ 400
2	Television sets #17-961	7	11/5/F	300	300	300	2,100
2	Radios #23-72	4	10/26/F	52	50	50	200
	Total Department Inventory						6,000
	TOTAL INVENTORY VALUE—ALL DEPARTMENTS 12/31/F						$35,000

*Replacement cost that would have to be paid if the item were being purchased on the inventory date (see lower of cost or market discussion in Chapter 7).

2. **Inventory costing**—After the physical count of goods on hand has been completed, each kind of merchandise must be assigned a **unit cost.** The quantity of each kind of merchandise is multiplied by the unit cost to derive the inventory amount (as illustrated in Exhibit 6–3). The sum of the inventory amounts for all merchandise on hand measures the total ending inventory amount for the business. Exhibit 6–3 reflects the computation of the ending inventory shown on the income statement for Campus Corner. In determining the value of inventory, the cost principle must be applied; therefore, unit purchase cost, as defined above, must be used. A problem arises if there are different unit costs for inventory items that otherwise are exactly the same. When this situation occurs, there are several ways to identify unit purchase cost for inventory purposes such as the first-in, first-out (FIFO), last-in, first-out (LIFO), or average cost approaches. These alternative approaches to costing inventories are discussed in detail in Chapter 7.

Management must deal with complex problems associated with planning and control of inventories. An excessive amount of inventory may tie up resources (i.e., cash) that could be employed more economically in other ways in the business. Insufficient inventory often results in lost sales. Decisions must be made concerning maximum and minimum levels of inventory that should be maintained; when to reorder; how much to reorder; and the characteristics of the items to stock, such as size, color, style, and specifications. Many of these issues are discussed in management accounting. From the viewpoint of the investor, creditor, and other interested parties, information concerning the investment in inventory frequently is important in decision making. Therefore, explanatory footnotes related to inventories frequently are included in the financial reports.

DATA PROCESSING—CLOSING ENTRIES FOR SALES REVENUE, COST OF GOODS SOLD, AND MERCHANDISE INVENTORY

Closing the sales revenue and bad debt expense accounts

This chapter introduced some new revenue and expense accounts related to the selling and purchasing functions. Because these accounts are **temporary** accounts, they must be closed at the end of the accounting period.

Sales Revenue is closed by recording a debit in that account and a credit in the Income Summary. Sales Discount Revenue is closed in the same way. Bad Debt Expense is closed by recording a credit in that account and a debit to the Income Summary. Sales Returns and Allowance (a contra revenue account) is closed by recording a credit to that account and a debit to the Income Summary. The closing entries for cost of goods sold (an expense) and the merchandise inventory amounts depend upon the inventory system (periodic versus perpetual) used.

Closing entries when a periodic inventory system is used

When a periodic inventory system is used, there is no Cost of Goods Sold account in the ledger. The merchandise inventory account requires two directly related closing entries: (1) an entry to close the **beginning inventory** amount to the Income Summary account and (2) an entry to transfer the **ending inventory** amount from the Income Summary account to the Inventory account. Campus Corner would make two closing entries for the merchandise inventories as follows:

December 31, 19F.

a. To close (transfer) the **beginning** merchandise inventory amount into Income Summary:

Income summary	40,000	
Merchandise inventory (beginning)		40,000

b. To transfer the **ending** merchandise inventory amount from the Income Summary account to the Merchandise Inventory account:

Merchandise inventory (ending)	35,000	
Income summary		35,000

The effects of these two entries (a) to replace the beginning inventory amount in the Merchandise Inventory account with the ending inventory amount and (b) to enter the beginning inventory amount in the Income Summary account as an **expense** (a debit) and to remove the ending inventory amount from the Income Summary account (a credit) as a cost transfer to the asset account Merchandise Inventory.

In addition, the Purchases account is closed to Income Summary as follows:

Income summary	55,000	
Purchases		55,000

The reason for the two closing entries for merchandise inventories under the **periodic inventory system** can be understood if you recall that under this system the ending inventory of the prior year (say, 1986) automatically is the beginning inventory for the current year (say, 1987) and that the Inventory account balance is unchanged throughout the year (because all purchases of merchandise are debited to the Purchases account rather than to the Inventory account). Therefore, at the end of the current year, the beginning inventory amount ($40,000 for Campus Corner) is still in the Inventory account at December 31, 19F. Simply, it must be transferred out as an expense and be replaced with the December 31, 19F, ending inventory amount ($35,000 for Campus Corner). The credit (i.e., $35,000) in entry (b) above is made to Income Summary because the beginning inventory and purchases have been closed to the Income Summary. When the ending inventory amount is transferred out of the Income Summary, the end result is that the Income Summary has been decreased by the amount of cost of goods sold (beginning inventory plus purchases minus ending inventory equals cost of goods sold). After completion of these closing entries, the Merchandise Inventory, Purchases, and Income Summary accounts for Campus Corner would appear as follows:

PERIODIC INVENTORY SYSTEM

Merchandise Inventory

12/31/19E (beginning)	40,000	(a) To close	40,000
(b) 12/31/19F (ending)	35,000		

Purchases

12/31/19F (balance)	55,000	(c) To close	55,000

Income Summary

Operating expenses (not shown)			Revenues (not shown)	
(a) 12/31/19E (beginning				
inventory)	40,000		(b) 12/31/19F (ending	
(c) (purchases)	55,000		inventory)	35,000

(Note that these three amounts net to $60,000,
the amount of cost of goods sold.)

These closing entries, along with all the other closing entries, are illustrated in the demonstration case (Rote Appliance Store, Inc.) at the end of this chapter.[10] This demonstration case should be studied carefully because it ties together all of the parts discussed in this chapter.

Closing entries when a perpetual inventory system is used

When a perpetual inventory system is used, the Merchandise Inventory account and Cost of Goods Sold account are affected by day-to-day transactions. Therefore, at the end of the accounting period, each of these accounts will reflect the correct up-to-date balance. Consequently, no adjusting or closing entries are needed for the Merchandise Inventory account; it reflects the end-

---

[10] There are several mechanical variations in how the closing entries can be made; all of them give the same end results. For example, some persons prefer to record the two inventory entries as adjusting, rather than closing, entries. Also, some persons prefer to use a temporary Cost of Goods Sold account in the closing process under a periodic inventory system; in this approach the two inventory amounts and purchases are first transferred to the Cost of Goods Sold account, which is then closed to Income Summary.

ing inventory amount that will be reported on the balance sheet. Because the Cost of Goods Sold account is an expense account, it will be closed. For example, Campus Corner would record the following closing entry under the perpetual inventory system:

December 31, 19F:

Income summary	60,000	
Cost of goods sold		60,000

Inventory shrinkage

Inventory shrinkage occurs as a result of theft, breakage, spoilage, and incorrect measurements. The measurement of inventory shrinkage is important for internal management purposes and, if large, is a major issue to investors and creditors. The dollar amount of shrinkage is reported on **internal** financial statements, but seldom, if ever, are such amounts significant enough to be reported **separately** on **external** financial statements. Accurate measurement of this loss is related directly to the inventory system used.

When a **periodic inventory** system is used, measurement of shrinkage loss is often difficult, and may be impossible. The inventory, as counted at the end of the period, does not, in itself, provide a basis for measurement of shrinkage. An implicit assumption underlying the periodic inventory model (i.e., Beginning inventory + Purchases − Ending inventory = Cost of goods sold) is that if an item is not in ending inventory, it must have been sold. Therefore, cost of goods sold includes inventory shrinkage.

Alternatively, a perpetual inventory system will provide data on shrinkage loss. The inventory record provides both cost of goods sold and the ending inventory. These data make it possible to measure shrinkage loss. To illustrate, assume the perpetual inventory records show cost of goods sold for the period, 12 units, $60,000 (Exhibit 6–2), and ending inventory of 7 units, $35,000. An inventory count at the end of the period showed 6 units on hand. In the absence of clerical error, an inventory shrinkage (probably due to theft) would be reported as 1 unit, and the loss amount would be $5,000 (assuming no insurance recovery). The entry to record the shrinkage, assuming a perpetual inventory system, would be:

Inventory shrinkage*	5,000	
Inventory		5,000
*Closed to Income Summary.		

DEMONSTRATION CASE

(Try to resolve the requirements before proceeding to the suggested solution that follows.)

Rote Appliance Store, Inc. has been operating for a number of years. It is a relatively small but profitable retail outlet for major appliances, such as refrigerators and air conditioners. Approximately 40 percent of the sales are on short-term credit. This case has been selected and simplified to demonstrate information processing when there are significant selling activities (the service activities have been deleted). The case has been structured to illustrate the application of both perpetual and periodic inventory systems with the same data. The annual accounting period ends December 31, 19D. Two independent cases will be assumed:

Case A—Perpetual inventory system is assumed.

Case B—Periodic inventory system is assumed.

The trial balance derived from the ledger at December 31, 19D, was:

	Unadjusted trial balance			
	Case A—Perpetual inventory system used		Case B—Periodic inventory system used	
Account titles	*Debit*	*Credit*	*Debit*	*Credit*
Cash...	$ 34,100		$ 34,100	
Accounts receivable...........................	5,000		5,000	
Allowance for doubtful accounts		$ 1,000		$ 1,000
*Merchandise inventory:				
January 1,19D			20,000	
December 31, 19D	16,000			
Store equipment.............................	30,000		30,000	
Accumulated depreciation,				
equipment		9,000		9,000
Accounts payable.............................		8,000		8,000
Income tax payable				
Capital stock, par $10		40,000		40,000
Retained earnings, January 1, 19D..............		9,000		9,000
Sales revenue.................................		102,000		102,000
Sales returns and allowances...................	2,000		2,000	
*Cost of goods sold	60,000			
*Purchases...................................			57,000	
*Purchase returns and allowances				1,000
Expenses (not detailed).......................	21,900		21,900	
Depreciation expense..........................				
Income tax expense				
	$169,000	$169,000	$170,000	$170,000

*These account balances are different between the two cases because of the effects of the two inventory systems used.

Data developed by Rote as a basis for the adjusting entries at December 31, 19D, were:

    a.   Credit sales in 19D amounted to $40,000; the average loss rate for bad debts is estimated to be 0.25 percent of credit sales.

b. The store equipment is depreciated on the basis of an estimated 10-year useful life with no residual value.

c. On December 31, 19D, the periodic inventory count of goods remaining on hand reflected $16,000.

d. The average income tax rate is 20 percent.

e. The beginning inventory, January 1, 19D, was as shown on the trial balance (Case B).

Required:

a. Based upon the above data, complete a worksheet at December 31, 19D, similar to that shown in Exhibit 5–3. If you prefer, you may omit the columns for Adjusted Trial Balance. **Prepare a separate worksheet for each separate case.**

b. Based upon the completed worksheets, present an income statement for each case. Use a single-step format for Case A and a multiple-step format for Case B.

c. Based upon the two worksheets, present, in parallel columns, the adjusting entries for each case at December 31, 19D.

d. Based upon the two worksheets, present, in parallel columns, the closing entries for each situation at December 31, 19D.

In preparing the worksheet when a **perpetual inventory** system is used, no new complications are presented. The inventory amount is extended across the worksheet as an asset because the balance in the Inventory account reflects the ending inventory when a perpetual inventory system is used. The expense—cost of goods sold—is extended to the Income Summary debit column along with the other expenses. See Exhibit 6–4.

In preparing the worksheet with a **periodic inventory system,** both the beginning and ending inventory amounts must be used. First, the beginning inventory amount must be extended horizontally as a debit to the Income Statement column (because it now is an expense). A special line, "Merchandise inventory, ending" is added to the bottom of the worksheet, and the ending inventory amount is entered on this line under Income Statement, credit. This amount also is listed on the same line under Balance Sheet, debit.[11]

---

[11]There are several mechanical ways of handling the inventories on the worksheet when a periodic inventory system is used. Some accountants view the inventory entries as closing rather than adjusting entries. The various approaches arrive at the same net result, and each has its particular mechanical advantages and disadvantages.

EXHIBIT 6–4   **Worksheets compared for perpetual and periodic inventory systems**

ROTE APPLIANCE STORE
Worksheet, December 31, 19D
Case A—Assuming Perpetual Inventory System Is Used

Account Titles	Trial Balance		Adjusting Entries*		Income Statement		Retained Earnings		Balance Sheet	
	Debit	Credit	Debit	Credit	Debit	Credit	Debit	Credit	Debit	Credit
Cash	34,100								34,100	
Accounts receivable	5,000								5,000	
Allowance for doubtful accounts		1,000		(a) 100						1,100
Merchandise inventory Dec. 31, 19D	16,000								16,000	
Store equipment	30,000								30,000	
Accumulated depreciation, equipment		9,000		(b) 3,000						12,000
Accounts payable		8,000								8,000
Income tax payable				(c) 3,000						3,000
Capital stock, par $10		40,000								40,000
Retained earnings, Jan. 1, 19D		9,000						9,000		
Sales revenue		102,000				102,000				
Sales returns and allowances	2,000				2,000					
Cost of goods sold	60,000				60,000					
Expenses (not detailed)	21,900		(a) 100		22,000					
Depreciation expense			(b) 3,000		3,000					
	169,000	169,000			87,000	102,000				
Income tax expense†			(c) 3,000		3,000					
Net income					12,000			12,000		
			6,100	6,100	102,000	102,000	–0–	21,000		
Retained earnings, Dec. 31, 19D							21,000			21,000
							21,000	21,000	85,100	85,100

*Note that a **simplifying mechanical change** is used—the "Adjusting Entries" total is not entered until **after** the income tax is computed and entered.
    †($102,000 − $87,000) × 20% = $3,000 income tax expense.

EXHIBIT 6–4 *(concluded)*

ROTE APPLIANCE STORE
Worksheet December 31, 19D
Case B—Assuming Periodic Inventory System Is Used

Account Titles	Trial Balance		Adjusting Entries*		Income Statement		Retained Earnings		Balance Sheet	
	Debit	Credit	Debit	Credit	Debit	Credit	Debit	Credit	Debit	Credit
Cash	34,100								34,100	
Accounts receivable	5,000								5,000	
Allowance for doubtful accounts		1,000		(a) 100						1,100
Merchandise inventory, Dec. 31, 19C	20,000				20,000					
Store equipment	30,000								30,000	
Accumulated depreciation, equipment		9,000		(b) 3,000						12,000
Accounts payable		8,000								8,000
Income tax payable				(c) 3,000						3,000
Capital stock, par $10		40,000								40,000
Retained earnings, Jan. 1, 19D		9,000						9,000		
Sales revenue		102,000				102,000				
Sales returns and allowances	2,000				2,000					
Purchases	57,000				57,000					
Purchase returns and allowances		1,000				1,000				
Expenses (not detailed)	21,900		(a) 100		22,000					
Depreciation expense			(b) 3,000		3,000					
Merchandise inventory, Dec. 31, 19D						16,000			16,000	
	170,000	170,000			104,000	119,000				
Income tax expense†			(c) 3,000		3,000					
Net income					12,000			12,000		
			6,100	6,100	119,000	119,000	–0–	21,000		
							21,000			21,000
							21,000	21,000	85,100	85,100

*Note that a **simplifying mechanical change** is used—the "Adjusting Entries" total is not entered until after the income tax is computed and entered.
†($119,000 − $104,000) × 20% = $3,000 income tax expense.

Requirement b:

ROTE APPLIANCE STORE, Inc.
Income Statement
For the Year Ended December 31, 19D
Case A—Perpetual Inventory System and Single-Step Format

Revenues:		
Sales	$102,000	
Less: Sales returns and allowances	2,000	
Net sales revenue		$100,000
Expenses:		
Cost of goods sold	60,000	
Expenses (not detailed for case purposes)...............................	22,000	
Depreciation expense	3,000	85,000
Pretax income..		15,000
Income tax expense ($15,000 × 20%)......................................		3,000
Net income		$ 12,000
EPS ($12,000 ÷ 4,000 shares)...		$3.00

ROTE APPLIANCE STORE, Inc.
Income Statement
For the Year Ended December 31, 19D
Case B—Periodic Inventory System and Multiple-Step Format

Gross sales revenue		$102,000
Less: Sales returns and allowances.......................................		2,000
Net sales revenues		100,000
Cost of goods sold:		
Inventory, January 1, 19D...	$ 20,000	
Purchases	57,000	
Purchase returns and allowances	(1,000)	
Goods available for sale..	76,000	
Less: Inventory, December 31, 19D	16,000	
Cost of goods sold		60,000
Gross margin on sales		40,000
Operating expenses:		
Expenses (not detailed for case purposes)...............................	22,000	
Depreciation expense	3,000	25,000
Pretax income..		15,000
Income tax expense ($15,000 × 20%)......................................		3,000
Net income		$ 12,000
EPS ($120,000 ÷ 4,000 shares)..		$3.00

Requirement c:

Adjusting Entries
December 31, 19D

	Case A		Case B	
	Perpetual inventory		*Periodic inventory*	
a. Expenses (estimated bad debt loss)	100		100	
Allowance for doubtful accounts.........		100		100
Bad debt loss estimated, $40,000 × 0.25% = $100.				
b. Depreciation expense......................	3,000		3,000	
Accumulated depreciation, equipment...........................		3,000		3,000
Depreciation for one year, $30,000 ÷ 10 years = $3,000.				
c. Income tax expense	3,000		3,000	
Income tax payable....................		3,000		3,000
Income tax for year, $15,000 × 20% = $3,000.				

Requirement d:

Closing Entries
December 31, 19D

		Case A		Case B	
		Perpetual inventory		*Periodic inventory*	
1.	Sales revenue...........................	102,000		102,000	
	Sales returns and allowances..........		2,000		2,000
	Income summary		100,000		100,000
	To transfer the revenue amounts to Income Summary.				
2.	Income summary	(Not applicable)		56,000	
	Purchase returns and allowances			1,000	
	Purchases...........................				57,000
	To transfer purchase amounts to Income Summary.				
3.	Income summary	(Not applicable)		20,000	
	Merchandise inventory (beginning).....				20,000
	To transfer beginning inventory to Income Summary.				
4.	Merchandise inventory (ending)...........	(Not applicable)		16,000	
	Income summary				16,000
	To transfer ending inventory from Income Summary.				
5.	Income summary	60,000		(Not applicable)	
	Cost of goods sold		60,000		
6.	Income summary	28,000		28,000	
	Expenses (not detailed)...............		22,000		22,000
	Depreciation expense.................		3,000		3,000
	Income tax expense		3,000		3,000
	To transfer expense amounts to Income Summary.				
7.	Income summary	12,000		12,000	
	Retained earnings....................		12,000		12,000
	To transfer net income to Retained Earnings.				

SUMMARY OF CHAPTER

This chapter discussed the measuring, recording, and reporting of the effects on income of the selling and purchasing activities of various types of business.

An important expense, cost of goods sold, was discussed. In conformity with the matching principle, the total cost of the goods sold during the period must be matched with the sales revenue earned during the period. The Cost of Goods Sold account measures the **cost** of merchandise that was sold while the Sales Revenue account measures the **selling price** of the same merchandise. When cost of goods sold is deducted from sales revenue for the period, the **difference is called gross margin on sales.** From this amount, the remaining expenses must be deducted to derive income.

The chapter also discussed and illustrated the effect on cost of goods sold of the beginning and ending inventory amounts. We observed that the ending inventory of one period is the beginning inventory of the next period. Two inventory systems were discussed for measuring the merchandise remaining on hand at the end of the period (ending inventory) and cost of goods sold for the period: (1) the perpetual inventory system, which is based on the maintenance of detailed and continuous inventory records for each kind of merchandise stocked; and (2) the periodic inventory system, which is based upon a physical inventory count of ending inventory and the costing of those goods in order to determine the proper amounts for cost of goods sold and ending inventory.

SUPPLEMENT 6A—DATA PROCESSING; CONTROL ACCOUNTS AND SUBSIDIARY LEDGERS

This supplement explains the use of control accounts and subsidiary ledgers that facilitate recordkeeping in situations where a large number of similar transactions occur. Their use does not involve accounting theory, principles, or standards but instead involves only the mechanics of processing. The use of control accounts and subsidiary ledgers will be explained and illustrated for accounts receivable; however, the procedure also is applicable in any situation that involves numerous transactions that are similar and require detailed recordkeeping, such as accounts payable and operational assets.

In the preceding discussions and illustrations, charge sales and services were credited to a revenue account with the corresponding debit to an account designated **Accounts Receivable.** Subsequently, upon payment, the Accounts Receivable account was decreased (a credit). Some businesses carry thousands of individual customers on a credit status. If a separate Accounts Receivable account was maintained in the general ledger for each customer, there would be thousands of receivable accounts in the general ledger. Instead, in most large businesses, the Accounts Receivable account is an aggregation of all of the individual customer accounts. However, to attain adequate control, and for

GENERAL LEDGER

Date 19A	Cash #101	Folio	Debit	Credit	Balance
Jan. 12		3	1,000		

	Accounts Receivable Control #102				
Jan. 5		1	2,400		2,400
7		2		140	2,260
12		3		1,000	1,260

	Sales #610				
Jan. 5		1		2,400	2,400

	Sales Returns #620				
Jan. 7		2	140		140

billing purposes, a business also must maintain detailed records concerning each customer's account.

Most large businesses maintain a **single control account** in the general ledger for Accounts Receivable and a **separate subsidiary ledger** that carries an individual account for each credit customer. Thus, in the above example, the **general ledger** would include Accounts Receivable as a **single control account** and the **subsidiary ledger** may include several thousand **individual receivable accounts.** At any given point, the **sum** of the individual account balances in the receivable subsidiary ledger should equal the single balance in the Accounts Receivable control account in the general ledger. The Accounts Receivable account in the general ledger is called a control account because it "controls" the subsidiary ledger. The individual customer accounts, as subdivisions of the control account, are subsidiary to the control account; thus the designation, subsidiary ledger.

SUBSIDIARY LEDGER

	Adams, J. K. 102.1					
Jan. 5		1	740			740
7	Return	2		140		600
12		3		400		200

	Baker, B. B. 102.2					
Jan. 5		1	120			120

	Ford, C. E. 102.3					
Jan. 5		1	340			340
12		3		340		-0-

	Moore, W. E. 102.4					
Jan. 5		1	320			320
12		3		220		100

	Price, V. T. 102.5					
Jan. 5		1	430			430
12		3		40		390

	Ward, B. L. 102.6					
Jan. 5		1	450			450

To illustrate the use of a control account with a subsidiary ledger for Accounts Receivable, we will assume several transactions for the Mayo Department Store. We will illustrate a manual system for instructional purposes, but control accounts and subsidiary ledgers also are used extensively with computerized systems. First, assume that on January 5, 19A, credit sales were made to six different customers. These sales could be recorded in the general journal as follows:

GENERAL JOURNAL   Page 1

Date	Account Titles and Explanation		Folio	Debit	Credit
Jan. 5	Accounts receivable		102	2,400	
	Sales revenue		610		2,400
	To record the following credit sales:				
	Adams, J. K.	$ 740	102.1		
	Baker, B. B.	120	102.2		
	Ford, C. E.	340	102.3		
	Moore, W. E.	320	102.4		
	Price, V. T.	430	102.5		
	Ward, B. L.	450	102.6		
	Total.............................	$2,400			

Posting of the above journal entry to the control account in the general ledger is indicated by entering the Accounts Receivable and Sales Revenue **account numbers** in the folio column in the usual manner. Posting to the individual customer accounts in the subsidiary ledger is indicated by entering an individual customer's account number in the folio column of the journal. Thus, the total amount was posted to the control account, Accounts Receivable (a debit total of $2,400), and the several single amounts were posted to the subsidiary ledger as illustrated earlier. Note that the debit-credit-balance form is used in our example of a subsidiary ledger rather than the T-account form that often is used for instructional purposes.

Now, assume that on January 7 one customer, J. K. Adams, returned some unsatisfactory merchandise purchased on January 5. Mayo accepted the goods and gave Adams credit on his account. The resultant journal entry was:

GENERAL JOURNAL   Page 2

Date	Account Titles and Explanation		Folio	Debit	Credit
Jan. 7	Sales returns		620	140	
	Accounts receivable		102		140
	To record the return of goods:				
	Adams, J. K.	$140	102.1		

The folio column reveals that the above entry has been posted in total to the control account in the general ledger and that the single amount has been posted to the individual customer account in the subsidiary ledger.

Now, let's complete the example by assuming subsequent collections on accounts from some of the customers. The collections are recorded in the journal entry given below. The folio column indicates that the entry has been posted in total to the control account and each single amount to the individual customer accounts in the subsidiary ledger.

GENERAL JOURNAL   Page 3

Jan. 12	Cash			101	1,000	
	Accounts receivable			102		1,000
	To record collections on accounts as follows:					
	Adams, J. K.	$ 400		102.1		
	Ford, C. E.	340		102.3		
	Moore, W. E.	220		102.4		
	Price, V. T.	40		102.5		
	Total	$1,000				

The subsidiary ledger should be reconciled frequently with the control account in order to determine whether errors were made in posting. This reconciliation is accomplished by summing the balances in the subsidiary ledger to determine whether that total agrees with the total shown by the control account in the general ledger. This check can be done simply by running an adding machine tape from the subsidiary ledger or by preparing a schedule or listing of the individual customer accounts balances. A reconciliation schedule for Mayo follows:

MAYO DEPARTMENT STORE
Schedule of Accounts Receivable
January 28, 19A

No.	Customer	Amount (per subsidiary)
102.1	Adams, J. K.	$ 200
102.2	Baker, B. B.	120
102.4	Moore, W. E.	100
102.5	Price, V. T.	390
102.6	Ward, B. L.	450
102	Total accounts receivable (per control account)	$1,260

In this instance, the subsidiary ledger total agrees with the balance in the control account. If there is disagreement, one or more errors are indicated; however, the mere fact of agreement does not necessarily mean there are no errors. A transaction could be posted to the wrong customer's account, and the two ledgers would still reconcile in total.

In the above situation, the **Sales Revenue** account also could have been established as a control account supported by a subsidiary ledger that would contain separate accounts for the sales of **each department** or for **each product.** Another common application of control accounts relates to **accounts payable** when there are numerous purchases on credit.

Control accounts are also useful when accounting for **operational assets.** For example, the Office Equipment account usually is included in the general ledger as a control account. In such instances, the control account is supported by a subsidiary ledger of office equipment that includes an account for each different kind of office equipment, such as copiers, typewriters, calculators, and furniture. These examples illustrate that the control account/subsidiary ledger procedure is an important element of the accounting information processing system of most enterprises.

A particular advantage of the use of subsidiary ledgers in a manual system is that it facilitates the subdivision of work. A person can be trained in a short time to maintain a subsidiary ledger because a knowledge of the broad field of accounting is not required for such routine recordkeeping tasks.

In the journal entries given above, the individual amounts relating to each individual customer account were listed in the Explanation column of the journal and then were posted to the subsidiary ledger. There are two approaches to simplifying this particular phase of the recordkeeping. Obviously, amounts could be transferred directly from the charge tickets to the subsidiary ledger accounts and thus avoid the detailed listing in the journal entry. This approach is used sometimes by small companies. Another simplifying approach involves the use of a related procedure known as **special journals.** This procedure is explained and illustrated in Supplement 8B.

Although our illustration used a manual approach to illustrate subsidiary ledgers, most companies of any size apply the procedure by means of electronic computers. The computer can be programmed to process credit sales, returns, collections on account, reconciliation of account balances, and a printout of monthly bills to be mailed to the customers.

SUPPLEMENT 6B—AGING ACCOUNTS RECEIVABLE

Usually as an account receivable gets older there is an increase in the probability that the account will be uncollectible. Therefore, an analysis of the age of accounts receivable provides management with valuable information concerning probable cash inflows, losses due to uncollectible accounts, and the general effectiveness of the credit and collection activities of the entity. Aging analysis of accounts receivable also is used by some companies to provide information needed to make the **adjusting entry** at the end of each period for estimated bad debt expense.

An aging analysis of the individual accounts receivable balances is done to **estimate** the amount of bad debts instead of estimating bad debt expense on the basis of credit sales for the period, as illustrated earlier in this chapter. The amount estimated to be uncollectible under the aging method is the balance that should be in the account "Allowance for Doubtful Accounts" at the end of the period. The **difference** between the **actual balance** in that account and the **estimated balance** is the amount recorded as bad debt expense in the adjusting entry at the end of the period.

To illustrate, assume the general ledger for Macon Appliance Store, whose fiscal year ended December 31, 19B, reflected the following account balances:

Accounts receivable.................. $ 40,000 (debit balance)
Allowance for doubtful accounts ...... 900 (credit balance)
Sales on credit for 19B 200,000

The adjusting entry for bad debt **expense** must be made at December 31, 19B. The company uses the **aging method** for determining the amount of the adjusting entry to record estimated bad debt expense. Consequently, the following aging analysis of accounts receivable was completed:

Aging Analysis of Accounts Receivable, December 31, 19B						
Customer	Total	Not Yet Due	1–30 Days Past Due	31–60 Days Past Due	61–90 Days Past Due	Over 90 Days Past Due
Adams, A. K.	$ 600	$ 600				
Baker, B. B.	1,300	300	$ 900	$ 100		
Cox, R. E.	1,400			400	$ 900	$ 100
Day, W. T.	3,000	2,000	600	400		
Zoe, A. B.	900					900
Total	$40,000	$17,200	$12,000	$8,000	$1,200	$1,600
Percent	100%	43%	30%	20%	3%	4%

The management, on the basis of experience and knowledge of specific situations, can use the above analysis as a basis for realistically estimating the probable **rates of uncollectibility for each age-group.** Assume the management **estimated** the following probable bad debt loss rates: not yet due, 1 percent; 1–30 days past due, 3 percent; 31–60 days, 6 percent; 61–90 days, 10 percent; over 90 days, 25 percent. The following estimating schedule can be prepared:

Estimate of Probable Uncollectible Accounts, December 31, 19B			
Age	Amount of Receivable	Percent Estimated to Be Uncollectible	Balance Needed in Allowance for Doubtful Accounts
Not yet due	$17,200	1	$ 172
1–30 days past due	12,000	3	360
31–60 days past due	8,000	6	480
61–90 days past due	1,200	10	120
Over 90 days past due	1,600	25	400
Total	$40,000		$1,532

The resultant adjusting entry on December 31, 19B, would be:

```
Dec. 31    Bad debt expense. . . . . . . . . . . . . . . . . . . . . . . . . . . . . . . . . . . . . . . . . . . . . . .    632
               Allowance for doubtful accounts . . . . . . . . . . . . . . . . . . . . . . . . . . .               632
           To adjust Allowance for Doubtful Accounts to the estimated
           balance needed.

           Computations
               Balance needed (per schedule above). . . . . . . . . . . . . . . . . . .     $1,532
               Balance before adjustment . . . . . . . . . . . . . . . . . . . . . . . . . . . . .        900
               Difference—adjustment needed (increase) . . . . . . . . . . . .        $  632
```

Some persons argue that the aging method approach to estimate the amount of bad debt expense does not apply the **matching principle** as effectively as the percent-of-credit-sales method discussed in the chapter. When the estimate is based on the amount of credit sales for the period from which uncollectible accounts ultimately will occur, bad debt expense is better matched with the current period's sales revenues.

In contrast, the aging method, because it is based on the ending balance in Accounts Receivable, tends to match bad debt expense with credit sales for a number of periods; hence, the matching principle may not be served well each period. However, the aging method produces a good measurement of the net realizable value of accounts receivable because it takes into account probable losses by actual age distribution of the amounts in each account.

In practice, the percent-of-credit-sales method appears to be used more widely.

IMPORTANT TERMS DEFINED IN THIS CHAPTER

Terms (alphabetically)	Keys words in definitions of important terms used in chapter	Page reference
Aging accounts receivable	Method to estimate uncollectible accounts based on the age of each account receivable.	290
Bad debt allowance method	Method that bases bad debt expense on an estimate of uncollectible accounts.	258
Bad debt loss	Expense associated with estimated uncollectible accounts receivable.	258
Gross margin on sales	As a dollar amount, net sales minus cost of goods sold; as a ratio, gross margin divided by net sales revenue.	253
Gross method to record revenue	Sales revenue is recorded without deducting the authorized cash discount.	256
Inventory shrinkage	Missing inventory caused by theft, breakage, spoilage, and incorrect measurements.	277
Markup	The difference between net sales revenue and cost of goods sold.	253
Net method to record revenue	Sales revenue is recorded after deducting the amount of any authorized cash discount.	256

Terms (alphabetically)	Keys words in definitions of important terms used in chapter	Page reference
Periodic inventory system	Ending inventory and cost of goods sold are determined at the end of the accounting period.	263
Perpetual inventory system	A detailed inventory record is maintained continuously during the accounting period.	263
Physical inventory count	Actual count of units in inventory.	263
Purchase discount	Cash discount received for prompt payment of an account payable.	271
Purchase returns and allowances	A deduction from the cost of purchases associated with unsatisfactory goods.	268
Sales discount	Cash discount offered to encourage prompt payment of an account receivable.	255
Sales returns and allowances	A contra revenue account which is associated with unsatisfactory goods.	261
Subsidiary ledger	A group of subaccounts that provides more detail than the general ledger control account.	286
Trade discount	A discount that is deducted from list price to derive the actual sales price.	257

QUESTIONS FOR DISCUSSION

Part A

1. In a company characterized by extensive selling and purchasing activities, the quantity of goods included in sales revenue also must be included in a particular expense amount. Explain the basis for this statement.

2. Explain the difference between gross sales and net sales.

3. What is gross margin on sales? How is the gross margin ratio computed (in your explanation, assume that net sales revenue was $100,000 and cost of goods sold was $60,000)?

4. Explain what is meant by sales discount. Use 1/10, n/30 in your explanation.

5. When merchandise, invoiced at $1,000, is sold on terms, 2/10, n/30, the vendor must make the following entry:

   Accounts receivable...............................
      Sales revenues ....

   What amounts should be used in this entry under the net method of recording sales discounts? Why is the net method preferred over the gross method?

6. A sale is made for $500; terms are 2/10, n/30. At what amount should the sale be recorded under the net method of recording sales discounts? Give the required entry with an explanation. Also, give the collection entry assuming it is after the discount period.

7. Because the actual time of cash collection is not relevant in determining the date on which a sale should be given accounting recognition, what factor is relevant?

8. Why is an estimate, instead of the actual amount of bad debts, used as the measure of periodic bad debt expense?

9. What is a contra account? Give two examples.

10. Define the book value of accounts receivable.

11. Why should estimated bad debt losses be based on credit sales rather than on total sales for the period?

12. What is the distinction between sales allowances and sales discounts?

13. Why are contra accounts used? Deal specifically with the case of allowance for doubtful accounts.

14. The estimated bad debt losses on sales for a period are treated as an expense in the chapter as they commonly are in published financial statements. Consider carefully the valuation of revenue and justify treating estimated bad debt losses on the credit sales for a period as a contra account to sales. Why might practice ignore your argument?

15. Sales discounts can be reported as *(a)* a contra revenue account, *(b)* an addition to selling expense, or *(c)* an interest expense. If the net method is theoretically correct as indicated in the chapter, what is the correct disclosure of sales discounts? Why?

Part B

16. Define goods available for sale. How does it differ from cost of goods sold?

17. Define beginning inventory and ending inventory.

18. Briefly distinguish between the perpetual and periodic inventory systems. Basically, how does each measure *(a)* inventory and *(b)* cost of goods sold?

19. Describe the periodic inventory model. Explain the source of each variable in the model.

20. Why is it necessary to take an actual physical inventory count at the end of the period when the periodic inventory system is used?

21. Under the cost principle, at what amount should a purchase be recorded? Be specific.

22. What is the purpose of a perpetual inventory record for each item stocked?

23. What accounts are debited and credited for a purchase of goods for resale *(a)* when a perpetual inventory system is used and *(b)* when a periodic inventory system is used?

24. What accounts are debited and credited for a sale of goods on credit *(a)* when a perpetual inventory system is used and *(b)* when a periodic inventory system is used?

25. Why is there no purchases account when the perpetual inventory system is used?

26. Why is transportation-in considered to be a cost of purchasing merchandise?

EXERCISES

Part A

E6–1. Supply the missing dollar amounts for the 19B income statement of Better Retail Company for each of the following independent cases:

	Case A	Case B	Case C	Case D	Case E
Sales revenue	$800	$800	$800	$?	$?
Selling expenses	?	190	80	120	180
Cost of goods sold	?	480	?	500	610
Income tax expense	?	30	30	20	40
Gross margin	400	?	?	?	390
Pretax income	100	40	?	80	?
Administrative expenses	100	?	60	100	90
Net income	80	?	120	?	80

E6–2. The following data were taken from the records of Reliable Appliances, Incorporated, at December 31, 19D:

Sales revenue	$150,000
Administrative expenses	15,000
Distribution (selling) expenses	20,000
Income tax rate	20%
Gross margin ratio	30%
Shares outstanding	4,000

Required:

Prepare a complete income statement for Reliable. Show all computations. (Hint: Set up side captions starting with sales revenue and ending with earnings per share; rely on the percents given.)

E6–3. The following data were taken from the records of Fun Center, Incorporated, at December 31, 19B:

Gross margin (40% ratio)	$24,000
Selling (distribution) expenses	9,000
Administrative expenses	?
Pretax income	10,000
Income tax rate, 17%	
Shares outstanding	2,000

Required:

Prepare a complete multiple-step income statement for Fun Center. Show all computations. (Hint: Set up the side captions starting with sales revenue and ending with earnings per share; rely on the percents given.)

E6–4. The following data were taken from the records of Leo Corporation on December 31, 19B:

Sales of merchandise for cash	$145,000
Sales of merchandise for credit	257,000
Sales returns and allowances	2,000
Selling expenses	100,000
Cost of goods sold	242,000
Administrative expenses	40,500

Items not included in above amounts:
  Estimated bad debt loss, 1% of net credit sales.
  Average income tax rate, 20 percent.
  Number of common shares outstanding,
  20,000.

Required:

a. Based on the above data, prepare a multiple-step income statement. There were no extraordinary items. Include a column for percentage analysis.

b. How much was the gross margin? What was the gross margin ratio? Explain what these two amounts mean.

E6–5. The following summarized data were provided by the records of Melody's Music Store, Incorporated, for the year ended December 31, 19B:

Sales of merchandise for cash	$124,000
Sales of merchandise on credit	80,000
Cost of goods sold	120,000
Distribution expenses	30,800
Administrative expenses	20,000
Sales returns and allowances	4,000

Items not included in above amounts:
  Estimated bad debt loss, 1½% of credit sales.
  Average income tax rate, 20 percent.
  Number of common shares outstanding,
  10,000.

Required:

a. Based upon the above data, prepare a multiple-step income statement. Include a Percentage Analysis column.

b. What was the amount of gross margin? What was the gross margin ratio? Explain.

E6–6. During the months of January and February, the WZH Corporation sold goods to three customers. The sequence of events was as follows:

Jan. 6 Sold goods for $800 to J. Doe and billed that amount subject to terms, 3/10, n/30.

6 Sold goods to R. Roe for $600 and billed that amount subject to terms, 2/10, n/30.

14 Collected cash due from J. Doe.

Feb. 2 Collected cash due from R. Roe.

28 Sold goods for $1,000 to B. Moe, and billed that amount subject to terms, 2/10, n/45.

Required:

a. Give the appropriate journal entry for each date. Assume a periodic inventory system is used and that the net method is used to record sales revenue.

b. Explain how each account balance as of February 28 should be reported, assuming that this is the end of the accounting period.

E6–7. The following transactions were selected from among those completed by Richard Retailers:

19B

Nov. 25 Sold 20 items of merchandise to Customer A at an invoice price of $2,000 (total); terms 3/10, n/30.

28 Sold 10 items of merchandise to Customer B at an invoice price of $4,000 (total); terms, 3/10, n/30.

30 Customer B returned one of the items purchased on the 28th; the item was defective and credit was given to the customer.

Dec. 6 Customer B paid the account balance in full.

30 Customer A paid in full for the invoice of November 25, 19B.

Required:

a. Give the appropriate journal entry for each of the above transactions assuming Richard Retailers uses the periodic inventory system and records sales revenue under the net method.

b. Assume it is December 31, 19B, end of the accounting period. Show how the various account balances would be reported on the balance sheet and the income statement.

E6–8. MK Company started business on January 1, 19A. During the year, 19A, the company's records indicated the following:

Sales on cash basis.....................	$200,000
Sales on credit basis..................	10,000
Collections on accounts receivable......	70,000

The manager of MK Company is concerned about accounting for the bad debts. At December 31, 19A, although no accounts were considered bad, several customers were considerably overdue in paying their accounts. A friend of the manager suggested a 1 percent bad debt rate on sales, which the manager decided to use at the start.

Required:

a. Assume you have been employed, on a part-time basis, to assist with the record-keeping for MK Company. The manager told you to set up bad debt expense of $3,000. Give the required entry.

b. Assume you were concerned about how the $3,000 was determined and the manager told you it was from another manager "who knew his business" and used 1 percent of sales. Do you agree with the $3,000? If you disagree, give the correct entry and explain the basis for your choice.

c. Show how the various accounts related to credit sales should be shown on the December 31, 19A, income statement and balance sheet.

E6–9. During 19G, West Ready-to-Wear Shop had sales revenue of $110,000, of which $40,000 was on credit. At the start of 19G, Accounts Receivable reflected a debit balance of $8,000 and the Allowance for Doubtful Accounts, a $500 credit balance. Collections on accounts receivable during 19G amounted to $33,000.

Data during 19G:

1. December 31, 19G, an account receivable (J. Doe) of $700 from a prior year was determined to be uncollectible; therefore, it was written off immediately as a bad debt.
2. December 31, 19G, on the basis of experience, a decision was made to continue the accounting policy of basing estimated bad debt losses on 2 percent of credit sales for the year.

Required:

a. Give the required journal entries for the two items on December 31, 19G (end of the accounting period).
b. Show how the amounts related to accounts receivable and bad debt expense would be reported on the income statement and balance sheet for 19G. Disregard income tax considerations.
c. On the basis of the data available does the 2 percent rate appear to be reasonable? Explain.

Part B

E6–10. Supply the missing dollar amounts for the 19B income statement of Joplin Retailers for each of the following independent cases:

Case	Sales Revenue	Beginning Inventory	Purchases	Total Available	Ending Inventory	Cost of Goods Sold	Gross Margin	Expenses	Pretax Income or (Loss)
A	900	100	700	?	200	?	?	200	?
B	900	180	750	?	?	?	?	100	0
C	900	140	?	?	300	650	?	100	?
D	900	?	600	?	210	?	?	150	50
E	900	?	650	?	100	?	100	?	(50)

E6–11. Supply the missing dollar amounts for the 19D income statement of Sweeney Company for each of the following independent cases:

	Case A	Case B	Case C
Sales revenue	6,000	6,000	6,000
Sales returns and allowances	150	?	?
Net sales revenue	?	?	?
Beginning inventory	9,000	9,500	8,000
Purchases	5,000	?	5,300
Freight-in	?	120	120
Purchase returns	40	30	?
Goods available for sale	?	14,790	13,370
Ending inventory	10,000	9,000	?
Cost of goods sold	?	?	5,400
Gross margin	?	110	?
Expenses	690	?	520
Pretax income	1,000	(500)	-0-

E6–12. The following list of transactions involving University Book Store were selected from the records of January 19B:

1. Sales: cash, $130,000; and on credit, $40,000 (terms, n/30).
2. Some of the merchandise sold on credit in 1 and subsequently returned for credit, $800.
3. Purchases: cash, $80,000; and on credit, $15,000 (terms, n/60).
4. Some of the merchandise purchased and subsequently returned for credit, $700.
5. Shipping costs paid in cash on the merchandise purchased, $400 (debit Freight-in).
6. Bad debt losses, on the basis of experience, are estimated to be 1 percent of credit sales net of sales returns and allowances.
7. An account receivable amounting to $150 was written off as uncollectible. The sale was made two years earlier.

Required:

a. Give the journal entry that would be made for each transaction, assuming the company uses a periodic inventory system.
b. Prepare an income statement for January 19B, through the caption "Gross margin on sales" and show the details of cost of goods sold. The December 31, 19A, inventory of merchandise was $75,000; and the physical inventory count of merchandise taken on January 31, 19B, amounted to $90,000.

E6–13. L & L Sport Shop sells merchandise on credit terms of 2/10, n/30. A sale invoiced at $800 was made to K. Williams on February 1, 19B. The full amount of the account was paid on time. L & L uses the net method of recording sales discounts.

Required:

a. Give the journal entry to record the credit sale.
b. Give the journal entry assuming the account was collected in full on February 9, 19B.
c. Give the entry assuming, instead, the account was collected in full on March 2, 19B.

On March 4, 19B, L & L purchased sporting goods from a supplier, on credit, invoiced at $6,000; the terms were 1/15, n/30. L & L uses the net method to record purchases.

Required:

d. Give the journal entry to record the purchase on credit. Assume a periodic inventory system.

e. Give the journal entry assuming the account was paid in full on March 12, 19B.

f. Give the journal entry assuming, instead, the account was paid in full on March 28, 19B.

E6–14. Arnold Company uses a perpetual inventory system. Because it is a small business and sells only five different high-cost items, a perpetual inventory record is maintained for each item. The following selected data relate to Item A for the month of January:

1. Beginning inventory—quantity 5, cost $77 each.
2. Purchased—quantity 4, cost $72 each; paid $20 total freight.
3. Sold—quantity 6, sales price $150 each.
4. Returns—one sold in (3) was returned for full credit.

Required:

a. Give the journal entries for the above transactions assuming a perpetual inventory system and cash transactions.

b. Prepare the perpetual inventory record for Item A.

c. For January, give the following amounts for Item A:

        a. Sales revenue.............. $_____
        b. Cost of goods sold .... $_____
        c. Gross margin on sales ...... $_____
        d. Ending inventory .... $_____

d. Is it possible to determine if there was any inventory shrinkage? Explain.

E6–15. Flower Company uses a perpetual inventory system that provides amounts for the period for (a) cost of goods sold and (b) ending inventory. Physical inventory counts are made from time to time to verify the perpetual inventory records. On December 31, 19B, the end of the accounting year, the perpetual inventory record for Item No. 18 showed the following (summarized):

	Units	Unit cost	Total cost
Beginning inventory.........................	500	$2	$1,000
Purchases during the period.................	900	2	1,800
Sales during the period (sales price $3.50)	800		

Required:

a. Give the journal entry to record the purchase of 900 units for cash during the period.

b. Give the journal entry to record the sales for cash during the period.

c. Assume a physical inventory count was made after the above transactions and it reflected 590 units of Item No. 18 on hand. Give any journal entry required.

d. Give the following amounts for 19B related to Item No. 18:

        1. Ending inventory .... units _____ $_____
        2. Cost of goods sold ...... units _____ $_____
        3. Shrinkage loss .... units _____ $_____

e. As a manager, would you investigate in this situation? How?

E6–16. During 19B, Iota Corporation's records reflected the following for one product stocked:

1.	Beginning inventory	1,000 units, unit cost $2
2.	Purchases.	8,000 units, unit cost $2
3.	Sales	7,000 units, unit sales price $3
4.	Purchase returns	10 units, for $2 per unit refund from the supplier
5.	Sales returns	5 units, for $3 per unit refund to the customer

Required:

a. All transactions were in cash; give the journal entries for the above transactions assuming:

Case A—A perpetual inventory system.

Case B—A periodic inventory system.

b. How would the amount of cost of goods sold be determined in each case?

c. Would you expect the cost of goods sold amount to be the same for Case A as for Case B? Why?

E6–17. The trial balance for Valley Store, Incorporated, at December 31, 19B (the end of the accounting year), is given below. Only selected accounts are given to shorten the case. The company uses a periodic inventory system. With the exception of the ending inventory, all of the accounts (before adjusting and closing entries) that you will need are listed in the trial balance.

Data developed as a basis for the adjusting entries at December 31, 19B, were:

a. Estimated bad debt expense for 19B was 1 percent of net credit sales of $12,000.

b. An inventory of store supplies on hand taken at December 31, 19B, reflected $50.

c. Depreciation on the store equipment is based on an estimated useful life of 10 years and no residual value.

d. Wages earned through December 31, 19B, not yet paid or recorded amounted to $500.

e. The beginning inventory is shown in the trial balance. A physical inventory count of merchandise on hand and unsold, at December 31, 19B, reflected $2,000.

f. Assume an average income tax rate of 20 percent.

Required:

Prepare a worksheet similar to the one in the demonstration case. If desired, you may omit columns for Adjusted Trial Balance and Retained Earnings. Enter the trial balance, adjusting entries, ending inventory, and complete the worksheet.

Debits		Credits	
Cash	$ 7,600	Allowance for doubtful	
Accounts receivable..............	3,000	accounts	$ 150
Merchandise inventory,		Accumulated depreciation	900
January 1, 19B.................	4,000	Accounts payable.................	5,000
Store supplies inventory..........	250	Wages payable	
Store equipment.................	3,000	Income tax payable	
Sales returns	150	Capital stock, par $10	6,000
Purchases......................	6,000	Retained earnings	1,870
Bad debt expense................		Sales revenue	13,000
Depreciation expense		Purchase returns	80
Freight-in (on purchases)..........	100		
Income tax expense..............			
Other operating expenses	2,900		
	$27,000		$27,000

E6–18. The trial balance for Home Appliances, Incorporated, at December 31, 19B (end of the accounting year), is given below. Only selected items have been used in order to shorten the case. The company uses a perpetual inventory system. All of the accounts you will need are listed in the trial balance.

Trial Balance
December 31, 19B

Account titles	Debit	Credit
Cash	$ 6,800	
Accounts receivable..................	12,000	
Allowance for doubtful accounts		$ 700
Merchandise inventory, ending	64,000	
Operational assets	40,000	
Accumulated depreciation		12,000
Accounts payable....................		8,000
Income tax payable		
Capital stock, par $10		60,000
Retained earnings, January 1, 19B......		14,300
Sales revenue		105,000
Sales returns and allowances	1,200	
Cost of goods sold...................	56,000	
Expenses (not detailed)...............	20,000	
Bad debt expense....................		
Depreciation expense		
Income tax expense..................		
....	$200,000	$200,000

Additional data developed for the adjusting entries:

a. Estimated bad debt expense is 2 percent of net credit sales. Net credit sales for 19B amounted to $35,000.
b. The operational assets are being depreciated $4,000 each year.
c. The average income tax rate is 20 percent.

Required:

Prepare a worksheet similar to the one in the demonstration case. If desired, you may omit columns for Adjusted Trial Balance and Retained Earnings. Enter the trial balance, adjusting entries, and complete the worksheet.

PROBLEMS/CASES

Part A

PC6–1. The following data were taken from the year-end records of Tip Top Company. You are to fill in all of the missing amounts. Show computations.

Income statement items		Case A		Case B
		Independent cases		
		Case A		Case B
Gross sales revenue		$110,000		$212,000
Sales returns and allowances		?		12,000
Net sales revenue		?		?
Cost of goods sold	(62%)	?		?
Gross margin on sales		?	(40%)	?
Operating expenses		18,000		?
Pretax income		?		35,000
Income tax expense (20%)		?		?
Income before extraordinary items		?		?
Extraordinary items	(gain)	5,000	(loss)	10,000
Less: Income tax (20%)		?		?
Net income		?		?
EPS (5,000 shares)		4.00		?

PC6–2. Adaire Equipment Company, Inc., sells heavy construction equipment. There are 10,000 shares of capital stock outstanding. The annual fiscal period ends on December 31. The following condensed trial balance was taken from the general ledger on December 31, 19D:

Account titles	Debit	Credit
Cash	$ 11,000	
Accounts receivable	20,000	
Allowance for doubtful accounts		$ 1,000
Inventory (ending)	90,000	
Operational assets	40,000	
Accumulated depreciation		8,000
Liabilities		17,000
Capital stock		100,000
Retained earnings, January 1, 19D		20,000
Sales revenue		208,000
Sales returns and allowances	8,000	
Cost of goods sold	110,000	
Selling expenses	37,000	
Administrative expenses	20,000	
Interest expense	3,000	
Extraordinary loss, unusual and infrequent storm damage	5,000	
Income tax expense*	10,000	
	$354,000	$354,000

*Assume a 40 percent average tax rate on both operations and the extraordinary loss.

Required:

a. Prepare a multiple-step income statement similar to the format in Exhibit 2–1. (Hint: Reflect the income tax effect of the extraordinary loss as is done with the extraordinary item in Exhibit 2–1.)

b. Prepare the following ratio analyses:
 1. Gross margin on sales ratio.
 2. Profit margin ratio (see Chapter 2).
 3. Return on investment; use owners' equity (see Chapter 2).
c. To compute (b) 2 and (b) 3, what amount did you use as the numerator? Explain why.
d. Briefly explain the meaning of each of the three ratios computed in (b).

PC6–3. Gnu Corporation is a local grocery store organized seven years ago as a corporation. At that time, a total of 10,000 shares of common stock was issued to the three organizers. The store is in an excellent location, and sales have increased each year. At the end of 19G, the bookkeeper prepared the following statement (assume all amounts are correct; also note the inappropriate terminology and format):

GNU CORPORATION
Profit and Loss
December 31, 19G

	Debit	Credit
Sales		$305,000
Cost of goods sold......................	$169,500	
Sales returns and allowances	5,000	
Selling expenses........................	60,000	
Administrative and general expenses	30,000	
Interest expense	500	
Extraordinary loss	4,000	
Income tax expense (on operations, $12,000 less $1,200 saved on the extraordinary loss)	10,800	
Net profit.............................	25,200	
	$305,000	$305,000

Required:

a. Prepare a multiple-step income statement similar to Exhibit 2–1. Assume an average 30 percent income tax rate.
b. Prepare the following ratio analyses:
 1. Profit margin on sales ratio (see Chapter 2).
 2. Gross margin on sales ratio.
 3. Return on investment; use owners' equity of $150,000 (see Chapter 2).
c. In computing ratios (b) 1 and (b) 3, what amount did you use for income? Explain why.
d. Generally, it is conceded that of the three ratios in (b), return on investment has the highest information content for the typical investor. Why?

PC6–4. The data below were selected from the records of Baldwin Company for the year ended December 31, 19C.

Balances January 1, 19C:
 Accounts receivable (various customers) $80,000
 Allowance for doubtful accounts 6,000

 Transactions during 19C:

1. Sold merchandise for cash, $200,000. Sold merchandise and made collections, on credit terms, 2/10, n/30, in the order given below (assume a unit sales price of $1,000 in all transactions and use the net method to record sales revenue):

2. Sold merchandise to T. Smith; invoice price, $18,000.
3. Sold merchandise to K. Jones; invoice price, $30,000.
4. T. Smith returned one of the units purchased in (2) above, two days after purchase date and received account credit.
5. Sold merchandise to B. Sears; invoice price, $20,000.
6. T. Smith paid his account in full within the discount period.
7. Collected $72,000 cash from customer sales on credit in prior year, all within the discount periods.
8. K. Jones paid the invoice in (3) above within the discount period.
9. Sold merchandise to R. Roy; invoice price, $10,000.
10. Three days after paying the account in full, K. Jones returned one defective unit and received a cash refund.
11. Collected $5,000 cash on an account receivable on sales in a prior year, after the discount period.
12. Baldwin wrote off a 19A account of $2,500 after deciding that the amount would never be collected.
13. The estimated bad debt rate used by Baldwin is 1 percent of *net* credit sales.

Required:

a. Give the journal entries for the above transactions, including the write-off of the uncollectible account and the adjusting entry for estimated bad debts. Assume a periodic inventory system. Show computations for each entry. (Hint: Set up T-accounts on scratch paper for Cash, Accounts Receivable by customer, Allowance for Doubtful Accounts, Sales Revenue, Sales Returns, Sales Discount Revenue, and Bad Debt Expense (this will provide the data needed for the next requirement).

b. Show how the accounts related to the above sale and collection activities should be reported on the 19C income statement and balance sheet.

PC6–5. The following transactions were selected from the records of Emerson Company:

July 15 Sold merchandise to Customer A at an invoice price of $4,000; terms 2/10, n/30.
20 Sold merchandise to Customer B at an invoice price of $3,000; terms 2/10, n/30.
21 Purchased inventory from Alpha Supply Company at an invoice price of $500; terms 3/10, n/45.
22 Purchased inventory from Beta Supply Company at an invoice price of $1,000; terms 1/10, n/30.
23 Received payment from Customer A, within the discount period.
25 Paid invoice from Alpha Supply Company, within the discount period.
Aug. 25 Received payment from Customer B, after the discount period.
26 Paid invoice from Beta Supply Company, after the discount period.

Required:

a. Give the appropriate journal entry for each of the above transactions. Assume that Emerson uses the periodic inventory system and records sales and purchases using the net method.

b. Give the appropriate journal entry for each of the above transactions. Assume that Emerson uses the periodic inventory system and records sales and purchases using the gross method.

PC6–6. (Based on Supplement 6B) Ready Equipment Company uses the aging approach to estimate bad debt expense at the end of each accounting year. Credit sales occur frequently on terms, n/60. The balance of each account receivable is aged on the basis of three time periods as follows: (a) not yet due; (b) up to one year past due; and (c) more than one year past due. Experience has shown that for each age group the average loss rate on the amount of the receivable at year-end due to uncollectibility is (a) 1 percent, (b) 5 percent, and (c) 30 percent.

At December 31, 19F (end of the current accounting year), the Accounts Receivable balance was $50,500, and the Allowance for Doubtful Accounts balance was $2,000. To simplify, only five customer accounts are used; the details of each on December 31, 19F, follow:

A. Able—Account Receivable

Date	Explanation	Debit	Credit	Balance
3/11/19E	Sale	15,000		15,000
6/30/19E	Collection		5,000	10,000
1/31/19F	Collection		3,000	7,000

C. Carson—Account Receivable

Date	Explanation	Debit	Credit	Balance
2/28/19F	Sale	21,000		21,000
4/15/19F	Collection		10,000	11,000
11/30/19F	Collection		3,000	8,000

M. May—Account Receivable

Date	Explanation	Debit	Credit	Balance
11/30/19F	Sale	18,000		18,000
12/15/19F	Collection		8,000	10,000

T. Tyler—Account Receivable

Date	Explanation	Debit	Credit	Balance
3/2/19D	Sale	5,000		5,000
4/15/19D	Collection		5,000	-0-
9/1/19E	Sale	12,000		12,000
10/15/19E	Collection		10,000	2,000
2/1/19F	Sale	19,000		21,000
3/1/19F	Collection		1,000	20,000
12/31/19F	Sale	1,500		21,500

Z. Ziltch—Account Receivable

Date	Explanation	Debit	Credit	Balance
12/30/19F	Sale	4,000		4,000

Required:

a. Set up an aging analysis schedule and complete it; follow the illustration given in Supplement 6B.

b. Compute the estimated collectible amount for each age category and in total.

c. Give the adjusting entry for bad debt expense at December 31, 19F.

d. Show how the amounts related to accounts receivable should be presented on the 19F income statement and balance sheet.

Part B

PC6–7. This problem is designed to demonstrate the accounting for cash discounts by both the vendor and purchaser. Observe the consistency between both parties to the same transactions—one party's sales discount is another party's purchase discount.

Assume the following summarized transactions between Company A, the vendor, and Company B, the purchaser. Use the letters to the left as the date notations. Assume each company uses a periodic inventory system and each uses the net method to record sales revenue and purchases.

1. Company A sold Company B merchandise for $10,000; terms, 2/10, n/30.
2. Prior to payment, Company B returned $1,000 (one tenth) of the merchandise for credit because it did not meet B's specifications.

Required:

Give the following journal entries in parallel columns for each party:

a. The sale/purchase transaction.
b. The return transaction.
c. Payment in full assuming it was made within the discount period.
d. Payment in full assuming, instead, it was made after the discount period.

Use a form similar to the following:

		Co. A—Vendor		Co. B—Purchase	
Date	Accounts	Debit	Credit	Debit	Credit

PC6–8. College Shop, Incorporated, is a student co-op. It has been operating successfully for a number of years. The board of directors is composed of faculty and students. On January 1, 19X, when this case starts, the beginning inventory was $200,000; the Accounts Receivable balance was $3,000; and the Allowance for Doubtful Accounts had a credit balance of $400. A periodic inventory system is used and purchases are recorded using the net method.

The following transactions (summarized) have been selected from 19X for case purposes:

1.	Merchandise sales for cash.	$340,000
2.	Merchandise returned by customers as unsatisfactory, for cash refund	1,400
	Merchandise purchased from vendors on credit; terms, 2/10, n/30:	
3.	May Supply Company invoice price, before deduction of cash discount	4,000
4.	Other vendors, invoice price, before deduction of cash discount.	115,000
5.	Purchased equipment for use in the store; paid cash	1,800
6.	Purchased office supplies for future use in the store; paid cash.	600

7. Freight on merchandise purchased; paid cash (set up a separate account for
    this item).. 500
    Accounts payable paid in full during the period as follows:
8. May Supply Company, paid after the discount period 4,000
9. Other vendors, paid within the discount period............................ 98,000

Required:

a. Prepare journal entries for each of the above transactions.
b. Give the closing entry required at December 31, 19X, for:
    1. Beginning inventory.
    2. Ending inventory (assume $130,000).
c. Prepare a partial income statement through gross margin on sales.
d. Explain why it was preferable to record purchases using the net method.

PC6–9. The transactions listed below were selected from those occurring during the month of
January 19D for Ranch Department Store, Incorporated. A wide line of goods is offered
for sale. Credit sales are extended to a few select customers; however, the usual credit
terms are n/EOM.

1. Sales to customers:
    Cash... $350,000
    On credit.. 20,000
2. Unsatisfactory merchandise returned by customers:
    Cash... 4,000
    Credit... 1,000
    Merchandise purchased from vendors on credit; terms, 1/20, n/30:
3. AB Supply Company, amount billed, before deduction of cash
    discount... 1,000
4. From other vendors, amount billed, before deduction of cash
    discount... 120,000
5. Freight paid on merchandise purchased; paid cash (set up a
    separate account for this item).. 2,000
6. Collections on accounts receivable 17,000
    The accounts payable were paid in full during the period as
    follows:
7. AB Supply Company, paid after the discount period 1,000
8. Other vendors, paid within the discount period................ 118,800
9. Purchased two new typewriters for the office; paid cash.......... 900
10. An account receivable from a customer from a prior year
    amounting to $300 was determined to be uncollectible and was
    written off.
11. At the end of January the adjusting entry for estimated bad debts is
    to be made. The loss rate, based on experience, is 1 percent of
    net credit sales for the period (i.e., on credit sales less credit
    returns).

Relevant account balances on January 1, 19D, were Accounts Receivable, $3,200 (debit);
and Allowance for Doubtful Accounts, $900 (credit). Total assets at the end of the pe-
riod, $250,000.

Required:

a. Prepare journal entries for the above transactions assuming a periodic inventory
    system is in use and record purchases using the net method.
b. Show how the following amounts should be reported on the January 19D income
    statement and balance sheet. Show computations.
    (1) Bad debt expense.

(2) Balance in accounts receivable.

(3) Balance in allowance for doubtful accounts.

c. Explain why bad debt expense should not be debited for the $300 uncollectible account written off in January.

PC6–10. Quick Distributing Company uses a perpetual inventory system for the items it sells. The following selected data relate to Item 10, a small but high-cost item stocked during the month of January 19B.

1. Beginning inventory—quantity, 70; cost, $50 each.
2. Purchases—quantity, 90; cost, $48 each plus $180 for transportation on the purchases.
3. Sales—quantity, 120; sale price, $95 each.
4. Returns—Quick accepted a return of two of the items sold in 3 because they were not needed by the customer and they had not been used.
5. At the end of January 19B a physical inventory count showed 37 items remaining on hand.

Required (assume all transactions were cash):

a. Prepare the perpetual inventory record for Item 10.
b. Give journal entries for each of the above transactions.
c. Prepare the income statement for January 19B through gross margin on sales as it related to Item 10. What was the gross margin ratio?
d. As the responsible manager, would you investigate the inventory shrinkage? How?
e. Assume that you observe quite often that the required items are out of stock. How can a perpetual inventory system be helpful in avoiding this problem?

PC6–11. Ditmore Company uses a perpetual inventory system. During the month of January 19D, the perpetual inventory record for Item A, which is one of the 23 items stocked, is shown below (summarized):

PERPETUAL INVENTORY RECORD

Date	Explanation	Goods Purchased		Goods Sold		Balance	
		Units	Total Cost	Units	Total Cost	Units	Total Cost
1	Beginning inventory					40	3,200
2	Purchase (at $80 each)	20	1600			60	4800
3	Sale (sales price $150 each)			31	2480	29	2320
4	Purchase return (one unit)	(1)	(80)			28	2240
5	Purchase (at $80 each)	30	2400			58	4640
6	Sale return (one unit)			(1)	(80)	59	4720
7	Sale (sales price $150 each)			29	4350	30	2400
8	Inventory shortage (two units)	(2)	(160)			28	2240

Required:

a. Complete the perpetual inventory record.
b. Give the journal entry for each transaction reflected in the perpetual inventory record (assume transactions are cash).
c. Complete the following tabulation:

Income statement:	
Sales.......................$	8850
Cost of goods sold	4720
Gross margin on sales	4130
Gross margin ratio	.46 =(17%)
Balance sheet:	
Inventory	2240

d. Explain how the inventory shortage should be reported.
e. As the responsible manager, would you investigate this situation? How?
f. Assume "stockout" has been a problem. What would you recommend?

PC6–12. The following transactions, relating to one product sold by Robertson Company, were completed in the order given during January:

a. Purchased—quantity, 120; cost, $20 each.
b. Sold—quantity, 100; $30 each.
c. Purchase return—returned one of the units purchased in *(a)* because it was the wrong size.
d. Sales return—accepted two units from a customer that were sold in *(b)*. The customer did not need them, and they were not damaged.
e. Inventories:
   Beginning inventory, January 1—30 units at total cost of $600.
   Ending inventory, January 31—per periodic inventory count, 51 units @ $20 = $1,020.
f. Cost of goods sold for January—98 units @ $20 – $1,960.

Required:

Give the journal entries that would be made for the above transactions assuming: Case A—a perpetual inventory system is used, and Case B—a periodic inventory system is used. To do this, set up the following form (assume cash transactions):

		Amounts			
		Perpetual		Periodic	
Date	Explanation	Debit	Credit	Debit	Credit
a.	To record the purchase				
b.	To record the sale				
c.	To record the purchase return				
d.	To record the sales return				
e.	To record the closing entries for inventories				
f.	To record the closing entry for cost of goods sold				
g.	To close purchases and purchase returns				

PC6–13. Roberta Retailers Inc., is completing the accounting information processing cycle for the year ended December 31, 19D. The worksheet given below has been completed through

the adjusting entries. (An optional column "Adjusted Trial Balance," may be helpful in completing the requirements.)

Required:

a.   Complete the following worksheet (periodic inventory system is used). Assume an average income tax rate of 20 percent.

b.   Give the closing journal entries at December 31, 19D. Close all revenue and expense accounts to Income Summary.

ROBERTA RETAILERS, INC.
Worksheet—December 31, 19D

Account Titles	Trial Balance		Adjusting Entries		Income Statement		Retained Earnings		Balance Sheet	
	Debit	Credit	Debit	Credit	Debit	Credit	Debit	Credit	Debit	Credit
Cash	25,700									
Accounts receivable	12,000									
Allowance for doubtful accounts		300		(a) 400						
Merchandise inventory Jan. 1, 19D	30,000									
Equipment	22,500									
Accumulated depreciation, equipment		7,500		(b) 1,500						
Other assets	20,000									
Accounts payable		8,000								
Interest payable				(c) 300						
Note payable, long term, 12%		10,000								
Capital stock, par $10		50,000								
Contributed surplus		7,500								
Retained earnings, Jan. 1, 19D		13,000								
Dividends declared (and paid (19D)	6,000									
Sales revenue		95,000								
Sales returns and allowances	1,000									
Purchases	52,000									
Freight-in	2,000									
Purchase returns and allowances		1,100								
Operating expense (not detailed)	20,300									
Bad debt expense			(a) 400							
Depreciation expense			(b) 1,500							
Interest expense	900		(c) 300							
Merchandise inventory, Dec. 31, 19D ($32,000)										
	192,400	192,400								
Income tax expense										
Income tax payable										
Net income										
Retained earnings, Dec. 31, 19D										

PC6–14.   A recent annual report for a large company contained the following information at the end of their fiscal year:

	Year 1	Year 2
Accounts receivable......................	$7,022,075,000	$7,336,308,000
Allowance for doubtful accounts	(86,605,000)	(96,989,000)
	$6,935,470,000	$7,239,319,000

A footnote to the financial statements disclosed that uncollectible accounts amounting to $55,000,000 were written off as bad during Year 1 and $69,000,000 during Year 2. Assume that the tax rate for the company was 40 percent.

Required:

a.   Determine the bad debt expense for Year 2 based on the facts given above.

b.   Working capital is defined as current assets minus current liabilities. How was the company's working capital affected by the write-off of $69,000,000 in uncollectible accounts during Year 2? What impact did the recording of bad debt expense have on working capital in Year 2?

c.   How was net income affected by the $69,000,000 write-off during Year 2? What impact did the recording of bad debt expense have on net income for Year 2?

PC6–15.   (Note: This is an extended problem designed to review Chapters 3, 4, 5, and 6). Quality Furniture Store, Inc., has been in operation for a number of years and has been quite profitable. The losses on uncollectible accounts and on merchandise returns are about the same as for other furniture stores. The company uses a perpetual inventory system. The annual fiscal period ended December 31, 19B, and the end-of-period accounting information processing cycle has been started. The following trial balance was derived from the general ledger at December 31, 19B.

Account titles	Debit	Credit
Cash	$ 28,880	
Accounts receivable.......................	36,000	
Allowance for doubtful accounts		$ 4,600
Merchandise inventory (ending)	110,000	
Store equipment...........................	20,000	
Accumulated depreciation		8,000
Accounts payable..........................		10,000
Income tax payable		
Interest payable		
Notes payable, long term (12%).............		50,000
Capital stock, par $10		70,000
Retained earnings, January 1, 19B...........		11,400
Sales revenue		441,000
Sales returns and allowances	25,000	
Cost of goods sold.........................	223,350	
Selling expenses...........................	102,700	
Administrative expenses	49,070	
Bad debt expense..........................		
Depreciation expense		
Interest expense...........................		
	$595,000	$595,000
Income tax expense........................		
Net income		

Data for adjusting entries:

a.   The bad debt losses due to uncollectible accounts are estimated to be $6,000.

b.   The store equipment is being depreciated over an estimated useful life of 10 years with no residual value.

c.   The long-term note of $50,000 was for a two-year loan from a local bank. The interest rate is 12 percent, payable at the end of each 12-month period. The note was dated April 1, 19B. (Hint: Accrue interest for nine months.)

d.   Assume an average 20 percent corporate income tax rate.

Required:

a. Based upon the above data, complete a worksheet similar to the one illustrated in the chapter for the demonstration case. If you prefer, you may omit columns for Adjusted Trial Balance and Retained Earnings. (Hint: Net income is $22,704).

b. Based upon the completed worksheet, prepare a multiple-step income statement and classified balance sheet.

c. Based upon the completed worksheet, prepared the adjusting and closing journal entries for December 31, 19B. Close all revenue and expense accounts to Income Summary.

PC6–16. (Note: This is an extended problem designed to review the materials discussed in Chapters 3, 4, 5, and 6.) Northwest Appliances, Incorporated, is owned by six local investors. It has been operating for four years and is at the end of the 19D fiscal year. For case purposes, certain accounts have been selected to demonstrate the information processing activities at the end of the year for a corporation that sells merchandise rather than services. The following trial balance, assumed to be correct, was taken from the ledger on December 31, 19D. The company uses a periodic inventory system.

Debits		Credits	
Cash	$ 18,000	Allowance for doubtful	
Accounts receivable.............	28,000	accounts	$ 600
Merchandise inventory,		Accumulated depreciation........	12,000
January 1, 19D	80,000	Accounts payable...............	15,000
Prepaid insurance	300	Notes payable,	
Store equipment.................	40,000	long term (12%)	30,000
Sales returns and		Capital stock, par $10	40,000
allowances	3,000	Retained earnings,	
Purchases......................	250,000	January 1, 19D	2,000
Freight-in.....................	11,000	Sales revenue	400,000
Operating expenses.............	76,300	Purchase returns	7,000
	$506,600		$506,600

Additional data for adjusting entries:

a. Credit sales during the year were $100,000; based on experience, a 1 percent loss rate on credit sales has been established.

b. Insurance amounting to $100 expired during the year.

c. The store equipment is being depreciated over a 10-year estimated useful life with no residual value.

d. The long-term note payable for $30,000 was dated May 1, 19D, and carries a 12 percent interest rate per annum. The note is for three years and interest is payable on April 30 each year.

e. Assume an average income tax rate of 30 percent.

f. Inventories:
   Beginning inventory, January 1, 19D (per above trial balance), $80,000.
   Ending inventory, December 31, 19D (per physical inventory count, $75,000).

Required:

a. Prepare a worksheet at December 31, 19D, similar to the one shown in the demonstration problem in the chapter. If you prefer, you may omit columns for Adjusted Trial Balance and Retained Earnings. To save time and space, all operating expenses have been summarized. However, you should set up additional expense accounts for depreciation, bad debts, interest, and income tax. Also, you will need additional liability accounts for interest payable and income tax payable. (Hint: Net income is $37,940.)

b. Based upon the complete worksheet, prepare a multiple-step income statement and classified balance sheet.

c. Based upon the completed worksheet, prepare the adjusting and closing journal entries at December 31, 19D. Close all revenue and expense accounts to Income Summary.

PC6–17. (Related to Supplement 6A) City Department Store, Incorporated, is a large department store located in a midwestern city with a population of approximately 200,000 persons. The store carries top brands and attempts to appeal to "quality customers." Approximately 80 percent of the sales are on credit. As a consequence, there is a significant amount of detailed recordkeeping related to credit sales, returns, collections, and billings. The accounts receivable records are maintained manually; however, the store is considering computerizing this phase of the accounting information system. Included in the general ledger is a control account for Accounts Receivable. Supporting the control account is an accounts receivable subsidiary ledger which has individual accounts for more than 20,000 customers. For case purposes, a few accounts and transactions with simplified amounts have been selected. The case requirement is intended to indicate the nature of the data processing work that City Store plans to computerize; however, here it will be completed manually.

On January 1, 19F, the Accounts Receivable control account (No. 52), in the general ledger, reflected a debit balance of $4,000 and the subsidiary ledger reflected the following balances:

52.1	Akins, A. K.	$400
52.2	Blue, V. R.	700
52.3	Daley, U. T.	900
52.4	Evans, T. V.	300
52.5	May, O. W.	800
52.6	Nash, G. A.	100
52.7	Roth, I. W.	600
52.8	Winn, W. W.	200

During the month of January, the following transactions and events relating to sales activities occurred (use the letter notation at the left for date):

a. Sales of merchandise on credit.

Akins, A. K.	$300
Blue, V. R.	250
Winn, W. W.	730
May, O. W.	140
Daley, U. T.	70
Roth, I. W.	370
Evans, T. V.	410

b. Unsatisfactory merchandise returned by customers:

Roth, I.W.	$ 30
Winn, W. W.	70
Akins, A. K.	20

c. Collections on accounts receivable:

Winn, W. W.	$800
May, O. W.	940
Akins, A. K.	200
Roth, I. W.	700
Blue, V. R.	750
Daley, U. T.	600

d. The account for G. A. Nash has been inactive for several years. After an investigation, the management decided that it was uncollectible; therefore, it is to be written off immediately.

e. The estimated loss rate is 2 percent of net credit sales (i.e., on credit sales less returns for credit).

Required:

a. Set up the general ledger control account for Accounts Receivable. Also, set up the general ledger account for Allowance for Doubtful Accounts (No. 53) with a credit balance of $600. Indicate the beginning balance as "Bal." and for convenience use T-accounts for these two accounts.

b. Set up an accounts receivable subsidiary ledger; use three columns—Debit, Credit, and Balance. Enter the beginning balances with the notation "Bal."

c. Prepare journal entries for each of the above transactions.

d. Post the entries prepared in (c) to the Accounts Receivable control account, Allowance for Doubtful Accounts, and the subsidiary ledger. Use folio numbers.

e. Prepare a schedule of accounts receivable to show how much each customer owed at the end of January.

f. Show how accounts receivable and the related allowance amounts would be reported in the January balance sheet.

PC6–18.

Required:

a. If a spreadsheet computer package is available set up the worksheet for PC6–13 by using columns for trial balance, adjustments, and adjusted trial balance. Complete the adjusted trial balance columns. (Hint: Use entries to adjust for inventories.)

b. Erase the numbers or use a blank form of the problem in Part A and fit the data for PC6–15 to it. Make whatever changes are necessary and compute the adjusted trial balance columns.

PC6–19. The purpose of this exercise is to solve PC6–17 using dBASE II. dBASE II is a popular data base program which runs on many brands of microcomputers. These instructions were written for dBASE II version 2.4 operating on an IBM PC. However, they should work with more versions of dBASE II and with dBASE III. These instructions will not work on the demonstration version of dBASE II because that program does not permit a sufficient number of records.

This exercise, together with others in this text, will provide you with some knowledge of how a data base program works. In particular, you will learn how to set up a data base, modify it, make interactive queries of it, and prepare reports using information in it. While a double-entry bookkeeping system could be written using dBASE II, it is not used in solving problems in this text because doing so would greatly increase the amount of work you would have to do.

To solve PC6–17 using dBASE II, do the following:

a.   Start the computer using the appropriate procedures.
b.   Set up a floppy disk to hold the data base files that you will create in this exercise. On an IBM PC, this can be done by doing as follows:
—put a system's disk in drive A,
—type FORMAT B: and press RETURN
—follow the instructions you get from the computer
c.   Put the dBASE II diskette in the default disk drive and
type: DBASE ... and press RETURN

In using dBASE II, you may not know the details of a particular command or you may want more information about a command than what is presented below. To get additional information,
type: HELP (return)   or HELP topic (return)
For example, to find out how editing keys work inside dBASE,
type: HELP FULL SCREEN (return)
A summary of dBASE II commands appears at the end of this exercise.
d.   Instruct the computer to create and use files on your floppy disk instead of the dBASE disk which should not and probably cannot be used for this.
type: SET DEFAULT TO B ...and press RETURN
e.   Because much of the data that we will be entering into the data base is of a repetitive nature, we want the computer to carry items forward from one record to the next. In order to have this happen,
type: SET CARRY ON   ... and press RETURN
f.   Create a data base file to contain accounts receivable records
type: CREATE ACCOUNTS ...and press RETURN
g.   After you have asked the computer to create a file, it will ask you for information about the fields in the file. For each field, you enter the name of the field, the type of field that it is (Numeric or Character), its width, and, in a numeric field, the number of places following the decimal point. When you are finished defining fields, merely press the RETURN key before entering the field name.

Our file will have five fields in it. It will have a 1-character field called TYPE, a 5-character field called MONTHDAY, a 2-character field called YEAR, 20-character field called ACCOUNT, and a 14-character, long numeric field with two places beyond the decimal point called AMOUNT. The specific information which you are to enter into the computer is presented below in lowercase letters followed by "(return)." In entering this information into the computer, you may use upper- and lowercase letters at your discretion. Be sure to press the RETURN key when you see "(return)."

ENTER RECORD STRUCTURE AS FOLLOWS:
FIELD   NAME,TYPE,WIDTH,DECIMAL PLACES
001   type,c,1 (return)
002   monthday,c,5 (return)
003   year,c,2 (return)
004   account,c,20 (return)
005   amount,n,14,2 (return)
006   (return)

h.   Having done this, the computer will ask if you want to enter data into the file. If you answer Y, the computer will prompt you for information about the first record. If you answer N, the computer will present a small dot to indicate that it is ready for the next dBASE II command.

type: Y

If you made a mistake in entering any of this data into the computer, you will have to (1) type "N" instead of "Y" above, (2) delete the file ACCOUNTS you just created, and (3) recreate the file by repeating steps f and g. To delete the file:

type: CLEAR ... and press RETURN

type: DELETE FILE ACCOUNTS ... and press RETURN

DO NOT delete the file unless you made a mistake entering the information set forth in step g.

i.   Now enter the following data into the file. If you want to stop entering data, merely press the RETURN key before entering any data into the first field of the record. At a future time, you can resume entering data by typing:

SET CARRY ON   ...and press RETURN
USE ACCOUNTS   ...and press RETURN
APPEND   ...and press RETURN

The computer will then allow you to add data to the end of your data base.

In entering data into the file, use the up and down arrow keys to move from one field to the next. Use the right and left arrow keys to move from one position in a field to another position in it. In a character field, as you type new data into it, you type over the information under the cursor. If after entering the new information, there are characters under or to the right of the cursor which should not be in the new record, you must use the space bar to make these characters blank. In a numeric field, you merely enter the new number into the field. You can ignore any part of an old number which appears in the field. To advance from one record to the next put the cursor in the last field of the record and press RETURN.

In entering data into the file, keep in mind that dBASE is case sensitive. Consequently, you should use upper- and lowercase consistently as you enter data. If, for example, you use both "S" and "s" to record type of transaction, you will make it much harder for yourself when you want to determine what are the total sales on account.

Now enter the following data into the computer:

Type	Monthday	Year	Account	Amount
B	01/01	85	AKINS, A.K.	400
B	01/01	85	BLUE, V.R.	700
B	01/01	85	DALEY, U.T.	900
B	01/01	85	EVANS, T.V.	300
B	01/01	85	MAY, O.W.	800
B	01/01	85	NASH, G.A.	100
B	01/01	85	ROTH, I.W.	600
B	01/01	85	WINN, W.W.	200
S	01/05	85	AKINS, A.K.	300
S	01/08	85	BLUE, V.R.	250
S	01/10	85	WINN, W.W.	730
S	01/12	85	MAY, O.W.	140
S	01/14	85	DALEY, U.T.	70
S	01/19	85	ROTH, I.W.	370
S	01/24	85	EVANS, T.V.	410
R	01/09	85	ROTH, I.W.	−30
R	01/15	85	WINN, W.W.	−70
R	01/15	85	AKINS, A.K.	−20
C	01/15	85	WINN, W.W.	−800
C	01/12	85	MAY, O.W.	−940
C	01/16	85	AKINS, A.K.	−200
C	01/20	85	ROTH, I.W.	−700
C	01/20	85	BLUE, V.R.	−750
C	01/25	85	DALEY, U.T.	−600
W	01/25	85	NASH, G.A.	−100

In this table, B stands for beginning balance, S for sales, R for sales returns and allowances, C for collections, and W for write-offs. Positive numbers represent debits and negative ones represent credits.

If you made a mistake in entering any of this information, do not worry, it is easy to correct it. To do so, when you have dBASE's period, ".", prompt,

type: EDIT n ... and press RETURN

where n is the number of the record you want to edit. Once you have corrected the information using the arrow keys and typing the correction in the appropriate place, press CONTROL and W simultaneously to exit the editor. In order to know what records need correction, you might use the DISPLAY ALL command set forth below.

Having entered all this information into the computer, you can make queries of the data in the file. However, before doing this you must tell the computer that you want to use the data base file you just created. To do so,

type: USE ACCOUNTS ...and press RETURN

Some of the commands you might give and their expected results are described below:

DISPLAY ALL

... displays all the records in the file

DISPLAY RECORD 10

...displays the 10th record in the file

SUM AMOUNT

...gives the balance of the receivables

SUM AMOUNT FOR TYPE-'S'

...gives the total sales for the period; in requesting information from the computer, you must use the same case (upper or lower) that you used in entering the information into the computer. Thus, if you used lowercase letters for TYPE, you would have to use 's' in searching for amounts

SUM AMOUNT FOR TYPE = 'S' TO SALES
SUM AMOUNT FOR TYPE = 'R' TO RETURNS
STORE (SALES − RETURNS)*.02 TO UNCOLE XP

...puts the total sales for the period in a variable called SALES, total returns in a variable called RETURNS, and 2 percent of net credit sales in a variable called UNCOLEXP; to see the amount of the expense, type: DISPLAY UNCOLEXP; to see the amounts in all the variables,

type: DISPLAY MEMORY

DISPLAY ALL FOR ACCOUNT = 'BLUE'

...displays all records for BLUE, V.R.

SUM AMOUNT FOR ACCOUNT = 'BLUE'

...computes the balance of BLUE's account

SUM AMOUNT FOR AMOUNT >= 0

...computes the total debits

COUNT ALL FOR AMOUNT > = 0

...gives the number of debit accounts

COUNT ALL

...gives the total number of records in the file

etc....

One can also prepare reports using information in the data base. For example, you may want to prepare a ledger listing for accounts receivable such as the following:

```
*    AKINS, A.K.
01/01      85 B      400.00
01/05      85 S      300.00
01/15      85 R      − 20.00
01/16      85 C     − 200.00
** SUBTOTAL **
                     480.00


*    BLUE, V.R.
01/01      85 B      700.00
01/08      85 S      250.00
01/20      85 C     − 750.00
** SUBTOTAL **
                     200.00


*    DALEY, U.T.
01/01      85 B      900.00
01/14      85 S       70.00
01/25      85 C     − 600.00
** SUBTOTAL **
                     370.00


etc....
** TOTAL **
                    2060.00
```

To do this, it is necessary to organize the file by ACCOUNT, YEAR, and MONTHDAY. Since dBASE II is only capable of sorting a file one field at a time, the file must be sorted three times. One first sorts the least significant field, that is, MONTHDAY, then the next least significant field, YEAR, and finally, the most significant field, ACCOUNT.

To do this, type the following commands. (Lowercase items are what you type. You may type this information in upper- and lowercase letters as you desire.)

. sort on monthday to tmp1 (return)
SORT COMPLETE
. use tmp1 (return)
. sort on year to tmp2 (return)
SORT COMPLETE
. use tmp2 (return)
. sort on account to ageinput (return)
SORT COMPLETE
. use ageinput (return)
. display structure (return)
STRUCTURE FOR FILE: C:AGEINPUT.DBF
NUMBER OF RECORDS: 00025
DATE OF LAST UPDATE: 09/27/85
PRIMARY USE DATABASE

FLD	NAME	TYPE	WIDTH	DEC
001	TYPE	C	001	
002	MONTHDAY	C	005	
003	YEAR	C	002	
004	ACCOUNT	C	020	
005	AMOUNT	N	014	002
** TOTAL **			00043	

The DISPLAY STRUCTURE command shows you that all 25 records have been copied to the file AGEINPUT.

If you made a mistake in doing the above, you have to delete all the files you created, tell the computer you want to use the data base ACCOUNTS which you previously created, and then redo your sorts. To do this type the following:

CLEAR (return)
USE ACCOUNTS (return)
DELETE FILE TMP1 (return)
DELETE FILE TMP2 (return)
DELETE FILE AGEINPUT (return)
SORT ON MONTHDAY TO TMP1 (return)
USE TMP1 (return)
SORT ON YEAR TO TMP2 (return)
USE TEMP2 (return)
SORT ON ACCOUNT TO AGEINPUT (return)
USE AGEINPUT (return)

Note: do not perform these commands unless it is necessary.

The AGEINPUT file can be used to generate the desired listing of receivables by creating a report. To tell the computer you want to use the data base called AGEINPUT and to create the report, do as follows (you should type the information which appears in lowercase using uppercase and lowercase as you desire; when only "(return)" appears in lowercase in the material below, it means that the default values that dBASE uses for the given item are satisfactory and so you only have to press the RETURN key):

. use ageinput (return)
. report (return)

ENTER REPORT FORM NAME: ledger (return)
ENTER OPTIONS, M= LEFT MARGIN, L= LINES/PAGE, W= PAGE WIDTH (return)
PAGE HEADING? (Y/N) (return)
DOUBLE SPACE REPORT? (Y/N) (return)
ARE TOTALS REQUIRED: (Y/N) y (return)
SUBTOTALS IN REPORT? (Y/N) y (return)
ENTER SUBTOTALS FIELD: account (return)
SUMMARY REPORT ONLY? (Y/N) n (return)
EJECT PAGE AFTER SUBTOTALS? (Y/N) n (return)
ENTER SUBTOTAL HEADING: (return)
COL   WIDTH,CONTENTS
001   8,monthday (return)
ENTER HEADING: (return)
002   2,year (return)
ENTER HEADING: (return)
003   10,type (return)
ENTER HEADING: (return)
004   15,amount (return)
ENTER HEADING: (return)
ARE TOTALS REQUIRED? (Y/N) y (return)
005   (return)

This series of steps causes the report to be printed to the screen. If the report looks okay, you can print a copy of it.

type: REPORT FORM LEDGER TO PRINT (return)

If the report does not look satisfactory, for example, because you entered something incorrectly, you can correct it by deleting the file that generates the report and repeating the steps mentioned above; that is,

type: DELETE FILE LEDGER (return)
        REPORT (return)
        (enter the information requested by the computer)

Create aging program

To prepare an aging of receivables report it is necessary to write a dBASE II program. In addition, since the only information thus far entered into the computer is January data, it is necessary to enter more data into the file.

To create the program, which we will call AGING, you can either use an editor or the MODIFY COMMAND name command. If you use an editor, edit a file called AGING.PRG and put the program listed below in that file. If you use MODIFY COMMAND, type MODIFY COMMAND AGING and press RETURN. The basic editing commands available to you when you use MODIFY COMMAND are presented at the end of this problem. (Program lines which start with * are comment lines and do not have to be typed.)

SET TALK OFF
*this stops dBASE from printing calculation results on the
*screen
SELECT PRIMARY
USE AGEDACCT
*establishes AGEDACCT as the primary file; this file will
*be used as the output file

```
SELECT SECONDARY
USE AGEINPUT
*the above two commands make AGEINPUT, the sorted account
*file, the secondary file. This file will be used for
*data input
GOTO   TOP
ERASE
@  10,10 SAY 'Enter current date:   (MM/DD/YY) ' ?
ACCEPT TO THISDATE
*the above commands place one at the first record in the
*secondary file, erases the screen, asks you to enter
*the date, takes the date you enter and stores it in a variable called THISDATE
STORE VAL($(THISDATE,7,2))   TO   THISYEAR
STORE VAL($(THISDATE,1,2))   TO   THISMONTH
*stores the last two and the first two characters of
*THISDATE as numbers in variables THISYEAR and THISMONTH
DO WHILE .NOT. EOF
*begins a while loop which executes until one reaches
*the end of file
   STORE ACCOUNT TO NAME
   *takes ACCOUNT from the input file and stores it in the
   *local variable NAME
   STORE 0 TO BALANCE
   STORE VAL($(MONTHDAY,1,2)) TO ACCTMONTH
   *puts the numeric value of the first two characters
   MONTHDAY in the local variable ACCTMONTH
   DO WHILE ACCOUNT=NAME .AND. .NOT. EOF
      STORE BALANCE+AMOUNT TO BALANCE
      STORE VAL(YEAR) TO TRANSYEAR
      STORE VAL($(MONTHDAY,1,2)) TO TRANSMONTH
      STORE TRANSMONTH+((TRANSYEAR − THISYEAR)*12) TO TRANSMONTH
      IF BALANCE <= 0
         STORE THISMONTH TO ACCTMONTH
         ENDIF
      IF BALANCE > 0 .AND. TYPE = 'C'
         STORE TRANSMONTH TO ACCTMONTH
         ENDIF
      IF BALANCE > 0 .AND. TYPE = 'S' .AND. TRANSMONTH < ACCTMONTH
         STORE TRANSMONTH TO ACCTMONTH
         ENDIF
      IF .NOT. EOF
         SKIP 1
         *if not end of file go to next record
         ENDIF
      ENDDO
      *ends the while loop
   ?NAME,' BALANCE IS ',BALANCE
   *displays the name and the account balance on the screen
   *while this statement is unnecessary, it lets you see
```

```
*what happens as you move from one account to the next:
*without such a statement, nothing will appear on the
*screen until all records have been processed; this may
*lead you to think that the program is not operating
IF BALANCE > 0
   STORE 0 TO DAYS90
   STORE 0 TO DAYS60
   STORE 0 TO DAYS30
   STORE 0 TO DAYSCUR
   STORE THISMONTH − ACCTMONTH TO DELTAMONTH
   DO CASE
   *this is a special type of IF statement
      CASE DELTAMONTH = 0
         STORE BALANCE TO DAYSCUR
      CASE DELTAMONTH = 1
         STORE BALANCE TO DAYS30
      CASE DELTAMONTH = 2
         STORE BALANCE TO DAYS60
      OTHERWISE
         STORE BALANCE TO DAYS90
      ENDCASE
   SELECT PRIMARY
   *selects the primary, the nonsecondary file for
   *data base commands; this is our output file
   APPEND BLANK
   *this adds a blank record to the end of the file
   REPLACE ACCOUNT WITH NAME, CURRENT WITH DAYSCUR
   REPLACE THIRTY WITH DAYS30, SIXTY WITH DAYS60
   REPLACE NINETY WITH DAYS90
   *these commands replace fields in the primary file
   *with values of various memory variables
   SELECT SECONDARY
   *selects the secondary file, our input file, for
   *data base commands
   ENDIF
ENDDO
SET TALK ON
RETURN
```

Additional data

Since the data previously entered into the file was only for the month of January, the following information should be entered into the computer. Before entering this information you should:

type: USE ACCOUNTS (return)

APPEND (return)

Enter the following information:

Type	Monthday	Year	Account	Amount
S	06/15	84	ADARS, N.I.	300
S	07/22	84	SCRISVI, J.G.	430
S	07/30	84	HAMAC, K.H.	900
C	08/18	84	ADARS, N.I.	−300
R	08/20	84	HAMAC, K.H.	−100
S	09/08	84	AHAS, H.T.	150
S	09/20	84	MORDGA, C.I.	800
S	10/01	84	ZERWI, F.A.	200
S	10/08	84	GERSH, A.H.	620
R	10/10	84	AHAS, H.T.	−25
S	10/18	84	ELKAN, T.O.	430
C	10/18	84	SCRISVI, J.G.	−120
C	11/08	84	ZERWI, F.A.	−150
C	11/14	84	AHAS, H.T.	−75
C	11/22	84	GERSH, A.H.	−400
S	12/09	84	AHAS, H.T.	80
C	12/14	84	MORDGA, C.I.	−550
S	12/15	84	ADARS, N.I.	250
C	12/20	84	ELKAN, T.O.	−350
S	12/28	84	TWELMON, K.C.	300

Having entered this data, the information should be sorted and put into the file AGEINPUT, as was done before. Because the files TMP1, TMP2, and AGEINPUT already exist, they must be deleted. To do so, do the following:

type: DELETE FILE TMP1 (return)

DELETE FILE TMP2 (return)

DELETE FILE AGEINPUT (return)

sort the files as previously done

if you wish, you can print out the account balances by
typing: REPORT FORM LEDGER (return)

Since the program uses the file AGEDACCT for output, it is necessary to create this file before running the program. Create the file by typing what appears in lowercase letters below.

create agedacct (return)

ENTER RECORD STRUCTURE AS FOLLOWS:

FIELD   NAME,TYPE,WIDTH,DECIMAL PLACES

001   account,c,20 (return)

002   current,n,14,2 (return)

003   thirty,n,14,2 (return)

004   sixty,n,14,2 (return)

005   ninety,n,14,2 (return)

006   (return)

INPUT DATA NOW? n

To run the aging program

type: do aging (return)

When prompted for the date enter 01/31/85 (return)

The following information will appear on the screen:

```
ADARS, N.I.        BALANCE IS    250.00
AHAS, H.T.         BALANCE IS    130.00
AKINS, A.K.        BALANCE IS    480.00
BLUE, V.R.         BALANCE IS    200.00
DALEY, U.T.        BALANCE IS    370.00
ELKAN, T.O.        BALANCE IS     80.00
EVANS, T.V.        BALANCE IS    710.00
GERSH, A.H.        BALANCE IS    220.00
HAMAC, K.H.        BALANCE IS    800.00
MAY, O.W.          BALANCE IS      0.00
MORDGA, C.I.       BALANCE IS    250.00
NASH, G.A.         BALANCE IS      0.00
ROTH, I.W.         BALANCE IS    240.00
SCRISVI, J.G.      BALANCE IS    310.00
TWELMON, K.C.      BALANCE IS    300.00
WINN, W.W.         BALANCE IS     60.00
ZERWI, F.A.        BALANCE IS     50.00
```

You can now use the newly created file to create an ageing report for receivables. To do this type what appears in lowercase letters below.

```
. clear (return)
. use agedacct (return)
. display structure (return)
STRUCTURE FOR FILE:     C:AGEDACCT.DBF
NUMBER OF RECORDS:      00015
DATE OF LAST UPDATE:    06/28/85
PRIMARY USE DATABASE
FLD     NAME      TYPE   WIDTH   DEC
001     ACCOUNT   C       020
002     CURRENT   N       014    002
003     THIRTY    N       014    002
004     SIXTY     N       014    002
005     NINETY    N       014    002
** TOTAL **                00077
```

Now create the report by typing what appears in lowercase letters below.

```
. report (return)
ENTER REPORT FORM NAME: age (return)
ENTER OPTIONS, M= LEFT MARGIN, L=LINES/PAGE, W=PAGE WIDTH (return)
PAGE HEADING? (Y/N) (return)
DOUBLE SPACE REPORT? (Y/N) (return)
ARE TOTALS REQUIRED? (Y/N) y (return)
SUBTOTALS IN REPORT? (Y/N) n (return)
COL      WIDTH,CONTENTS
001         15,ACCOUNT (return)
ENTER HEADING: account name (return)
002         10,current (return)
ENTER HEADING: 0-30 days (return)
ARE TOTALS REQUIRED? (Y/N) y (return)
003         10,thirty (return)
ENTER HEADING: 30-60 days (return)
```

ARE TOTALS REQUIRED? (Y/N) y (return)
004   10,sixty (return)
ENTER HEADING: 60-90 days (return)
ARE TOTALS REQUIRED? (Y/N) y (return)
005   10,ninety (return)
ENTER HEADING: 90 plus days (return)
ARE TOTALS REQUIRED? (Y/N) y (return)
006   10,current + thirty + sixty + ninety (return)
ENTER HEADING: total (return)
ARE TOTALS REQUIRED? (Y/N) y (return)
007   (return)

(Column 006 above is a computed field. In a computed field, the column width is followed by an arithmetic expression which can involve constants or record variables. In this case the sum of the accounts receivable is computed.)

Having entered the RETURN in column 7, the following report will be generated on the computer's screen:

PAGE NO. 00001
06/28/85

account name	0–30 days	30–60 days	60–90 days	90 plus days	total
ADARS, N.I.	0.00	250.00	0.00	0.00	250.00
AHAS, H.T.	0.00	0.00	130.00	0.00	130.00
AKINS, A.K.	480.00	0.00	0.00	0.00	480.00
BLUE, V.R.	200.00	0.00	0.00	0.00	200.00
DALEY, U.T.	370.00	0.00	0.00	0.00	370.00
ELKAN, T.O.	0.00	80.00	0.00	0.00	80.00
EVANS, T.V.	710.00	0.00	0.00	0.00	710.00
GERSH, A.H.	0.00	0.00	220.00	0.00	220.00
HAMAC, K.H.	0.00	0.00	0.00	800.00	800.00
MORDGA, C.I.	0.00	250.00	0.00	0.00	250.00
ROTH, I.W.	240.00	0.00	0.00	0.00	240.00
SCRISVI, J.G.	0.00	0.00	0.00	310.00	310.00
TWELMON, K.C.	0.00	300.00	0.00	0.00	300.00
WINN, W.W.	60.00	0.00	0.00	0.00	60.00
ZERWI, F.A.	0.00	0.00	50.00	0.00	50.00
** TOTAL **					
	2060.00	880.00	400.00	1110.00	4450.00

Having created this report, you can now print it.
type: REPORT FORM AGE TO PRINT (return)

Summary of dBase Editing Commands

Full-screen cursor movement codes
down arrow moves cursor DOWN to the next field
up arrow moves cursor UP to the previous field
right arrow moves cursor AHEAD one character
left arrow moves cursor BACK one character
ctrl-G deletes character under cursor
<Rubout> or <DEL> deletes character to left of cursor
ctrl-Y blanks out current field to right of cursor
ctrl-V toggles between overwrite and INSERT modes
ctrl-W save changes and returns to "." prompt

In edit mode

ctrl-U toggles the record DELETE mark on and off

ctrl-C writes current record to disk and ADVANCES to next record

ctrl-R writes current record to disk and BACKS to previous record

ctrl-Q ignores changes to current record and returns to "." prompt

ctrl-W writes all changes to disk and returns to "." prompt

In modify mode

ctrl-T DELETES current line, moves all lower lines up

ctrl-N INSERTS new line at cursor position

ctrl-C scrolls down a half page

ctrl-W writes all changes to disk and returns to "." prompt

ctrl-Q ignores all changes and returns

In append mode

<enter> terminates APPEND when cursor is in first position of first field

ctrl-W writes record to disk and moves to next record

ctrl-Q ignores current record and returns to "." prompt

Control key strokes operable when not in full screen

ctrl-P toggles your printer ON and OFF

ctrl-R repeats last executed command

ctrl-X clears the command line without executing command

Summary of dBase II Commands

—?: displays an expression, variable, or field.

—??: displays an expression list without a preceding line feed.

—@: displays user formated data on screen or printer.

—ACCEPT: allows input of character strings into memory variables.

—APPEND: append information from another dBASE II
  database or files in Delimited or System Data format.

—BROWSE: full screen window viewing and editing of database.

—CANCEL: cancels command file execution.

—CHANGE: Non-Full-Screen edit of fields of database.

—CLEAR: closes databases in use and releases current memory variables.

—CONTINUE: continue the searching action of a LOCATE command.

—COPY: creates a copy of an existing database.

—COUNT: counts the number of records in file which meet some criteria.

—CREATE: creates new database.

—DELETE: deletes a file or marks records for deletion.

—DISPLAY: display files, database records or structure, memory variables, or status.

—DO: executes command files or structured loops in same.

—EDIT: initiates edit of records in a database.

—EJECT: ejects a page on the printer.

—ELSE: alternate path of command execution within IF.

—ENDCASE: terminates a CASE command.

—ENDDO: terminates DO WHILE command.

—ENDIF: terminates an IF command.

—ENDTEXT: terminates a TEXT command

—ERASE: clears the screen.

—FIND: positions to record corresponding to key in index file.

—GO or GOTO: positions to specific record or place in file.

—HELP: access help file overview or specific help file entry.
—IF: allows conditional execution of commands.
—INDEX: creates an index file.
—INPUT: allows input of expressions into memory variables.
—INSERT: insert new record in database.
—JOIN: joins output of two databases.
—LIST: lists files, database records or structure, memory variables, and status.
—LOCATE: find a record that fits a condition.
—LOOP: skips to beginning of DO WHILE command.
—MODIFY: create and/or edit command file or modify structure of existing database.
—NOTE or *: allows insertion of comments in command file.
—PACK: erases records marked for deletion.
—QUIT: exits dBASE and returns to operating system.

(Prepared by C. Dirksen)

Costing Methods for Measuring Inventory and Cost of Goods Sold

PURPOSE OF THIS CHAPTER

In the previous chapters, we assumed that the unit cost of items that were purchased for inventory remained stable. In reality, however, the unit cost of inventory items often will change each time a new purchase order is placed. When unit cost changes in this manner, the accountant must answer two difficult questions at the end of the accounting period: (1) What quantity (units) of goods and what cost (dollars) should be assigned to **ending inventory?** (2) What quantity of goods and what cost should be assigned to **cost of goods sold?**

This chapter discusses the generally accepted accounting answers to these two questions and their implementation in an information processing system. The discussions and illustrations will be presented in two parts as follows:

Part A—Measuring ending inventory and cost of goods sold with a periodic inventory system

Part B—Application of a perpetual inventory system and selected inventory costing problems

Part A—Measuring Ending Inventory and Cost of Goods Sold with a Periodic Inventory System

INVENTORY EFFECTS ON THE MEASUREMENT OF INCOME

A close relationship exists between ending inventory and cost of goods sold. When the periodic inventory system (Chapter 6) is used, inventory items not in the ending inventory are assumed to have been sold. Thus, the measurement of ending inventory affects both the balance sheet (assets) and the income statement (cost of goods sold and net income). The amount of inventory, measured at the end of the accounting period, affects not only the accounting income for that period but also the amount of income for the **following accounting period.** This two-period effect is due to the fact that the ending inventory for one period is the beginning inventory for the next accounting period. To illustrate these effects, assume that the 19A and 19B income statements for Company X reflected pretax incomes of $5,000 and $6,500, respectively, measured as follows:

	19A		19B	
Sales revenue..................		$100,000		$110,000
Cost of goods sold:*				
Beginning inventory	$ –0–		$10,000	
Purchases...................	70,000		58,000	
Goods available for sale	70,000		68,000	
Ending inventory	10,000		–0–	
Cost of goods sold ...		60,000		68,000
Gross margin.................		40,000		42,000
Expenses.....................		35,000		35,500
Pretax income		$ 5,000		$ 6,500

*See Chapter 6: BI + P − EI = CGS.

Observe that the ending inventory, as measured and reported at December 31, 19A, amounted to $10,000. This amount also is reported as the beginning inventory of 19B.

To illustrate inventory effects on **pretax** income, assume that an error was made in measuring the ending inventory at December 31, 19A, because the recorded amount should have been $11,000 (i.e., $1,000 more than shown above). The $1,000 understatement of the ending inventory could have been due to either one or a combination of the following factors:

1. In physically counting the inventory items, some items were left out incorrectly. They had a cost of $1,000.
2. Although the physical count of items was correct, in determining the total cost of inventory, a higher unit cost should have been used. This higher cost would have increased the amount of the inventory by $1,000.

We now will see how this $1,000 understatement of the 19A ending inventory affected the pretax income amounts for each of the two years. The income statement may be restated to reflect the correct inventory amount as follows:

	19A	19B
Sales revenue	$100,000	$110,000
Cost of goods sold:		
Beginning inventory	$ –0–	$11,000
Purchases.................	70,000	58,000
Goods available for sale	70,000	69,000
Ending inventory...........	11,000	–0–
Cost of goods sold.......	59,000	69,000
Gross margin..............	41,000	41,000
Expenses	35,000	35,500
Pretax income	$ 6,000	$ 5,500

Observe that in comparison with the preceding income statements, pretax income for 19A is more by $1,000 and less by the same amount for 19B. Thus, a comparison of the two sets of income statements demonstrates the following generalizations:

1. **In the period of the change**—An increase in the amount of the ending inventory for a period decreases cost of goods sold by the same amount, which in turn increases pretax income for that period by the same amount. To the contrary, a decrease in the amount of ending inventory increases cost of goods sold, which in turn decreases pretax income for that period by the same amount.

2. **In the next period**—An increase in the amount of the ending inventory for a period increases the beginning inventory for the next period. The increase in beginning inventory increases cost of goods sold which decreases the pretax income of the next period by the same amount. To the contrary, a decrease in the amount of the ending inventory for a period decreases cost of goods sold of the next period which increases pretax income of the **next period** by the same amount.

There is a direct relationship between ending inventory and pretax income. Conversely, there is an inverse relationship between beginning inventory and pretax income.

The above illustration was presented to indicate the importance of careful measurement of inventory. Care must be exercised in (1) measuring the **quantity** of items that should be included in the inventory and (2) applying the dollar **unit cost** to the units included in the ending inventory.

ITEMS TO BE INCLUDED IN INVENTORY

Inventory usually includes tangible property that is: (1) held for sale in the normal course of business or (2) to be consumed in producing goods or services for sale. Inventory is reported on the balance sheet as a current asset because it normally will be consumed or converted into cash within one year or within the next operating cycle of the business, whichever is the longer. Inventory is less liquid (i.e., less readily convertible to cash) than accounts receivable; therefore, inventory usually is listed below accounts receivable on the balance sheet.

The kinds of inventory normally held depend upon the characteristics of the business:[1]

Retail or Wholesale Business:

Merchandise inventory—goods (or merchandise) held for resale in the normal course of business. The goods usually are acquired through purchase in a completely manufactured condition and are ready for sale without further processing.

Manufacturing Business:[2]

Finished goods inventory—goods manufactured by the business, completed and ready for sale.

Work in process inventory—work (or goods) in the process of being fabricated or manufactured but not yet completed as finished goods. Work in process inventory, when completed, becomes finished goods inventory.

Raw materials inventory—items acquired by purchase, growth (such as food products), or extraction of natural resources for the purpose of processing into finished goods. Such items are accounted for as raw materials inventory until used. When used, their cost is included in the work in process inventory (along with direct labour and factory overhead costs). The flow of inventory costs in a manufacturing environment can be diagrammed as follows:

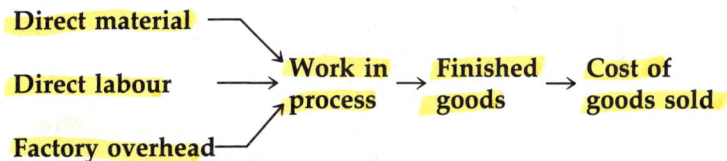

The work in process inventory includes the cost of raw materials used and the **direct labour** incurred in the manufacturing process and the factory overhead costs. Direct labour cost represents the earnings of employees who work directly on the products being manufactured. Factory overhead costs include all manufacturing costs that are not direct material or direct labour costs. For example, the salary of the plant supervisor would be included in factory overhead.

---

[1]Supplies on hand may be reported as prepaid expenses or totaled with raw materials where they are used to manufacture a product.

[2]Management accounting presents a complete discussion of inventory measurement and accounting in a manufacturing environment.

The discussions that follow focus on merchandise and finished goods inventories.

In measuring the **physical quantity** of goods in the inventory, a company should include all items to which it has **ownership,** regardless of their locations. In business transactions involving purchase and sale, accounting focuses on the passage of ownership. Usually when ownership passes, one party records a sale and the other party records a purchase. In a purchase/sale transaction, the basic guideline is that ownership to the goods passes at the **time intended by the parties** to the transaction. Usually, ownership passes when the goods are delivered by the seller to the buyer; however, there are situations in which this is not the case.

The terms of sale have conditions that can affect the passage of title to the goods to the buyer. Three conditions are generally encountered either explicitly in the terms of sale or implicitly in the usual trade relations between the buyer and seller. Conditions of quantity of delivery, time of delivery and place of delivery, if not followed by the seller, can lead to a rescinding of the contract by the buyer. Two common shorthand notations for terms which signify the relative conditions to be followed are: (1) FOB (free on board) at a location specified which signifies the seller's responsibility to place the goods on the type of transport specified and have the goods delivered at the seller's expense to the location specified, such as FOB Halifax. (2) CIF (cost, insurance, freight) signifies the seller agrees the price includes insurance in the name of the buyer, shipping, and freight to the location specified, such as CIF Ottawa.[3] The 1980 Incoterms statement by the International Chamber of Commerce of Paris, France, outlines the more generally accepted shipping terms. FOR or FOT stand for free on rail car or free on a truck at a specific departure point. FOS stands for free alongside a ship at a particular port. Ex QUAY implies port, import costs, and taxes are paid to a specific port. At this point it is worth noting that the term FOB destination commonly found in accounting textbooks is no longer an accepted term by transportation authorities. CIF or C&F at port of destination is now used in place of the older term. Because the terms and conditions such as FOB, CIF and COD (cash on delivery) are only part of the sales terms that govern the passage of title to the goods to the buyer, the accountant must be careful to understand these terms in order to appropriately record the sale.

The passage-of-ownership guideline is a facet of the revenue principle, previously discussed (Exhibit 2–6). The passage-of-ownership guideline has a legal basis and prevails in the accounting process with respect to both the sale and purchase of goods. In the absence of the passage-of-ownership guideline, the financial statements could be manipulated to overstate revenue by entering all **sales orders** received up through the last day of the period, regardless of the fact that ownership to the goods ordered may not have passed to the

[3]J. E. Smyth, and D. A. Soberman, *The Law and Business Administration in Canada,* 4th ed. (Scarborough, Ont.: Prentice-Hall Canada, 1983), pp. 362–78.

buyer. Conversely, costs could be manipulated by not recording purchases even though ownership to the goods has passed.

When a company has possession of goods that it does not own, those goods should be excluded from the inventory. This situation often occurs when goods are on **consignment** for sale on a commission basis. The supplier (known as the consignor) legally retains ownership to the goods on consignment, although the goods are in the physical possession of the party that will sell them (known as the consignee). The consignor, although the goods are not in his or her physical possession, should include them in the ending inventory. The consignee, although having possession of the goods, should exclude them from the ending inventory because ownership still resides with the consignor.

In summary, in identifying the individual items to be included in the ending inventory at a specific date, ownership, rather than physical possession is the controlling consideration. The inventory should include all of the goods to which the entity has legal ownership.

MEASURING INVENTORY COST

In Chapter 6 we discussed the application of the cost principle to the purchase of goods for resale. Goods in inventory are recorded in accordance with the **cost principle** as follows:

> In the case of merchandise purchased for resale, or of raw materials which are to enter into production, cost may be said to be "laid-down" cost; for example, an invoice cost (in terms of Canadian dollars) plus customs and excise duties and freight and cartage. In the case of work in process and finished goods, cost will include the laid-down cost of material plus the cost of direct labour applied to the product and ordinarily the applicable share of overhead expense properly chargeable to production.[4]

In accordance with the cost principle, indirect expenditures related to the purchase of goods, such as freight, insurance, and storage, theoretically should be included in measuring the purchase cost of the goods acquired. However, because these incidental amounts frequently are not **material in amount** (see the materiality concept, Exhibit 2–6) when related to the total purchase cost, and because there often is no convenient method of apportioning such costs to each item of goods, they may not be assigned to the inventory cost. Thus, for practical reasons, some companies use the **net invoice price** when assigning a unit cost to goods included in the ending inventory and record the indirect purchase expenditures as a separate cost which is added to cost of goods sold. Abnormal costs such as those arising from rehandling, or idle facilities can and should be eliminated from the inventory cost.

Chapter 6 discussed the assignment of **dollar cost** to (a) the ending inventory and (b) cost of goods sold in situations in which there were no changes in unit purchase (or manufacturing) cost during the period (including the begin-

---

[4]*CICA Handbook*, Section 3030.

EXHIBIT 7–1
Illustrative
inventory data

SUMMER RETAIL STORE
19A Illustrative Data—Beginning Inventory, Purchases, and Sales

Transactions	Symbol	Number of units	Unit cost	Total cost	
Beginning inventory January 1, 19A (carried over from last period).....................	BI	100	$6		$ 600
Purchases during 19A:					
January 3, first purchase	P	50	7	$ 350	
June 12, second purchase....................	P	200	8	1,600	
December 20, third purchase	P	120	9	1,080	
Total purchases during 19A..............		370			3,030
Goods available for sale during the year		470			3,630
Goods sold during 19A:					
January 6 (unit sales price, $10)	S	40			
June 18 (unit sales price, $12).................	S	220			
December 24 (unit sales price, $14)...........	S	60			
Total sales during 19A		320			?
Ending inventory December 31, 19A (units 470 − 320).........................	EI	150			?

ning inventory). This chapter expands those discussions to the typical situation in which the cost per unit of the goods stocked changes during the annual accounting period. To illustrate the typical situation, assume Summer Retail Store stocks a product that reflected the beginning inventory, merchandise purchases, and sales data given in Exhibit 7–1.

When there is a change in the unit cost of items purchased for inventory, an accounting allocation problem must be resolved before the financial statements can be prepared. In the case of Summer Retail Store, the accounting problem is: of the $3,630 total cost of **goods available for sale,** how much should be apportioned to cost of goods sold (i.e., for the 320 units sold) and how much should be apportioned to the ending inventory (i.e., 470 units − 320 units = 150 units). The answer to this problem necessarily involves assignment of the four unit cost amounts ($6, $7, $8, and $9), or some combination of them, to the ending inventory and to cost of goods sold. This part of the chapter discusses the alternative methods used for making this allocation (assignment) of costs.

Chapter 6 presented two alternative inventory systems used to accumulate data to facilitate determination of (a) the ending inventory and (b) cost of goods sold. To review, the two alternative inventory systems are:[5]

1. **Periodic inventory system**—This system accumulates total merchandise acquisition cost (including the beginning inventory), and at the **end of the accounting period,** the ending in-

---

[5]Often a single company will use one of the systems for certain items stocked and the other system for the remaining items. The choice usually depends upon such factors as the nature of the item (size), unit cost, number of units stocked, and cost to implement the system.

ventory is measured by means of a physical inventory count of all goods remaining on hand. The units counted on hand then are valued (costed) in dollars by using appropriate unit purchase cost amounts (for example, from above, some combination of $6, $7, $8, and $9). The periodic inventory system measures **cost of goods sold** as a residual amount; that is:

$$BI + P - EI = CGS$$

2. **Perpetual inventory system**—This system maintains a detailed daily inventory record throughout the period for each item stocked. This record includes (a) the beginning inventory, (b) each purchase, (c) each issue (i.e., sales), and (d) a continuous (perpetual or running) balance of the inventory. Thus, this system measures cost of goods sold and ending inventory without a physical inventory count at the end of each accounting period. Under this system, the **ending inventory** can be viewed as a residual amount; that is:

$$BI + P - CGS = EI$$

The discussions that follow in Part A of this chapter present several alternative inventory costing methods under the assumption that the **periodic inventory system** is used. Part B of this chapter discusses these methods with a perpetual inventory system. The four generally accepted **inventory costing methods** commonly used are:

1. Weighted average.
2. First-in, first-out (FIFO).
3. Last-in, first-out (LIFO).
4. Specific identification.

The primary objective of the inventory costing methods is not limited to measurement of the amount of goods on hand in order to obtain the balance sheet amount, but the objective also is to measure cost of goods sold, which is important in the measurement of income.

APPLICATION OF THE INVENTORY COSTING METHODS WITH THE PERIODIC INVENTORY SYSTEM

The four inventory costing methods listed above are **alternative allocation methods** for assigning the total amount of goods available for sale (BI + P) between (a) ending inventory (reported as an asset at the end of the period) and (b) cost of goods sold (reported as an expense of the period). For illustration, refer to the data for Summer Retail Store given in Exhibit 7–1. These two allocated amounts are given below. They were calculated using the weighted-average inventory costing method. At this point you need not be concerned about how the two amounts were calculated.

	Units	Amount
Goods available for sale (total amount to be allocated).........	470	$3,630
Cost allocation:		
Ending inventory (determined by inventory count and then costed at weighted-average unit cost)..............	150	1,158
Cost of goods sold (residual amount).................	320	$2,472

The amount of **goods available for sale** ($3,630) was allocated between **ending inventory** ($1,158) and **cost of goods sold** ($2,472), and the sum of these two amounts (and the related units as well) necessarily must be the same as goods available for sale. This cost allocation procedure also is portrayed graphically in Exhibit 7–2.

Each of the four inventory costing methods listed above will be discussed and illustrated using the data for Summer Retail Store given in Exhibit 7–1.

The total amount of cost to be allocated (cost of goods available for sale) is provided directly by the accounting records under either the periodic inventory system or the perpetual inventory system. The **periodic inventory system** requires computation of the ending inventory by means of a physical count of the goods remaining on hand (which then are costed in dollars by applying one of the inventory costing methods), and cost of goods sold is computed as a residual amount; the amount that remains after ending inventory is subtracted from cost of goods available for sale.

EXHIBIT 7–2
Graphic illustration of cost allocation

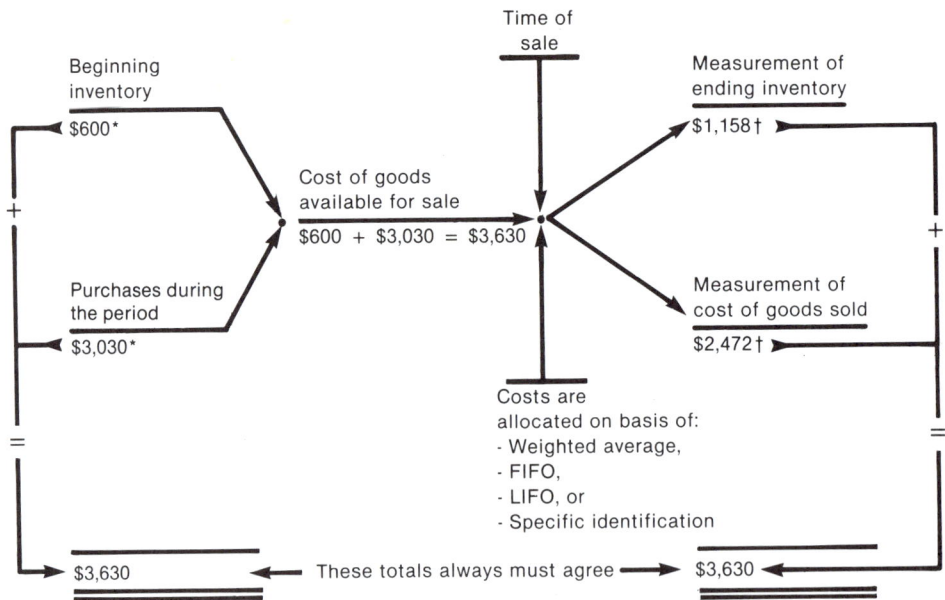

*Data from Exhibit 7-1.
†Based on the weighted-average cost method.

INVENTORY COSTING METHODS ILLUSTRATED

A choice among the inventory costing methods is necessary only when there are different unit costs in the beginning inventory and/or purchases during the current period. (If unit costs are stable, all of the methods provide exactly the same amounts.) The choice among the inventory costing methods is not based on the physical flow of goods on and off the shelves. Although the actual **physical flow** of goods usually is first-in, first-out (FIFO), a company can use any of the four inventory costing methods. Generally accepted accounting principles only require that the inventory costing method used be rational and systematic.

A company is not required to use the same inventory costing method for all inventory items, and no particular justification is required for the selection of one or more of the acceptable methods. However, a change in method is viewed as significant and requires special disclosures in the footnotes to the financial statements.

Weighted-average inventory costing method

The weighted-average method requires computation of the weighted-average unit cost of the goods available for sale. In a periodic inventory system, the computed unit cost is applied to the **number of units** in inventory determined by the physical inventory count to derive the total cost of ending inventory. Cost of goods sold is determined by subtracting the ending inventory amount from the amount of goods available for sale. To illustrate, the weighted-average method would be applied by Summer Retail Store (Exhibit 7–1) as follows under a **periodic** inventory system.[6]

Step 1—Computation of the weighted-average unit cost for the period:

$$\frac{\text{Total goods available for sale—at cost}}{\text{Total goods available for sale—units}} = \frac{\$3,630}{470} = \$7.72 \quad \left\{ \begin{array}{l} \textbf{Weighted-} \\ \textbf{average} \\ \textbf{cost per} \\ \textbf{unit for} \\ \textbf{the period} \end{array} \right.$$

Step 2—Allocation of the cost of goods available for sale under the periodic inventory system:

	Units	Amount
Goods available for sale (Exhibit 7–1)	470	$3,630
Ending inventory (150 units × $7.72)	150	1,158*
Cost of goods sold (residual amount)	320	$2,472†

*Reported on the balance sheet.
†Reported as an expense on the income statement. This amount can be verified as 320 units × $7.72 = $2,470 (a $2 rounding error).

---

[6]When an average cost is used, uneven unit cost usually are rounded to the nearest cent. The rounded unit cost amount is used to compute the ending inventory amount which allocates any rounding error to cost of goods sold. Under the perpetual inventory system, a moving average unit cost (rather than the weighted-average unit cost) usually is used (see Part B).

The weighted-average cost method is rational, systematic, easy to apply, and not subject to manipulation. It weights the number of units purchased and unit costs that prevailed during the period (including the beginning inventory). Thus, it is representative of costs during the entire period (including the beginning inventory) rather than of the cost only at the beginning, end, or at one point during the period.[7] Representative costs are reported on both the balance sheet (ending inventory) and the income statement (cost of goods sold).

First-in, first-out inventory costing method

The first-in, first-out method, frequently referred to as **FIFO, assumes that the oldest units (i.e., the first costs in) are the first units sold (i.e., the first costs out).** In other words, the units in the beginning inventory are treated as if they were sold first, the units from the first purchase sold next, and so on until the units left in the ending inventory all come from the most recent purchases. FIFO allocates the oldest unit costs to cost of goods sold and the most recent unit costs to the ending inventory.

Frequently, FIFO is justified on the basis that it is consistent with the actual physical flow of the goods. In most businesses, the first goods placed in stock tend to be the first goods sold. However, FIFO can be applied regardless of the actual physical flow of goods because the objective of FIFO is to allocate costs to ending inventory and to cost of goods sold in a systematic and rational manner.

To illustrate, the FIFO method would be applied by Summer Retail Store (Exhibit 7–1) as follows under a **periodic** inventory system:

	Units	Unit cost	Total cost
Goods available for sale (Exhibit 7–1)	470		$3,630
Valuation of ending inventory (FIFO):			
At latest unit costs, 150 units:			
From December 20 purchase (latest)	120	$9	$1,080
From June 12 purchase (next latest).................	30	8	240
Valuation, FIFO basis	150		1,320*
Cost of goods sold (residual FIFO amount)......	320		$2,310†

*Report on balance sheet.
†Report as an expense on income statement. This amount can be verified as follows: Units sold at oldest costs—100 units @ $6 = $600, plus 50 units @ $7 = $350, plus 170 units @ $8 = $1,360, which sum to $2,310.

The FIFO method is rational, systematic, easy to apply, and not subject to manipulation. On the balance sheet, the FIFO ending inventory amount is costed on the basis of the most recent unit costs and, therefore, it is likely to be a realistic valuation prevailing at the balance sheet date. In contrast, on the income statement, cost of goods sold is at the oldest unit costs, which may not reflect the current cost of items which were sold. The significance of the impact of FIFO, on the income statement (i.e., cost of goods sold and income) and the

---

[7] A weighted-average unit cost rather than a simple average of the unit costs must be used. For example, ($6 + $7 + $8 + 9) ÷ 4 = $7.50 would be incorrect because it does not consider the number of units at each unit cost.

balance sheet (i.e., the ending inventory amount under current assets) depends on the extent to which unit costs increase or decrease during the period. Comparative effects are illustrated later.

Last-in, first-out inventory costing method

The last-in, first-out method, frequently referred to as **LIFO, assumes that the most recently acquired goods are sold first.** Regardless of the physical flow of goods, LIFO treats the costs of the most recent units purchased as cost of goods sold, which leaves the unit costs of the beginning inventory and the earlier purchase cost in the ending inventory. The LIFO flow assumption is the exact opposite of the FIFO flow assumption.

That is, under LIFO, the total ending inventory cost is measured at the oldest unit costs and cost of goods sold is measured at the newest unit costs.

To illustrate, the LIFO method would be applied by Summer Retail Store (Exhibit 7–1) as follows under a **periodic** inventory system.

	Units	Unit cost	Total cost
Goods available for sale (Exhibit 7–1)	470		$3,630
Valuation of ending inventory (LIFO):			
At oldest unit costs, 150 units:			
From beginning inventory (oldest)..................	100	$6	$600
From January 3 purchase (next oldest)	50	7	350
Valuation, LIFO basis	150		950*
Cost of goods sold (residual LIFO amount)	320		$2,680†

*Report on balance sheet.
†Report as an expense on the income statement. This amount can be verified as follows: Units sold at latest costs—120 units @ $9 = $1,080, plus 200 units @ $8 = $1,600, which sum to $2,680.

The LIFO method is rational and systematic. However, it is subject to manipulation by buying (or not buying) goods at the end of a period when unit costs have changed, which makes it possible to manipulate cost of goods sold and, hence, reported income. On the income statement, LIFO cost of goods sold is based on the latest unit costs, which is a realistic measurement of the current cost of items which were sold. In contrast, on the balance sheet, the ending inventory amount is based on the oldest unit costs which may be an unrealistic valuation. The comparative impact of LIFO will be discussed later.[8]

Specific identification inventory costing method

Specific identification is another method of allocating the cost of goods available for sale to cost of goods sold and the ending inventory by keeping track of the purchase cost of each item. This is done either by coding the purchase cost on each unit before placing it in stock or by keeping a separate record of the unit and identifying it with a serial number. When a sale is made, the cost

---

[8] The discussion assumes an item-by-item application of LIFO and costing of goods sold currently throughout the period. Other approaches to the computation of LIFO are possible but the results are approximately the same as the item-by-item approach used here. It should be noted, as well, that LIFO is not popular in Canada because it is not allowed for Canadian income tax computations.

of that specific unit is identified and recorded. For example, using the data given in Exhibit 7–1, if the 40 units sold on January 6 were selected specifically from the units that were purchased at $6 each (i.e., from the beginning inventory), the cost of goods sold amount for that particular sale would be measured as 40 units × $6 = $240. Alternatively, if 20 of the units were selected from those that cost $6 each (from the beginning inventory) and the other 20 from those that cost $7 each (from the January 3 purchase), cost of goods sold would be measured as (20 units × $6) + (20 units × $7) = $260.

The specific identification method would be rather tedious and impractical where (1) unit costs are low, (2) unit costs change frequently, or (3) a large number of different items are stocked. On the other hand, where there are "big-ticket" items such as automobiles and expensive jewelry, it is especially appropriate because each item tends to be different from the other items. In such situations, it is rational because the **selling price** usually is based on a markup over specific cost. However, the method may be manipulated when the units are identical because one can affect the cost of goods sold and the ending inventory accounts by "picking and choosing" from among the several available unit costs, even though the goods are identical in other respects. To illustrate, in the above example, cost of goods sold was either $240 or $260, depending on the choices made. In that example, income would be different by $20, depending on an arbitrary selection from a group of identical items.

COMPARISON OF THE INVENTORY COSTING METHODS

Each of the four alternative inventory costing methods is in accordance with generally accepted accounting principles, although each may produce significantly different income and asset (i.e., ending inventory) amounts. To illustrate this difference, the comparative results for Summer Retail Store are as follows:

	Sales revenue	Cost of goods sold	Gross margin	Balance sheet (inventory)
Weighted average......	$3,880	$2,472	$1,408	$1,158
FIFO.................	3,880	2,310	1,570	1,320
LIFO (end of period)...	3,880	2,680	1,200	950

From the above results, we see that when unit costs are changing, each method tends to give different income and different inventory amounts. Observe that the difference in **pretax income** among each of the methods is the same as the difference in the inventory amounts. The method that provides the highest ending inventory amount also provides the highest income amount and vice versa. The weighted-average cost method tends to give income and inventory amounts that fall between the FIFO and LIFO extremes.

We will focus now on a comparison of the FIFO and LIFO methods because they usually represent the extreme, and opposite, effects. Note in the comparison above that unit costs were **increasing** and that LIFO provided the lower income and inventory amounts, whereas FIFO provided the higher income and inventory amounts. In comparing the effects of LIFO with FIFO, it is important to note that the comparative effects will depend upon the direction of change in unit cost. When unit costs are rising, LIFO will result in lower income and a lower inventory valuation than will FIFO. Conversely, when unit costs are declining, LIFO will result in higher income and higher inventory valuation than will FIFO. These effects occur because LIFO will cause the newer unit costs to be reflected on the income statement whereas FIFO will cause the older unit costs to be reflected on the income statement.

Many accountants believe that the best inventory costing method is the one that best reflects the sales pricing policy of the company, and many companies do price units for sale in each of the ways implied by these four costing methods. Other accountants believe that the choice of method should be based upon whether the measurement emphasis should be on the income statement or on the balance sheet. Those who believe that the income statement should be accorded primary emphasis tend to defend LIFO because it matches the most recent purchase cost with current sales revenue. To the contrary, those who prefer to emphasize the balance sheet tend to prefer FIFO because it reports the ending inventory on the balance sheet at the most current cost price. Because of these considerations, it is not difficult to understand why the accounting profession has accepted several alternative inventory costing methods.

COMPARABILITY PRINCIPLE (CONSISTENCY)

The previous section emphasized that different income statement and balance sheet amounts result from the use of different inventory costing methods. These differences in reported financial data cause problems for statement users in comparing companies that use different accounting methods. Problems are also created when an individual business changes accounting methods over time. The comparability principle (Exhibit 2–6)[9] is applied to maximize comparability when accounting alternatives are permitted. The comparability principle holds that in the accounting process all concepts, principles, and measurement approaches should be applied in a similar or consistent way from one period to the next in order to assure that the data reported in the financial statements are reasonably comparable over time. This principle prevents arbitrary changes from one accounting or measurement approach to another. The comparability principle is not inflexible. It permits changes in accounting when the changes tend to improve the measurement of financial results and financial position if the user of the statements is informed of the change.

---

[9]Careful reading of Exhibit 2–6 will indicate that the definition of the comparability principle is broader than its usage in this section. The more restricted interpretation presented in this chapter concentrates on the consistency aspect of the definition of comparability. This usage of the principle is consistent with how it is applied in Canadian practice.

In respect to inventories, a business is not permitted to change from one inventory costing method to another from period to period. Changing from one inventory costing method to another is a major event, and such a change requires full disclosure as to the reason for the change and the accounting effects.

Part B—Application of a Perpetual Inventory System and Selected Inventory Costing Problems

Recall that in Chapter 6, Part B, the periodic and perpetual inventory systems were discussed and illustrated. Regardless of which of the two alternative inventory systems is used, one or more of the inventory costing methods (discussed in Part A) must be applied. The discussions and illustrations in Part A of this chapter assumed a periodic inventory system (i.e., in this system the units in the ending inventory are determined by a physical inventory count, and then the units found to be on hand are valued in dollars by applying one of the inventory costing methods).

This part of the chapter discusses and illustrates **application of each of the inventory costing methods with a perpetual inventory system.** Separate discussion of the two systems is essential because:

a.   The timing of the application of the inventory costing methods between the two systems causes some differences in the allocated amounts. The periodic inventory system costs inventory units at the end of the period, whereas the perpetual inventory system costs units on a day-to-day basis.

b.   The accounting entries vary between the two systems.

c.   The inventory controls that are available with the two systems vary.

d.   Recent developments of computers of various capabilities have encouraged a high percent of large, medium, and even small businesses to change to the perpetual inventory system for numerous items in their inventories.

APPLICATION OF THE INVENTORY COSTING METHODS WITH A PERPETUAL INVENTORY SYSTEM

A perpetual inventory system requires the maintenance of a day-to-day **perpetual inventory record** for each kind of goods or merchandise stocked and sold. This record is designed to show units, unit costs, and dollar amounts, at all times, for (a) beginning inventory, (b) goods received (purchases), (c) goods sold (issues), and (d) balance of goods on hand (ending inventory). Each purchase and each sale transaction is entered in the perpetual inventory record when it occurs. The perpetual inventory record is designed so that cost of goods sold and the ending inventory are measured on a perpetual or continuous basis.

In the discussions to follow, a **perpetual inventory record** will be illustrated for each of the four inventory costing methods. To illustrate each application, we will use the data for Summer Retail Store given in Exhibit 7–1. The manual system is used for instructional purposes. The beginning inventory of 100 units at a unit cost of $6 would have been carried over in the records from the prior period. Recall from Chapter 6 that each purchase would be recorded as follows and, at the same time, entered on the perpetual inventory record (see Exhibit 7–3):

Jan. 3 Inventory (50 units @ $7) 350	
Cash (or accounts payable)	350

EXHIBIT 7–3
Moving weighted-average method—perpetual inventory system

PERPETUAL INVENTORY RECORD

Item __Item A__   Cost Basis __Moving average__
Location __320__   Minimum
Code __13__   Level __100__
Maximum
Level __300__

Date	Received (purchases)			Issued (sales)			Inventory Balance		
	Units	Unit Cost	Total Cost	Units	Unit Cost	Total Cost	Units	Unit Cost	Total Cost
1/1 bal.							100	6.00	600
1/3	50	7.00	350				150	6.33*	950
1/6				40	6.33	253	110	6.33	697
6/12	200	8.00	1,600				310	7.41*	2,297
6/18				220	7.41	1,630	90	7.41	667
12/20	120	9.00	1,080				210	8.32*	1,747
12/24				60	8.32	499	150	8.32	1,248
Total cost of goods sold						2,382			
Total ending inventory									1,248

*New moving weighted-average unit cost computed.

A sale generates two companion entries when a perpetual inventory system is used; one at sale price and one at cost:

```
Jan. 6  Cash ......................................................  400
             Sales revenue (40 units @ $10)............................        400

        Cost of goods sold (FIFO basis)..............................  240
             Inventory (40 units @ $6) ...................................        240
```

Weighted-average inventory costing method

When the weighted-average cost method is applied with a perpetual inventory system, a **moving weighted-average** unit cost is used because the cost of goods sold amount is measured and recorded at the **time of each sale.** Instead, if one were to apply the concept of an **annual** weighted average, the recording of cost of goods sold would be delayed until year-end, which is the only time an annual average unit cost can be computed.

In applying a moving weighted average, a **new** average unit cost is computed at the time of **each purchase.** Cost of goods sold and the remaining inventory are measured at the then prevailing moving average unit cost. An illustration of a perpetual inventory record on a moving weighted-average basis for the data given in Exhibit 7–1 is shown in Exhibit 7–3. The moving weighted-average unit cost was recomputed three times during the period because there were three purchases. Units sold are removed from the inventory record at the then moving average unit cost. For example, the moving weighted-average unit cost was computed on the date of the first purchase as follows:

	Units	Cost
Beginning inventory	100	$600
Purchase, January 3....................	50	350
Totals.........................	150	$950

Moving average unit cost:
$950 ÷ 150 units = $6.33 per unit.

The companion entries for the sale on January 6 would reflect sales revenue of $400 and cost of goods sold of $253 (from the perpetual inventory record) as follows:

```
Jan. 6  Cash ......................................................  400
             Sales revenue (40 units @ $10)............................        400

        Cost of goods sold (moving average basis)......................  253
             Inventory.............................................        253
        From Exhibit 7–3.
```

**EXHIBIT 7–4
FIFO method—
perpetual inventory
system**

PERPETUAL INVENTORY RECORD

(heading—same as in Exhibit 7–3, except cost basis—FIFO)

Date	Received (purchases)			Issued (sales)			Inventory Balance*		
	Units	Unit Cost	Total Cost	Units	Unit Cost	Total Cost	Units	Unit Cost	Total Cost
1/1 bal.							100	6	600
1/3	50	7	350				100	6	600
							50	7	350
1/6				40	6	240	60	6	360
							50	7	350
6/12	200	8	1,600				60	6	360
							50	7	350
							200	8	1,600
6/18				60	6	360			
				50	7	350			
				110	8	880	90	8	720
12/20	120	9	1,080				90	8	720
							120	9	1,080
1/24				60	8	480	30	8	240
							120	9	1,080
Total cost of goods sold						2,310			
Total ending inventory									1,320

*Maintained by FIFO unit cost inventory layers.

**FIFO inventory
costing method**

When the FIFO method is applied with a perpetual inventory system, after each issue the remaining units on hand must be "layered" by the different unit costs which frequently are referred to as "inventory cost layers." The identification of inventory cost layers is necessary because goods are removed from the perpetual inventory record in FIFO order; that is, the oldest unit cost is taken off first. An illustration of a perpetual inventory record on a FIFO basis is shown in Exhibit 7–4. Each purchase and each sale of goods is entered in the inventory record at the time of the transaction. At each transaction date, the balance column on the perpetual inventory record is restated to show the units and amount on hand for each different unit cost. At the same time, each transaction would be recorded in the journal. For example, the two companion journal entries to record the sales of June 18 are:

June 18	Cash	2,640	
	Sales revenue (220 units @ $12)		2,640
	Cost of goods sold (FIFO basis)	1,590	
	Inventory		1,590
	From Exhibit 7-4, $360 + $350 + $880 = $1,590.		

EXHIBIT 7-5
LIFO method,
costed currently—
perpetual inventory
system

PERPETUAL INVENTORY RECORD

(heading—same as in Exhibit 7-3, except cost basis—LIFO)

Date	Received (purchases)			Issued (sales)			Inventory Balance*		
	Units	Unit Cost	Total Cost	Units	Unit Cost	Total Cost	Units	Unit Cost	Total Cost
1/1 bal.							100	6	600
1/3	50	7	350				100	6	600
							50	7	350
1/6				40	7	280	100	6	600
							10	7	70
6/12	200	8	1,600				100	6	600
							10	7	70
							200	8	1,600
6/18				200	8	1,600			
				10	7	70			
				10	6	60	90	6	540
12/20	120	9	1,080				90	6	540
							120	9	1,080
12/24				60	9	540	90	6	540
							60	9	540
Total cost of goods sold						2,550			
Ending inventory									1,080

*Maintained by LIFO unit cost inventory layers.

LIFO inventory costing method

When the LIFO method is applied with a perpetual inventory system, the inventory cost layers must be identified separately on the perpetual inventory record, as was the case with FIFO. This identification is necessary so that the units (and their unit costs) can be removed at the time of sale from the inventory record in the inverse order that they came in. Unit costs are removed from the perpetual inventory record at the time of each issue which means that the **timing of costing is during the period rather than at the end of the period.** A perpetual inventory record on a LIFO basis is illustrated in Exhibit 7–5.

Specific identification inventory costing method

When the specific identification method is applied with a perpetual inventory system, the item-by-item choice (for entry in the perpetual inventory record and in the accounts) should be made at the time of sale rather than later (which is possible under the periodic inventory system). Application of the specific identification costing method in a perpetual inventory system is accomplished in a manner similar to the preceding illustrations.

COMPARISON OF PERIODIC AND PERPETUAL INVENTORY SYSTEMS

There are two important implementation differences between the periodic inventory system and the perpetual inventory system, viz:

a. The perpetual system requires more clerical effort than the periodic system.

b. The periodic system requires a year-end physical inventory whereas the perpetual system does not.

In the past, most businesses used the periodic inventory system because of its relative low cost and convenience, but recent advances in computer technology have produced a significant reduction in the cost of maintaining a perpetual inventory system. As a result, many businesses have adopted the perpetual system. The perpetual system offers the advantage of providing management with inventory information which is always up to date and the status of the inventory is readily available.

The periodic and perpetual inventory systems may produce different valuations of cost of goods sold and ending inventory because of differences with respect to the timing of the costing of cost of goods sold and inventory. The **periodic** inventory system costs ending inventory and cost of goods sold at the **end** of the accounting period. In contrast, the **perpetual** inventory system costs inventory and cost of goods sold **throughout** the accounting period.

The FIFO inventory method results in identical valuations of ending inventory and cost of goods sold under both the periodic and perpetual inventory systems. The results are identical because of the basic FIFO assumption that the first goods into inventory are the first goods taken out of inventory, and that order always is maintained. To illustrate, compare the following FIFO results for Summer Retail Store:

FIFO	Perpetual inventory system	Periodic inventory system
Source........................	Exhibit 7–4	
Ending inventory..............	$1,320	$1,320
Cost of goods sold.............	2,310	2,310
Total goods available......	$3,630	$3,630

In contrast, results typically will be different under periodic and perpetual systems when either the LIFO or the average inventory costing method is used. The results will be different under the **average cost** method because the **periodic** inventory system applies an **annual** weighted average for cost allocation whereas the **perpetual** inventory applies a series of **moving** averages throughout the accounting period.

Results will be different under the **LIFO** method because **at the end** of the accounting period the **periodic** inventory system allocates the most recent purchase cost to cost of goods sold. In contrast, the **perpetual** system allocates the most recent purchase costs to cost of goods sold **during** the accounting period on the date that each sales transaction occurs.

To illustrate the differences that can occur between LIFO and weighted average, compare the following results for Summer Retail Store:

LIFO	Perpetual inventory system	Periodic inventory system
Source........................	Exhibit 7–5	
Ending inventory..............	$1,080	$ 950
Cost of goods sold.............	2,550	2,680
Total goods available......	$3,630	$3,630
Weighted Average		
Source........................	Exhibit 7–3	
Ending inventory..............	$1,248	$1,158
Cost of goods sold.............	2,382	2,472
Total goods available......	$3,630	$3,630

To summarize, the four **inventory costing methods** (weighted average, FIFO, LIFO, and specific identification) are alternative methods of measuring the valuation of ending inventory and cost of goods sold. Each method assumes a different flow of unit costs during the accounting period; therefore, each method tends to produce different results. The **periodic** and **perpetual inventory systems** are two different accounting approaches for applying the inventory costing methods to measure cost of goods sold and ending inventory. The periodic inventory system assumes **cost allocation at the end of the accounting period** (using one of the four inventory costing methods), while the perpetual inventory system assumes **cost allocation currently during the accounting period** (again, using one of the inventory costing methods). Because of these two different timing assumptions, the two systems tend to give different valuations of ending inventory and cost of goods sold under the weighted average, LIFO, and specific identification costing methods, but valuations are always the same under FIFO.

SELECTED INVENTORY PROBLEMS

The remaining discussions in this chapter relate to three issues that may directly affect the valuation of the ending inventory reported on the balance sheet and the amount of income reported on the income statement; they are (a) lower of cost or market (LCM) valuation, (b) damaged items, and (c) estimating the ending inventory.

Inventories at lower of cost or market (LCM)

We have emphasized that inventories should be measured at their unit purchase cost in accordance with the cost principle. However, when the goods remaining in the ending inventory can be replaced with identical goods at a lower cost, the lower unit cost should be used as the inventory valuation. This rule is known as measuring inventories on a **lower of cost or market (LCM) basis.** It is a departure from the cost principle in favour of conservatism (see Exhibit 2–6). The LCM basis recognizes a "holding" loss in the period in which the replacement cost of an item dropped, rather than in the period in which the item actually is sold. The holding loss is the difference between purchase cost and the subsequent lower replacement cost. To illustrate, assume that an office equipment dealer has 10 new electronic calculators remaining in the 19B ending inventory. The calculators were purchased for $450 each and were marked to sell at $499.95. At the date of the ending inventory, however, the same new calculators can be purchased for $400 and will be marked to sell for $429.95. The 10 calculators should be valued in the ending inventory at the lower of cost ($450) or current market ($400). The LCM basis costs the ending inventory at $400 per unit. There are several effects associated with using a replacement cost of $400 against using the original purchase cost of $450 for the 10 calculators included in the ending inventory. By valuing them at $50 per unit below their purchase cost, 19B pretax income will be $500 (i.e., 10 × $50), less than it would have been had they been valued in the inventory at $450 per unit. This $500 loss in the economic value of the inventory (i.e., the holding loss) was due to a decline in the replacement cost. Because the loss is included in the cost of goods sold, 19B pretax income will be reduced by $500 in the period in which the replacement cost dropped (19B) rather than in the later period when the goods actually are sold. The $500 loss also reduces the amount of inventory that is reported on the 19B balance sheet. These effects are demonstrated in Exhibit 7–6. LCM usually is applied to all inventories on an item-by-item basis rather than on the aggregate inventory as a whole.[10]

---

[10]In contrast, if the replacement cost had increased to, say, $500 each, there would have been a **holding gain** of 100 units × $50 = $500. Generally accepted accounting principles do not permit recognition of holding gains because revenue is recognized only at date of sale of the goods. Because of the unfavourable connotations, holding gains are called windfall profits in the political arena. In view of the various possible values for market such as replacement cost, net realizable value or net realizable value less normal profit margin, the *CICA Handbook*, Section 3030.11, recommends disclosure of the specific market value used.

EXHIBIT 7–6
Effect of inventory measurement at LCM

| | Inventory measured at— | |
	Cost (FIFO)	LCM
Sales revenue	$41,500	$41,500
Cost of goods sold:		
Beginning inventory	$ 5,000	$ 5,000
Add purchases	20,000	20,000
Goods available for sale	25,000	25,000
Less ending inventory (10 calculators):		
At purchase cost of $450	4,500	
At LCM of $400		4,000
Cost of goods sold	20,500	21,000
Gross margin on sales	21,000	20,500
Expenses	15,000	15,000
Pretax income	$ 6,000	$ 5,500

Damaged and deteriorated goods

Merchandise on hand that is damaged, obsolete, or shopworn should not be measured and reported at original cost but at present **net realizable value** when it is below cost.

Net realizable value is the **estimated amount** that will be realized when the goods actually are sold in their deteriorated condition, less all repair and sale costs.

To illustrate net realizable value, assume a retail store has on hand two television sets that have been used as demonstrators and cannot be sold as new sets (i.e., they are shopworn). When purchased, the sets cost $300 each. In the light of their present condition, realistic estimates are:

	Per set
Estimated sales price in present condition	$175
Estimated repair costs of $20 and sales costs of $15	35
Estimated net realizable value	$140

On the basis of these estimates, the two television sets would be included in the inventory at $140 each, rather than at the original cost of $300 each. Net realizable value is used, rather than cost, because it records the loss in the period in which it occurred rather than in the period of sale and does not overstate the asset.

If a **periodic** inventory system is used, the item is included in the ending inventory of **damaged goods** at its estimated net realizable value, and the loss is reflected in cost of goods sold. However, if a **perpetual** system is used, the following entry would be made:

Inventory of damaged goods (2 × $140)	280	
Loss on damaged goods (an expense) ($600 − $280)	320	
Inventory (2 × $300)		600

The perpetual inventory record also would be changed to reflect this entry.[11]

Estimating ending inventory and cost of goods sold

When a periodic **inventory system** is used, a physical inventory count must be taken to determine the amount of the ending inventory. Taking a physical inventory is a time-consuming task in many businesses. As a consequence, physical inventories may be taken only once a year. Nevertheless, managers often desire financial statements for internal use on a monthly or, at least, a quarterly basis. When a periodic inventory system is used, some businesses **estimate** the ending inventory for the monthly or quarterly financial statements rather than taking a physical inventory. The **gross margin method** is used for this purpose. The method uses an **estimated gross margin ratio** as the basis for the computation.

The gross margin ratio is derived by dividing the gross margin amount by net sales revenue. The gross margin method assumes that the **gross margin ratio** for the current period should be essentially the same as it was in the recent past. Therefore, the average gross margin ratio from one or more prior periods is used as an estimate of the ratio for the current period. This estimated ratio then can be used to compute **estimated amounts** for (1) gross margin on sales, (2) cost of goods sold, and (3) ending inventory.

To illustrate the gross margin method, assume Patz Company uses the periodic inventory system and is preparing **monthly** financial statements at January 31, 19D. The accounting records provide the sales revenue, beginning inventory, purchases, and expense amounts listed below.

PATZ COMPANY
Income Statement
For the Month Ended January 31, 19D

Sales revenue		$100,000*
Cost of goods sold:		
Beginning inventory	$15,000*	
Add purchases	65,000	
Goods available for sale	80,000	
Less ending inventory	?	
Cost of goods sold.........		?
Gross margin on sales.............		?
Expenses		30,000*
Pretax income		$?

*Provided by the accounts.

---

[11]The subsequent entries may be as follows:

a. To record actual repair costs of $25:

Inventory of damaged goods	25	
Cash..		25

b. To record sale of the two sets for $360 (less actual selling costs of $15):

Cash ($360 − $15)...	345	
Selling expense	15	
Inventory ($280 + $25)		305
Gain on sale of damaged goods...........................		55

The amount of the ending inventory at the end of January is to be **estimated** rather than determined by physical count. Assume that the yearly net sales for 19C amounted to $1,000,000 and gross margin was $400,000; therefore, the actual gross margin ratio for 19C was $400,000 ÷ $1,000,000 = .40. Management has decided that this ratio is a realistic estimate for use during 19D. Using the .40 as our estimate for 19D, we can compute an **estimated** inventory valuation. The computational steps, in lettered sequence, are shown below to estimate the ending inventory for January and to complete the estimated income statement.

PATZ COMPANY
Income Statement
For the Month Ended January 31, 19D (estimated)

			Computations (sequence a, b, c)
Sales revenue.....................		$100,000	Per accounts
Cost of goods sold:			
Beginning inventory..............	$15,000		Per accounts
Add purchases...................	65,000		Per accounts
Goods available for sale.......	80,000		
Less ending inventory...........	20,000		*c.* $ 80,000 − $60,000 = $20,000
Cost of goods sold		60,000	*b.* $100,000 − $40,000 = $60,000*
Gross margin on sales		40,000	*a.* $100,000 × .40 = $40,000
Expenses.........................		30,000	Per accounts
Pretax income		$ 10,000	

*Or alternatively, $100,000 × (1.00 − .40) = $60,000.

The balance sheet can be completed by reporting the $20,000 estimated ending inventory amount as a current asset.

The gross margin method (sometimes called gross profit method) has several other uses apart from making possible preparation of the monthly or quarterly financial statements without a physical count of the ending inventory. Auditors and accountants may use this method to test the reasonableness of the amount of the inventory determined by other means. If the current gross margin ratio has changed materially from the recent past, it may suggest an error in the ending inventory. The method also is used in the case of a casualty loss (i.e., when an inventory of goods is destroyed or stolen and its valuation must be estimated for settlement purposes with an insurance company.)[12]

DEMONSTRATION CASE A

(Try to resolve the requirements before proceeding to the suggested solution that follows.)

---

[12]Another method, known as the retail inventory method, is used widely to estimate the ending inventory by department stores. It is essentially the same as the gross margin method, but differs in detail. Discussion of it is deferred to more advanced courses.

This case focuses on the effects of an error in the amount of the ending inventory. It does not introduce any new accounting concepts or procedures.

Metal Products, Incorporated, has been operating for eight years as a distributor of a line of metal products. It is now the end of 19C, and for the first time the company will undergo an audit by an independent PA. The company uses a **periodic** inventory system. The annual income statements, prepared by the company, were:

| | For the year ended December 31 | |
	19C	19B
Sales revenue	$800,000	$750,000
Cost of goods sold:		
Beginning inventory	40,000	45,000
Add purchases	484,000	460,000
Goods available for sale	524,000	505,000
Less ending inventory	60,000	40,000
Cost of goods sold.......	464,000	465,000
Gross margin on sales..............	336,000	285,000
Operating expenses................	306,000	275,000
Pretax income	30,000	10,000
Income tax expense (20%)	6,000	2,000
Net income	$ 24,000	$ 8,000

During the early stages of the audit, the independent PA discovered that the ending inventory for 19B was understated by $15,000.

Required:

a. Based on the above income statement amounts, compute the gross margin ratio on sales for each year. Do the results suggest an inventory error? Explain.

b. Reconstruct the two income statements on a correct basis.

c. Answer the following questions.
  (1) What are the correct gross margin ratios?
  (2) What effect did the $15,000 understatement of the ending inventory have on 19B pretax income? Explain.
  (3) What effect did the inventory error have on 19C pretax income? Explain.
  (4) How did the inventory error affect income tax expense?

Suggested solution

Requirement a. Gross margin ratios as reported:

$$19B: \$285,000 \div \$750,000 = .38$$
$$19C: \$336,000 \div \$800,000 = .42$$

The change in the gross margin ratio from .38 to .42 suggests the possibility of an inventory error in the absence of any other explanation.

Requirement b. Income statements corrected:

	For the year ended December 31	
	19C	19B
Sales revenue	$800,000	$750,000
Cost of goods sold:		
Beginning inventory	55,000*	45,000
Add purchases	484,000	460,000
Goods available for sale	539,000	505,000
Less ending inventory	60,000	55,000*
Cost of goods sold.......	479,000	450,000
Gross margin on sales.............	321,000	300,000
Operating expenses...............	306,000	275,000
Pretax income....................	15,000	25,000
Income tax expense (20%)	3,000	5,000
Net income	$ 12,000	$ 20,000

*Increased by $15,000.

Requirement c:

1. Correct gross margin ratios:

    $$19B: \$300,000 \div \$750,000 = .400$$
    $$19C: \$321,000 \div \$800,000 = .401$$

    The inventory error of $15,000 was responsible for the difference in the gross margin ratios reflected in Requirement (a). The error in the 19B ending inventory affected gross margin for both 19B and 19C, in the opposite direction, but by the same amount ($15,000).

2. Effect on pretax income in 19B: **Ending inventory understatement** ($15,000) caused an **understatement of pretax income** by the **same amount.**

3. Effect on pretax income in 19C: Beginning inventory **understatement** (by the same $15,000 since the inventory amount is carried over from the prior period) caused an **overstatement** of pretax income by the same amount.

4. Total income tax expense for 19B and 19C combined was the same ($8,000) regardless of the error. However, there was a shift of $3,000 ($15,000 × 20 percent) income tax expense from 19B to 19C.

Observation—An ending inventory error in one year affects pretax income of that year by the amount of the error and in the next year affects the new pretax income by the same amount but in the opposite direction.

DEMONSTRATION CASE B

(Try to resolve the requirements before proceeding to the suggested solution that follows.)

This case presents the effects on ending inventory, cost of goods sold, and the related accounting entries of a **periodic** inventory system compared with a **perpetual** inventory system assuming the LIFO inventory costing method is applied in each system.

Balent Appliances distributes a number of high-cost household appliances. One product, microwave ovens, has been selected for case purposes. Assume the following summarized transactions were completed during the accounting period in the order given below (assume all transactions are cash).

		Units	Unit cost
a.	Beginning inventory..........................	11	$200
b.	Sales (selling price $420)	8	?
c.	Sales returns (can be resold as new)	1	200
d.	Purchases	9	220
e.	Purchase returns (damaged in shipment)......	1	220

Required:

    a. Compute the following amounts assuming application of the LIFO inventory costing method:

	Ending inventory		Cost of goods sold	
	Units	Dollars	Units	Dollars
(1) Periodic inventory system (costed at end of period).........	___	___	___	___
(2) Perpetual inventory system (costed during period)...........	___	___	___	___

    b. Give the indicated journal entries for transactions (b) through (e) assuming:

        (1) Periodic inventory system.

        (2) Perpetual inventory system.

Suggested solution

Requirement a:

		Ending inventory		Cost of goods sold	
		Units	Dollars	Units	Dollars
1.	Periodic inventory system (costed at end of the period)	12	$2,420	7	$1,540
2.	Perpetual inventory system (costed during the period)	12	2,560	7	1,400

Computations:

Goods available for sale: (11 units @ $200 = $2,200) + (8 units @ $220 = $1,760) = $3,960.

1. Periodic LIFO inventory (costed at end):
   Ending inventory: (11 units @ $200 = $2,200) + (1 unit @ $220 = $220) = $2,420.
   Cost of goods sold: (Goods available, $3,960)—(Ending inventory, $2,420) = $1,540.

2. Perpetual LIFO inventory (costed during period):
   Ending inventory: (8 units @ $220 = $1,760) + (4 units @ $200 = $800) = $2,560.
   Cost of goods sold: 7 units @ $200 = $1,400.

Requirement b. Journal entries:

1. Periodic Inventory System			2. Perpetual Inventory System		
b. Sales:					
Cash (8 × $420)	3,360		Cash	3,360	
Sales revenue		3,360	Sales revenue		3,360
			Cost of goods sold	1,600	
			Inventory (8 × $200)		1,600
c. Sales returns:					
Sales returns	420		Sales returns	420	
Cash (1 × $420) . .		420	Cash		420
			Inventory (1 × $200)	200	
			Cost of goods sold . . .		200
d. Purchases:					
Purchases	1,980		Inventory	1,980	
Cash (9 × $220) . .		1,980	Cash		1,980
e. Purchase return:					
Cash	220		Cash	220	
Purchase returns . .		220	Inventory		220

SUMMARY OF CHAPTER

This chapter focused on the problem of measuring cost of goods sold and ending inventory when unit costs change during the period. Inventory should include all the items remaining on hand for resale to which the entity has ownership. Costs flow into inventory when goods are purchased (or manufactured) and flow out (as expense) when the goods are sold or disposed of otherwise. When there are several unit cost amounts representing the inflow of goods for the period, a rational and systematic method must be used to allocate unit cost amounts to the units remaining in inventory and to the units sold (cost of goods sold). The chapter discussed and illustrated four different inventory costing methods and their applications in both a perpetual inventory system and a periodic inventory system. The methods discussed were weighted-average cost, FIFO, LIFO, and specific identification. Each of the inventory costing methods is in accordance with generally accepted accounting principles. The selection of a method of inventory costing is particularly important because it will affect reported income and the inventory valuation reported on the balance sheet. In a period of rising prices, FIFO gives a higher income than does LIFO; in a period of falling prices, the opposite result occurs.

Damaged, obsolete, and deteriorated items in inventory should be assigned a unit cost that represents their current estimated net realizable value. Also, the ending inventory of new items (not damaged, deteriorated, or obsolete) should be measured on the basis of the lower of actual cost or replacement cost (i.e., LCM basis).

This chapter explained another fundamental accounting principle (Exhibit 2–6) known as the comparability principle which holds that all accounting concepts, principles, and measurement approaches should be applied in a consistent manner from period to period.

IMPORTANT TERMS DEFINED IN THIS CHAPTER

Terms (alphabetically)	Key words in definitions of important terms used in chapter	Page reference
Comparability principle (consistency)	Accounting methods should be consistently applied from one period to the next.	343
Consignments	Goods in possession of a seller but legal title is retained by the supplier.	335
Finished goods inventory	Manufactured goods that are completed and ready for sale.	333
First-in, first-out	Inventory costing method that assumes the oldest units are the first units sold.	340
Gross margin method	Method to estimate ending inventory based on the gross margin ratio.	353
Last-in, first-out	Inventory costing method that assumes the newest units are the first units sold	341
Lower of cost or market	Departure from cost principle that serves to recognize a "holding" loss when replacement cost drops below cost.	351
Merchandise inventory	Goods held for resale in the ordinary course of business.	333

Terms (alphabetically)	Key words in definitions of important terms used in chapter	Page reference
Moving weighted average	Weighted-average inventory costing method applied in the perpetual inventory system.	346
Net realizable value	Estimated amount to be realized when goods are sold, less repair and disposal costs.	352
Periodic inventory system	Ending inventory and cost of goods sold are determined at the end of the accounting period; a physical inventory count must be taken.	336
Perpetual inventory system	A detailed daily inventory record is updated continuously during the accounting period; provides ending inventory and cost of goods sold.	337
Raw materials inventory	Items acquired for the purpose of processing into finished goods.	333
Specific identification	Inventory costing method that identifies the cost of the specific item that was sold.	341
Weighted average	Inventory costing method used with a periodic inventory system that averages all purchase costs to calculate a weighted-average unit cost on an annual basis.	339
Work in process inventory	Goods in the process of being manufactured that are not yet complete.	333

QUESTIONS FOR DISCUSSION

Part A

1. Assume the 19A ending inventory was understated by $100,000. Explain how this error would affect the 19A and 19B pretax income amounts. What would be the effects if the 19A ending inventory were overstated by $100,000 instead of understated?

2. Match the type of inventory with the type of business in the following matrix:

Type of Inventory	Type of Business	
	Trading	Manufacturing
Merchandise		
Finished goods		
Work in process		
Raw materials		

3. Why is inventory an important item to both internal management and external users of financial statements?

4. What are the general guidelines for deciding which items should be included in inventory?

5. In measuring cost of goods sold and inventory, why is passage of ownership an important issue? When does ownership to goods usually pass? Explain.

6. Identify the two parties to a consignment. Which party should include the goods on consignment in inventory? Explain.

7. Explain the application of the cost principle to an item in the ending inventory.

8. When a perpetual inventory system is used, unit costs of the items sold are known at the date of each sale. In contrast, when a periodic inventory system is used, unit costs are known only at the end of the accounting period. Explain why these statements are correct.

9. The periodic inventory model is BI + P − EI = CGS, and the perpetual inventory model is BI + P − CGS = EI. Explain the significance of the difference between these two models.

10. The chapter discussed four inventory costing methods. List the four methods and briefly explain each.

11. The four inventory costing methods may be applied with either a periodic inventory system or a perpetual inventory system. Briefly explain how the methods are applied in each system.

12. Explain how income can be manipulated when the specific identification inventory costing method is used.

13. Contrast the effects of LIFO versus FIFO on reported assets (i.e., the ending inventory) when (a) prices are rising and (b) prices are falling.

14. Contrast the income statement effect of LIFO versus FIFO (i.e., on pretax income) when (a) prices are rising and (b) prices are falling.

15. The term **articulation,** defined early in Chapter 4, describes the linking together of four financial statements: income statement, retained earnings, balance sheet, and the statement of changes in financial position. Speculate with a specific example from inventories what measurement difficulties this articulation requirement might pose for the conceptual foundations of accounting. (Hint: Refer to the definition of expenses in Exhibit 2–6 and the definition of assets.)

Part B

16. What is the purpose of a perpetual inventory record? List the four main column headings and briefly explain the purpose of each.

17. When a perpetual inventory system is used, a **moving weighted average** is used. In contrast, when a periodic inventory system is used, an **annual weighted average** is used. Explain why the different averages are used.

18. The weighted-average inventory costing method usually produces different results when a perpetual inventory system is used rather than a periodic inventory system. Explain why.

19. Explain briefly the application of the LCM concept to the ending inventory and its effect on the income statement and balance sheet when market is lower than cost.

20. When should net realizable value be used in costing an item in the ending inventory?

21. The chapter discussed the gross margin method to estimate inventories. Briefly explain this method and indicate why it is used.

22. Briefly explain the comparability principle. How might it relate to the inventory costing methods?

23. If you were given the task of programming a perpetual inventory into a computer, what method of inventory cost allocation would you prefer, FIFO, LIFO, or average? Why?

24. The *CICA Handbook*, Section 3030.09 suggests the selection of the appropriate inventory cost allocation method should be made according to whether FIFO, LIFO, average, or specific produces the fairest matching of cost of goods sold with revenues.

   LIFO matches current purchase or manufacturing costs against current sales prices. Yet LIFO is not a popular method in Canada. Why?

25. Application of lower of cost and market valuation to inventory valuation is suggested as a departure from the cost principle in favour of conservation. Suggest another justification for LCM in terms of the definition of what constitutes an asset.

26. Is the use of lower of cost and market method for valuing inventories a violation of the comparability principle? Explain.

EXERCISES

Part A

E7–1. Handy Corporation prepared the two income statements that follow (simplified for illustrative purposes):

	First quarter 19B		Second quarter 19B	
Sales revenue		$10,000		$13,000
Cost of goods sold:				
Beginning inventory	$ 2,000		$ 3,000	
Purchases......................	9,000		10,000	
Goods available for sale	11,000		13,000	
Ending inventory................	3,000		4,000	
Cost of goods sold.......		8,000		9,000
Gross margin.....................		2,000		4,000
Expenses		1,000		1,000
Pretax income....................		$ 1,000		$ 3,000

During the third quarter it was discovered that the ending inventory for the first quarter should have been $3,500.

Required:

a. What effect did this error have on the combined pretax income of the two quarters? Explain.
b. Did this error affect the EPS amounts for each quarter? Explain.
c. Prepare corrected income statements for each quarter.
d. Set up a schedule which reflects the comparative effects of the correct and incorrect amounts.

E7–2. Fashion Clothing Store purchased 100 new shirts and recorded a total cost of $2,940 determined as follows:

Invoice cost	$2,000
Less: Cash discount 2%	
Shipping charges	530
Import taxes and duties	110
Interest paid in advance (15%) on $2,000	
borrowed to finance the purchase	300
	$2,940

Give the journal entry(s) to record this purchase assuming a periodic inventory system. Show computations.

E7–3. The records at the end of January 19B for Newman Company showed the following for a particular kind of merchandise:

Transactions	Units	Total cost
Inventory, December 31, 19A....................	30	$390
Purchase, January 9, 19B.......................	60	900
Sale, January 11, 19B (at $35 per unit)	50	
Purchase, January 20, 19B......................	35	490
Sale, January 27, 19B (at $36 per unit)	41	

Required:

Assuming a periodic inventory system, compute the amount of (1) goods available for sale, (2) ending inventory, and (3) cost of goods sold at January 31, 19B, under each of the following inventory costing methods (show computations and round to the nearest dollar):

a. Weighted-average cost.
b. First-in, first-out.
c. Last-in, first-out.
d. Specific identification (assume the sale on January 11 was "identified" with the purchase of January 9, the sale of January 27 was "identified" with the purchase of January 20, and any excess identified with the beginning inventory).

E7–4. Dean Company uses a periodic inventory system. At the end of the annual accounting period, December 31, 19B, the accounting records provided the following information for Product Z:

Transaction	Units	Unit cost
1. Inventory, December 31, 19A...............	2,000	$20
For the year 19B:		
2. Purchase, April 11.........................	2,000	22
3. Sale, May 1 (@ $50 each)	3,000	
4. Purchase, June 1	6,000	24
5. Sale, July 3 (@ $53 each)..................	4,000	
6. Operating expenses (excluding income tax expense), $140,000.		

Required:

a. Prepare a separate income statement through pretax income that details cost of goods sold for:
Case A—Annual weighted average.
Case B—FIFO.

Case C—LIFO.

Case D—Specific identification assuming two thirds of the first sale was "selected" from the beginning inventory and one third was "selected" from the items purchased on April 11, 19B. The second sale was "selected" from the purchase of June 1, 19B.

For each case, show the computation of the ending inventory. (Hint: Set up adjacent columns for each case.)

b. For each case, compare the pretax income and the ending inventory amounts. Explain the similarities and differences.

E7–5. Use the data given in Exercise 7–3 for this exercise (assume cash transactions and a periodic inventory system).

Required:

a. Compute (a) goods available for sale, (2) cost of goods sold, and (3) ending inventory for Case A—FIFO, and Case B—LIFO.

b. In parallel columns, give the journal entries for each purchase and sale transaction, assuming a periodic inventory system is used for each case. Set up captions as follows:

	FIFO		LIFO	
Accounts	Debit	Credit	Debit	Credit

c. Prepare an income statement through gross margin and explain why the FIFO and LIFO ending inventory, cost of goods sold, and gross margin amounts are different.

d. Which inventory costing method may be preferred for income tax purposes? Explain.

E7–6. During January 19B, Dixon Company reported sales revenue of $400,000 for the one item stocked. The inventory for December 31, 19A, showed 7,500 units on hand with a cost of $165,000. During January 19B, two purchases of the item were made: the first was for 1,500 units at $24 per unit; and the second was for 7,600 units at $25 each. The periodic inventory count reflected 8,600 units remaining on hand on January 31, 19B. Total operating expense for the month was $84,900.

Required:

a. On the basis of the above information, complete the 19B summary income statements under FIFO and LIFO. Use a single list of side captions including computation of cost of goods sold. Set up three separate column headings as follows: Units, FIFO, and LIFO. Show your computations of the ending inventory.

b. Which method gives the higher pretax income? Why?

c. Which method gives the more favourable cash flow effects? By how much, assuming a 20 percent tax rate?

E7–7. King Company uses a periodic inventory system. Data for 19B were: beginning merchandise inventory (December 31, 19A), 1,600 units @ $15; purchases, 6,000 units @ $18; expenses (excluding income taxes), $51,800; ending inventory per physical count at December 31, 19B, 1,500 units; sales price per unit, $33; and average income tax rate of 20 percent.

Required:

a.   Prepare income statements under the FIFO, LIFO, and weighted-average costing methods. Use a format similar to the following:

| | | Inventory costing method | | |
Income statement	Units	FIFO	LIFO	Weighted average
Sales revenue	___	$___	$___	$___
Cost of goods sold:				
Beginning inventory	___	___	___	___
Purchases......................	___	___	___	___
Goods available for sale	___	___	___	___
Ending inventory................	___	___	___	___
Cost of goods sold.......	___	___	___	___
Gross margin.....................	___	___	___	___
Expenses		___	___	___
Pretax income....................		___	___	___
Income tax expense.............		___	___	___
Net income		___	___	___

b.   Comparing FIFO and LIFO, which method is preferable in terms of (1) net income and (2) cash flow? Explain.

c.   What would be your answer to Requirement *(b)* assuming prices were falling? Explain.

E7–8.   Following is partial information for the income statement of Prelim Company under three different inventory costing methods assuming a periodic inventory system:

	FIFO	LIFO	Weighted average
Unit sales price, $30			
Cost of goods sold:			
Beginning inventory (480 units)	$ 9,600	$ 9,600	$ 9,600
Purchases (520 units)...........	13,000	13,000	13,000
Goods available for sale			
Ending inventory (530 units)			
Cost of goods sold			
Expenses, $1,500................			

Required:

a.   Compute cost of goods sold under the FIFO, LIFO, and weighted-average inventory costing methods.

b.   Prepare an income statement through pretax income for each method.

c.   Rank the three methods in order of favourable cash flow and explain the basis for your ranking.

Part B

E7–9.   Eastern Company uses a perpetual inventory system and FIFO. The inventory records reflected the following for January 19B:

Transactions	Units	Unit cost
Beginning inventory, January 1	100	$1.00
Purchase, January 6	200	1.10
Sale, January 10 (at $2.40 per unit)	110	
Purchase, January 14	100	1.30
Sale, January 29 (at $2.60 per unit)	160	

Required:

a. Prepare the perpetual inventory record for January. See Exhibit 7–3 for an example of a perpetual inventory record.

b. Give journal entries indicated by the above data for January (assume cash transactions).

c. Prepare a summary income statement for January through gross margin.

E7–10. At the end of the accounting period, the inventory records of Cain Company reflected the following:

Transactions (in order of date)	Units	Unit cost
Beginning inventory	500	$10
1. Purchase No. 1	600	12
2. Sale No. 1 (@ $23 per unit)	(700)	
3. Purchase No. 2	800	14
4. Sale No. 2 (@ $25 per unit)	(500)	
Ending inventory	700	

Required:

a. Compute goods available for sale in units and dollars.

b. Compute the (1) ending inventory valuation and (2) cost of goods sold assuming a **periodic** inventory system under the LIFO inventory costing method.

c. For comparative purposes compute the (1) ending inventory valuation and (2) cost of goods sold assuming a **perpetual** inventory system under the LIFO inventory costing method. To do this prepare a perpetual inventory record and cost each sale when made. See Exhibit 7–3 for an example of a perpetual inventory record.

d. Compare the results of *(b)* and *(c)* and explain why the valuations of ending inventory and cost of goods sold are different as between the periodic and perpetual inventory systems.

E7–11. Use the data given in Exercise 7–3 for this exercise (assume cash transactions, a perpetual inventory system, and moving average cost).

Required:

a. Prepare the perpetual inventory record for January on a moving average basis. Round to the nearest cent on unit costs and the nearest dollar on total cost. See Exhibit 7–3 for an example of a perpetual inventory record.

b. Give the journal entry to record the purchase of January 9.

c. Give the journal entries to record the sale on January 11.

d. Prepare a summarized income statement through gross margin for January.

e. Explain why a moving average rather than a weighted average for the period was used.

f. When the average cost method is used, would the ending inventory and cost of goods sold amounts usually be different between periodic and perpetual inventory systems? Explain why.

E7–12. Garden Company uses a perpetual inventory system and applies FIFO inventory costing. The data below were provided by the accounting records for 19B:

Transactions (in order of date)	Units	Unit cost	Total cost
Beginning inventory	100	$10	$1,000
1. Purchase No. 1	300	12	3,600
2. Sale No. 1 (@ $21 each)	(200)		
3. Purchase No. 2	400	$14	5,600
4. Sale No. 2 (@ $23 each)	(200)		
Ending inventory	400		

Required:

a. Compute the valuation of (1) cost of goods sold and (2) ending inventory assuming a perpetual inventory system and application of the FIFO inventory costing method.

b. Give the entries to record transactions 1 and 2 assuming FIFO:

Case A—A perpetual inventory system.
Case B—A periodic inventory system.

Use adjacent amount columns for each system and assume cash transactions.

c. Explain why the entries are different between the perpetual and periodic inventory systems.

E7–13. Contemporary Sound Company is preparing the annual financial statements at December 31, 19D. Two different types of tape recorders that were used as demonstrators remained on hand at year-end. These items will be sold as damaged (used) merchandise; therefore, they must be removed from the ending inventory of new merchandise. The company uses a perpetual inventory system. These items will be included in the inventory of damaged goods. Data on the tape recorder models are:

	Model 2–206	Model 112A
Quantity damaged	1	2
Actual unit cost	$400	$300
Regular sales price	700	500
Estimated unit market value in present condition	380	250
Estimated unit cost to sell	60	35

Required:

a. Compute the valuation of each item that should be used for 19D inventory purposes. Show computations.

b. Give the required entry(s) to reflect the appropriate inventory valuations in the accounts.

E7–14. Arthur Company is preparing the annual financial statements dated December 31, 19B. Ending inventory information about the five major items stocked for regular sale is:

		Ending inventory, 19B	
Item	*Quantity on hand*	*Unit cost when acquired (FIFO)*	*Replacement cost (market) at year-end*
A	50	$20	$18
B	100	45	45
C	20	60	62
D	40	40	40
E	1,000	10	8

Required:

a. Compute the valuation that should be used for the 19B ending inventory using the LCM rule applied on an item-by-item basis. (Hint: Set up columns for Item, Quantity, Total Cost, Total Market, and LCM Valuation.)
b. Compute the valuation of ending inventory using the LCM rule applied to total cost and total market value of the inventory.
c. Which method *(a)* or *(b)* is preferable? Why?

E7–15. Rocky Retail Company prepares annual financial statements each December 31. The company uses a periodic inventory system. This system requires an annual detailed inventory count of all items on the store shelves and items stored in a separate warehouse. However, the management also desires quarterly financial statements but will not take a physical inventory count four times during the year. Accordingly, they use the gross margin method to estimate the ending inventory for the first three quarters.

At the end of the first quarter, March 31, 19D, the accounting records provided the following information:

1. Beginning inventory, January 1, 19D....................	$ 60,000
Data for the first quarter of 19D:	
2. Sales revenue.......................................	305,000
3. Return sales	5,000
4. Purchases	196,000
5. Freight-in...	4,000
6. Operating expenses (excluding income tax expense)	50,000
7. Estimated average income tax rate, 20%.	
8. Estimated gross margin ratio, 40%	

Required:

Based on the above information, prepare a detailed income statement for the first quarter of 19D. Show all computations.

E7–16. On November 2, 19C, a fire destroyed the inventory of Dixon Retail Store. The accounting records were not destroyed; therefore, they provided the following information:

	19A	*19B*	*19C to date of fire*
Sales revenue..............	$120,000	$142,000	$120,000
Cost of goods sold	73,200	85,200	?
Gross margin on sales	46,800	56,800	?
Expenses..................	34,800	42,800	37,000
Pretax income	$ 12,000	$ 14,000	?
Ending inventory	$ 20,000	$ 22,000	?
Purchases during year......	70,000	87,200	68,000

Required:

a. Based on the data available, prepare an estimated income statement for 19C up to the date of the fire. Show details for the cost of goods sold. Disregard income taxes and show computations.

b. What amount of loss on the inventory should be submitted to the insurance company (a casualty loss insurance policy is in effect)? Write a brief statement in support of the amount of indemnity claimed.

PROBLEMS/CASES

Part A

PC7–1. The income statement for Mellon Company summarized for a four-year period shows the following:

	19A	19B	19C	19D
Sales revenue..................	$1,000,000	$1,200,000	$1,300,000	$1,100,000
Cost of goods sold	600,000	610,000	870,000	650,000
Gross margin.................	400,000	590,000	430,000	450,000
Expenses.....................	300,000	328,000	362,000	317,000
Pretax income	100,000	262,000	68,000	133,000
Income tax expense (30%)	30,000	78,600	20,400	39,900
Net income...................	$ 70,000	$ 183,400	$ 47,600	$ 93,100

An audit revealed that in determining the above amounts, the ending inventory for 19B was overstated by $50,000. The company uses a periodic inventory system.

Required:

a. Recast the above income statements on a correct basis.
b. Did the error affect cumulative net income for the four-year period? Explain.
c. Did the error affect cash inflows or outflows? Explain.

PC7–2. Arch Company has just completed a physical inventory count at year-end, December 31, 19B. Only the items on the shelves, in storage, and in the receiving area were counted and costed on a FIFO basis. The inventory amounted to $90,000. During the audit, the independent CA developed the following additional information:

a. Goods costing $400 were being used by a customer on a trial basis and were excluded from the inventory count at December 31, 19B.
b. Goods in transit on December 31, 19B, from a supplier, with terms CIF destination, cost, $700. Because these goods had not arrived, they were excluded from the physical inventory count.
c. On December 31, 19B, goods in transit to customers, with terms FOB shipping point, amounted to $900 (expected delivery date January 10, 19C). Because the goods had been shipped, they were excluded from the physical inventory count.
d. On December 28, 19B, a customer purchased goods for cash amounting to $1,500 and left them "for pickup on January 3, 19C." Arch Company had paid $800 for the goods and, because they were on hand, included the latter amount in the physical inventory count.

e. Arch Company, on the date of the inventory, received notice from a supplier that goods ordered earlier, at a cost of $2,400, had been delivered to the transportation company on December 27, 19B; the terms were FOB shipping point. Because the shipment had not arrived by December 31, 19B, it was excluded from the physical inventory.

f. On December 31, 19B, Arch Company shipped $750 worth of goods to a customer, CIF destination. The goods are expected to arrive at their destination no earlier than January 8, 19C. Because the goods were not on hand, they were not included in the physical inventory count.

g. One of the items sold by Arch Company has such a low volume that the management planned to drop it last year. In order to induce Arch Company to continue carrying the item, the manufacturer-supplier provided the item on a consignment basis. At the end of each month, Arch Company (the consignee) renders a report to the manufacturer on the number sold and remits cash for the cost. At the end of December 19B, Arch Company had five of these items on hand; therefore, they were included in the physical inventory count at $2,000 each.

Required:

Begin with the $90,000 inventory amount and compute the correct amount for the ending inventory. Explain the basis for your treatment of each of the above items. (Hint: The correct amount is $82,750. Set up three columns: Item, Amount, and Explanation.)

PC7–3. Wyman Company uses a periodic inventory system. At the end of the annual accounting period, December 31, 19E, the accounting records for the most popular item in inventory showed:

Transaction	Units	Unit cost
Beginning inventory, January 1, 19E	300	$20
Transactions during 19E:		
1. Purchase, February 20	500	22
2. Sale, April 1 (@ $40 each)	(600)	
3. Purchase, June 30	400	24
4. Sale, August 1 (@ $42 each)	(200)	
5. Return sale, August 5, (related to transaction 4)	10	

Required:

Compute the amount of (1) goods available for sale, (2) ending inventory, and (3) cost of goods sold at December 31, 19E, under each of the following inventory costing methods (show computations and round to the nearest dollar):

a. Weighted-average cost.
b. First-in, first-out.
c. Last-in, first-out.
d. Specific identification, assuming the April 1, 19E, sale was "selected" one third from the beginning inventory and two thirds from the purchase of February 20, 19E. Assume the sale of August 1, 19E, was "selected" from the purchase of June 30, 19E.

PC7–4. At the end of January 19B, the records at Quebec Company showed the following for a particular item that sold at $20 per unit:

Transactions	Units	Amount
Inventory, January 1, 19B	500	$3,000
Sale, January 10.................	(400)	
Purchase, January 12	600	4,200
Sale, January 17.................	(550)	
Purchase, January 26	310	2,790
Purchase return, January 28	(10)	Out of Jan. 26 purchase

Required:

a. Assuming a periodic inventory system, prepare a summarized income statement through gross margin on sales under each method of inventory: (1) weighted-average cost, (2) FIFO, (3) LIFO, and (4) specific identification. For specific identification, assume the first sale was out of the beginning inventory and the second sale was out of the January 12 purchase. Show the inventory computations in detail.

b. Between FIFO and LIFO, which method will derive the higher pretax income? Which would derive the higher EPS?

PC7–5. Speculative Company sells large computers that it acquires from a foreign source. During the year 19W, the inventory records reflected the following:

	Units	Unit cost	Total cost
Beginning inventory	10	$25,000	$250,000
Purchases....................	30	20,000	600,000
Sales (35 units @ $45,000)			

The company uses the LIFO inventory costing method. On December 28, 19W, the unit cost of the computer was decreased to $18,000. The cost will be decreased again during the first quarter of the next year.

Required:

a. Complete the following income statement summary using the LIFO method and the periodic inventory system (show computations):

Sales revenue...........	$_____
Cost of goods sold	_____
Gross margin...........	_____
Expenses..............	400,000
Pretax income	$_____
Ending inventory	$_____

b. The management, for various reasons, is considering buying 20 additional units before December 31, 19W, at $18,000 each. Restate the above income statement (and ending inventory) assuming this purchase is made on December 31, 19W.

c. How much did pretax income change because of the decision on December 31, 19W? Is there any evidence of income manipulation? Explain.

PC7–6. Big Top Corporation reported the following summarized annual data at the end of 19X:

	(millions)
Sales revenue	$950
Cost of goods sold*	540
Gross margin...........	410
Expenses	200
Pretax income	$210

*Based on ending FIFO inventory of $150 million. On a LIFO basis this ending inventory would have been $80 million.

Before issuing the preceding statement the company decided to change from FIFO to LIFO for 19X because "it better reflects our operating results." The company has always used FIFO.

Required:

a. Restate the summary income statement on a LIFO basis.
b. How much did pretax income change due to the LIFO decision for 19X? What caused the change in pretax income?
c. If you were a shareholder, what would be your reaction to this change? Explain.

PC7–7. This case demonstrates the effect on income of (a) rising prices and (b) falling prices in comparing FIFO with LIFO. Income is to be evaluated under four different situations as follows:

Prices are rising:
Situation A—FIFO is used.
Situation B—LIFO is used.

Prices are falling:
Situation C—FIFO is used.
Situation D—LIFO is used.

The basic data common to all four situations are sales, 600 units for $5,600; beginning inventory, 500 units; purchases, 500 units; ending inventory, 400 units; and operating expenses, $3,000. The following tabulated income statements for each situation have been set up for analytical purposes:

	Prices rising		Prices falling	
	Situation A FIFO	Situation B LIFO	Situation C FIFO	Situation D LIFO
Sales revenue	$5,600	$5,600	$5,600	$5,600
Cost of goods sold:				
Beginning inventory	1,000	?	?	?
Purchases	1,500	?	?	?
Goods available for sale	2,500	?	?	?
Ending inventory	1,200	?	?	?
Cost of goods sold	1,300	?	?	?
Gross margin	4,300	?	?	?
Expenses	3,000	3,000	3,000	3,000
Pretax income	1,300	?	?	?
Income tax expense (20%)	260	?	?	?
Net income	$1,040	?	?	?

Required:

a. Complete the above tabulation for each situation. In Situations A and B (prices rising), assume the following: beginning inventory, 500 units @ $2 = $1,000; and purchases, 500 units @ $3 = $1,500. In Situations C and D (prices falling), assume the opposite; that is, beginning inventory, 500 units @ $3 = $1,500; and purchases, 500 units @ $2 = $1,000. Use periodic inventory procedures.
b. Analyze the relative effects on pretax income and on net income as demonstrated by Requirement (a) when prices are rising and when prices are falling.
c. Analyze the relative effects on the cash position for each situation.
d. Would you recommend FIFO or LIFO? Explain.

Part B

PC7–8. The income statements for four consecutive years for Clean Company reflected the following summarized amounts:

	19A	19B	19C	19D
Sales revenue...........	$60,000	$70,000	$80,000	$65,000
Cost of goods sold	36,000	38,300	50,100	39,000
Gross margin...........	24,000	31,700	29,900	26,000
Expenses..............	15,000	16,700	19,100	15,800
Pretax income	$ 9,000	$15,000	$10,800	$10,200

Subsequent to development of the above amounts, it has been determined that the physical inventory taken on December 31, 19B, was overstated by $4,000.

Required:

a. Recast the above income statements to reflect the correct amounts, taking into consideration the inventory error.
b. Compute the gross margin ratio for each year (1) before the correction and (2) after the correction. Do the results lend confidence to your corrected amounts? Explain.
c. What effect would the error have had on the income tax expense assuming a 20 percent average rate?

PC7–9. Manitoba Company has completed taking the periodic inventory count of merchandise remaining on hand at the end of the fiscal year, December 31, 19D. Questions have arisen concerning inventory costing for five different items. The inventory reflected the following:

	Units	Original unit cost
Item A—The two units on hand are damaged because they were used as demonstrators. The company estimated that they may be sold at 20 percent below cost and that disposal costs will amount to $60 each.	2	$260
Item B—Because of a drop in the market, this item can be replaced from the original supplier at 10 percent below the original cost. The sale price also was reduced.	20	70
Item C—Because of style change, it is highly doubtful that the four units can be sold; they have no scrap value.	4	20
Item D—This item no longer will be stocked; as a consequence it will be marked down from the regular sale price of $110 to $50. Cost of selling is estimated to be 20 percent of the original cost.	3	80
Item E—Because of high demand and quality, the cost of this item has been raised from $120 to $144; hence, all replacements for inventory in the foreseeable future will be at the latter price.	15	120

The remaining items in inventory pose no valuation problems: their costs sum to $50,000.

Required:

Compute the total amount of the ending inventory including the damaged goods. List each of the above items separately and explain the basis for your decision with respect to each item.

PC7–10. Pepper Hardware Store uses a perpetual inventory system. This problem will focus on one item stocked, designated as Item A. The beginning inventory was 2,000 units @ $4. During January, the following transactions occurred that affected Item A:

Jan. 5 Sold 500 units at $10 per unit.
     10 Purchased 1,000 units at $5 per unit.
     16 Sold 1,800 units at $10 per unit.
     18 Purchased 2,300 units for $13,800.
     24 Sold 600 units at $12 per unit.

Required (assume cash transactions):

a. Prepare a perpetual inventory record for January on (1) a FIFO basis and (2) a LIFO basis.
b. Give the entry for each basis for the purchase on January 10.
c. Give the entries for each basis for the sale on January 16.
d. Complete the following financial statement amounts for each basis:

	January	
	FIFO	LIFO
Income statement:		
Sales revenue..................	$?	$?
Cost of goods sold	?	?
Gross margin.................	?	?
Expenses....................	12,000	12,000
Pretax income	?	?
Balance sheet:		
Current assets:		
Merchandise inventory	?	?

e. Which method derives the higher pretax income? Under what conditions would this comparative effect be the opposite?
f. Assuming a 20 percent average tax rate, which method would provide the more favourable cash position? By how much? Explain.
g. Which basis would you recommend for Pepper? Why?

PC7–11. Carbo Company uses a perpetual inventory system. Below is a perpetual inventory record for the period for one product sold at $6 per unit.

PERPETUAL INVENTORY RECORD

Date							
a.						400	1,200
b.	800	3.30				1,200	
c.				500	1,600	700	2,240
d.	300		1,050				3,290
e.				200		800	2,632
f.				300	987	500	
g.	100	3.65				600	

Required:

1. Complete the column captions for the perpetual inventory record.
2. What inventory costing method is being used?
3. Enter all of the missing amounts on the perpetual inventory record.
4. Complete the following tabulation:

		Units	Per unit	Amount
a.	Beginning inventory.........			
b.	Ending inventory............			
c.	Total purchases			
d.	Total cost of goods sold			

5. Give the entry(s) for date *(b)*.
6. Give the entry(s) for date *(c)*.
7. Complete the following tabulation:

	Assumption	Cost of goods sold	Ending inventory
a.	FIFO.........................		
b.	LIFO (end of period)		
c.	Annual weighted average (for the period)...............		

8. Assume a periodic inventory taken at the end of the period reflected 590 units on hand. Give any entry(s) required. (Disregard Requirement 7.)
9. Disregard Requirements 7 and 8 and assume that on date *(h)* 10 units of the inventory were returned to the supplier and a cash refund of $2.90 per unit was recovered. Give the required entry.

PC7–12. Kent Company executives are considering their inventory policies. They have been using the moving average method with a perpetual inventory system. They have requested an "analysis of the effects of using FIFO versus LIFO." Selected financial statement amounts (rounded) for the month of January 19B based upon the moving average method are as follows:

	Units	Amounts
Income statement:		
Sales revenue...............	180	$10,600
Cost of goods sold..........	180	5,710
Gross margin on sales.......		4,890
Less: Expenses		1,700
Pretax income		$ 3,190
Balance sheet:		
Merchandise inventory......		$ 2,620

Transactions during the month were:

Beginning inventory 50 units @ $30.

Jan. 6 Sold 40 units @ $55.
     9 Purchased 100 units @ $32.
   16 Sold 80 units @ $60.
   20 Purchased 110 units @ $33.
   28 Sold 60 units @ $60.

Required:

a. Copy the above statement data and extend each item to the right by adding columns for FIFO and LIFO (costed currently using perpetual inventory system). This statement will provide one basis for analyzing the different results among the three inventory costing methods.

b. Which inventory costing method produces the highest pretax income? Explain.

PC7–13. Vista Company prepared their annual financial statements dated December 31, 19B. The company uses a periodic inventory system and applies the FIFO inventory costing method; however, the company neglected to apply LCM to the ending inventory. The preliminary 19B income statement is summarized below:

Sales revenue		$310,000
Cost of goods sold:		
Beginning inventory	$ 40,000	
Purchases.............................	206,000	
Goods available for sale	246,000	
Ending inventory (FIFO cost)	50,000	
Cost of goods sold..............		196,000
Gross margin............................		114,000
Operating expenses......................		58,000
Pretax income		56,000
Income tax expense (25%)		14,000
Net income		$42,000

Assume you have been asked to restate the 19B financial statements to incorporate LCM. You have developed the following data relating to the 19B ending inventory:

		Acquisition cost		Current replacement unit cost
Item	Quantity	Unit	Total	(market)
A	2,000	$ 2	$ 4,000	$ 2
B	3,000	6	18,000	5
C	4,000	4	16,000	5
D	1,000	12	12,000	10
			$50,000	

Required:

a. Restate the above income statement to reflect LCM valuation of the 19B ending inventory. Apply LCM on an item-by-item basis and show computations.

b. Compare and explain the LCM effect on each amount that was changed in (a).

c. What is the conceptual basis for applying LCM to merchandise inventories?

d. Thought question: What effect did LCM have on the cash flow of 19B? What will be the long-term effect on cash flow?

PC7–14. On April 15, 19B, Lowlands Company suffered a major flood that damaged their entire merchandise inventory. Fortunately, Lowlands carried a casualty insurance policy that covered floods. The accounting records were not damaged; therefore, they provided the following information for the period January 1 through April 14, 19B:

Merchandise inventory,
December 31, 19A . . . . $ 21,000

Transactions through April 14, 19B:
Purchases   70,000
Purchase returns   2,000
Freight-in   1,000
Sales   103,000
Sales returns   3,000

Required:

For insurance indemnity purposes you have been asked to estimate the amount of the inventory loss. Your analysis to date indicates that (a) a 35 percent gross margin rate is reasonable and (b) the damaged merchandise can be sold to a local salvage company for approximately $2,000 cash.

What amount should be presented to the insurance company as a claim for insurance indemnity? Show computations.

PC7–15. The president of ET Company has been presented with the March 19B financial statements. They reflect data for three months as summarized below:

	Income statements			
	January	*February*	*March*	*Quarter*
Sales revenue	$100,000	$106,000	$90,000	$296,000
Cost of goods sold	61,000	59,360	?	?
Gross margin on sales	39,000	46,640	?	?
Expenses	32,000	33,500	32,000	97,500
Pretax income	$ 7,000	$ 13,140	?	?
Gross margin ratio	.39	.44	.40 (estimated)	
Ending inventory	$ 14,000	$ 16,000		

The company uses a periodic inventory system. Although monthly statements are prepared, a monthly inventory count is not made. Instead, the company uses the gross margin method for monthly inventory purposes.

Required:

a. Complete computations in the following tabulation to estimate the results for March.

	Amounts	*Computations*
Cost of goods sold:		
Beginning inventory	$16,000	From records
Purchases	51,000	From records
Goods available for sale	?	?
Ending inventory	?	?
Cost of goods sold	?	

b. Complete the income statements given above (March and Quarter). Disregard income tax.
c. What level of confidence do you think can be attributed to the results for March? Explain.
d. Would you recommend continued use of the method for the company? Explain.

PC7–16. The 1981 annual report of Standard Oil Company (Indiana) contained the following footnote:

During both 1981 and 1980, the company reduced certain inventory quantities which were valued at lower LIFO costs prevailing in prior years. The effect of these reductions was to increase aftertax earnings by $71 million, or $.24 per share, and $74 million, or $.25 per share, in 1981 and 1980, respectively.

Required:

a. Explain why the reduction in inventory quantity increased aftertax earnings (net income) for Standard Oil.
b. If Standard Oil had used FIFO, would the reductions in inventory quantity in 1980 and 1981 have increased aftertax earnings? Explain.

PC7–17. Several years ago, the financial statements of Lafayette Radio Electronics Corporation contained the following footnote:

Subsequent to the issuance of its financial statements, the company discovered a computational error in the amount of $1,046,000 in the calculation of its year-end inventory which resulted in an overstatement of ending inventory.

Assume that Lafayette reported an incorrect net income amount of $3,101,000 for the year in which the error occurred and that the income tax rate is 40 percent.

Required:

a. Compute the amount of net income that Lafayette should report after correcting the inventory error. Show computations.
b. Assume that the inventory error had not been discovered. Identify the financial statement accounts that would have been incorrect for the year the error occurred and for the subsequent year. State whether each account was understated or overstated.

PC7–18. The 1981 annual report for General Motors Corporation included the following footnote:

Inventories are stated generally at cost, which is not in excess of market. The cost of substantially all domestic inventories was determined by the last-in, first-out (LIFO) method. If the first-in, first-out (FIFO) method of inventory valuation had been used by the corporation for U.S. inventories, it is estimated they would be $2,077.1 million higher at December 31, 1981, compared with $1,784.5 million higher at December 31, 1980.

In 1981, GM reported net income (after taxes) of $320.5 million. On December 31, 1981, the balance of the GM retained earnings account was $15,340 million.

Required:

a. Determine the amount of net income that GM would have reported in 1981 if the FIFO method had been used (assume a 48 percent tax rate and that LIFO was allowed for income tax purpose.)
b. Determine the amount of retained earnings that GM would have reported on December 31, 1981, if the FIFO method had always been used (assume a 48 percent tax rate and that LIFO was allowed for income tax purpose.)
c. Use of the LIFO method reduced the amount of taxes that GM had to pay for 1981 compared with the amount that would have been paid if FIFO had been used. Calculate the amount of this reduction (assume a 48 percent tax rate and that LIFO was allowed for income tax purposes.)

PC7–19. Refer to the financial statements of Consolidated-Bathurst given in Special Supplement B immediately preceding the Index. Respond to the following questions:

1. What inventory costing method was used by C-B?
2. The total amount of inventories at the end of 1984 was $331.3. Determine the breakdown of the inventory amounts.
3. What was the cost of sales in terms of current costs?
4. What is the "current cost" of the inventory on the 1984 balance sheet?
5. What accounts for the $8 million increase in current cost inventory over historical cost for 1984?

PC7–20. To solve this problem using a data base computer program, you must do the following:

a. Create an inventory master file and enter data into it.
b. Index the file so that you can easily find specific records in it.
c. Query the data base to discover information about various inventory items.
d. Create a report of all inventory items.
e. Write programs to update the inventory account for purchases and sales.
f. Update the inventory for a variety of transactions using these programs.
g. Prepare an updated inventory report.

a,b,c. Create and Query An Inventory Masterfile

Before creating your inventory master file, be sure to set the default drive to drive B. Refer to Problem 6–19 when necessary for detailed assistance.

Records in the inventory master file have four fields, these fields together with suggested field names are:

1. Account number (account).
2. Description (item).
3. Unit price (using average cost; keep at least four places following the decimal point), (unitprice).
4. Quantity of goods on hand, (quantity).

The following data is to be entered into the file:

Product no.	Description	Unit price	Quantity
1254............	BULO	37.32	897
1416............	CRIUN	46.14	780
1456............	DETHEN	62.81	840
1482............	HATHO	71.98	945
1564............	LEMEO	34.10	480
1611............	MERUP	31.39	277
1615............	RETLO	99.07	950
1785............	SHANEE	68.99	703
1934............	SOOP	18.41	930
1994............	THODO	29.07	225

Having entered this information, query the data base to display all records for DETHEN. If ITEM is the name given to the variable containing the description of inventory items (DESCRIPTION cannot be used since variable names can only be 10 characters long), you would do this as follows:

type: DISPLAY ALL FOR ITEM = 'DETHEN' (return)

An alternative method of finding records is to index the file on a field in the file; for example, on ITEM. Having done this, you can ask the computer to FIND DETHEN, and it will find the appropriate account. To index the file,

type: INDEX ON ITEM TO INVEN (return)

this causes the file to be indexed on the variable ITEM. The index will be put in a file called INVEN.NDX.

The computer will respond with:

00010 RECORDS INDEXED

Now, you can find the account DETHEN and display it by typing:

    FIND DETHEN (return)
    DISPLAY (return)

The computer now prints:

    00003   1456 DETHEN   62.8100   840

If you had typed:

        FIND dethen (return)
    or FIND DETHAN (return)

the computer would have responded:

    NO FIND

because it could not find an appropriate record. In the first situation, it could not find the record because the ITEM name is uppercase, not lowercase. In the second situation, it could not find the item because the name was misspelled.

If you type:

    FIND SHAN (return)
    DISPLAY (return)

The computer will display:

00008   1785 SHANEE   68.9900   703

since this is the first record in the file with SHAN at its beginning.

In the future when you want to use the data base file with its index, you type:

        USE INVEN INDEX INVEN (return)

if both the data base file and the index file are called INVEN.

d. Create Inventory Report

Create an inventory report which looks like:

		Inventory report		
Product	*Item id*	*Cost/unit*	*Units*	*Balance*
BULO	1254	37.3200	897	33476.0400
CRIUN	1416	46.1400	780	35989.2000
DETHEN	1456	62.8100	840	52760.4000
HATHO	1482	71.9800	945	68021.1000
LEMEO	1564	34.1000	480	16368.0000
MERUP	1611	31.3900	277	8695.0300
RETLO	1615	99.0700	950	94116.5000
SHANEE	1785	68.9900	703	48499.9700
SOOP	1934	18.4100	930	17121.3000
THODO	1994	29.0700	225	6540.7500
TOTAL				381588.2900

The last column in the report is a computed field. You can get it by entering the field width, comma, and the cost per unit variable; for example unitprice, times the quantity variable. The multiplication symbol in dBASE II is the asterisk, *. If the cost per unit variable is UNITPRICE and the units variable is QUANTITY, you would type

20,UNITPRICE * QUANTITY (return)

e. Create Programs to Update Inventory

The programs to update the inventory should do the following:

a. Update the quantity of inventory in the inventory master file.
b. Update the inventory's cost using the average costing method if the transaction is a purchase of goods.
c. Update cumulative sales and purchase information.

Before one can update cumulative information, one has to first create this information and then save it. You can do this by setting the variables which will store the cumulative information to zero and then saving this information to a file. This is done by typing the following:

a. RELEASE ALL (return)—this clears local memory
b. STORE 0 TO SALES (return)
c. STORE 0 TO CGS (return)
d. STORE 0 TO PROFIT (return)
e. STORE 0 TO PURCHASES (return)
   these statements initialize the variables to 0
f. SAVE TO INVEN (return)—this saves the value of these variables in a file called INVEN.MEM

The saved file can be brought into the computer's memory by typing:
RESTORE FROM INVEN (return)

The programs you write should assume that the user of the program will first locate the record for a specific inventory item. The user will look at the record and then record a purchase or a sale for the item or do nothing. In recording a transaction, the program will update the item's quantity and, on a purchase, its unit price. In addition, the program will update the cumulative variables for sales, cost of goods sold, profit, and purchases.

The program should RESTORE the local variable memory file near its beginning and SAVE it near its end. Below are parts of a program to record sales. Comment lines begin with * and do not have to be typed. Other lowercase lines are not valid dBASE II command lines. Instead they explain what a dBASE II command should do. You must write the actual dBASE II command(s).

The sales program should be called SALE and, if using an editor to create it, be created in a file called SALE.PRG.

```
SET TALK OFF
RESTORE FROM INVEN
INPUT 'ENTER UNITS SOLD ' TO UNITSSOLD
INPUT 'ENTER PRICE PER UNIT ' TO SALEPRICE
* INPUT followed by words in quotes will cause the computer
* to prompt the person running the program with what appears
* in quotes; the word following TO is the name of the
* variable where the numeric input will be stored
```

compute the total sales amount and store it in THISSALE
compute the total cost of this sale and store it in THISCOST
compute the total profit on this sale and store it in THISPROFIT
STORE QUANTITY – UNITSSOLD TO NEWQUANT
* if QUANTITY is the name of the field which holds the
* quantity of the ITEM then the above statement puts the
* quantity less the units sold; that is, the new quantity, in
* a new variable called NEWQUANT
update the local variables SALES, CGS, and PROFIT
REPLACE QUANTITY WITH NEWQUANT
* this statement replaces QUANTITY in the record with the
* value of NEWQUANT
RELEASE NEWQUANT
* this statement releases the local variable NEWQUANT
DISPLAY MEMORY
* this statement displays the value of all local variables
DISPLAY
* this statement displays the revised record
RELEASE UNITSSOLD,SALEPRICE,THISSALE,THISCOST,THISPROFIT
* this statement releases all local variables except those
* which hold cumulative totals; that is, SALES, CGS, PROFIT,
* and PURCHASES
SAVE TO INVEN
* this statement saves the updated local variables
SET TALK ON
RETURN

Having written this program to record sales, write another program called PUR-CHASE. The SALE program which you wrote, can be used as a guide.

The purchase program must increase the QUANTITY field of the record, that is, it must change the UNIT PRICE field using the average cost method, and must update the PURCHASES local variable. In addition, the program should do many of the things done in the SALE program, that is, present information on the current purchase and release all local variables other than SALES, CGS, PROFIT, and PURCHASES before saving the cumulative totals.

f. g. Update Inventory and Prepare a Revised Report

Use the programs which you created, to record the following transactions:

Transaction	Item affected	Price	Units
PURCHASE	LEMEO	33.42	400
SALE	CRIUN	84.90	10
PURCHASE	DETHEN	71.61	200
SALE	CRIUN	114.43	18
PURCHASE	SHANEE	64.17	200
SALE	LEMEO	66.84	240
PURCHASE	SOOP	18.05	200
PURCHASE	RETLO	115.92	230
SALE	SHANEE	131.09	903
SALE	CRIUN	76.14	35
SALE	CRIUN	87.21	163
PURCHASE	RETLO	114.93	400
PURCHASE	MERUP	36.42	800
SALE	CRIUN	73.83	546
PURCHASE	SHANEE	65.55	200

When the transaction is a sale, the price is the sales price of the goods sold. When the transaction is a purchase, the price is the cost of the goods acquired.

To update the inventory,

type: FIND item name (return)
        DISPLAY (return)

  e.g.,   FIND LEMEO (return)
        DISPLAY (return)

this will find and display the appropriate record, then if the transaction is a sale,

   type: DO SALE (return)

else

   type: DO PURCHASE (return)

and enter the information requested by the program.

Having entered all this data into the computer, prepare an inventory report like you did before.

(Prepared by C. Dirksen)

PC7–21 ARB Limited, is a Canadian company engaged in a wholesaling business and currently distributes three major product lines. Over the years, the company has distributed several other product lines, only to discontinue them when the competition became too intense. During the past three years, one of its product lines, product line X, has suffered a continual decline in sales volume and has had a negative effect on the company's operating profits. At December 31, 1985, a significant portion of the inventory of product line X was about two years old.

In October 1985, management decided to discontinue distribution of product line X and, accordingly, notified the company's customers that it would continue to sell the inventory then on hand but would no longer accept orders for items which would have to be purchased from a manufacturer. After this notice was sent to the company's customers, sales volume of product line X declined even further. Therefore, management decided in early 1986 to sell this inventory in bulk to one of the company's competitors.

The company's preliminary financial position and operating results before any write-down of inventory are shown in the attached Exhibits.

In order to meet its debt agreement, audited financial statements must be provided to the bank by February 18, 1986. Your firm has been the auditor of the company for the last five years.

Early in 1986, when you arrive at the client's premises to finalize the audit of the December 31, 1985 financial statements, management informs you that they are attempting to sell the inventory of product line X in bulk. Management informs you that they are currently negotiating the sale with one competitor and that the asking price is $1,100,000, which they are confident they will get. They are unwilling to permit you to review any documentation supporting the current negotiations because of a commitment that they have made not to disclose the purchaser's identity. They also inform you that the only firm written offer received so far is from a second competitor and the amount of this offer is $800,000. They are prepared to provide you with a copy of this offer.

Management agrees that the inventory value for product line X is overstated and that a write-down is necessary. They argue that the value of the inventory was impaired at the beginning of 1985 and, although the formal decision to cease distribution of product line X was not made until 1985, the economic event occurred in 1984. To support their argument, they point out that most of the inventory is about two years old and must have been overvalued at the beginning of 1985 as demonstrated by the losses incurred during the year on sales of the product line.

Based on these facts, management concludes that a write-down of $500,000 (i.e., to the amount of $1,100,000 currently being negotiated) is all that is required and that the write-down should be treated as a charge against 1984 income. Management believes that this was abnormal in magnitude and nature to the company's regular business and that it pertains to the disposal of a major product line, and, therefore, it should be treated as an extraordinary item. Management is prepared to make any disclosure you consider appropriate in the notes to the financial statements, but, will not change their position on these matters.

Required:

Discuss the accounting considerations in this situation and how they should affect the 1985 financial statement.

(CICA Adapted)

ARB LIMITED
Balance Sheet
As at December 31, 1985

Current assets excluding inventories	$ 1,500,000
Inventories:	
Product line C	1,600,000
Other product lines......................................	3,900,000
Fixed assets:	
Land and warehouses—net	6,000,000
	$13,000,000
Current liabilities..	$ 2,500,000
Long-term debt:	
9¾% sinking fund bonds repayable at $500,000 per year	6,000,000
Deferred income taxes	1,000,000
Shareholders' equity:	
Share capital (1 million common shares)....................	1,000,000
Retained earnings	2,500,000
	$13,000,000

ARB LIMITED
Retained Earnings
For the Year Ended December 31, 1985

Retained earnings, beginning of year	$2,000,000
Net income	825,000
Dividends..	(325,000)
Retained earnings, end of year..	$2,500,000

ARB LIMITED
Statement of Income
For the Year Ended December 31, 1985

	Product lines			
	A	*B*	*C*	*Total*
Sales	$4,500,000	$3,000,000	$1,500,000	$9,000,000
Cost of sales	2,400,000	1,200,000	1,400,000	5,000,000
Gross margin	2,100,000	1,800,000	100,000	4,000,000
Direct operating expenses	400,000	300,000	200,000	900,000
	$1,700,000	$1,500,000	$ (100,000)	3,100,000
Unallocated expenses				
Interest on long-term debt		$633,750		
Other		816,250		1,450,000
Income before income taxes				1,650,000
Income taxes (including $200,000 deferred)				825,000
Net income				$ 825,000

Note: Net income for the years ending December 31, 1981 to 1984 was $750,000, $800,000, $700,000 and $925,000 respectively.

8

Cash, Short-Term Investments in Securities, and Receivables

PURPOSE OF THIS CHAPTER

This chapter discusses the measurement and reporting of a group of assets known as **liquid assets:** cash, short-term investments in securities, and receivables. They are designated as liquid assets because of a primary characteristic: they are either cash or close to conversion to cash. Thus, they meet the definition of a current asset.

To explain the features and accounting problems peculiar to liquid assets, this chapter is divided into three parts as follows:

Part A—Safeguarding and reporting cash

Part B—Measuring and reporting short-term investments

Part C—Measuring and reporting receivables

This chapter also includes the following Supplements:

Supplement 8A—Petty cash

Supplement 8B—Special journals

Part A—Safeguarding and Reporting Cash

CASH DEFINED

Cash is defined as money and any instrument that banks normally will accept for deposit and immediate credit to the depositor's account, such as a cheque, money order, or bank draft. Following this definition, cash excludes such items as notes receivable, IOUs, and postage stamps (a prepaid expense). Cash usually is divided into three categories: cash on hand, cash deposited in banks, and other instruments that meet the definition of cash. It is not unusual for a business to have several bank accounts. Even though a separate cash account may be maintained for each bank account, all cash accounts are combined as one amount for financial reporting purposes.

Because cash is the most liquid asset and is received and used continuously, it imposes heavy responsibilities on the management of an entity. These cash management responsibilities may be summarized as follows:

1. Safeguarding to prevent theft, fraud, loss through miscounting, and so on.
2. Accurate accounting so that relevant reports of cash inflows, outflows, and balances may be prepared periodically.
3. Control to assure that a sufficient amount of cash is on hand to meet (a) current operating needs, (b) maturing liabilities, and (c) unexpected emergencies.
4. Planning to prevent excess amounts of idle cash from accumulating. Idle cash produces no revenue; therefore, it often is invested in securities to derive a return (i.e., revenue) pending a future need for the cash.

INTERNAL CONTROL OF CASH

Internal control refers to those policies and procedures of an entity designed primarily to safeguard all of the assets of the enterprise. Internal control procedures should extend to all assets: cash, receivables, investments, operational assets, and so on. An important phase of internal control focuses on cash. Effective internal control of cash normally should include:

Separation of functions and routines:

1. Complete separation of the **functions** of receiving cash from disbursing cash.
2. Complete separation of the recording **procedures** for cash receipts from cash disbursements.
3. Complete separation of (a) the **physical** handling of cash from (b) all phases of the **accounting** function.
4. Require that all cash receipts be deposited in a bank daily. Keep any cash held on hand (for making change) under strict control.

5. Require that all cash payments be made by prenumbered cheques with a separate approval of the expenditures and separate approval of the cheques in payment.

Responsibilities assigned to individuals:

6. Assign the cash receiving and cash paying responsibilities to different individuals.
7. Assign the cash handling and cash record-keeping responsibilities to different individuals.
8. Assign the cash payment approval and cheque signing responsibilities to different individuals.
9. Assign responsibilities for the cash function and the accounting function to different individuals.

The separation of individual responsibilities and the use of prescribed policies and procedures are particularly important phases in the control of cash. A clearcut separation of duties and responsibilities among persons would deter theft because collusion would be required among two or more persons to steal cash and then conceal the theft in the accounting records. Prescribed procedures are designed so that the work done by one individual automatically is checked by the results reported by other individuals.

To indicate how easy it is to conceal a cash theft when internal control is lacking, two examples are provided:

Example 1—An employee handles both cash receipts and the recordkeeping. Cash amounting to $100 was collected from J. Doe in payment of an account receivable. An employee pocketed the cash and made an entry for $100 crediting Accounts Receivable (J. Doe) and debiting Allowance for Doubtful Accounts.

Example 2—Occasionally an employee with cash payment authority could send a fictitious purchase invoice through the system. The cheque, payable to a fictitious person, would not be mailed, but instead it would be cashed by the employee.

In each example, the accounting records would not reveal the theft, and the financial statements would not provide any evidence that a theft had occurred. The theft in Example 2 could have been prevented with simple internal control procedures.

All cash disbursements should be made with prenumbered cheques. Ideally for cash payments there should be separate routines and responsibilities specified for (1) payment approvals, (2) cheque preparation, and (3) cheque signing. When procedures similar to these are followed, it is difficult to conceal a fraudulent cash disbursement without the collusion of two or more persons. The level of internal control, which is subject to close scrutiny by the outside independent auditor, increases the reliability that users can accord the financial statements of the business.

BANK STATEMENTS TO DEPOSITORS

When a depositor opens a bank account, a **signature card** must be completed that lists the names and signatures of persons authorized to sign cheques drawn against the account. When a deposit is to be made, the depositor must fill out a **deposit slip** that includes the name of the account, the account number, and a listing of the coins, currency, and cheques deposited. In recent years, most banks have converted almost exclusively to personalized cheques; that is, the name, address, and bank account number of the depositor are preprinted on each cheque. Obviously, the use of personalized cheques is an important safety feature for all parties concerned.

Each month, the bank provides the depositor with a **bank statement** that lists (1) each deposit recorded by the bank during the period, (2) each cheque cleared by the bank during the period, and (3) a running balance of the depositor's account. The bank statement also will reflect any bank charges or deductions (such as service charges) made directly to the depositor's account by the bank. Also included with the bank statement are copies of the deposit slips and all cheques that cleared through the bank during the period covered by the statement. A typical bank statement (excluding the deposit slips and canceled cheques) is shown in Exhibit 8–1.

Exhibit 8–1 lists three items that need explanation. First, observe that on June 20, listed under "Cheques and Debits," is a deduction for $18 coded with "NC."[1] This code indicates an "NSF cheque charge" (in slang, a "hot" or "rubber" cheque); NSF stands for Not Sufficient Funds. A cheque for $18 was received from a customer, R. Ree, which then was deposited by J. Doe Company with its bank, the Northern Bank. The bank processed the cheque through banking channels to Ree's bank. Ree's account did not have sufficient funds to cover it; therefore, Ree's bank returned it to the Northern Bank which then charged it back to J. Doe Company. The NSF cheque is now a receivable; consequently, J. Doe Company must make an entry debiting Accounts Receivable (R. Ree) and crediting Cash for the $18.

The second item on Exhibit 8–1 that requires explanation is the $6 listed on June 30 under "Cheques and Debits" and coded "SC." This is the code for **bank service charges.** The bank statement included a memo by the bank explaining this service charge (which was not supported by a cheque). J. Doe Company must make an entry to reflect this $6 decrease in the bank balance as a debit to an appropriate expense account, such as Bank Service Expense, and a credit to Cash.

The third item that needs explanation is the $100 listed on June 12 under "Deposits" and coded "CM" for "credit memo." J. Doe Company had asked the bank to collect a note receivable held by Doe that had been received from a customer. The bank collected the note and increased the depositor account

---

[1] These codes vary among banks.

**EXHIBIT 8–1
Example of a bank
statement**

```
            NORTHERN
            BANK

         J. Doe Company
         1000 Blank Road
         Anywhere
```

ACCOUNT NUMBER	STATEMENT DATE	PAGE NO.
877-9 58 61	30-6-86	1

STATEMENT OF ACCOUNT

Please examine statement and cheques promptly. If no error is reported within ten days, the account will be considered correct. Please report change of address. For questions or problems call Northern Bank.

ON THIS DATE	YOUR BALANCE WAS	DEPOSITS ADDED NO.	AMOUNT	CHEQUES AND DEBITS SUBTRACTED NO.	AMOUNT	SERVICE COST	RESULTING BALANCE
1-6-86	7 562 40	5	4 050 00	23	3 490 20	6 00	8 122 20

CHEQUES AND DEBITS			DEPOSITS	DATE	DAILY BALANCE
500 00			3 000 00	1-6-86	7 562 40
55 00	5 00	40 00		2-6-86	10 562 40
100 00				4-6-86	10 062 40
8 20	16 50	160 00	500 00	5-6-86	9 962 40
2 150 00	10 00		*100 00CM	8-6-86	10 362 40
7 50	15 30			10-6-86	10 177 70
35 00	1 50		150 00	12-6-86	8 117 70
40 20	15 00	6 00		16-6-86	8 094 90
*18 00NC				17-6-86	8 208 40
125 50	80 00	2 00	300 00	18-6-86	8 147 20
18 90				20-6-86	8 129 20
7 52	19 60			21-6-86	7 921 70
15 00	32 48			24-6-86	8 202 80
*6 00SC				27-6-86	8 175 68
				28-6-86	8 128 20
				30-6-86	8 122 20

Code:
CM   Credit Memo—Customer note collected
NC   Not sufficient funds
SC   Service charge

IMPORTANT: SEE REVERSE SIDE OF STATEMENT.

of J. Doe Company. The bank service charge (SC) included the collection service cost. J. Doe Company must record the collection by making an entry to debit Cash and credit Note Receivable for the $100.

CASH ACCOUNTS IN THE LEDGER

Typically, a balance sheet reports cash as the first current asset because it is the most liquid of all assets. The amount of cash reported on a balance sheet is the total amount of cash at the end of the last day of the accounting period. The total amount of cash reported is the end-of-period total of—

1. Cash on deposit in all chequing accounts subject to current chequing privileges (offset by any overdrafts).[2]

[2]Adjusted for deposits in transit and outstanding cheques (discussed later).

2. **Cash on hand** (not yet transmitted to a bank for deposit).
3. **Cash held in all petty cash funds.**

Typically, a company will have a separate account in the **ledger** for each separate bank account.[3] Often companies maintain a daily minimum amount of **cash on hand.** Although such amounts are included in debits to the **regular Cash account,** those amounts have not yet been deposited because they represent *(a)* amounts of cash received since the last deposit was made and/or *(b)* a stable amount of cash needed for making change to start the next day.

Frequently, a **petty cash system** is maintained for the purpose of making separate **small cash payments** (not making change) in lieu of writing a separate cheque for each such item. This system necessitates the use of another separate cash account, usually called Petty Cash (discussed later).

BANK RECONCILIATION

Bank reconciliation is a term usually used to identify the process of comparing (reconciling) the **ending** cash balance reflected in a **company's Cash account** and the **ending** cash balance reported by the bank on the monthly **bank statement.** A bank reconciliation serves two primary accounting purposes:

a. Checks on the accuracy of both the ending balances of the company's Cash account and ending balance reported on the bank statement.
b. Identifies certain transactions that have not been recorded in the company's accounts, although they appear on the bank statement (and vice versa).

A bank reconciliation should be completed for each separate chequing account (i.e., for each bank statement received from each bank) at the end of each month.

Usually, the ending cash balance in the bank as shown on the bank statement will not agree with the ending cash balance shown by the related Cash ledger account on the books of the depositor. For example, assume the Cash ledger account at the end of June 1986 of J. Doe Company reflected the following (Doe has only one chequing account):

Cash

| June 1 | Balance | 7,010.00* | June | Cheques written | 3,800.00 |
| June | Deposits | 5,750.00 | | | |

(Ending balance, $8,960.00)

*Including $200 undeposited cash held for change.

[3] Larger companies often carry one Cash control account in the ledger which is supplemented with a series of separate cash subsidiary accounts for the depository banks. Refer to Supplement 6A.

The $8,122.20 **ending cash balance** shown on the **bank statement** (Exhibit 8–1) is different from the $8,960.00 **ending book balance** of cash shown on the **books of the J. Doe Company** because (1) some transactions affecting cash were recorded in the books of depositor Doe but were not reflected on the bank statement, and (2) some transactions were reflected on the bank statement but had not been recorded in the books of the depositor, Doe. The most common causes of a difference between the ending bank balance and the ending book balance of cash are:

1. **Outstanding cheques**—cheques written by the depositor and recorded in the depositor's ledger as credits to the Cash account that have not cleared the bank (hence they are not listed on the bank statement as a deduction from the bank balance). The outstanding cheques are identified by comparing the canceled cheques returned with the bank statement and with the record of cheques (such as the cheque stubs) maintained by the depositor.

2. **Deposits in transit**—deposits taken or mailed to the bank by the depositor and recorded in the depositor's ledger as debits to the Cash account that have not been recorded by the bank (hence they are not reflected on the bank statement as an increase in the bank balance). Deposits in transit usually happens when deposits are made one or two days before the close of the period covered by the bank statement. These are known as deposits in transit and are determined by comparing the deposits listed on the bank statement with the copies of the deposit slips retained by the depositor.

3. **Bank service charges**—explained in "Bank Statements to Depositors" section above.

4. **NSF cheques**—explained in "Bank Statements to Depositors" section above.

5. **Errors**—both the bank and the depositor may make errors, especially when the volume of cash transactions is large.

In view of these factors, a **bank reconciliation** should be made by the depositor (whether for a business or a personal account) immediately after each bank statement is received. A bank reconciliation is an important element of internal control and is needed for accounting purposes. To encourage bank reconciliation by depositors, many banks provide a format on the back of the bank statement for such purposes. Instructions for completing a bank reconciliation also may be given. A typical form is shown in Exhibit 8–2.

Bank reconciliation illustrated

The bank reconciliation for the month of June prepared by J. Doe Company to reconcile the **ending bank balance** (Exhibit 8–1, $8,122.20) with the **ending book balance** ($8,960) is shown in Exhibit 8–3. On the completed reconciliation, Exhibit 8–3, the **true** (correct) cash balance is $9,045, which is different from both the reported bank and book balances before the reconciliation.

EXHIBIT 8–2
Sample form and instructions for a bank reconciliation

CHEQUES OUTSTANDING	
NO.	AMOUNT
TOTAL	

THIS IS PROVIDED TO HELP YOU BALANCE
YOUR BANK STATEMENT

BANK BALANCE
SHOWN ON THIS STATEMENT $_____

ADD + (IF ANY)
DEPOSITS NOT SHOWN
ON THIS STATEMENT _____

TOTAL _____

SUBTRACT – (IF ANY)
CHEQUES OUTSTANDING _____

BALANCE $ _____
SHOULD AGREE WITH YOUR CHEQUEBOOK BALANCE

THIS IS PROVIDED TO HELP YOU BALANCE
YOUR CHEQUEBOOK

CHEQUEBOOK BALANCE
$_____

SUBTRACT – (IF ANY)
ACTIVITY CHARGE _____

SUB-TOTAL _____

SUBTRACT – (IF ANY)
OTHER BANK CHARGES _____

BALANCE $ _____
SHOULD AGREE WITH YOUR STATEMENT BALANCE

IF YOUR ACCOUNT DOES NOT BALANCE
PLEASE CHECK THE FOLLOWING CAREFULLY

☐ HAVE YOUR CORRECTLY ENTERED THE AMOUNT OF
EACH CHEQUE ON YOUR CHEQUEBOOK STUB?

☐ ARE THE AMOUNTS OF YOUR DEPOSIT ENTERED ON
CHEQUEBOOK STUBS THE SAME AS IN YOUR STATE-
MENT?

☐ HAVE YOU CHECKED ALL ADDITIONS AND SUBTRAC-
TIONS ON YOUR CHEQUEBOOK STUBS?

☐ HAVE YOU DEDUCTED ALL BANK CHARGES FROM YOUR
STUBS?

☐ HAVE YOU CARRIED THE CORRECT BALANCE FORWARD
FROM ONE CHEQUEBOOK STUB TO THE NEXT?

☐ HAVE ALL CHEQUES BEEN DEDUCTED FROM YOUR
STUBS?

EXHIBIT 8–3
Bank reconciliation illustrated

J. DOE COMPANY
Bank Reconciliation
For the Month Ending June 30, 1986

Depositor's Books		Bank Statement	
Ending cash balance per books	$8,960.00	Ending cash balance per bank statement	$ 8,122.20
Additions:		Additions:	
Proceeds of customer note collected by bank	100.00	Deposit in transit	1,800.00
Error in recording cheque No. 137	9.00	Cash on hand	200.00
	9,069.00		10,122.20
Deductions:		Deductions:	
NSF cheque of R. Ree . $18.00		Outstanding changes.........	1,077.20
Bank service charges .. 6.00	24.00		
Ending true cash balance	$9,045.00	Ending true cash balance	$ 9,045.00

Although the layout of a bank reconciliation can vary, the most simple and flexible one follows a balancing format with the "Depositor's Books" and the "Bank Statement" identified separately. This format starts with two different amounts: (1) the reported **ending balance per books** and (2) the reported **ending balance per bank statement.** Provision then is made for additions to, and subtractions from, each balance so that the last line reflects the same correct cash balance (for the bank and the books). This correct balance represents the amount that **should be** reflected in the Cash account **after the reconciliation.** In this example it is also the amount of cash that should be reported on the balance sheet because J. Doe Company has only one chequing account and no petty cash system. J. Doe Company followed these steps in completing the bank reconciliation:

1. **Identification of the outstanding cheques**—A comparison of the cancelled cheques returned by the bank with the records of the company of all cheques drawn revealed the following cheques still outstanding (not cleared) at the end of June:

Cheque No.	Amount
101	$ 145.00
123	815.00
131	117.20
Total	$1,077.20

This total was entered on the reconciliation as a **deduction** from the bank account because the cheques will be deducted by the bank when they clear the bank.

2. **Identification of the deposits in transit**—A comparison of the deposit slips on hand with those listed on the bank statement revealed that a deposit made on June 30 for $1,800 was not listed on the bank statement. This amount was entered on the reconciliation as an **addition** to the bank account because it will be added by the bank when the deposit is recorded by the bank.

3. **Cash on hand**—On the date of the bank statement, cash on hand (i.e., undeposited cash held for making change) amounted to $200. This amount is included in the company's Cash account but was not included in the bank statement balance (it was not deposited); therefore, it must be entered on the reconciliation as an addition to the bank balance (as it would be, if deposited).

4. Items on bank statement not yet recorded in the books of J. Doe Company; refer to Exhibit 8–4.

   a. Proceeds of note collected, $100—entered on the bank reconciliation as an **addition** to the book balance; it already has been included in the bank balance. A journal entry is

**EXHIBIT 8–4
Entries from bank
reconciliation
(Exhibit 8–3)**

Accounts of J. Doe Company:

a. Cash... 100
      Note receivable   100
      To record note collected by bank.

b. Accounts receivable 18
      Cash...   18
      To record NSF cheque.

c. Bank service expense... 6
      Cash...   6
      To record service fees charged by bank.

d. Cash... 9
      Accounts payable (name)   9
      To correct error made in recording a cheque payable to a creditor.

Cash account of J. Doe Company:

The Cash account prior to reconciliation was given earlier. After the above journal entries are posted, the Cash account is as follows:

Cash (after recording results of bank reconciliation)

June 1	Balance	7,010.00	June	Cheques written	3,800.00
June	Deposits	5,750.00	June 30	NSF cheques*	18.00
June 30	Note collected*	100.00	June 30	Bank service charge*	6.00
June 30	Correcting entry*	9.00			

(True cash balance, $9,045.00)

*Based on the bank reconciliation.

required to increase the Cash account balance and decrease the Note Receivable balance for this item.

b. NSF cheque of R. Ree, $18—entered on the bank reconciliation as a **deduction** from the book balance; it already has been deducted from the bank statement balance. A journal entry is required to reduce the Cash account balance for this item and to increase the receivable account.

c. Bank service charges, $6—entered on the bank reconciliation as a **deduction** from the book balance; it already has been deducted from the bank balance. A journal entry is required to reduce the Cash account balance for this item and to increase an expense account.

5. **Error**—At this point J. Doe Company found that the reconciliation did not balance by $9. Because this amount is divisible by 9, they suspected a transposition. (A transposition, such as writing 27 for 72, always will cause an error that is exactly di-

visible by 9.) Upon checking the journal entries made during the month, they found that a cheque was written by J. Doe Company for $56 to pay an account payable for that amount. The cheque was recorded in the company's accounts as $65. The incorrect entry made was a debit to Accounts Payable and a credit to Cash for $65 (instead of $56). Therefore, $9 (i.e., $65–$56) must be **added** to the book cash balance on the reconciliation; the bank cleared the cheque for the correct amount, $56. The following correcting entry must be made in the accounts: Cash, debit $9; and Accounts Payable, credit $9.

Note in Exhibit 8–3 that the "Depositor's Books" and the "Bank Statement" parts of the bank reconciliation now agree at a **true cash balance** of $9,045. This is the amount that will be included in the cash amount reported on a balance sheet prepared at the end of the period.

A bank reconciliation as illustrated in Exhibit 8–3 accomplishes two major objectives:

1. Checks the accuracy of the bank balance and the company cash records which involves development of the **true cash balance.** The true cash balance is the amount of cash that must be in the Cash account for financial reporting purposes (i.e., the balance sheet) and the amount that would be in the bank if all cash items were recognized by the bank.

2. Identifies any previously unrecorded transactions or changes that are necessary to cause the company's Cash account(s) to reflect the **true cash balance.** These transactions or changes require journal entries. The explanations given above of the development of the bank reconciliation of J. Doe Company cite such transactions and changes. Therefore, the entries shown in Exhibit 8–4, taken directly from the "Depositor's Books" part of the bank reconciliation, (Exhibit 8–3) must be entered into the company's records.

Observe that all of the additions and deductions on the "Depositor's Books" side of the reconciliation require journal entries to update the Cash account. The additions and deductions on the "Bank Statement" side do **not** require journal entries because they will work out automatically when they clear the bank. The cash amount reported on the balance sheet and reflected in the Cash account will be the **true cash balance** only if the proper journal entries are made after the bank reconciliation is completed.

The importance of the bank reconciliation procedure in generating entries to **update** the Cash account should not be overlooked. This feature is important in measuring the true cash balance that should be reported on the balance sheet.

CASH OVER AND SHORT

Regardless of the care exercised, errors in handling cash inevitably occur when a large number of cash transactions is involved. These errors cause cash shortages or cash overages at the end of the day when the cash is counted and compared with the cash records for the day. Cash overages and shortages must be recorded in the accounts. To illustrate, assume that at the end of a particular day the count of cash from sales amounted to $1,347.19 but the cash register tapes for sales totaled $1,357.19—a **cash shortage** of $10 is indicated. The sales for the day should be recorded as follows:

Cash	1,347.19	
Cash over and short	10.00	
Sales		1,357.19
To record cash sales and cash shortage.		

In the case of a cash **overage,** the Cash Over and Short account would be credited. Sales revenue should be recorded for the correct amount reflected on the register tapes regardless of any cash overage or shortage. Sometimes the bank reconciliation will divulge a cash shortage or overage that must be reflected under the "books" portion of the reconciliation and recorded in an accounting entry. At the end of the period, the Cash Over and Short account, in the case of a cumulative debit balance, usually is reported as miscellaneous expense. If a credit balance exists, it is reported as miscellaneous revenue.

PETTY CASH

The discussion of internal control explained that all major disbursements of cash should be made by **prenumbered cheques.** Many businesses find it inconvenient and expensive in terms of paperwork and employee time to write cheques for small payments for items such as taxi fares, newspapers, and small amounts of supplies. To avoid this inconvenience and expense, businesses frequently establish a **petty cash fund** to handle small miscellaneous cash payments. To establish a petty cash fund, a cheque should be drawn "Pay to the order of the custodian of Petty Cash" for the amount needed in the fund and cashed. Small cash payments, supported by written receipts, are made from this fund, and no journal entry is made at the time of payment. When the petty cash fund runs low and at the end of each accounting period, the expenditures from the fund are summarized and an accounting entry is made to reflect the payments from the fund (as a debit to expenses) and to record the cheque written to reimburse the fund for the total amount spent. For balance sheet reporting, the amount in the Petty Cash account must be added to the other cash balances. The details of accounting for a petty cash fund are discussed and illustrated in Supplement 8A to this chapter.

COMPENSATING BALANCES

A **compensating balance** exists when the bank requires the business to maintain a minimum amount in its bank account. A compensating balance may be required by the bank explicitly (by a loan agreement), or implicitly (by informal understanding), as part of a credit-granting arrangement. Often, it is difficult for the independent auditor to know whether or not an informal understanding exists. Information on compensating balances is important to statement users because there are two major effects on the business: (1) a compensating balance requirement imposes a restriction on the amount of cash readily available in the chequing account; and (2) if it arises in connection with a loan, the compensating balance increases the real rate of interest on the loan because not all of the cash borrowed can be used (i.e., the minimum must remain on deposit).

Information concerning a compensating balance must be reported in the notes to the financial statements because of its importance to statement users.

DATA PROCESSING OF CASH

Small businesses usually process cash transactions manually. In contrast, large businesses often process cash information by means of electronic computers. However, the recent development of microcomputers, and the software needed for processing accounting information, has brought computer processing of cash information within the cost-benefit range of small and medium-sized businesses. The basic data activities of accounting are broadly the same whether manual, mechanical, or electronic approaches are used. For most instructional situations, the basic characteristics of accounting information processing are best viewed in terms of a manual system.

Supplement 8B to this chapter presents one information processing procedure known as **special journals.** Two of these special journals relate to information processing of cash inflows (i.e., cash receipts journal) and cash outflows (i.e., cash payments journal). Supplement 8B illustrates the manual system for the special journals; however, computerized systems for these cash activities follow in essentially the same manner.

Part B—Measuring and Reporting Short-Term Investments

To employ idle cash, primarily to earn investment revenue, a company may invest in commercial paper (such as term deposits), or in the capital stocks (equity securities) or bonds (debt securities) of another company. Such investments are facilitated because term deposits are sold by local banks, and the shares and bonds of most of the large corporations are "listed" on the Canadian stock exchanges. Capital stock of smaller unlisted companies frequently can be bought and sold "over the counter" or between individuals and companies directly.

When bonds of another company are acquired, the purchaser has become a creditor of the issuing company because bonds represent debt owed by the other company similar to a long-term note payable. As the holder of a bond, the investor is entitled to receive interest on the principal of the bond and the principal if held to maturity. In contrast, when shares of capital stock are purchased as an investment, the purchaser becomes one of the owners (frequently called shareholders or equityholders) of the company that issued the shares. As an owner, the shareholder receives dividends when they are declared and paid by the other company. Most capital stock confers voting rights, which means the shareholder is provided an opportunity to exercise some control over the issuing company. The amount of control depends upon the number of voting shares owned by the shareholder in relation to the total number of such shares outstanding.

Investments made by one company in the shares or bonds of another company may be either (1) short-term investments (sometimes called temporary investments) or (2) long-term investments (sometimes called permanent investments). This chapter discusses the measurement and reporting of short-term investments; long-term investments are discussed in Chapter 13.

SHORT-TERM INVESTMENTS DEFINED

To be classified as a short-term (or temporary) investment, a security (e.g., a share or bond) must meet a twofold test of (1) marketability and (2) an expected short-term holding period. Marketability means that the security must be traded regularly in a market so that there is a continuous market available and a determinable market price. Therefore, short-term investments usually are listed shares and bonds, or short-term government securities. A short-term holding period means that it must be the intention of the management to convert the securities into cash in the near future for normal operating purposes.[4] Short term refers to the longer of the normal operating cycle of the business or one year as specified in the definition of current assets. The distinction between short-term and long-term investments is important because (1) there are accounting differences that must be observed and (2) short-term investments must be classified as a current asset, whereas the long-term investments are reported under a noncurrent caption, "Investments and funds."

---

[4]We shall see later that long-term investments also include marketable securities. Thus, the basic distinction between short-term and long-term investments hinges primarily on the intention of management in respect to their expected disposal date. As a result, the same kind of security may be a short-term investment in one company and a long-term investment in another company, depending upon the intentions of the respective managements.

MEASUREMENT OF SHORT-TERM INVESTMENTS

In accordance with the cost principle, short-term investments, when acquired, are measured and recorded at their cost. Cost includes the market price paid plus all additional costs incurred to purchase the security. To illustrate, assume Brown Corporation had approximately $50,000 in cash that would not be needed for operations for six or more months. In December, Brown purchased 1,000 shares of Arctic Telephone and Telegraph (AT&T) for $56,000, including all broker's fees, transfer costs, and taxes related to the purchase. This transaction would be recorded as shown in Exhibit 8–5.

Short-term investments held at the end of the accounting period are reported, at the **lower of cost or market** (LCM) on the balance sheet as a current asset (lower of cost or market is discussed in the next section). The **current market value** at the date of the balance sheet should be shown parenthetically. For example, at the end of the accounting period, December 31, 19A, Brown Corporation would report the short-term investment of AT&T shares, assuming a market value **above** cost of $57 per share, as shown in Exhibit 8–5.

When a cash dividend is received on capital stock (an equity security), or interest is received on a debt security held as a short-term investment, Cash is debited for the amount received, and a revenue account, such as Investment Revenue, is credited for the same amount. To illustrate, assume Brown Corporation received a cash dividend of $.70 per share on the AT&T stock on February 2, 19B. This transaction would be recorded by Brown as shown in Exhibit 8–5.

EXHIBIT 8–5
Accounting for short-term investments illustrated

December 1, 19A—Purchase of 1,000 shares of AT&T common stock for $56,000 including all transfer costs:

Short-term investments (1,000 shares @ $56)	56,000	
Cash		56,000

December 31, 19A (end of the accounting period)—on this date the AT&T stock was selling at $57 (i.e., above acquisition cost)*

Balance sheet at December 31, 19A:
Current assets:

Cash (assumed amount)	$62,000
Short-term investments at cost (current market value, $57,000)	56,000

February 2, 19B—Received a quarterly cash dividend on the AT&T stock of $.70 per share:

Cash (1,000 shares @ $.70 per share)	700	
Investment revenue		700

April 5, 19B—Sold 250 shares of the AT&T stock at $58 per share (cash).

Cash (250 shares @ $58)	14,500	
Short-term investments (250 shares @ $56)		14,000
Gain on sale of investments		500

*See next section on LCM when the market price is less than the acquisition price.

When a short-term investment is sold, the difference between the sale price and the cost of the security is recorded as a gain, or loss, as illustrated in Exhibit 8–5.

When a company owns short-term equity securities in several other companies, the securities held are referred to collectively as a **short-term portfolio of equity securities.** If debt securities also are held, they are considered by some authorities to be a separate **portfolio** of **debt securities.** Each portfolio of short-term investments is managed (i.e., acquired, held, and sold) with the objective of maximizing the return while minimizing the risk. Thus the **investment portfolio** is accounted for as a whole rather than as a number of separate investments.

Short-term investments valued at lower of cost or market (LCM)

Although short-term investments are measured and recorded at cost when acquired and are measured thereafter in conformity with the cost principle, there is an important exception related **only** to equity securities. The exception occurs when the **current** market value of the **short-term portfolio of equity securities** drops below the recorded acquisition cost.[5]

Chapter 7, relating to inventories of merchandise, explained that items of merchandise in the inventory for which the **current replacement cost** had dropped below acquisition cost should be measured on a lower of cost or market (LCM) basis. The same principle applies to the **short-term portfolio of equity securities.** Because of a drop in market value, the short-term portfolio of equity securities has lost a part of its value as a short-term source of **cash.** The drop in value is viewed as a **holding or unrealized loss** that should be recognized in the period in which the drop occurred. However, a holding gain is **not** recorded when the current market value is **above** the acquisition cost. The LCM basis is an exception to the **cost principle.** The LCM basis is applied because the **conservatism exception** (see Exhibit 2–6) is permitted to override the cost principle.

For short-term investments at the end of the accounting period, any difference between their cost and a **lower** end-of-period market value is recorded as a debit to an **expense** account called Unrealized Loss on Short-Term Investments and a credit to an **asset contra** account called Allowance to Reduce Short-Term Investments to Market. Thus, this entry records the holding (market) loss as an expense in the period in which the market dropped and revalues the short-term investment on an LCM basis.

To illustrate a situation where market is **lower** than cost at the end of the accounting period, we return to Brown Corporation (and continue the situation in Exhibit 8–5). Recall that at the end of 19B, Brown Corporation still owned 750 shares of the AT&T common stock acquired at $56 per share (i.e., total cost is, $42,000). At the end of 19B, the AT&T shares were selling on the stock

---

[5]*CICA Handbook,* Section 3010, suggests the use of market for this situation but does not specify how market should be applied. It should be noted here that LCM is applicable to investments in debt securities as well as shares.

exchange at $55 per share, which was $1 per share less than cost. Therefore, the LCM valuation must be applied to it. This means that an **unrealized** loss of $750 must be recorded and reported as shown in Exhibit 8–6.

The illustration presented in Exhibit 8–6 involved only one stock investment (AT&T) in the investment portfolio. Often the portfolio includes several different equity securities. In such cases, LCM is based upon the **total portfolio cost versus total portfolio market** amount rather than on an item-by-item basis. Even though the *CICA Handbook* is silent on this point, it is reasonable to expect the portfolio basis would be used in Canada. To illustrate, assume Cox Company has three separate shares, A, B, and C (rather than one) in its short-term **investment portfolio.** The measurement at the end of the accounting period would be derived as follows:

	Portfolio	
Security	Acquisition cost	Current market
A Company common shares	$10,000	$ 9,000
B Company preferred shares......	23,000	22,000
C Company common shares	7,000	8,000
Total portfolio...............	$40,000	$39,000

Under the LCM basis, the Short-Term Investments account of Cox Company

EXHIBIT 8–6
Recording and reporting short-term equity investments at LCM

Entries:
December 31, 19B (end of accounting period)—AT&T common stock held as a short-term investment; 750 shares, cost $56, current market, $55 per share.

Unrealized loss on short-term investments	750*	
Allowance to reduce short-term investments to market		750

Computation:
Cost (750 shares @ $56)	$42,000
Market (750 shares @ $55)	41,250
Unrealized loss	$ 750

Financial statements:
Balance sheet at December 31, 19B:
Current assets:
Short-term investments (at cost)......................	$42,000	
Less: Allowance to reduce short-term investments to market..	750	$41,250

or alternatively:

Current assets:
Short-term investment, at LCM (cost $42,000)	$41,250

Income statement for year ended December 31, 19B:
Expenses:
Unrealized loss on short-term investments	$750

would be written down to $39,000 by recognizing a $1,000 unrealized loss as follows:[6]

Unrealized loss on short-term investments	1,000	
Allowance to reduce short-term investments to market		1,000

When investments are **sold** that previously have been written down to a lower market (i.e., LCM), the gain or loss is measured as the difference between the sale price and the original purchase cost regardless of any balance in the allowance account. Any balance in the allowance account at the end of the accounting period is adjusted (up or down) to reflect any difference between total portfolio cost and a lower total portfolio market of the short-term investments held at the end of the accounting period.

To illustrate, assume that Cox Company sold all of the portfolio on January 15, 19C, for $39,400 cash. This transaction would be recorded as follows:[7]

Cash..	39,400	
Loss on sale of short-term investments...........................	600	
Short-term investments (at cost)		40,000

TERM DEPOSITS

In recent years, a common short-term investment strategy to employ idle cash has been to deposit the money for a fixed period of time. A "term deposit" is an investment contract an investor may purchase from a bank for cash. The contract specifies (1) a limited period of time for the investment, such as 90 days, 6 months, 1 year, and so on; and (2) a guaranteed interest rate. Generally, the larger the amount of the deposit (the amount invested), the higher the interest rate. The interest rate also tends to be higher for longer

---

[6]In contrast, when the LCM rule is applied to merchandise inventories, the item-by-item basis usually is used because merchandise is not viewed "as a single item" but as separate items.

[7]Assuming no short-term investments were held at the end of 19C, the following entry would be made:

December 31,19C:

Allowance to reduce short-term investments to market..................	1,000	
Recovery of unrealized loss on short-term investments*		1,000

*Some accountants prefer the title: "Unrealized Gain on Short-Term Investments."

Note that the LCM effect is to record a holding loss in the period that the market dropped below cost and to record an offset (a holding gain) in the period of sale. This anomalous effect occurs because LCM is not consistent with either cost basis accounting or market value accounting for investments.

time periods to maturity. Then, term deposits and similar commercial paper often are used for the short-term employment of idle cash because of the relatively high interest return and the liquidity factor.

Term deposits require that at the end of the accounting period, an adjusting entry is made for any accrued interest earned but not yet collected. Term deposits are accounted for separately from cash. The interest earned is reported on the income statement as **investment revenue.** For external reporting purposes, term deposits are reported on the balance sheet as a current asset as shown here:

Current assets:
Cash.............. $200,000
Term deposit...... 300,000

ADJUSTING ENTRIES FOR INVESTMENT REVENUE

At the end of the accounting period, **no adjusting entry is made for dividend revenue** on capital stock held as an investment because dividends (1) do not accrue on the basis of time and (2) are not paid unless formally declared by the board of directors of the issuing corporation. In contrast, when term deposits, bonds, or other **debt securities are held, an adjusting entry is required** for accrued interest revenue as for each debt security because interest is a legal liability that increases in amount with the passage of time. Accrual of interest is illustrated in Chapter 4 and in Part C of this chapter.

Part C—Measuring and Reporting Receivables

RECEIVABLES DEFINED

Broadly, receivables encompass all claims of the entity against other entities or persons for money, goods, or services. In most businesses there are two types of receivables: trade receivables and special (nontrade) receivables. Either type may include both short-term receivables (i.e., classified as current assets) and long-term receivables (i.e., classified as long-term investments or other assets). For example, a balance sheet may report the following receivables:

Current assets:
Trade accounts receivable $40,000
   Less: Allowance for doubtful accounts...... 3,000 $37,000
Trade notes receivable, short term............ 5,000
Special receivables:
   Due from employees...................... 400
   Equipment note receivable, short term...... 600

Long-term investments:
   Note receivable, long term.................. 10,000
   Special receivable, long term................ 8,000

Other assets:
   Utility deposits........................... 2,000
   Due from company officers................. 1,000

TRADE RECEIVABLES

Trade receivables include trade accounts receivable, usually called **accounts receivable,** and trade notes receivable. Either may be short or long term, although the latter is relatively rare in most situations. Trade receivables arise from the regular operating activities of the business; that is, from the sale of merchandise and/or services.

Trade accounts receivable and the contra account, Allowance for Doubtful Accounts, were discussed in detail in Chapter 6.

Many businesses **factor** their accounts receivable instead of holding them until the due date for collection. "Factoring" is a term used for the sale of accounts receivable to a financial institution, which usually occurs on the date that the goods and/or services are sold. Factoring is used because the company immediately receives the cash for sales; however, the rate of interest for factoring arrangements tends to be high. A discussion of the detailed accounting involved for factoring is beyond the objectives of this book.

SPECIAL RECEIVABLES

Special (or nontrade) receivables arise from transactions other than the sale of merchandise and/or services. Special receivables may be short or long term and should be given descriptive titles similar to those illustrated above. They should not be included in the caption "Accounts receivable." Other than for appropriate classification on the balance sheet, special receivables seldom involve unusual measurement or reporting problems.

NOTES RECEIVABLE

Notes receivable may be either **trade** notes receivable or **special** notes receivable, depending upon the source of the note. A promissory note is an unconditional promise in writing (i.e., a formal document) to pay (1) a specified sum of money on demand or at a definite future date known as the maturity or due date and (2) specified interest at one or more future dates. The person who signs a promissory note is known as the **maker,** and the person to whom payment is to be made is known as the **payee.** The maker views the note as a "note payable," whereas the payee views the note as a "note receivable." A note receivable involves two distinctly different amounts: (1) **principal,** which is the amount that the interest amount is based upon and (2) **interest,** which is the specified amount charged for use of the principal. The **face amount** of a note is the amount specified on the note that is payable at maturity.

Interest calculations on notes

Interest represents the time value of money; that is, the cost of using money over time. To the payee of a promissory note, interest is **revenue;** while to the maker it is **expense.** The formula for computing interest is:

$$\text{Principal} \times \frac{\text{Annual rate of interest}}{\text{}} \times \frac{\text{Fraction of year}}{\text{}} = \frac{\text{Interest amount}}{\text{}}$$

It is important to remember that **interest rates** are usually quoted on an **annual basis** and, therefore, must be restated for time periods of less than one year. Thus, the interest on a $10,000, 12 percent, 90-day promissory note would be calculated as follows:

$$\$10,000 \times .12 \times 93^*/365 = \$306$$

*Note: 90 + 3 days of grace.

When a note specifies a number of days, the exact days must be counted on the calendar to determine the due date and then related to the number of days in the year.[8]

All commercial notes involve interest, either explicitly or implicitly, because money borrowed, or loaned, has a time value that cannot be avoided.[9]

Accounting for notes receivable

Notes receivable usually arise as a result of a business selling merchandise or services. Although most businesses use open accounts (i.e., accounts receivable), those selling high-priced items on credit frequently require notes from their customers. To illustrate, assume Jackson Company received a $10,000, 12 percent, interest-bearing note from a customer as a result of the sale of goods; the payee would record it on the date of the sale as follows:

Notes receivable (trade)...	10,000	
Sales revenue...		10,000

To record 90-day, 12 percent, interest-bearing note received from customer.

Note: Assuming the note was in settlement of an open account receivable, which frequently happens, the credit would have been to Accounts Receivable instead of to Sales Revenue.

When **collection** is made at **maturity date** 93 days later, the entry to record the principal amount and the interest would be:

---

[8]For simplicity throughout this book, interest dates are given in a manner that avoids the needless counting of exact days on a calendar. Most lending institutions use 365 days in the calculations. Interest rates will be yearly rates. Notice the law in Canada adds three days of grace to the usual term of the note.

[9]An **interest-bearing note** explicitly specifies a stated rate of interest (such as 12 percent) on the face of the note, and the interest is to be paid in addition to the **face amount** of the note. In contrast, a **noninterest-bearing note** does not explicitly state an interest rate on the note because the interest charge is included in the face amount of the note (i.e., the interest is implicit).

```
Cash................................................................   10,306
    Notes receivable (trade)....................................            10,000
    Interest revenue ..........................................               306
To record collection of a 90-day, 12 percent, interest-bearing note
receivable of $10,000 plus interest ($10,000 × .12 × 93/365 = $306).
```

Default of a note receivable

A note receivable that is not collected at maturity is said to be **dishonoured** or **defaulted** by the maker. Immediately after default, an entry should be made by the payee transferring the amount due from the Notes Receivable account to a special account such as Special Receivable—Defaulted Trade Notes. The maker is responsible for both the unpaid principal and the unpaid interest; therefore, the receivable account should reflect the full amount owed to the payee. To illustrate, assuming the above note receivable was defaulted by the maker, the entry in the accounts of Jackson Company (the holder or payee) would be:[10]

```
Special receivable—defaulted trade notes.........................   10,306
    Notes receivable (trade)....................................            10,000
    Interest revenue ..........................................               306
To record the principal and interest earned on defaulted note.
```

Special Receivable—Defaulted Trade Notes is reported as a current or non-current asset depending upon the probable collection date.

Discounting a note receivable

Many businesses prefer a note receivable rather than an open account receivable from customers involved in large amounts of credit. The primary reasons are (1) the note provides formal evidence of the receivable and (2) notes, if negotiable, often can be sold to a financial institution, such as a bank, or to individuals to obtain needed cash **before** the maturity date. Selling a note receivable to a financial institution frequently is referred to as **discounting** a note receivable.

Promissory notes almost always are negotiable. **A negotiable instrument** is one that can be transferred by endorsement (there are other technical legal requisites for negotiability). The most common negotiable instrument is a cheque. Notes and a number of other instruments can be transferred by endorsement.

---

[10]From date of default, the amount due at that date (principal plus interest) continues to draw interest at the stipulated rate. There may be a question about the propriety of recognizing the interest revenue until collection is made when there is a reasonable probability that collection will not be made.

An endorsement may be made simply by signature of the holder, in which case it is said to be "with recourse." **With recourse** means that in case of default, as in the case of a "hot" cheque (i.e., one that the depositor's bank has turned down because of insufficient funds in the depositor's account), the endorser is liable for repayment. In contrast, an endorsement may be made "without recourse" by writing this phrase on the instrument before the endorsement signature. **Without recourse** means that the endorser cannot be held liable contractually in the case of default by the maker. Entities and individuals will seldom accept endorsements without recourse; that is, a discounted note receivable usually is endorsed with recourse and, as a result, the financial institution can rely on both the maker and the endorser. An endorsement with recourse makes the endorser **contingently liable;** that is, if the maker does not pay the note at maturity, the endorser must do so. The **reporting principle** (Exhibit 2–6) requires that such contingent liabilities be reported on the financial statements. Reporting usually requires a note to the financial statements, as illustrated later in this chapter.

The sale of a note receivable provides the payee with immediate cash and causes the transfer of the asset (note receivable) to the lender. A difference between the interest specified on the note and the interest charged by the purchaser of the note must be recorded as interest by the payee.

To illustrate the discounting of a note receivable, assume that Jackson Company held the $10,000, 12 percent, 90-day interest-bearing note receivable for 30 days, then sold it to the Northern Bank at a **discount rate** of 15 percent per annum. The discount rate is the annual rate of interest required by the bank and may be more or less than the interest rate specified on the note. The discount rate is applied to the **maturity value** of the note, that is, the principal amount of the note **plus** the amount of interest due at maturity. The discount rate of interest is applied to the number of days the bank will hold the note (in this case, 63 days). Computation of the amount of cash the bank will pay for the note is:

Discounting a note receivable:

Note: Principal, $10,000; annual interest rate, 12%; term, 90 days.
Discounted: Thirty days after date; discount rate, 15% per year.

Principal amount	$ 10,000.00
Plus: Interest due at maturity ($10,000 × .12 × 93/365)	306.00
Maturity value—amount subject to discount rate	10,306.00*
Less: Discount—interest charged by bank ($10,306 × .15 × 63/365)	267 *
Cash proceeds—amount the bank pays for the note	$ 10,039.00*

*Rounded.

The discounting or sale of the above note receivable would be recorded by the payee (Jackson Company) as follows:[11]

---

[11]The credit of $39 to Interest Revenue may be explained as follows: Had the note been held to maturity, the payee would have earned $306 interest revenue; however, the bank charged interest amounting to $267. The difference is $39, which is the net interest earned by the payee for holding it 30 of the 93 days. The discount rate is applied to the maturity value of the note because that is the amount the bank will advance, less the interest required by the bank.

Cash	10,039.00	
Notes receivable(trade)		10,000.00
Interest revenue		39.00
To record discounting of note receivable.		

Even though the note was sold, the financial institution has recourse against the endorser in case of default by the maker. Therefore, in accordance with the reporting principle, the endorser (Jackson Company) must disclose the **contingent liability** related to the note by means of a footnote to the financial statements similar to the following:

Note: At December 31, 19B, the company was contingently liable for notes receivable discounted in the amount of $10,306.

EXCEPTIONS TO ACCOUNTING PRINCIPLES

In the preceding chapters, the terms **materiality** (or material amount) and **conservatism** were used often. The conservatism exception was cited earlier as the reason for using the LCM basis in measuring inventory and short-term investments. The terms **materiality** and **conservatism** modify the **implementation principles** listed in Exhibit 2–6. In that exhibit, three exceptions to the implementation principles were identified and outlined; they are: (1) materiality, (2) rational conservatism, and (3) industry peculiarities.

Although accounting recognizes that measurement and compliance with the fundamental accounting concepts, assumptions, and principles (Exhibit 2–6) are essential, from a practical point of view the benefits of extremely high accuracy in measurement and absolute compliance with concepts sometimes are offset by purely practical considerations. Under certain **limited conditions**, an exception may be permitted to override one or more of the other principles. These conditions are specified for the following three exceptions:

1. **Materiality**—The fundamental accounting principles must be followed without exception for each transaction when the amount involved in the transaction is **material** (i.e., significant) in relationship to its overall effect on the financial statements. Although amounts **not** material must be accounted for, they **need not be accorded theoretically correct treatment.** For example, a pencil sharpener that cost $7.99 and has a five-year estimated life need not be depreciated under the matching principle; rather the $7.99 may be expensed in the period of acquisition because the amount involved is not material. The clerical cost alone of recording depreciation over the five-year period would exceed, by far, the cost of the asset. Addition-

ally, the $1.60 annual depreciation amount would not affect any important decisions by statement users.

2. **Rational conservatism**—This concept holds that where more than one accounting or measurement alternative is permissible for a transaction, the one having the **least favourable immediate effect on income or owners' equity usually should be selected.** For example, the LCM basis is used in measuring the amount of short-term investments and merchandise inventory. In this case, conservatism overrides the cost principle so that a holding loss (but not a gain) that occurs before the asset is sold is recorded and reported.

3. **Industry peculiarities**—This concept holds that the **unique characteristics of an industry may require use of special accounting approaches and measurement procedures in order to produce realistic financial reporting.** For example, in the mutual fund industry, investment portfolios are accounted for and reported at market value (rather than at LCM or at cost). In the insurance industry, government regulations specify some departures from LCM.

DEMONSTRATION CASE

(Try to resolve the requirements before proceeding to the suggested solution that follows.)

Dotter Equipment Company has been selling farm machinery for more than 30 years. The company has been quite successful in both sales and repair services. A wide range of farm equipment, including trucks, is sold. The company policy is to seek "high volume and quality service, at the right price." Credit terms with varying conditions are typical. Although most of the credit granted is carried by several financial institutions, Dotter will carry the credit in special circumstances. As a result, the company occasionally accepts a promissory note and keeps it to maturity. However, if a cash need arises, some of these notes may be sold (i.e., discounted) to the local bank with which Dotter has its chequing account. This case focuses on two farm equipment notes that were received during 19D. By following these notes from date of sale of farm equipment to final collection, we can see the various measurement problems posed and the accounting for them. The accounting period ends December 31, 19D.

The series of transactions in respect to the two notes follows:

Equipment Note No. 1:

19D

Jan. 15 Sold a farm tractor to S. Scott for $20,000 and received a 25 percent cash down payment plus a $15,000 equipment note receivable for the balance. The note was due in nine months and was interest bearing at 12 percent per annum. A mortgage on the tractor was executed as a part of the agreement.

Apr. 15 The Scott equipment note was sold to the local bank at a 13 percent per annum discount rate. Dotter endorsed the note, with recourse, and the proceeds were deposited in Dotter's chequing account.

Oct. 15 Scott paid the bank the face amount of the note plus the interest, $15,000 + ($15,000 × .12 × $\frac{9}{12}$) = $16,350. (As mentioned in footnote 8, for simplicity of exposition, days of grace are ignored.)

Required:

    a. Give appropriate journal entries for Dotter Equipment Company on each of the three dates. Show the interest computations and give an explanation for each entry.

    b. Assume that instead of payment on October 15, 19D, S. Scott defaulted on the note. When notified by the bank, Dotter paid the note and interest in full. Give the appropriate entry for this assumption and one for the further assumption that Scott later paid Dotter in full on December 1, 19D.

Equipment Note No. 2:

19D

Oct. 1 Sold a farm truck to B. Day for $7,000; received a down payment of $1,000 and set up an account receivable for the balance; terms, n/30.

Nov. 1 Day came in and wanted an extension on the account receivable "until he sold some equipment." After some discussion it was agreed to settle the account receivable with a six-month, 12 percent, interest-bearing note. Day signed the $6,000 note and a mortgage on this date.

Dec. 31 End of the accounting period. An adjusting entry is required.

19E

Jan. 1 Start of the new accounting period.

May 1 On this due date, Day paid the face amount of the note plus interest in full. The note was marked paid, and the mortgage was cancelled by Dotter.

Required:

    c. Give appropriate journal entries on each date, including any adjusting entries at year-end and the entry on maturity date. Omit closing entries at year-end. Explain what could be done on January 1, 19E, to simplify subsequent accounting. Provide a brief explanation with each entry.

Suggested solution

The solutions for Requirements *(a)*, *(b)*, and *(c)* are given in Exhibits 8–7 and 8–8.

EXHIBIT 8–7
Accounting for discounted and defaulted notes receivable illustrated

Requirement *a*. Equipment Note No. 1:

January 15, 19D—Note executed:

Cash	5,000.00	
Equipment notes receivable	15,000.00	
Sales revenue		20,000.00

Sale of tractor to S. Scott for cash and equipment note; terms of note, nine months, 12 percent interest, including a mortgage.

April 15, 19D—Note discounted:

Cash	15,287.25	
Equipment notes receivable		15,000.00
Interest revenue		287.25

Discounted Scott equipment note receivable at bank discount rate of 13 percent.

Proceeds computed:

Principal amount	$15,000.00
Interest to maturity ($15,000 × .12 × 9/12)	1,350.00
Maturity value	16,350.00
Discount ($16,350 × .13 × 6/12)	(1,062.75)
Cash proceeds	$15,287.25

October 15, 19D—Maturity date of note:

No entry required; Scott paid the bank that owned the note. During the period from April 15, 19D, until the note was paid, Dotter was contingently liable for the note because of the possibility that Scott would default.

Requirement *b*. Note defaulted:

October 15, 19D—Under the assumption that Scott defaulted on the note on due date, Dotter would have to pay the principal plus interest in full.

Special receivable (defaulted note—S. Scott)	16,350.00	
Cash		16,350.00

Scott note defaulted; payment to bank of the $15,000 principal plus interest ($15,000 × .12 × 9/12 = $1,350).

December 1, 19D—Scott paid Dotter the full amount of the note plus interest.

Cash	16,350.00	
Special receivable (defaulted note, S. Scott)		16,350.00

Payment received in full on Scott note in default.

Note: Dotter could also have assessed Scott interest at the legal rate on the $16,350 amount overdue; in this case, there would be a credit to Interest Revenue.

EXHIBIT 8–8 **Accounting for interest accrual on notes receivable illustrated**	

Requirement *c*. Equipment Note No. 2:

October 1, 19D—Sale and account receivable:

Cash...	1,000	
Accounts receivable	6,000	
Sales revenue..		7,000
Sold truck to B. Day; terms of the receivable, n/30.		

November 1, 19D—Note executed:

Equipment notes receivable	6,000	
Accounts receivable		6,000
Settled account receivable with a six-month, 12 percent interest-bearing note.		

December 31, 19D—Accrual (end of accounting period):

Interest receivable...	120	
Interest revenue		120
Adjusting entry for two months' interest accrued at 12 percent on Day equipment note ($6,000 $\times$ .12 $\times$ $^2/_{12}$ = $120).		

January 1, 19E—Start of next accounting period:
   No entry is required on this date; however, a reversal of the adjusting entry could be made to facilitate the subsequent entry when the interest is collected on April 30, 19E. The optional reversing entry would be (see Supplement 5A).

Interest revenue	120	
Interest receivable..		120
Reversing entry on Day note.		

April 30, 19E—Maturity date (assuming no reversing entry was made on January 1, 19E):

Cash $6,000 + ($6,000 $\times$ .12 $\times$ $^6/_{12}$)	6,360	
Note receivable (principal amount)............................		6,000
Interest revenue ($6,000 $\times$ .12 $\times$ $^4/_{12}$)		240
Interest receivable..		120

SUMMARY OF CHAPTER

This chapter discussed the measurement and reporting of cash, short-term investments, and receivables. Because cash is the most liquid of all assets and is flowing continually into and out of a business, it can be one of the most critical control problems facing the managers. Also, it may be of critical importance to decision makers who rely on financial statements for relevant information. The measurement and reporting of cash includes such problems as controlling and safeguarding cash, reconciling bank balances, petty cash, and recording the cash inflows and outflows.

The use of short-term investments to employ idle cash was discussed. Marketability and the intention of management in respect to the holding period are fundamental in the classification of an investment as short term as opposed to long term. Short-term investments are accounted for in accordance with the

cost principle; however, in accordance with the conservatism exception, the LCM basis is applied to the short-term investment portfolio at the end of each accounting period. Long-term investments are discussed in Chapter 13.

Receivables include trade receivables (usually called accounts receivable), special receivables, and notes receivable. Each of these should be accounted for separately. Interest calculations and discounting of notes receivable were discussed and illustrated.

The chapter emphasized the importance of careful measurement of these liquid assets and the importance of examining their characteristics before classifying them as current assets for reporting purposes. Financial statement users often are faced with decisions in which these liquid assets are critical; therefore, they should be measured properly and reported adequately.

SUPPLEMENT 8A—PETTY CASH

A petty cash fund is established to avoid the inconvenience and cost of writing cheques for the many small payments that occur daily in some businesses. This Supplement discusses and illustrates the detailed accounting and record-keeping for a petty cash fund (also called an imprest fund).

Establishing the petty cash fund. To establish a petty cash fund, a cheque should be written for the estimated amount needed to meet the expected payments, say, for an average month. The cheque, made payable to "the Custodian of Petty Cash," is cashed, and the money kept in a safe place under the direct control of a **designated individual** known as the **custodian.** The entry to set up a **separate Cash account** and to record the initial cheque would be:

Petty cash...	100	
Cash		100
To record establishment of a petty cash fund.		

Disbursements from the petty cash fund. The policies of the petty cash fund should require that the custodian maintain a perpetual record of all disbursements and the amount of cash on hand. No entry is made in the regular ledger accounts at the time each payment is made from the petty cash fund by the custodian. Instead, the custodian maintains a separate **petty cash record** in which each disbursement is recorded when made. This record is supported by documentation, such as a signed bill, voucher, or receipt for each payment made. As an internal control feature, occasional surprise audits of the fund and the records of disbursements should be conducted. "Borrowing" from the fund by the custodian or others should not be allowed. Careless handling of petty cash often leads to theft.

Replenishment of the petty cash fund. When the amount of cash held by the custodian gets low, and at the end of each accounting period, the fund should be reimbursed (or replenished) with an amount of cash sufficient to restore it to the original amount (to $100 in the example). Reimbursement is accomplished by having the custodian turn in the petty cash record and the supporting documents to the accountants. On the basis of these records, a cheque to "The Custodian of Petty Cash," is written for the amount of cash needed for replenishment which is the same as the sum of the expenditures reported by the custodian. The cheque is cashed by the custodian, which increases the cash held to the original amount ($100 in the example). A journal entry is made to credit Cash for the amount of the cheque and to debit expenses. The petty cash documents turned in by the custodian provide the underlying support for this journal entry.

To illustrate, assume that by the end of the month, there remained $8.50 petty cash on hand of the $100. This means that cash expenditures by the custodian amounted to $91.50 for the month. Assuming no shortage or overage, the bills, vouchers, and receipts accumulated by the custodian should sum to this amount. These documents provide support for the additional cheque to petty cash for $91.50.

The detailed data for recording the replenishment cheque in the following journal entry are based on the supporting documents:

Telephone expense	12.40	
Office supplies expense	6.32	
Postage expense	21.45	
Delivery expense	6.33	
Taxi fare expense	14.87	
Repair expense, office equipment	15.00	
Coffee expense	10.04	
Miscellaneous expense	5.09	
Cash		91.50

It should be emphasized that the Petty Cash account is debited **only** when the petty cash fund is first established and when the fund amount is increased on a permanent basis. The Petty Cash account carries a stable balance at all times ($100 in the above example). Expense accounts, not Petty Cash, are debited, and the **regular** Cash account is credited when the fund is replenished. Therefore, there will be no further entries in the petty cash fund once it is established unless it is decided by management to discontinue the fund or to increase or decrease the original amount on a permanent basis. The fund must be replenished (a) when the balance of cash in the fund is low, and (b) always at the end of the accounting period, whether low or not. Replenishment at the end of the accounting period is necessary in order to (a) record the expenses incurred by the fund up to the date of the financial statements and *(b)* have the same amount of cash on hand that is shown in the Petty Cash account and included on the balance sheet. The petty cash fund should be subject to rigid internal control procedures to remove all temptations to misuse it.

SUPPLEMENT 8B—SPECIAL JOURNALS

In the preceding chapters we have used the **general journal** to record all transactions in chronological order (i.e., by order of date). The general journal is flexible in that any transaction can be recorded in it. However, it is inefficient if used for recording transactions that have a high rate of occurrence, such as credit sales, credit purchases, cash receipts, and payments. The **general** journal is inefficient in three ways: (1) the same journal entry must be recorded repeatedly (except for changed amounts), (2) a large number of journal entries must be posted to the ledger, and (3) division of labour is difficult with a single journal. Special journals are designed to reduce these inefficiencies as demonstrated below.

In discussing and illustrating special journals, we emphasize that no accounting principles or concepts are involved—we are dealing simply with the **mechanics** of data processing. Although special journals can, and should, be designed to meet a special need when a particular type of data processing problem arises, we will limit this discussion to the four special journals that often are used: credit sales, credit purchases, cash receipts, and cash payments.

Credit sales journal. This journal is designed to accommodate **only credit sales.** Cash sales are entered in the cash receipts journal as explained below. You will recall that the journal entry to record a credit sale (assuming a periodic inventory system) is:[12]

Jan. 3 Accounts receivable (customer's name)	100	
Sales		100
To record credit sale; Invoice No. 324; terms, n/30.		

The credit sales journal is designed specifically to simplify (1) recording only this kind of entry and (2) subsequent posting to the ledger. The design of a credit sales journal is shown in Exhibit 8–9. Observe the **saving** in space, time, and accounting expertise required to journalize a credit sale (all of these are minimized).

---

[12]For instructional purposes, we will utilize simplified amounts, a limited number of transactions and customers, T-accounts, and a manual system. In many companies these procedures are computerized.

EXHIBIT 8–9
Credit sales journal and accounts receivable subsidiary ledger illustrated

		CREDIT SALES JOURNAL			Page _9_	
Date		Customer	Terms	Invoice Number	Folio	Amount
Jan.	3	Adams, K. L.	n/30	324	34.1	100
	4	Small, C. C.	n/30	325	34.6	60
	6	Baker, C. B.	n/30	326	34.2	110
	10	Roe, R. R.	n/30	327	34.5	20
	11	Mays, O. L.	n/30	328	34.3	200
	16	Roe, R. R.	n/30	329	34.5	90
	18	Null, O. E.	n/30	330	34.4	30
	20	Baker, C. B.	n/30	331	34.2	180
	21	Small, C. C.	n/30	332	34.6	150
	31	Null, O. E.	n/30	333	34.4	260
		Total				1,200
		Posting				(34)(81)

ACCOUNTS RECEIVABLE SUBSIDIARY LEDGER

Adams, K. L.			34.1
Jan. 3		9	100

Baker, C. B.				34.2
Jan. 6		9	110	
20		9	180	290

Mays, O.L.			34.3
Jan. 11		9	200

Null, O. E.				34.4
Jan. 18		9	30	
31		9	260	290

Roe, R. R.				34.5
Jan. 10		9	20	
16		9	90	110

Small, C. C.				34.6
Jan. 4		9	60	
21		9	150	210

GENERAL LEDGER

Accounts Receivable (control)		34
Jan. 31 9	1,200	

Sales Revenue		81
	Jan. 31 9	1,200

Posting the credit sales journal. Posting the special credit sales journal involves two distinct phases. First, the **individual charges** (i.e., debits) must be posted daily to the customers' individual accounts in the **accounts receivable subsidiary ledger** (see Chapter 6, Supplement 6A). This task may be divided among several employees. Second, periodically (usually weekly or monthly), the **totals** are posted to the **general ledger** accounts: Accounts Receivable (debit) and Sales Revenue (credit). In this activity, there is a significant saving in time compared with posting each transaction to the general ledger.

Posting on a daily basis to the **subsidiary ledger,** as shown in Exhibit 8–9, is indicated in the folio column by entering the account number for each individual customer. Daily posting to the subsidiary ledger is necessary because the customer may, on any day, want to pay the current balance then owed.

The second phase in posting the sales journal is to transfer to the general ledger the total credit sales for the month. Thus, the $1,200 total will be posted to the general ledger as (1) a debit to the Accounts Receivable **control account** and (2) as a credit to the Sales Revenue account. This posting is shown in Exhibit 8–9; note in the credit sales journal that two ledger account numbers were entered for the $1,200 total to indicate the posting procedure.

The credit sales journal can be adapted readily to fill special needs. For example, sales taxes could be recorded by adding a column headed "Sales Taxes Payable," and separate sales columns can be added to accumulate sales by department or product. You should observe the following efficiencies attained: (1) recording in the credit sales journal is much less time consuming than separately entering each credit sale in the general journal; (2) posting is reduced significantly by transferring the **total** to the general ledger as opposed to posting separate debits and credits for each sales transaction; (3) the opportunity for division of labour; and (4) additional information (such as sales revenue by department) can be recorded easily.

Credit purchases journal. Following exactly the same pattern as described above, a credit purchases journal may be designed as shown below to accommodate the entry common to all purchases on credit, viz:

Jan. 8   Purchases*...   392
             Accounts payable, C. B. Smith...........................   392
             To record purchase on credit from C. B. Smith, Purchase Order
         No. 139; invoice dated January 5, 19B; terms 2/10, n/30. Recorded net of
         discount, $400 × .98 = $392.
             *This debit assumes a periodic inventory system; if a perpetual system is used this
         account would be Merchandise Inventory.

Only credit purchases are recorded in the credit purchases journal. Cash purchases are entered in the cash payments journal as illustrated later. The design of a purchases journal generally is as shown in Exhibit 8–10.

Observe that purchases are recorded net of the purchase discount as explained in Chapter 6. The cash payments journal will be used to record the subsequent payment of cash for the purchase including situations where the purchase discount is lost.

Exhibit 8–10 was not completed in detail for illustrative purposes because it follows essentially the same pattern already illustrated for the sales journal, both in respect to entries therein and the two phases in posting. Daily posting

EXHIBIT 8–10
Credit purchases
journal illustrated

		CREDIT PURCHASES JOURNAL					Page 4
Date		Creditor's Account	Purchase Order No.	Date of Invoice	Terms	Folio	Amount
Jan.	8	Smith, C. B.	139	Jan. 5	2/10, n/30	51.8	392
		Etc.					
		Total					784
		Posting					(6)(51)

would involve transfer to the creditors' individual accounts in the **accounts payable subsidiary ledger.** Periodically, the total would be posted to the **general ledger** as (1) a debit to the Purchases account and (2) a credit to the Accounts Payable control account. The efficiencies cited for the sales journal also are realized by a purchases journal.

Cash receipts journal. The design of a special journal to accommodate **all, and only, cash receipts** is more complex because there are a number of different accounts that are **credited individually** when the Cash account is debited. To resolve this problem, more than one **credit** column is necessary to accommodate the various credits. The number and designation of the debit and credit columns will depend upon the character of the repetitive cash receipts transactions in the particular business.

A typical cash receipts journal with some usual transactions recorded is shown in Exhibit 8–11. Notice in particular that there are separate debit and credit sections. Each column illustrated is used as follows:

1. **Cash debit**—This column is used for **each** debit to cash. The column is totaled at the end of the month and posted as one debit amount to the Cash account in the general ledger. The posting number at the bottom indicates the total was posted to account number "12," which is the Cash account.[13]
2. **Accounts Receivable credit**—This column is used to enter the individual amounts collected on trade accounts which must be

---

[13]This design assumes that the company correctly records credit sales at net of discounts. If credit sales are recorded at "gross," then a Sales Discount debit column also would be needed in this special journal.

EXHIBIT 8–11   **Cash receipts journal illustrated**

Date		Explanation	DEBITS	CREDITS				
			Cash	Account Title	Folio	Accounts Receivable	Sundry Accounts	Cash Sales
Jan.	2	Cash sales	1,237					1,237
	3	Cash sales	1,482					1,482
	4	Sale of land	2,500	Land	43		2,000	
				Gain on sale of land	91		500	
	4	Cash sales	992					992
	6	Invoice #324	100	Adams, K. L.	34.1	100		
	6	Cash sales	1,570					1,570
	10	Bank loan, 12%	1,000	Notes payable	54		1,000	
	15	Invoice #328	200	Mays, O. L.	34.3	200		
	26	Cash sales	1,360					1,360
	31	Invoice #326	110	Baker, C. B.	34.2	110		
	31	Cash sales	1,810					1,810
		Totals	12,361			410	3,500	8,451
		Posting	(12)			(34)	(NP)	(81)

CASH RECEIPTS JOURNAL — Page 14

posted to the individual customer accounts in the **accounts receivable subsidiary ledger** (as indicated by the posting numbers in the folio columns). The **total** of this column is posted at the end of the month as a credit to the Accounts Receivable **control** account in the general ledger as indicated by the posting number "34."

3. **Sundry Accounts credit**—This column is used for recording credits to all accounts other than those for which special credit columns are provided (in this example Accounts Receivable and Sales Revenue). The titles of the accounts to be credited are entered under the column "Account Title." Because the Sundry Accounts column represents a number of **accounts,** the **total** is not posted; rather, each individual amount must be posted as a credit directly to the indicated general ledger account. Account numbers entered in the related folio column indicate the posting.

4. **Cash Sales credit**—This column is used to record **all cash sales.** The total at the end of the month is posted as a credit to the Sales Revenue account in the general ledger.

Posting the cash receipts journal involves the same two phases explained previously for the credit sales and credit purchases journals. The **daily posting** phase encompasses posting the individual credits to the accounts receivable subsidiary ledger. The **second phase** involves posting the totals periodically to

EXHIBIT 8–11
(concluded)

Jan. 2	Cash..	1,237	
	Sales revenue......................................		1,237
	To record total cash sales for the day.		
3	Cash..	1,482	
	Sales revenue......................................		1,482
	To record total cash sales for the day.		
4	Cash..	2,500	
	Land		2,000
	Gain on sale of land................................		500
	To record sale of land for $2,500 that originally cost $2,000.		
4	Cash..	992	
	Sales revenue......................................		992
	To record total cash sales for the day.		
6	Cash..	100	
	Accounts receivable		100
	To record total collection of K. L. Adams account for Invoice No. 324 (no discount).		
6	Cash..	1,570	
	Sales revenue......................................		1,570
	To record total cash sales for the day.		
10	Cash..	1,000	
	Notes payable		1,000
	To record bank loan, 90-day, 12 percent.		
15	Cash..	200	
	Accounts receivable		200
	To record collection of O. L. Mays account for Invoice No. 328 (no discount).		
26	Cash..	1,360	
	Sales revenue......................................		1,360
	To record total cash sales for the day.		
31	Cash..	110	
	Accounts receivable		110
	To record total collection of C. B. Baker account for Invoice No. 326 (no discount).		
31	Cash..	1,810	
	Sales revenue. :....................................		1,810
	To record total cash sales for the day.		

the accounts in the general ledger, with the exception of the column total for "Sundry Accounts," as explained above.

The individual accounts shown in the "Sundry Accounts" column can be posted daily or at the end of the month. Posting through January is indicated by account code numbers in the illustrated cash receipts journal.

The representative entries shown in the illustrated cash receipts journal are summarized in Exhibit 8–11, in **general journal form,** for convenience in assessing the increased efficiencies of the cash receipts journal approach in journalizing and posting a large number of individual cash transactions.

Other debit and credit columns can be added to the cash receipts journal to accommodate repetitive transactions that also involve cash receipts.

Cash payments journal.   The special cash payments journal (often called the cheque register) is designed to accommodate efficiently the recording of **all (and only) cash payments.** The basic credit column is for Cash; columns for debits are incorporated into the format to accommodate repetitive transactions that involve cash payments. The cash payments journal also must include a column for "Sundry Accounts, Debits" to accommodate the nonrecurring transactions involving cash payments for which a special debit column is not provided.

A typical cash payments journal with some usual transactions recorded is shown in Exhibit 8–12. Observe that in common with the cash receipts journal, there are separate debit and credit sections. Each column illustrated is used as follows:

1. **Cash credit**—This column is for **every credit** to the Cash account. The column is totaled at the end of the month and posted as a credit to the Cash account in the general ledger.
2. **Accounts Payable debit**—This column is used to enter the individual amounts paid on accounts payable. The individual amounts are posted as debits to the **accounts payable subsidiary ledger** (as indicated by the account numbers under folio), and the total at the end of the month is posted as a debit to the Accounts Payable control account in the general ledger.
3. **Sundry Accounts debit**—This column is used to record all accounts debited for which special columns are not provided (in this example Accounts Payable and Purchases are provided). The titles of the accounts to be debited are entered under the column "Account Title." Because this column represents a number of accounts, the total cannot be posted; rather, each individual amount is posted as a debit directly to the indicated general ledger account.
4. **Cash Purchases debit**—All cash purchases are entered in this column. The total at the end of the month is posted as a debit to the Purchases account in the ledger.

Posting the cash payments journal involves two phases: (1) **daily posting** of the individual credit amounts to the **accounts payable subsidiary ledger;** and (2) **periodic posting** of the totals to the **general ledger,** with the exception of the total of "Sundry Accounts." The posting of the individual amounts in the "Sundry Accounts" column can be done during the period, say, daily.

EXHIBIT 8–12   **Cash payments journal illustrated**

			CREDITS	DEBITS				
Date	Cheque No.	Explanation	Cash	Account Title	Folio	Accounts Payable	Sundry Accounts	Cash Purchases
Jan. 2	101	Purchased mdse.	1,880					1,880
4	102	Invoice #37	2,970	Ray Mfg. Co.	51.3	2,970		
5	103	Jan. rent	1,200	Rent expense	71		1,200	
8	104	Purchased mdse.	250					250
10	105	Freight on mdse.	15	Freight in	63		15	
14	106	Invoice #42	980	Bows Supply Co.	51.1	980		
15	107	Paid note, plus	2,200	Notes payable	54		2,000	
		interest		Interest expense	79		200	
20	108	Insurance premium	600	Prepaid insurance	19		600	
26	109	Purchased mdse.	2,160					2,160
29	110	Invoice #91—after	500	Myar Corp.	51.2	490		
		discount period		Discount lost	80		10	
31	111	Wages	1,000	Wage expense	76		1,000	
		Totals	13,755			4,440	5,025	4,290
		Posting	(12)			(51)	(NP)	(61)
Feb. 1		Etc.						

CASH PAYMENTS JOURNAL   Page ____16

The illustrative transactions entered in the cash payments journal (Exhibit 8–12) were:

Jan. 2   Issued Cheque No. 101 for cash purchase of merchandise costing $1,880.

4   Issued Cheque No. 102 to pay account payable owed to Ray Manufacturing Company within the discount period. Discount allowed, 1 percent; Invoice No. 37, $3,000.

5   Issued Cheque No. 103 to pay January rent, $1,200.

8   Issued Cheque No. 104 for cash purchase of merchandise costing $250.

10   Issued Cheque No. 105 for freight-in on merchandise purchased, $15.

14   Issued Cheque No. 106 to pay account payable owed to Bows Supply Company within the discount period. Discount allowed, 2 percent; Invoice No. 42, $1,000.

15   Issued Cheque No. 107 to pay $2,000 note payable plus 10 percent interest for one year.

20   Issued Cheque No. 108 to pay three-year insurance premium, $600.

26   Issued Cheque No. 109 for cash purchase of merchandise costing $2,160.

29   Issued Cheque No. 110 to pay account payable to Myar Corporation; terms, 2/10, n/30; Invoice No. 91, $500. Therefore, accounts payable to Myar was credited for $490 at the purchase date (see Chapter 6). The payment was made after the discount period; hence, the full invoice price of $500 was paid and purchase discount lost of $10 was recorded.

31   Issued Cheque No. 111 to pay wages amounting to $1,000.

Additional debit and credit columns can be added to the cash payments journal to accommodate other repetitive transactions involving cash disbursements.

Many companies control expenditures with a **voucher system** for controlling expenditures rather than with the credit purchases and the cash payments journals. A voucher system is particularly adaptable to computerized accounting and provides tight control mechanisms on the sequence of events for each transaction from incurrence until final cash payment. The voucher system is explained and illustrated in Chapter 10.

In summary, special journals do not involve new accounting principles or concepts. Rather, they represent a mechanical technique designed to increase efficiency in the data processing cycle. Special journals are not standardized; they should be designed especially to fit each particular situation. Although a manual approach has been illustrated for instructional purposes, many companies have computerized the procedures represented by special journals. In computerized systems, essentially the same mechanics illustrated for the manual system are accomplished by the computer.

IMPORTANT TERMS DEFINED IN THIS CHAPTER

Terms (alphabetically)	Key words in definitions of terms used in chapter	Page reference
Bank reconciliation	Process of verifying the accuracy of both the bank statement and the cash accounts of the business.	391
Bank statement	Monthly report from a bank that shows deposits recorded, cheques cleared, and a running bank balance.	389
Cash	Money and any instrument that banks will accept for immediate increase in depositor's chequing account.	387
Cash over and short	Difference between the amount of cash held at a particular time and the amount the cash records call for.	397
Compensating balances	Exists when a bank requires that a specified minimum cash balance must be maintained in the depositor's account.	398
Conservatism in accounting	When more than one alternative is acceptable in accounting, use the one that has the least short-term favourable effect on income and owners' equity.	401
Contingent liability	An endorser (on a negotiable instrument) is liable for its payment if the maker defaults; a contingent liability exists for the endorser.	408
Default of note receivable	Failure of the maker (payor) of a note to pay it by its maturity date.	407

Terms (alphabetically)	Key words in definitions of terms used in chapter	Page reference
Deposits in transit	Deposits made by a depositor that have not yet been reported on the bank statement.	392
Discounting a note receivable	Sale of a note receivable to another party prior to its maturity date.	407
Exceptions to accounting principles	Implementation principles may be modified in application for *(a)* immaterial amounts, *(b)* conservatism, and *(c)* industry peculiarities.	409
Holding (unrealized) loss	Difference between original purchase cost of an investment and its current market value; if market value is **lower,** there is an unrealized loss (if not sold).	401
Internal control	Policies and procedures of a business designed to safeguard the assets of the business.	387
Investment portfolio	A group of securities (shares or bonds) held as an investment; grouped to be accounted for as one unit.	402
Lower of cost or market	Valuation of an investment at either *(a)* original cost or *(b)* current market, whichever is lower.	401
Materiality	Small amounts involved in transactions must be recorded; however, the theoretically correct way may, but need not, be followed; use a simple accounting approach.	409
Negotiable instrument	A formal (written) instrument that specifies the terms of a debt; it is **transferable by endorsement.**	407
Notes receivable	A written promise that requires another party to pay the business under specified conditions (amount, time, interest).	405
Outstanding cheques	Cheques written by a depositor that have not yet been cleared (cashed) by the depositor's bank.	392
Petty cash	A small amount of cash set aside for making small cash payments instead of writing cheques.	397
Receivables, short-term	Short-term notes and accounts owed to the business by regular trade customers.	404
Short-term investment	An investment that *(a)* is marketable and *(b)* will have a short-term holding period.	399
Special receivables	Receivables that arise from transactions other than merchandise and services sold.	405
Term deposit	An investment contract that can be purchased from banks; specifies amount, time, and interest rate.	403
Trade receivables	Another name for accounts receivable; open accounts owed to the business by trade customers.	405

QUESTIONS FOR DISCUSSION

Part A

1. Define cash in the context of accounting and indicate the types of items that should be included and excluded. Identify typical categories of cash.

2. Outline the primary characteristics of an effective internal control system for cash.

3. Why should cash-handling and cash-recording activities be separated? Generally, how is this separation accomplished?

4. What are the purposes and nature of a bank reconciliation? Specifically, what balances are reconciled?

5. Briefly explain how the **total** amount of cash reported on the balance sheet is determined.

6. What is the purpose of petty cash? How is it related to the regular Cash account?

Part B

7. Define a short-term investment. What is the twofold test for classification of an investment as short term?

8. Is a marketable security always classified as a short-term investment? Explain.

9. How does the cost principle apply in accounting for short-term investments in (a) debt securities and (b) equity securities?

10. What is the rationale for application of the LCM basis to the short-term investment portfolio of equity securities?

11. Explain the purpose and nature of the account, Allowance to Reduce Short-Term Investments to Market.

12. The revenue recognition principle (as discussed in Chapter 4) was defined to provide guidance as to when revenue should be recognized in the income statement. Indicate how a company should record interest on a note defaulted on by its customer using this principle.

Part C

13. Distinguish between accounts receivable and special receivables.

14. Define a promissory note indicating the designation of the parties and explain what is meant by principal, maturity date, face amount, and interest rate.

15. Distinguish between an interest-bearing and noninterest-bearing note.

16. What is a negotiable note?

17. What is a defaulted note? Who is responsible for its payment? Explain.

18. What is meant by discounting a note receivable?

19. What is a contingent liability? How does one arise in respect to a note receivable?

20. Identify and briefly explain the three recognized exceptions to the implementing accounting principles.

21. Short-term investments by most companies are valued at the lower of cost or market while accounts receivable are valued at their realizable amount. What is the difference in nature between these two classifications of assets that might warrant the difference in the two valuations?

EXERCISES

Part A

E8–1. National Company operates several branches and, as a consequence, has cash on hand at several locations as well as several bank accounts. The general ledger at the end of 19A showed the following accounts: Petty Cash–Home Office, $500; City Bank–Home Office, $57,300; Cash Held for Making Change, $1,000 (included in the regular Cash Account balance); Petty Cash—Branch A, $100; National Bank—Branch A, $4,458; Petty Cash—Branch B, $200; Southwest Bank—Branch B, $864; Petty Cash—Branch C, $100; State Bank—Branch C, $965; and Metropolitan Bank—Certificate of Deposit, $7,500; and post-dated cheques held that were received from two regular customers, $600.

The four bank balances given represent the true cash balances as reflected on the bank reconciliations.

Required:

What cash amount should be reported on National's 19A balance sheet? Explain the basis for your decisions on any questionable items.

E8–2. Bye Service Company prepared a December 31, 19B, balance sheet that reported cash, $5,849. The following items were found to have been included in the reported cash balance:

	Balance per bank statement at City Bank	$4,934*
a.	A deposit made to the local electric utility	600
b.	Postage stamps on hand	40
c.	Cheque signed by a customer, returned NSF	30
d.	Petty cash on hand	150
e.	IOUs signed by employees	80
f.	Cheque signed by the company president for an advance to him; to be held until he "gives the word to cash it."	1,000
g.	Money orders on hand (received from customers)	45
h.	A signed receipt from a freight company that involved a $10 overpayment to them. They have indicated "a cheque will be mailed shortly."	10
i.	A money order obtained from the post office to be used to pay for a special purchase upon delivery; expected within the next five days	160
	Total cash shown on the 19B balance sheet	$7,049

*Items not considered: deposit in transit, $300; cheques outstanding, $175; and cash held for making change, $100 (all included in the regular Cash account).

Required:

a. The reported cash balance has been questioned. Compute the correct cash amount that should be reported on the balance sheet. Give appropriate reporting for any items that you exclude. (Hint: Set up a form similar to the above.)

b. Assume the company carries two cash accounts in the general ledger—Cash and Petty Cash. What is the correct balance that should be reflected in each cash account at December 31, 19B (end of the accounting period)? Show computations.

E8–3. Baker Company has just received the June 30, 19B, bank statement and the June ledger accounts for cash, which are summarized on the next page:

Bank Statement

	Cheques	Deposits	Balance
Balance, June 1, 19B			$ 4,900
Deposits during June		$17,000	21,900
Cheques cleared through June	$17,700		4,200
Bank service charges..............	20		4,180
Balance, June 30, 19B			4,180

Cash

June 1	Balance	4,500	June	Cheques written	18,100
June	Deposits	19,000			

Petty Cash

June 30	Balance	200	

Required:

a. Reconcile the bank account, assuming that a comparison of the cheques written with the cheques that have cleared the bank show outstanding cheques of $900 and that cash on hand (for making change) on June 30 is $100 (included in the Cash account). Some of the cheques that cleared in June were written prior to June; there were no deposits in transit carried over from May, but there is a deposit in transit at the end of June.

b. Give any journal entries that would be made as a result of the bank reconciliation.

c. What is the balance in the Cash account after the reconciliation entries?

d. What total amount of cash should be reported on the balance sheet at June 30?

E8–4. The September 30, 19D, bank statement for Dotson Company and the completed September ledger accounts for cash are summarized below:

Bank Statement

	Cheques	Deposits	Balance
Balance, September 1, 19D			$ 5,100
Deposits recorded during September		$27,000	32,100
Cheques cleared during September	$27,300		4,800
NSF cheques—J. J. Jones................	80		4,720
Bank service charges...................	23		4,597
Balance, September 30, 19D			4,597

Cash

Sept. 1	Balance	5,300	Sept.	Cheques written	27,800
Sept.	Deposits	29,500			

Petty Cash

Sept. 30	Balance	100	

Cash on hand for making change (included in the Cash account) on September 1 and September 30 amounted to $200. There were no outstanding cheques and no deposits in transit carried over from August; however, there are deposits in transit and cheques outstanding at the end of September.

Required:

a. Reconcile the bank account. (Hint: Audit carefully because you may find an error made by either the bank or the company.)
b. Give any journal entries that would be made as a result of the bank reconciliation.
c. What should be the balance in the Cash account after the reconciliation entries?
d. What total amount of cash should Dotson report on the September 30 balance sheet?

E8–5. The March 31, 19C, bank statement for Diamond Company and the March ledger accounts for cash are summarized below:

Bank Statement

	Cheques	Deposits	Balance
Balance, March 1, 19C			$ 8,600
Deposits during March..............		$28,000	36,600
Note collected for depositor			
(including $60 interest)............		1,060	37,660
Cheques cleared during March.......	$32,200		5,460
Bank service charges................	35		5,425
Balance, March 31, 19C			5,425

Cash

Mar. 1	Balance	8,320	Mar.	Cheques written	32,500
Mar.	Deposits	31,000			

Petty Cash

Mar. 31	Balance	200		

A comparison of March deposits recorded with deposits on the bank statement showed deposits in transit of $3,000. Similarly, outstanding cheques at the end of March were determined to be $900. Cash on hand (not petty cash) for making change (included in the Cash account) was $300 at March 31.

Required:

a. Prepare a bank reconciliation for March. (Hint: A cash overage or shortage is involved; however, the bank figures have been verified as correct.)
b. Give any journal entries that should be made by Diamond based on the reconciliation.
c. What amount should be reflected as the ending balance in the Cash account after the reconciliation entries? What total amount of cash should be reflected on Diamond's balance sheet at the end of March?

Part B

E8–6. Perry Company, in July 19B, had accumulated excess cash that would not be needed for 10 to 15 months. To employ the idle cash profitably, the management decided to purchase some shares as a short-term investment. The following related transactions occurred:

19B

July 30   Purchased 5,000 shares of the common stock of Sharp Corporation on the Toronto stock exchange. The cash price, including fees and transfer costs related to the acquisition, amounted to $20,000.

Dec. 15   Received a cash dividend of $.30 per share on the Sharp shares.

     30   Sold 1,000 of the Sharp shares at $5 per share for cash.

Required:

a.   Give appropriate journal entries for Perry Company on each date for this short-term investment. The accounting period of Perry Company ends on December 31.

b.   Show how this short-term investment should be reported on the balance sheet at December 31, 19B. Assume the same market value as on December 30.

E8–7.   Darby Company, to put some idle cash to work, decided to purchase some common shares in Bay Corporation as a short-term investment. The following related transactions reflect what happened after this decision:

19B

Feb. 1   Purchased 7,000 shares of Bay Corporation common stock at a cash cost of $42,000.

Aug. 15   Received a cash dividend on the Bay shares of $0.30 each.

Dec. 30   Sold 3,000 shares of the Bay at $5.80 per share.

     31   End of the accounting year. Bay shares were selling at $5.75 each.

Required:

a.   Give appropriate journal entries for Darby Company on each date (including December 31) for the investment in Bay shares. Darby Company had no other short-term investments.

b.   Show how the effects of this short-term investment should be reported on the financial statements at December 31, 19B.

c.   Give the entry on January 15, 19C, assuming the remaining shares were sold at $5.50 per share.

d.   Explain what Darby Company should do about the allowance account on December 31, 19C, assuming no short-term investments are held on that date.

E8–8.   White Company, to use some idle cash in March 19B, acquired 200 shares of common stock in each of three corporations at the following costs: Corporation A, $8,000; Corporation B, $6,000; and Corporation C, $12,000. At the end of the annual accounting period, December 31, 19B, the quoted market prices per share were: Corporation A, $40; Corporation B, $25; and Corporation C, $61.

Required:

a.   Give the journal entry by White Company to record the acquisition of these short-term investments in equity securities.

b.   Give the entry to record cash dividends of $1,200 received on the short-term investments in November 19B.

c.   Give the entry to reflect the investments at LCM at December 31, 19B. Show computations.

    d. Show how the investments would be reported on the financial statements at December 31, 19B.

    e. Give the entry on January 5, 19C, assuming all of the shares were sold for $25,000 cash.

    f. Give any entry required at December 31, 19C, assuming no short-term equity investments are held at that time (disregard any closing entries).

E8–9. Cable Company, to put some idle cash to work, purchased a debt security as a short-term investment at a cash cost of $20,000 on August 1, 19B. The security (due in 12 months) earns 9 percent annual interest on its principal amount of $20,000, payable on the date of maturity. At the end of the annual accounting period (December 31), the same security could be purchased for $21,600 cash.

    a. Give all of the journal entries for Cable Company that are indicated on the following dates and provide an explanation for each date:

        (1) August 1, 19B.

        (2) December 31, 19B.

        (3) July 31, 19C.

    b. Show how the security would affect the 19B financial statements.

Part C

E8–10. Approximately 40 percent of the merchandise sold by Gordon Company is sold on credit. Accounts receivable that are overdue, if material in amount, are "converted" to notes receivable when possible. This case traces one sale through accounts receivable, to notes receivable, and to final collection. The related transactions during 19B were:

Jan. 10 Sold merchandise on account to B. A. Cable for $10,000; terms, n/30.

Mar. 1 The account was unpaid; therefore, Gordon Company asked Cable to sign a six-month, 12 percent, interest-bearing note for the account. Cable executed the note on this date.

Aug. 31 Cable paid the principal of the note plus interest.

Required:

    a. Give the journal entry that Gordon should make on each of the three dates.

    b. Give the journal entry that would have been made on September 1, 19B, assuming Cable defaulted.

    c. Give the journal entry assuming the default in *(b)* and also that Cable paid the note in full on September 15, 19B (no additional interest was paid).

E8–11. Hoosier Company sells a line of products that has a high unit sales price. Credit terms are traditional in the industry; accordingly, Hoosier frequently takes a promissory note for the sale price. This exercise follows one promissory note, taken at date of sale, through final collection. The accounting year ends December 31. The transactions and events were:

19B

Dec. 1 Sold merchandise to B. T. Hamm on a three-month, 12 percent, interest-bearing note for $3,000.

    31 End of accounting year, adjusting entry.

19C
Jan. 1 Start of new accounting period.
Mar. 1 Collected the note plus interest.

Required:

a. Give appropriate journal entries for Hoosier Company at each of the four dates; if none, so state.
b. With respect to the note, what item(s) and amount(s) would be reported on the 19B income statement?
c. With respect to the note, what item(s) and amount(s) would be reported on the balance sheet at December 31, 19B?

E8–12. Jones Company frequently sells merchandise on a promissory note, which later is sold (i.e., discounted) to the local bank to obtain cash needed before maturity date. The following transactions relate to one note that followed this pattern:

19B
Apr. 1 Sold merchandise for $9,000 to R. C. Day; took a six-month, 12 percent, interest-bearing note.
June 1 Discounted the note at the local bank at an 11 percent discount rate; received the cash proceeds upon endorsement of the note to the bank.
Oct. 1 Due date of the note plus interest.

Required:

a. Give appropriate journal entries at each of the three dates, assuming Day paid the bank for the note on its due date.
b. Give the appropriate journal entry on October 1, 19B, assuming Day defaulted on the note and Jones Company had to make payment plus a $20 protest fee. This protest fee will be charged to Day.
c. Give the appropriate journal entry assuming Day paid Jones in full on October 5, 19B (no additional interest was received).

E8–13. (Based on Supplement 8A) On January 1, 19B, Kingston Company established a petty cash fund amounting to $200 by writing a cheque to "the Custodian of Petty Cash." The fund was assigned to J. Wright, an employee, to administer as custodian. At the end of January there was $10 cash remaining in the fund. Signed receipts for expenditures during January were summarized as follows: postage, $63; office supplies, $28; transportation, $51; newspapers, $34; and miscellaneous (coffee for the office), $14.

Required:

a. Give the journal entry to establish the petty cash fund on January 1, 19B.
b. Give the journal entry to replenish the fund on January 31, 19B.
c. What balance would be reflected in the Petty Cash account in the ledger at January 31? Explain.
d. How would petty cash be reported on the balance sheet at January 31, 19B?
e. What effect did the petty cash fund activities have on the January 19B income statement?
f. Assume it is January 5, 19C, and the management has decided to increase the petty cash fund to $250. Give the required journal entry.

PROBLEMS/CASES

Part A

PC8–1. Careless Company has one trusted employee who, as the owner said, "handles all of the bookkeeping and paperwork for the company." This employee also is responsible for counting, verifying, and recording cash receipts and payments, such as making the weekly bank deposit, preparing cheques for major expenditures (signed by the owner), making small expenditures from the cash register for daily expenses, and collecting accounts receivable. The owner asked the local bank for a $25,000 loan, whereupon the bank asked that an audit be performed covering the year just ended. The independent auditor (a local CA), in a private conference with the owner, presented some evidence of the following activities of the trusted employee during the past year:

1. Cash sales sometimes were not entered in the cash register, and the trusted employee pocketed approximately $40 per month.
2. Cash taken from the cash register (and pocketed by the trusted employee) was replaced with **expense memos** with fictitious signatures (approximately $10 per day).
3. A $500 collection on an account receivable of a valued out-of-town customer was pocketed by the trusted employee and was covered by making a $500 entry as a debit to Returned Sales and a credit to Accounts Receivable.
4. A $700 collection on an account receivable from a local customer was pocketed by the trusted employee and was covered by making a $700 entry as a debit to Allowance for Doubtful Accounts and a credit to Accounts Receivable.

Required:

a. What was the approximate amount stolen during the past year?
b. What would be your recommendations to the owner?

PC8–2. Hall Manufacturing Company is a relatively small local business that specializes in the repair and renovation of antique jewelry, brass objects, and silverware. The owner is an expert craftsman. Although a number of skilled workers are employed, there is always a large backlog of work to be done. A long-time employee, who serves as clerk-bookkeeper, handles cash receipts, keeps the records, and writes cheques for disbursements. The cheques are signed by the owner. Small amounts are paid in cash by the clerk-bookkeeper, subject to a month-end review by the owner. Approximately 100 regular customers regularly are extended credit, that typically amounts to less than $500. Although credit losses are small, in recent years the bookkeeper had established an Allowance for Doubtful Accounts, and all write-offs were made at year-end. During January 19E (the current year), the owner decided to start construction as soon as possible of a building for the business that would provide many advantages over the presently rented space and would have space usable for expansion of facilities. As a part of the considerations in financing, the financing institution asked for "19D audited financial statements." The company records never had been audited. Early in the audit, the independent CA found numerous errors and one combination of amounts, in particular, that caused concern.

There was some evidence that a $1,500 job completed by Hall had been recorded as a receivable (from a new customer) on July 15, 19D. The receivable was credited for a

$1,500 cash collection a few days later. The new account never was active again. The auditor also observed that shortly thereafter three write-offs of Accounts Receivable balances had been made to Allowance for Doubtful Accounts as follows: Jones, $250; Adams, $750; and Coster, $500; all of whom were known as regular customers. These write-offs drew the attention of the auditor.

Required:

a. Can you determine what caused the CA to be concerned? Explain. Should the CA report his suspicions to the owner?

b. What recommendations would you make in respect to internal control procedures for this company?

PC8–3. The bookkeeper at Laizee Company has not reconciled the bank statement with the Cash account, saying, "I don't have time." You have been asked to prepare a reconciliation and review the procedures with the bookkeeper.

The April 30, 19D, bank statement and the April ledger accounts for cash showed the following (summarized):

Bank Statement

	Cheques	Deposits	Balance
Balance, April 1, 19D..............			$23,550
Deposits during April		$38,000	61,550
Note collected for depositor			
(including $90 interest)		1,090	62,640
Cheques cleared during April	$44,700		17,940
NSF cheque—A. B. Cage	140		17,800
Bank service charges	30		17,770
Balance, April 30, 19D............			17,770

Cash

Apr.	1	Balance	22,850	Apr.	Cheques written	44,500
Apr.		Deposits	42,000			

Petty Cash

Apr. 30	Balance	200	

A comparison of cheques written before and during April with the cheques cleared through the bank reflected outstanding cheques at the end of April of $600. No deposits in transit were carried over from March, but there was a deposit in transit at the end of April. Cash on hand, held for change, at the end of April was $100 (included in the regular Cash account).

Required:

a. Prepare a detailed bank reconciliation for April.

b. Give any required journal entries as a result of the reconciliation. Why are they necessary?

c. What were the balances in the cash accounts in the ledger on May 1, 19D?

d. What total amount of cash should be reported on the balance sheet at the end of April?

PC8–4. The August 19B bank statement for Western Company and the August 19B ledger accounts for cash are given below:

Bank Statement

	Cheques	*Deposits*	*Balance*
Aug. 1......			$16,000
2......	$ 300		15,700
3......		$7,000	22,700
4......	400		22,300
5......	200		22,100
9......	900		21,200
10......	300		20,900
15......		9,000	29,900
21......	700		29,200
24......	21,000		8,200
25......		8,000	16,200
30......	800		15,400
31......		2,180*	17,580
31......		30†	17,550

*$2,000 note collected plus interest.
†Bank service charge.

26,180

24,630

Cash

			Cheques written:		
Aug. 1 Balance	15,250		Aug. 2		300
Deposits:			4		900
Aug. 2	7,000		15		600
12	9,000		17		550
24	8,000		18		800
31	6,000		18		700
			23		21,000

36,000

45,250

45,1

24,850

Petty Cash

Aug. 31 Balance	100

Cash on hand for making change at the end of August amounted to $150 (included in the regular Cash account). There were three outstanding cheques at the end of July: $200, $400, and $300. There were no deposits in transit at the end of July.

Required:

a. Determine the deposits in transit at the end of August.
b. Determine the outstanding cheques at the end of August.
c. Prepare a bank reconciliation for August.
d. Give any journal entries that should be made as a result of the bank reconciliation by Western Company. Why are they necessary?
e. After the reconciliation journal entries are posted, what balances would be reflected in the cash accounts in the ledger?

f. What total amount of cash should be reported on the August 31, 19B, balance sheet?

PC8–5. The December 31, 19B, bank statement for Never-out Company and the December 19B ledger accounts for cash are given below.

Bank Statement

Date	Cheques	Deposits	Balance
Dec. 1			$41,000
2	400, 150	16,000	56,450
4	7,000, 80		49,370
6	120, 180, 1,500		47,570
11	900, 1,200, 90	21,000	66,380
13	450, 700, 1,900		63,330
17	17,000, 2,000		44,330
23	40, 23,500	36,000	56,790
26	1,800, 2,650		52,340
28	2,200, 4,800		45,340
30	13,000, 1,890, 200*	19,000	49,250
31	1,650, 1,200, 28‡	6,360†	52,732

*NSF cheque, J. Doe, a customer.
†Note collected, principal, $6,000 plus interest.
‡Bank service charge.

Cash

Dec. 1 Balance	55,850	Cheques written during December:		
Deposits:		40	5,000	2,650
Dec. 11	21,000	13,000	4,800	1,650
23	36,000	700	1,890	2,200
30	19,000	4,400	1,500	7,000
31	17,000	1,200	120	150
		180	80	450
		17,000	23,500	2,000
		90	900	1,900
		1,800	1,200	

Petty Cash

Dec. 31 Balance	150	

The November 19B, bank reconciliation showed the following: True cash balance at November 30, $55,700: deposits in transit on November 30, $16,000; and outstanding cheques on November 30, $400 + $900 = $1,300. At the end of December 19B, cash held on hand for making change amounted to $150 (included in the regular Cash account).

Required:

a. Determine the deposits in transit December 31, 19B.

b. Determine the outstanding cheques at December 31, 19B.

c. Prepare a bank reconciliation at December 31, 19B.

d. Give any journal entries that should be made as a result of the bank reconciliation made by Never-out Company. Why are they necessary?

e. After the reconciliation journal entries, what balances would be reflected in the cash accounts in the ledger?

   f. What total amount of cash should be reported on the December 31, 19B, balance sheet?

Part B

PC8–6. Davis Company, to use idle cash, usually acquires common shares as a short-term investment. This case focuses on the purchase of common shares from three different companies during 19B. The annual accounting period ends December 31. The sequence of transactions was:

19B

Apr. 2 Purchased (with cash) the following common shares as a short-term investment:

Corporation	Number of shares	Total price per share
X.........	300	$50
Y.........	400	70
Z.........	500	90

Sept. 8 Received a cash dividend of $2 per share on Corporation Z shares.

Dec. 30 Sold the shares of Corporation Y for $76 each.

Dec. 31 Quoted market prices on this date were: Corporation X shares, $53; Corporation Y shares, $75; and Corporation Z shares, $86.

Required:

 a. Give the journal entry for Davis Company on each date.

 b. Illustrate how the effects of these investments would be reflected on the 19B income statement and the balance sheet at December 31, 19B.

 c. What was the amount of the 19B holding loss? Explain what this means.

 d. Assume it is December 31, 19C, and that all of the X and Z shares still are held and that their market values per share are X, $51; and Z, $88. Give the required LCM entry. (Hint: Leave the correct balance in the Allowance account.)

PC8–7. On July 1, 19D, CAL Corporation purchased, as a short-term investment, ten $1,000, 10 percent bonds of Lower Corporation at par (i.e., at $1,000 each). The bonds mature on June 30, 19G. Annual interest is payable on June 30 each year. The accounting period for CAL Corporation ends on December 31.

Required:

 a. Give the journal entries required for CAL Corporation on the following dates (if no entry is required, explain why): July 1, 19D, and December 31, 19D (adjusting entry).

 b. At the end of 19D, the bonds were quoted on the market at $990 each. Give any LCM basis journal entry required on December 31, 19D. If none is required, explain why.

 c. Show how this investment would be reported on the 19D balance sheet and income statement.

 d. Give the journal entry required on June 30, 19E.

PC8–8. Superior Manufacturing Company produces and sells one main product. Demand is seasonal, and the unit sales price is high. Superior's accounting year ends December 31. Typically, in the busy months of the demand cycle, the company collects large amounts of cash, which is idle during the slow months. As a consequence, the company consistently acquires short-term investments to earn a return on what otherwise would be idle cash. Recently, the company purchased 1,000 common shares in each of two other corporations—Corporations A and B. The prices per share, including fees and related costs, were A, $30; and B, $70. In addition, Superior purchased a $10,000 bond of James Corporation. The bond pays 9 percent annual interest on each March 31. The bond was purchased on April 1, 19B, for $10,000 cash (i.e., at par).

The sequence of transactions was:

19B
Apr. 1 Purchased the 2,000 common shares and the $10,000 bond. (Hint: Account for the shares and bond portfolios separately.)
Oct. 3 Received a cash dividend of $0.60 per share on the stock of Corporation B.
Nov. 30 Sold 600 shares of Corporation A at $26 per share and 600 shares of Corporation B at $75 per share.
Dec. 31 End of the accounting period. The market prices on this date were A shares, $29; B shares, $68; and James bonds, 100 (i.e., at par). (Hint: Do not overlook accrued interest.)

Required:

a. Give the journal entries for Superior at each of the four dates given above. Omit any closing entries.
b. Show how the effects of the investment would be reported on the balance sheet at December 31, 19B.
c. What items and amounts would be reported on the 19B income statement?

Part C

PC8–9. Doan Company sells approximately 60 percent of its merchandise on credit; terms, n/30. Occasionally, a promissory note will be received as a part of the collection process of a delinquent account. This case focuses on two different sales that ended with promissory notes. The annual accounting period ends December 31. The sequence of transactions was:

Note No. 1:

19B
Feb. 15 Sold merchandise for $3,000 to A. B. Lee; received $1,000 cash, and the balance was debited to Accounts Receivable.
Apr. 1 Received an interest-bearing note in settlement of the overdue account of Lee. Terms of the note were four months, 12 percent interest.
July 31 Due date for note; Lee defaulted.
Oct. 1 Lee paid the defaulted note plus interest, plus 8 percent interest on the defaulted amount for the period July 31–October 1. The 8 percent is the legal rate of interest on overdue obligations.

Note No. 2:

19B
Oct. 1 Sold merchandise for $3,600 to J. K. Pope, received $600 cash, and the balance was charged to Accounts Receivable (terms, n/EOM).

Nov. 1 Received an interest-bearing note in settlement of the overdue account from Pope. The terms of the note were three months, 12 percent interest.

Dec. 31 End of fiscal period.

19C

Jan. 1 Start of new accounting period.

      30 Maturity date of the note. Pope paid the principal plus interest.

Required:

a. Note No. 1—Give the required journal entries for Doan Company on each date. Show interest calculations. Omit any closing entries.

b. Note No. 2—Give the required journal entries for Doan Company on each date. Show interest calculations. Omit any closing entries.

c. Note No. 2—How much interest revenue will be reported on the 19B income statement of Doan Company?

d. Note No. 2—How will this note affect the 19B balance sheet of Doan Company?

PC8–10. Farmer Company sells heavy machinery. Credit terms are customary and usually involve promissory notes and a mortgage on the machinery sold. Down payments of 20 percent to 33⅓ percent are required. The annual accounting period ends December 31. This problem focuses on two different promissory notes that were received in 19B. The transactions were:

Note No. 1:

19B

Feb. 1 Sold equipment to W. D. Fort for $30,000; received a 20 percent cash down payment and a four-month, 12 percent, interest-bearing note for the balance.

Mar. 1 Sold the note to the local bank at a 10 percent discount rate; endorsed the note to the bank and received the cash proceeds.

June 1 Due date of the note plus interest; Fort paid the note and interest in full.

Required:

a. Give the journal entry for Farmer Company on each of the three dates. Show interest computations. Assume that Fort paid the bank the principal plus interest on the due date.

b. Give the journal entry on the due date, June 1, 19B, assuming instead that Fort defaulted on the note and Farmer paid the local bank the face amount of the note plus interest, and plus a $25 protest fee.

c. How much interest revenue will be reported on the 19B income statement for Note No. 1?

Note No. 2:

19B

Dec. 1 Sold equipment to W. T. Owens for $20,000; received $5,000 cash down payment and a three-month, 12 percent, interest-bearing note for the balance.

     31 End of accounting period.

19C

Jan. 1 Start of new accounting period.

Mar. 1 Due date of the principal plus interest; Owens paid the note plus interest in full.

Required:

d. Give the journal entry for Farmer Company on each of the four dates (omit any closing entries). State any assumptions you make.

e. How much interest revenue (Note No. 2) will be reported on the 19B income statement?

f. Show how Note No. 2 should be reported on the balance sheet at December 31, 19B.

PC8–11. (Based on Supplement 8B) York Company completes a variety of transactions each year. A number of them are repetitive in nature; therefore, the company maintains five different journals: general, credit sales, credit purchases, cash receipts, and cash payments. Selected transactions are listed below that are to be appropriately entered in these journals. To shorten this case amounts have been simplified and the number of transactions limited. All credit sales and credit purchases are recorded net of discount.

Selected transactions are listed below. (use the letter to the left in lieu of the date and use the letter *v* for the last day of the period):

a. Sold merchandise to K. K. May at invoice cost of $250; terms, 2/10, n/20; Invoice No. 38.

b. Received merchandise from Sable Company at invoice cost of $300; credit terms, 1/10, n/20; Purchase Order No. 17.

c. Sold merchandise to B. B. Wise for $200 on credit; terms, 2/10, n/20; Invoice No. 39.

d. Received merchandise from Rex Supply Company at an invoice cost of $200 on credit; terms, 1/10, n/20; Purchase Order No. 18.

e. Sold merchandise to A. B. Cox for $150.

f. Received merchandise from Baker Manufacturing Company at a cost of $360; paid cash (number the cheques consecutively starting with No. 81).

g. Purchased an operational asset (machinery) at a cost of $3,000; gave a 90-day, 12 percent, interest-bearing note payable for the purchase price.

h. Sold a tract of land for $9,000 which previously was used by the company as a parking lot and originally cost $3,000; collected cash.

i. Collected the account receivable from B. B. Wise within the discount period; Invoice No. 39.

j. Paid $600 for a three-year insurance policy on operational assets.

k. Obtained a $5,000 bank loan; signed a one-year, 12 percent, interest-bearing note payable.

l. Paid the account payable to Rex Supply Company within the discount period.

m. Paid monthly rent, $650.

n. Sold merchandise for cash, $1,400.

o. Purchased merchandise for cash, $980.

p. Sold merchandise on credit to C. C. Coe for $700; terms, 2/10, n/20; Invoice No. 40.

q. Received merchandise on credit from Stubbs Company at an invoice cost of $400; terms, 2/10, n/30; Purchase Order No. 19.

r. Collected the account receivable from K. K. May after the discount period.

s. Paid the account payable to Sable Company after the discount period.

t. Paid monthly salaries, $2,400.

u. By year-end, six months of the prepaid insurance had expired.

Use the following general ledger account code numbers for posting: Cash, 11; Accounts Receivable, 14; Prepaid Insurance, 16; Machinery, 17; Land, 19; Accounts Payable, 21; Notes Payable, 22; Purchases, 31; Purchase Discounts Lost, 33; Sales Revenue, 41; Sales Discount Revenue, 43; Expenses, 51; and Gain on Sale of Operational Assets, 53. For journals, use the following page numbers: General, 15; Credit Sales, 18; Credit Purchases, 14; Cash Receipts, 21; and Cash Payments, 34.

Required:

1. Draft a format for each of the five journals, including a general journal, following the illustrations included in Supplement 8B. Include folio columns.

2. Set up separate T-accounts for each of the general ledger accounts listed above.

3. Set up separate T-accounts (with account numbers) for the subsidiary ledgers as follows:

Accounts receivable (14)	*Accounts payable (21)*
Coe— 14.1	Sable— 21.1
May— 14.2	Stubbs—21.2
Wise— 14.3	Rex— 21.3

4. Enter each transaction in the appropriate journal.

5. Indicate all postings to the **subsidiary ledgers** by entering appropriate account numbers in the folio columns.

6. Total each money column in the special journals and indicate all postings to the **general ledger** accounts by entering the account code numbers in the folio columns and below total amounts posted. Use the account code numbers given above.

PC8–12. Refer to the financial statements of Consolidated-Bathurst in Special Supplement B immediately preceding the Index. Respond to the following questions using the 1984 financial statements:

1. How much did cash and short-term deposits change during 1984?

2. How much cash was invested in additions to property, plant, and equipment during 1984?

3. How much did the company have invested in investments in securities? Explain the basis for the classification of these securities.

4. Did the company make a journal entry for lower of cost or market on the marketable securities? Explain.

5. Complete the following schedule:

	1984	1983
Accounts receivable	_____	_____
Less: Allowance for doubtful accounts	_____	_____
Accounts receivable expected to be collected	_____	_____

6. What was the book value of accounts receivable at the end of 1984?

7. Assume bad debts of $1.1 million were written-off during 1984. Give the journal entry that C-B would have made.

8. How much did the allowance for doubtful accounts increase during 1984?

9. Assuming bad debt expense was $2.3 million in 1984, give the journal entry that C-B would have made for bad debt expense for 1984.

10. What was the percentage of the bad debt expense to sales to customers for 1984? Do you think a user would want to know this percentage?

PC8–13. Your audit client, Quebec Furniture Ltd. (QFL), which employs 250 people and manufactures furniture has recently acquired a minicomputer to replace its two mechanical bookkeeping machines. The bookkeeping machines are being used for all accounting operations, including the preparation of journals and ledgers and various documents such as sales invoices, purchase orders, cheques, and customer statements. QFL has also contracted with a local programming firm to provide a complete set of standardized accounting programs designed for small manufacturing firms. This set of computer programs performs the following functions:

1. Customer order entry.
2. Customer shipments and invoicing.
3. Accounts receivable and customer remittances.
4. Sales analysis.
5. Purchase order entry.
6. Receipts from vendors and vendor invoice processing.
7. Accounts payable and cash disbursements.
8. Inventory control.
9. Production scheduling and reporting.
10. Cost accounting.
11. Payroll.
12. Fixed assets.
13. General ledger and financial statements.
14. Generalized information retrieval and report writing.

The minicomputer has just been delivered and the programming firm's representatives are working on the installation of the set of standardized accounting programs. The minicomputer hardware consists of three visual display terminals with attached keyboards, a 150-line/minute printer, a 50-million byte magnetic disk drive, a 10-million byte magnetic tape cassette drive, and 64,000-byte central processing unit. The minicomputer vendor's system software resides in 32,000 bytes of primary storage in the central processing unit and consists of a realtime program scheduler, an input/output control program, a BUSINESS BASIC language interpreter, and various utility programs for common data processing purposes (sort, merge, and copy data files, list programs, etc.).

The minicomputer hardware and the programming firm's software are designed so that all data input will be submitted through the keyboards attached to the visual display terminals. These terminals will also be used to call for information to be displayed on the terminal screen, to initiate the execution of computer programs which produce reports based on the data in the computer files, and to enter new programs or changes to existing programs. Data submitted to the minicomputer will either be processed immediately against master file records maintained on the magnetic disk drive or stored temporarily on the magnetic disk drive for subsequent batch processing against master file data.

The magnetic disk drive, which contains a fixed disk pack, will also contain the accounting programs being supplied by the programming firm. The magnetic tape cassette drive will serve as the means of providing backup copies of the data and programs stored on the fixed magnetic disk pack.

The set of accounting programs are "standardized modules" and must be tailored to each specific user firm's requirements. The tailoring process consists of modifying the programs:

1. To print outputs in a format desired by the user.
2. To insert various terms and tax rates applicable to the user (e.g., sales on a 2 percent-10, net-30).
3. To insert the user's account codings and additional custom programs desired by the user.

These programs are written in BUSINESS BASIC, a high-level computer programming language noted for its simplicity. The generalized information retrieval and report writing feature allows a nonprogrammer to enter simple English-like commands through a visual display terminal to extract information and print exception reports based on any selection parameters specified by the user.

The only office staff at QFL are five clerical and bookkeeping personnel. There is no qualified accountant as QFL has relied on your firm for assistance in all accounting matters. Management consists of the owner/manager, a production manager, and several production foremen. Your firm has provided monthly accounting services leading to the preparation of monthly financial statements. The bookkeeping machine operator is being trained to be the senior data entry operator and to handle the relatively simple operations of turning on the minicomputer, setting up forms on the printer, and backing up data files and programs on the magnetic disk to magnetic tape cassette. QFL's owner/manager hopes that the use of a minicomputer will allow the firm to reduce the office staff to three: a senior data entry operator, a junior clerk, and a secretary/receptionist.

One of the main reasons why QFL's owner/manager decided to buy this minicomputer was that its operation would not require the hiring of any full-time computer people. Both he and the senior bookkeeping machine operator have attended a five-day course on programming and operating the equipment which he believes will be sufficient for either he or the operator to make any simple program changes that may be required at a future date. He plans to rely on the programming services firm for any major program changes that may be required in the future.

Required:

Discuss any significant control problems that may be created by the introduction of the minicomputer at QFL and recommend to the owner/manager steps to reduce their significance.

(CICA Adapted)

PC8–14. Cape Briton Supplies Ltd. (CBS), a client of yours, has recently installed a computerized sales/order entry system. The controller of CBS, Mr. Byte, has been reading articles and reports concerning computer fraud. He is concerned that the new system does not have appropriate controls to minimize the risks to the company. He has asked you to review the system in the normal course of your audit engagement.

CBS is a wholesale distributor of building products. It has a head office, three separate sales branches and four separate warehouse locations. Each warehouse has significant inventory levels and approximately 2,500 different items. Annual sales are $80 million and the accounts receivable balance is $25 million. There are 5,000 customer accounts.

A schematic of the hardware configuration is outlined in Exhibit I.

The central processor is located at the head office and includes a megabyte of storage with supporting disk drive capacity, telecommunication interface, tape drives, master printer and master terminal. Other terminals are located in the following sites:

> Accounting department—2;
> Order desk—head office—3;
>   —branches—2 at each sales branch for a total of 6;
> Warehouses—1 at each of 4 warehouses.

Printers are located in each warehouse for the printing of shipping documents as well as in the accounting department and in the computer room.

Historically, the computer operations at CBS have been well controlled. A review of the existing environment or general computer controls has revealed that controls over implementation, program and data files, physical operations and the operating system are adequate.

The system was designed to speed up the order entry processing/shipping function, and improve inventory and accounts receivable management.

Clerks at the terminal locations take orders over the phone or from salesmen's written orders. The clerks call a "menu" to the screen and prepare the required order. Input includes customer numbers, product numbers, quantity, special shipping instructions and branch location code. The computer edits the input data for correct format, valid dates, valid customer, product, and location codes, credit limits and inventory availability.

The accounts receivable file contains the data elements listed in Exhibit II.

For all orders clearing the edits, a sales order is produced in two copies at the warehouse location. A computer file of outstanding sales orders is created. The warehouse clerks take the orders and fill them. One copy of the sales order serves as the packing slip. The other copy is sent to accounting for filing by customer number.

The following action results when edit checks are not successful:

1. Invalid product, customer or location codes and invalid dates are immediately identified to the operator for reentry.
2. Where the product is not available at the location identified, the inventory file of other locations is searched. If the product is available at the alternate location, a sales order is produced with instructions to ship only the relevant item.
3. Where inventory is not available at any location, a record is created in the backorder file and a printout of the order is sent to the purchasing department for follow-up.
4. Where the credit limit is exceeded, the order is printed out in the accounting department for credit override approval.

When an order is complete and shipped, the warehouse clerk keys in this fact in the warehouse terminal and the order is flagged as shipped on the outstanding sales order file.

In the case of partial shipments from a warehouse, the clerk codes the order as partial and indicates items shipped. This is noted on the outstanding order file and when these items have been shipped, the program changes the code on the outstanding order file to read complete.

**EXHIBIT I
Schematic of
hardware
configuration**

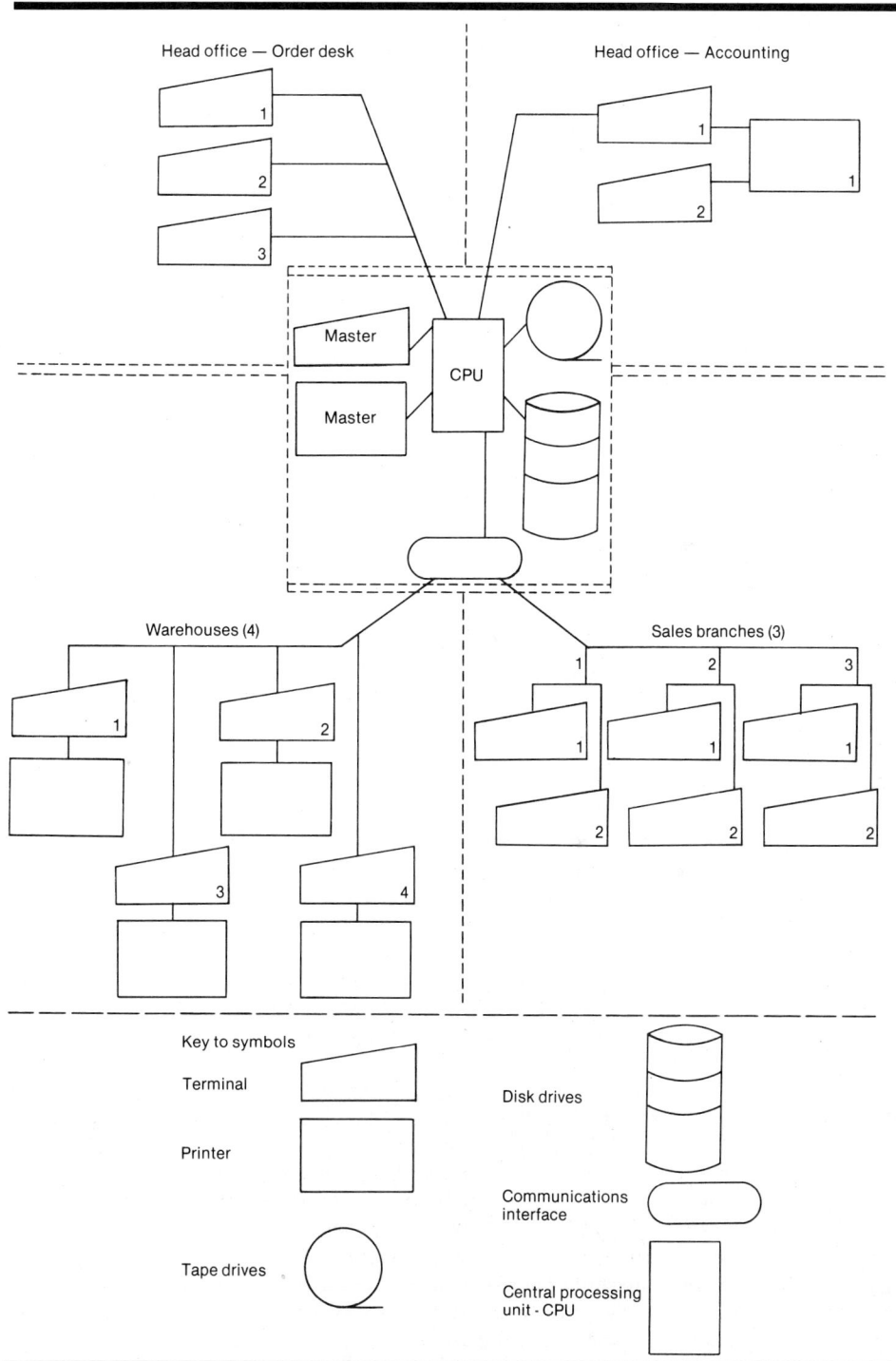

Head office — Order desk

Head office — Accounting

1

2

3

1

2

1

Master

Master

CPU

Warehouses (4)

1

2

3

4

Sales branches (3)

1

2

3

1

1

1

2

2

2

Key to symbols

Terminal

Printer

Tape drives

Disk drives

Communications
interface

Central processing
unit - CPU

EXHIBIT II
Accounts receivable
file layout

Field name	No. of characters and field characteristics	Description
1. Acc-Number	9(10)	Customer number
2. Division	9(2)	Sales branch
3. Cust-Name	X(25)	Name
4. Address	X(50)	Address
5. Credit-Lim	9(7)	Credit limit
6. Total-Due	S9(7)V99	Total A/R
7. Current-Bal	S9(7)V99	
8. Bal-30-60	S9(7)V99	
9. Bal-60-90	S9(7)V99	Age of invoices on file
10. Bal-Over-90	S9(7)V99	
	S9(7)V99	
11. Invoice-No.*	9(5)	Individual invoice number
12. Invoice-Date	9(6)	Date of invoice
13. Invoice-Amt	S9(7)V99	Amount of invoice
14. Credit-No.*	9(5)	Credit note number
15. Credit-Date	9(6)	Date of credit note
16. Credit-Amt	S9(7)V99	Amount of credit note
17. Unallocated-Cash	S9(7)V99	Cash not matched with invoices

Note: S—designates that the field is signed.
    V—represents a decimal point.
    X—indicates an alphanumeric field.
    9—indicates a numeric field.
    *—file contains as many items as exist that are not matched with cash.

For example: 9(6) represents a numeric field of six characteristics.

For orders for which inventory is not available, a back order is created and identified on the outstanding order file. When all items other than the back-order items are keyed in as shipped, the program codes the order complete and it enters the billing cycle.

At the end of each day, the outstanding order file is processed and all shipments coded complete enter the billing program which creates an invoice and updates the accounts receivable and sales files.

When goods are received at a warehouse, the warehouse clerk enters the data. The system searches the back-order file and immediately creates sales orders for the items in back order. It then follows the normal processing cycle.

The inventory file contains the data elements described in Exhibit III. The warehouse clerks have access through terminals to inventory files and are encouraged to make adjustments to the records through the terminals, if in filling an order they find inventory overages or shortages. Cyclical counts of inventory are carried out by designated warehouse clerks who adjust records as required through the terminals. In order to carry out the credit checks at the input stage of the sales order system, the program accesses the price file, prices the order and calculates the total. It then accesses the receivable file to obtain the current balance, adds the order value and compares the total to the credit limit. To save processing time, only orders in excess of $200 are subject to the credit check.

If a customer account is not on file, as determined at the edit stage, the order is printed out at the accounting office printer and a credit investigation is done by credit clerks. When the customer is approved for credit, the credit clerk goes to the terminal

EXHIBIT III
Inventory file
layout

	Field name	No. of characters and field characteristics	Description
1.	Product-Number	9(10)	Individual item identification code
2.	Warehouse-Code	9(2)	Warehouse location
3.	Product-Group	9(2)	
4.	Product-Description	X(40)	
5.	Date-Cost	9(6)	Last date cost changed (YYMMDD)
6.	Recent-Cost	S9(6)V99	Most recent unit cost
7.	Prior-Cost	S9(6)V99	Previous unit cost
8.	Selling-Price	S9(6)V99	Current selling price
9.	Date-Selling Price	9(6)	Date of last selling price change (YYMMDD)
10.	Quantity-On-Hand	S9(6)	Inventory in warehouse
11.	Quantity-On-Order	S9(6)	Inventory on order
12.	Economic-Order	S9(6)	Economic order quantity
13.	Order-Point	S9(6)	Minimum stock level/reorder level
14.	Quantity-Previous-Y/E	S9(6)	Closing inventory previous year (units)
15.	Current-Year's-Sales-Units	S9(6)	Number of units sold current year
16.	Previous-Year's Sales	S9(7)V99	Total sales previous financial year
17.	Previous-Year's-Sales-Units	S9(6)	Total units sold previous financial year
18.	Date-Last-Count	9(6)	Last cyclical count date (YYMMDD)
19.	Adjustment-Last-Count	S9(7)V99	Adjustment on last cyclical count
20.	Net-Adjustment-Year	S9(7)V99	Net adjustments made during the year
21.	Date-Last-Receipt	9(6)	Date of last receipt (YYMMDD)
22.	Quantity-Last-Receipt	S9(6)	Quantity received on last receipt
23.	Supplier-Number	9(8)	Designated supplier
24.	Date-Last-Shipment	9(6)	Date of last shipment (YYMMDD)
25.	Quantity-Last-Shipment	S9(6)	Quantity shipped in last sale

Note: S—designates that the field is signed (i.e., positive or negative)
 V—represents a decimal point
 X—indicates an alphanumeric field
 9—indicates a numeric field

and creates the customer file with the appropriate credit limit. The order is sent back to the sales order clerks for processing in the normal fashion.

The credit manager can approve sales over the credit limit. He receives these sales order copies and reviews them. When he authorizes a sale over the credit limit, he signs the order copy and resubmits it to the sales order clerks. With a special code, they bypass the credit check and the order is processed normally.

At the end of each week, the outstanding order file is processed and a printout is produced. On Monday morning, the warehouse managers review the outstanding list.

Payments on account are received by a cash receipts clerk who takes an adding machine tape of the receipts and codes the tapes for customer number. She prepares a bank deposit slip in duplicate, and gives the payments and original deposit slip to a messenger who makes the bank deposit. She then enters the payments by customer number into the terminal for updating of the receivables file. Independently, another clerk checks the stamped bank deposit slip to the adding machine tape to ensure all receipts were deposited. A daily cash listing is printed on the accounting office printer so that the cash receipts clerk can respond to any customer queries.

At month end, the following reports are printed:

Accounts Receivable Aged Trial Balance
Sales Analysis—by warehouse
                    —by salesman
                    —by product
Inventory Adjustment listing
Cash Receipts listing

These listings are used to update general ledger control accounts. Accounts receivable are reconciled to the general ledger by a clerk who is independent of the accounts receivable, inventory, and cash receipts functions.

Required:

Identify the control weaknesses in the sales/order entry and cash receipts system as described and suggest ways in which the company might correct the weaknesses.

(CICA Adapted)

PC8–15. *Required:*

Write a computer program to solve Problem PC8–5. Your program should result in a bank reconcilation report which should resemble the following:

RECONCILIATION OF BANK STATEMENT

BANK BALANCE	52732
DEPOSITS IN TRANSIT	17000
OUTSTANDING CHEQUES	− 10300
CASH ON HAND	150
BANK ERRORS	0
TRUE BALANCE	59582

RECONCILIATION OF BOOK CASH BALANCE

BOOK BALANCE	53450
NOTES COLLECTED	6360
SERVICE CHARGE	− 28
NSF CHEQUES	− 200
BOOK ERRORS	0
TRUE BALANCE	59582
DIFFERENCE	0

If the computer language you use allows you to make the report look better than the one presented above, then do improve on it.

There are many different ways by which a computer could prepare a report like this one. The computer could get its data from a file or, in the BASIC language, from READ and DATA statements. Alternatively, the computer could prompt the user for each piece of information needed.

You should seriously consider the pros and cons of these various alternatives.

The objective is to write a simple program which will help someone who does not know much about bank reconciliations to use the computer to prepare such a report. Therefore, the program should be written to solve the problem by prompting the user for input.

Here are some hints to help write the program:

1. Study the material in the text to determine the major items that should appear in a bank reconciliation.
2. For each item for which data has to be entered into the computer, for example, the cash balance according to the bank statement, write an appropriate prompt to the terminal screen and ask for the desired information.
3. Store the information received in response to prompts in appropriate variables.
4. Organize the information received from the user of the program into the proper format and print out the Bank Reconciliation.
5. In writing your program, it is not necessary to have it allow the user to correct a bank reconciliation that does not balance; it is acceptable to require that the program's user reenter all the requested information; however, you should give some thought to how you might allow the user to correct various values in the statement that may have been incorrectly entered into the computer.

After solving Problem PC8–5 using your program, solve Problem PC8–4 using the same program.

(Prepared by C. Dirksen)

9

Operational Assets—Plant and Equipment, Natural Resources, and Intangibles

PURPOSE OF THIS CHAPTER

Operational assets are the **noncurrent assets** that a business retains more or less permanently (not for sale) for use (physical substance or in terms of rights) in the course of **normal ongoing operations.** Operational assets include land in use, plant and equipment, furniture and fixtures, natural resources, and certain intangibles (such as a patent) used in operating the business. Operational assets also are referred to as "fixed" assets, "long-lived" assets, or "property, plant, and equipment." The degree of efficiency in the utilization of the operational assets influences the earnings of the business. The types and costs of the operational assets, their ages and states of repair, and the future demands for funds needed to replace them influence many important decisions. The expense of maintaining and operating these assets often has a major effect on income.

An operational asset is acquired by a business because of the future services potentially available from the asset to create future revenue through use by the entity. Thus, such an asset can be viewed as a bundle of services that is purchased in **advance of usage** for creating revenue. As those services are used, as in the use of a machine, the **prepaid cost** of the services, in part, is allocated as an **expense** of each of the periods of utilization. To illustrate, assume a truck is purchased at a cost of $10,000 for use in the business. The cost is debited to an asset account and, assuming a five-year useful life, each year a part of the cost of the asset is apportioned to expense. This periodic apportionment of the prepaid costs of operational assets to expense is known as **depreciation, depletion, or amortization,** depending upon the characteristics of the particular asset.

The financial statements report information in respect to operational assets. The economic impact of operational assets on the balance sheet, income statement, and statement of changes in financial position is useful information for decision makers.

The purpose of this chapter is to discuss and illustrate the measuring, accounting, and reporting of operational assets (a) at acquisition, (b) during subsequent use, and (c) at disposition. To accomplish this purpose the chapter is subdivided as follows:

Part A—Property, plant and equipment, and depreciation

Part B—Repairs and maintenance, natural resources, and intangible operational assets

Supplement 9A—Trading in assets

CLASSIFICATION OF OPERATIONAL ASSETS

Typical business operations require a combination of assets with different characteristics and purposes. Each type of asset—be it current, long-term investments, or operational—serves a particular purpose not served by the other types of assets. The optimum combination of assets varies with each business, and its determination is a major responsibility of the management. An objective of the financial statements is to report the different assets classified by types and the amount of resources committed to each type. For measuring and reporting purposes, operational assets may be classified broadly as:

1. **Tangible operational assets**—the long-lived tangible assets (i.e., having physical substance) acquired for continued use in carrying on the normal operations of the business and not intended for resale. Examples are land, buildings, equipment, furniture, tools, vehicles, and mineral deposits. There are three kinds of tangible operational assets: *(a)* land—not subject to depreciation; *(b)* plant, equipment, and fixtures—subject to periodic **depreciation;** and *(c)* natural resources—the wasting assets used in the operation of the business, such as coal mines, gravel pits, oil wells, and timber tracts. Natural resources are subject to **depletion.**
2. **Intangible operational assets**—the assets that do not have physical substance that are held by the business because of the **special rights** they confer. Examples are patents, copyrights, franchises, licenses, and trademarks. Intangible assets are subject to periodic **amortization.**

PRINCIPLES UNDERLYING ACCOUNTING FOR OPERATIONAL ASSETS

The primary phases of accounting for operational assets are:

1. Measuring and recording the cost of the asset at **acquisition** date.
2. After acquisition, measuring the expense of **using** the asset during its useful life.
3. Recording **disposals** of operational assets.

At the date of acquisition, an operational asset is measured and recorded in conformity with the **cost principle.** After acquisition, a portion of the cost of an operational asset (except land) is matched periodically with the revenues earned during its useful life in accordance with the **matching principle.**

Part A—Property, Plant and Equipment, and Depreciation

MEASURING AND RECORDING ACQUISITION COST

Under the **cost principle** (Exhibit 2–6), all reasonable and necessary costs incurred in acquiring an operational asset, placing it in its operational setting and preparing it for use, less any cash discounts, should be recorded in an appropriately designated asset account. Cost is measured at the **net cash equivalent** paid or to be paid. **Acquisition cost can be determined readily when an operational asset is purchased for cash.** For example, the acquisition cost of a machine on January 1, 19A, may be measured as follows:

Invoice price of the machine...............................	$10,000
Less: Cash discount allowed ($10,000 × .02)...............	200
Net cash invoice price	9,800
Add: Transportation charges paid by purchaser............	150
Installation costs paid by purchaser..................	200
Sales tax paid ($10,000 × .08)*......................	800
Cost—amount debited to the Machinery account............	$10,950

*Assumed rate of 8 percent.

The acquisition of this operational asset would be recorded as follows:

January 1, 19A:

Machinery..	10,950	
Cash..		10,950

The $10,950 cost of the machine is unaffected by whether the cash discount ($200) actually is taken by the purchaser. If it is not taken, the discount is **interest expense.**

When an operational asset is purchased and a **noncash** consideration is included in part, or in full, payment for it, the cash equivalent cost is measured as any cash paid plus the **market value** of the noncash consideration given. Alternatively, if the market value of the noncash consideration cannot be reasonably determined, the market value of the asset purchased is used for measurement purposes. To illustrate, assume a tract of timber (a natural resource) was acquired by Fast Corporation. Payment in full was made as follows: $28,000 cash plus 2,000 shares of Fast Corporation capital stock (nopar).[1] At the date of the purchase, Fast stock was selling at $12 per share. The cost of the tract would be measured as follows:

---

[1]See Chapter 12 for discussion of capital stock.

Cash paid..	$28,000
Market value, noncash consideration given	
(2,000 shares nopar stock @ $12).......................	24,000
	52,000
Title fees, legal fees, and other costs paid in cash	
(incidental to the acquisition)	1,000
Cost—amount debited to the asset account..................	$53,000

The journal entry to record the acquisition of this natural resource would be:

January 1, 19A:

Timber tract (#20)	53,000	
Cash..		29,000
Capital stock, nopar (2,000 shares @ $12)		24,000

When land is purchased, all of the incidental costs paid by the purchaser, such as title fees, sales commissions, legal fees, title insurance, delinquent taxes, and surveying fees, should be included in the cost of the land. Because land is not subject to depreciation, it must be recorded and reported as a separate operational asset.

Not infrequently, an old building or used machinery is purchased for operational use in the business. Renovation and repair costs incurred by the purchaser **prior to use** should be debited to the asset account as a part of the cost of the asset. Repair costs incurred **after** the asset is placed in use usually are normal operating expenses.

Basket purchases

When two or more kinds of operational assets are acquired in a single transaction and for a single lump sum, the cost of each kind of asset acquired must be **measured and recorded separately.** For example, when a building and the land on which it is located are purchased for a lump sum at least two separate accounts must be established: one for the building (which is subject to depreciation) and one for the land (which is not subject to depreciation). This means that the single sum must be apportioned between the land and the building on a **rational** basis.

Relative market value of the several assets at the date of acquisition is the most logical basis on which to allocate the single lump sum. Appraisals or tax assessments often have to be used as indications of the market values. To illustrate, assume Fox Company paid a total of $300,000 cash to purchase a building suitable for an additional plant and the land on which the building is located. The separate, true market values of the building and land were not known; therefore, a professional appraisal was obtained that showed the following **estimated** market values: building, $189,000; and land, $126,000 (appar-

EXHIBIT 9–1
Recording a basket
purchase of an
operational asset

Situations:

Fox Company purchased a building and the related land for $300,000 cash. Estimated
current market values: building, $189,000; and land, $126.000.

Allocation of acquisition cost:

	Appraised value		Apportionment of lump-sum acquisition cost	
Asset	Amount	Ratio	Computation	Apportioned cost
Building	$189,000	.60*	$300,000 × .60 =	$180,000
Land	126,000	.40†	300,000 × .40 =	120,000
	$315,000	1.00		$300,000

*$189,000 ÷ $315,000 = .60.
†$126,000 ÷ $315,000 = .40.

Entry to record the acquisition:

```
Plant building ............................................    180,000
Land—plant site..........................................    120,000
    Cash .................................................                300,000
```

ently the buyer got a good deal). The apportionment of the $300,000 purchase
price and the journal entry to record the acquisition are illustrated in Exhibit
9–1.

**Capitalization
of interest as a
cost of
operational
assets**

In the preceding paragraphs we have discussed application of the **cost principle** in determining the acquisition cost of an operational asset. *FASB Statement 34* provides for the inclusion of **interest cost** as a part of the acquisition
cost of an operational asset under very limited conditions. A basic concept of
accounting is that interest on borrowed funds must be recorded and reported
as interest **expense** on the income statement when incurred. Interest is incurred on funds borrowed because of the **passage of time** (rather than when
the related cash is paid); that is, interest is the **time cost of money.**

When an operational asset is purchased and a loan is incurred as all, or part,
of the payment, periodic interest on the debt is recorded and reported as interest **expense** over the term of the loan. However, *FASB Statement 34* provides
an exception to this principle. The exception is that interest cost must be capitalized as a part of the cost of acquiring assets that require a period of time to
get them ready for their intended use. **In such situations, interest on the average expenditures incurred during the construction or acquisition period is
recorded as a part of the cost of the operational asset.** Interest is included in
the cost of the asset (*a*) **only** during the construction or acquisition period and
(*b*) not in excess of total interest cost incurred by the entity during the period.

It is not necessary that the debts of the company be related to the construction of the operational asset.[2]

To illustrate capitalization of interest during construction, assume that on January 1, 19A, Byers Corporation signed a contract that required Dow Construction Company to build a new plant building at a contract price of $1 million. The construction period started March 1, 19A, and the building was substantially complete and ready for its intended use on December 31, 19A (end of the 10-month construction period). Byers Corporation was required to make the following quarterly cash progress payments on the contract during 19A:

	Date of payment	Amount
a.	March 31, 19A...............	$ 120,000
b.	June 30, 19A.................	220,000
c.	September 30, 19A............	480,000
d.	December 31, 19A.............	180,000
	Total....................	$1,000,000

To make the progress payments, Byers Corporation borrowed 60 percent of each payment from a financial institution at 10 percent annual interest; the remaining cash needed was from within Byers Corporation. Total interest cost incurred by Byers during the period was $70,000 (at an average rate of 10 percent).

Upon completion, December 31, 19A, Byers Corporation should reflect the following acquisition cost in the operational asset account, Plant Building:

Contract price (paid in full)......................			$1,000,000
Add interest during the construction period:			
a. $120,000 × .10 × 9/12 = ...		$ 9,000	
b. $220,000 × .10 × 6/12 = ...		11,000	
c. $480,000 × .10 × 3/12 = ...		12,000	
d. $180,000—no interest......................		–0–	32,000*
Total acquisition cost			$1,032,000

*Note that this amount was not based on the specific borrowings of 60 percent but on the expenditures. The amount cannot exceed the $70,000 total interest cost for the period (19A).

FASB Statement 34 provides the following guidelines that must be observed:

1. Interest is capitalized **only** during the construction period.

---

[2]FASB, *Statement of Financial Accounting Standards No. 34,* "Capitalization of Interest Cost" (Stamford, Conn., October 1979). Under this *Statement,* interest cannot be capitalized for assets that are (1) in use or ready for their intended use, or (2) not used in the earnings activities of the entity. *Statement 34* specifies the qualifying assets as follows: "Assets that are constructed or otherwise produced for an enterprise's own use (including assets constructed or produced for the enterprise by others for which deposits or progress payments have been made)."

CICA Handbook, Section 3060, is silent on this topic. Therefore, Canadian accounting practice can vary in the treatment of interest during the construction or acquisition period.

2. Interest is computed on the average expenditures during the construction period.
3. The applicable borrowing interest rate for the company is used.
4. Interest is computed regardless of the source of the funds (borrowed or obtained from normal operations of the entity).
5. Interest added to the cost of the operational assets cannot exceed the total amount of total interest cost incurred by the entity in that period (for all purposes).

GOVERNMENT ASSISTANCE

Governments at all levels in Canada provide assistance to businesses in a variety of forms. Low-interest loans, tax write-offs, forgivable loans, property tax reductions, sales tax rebates, subsidies to reduce various operating costs, and cash grants to reduce the construction or acquisition cost of fixed assets are some common examples. To account for such a complex array of assistance can present difficulties for the accountant. Careful analysis of each case is required.

Two general rules can help guide the accountant. Grants or rebates that reduce operating expenses of the current period should be treated as such. Assistance that reduces the cash cost of acquiring or constructing fixed assets should reduce the cost of the fixed asset and correspondingly reduce the subsequent depreciation.[3] Sales tax rebates and loans, when the company has become eligible for forgiveness, are treated in the same way as a cash grant.

The receipt of a federal government cash grant of $50,000 by Fox (see Exhibit 9–1) would be accounted for as follows:

Grant receivable from government of Canada.....................	50,000	
Plant building		30,000
Land—plant site		20,000
To record the approved grant of $50,000 allocated 60 percent to buildings and 40 percent to land.		
Cash...	50,000	
Grant receivable from government of Canada		50,000
To record the receipt of the cheque from the government.		

---

[3]*CICA Handbook,* Section 3800.26, permits an alternative treatment for assistance involved in the acquisition of fixed assets. Further elaboration will not be presented because the effect is also to reduce depreciation expense and this alternative is not commonly used in Canada. *Financial Reporting in Canada,* 15th ed. (Toronto, Ont.: Canadian Institute of Chartered Accountants, 1983), p. 47.

MATCHING THE COST OF AN OPERATIONAL ASSET WITH FUTURE REVENUES

The acquisition cost of an operational asset that has a limited useful life represents the **prepaid cost** of a bundle of **future** services or benefits (i.e., future economic usefulness to the entity). The **matching principle** (Exhibit 2–6) requires that the acquisition cost of operational assets (other than land) be apportioned as expense to the periods in which revenue is earned as a result of using those assets. Thus, the acquisition cost of this kind of operational asset is matched in a systematic and rational manner in the future with the future revenues to which it contributes by way of services and benefits.

We should make clear the distinction among three different terms that are used to describe the cost apportionment required by the matching principle as follows:

1. **Depreciation**—the systematic and rational apportionment of the acquisition cost of **tangible operational assets** (other than natural resources) to future periods in which the services or benefits contribute to revenue. Example—depreciation of the $10,950 cost of a machine over its estimated useful life of 10 years and no residual value:

   December 31, 19B:

Depreciation expense ($10,950 ÷ 10 years)	1,095	
Accumulated depreciation, machinery		1,095

2. **Depletion**—the systematic and rational apportionment of the acquisition cost of **natural resources** to future periods in which the use of those natural resources contributes to revenue. Example—depletion of the $53,000 cost of a timber tract over the estimated period of cutting based on "cutting" rate of approximately 20 percent per year:

   December 31, 19B:

Depletion expense ($53,000 × .20)	10,600	
Timber tract (No. 20)		10,600
Note: A contra account could be used such as Accumulated Depletion.		

3. **Amortization**—the systematic and rational apportionment of the acquisition cost of **intangible operational assets** to future periods in which the benefits contribute to revenue. Example— amortization of the $8,500 cost of a patent over its estimated economic useful life to the entity of 17 years:

December 31, 19B:

Patent expense ($8,500 ÷ 17 years)   500
    Patents   500
    Note: A contra account could be used such as Accumulated Patent
    Amortization.

The three terms—depreciation, depletion, and amortization—relate to the same basic objective; namely, the apportionment of the acquisition cost of an operational asset to the future periods in which the benefits of its use contribute to earning revenue.

The amounts of depreciation, depletion, and amortization measured and recorded during each period are reported as expenses or costs for the period. The amounts of depreciation, depletion, and amortization **accumulated since acquisition date** are reported on the balance sheet as deductions from the assets to which they pertain. To illustrate, an operational asset, such as the machine illustrated above, would be reported on the balance sheet (at the end of the second year in the example) as follows:

Balance Sheet
At December 31, 19B

Property, plant, and equipment:
    Machinery $10,950
    Less: Accumulated depreciation 2,190 $8,760*

or
Machinery (less accumulated depreciation, $2,190) $8,760*

*Called book value or carrying value.

We emphasize that the amounts for operational assets reported on the balance sheet do not represent their market values at the balance sheet date; rather, the amounts are book, or carrying, values. The **book, or carrying value** of an operational asset is its acquisition cost, less the accumulated apportionments to expense of that cost from acquisition date to the date of the balance sheet. Recording and reporting depreciation is a process of **cost allocation;** it is not a process of determining the current market value of the asset. Under the **cost principle,** the cost of an operational asset is measured and recorded at acquisition date at its current market value. The cost is not remeasured on a market value basis at subsequent balance sheet dates, rather, the acquisition cost is reduced by the accumulated expense allocation for depreciation, depletion, or amortization.

OPERATIONAL ASSETS SUBJECT TO DEPRECIATION

Two classifications of operational assets were identified at the beginning of this chapter. In this section, the discussion will be limited to those tangible operational assets subject to depreciation. The classification, **tangible operational assets,** includes all kinds of buildings, machinery, furniture, and other equipment used in the operation of the business. Although the term **fixed** asset is used sometimes, more descriptive terms such as **property, plant, and equipment** and **land, plant, and equipment** are used in most published financial statements.

Buildings, machinery, furniture, and other tangible operational assets (except land) decrease in economic utility to the user because of a number of causative factors, such as wear and tear, the passage of time, effects of the elements (such as the weather), obsolescence (i.e., becoming out-of-date), technological changes, and inadequacy. These causative factors always impact on such assets during the periods in which the assets are being used to generate revenues. Thus, under the **matching principle,** at the end of each accounting period an **adjusting entry** is needed to record these expense-causing factors. In developing the adjusting entry, accounting principles require that a **rational and systematic** measurement approach be used to match the acquisition cost of tangible operational assets with periodic revenues.[4]

Because of the wide diversity of operational assets subject to depreciation and the varying effects of the causative factors listed above, a number of **depreciation methods** have been developed that are acceptable for both accounting and income tax purposes. In the paragraphs to follow, we will discuss and illustrate the methods of measuring and recording depreciation that are usually used.

Each of the depreciation methods requires three amounts for each asset: (1) **actual acquisition cost,** (2) **estimated net residual value,** and (3) **estimated useful life.** It is important to observe that of these three amounts, two are **estimates** (residual value and useful or service life); thus, the periodic amount of depreciation expense that is recorded and reported is an **estimate.** To illustrate, depreciation expense may be measured as follows:

Acquisition cost	$625
Less: Estimated residual value	25
Amount to be depreciated over useful life	$600
Estimated useful life	3 years
Annual depreciation expense: $600 ÷ 3 =	$200

---

[4]*Terminology for Accountants,* 3d. ed. (Toronto, Ont.: Canadian Institute of Chartered Accountants, 1983), p. 52, defines depreciation accounting as "an accounting procedure in which the cost or other recorded value of a fixed asset less estimated residual (if any) is distributed over its estimated useful life in a systematic and rational manner. It is a process of allocation, not valuation."

Estimated residual value[5] must be deducted from acquisition cost because it represents that part of the acquisition cost that is expected to be recovered by the user upon disposal of the asset at the end of its estimated useful life to the entity. **Residual value is the total estimated amount to be recovered less** any estimated costs of dismantling, disposal, and selling. Because disposal costs may approximately equal the gross residual amount recovered, many depreciable assets are assumed to have no residual value. It is important to realize that the estimated net residual value is not necessarily the value of the asset as salvage or scrap, rather, it may be the value to another user at the date on which the **current owner** intends to dispose of it. For example, a company whose policy is to replace all trucks at the end of three years normally would use a higher estimated residual value than would a user of the same kind of truck whose policy is to replace the trucks at the end of five years.

Estimated useful or service life should be viewed as the useful **economic** life to the **present owner** rather than as the total economic life to all potential users. In the truck example above, for accounting purposes, one owner would use a three-year estimated useful life, whereas the other owner would use a five-year estimated useful life.

Estimates are necessary to allocate a known cost amount (the acquisition cost of an operational asset) over a number of future periods during which the asset will contribute to the earning of revenues. The allocation must be made at the end of each period because it would not be very useful in the measurement of periodic income to defer all cost allocations until the date of disposal of an operational asset which is "used up."

The determination of an estimated useful life of an operational asset must conform to the **continuity assumption** (see Exhibit 2–6). This assumption holds that the business will continue as a going concern; that is, that the business will continue indefinitely to pursue its commercial objectives (it will not liquidate in the foreseeable future). This assumption prevents a business from estimating the life of an operational asset to be less than its potential life because of some conjecture that the business will liquidate in the near future.

DEPRECIATION METHODS

Several **methods of depreciation** will be discussed and illustrated in this section. For this purpose we will use the common set of facts and notations shown in Exhibit 9–2.

The several depreciation methods commonly used are identical in basic concept; that is, each method allocates a portion of the cost of a depreciable asset to each of a number of future periods in a systematic and rational manner. The methods vary among themselves as to the allocation pattern to each of the future periods.

---

[5]Residual value also is called scrap value or salvage value; however, "residual value" is a more descriptive term because the asset may not be scrapped or sold as salvage upon disposition—a subsequent buyer may renovate it and reuse it for years.

EXHIBIT 9–2
Illustrative data for
depreciation

	Symbols	Illustrative amounts
Acquisition cost of a particular operational asset (a productive machine).........................	C	$625
Estimated net residual value at end of useful life	RV	$ 25
Estimated service life:		
Life in years.......................................	N*	3
Life in units of productive output	P*	10,000
Depreciation rate	R	
Dollar amount of depreciation expense per period	D	
*Lowercase letters will be used for the current period.		

The discussions to follow will define, illustrate, and evaluate the following commonly used depreciation methods.[6]

    1. Straight-line.
    2. Productive output (units of production).
    3. Sum-of-the-years'-digits.
    4. Diminishing balance.

Straight-line depreciation method

The straight-line method has been used widely because of its simplicity and apparent relationship to the pattern of use of the utility of many kinds of depreciable assets. Under this method, an **equal portion** of the acquisition cost less the estimated residual value is allocated to each accounting period during the estimated useful life. Thus, the annual depreciation expense is measured as follows (refer to Exhibit 9–2):

$$D = \frac{C - RV}{N} \quad \text{or} \quad D = \frac{\$625 - \$25}{3 \text{ years}} = \$200 \text{ depreciation expense per year}$$

A depreciation schedule covering the entire useful life of the machine can be developed as follows:

Depreciation Schedule—Straight-Line Method

Year	Periodic depreciation expense	End of year Balance in accumulated depreciation	Book value
At acquisition			$625
1.................	$200	$200	425
2.................	200	400	225
3.................	200	600	25
	$600		

The adjusting entry for depreciation expense on this machine would be the same for each of the three years of the useful life, viz:

---

[6]*Financial Reporting in Canada*, 15th ed. (Toronto, Ont.: Canadian Institute of Chartered Accountants, 1983), p. 174 reports 262 of 316 companies surveyed use either a straight line method or a straight-line method in combination with some other method.

Sum-of-the-years' digits is not a popular method of depreciation in Canada. It is discussed in this chapter so it can be used for illustrative purposes.

Adjusting entry	Year 1		Year 2		Year 3	
Depreciation expense	200		200		200	
Accumulated depreciation, machinery		200		200		200

Observe that (a) **depreciation expense** is a constant amount for each year (often called a fixed expense), (b) **accumulated** depreciation increases by an equal amount each year, and (c) **book value** decreases by the same amount each year. This is the reason for the designation, straight line.

The straight-line method is simple, rational, and systematic (i.e., logical, stable, consistent, and realistically predictable from period to period). It is especially appropriate where the asset is used essentially at the same rate each period. It implies an approximately equal decline in the economic usefulness of the asset each period. For these reasons, it is a very popular method (see footnote 6).

Productive-output method

The productive-output method, sometimes called the units-of-production method, is based upon the assumption that the revenue-generating benefits derived each period from a depreciable asset are related directly to the periodic output of the asset. For example, many accountants believe that certain equipment, such as a machine, should be depreciated on the basis of units produced each period (i.e., based on a measure of output) rather than on the mere passage of time as is assumed by the straight-line method. These accountants believe that many productive assets contribute to the earning of revenues only when they are used productively, not merely because time has passed.

The productive-output method relates acquisition cost less estimated residual value to the estimated productive output; therefore, a depreciation rate per unit of output is computed as follows (refer to Exhibit 9–2):

$$R = \frac{C - RV}{P} \quad \text{or} \quad R = \frac{\$625 - \$25}{10,000 \text{ units}} = \$0.06 \text{ depreciation rate per unit of output}$$

Assuming 3,000 units of actual output from the illustrative machine in Year 1, depreciation expense for Year 1 would be:

$$D = R \times p \quad \text{or} \quad D = \$.06 \times 3,000 = \$180 \text{ depreciation expense}$$

Assuming actual output to be 5,000 units in Year 2 and 2,000 units in Year 3, a depreciation schedule could be developed as follows:

Depreciation Schedule—Productive-Output Method

Year	Periodic depreciation expense		End of year Balance in accumulated depreciation	Book value
At acquisition				$625
1.	(3,000 × $.06)	$180	$180	445
2.	(5,000 × .06)	300	480	145
3.	(2,000 × .06)	120	600	25
		$600		

The **adjusting entry** for depreciation at the end of each year would be:

Adjusting entry	Year 1		Year 2		Year 3	
Depreciation expense	180		300		120	
Accumulated depreciation, machinery		180		300		120

Observe that depreciation expense, accumulated depreciation, and book value vary from period to period directly with the periodic outputs; thus, when the productive-output method is used, depreciation expense is said to be a variable expense.

The productive-output method is simple, rational, and systematic. It is appropriate where output of the asset can be measured realistically and where the economic utility of the asset to the entity tends to decrease with productive use rather than with the passage of time. Also, when the productive use varies significantly from period to period, a more realistic **matching** of expense with revenue is attained.

Accelerated depreciation methods

Accelerated depreciation is based upon the notion that there should be relatively large amounts of depreciation expense reported in the early years of the useful life of the asset and correspondingly reduced amounts of depreciation expense in the later years. The basis for this conclusion is that a depreciable asset is more efficient in earning revenue in the early years than in the later years of its life. Also, repair expense tends to be lower in the early years and higher in the later years. Therefore, it is contended that the **combined effect** of decreasing depreciation expense and increasing repair expense is relatively constant from period to period over the life of the asset as illustrated below:

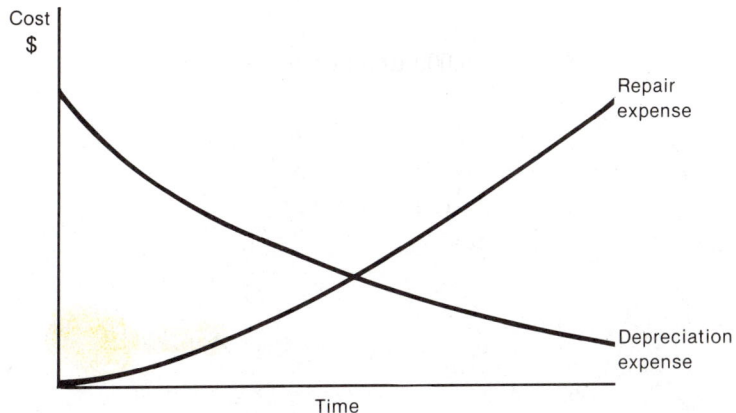

Accelerated capital cost allowance (the tax term for depreciation) has considerable appeal from the **income tax** viewpoint. Higher capital cost allowance means a lower reported taxable income amount in the early years which causes income tax expense to be less. Of course, the effect reverses in the later years; however, an early tax deduction is to be preferred over a later tax deduction because of the **time value of money.**[7]

It is worth noting that the income tax rules permit a company to use its own depreciation procedures while using capital cost allowance for its tax return. Capital cost allowance rates are maximums thus permitting companies to deduct less if they wish. There are several variations of accelerated depreciation; however, the two accelerated methods that will be illustrated are the sum-of-the-years'-digits method and the diminishing balance method.

Sum-of-the-years'-digits method. The sum-of-the-years'-digits (colloquially known as the rule of 78) method, sometimes abbreviated as the SYD method, is used primarily because it is simple and produces a significantly accelerated effect compared to straight-line depreciation. Depreciation expense each year is computed by multiplying the acquisition cost, **less** estimated residual value, by a fraction that is successively **smaller** each year. Each of the decreasing fractions is determined by using the sum of the digits comprising the estimated useful life as the denominator and the specific year of life in **inverse order** as the numerator. The computations may be demonstrated as follows using the illustrative data given in Exhibit 9–2.

> To compute the denominator:[8]
> Sum of digits (comprising the useful life): 1 + 2 + 3 = 6.
> Numerators:
> Digits (specific year of life) in inverse order: 3, 2, 1.
> To compute the depreciation fraction:
> Year 1, ³⁄₆; Year 2, ²⁄₆; Year 3, ¹⁄₆ (total ⁶⁄₆)

The accelerated effects of the SYD method can be observed in the following depreciation schedule:

---

[7]The time value of money refers to interest that can be earned on money invested or used in the business.

[8]The denominator (i.e., sum of the digits) can be computed by using the formula:

$$SYD = n\left(\frac{n+1}{2}\right)$$

For example, a five-year life would be:

$$SYD = 5\left(\frac{5+1}{2}\right) = 15$$

Depreciation Schedule—Sum-of-the-Years'-Digits Method

Year	Computations	Periodic depreciation expense	Balance in accumulated depreciation (End of year)	Book value (End of year)
At acquisition				$625
1.	$600 × 3/6 =	$300	$300	325
2.	600 × 2/6 =	200	500	125
3.	600 × 1/6 =	100	600	25
Total		$600		

The **adjusting entry** for depreciation expense by year would be:

Adjusting entry	Year 1	Year 2	Year 3
Depreciation expense	300	200	100
Accumulated depreciation, machinery	300	200	100

Observe that, compared to straight-line results, depreciation expense under the SYD method is higher in the earlier years and lower in the later years. The total amounts of depreciation expense over the entire life of the asset are the same under both methods.

The SYD method is relatively simple to apply and is considered to be "rational and systematic"; therefore, it is acceptable under generally accepted accounting principles.

Diminishing balance method. All depreciable assets are, for income tax purposes, grouped into one of a number of classes. Each class of assets is permitted a maximum capital cost of allowance rate. Commonly the classes use the diminishing balance method of calculating the maximum yearly deduction for tax purposes. Estimated residual values are ignored for these calculations. These rates vary at the present time from a high of 100 percent to a low of 4 percent depending upon the type of property, the date of acquisition, and the type of business.[9] To illustrate, the following presents a few common classes and their rates:

Class	General type of asset	Rate (percent)
3	Brick building	5
8	Equipment	20
10	Automobiles	30

---

[9] Currently the income tax regulations permit a maximum of 50 percent of the allowable capital cost allowance to be deducted in the year of acquisition regardless of the date the asset is acquired during the year.

Because the DB method is used to calculate capital cost allowance for income tax determinations, it is often used for computing depreciation expense for accounting purposes. Care is needed, however, because some CCA rates are used as economic incentives by the government and thus produce unreasonable accounting depreciation.

Capital cost allowance (CCA) is computed by multiplying the **CCA rate** (illustrated above) by the **undepreciated capital cost of the asset** (i.e., its current book value) ignoring residual value. Because the estimated residual value is ignored, the undepreciated balance of the asset at the end of the last year of its life may be **higher or lower** than the residual value.

Computation of DB depreciation expense is illustrated below using the data given in Exhibit 9–2 and assuming class 8, equipment rate.

> To compute CCA tax expense (Year 1):
> Current carrying value of the asset, $625 \times .20 \times \frac{1}{2} = \$62.50$.

The effects of the DB method are illustrated in the following schedule:

Depreciation Schedule—Capital Cost Allowance Method

			End of year
Year	Computations	Periodic CCA	Undepreciated capital cost (book value)
At acquisition			$625
1............	.20 × $625 × ½	$ 62.50	562.50
2............	.20 × $562.50	112.50	450.00
3............	.20 × $450	90.00	360.00*

*For income tax purposes, the undepreciated capital cost of $360 would be added to the cost of the new machine acquired to replace the old one and capital cost allowance would be continued on the new total. The effect of this treatment is to depreciate the $360 after the asset has been sold. If the class of assets was empty (no assets acquired or remaining) the $360 less the residual value of $25 would be a tax expense in Year 3. For accounting purposes, a loss on disposal of $360 − $25 would be appropriate although such a large loss would suggest the use of the CCA rate is inappropriate.

The adjusting entry for depreciation at each year-end would be:

Adjusting entry	Year 1	Year 2	Year 3
Depreciation expense.........	62.50	112.50	90
Accumulated depreciation, machinery	62.50	112.50	90

To date, the accounting profession has not provided officially definitive guidelines for selection of a depreciation method that would be preferable for each type of depreciable asset. Therefore, each one of the several methods can

EXHIBIT 9–3
Depreciation
methods compared
graphically
(including a typical
repair curve)

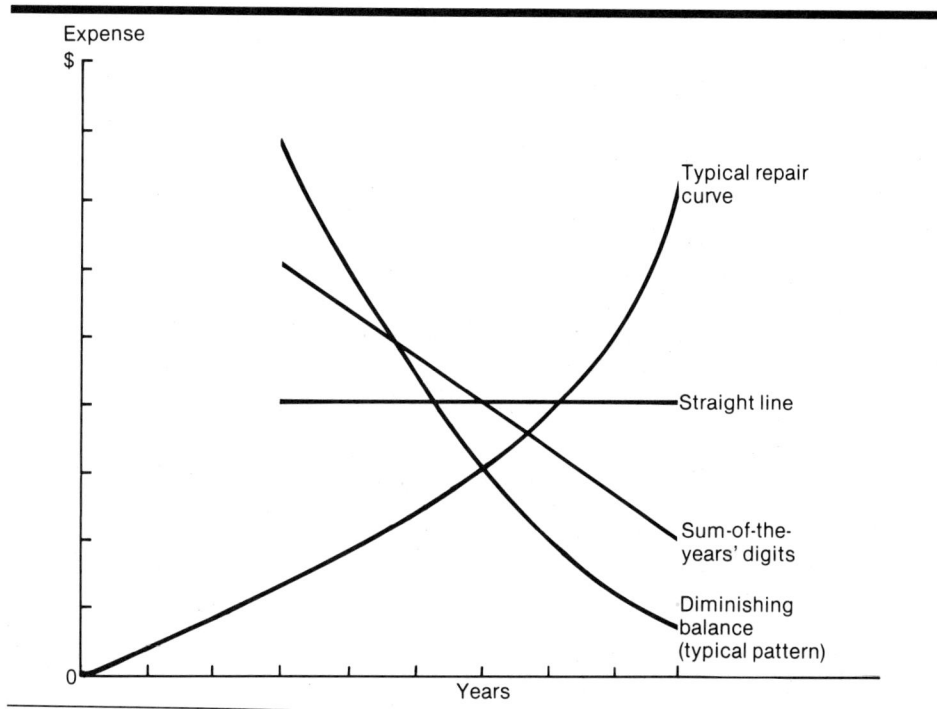

be characterized as an acceptable alternative for financial reporting purposes, which means that any of the above depreciation methods may be used regardless of the characteristics of the operational asset and the way it is used. Exhibit 9–3 further illustrates the significant differences among the three most commonly used depreciation methods.

GAAP requires that the depreciation method selected must be "rational and systematic" and that it should reliably measure net income of the company considering the circumstances in which the asset is used. Thus, it is usual for a company to use more than one depreciation method.

DEPRECIATION EFFECTS ON INCOME AND CASH FLOW

Although each of the four depreciation methods produces different amounts of depreciation expense each accounting period of the life of an asset, the **total** amount of depreciation expense recorded over the life of the asset is the same (i.e., its acquisition cost less any residual value), except for the DB method in some cases. Because each method produces a different pattern of depreciation expense, during the life of the asset each one will cause different periodic amounts to be reported for (a) pretax income, (b) income tax expense, (c) net income, (d) retained earnings, and (e) book value of the asset. Depreciation often is confusing to users of financial statements because of these varied effects, particularly as they relate to net income and cash flows (i.e., the receipts and payments of cash). Exhibit 9–4 illustrates the effects of depreciation on (a) the income statement and (b) cash flows under the SL and SYD methods. The SYD method is used as a substitute for capital cost allowance (DB depreciation) in order to simplify the presentation.

Effects of depreciation on the income statement

Depreciation is an expense on the income statement so pretax income depends on the depreciation approach used for accounting purposes (refer to Exhibit 9–4, Panel B). Capital cost allowance is used to calculate the income taxes payable to the government (refer to Exhibit 9–4, Panel C). The differences between the taxes calculated using the accounting depreciation and the taxes calculated using capital cost allowance is accounted for as a deferred income tax credit or deferred income tax debit. This difference represents one of

EXHIBIT 9–4   Illustration of depreciation effects on net income and cash flow

Panel A—Data assumed (refer to Exhibit 9–2):

Revenues (all cash): Year 1, $5,000; Year 2, $6,000; Year 3, $7,000.

	Year 1	Year 2	Year 3
Depreciation expense:			
SL (straight line)	$ 200	$ 200	$ 200
SYD	300	200	100
Remaining expenses (all cash)	2,800	3,300	3,800
Income tax rate, 20%.			

Panel B—Income statements comparing SL and SYD:

	Year 1		Year 2		Year 3	
Accrual basis	SL	SYD	SL	SYD	SL	SYD
Revenues (cash)	$ 5,000	$ 5,000	$ 6,000	$ 6,000	$ 7,000	$ 7,000
Depreciation expense (noncash)	(200)	(300)	(200)	(200)	(200)	(100)
Remaining expenses (cash)	(2,800)	(2,800)	(3,300)	(3,300)	(3,800)	(3,800)
*Pretax income	2,000	1,900	2,500	2,500	3,000	3,100
†Income tax expense (20%)	(400)	(380)	(500)	(500)	(600)	(620)
Net income	$ 1,600	$ 1,520	$ 2,000	$ 2,000	$ 2,400	$ 2,480

*Amounts differ between SL and SYD because of the depreciation expense.
†Income tax expense is computed on the basis of pretax income.

Panel C—Depreciation effects on cash flow comparing SL and SYD:

	Year 1		Year 2		Year 3	
Cash flow basis	SL	SYD	SL	SYD	SL	SYD
Revenues (all cash)	$ 5,000	$ 5,000	$ 6,000	$ 6,000	$ 7,000	$ 7,000
Depreciation expense (noncash)	–0–	–0–	–0–	–0–	–0–	–0–
Remaining expenses (all cash)	(2,800)	(2,800)	(3,300)	(3,300)	(3,800)	(3,800)
*Pretax cash inflow	2,200	2,200	2,700	2,700	3,200	3,200
†Income tax payment	(380)	(380)	(500)	(500)	(620)	(620)
Aftertax cash inflow	$ 1,820	$ 1,820	$ 2,200	$ 2,200	$ 2,580	$ 2,580

*Same regardless of depreciation method used.
†For simplicity the example assumes SYD depreciation equals the capital cost allowance claimed for income tax purposes. The difference between taxes paid and tax expense is a tax allocation timing difference discussed in Chapter 10.

the major timing differences that must be accounted for as part of the tax allocation procedures to be discussed in Chapter 10.

Effects of depreciation on cash flow

When an operational asset is acquired, there is a cash **outflow** (i.e., payment) for its acquisition (and/or later cash outflows for any related debt). Subsequent journal entries for depreciation do not involve cash outflows because the expense lags the cash outflow already made. Therefore, depreciation expense does not represent a current cash outflow; it is a noncash expense on the income statement. However, capital cost allowance does affect cash flow each period because it **reduces** the amount of income tax that otherwise would be paid. In this way it reduces the amount of cash outflow for income tax (this reduction often is called a "tax saving" or "tax shield."). Thus, if capital cost allowance is increased for the period the cash outflow for income tax is decreased. This cash flow effect is illustrated in Exhibit 9–4, Panel C. Observe in Panel C, for all years, that the **aftertax cash inflow** is the same under SYD as it is under SL even though Panel B shows **net income to be lower** under SYD than under SL except for the last year. In summary, as the amount of depreciation expense is increased net income is decreased. Cash inflow is increased (i.e., tax saving) as CCA is increased.

Finally, let's consider some misleading terminology that often is used. Analysts and others often say that "cash is provided by depreciation." Depreciation is not a source of cash, and the accumulated depreciation amount does not represent cash or a fund of cash available to replace the operational asset when it is disposed of. Accumulated depreciation is a contra asset account (not cash). Exhibit 9–4, Panel C, demonstrates that (a) the aftertax cash inflow (bottom line) is the result of sales to customers, less cash expenses, and (b) capital cost allowance reduces cash outflow because less income taxes are paid. A significant long-term effect of depreciation expense is a reduction of the cumulative balance of retained earnings. A lower balance in retained earnings in some situations possibly could reduce cash dividends. If cash dividends were reduced there would be a decrease in cash outflows.[10]

DEPRECIATION FOR INTERIM PERIODS

The preceding illustrations assumed that depreciation expense for a full year is recorded at the end of each year by means of an adjusting entry. Some businesses record depreciation for interim periods, such as monthly, quarterly, or semiannually. Also, a depreciable asset may be acquired or disposed of during the year which requires that depreciation expense be recorded for periods of less than one year. It is customary to compute depreciation on a proportional basis to either the nearest month, quarter, or six-month period. For example, depreciation for a month may be assumed to start or end at the nearest first of the month. For all of the methods illustrated, except productive output,

---

[10]Chapter 10 discusses the reporting implications of the use of different depreciation methods for financial reporting and tax purposes.

monthly depreciation usually is determined by computing the annual amount of depreciation as illustrated, then dividing by 12 to obtain the monthly amount.[11] To illustrate, in Exhibit 9–4, sum-of-the-years'-digits (SYD) depreciation for the first year was determined to be $300. Assume the asset was acquired on August 12, 19A, with a December 31 fiscal year ending. The depreciation expense for 19A would be (nearest-month basis):

$$\frac{\$300}{12} \times 5 \text{ months} = \$125$$

CHANGES IN DEPRECIATION ESTIMATES

Recall that depreciation is based on two estimates—useful life and residual value—which are made at the time a depreciable asset is acquired. Sometimes it is necessary to revise one, or both, of these initial estimates as experience with the asset accumulates. When it becomes clear that either estimate should be revised (to a material degree), the undepreciated balance, less any residual value, at that date should be apportioned, based on the new estimate, over the remaining estimated life. In accounting this is called a "change in estimate."

To illustrate, assume the following for a particular machine:

Cost of machine when acquired $33,000
Estimated life .... 10 years
Estimated residual value .... $ 3,000
Accumulated depreciation through Year 6
  (assuming the straight-line method is used) $18,000

Shortly after the start of Year 7, the initial estimates were changed to the following:

Revised estimated total life .... 14 years
Revised estimated residual value $1,000

No entry is required when this decision is reached. However, the **adjusting entry at the end of Year 7** would be:

Depreciation expense..	1,750	
Accumulated depreciation		1,750
Computations:		
Acquisition cost......................................	$33,000	
Accumulated depreciation, Years 1–6	18,000	
Undepreciated balance..............................	15,000	
Less: Revised residual value.......................	1,000	
Balance to be depreciated	$14,000	
Annual depreciation:		
$14,000 ÷ (14 years − 6 years) = ...	$ 1,750	

---

[11]Under the productive-output method, monthly depreciation is derived by multiplying the unit depreciation rate by the output for the particular month.

Under GAAP, changes in accounting estimates and depreciation methods should be made only when the new estimate or accounting method "better measures" the periodic income of the business.[12] The **comparability principle** (Exhibit 2–6) requires that accounting information reported in the financial statements should be comparable across accounting periods and among similar entities. This principle exerts a significant constraint on changing depreciation estimates and methods unless the effect is to improve the measurement of depreciation expense and, hence, net income.

Part B—Repairs and Maintenance, Natural Resources, and Intangible Operational Assets

REPAIRS AND MAINTENANCE

Subsequent to the acquisition of a tangible operational asset, related cost outlays often must be made for such items as ordinary repairs and maintenance, major repairs, replacements, and additions. The central measurement problem is determination of which expenditures should be recorded as expenses of the period when incurred, and which should be recorded as assets (i.e., as a prepayment) to be matched with **future** revenues. The term **expenditure** means the payment of cash or the incurrence of a debt for an asset or service received. The purchase of a machine or a service, such as repairs on a truck, may be for cash or on credit. In either case, there is an expenditure.

In measuring the cost of using operational assets, **two** basic types of expenditures are involved. The two types of expenditures are called capital expenditures and revenue expenditures.

Capital expenditures

Capital expenditures for the acquisition of an asset or for the expansion or improvement of an asset already owned. A capital expenditure benefits one or more accounting periods **beyond the current period;** therefore, capital expenditures are recorded in appropriate asset accounts. For example, a plant **addition** that cost $90,000 would be recorded as follows:

Plant...	90,000	
Cash...		90,000

Revenue expenditures

Revenue expenditures for **normal operating** items such as ordinary repairs, maintenance, and salaries benefit **only** the current period; therefore, when revenue expenditures are incurred, they are debited directly to appropriate ex-

---

[12]*CICA Handbook,* Section 1506, distinguishes between a change in estimate which is treated like the above example and a change in accounting policy. A change in accounting policy results in a retroactive revision. This matter will be discussed further in Chapter 12.

pense accounts.[13] For example, the payment of $600 for ordinary repairs to the plant would be recorded in the current period as follows:

Repair expense	600	
Cash		600

Each expenditure made subsequent to the acquisition of an operational asset must be evaluated carefully to classify it as either a capital or revenue expenditure. The distinction between capital and revenue expenditures is essential to conform with the matching principle. The expenditures must be matched with the periodic revenues to which they relate. The purpose and nature of the expenditure is the controlling factor in its classification. For practical applications, materiality is also an important factor in determining the appropriate treatment. In the next few paragraphs we will discuss the usual types of outlays subsequent to acquisition of a tangible operational asset.

Extraordinary repairs

Extraordinary repairs are classified as **capital expenditures;** therefore, an extraordinary repair is debited to the related **asset** account and depreciated over the **remaining** life of that asset. **Extraordinary repairs** occur infrequently, involve relatively large amounts of money, and tend to increase the economic usefulness of the asset in the future because of either greater efficiency or longer life, or both. They are represented by major overhauls, complete reconditioning, and major replacements and betterments. For example, the complete replacement of a roof on the factory building would constitute an extraordinary repair, whereas patching the old roof would constitute an ordinary repair.

To illustrate the accounting for extraordinary repairs, assume a machine that originally cost $40,000 is being depreciated on a straight-line basis over 10 years with no estimated residual value. At the beginning of the seventh year, a major reconditioning was completed at a cost of $12,700. The estimated useful life was changed from 10 years to 13 years (i.e., a change in estimate). A typical sequence of entries would be:

At acquisition of the asset:

Machinery.	40,000	
Cash.		40,000
Purchase of machinery.		

---

[13]The term *revenue* expenditure is widely used. It suggests that the expenditure is to be deducted in the current period from revenue in deriving income. However, a term such as expense expenditure would be more descriptive.

Depreciation—annually at end of Years 1 through 6:

Depreciation expense...	4,000	
Accumulated depreciation, machinery.........................		4,000
Adjusting entry to record annual depreciation ($40,000 ÷ 10).		

Extraordinary repair—at start of seventh year:[14]

Machinery..	12,700	
Cash...		12,700
Expenditure for major repair.		

Revised depreciation—annually at end of Years 7 through 13:

Depreciation expense...	4,100		
Accumulated depreciation, machinery.........................		4,100	
Adjusting entry to record annual depreciation.			
Computation:			
Original cost...........................	$40,000		
Depreciation, Years 1–6	24,000		
Book value remaining		$16,000	
Extraordinary repair....................		12,700	
Balance to be depreciated			
over remaining life...................		$28,700	
Annual depreciation: $28,700 ÷ (13 − 6) years = $4,100			

Additions

Additions are extensions to, or enlargements of, existing assets, such as the addition of a wing to a present building. These represent **capital expenditures;** therefore, the cost of such additions should be debited to the existing account for the asset and depreciated over the remaining life of the asset to which the cost is related. However, if the life of the addition is shorter than the life of the

---

[14]Some accountants prefer to debit the related asset account, as illustrated above, only when the major repair increases the efficiency above normal. In contrast, when it is estimated that only the useful life is extended, those accountants instead would debit the related accumulated depreciation account. This distinction usually is not made because it is difficult to apply practically. Also, subsequent book value and depreciation expense would be the same regardless of which account is debited because the remaining book value to be depreciated would be the same in either instance.

related asset, the addition should be depreciated over its remaining life (less any residual value).

Ordinary repairs and maintenance

Ordinary repairs and maintenance always are classified as **revenue expenditures** and debited to an appropriate **expense** account in the period in which incurred. **Ordinary repairs and maintenance** are those relatively small recurring outlays essential to keep a tangible operating asset in **normal** operating condition. Ordinary repairs do not add materially to the economic value of the asset or to its estimated useful life. Rather, they tend to restore and repair the effects of normal wear and tear that occur with usage. As a consequence, normal repair and maintenance tend to assure that the expected useful life and operating efficiency of the asset will be maintained. These reasons justify the matching of current repair and maintenance expenditures (i.e., expense) with revenues of the current period.

NATURAL RESOURCES

Natural resources, such as a mineral deposit, oil well, or timber tract, often are referred to as "wasting assets" because they are consumed physically, or **depleted,** as used. When acquired or developed, a natural resource is measured and recorded in the accounts in accordance with the **cost principle.** As the natural resource is consumed or used up, the acquisition cost, in accordance with the **matching principle,** must be apportioned among the various periods in which the resulting revenues are recognized. The term **depletion** is used to describe this process of periodic cost allocation over the period of use of a natural resource. A **depletion rate** per unit of the resource produced is computed by dividing the total acquisition and development cost (less any estimated residual value, which is rare) by the **estimated** units that can be withdrawn economically from the resource. The depletion rate, thus computed, is multiplied each period by the **actual** number of units withdrawn. This procedure is the same as the productive-output method of calculating depreciation.

To illustrate accounting for a natural resource, assume that a gravel pit was developed at a cost of $80,000 and that a reliable estimate was made that 100,000 cubic meters of gravel could be withdrawn economically from the pit. The **depletion rate per unit** would be computed as follows (assuming no residual value):

$$\text{\$80,000} \div \text{100,000 cubic yards} = \text{\$.80 per cubic meter (depletion}$$
$$\text{rate per unit)}$$

Depletion expense for the first year, assuming 5,000 cubic meters of gravel were withdrawn during the year, would be recorded by means of the following adjusting entry.[15]

---

[15]Consistent with the procedure for recording depreciation, an Accumulated Depletion account may be used. However, as a matter of precedent, the asset account itself usually is credited directly for the periodic depletion. Either procedure is acceptable. The same is true for intangible operational assets, discussed in the next section.

```
Depletion expense ..............................................  4,000
    Gravel pit .................................................         4,000
  Depletion for the year, 5,000 cubic meters × $.80 = $4,000.
```

At the end of the first year, this natural resource should be reported as follows:

Balance Sheet

Operational assets:
    Gravel pit (cost, $80,000 − $4,000 accumulated depletion)...... $76,000

Because it is difficult to estimate the recoverable units from a natural resource, the depletion rate often must be revised. This is a "change in estimate"; therefore, the undepleted acquisition cost is spread over the estimated remaining recoverable units by computing a new depletion rate. For example, assume in Year 2 that the estimate of recoverable units remaining was changed from 95,000 to 150,000 cubic meters. The depletion rate to be applied to the cubic meters of gravel withdrawn in Year 2 would be:

($80,000 − $4,000) ÷ 150,000 cubic meters = $.51 per cubic meter

When buildings and similar improvements are constructed in connection with the development and exploitation of a natural resource, they should be recorded in separate asset accounts and **depreciated**—not depleted. Their estimated useful lives cannot be longer than the time required to exploit the natural resource unless they have a significant use-value after the resource is depleted.

INTANGIBLE OPERATIONAL ASSETS

An intangible operational asset, like any other asset, has value because of certain rights and privileges conferred by law upon the owner of the asset. However, an intangible asset has no material or physical substance as do tangible assets such as land and buildings. Thus, intangible assets are characterized by their lack of physical substance and the special rights that ownership confers. Examples of intangible operational assets are patents, copyrights, franchises, licenses, trademarks, and goodwill. The acquisition of an intangible asset usually requires the expenditure of resources. For example, an entity may purchase a patent from the inventor. The cost of an intangible asset should be measured and recorded in the accounts and reported on the financial statements of the entity in the same way as a tangible asset.[16]

---

[16]Intangible operational assets often are referred to as intangible assets.

At acquisition, an intangible operational asset is recorded at its cash equivalent cost in accordance with the **cost principle.** Cost is defined as the sum of all expenditures made to acquire the rights or privileges.

Each type of intangible operational asset should be recorded in a separate asset account when acquired. To illustrate, assume that on January 1, 19A, Mason Company purchased a patent from its developer, J. Doe, at a cash price of $17,000. The acquisition of this intangible asset would be recorded as follows:

January 1, 19A:

Patents..	17,000	
Cash..		17,000
Purchase of patent rights from J. Doe.		

Under the cost principle, an intangible right or privilege, although it may have value, is not recorded unless there has been an identifiable expenditure of resources to acquire or develop it. For example, the demise of a competitor's patent may cause the company's patent to be more valuable. This increase in value would not be recorded because there was no expenditure of resources incident to the increase in value.

Research and development (R&D) costs are separated into two types: research and development. Research costs are expenses even though they may result in a patent or a product which has future value. Development costs, on the other hand, can be capitalized as an asset if a set of criteria can be satisfied which indicate they have future value.[17]

Amortization of intangible operational assets

Intangible operational assets normally have limited lives; however, they seldom, if ever, have a residual value. Intangible assets have a limited life because the rights or privileges that give them value terminate or simply disappear. Therefore, the acquisition cost of an intangible operational asset must be written off over its estimated economic life. This systematic write-off usually is called **amortization.**

Each intangible asset should be amortized over its estimated economic life. Arbitrary and immediate write-off of an intangible asset is not an acceptable practice.

Although an intangible asset may be amortized by using any "systematic and rational" method that reflects the actual expiration of its economic usefulness, the **straight-line** method is used almost exclusively.

---

[17]The criteria that must be met in order to capitalize development costs are set forth in *CICA Handbook*, Section 3450.21. They are technical feasibility, management intention to develop, a defined future market, and adequate resources available or obtainable to carry out the development.

Patents.   A patent, when acquired, is recorded at its cash equivalent cost in accordance with the **cost principle.** Subsequent to acquisition, a patent is **amortized,** in accordance with the **matching principle,** over the shorter of its economic life or its remaining legal life (of the 17 years from date of grant). To illustrate, assume the patent acquired by Mason Company, recorded above, had an estimated 10-year remaining economic life. At the end of 19A, the **adjusting entry** to record amortization for one year would be:

December 31, 19A:

Patent expense..	1,700	
Patents...		1,700
Adjusting entry to record amortization of patent over the estimated economic life of 10 years ($17,000 ÷ 10 years = $1,700).		

The amount of patent amortization expense recorded for 19A is reported on the income statement as an operating expense. The patent would be reported on the December 31, 19A, balance sheet as follows:

> Intangible assets:
>   Patents (cost, $17,000, less amortization)........ $15,300

Copyrights.   A copyright is similar to a patent. A copyright gives the owner the exclusive right to publish, use, and sell a literary, musical, or artistic piece of work for a period not exceeding 50 years beyond the author's death. The same principles, guidelines, and procedures used in accounting for and reporting the cost of patents also are appropriate for copyrights.

Franchises and licenses.   Franchises and licenses frequently are granted by governmental and other units for a specified period and purpose. For example, a province may grant one company a franchise to operate a bus service, or a company may sell franchises, such as the right for a local outlet to operate a Canadian Tire store. Franchises and licenses usually require the expenditure of resources by the franchisee to acquire them; therefore, they represent intangible operational assets that should be accounted for as illustrated earlier for patents.

Leaseholds.   Leasing is a common type of business contract whereby the owner (or lessor) for a consideration known as rent, extends to another party (the lessee) certain rights to use specified property. Leases may vary from simple arrangements, such as the month-to-month lease of an office or the daily rental of an automobile, to long-term leases having complex contractual arrangements. The rights granted to a lessee frequently are referred to as a **leasehold.**

Long-term leases sometimes require a lump-sum advance rental payment by the lessee. In such cases, the lessee should record the advance payment as a debit to an intangible asset account (frequently called Leaseholds) and amortize it to expense over the contractual life of the lease. The true amount of annual rent expense includes the amortization of the leasehold; therefore, the annual amortization is debited to Rent Expense. To illustrate, assume that Favour Company leased a building for its own use on January 1, 19A, under a five-year contract that required, in addition to the monthly rental payments of $2,000, a single payment in advance of $20,000. The advance payment would be recorded as follows:

January 1, 19A:

Leasehold (or Rent paid in advance)	20,000	
Cash..		20,000
Rent paid in advance.		

At the end of 19A, and at the end of each of the remaining four years, the following **adjusting** entry would be made to reflect amortization of this intangible asset.[18]

December 31, 19A:

Rent expense	4,000	
Leasehold		4,000
Adjusting entry to record amortization of leasehold over five years ($20,000 ÷ 5 years = $4,000).		

The $2,000 monthly rental payments would be debited to Rent Expense when paid each month. Thus, the 19A income statement would report rent expense of $28,000 [i.e., ($2,000 × 12) + $4,000 = $28,000]. The December 31,

---

[18]This discussion presumes the normal or **operating** type of lease. In some instances, a lease is in effect a sale/purchase agreement. Such leases, known as financing leases, involve complex accounting problems that are deferred to more advanced accounting books.

19A, balance sheet would report an asset, Leasehold, of $16,000 (i.e., Cost, $20,000 − Amortization, $4,000 = $16,000).

Leasehold improvements. In most instances, when buildings, improvements, or alterations are constructed by the **lessee** on leased property, such assets legally revert to the owner of the property at the end of the lease. The lessee has full use of such improvements during the term of the lease, therefore, they should be recorded as an intangible operating asset, "Leasehold Improvements." These expenditures should be amortized over the estimated useful life of the related improvement or the remaining life of the lease, whichever is shorter.

Goodwill. Usually, when a successful business is sold as a unit, the price will be somewhat in excess of the sum of the market values of its recorded assets less its liabilities. A business may command an excess price because an intangible operational asset called goodwill attaches to a successful business.

Goodwill represents the potential of a business to earn above a normal rate of return on the recorded assets less the liabilities. Goodwill arises from such factors as customer confidence, reputation for dependability, efficiency and internal competencies, quality of goods and services, and financial standing. From the date of organization, a successful business continually builds goodwill. In this context, the goodwill is said to be "generated internally at no identifiable cost." On the other hand, when a business is purchased as an entity, the purchase price will include a payment for any goodwill that exists at that time. **In conformance with the cost principle, goodwill is recorded as an intangible operational asset only when it actually is purchased.**

To illustrate, assume Richard Roe purchased the College Men's Store on January 1, 19A, for $200,000 cash. At the date of purchase, it was determined that the recorded assets had a total **market value** of $160,000, comprised of the market values of inventory, $110,000; fixtures, $35,000; prepaid rent, $1,000; and other assets, $14,000. Roe did not accept any of the store's liabilities. The purchase would be recorded by Roe as follows:

January 1, 19A:

Inventory	110,000	
Furniture and fixtures	35,000	
Prepaid rent	1,000	
Other assets	14,000	
Goodwill	40,000	
Cash		200,000
Purchase of College Men's Store.		

The intangible asset—goodwill—must be amortized to expense over its estimated economic life not to exceed 40 years.[19] Assuming a 40-year economic life, the amortization for 19A would be recorded in an **adjusting entry** as follows:

December 31, 19A:

Goodwill amortization (expense)...............................	1,000	
Goodwill...		1,000
Adjusting entry to record goodwill amortization for one year based on 40-year economic life ($40,000 ÷ 40 years = $1,000).		

Many other types of intangible assets may be observed in financial statements. Examples are formulas, processes, and film rights. These types are accounted for, and reported, in a manner similar to that illustrated above.

DEFERRED CHARGES

An asset category called **deferred charges** is reported occasionally on balance sheets. A deferred charge, like a prepaid expense, is an **expense paid in advance;** that is, goods or services were acquired that will be used to earn future revenues. A deferred charge is a **long-term** prepaid expense and, therefore, cannot be classified as a current asset. A prepaid expense is a short-term prepayment and, for this reason, is classified as a current asset. Thus, the only difference between the two is time. For example, $1,000 was expended for issuing a five-year debt issue at the start of Year 1. The report of this cost at the end of Year 1 would be as follows:

Income statement:
    Debt expense...................... $200
Balance sheet:
    Deferred charges:
        Unamortized debt issue costs...... 800

Common examples of deferred charges are bond issuance costs (Chapter 11), start-up costs, organization costs, and plant rearrangement costs. In conformance with the matching principle, deferred charges are amortized to ex-

---

[19]*CICA Handbook*, Section 1580.58, suggests this treatment for goodwill arising on the purchase of one company by another company (called a business combination). Chapter 14 will discuss this issue in more detail. The treatment of goodwill in a more general setting such as the one illustrated above is not mandated in the *CICA Handbook* but would likely follow the rules for business combinations.

pense each period over the future periods benefited. Conceptually, organization costs which represent the various costs involved in forming a limited company have an unlimited life. But for practical purposes they are commonly amortized over a short period of time.

DISPOSAL OF OPERATIONAL ASSETS

Operational assets may be disposed of in two ways: voluntarily by sale, trade-in, or retirement; or involuntarily as a result of a casualty, such as a storm, fire, or accident. Whatever the nature of the disposal, the cost of the asset and any accumulated depreciation, depletion, or amortization must be removed from the accounts at the date of disposal. The difference between any resources received upon disposal of an operational asset and the **book value** of the asset at the date of disposal represents a "gain or loss on disposal of operational assets." This gain (or loss) is not revenue (or expense) because it is from "peripheral or incidental" activities rather than from normal operations (see Exhibit 2–6). To illustrate, assume a machine is sold for $3,500 cash when the account balances showed: Machine, $10,000; and Accumulated Depreciation, Machine, $7,000 (i.e., a book value of $3,000). The entry to record this **voluntary** disposal would be:

Cash...	3,500	
Accumulated depreciation, machine	7,000	
Machine..		10,000
Gain on disposal of operational asset		500
Gain computed:		
Sale price... $3,500		
Book value at date of sale ($10,000 − $7,000) 3,000		
Difference − gain.............................. $ 500		

When an operational asset is disposed of at any date other than the end of the accounting period, it may be necessary to record depreciation, depletion, or amortization for the fraction of the year to the date of disposal. After this entry is made, the entry to record the disposal must be recorded. A gain or loss on involuntary disposals of operational assets is reported on the income statement; the asset and the related accumulated depreciation would no longer be reported on the balance sheet. Exhibit 9–5 illustrates the acquisition, depreciation, and **involuntary disposal** of an operational asset (a heavy-duty truck).

EXHIBIT 9–5
Involuntary disposal of an operational asset

Situation of Bye Company:

January 1, 19A—Purchased a heavy-duty truck for $38,000 cash; estimated useful life eight years and $6,000 residual value (straight-line depreciation).

December 31—End of accounting year.

June 30, 19D—The truck was wrecked and the insurance company paid a claim of $21,000 (i.e., the replacement cost of the truck at the date of the wreck).

Entries during the life of the truck:

January 1, 19A—To record purchase of the truck:

Truck	38,000	
Cash		38,000

December 31—To record annual depreciation 19A–19C:

	19A		19B		19C	
Depreciation expense	4,000		4,000		4,000	
Accumulated depreciation		4,000		4,000		4,000

Computation: ($38,000 − $6,000) ÷ 8 years = $4,000.

June 30, 19D—Entries on date of disposal (wreck):

1. To record depreciation for six months (to date of wreck):

Depreciation expense	2,000	
Accumulated depreciation		2,000

Computation: $4,000 × 6/12 = $2,000.

2. To record the involuntary disposal of the asset and the insurance indemnity:

Cash (insurance indemnity).	21,000	
Accumulated depreciation ($4,000 × 3) + $2,000	14,000	
Casualty loss on operational assets	3,000	
Truck.		38,000

DEMONSTRATION CASE

(Try to resolve the requirements before proceeding to the suggested solution that follows.)

Diversified Industries has been in operation for a number of years. It started as a construction company, and in recent years it has expanded into a number of related activities, including heavy construction, ready-mix concrete, sand and gravel, construction supplies, and earth-moving services.

The transactions given below were selected from those completed during 19D. They focus on the primary issues discussed in this chapter. Amounts have been simplified for case purposes.

19D

Jan. 1 The management decided to purchase a building that was approximately 10 years old. The location was excellent, and there was adequate parking space. The company bought the building and the land on which it was situated for $305,000 cash. A reliable appraiser appraised the property at the following market values: land, $126,000; and building, $174,000.

Jan. 12 Paid renovation costs on the building amounting to $38,100.

June 19 Purchased a third location for a gravel pit (designated No. 3) at a cost of $50,000 cash. The location had been carefully surveyed, and it was estimated that 100,000 cubic meters of gravel could be removed from the deposit.

July 10 Paid $1,200 ordinary repairs on the building.

Aug. 1 Paid $10,000 for costs of preparing the gravel pit, acquired in June 19D, for exploitation.

December 31, 19D (end of the annual accounting period)—the following data were developed as a basis for the adjusting entries:

    a. The building will be depreciated on a straight-line basis over an estimated useful life of 30 years. The estimated residual value is $35,000.

    b. During 19D, 12,000 cubic meters of gravel were removed from gravel pit No. 3. Use an Accumulated Depletion account.

    c. The company owns a patent right that is used in operations. The Patent account on January 1, 19D, reflected a balance of $3,300. The patent has an estimated remaining life of six years (including 19D).

Required:

    1. Give the journal entries for the five transactions completed during 19D.

    2. Give the adjusting entries on December 31, 19D.

    3. Show the December 31, 19D, balance sheet classification and amount for each of the following items: land, building, gravel pit, and patent.

Suggested solution

Requirement 1. Entries during 19D:

January 1, 19D:

Land (building site)	128,100	
Building...	176,900	
Cash...		305,000

Allocation of purchase price based on appraisal:

Item	Appraisal value	Percent	Computation	Allocation
Land	$126,000	42	× $305,000 =	$128,100
Building	174,000	58	× 305,000 =	176,900
Totals . .	$300,000	100		$305,000

January 12, 19D:

Building.	38,100	
Cash.		38,100
Renovation costs on building prior to use.		

June 19, 19D:

Gravel pit (No. 3)	50,000	
Cash.		50,000
Purchased gravel pit; estimated production, 100,000 cubic meters.		

July 10, 19D:

Repair expense	1,200	
Cash.		1,200
Ordinary repairs.		

August 1, 19D:

Gravel pit (No. 3)	10,000	
Cash.		10,000
Preparation costs.		

Requirement 2. Adjusting entries, December 31, 19D:

---

a.   Depreciation expense, building   6,000
    Accumulated depreciation.....................................   6,000

    Computations:
      Cost ($176,900 + $38,100) $215,000
        Less: Residual value   35,000
      Cost to be depreciated $180,000

    Annual depreciation: $180,000 ÷ 30 years = $6,000.

b.   Depletion expense..   7,200
    Accumulated depletion, gravel pit (No. 3)   7,200

    Computations:
      Cost ($50,000 + $10,000) $60,000
    Depletion rate:
      $60,000 ÷ 100,000 cubic meters = $.60
    Depletion expense:
      $.60 × 12,000 cubic meters = $7,200

c.   Patent expense...   550
    Patent...   550

    Computation:
      $3,300 ÷ 6 years = $550.

Requirement 3. Balance sheet, December 31, 19D:

Assets

Operational assets:
  Land $128,100
  Building $215,000
    Less: Accumulated depreciation......   6,000   209,000
  Gravel pit..........................   60,000
    Less: Accumulated depletion.........   7,200   52,800
    Total operational assets............ $389,900

Intangible assets:
  Patent ($3,300 − $550)   2,750

SUMMARY OF CHAPTER

This chapter discussed accounting for operational assets, which are the noncurrent assets that a business retains for long periods of time for use in the course of normal operations rather than for sale. They include tangible assets and intangible assets. At acquisition, operational assets are measured and recorded in the accounts at cost, in conformity with the cost principle. Cost includes the cash equivalent purchase price plus all reasonable and necessary expenditures made to acquire and prepare the asset for its intended use.

An operational asset represents a bundle of future services and benefits that has been paid for in advance. As an operational asset is used, this bundle of future services gradually is used to earn revenue. Therefore, in accordance with the matching principle, the asset cost (less any estimated residual value) is allocated to periodic expense over the periods benefited. In this way, the expense associated with the use of operational assets is matched with the revenues earned. This allocation process is known as depreciation in the case of property, plant, and equipment; as depletion in the case of natural resources; and as amortization in the case of intangibles.

Three methods of depreciation are widely used: straight line, productive output, and diminishing balance.

Expenditures related to operational assets are classified either as:

1. **Capital expenditures**—those expenditures that provide benefits for one or more accounting periods beyond the current period; consequently, they are debited to appropriate asset accounts and depreciated, depleted, or amortized over their useful lives; or

2. **Revenue expenditures**—those expenditures that provide benefits during the current accounting period only; consequently, they are debited to appropriate current expense accounts when incurred.

Ordinary repairs and maintenance costs are revenue expenditures, whereas extraordinary repairs and additions are capital expenditures.

Operational assets may be disposed of voluntarily by sale or retirement, or involuntarily through casualty, such as storm, fire, or accident. Upon disposal, such assets must be depreciated, depleted, or amortized up to the date of disposal. The disposal transaction is recorded by removing the cost of the old asset and the related accumulated depreciation, depletion, or amortization amount from the accounts. A gain or loss on disposal of an operational asset will result when the disposal price is different from the book value of the old asset. Special rules apply to the trade in of an asset as all, or part, of the consideration given for another asset (trade-ins are discussed in Supplement 9A).

SUPPLEMENT 9A—TRADING IN ASSETS

It is not unusual when acquiring an asset to trade in another asset. Although there may be a direct trade of two assets, the typical case involves the trading in of an old asset plus the payment of cash for the difference (often called boot). In such transactions, the asset acquired must be recorded in the accounts and the old asset removed from the accounts.

Accounting for the exchange of one asset for another asset depends on two factors.[20]

---

[20]*APB Opinion 29*, ''Accounting for Nonmonetary Transactions'' (New York, May 1973), specifies the appropriate accounting for transactions that involve the exchange of assets when either or both of these factors are present. The *CICA Handbook* is silent on this point.

1. Whether the two assets are similar or dissimilar.
2. Whether cash for the difference (boot) is paid or received.

The trading in of an old truck for another truck would involve similar assets. In contrast, the trading in of a plot of land for a new truck would involve dissimilar assets.

The basic principle for recording the exchange of assets can be stated as follows: If the assets exchanged are **similar,** the exchange should be recorded on a "book value" basis because there is no completed earning process.[21] If the assets exchanged are **dissimilar,** the exchange should be recorded on a "market value" basis because there is a completed earning process.

Exhibit 9–6 illustrates accounting for the acquisition of an asset when another asset is given as a trade-in. Four independent cases are illustrated as follows:

Case	*Situation*
A	**Similar** assets are exchanged; **no cash boot** is paid.
B...........	**Dissimilar** assets are exchanged; **no cash boot** is paid.
C	**Similar** assets are exchanged; **cash boot** is paid.
D	**Dissimilar** assets are exchanged; **cash boot** is paid.

The four cases illustrated in Exhibit 9–6 are sufficient for our objective to explain the exchange of assets. Sometimes the terms of the transaction involving a trade-in also includes the **receipt** of cash boot, in which case the recording becomes more complex.

Under the cost principle, an asset, when acquired, never should be recorded at an amount greater than its cash equivalent price. In some instances, this constraint must be carefully considered because it will serve to reduce a gain (or increase a loss) on disposal. The difficulty will generally be encountered in determining the cash equivalent of the asset given up in the transaction.

In the illustration in Exhibit 9–6, the market value of the old Asset O was $200 in excess of its book value [i.e., $2,200 − ($5,000 − $3,000)]. Therefore, in Cases B and D (relating to dissimilar assets), this amount was recorded as a gain. In contrast, if the market value of the old Asset O were $1,900 (i.e., $100 below book value), a loss of $100 would be reported in Cases B and D. A loss would be recorded for Cases A and C (similar assets) when the market value of either asset is below book value because it indicates an impairment of value.

---

[21]In the case of an exchange of similar productive assets, because the asset acquired performs essentially the same productive function as the asset given up, the exchange is only one step in the earning process. The earning process in these situations is completed when the goods or services are sold that the similar productive assets helped to produce. In contrast, in the case of an exchange of dissimilar productive assets, the earning process is completed because the productive function of the productive asset given up is terminated. The asset acquired serves a different economic purpose for the entity and begins a new earning process of its own.

EXHIBIT 9–6
Trading in used
assets illustrated

Situation of Company T:

Transaction: Company T acquired Asset N, and traded in Asset O. At the date of the transaction, the accounts of Company T reflected the following:

Asset O:
Cost when acquired............	$5,000
Accumulated depreciation......	3,000
Estimated market value........	2,200

Asset N:
Market value.................	2,250

Case A—Similar assets are exchanged; **no** cash boot paid.

Principle applied: The asset acquired is recorded at the **book value** of the asset traded in.

Asset N	2,000	
Accumulated depreciation, Asset O	3,000	
Asset O		5,000

Case B—Dissimilar assets are exchanged; **no** cash boot paid.
Principle applied: The asset acquired is recorded at the **market value** of the asset traded in.

Asset N	2,200	
Accumulated depreciation, Asset O	3,000	
Asset O		5,000
Gain on disposal of operational asset...........................		200

Case C—Similar assets are exchanged; **$50** cash boot is paid.

Principle applied: The asset acquired is recorded at the **book value** of the asset traded in **plus the cash boot** paid.

Asset N ($2,000 + $50)	2,050*	
Accumulated depreciation, Asset O	3,000	
Asset O		5,000
Cash		50

*This amount cannot exceed the cash equivalent of the asset acquired.

Case D—Dissimilar assets are exchanged; **$50** cash boot is **paid.**

Principle applied: The asset acquired is recorded at the **market value** of the asset traded in **plus the cash boot** paid.

Asset N ($2,200 + $50)	2,250*	
Accumulated depreciation, Asset O	3,000	
Asset O		5,000
Cash		50
Gain on disposal of operational asset...........................		200

*This amount cannot exceed the cash equivalent of the asset acquired.

IMPORTANT TERMS DEFINED IN THIS CHAPTER

Terms (alphabetically)	Key words in definitions of important terms used in chapter	Page reference
Acquisition cost	Net cash equivalent amount paid for an asset.	452
Amortization	Systematic and rational apportionment of the cost of an intangible operational asset over its useful life.	458
Basket purchase	Acquisition of two or more assets in a single transaction for a single lump sum.	453

Terms (alphabetically)	Key words in definitions of important terms used in chapter	Page reference
Book (or carrying) value	Acquisition cost of an operational asset less accumulated depreciation, depletion or amortization.	458
Capital expenditures	Expenditures that are debited to an asset account; the acquisition of an asset.	471
Capitalization of interest	Interest expenditures included in the cost of an operational asset; interest capitalized during construction period.	454
Copyrights	Exclusive right to publish, use, and sell a literary, musical or artistic work.	477
Deferred charges	An expense paid in advance of usage of the goods or services; long-term prepayment.	480
Depletion	Systematic and rational apportionment of the cost of a natural resource over the period of exploitation.	457
Depreciation	Systematic and rational apportionment of the cost of a tangible operational asset over its useful life.	457
Diminishing balance	The method used to calculate capital cost allowance for income tax purposes.	465
Estimated residual value	Estimated amount to be recovered, less disposal costs, at the end of the estimated useful life of an operational asset.	460
Estimated useful life	Estimated service life of an operational asset to the present owner.	459
Extraordinary repairs	Major, high cost, and long-term repairs; debited to an asset account (or accumulated depreciation); a capital expenditure.	472
Goodwill	Acquisition cost of the purchase of a business that is in excess of the market value of the net assets of the business purchased.	479
Government assistance	Amounts provided by various governments to assist businesses usually in the form of operating expense reductions or fixed asset cost reductions.	456
Intangible operational assets	Assets used in the operations of a business that have special rights but not physical substance.	451
Leasehold improvements	Expenditures by the lessee on leased property that have use value beyond the current accounting period.	479
Leaseholds	Rights granted to a lessee under a lease contract.	477
Operational assets	Tangible and intangible assets owned by a business and used in its operations.	451
Productive-output depreciation	Cost of an operational asset is allocated over its useful life based upon the periodic output related to total estimated output.	462
Repairs and maintenance	Expenditures for normal operating upkeep of operational assets; debit expense for ordinary repairs.	471
Residual value	Estimated amount to be recovered, less disposal costs, at the end of the estimated useful life of an operational asset.	460
Revenue expenditures	Expenditures that are debited to an expense account; the incurrence of an expense.	471
Straight-line depreciation	Cost of an operational asset is allocated over its useful life in equal periodic amounts.	461
Sum-of-years'-digits depreciation	Cost of an operational asset is allocated over its useful life based upon a fraction where the denominator is the total of all of the useful years and the numerator is the year of life in inverse order.	464
Tangible operational assets	Assets used in the operations of a business that have physical substance.	451

QUESTIONS FOR DISCUSSION

Part A

1. Define operational assets. Explain how they may be considered as a "bundle of future services."

2. What are the classifications of operational assets? Briefly explain each.

3. Relate the cost principle to accounting for operational assets.

4. Describe the relationship between the matching principle and accounting for operational assets.

5. Define and illustrate the book value of a three-year-old operational asset that cost $11,500, has an estimated residual value of $1,500 and an estimated useful life of five years. Relate book value to market value.

6. Under the cost principle, what amounts usually should be included in the acquisition cost of an operational asset?

7. What is a "basket purchase"? What measurement problem does it pose?

8. Briefly explain the circumstances under which interest cost must be included in the acquisition cost of an operational asset.

9. Briefly distinguish among depreciation, depletion, and amortization.

10. In computing depreciation, three values must be known or estimated; identify and explain the nature of each.

11. Estimated useful life and residual value of an operational asset relate to the current owner or user rather than to all users. Explain this statement.

12. What kind of a depreciation-expense pattern is provided under the straight-line method? When would its use be particularly appropriate?

13. What kind of depreciation-expense pattern emerges under the productive-output method? When would its use be particularly appropriate?

14. What are the arguments in favour of accelerated depreciation?

15. Explain how monthly depreciation should be computed when the sum-of-the-years'-digits method is used for an asset having a 10-year life.

16. When an asset is acquired by giving up a noncash asset (noncash consideration), the preferred value for the new asset is the market value of the noncash asset rather than the market value of the asset purchased. Why?

17. What accounting principle could justify treating a government grant received for the construction of a new building as a reduction of the asset value recorded?

Part B

18. Distinguish between capital expenditures and revenue expenditures.

19. Distinguish between ordinary and extraordinary repairs. How is each accounted for?

20. Over what period should an addition to an existing operational asset be depreciated? Explain.

21. Define an intangible operational asset.

22. What period should be used to amortize an intangible operational asset?

23. Define goodwill. When is it appropriate to record goodwill as an intangible operational asset?

24. Distinguish between a leasehold and a leasehold improvement.

25. Over what period should a leasehold improvement be amortized? Explain.

26. Compare the accounting for a prepaid expense with a deferred charge.

27. When an operational asset is disposed of **during** the accounting period, two separate entries usually must be made. Explain this statement.

28. Why are ordinary repair costs incurred prior to the use of an asset debited to the asset account while ordinary repair costs incurred after the asset is placed in use are debited to operating expenses?

29. Why are research costs expensed while development costs may be capitalized?

30. Why are purchases of assets where a trade-in is used treated differently than a straight cash purchase of an asset?

EXERCISES

Part A

E9–1. For each asset listed below, enter a code letter to the left to indicate the allocation procedure for each asset. Use the following letter codes:

A—Amortization   P—Depletion
D—Depreciation   N—None of these

_____	1.	Land	_____ 11.	Copyright
_____	2.	Patent	_____ 12.	Investment in common stock
_____	3.	Building	_____ 13.	Mineral deposit
_____	4.	Cash	_____ 14.	Machinery
_____	5.	Oil well	_____ 15.	Licence right
_____	6.	Trademark	_____ 16.	Deferred charge
_____	7.	Goodwill	_____ 17.	Inventory of goods
_____	8.	Postage stamps	_____ 18.	Timber tract
_____	9.	Franchise	_____ 19.	Tools
_____	10.	Plant site in use	_____ 20.	Gravel pit

E9–2. A machine was purchased by Ryan Company on March 1, 19A, at an invoice price of $20,000. On date of delivery, March 2, 19A, Ryan Company paid $10,000 on the machine and the balance was an open account at 12 percent interest. On March 3, 19A, $200 was paid for freight on the machine, and on March 5 installation costs relating to the machine were paid amounting to $600. On October 1, 19A, Ryan Company paid the balance due on the machine plus the interest.

Required:

a. Give the journal entries on each of the above dates through October 19A.
b. Give the adjusting entry for straight-line depreciation at the end of 19A, assuming an estimated useful life of 10 years and an estimated residual value of $2,800. Depreciate to the nearest month. The accounting period ends December 31, 19A.
c. What would be the book value of the machine at the end of 19B?

E9–3. Raul Company purchased a building and the land on which it is located for a total cash price of $480,000. In addition, they paid transfer costs of $1,000. Renovation costs on the building amounted to $9,250. An independent appraiser provided market values of building, $363,750; and land, $121,250.

Required:

a. Apportion the cost of the property on the basis of the appraised values. Show computations.
b. Give the journal entry to record the purchase of the property, including all expenditures. Assume that all transactions were for cash and that all purchases occurred at the start of Year 1.
c. Give the journal entry to record straight-line depreciation at the end of one year assuming an estimated 20-year useful life and a $20,000 estimated residual value.
d. What would be the book value of the property at the end of Year 2?

E9–4. On January 1, 19A, Stonewall Corporation purchased land at a cost of $120,000 and paid transfer fees of $6,000. Clearing the land, and planning for the building construction was started immediately. Construction of an office building for company use was started on April 1, 19A. The company borrowed approximately 80 percent of the funds to purchase the land and construct the office building at a 12 percent interest rate. The remaining cash needed was paid from company funds. Total interest cost for 19A was $36,000. The company made the following cash expenditures at the dates indicated:

January 1, 19A, down payment on the land (20%)..............	$ 24,000
January 1, 19A, transfer costs on the land	6,000
March 1, 19A, fees for preliminary surveys and work prior to start of construction	12,000
Progress payments to contractor for construction costs:	
May 31, 19A, No. 1	200,000
August 31, 19A, No. 2......................................	300,000
November 30, 19A, No. 3 (end of the construction period)......	200,000

Required:

a. Compute the cost of the tangible operational asset with separate amounts for the land and building. Assume the construction period started on April 1, 19A. Show computations.
b. How much interest expense should be reported on the 19A income statement?

E9–5. Astro Corporation purchased an automobile at a cost of $1,350. The estimated useful life was four years, and the residual value, $150. Assume that the estimated productive life of the auto is 50,000 kilometers and each year's use was Year 1, 20,000; Year 2, 15,000; Year 3, 9,000; and Year 4, 6,000.

Required:

a. Determine the amount for each cell in the following table. Show your computations and round to the nearest dollar.

Year	Depreciation Expense			
	Straight Line	Productive Output	Sum-of-the-Years'-Digits	Class 10 Capital Cost Allowance
1				
2				
3				
4				
Total				

b. Assuming the auto was used directly in the production of one of the products manufactured and sold by the company, what factors might be considered in selecting a preferable depreciation method in terms of the matching principle?

E9–6. Vance Company purchased a machine that cost $18,000. The estimated useful life was five years, and the estimated residual value, $3,000. Assume the estimated useful life in productive units is 50,000. Units actually produced were Year 1, 9,000; and Year 2, 11,000.

Required:

a. Determine the appropriate amounts to complete the table below. Show computations.

	Depreciation expense		Book value at end of	
Method of depreciation	Year 1	Year 2	Year 1	Year 2
Straight line	____	____	____	____
Productive output.	____	____	____	____
Sum-of-the-years'-digits	____	____	____	____
20% capital cost allowance	____	____	____	____

b. Which method would result in the lowest EPS for Year 1? for Year 2?

E9–7. East Company acquired, and paid for, a machine that cost $5,300 on July 1, 19B. The estimated useful life is four years, and the estimated residual value is $500. The accounting period ends December 31.

Required:

a. Compute monthly depreciation expense for July 19B and July 19C assuming (a) the straight-line method and (b) the SYD method.
b. Assume cash revenues of $40,000 and cash expenses of $30,000 for the year 19B and an income tax rate of 20 percent. Complete the following tabulation for 19B:

	Straight Line	Sum-of-the-Years'-Digits
Revenues		
Expenses		
Depreciation expense		
Pretax income		
Income tax expense		
Net income		

c. Which method produced the higher net income? By how much? Explain why the net incomes differ (use amounts).

E9–8.   Belt Company owns the office building occupied by its administrative office. The office building was reflected in the accounts on the December 31, 19O, balance sheet as follows:

> Cost when acquired.............................. $250,000
> Accumulated depreciation (based on straight-line
>   depreciation, an estimated life of 30 years,
>   and a $40,000 residual value) 105,000

During January 19P, on the basis of a careful study, the management decided that the total estimated useful life should be changed to 25 years (instead of 30) and the residual value reduced to $35,000 (from $40,000).

Required:

a. Give the adjusting entry for straight-line depreciation at the end of 19P. Show computations.
b. Explain the rationale for your response to (a).

Part B

E9–9.   For each item listed below, enter the appropriate letter to the left to indicate the type of expenditure. Use the following:

> A—Capital expenditure
> B—Revenue expenditure
> C—Neither

_____ 1. Paid $500 for ordinary repairs.
_____ 2. Paid $6,000 for extraordinary repairs.
_____ 3. Addition to old building; paid cash, $10,000.
_____ 4. Routine maintenance; cost, $300; on credit.
_____ 5. Purchased a machine, $6,000; gave long-term note.
_____ 6. Paid $2,000 for organization costs.
_____ 7. Paid three-year insurance premium, $600.
_____ 8. Purchased a patent, $3,400 cash.
_____ 9. Paid $10,000 for monthly salaries.
_____ 10. Paid cash dividends, $15,000.

E9–10.   Quebec Company operates a small manufacturing facility as a supplement to its regular service activities. At the beginning of 19L, an operational asset account for the company showed the following balances:

> Manufacturing equipment $70,000
> Accumulated depreciation through 19K 48,400

During 19L, the following expenditures were incurred for repairs and maintenance:

> 1. Routine maintenance and repairs on the equipment $1,000
> 2. Major overhaul of the equipment 6,400

The equipment is being depreciated on a straight-line basis over an estimated life of 15 years and a $4,000 estimated residual value. The annual accounting period ends on December 31.

Required:

a.   Give the adjusting entry for depreciation on the manufacturing equipment that was made at the end of 19K. Starting with 19L, what is the remaining estimated life?

b.   Give the journal entries to record appropriately the two expenditures for repairs and maintenance during 19L.

c.   Give the adjusting entry that should be made at the end of 19L for depreciation of the manufacturing equipment assuming no change in the estimated life or residual value. Show computations.

E9–11.   At the end of the annual accounting period, December 31, 19C, the records of Wang Company reflected the following:

> Machine A:
> Cost when acquired $34,000
> Accumulated depreciation 12,000

During January 19D, the machine was renovated extensively including several major improvements at a cost of $8,000. As a result, the estimated life was increased from 8 years to 10 years, and the residual value was increased from $2,000 to $5,500. ↘capital Expense

Required:

a.   Give the journal entry to record the renovation. How old was the machine at the end of 19C?

b.   Give the adjusting journal entry at the end of 19D to record straight-line depreciation for the year.

c.   Explain the rationale for your entries given in (a) and (b).

E9–12.   In February 19A, Rapid Extractive Industries paid $450,000 for a mineral deposit. During March, $150,000 was spent in preparing the deposit for exploitation. It was estimated that 800,000 total cubic meters could be extracted economically. During 19A, 40,000 cubic meters were extracted. During January 19B, another $90,000 was spent for additional developmental work. After conclusion of the latest work, the estimated remaining recovery was increased to 1 million cubic meters over the remaining life. During 19B, 35,000 cubic meters were extracted.

Required:

Give the appropriate journal entry on each of the following dates:

a.   February 19A, for acquisition of the deposit.
b.   March 19A, for developmental costs.
c.   Year 19A, for annual depletion assuming the company uses a contra account (show computations).
d.   January 19B, for developmental costs.
e.   Year 19B, for annual depletion (show computations).

E9–13.   Reo Manufacturing Company had three intangible operational assets at the end of 19F (end of the fiscal year):

1.   Patent—Purchased from J. Ray on January 1, 19F, for a cash cost of $4,260. Ray had registered the patent five years earlier on January 1, 19A. Amortize over the remaining legal life.
2.   A franchise acquired from the local community to provide certain services for 10 years starting on January 1, 19F. The franchise cost $26,000 cash.
3.   On January 1, 19F, the company leased some property for a five-year term. Reo immediately spent $4,800 cash for long-term improvements (estimated useful life, eight years, and no residual value). At the termination of the lease, there will be no recovery of these improvements.

Required:

a.   Give the journal entry to record the acquisition of each intangible. Provide a brief explanation with the entries.
b.   Give adjusting journal entry at December 31, 19F, for amortization of each intangible. Show computations. The company does not use contra accounts.
c.   Show how these assets, and any related expenses, should be reported on the financial statements for 19F.

E9–14.   MB Company acquired three intangible operational assets during 19C. The relevant facts were:

1.   On January 1, 19C, the company purchased a patent from C. Cox for $2,550 cash. Cox had developed the patent and registered it on January 1, 19A. Amortize over the remaining legal life.
2.   On January 1, 19C, the company purchased a copyright for a total cash cost of $9,500 and the remaining legal life was 25 years. The company executives estimated that the copyright would be of no value by the end of 20 years.
3.   MB Company purchased a small company in January 19C at a cash cost of $100,000. Included in the purchase price was $16,400 for goodwill; the balance was for plant, equipment, and fixtures (no liabilities were assumed). Amortize the goodwill over the maximum period permitted.

Required:

a.   Give the journal entry to record the acquisition of each intangible.
b.   Give the adjusting journal entry that would be required at the end of the annual accounting period, December 31, 19C, for each intangible. The company uses contra accounts. Include a brief explanation and show computations.
c.   What would be the book (carrying) value of each intangible at the end of 19D?

E9–15. Vol Company conducts operations in several different localities. In order to expand into still another city, the company obtained a 10-year lease, starting January 1, 19D, on a very good downtown location. Although there was a serviceable building on the property, the company had to construct an additional structure to be used for storage purposes. The 10-year lease required a $12,000 cash advance rental payment, plus cash payments of $1,000 per month during occupancy. During January 19D, the company spent $30,000 cash constructing the additional structure. The new structure has an estimated life of 12 years with no residual value (straight-line depreciation).

Required:

a. Give the journal entries for Vol Company to record the payment of the $12,000 advance on January 1, 19D, and the first monthly rental.
b. Give the journal entry to record the construction of the new structure.
c. Give any adjusting entries required at the end of the annual accounting period for Vol Company on December 31, 19D, in respect to (1) the advance payment and (2) the new structure. Show computations.
d. What is the total amount of expense resulting from the lease for 19D?

E9–16. Rye Company is in the process of preparing the balance sheet at December 31, 19B. The following are to be included:

Prepaid insurance..............................	$ 450
Long-term investment in common shares of	
X Corporation, at cost (market $6,200)	6,000
Patent (at cost)	3,400
Accumulated amortization, patent...............	800
Accounts receivable............................	20,000
Allowance for doubtful accounts	600
Franchise (at cost)..............................	1,400
Accumulated amortization, franchise	700
Land—site of building...........................	10,000
Building	280,000
Accumulated depreciation, building	150,000

Required:

Show how each of the above assets would be reflected on the Rye Company balance sheet at December 31, 19B. Use the following subcaptions: Current assets, Investments and funds, Tangible operational assets, and Intangible operational assets. The company uses the "accumulated" accounts as listed above. (Hint: Intangible operational assets sum to $3,300 on the balance sheet.)

E9–17. Stanley Company sold a small truck that had been used in the business for three years. The records of the company reflected the following:

Delivery truck.................	$12,000
Accumulated depreciation......	10,000

Required:

a. Give the journal entry for disposal of the truck assuming the sales price was $2,000.
b. Give the journal entry for the disposal of the truck assuming the sales price was $2,200.
c. Give the journal entry for the disposal of the truck assuming the sales price was $1,800.

d. Summarize any underlying principles that can be observed from the three different situations on the preceding page.

E9–18. The records of the Queen Company on December 31, 19D, reflected the following data in respect to a particular machine:

Machine, original cost. $27,000
Accumulated depreciation 16,000*

*Based on a six-year estimated useful life, a $3,000 residual value, and straight-line depreciation.

On April 1, 19E, the machine was sold for $10,700 cash. The accounting period ends on December 31.

Required:

a. How old was the machine on January 1, 19E? Show computations.
b. Give the journal entry, or entries, incidental to the sale of the machine.

E9–19. On August 31, 19C, a delivery truck owned by Prince Corporation was a total loss as the result of an accident. On January 1, 19C, the records reflected the following:

Truck (estimated residual value, 10% of cost). $10,000
Accumulated depreciation (straight line, two years) 3,000

The truck was insured; therefore, Prince Corporation collected $6,300 cash from the insurance company on October 5, 19C.

Required:

a. Based on the data given, compute the estimated useful life and the estimated residual value of the truck.
b. Give all of the journal entries with respect to the truck from January 1 through October 5, 19C. Show computations.

E9–20. (Based on Supplement 9A) Mason Company owned a particular machine (designated Machine O for case purposes) which no longer met the needs of the company. On December 31, 19F, the records reflected the following:

Machine O:
Original cost $30,000
Accumulated depreciation 17,000

On January 3, 19G, the company acquired another machine (Machine N) and traded in Machine O. On this date, a reliable estimate of the market value of Machine O was $15,000.

Required:

a. Give the journal entry by Mason to record the transaction completed on January 3, 19G, for each of the following independent cases:

Case A—The machines were similar, and no cash difference was paid or received by Mason.

Case B—The machines were dissimilar, and no cash difference was paid or received by Mason.

b. For each case, explain the underlying reason for the amount that you recorded as the cost of Machine N.

E9–21. (Based on Supplement 9A) Use the facts and requirements given in Exercise 9–20 except that for each case assume Mason paid a $1,000 cash difference (boot). The market value of Machine N was $16,100.

PROBLEMS/CASES

Part A

PC9–1. White Company purchased three used machines from J. Evers for a cash price of $39,000. Transportation costs on the machines amounted to $1,000. The machines immediately were overhauled, installed, and started operating. The machines were essentially different; therefore, each had to be recorded separately in the accounts. An appraiser was employed to estimate their market values at date of purchase (prior to the overhaul and installation). The book values reflected on Evers' books also are available. The book values, appraisal results, installation costs, and renovation expenditures were:

	Machine A	Machine B	Machine C
Book value—Evers...............	$5,000	$ 9,000	$6,000
Property appraisal	6,000	15,000	9,000
Installation costs.................	200	400	100
Renovation costs prior to use	800	500	600

Required:

a. Compute the cost of each machine by making a realistic allocation. Explain the rationale for the allocated basis used.

b. Give the journal entry to record the purchase of the three machines assuming all payments were cash. Set up a separate asset account for each machine.

c. Give the entry to record depreciation expense at the end of Year 1, assuming:

		Estimates	
Machine	Life	Residual value	Depreciation method
A	6	$ 300	Straight line
B	4	2,900	SYD
C	5	1,700	Class 8, 20% CCA

PC9–2. Bye Company purchased a machine that cost $34,375. The estimated useful life is 10 years, and the estimated residual value is 4 percent of cost. The machine has an estimated useful life in productive output of 110,000 units. Actual output was Year 1, 15,000; and Year 2, 12,000.

Required:

a. Determine the appropriate amounts for the table below. Show your computations.

	Depreciation expense		Book value at end of	
Depreciation method	Year 1	Year 2	Year 1	Year 2
Straight line..................	$_____	$_____	$_____	$_____
Productive output	_____	_____	_____	_____
Sum-of-the-years'-digits	_____	_____	_____	_____
Class 8, 20% CCA	_____	_____	_____	_____

b. Give the adjusting entries for Years 1 and 2 under each method.

c. In selecting a depreciation method, some companies assess the comparative effect on **cash flow** and EPS. Briefly comment on the depreciation methods in terms of cash flow and EPS effects.

PC9–3. Stable Corporation purchased an operational asset on January 1, 19A, at a cash cost of $34,000. The estimated useful life is five years, and the estimated residual value is $4,000. Assume a constant 30 percent income tax rate; all paid in cash.

The company is deciding to use either straight-line (SL) depreciation or class 10, 30% CCA. The five-year projected all-cash incomes (before depreciation and income tax) are shown in the second column below.

Schedule to Compare Projected SL and DB Results

Year	Income (all-cash) before Depreciation and Income Tax	Depreciation Expense (dollars)		Income Tax Expense (dollars)		Net income (dollars)		Net Cash Inflow (dollars)	
		SL	CCA	SL	CCA	SL	CCA	SL	CCA
1	$ 40,000	6,000	5,100	10,200	10,470	23,800	24,430	29,530	29,530
2	40,000								
3	40,000								
4	40,000								
5	40,000								
Total	200,000	30,000		51,000		119,000		148,118	

Required:

a. Complete the above schedule. Round to nearest dollars. (Hint: Use total line to prove your computations.)

b. Briefly explain how to compute the last two columns (cash flow).

c. Identify and briefly explain any generalizations that can be made from the columns for (1) depreciation, (2) income tax, (3) net income, and (4) cash flow.

d. Which method would you recommend in this particular situation? Explain the basis for your recommendation.

PC9–4. (This PC is comprehensive and challenging.) Slick Corporation acquired a large machine for use in its productive activities at a cash cost of $189,000. The machine was acquired on January 1, 19A, at which time its estimated useful life was 500,000 units of output over a period of 10 years. The estimated residual value was $24,000. Assume a 40 percent income tax rate for Slick.

The top management of Slick is considering using either straight-line (SL), productive-output (PO), or SYD depreciation. The management also is developing a 10-year profit plan. The 10-year projected all-cash incomes (before depreciation and income tax) are shown in the first column below.

Required:

a.   Complete the following tabulation (round to nearest $1):

Year	Income (all-cash) before Depreciation and Income Tax		Depreciation Expense (dollars)			Income tax Expense (dollars)			Net Income (loss) (dollars)		
	Units	Dollars	SL	PO	SYD	SL	PO	SYD	SL	PO	SYD
1	70,000	96,500	16,500	23,100	30,000	32,000	29,360	26,600	48,000	44,040	39,900
2	75,000	103,400									
3	80,000	102,300									
4	75,000	103,400									
5	60,000	82,700	16,500	19,800	18,000	26,480	25,160	25,880	39,720	37,740	38,820
6	60,000	82,700									
7	50,000	69,000									
8	20,000	27,600	16,500	6,600	9,000	4,440	8,400	7,440	6,660	12,600	11,160
9	8,000	11,000									
10	2,000	2,400	16,500	660	3,000	(5,640)	696	(240)	(8,460)	1,044	(360)
Total	500,000	681,000	165,000	165,000	165,000	206,400	206,400	206,400	309,600	309,600	309,600

b.   List, and briefly explain any generalizations that you can make from the columns for (1) depreciation expense, (2) income tax expense, and (3) net income.

c.   Which method would you recommend in this situation? Explain the basis for your recommendation.

PC9–5.   (This PC is comprehensive and challenging.) On January 1, 19A, Brown Corporation purchased a special machine for use in the business that cost $33,000. The machine has a three-year useful life and a residual value of $3,000. The company is considering using either the straight-line method (SL) or class 29, 50 percent CCA on a straight-line basis. Assume an average income tax rate of 30 percent and that it is paid in full in cash.

Required:

a.   You have been asked to prepare an analysis of the effects of SL versus CCA depreciation on the projected financial statements and cash flows over the life of the machine (19A–19C). Accordingly, you have decided to complete the following schedules—one set based on straight-line depreciation and another set based on 50 percent straight-line CCA.

	Year 1	Year 2	Year 3
Income statements:			
Revenues (all-cash)	$90,000	$95,000	$99,000
Expenses (all-cash)...............	(60,000)	(62,000)	(63,000)
Depreciation expense			
Pretax income....................			
Income tax expense..............			
Net income			
EPS (5,000 shares)			
Balance sheets:			
Operational assets:			
Machine......................			
Accumulated depreciation......			
Book value..................			
Cash flows:			
Revenues			
Expenses			
Depreciation expense			
Income tax......................			
Net cash inflow			

Requirement b.

Complete the following summary based upon your answer to Requirement *(a):*

Items Compared	Year 1		Year 2		Year 3		Total (both methods)
	SL	CCA	SL	CCA	SL	CCA	
1. Net income							
2. Machine, book value							
3. Net cash inflow							

Requirement c.

List, and briefly explain, any generalizations that you can make about the three items summarized in Requirement *(b):* (1) net income, (2) machine book value, and (3) net cash inflow.

Requirement d.

Which method would you recommend? Explain the basis for your recommendation.
Instructional note: This problem assumes a constant income tax rate in order to focus on the different effects of SL versus CCA depreciation. Also, the time period is limited to a three-year useful life only to reduce the computational burden.

PC9–6. Erie Company owns an existing building that was constructed at an original cost of $300,000. It is being depreciated on a straight-line basis over a 20-year estimated useful life and has a $60,000 estimated residual value. At the end of 19H, the building had been depreciated for a full eight years. In January 19I, a decision was made, on the basis of new information, that a total estimated useful life of 30 years, and a residual value of $39,000 would be more realistic. The accounting period ends December 31.

Required:

a. Compute the amount of depreciation expense recorded in 19H and the book value of the building at the end of 19H.
b. Compute the amount of depreciation that should be recorded in 19I. Show computations. Give the adjusting entry for depreciation at December 31, 19I.

Part B

PC9–7. Rice Company found it necessary to make extensive repairs on its existing building and to add a new wing. The existing building originally cost $300,000; and by the end of 19J, it was half depreciated on the basis of a 20-year estimated useful life and no residual value. During 19K, the following expenditures were made that were related to the building:

1. Ordinary repairs and maintenance expenditures for the year, $9,000 cash.
2. Extensive and major repairs to the roof of the building, $20,000 cash. These repairs were completed on June 30, 19K.
3. The new wing was completed on June 30, 19K, at a cash cost of $170,000. The wing had an estimated useful life of 10 years and no residual value.

Required:

a. Give the journal entry to record each of the 19K transactions.
b. Give the adjusting entry that would be required at the end of the annual accounting period, December 31, 19K, for the building after taking into account your entries in (a) above. Assume straight-line depreciation. The company computes depreciation based on the nearest month.
c. Show how the assets would be reported on the December 31, 19K, balance sheet. (Hint: Depreciation expense for 19K is $25,000.)

PC9–8. PGI Company has five different intangible operational assets to be accounted for and reported on the financial statements. The management is concerned about the amortization of the cost of each of these intangibles. Facts concerning each intangible are:

1. Patent—The company purchased a patent at a cash cost of $26,000 on January 1, 19E. The patent had a legal life of 17 years from date of registration, which was January 1, 19A. Amortize over the remaining legal life.
2. Copyright—On January 1, 19E, the company purchased a copyright at a cash cost of $15,000. The legal life remaining from that date is 30 years. It is estimated that the copyrighted item will have little or no value by the end of 25 years.
3. Franchise—The company obtained a franchise from X Company to make and distribute a special item. The franchise was obtained on January 1, 19E, at a cash cost of $10,000 and was for a 10-year period.
4. License—On January 1, 19D, the company secured a license from the city to operate a special service for a period of five years. Total cash expended in obtaining the license was $8,000.
5. Goodwill—The company started business in January 19C by purchasing another

business for a cash lump sum of $400,000. Included in the purchase price was the item "Goodwill, $80,000." PGI executives stated that "the goodwill is an important long-term asset to us." Amortize over the maximum period permitted.

Required:

a. You have been asked to analyze each intangible and give the journal entry to record each of the five acquisitions.
b. Give the adjusting entry for each intangible asset that would be necessary at the end of the annual accounting period, December 31, 19E. Provide a brief explanation and show computations. If no entry is required for a particular item, explain the basis for your conclusion.
c. Determine the book value of each intangible on January 1, 19G. (Hint: The total book value for the five intangibles is $119,000.)

PC9–9.   On January 1, 19A, Investor Corporation was organized by five individuals for the purpose of purchasing and operating a successful business known as Kampus Korner. The name was retained, and all of the assets, except cash, were purchased for $300,000 cash. The liabilities were not assumed by Investor Corporation. The transaction was closed on January 5, 19A, at which time the balance sheet of Kampus Korner reflected the book values shown below:

KAMPUS KORNER
January 5, 19A

	Book value	*Market value**
Accounts receivable (net)...............	$ 30,000	$ 30,000
Inventory............................	180,000	175,000
Operational assets (net)...............	19,000	50,000
Other assets	1,000	5,000
Total assets	$230,000	
Liabilities...........................	$ 80,000	
Owner's equity	150,000	
Total liabilities and owners' equity	$230,000	

*These values for the assets purchased were provided to Investor Corporation by an independent appraiser.

As a part of the negotiations, the former owners of Kampus Korner agreed not to engage in the same or similar line of business in the same general region.

Required:

a. Give the journal entry by Investor Corporation to record the purchase of the assets of Kampus Korner. Include goodwill.
b. Give the adjusting journal entries that would be made by Investor Corporation at the end of the annual accounting period, December 31, 19A, for:

   (1) Depreciation of the operational assets (straight line) assuming an estimated remaining useful life of 20 years and no residual value.
   (2) Amortization of goodwill assuming the maximum amortization period is used.

PC9–10.   During 19K Wilson Company disposed of three different assets. On January 1, 19K, prior to their disposal, the accounts reflected the following:

Assets	Original cost	Residual value	Estimated life	Accumulated depreciation (straight line)
Machine A......	$20,000	$2,000	10 years	$12,600 (7 years)
Machine B	35,400	3,000	9 years	21,600 (6 years)
Machine C......	65,200	6,400	14 years	46,200 (11 years)

The machines were disposed of in the following ways:

Machine A—Sold on January 1, 19K, for $6,400 cash.

Machine B—Sold on May 1, 19K, for $13,200; received cash, $3,200, and a $10,000 interest-bearing (12 percent) note receivable due at the end of 12 months.

Machine C—On July 2, 19K, this machine suffered irreparable damage from an accident. On July 10, 19K, it was given to a salvage company at no cost. The salvage company agreed to remove the machine immediately at no cost. The machine was insured, and $18,000 cash was collected from the insurance company.

Required:

Give all journal entries incidental to the disposal of each machine assuming the fiscal year-end is December 31. Explain the accounting rationale for the way that you recorded each disposal.

PC9–11. (Note: This is a comprehensive PC to test your analytical ability.)

It is the end of the annual fiscal period, December 31, 19F, for Modern Company. The following items must be resolved before the financial statements can be prepared:

1. On January 1, 19F, a used machine was purchased for $5,000 cash. This amount was debited to an operational asset account, Machinery. Prior to use, cash was expended for (a) overhauling the machine, $600, and (b) for installation, $150; both of these amounts were debited to Expense. The machine has an estimated remaining useful life of five years and a 10 percent residual value. Straight-line depreciation will be used.

2. A small warehouse (and the land on which it is located) was purchased on January 1, 19F, at a cash cost of $40,000 which was debited to an operational asset account, Warehouse. The property was appraised for municipal tax purposes near the end of 19E as follows: warehouse, $21,250; and land, $8,250. The warehouse has an estimated remaining useful life of 10 years and a 10 percent residual value. Straight-line depreciation will be used.

3. During the year 19F, usual recurring repair costs of $1,200 were paid. During January 19F, major repairs (on the warehouse purchased in 2 above) of $1,000 were paid. Repair expense was debited $2,200, and Cash was credited.

4. On June 30, 19F, the company purchased a patent for use in the business at a cash cost of $2,040. The patent was dated July 1, 19A. The Patent account was debited.

5. On December 31, 19F, the company acquired a new truck that had a list price of $15,000 (estimated life, five years; residual value, $2,000). The company paid for the truck with cash, $7,000, and issued to the seller 600 shares of its own capital stock, par $10, and market value $12 per share.

Required:

a. Give the journal entry or entries that should be made to correct the accounts at December 31, 19F, before the adjusting entries are made. If none is required, so state.

b. Give the adjusting journal entry at December 31, 19F, after the corrections in Requirement *(a)* have been made.

PC9–12.   (Special case for discussion)   The quotation below was taken directly from *Forbes* magazine (November 22, 1982, p. 178). You are to study it carefully and identify at least two primary accounting issues. Be prepared to discuss all aspects of this article.

> One of the old standbys for financial officers when times got tough has always been to try to pick up earnings by slowing depreciation charges.
>
> Last year's Accelerated Cost Recovery System only made that easier by effectively permitting companies to depreciate plant and equipment at different rates for tax and accounting purposes. Says Ronald Murray, Coopers & Lybrand's director of accounting and SEC technical services: "Now you can have a slower book depreciation schedule, which helps financial statements, and yet still stay with fast depreciation for tax purposes, which helps cash flow."
>
> Changing depreciation schedules can make quite a difference for a company. Inland Steel, which recently slowed down its depreciation, will reduce this year's losses by $43 million, or $1.20 per share (Inland made only $57 million last year).
>
> "We realized that, compared to our competitors, our conservative method of depreciation might have hurt us with investors because of its negative impact on net earnings," comments RTE Controller Douglas Haag. Says Duane Borst, Inland Steel's comptroller: "Why should we put ourselves at a disadvantage by depreciating more conservatively than other steel companies do?"
>
> Up until recently, of course, most corporations were pushing for faster depreciation to escape the ravages of inflation. Now, by dragging out their depreciation schedules, firms may run the risk of repeating the errors of the automobile and steel industries, which found themselves hard pressed to replace assets because of years of underdepreciation.
>
> The easiest way to lower depreciation charges is to switch from accelerated depreciation to straight line, where the same sum gets written off every year.
>
> Those companies who want to lower their depreciation even further in hard times can switch to the units-of-production method, where charges are tied not to time but to production volume. In this way a plant running at 40 percent of capacity generates 60 percent lower depreciation charges. Ernst & Whinney's Denny Beresford, partner in charge of accounting standards, expects that more companies will follow the lead of Inland Steel and Asarco by switching to units-of-production depreciation.
>
> For the investor, several questions remain so far unresolved. What about the problem of technological obsolescence, for example? Any slow method of depreciation might well encourage management to keep a piece of machinery in operation long after far superior replacements become available. The risk is great with units of production, especially in slow times.
>
> Beresford raises a related issue: quality of earnings. "Some people would view a company that uses accelerated depreciation as being more conservative in its financial reporting and thus having a higher quality of earnings," he comments. IBM, for example, is still using the so-called sum-of-the-years digits method, which

raises depreciation charges dramatically in the early years of an asset's life and then slows down as time goes on. As Beresford puts it: "A company changing away from accelerated to straight line might be viewed by some people as reporting at that time lower quality earnings."

It's worth watching.

Slowdown				
Below, a look at nine companies that switched some or all depreciation schedules and the effect of earnings.				
Company	Switch	Year	Addition to net income (per share)	Earnings per share
Asarco	s.l. to u.o.p.	1980	$0.38	$8.02
Bell & Howell	acc. to s.l.	1981	0.04	3.83
Burlington Industries	acc. to s.l.	1981	0.15	3.98
Chrysler	acc. to s.l.	1981	0.52	−7.18
Cone Mills	acc. to s.l.	1981	0.10	5.87
Harsco	acc. to s.l.	1981	0.08	3.15
Inland Steel	s.l. to u.o.p.	1982	1.20	NA
McGraw-Edison	acc. to s.l.	1981	0.13	5.11
JP Stevens	acc. to s.l.	1980	0.06	1.43
Abbreviations: s.l. stands for straight line; acc. for accelerated; u.o.p. for units of production. NA Not available.				

PC9–13. Refer to the financial statements of Consolidated-Bathurst in Special Supplement B immediately preceding the Index. Respond to the following questions for 1984.

1. What amount was reported in 1984 for "accumulated depreciation"?
2. Generally what methods of depreciation were used?
3. What total amount of "depreciation" expense was reported for 1984?
4. Give your explanation of why depreciation expense was added to net income in the computation of "cash flow from operations" on the SCFP.
5. Were any deferred charges reported on the balance sheet? If deferred charges are not reported separately, what amount on the balance sheet would include them?
6. How much interest did the company capitalize?
7. What were the amounts of (a) total interest costs and (b) interest expense reflected on the income statement?
8. What segment (line of business) of the company had the highest amount of identifiable assets at year-end 1984?
9. What segment (line of business) of the company had the highest amount of "depreciation and amortization" in 1984?
10. Of the total "Identifiable assets at year-end," what percent was outside Canada in 1984?

PC9–14. (Based on Supplement 9A) Quick Manufacturing Company operates a number of machines. One particular bank of machines consists of five identical machines acquired on the same date. At the beginning of 19G the operational asset account for the five machines showed the following:

Machinery (Type A, five machines)............... $200,000
Accumulated depreciation (Type A machines)..... 108,000*
*Based on 10-year estimated useful life and $4,000 residual value per machine and straight-line depreciation.

One of the machines (Type A) was disposed of on September 1, 19G.

Required:

a. How old were the Type A machines at January 1, 19G? Show computations.
b. What was the book value of the machine at date of disposal? Show computations. The company computes depreciation to the nearest full month.
c. Give all journal entries to record the disposal of the machine under two independent assumptions:
  (1) It was sold outright for $14,000 cash.
  (2) It was exchanged for a new machine having a "quoted" price of $47,000; however, it was determined that it could be purchased for $44,000 cash. The old machine was traded in, and $30,000 was paid in cash. Assume the machines were similar. No reasonable market value was determinable for the old machine.

PC9–15. Every Friday afternoon, the audit staff of the firm of TD & Co., Chartered Accountants, meets to discuss various technical and professional client matters. These meetings are used for training, planning audits or discussing the results of audit work.

CL Ltd., a new client, was the subject of discussion at one of these meetings. Roy Gray, an audit manager with TD & Co., had made several visits to CL. During these visits, Jeff Jax, the president, had explained the operations of his company at some length. He had also described some of CL's accounting practices, including its revenue recognition policies. At this Friday afternoon meeting, Gray relayed portions of his conversations with Jax and provided background information on the company.

CL, a favourite of the investment community, is a public company with shares listed on Canadian stock exchanges. Its shares, originally issued at $4.50 five years ago, have recently been trading in the $25 to $30 range. Jeff Jax owns 65 percent of the voting shares of CL.

Five months ago, Jax approached the senior partner of TD & Co. stating that he had heard of the firm's excellent reputation and wanted the firm as auditor. Jax indicated that CL was growing quickly and that he wanted TD & Co. to handle all financial affairs for both CL and Jax personally.

Jax indicated that due to the significance of debt financing, maintaining good relations with CL's various lenders was important. He did not want any difficulties with them resulting from disputes over the financial statements. Also, Jax made it clear that he wanted to maintain the company's rising profit picture. He said it correctly portrayed the growth and innovation of the company and facilitated further expansion.

CL manufactures the hardware and develops the software for Computo, a full line of microcomputers for home and small office applications. Even though CL is faced with strong competition from the well-known products of Tandy, Apple, IBM and others, Jax expects great expansion ahead through franchising and special contracts.

CL operates five company stores in three major cities. In order to expand into more cities and increase its share of the market, CL sells store franchises. The number of franchise stores dealing exclusively in the Computo line is growing quickly. The franchisee is granted the exclusive right to the Computo name and products for a store in a specific area. CL is required to supply advice on store location, and to provide technical training, advertising and other specified franchise support activities. Each store handles only the Computo line of microcomputer products, but noncompeting lines of electronic merchandise can also be carried.

New, advanced products with good consumer acceptance are continually emerging as a result of the major expenditures on research and development during the past few years. CL's revenues were growing as the following financial statement excerpts indicate:

	Year Ended December 31, 1985	Year Ended December 31, 1984
	($000)	($000)
Sales of franchises............	$4,520	$2,459
Sales of equipment	2,896	2,270
Continuing fees	898	549
Software and other sales	3,066	1,781

Franchises are sold for a franchise price ranging from $80,000 to $150,000 depending on store location. Terms of payment include a down payment and a series of notes payable to CL with terms ranging from 5 to 10 years. The notes bear interest at rates significantly below the market rate at the time the agreement is signed. The financial arrangements are intended to help the new franchisees become established. CL recognizes the franchise price as revenue when contracts with franchisees are signed. Jax stated that the notes receivable are recorded by CL at face value to conform to generally accepted accounting principles.

Continuing fees are charged as a percentage of each franchisee's monthly sales of the Computo line. These fees are recorded on an accrual basis each month when reports are received from the franchisees. Revenue from both equipment and software sales is recognized when shipments are made from CL's plant.

In common with other growing firms, CL has a large proportion of its financing in the form of debt (is highly leveraged) and owes slightly over $10 million at an average interest rate of nearly 17 percent. A substantial part of the proceeds from this debt was used to finance research and development activities. A second major portion was used to finance two special projects. The remainder was used to finance the manufacturing assets for the Computo line.

In 1985, research costs and development costs other than interest, were close to $2 million each. CL had capitalized nearly 90 percent of the total $4 million to match these costs with the applicable future revenues. In addition, CL capitalized the interest on the debt applicable to the research and development expenditures. In Jax's opinion, all these costs would have a highly beneficial effect on CL in the future.

Jax was uncertain about what accounting policy he should use for the interest charges on debt relating to CL's two new special projects. He thought these interest charges probably should be capitalized because the benefits and revenues would flow in a future period.

One project is the design and construction by CL's engineers of a manufacturing facility for a line of video games. This project has been underway for nine months and will be completed in the next fiscal year. Production and marketing of the video games will commence immediately upon completion of the facility. The other project is the manufacturing of a large number of special-design, computerized components for Canadian Armed Forces equipment. All of the design costs and about 30 percent of the production costs will be incurred in this fiscal year. Delivery of the components will be made next year.

The interest on the debt related to the manufacturing assets for the Computo line was expensed because Jax said that it would not benefit future periods.

Considerable discussion of CL's financial and accounting affairs took place during the Friday afternoon meeting. Gray closed the meeting by summarizing the issues raised and requesting you to prepare a written report on the accounting issues. He asked you to recommend and justify the accounting policies that should be followed.

Required:

Prepare the report for Roy Gray on the accounting issues you believe are important for him to consider.

(CICA Adapted)

PC9–16. Use the information provided in Problem 9–4 and the form of the table presented therein to prepare a computer spreadsheet using any standard computer package and analyze the following questions.

Required:

a. Assume the machine has a 10-year life (500,000 units) but may be classified as a class 29 machine for income tax purposes. This would entitle Slick Corporation to a 50 percent straight-line capital cost allowance write-off up to the maximum of the capital cost of the machine.

What would be the cash flow for years 1 to 10?

b. Assume the machine can be classified as class 8, 20 percent declining balance, for income tax purposes. Assume also the machine is not replaced at the end of its life. What would be the cash flow for years 1 to 10?

c. How much cash is provided to Slick Corporation as a result of the accelerated tax write-off provided by class 29?

d. Assume the marketing department decides to adjust the sales price downward in year 6 and subsequent years by 15 percent which in turn is expected to increase the sales volume by 20 percent. To assist computations assume the costs per unit will not change as a result of the volume change and that the life of the machine is limited by its production.

What is the effect of this marketing decision on cash flows using the class 8 capital cost allowance assumption in order to compute income taxes?

10

Measuring and Reporting Liabilities

PURPOSE OF THIS CHAPTER

A business generates or receives resources from three distinct sources: *(a)* capital contributions by owners, *(b)* sale of goods and services, and *(c)* extension of credit by creditors. Creditors provide resources to the business through cash loans and by providing property, goods, and services to the entity on credit. The borrowing activities of the entity create **liabilities** that are defined as probable future sacrifices of economic benefits arising from present obligations of a particular enterprise to transfer assets or provide services to other entities in the future as a result of past transactions or events.[1]

From the point of view of the user of the financial statements, the liabilities reported on the balance sheet, and the related expense incurred from borrowing (i.e., interest expense), reported on the income statement, are often important factors in evaluating the financial performance of an entity. Usually there are a number of different kinds of liabilities and a wide range of creditors; therefore, those interested in the business necessarily must rely on the financial statements for relevant information on these important financial activities of an entity. The accounting model, coupled with the audit made by an independent accountant, provides the user with reliable evidence that all liabilities are identified, properly measured, and fully reported.

This chapter discusses the measurement and reporting problems associated with the various classifications of liabilities. Throughout this chapter, the discussions emphasize (1) identification of liabilities, (2) measurement of the amount of each liability, (3) accounting for the various types of liabilities, and (4) appropriate reporting. To accomplish this purpose, the chapter is divided into two parts:

Part A—Accounting for, and reporting, liabilities

Part B—Present value and future value concepts

This chapter includes the following supplements:

Supplement 10A—Payroll accounting

Supplement 10B—The voucher system

---

[1]FASB, *Statement of Financial Concepts No. 3,* "Elements of Financial Statements of Business Enterprises" (Stamford, Conn., December 1980). *Terminology for Accountants,* 3d ed. (Toronto, Ont.: The Canadian Institute of Chartered Accountants, 1983), p. 87, has a similar definition of a liability.

Part A—Accounting for, and Reporting, Liabilities

Although there are various ways to classify liabilities, for accounting and reporting purposes the following classifications typically are used:

1. Current liabilities:
   a. Accounts payable.
   b. Short-term notes payable.
   c. Other short-term obligations.
2. Long-term liabilities:
   a. Long-term notes payable and mortgages.
   b. Bonds payable.
   c. Other long-term obligations.

Bonds payable will be discussed in Chapter 11. Each of the other classifications will be discussed and illustrated in this chapter.

MEASURING LIABILITIES

Usually a liability involves the payment of the two distinctly different amounts; (a) the **principal** of the debt and (b) the **interest** on the principal. To illustrate, assume that you borrowed $1,000 cash on January 1, 19A, and signed a $1,000 note payable that specified 10 percent interest and a time to maturity (repayment) of one year. You would receive $1,000 cash and repay $1,100 ($1,000 principal plus $100 interest). In this situation, this liability would be measured and recorded on January 1, 19A, at its principal amount. The transaction would be recorded as follows:

January 1, 19A:

Cash..	1,000	
Note payable		1,000

Fundamentally, liabilities are measured in accordance with the **cost principle.** The amount of a liability, when initially incurred, is equivalent to the cash received when the transaction occurred. Difficulties can arise, however, when a noncash asset is received for which an obvious value is not available. Here, a value for the liability may have to be established by using the present value techniques to be discussed later in this chapter. In most cases, liabilities are measured, recorded, and reported at their **principal** amounts, which is usually the same as the face amount or maturity value. However, there are two important exceptions to the general case:

1. Noninterest-bearing notes—some notes do not specify a rate of interest but nevertheless there is **implicit** interest. To illustrate,

assume you borrow $1,000 cash on January 1, 19A, and agree to repay $1,100 in one year. You sign a $1,100 note that does not specify an interest rate (this is a noninterest-bearing note). The difference between the cash you borrow and the amount you repay ($1,100 − $1,000 = $100) is implicit interest.

2. Liabilities with a **stated** interest rate that is either higher or lower than the **going** or **market** rate for the transaction. To illustrate, the stated rate on the above note may be 6 percent and the going or market rate 10 percent. Measuring liabilities with an effective interest rate that is different than the stated interest rate requires application of present value concepts (discussed in Part B of this chapter). In most situations, the stated and effective interest rates for liabilities will be the same; in these situations, the liabilities are measured at their **principal** amounts.

CURRENT LIABILITIES

Current liabilities are defined as short-term obligations that will be paid within the **current operating cycle** of the business or within one year of the balance sheet date, whichever is the longer. This definition presumes that current liabilities will be paid with assets that are classified as current assets on the same balance sheet.[2]

An important financial relationship is the dollar difference between total current assets and total current liabilities. This difference is called **working capital.** The relationship between current assets and current liabilities also is measured as a ratio known as the current ratio (or the working capital ratio). The current ratio is computed by dividing total current assets by total current liabilities. To illustrate, assume the balance sheet for Howe Company on December 31, 19B, reported total current assets of $900,000 and total current liabilities of $300,000 The amount of working capital would be $900,000 − $300,000 = $600,000. The current ratio would be $900,000 ÷ $300,000 = 3.00, or 3 to 1. A current ratio of 3 to 1 means that, at the balance sheet date, there were $3 of current assets for each $1 of current liabilities. These relationships often assist creditors and others in assessing the ability of a company to meet its short-term obligations.[3]

Accounts payable

Trade accounts payable are created by purchases of goods for resale and services made in the normal course of business. The term **accounts payable** is used in accounting to mean **trade** accounts payable. Typical journal entries associated with creating and paying an account payable are:

[2]Current assets and current liabilities were defined and discussed in Chapter 2. Current assets are defined as cash and other resources reasonably expected to be realized in cash or sold or consumed within one year from the date of the balance sheet or during the **normal operating cycle,** whichever is the longer.

[3]Interpretation of financial ratios is discussed in Chapter 16.

March 6, 19B (purchase on credit, periodic inventory system):

```
Purchases.......................................................  980
     Accounts payable.............................................         980
     Purchase of merchandise on credit; terms, 2/10, n/30. (Invoice price,
     $1,000 × .98 = $980.)
```

March 11, 19B (payment of liability):[4]

```
Accounts payable................................................  980
     Cash .......................................................         980
     Payment of account payable within the discount period.
```

Accrued expenses

Accrued expenses (also called accrued liabilities) arise when there are expenses that have been incurred but have not yet been paid or recorded at the end of the accounting period. These liabilities are recorded as adjusting entries. To illustrate a typical accrued expense, assume that on December 31, 19B, the annual amount of property taxes for 19B was determined to be $1,600, which had not been paid or recorded. At the end of the accounting period, December 31, 19B, the expense and related liability must be recorded and reported, although the amount will not be paid until January 15, 19C.[5] Therefore, the following **adjusting entry** must be made:

December 31, 19B (adjusting entry):

```
Property tax expense .............................................  1,600
     Property taxes payable........................................          1,600
     Adjusting entry to record property taxes incurred in 19B yet not
     recorded or paid.
```

---

[4]In case of payment after the discount period, the entry would be:

```
Accounts payable...................................................  980
Purchase discounts lost (or Interest expense) ...........................   20
     Cash ........................................................         1,000
```

[5]If these taxes already had **been paid** (i.e., Expense debited and Cash credited), there would be no accrued liability to record at year-end. Similarly, if these taxes already had been recorded but not paid (i.e., Expense debited and Taxes Payable credited), there would be no need to make an adjusting entry at year-end.

The entry in 19C for payment of the above liability would be:

January 15, 19C:

Property taxes payable...	1,600	
Cash...		1,600
Payment of liability for property taxes accrued in 19B.		

Payroll liabilities

When employees perform services, the employer incurs an obligation that is not satisfied until the employees are paid on a weekly or monthly payroll basis. In previous chapters, accounting for wage and salary expense was simplified by disregarding payroll taxes and payroll deductions; we will now discuss these additional complications.

In addition to the obligation to the employee for salary or wages, the employer incurs other liabilities that are related directly to the payment of salaries and wages. These additional liabilities usually arise as a result of federal and provincial laws, and contractual obligations (such as pension plans and union dues). Some of these liabilities are paid by the **employees** through the employer (as payroll deductions); others must be paid by the **employer** and thus are additional expenses to the business.

The take-home pay of most employees is considerably less than the gross salary or wages because of **payroll deductions** for such items as employee income taxes withheld, Canada Pension Plan (CPP) that must be paid by the employee, and other employee deductions such as insurance and union dues. The employer is required to pay the amounts, deducted from the wages, to the designated governmental agencies and other organizations such as the union. From the date of the payroll deduction until the date of payment to the agencies or organizations, the employer must record and report the **current liabilities** that are owed to the designated taxing agencies and other parties. A typical journal entry for a $100,000 payroll would be as follows:

January 31, 19B:

```
Salaries expense ...............................................    60,000
Wages expense ................................................    40,000
    Liability for income taxes withheld—employees...............              21,000
    Liability for union dues withheld—employees ................                 400
    Unemployment insurance withheld...........................               2,350
    CPP contributions withheld .................................               1,455
    Cash (take-home pay) .......................................              74,795
To record the payroll including employee deductions (see
Supplement 10A).
```

In addition to the payroll taxes that the **employees** must pay through the employer, the **employer** is required by law to pay additional specified payroll taxes, such as the employer's share of the Canada Pension Plan and Unemployment Insurance (UI). These taxes constitute an operating expense for the business. Therefore, a second entry related to the payroll is needed to record the payroll taxes to be paid by the employer. A typical entry, related to the above payroll, would be as follows:

January 31, 19B:

```
Payroll tax and benefits expense ..................................    5,545*
    Unemployment insurance payable (2,350 × 1.4)................               3,290
    Canada Pension Plan payable ..............................               1,455
    Workmen's compensation payable ..........................                 800
Employer payroll taxes for January payroll.
    *Total payroll expense: $100,000 + $5,545 = $105,545.
```

The six current liabilities recorded in the two entries immediately above will be paid in the near future when the company remits the requisite amounts of cash to the appropriate taxing agencies and other parties. Details involved in payroll accounting are discussed and illustrated in Supplement 10A to this chapter. Payroll accounting does not entail any new accounting concepts or principles; however, a significant amount of clerical detail is involved.

Deferred revenues

Deferred revenues (frequently called unearned revenues or revenues collected in advance) arise when revenues are collected during the current period that will not be earned until a later accounting period (see Chapter 4).

Deferred revenues create a liability because cash has been collected but the related revenue has not been earned by the end of the accounting period; therefore, there is a **current obligation** to render the services or to provide the goods in the future. To illustrate, assume that on November 15, 19B, rent revenue collected amounted to $6,000, which was recorded as a debit to Cash and a credit to Rent Revenue. Assume further that at the end of 19B it was determined that $2,000 of this amount was for January 19C rent. Thus, there is a current liability of $2,000 for deferred rent revenue that must be recognized. The sequence of entries for this situation would be as follows:

November 15, 19B (collection of rent revenue):

Cash...	6,000	
Rent revenue		6,000
Collection of rent revenue.[6]		

December 31, 19B (adjusting entry for unearned rent revenue):

Rent revenue	2,000	
Rent revenue collected in advance (deferred revenue)		2,000
Adjusting entry to record unearned rent revenue at the end of the accounting period.		

LONG-TERM LIABILITIES

Long-term liabilities encompass all obligations of the entity not properly classified as current liabilities. Long-term liabilities often are incurred in conjunction with the purchase of operational assets or the borrowing of large amounts of cash for asset replacements and major expansions of the business. Long-term liabilities usually are represented by long-term notes payable or bonds payable. A long-term liability often is supported by a mortgage on specified assets of the borrower **pledged** as security for the liability. A mortgage involves a separate document that is appended to the note payable. A liability supported by a mortgage is said to be a "**secured** debt." An **unsecured** debt is one for which the creditor relies primarily on the integrity and general earning power of the borrower.

Long-term liabilities are reported on the balance sheet under a separate caption below "Current liabilities." As a long-term debt approaches the maturity

---

[6]On November 15, 19B, the credit could have been made to Rent Revenue Collected in Advance, in which case the adjusting entry to give the same results on December 31, 19B, would be

Rent revenue collected in advance..	4,000	
Rent revenue		4,000

date, the portion of it that is to be paid in the next current period is reclassified as a current liability. To illustrate, assume a five-year note payable of $50,000 was signed on January 1, 19A. Repayment is to be in two installments as follows: December 31, 19D, $25,000; and December 31, 19E, $25,000. The December 31, 19B, 19C, and 19D balance sheets would report the following:

```
December 31, 19B:
  Long-term liabilities:
    Note payable ..........................     $50,000
December 31, 19C:
  Current liabilities:
    Maturing portion of long-term note ......    25,000
  Long-term liabilities:
    Long-term note ........................      25,000
December 31, 19D:
  Current liabilities:
    Maturing portion of long-term note ......    25,000
```

Notes payable may be either short term or long term. A short-term note payable usually has a maturity date within one year from the balance sheet date and often arises as a result of borrowing cash or from purchasing merchandise or services on credit. Bonds payable (see Chapter 11) always are long-term liabilities, except for any currently maturing portion as illustrated above for the long-term note payable.

Notes payable   A note payable (short or long term) is a written promise to pay a stated sum at one or more specified dates in the future. A note payable may require a single-sum repayment at the due or maturity date or it may call for installment payments (known as an annuity). To illustrate installment payments, consider the purchase of a sailboat for $3,000, with a $1,000 cash down payment and a note payable for the balance which specifies 12 equal monthly payments that include principal and interest.

Notes payable require the payment of interest and, hence, the recording of interest expense. Interest expense is incurred on liabilities because of the **time value of money.** The word **time** is significant because the longer borrowed money is held, the larger the total dollar amount of interest expense. Thus, one must pay more interest for a two-year loan of a given amount, at a given **interest rate,** than for a one-year loan. To the borrower, interest is an **expense;** whereas to the lender (creditor), interest is a **revenue.** In calculating interest, three variables must be considered: (1) the principal, (2) the interest rate, and (3) the duration of time. Therefore the interest formula is:

$$\text{Interest} = \text{Principal} \times \text{Rate} \times \text{Time}$$

To illustrate, assume $10,000 cash was borrowed by Baker Company on November 1, 19A, and a six-month, 12 percent, interest-bearing note payable was given. The interest is payable at the due date of the note. The computation of interest expense would be: $10,000 \times .12 \times 6/12 = \$600$. This note would be recorded in the accounts as follows:

November 1, 19A:

```
Cash...........................................................  10,000
    Note payable, short term ...................................              10,000
    Borrowed on short-term note; terms, six months at 12 percent per
    annum; interest is payable at maturity.
```

Interest is an expense of the period when the money is used (unpaid); therefore it is measured, recorded, and reported on a **time basis** rather than when the cash actually is paid or borrowed. This concept is based on legal as well as on economic considerations. For example, were the $10,000 loan cited above to be paid off in two months instead of in six months, interest amounting to $10,000 \times .12 \times 2/12 = \$200$ would have to be paid.

The **adjusting entry** for accrued interest payable would be made at the end of the accounting period on the basis of time expired from the last interest date or from the date of the note. To illustrate, assume the accounting period ends December 31, 19A. Although the $600 interest for the six months will not be paid until April 30, 19B, two months' unpaid interest (i.e., November and December 19A) must be accrued by means of the following adjusting entry by Baker Company:

December 31, 19B:

```
Interest expense ..................................................  200
    Interest payable ...............................................              200
    Adjusting entry to accrue two months' interest ($10,000 × .12 × 2/12 =
    $200).
```

At maturity date the payment of principal plus interest for six months would be recorded as follows:[7]

April 30, 19C:

---

[7]This journal entry assumes no reversing entry was made on January 1, 19C. (See Supplement 5A.) If a reversing entry of the accrual had been made on January 1, 19C, the payment entry would have been:

```
Note payable, short term.........................................  10,000
Interest expense .................................................     600
    Cash ........................................................              10,600
```

```
        Note payable, short term ........................................  10,000
        Interest payable (per prior entry) ..............................     200
        Interest expense ($10,000 × .12 × 4/12).........................     400
            Cash ($10,000 + $600 interest) .............................            10,600
        To record payment of note payable including interest.
```

Accounting for a note payable is the same whether it is classified as a current or as a long-term liability. Accounting for a note payable also is the same regardless of the purpose for which the note was executed.

Lease liabilities   Leases are classified for accounting purposes as operating leases and capital leases.

1. **Operating lease**—a lease in which the owner (called the lessor), for a stated rental, grants the user (called the lessee) the right to use property under specified conditions. The lessor is responsible for the cost of ownership (such as taxes, insurance, and major maintenance), and the lessee pays a monthly rental (and usually the utilities). The lease of an automobile on a daily basis and office space on a monthly basis are typical of operating leases. When the monthly rent is paid, the lessor records rent revenue and the lessee records rent expense. Any unpaid rentals constitute a current liability.

2. **Capital lease**—a lease contract in which the lessor transfers most of the **risks and rewards of ownership** to the lessee during the lease term. Thus, the lessee assumes most of the costs of ownership (such as taxes, insurance, and maintenance) and, in addition, pays a periodic rental. For accounting purposes this type of lease is viewed as a **sale** of the leased property by the lessor and a **purchase** of it by the lessee. Therefore, when a capital lease is signed, the lessor records a sale of the property (on the installment basis) and the lessee records a purchase of it that involves recognition of a long-term liability. Accounting for capital leases requires the use of present value concepts (discussed in Part B of this chapter).

Deferred income tax   Throughout the preceding chapters, we discussed and illustrated income taxes paid by corporations. In those illustrations, income tax expense was reflected on the income statement and income tax payable was reflected as a liability on the balance sheet. In addition to income tax payable, most corporate balance sheets report another tax item called **deferred income tax.**

The concept of deferred income tax is that **income tax expense** should be based on the **taxable** income reported on the income statement, while **income** tax payable necessarily must be based on the taxable income per the tax return (i.e., as specified in the tax laws). Often there is a difference between the time when certain revenues or expenses (which affect income taxes) appear on the income statement and when they appear on the tax return. Thus, a deferred income tax amount will result whenever there is a timing difference between when a taxable revenue or tax deductible expense appears on the income statement and when it appears on the tax return. Deferred taxes are created only by timing differences; therefore, deferred taxes will always "reverse" or "turn-around." To illustrate a deferred tax reversal, consider a $10,000 taxable revenue that is reported on the 19A income statement but not on the 19A tax return. This timing difference will result in the recording of a deferred tax credit in 19A. In 19B, when the $10,000 taxable revenue is reported on the tax return (but not on the income statement), the deferred tax amount is reduced to zero (i.e., it "reverses"). In a similar manner, when a tax deductible expense is on the income statement and the tax return in different periods, a timing difference must be accounted for. Accounting for deferred income taxes is illustrated in Exhibit 10–1.

Observe in Exhibit 10–1 that income tax expense for Web Corporation (on the income statement) does not agree with income tax payable on the balance sheet in years 19A and 19C. However, the totals for the three years agree ($27,000).

The difference between "Income tax expense" on the income statement and "Income tax payable" on the balance sheet in Exhibit 10–1 was due to a single expense—depreciation. Web Corporation purchased a depreciable asset at the beginning of 19A that cost $12,000 and had a useful life of three years with no residual value. The company used straight-line depreciation in its accounts (and on its income statement) and capital cost allowance on its tax return. This timing difference caused a difference between income tax expense and income tax payable as shown in Exhibit 10–1.

Deferred income tax is recorded when a difference exists between income tax expense and income tax payable. Web Corporation would record deferred tax each year as shown in Exhibit 10–1.

The $300 deferred income tax amount for 19A would be classified as an asset on the balance sheet, the $300 cumulative deferred income tax for 19B would be classified as a liability, and no deferred income tax would be reported in 19C. This effect occurred because the disadvantage (of capital cost allowance being $1,000 less than depreciation) in 19A was reversed in 19B when the capital cost allowance became $2,000 greater than the depreciation expense. The cumulative net balance of $300 credit in 19B was again reversed in 19C. Recall that regardless of the method of depreciation used, only the cost of the asset (less any residual value) can be depreciated for accounting purposes ($12,000 in the example above). Also, this illustration demonstrates what has been noted before—the potential economic advantage of capital cost allowance over straight-line depreciation is only the time value of money. That is, the tax savings resulting from using capital cost allowance in early years can be invested to earn a certain return during 19C.

EXHIBIT 10–1   **Deferred income taxes illustrated**

Situation—Web Corporation:

a.   Depreciation—Straight-line depreciation on income statement and capital cost allowance on income tax return:

	19A	19B	19C
Income statement:			
Income before depreciation expense			
and before income tax expense	$34,000	$34,000	$34,000
Depreciation expense	4,000	4,000	4,000
Pretax income	30,000	30,000	30,000
Income tax expense (30%)	9,000	9,000	9,000
Net income	$21,000	$21,000	$21,000
Balance sheet (December 31);			
Liability:			
Income tax payable	$ 9,300	$ 8,400	$ 9,300
Deferred income tax		300Dr*	300Cr*

*Cumulative balance (as a deferred charge or deferred credit).

Computation of income tax and income tax payable as reported above:

a.   Depreciation expense computed:

Year	Straight-line depreciation (for income statement)	Capital cost allowance class 29 (for tax purposes)
19A	$4,000	$3,000
19B	4,000	6,000
19C	4,000	3,000

b.   Computation of tax **expense** as reported on the income statement:

	19A	19B	19C
Income before depreciation expense and before income tax expense	$34,000	$34,000	$34,000
Less: Depreciation expense (straight line)	4,000	4,000	4,000
Amount subject to tax	30,000	30,000	30,000
Income tax expense (30%)	$ 9,000	$ 9,000	$ 9,000 ←

c.   Computation of income tax **payable** as reported on the tax return:

Compare these amounts*

	19A	19B	19C
Income before depreciation expense and before income taxes	$34,000	$34,000	$34,000
Less: Capital cost allowance	3,000	6,000	3,000
Amount subject to tax	31,000	28,000	31,000
Income tax **payable** (30%)	$ 9,300	$ 8,400	$ 9,300 ←

Entries to record income taxes:

	19A		19B		19C	
Income tax expense (from income statement)	9,000		9,000		9,000	
Income tax payable (from tax return)		9,300		8,400		9,300
Deferred income tax (the difference)	300			600	300	

Deferred tax amounts often are very large. For example, Consolidated-Bathurst recently reported a deferred income tax balance of $215,211,000 which represented 27 percent of their total liabilities.

It is possible to have a debit balance in deferred income taxes, but such a situation is not typical because the tax law usually does not require "early" tax payments. If the deferred income tax account has a debit balance, it would be reported under assets on the balance sheet as a prepaid expense (if short term) or deferred charge (if long term).

Section 3470 of the *CICA Handbook* on "Corporate Income Taxes," specifies that deferred income tax shall be recorded **only** when there is a timing difference between the income statement and the tax return. A timing difference occurs only when an item of revenue or expense will be included on **both** the income statement and the tax return in different years so that the deferred tax effect automatically will reverse (as illustrated in Exhibit 10–1). Another type of difference between the income statement and tax return amounts is called a **permanent difference.** A permanent difference does not create deferred income tax because the revenue or expense appears on either the income statement or the tax return, but not both. For example, part of capital gains which is not taxed is included on the income statement of the recipient, but is not reported on the recipient's federal income tax return as income for tax purposes.

On the balance sheet, the total amount of deferred income tax must be reported in part in the current liability (or asset) section and in part in the long-term liability (or asset) section depending upon the classification of the specific asset that gave rise to the deferred tax amount. Thus, the deferred income tax amount for Web Corporation would be classified as noncurrent because it was related to a noncurrent asset.

This discussion of deferred income taxes was presented so that you will understand the nature of deferred income tax reported on the balance sheets of most medium and large corporations. Income tax payable (as a liability) is easy to comprehend; however, many statement users have difficulty understanding the other tax item—deferred income tax.

The conceptual nature of deferred taxes is a complex matter that has been debated for years among practitioners and academics. The justification for deferred taxes in the professional pronouncements is the need to match income tax expense with the accounting income that was earned in a fiscal period. The conceptual difficulty is that the resulting balance sheet deferred tax debits and credits cannot be easily justified as assets or liabilities. The result of this difficulty is to have deferred charges or credits that are classified as assets or liabilities yet do not satisfy the criteria of an asset or a liability such as the ones set out in Exhibit 2–6.

CONTINGENT LIABILITIES

A contingent liability is defined as a potential liability that has arisen as a result of an event or transaction that **already has occurred,** but its conversion to an effective liability is dependent upon the occurrence of one or more **future events or transactions** (i.e., a future contingency). To illustrate, assume that in 19B Baker Company was sued for $100,000 damages arising from an accident involving one of the trucks owned by the company. The suit is scheduled for trial during March 19C. Whether an effective liability is created will depend upon the decision of the court at the termination of the trial. When financial statements are prepared at December 31, 19B, a contingent liability must be disclosed. Because of the accident, the company is contingently liable for the payment of damages.

A contingent liability is **not** recorded in the accounts unless a loss is probable. Rather, it is reported in a note to the financial statements. For example, the contingent future liability arising from the Baker Company lawsuit may be disclosed by a note to the 19B balance sheet similar to the following:

> The company is contingently liable for $100,000 because of a lawsuit based on an accident involving a company vehicle. Legal counsel believes that the suit is lacking in merit. Trial is scheduled for March 19C.

CONTROLLING EXPENDITURES

The purchase of merchandise, services, and operational assets often requires that either a short-term or long-term liability be recorded. As a consequence, a large number of cash payments on liabilities typically are made in a business. In most companies, control over cash expenditures is essential to prevent the misapplication of cash in the cash-disbursement process. In a very small business it is often possible for the owner to give personal attention to each transaction when it is incurred and to make each cash payment. This personal attention may assure that the business is getting what it pays for, that cash is not being disbursed carelessly, and that there is no theft or fraud involving cash.

As a business grows and becomes more complex, the owner or top executive cannot devote personal attention to each transaction involving the processing of cash disbursements. In such situations these activities must be assigned to various employees. The assignment of these responsibilities to others creates a need for systematic and effective procedures for the control of cash expenditures. This is an important facet of the internal control of a well-designed accounting system.

In Chapter 8, the essential features of effective **internal control** were discussed, with emphasis on the control of cash receipts. Similar internal control procedures were discussed in respect to cash disbursements: the separation of duties, disbursement of cash by cheque, petty cash, and the two special journals—the purchases journal and the cash disbursements journal. In larger companies and in computerized accounting systems, the method usually used for maintaining control over cash expenditures is known as the **voucher system.** This system replaces the cash disbursements journal procedures that were explained in Supplement 8B.

The voucher system

The voucher system is designed to establish strict control over transactions that create a legal obligation to make an expenditure of cash. The system requires that a **written authorization,** called a **voucher,** be approved by one or more designated managers at the time each such transaction occurs. An approved voucher is required regardless of whether the transaction involves the purchase of merchandise or services, the acquisition of operational assets, the payment of a liability, or an investment. The system permits cheques to be issued only in payment of properly prepared and approved vouchers. Cheque writing is kept completely separate from the voucher-approval, cheque-approval, and cheque-distribution procedures.

The voucher system requires that every obligation be supported by a previously approved voucher and that each transaction be recorded when incurred. The incurrence of each obligation is treated as an independent transaction, and each payment of cash is treated as another independent transaction. This sequence of voucher approval, followed by payment by cheque, is required even in strictly cash-disbursement transactions. To illustrate, the **cash** purchase of merchandise for resale would be recorded under the voucher system as follows:

1. To record the incurrence of an obligation (with a periodic inventory system):

Purchases	1,000	
Vouchers payable		1,000

2. To record payment of the obligation by cheque (immediately thereafter):

Vouchers payable	1,000	
Cash		1,000

In a voucher system, the account designated **Vouchers Payable** replaces the account entitled Accounts Payable; but "Accounts payable," as the designation on the balance sheet, continues to be used.

The primary objective of the voucher system is to attain continuous control over each step in an expenditure from the incurrence of an obligation to the final disbursement of cash to satisfy the obligation. Thus, every single transaction leading to a cash payment, and the cash payment itself, is reviewed systematically, then subjected to an approval system based on separately designated responsibilities. Supplement 10B discusses and illustrates the **mechanics** of the voucher system.

Part B—Present Value and Future Value Concepts

CALCULATION OF PRESENT VALUE AND FUTURE VALUE AMOUNTS

The measuring and reporting of liabilities, when they are first recorded in the accounts and during the periods they are outstanding, often involve application of the concepts of present value and future value. These concepts also are used in measuring the effects of long-term investments in bonds, leases, pension plans, and sinking funds. Most of these applications in accounting involve either measurement of a liability or a receivable, or the establishment of a fund of cash to be used in the future for some special purpose (such as the retirement of debt).

The concepts of present value and future value focus on the time value of money, which is another name for interest. The time value of money refers to the fact that a dollar received today is worth more than a dollar to be received one year from today (or at any other later date) because a dollar received today can be invested say at 10 percent, so that it grows to $1.10 in one year. In contrast, if the dollar is to be received one year from today, one is denied the opportunity to earn the $.10 interest revenue for the year. The difference between the $1 and $1.10 is due to interest that can be earned during the year. Interest is the cost of the use of money for a specific period of time, just as rent represents the cost for use of a tangible asset for a period of time. Interest may be specified (i.e., stated explicitly), as in the case of an interest-bearing note, or it may be unspecified, as in a noninterest-bearing note (but interest is paid nonetheless; i.e., it is implicitly there).

To illustrate the application of the time value of money, assume a machine is purchased for $20,000. The purchaser is allowed to pay the $20,000 at the end of two years, and there is an implied interest rate of 12 percent (which is the market rate of interest). The $20,000 to be paid represents the current cash equivalent amount of the debt **plus** the interest that will be paid during the two years. Under the cost principle, the machine account should be debited for the present value (current cash equivalent) of the debt, or $15,944.

There are four different types of problems related to the time value of money; they are identified in Exhibit 10–2. Each type of problem is based on the interest formula that was discussed in Part A of this chapter, viz:

$$\text{Interest} = \text{Principal} \times \text{Rate} \times \text{Time}$$

In **future value** problems, you will be given the amount of cash (principal) to be invested and you will be asked to use the basic interest formula to calculate the amount of principal plus interest that will be available at some future date. In contrast, **present value** problems involve a simple rearrangement of the basic interest formula. In present value problems, you will be given the amount that will be available at some future date (principal plus interest) and you will be asked to calculate the current cash equivalent of that amount.

Tables have been developed to avoid the detailed arithmetic calculations that are required in present value and future value computations. These tables pro-

EXHIBIT 10–2
Symbols representing the four types of present value and future value problems

	Symbol	
Payment or Receipt	*Present value*	*Future value*
Single amount	*p*	*f*
Annuity (equal payments or receipts for a series of equal time periods)	*P*	*F*

vide values for each of the four types of problems for different periods of time (*n*) and at different rates of interest (*i*). The values given in the tables are based on payments of $1, so if a problem involves payments other than $1, it is necessary to multiply the value from the table by the amount of the payment.[8] To illustrate these concepts, we will examine each of the four types of present value and future value problems.

Future value of a single amount (f)

The future value is the sum to which an amount will increase at *i* interest rate for *n* periods. The future sum will be the **principal plus compound interest.** The future value concept is based upon compound interest so that the amount of interest for each period is calculated by multiplying the interest rate by the principal plus any interest that accrued in prior years but was not paid out.

To illustrate, assume that on January 1, 19A, $1,000 was deposited in a savings account at 10 percent annual interest, compounded annually. At the end of three years, that is, on December 31, 19C, the $1,000 that was deposited would increase to $1,331 as follows:

	Amount at start of year	+	*Interest during the year*	=	*Amount at end of year*
Year 1	$1,000	+	$1,000 × .10 = $100	=	$1,100
Year 2	1,100	+	1,100 × .10 = 110	=	1,210
Year 3	1,210	+	1,210 × .10 = 121	=	1,331

However, we can avoid the detailed arithmetic by referring to Table 10–1, **Future value of $1.** For *i* = 10 percent, *n* = 3, we find the value 1.331; therefore, we can compute the balance at the end of Year 3 as $1,000 × 1.331 = $1,331. The increase of $331 was due to the time value of money; it would be interest revenue to you and interest expense to the savings institution. With any positive interest rate, the future value of $1 always will be greater than $1. Exhibit 10–3 presents a summary of this future value concept.

---

[8]Present value and future value problems assume cash flows. The basic concepts are the same for cash inflows (receipts) and cash outflows (payments). Thus, there are no fundamental differences between present value and future value calculations for cash payments versus cash receipts.

EXHIBIT 10–3
Time value of money determinations

Table No.	Designation	Definition and graphic representation	Table formula
10–1	Future value of $1 (f) $n = 3$ $i = 10\%$	The future value of $1 at the end of n periods at i compound interest rate. This is simply the principal plus compound interest.	$(1 + i)^n$

Present time

$1   1   2   3   Future value of $1 $1.33

| 10–2 | Present value of $1 (p) $n = 3$ $i = 10\%$ | The present value (now) of $1 due n periods hence, discounted at i compound interest rate. This is simply a future amount with compound discount subtracted from it. | $\dfrac{1}{(1 + n)^n}$ |

Present value of $1

$.75   1   2   3   Future principal $1

| 10–3 | Future value of annuity of $1 (F) $n = 3$ $i = 10\%$ | The future value of n periodic contributions (i.e., rents) of $1 each plus accumulated compound interest at i rate. The first rent is at the end of the current period and the future value is on the date of the last rent. | $\dfrac{(1 + i)^n - 1}{i}$ |

Present time   Future value of n rents of $1 each

1   2   3 $1 $1 $1 $3.31

| 10–4 | Present value of annuity of $1* (P) $n = 3$ $i = 10\%$ | The present value (now) of n periodic rents of $1 each to be received (or paid) each period, discounted at i compound discount rate per period. The first rent is at the end of the first period. | $\dfrac{1 - \dfrac{1}{(1 + i)^n}}{i}$ |

Present value of n rents of $1   Future time

1   2   3 $1 $1 $1

$2.49

*Observe that these are **ordinary** annuities; that is, they are often called end-of-period annuities. Thus, for F, the future amount is on the date of the last rent; and for P, the present value is at the beginning of the period of the first rent. Annuities **due** assume the opposite; that is, they are "beginning-of-period" annuities. Ordinary annuity values can be converted to annuities due simply by multiplication of $(1 + i)$. Annuities due are discussed at the next level of accounting sophistication, intermediate accounting.

TABLE 10–1
Future value of $1,
$f = (1 + i)^n$

Periods	2%	3%	3.75%	4%	4.25%	5%	6%	7%	8%
0	1.	1.	1.	1.	1.	1.	1.	1.	1.
1	1.02	1.03	1.0375	1.04	1.0425	1.05	1.06	1.07	1.08
2	1.0404	1.0609	1.0764	1.0816	1.0868	1.1025	1.1236	1.1449	1.1664
3	1.0612	1.0927	1.1168	1.1249	1.1330	1.1576	1.1910	1.2250	1.2597
4	1.0824	1.1255	1.1587	1.1699	1.1811	1.2155	1.2625	1.3108	1.3605
5	1.1041	1.1593	1.2021	1.2167	1.2313	1.2763	1.3382	1.4026	1.4693
6	1.1262	1.1941	1.2472	1.2653	1.2837	1.3401	1.4185	1.5007	1.5869
7	1.1487	1.2299	1.2939	1.3159	1.3382	1.4071	1.5036	1.6058	1.7138
8	1.1717	1.2668	1.3425	1.3686	1.3951	1.4775	1.5938	1.7182	1.8509
9	1.1951	1.3048	1.3928	1.4233	1.4544	1.5513	1.6895	1.8385	1.9990
10	1.2190	1.3439	1.4450	1.4802	1.5162	1.6289	1.7908	1.9672	2.1589
20	1.4859	1.8061	2.0882	2.1911	2.2989	2.6533	3.2071	3.8697	4.6610

Periods	9%	10%	11%	12%	13%	14%	15%	20%	25%
0	1.	1.	1.	1.	1.	1.	1.	1.	1.
1	1.09	1.10	1.11	1.12	1.13	1.14	1.15	1.20	1.25
2	1.1881	1.2100	1.2321	1.2544	1.2769	1.2996	1.3225	1.4400	1.5625
3	1.2950	1.3310	1.3676	1.4049	1.4429	1.4815	1.5209	1.7280	1.9531
4	1.4116	1.4641	1.5181	1.5735	1.6305	1.6890	1.7490	2.0736	2.4414
5	1.5386	1.6105	1.6851	1.7623	1.8424	1.9254	2.0114	2.4883	3.0518
6	1.6771	1.7716	1.8704	1.9738	2.0820	2.1950	2.3131	2.9860	3.8147
7	1.8280	1.9487	2.0762	2.2107	2.3526	2.5023	2.6600	3.5832	4.7684
8	1.9926	2.1436	2.3045	2.4760	2.6584	2.8526	3.0590	4.2998	5.9605
9	2.1719	2.3579	2.5580	2.7731	3.0040	3.2519	3.5179	5.1598	7.4506
10	2.3674	2.5937	2.8394	3.1058	3.3946	3.7072	4.0456	6.1917	9.3132
20	5.6044	6.7275	8.0623	9.6463	11.5231	13.7435	16.3665	38.3376	86.7362

TABLE 10–2
Present value of $1,
$$p = \frac{1}{(1 + i)^n}$$

Periods	2%	3%	3.75%	4%	4.25%	5%	6%	7%	8%
1	0.9804	0.9709	0.9639	0.9615	0.9592	0.9524	0.9434	0.9346	0.9259
2	0.9612	0.9426	0.9290	0.9246	0.9201	0.9070	0.8900	0.8734	0.8573
3	0.9423	0.9151	0.8954	0.8890	0.8826	0.8638	0.8396	0.8163	0.7938
4	0.9238	0.8885	0.8631	0.8548	0.8466	0.8227	0.7921	0.7629	0.7350
5	0.9057	0.8626	0.8319	0.8219	0.8121	0.7835	0.7473	0.7130	0.6806
6	0.8880	0.8375	0.8018	0.7903	0.7790	0.7462	0.7050	0.6663	0.6302
7	0.8706	0.8131	0.7728	0.7599	0.7473	0.7107	0.6651	0.6227	0.5835
8	0.8535	0.7894	0.7449	0.7307	0.7168	0.6768	0.6274	0.5820	0.5403
9	0.8368	0.7664	0.7180	0.7026	0.6876	0.6446	0.5919	0.5439	0.5002
10	0.8203	0.7441	0.6920	0.6756	0.6595	0.6139	0.5584	0.5083	0.4632
20	0.6730	0.5534	0.4789	0.4564	0.4350	0.3769	0.3118	0.2584	0.2145

Periods	9%	10%	11%	12%	13%	14%	15%	20%	25%
1	0.9174	0.9091	0.9009	0.8929	0.8850	0.8772	0.8696	0.8333	0.8000
2	0.8417	0.8264	0.8116	0.7972	0.7831	0.7695	0.7561	0.6944	0.6400
3	0.7722	0.7513	0.7312	0.7118	0.6931	0.6750	0.6575	0.5787	0.5120
4	0.7084	0.6830	0.6587	0.6355	0.6133	0.5921	0.5718	0.4823	0.4096
5	0.6499	0.6209	0.5935	0.5674	0.5428	0.5194	0.4972	0.4019	0.3277
6	0.5963	0.5645	0.5346	0.5066	0.4803	0.4556	0.4323	0.3349	0.2621
7	0.5470	0.5132	0.4817	0.4523	0.4251	0.3996	0.3759	0.2791	0.2097
8	0.5019	0.4665	0.4339	0.4039	0.3762	0.3506	0.3269	0.2326	0.1678
9	0.4604	0.4241	0.3909	0.3606	0.3329	0.3075	0.2843	0.1938	0.1342
10	0.4224	0.3855	0.3522	0.3220	0.2946	0.2697	0.2472	0.1615	0.1074
20	0.1784	0.1486	0.1240	0.1037	0.0868	0.0728	0.0611	0.0261	0.0115

Table 10–3
Future value of annuity of $1 (ordinary),
$$F = \frac{(1 + i)^n - 1}{i}$$

Period rents*	2 %	3 %	3.75 %	4 %	4.25 %	5 %	6 %	7 %	8 %
1	1.	1.	1.	1.	1.	1.	1.	1.	1.
2	2.02	2.03	2.0375	2.04	2.0425	2.05	2.06	2.07	2.08
3	3.0604	3.0909	3.1139	3.1216	3.1293	3.1525	3.1836	3.2149	3.2464
4	4.1216	4.1836	4.2307	4.2465	4.2623	4.3101	4.3746	4.4399	4.5061
5	5.2040	5.3091	5.3893	5.4163	5.4434	5.5256	5.6371	5.7507	5.8666
6	6.3081	6.4684	6.5914	6.6330	6.6748	6.8019	6.9753	7.1533	7.3359
7	7.4343	7.6625	7.8386	7.8983	7.9585	8.1420	8.3938	8.6540	8.9228
8	8.5830	8.8923	9.1326	9.2142	9.2967	9.5491	9.8975	10.2598	10.6366
9	9.7546	10.1591	10.4750	10.5828	10.6918	11.0266	11.4913	11.9780	12.4876
10	10.9497	11.4639	11.8678	12.0061	12.1462	12.5779	13.1808	13.8164	14.4866
20	24.2974	26.8704	29.0174	29.7781	30.5625	33.0660	36.7856	40.9955	45.7620

Period rents*	9 %	10 %	11 %	12 %	13 %	14 %	15 %	20 %	25 %
1	1.	1.	1.	1.	1.	1.	1.	1.	1.
2	2.09	2.10	2.11	2.12	2.13	2.14	2.15	2.20	2.25
3	3.2781	3.3100	3.3421	3.3744	3.4069	3.4396	3.4725	3.6400	3.8125
4	4.5731	4.6410	4.7097	4.7793	4.8498	4.9211	4.9934	5.3680	5.7656
5	5.9847	6.1051	6.2278	6.3528	6.4803	6.6101	6.7424	7.4416	8.2070
6	7.5233	7.7156	7.9129	8.1152	8.3227	8.5355	8.7537	9.9299	11.2588
7	9.2004	9.4872	9.7833	10.0890	10.4047	10.7305	11.0668	12.9159	15.0735
8	11.0285	11.4359	11.8594	12.2997	12.7573	13.2328	13.7268	16.4991	19.8419
9	13.0210	13.5795	14.1640	14.7757	15.4157	16.0853	16.7858	20.7989	25.8023
10	15.1929	15.9374	16.7220	17.5487	18.4197	19.3373	20.3037	25.9587	33.2529
20	51.1601	57.2750	64.2028	72.0524	80.9468	91.0249	102.4436	186.6880	342.9447

*There is one rent each period.

TABLE 10–4
Present value of annuity of $1 (ordinary),
$$P = \frac{1 - \frac{1}{(1 + i)^n}}{i}$$

Period rents*	2 %	3 %	3.75 %	4 %	4.25 %	5 %	6 %	7 %	8 %
1	0.9804	0.9709	0.9639	0.9615	0.9592	0.9524	0.9434	0.9346	0.9259
2	1.9416	1.9135	1.8929	1.8861	1.8794	1.8594	1.8334	1.8080	1.7833
3	2.8839	2.8286	2.7883	2.7751	2.7620	2.7232	2.6730	2.6243	2.5771
4	3.8077	3.7171	3.6514	3.6299	3.6086	3.5460	3.4651	3.3872	3.3121
5	4.7135	4.5797	4.4833	4.4518	4.4207	4.3295	4.2124	4.1002	3.9927
6	5.6014	5.4172	5.2851	5.2421	5.1997	5.0757	4.9173	4.7665	4.6229
7	6.4720	6.2303	6.0579	6.0021	5.9470	5.7864	5.5824	5.3893	5.2064
8	7.3255	7.0197	6.8028	6.7327	6.6638	6.4632	6.2098	5.9713	5.7466
9	8.1622	7.7861	7.5208	7.4353	7.3513	7.1078	6.8017	6.5152	6.2469
10	8.9826	8.5302	8.2128	8.1109	8.0109	7.7217	7.3601	7.0236	6.7101
20	16.3514	14.8775	13.8962	13.5903	13.2944	12.4622	11.4699	10.5940	9.8181

Period rents*	9 %	10 %	11 %	12 %	13 %	14 %	15 %	20 %	25 %
1	0.9174	0.9091	0.9009	0.8929	0.8850	0.8772	0.8696	0.8333	0.8000
2	1.7591	1.7355	1.7125	1.6901	1.6681	1.6467	1.6257	1.5278	1.4400
3	2.5313	2.4869	2.4437	2.4018	2.3612	2.3216	2.2832	2.1065	1.9520
4	3.2397	3.1699	3.1024	3.0373	2.9745	2.9137	2.8550	2.5887	2.3616
5	3.8897	3.7908	3.6959	3.6048	3.5172	3.4331	3.3522	2.9906	2.6893
6	4.4859	4.3553	4.2305	4.1114	3.9975	3.8887	3.7845	3.3255	2.9514
7	5.0330	4.8684	4.7122	4.5638	4.4226	4.2883	4.1604	3.6046	3.1611
8	5.5348	5.3349	5.1461	4.9676	4.7988	4.6389	4.4873	3.8372	3.3289
9	5.9952	5.7590	5.5370	5.3282	5.1317	4.9464	4.7716	4.0310	3.4631
10	6.4177	6.1446	5.8892	5.6502	5.4262	5.2161	5.0188	4.1925	3.5705
20	9.1285	8.5136	7.9633	7.4694	7.0248	6.6231	6.2593	4.8696	3.9539

*There is one rent each period.   A computer can easily refine any of the tables.

Present value of a single amount (p)

Present value of a single amount is the value now (i.e., the present) of an amount to be received at some date in the future. It can be said to be the inverse of the future value concept. To compute the present value of a sum to be received in the future, the future sum is subjected to compound discounting at i interest rate for n periods. In compound discounting, the interest is subtracted rather than added, as in compounding (as was demonstrated in the discussion of the future value concept). To illustrate discounting, assume that today is January 1, 19A, and that you will receive $1,000 cash on December 31, 19C; that is, three years from now. Assuming an interest rate of 10 percent per year, how much would the $1,000 be worth today; that is, what is its present value (today, on January 1, 19A)? We could set up a discounting computation, year by year, that would be the inverse to the tabulation of interest. However, to facilitate the computation, we can refer to the **Present value of $1 table,** Table 10–2. For i = 10 percent, n = 3, we find the present value of $1 is 0.7513. The $1,000, to be received three years hence, has a present value of $1,000 × 0.7513 = $751.30. The difference (i.e., the discount) of $248.70 is due to the time value of money; it is the interest. The concept of the present value of $1 is summarized in Exhibit 10–3.

Future value of an annuity (F)

Basically, the future value of an **annuity** is the same as the future value of a single amount, except for the addition of the concept of an annuity. The word annuity refers to a series of periodic payments characterized by (1) an **equal amount each period** (for two or more future consecutive periods), (2) **equal length of each consecutive period,** and (3) an **equal** interest rate each period. The future value of an annuity involves **compound interest** on each periodic amount. To illustrate, assume that you decide to deposit (i.e., contribute) $1,000 cash in a savings account each year for three years at 10 percent interest per year (i.e., a total of $3,000). The first $1,000 deposit is made on December 31, 19A; the second one on December 31, 19B; and the third and last one on December 31, 19C. How much would you have in the savings account at the end of Year 3, that is, immediately after the third (and last) deposit on December 31, 19C? In this situation, the first $1,000 deposit would draw compound interest for two years (for a total principal and interest of $1,210); the second deposit would draw interest for one year (for a total principal and interest of $1,100); and the third deposit would draw no interest because it was made on the last day of the final year in the savings plan. Thus, the total amount in the savings account at the end of three years, would be $3,310 ($1,210 + $1,100 + $1,000). We could compute separately the interest on each deposit to derive the future value of this annuity. However, we can refer to Table 10–3, **Future value of annuity of $1.** For i = 10 percent, n = 3, we find the value 3.31.[9] Therefore, the total of your three deposits (of $1,000 each) would have in-

---

[9]The equal amounts for each period in annuities often are referred to in the literature as "rents."

creased to $1,000 × 3.31 = $3,310 on December 31, 19C. The increase of $310 was due to the time value of money; it is interest revenue to you on the $3,000. This concept is summarized in Exhibit 10–3.

Present value of an annuity *(P)* The present value of an annuity is the value now (i.e., the present time) of a series of **equal amounts** (i.e., rents) to be received each period for some specified number of periods in the future. It can be said to be the inverse of the future value of an annuity explained immediately above. It involves compound **discounting** of each of the equal periodic amounts.

To illustrate, assume now is January 1, 19A, and that you are to receive $1,000 cash on each December 31, 19A, 19B, and 19C. How much would the sum of these three $1,000 future amounts be worth now, on January 1, 19A (i.e., the present value), assuming an interest rate of 10 percent per year? We could calculate laboriously the discounting on each rent as follows:

Year	Amount	Value from Table 10–2 i = 10 percent		Present value
1......	$1,000	×	.9091 (n = 1) =	$ 909.10
2......	1,000	×	.8264 (n = 2) =	826.40
3......	1,000	×	.7513 (n = 3) =	751.30
			Total present value	$2,486.80

We can compute the present value more readily by referring to Table 10–4, **Present value of annuity of $1.** For i = 10 percent, n = 3 rents, we find the value 2.4869. Therefore, your three $1,000 amounts to be received in the future have a total present value of $1,000 × 2.4869 = $2,487. The difference of $513 ($3,000 − $2,487) was due to the interest discount factor. This concept is summarized in Exhibit 10–3.

To conclude this section, observe that the preceding illustrations assumed annual interest rates and annual periods for compounding and discounting. While interest rates almost always are quoted on an annual basis, interest compounding periods often are less than one year (such as semiannually or quarterly). When interest periods are less than a year, the values of **n** and **i** must be restated to be consistent with the length of the interest period. To illustrate, 12 percent interest compounded annually for five years requires use of n = 5 and i = 12. If compounding is quarterly, the interest period is one quarter of a year (i.e., four periods per year), and the quarterly interest rate would be one quarter of the annual rate (i.e., 3 percent per quarter); therefore, 12 percent interest compounded quarterly for five years requires use of n = 20 and i = 3.

MEASUREMENT AND ACCOUNTING APPLICATIONS OF FV AND PV

There are numerous transactions where the concepts of future and present value are used for accounting measurements. Below are cited four different situations where these concepts must be employed.

Case A:

On January 1, 19A, Company A set aside $150,000 cash in a special building fund (an asset) to be used at the end of five years to construct a new building. The fund is expected to earn 10 percent interest per year, which will be added to the fund balance each year. On the date of deposit the company made the following entry:

January 1, 19A:

Special building fund...	150,000	
Cash..		150,000

Required:

1. What will be the balance of the fund at the end of the fifth year?

   Answer: This situation requires application of the future value of a single amount.

   Principal × Table 10–1 value (i = 10%; n = 5) = Future value
   $150,000 × 1.6105   = $241,575

2. How much interest revenue was earned on the fund during the five years?

   Answer:

   $241,575 − $150,000 = $91,575

3. What entry would be made on December 31, 19A, to record the interest revenue for the first year?

   Answer: Interest for one year on the fund balance is added to the fund and recorded as follows:

December 31, 19A:

Special building fund.........................	15,000	
Interest revenue ($150,000 × .10)..........		15,000

4. What entry would be made on December 31, 19B, to record interest revenue for the second year?

Answer:

December 31, 19B:

```
Special building fund. . . . . . . . . . . . . . . . . . . . . . .     16,500
      Interest revenue . . . . . . . . . . . . . . . . . . . . . . . .          16,500
      ($150,000 + $15,000) × .10 = $16,500.
```

Case B:

On January 1, 19A, Company B purchased a new machine at a list price of $20,000, which was payable at the end of two years with no interim interest payments. The going rate of interest was 12 percent.

Required:

1. The company accountant is preparing the following journal entry:

January 1, 19A:

```
Machinery. . . . . . . . . . . . . . . . . . . . . . . . . . . . . . . . .     $ ?
      Account payable (special) . . . . . . . . . . . . . . . . . . .          $ ?
```

What amount should be recorded in this entry?

Answer: This situation requires application of the present value of a single amount. Under the cost principle, the cost of the machine is its current cash equivalent price, which is the present value of the future payment. The present value of the $20,000 is computed as follows:

Future amount × Table 10–2 ($i = 12\%; n = 2$) = Present value
$20,000 × 0.7972   = $15,944

Therefore, the journal entry would be as follows:

January 1, 19A:

```
Machinery . . . . . . . . . . . . . . . . . . . . . . . . . . . . . .     15,944
      Account payable (special). . . . . . . . . . . . . . . . .          15,944
```

2. What journal entry would be made at the end of the first and second years for interest expense on the accounts payable?

   Answer: Interest expense for each year on the amount in the Account Payable account would be recorded by means of an adjusting entry, as follows:

December 31, 19A:

Interest expense	1,913	
Account payable (special)....................		1,913
$15,944 \times .12 = \$1,913$.....................		
Note: The account payable would be reported on the 19A balance sheet at $15,944 + \$1,913 = \$17,857$.		

December 31, 19B:

Interest expense	2,143	
Account payable (special)....................		2,143
$(\$15,944 + \$1,913) \times .12 = \$2,143$.		

The effect of these two entries is to increase the balance in Account Payable for the new accrued interest payable at maturity date. By maturity date, the balance will have been increased to the maturity amount, $20,000, which is the total amount payable at due date. Interest expense was $1,913 + $2,143 = $4,056, or alternatively, $20,000 − $15,944 = $4,056.

3. What journal entry would be made to record payment of the note on December 31, 19B (the maturity date)?

   Answer: At this date the amount to be paid is the balance of Account Payable, which is the same as the maturity amount on the due date, that is, $15,944 + $1,913 + $2,143 = $20,000.[10]

The journal entry to record full payment of the debt would be:

December 31, 19B:

Account payable (special)......................	20,000	
Cash.....................................		20,000

Case C:

Company C decided to make five equal annual deposits of $30,000 with a financial institution to accumulate a debt retirement fund. The deposits will be made each December 31, starting December 31, 19A. The fifth and last deposit will be made December 31, 19E. The financial institution will pay 8 percent annual compound interest, which will be added to the fund at the end of each year.

1. What entry should be made to record the first deposit?
    Answer:

    December 31, 19A:

---

[10]These entries also could be made as follows with the same results:

January 1, 19A:

Machinery	15,944	
Discount on account payable	4,056	
Account payable (special)...		20,000

December 31, 19A:

Interest expense ($15,944 × .12)	1,913	
Discount on account payable		1,913

At the end of 19A, the liability would be reported at net as $20,000 − $2,143 = $17,857.

December 31, 19B:

Interest expense ($17,857 × .12)	2,143	
Accounts payable (special)...	20,000	
Cash		20,000
Discount on account payable		2,143

```
 Debt retirement fund.........................   30,000
        Cash....................................            30,000
```

2. What will be the balance in the fund immediately after the fifth and last deposit (i.e., on December 31, 19E)?
    Answer: This situation requires application of future value of an annuity.

    Rent   × Table 10–3 ($i = 8\%$; $n = 5$) = Future value
    $30,000 × 5.8666   = $175,998

3. What entries would be made at the end of 19B?
    Answer:

    a. Interest for one year on the fund balance would be added to the fund and recorded as follows:

    December 31, 19B:

    ```
     Debt retirement fund...........................   2,400
            Interest revenue ($30,000 × .08).............        2,400
    ```

    b. The second deposit would be recorded as follows:

    December 31, 19B:

    ```
     Debt retirement fund ....................   30,000
            Cash ..............................            30,000
    ```

4. What would be the amount of interest revenue to be recorded at the end of the 19C?
    Answer: Interest would be computed on the increased fund balance as follows:

    ($30,000 + $2,400 + $30,000) × .08 = $4,992

Case D:

On January 1, 19A, Company D purchased a new machine at a cash price of $40,000. The company was short of cash so arrangements were made to execute a $40,000 note payable to be paid off in three equal annual installments. Each installment includes principal plus interest on the unpaid balance at 11 percent per year. The equal annual installments are due on December 31, 19A, 19B, and 19C. The acquisition was recorded as follows:

January 1, 19A:

Machinery.............................	40,000	
Notes payable.......................		40,000

Required:

1. What would be the amount of each equal annual installment?
   Answer: The $40,000 is the amount of the debt today; hence, $40,000 is the present value of the three future installment payments required. Therefore, $n = 3$, $i = 11$ percent, and the present value is $40,000. To compute the amount of each equal payment required, the present value of an annuity must be used as follows:

   Payment × Table 10–4 value ($i = 11\%$; $n = 3$) = Present value
   Substituting:
   Payment × 2.4437 = $40,000
   Payment = $40,000 ÷ 2.4437
   **   = $16,369 (amount of each annual payment)**

2. What was the amount of interest expense in dollars?
   Answer:

   ($16,369 × 3) − $40,000 = $9,107

3. What journal entry should be made at the end of each year to record the payment on this $40,000 note payable?
   Answer:

   a. To record the first installment payment on the note:

   December 31, 19A:

Note payable	11,969	
Interest expense ($40,000 × .11)	4,400	
Cash (computed above)..............		16,369

b. To record the second installment payment on the note:

December 31, 19B:

```
Note payable ..........................     13,285
Interest expense ($40,000 − $11,969) × .11    3,084
    Cash (computed above)..............              16,369
```

c. To record final installment payment on the note:

December 31, 19C:

```
Note payable ..........................     14,746
Interest expense........................     1,623
    Cash (computed above)..............              16,369
Interest: ($40,000 − $11,969 − $13,285) × .11 = $1,623
(rounded to accommodate rounding errors).
```

4. Prepare a **debt payment schedule** that shows the effect on interest expense and the unpaid amount of principal each period.

Debt Payment Schedule

Date	Payment of cash (cr.)	Interest expense (dr.)	Reduction of principal (dr.)	Unpaid principal
1/1/A..				40,000
12/31/A.....................................	16,369[a]	4,400[b]	11,969[c]	28,031[d]
12/31/B.....................................	16,369	3,084	13,285	14,746
12/31/C.....................................	16,369	1,623*	14,746	−0−
Total.............................	49,107	9,107	40,000	

*To accommodate rounding error.
Sequential computations:
  [a]Annual payment: Computed above.
  [b]Interest expense: Unpaid principal, $40,000 × .11 = $4,400.
  [c]Reduction of principal: Annual payment, $16,369 − Interest, $4,400 = $11,969.
  [d]New unpaid balance: Prior Balance, $40,000 − Reduction, $11,969 = $28,031.

Observe in the debt payment schedule that of each successive payment an increasing amount is payment on principal and a decreasing amount is interest expense. This effect occurs because the interest each period is based on a lower amount of unpaid principal.

Although there are many other applications of the concept of the time value of money in the recording and reporting processes, the above examples are typical. The application of present value and future value concepts to capital budgeting is deferred to management accounting.

PRESENT VALUE CONCEPTS AND LEASE LIABILITIES

A lease is a contract that specifies that a particular asset will be leased by the owner (i.e., the lessor) to another party (i.e., the lessee) under certain agreements. For accounting purposes, leases are classified as **operating leases** (usually short term) or **capital leases** (usually long term).

Significantly different accounting approaches are required for operating leases than for capital leases. Because of the importance of these differences, the *CICA Handbook,* Section 3065, established three criteria to differentiate capital leases from operating leases. If **any one** of the three criteria is met by the lease contract, the lease **must** be accounted for as a **capital** lease by the lessee; all other leases must be accounted for as **operating** leases. The three criteria for a **capital lease** may be summarized as follows: (1) the leased property transfers to the lessee by the end of the lease term either by the terms of the lease contract or what is termed a bargain purchase option, (2) the lease term is at least 75 percent of the estimated useful life of the leased asset, and (3) the present value of the minimum lease payments is at least 90 percent of the market value of the leased asset on the date of the lease contract.[11]

The three criteria provide the basis for establishing whether or not the transaction is "in substance" a purchase of an asset. If the accountant deems the transaction to be "in substance" a purchase by the lessee, then the transaction is recorded in the same way as the purchase of a long-term asset with the money received from a long-term loan. Such practice provides a classic illustration of a victory of "substance" over "form" because a lease is a lease in form, not a purchase.

Basically, accounting for an **operating lease** requires a journal entry for each rental payment (i.e., for the lessee, debit Rent Expense and credit Cash). In contrast, accounting for a **capital lease** assumes that the **lessor sold** the leased asset and the **lessee purchased** it. This assumption means that when the lease contract is signed, the **lessee** will debit an asset and credit a long-term lease liability.

A typical operating and a typical capital lease are illustrated in Exhibit 10–4. On January 1, 19A, Daly Construction Company must acquire a heavy-duty machine ready to operate. The machine has a cash price of $100,000, and it has a five-year estimated useful life and no residual value. Daly's top management, in the face of a serious cash problem, is considering three alternative ways of acquiring the machine: *(a)* purchase by signing a note for the full purchase price, *(b)* lease the machine on an **operating** lease, and *(c)* lease the machine on a **capital** lease. The basic entries for each alternative are presented in Exhibit 10–4. Let's examine each alternative.

---

[11]*CICA Handbook,* Section 3065, also specifies the rules for determining how the lessor should account for a lease. This topic will be discussed in advanced courses.

EXHIBIT 10–4
Operating and
capital leases
illustrated

Situation:
   Daly Construction Company intends to acquire a heavy-duty machine that will cost
      $100,000 cash equivalent price. Estimated useful life of the machine is five years and
      no residual value. Daly is considering three alternatives: *(a)* purchase by signing
      note, *(b)* rent on an operating lease, and *(c)* rent on a capital lease.

Alternative *a*:
   On January 1, 19A, purchased the machine for $100,000 and signed a two-year 15-
      percent note that requires equal month-end payments (24) of $4,849.

   Journal entries:

   Purchase, January 1, 19A:

Machinery...	100,000	
Note payable, long term		100,000

   Payment on note, January 31, 19A:

Interest expense ($100,000 × $1¼%)......................	1,250	
Note payable ($4,849 − $1,250).........................	3,599	
Cash (per note)		4,849

Alternative *b*:
   Lease on a month-to-month **operating lease;** month-end rental payments of $6,000, as
      required by lessor.

   Journal entries:

   January 31, 19A:

Machinery rental expense................................	6,000	
Cash (per lease agreement)		6,000

Alternative *c*:
   Lease on a **capital lease** that requires month-end payments of $3,321 for 36 months (the
      implied interest rate is 12 percent). Daly is required by the lease to pay all
      ownership costs.

   Journal entries:

   January 1, 19A—Inception date of the lease (record as a purchase):

Machinery (under capital lease)..........................	100,000	
Liability, capital lease................................		100,000

   Computation:
      Present value = Payments × Table 10–4 ($i = 1\%; n = 36$)
                    = $3,321 × 30.0175*
                    = $100,000 (rounded)

   January 31, 19A, first monthly rental payment:

Interest expense ($100,000 × 1%)........................	1,000	
Liability, capital lease ($3,321 − $1,000)...................	2,321	
Cash (per lease contract).............................		3,321

   *This value is given for illustrative purposes. Table 10–4 does not contain values for 36 periods.

Alternative *a*. Purchase the machine and sign a two-year interest-bearing
note; 15 percent interest and principal payable each month-end (i.e., 24
equal payments). On January 1, 19A, Daly would record the purchase
at cost and a liability as illustrated in Exhibit 10–4. Equal monthly payments of principal plus interest ($4,849) are to be made; the journal

entry to record the first payment is illustrated in Exhibit 10–4. Under this alternative Daly would own the machine; therefore, Daly would record depreciation expense, and all other expenses incurred, such as maintenance, insurance, and taxes.

Alternative *b*. Lease the machine on a month-to-month **operating lease** at a monthly rental of $6,000 (as determined by the lessor), payable at each month-end. Under this alternative Daly would not own the machine; therefore, the only journal entries to be recorded by Daly would be for the monthly rental payments as illustrated in Exhibit 10–4. Under this alternative Daly would have to continue lease payments as long as the machine is used and would never own the machine.

Alternative *c*. Lease the machine on a three-year **capital lease.** The contract requires Daly to pay 36 month-end rentals of $3,321, computed by the **lessor** to earn 12 percent on the $100,000 cash equivalent price. In addition, Daly is required to pay most of the "ownership" costs, such as maintenance insurance and taxes. The lessee learned that the rental of $3,321 was based on 12 percent interest; therefore, the **lessee** computed the **present value** of the future lease rentals as follows:

Present value = Rents (payments) × Table 10–4 (*i* = 1%; *n* = 36)
= $3,321 × 30.1075 (given; Table 10–4
does not contain values for 36 periods)
= $100,000 (rounded)

Because a **capital lease** is viewed in accounting as a sale of the asset by the lessor to the lessee, Daly (the lessee) would record a purchase of the machine on the date of the lease contract for $100,000 (its present value).

On January 1, 19A, Daly would debit machinery and credit a lease liability for $100,000 as illustrated in Exhibit 10–4. Each of the 36 month-end lease payments would be recorded, in part as payment of principal and in part as payment of interest expense. Exhibit 10–4 illustrates entries at the inception of the lease (i.e., a "purchase" of the machine is recorded) and the first interest payment on January 31, 19A.

Because Daly is assumed to "own" the machine during the lease term, Daly will record depreciation expense and all other "ownership" expenses incurred, such as maintenance, insurance, and taxes. Under this alternative, Daly will own the machine after the last rental payment with no further obligations to the lessor.

The above example is not intended to suggest which alternative is the "best" for Daly. Such a determination would necessitate considerably more information than given. Rather, it is intended to differentiate between the required accounting approaches for an operating lease versus capital lease. The basic difference requires the application of **present value** determination for **capital leases.**

PRESENT VALUE CONCEPTS AND NOTES PAYABLE

A note may be designated as either "interest bearing" or as "noninterest bearing." Nevertheless, all commercial notes involve interest, either explicitly or implicitly, because money loaned, or borrowed, has a time value that cannot be avoided.

An **interest-bearing note** is one that explicitly specifies (1) a stated rate of interest (such as 12 percent) on the note itself, and (2) that the interest is to be paid at maturity, or in future installments, **in addition to the face or principal amount** of the note. For example, a $30,000, 12 percent, one-year, **interest-bearing** note would (1) provide the borrower with $30,000 cash, (2) have a face or principal amount of $30,000, and (3) require the payment of the principal ($30,000) plus interest for one year ($3,600)—a total of $33,600.

In contrast, a **noninterest-bearing note** is one that has implicit interest; that is, it is a note that (1) does not specify a rate of interest on the note itself but (2) includes the interest in the face amount of the note. For example, a $33,600,

EXHIBIT 10–5
Interest-bearing and noninterest-bearing notes illustrated

Transactions	Interest-bearing		Noninterest-bearing	
a. November 1, 19A, date of note:				
Cash	30,000		30,000	
Discount on note payable			3,600	
Note payable, short term		30,000		33,600
(12% interest; term, one year).				
b. December 31, 19A, end of accounting period:				
Interest expense (two months)	600		600	
Interest payable		600		
Discount on note payable				600
Adjusting entry for 2 months' accrued interest; $30,000 \times .12 \times 2/12 = \$600$.				
c. October 31, 19B, maturity date of note:*				
Note payable	30,000		33,600	
Interest expense (10 months)	3,000		3,000	
Interest payable	600			
Discount on note payable				3,000
Cash		33,600		33,600
Payment of note at maturity.				

*It would have simplified this entry if a **reversing entry** of the accrual of December 31, 19A, had been made on January 1, 19B.

one-year, noninterest-bearing note (assuming an implicit rate of interest of 12 percent) (1) would provide the borrower $30,000 cash (i.e., $33,600 − $3,600 implicit interest) and (2) would require the payment of only the face amount of the note at maturity date ($33,600). Observe that the implicit interest is included in the face amount of the note. In each case, the note is recorded at the present value of the future cash payments:

$$PV = \textbf{Future amount} \times \textbf{Table 10–2 } (i = 12\%; n = 1)$$
$$= \$33,600 \times .8929$$
$$= \$30,000 \text{ (rounded)}$$

The journal entries for the two different types of notes payable (cited above) are given in Exhibit 10–5.

The illustration in Exhibit 10–5 suggests the important concepts in the measurement of liabilities and interest expense. The concept of **present value** is important in the measurement of liabilities. The present value of a note is the value today of its future cash flows. In the case of the interest-bearing note, the present value, the face amount, and the principal are the same at all dates, that is, $30,000 (at 12 percent). In the case of the noninterest-bearing note, the present value on the date of the note (November 1, 19A) is $30,000, the amount of cash received; however, the face amount is $33,600.

SUMMARY OF CHAPTER

This chapter discussed accounting for three types of obligations: current, long-term, and contingent liabilities. Accounting for bonds payable is discussed in Chapter 11. Liabilities are obligations of either a known or estimated amount. Detailed information concerning the liabilities of an entity is especially important to many decision makers, whether internal or external to the enterprise, because liabilities represent claims against the resources of an entity. Decision makers often may be unable to identify the kinds and amounts of liabilities without reliable financial statements. The existence and amount of liabilities sometimes are easy to conceal from outsiders. The accounting model and the verification by the independent auditor constitute the best assurance that all liabilities are disclosed.

Current liabilities are obligations that will be paid from the resources reported on the same balance sheet as current assets. Thus, they are short-term obligations that will be paid within the coming year or within the normal operating cycle of the business, whichever is longer. All other liabilities (except contingent liabilities) are reported as long-term liabilities. A contingent liability is not an effective liability; it is a potential claim due to some event or transaction that has happened already, but whether it will materialize as an effective liability is not certain because that depends upon some future event or transaction. Contingent liabilities must be disclosed fully on the financial statements. Disclosure usually is by a note to the financial statements.

SUPPLEMENT 10A—PAYROLL ACCOUNTING[12]

Payroll accounting does not involve any new accounting concepts or princi-ples, but payroll accounting deserves additional discussion because of the ne-cessity to pay employees for their services promptly and correctly. In addition, detailed payroll accounting is necessary to fulfill legal requirements under fed-eral and provincial laws with respect to withholdings for income taxes, Canada or Quebec Pension Plan, and unemployment insurance. Further, the manage-ment of an enterprise, for planning and control purposes, needs detailed and accurate cost figures for wages and salaries. Frequently, salaries and wages constitute the largest category of expense in an enterprise. As a consequence of the large amount of detailed recordkeeping that is required, payroll account-ing is often computerized, including the production of individual cheques for the employees.

A detailed payroll record must be maintained for each employee. The pay-roll record varies with the circumstances in each company; however, it must include for each individual such data as social insurance number, number of dependents (for income tax withholding), rate of pay, a time record (for hourly paid employees), deductions from gross pay, and so on.

To understand payroll accounting, a distinction must be made between (1) payroll deductions and taxes that must be paid by the **employee** (i.e., deducted from the employee's gross earnings); and (2) payroll taxes that must be paid by the **employer.** Both types of payroll amounts must be transmitted to the governmental unit or other party to whom the amounts are owed. Payroll taxes and deductions apply only in situations where there is an employer-employee relationship. Independent contractors that are not under the direct supervision of the client, such as outside lawyers, independent accountants, consultants, and building contractors, are not employees; hence; amounts paid to them are not subject to payroll taxes and related deductions.

An employee usually receives take home pay that is much less than the gross earnings for the period. This is due to two types of payroll deductions:

1. Required deductions for taxes that must be paid by the em-ployee as specified by provincial and federal laws.
2. Optional deductions authorized by the employee for special purposes.

Required deductions

There are three categories of taxes that the employee must pay and thus must be deducted from the employee's gross earnings; they are income taxes, Canada or Quebec Pension Plan contributions and unemployment insurance premiums. The employer must remit the total amount deducted to the appro-priate government agency.

---

[12]This section of the chapter was revised by E. Scott.

Employee income taxes. Practically every employee must prepare an annual federal income tax return. Wages and salaries earned during the year must be reported on the income tax return as income. Federal and Quebec laws require the employer to deduct an appropriate amount of income tax each period from the gross earnings of each employee. The amount of the deduction for income tax is determined from a tax table (provided by the Revenue Canada, Taxation) based upon the earnings and number of exemptions (for self and dependents) of the employee. The amount of income tax withheld from the employee's wages is recorded by the employer as a current liability between the date of deduction and the date the amount withheld is remitted to the government.

Employee Canada Pension Plan contributions. The Canada Pension Plan provides retirement and disability benefits for those who have contributed to the plan over their working life. Funding comes from contributions by both employees and employers at the rate of 1.8 percent of "annual pensionable earnings" from each party.[13] The employer is required to make the appropriate deductions from employees each pay period and then make remittances to the federal government.

Employee unemployment insurance premiums. The Federal Unemployment Insurance Act also requires that employers deduct premiums from employees on the basis of 2.35 percent of their "insurable earnings" (with the employer adding an additional contribution).[14] Eligibility for benefits is based on a "record of employment" form provided by the employer.

For each of the three types of payroll taxes described above, the total amount withheld must be paid to Revenue Canada, Taxation by the 15th day of the month following the month in which the remuneration was paid. Remittance forms to accompany each payment are provided by Revenue Canada, Taxation.

To identify the amounts withheld for each employee, an annual statement (T4 Summary) is filed with Revenue Canada on or before February 28, covering the preceding calendar year. Individual statements (T4 Supplementary) are provided to each employee at the same time.

The Province of Quebec similarly requires separate withholding, reporting, and remittance for provincial income tax and the Quebec Pension Plan.

---

[13]Annual "pensionable earnings" in 1985 are those earnings in excess of $2,300 up to a maximum of $23,400. Monthly contributions, for example, by the employee are 1.8 percent of actual earnings for the month less 1/12 of the $2,300, and are determined from tables provided by Revenue Canada, Taxation. Once the maximum contributions have been made, no further contributions are required in the year for that employee.

Individuals who are "self-employed" (in business as proprietors or partners) must make both the employee's and employer's share of the contributions annually.

[14]"Insurable earnings" in 1985 are those annual earnings up to $23,920. If earnings are $4,784 or less annually ($498.66 monthly) they are exempt. Deduction tables are provided showing the amount of deductions for various amounts of earnings. (The maximum and minimum earnings are prorated by the length of the period in these tables.)

Optional deductions

Many companies encourage programs of voluntary deductions from earnings by employees. Typical of these voluntary deductions are savings funds, insurance premiums, charitable contributions, supplementary retirement programs, repayment of loans, share purchase plans, and the purchase of Canada savings bonds. The employer agrees to make these deductions, subject to employee authorization, as a matter of convenience to the employees. The amounts deducted are remitted in a short time to the organization or agency in whose behalf the deduction was authorized. Another type of deduction is for union dues as specified in the union contract. In some cases, this deduction may not be voluntary on an individual basis. The employer is required to remit the deductions, along with the employee list, to the union each month. Where the employer also agrees to contribute amounts, an employee benefits expense is incurred.

Accounting for employee deductions

The employer must maintain detailed and accurate records of all deductions from the earnings of each employee. From the employer's viewpoint, the employee deductions are **current liabilities** from the date of the payroll deduction to the date of remittance to the government or other entity.

To illustrate the basic accounting entry to be made for the payment of a payroll and the accrual of liabilities for the **employee** deductions, assume that Real Company accumulated the following data in the detailed payroll records for the month of January 19B:

Gross earnings:
Salaries $60,000
Wages (hourly paid employees) 40,000
Income taxes withheld 21,000
Union dues, withheld 400
Unemployment insurance withheld .. 2,350
Canada Pension Plan contributions
    withheld 1,455

The entry to record the payroll and employee deductions would be:

January 31, 19A:

Salaries expense 60,000
Wages expense 40,000
    Liability for income taxes withheld—employees 21,000
    Liability for union dues withheld—employees 400
    Unemployment insurance withheld 2,350
    CPP contributions withheld 1,455
    Cash (take-home pay) 74,795
Payroll for January, including employee payroll deductions.

Employer-paid payroll taxes

Remember that the payroll taxes illustrated above are those levied on the **employees.** The employer simply serves as a tax collector with respect to them. Specific payroll taxes also are levied on the employer. These taxes represent **operating expenses** of the business. The liability for these taxes is extinguished when the taxes are remitted to the designated agencies of the provincial and federal governments. Usually, three different payroll taxes must be paid by the employer—Canada Pension Plan, unemployment insurance, and provinicial workmen's compensation.

Employer Canada Pension Plan contributions. As previously noted, the employer must match the employee's contributions to the Canada or Quebec Pension Plan by equal amounts.

Employer unemployment insurance premiums. The employer must also contribute to the unemployment insurance fund. The employer's premium is 1.4 times the amount of the employee's premiums in most cases.

Workmen's compensation. Provincial legislation requires employers to pay insurance premiums on behalf of employees who may be injured or disabled in work-related activities. The premiums are paid to a provincial board which administers the program, and the amount of premium depends upon such factors as the type of employment, the amount of pay and the claims experience.

Accounting for employer payroll taxes

Payroll taxes paid by the employer are debited to an expense account and credited to a current liability when the payroll is paid each period. To illustrate, the January entry for the employer's payroll taxes for Real Company would be as follows assuming a workmen's compensation premium of $800:

Payroll and benefits expense	5,545*	
Unemployment insurance payable ($2,350 × 1.4)...............		3,290
Canada Pension Plan payable		1,455
Workmen's compensation payable		800
To record employer payroll taxes.		
*Total payroll expenses, $100,000 + 5,545 = $105,545.		

When the taxes are remitted to the governments, the liability accounts are debited and Cash is credited.

SUPPLEMENT 10B—THE VOUCHER SYSTEM

The voucher system is designed to attain strict control over cash expenditures from the point an obligation is incurred (by means of purchase of merchandise for resale, services, operational assets, investments, etc.) through the payment of cash. The incurrence of an obligation and the payment of cash to satisfy it are viewed as separate and independent transactions. When a voucher system is used, an account called **Vouchers Payable** is often used to replace the **Accounts Payable** account in the ledger. Similarly, a **voucher register** and a **cheque register** replace the purchases journal and the cash disbursements journal, respectively (see Supplement 8B).

The basic document in the voucher system is the **voucher.** A voucher is a form, prepared and used within the business, on which a transaction is (1) summarized and supported adequately, (2) approved, (3) analyzed for recording, and (4) approved for payment. Thus, it is a comprehensive document that follows a transaction from the transaction date to the final cash payment. A voucher is prepared for **each** transaction involving the payment of cash, such as the purchase of assets, the use of services, the incurrence of expenses, and the payment of debt. The form of a voucher varies between companies because it should be designed to meet the specific internal requirements of the individual company. For control purposes, all voucher forms and cheques should be numbered consecutively when printed.

Each voucher, after approval, is entered in the voucher register in order of number. The voucher register is designed to record the basic information from the voucher, including the accounts to be debited and credited.

To illustrate the mechanics of a voucher system, we will follow a purchase of merchandise for resale through the system from the **order date** to the final cash payment date. Each step in the sequence may be illustrated and explained as follows:

19A

Jan. 10   Merchandise ordered from Box Supply Company, cost $1,000; terms, n/15. A purchase order is prepared and approved.

12   Merchandise ordered from Box Supply Company on January 10 is received; invoice is received. Voucher No. 47 is drawn and the purchase order is attached (see Exhibit 10–6). Goods are checked for quantity and condition; a receiving report is prepared.

12   Receiving report and invoice sent to accounting department; they are attached to the voucher. Voucher is approved, and then recorded in the voucher register (see Exhibit 10–7).

26   Voucher is approved by designated manager for payment on January 27 and sent to disbursements department; Cheque No. 90 is prepared.

27   Cheque No. 90 is signed by treasurer and mailed.

28   The accounting department enters Cheque No. 90 in the cheque register (see Exhibit 10–8); enters payment notation in the voucher register (see Exhibit 10–7); and files the voucher in the **Vouchers Paid File.**

For illustrative purposes, two more transactions are recorded in the voucher register, one of which remains unpaid.

EXHIBIT 10–6
Voucher

Voucher No. ___47___

MAY DEPARTMENT STORE
Windsor, Ont.

Date of Voucher _____Jan. 12, 19A_____   Date Paid ___Jan 27, 19A___

Pay to: _____Box Supply Company_____   Cheque No. ____90____

_____1119 Brown Street_____

_____Anywhere, Canada_____

For the following goods or services: (attach all supporting documents)

Date Incurred	Terms	Explanation of Details	Amount
Jan. 12	n/15	Merchandise, Dept. 8 Invoice No. 17-8132 Receiving Report No. 123	1,000.00
		Net payable	1,000.00

Approvals:

      Voucher Approval: Date ___1/12/A___ Signature _____R. C. Roe_____

      Payment Approval: Date ___1/26/A___ Signature _____A. B. Doe_____

Accounting Analysis:

Account Debited:	Acct. No.	Amount
Purchases	91	1,000.00
Office Supplies		
Sales Salaries		
Operational Assets		
Etc.		
Total, Voucher Payable Credit 41	1,000.00

EXHIBIT 10–7   **Voucher register**

Date	Vou. No.	Payee	Payment Date	Cheque No.	Vouchers Payable (Credit)	Purchases (Debit)	Selling Expense Control Account Code	Folio	Amount (Debit)	Adm. Expense Control Account Code	Folio	Amount (Debit)	Other Accounts to Be Debited Account Name	No.	Folio P	Amount (Debited)
Jan. 12	47	Box Supply Co.	1/27	90	1,000.00	1,000.00										
Jan. 14	48	John Day salary	1/15	89	600.00		64	√	600.00							
Jan. 31	98	Capital Nat'l Bank-note			2,160.00								Notes payable	44	√	2,000.00
													Interest expense	82	√	160.00
		Totals			27,605.00	14,875.00			7,410.00			3,160.00				2,160.00
		Posting notations			(41)	(91)			(60)			(70)				(√)

At the end of the month the voucher register and the cheque register are totaled and the equality of the debits and credits is verified. Posting to the ledger from these two special journals follows the same pattern explained in Supplement 8B, for the special journals illustrated there. Posting involves two separate phases:

1. Current posting—During the period, and perhaps daily, the details in the Voucher Register columns are posted to (a) the selling expense subsidiary ledger (under the selling expense control); (b) the administrative expense subsidiary ledger (under the administrative expense control); and (c) other accounts to be debited. No current posting is required from the cheque register as illustrated.

2. Monthly posting—The totals from the voucher register, except for the "Other Accounts to Be Debited" are posted at the end of each month. The account number to which each total is posted is entered below the amount. The column for "Other Accounts to Be Debited" was posted individually; hence, the total should not be posted. The totals from the cheque register are posted to the accounts at the end of each month as indicated by the account numbers entered below the total.

EXHIBIT 10–8
Cheque register

Date		Payee	Voucher No. Paid	Cheque No.	Vouchers Payable (Debit)*	Cash (Credit)*
Jan.	15	John Day	48	89	600.00	600.00
	27	Box Supply Co.	47	90	1,000.00	1,000.00
	31	Totals			18,751.00	18,751.00
		Posting notation			(41)	(11)

*These two columns could be combined.

The balance in the ledger account Vouchers Payable is reported on the balance sheet as a liability and is designated as Accounts Payable. The amount should be allocated and classified between current and long-term liabilities, depending on due dates.

The Vouchers Payable account is a control account, the balance of which represents all of the **unpaid** vouchers at any given time. The total of all vouchers in the **Unpaid Voucher File** must agree with the balance of the Vouchers Payable account; therefore, the Vouchers Payable account replaces the Accounts Payable control account in the ledger (see Supplement 6A).

In studying the mechanics of the voucher system, as illustrated above, you should not overlook its most important aspect—the high degree of **internal control** attained through formalization of the sequence of acquiring operational assets, services, and merchandise, and in making the cash payments. The internal control feature rests upon (1) clear-cut separation and designation of specific approval responsibilities, (2) a prescribed routine for carrying out these responsibilities, and (3) accounting for the results.

Although a manual approach was illustrated, these routines are adapted easily to the computer. A computer program can be designed to accomplish the same steps and procedures illustrated above. Most companies of any size have computerized the voucher system in order to attain a high degree of control over expenditures and to accelerate the processing of a large volume of transactions, including cash disbursements.

IMPORTANT TERMS DEFINED IN THIS CHAPTER

Terms (alphabetically)	Key words in definitions of important terms used in chapter	Page reference
Accrued expenses	Expenses that have been incurred but have not yet been paid or recorded at the end of the accounting period; a liability.	515
Annuity	A series of periodic cash receipts or payments that are equal in amount.	532
Capital lease	A lease that is viewed as a purchase/sale, for accounting purposes.	521
Contingent liability	Potential liability that has arisen as the result of a past event; not an effective liability.	524
Current liabilities	Short-term obligations that will be paid within the current operating cycle or one year, whichever is longer.	514
Deferred income tax	Difference between income tax expense and income tax liability, caused by timing differences.	521
Deferred revenues	Revenues that have been collected but not earned; a liability.	517
Future value	The sum to which an amount will increase as the result of compound interest.	527
Interest-bearing note	A note that explicitly specifies a stated rate of interest.	544
Liabilities	Probable future sacrifices of economic benefits that arise from past transactions.	512
Long-term liabilities	All obligations not properly classified as current liabilities.	518

Terms *(alphabetically)*	*Key words in definitions of important* *terms used in chapter*	*Page* *reference*
Noninterest-bearing note	A note that does not explicitly state a rate of interest but has implicit interest; interest is included in the face amount of the note.	513
Operating lease	A rental agreement between a lessor and lessee that is not viewed in accounting as a purchase/sale.	521
Permanent difference	An income tax difference that does not give rise to deferred taxes.	524
Present value	The value now of an amount to be received in the future.	527
Time value of money	Interest that is associated with the use of money over time.	519
Timing difference	An income tax difference that causes deferred taxes; will reverse or turn around in the future.	522
Working capital	The dollar difference between total current assets and total current liabilities.	514
Working capital ratio	The ratio of total current assets divided by total current liabilities; also known as the current ratio.	514

QUESTIONS FOR DISCUSSION

Part A

1. Define a liability and distinguish between a current liability and a long-term liability.

2. How can external parties be informed in respect to liabilities of an enterprise?

3. Liabilities are measured and reported at their current cash equivalent amount. Explain.

4. A liability is a known obligation of either a definite or estimated amount. Explain.

5. Define working capital. How is it computed?

6. What is the current ratio? What is another name for the current ratio? How is the current ratio related to the classification of liabilities?

7. Define an accrued liability. What kind of an entry usually reflects an accrued liability?

8. Define a deferred revenue and explain why it is a liability.

9. Define a note payable and distinguish between a secured and an unsecured note.

10. Distinguish between an interest-bearing note and a noninterest-bearing note.

11. Define deferred income tax. Explain why deferred income tax is said to reverse, or turn around, in subsequent periods.

12. What is a contingent liability? How is a contingent liability reported?

13. Briefly explain the primary purpose of a voucher system.

14. Compare the conceptual valuation rules for accounts receivable with those of accounts payable.

Part B

15. Briefly explain what is meant by the time value of money.

16. Explain the basic difference between future value and present value.

17. What is an annuity?

18. Complete the following schedule:

Concept	Symbol	Table Values		
		$n = 4; i = 5\%$	$n = 7; i = 10\%$	$n = 9; i = 15\%$
FV of $1				
PV of $1				
FV of annuity of $1				
PV of annuity of $1				

19. What is a lease liability?

20. What is meant by a capital lease?

21. The Halifax Schooners Baseball Ltd. obtains a new pitching machine by leasing the machine from a supplier under terms that require its disclosure as a capital lease. The team also hires a star player for a substantial salary on a five-year contract. Why would the pitching machine be treated differently for accounting purposes than the employee contract?

EXERCISES

Part A

E10–1. Banks Company is preparing its 19B balance sheet. The company records reflect the following related amounts:

Total current assets.........................	$157,100
Total all remaining assets	665,000
Liabilities:	
Note payable (10%, due in 5 years)	22,000
Accounts payable	60,000
Income tax payable......................	15,000
Liability for withholding taxes.............	4,000
Rent revenue collected in advance	3,000
Bonds payable (due in 15 years)	200,000
Wages payable...........................	6,000
Property taxes payable....................	2,000
Note payable, 12% (due in 6 months)	5,000
Interest payable.........................	100

Required:

a. Compute total owners' equity.

b. Compute (1) working capital in dollars and (2) the working capital ratio (show computations).

c. Compute the amount of interest expense for 19B on the 10 percent note assuming it was dated October 1, 19B.

E10–2. During 19B, the two transactions given below were completed by Post Company. The annual accounting period ends December 31.

1. Wages paid and recorded during 19B amounted to $70,000; however, at the end of December 19B, there were two days' wages unpaid and unrecorded because the weekly payroll will not be paid until January 6, 19C. Wages for the two days amounted to $700.
2. On December 10, 19B, Post Company collected rent revenue amounting to $600 on some office space that it rented to another party. The rent collected was for the month from December 10, 19B, to January 10, 19C, and was credited to Rent Revenue.

Required:

a. Give (1) the adjusting entry required on December 31, 19B, and (2) the January 6, 19C, journal entry for payment of any unpaid wages from December 19B.
b. Give (1) the journal entry for the collection of rent on December 10, 19B, and (2) the adjusting entry on December 31, 19B (compute rent to the nearest 10 days).
c. Show how any liabilities related to the above transactions should be reported on the balance sheet at December 31, 19B.

E10–3. Corning Manufacturing Company has completed the payroll for January 19B, reflecting the following data:

Salaries and wages earned	$80,000
Employee income taxes withheld	11,000
Union dues withheld	1,100
Canada Pension Plan contributions withheld	1,356
Unemployment insurance premiums withheld	1,880
Private pension plan contributions withheld	3,360

The employer was required to pay the following additional amounts for the January payroll:

Canada Pension Plan	1,356
Unemployment insurance	2,632
Workmen's compensation	700
Matching share to private pension plan	3,360

Required:

a. Give the journal entry to record payment of the payroll.
b. Give the journal entry to record employer payroll taxes.
c. Give the journal entry in February 19B to record payment of all payroll liabilities by the employer.
d. What was the amount of additional labour expense to the company due to tax laws and benefit contracts? Explain. What was the employees' take-home pay? Explain.

(Revised by E. Scott)

E10–4. On November 1, 19A, Quality Auto Parts Company borrowed $40,000 cash from the City Bank for working capital purposes and gave an interest-bearing note with a face amount of $40,000. The note was due in six months, and the interest rate was 12 percent per annum payable at maturity.

Required:

a. Give the journal entry to record the note on November 1.
b. Give the adjusting entry that would be required at the end of the annual accounting period, December 31, 19A.
c. Give the journal entry to record payment of the note and interest on the maturity date, April 30, 19B (disregard reversing entries).

E10–5. Trend Company sells a wide range of goods through two retail stores that are operated in adjoining cities. Most purchases of goods for resale are on invoices with credit terms of 2/10, n/30. Occasionally, a short-term note payable is executed to obtain cash for current use. The following transactions were selected from those occurring during 19B:

1. On January 10, 19B, purchased merchandise on credit, $14,000; terms, 2/10, n/30. Record at net (see Chapter 6); the company uses the periodic inventory system.
2. On March 1, 19B, borrowed $30,000 cash from City Bank and gave an interest-bearing note payable: face amount, $30,000; due at the end of six months, with an annual interest rate of 12 percent payable at maturity.

Required:

a. Give the journal entry for each of the above transactions. Record purchases and accounts payable at net.
b. Give the journal entry assuming the account payable of January 10, 19B, was paid within the discount period.
c. Give the journal entry assuming the account payable of January 10, 19B, was paid after the discount period.
d. Give the journal entry for the payment of the note payable plus interest on the maturity date.

E10–6. The comparative income statement of Telex Company at December 31, 19B, reflected the following data (summarized and excluding income taxes):

	Annual income statement for	
	19A	19B
Sales revenue	$50,000	$60,000
Expenses	40,000	48,000
Pretax income	$10,000	$12,000

Included on the 19B income statement given above was an expense amounting to $6,000 that was deductible on the income tax return in 19A rather than in 19B. Assume an average tax rate of 20 percent.

Required:

a. For each year compute (1) income tax expense, (2) income tax payable, and (3) any deferred tax.
b. Give the journal entry for each year to record income tax, including any deferred tax.
c. Show how the income tax liabilities would be shown on the balance sheet for each year assuming the tax is paid the following April.

E10–7. The comparative income statement for Blues Company for the years ended December 31, 19A, and 19B, reflected the following data (summarized and excluding income taxes):

	Annual income statement for	
	19A	19B
Revenues	$90,000	$94,000
Expenses	75,000	78,000
Pretax income	$15,000	$16,000

Included on the 19B income statement given above was a revenue item amounting to $5,000 that was included on the income tax return for 19A rather than in 19B. Assume an average income tax rate of 20 percent.

Required:

a. For each year, compute (1) income tax expense, (2) income tax payable, and (3) deferred income tax. (Hint: Deferred income tax will have a debit balance for 19A.)
b. Give the journal entry for each year to record income tax, including any deferred tax.
c. Show how income tax would be reported on the balance sheet each year assuming the tax is paid the following April.

E10–8. Green Corporation reported the following income statement data (summarized):

	Income statement for year ended December 31		
	19A	19B	19C
Revenues	$150,000	$150,000	$150,000
Expenses (including depreciation)	110,000	110,000	110,000
Pretax income	$ 40,000	$ 40,000	$ 40,000

Depreciation expense included on the income statement was computed as follows:

Machinery cost (acquired on January 1, 19A), $60,000; estimated useful life, three years, no residual value; annual depreciation (straight line) $60,000 ÷ 3 years = $20,000.

The company claims maximum capital cost allowances under class 29 rules at the rates of 25 percent, 50 percent, and 25 percent, respectively, for each of the years 19A, 19B, and 19C. The company has an average income tax rate of 30 percent.

Required:

a. For each year, compute (1) income tax expense for the income statement and (2) income tax payable for the tax return (show computations).
b. Give the journal entry for each year to record income tax including any deferred income tax.
c. What kind of "tax difference" was involved? Explain.
d. What advantage was gained by using capital cost allowance at the maximum rates on the tax return, if any?

Part B

E10–9. On January 1, 19A, Hyper Company, completed the following transactions (assume a 12 percent annual interest rate):
1. Deposited $10,000 in a special fund (designated Fund A).
2. Decided to establish a special fund (designated Fund B) by making six equal annual deposits of $2,000 each.
3. Decided to establish a special fund (designated Fund C) by depositing a single amount that will increase to $50,000 by the end of Year 7.
4. Decided to deposit a single sum in a special fund (designated Fund D) that will provide 10 equal annual year-end payments of $10,000 to a retired employee (payments starting December 31, 19A).

Required (show computations and round to the nearest dollar):
a. What will be the balance of Fund A at the end of Year 9?
b. What will be the balance of Fund B at the end of Year 6?
c. What single amount must be deposited in Fund C on January 1, 19A?
d. What single sum must be deposited in Fund D on January 1, 19A?

E10–10. On January 1, 19A, you deposited $5,000 in a savings account. The account will earn 9 percent annual compound interest, which will be added to the fund balance at the end of each year. You recorded the deposit as follows:

Savings account	5,000	
Cash		5,000

Required:
a. What will be the balance in the savings account at the end of 10 years (round to the nearest dollar)?
b. What is the time value of the money in dollars for the 10 years?
c. How much interest revenue did the fund earn in 19A? 19B?
d. Give the journal entry to record interest revenue at the end of 19A and 19B.

E10–11. On December 31, 19A, Parent decided to deposit an amount in a savings account that will provide $20,000 four years later to send Offspring to Super University. The savings account will earn 8 percent which will be added to the fund each year-end.

Required (show computations and round to the nearest dollar):
a. How much must Parent deposit on January 1, 19A?
b. Give the journal entry that Parent should make on January 1, 19A.
c. What is the time value of the money for the four years?
d. Give the journal entry Parent should make on (1) December 31, 19A, and (2) December 31, 19B.

E10–12. On each December 31, you plan to deposit $600 in a savings account. The account will earn 9 percent annual interest, which will be added to the fund balance at year end. The first deposit will be made December 31, 19A.

Required (show computations and round to the nearest dollar):
a. Give the required journal entry on December 31, 19A.
b. What will be the balance in the savings account at the end of the 10th year (i.e., 10 deposits)?

    c.   What is the time value of money in dollars for the 10 deposits?

    d.   How much interest revenue did the fund earn in 19B? 19C?

    e.   Give all required journal entries at the end of 19B and 19C.

E10–13.   You have decided to take a trip around the world upon graduation, four years from now (January 1, 19A). Your grandfather desires to deposit sufficient funds for this purpose in a savings account for you. On the basis of a carefully drawn budget you estimate the trip now would cost $8,000. To be generous, your grandfather decided to deposit $2,200 in the fund at the end of each of the next four years. The savings account will earn 7 percent annual interest, which will be added to the savings account at each year-end.

    Required (show computations and round to the nearest dollar):

    a.   Give the required journal entry on December 31, 19A, to record the first deposit.

    b.   What will be the balance in the fund at the end of Year 4 (i.e., four deposits)?

    c.   What is the time value of the money for the four years?

    d.   How much interest revenue would the fund earn in 19A, 19B, and 19C?

    e.   Give the journal entries at the end of 19B and 19C.

E10–14.   You have an opportunity to purchase the royalty interest of a landowner in an oil well. Your best estimate is that the net royalty income will average $30,000 per year for five years. There will be no residual value at that time. Assume the cash inflow is at each year-end and that, considering the uncertainty in your estimates, you expect to earn 20 percent per year on the investment.

    Required:

    a.   What should you be willing to pay for this investment on January 1, 19A? Show computations and round to nearest dollar.

    b.   Give the required journal entry (cash paid in full) on January 1, 19A.

    c.   Give the required journal entry on December 31, 19A, assuming the net cash received was 10 percent above your estimate.

E10–15.   On November 1, 19A, Design Furniture Company borrowed $40,000 cash from the City Bank for working capital purposes and gave a noninterest-bearing note payable. The note was due in six months, and the face amount was $42,400. The going rate of interest was 12 percent per year.

    Required:

    a.   Give the journal entry to record the note on November 1, 19A.

    b.   Give the adjusting entry that would be required at the end of the annual accounting period, December 31, 19A.

    c.   Show how the note should be reported on the December 31, 19A, balance sheet.

    d.   Give the journal entry to record payment of the note at maturity on April 30, 19B (disregard reversing entries).

E10–16.   Assume you needed to borrow exactly $3,600 cash for one year. The City Bank charges 12 percent interest per annum on such loans. You are to respond to the following questions (show computations):

    Required:

    a.   What would be the face amount of the note assuming the bank agreed to accept an interest-bearing note?

b. What would be the face amount of the note assuming the bank insisted on a non-interest-bearing note?
c. Give the journal entries to record the note in (a) and (b). Set the entries in parallel columns.
d. Give the journal entries at date of maturity in (a) and (b).

PROBLEMS/CASES

Part A

PC10–1. Webster Company completed the transactions listed below during 19B. The annual accounting period ends December 31, 19B.

Jan.   8   Purchased merchandise for resale at an invoice cost of $15,000; terms, 2/10, n/60. Record at net (see Chapter 6); assume a periodic inventory system.
      17   Paid invoice of January 8.
Apr.   1   Borrowed $20,000 from the National Bank for general use; executed a 12-month, 12 percent, interest-bearing note payable.
June   3   Purchased merchandise for resale at an invoice cost of $30,000; terms, 1/20, n/30; record at net.
July   5   Paid invoice of June 3.
Aug.   1   Rented two rooms in the building owned by Webster and collected six months' rent in advance amounting to $1,800. Record the collection in a way that will not require an adjusting entry at year-end.
Dec. 20   Received a $200 deposit from a customer as a guarantee to return a large trailer "borrowed" for 30 days.
      31   Wages earned but not paid on December 31 amounted to $4,000 (disregard payroll taxes).

Required:

a. Prepare journal entries for each of the above transactions.
b. Prepare all adjusting entries required on December 31, 19B.
c. Show how all of the liabilities arising from the above transactions would be reported on the balance sheet at December 31, 19B.

PC10–2. Arbor Company completed the transactions listed below during 19A. The annual accounting period ends December 31.

May   1   Purchased an operational asset (fixtures) for $60,000; paid $20,000 cash and gave a 12-month, 12 percent, interest-bearing note payable for the balance.
June 5   Purchased an operational asset (machine) at an invoice cost of $10,000; terms, 3/10, n/60.
     14   Paid invoice of June 5.
Sept. 1   Collected rent revenue on some office space rented to another company; the rent of $6,000 was for the next six months. Record the collection so as to avoid an adjusting entry at the end of 19A.
Dec. 31   Received a tax bill for property tax for 19A in the amount of $900; the taxes are payable no later than March 1, 19B.

Required:

a.   Give the journal entries for each of the above transactions.
b.   Prepare any adjusting entries required on December 31, 19A (exclude depreciation).
c.   Show how all liabilities arising from the above transactions would be reported on the balance sheet at December 31, 19A.

PC10–3.   Hi-Fi Retailers sold a Super-set stereo to a customer for $2,000 cash on December 30, 19A. Hi-Fi gave the customer a one-year guarantee on the Super-set. Experience with this set by Hi-Fi indicates that to maintain the warranty would cost approximately 5 percent of the sales price.

Assume a perpetual inventory system and that the Super-set cost Hi-Fi Retailers $900.
Actual cash for warranty expenditures (parts and labour) to make good the warranty on the set during 19B amounted to $95.

Required:

a.   Give the journal entry or entries required on December 30, 19A. Explain the basis for your entries.
b.   Give the journal entry or entries required on December 31, 19A, end of the annual accounting period. Explain the basis for your responses. (Hint: Consider the liability for warranty work.)
c.   Show how the income statement and balance sheet for 19A would reflect the above data.
d.   Give the journal entry to record the repair made to the set in 19B. Discuss any issues that are evident.

PC10–4.   On April 1, 19A, Perduyn Company purchased equipment at a cost of $110,000. A cash down payment in the amount of $30,000 was made. An interest-bearing note (including a mortgage on the equipment) for $80,000 was given for the balance. The note specified 14 percent annual interest. Two payments on principal of $40,000 each plus interest on the unpaid balance on March 31, 19B, and March 31, 19C, are required. (Note: These will be unequal cash payments.)

Required:

a.   Give the journal entries on April 1, 19A, and December 31, 19A (end of the annual accounting period).
b.   Show how the liabilities related to the purchase should be shown on the Perduyn balance sheet on December 31, 19A.
c.   Give the journal entry on March 31, 19B.

PC10–5.   Radney Company is in the process of preparing comparative statements at December 31, 19B. The records reflect the following summarized income statement data, exclusive of income tax expense:

	19A	19B
Revenues	$180,000	$190,000
Expenses	(110,000)	(129,000)
Extraordinary item	(10,000)	4,000
Income before income tax	$ 60,000	$ 65,000

Included in the 19B revenues of $190,000 is a revenue item amounting to $20,000 that was included on the income tax return for 19A rather than 19B. Also included in the 19B expenses of $129,000 was an expense item amounting to $6,000 that was deducted on the income tax return for 19A rather than 19B. Assume an average 20 percent income tax rate. Assume there were no deferred income taxes in the extraordinary items.

Required:

a. For each year, compute (1) income tax expense, (2) income tax liability, and (3) deferred income tax.
b. Give the journal entry for each year to record income tax expense, including any deferred income taxes.
c. Restate the above comparative income statement, including the appropriate presentation of income tax for each year. (Hint: Allocate income tax expense between operations and extraordinary items.)
d. What kind of "tax difference" was represented by the two items? Explain.

PC10–6. At December 31, 19B, the records of Laymon Corporation provided the following pretax information:

1. Revenues $150,000
2. Expenses (including $13,000 depreciation expense) 113,000
3. Depreciation expense was computed as follows for income statement purposes:
   Operational asset cost (acquired January 1, 19A) 52,000
   Four-year useful life (no residual value).
   Depreciation expense per year $52,000 ÷ 4 years 13,000
4. Extraordinary loss... 10,000
5. The revenues given in 1 include $5,000 of tax-free dividends on tax-deferred preferred shares.
6. Assume an average income tax rate of 20 percent on both ordinary income and extraordinary income.
7. Class 29 capital cost allowance on the operational asset will be used on the income tax return, and straight-line depreciation on the income statement.

Required:

a. Compute income tax expense.
b. Compute income tax on the tax return.
c. Give the journal entry to record income tax including any deferred income tax.
d. Prepare a single-step income statement.
e. What kind of "tax differences" were involved? Explain the basis for your treatment of them.

Part B

PC10–7. On January 1, 19A, Illustrative Company completed the following transactions (assume a 10 percent annual interest rate):

1. Deposited $30,000 in a special debt retirement fund. Interest will be computed at six-month intervals and added to the fund at those times (i.e., semiannual compounding). (Hint: Think carefully about n and i.)
2. Decided to establish a plant addition fund of $150,000 to be available at the end of Year 5. A single sum will be deposited on January 1, 19A, that will grow to the $150,000.
3. Decided to establish a pension retirement fund of $400,000 by the end of Year 6 by making six equal annual deposits each at year-end, starting on December 31, 19A.

4. Decided to purchase a $100,000 machine on January 1, 19A, and pay cash, $25,000. A three-year note payable is signed for the balance. The note will be paid in three equal year-end payments starting on December 31, 19A.

Required (show computations and round to the nearest dollar):

a. In transaction 1 above, what will be the balance in the fund at the end of Year 4? What is the total amount of interest revenue earned?
b. In transaction 2 above, what single sum amount must the company deposit on January 1, 19A? What is the total amount of interest revenue earned?
c. In transaction 3 above, what is the required amount of each of the six equal annual deposits? What is the total amount of interest revenue earned?
d. In transaction 4 above, what is the amount of each of the equal annual payments that must be paid on the note? What is the total amount of interest expense?

PC10–8. Giant Company has decided to build another plant during 19C that they estimate will cost $800,000. At the present time, January 1, 19A, they have excess cash, some of which they may decide to set aside in a special savings account to defray $600,000 of the plant cost. The savings account would earn 10 percent annual interest which would be credited to the savings account each year-end.

Required (show computations and round to the nearest dollar):

a. What single amount would have to be deposited in the savings account on January 1, 19A, to create the desired amount by the end of 19C?
b. What will be the time value of the money by the end of 19C?
c. How much interest revenue will be earned each year?
d. Give the following journal entries:
   (1) Interest earned at each year-end.
   (2) Use of the fund to pay on the plant (completed December 31, 19C).

PC10–9. On January 1, 19A, Delta Construction Company signed a construction contract with Dawn Company. Delta Company was required to deposit with an independent trustee $50,000 cash as a performance guarantee on a construction project. The trustee agreed to pay 7 percent annual interest on the fund and to add it to the fund balance at each year-end. At the end of the third year, the construction project was completed satisfactorily and the trustee returned the balance of the fund to Delta Construction Company. The entry by Delta Construction Company to record the deposit was as follows:

Performance fund 50,000
    Cash   50,000

Required (show computations and round to the nearest dollar):

a. What was the balance of the fund at the end of the three years?
b. What was the time value of the money for the three years?
c. How much interest revenue did the fund earn each year?
d. Give the following journal entries for Delta Construction Company:
   (1) To record interest revenue at each year-end.
   (2) To record receipt of the fund balance at the end of 19C.

PC10–10. On January 1, 19A, the management of Flood Company agreed to set aside a special fund in order to provide sufficient cash to pay off the principal amount of a $55,000 long-term debt that will be due at the end of five years. The single deposit will be made with an independent party (a bank), which will pay 8 percent annual interest on the fund balance. The interest will be added to the fund balance at each year-end.

Required (show computations and round to the nearest dollar):

a. How much must be deposited as a single sum on January 1, 19A, to satisfy the agreement?

b. What was the time value of the money in dollars for the five years?

c. How much interest revenue would the fund earn in 19A? 19B?

d. Give the journal entries for Flood Company:
    (1) To record the deposit on January 1, 19A.
    (2) To record the interest revenue for 19A and 19B (separately).
    (3) To record payment of the maturing liability at the end of the fifth year.

PC10–11. On December 31, 19A, the management of Moe Company agreed to set aside, in a special fund, sufficient cash to pay the principal amount of a $50,000 debt which will be due on December 31, 19D. Moe Company will make four equal annual deposits on each December 31, 19A, 19B, 19C, and 19D. The fund balance will earn 10 percent annual interest, which will be added to the balance of the fund at each year-end. The fund trustee will pay the loan principal (to the creditor) upon receipt of the last fund deposit.

Required (show computations and round to the nearest dollar):

a. How much must be deposited each December 31? (Hint: Use Table 10–3 and divide instead of multiply.)

b. What will be the time value of the money in dollars for the fund?

c. How much interest revenue will the fund earn in 19A, 19B, 19C, and 19D?

d. Give the journal entries for the following for Moe Company:
    (1) For the first deposit on December 31, 19A.
    (2) For all amounts at the ends of 19B and 19C.
    (3) For payment of the debt on December 31, 19D.

PC10–12. On January 1, 19A, Big Company sold to Small Company a new machine for $40,000. A cash down payment of $10,000 was made by Small Company. A $30,000, 12 percent note was signed by Small Company for the balance due. The note is to be paid off in three equal installments due on December 31, 19A, 19B, and 19C. Each payment is to include principal plus interest on the unpaid balance. The purchase was recorded by Small as follows:

January 1, 19A:

Machine	40,000	
Cash		10,000
Note payable...		30,000

Required (show computations and round to the nearest dollar):

a. What is the amount of the equal annual payment that must be made by Small Company? (Hint: Use Table 10–4 and divide instead of multiply.)

b. What was the time value of the money, in dollars, on the note?

c. Complete the following debt payment schedule:

Date	Cash Payment	Interest Expense	Reduction of Principal	Unpaid Principal
1/1/19A				
12/31/19A				
12/31/19B				
12/31/19C				
Total				

    d. Give the journal entries for each of the three payments.

    e. Explain why interest expense decreased in amount each year.

PC10–13.   On January 1, 19A, you purchased a new Super-Whiz automobile for $15,000. You paid a $5,000 cash down payment and signed a $10,000 note, payable in four equal installments on each December 31, the first payment to be made on December 31, 19A. The interest rate is 14 percent per year on the unpaid balance. Each payment will include payment on principal plus the interest.

Required:

    a. Compute the amount of the equal payments that you must make (Hint: Use Table 10–4.)

    b. What is the time value of the money in dollars for the installment debt?

    c. Complete a schedule using the format below.

DEBT PAYMENT SCHEDULE

Date	Cash Payment	Interest Expense	Reduction of Principal	Unpaid Principal
1/1/A				
12/31/A				
12/31/B				
12/31/C				
12/31/D				
Total				

    d. Explain why the amount of interest expense decreases each year.

    e. Give the journal entries on December 31, 19A, and 19B.

PC10–14.   This problem was designed to illustrate and compare the accounting for (*a*) an interest-bearing note payable and (*b*) a noninterest-bearing note payable. The annual accounting period ends December 31 in both cases. Cove Company executed a note payable to Canadian Bank for a loan of cash on April 1, 19A. The loan was for 12 months with a maturity date of March 31, 19B. The bank charges a 12 percent annual rate on loans of this type. The amount of cash borrowed was $20,000. We will assume:

Case A—The note was interest bearing—that is, the principal plus the interest is payable at maturity. The face amount of the note was $20,000.

Case B—The note was noninterest bearing—that is, the interest was on the cash received and was included in the face amount of the note.

Required:

a. Record the issuance of the note on April 1, 19A, under each of the two cases. Your solution can be simplified by setting up five columns: Account Titles; Case A (debit and credit), and Case B (debit and credit). Thus, the two cases can be presented in your solution in parallel columns.

b. Give the journal entry to record the adjusting entry that would be required for each case on December 31, 19A.

c. Give the journal entry to record payment of the note under each case at maturity, March 31, 19B; disregard any reversing entries.

d. In respect to each case show the following:
   (1) Liabilities that would be reported on the balance sheet at December 31, 19A.
   (2) Interest expense that would be reported on the income statements for 19A and 19B (separately).

PC10–15. Several years ago, Rapid Service Company borrowed a large amount of money from First Canadian Bank. At the time the loan was approved, Rapid Service agreed not to borrow any additional money from any other sources until the First Canadian loan was repaid. As the result of continued growth, Rapid Service must acquire a large computer during the current year. Unfortunately, Rapid Service does not have sufficient cash to purchase the computer or to repay the loan to First Canadian. You have been engaged as a consultant to Rapid Service. The president of Rapid Service, Allison Payne, described the problem during your first meeting:

The computer can be purchased from Super Computer Company for $500,000, but we don't have the cash and the bank won't let us borrow any more money. However, the computer company has agreed to lease the computer to us on a 10-year lease which is the expected useful life of the computer with no residual value. Annual lease payments of $81,372 would be paid based on an interest rate of 10 percent. I think that this lease deal will solve our problem because we will not violate our agreement with First Canadian as long as we don't report any additional debt on the balance sheet. But I have to admit that I don't understand accounting. What do you think?

In order to help the president understand the required accounting treatment, the president could consider three alternative situations:

Alternative No. 1—Rapid Service could purchase the computer but would have to borrow $500,000 with a note payable to the computer company at 10 percent interest for 10 years. Annual year-end payments for principal and interest amount to $81,372.

Alternative No. 2—Rapid Service could rent the computer on a monthly lease basis. The terms of the lease cause it to be considered an operating lease. Annual rent payments would be $125,000 at each year-end.

Alternative No. 3—Rapid Service could acquire the computer on a long-term lease basis. At the expiration date of the lease, the computer would be returned to Super Computer Company. The terms of the lease cause it to be considered a capital lease. The lease payments would be $81,372.

Required:

a. Assume that the computer was acquired on January 1, 19D, which is the beginning of the accounting period. Prepare journal entries to record the acquisition of the computer by Rapid Service under each of the three alternatives.
b. Assume Rapid Service makes cash payments under each alternative on December 31 of each year. Prepare the required journal entries on December 31, 19D (include adjusting entries, if required). Rapid Service uses straight-line depreciation for all assets.
c. Would the capital lease alternative, described by the president, permit Rapid Service to acquire the computer and to conform to GAAP?
d. What are the primary problems of alternatives 1 and 2?

PC10–16. In recent years, it was possible to buy a savings bond for $18.75. When the bond was "cashed in" at the end of five years, the government would pay $25.

Required (show computations):

a. Determine the approximate annual interest rate that the government paid on the savings bonds (Hint: This is a present value problem where you are given the time to maturity, the future cash inflow [$25] and the present value [$18.75] but not the interest rate.)
b. If you want to earn 6 percent on your savings and the government agreed to pay you $25 at the end of five years if you purchase a savings bond, what price would you be willing to pay for the savings bond at the beginning of Year 1?

PC10–17. Walter Carrington, a home builder, published an advertisement that offered for sale "a $120,000 house with a zero interest rate mortgage." If the purchaser made monthly payments of $2,000 for five years ($120,000 ÷ 60 months), there would be no additional charge for interest. When the offer was made, mortgage interest rates were 12 percent. PV for $n = 60$, and $i = 1\%$ is 44.9550.

Required:

a. Did Walter Carrington actually provide a mortgage at zero interest?
b. Estimate the true price of the home that was advertised. Assume that the $2,000 monthly payment was based on an implicit interest rate of 12 percent.

PC10–18. (Based on Supplement 10A.)   Tappen Company has completed the salaries and wages payroll for March 19A. Details provided by the payroll were:

Salaries and wages earned	$200,000*
Employee income taxes withheld	42,000
Union dues withheld	2,000
Insurance premiums withheld	900
Canada Pension Plan contributions	3,424
Unemployment insurance premiums withheld 2.35 per cent	

*Subject in full to payroll taxes.

Required:

a. Give the journal entry to record the payroll for March, including employee deductions. Show computations.

b. Give the journal entry to record the employer's payroll taxes.

c. Give a combined journal entry to reflect remittance of amounts owed to governmental agencies and other organizations.

d. What was the total labour cost for Tappen Company? Explain. What percentage of the payroll was take-home pay? Explain.

PC10–19. (Based on Supplement 10B.) Holt Company uses a voucher system to attain control of expenditures. The following transactions have been selected from December 19B for case purposes. The accounting year ends December 31.

You are to design a voucher register and a cheque register similar to those shown in Supplement 10B. The transactions that follow will be entered in these two special journals.

Dec. 2 Purchased merchandise from AB Wholesalers for resale, $2,000; terms, 2/10, n/30; record purchases at net and assume a periodic inventory system (see Chapter 6); Invoice No. 14; start with Voucher No. 11.

7 Approved contract with Ace Plumbing Company for repair of plumbing, $450; account, Building Repairs, No. 77

11 Paid Voucher No. 11; start with Cheque No. 51.

22 Purchased store supplies for future use from Crown Company; Invoice No. 21 for $90; account, Stores Supplies Inventory, No. 16.

23 Advertising for pre-Christmas sale $630; bill received from Daily Press and payment processed immediately; account, Advertising Expense, No. 54.

31 Monthly payroll voucher, total $2,500; $1,500 was selling expense (Sales Salaries, No. 52) and $1,000 was administrative expense (Administrative Salaries, No. 62). The voucher was supported by the payroll record; therefore, one voucher was prepared for the entire payroll. The voucher was approved for immediate payment. Six cheques with consecutive numbers were issued.

Required:

a. Enter the above transactions in the voucher register and the cheque register.

b. Total the special journals and check the equality of the debits and credits. Set up T-accounts and post both registers. Complete all posting notations. The following accounts may be needed:

Account titles	Account No.
Cash	01
Store supplies inventory	16
Vouchers payable	30
Purchases	40
Selling expense control	50
Subsidiary ledger:	
Sales salaries	52
Advertising expense	54
Administrative expense control	60
Subsidiary ledger:	
Administrative salaries	62
Building repairs	77

c.   Reconcile the Vouchers Payable account balance with the Unpaid Vouchers File at the end of December.

PC10–20. TS Limited, a well-known public company, operates a chain of department stores across Canada. These stores are in leased premises in shopping centres. TS Ltd. is required to file annually with several provincial securities commissions. The company has a long history of marginal profitability.

Management personnel are paid bonuses calculated as a percentage of the excess of net income in the financial statements over the budgeted net income. Budgets are approved by the board of directors.

The company has entered into certain contractual arrangements, including bank loan agreements, promissory notes, and mortgages. These arrangements have restrictions as to the amount of debt permitted in relation to shareholders' equity. At December 31, 1985, the company's most recent year-end, the company came close to being in default of the debt/equity restrictions.

TS Ltd. has a store in premises leased from Suburban Shopping Centres Limited (SSC) and accounts for the contract as a capital lease. In 1985, SSC paid TS Ltd. $3 million and agreed to renovate the exterior of TS Ltd.'s store. In exchange, TS Ltd. agreed: (1) to renovate the interior of the store; (2) to pay an additional $180,000 rent per annum for the remaining 12 years of the lease; and (3) to allow SSC to further develop the centre including the rental of space to one of TS Ltd.'s competitors.

TS Ltd.'s auditors, CW & Co., became aware of this transaction during the interim audit in September, 1985. At that time, a dispute arose between CW & Co. and the management of TS Ltd. with respect to the appropriate accounting treatment for the transaction. This dispute ultimately led to the replacement of CW & Co. by another firm of auditors, GA & Co. GA & Co. agreed to accept management's viewpoint and in March 1986, rendered an opinion on the December 31, 1985 financial statements. The statements showed that TS Ltd. had a net income of $1 million for the 1985 fiscal year. A note to the financial statements stated the following:

> The gain on disposition of a leasehold right arose as a result of a payment received from a lessor in exchange for the company's agreement to allow the expansion of a shopping centre in which it operates a department store. In November 1985, the company filed with the securities commissions reporting a change in independent public accountants. The company's former auditors, CW & Co., disagreed with the company's method of accounting for the transaction and were of the opinion that the gain should be amortized to income over the remaining term of the lease. Management, with the concurrence of the audit committee of the board of directors and the company's current auditors, GA & Co., believes its accounting treatment (i.e., recognizing the gain immediately) is preferable based on the substance of the transaction and the intent of the parties. Had the accounting treatment suggested by the company's former auditors been followed, net income for 1985 would have been $1.6 million ($.50 per share) less than reported.

The company's 1985 statement filed with the securities commissions stated the following:

> Under an amendment to a capital lease, the lessor of a shopping centre in which the company operates a store, developed plans to expand the shopping centre to become an integrated regional mall. The company consented to this development in exchange for $3 million. Further, the amendment provided that the lessor refurbish the

exterior of the company's store and the company agreed to proceed diligently to alter, modernize, and refixture the interior of the store. No amount to be expended was specified. As a result of the lessor's enhancement of the centre and refurbishing of the exterior of the store, the company agreed to pay an increase in rent of $180,000 per annum for the remaining 12 of the original 30 years of the lease term (such increased rental does not apply to subsequent renewal option periods). Management concluded that the appropriate accounting treatment was to recognize income of approximately $1.6 million in the 1985 fiscal year, representing the difference between the $3 million and the present value of the increased rental. The present value was calculated using the implicit rate of the original lease which was 8 percent. The lease obligation and asset were recorded at that rate several years ago. This accounting treatment was ratified by the audit committee of the board of directors of the company.

In support of its accounting treatment, TS Ltd.'s management argued that the use of an 8 percent implicit interest rate resulted in conservative recognition of income. Had the 18 percent current borrowing rate been used, the gain on disposition would have been $2.1 million. Furthermore, they suggested that a complete note disclosure would ensure that its accounting treatment was acceptable.

A financial analyst suggested that a third alternative might have better described the true nature of the transaction. It could be considered to consist of two separate events. The first event is the selling of an exclusive right for $3 million. The second event is the improvement of the exterior of TS Ltd.'s store by the lessor, in return for higher rentals over the next 12 years. This view may be summarized by the following journal entries:

Cash	3,000,000	
Gain on disposition of leasehold right		3,000,000
To record the sale of an exclusive right.		
Leased asset, capitalized	1,400,000	
Present value of lease obligation		1,400,000
To record an increase in future lease payments as a result of the lessor's improvements to the exterior of the store.		

Required:

Discuss the accounting issues involved in this situation. Assess the various viewpoints involved as part of the discussion.

(CICA Adapted)

PC 10–21. On January 1, 19A, assume you purchased a new automobile for $15,000. You paid $5,000 cash down payment and signed a $10,000 note, payable in equal monthly installments of principal and interest on the last day of each month for four years from the date of purchase. The interest rate is 12 percent per year on the monthly unpaid balance.

Required:

a. Using a computer spreadsheet, prepare a debt payment schedule of the form illustrated in Problems PC10–12 or PC10–13.

b. What would the sales price of the automobile be if the dealer advertised interest rates of 6 percent per annum when the market rate of interest (what it wanted) was 12 percent? Compute the payment schedule for the 6 percent loan. (Hint: To determine sales price, equate future values of selling prices, one price unknown, at the end of 48 months. Solve for the unknown.)

c. How many dollars would you save if you paid the note over two years rather than four years assuming a 12 percent interest rate? (Hint: Modify your spreadsheet in Part a).

PC10–22.   You are to do the following:

a. Create an employee master file and enter data into it.

b. Create a file to record the hours worked by nonsalaried employees during a weekly pay period.

c. Put the actual hours worked during a given pay period in this file.

d. Write a program to update the employee master file and prepare a payroll summary file which can be used in generating payroll reports.

e. Prepare payroll summary reports.

f. Add and delete records from the payroll file.

g. Rerun the payroll program and prepare revised reports.

a. Create Employee Master File

The employee master file consists of nine fields. These are:

1. Name of employee.
2. Type of employee, *S* is salaried, *H* is hourly.
3. Pay rate, weekly rate for salaried employees and hourly rate for hourly employees.
4. Weekly deductions; for example, union dues, United Way contributions, etc.
5. Year to date earnings.
6. Year to date deductions for income tax.
7. Year to date deductions for the Canada Pension Plan.
8. Year to date deductions for unemployment insurance.
9. Year to date deductions for weekly deductions (item 4).

The following information should be entered into the file:

Name	Class	Rate	Deductions	ytdearn	ytdtax	ytdcpp	ytduic	ytdded
AFJEC, Q.A....................	H	20.00	0.00	$ 8,540.00	$2,562.00	153.72	200.69	0.00
ANSAG, N.D.	H	15.00	37.00	7,545.00	1,886.25	135.81	177.31	518.00
ARIOQ, D.D.	S	800.00	33.00	11,200.00	3,360.00	201.60	263.20	462.00
AWASL, C.T....................	H	15.00	0.00	9,435.00	2,830.50	169.83	221.72	0.00
BETHO, H.D....................	S	800.00	47.00	11,200.00	3,360.00	201.60	263.20	658.00
CHALDDRE, I.S.................	H	8.00	0.00	1,976.00	197.60	35.57	46.44	0.00
EDEGAR, O.A.	H	10.00	51.00	2,350.00	235.00	42.30	55.23	714.00
HANAN, S.I.	H	10.00	38.00	5,360.00	1,072.00	96.48	125.96	532.00
KNAST, A.T.	S	320.00	0.00	4,480.00	896.00	80.64	105.28	0.00
LEBA, C.W.	H	8.00	45.00	4,848.00	969.60	87.26	113.93	630.00
MISH, A.H.	H	15.00	43.00	8,025.00	2,006.25	144.45	188.59	602.00
NEBUBAB, A.D.	H	20.00	0.00	4,340.00	868.00	78.12	101.99	0.00
NECLI, T.B.	H	7.00	11.00	1,008.00	0.00	18.14	23.69	154.00
SHAVE, H.D....................	H	8.00	39.00	4,768.00	953.60	85.82	112.05	546.00
SHIPTON, D.U..................	H	20.00	26.00	12,240.00	3,672.00	220.32	287.64	364.00
SPELD, Y.O....................	H	15.00	63.00	5,340.00	1,068.00	96.12	125.49	882.00
TYRUN, M.S....................	H	20.00	24.00	3,140.00	628.00	56.52	73.79	336.00
WIFUL, P.A....................	H	7.00	54.00	3,913.00	782.60	70.43	91.96	756.00
WILCOM, W.I.	S	280.00	0.00	3,920.00	784.00	70.56	92.12	0.00
WORJER, T.P.	S	320.00	0.00	4,480.00	896.00	80.64	105.28	0.00

b.c. Create Hours Worked File and Enter Hours Worked

There are many ways you could create the hours worked file. One method is to copy the records in the master file for hourly employees to a temporary file. After doing this, a second file is created which has only two fields in it: employee name and hours worked. The temporary file is then appended to this second file.

If PAYMAST is the name of the master file and if CLASS is the variable which indicates whether a person is a salaried or an hourly employee, you could create the new file (called HRWORK in this example) by typing:

. use paymast (return)
. copy to hrwork for class = 'H' (return)

To create the new file, called PAYHOURS, type what appears in lower case letters below:

. create payhours (return)
ENTER RECORD STRUCTURE AS FOLLOWS:
FIELD   NAME,TYPE,WIDTH,DECIMAL PLACES
001   name,c,20 (return)
002   hours,n,10 (return)
003   (return)
INPUT DATA NOW? n

The "n" here means no. The reason for no is the use of the append routine rather than the input data routine.

To put the names which are in the temporary file into the payhours file type:

. use payhours (return)
. append from hrworked (return)

To put the hours worked in the current period into the file payhours type:

. edit 1 (return)

Then put the appropriate number of hours in the hour field of each record. Do this by merely pressing the RETURN key until you are in the hour field, then enter the number of hours, press RETURN. Continue revising records until the last record has been updated. You will then automatically leave edit mode.

The following hours worked data should be entered into the file payhours:

Employee	Hours Worked
AFJEC, Q.A.	35
ANSAG, N.D.	37
AWASL, C.T.	44
CHALDDRE, I.S.	18
EDEGAR, O.A.	18
HANAN, S.I.	43
LEBA, C.W.	42
MISH, A.H.	36
NEBUBAB, A.D.	17
NECLI, T.B.	3
SHAVE, H.D.	43
SHIPTON, D.U.	42
SPELO, Y.O.	27
TYRUN, M.S.	3
WILFUL, P.A.	38

d. Write Payroll Update Program

The program that you write should conform to the following general logic:

1. Initialize.

    Do while there are more records to process.

2. Process payroll.

    Advance to next record in file.

3. Closing.

The initialize portion of the program should:

a. Copy the payroll master file to a temporary file which will be used by the program; in the closing portion of the program, you will delete all the records in the original payroll master file and will put updated information into it; for example, if the primary file is PAYMAST and the temporary file is TMPMAST, you would:

    use paymast
    copy to tmpmast

    These commands, when executed by the program, will put all the information in the file PAYMAST into the file TMPMAST.

b. Make the copy of the master file your primary file and the file with the hours worked in the current period the secondary file; for example:

    select primary
    use tmpmast
    select secondary
    use payhours

    These commands, when executed, will permit us to combine the information in these two files into one file.

c. Set up the temporary master file so that it contains the hours worked information for hourly employees in addition to their payroll master file information. If the field with the names of employees is NAME in both the payroll hour file (called PAY-HOURS) and in the temporary payroll master file (called TMPMAST) then the following line should be included in your payroll program:

join to tmpmast for p.name = s.name

When this command is executed, the temporary master file, TMPMAST, will contain information only for hourly employees. For each of these employees, the file will have both the information in the original payroll master file and the information in the hours worked file.

d. Add information on salaried employees to the temporary payroll master file (TMPMAST). This information will be copied from the original payroll master file (PAYMAST). If the field in the temporary master file which indicates whether an individual is a salaried or an hourly employee is CLASS then the following lines should be in your programs:

use tmpmast
append from paymast for class = 'S'

The first command causes the computer to use the temporary payroll master file. The second command puts all employees with a class of "S" at the end of this file. After these commands are executed the temporary master file begins with a listing of all hourly employees followed by a listing of all salaried employees. For the hourly workers, the file contains hours worked and payroll master file information. For salaried employees, the file contains zero hours worked and payroll master file.

e. Sort the temporary master file (called TMPMAST) by employee name to another temporary master file (called TMASTER) so that the master file information will be organized alphabetically. This can be done by adding the following line to your program:

sort on name to tmaster

f. Delete the original temporary master file, TMPMAST; for example, by adding the following line to your program:

use
delete file tmpmast

The first line, when executed, closes the original temporary master file and the second line deletes it.

g. Select the payroll summary file (called PAYSUM in this example) as your primary file and new temporary master file (TMASTER) as your secondary file. This can be done by adding the following lines to your program:

use paysum
select secondary
use tmaster
goto top

The GOTO TOP line is included to position the secondary file, TMASTER, at its beginning. These commands will make the output file (PAYSUM) the primary file and the input file (TMASTER) the secondary file.

The closing routine portion of the program should:

a. Use the original payroll master file.
b. Delete all records from it; this can be done by putting the following lines in your program when the original master file has been selected for use:

delete all
pack

c.   Append records from the temporary master file to the payroll master file; if the temporary payroll master file is called TMASTER, you would have a line in the closing routine which reads:

   append from tmaster

d.   Delete the temporary master file used in the program; if the temporary file was called TMASTER, you would have the following line in your closing routine:

   delete file tmaster

The process payroll portion of the program should:

a.   Compute the gross pay of each employee; for salaried employees this is their rate; for hourly employees it is their rate times the number of hours worked for all hours less than or equal to 40 and their rate times 1.5 times the hours they work over 40.
b.   Compute the total taxes of individual employees according to the following schedule:

	Tax rate (percent)
Weekly gross pay	
Less than $100	0%
$100 or more and less than 200 . . .	10
$200 or more and less than 400 . . .	20
$400 or more and less than 600 . . .	25
$600 or more	30

c.   Compute the total Canada Pension Plan payment, 1.8 percent of gross pay to a maximum of $379.80 per year
d.   Compute the total unemployment insurance payment, 2.35 percent of gross pay to a maximum of $562.12
e.   Compute the total other deductions, the lesser of the amount specified as payroll deductions or the amount of pay left after deducting taxes, CPP, and UIC from gross pay
f.   Replace the year-to-date figures in the sorted temporary master file with the original amounts plus the amounts for the current pay period.
g.   Select the payroll summary file, the secondary file, append a record to it, and replace all of the fields in this appended record.

The payroll summary file must be created before you can run the payroll program. The summary file should have the following fields in it:
  1.   Employee name.
  2.   Regular time hours worked, zero for salaried employees.
  3.   Overtime hours worked, zero for salaried employees.
  4.   Gross wages for all salaried employees.
  5.   Gross wages for all hourly employees.
  6.   Gross wages.
  7.   Income taxes deducted from gross pay.
  8.   Canada Pension Plan payments.
  9.   Unemployment insurance payments.
 10.   Other payroll deductions.
 11.   Net pay.

e. Preparation of Desired Reports

Use your payroll summary file; that is, your payroll program's output file to create a report like the one that follows:

Employee	Gross pay	Taxes	CPP	UIC	Deductions	Net pay
AFJEC, Q.A.	$ 700.00	$210.00	$12.60	$16.45	$ 0.00	$ 460.95
ANSAG, N.D.	555.00	138.75	9.99	13.04	37.00	356.21
ARIOQ, D.D.	800.00	240.00	14.40	18.80	33.00	493.80
AWASL, C.T.	690.00	207.00	12.42	16.21	0.00	454.36
BETHO, H.D.	800.00	240.00	14.40	18.80	47.00	479.80
CHALDDRE, I.S.	144.00	14.40	2.59	3.38	0.00	123.62
EDEGAR, O.A.	180.00	18.00	3.24	4.23	51.00	103.53
HANAN, S.I.	445.00	111.25	8.01	10.45	38.00	277.28
KNAST, A.T.	320.00	64.00	5.76	7.52	0.00	242.72
LEBA, C.W.	344.00	68.80	6.19	8.08	45.00	215.92
MISH, A.H.	540.00	135.00	9.72	12.69	43.00	339.59
NEBUBAB, A.D.	340.00	68.00	6.12	7.99	0.00	257.89
NECLI, T.B.	21.00	0.00	0.37	0.49	11.00	9.12
SHAVE, H.D.	356.00	71.20	6.40	8.36	39.00	231.02
SHIPTON, D.U.	860.00	258.00	15.48	20.21	26.00	540.31
SPELO, Y.O.	405.00	101.25	7.29	9.51	63.00	223.94
TYRUN, M.S.	60.00	0.00	1.08	1.41	24.00	33.51
WIFUL, P.A.	266.00	53.20	4.78	6.25	54.00	147.76
WILCOM, W.I.	280.00	56.00	5.04	6.58	0.00	212.38
WORJER, T.P.	320.00	64.00	5.76	7.52	0.00	242.72
TOTAL	$8,426.00	$2,118.85	$151.64	$197.97	$511.00	$5,446.43

Using the same file prepare a report as follows:

Employee	Reg. hours	Overtime	Hourly pay	Salary
AFJEC, Q.A.	35.00	0.00	$ 700.00	$ 0.00
ANSAG, N.D.	37.00	0.00	555.00	0.00
ARIOQ, D.D.	0.00	0.00	0.00	800.00
AWASL, C.T.	40.00	4.00	690.00	0.00
BETHO, H.D.	0.00	0.00	0.00	800.00
CHALDDRE, I.S.	18.00	0.00	144.00	0.00
EDEGAR, O.A.	18.00	0.00	180.00	0.00
HANAN, S.I.	40.00	3.00	445.00	0.00
KNAST, A.T.	0.00	0.00	0.00	320.00
LEBA, C.W.	40.00	2.00	344.00	0.00
MISH, A.H.	36.00	0.00	540.00	0.00
NEBUBAB, A.D.	17.00	0.00	340.00	0.00
NECLI, T.B.	3.00	0.00	21.00	0.00
SHAVE, H.D.	40.00	3.00	356.00	0.00
SHIPTON, D.U.	40.00	2.00	860.00	0.00
SPELO, Y.O.	27.00	0.00	405.00	0.00
TYRUN, M.S.	3.00	0.00	60.00	0.00
WIFUL, P.A.	38.00	0.00	266.00	0.00
WILCOM, W.I.	0.00	0.00	0.00	280.00
WORJER, T.P.	0.00	0.00	0.00	320.00
TOTAL	432.00	14.00	$5,906.00	$2,520.00

Use the payroll master file to create a report as shown:

Employee	Class	Pay rate	Deductions
AFJEC, Q.A.	H	$ 20.00	$ 0.00
ANSAG, N.D.	H	15.00	37.00
ARIOQ, D.D.	S	800.00	33.00
AWASL, C.T.	H	15.00	0.00
BETHO, H.D.	S	800.00	47.00
CHALDDRE, I.S.	H	8.00	0.00
EDEGAR, O.A.	H	10.00	51.00
HANAN, S.I.	H	10.00	38.00
KNAST, A.T.	S	320.00	0.00
LEBA, C.W.	H	8.00	45.00
MISH, A.H.	H	15.00	43.00
NEBUBAB, A.D.	H	20.00	0.00
NECLI, T.B.	H	7.00	11.00
SHAVE, H.D.	H	8.00	39.00
SHIPTON, D.U.	H	20.00	26.00
SPELO, Y.O.	H	15.00	63.00
TYRUN, M.S.	H	20.00	24.00
WIFUL, P.A.	H	7.00	54.00
WILCOM, W.I.	S	280.00	0.00
WORJER, T.P.	S	320.00	0.00

Also use the payroll master file to create a report of year to date figures for employees as shown below:

Employee	Earnings	Taxes	CPP	UIC	Deductions	Net pay
AFJEC, Q.A.	$ 9,240.00	$2,772.00	$166.32	$217.14	$ 0.00	$ 6,084.54
ANSAG, N.D.	8,100.00	2,025.00	145.80	190.35	555.00	5,183.85
ARIOQ, D.D.	12,000.00	3,600.00	216.00	282.00	495.00	7,407.00
AWASL, C.T.	10,125.00	3,037.50	182.25	237.93	0.00	6,667.32
BETHO, H.D.	12,000.00	3,600.00	216.00	282.00	705.00	7,197.00
CHALDDRE, I.S.	2,120.00	212.00	38.16	49.82	0.00	1,820.02
EDEGAR, O.A.	2,530.00	253.00	45.54	59.46	765.00	1,407.00
HANAN, S.I.	5,805.00	1,183.25	104.49	136.41	570.00	3,810.85
KNAST, A.T.	4,800.00	960.00	86.40	112.80	0.00	3,640.80
LEBA, C.W.	5,192.00	1,038.40	93.45	122.01	675.00	3,263.14
MISH, A.H.	8,565.00	2,141.25	154.17	201.28	645.00	5,423.30
NEBUBAB, A.D.	4,680.00	936.00	84.24	109.98	0.00	3,549.78
NECLI, T.B.	1,029.00	0.00	18.51	24.18	165.00	821.31
SHAVE, H.D.	5,124.00	1,024.80	92.22	120.41	585.00	3,301.57
SHIPTON, D.U.	13,100.00	3,930.00	235.80	307.85	390.00	8,236.35
SPELO, Y.O.	5,745.00	1,169.25	103.41	135.00	945.00	3,392.34
TYRUN, M.S.	3,200.00	628.00	57.60	75.20	360.00	2,079.20
WIFUL, P.A.	4,179.00	835.80	75.21	98.21	810.00	2,359.78
WILCOM, W.I.	4,200.00	840.00	75.60	98.70	0.00	3,185.70
WORJER, T.P.	4,800.00	960.00	86.40	112.80	0.00	3,640.80
TOTAL	$126,534.00	$31,146.25	$2,277.57	$2,973.53	$7,665.00	$82,471.65

f. Delete Records From and Add Records to Payroll Master File

In this problem, we want to delete the records for employees NECLI and SPELO from the payroll master file and we want to add records for employees COMT and PASHU.

To delete the desired records, select the payroll master file for use, locate the appropriate records in the file and delete them. If the payroll master file is called PAYMAST and NAME is the field in this file which holds employee names, you can eliminate the desired records by typing what appears below.

use paymast (return)
display for name = 'NECLI' (return)
delete record 13 (return)
display for name = 'SPELO' (return)
delete record 16 (return)

The reason you delete records 13 and 16 is because when we asked the computer to display the records we wanted to delete, it displayed the record number 13 for NECLI and record number 16 for SPELO.

If you display all the records in the file after deleting these two records, you will still see the records listed. However, next to each of these employee's names, you will see an asterisk. The asterisk indicates that the record has been marked for deletion. However, the record will not be irretrievably deleted from the file until you PACK the file.

To permanently eliminate these records, type:

pack (return)

Now, if you display all the records in the file, you will no longer see NECLI or SPELO in the file.

To add records to the file, first determine where the records should be placed in the file and then insert the records in the appropriate locations.

In this problem, we want to add two records to the file. The following summarizes the information associated with these records:

1. COMT, A.T. earns $10 an hour and has no other deductions,
2. PASHU, J.S. earns $20 an hour and has $40 per week of other deductions.

Use the DISPLAY command to determine where the new records should be placed in the file. Doing this, we determine that COMT's record should be placed between the 6th and 7th record and that PASHU's should be placed between records 13 and 14. If NAME is the field which holds the names of company employees, then typing the following will add the records to the payroll master file in their appropriate places.

display for name = 'C' (return)
display record 7 (return)
insert before (return)
    now provide the information for COMT
display for name = 'P' (return)
display for name = 'O' (return)
display for name = 'N' (return)
display record 13 (return)
insert (return)
    now provide the information for PASHU

If you display all the information in the payroll master file, you will see that the records for COMT and PASHU have been added to the file in their appropriate places.

g. Rerun Payroll Program for the Next Period

In running the payroll program for a second time, you must eliminate any data in the various payroll files which have to do with previous payroll periods.

First, delete the temporary file used in creating the one which has the names of hourly employees in it. If the temporary file is HRWORK then type:

delete file hrwork (return)

Second, recreate the file with the names of hourly employees in it. CLEAR your files, select the payroll master file (PAYMAST in the example below), copy the master file information to the temporary file deleted above. If the field which indicates whether an employee is an hourly or a salaried employee is called CLASS, then type:

```
clear (return)
use paymast (return)
copy to hrwork for class = 'H' (return)
```

Third, use the file which contains the number of hours worked by employees during a given period (PAYHOURS in the example below) and delete all the records in it. Having done this use the APPEND command to put the names of the current period's hourly employees in this file. Now, EDIT the file and put the hours worked by employees in the current period in the file. To do this, type:

```
use payhours (return)
delete all (return)
pack (return)
append from hrwork (return)
edit 1 (return)
```

Now place the following hours worked information into this file:

Employee	Hours worked
AFJEC, Q.A.	40
ANSAG, N.D.	35
AWASL, C.T.	43
CHALDDRE, I.S.	33
COMT, A.T.	28
EDEGAR, O.A.	0
HANAN, S.I.	40
LEBA, C.W.	47
MISH, A.H.	31
NEBUBAB, A.D.	0
PASHU, J.S.	38
SHAVE, H.D.	39
SHIPTON, D.U.	46
TYRUN, M.S.	10
WIFUL, P.A.	32

Finally, use the payroll summary file, delete all the records in it, and CLEAR your files. If the payroll summary file is PAYSUM, you would type:

```
use paysum (return)
delete all (return)
pack (return)
clear (return)
```

Having done this, you can now rerun the payroll program and generate the same reports that you generated for the previous payroll.

(Prepared by C. Dirksen)

PC10–23. The following questions are based on the 1984 financial statements of Consolidated-Bathurst Inc. presented in Supplement B.

a. In footnote 10, the company states it classified $66,070,000 of bank loans and notes as long-term debt. How was this classification justified?

b. How much did C-B expense for current and deferred income taxes in 1984?

c. The statutory income tax rate for 1984 was 45.5 percent for C–B. What was the income tax rate used to determine the income tax expense?

d. How did C–B classify deferred income taxes on the balance sheet? How did it justify this classification?

e. How much did C–B owe on its capital leases as at December 31, 1984? What was the numerical makeup of this amount? Is the value the same as stated in its statement of accounting policies?

11

Measuring and Reporting Bonds Payable

PURPOSE OF THIS CHAPTER

The issuance of bonds is a primary way to obtain resources for long-term growth and expansion by businesses, nonprofit organizations (such as universities), and public subdivisions (such as municipalities and water utilities). Bonds are long-term debt instruments. When bonds are issued (i.e., sold), they become an investment to the buyer and an obligation of the issuer. Accounting for bonds is complex because of the wide range of characteristics they possess. Both the issuing entity and the investor need to understand the characteristics of bonds and their varying economic effects. Accounting seeks to measure and report these economic effects.

Because of the special characteristics of bonds and the related accounting complexities, we give bonds separate consideration. The purposes of this chapter are to discuss the characteristics of bonds payable and to explain the accounting approaches used to measure, record, and report their economic impact on the entity. To provide flexibility the chapter is divided into two parts:

Part A—Fundamentals of measuring, recording, and reporting bonds payable

Part B—Some special problems in accounting for bonds payable

Part A—Fundamentals of Measuring, Recording, and Reporting Bonds Payable

CHARACTERISTICS OF BONDS PAYABLE

Funds required for long-term purposes, such as the acquisition of high-cost machinery or the construction of a new plant, are often obtained by issuing long-term debt instruments, such as long-term notes payable (discussed in Chapter 10) or bonds payable. Bonds payable may be secured by a mortgage on specified assets, or the bonds may be unsecured. Bonds commonly are issued in denominations of $1,000 or $10,000 and, occasionally, in denominations of $100,000. They usually are negotiable (i.e., transferable by endorsement), and the bonds of most large companies are bought and sold by investors on the major stock exchanges.[1] A typical bond certificate is shown in Exhibit 11–1.

The **principal** of a bond is the amount payable at the maturity or due date as specified on the bond certificate. This amount also is called its **par value, maturity value,** or its **face amount.** Throughout the life of a bond, the issuing company makes periodic interest payments, usually semiannually, to the bondholders.

A company desiring to sell a bond issue must draw up a **bond indenture** (or **bond contract**) that specifies the legal provisions of the bonds, such as the maturity date, rate of interest to be paid, date of each interest payment, and any conversion privileges (explained later). When a bond is issued, the investor receives a **bond certificate** (i.e., a bond). All of the bond certificates for a single bond issue are identical. Specified on the face of each certificate are the same maturity dates, interest rate, interest dates, and other provisions. Usually when a company issues bonds, an **underwriter** is engaged to sell the bonds to the public. A third party, called the **trustee,** usually is appointed to represent the bondholders. The duties of an independent trustee are to ascertain whether the issuing company fulfills all of the provisions of the bond indenture.

SPECIAL CHARACTERISTICS OF BONDS

A particular bond issue will have a combination of characteristics that will be specified in the bond indenture. The issuing company often will add special characteristics to a bond issue in order to make the bond more attractive to potential investors. Bonds may be classified in a number of ways, depending upon their characteristics. Typical bond characteristics and their related classifications are presented in Exhibit 11–2.

---

[1] In addition to bonds that are issued by corporations, bonds also are issued by governmental units such as federal and provincial governments, cities, and by other nonprofit institutions. The discussions in this chapter apply to both types, although we will focus mainly on those issued by corporations.

**EXHIBIT 11–1
Typical bond
certificate**

$1000

DEBENTURE

$1000

DEBENTURE
75- C1262

CANADA — PROVINCE OF NOVA SCOTIA

THE CITY OF HALIFAX

DEBENTURE

GENERAL PURPOSES – 1975

Issued under authority of Chapter 193 of the Revised Statutes of Nova Scotia, 1967,
and of a resolution passed by the City Council of The City of Halifax on the 23rd day of
April, A.D. 1975.

THE CITY OF HALIFAX

WILL PAY IF UNREGISTERED TO THE BEARER HEREOF, OR IF REGISTERED TO THE REGISTERED
HOLDER HEREOF, THE SUM OF

ONE THOUSAND DOLLARS

IN LAWFUL MONEY OF CANADA AT THE OFFICE OF THE CITY TREASURER OF THE CITY OF
HALIFAX, AT HALIFAX, NOVA SCOTIA, OR AT THE PRINCIPAL OFFICE OF THE ROYAL BANK OF
CANADA IN ANY OF THE CITIES OF HALIFAX, NOVA SCOTIA; SAINT JOHN, NEW BRUNSWICK;
MONTREAL, PROVINCE OF QUEBEC; TORONTO, ONTARIO ; WINNIPEG, MANITOBA; AND
VANCOUVER, BRITISH COLUMBIA; IN CANADA, AT THE OPTION OF THE HOLDER IN

TEN YEARS (1st MAY, 1985)

FROM THE DATE HEREOF, AND WILL PAY INTEREST UPON THE SAID SUM AT THE RATE OF
— NINE AND THREE-QUARTERS PER CENTUM PER ANNUM —

PAYABLE HALF-YEARLY AT THE SAID OFFICES, AT THE OPTION OF THE HOLDER UPON THE
FIRST DAYS OF MAY AND NOVEMBER IN EACH YEAR, UPON PRESENTATION AND SUR-
RENDER OF THE COUPONS HERETO ATTACHED.

ISSUED AT HALIFAX IN THE COUNTY OF HALIFAX THIS FIRST DAY OF MAY, A.D. 1975.

_____
City Clerk

_____
Mayor

EXHIBIT 11–2
**Bond characteristics
and classifications**

Bond Classification	Bond Characteristic
1. **On the basis of collateral:**	
a. Unsecured bonds (often called debentures).	a. Bonds that do **not** include a mortgage or pledge of specific assets as a guarantee of repayment at maturity.
b. Secured bonds (often designated on the basis of the type of asset pledged, such as a real estate mortgage).	b. Bonds that include the pledge of specific assets as a guarantee of repayment at maturity.
2. **On the basis of repayment of principal:**	
a. Ordinary or single-payment bonds.	a. The principal is payable in full at a single specified maturity date in the future.
b. Serial bonds.	b. The principal is payable in installments on a series of specified maturity dates in the future.
3. **On the basis of early retirement:**	
a. Callable bonds.	a. Bonds that may be called for early retirement at the option of the **issuer**.
b. Redeemable bonds.	b. Bonds that may be turned in for early retirement at the option of the **bondholder**.
c. Convertible bonds.	c. Bonds that may be converted to other securities of the issuer (usually common stock) at the option of the **bondholder**.
4. **On the basis of the payment of interest:**	
a. Registered bonds.	a. Payment of interest is made by cheque and mailed direct to the bondholder whose name must be on file (i.e., in the bond register).
b. Coupon bonds.	b. Bonds with a printed coupon attached for each interest payment. The bondholder "clips" the coupon on the interest date and deposits it in a bank like a cheque, or mails it to the issuing company which, in turn, mails the interest cheque direct to the person and address shown on the completed coupon. The interest rate on coupon bonds often is called the coupon rate.

ADVANTAGES OF ISSUING BONDS

The advantages of issuing bonds instead of capital stock stem from the fact that the bondholders are **creditors** and not owners (as are shareholders). A bondholder does not share in the management, the accumulated earnings, or the growth in assets, as does the shareholder. Payments to bondholders are limited to (1) the amount of interest specified on the bond and (2) the principal or face amount of the bond at maturity. Interest payments to bondholders are a tax-deductible expense, but dividend payments to owners are not tax deductible. This fact may reduce the net (i.e., aftertax) cost of funds acquired by issuing bonds.

Use of creditors' funds often increases the rate of return to owners' equity. This enhancement of the return to owners is called **financial leverage.** When leverage is positive, an important financial advantage to the shareholders occurs. Financial leverage is **positive** when the net aftertax interest rate on borrowed funds is **less** than the aftertax rate of return earned by the company on total assets.

To illustrate, assume Spicewood Corporation earned a 15 percent return (after income tax) on total assets (i.e., net income, $75,000 ÷ total assets, $500,000 = .15) and that the interest on total debt was 9.0 percent (i.e., interest expense, $18,000 ÷ total debt, $200,000 = .09). The income tax rate for Spicewood Corporation is assumed to be 40 percent. The $18,000 interest expense reduced both taxable income and Spicewood's tax liability. The **net interest cost** of the debt was the interest expense ($18,000) minus the tax savings associated with the interest expense ($18,000 × .40 = $7,200). Thus, Spicewood's aftertax interest cost was $10,800 (i.e., $18,000 − $7,200). There was positive financial leverage in this situation because the creditors provided funds for 5.4 percent aftertax interest ($10,800 ÷ $200,000 = .054) and the company is earning 15 percent on those (and the other) assets. Because the only return paid to the creditors is 5.4 percent aftertax interest, the difference between 15 percent and 5.4 percent (of the $200,000) increases net income, which in turn accrues to the long-term benefit of the company and, therefore, to the shareholders. Exhibit 11–3 presents two comparative cases for Spicewood Corporation to illustrate the cause and economic effects of financial leverage. Case A assumes that the company has total assets of $500,000, which were provided in full by shareholders (i.e., it has no debt). In contrast, Case B assumes that of the total amount of assets, $300,000, was provided by shareholders and the remaining $200,000 was provided by creditors (i.e., debt). For illustrative purposes, the other variables are held constant in order to demonstrate the cause and economic effects of using debt to help finance a business.

Observe in Exhibit 11–3, Case A, that return on total assets and return on shareholders' equity are the same (15 percent) because there was no debt. There is no financial leverage because it is caused only by debt. In contrast, in Case B, the $200,000 of debt caused return on shareholders' equity (21 percent) to be higher than the return on total assets (15 percent); thus there was **positive financial leverage,** which is measured as the difference between the return on shareholders' equity and the return on total assets (i.e., 21% − 15% = 6%). This illustration demonstrates that financial leverage is caused by the existence of debt and that the economic effect of financial leverage can be measured. Financial leverage will be positive when the overall earnings rate of the company is more than the average aftertax interest rate on debt. **Negative financial leverage** will exist if the overall earnings rate is less than the average aftertax

EXHIBIT 11–3
Effects of financial
leverage

	Spicewood Corporation	
	Case A: No debt	**Case B: Debt, $200,000 @ 9 Percent**
Balance sheet:		
Total assets	$ 500,000	$ 500,000
Total debt (9% interest)	–0–	200,000
Shareholders' equity,		
(10,000 shares)	$ 500,000 (6,000 shares)	$ 300,000
Income statement:		
Revenues	$ 300,000	$ 300,000
Operating expenses........	(175,000)	(175,000)
Income tax (40%)	(50,000)	(50,000)
Interest expense	$200,000 × 9% = $18,000	
(net of income tax).......	–0– Less: $18,000 × 40%	
Net income	$ 75,000 = (7,200)	(10,800)
		$ 64,200
Analysis:		
a. Return on total assets	[($64,200 + $10,800)	
($75,000 ÷ $500,000) ..	15% ÷ $500,000]*	15%
b. Return on shareholders'		
equity ($75,000		
÷ 500,000)	15% ($64,200 ÷ $300,000)........	21%
c. Financial leverage		
([b] − [a])†	–0–	6%
d. EPS ($75,000 ÷ 10,000		
shares).............	$7.50 ($64,200 ÷ 6,000 shares)	$ 10.70

*Interest on debt, net of income tax, is added back to derive total return to all fund
providers (also see Chapter 15).
†Also see discussion of financial leverage in Chapter 16.

interest rate on debt. The significance of the economic effect of financial leverage depends upon (1) the difference between the aftertax interest rate and the
earnings rate on total assets and (2) the relative amount of total assets provided
by creditors.

Despite the advantages of financial leverage, sound financing of a large business requires a realistic **balance** between the amount of debt (including bonds
payable) and owners' equity (i.e., common and preferred shares and retained
earnings). For example, in Case A, there was no debt, which is the most conservative position. In Case B, the $200,000 of debt was 40 percent of total assets
employed (not an unusual situation). However, if Spicewood Corporation had
$400,000 debt, the 80 percent debt to total assets would be considered too high
in most situations. It would be considered too high because interest payments
to bondholders are **fixed charges.** Interest payments legally must be paid each
period, regardless of whether the corporation earns income or incurs a loss. In
contrast, dividends usually are paid to shareholders only if earnings are satisfactory. Each year, some companies go bankrupt because of their inability to
make required interest payments to creditors.

MEASURING BONDS PAYABLE AND BOND INTEREST EXPENSE

The accounting approach used to measure, record, and report bonds payable is based primarily on the **cost** and **matching principles.** When a bond is issued (i.e., sold), the proceeds include the net cash received, plus the market value of any noncash resources received. Under the cost principle, bonds payable are recorded at their **issue price,** which is their **current cash equivalent amount** (the present value of the future cash flows). Subsequent to the issuance of the bonds, the present value will change from period to period if the bond was issued at a discount or at a premium.

Bonds may be sold at **par;** that is, at the face or maturity amount (these are alternative terms for the same amount). If sold above par, bonds are said to have been issued at a **premium.** If sold below par, bonds are said to have been issued at a **discount.** To illustrate, if the issuing corporation received $1,000 cash for a bond with a $1,000 face, maturity, or par value, there would be no premium or discount. Alternatively, if the corporation received $967 for the bond, there would be a discount of $33; or if $1,035 cash were received, there would be a premium of $35. Typically, bond prices are quoted on the security exchanges as a **percent** of the par amount. A bond quoted at 100 sells at par; if quoted at 96.7, it sells at a discount of 3.3 percent below its par; if quoted at 103.5, it sells at a premium of 3.5 percent above its par.

Interest rates on bonds

A bond specifies an **annual rate of interest** based on the par value (face or maturity amount) of the bond. This rate is called variously the **stated, coupon, nominal,** or **contract rate.** Interest is usually paid on a semiannual basis; thus, an 8 percent bond of $1,000 par will pay semiannual **cash** interest of 4 percent (8 percent ÷ 2 = 4 percent) or $40 (i.e., $1,000 × .04 = $40) each six months regardless of whether the bond sold at par, a discount, or a premium. The **stated** rate is set by the issuing company to approximate the market rate of interest when the bond issue is authorized. It is printed on each bond certificate and does not change over the term of the bond.

The stated rate establishes the fixed amount of cash interest that will be paid each interest period over the entire life of the bond regardless of the issuing price of the bond. However, bonds sell at a market rate of interest that often is different from the stated rate. Whether a bond sells at par, at a discount, or at a premium is determined by the forces of supply and demand in the capital markets. The **market rate** of interest on a bond is the rate that borrowers (issuers) are willing to pay and lenders (investors) are willing to accept on their money taking into consideration the perceived level of risk involved. Market rates tend to fluctuate from day to day, but the stated rate of interest is fixed by contract for the life of the bond. As a result, the market price of a bond will be affected by changes in the market rate of interest.

When the **market** and **stated rates of interest are the same,** a bond will sell at **par.** When the market rate for a bond is **higher** than the stated rate, the bond will sell at a **discount;** and when the market rate is **lower** than the stated rate, a bond will sell at a **premium.**

When a bond is issued at a **discount,** the issuer receives less cash than will be paid at maturity date. When a bond is issued at a **premium,** the issuer receives more cash than will be paid at maturity. The difference between the market and stated rates of interest on a bond causes a different cash flow on issue date than on maturity date. The specified cash flow for interest on each interest payment date is determined by the stated rate of interest times the par and is not changed by the issue price of the bond.

Each period bond interest is measured, recorded, and reported in conformance with the **matching principle.** Interest is incurred on the basis of passage of time. At the end of each period, the amount of interest unpaid must be accrued and reported as expense so that it will be matched with the revenues in the period in which it was incurred. The measurement and reporting of interest on bonds is similar to interest on notes receivable and notes payable. When bonds are issued at a premium or discount, however, an additional measurement problem arises because these affect both the price of the bond and the amount of **interest expense** (but not the periodic **cash** payment of interest).

Accounting for bonds and bond interest is illustrated in Exhibit 11–4 under three independent situations: (1) bonds issued at par, (2) bonds issued at a discount, and (3) bonds issued at a premium.

Bonds sold at par

Bonds sell at their par value when buyers (investors) are willing to invest in them at the stated interest rate on the bond. To illustrate, assume that on January 1, 19A, Mason Corporation issued $400,000 of the bonds payable and received $400,000 in cash for them. The bonds were dated to start interest on January 1, 19A. The entry by Mason Corporation to record the issuance of the bonds is given in Exhibit 11–4 (bonds issued at par).

Subsequent to the sale of the bonds, interest at 5 percent (i.e., 10 percent per year) on the face amount of the bonds must be paid each June 30 and December 31 until maturity. The entries to record the interest payments during 19A are given in Exhibit 11–4.

At the end of the accounting period, December 31, 19A, the financial statements would report bond interest expense and a long-term liability, as illustrated in Exhibit 11–4.

In this example, Mason Corporation received $1,000 cash for each $1,000 bond sold and will pay back $1,000, principal + ($50 × 20, semiannual interest payments) = $2,000. The $1,000 difference is the amount of interest expense for the 10 years; therefore, the interest cost was $100 per year and the yield or effective rate of interest was $100 ÷ $1,000 = 10 percent per year. The stated rate called for on the bond also was 10 percent.

The $1,000 cash that Mason Corporation received when each bond was sold is the present value of the future cash flows associated with the bond (refer to Chapter 10, Part B) computed as follows:

		Present value
a.	Principal: $1,000 × $p_{n=20;\ i=5\%}$ (Table 10–2, .3769) =	$ 377
b.	Interest: $50 × $P_{n=20;\ i=5\%}$ (Table 10–4, 12.4622) =	623
	Issue (sale) price of one Mason bond	$1,000

EXHIBIT 11–4   Accounting for bonds payable illustrated

Situation:

Mason Corporation approved the following bond issue on January 1, 19A: Bonds payable authorized, 500 bonds, $1,000 par per bond, 10 percent interest (payable semiannually each June 30 and December 31), maturity in 10 years on December 31, 19J.

Mason's accounting period ends December 31.

Bonds issued at par:

On January 1, 19A, Mason issued 400 of the bonds at par (i.e., an effective rate of 10 percent) and received $400,000 cash.

Entries throughout 19A:

January 1, 19A—To record issuance of the bonds at par.

Cash (400 bonds × $1,000)	400,000	
Bonds payable (400 bonds)		400,000

Interest payments during 19A:

	June 30, 19A		December 31, 19A	
Bond interest expense..	20,000		20,000	
Cash ($400,000 × 5%).......................................		20,000		20,000

Financial statement for 19A:

Income statement:	
Bond interest expense..	$ 40,000
Balance sheet:	
Long-term liabilities:	
Bonds payable, 10% (due December 31, 19J)..	400,000

Bonds issued at a discount:

On January 1, 19A, Mason issued 400 ($400,000 par) of the bonds at an effective interest rate of 12 percent (i.e., at a price of 88.5) and received $354,000 cash.

Entries throughout 19A:

January 1, 19A—To record issuance of the bonds at a discount:

Cash (400 bonds × $885)...	354,000	
Discount on bonds payable [400 bonds × ($1,000 − $885)].........................	46,000*	
Bonds payable (400 bonds × $1,000)		400,000*

*Note: In effect, the bonds are recorded at their issue price because the liability is reported on the balance sheet net of these two balances.

Interest payments during 19A:

	June 30, 19A		December 31, 19A	
Bond interest expense..	22,300		22,300	
Discount on bonds payable, straight-line amortization				
($46,000 ÷ 20 periods)		2,300		2,300
Cash ($400,000 × .05)...		20,000		20,000

EXHIBIT 11–4   *(concluded)*

Financial statements for 19A:

Income statement.
  Bond interest expense ($22,300 × 2)... $ 44,600

Balance sheet:
  Long-term liabilities:
    Bonds payable 10%, due December 31, 19J................................... $400,000
      Less unamortized discount 41,400*   358,600

Or, alternatively:

  Bonds payable, 10%, due December 31, 19J
    (maturity amount, $400,000, less unamortized discount)........................ 358,600†

*$46,000 − $2,300 − $2,300 = $41,400.
†This amount is called the net liability.

Bonds issued at a premium:
  On January 1, 19A, Mason issued 400 ($400,000 par) of the bonds at an effective interest rate of 8½ percent (i.e., at a price of 110) and received $440,000 cash.

Entries throughout 19A:

Cash (400 bonds × $1,100) 440,000
  Premium on bonds payable [400 bonds × ($1,100 − $1,000)] 40,000
  Bonds payable (400 bonds × $1,000) 400,000

Interest payments during 19A:

	June 30, 19A	December 31, 19A
Bond interest expense...	18,000	18,000
Premium on bonds payable, straight-line		
amortization ($40,000 ÷ 20 periods)...............................	2,000	2,000
Cash ($400,000 × .05)...	20,000	20,000

Financial statements for 19A:

Income statement:
  Bond interest expense ($18,000 × 2) .... $ 36,000

Balance sheet:
  Long-term liabilities:
    Bonds payable, 10%, due December 31, 19J.................................. $400,000
      Add unamortized premium 36,000*   436,000

Or, alternatively:

  Bonds payable, 10%, due December 31, 19J
    (maturity amount, $400,000, plus unamortized premium) .... 436,000†

*$40,000 − $2,000 − $2,000 = $36,000.
†This amount is called the net liability.

Payment of principal (face) amount at maturity date (all three situations):

December 31, 19J:

Bonds payable 400,000
  Cash 400,000

When the effective rate of interest is equal to the stated rate of interest, the present value of the future cash flows associated with a bond will **always** equal the bond's par amount.

Bonds sold at a discount

Bonds sell at a discount when the buyers (investors) are willing to invest in them only at a yield or market rate of interest that is **higher** than the stated interest rate on the bonds. To illustrate, assume the capital market established a 12 percent market rate of interest for the 10-year Mason bonds (Exhibit 11–4) with a stated rate of 10 percent, payable semiannually, which means the bonds would sell at a **discount.** At a 12 percent market rate, how much cash would a $1,000 bond of Mason Company generate if sold on January 1, 19A? To compute the cash issue (sale) price of one bond requires computation of the present value, at the **market rate,** of the two future cash flows specified on the bond: (a) the principal ($n = 20$, $i = 6\%$) and (b) the cash interest paid each semiannual interest period ($n = 20$, $i = 6\%$). Thus, the cash issue (sale) price of one Mason bond would be computed as follows (refer to Chapter 10, Part B):

		Present value
a.	Principal: $1,000 × $p_{n=20;\ i=6\%}$ (Table 10–2, .3118) =	$312
b.	Interest: $50 × $P_{n=20;\ i=6\%}$ (Table 10–4, 11.4699) =	573
	Issue (sale) price of one Mason bond..............	$885*

*Thus, the issue price would be 88.5.

The cash issue price of the 400 bonds issued by Mason would be $354,000 (i.e., 400 bonds × $885).

When a bond is sold at a discount (i.e., $115 discount per bond in the above example), the Bonds Payable account is credited for the face or maturity amount and the discount is recorded as a debit to Discount on Bonds Payable. To illustrate, the issuance of 400 of the bonds of Mason Company at a cash sale price of $885 per bond (i.e., a 12 percent market rate) would be recorded as shown in Exhibit 11–4 (bonds issued at a discount).

The journal entry to record the issuance of the bonds (Exhibit 11–4) recorded the amount of the discount in a separate contra liability account (Discount on Bonds Payable) as a **debit.** The discount must be accorded special treatment on the income statement (in measuring interest expense) and on the balance sheet, which reports the bonds payable at their **carrying value** (maturity amount less any **unamortized** discount).

Measuring and recording interest expense (on bonds sold at a discount)

The computation and related entry given in Exhibit 11–4 indicate that each of the 10 percent Mason bonds issued at a 12 percent market rate commanded $885 cash and a discount of $115 (i.e., $1,000 − $885). During the 10-year term of the bonds, Mason must make 20 semiannual interest payments of $50 each (i.e., $50 × 20 = $1,000 total interest) and at maturity must pay back the $1,000 cash principal. Therefore, in addition to the cash interest of $1,000, $115 more cash per bond is paid back than was borrowed. This, $115 discount on each bond causes the yield or effective rate to be 12 percent (instead of the 10 percent stated on the bonds). The discount is an adjustment of the amount of interest expense that will be **reported** each accounting period on the income statement. Bond discount, in the economic sense, represents an **increase in bond interest expense.** To give accounting effect to bond discount in periods subsequent to issuance, the $46,000 debit to Discount on Bonds Payable (in Exhibit 11–4), must be apportioned to each semiannual interest period as an increase in bond interest expense from the date of issuance to maturity date. There are two different methods for doing this: (1) **straight-line amortization** and (2) **effective-interest amortization.** Straight-line amortization is easy to understand and compute; however, it is conceptually deficient. Effective-interest amortization requires use of the present value concepts (discussed in Part B of Chapter 10). The effective-interest method is required; however, it or the straight-line method may be used when the difference between the two results is not material in amount each year. Although the difference may appear material for Mason Company, we will introduce the subject with straight-line amortization because it is easy to follow. The more complex **effective-interest method** will be presented in Part B of this chapter.

Straight-line amortization. To amortize the $46,000 bond discount over the period from date of issuance to maturity date on a straight-line basis, an equal dollar amount is allocated to each interest period. Since there are 20 six-month interest periods, the computation would be: $46,000 ÷ 20 periods = $2,300 amortization on each semiannual interest date. Therefore, the payments of interest on the bonds during 19A would be recorded as shown in Exhibit 11–4 (bonds issued at a discount).[2]

Conceptually, it can be argued that unamortized bond discount and unamortized bond premium should be disclosed as presented in Exhibit 11–4; that is, as a contra account to bonds payable or as an addition (adjunct) account to the par (face) amount. This disclosure implies the net liability should always equal the present value of all future cash payments using the market rate of interest existing when the bond was issued if the effective-interest method of amortization is used. If the straight-line method of amortization is used, the net liability will only approximate this present value. The *CICA Handbook* is silent on the disclosure of premiums, but Section 3070 permits the disclosure of bond discounts as a deferred charge in the asset section of the balance sheet.

---

[2]The amount of interest expense recorded each semiannual period may be confirmed as follows:

Cash to be paid out by the borrower:	
Par amount of the bonds—payable at maturity	$400,000
Interest payments ($20,000 × 20 semiannual payments)	400,000
Total cash payments	800,000
Cash received by the borrower	354,000
Total interest expense over 10 years	$446,000
Interest expense per semiannual period ($446,000 ÷ 20 periods)	$ 22,300

(Alternatively, $20,000 cash interest + $2,300 discount amortization = $22,300.)

The apparent lack of concern about the rules of disclosure is likely to result from the fact that careful consideration of the stated or coupon rate of interest in terms of the market rate will cause the discount or premium to be small relative to the proceeds from the bond issue.

Each succeeding year the unamortized discount will **decrease** by $4,600, and as a consequence, the net liability will **increase** each year by $4,600. At the maturity date of the bonds, the unamortized discount (i.e., the balance in the Discount on Bonds Payable account) will be **zero.** At that time the maturity or face amount of the bonds and the current net liability amount will be the same (i.e., $400,000).

While bond discount amortization is treated as an addition to interest expense for the period, income tax laws place restrictions on the timing and the amount of a deduction that may be claimed as an expense in computing income tax for the year. While the provisions are somewhat technical, the effect is to create a timing difference (see Chapter 10, a deferred tax debit) for the amount of the bond amortization recorded for accounting purposes if the discount is small. For tax purposes the discount can be claimed as an expense only in the year the principal is paid. If the discount is too large, only one half of the discount can be expensed when the principal is paid at maturity or at redemption. This rule would create a permanent tax allocation difference for the one half that is disallowed as a deduction and a timing tax allocation difference for the remainder.

Bonds sold at a premium

Bonds sell at a premium when the buyers (investors) are willing to invest in bonds at a market or yield rate of interest that is **lower** than the stated interest rate on the bonds. To illustrate, assume the capital market established an 8½ percent market rate of interest for the 10-year Mason bonds (Exhibit 11–4, stated rate, 10 percent, payable on semiannual basis), which means the bonds would sell at a **premium.** Computation of the cash issue (sale) price of one Mason bond would be as follows (refer to Chapter 10, Part B):

		Present value
a.	Principal: $1,000 $\times p_{n=20;\ i=4\ 1/4\%}$ (Table 10–2, .4350) =	$ 435
b.	Interest: $50 $\times P_{n=20;\ i=4\ 1/4\%}$ (Table 10–4, 13.2944) =	665
	Issue (sale) price of one Mason bond	$1,100

The cash issue price (110) of the 400 bonds issued by Mason would be $440,000 (i.e., 400 bonds $\times$ $1,100).

When a bond is sold at a premium (e.g., $100 premium per bond in the above example), the Bonds Payable account is credited for the par amount, and the premium is recorded as a credit to Premium on Bonds Payable. To illustrate, the issuance of 400 of the bonds of Mason Company at a cash sale price of $1,100 each (i.e., at an 8½ percent market rate) would be recorded as shown in Exhibit 11–4 (bonds issued at a premium).

Measuring and recording interest expense (bonds sold at a premium)

   The premium of $40,000 recorded by Mason must be apportioned to each of the 20 interest periods. The effective-interest method usually must be used to make the allocation; however, the straight-line method may be used if the results are not different materially from the other method. For illustrative purposes, the straight-line method is used because of its simplicity. The amortization of premium each semiannual interest period would be: $40,000 ÷ 20 periods = $2,000. Therefore, the payments of interest on the bonds during 19A would be recorded as shown in Exhibit 11–4 (bonds issued at a premium).[3]

   In the journal entry to record the sale and issuance of the bonds by Mason, the premium was recorded in a separate account, Premium on Bonds Payable, as a **credit.** The premium has the effect of **decreasing** interest expense; therefore, in each period a portion of it is amortized to interest expense. Observe that in the illustration in Exhibit 11–4 (bonds issued at a premium), Bond Interest Expense was reduced by $2,000 each semiannual period because straight-line amortization was assumed. At the end of 19A, the financial statements of Mason Company would report interest expense and bonds payable as shown in Exhibit 11–4.

   At maturity date, after the last interest payment, the bond premium of $40,000 will be amortized fully and the maturity or face amount of the bonds and the current net liability of the bonds will be the same (i.e., $400,000). At maturity, December 31, 19J, the bonds will be paid off in full, resulting in the same entry whether originally sold at par, a discount, or a premium, as illustrated at the bottom of Exhibit 11–4.

   Bond premium amortizations are treated as a reduction of interest expense for accounting purposes. For income tax purposes, they are ignored when computing the income tax payable by the corporation. Therefore, tax allocation (see Chapter 10) would treat the premium amortization as a permanent difference between the accounting income and the taxable income. This treatment implies the credit for the bond premium amortization is not included when computing income tax expense for the income statement.

   The effect of amortization of bond discount and bond premium on a $1,000 bond is shown graphically in Exhibit 11–5.

---

[3]The amount of interest expense recorded each semiannual period may be confirmed as follows:

Cash paid out by the borrower:

Par amount of bonds at maturity	$400,000
Interest payments ($20,000 × 20 periods).	400,000
Total cash payments.	800,000
Cash received by the borrower	440,000
Total interest expense over 10 years.	$360,000
Interest expense per semiannual period ($360,000 ÷ 20 periods).	$ 18,000

(Alternatively, $20,000 cash interest − $2,000 premium
   amortization = $18,000.)

EXHIBIT 11-5
Graphic illustration
of straight-line
amortization of
bond premium and
discount

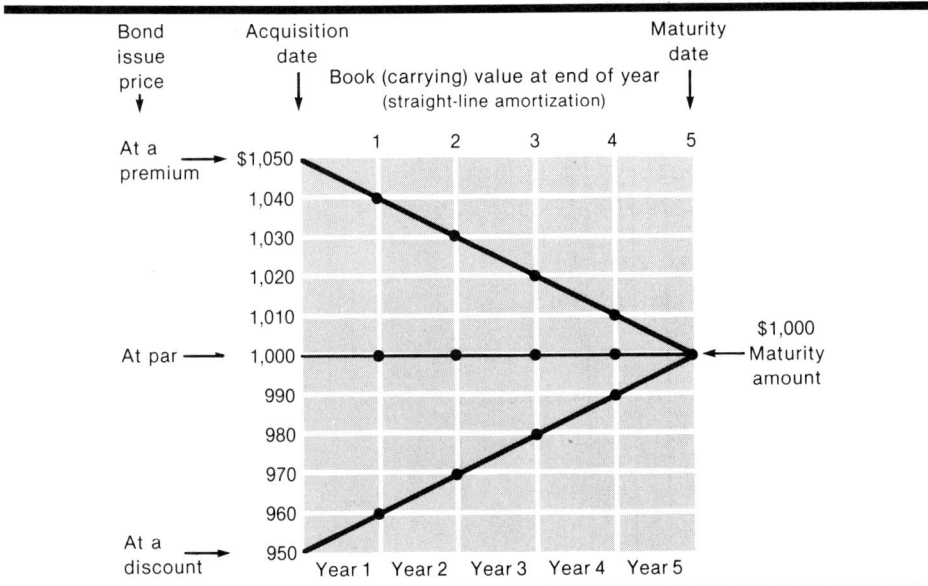

The preceding discussion has focused on the fundamental issues in measuring and reporting bonds payable. This discussion has provided the background essential to understanding the economic impact of bonds payable on the issuing company and its reporting on the periodic financial statements. The next part of the chapter discusses some complexities often encountered in accounting for bonds payable.

Part B—Some Special Problems in Accounting for Bonds Payable

This part of the chapter focuses primarily on four special problems commonly encountered in accounting for bonds payable. These four problems are (1) accounting for bonds sold between interest dates, (2) adjusting entries for accrued bond interest, (3) bond sinking funds, and (4) effective-interest amortization.

ACCOUNTING FOR BONDS SOLD BETWEEN INTEREST DATES

The bond certificates specify the **date** and **amount** of each cash interest payment. Although bonds may be sold on an interest date, usually market factors cause them to be sold **between** interest dates. Nevertheless, the exact amount of interest specified on the bond certificate for each interest date will be paid, regardless of whether a bond is sold on an interest date or between interest dates. Therefore, when bonds are sold between two interest dates, the investor (i.e., the buyer) must pay the interest that has accrued **since the last interest date** in addition to the market price of the bond. The amount of the next interest payment will be for a **full** interest period; therefore, the accrued interest is effectively returned to the buyer. The net effect is that the investor will realize interest revenue only for the number of months the bonds were held from the date of sale. Similarly, the issuing corporation will incur interest expense for the same period. This situation represents two complexities in accounting for bonds: (1) the amount of accrued interest charged to the buyer must be included in the journal entry of the issuer to record the sale of bonds; and (2) any premium or discount must be amortized by the issuer over the remaining period that the bonds will be outstanding; that is, the period from date of sale to date of maturity of the bonds.

In this section, we will illustrate the four special problems in accounting for bonds with data for Mendez Corporation, given at the top of Exhibit 11–6. Mendez Corporation issued bonds on August 1, 19A, which was two months after the date of the bonds (June 1, 19A). The time scale given in Exhibit 11–6 will be helpful in analyzing the effect of different dates on the accounting for the bond issue.

On August 1, 19A, date of the issuance of the 100 bonds, Mendez Corporation would receive cash for the sale price of the bonds, **plus** two months' accrued interest (June 1, 19A to July 31, 19A), computed as follows (refer to the bond time scale, Exhibit 11–6):

Market price (for 100 bonds)...........................	$96,460
Add accrued interest for 2 months (June and July):	
$100,000 × 12% × 2/12.............................	2,000
Total cash received	$98,460

The bond investors must pay two months of accrued interest to Mendez because the bond indenture (contract) requires that Mendez pay a full six months of interest on the next interest date (i.e., November 30). On the first interest date, the bonds will have been outstanding for only four months (August 1 through November 30). Therefore, on November 30, 19A, the investors will have earned four months' interest revenue and the issuer (Mendez) will have incurred four months' interest expense. The payment of two months' accrued interest when the bonds are purchased is an offset that causes interest to be adjusted to a four-month basis for both the investor and the issuer.

The journal entry by the issuer, Mendez Corporation, to record the issuance of the 100 bonds payable is shown in Exhibit 11–6. In that entry, Bond Interest Expense was credited for $2,000 accrued interest collected because that amount will be refunded to the investor when the next interest payment is made. That interest payment will be recorded as a credit to Cash and a debit to Bond Interest Expense (Exhibit 11–6).

The $3,540 recorded in the Discount on Bonds Payable account is amortized over the **period outstanding** of 118 months; therefore, straight-line amortization would be $3,540 ÷ 118 months = $30 per month. The entry to record the first interest payment would include amortization of discount only for the four

EXHIBIT 11–6
Some special
problems in
accounting for
bonds payable
illustrated

Situation:

Mendez Corporation approved the following bond issue on June 1, 19A:

Bonds payable authorized, 200 bonds, $1,000 par per bond, 12 percent interest (payable each May 31 and November 30), maturity in 10 years on May 31, 19J.

Mendez's accounting period ends December 31.

Bonds issued: 100 bonds (par $100,000) issued on August 1, 19A, for $96,460.

Analysis of the situation (graphic time scale):

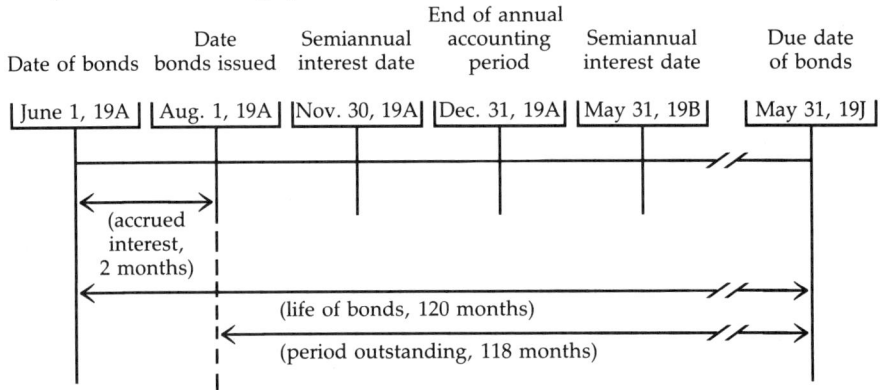

			End of annual		
	Date	Semiannual	accounting	Semiannual	Due date
Date of bonds	bonds issued	interest date	period	interest date	of bonds
June 1, 19A	Aug. 1, 19A	Nov. 30, 19A	Dec. 31, 19A	May 31, 19B	May 31, 19J

←→ (accrued interest, 2 months)

(life of bonds, 120 months)

(period outstanding, 118 months)

Current 19A entries:

August 1, 19A—Issuance of the bonds (par $100,000) for $96,460 plus two months' accrued interest prior to issuance date, $2,000.

Cash ($96,460 + $2,000)	98,460	
Discount on bonds payable ($100,000 − $96,460).	3,540	
Bonds payable (100 bonds × $1,000 par)		100,000
Bond interest expense ($100,000 × .12 × 2/12).		2,000

November 30, 19A—First interest payment (issue to maturity date, 118 months):

Bond interest expense	6,120	
Discount on bonds payable (straight-line;		
$3,540 × 4/118 mos.)		120
Cash ($100,000 × .06)		6,000

Adjusting entry:

December 31,19A—For 1 month interest since last interest date:

Bond interest expense ($1,000 + $30 amortization)	1,030	
Discount on bonds payable ($3,540 × 1/118 mos.).		30
Bond interest payable ($100,000 × .12 × 1/12)		1,000

T-accounts for 19A:

Bond Interest Expense				Discount on Bonds Payable			
11/30/19A	6,120	8/1/19A	2,000	8/1/19A	3,540	11/30/19A	120
12/31/19A	1,030					12/31/19A	30

(Balance 12/31/19A, $5,150; close to Income Summary and report on income statement.)

(Balance 12/31/19A, $3,390; report on balance sheet as a deduction [contra] to Bonds payable.)

months that the bonds have been outstanding. Therefore, the first interest payment would be recorded as illustrated in Exhibit 11–6.

After journal entries are made to record the collection of accrued interest (August 1, 19A) and the payment of interest (November 30, 19A), the Bond Interest Expense account will reflect a debit balance of $4,120. This amount is equivalent to four months' interest (i.e., $100,000 × 12% × 4/12 = $4,000) plus four months' amortization of discount (i.e. $30 × 4 = $120). The Bond Interest Expense Account would appear as follows:

Bond Interest Expense

11/30/19A	6,120	8/1/19A	2,000

(Balance, 11/30/19A, $4,120)

ADJUSTING ENTRY FOR ACCRUED BOND INTEREST

In Chapter 10, we discussed the **adjusting entry** that must be made for any interest expense accrued since the last interest payment date for a note payable. The same adjustment procedure must be applied to bonds payable. However, in the case of bonds, the adjusting entry must include **both** the accrued interest and amortization of any bond discount or premium. To illustrate, Mendez Corporation (Exhibit 11–6) recorded an interest payment on November 30, 19A; therefore, on December 31, 19A, there is accrued interest for one month. Bond discount also must be amortized for one more month. The adjusting entry at December 31, 19A, is illustrated in Exhibit 11–6.

After the adjusting entry is posted on December 31, 19A, the Bond Interest Expense account will reflect a debit balance of $5,150, which represents interest expense for the five months that the bonds have been outstanding during 19A (August 1 to December 31). The Bond Interest Expense account for 19A is illustrated at the bottom of Exhibit 11–6. The ending balance of $5,150 can be verified as follows:

Interest: $100,000 × 12% × 5/12..........	$5,000
Add discount amortized: $30 × 5.........	150
Total interest expense for 19A......	$5,150

Bond Interest Expense is closed to Income Summary at the end of the accounting period and is reported on the 19A income statement. The Bond Discount account for 19A is reported on the balance sheet as follows:

Long-term liabilities:	
Bonds payable........................	$100,000
Less: Discount on Bonds payable......	3,390
	$96,610

Bond Sinking Funds

On the maturity date of bonds payable, the issuing company must have available a large amount of cash to pay off the bondholders. Such a demand for a large amount of cash might place the issuing company in a severe financial strain. In order to avoid this situation, some companies build up a separate

cash fund by making equal annual contributions over a period of time in advance of the bond maturity date. Such a separate cash fund customarily is called a **bond sinking fund.** A bond sinking fund is an asset that is invested pending the due date of the bonds; it is reported on the balance sheet under the caption "Investments and funds."

A bond sinking fund also adds a measure of security for the bondholders because it assures them that funds will be available for retirement of the bonds at their maturity date. Each cash contribution to the fund usually is deposited with an independent trustee (a designated third party such as bank or another financial institution). The trustee invests the funds received and adds the fund earnings to the fund balance each year. Interest earned on a sinking fund is recorded as an increase in the fund balance (a debit) and as interest revenue (a credit). Thus, a bond sinking fund typically has the characteristics of a regular savings account such as was illustrated in Chapter 10, Part B. At the maturity date of the bonds, the balance of the fund is used to pay the bondholders. Any excess cash is returned to the issuing corporation, or, in the case of a deficit, it must be made up by the issuer.

Exhibit 11–7 illustrates a bond sinking fund for Mendez Corporation. The fund will be built up over the last five years that the bonds are outstanding by making five equal annual deposits each May 31, starting in 19F. The sinking fund contributions will be deposited with City Trust Co., as trustee, which will pay 8 percent annual interest on the fund balance each May 31. The amount of each deposit required can be calculated using the time value of money concepts discussed and illustrated in Chapter 10, Part B. If the fund earned no interest, obviously each deposit would have to be $20,000 (i.e., $100,000 ÷ 5 contributions = $20,000). Instead of $20,000, the annual deposit required is less than $20,000 because the interest earned each year will be added to the fund balance. The required annual deposit was determined to be $17,046, as illustrated in Exhibit 11–7.

The journal entries for May 31, 19F, and 19G, for the sinking fund are illustrated in Exhibit 11–7.[4] Observe that the fund is increased by **both** the annual deposits and the accumulation of interest. Identical journal entries with different interest amounts would be made for each of the five years of the accumulation period. The interest amounts increase each year because of the increasing balance in the fund. At the maturity date of the bonds, payment will be made to the bondholders using the cash accumulated in the sinking fund. The journal entry to retire the bonds payable is illustrated in Exhibit 11–7.

Often it is useful to develop a fund accumulation schedule as shown in Exhibit 11–7. Observe that the schedule provides data for (1) the entry on each interest date and (2) the buildup of the fund to maturity date.

Some bond indentures for sinking-fund bonds will permit the organization to use the cash placed in the sinking fund to buy the bonds of the issuing

---

[4]In connection with such funds, a company also may restrict, or appropriate, an equivalent amount of retained earnings as a dividend restriction. The restriction of retained earnings by a corporation is discussed in Chapter 12.

EXHIBIT 11–7
Accounting for a
bond sinking fund

Situation:

Mendez Corporation plans to accumulate a bond sinking fund sufficient to retire the $100,000 bond issue outstanding on maturity date, May 31, 19J (see Exhibit 11–6). Five equal annual deposits are to be made each May 31, starting in 19F. Expected earning rate on the fund is 8 percent.

Computation of periodic deposits ($n = 5$, years F through J; $i = 8\%$):

Computation (application of future value of annuity of $1):
  Future value $=$ Periodic rent $\times F_{=6;\ i=\ 9\%}$
  Substituting:
  $\$100{,}000 = \quad ? \quad \times 5.8666$ (Table 10–3)
  Periodic rent $= \$100{,}000 \div 5.8666$
  $ = \underline{\$\ 17{,}046}$

Entries—for first year of the fund and the second deposit):
  May 31, 19F—To record the first deposit by Mendez:

Bond sinking fund..	17,046	
Cash (computed above)		17,046

  May 31, 19G—To record interest revenue for 1 year added to the fund:

Bond sinking fund (observe, not the cash account)...............	1,364	
Interest revenue ($17,046 $\times$ .08)		1,364

  May 31, 19G—To record the second deposit by Mendez:

Bond sinking fund..	17,046	
Cash (computed above)		17,046

Entry at maturity date, (May 31, 19J) to retire the bonds:

Bonds payable..	100,000	
Bond sinking fund...		100,000

Sinking fund accumulation schedule (Deposits, $17,046; $n = 5$; $i = 8\%$):

Date	Cash Deposit (Credit Cash)	Interest Revenue (Credit)	Fund Increase (Debit Fund)	Accumulated Fund Balance
5/31/19F	17,046[a]		17,046	17,046
5/31/19G	17,046	17,046 $\times$ .08 = 1,364[b]	18,410[c]	35,456[d]
5/31/19H	17,046	35,456 $\times$ .08 = 2,836	19,882	55,338
5/31/19I	17,046	55,338 $\times$ .08 = 4,427	21,473	76,811
5/31/19J	17,046	76,811 $\times$ .08 = 6,143*	23,189	100,000
Totals	85,230	14,770	100,000	

*Rounded $2 to accommodate prior rounding errors.
[a]Computed above.
[b]Interest earned on beginning balance in the fund each period at 8 percent.
[c]Period deposit ($17,046) plus interest earned ($1,364) = $18,410 (etc.).
[d]Prior balance ($17,046) plus increase in fund ($18,410) = $35,456 (etc.).
Note: This is an ordinary annuity (i.e., end-of-period contributions.)

organization on the open market. The bonds would then be canceled and the bond liability reduced correspondingly. Such an approach would mean that the sinking fund would not be an asset because each purchased bond can be offset against the outstanding liability using what is termed the *right of offset*. The accounting entries for such a procedure will be discussed in advanced courses.

EFFECTIVE-INTEREST AMORTIZATION ON BONDS PAYABLE

Effective-interest amortization of bond discount or bond premium is the only conceptually sound method for measuring both (1) the effective-interest expense on bonds and (2) the carrying amount of the bonds (at the current net liability amount). This approach uses the concept of present value discussed in Chapter 10, Part B.

The straight-line approach is permitted when the difference in amortization results is not material in amount. Conceptually, the effective-interest method is similar to the debt repayment which was discussed in Chapter 10. Each equal payment made on the debt consists of two parts: (1) a payment of principal and (2) a payment of interest.

A simplified case is used to illustrate effective-interest amortization and the related journal entries. The facts for the example are presented in Exhibit 11–8.

The sale price of the West Corporation bonds is the present value of the future cash flows associated with the bonds. The difference between the total par value of the bonds ($10,000) and the present value of the bonds ($8,558) is the discount ($1,442) which must be amortized over the life of the bonds. The journal entry to record the issuance of the bonds is shown in Exhibit 11–8.

When the effective-interest amortization method is used, the amount of interest expense and the amount of discount or premium that is amortized **change** each interest period. The amount of cash interest paid does not change because it is based on the stated rate of interest that is specified by the bond contract. The amounts for each journal entry to record the payment of interest must be computed uniquely. An organized approach to this computation is based on the preparation of a **debt payment schedule.** The schedule provides the amortization and interest expense amounts that must be recorded each interest period, as illustrated in Exhibit 11–8. The journal entries to record periodic interest are based on the amounts contained in the debt payment schedule. The journal entries for West Corporation are illustrated in Exhibit 11–8.

The effective-interest amortization method is preferred conceptually because it measures the effective, or true, interest expense each period. To illustrate, West Corporation borrowed $8,558 on January 1, 19A, at a market interest rate of 12 percent. The interest expense for the first year should be $1,027 (i.e., 12% × $8,558 = $1,027) which is the amount recorded in the journal entry for 19A in Exhibit 11–8. In contrast, if the straight-line method had been used, the amortization of the bond discount would have been $288 (i.e., $1,442 ÷ 5 = $288), and interest expense would have been $1,088 (i.e., $288 + $800 =

EXHIBIT 11–8
Effective-interest amortization on bonds payable

Situation: West Corporation sold ten, $1,000 bonds as follows:

Bonds payable authorized (10 bonds at $1,000 par each)	$10,000
Date printed on each bond.	January 1, 19A
Maturity date (five-year term)	December 31, 19E
Interest, **payable per annum** each December 31	8%
Issued (sold) all of the bonds.	January 1, 19A
Market interest rate	12%
Sale price (at a discount).	$8,558*
End of the accounting period for West	December 31

*Issue price computed as follows:
$10,000 × $P_{n=6;\ i=12\%}$ (Table 10–2 = .5674) = $5,674
$800 × $p_{n=6;\ i=12\%}$ (Table 10–4 = 3.6048) = 2,884
$8,558

Entry: To record issuance (sale) of the bonds at a discount:

January 1, 19A:

Cash (computed above)	8,558	
Discount on bonds payable ($10,000 − $8,558)	1,442	
Bonds payable (10 bonds × $1,000 par)		10,000

Bond payment schedule, effective-interest amortization:

(a) Date	(b) Cash Interest Paid on Each Interest Date ($10,000 × 8%)	(c) Interest Expense (based on beginning unpaid liability at market rate of 12%)	(d) Effective-Interest Amortization (increase of liability)*	(e) Net Liability (unpaid balance)
1/1/19A				8,558
12/31/19A	800	8,558 × .12 = 1,027	227	8,785
12/31/19B	800	8,785 × .12 = 1,054	254	9,039
12/31/19C	800	9,039 × .12 = 1,085	285	9,324
12/31/19D	800	9,324 × .12 = 1,119	319	9,643
12/31/19E	800	9,643 × .12 = 1,157	357	10,000
Subtotal	4,000	5,442	1,442	
12/31/19E	10,000†		10,000	–0–

*Adjusts the net liability to the maturity amount.
†Payment of principal.

Periodic entries to record interest paid and discount amortization:

	19A	19B	19C	19D	19E
Bond interest expense.	1,027	1,054	1,085	1,119	1,157
Discount on bonds payable . .	227	254	285	319	357
Cash.	800	800	800	800	800

Financial statements:

Income statement:

	19A	19B	19C	19D	19E
Bond interest expense	$1,027	$1,054	$1,085	$1,119	$1,157

Balance sheet:

	19A	19B	19C	19D	19E
Bonds payable (maturity amount $10,000) minus unamortized discount	8,785	9,039	9,324	9,643	–0–

$1,088). The straight-line method is acceptable only if its use results in amounts that are not materially different from effective-interest amounts.

The net liability measured and reported on the balance sheet under the effective-interest method is the present value of the remaining cash flows associated with the bond, which is the conceptually preferred amount. The straight-line method approximates this amount and is acceptable if there is not a material difference between the two amounts.

To summarize, effective-interest amortization conceptually is superior to straight-line amortization because, for each period, consistent with the issue price of the bonds, it measures (1) the true amount of interest expense each period on the income statement and (2) the true current net carrying amount of the bonds outstanding (net liability) on the balance sheet each period. Straight-line amortization provides approximations of these amounts and can be used only when the difference between the two methods is deemed not material (refer to exception principle, materiality). In such situations, straight-line amortization is often used because it is less complex.

DEMONSTRATION CASE

(Try to resolve the requirements before proceeding to the suggested solution that follows.)

In order to raise funds to construct a new plant, the management of Reed Company decided to issue bonds. Accordingly, a proposed bond indenture was submitted to the board of directors and approved. The provisions in the bond indenture and specified on the bond certificates were:

Par value of bonds to be issued ($1,000 bonds) $600,000
Date of bond issue—February 1, 19A, due in 10 years on January 31, 19K.
Interest—10% per annum, payable 5% on each July 31 and January 31.

The bonds were sold on June 1, 19A, at 102½ plus accrued interest. The annual accounting period for Reed Company ends on December 31.

Required:

a. How much cash was received by Reed Company from the sale of the bonds payable on June 1, 19A? Show computations.

b. What was the amount of premium on the bonds payable? Over how many months should it be amortized?

c. Compute the amount of amortization of premium per month and for each six-month interest period; use straight-line amortization. Round to the nearest dollar.

d. Give the journal entry on June 1, 19A, to record the sale and issuance of the bonds payable.

e. Give the journal entry for payment of interest and amortization of premium for the first interest payment on July 31, 19A.

f. Give the adjusting entry required on December 31, 19A, at the end of the accounting period.

g. Give the optional reversing entry that could be made on January 1, 19B.

h.   Give the journal entry to record the second interest payment and the amortization of premium on January 31, 19B.

i.   Show how bond interest expense and bonds payable would be reported on the financial statements at December 31, 19A.

Suggested solution

Requirement a:

Sales price of the bonds: ($600,000 × 102.5%).................	$615,000
Add accrued interest for four months (February 1 to	
May 31) ($600,000 × 10% × 4/12)...........................	20,000
Total cash received for the bonds	$635,000

Requirement b:

Premium on the bonds payable ($600,000 × 2.5%)	$ 15,000
Months amortized: From date of sale, June 1, 19A,	
to maturity date, January 31, 19K.	
120 months − 4 months =...............................	116 months

Requirement c:

Premium amortization: $15,000 ÷ 116 months = $129 per month, or $774 each six-month interest period (straight line).

Requirement d:

June 1, 19A:

Cash (per Requirement [a] above).............................	635,000	
Premium on bonds payable (per Requirement [b] above)......		15,000
Interest expense (per Requirement [a] above)		20,000
Bonds payable		600,000
To record sale of bonds payable at 102½ plus accrued interest for four months, February 1 to May 31, 19A.		

Requirement e:

July 31, 19A:

Bond interest expense	29,742	
Premium on bonds payable ($129 × 2 months)	258	
Cash ($600,000 × 5%).......................................		30,000
To record payment of semiannual interest and to amortize premium for two months, June 1 to July 31, 19A.		

Requirement f:
December 31, 19A:

```
Bond interest expense .........................................  24,355
Premium on bonds payable ($129 × 5 months) ...................     645
   Bond interest payable ($600,000 × 10% × 5/12)...............           25,000
   Adjusting entry for five months' interest accrued plus
   amortization of premium, August 1 to December 31, 19A.
```

Requirement g:
January 1, 19B:

```
Bond interest payable .........................................  25,000
   Premium on bonds payable ..................................              645
   Bonds interest expense ....................................           24,355
   Reversing entry; optional.
```

Requirement h:
January 31, 19B (assuming reversing entry [g] was made):[5]

```
Bond interest expense ........................................  29,226
Premium on bonds payable (per Requirement [c]) ................     774
   Cash ($600,000 × 10% × 6/12) .............................           30,000
   To record payment of semiannual interest and to amortize
   premium for six months.
```

---

[5]If no reversing entry was made on January 1, 19B, this entry would be:

```
Bond interest payable ...............................................  25,000
Premium on bonds payable.............................................     129
Bond interest expense................................................   4,871
   Cash .............................................................           30,000
```

Requirement i:

Interest expense to be reported on the 19A income statement should be for the period outstanding during the year (i.e., for seven months, June 1 through December 31). Interest expense, per the above entries, is $29,742 + $24,355 − $20,000 = $34,097; or, alternatively, ($600,000 × 10% × 7/12 = $35,000) minus ($129 × 7 months = $903) = $34,097.

Income statement for 19A:

Interest expense	$ 34,097

Balance sheet, December 31, 19A:

Long-term liabilities:

Bonds payable, 10% (due January 31, 19K)	$600,000	
Add unamortized premium*	14,097	614,097

*$15,000 − ($258 + $645) = $14,097.

SUMMARY OF CHAPTER

This chapter discussed bonds payable, which represent one of the primary ways to obtain funds to acquire long-term assets and to expand a business. An important advantage of bonds payable is that the cost of borrowing the funds—interest expense—is deductible for income tax purposes which reduces the interest cost to the business.

Bonds may be sold at their par (or face) amount; at a premium; or at a discount, depending upon the stated interest rate on the bonds compared with the market (or yield) rate of interest that the bond buyers demand and the issuer will accept. In each case, bonds are measured, recorded, and reported at their current cash equivalent amount. The price of a bond varies based on the relationship between the market and stated rates of interest. If the market rate is higher than the stated rate on the bond, the bonds will sell at a discount. Conversely, if the market rate is lower than the stated rate of the bond, the bonds will sell at a premium.

Discounts and premiums on bonds payable are adjustments of the cash interest payments made by the issuing company during the term of the bonds. As a consequence, discount or premium on bonds payable is amortized to interest expense over the time from issue date to maturity date.

To assure that funds are available to retire bonds payable at maturity, a company may set aside cash in advance by means of periodic contributions to a bond sinking fund. Such a fund is similar to a savings account. The bond sinking fund usually is administered by an independent third party, such as a bank (called the trustee). Interest earned on the fund balance is added to the fund each period. At the maturity date of the bonds, the fund is used to pay the bondholders. Such a fund is reported on the balance sheet under the caption "Investments and funds." Interest earned on the fund is reported on the income statement as "Interest revenue."

IMPORTANT TERMS DEFINED IN THIS CHAPTER

Terms (alphabetically)	Key words in definitions of important terms used in chapter	Page reference
Bond certificate	The physical bond document; an example is presented in Exhibit 11–1.	583
Bond discount	A bond that is sold for less than par.	592
Bond premium	A bond that is sold for more than par.	594
Bond principal	The amount payable at the maturity of the bond; face amount.	583
Bond sinking fund	A cash fund accumulated for repayment of a bond upon maturity.	600
Callable bond	Bond that may be called for early retirement at the option of the issuer.	585
Convertible bond	A bond that may be converted to other securities of the issuer (usually common shares).	585
Coupon rate of interest	Another name for the stated rate of interest; particularly on coupon bonds.	588
Debenture	An unsecured bond; no assets specifically pledged to guarantee repayment.	585
Effective-interest amortization	Theoretically preferred method to amortize a bond discount or premium.	602
Face amount	Another name for bond principal.	583
Financial leverage	Use of creditors' funds to increase the rate of return on owners' equity; occurs when the interest rate on debt is lower than the earnings rate on total assets.	586
Indenture	Bond contract that specifies the legal provisions of the bond.	583
Net interest cost	Interest cost, less the tax savings associated with interest expense.	586
Par value	Another name for bond principal or maturity amount.	583
Redeemable bond	Bond that may be turned in for early retirement at the option of the bondholder.	585
Stated rate	The rate of cash interest per period specified in the bond contract.	588
Straight-line amortization	Simplified method to amortize a bond discount or premium.	593
Trustee	An independent party appointed to represent the bondholders.	583

QUESTIONS FOR DISCUSSION

Part A

1. What are the primary characteristics of a bond? For what purpose are bonds usually issued?

2. What is the difference between a bond indenture and a bond certificate?

3. Distinguish between secured and unsecured bonds.

4. Distinguish among callable, redeemable, and convertible bonds.

5. Distinguish between registered and coupon bonds.

6. From the perspective of the issuer, what are some advantages of issuing bonds, as compared with issuing capital stock?

7. As the tax rate increases, the net cost of borrowing money decreases. Explain.

8. Briefly explain financial leverage. Can financial leverage be negative?

9. At the date of issuance, bonds are recorded at their current cash equivalent amount. Explain.

10. What is the nature of the discount and premium on bonds payable?

11. What is the difference between the stated interest rate and the effective interest rate on a bond?

12. Distinguish between the stated and effective rates of interest on a bond (a) sold at par, (b) sold at a discount, and (c) sold at a premium.

Part B

13. Why are bond discounts and premiums amortized over the outstanding life of the related bonds payable rather than the period from the date of the bonds to their maturity date?

14. What is meant by the "current net liability" of a bond payable?

15. Why is the lender (i.e., the purchaser of a bond) charged for the accrued interest from the last interest date to the date of purchase of the bonds?

16. What is a bond sinking fund? How should a bond sinking fund be reported in the financial statements?

17. Explain the basic difference between straight-line amortization and effective-interest amortization of bond discount or premium. Explain when each method should, or may, be used.

EXERCISES

Part A

E11–1. On January 1, 19A, Orange Corporation borrowed $90,000 on a three-year note payable. The interest rate is 12 percent per annum, payable each year. The company computed its return on total assets [i.e., Net income (before interest but after income taxes) ÷ (Liabilities + Owners' equity)] to be 20 percent. The average income tax rate for the company is 40 percent.

Required:

a. What amount of interest would be paid the first year?
b. Considering the effect of income tax, what would be the net interest cost and the net interest rate?

c. Would financial leverage be present in this situation? Explain.

d. List two primary advantages to Orange Corporation in favour of the note payable versus selling more of its unissued capital stock to obtain needed funds.

E11–2. London Corporation is planning to issue $100,000, five-year, 10 percent bonds. Interest is payable semiannually each June 30 and December 31. Assume all of the bonds will be sold on January 1, 19A, and that they will mature on December 31, 19E.

Required (round to the nearest dollar):

a. Compute the issue (sale) price on January 1, 19A, for each of the following three independent cases (show computations).
   Case A—The market (yield) rate is 10 percent.
   Case B—The market (yield) rate is 8 percent.
   Case C—The market (yield) rate is 12 percent.

b. Give the journal entry to record the issuance for each case.

E11–3. Jacob Corporation had $200,000, 10-year, coupon bonds outstanding on December 31, 19A (end of the accounting period). Interest is payable each June 30 and December 31. The bonds were issued (sold) on January 1, 19A. The 19A annual financial statements reflected the following:

> **Income statement:**
> Bond interest expense (straight-line amortization)...... $ 18,600
>
> **Balance sheet:**
> Bonds payable (net liability).........................   194,600

Required (show computations):

a. What was the issue price of the bonds?

b. What was the coupon rate on the bonds?

c. Prepare computations which will show that the above amounts of (1) interest expense and (2) bonds payable (net liability) are correct.

E11–4. The summarized information below was taken from the 19B annual financial statements of two competing companies in the same industry (assume 50,000 shares of common stock outstanding):

	Company A	Company B
	Thousands of dollars	
Balance sheet:		
Total assets	$900	$900
Total liabilities (10% interest)	400	600
Income statement:		
Total revenues	480	421
Total expenses (including income tax)	300	400
Tax rate	40%	20%

Required:

a. Complete a tabulation similar to the following (show computations):

Item	Company A	Company B
Earnings per share		
Return on shareholders' equity		
Return on total assets		
Financial leverage		

b. Interpret and compare the financial leverage figures for the two companies.

E11–5. Adams, Incorporated, sold a $150,000, 8 percent bond issue on January 1, 19A, for $140,372 (9 percent market rate). The bonds were dated January 1, 19A, and pay interest each December 31. The bonds mature 10 years from January 1, 19A.

Required:

a. Give the journal entry to record the issuance of the bonds.
b. Give the journal entry to record the interest payment on December 31, 19A. Assume straight-line amortization.
c. Show how the bond interest expense and the bonds payable should be reported on the December 31, 19A, annual financial statements.
d. Verify the sales price of $140,372 (show computations).

E11–6. Keller Corporation sold a $60,000, 14 percent bond issue on January 1, 19A, for $66,782 (at a market rate of 12 percent). The bonds were dated January 1, 19A, and interest is paid each December 31. The bonds mature 10 years from January 1, 19A.

Required:

a. Give the journal entry to record the issuance of the bonds.
b. Give the journal entry for the interest payment on December 31, 19A. Assume straight-line amortization.
c. Show how the bond interest expense and the bonds payable should be reported on the December 31, 19A, annual financial statements.
d. Verify the issue (sale) price of $66,782 (show computations).

E11–7. In order to obtain cash to purchase operational assets, Day Corporation, whose annual accounting period ends on December 31, issued the following bonds:

Date of bonds: January 1, 19A.
Maturity amount and date: $100,000, due in 10 years (December 31, 19J).
Interest: 11 percent per annum payable each December 31.
Date sold: January 1, 19A.

Required:

a. Give the journal entry to record the issuance and the first two interest payments under each of three different independent assumptions (assume straight-line amortization):
(1) The bonds sold at par.
(2) The bonds sold at 96.
(3) The bonds sold at 104.

b. Provide the following amounts to be reported on the 19A financial statements:

		Assumption 1	Assumption 2	Assumption 3
1.	Interest expense	$_____	$_____	$_____
2.	Bonds payable........................	_____	_____	_____
3.	Unamortized premium or discount	_____	_____	_____
4.	Net liability	_____	_____	_____
5.	Stated rate of interest	_____	_____	_____
6.	Cash interest paid	_____	_____	_____

   c.   Explain why items 1 and 6 are different in Requirement *(b)*.

Part B

E11–8.   Dymo Corporation authorized the issuance of $300,000, 9 percent, 10-year bonds. The date printed on the bond certificates is January 1, 19A, and the interest is payable each June 30 and December 31.

On September 1, 19A, the company issued (sold) $200,000 of the bonds at 96 plus any accrued interest.

Required:

a.   How much cash did Dymo Corporation receive on September 1, 19A? Show computations.

b.   Give the journal entry to record the issuance.

c.   How much net cash interest did Dymo Corporation pay during 19A on the $200,000 issuance? Show computations.

E11–9.   White Corporation issued the following bonds:

Bonds payable authorized......................	$60,000
Date on each bond	Jan. 1, 19A
Maturity date (10 years)	Dec. 31, 19J
Interest, 10% per year, payable each December 31.	

White sold all of the bonds on March 1, 19A, and received $62,180 cash which included the accrued interest.

Required:

a.   What was the amount of discount or premium?

b.   Over what period of time should the discount or premium be amortized?

c.   What would be the amortization amount per month assuming straight-line amortization?

d.   Give the journal entry to record the issuance.

e.   Give the journal entry on first interest payment date.

f.   What amount should be reported as interest expense for 19A?

g.   What amount of net liability should be shown on the balance sheet at December 31, 19A?

E11–10.   Dopuch Corporation issued $10,000, 9 percent bonds dated April 1, 19A. Interest is paid each March 31. The bonds mature in three years on March 31, 19D. The bonds were sold on June 1, 19A, for $9,660 plus accrued interest. The accounting period ends each December 31.

Required:

a. Give the journal entry to record the issuance on June 1, 19A.
b. Give the adjusting entry required on December 31, 19A; use straight-line amortization.
c. What amount of interest expense should be reported on the income statement for 19A?
d. Show how the bonds should be reported on the balance sheet at December 31, 19A?
e. Give the journal entry to record the first interest payment on March 31, 19B.

E11–11. Tower Corporation has a $100,000 bond issue outstanding that is due four years hence. It desires to set up a bond sinking fund for this amount by making five equal annual contributions. The first contribution will be made immediately and the last one on the due date (i.e., an ordinary annuity). The corporation will deposit the annual contributions with a trustee that will increase the fund at the end of each year for 8 percent on the fund balance that existed at the beginning of the year.

Required:

a. Compute the annual contribution (rent) to the fund.
b. Give the journal entry for the first and second contributions, including interest.
c. Show how the effects of the fund would be reported on the financial statements at the end of the second year.

E11–12. Small Company has a $90,000 debt that will be due at the end of three years. The management has decided to deposit three equal year-end amounts of $27,723 in a debt retirement fund (i.e., an ordinary annuity). The fund balance will earn 8 percent interest which will be added to the fund at each year-end.

Required:

a. Prepare a fund accumulation schedule similar to Exhibit 11–7. Round to the nearest dollar and show computations.
b. Give the journal entry(s) at the end of the second year to record the increase in the fund.
c. Show how the $27,723 was computed.
d. Did the earnings on the fund increase the balance of the company's cash account? Explain.

E11–13. Jolly Corporation issued a $1,000 bond on January 1, 19A. The bond specified an interest rate of 8 percent payable at the end of each year. The bond matures at the end of 19C. It was sold at a market rate of 9 percent per year. In respect to the issuance of the bond, the following schedule was completed:

Date	Cash	Interest	Amortization	Balance
Jan. 1, 19A (issuance)				$ 975
End of Year A.............	$80	$88	$8	983
End of Year B	80	88	8	991
End of Year C.............	80	89	9	1,000

Required:

Respond to the following questions:

a. What was the issue price of the bond?
b. Did the bond sell at a discount or a premium? How much?

c.   What amount of cash was paid each year for bond interest?
d.   What amount of interest expense should be shown each year on the income statement?
e.   What amount(s) should be shown on the balance sheet for bonds payable at each year-end (for Year C, show the balance just before retirement of the bond)?
f.   What method of amortization was used?
g.   Show how the following amounts were computed for Year A: (1) $80, (2) $88, (3) $8, and (4) $983.
h.   Is the method of amortization used preferable? Explain why.

E11–14.   Butle Company issued a $10,000, 11 percent, three-year bond on January 1, 19A. The bond interest is paid each December 31. The bond was sold to yield 10 percent (issue price, $10,249).

Required:

a.   Complete a bond payment schedule.
b.   Give the interest and amortization entry at the end of 19B.
c.   Show how the $10,249 issue price was computed.

PROBLEMS/CASES

Part A

PC11–1.   The financial statements of Stickney Corporation for 19A reflected the following:

Income Statement

Revenues.	$200,000)
Expenses.	(139,000)
Interest expense	(1,000)
Pretax income	60,000
Income taxes (40%).	(24,000)
Net income.	$ 36,000

Balance Sheet

Assets	$150,000
Liabilities (average interest rate, 10%)	$ 10,000
Common stock, par $10.	100,000
Retained earnings.	40,000
	$150,000

To demonstrate financial leverage, assume that Stickney Corporation during 19A had $60,000 liabilities (instead of $10,000) and common stock of $50,000 (5,000 shares) instead of $100,000 (10,000 shares). That is, more debt was used to finance the business.

Required:

a.   Complete a table similar to the following to demonstrate the economic effects of financial leverage.

Item	Actual results for 19A	Results assuming an increase in debt of $50,000
a. Total debt............................	_____	_____
b. Total assets	_____	_____
c. Total shareholders' equity	_____	_____
d. Interest expense (total @ 10%)..........	_____	_____
e. Net income	_____	_____
f. Return on total assets	_____	_____
g. Earnings available to shareholders:		
(1) Amount..........................	_____	_____
(2) Per share.........................	_____	_____
(3) Return on shareholders' equity	_____	_____

    b. Write an explanation of the advantages and disadvantages of higher debt financing (i.e., higher leverage) in this particular situation.

PC11–2. On January 1, 19A, Beckwith Corporation sold and issued $100,000, 8 percent, five-year bonds. The bond interest is payable annually each December 31. Assume the bonds were sold under three separate and independent cases: Case A, at par; Case B, at 95; and Case C, at 105.

Required:

    a. Complete a tabulation similar to the following for each separate case assuming straight-line amortization of discount and premium. Disregard income tax.

	At Start of 19A	At End of 19A	At End of 19B	At End of 19C	At End of 19D	At End of 19E	
						Prior to Payment of Principal	Payment of Principal
Case A—Sold at par (100): Pretax cash inflow	$	$	$	$	$	$	$
Pretax cash outflow							
Interest expense on income statement							
Net liability on balance sheet							
Case B—Sold at a discount (95): Pretax cash inflow							
Pretax cash outflow							
Interest expense on income statement							
Net liability on balance sheet							
Case C—Sold at a premium (105): Pretax cash inflow							
Pretax cash outflow							
Interest expense on income statement							
Net liability on balance sheet							

b. For each separate case, calculate each of the following:
  (1) Total pretax cash outflow.
  (2) Total pretax cash inflow.
  (3) Difference—net pretax cash outflow.
  (4) Total pretax interest expense.
c. (1) Explain why the net pretax cash outflows differ among the three cases.
  (2) For each case, explain why the net pretax cash outflow is the same amount as total interest expense.

PC11–3. Southwick Corporation sold a $200,000, 8 percent bond issue on January 1, 19A. The bonds pay interest each December 31, and will mature 10 years from January 1, 19A. For comparative study and analysis, assume three separate cases (show computations, assume straight-line amortization, and disregard income tax unless specifically required):

Case A—The bonds sold at par.
Case B—The bonds sold at 97.
Case C—The bonds sold at 103.

	Case A	Case B	Case C
1. Cash inflow at issue (sale) date			
2. Total cash outflow through maturity date			
3. Difference—total interest expense			
Income statement for 19A:			
4. Bond interest expense, pretax.................			
Balance sheet at December 31, 19A:			
Long-term liabilities:			
5. Bonds payable, 8%			
6. Unamortized discount........................			
7. Unamortized premium			
8. Net liability			
9. Stated interest rate..........................			
10. Total interest expense, net of income tax (40% tax rate)			

Required:

a. Complete a schedule similar to the one outlined above.
b. Give the journal entries for each case on January 1, 19A, and December 31, 19A (excluding closing entries).
c. For each case, explain why items 3, 4, and 10 of Requirement *(a)* are the same, or different.

PC11–4. Ward Company issued bonds with the following provisions:

Maturity value: $300,000.
Interest: 11% per annum payable semiannually each June 30 and December 31.
Terms: Bonds dated January 1, 19A, due five years from that date.

The annual accounting period for Ward ends December 31. The bonds were sold on January 1, 19A, at a 10 percent market rate.

Required:

a. Compute the issue (sale) price of the bonds (show computations).
b. Give the journal entry to record issuance of the bonds.

c. Give the journal entries at the following dates (assume straight-line amortization): June 30, 19A; December 31, 19A; and June 30, 19B.

d. How much interest expense should be reported on the income statement for 19A? Show how the liability related to the bonds would be reported on the December 31, 19A, balance sheet.

PC11–5. Hi-Risk Company issued $75,000 bonds, due in five years, at 11 percent interest. The bonds were dated January 1, 19A, and interest is payable each June 30 and December 31.

   The bonds were sold on January 1, 19A, to yield 12 percent interest. The annual accounting period ends December 31.

Required:

a. Compute the issue (sale) price of the bonds (show computations).

b. Give the journal entry to record the issuance of the bonds on January 1, 19A.

c. Give the journal entry to record the first interest payment and amortization of discount on June 30, 19A. Assume straight-line amortization.

d. Give the amounts that should be reported on the 19A financial statements for:
    Interest expense.
    Bonds payable.
    Unamortized discount or premium.
    Net liability.

e. What would be the aftertax net interest cost for 19A (dollars and percent) assuming a 30 percent tax rate? Show computations.

Part B

PC11–6. Raynard Corporation authorized the following bond issue:

Bonds payable authorized ($1,000 bonds)	$100,000
Date printed on each bond	Jan. 1, 19A
Maturity date (10 years)	Dec. 31, 19J
Interest, 9% per year, payable each June 30 and December 31.	

During 19A, Raynard Corporation issued (sold) the following bonds:

Date		Issuance (sale)		Market price (does not include any accrued interest)
Jan. 1, 19A	#1	10 bonds		100
May 1, 19A	#2	20 bonds		94
Sept. 1, 19A . . .	#3	30 bonds		106

Required:

a. Complete a schedule for Raynard Corporation similar to the following (show computations, round to the nearest dollar, and disregard income tax):

	Cash received			Cash disbursed		
Date	#1	#2	#3	#1	#2	#3
Jan. 1, 19A						
May 1, 19A						
June 30, 19A						
Sept. 1, 19A						
Dec. 31, 19A						

> *b.* Give a separate journal entry to record each of the three issuances.
>
> *c.* How much net cash interest was paid during 19A to the investors in each of the three issuances? Show computations.

PC11–7. Cody Corporation authorized a $300,000, 10-year bond issue dated July 1, 19A. The bonds pay 8 percent interest each June 30. The accounting period ends December 31. Assume the bonds were sold on August 1, 19A, under three different assumptions as follows:

> Case A—Sold at par.
> Case B—Sold at 98.
> Case C—Sold at 102.

Required:

Complete a schedule for Cody Corporation similar to the following assuming straight-line amortization. Show computations.

	Case A par	Case B 98	Case C 102
1. Cash received at issuance (sale) date	$_____	$_____	$_____
2. Cash received for accrued interest at issuance date	_____	_____	_____
3. Amount of premium or discount at issuance date	_____	_____	_____
4. Stated rate of interest (annual)	_____%	_____%	_____%
5. Net cash interest paid during 19A	$_____	$_____	$_____
6. Interest expense reported for 19A	_____	_____	_____
7. Bonds payable reported at end of 19A	_____	_____	_____
8. Unamortized premium or discount reported at end of 19A	_____	_____	_____
9. Net liability reported at end of 19A	_____	_____	_____
10. Interest payable reported at end of 19A	_____	_____	_____

PC11–8. In order to expand to a new region, Goode Manufacturing Company decided to construct a new plant and warehouse. It was decided that approximately 60 percent of the resources required would be obtained through a $600,000 bond issue. Accordingly, the company developed and approved a bond indenture with the following provisions:

> Date of bonds . . . .   Mar. 1, 19A, due in 10 years
> Amount authorized . . . . . . $600,000 (par amount)
> Interest . . . .   10% per annum, payable 5% each Feb. 28 and Aug. 31

The annual accounting period ends on December 31. The bonds were issued (sold) on May 1, 19A, at 102.36.

Required:

   a. How much cash was received by Goode on May 1, 19A?

   b. What was the amount of the premium? Over how many months will it be amortized?

   c. Complete the following tabulation (use straight-line amortization):

	Per month
Interest payment	$_____
Premium amortization	$_____
Interest expense	$_____

   d. Give journal entries, if any, at each of the following dates: May 1, 19A; August 31, 19A; December 31, 19A; January 1, 19B; and February 28, 19B.

   e. In respect to the financial statements for December 31, 19A:

     (1) How much interest expense should be reported on the income statement?

     (2) Show how the liabilities related to the bonds should be reported on the balance sheet.

PC11–9. On January 1, 1970, Hamilton Corporation issued $500,000, 6 percent bonds due at the end of 20 years (December 31, 1989). The bonds specified semiannual interest payments on each June 30 and December 31. The bonds originally sold at par. Additionally, the bond indenture called for the establishment of a bond sinking fund to be accumulated over the last five years by making five equal annual deposits on each December 31, starting in 1985. Interest on the fund balance at 8 percent is to be added to the fund at year-end.

Required:

   a. Give the journal entry for issuance of the bonds on January 1, 1970.

   b. Give the journal entry for the semiannual interest payment on the bonds on June 30, 1985.

   c. Give the journal entry on December 31, 1985, for the first $85,228 contribution of cash to the sinking fund. Show how this amount was computed.

   d. Give the sinking fund entry at the end of 1986.

   e. Prepare a fund accumulation schedule.

   f. Give the journal entry to record retirement of the bonds at maturity assuming the total bond sinking fund accumulation is $500,000.

PC11–10. To obtain funds to acquire additional long-term assets, National Company approved the following bond indenture:

    Maturity value authorized: $600,000 (in $1,000 denominations).

    Interest: 8% per annum, payable 4% each May 31 and November 30.

    Maturity: Ten years from June 1, 19A.

    Bond sinking fund: Starting on July 1 of the eighth bond year, deposit $150,000 annually (three deposits) into a bond sinking fund under the control of Trustee X. Interest earned by the fund will be deposited in the fund. The bond sinking fund will be used only to retire the bonds at maturity.

The annual accounting period for National Company ends on December 31. The bonds were sold on August 1, 19A for $625,700, an amount that included two months' accrued interest (June 1 to July 31).

Required:

a.   Give the journal entry to record the issuance of the bonds on August 1, 19A.
b.   Give the journal entries at the following dates (assume straight-line amortization):
   (1)   First interest date.
   (2)   End of first annual accounting period (19A).
   (3)   Beginning of second accounting period (19B).
   (4)   Second interest date.
c.   In respect to the 19A financial statements.
   (1)   How much interest expense would be reported on the 19A income statement?
   (2)   Show how the liabilities related to the bonds would be reported on the December 31, 19A, balance sheet.
d.   Give the journal entry to record:
   (1)   The first contribution to the sinking fund.
   (2)   Interest earned on the sinking fund by December 31, bond Year 8, 6,000 (net of fund expenses).
e.   Give the journal entry to retire the bond issue at the end of the 10th bond year assuming the bond sinking fund has a balance of $510,000. (Note: The fund earnings rate varied from year to year.)

PC11–11.   Foster Corporation issued bonds and received cash in full for the issue price. The bonds were dated and issued on January 1, 19A. The stated interest rate was payable at the end of each year. The bonds mature at the end of four years. In respect to the issuance of the bonds, the following schedule has been completed:

Date	Cash	Interest	Amortization	Balance
Jan. 1, 19A				$5,173
End of Year 19A	$350	$310	$40	5,133
End of Year 19B	350	308	42	5,091
End of Year 19C	350	305	45	5,046
End of Year 19D	350	304	46	5,000

Required:

Respond to the following questions:
a.   What was the maturity amount of the bonds?
b.   How much cash was received at date of issuance (sale) of the bonds?
c.   Was there a premium or a discount? If so, which and how much?
d.   How much cash will be disbursed for interest each period and in total for the full life of the bond issue?
e.   What method of amortization is being used? Explain.
f.   What is the stated rate of interest?
g.   What is the yield rate of interest?
h.   Show how the following amounts for 19C were computed: (1) $350, (2) $305, (3) $45, and (4) $5,046.
i.   What amount of interest expense should be reported on the income statement each year?
j.   Show how the bonds should be reported on the balance sheet at the end of each year (show the last year immediately before retirement of the bonds).
k.   Why is the method of amortization being used preferable to other methods? When must it be used?

PC11–12. On December 31, 19F, Steady Company had bonds outstanding of $120,000, par (8 percent annual interest payable each December 31). The bonds will mature at the end of 19J. Anticipating the maturity date, the maturity amount, and some possible miscellaneous related costs, Steady Company decided to accumulate a bond sinking fund of $122,102 so that cash will be available to pay the bonds on maturity date. Steady will make five equal annual deposits on December 31, 19F, G, H, I, and J. The trustee will handle the fund and will increase its balance by 10 percent at each year-end starting in 19G.

Required:

a. Compute the amount of each of the five equal deposits that Steady Company must make to accumulate $122,102.
b. Give the journal entry to record the first deposit by Steady Company (December 31, 19F).
c. Prepare a fund accumulation schedule for the five annual deposits.
d. Give the journal entry that Steady Company should make on December 31, 19G.
e. Assume it is December 31, 19J.
   (1) Give the journal entry that Steady Company should make to record the payment of the bond principal.
   (2) What balance remains in the bond sinking fund? What disposition should Steady Company make of this amount?

PC11–13. In some parts of the world, companies issue "zero coupon" bonds. For example, bonds with a face value (maturity value) of $400,000 due in 1989 (eight years after issuance) were issued early in 1981. At the time the bonds were sold to the public, similar bonds paid a 15 percent effective (true) interest. A discussion of such bonds might state, "It's easy to see why corporations like to sell bonds that don't pay interest. But why would anybody want to buy that kind of paper (bond)?"

Required:

a. Explain why an investor would buy "zero coupon" bonds. If investors could earn 15 percent on similar investments, how much should they be willing to pay for such a bond with a par value of $1,000 (due eight years after issuance)?
b. Assume that the bonds were sold on May 1, 1981, the first day of the term (life) of the bond issue. Give the journal entry to record the sale of the bonds for cash.
c. Assume that the accounting period for the company ends on December 31 each year. Give the journal entry required on December 31, 1981, to record accrued interest expense. If none is required, state why.

PC11–14. Tumbleweed Corporation manufactures electronic equipment. Tumbleweed authorized bonds on January 1, 19A, with the following terms:

Maturity (par) value: $500,000.
Interest: 9% per annum payable each December 31.
Maturity date: December 31, 19E.

The bonds were sold at an effective interest rate of 13 percent. Tumbleweed received $429,674 when the bonds were issued on January 1, 19A.

Required:

a. Show how the bond issue price of $429,674 was determined. Give the entry to record this bond issue.
b. Assume that Tumbleweed used the straight-line approach to amortize the discount on the bond issue. Compute the following amounts for each year (19A–19E):
    (1) Cash payment for bond interest.
    (2) Bond interest expense.
    (3) Bond interest expense as a percent of the net liability of the bonds at the beginning of each year.
c. Assume that Tumbleweed used the effective-interest method to amortize the discount on the bond. Compute the amounts listed in Requirement *(b)*, above.
d. Which method should be used by Tumbleweed to amortize the bond discount?

PC11–15. MB Mining Limited is a federally incorporated company with shares traded on Canadian stock exchanges. The company has a number of public issues of bonds outstanding and a bond indenture that contains restrictions regarding the ratio of shareholders' equity. In addition, top executives of MML receive bonuses based upon net income measured in accordance with generally accepted accounting principles.

MBM operates several silver mines in Canada. In 1980, 3.6 million ounces of silver were produced at the mines. Independent mining engineers have estimated that as of January 1, 1981, the company's proven and probable silver reserves are about 24.3 million recoverable ounces.

In April 1981, MBM issued to the public $25 million of 8½ percent silver-indexed bonds due April 15, 1996. The bonds were issued at par. Each $1,000 face value bond is payable at maturity in $1,000 cash or 50 ounces of silver at the holders' option. The bonds are secured by an agreement entitling the trustee to receive, upon default, and on behalf of the bondholders, 3.7 percent of the annual mining production of MBM, Limited to not more than an aggregate of 50 ounces of silver per outstanding bond.

The transaction may be viewed as an issuance of convertible debt. Debt securities are often issued with a conversion feature which permits the holder to convert a bond into a predetermined number of shares of common stock, whereas MBM bonds permit the holders to convert a bond into a predetermined number of ounces of silver. This option on silver allowed MBM to issue the bonds initially at a substantially higher price than it could have obtained for a bond with an 8½ percent interest rate but without the option on silver. Major considerations in deciding how MBM should account for the proceeds from the issuance of the convertible debt are:

1. The valuation of the liability at the date of issuance and subsequently.
2. The measurement of interest expense in each period the debt is outstanding.
3. The treatment of the bond retirement at maturity.

One possibility for accounting for the bonds at issuance, though not one proposed by management, is to view the convertible debt as possessing the characteristics of both a debt and a option on silver. Consistent with this view, a portion of the proceeds could be allocated to the call option and credited to a separate account. The amount so allocated would be a measure of the excess of the fair value of the bond liability expected at maturity over its par value. The remainder of the proceeds would be allocated to the debt. To reflect the bond liability at its par value, the recording of a bond discount would be required. The amount assigned to the options could be measured as the excess of the amount received for the bonds over the estimated price that could have been obtained for similar bonds without the option on silver since estimation can be made with reasonable accuracy. The amount recorded in the deferred credit account would be included in the liabilities of the company's balance sheet. The following entry reflects this interpretation (all amounts are hypothetical):

```
Cash........................................................  1,000
Discount on silver-indexed bond ................................   300
    Silver-indexed bond payable ...................................         1,000
    Deferred credit—option on silver .............................           300
    To record the issuance of one silver-indexed bond.
```

Consistent with this method, the bond discount would be amortized to interest expense in each year the debt is outstanding. The deferred credit would be adjusted upward or downward each year to reflect changes in the fair value of the option on silver because of changes in the market price of silver. Any such adjustment would be charged or credited to interest expense in each year.

The entry at maturity, assuming the market price of silver is $40 per ounce, at that time, is as follows (all amounts are hypothetical):

```
Silver-indexed bond payable .....................................  1,000
Deferred credit—option on silver .................................  1,000
    Revenue from the sale of silver................................         2,000
    To record the delivery of 50 ounces of silver to the trustee to satisfy
    the debt obligation on one silver-indexed bond.
```

Alternatively, the management of MBM has proposed another method to record the silver-indexed bond in a manner consistent with a "debt only" view of the transaction. The bonds would be recorded at their face value. Interest expense reported in each period would reflect the coupon rate of interest. If bondholders elect to take silver as payment at maturity, management proposes to record the delivery to the trustee as a sale of silver at $20 per ounce.

This method would result in the following journal entry at maturity (all amounts are hypothetical):

```
Silver-indexed bond payable .....................................  1,000
    Revenue from the sale of silver................................         1,000
    To record the delivery of 50 ounces of silver to the trustee to satisfy
    the debt obligation on one silver-indexed bond.
```

Under management's proposed method, MBM would realize, at maturity, a loss or profit from the delivery of silver depending on whether or not the cost of producing silver exceeds $20 per ounce at maturity. If the market price of silver at maturity falls below $20 per ounce, bondholders will take cash rather than silver to satisfy the debt obligation, so that all of the company's silver production would be sold in the normal course of operation.

The silver-indexed bonds of MBM reflect an unusual and unique response to inflation—namely, providing bondholders with a hedge against inflation. As inflation continues at or near double-digit rates, we are likely to see an increased number of debt obligations similar to that of MBM which are convertible into various commodities such as silver, gold or oil, all of which give the bond holder the opportunity to share in the appreciation of nonmonetary assets over long periods of time. These types of complicated option contracts are likely to put considerable pressure and strain on transaction or exchange-based accounting, since such transactions or exchanges may effectively be held open for many years.

Required:

Discuss the accounting treatment of the bonds of MBM Ltd.

(CICA Adapted)

PC11–16. GR Corporation authorized a 10-year bond dated January 1, 19A that has an annual coupon rate of interest of 9 percent payable each June 30 and December 31. Two hundred thousand dollars were issued for $194,000 on January 1, 19A.

Required:

Using a computer spreadsheet package determine the following:
a. The effective rate of interest.
b. The amortization schedule for the 10 years using the effective-interest method of amortization.
c. How much the company would have to deposit at the beginning of Year 8 to pay off the bonds at the end of Year 10 assuming the original effective interest rate was still in effect and if the effective-interest rate was 15 percent per year.

(Hint: If your spreadsheet package does not contain interest functions, use the formulas in Chapter 10.)

PC11–17. The questions that follow are based on the 1984 financial statements of Consolidated-Bathurst Inc. presented in Supplement B at end of book.
a. List the various types of long-term debt outstanding during 1984.
b. Determine the effective interest rate on all interest-bearing obligations outstanding during 1984 (Hint: To simplify the calculation, use the year-end amounts for 1984 debt.) How much interest was charged to the long-term assets?
c. What amounts, if any, were amortized to expense during the period relating to the long-term debt? (Disregard foreign exchange translation losses or gains.)
d. How did C–B disclose its sinking funds on its debentures or bonds?

12

Measuring and Reporting Owners' Equity

PURPOSE OF THIS CHAPTER

Owners' equity is defined as the excess of total assets over total liabilities. It is a residual amount that represents the **book value** of the owners' interest in the business enterprise. Because of the **reporting principle** (Exhibit 2–6) and certain legal differences, owners' equity appears somewhat differently on the balance sheet (and in the accounts) of sole proprietorships, partnerships, and corporations. Given the same set of transactions, however, the **total amount** of owners' equity on a given date would be the same (except for income tax effects) regardless of the type of business organization. The accounting entries and financial reporting for the three types of business organizations essentially are the same in all situations, **except for those entries that directly affect owners' equity.** This commonality exists because the underlying fundamental accounting concepts apply equally to each of the three types of business organizations.

This chapter discusses the accounting for, and reporting of, owners' equity. It focuses primarily on corporations because they constitute the most prominent type of accounting entity.

To accomplish the above purposes, the chapter is divided into two parts:

Part A—Shareholders' equity

Part B—Accounting for dividends and retained earnings and for unincorporated businesses

Supplement 12A—Participating dividend preferences on preferred shares

Supplement 12B—Accounting for owners' equity for sole proprietorships and partnerships

Part A—Shareholders' Equity

NATURE OF A CORPORATION

A corporation is a separate legal entity, authorized by law, with certain rights and duties as if it were a distinct individual, although it is owned by a number of persons and perhaps other entities. Ownership in the corporation is evidenced by shares of capital stock. The life of a corporation is unaffected by changes in the group of individuals, or other entities, that own it.

In terms of volume of business, the corporation is the dominant type of business organization in Canada because the corporate form has three important advantages over the sole proprietorship and the partnership. First, the corporate form facilitates the bringing together of large amounts of funds through the sale of ownership interests (capital stock) to the public. Second, it facilitates the transfer of separate ownership interests because the shares can be transferred easily to others. Third, it provides the investor or shareholder with limited liability.[1]

In contrast to a sole proprietorship or a partnership, a corporation is recognized in law as a separate legal entity. Legally, as a distinct entity, the corporation enjoys a continuous existence separate and apart from its owners. It may own assets, incur liabilities, expand and contract in size, sue others, be sued, and enter into contracts independently of the shareholder owners.

STRUCTURE OF A CORPORATION

Ownership of a corporation is evidenced by shares of capital stock that are freely transferable without affecting the corporation. The owners of a corporation are known as shareholders or stockholders.

The federal government and all provinces have laws that govern the organization and operation of limited companies incorporated within their jurisdiction. The specific provisions vary from act to act. To form a corporation in the majority of Canadian provinces and federally, an article of incorporation is filed by the incorporators or their representatives which results in the receipt of a charter from the jurisdiction. This charter is called a certificate of incorporation. Other jurisdictions use terms such as letters patent or memorandum of association for the charter.

The charter sets forth the name, objectives, type of shares to be issued, and any restrictions on the transfer of shares. Bylaws are used to clarify the detailed relationships among various classes of shareholders and to specify other specific rules governing the operation of the company. The governing body of a corporation is the board of directors, a body elected by the shareholders.

When a person acquires shares of capital stock, a share certificate is received

---

[1] In case of insolvency of a corporation and the absence of any special agreement, the creditors have recourse for their claims only to the assets of the corporation. Thus, the shareholders stand to lose, as a maximum, only their equity in the corporation. In contrast, in the case of an ordinary partnership or sole proprietorship, creditors have recourse to the personal assets of the owners if the assets of the business are insufficient to meet the outstanding debts of the business.

EXHIBIT 12–1 Common share certificate

BELL CANADA

INCORPORATED BY ACT OF THE PARLIAMENT OF CANADA, APRIL 29, 1880
CONSTITUÉE PAR UNE LOI DU PARLEMENT DU CANADA, LE 29 AVRIL 1880

SEE REVERSE AS TO ABBREVIATIONS

VOIR ABRÉVIATIONS AU VERSO

CUSIP 078149 10 1

This certifies that
Ceci certifie que

100****
*100***
100
***100*
****100

is the holder of
est le détenteur de

ONE HUNDRED

FULLY PAID AND NON-ASSESSABLE COMMON SHARES OF THE PAR VALUE OF EIGHT AND ONE-THIRD DOLLARS ($8 1/3) EACH IN THE CAPITAL STOCK OF

The Bell Telephone Company of Canada, transferable only on the books of the Company in person or by duly authorized Attorney upon surrender of this Certificate properly endorsed. This certificate is not valid until countersigned by a Transfer Clerk or Transfer Agent and registered by the Registrar.

In Witness Whereof the said Company has caused this Certificate to be signed by its duly authorized officers.

ACTIONS ORDINAIRES ENTIÈREMENT PAYÉES ET NON RÉPARTISSABLES D'UNE VALEUR AU PAIR DE HUIT DOLLARS ET UN TIERS ($8 1/3) CHACUNE, DU CAPITAL-ACTIONS DE

La Compagnie de Téléphone Bell du Canada, transférables dans les livres de la compagnie seulement par le détenteur en personne ou par procureur dûment autorisé sur remise de ce certificat dûment endossé. Ce certificat n'est valide qu'après avoir été contresigné par un commis aux transferts ou un agent des transferts et inscrit aux registres par le comptable des transferts.

En Foi De Quoi ladite compagnie a fait signer ce certificat par ses représentants dûment autorisés.

LE VICE-PRÉSIDENT ET TRÉSORIER

VICE PRESIDENT & TREASURER

15 05 79

DAY MONTH YEAR
JOUR MOIS ANNÉE

LE PRÉSIDENT,

PRESIDENT

COUNTERSIGNED - CONTRESIGNÉ
BELL CANADA

REGISTERED - INSCRIT AUX REGISTRES
MONTREAL TRUST COMPANY
COMPAGNIE MONTRÉAL TRUST
REGISTRAR - COMPTABLE DES TRANSFERTS.

TRANSFER CLERK - COMMIS AUX TRANSFERTS.

THIS CERTIFICATE MAY BE PRESENTED FOR TRANSFER AT THE COMPANY TRANSFER OFFICE IN MONTREAL OR TORONTO, THE PRINCIPAL OFFICE OF THE ROYAL TRUST COMPANY IN ST. JOHN'S, NFLD., HALIFAX, CHARLOTTETOWN, SAINT JOHN, N.B., WINNIPEG, REGINA, CALGARY, VANCOUVER OR LONDON, ENGLAND, OR AT THE PRINCIPAL OFFICE OF MORGAN GUARANTY TRUST COMPANY OF NEW YORK IN NEW YORK, N.Y.

AUTHORIZED OFFICER - REPRÉSENTANT AUTORISÉ.

CE CERTIFICAT EST TRANSFÉRABLE AUX GUICHETS DES TRANSFERTS DE LA COMPAGNIE À MONTRÉAL OU À TORONTO, AU BUREAU PRINCIPAL DE LA COMPAGNIE TRUST ROYAL, À ST JEAN, T.-N., HALIFAX, CHARLOTTETOWN, SAINT JEAN, N.B., WINNIPEG, REGINA, CALGARY, VANCOUVER OU LONDRES, ANGLETERRE, OU AU BUREAU PRINCIPAL DE LA MORGAN GUARANTY TRUST COMPANY OF NEW YORK, À NEW YORK, N.Y.

as evidence of an ownership interest in the corporation. The certificate designates the name of the shareholder, date of purchase, type of shares, number of shares represented, and description of the characteristics of the shares. Exhibit 12–1 shows a share certificate for 100 shares of common stock. On the back of the certificate are instructions and sections to be completed when the shares are sold or transferred to another party.

Shareholders, in the absence of other agreements, have the following basic rights:

1. Vote in shareholders' meeting (or by proxy) on major issues in respect to management of the corporation.[2]
2. Participate proportionately with other shareholders in distribution of profits of the corporation.
3. Share proportionately with other shareholders in the distribution of entity assets upon liquidation.
4. Right to receive minimum information as part of the annual financial statements and to inspect certain specified documents such as the minute book of shareholders' meetings, the register of share transfers, the charter, the bylaws, and register of shareholders and directors. Formal court procedures are required to permit examination of the accounting books and records of the company.

Shareholders exercise their control of a corporation by voting in the annual meeting of the shareholders. The usual organizational structure of a corporation is shown in Exhibit 12–2.

EXHIBIT 12–2 Typical organizational structure of a corporation

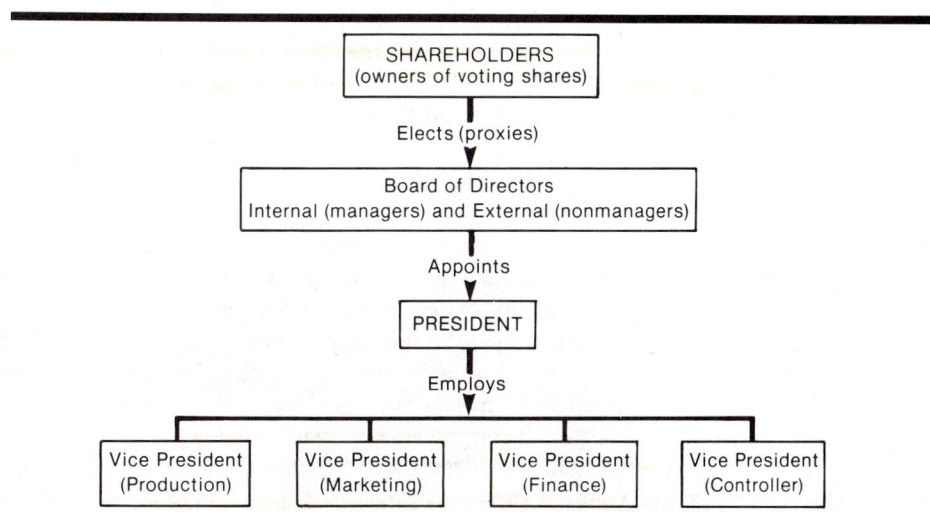

SHAREHOLDERS (owners of voting shares)

Elects (proxies)

Board of Directors Internal (managers) and External (nonmanagers)

Appoints

PRESIDENT

Employs

Vice President (Production) | Vice President (Marketing) | Vice President (Finance) | Vice President (Controller)

---

[2]A voting proxy is a written authority given by a shareholder that gives another party the right to vote the shareholders' shares in the annual meeting of the shareholders. Typically, proxies are solicited by, and given to, the president of the corporation.

EXHIBIT 12–3
Issued and
outstanding shares

Definition	Illustration
Issued number of shares: The total cumulative number of shares that has been issued to date by the corporation.	To date, Tye Corporation sold and issued **30,000** shares of its capital stock.
Subscribed number of shares: Shares sold on credit and not yet issued.	Tye Corporation sold 1,000 shares on credit; the shares will be issued when the sale price is collected in full. Subscribed shares = 1,000.
Outstanding number of shares: The number of shares currently owned by shareholders.	Tye Corporation: Outstanding shares **30,000***

*Observe that outstanding shares and issued shares are the same (i.e., 30,000 shares) in this situation. **Treasury stock** (i.e., shares that have been issued then subsequently repurchased by the issuing corporation) will be presented later. When treasury stock is held, the number of shares issued and the number outstanding will differ by the number of shares of treasury stock held (treasury stock is included in "issued" but not in "outstanding").

The province of Manitoba is the only Canadian province currently requiring the authorization of shares in the charter before they can be issued.

ISSUED AND OUTSTANDING CAPITAL STOCK

Accounting for, and reporting of, capital stock involves the terms: issued and outstanding shares of capital stock. Subsequent to the granting of the charter, the number of shares issued, and the number of shares outstanding are determined by the share transactions of the corporation. Exhibit 12–3 defines and illustrates the three terms usually used in respect to corporate shares.

TYPES OF CAPITAL STOCK

The capital stock of a corporation may consist of only one kind of share, which would be known as **common shares;** or it may consist of two kinds of shares—common shares (which must be issued) and **preferred shares.**

In addition, companies may have various classes of shares, called simply Class A, Class B, and so on, which contain various rights and privileges. For ease of description, the term **preferred** and **common** will be used in subsequent discussions. Common shares may be viewed conveniently as the "usual" or "normal" shares of the corporation. In contrast, preferred shares (if issued) are distinguished because they grant certain **preferences** that the common shares do not have. These preferences usually specify, as a minimum, that the preferred shareholders must receive their dividends **before** any dividends can be declared or paid to the common shareholders. Because of the important differences between common and preferred shares, they are identified separately in accounting and reporting (and on the stock exchanges).

Common shares   When only one class of shares is issued, it must be common. It always has voting rights and often is called the **residual equity** because it ranks **after** the preferred shares for dividends and assets distributed upon dissolution or liquidation of the corporation. Because common shares do not have a dividend rate comparable with that associated with preferred, they have the possibility of higher dividends (after the preferred dividends are paid) and increases in market value. The two primary classifications of common shares are par value and nopar value.

Par value and nopar value shares. Many years ago, all capital stock had to specify a par value. Par value is a **nominal** value per share established for the shares in the charter of the corporation and is printed on the face of each share certificate. Shares that are sold by the corporation to investors above par value are said to sell at a **premium;** whereas, shares sold below par are said to sell at a **discount.** Generally, the laws of all jurisdictions forbid the initial sale of shares by the corporation to investors below par value.[3] Originally, the concept of par value was established as a protection to creditors and investors by specifying a "cushion" of assets that could not be impaired. Par value has no relationship to market value, and the original idea that it represented a financial cushion was ill-conceived. Today, par value, when specified, only serves to identify the stated or **legal capital** of the corporation (otherwise, it has no particular significance).

The par value concept proved to be ineffective in protecting either creditors or shareholders. For that reason, many jurisdictions enacted legislation permitting **nopar value** shares. Nopar value common shares do not have an amount per share specified in the charter; therefore, they may be issued at any price without involving a **discount or premium.** Nopar value shares avoid giving the impression of a market value. When nopar shares are used by a corporation, the legal, or stated, capital is as defined by law.

In recent years, when a par value share is used, the par value typically is set at a very low amount (such as $1 per share) and the issuing (asking) price is set much higher (such as $10 per share). This arrangement reduces significantly the possibility of a discount. Companies are generally prohibited from issuing shares for an amount below their par value (at a discount) so that creditors and shareholders are not misled by relying on the par value.

The term **legal capital** is defined by the law of incorporation. It varies among areas; however, legal capital usually is viewed as the par value of the

---

[3]The discussions throughout this chapter in respect to the sale of capital stock refer to the **initial** sale of the shares by the corporation rather than to later sales between investors as is the common situation in the day-to-day transactions of the stock markets. Because the sale of shares by a corporation at a discount is generally not legal, no further discussion of it is included. The sale of shares among **individuals** is not recorded in the accounts of the corporation.

shares outstanding (in the case of par value shares), or in the case of nopar value shares, the stated value set by the company or the amount for which the shares were sold originally. We shall see later that legal capital usually cannot be used as the basis for dividends. The share certificate shown in Exhibit 12–1 represents a common share, par $8.33.

Preferred shares   When shares other than common are issued, the additional class is sometimes called **preferred shares.** A sample preferred share certificate is presented in Exhibit 12–4. Preferred shares have some characteristics that make them different from the common shares. The usual characteristics of preferred shares are:

       1. Dividend preferences.
       2. Conversion privileges.
       3. Asset preferences.
       4. Nonvoting specifications.

Preferred shares have both favourable and unfavourable characteristics.[4] For example, the nonvoting characteristic is an unfavourable characteristic. Preferred shares may be par or nopar value. For example, the charter of Tye Corporation may have specified "nonvoting, 6 percent **preferred shares,** par value $10 per share" in addition to the common shares. In this situation, the annual preferred dividend preference would be 6 percent of par, or $.60 per share. In contrast, if the preferred shares are nopar value, the preferred dividend preference would be specified as $.60 per share.

A corporation may choose to issue more than one class of shares to (1) obtain favourable control arrangements from its own point of view, (2) issue shares with restricted voting privileges, and (3) appeal to a wide range of investors with the special provisions of the preferred shares.

The dividend preferences of preferred shares take precedence over the common shares, up to a specified limit. Preferred shares that have a cumulative dividend feature have to be paid their required dividend each year or the arrears paid before a dividend can be paid to the common shareholders. Dividend preferences will be discussed and illustrated later in Part B of the chapter. The other features of preferred shares are explained below.

Convertible preferred shares. **Convertible preferred shares** provide preferred shareholders the option to exchange their preferred shares in return for **common** shares of the corporation. The terms of the conversion will specify dates and a conversion ratio. To illustrate, a charter could read: "Each share of preferred stock, at the option of the shareholder, can be converted to two shares of the nopar common stock anytime after January 1, 19A."

---

[4]A majority of corporations issue only common shares. Large corporations tend to have both common and preferred in their financial structures. Some large companies also issue more than one class of preferred shares in addition to the common shares.

EXHIBIT 12–4   Sample of preferred share certificate

✖I50✖ SHARES

SOBEYS STORES LIMITED

Incorporated under the Companies Act of Nova Scotia

AUTHORIZED CAPITAL

750,000 Class A Common Shares without nominal or par value, 500,000 Class B Common Shares without nominal or par value and $5,000,000 divided into 250,000 Preference Shares of the par value of $20.00 each, of which Preference Shares 75,000 are designated 6¼ % Cumulative Redeemable Preference Shares, 1966 Series

THIS IS TO CERTIFY THAT

✖I50✖

SOBEYS STORES LIMITED

is the registered holder of ....
fully paid and non-assessable 6¼ % Cumulative Redeemable Preference Shares, 1966 Series of the par value of $20.00 each in the capital stock of

transferable only on the books of the Company by such registered holder in person or by attorney duly authorized in writing upon surrender of this certificate properly endorsed.

The preferences, rights, conditions, restrictions, limitations and prohibitions attaching to the classes of shares in the capital stock of the Company are fully set forth on the reverse side of this certificate.

This certificate is not valid until countersigned by the Transfer Agent and Registrar of the Company.

IN WITNESS WHEREOF the Company has caused its corporate seal to be hereto affixed and this certificate to be signed by its duly authorized officers this .... **DEC 17 1982**

Secretary

President

Authorized Officer

By _Ben Ancera_

Transfer agent and Registrar

Countersigned and Registered
MONTREAL TRUST COMPANY,
Montreal   Saint John   Halifax

Asset preferences of preferred shares. Two **asset preferences** almost always are specified on preferred shares. One is a preference price that the corporation must pay to the shareholders if the preferred shares are **callable.** The timing of the call is determined by the corporation. The call price almost always is higher than the par value. Upon call of the preferred shares, the preferred shareholders would receive cash equal to, but no more than, the asset preference of their shares before any distributions could be made to the common shareholders. To illustrate, in the above example (Tye Corporation), the asset preference could have been specified at $15 per share. At this preference rate, a holder of the preferred shares would be entitled to receive $15 per share upon ''call'' by the corporation.

The other asset preference on the preferred shares occurs when the corporation **dissolves** (e.g., in case of termination of operations). Preferred shares almost always have a specified preference amount per share that must be paid upon dissolution to the preferred shareholders before any assets can be distributed to the common shareholders. Usually, the preference amount also is the maximum that would be paid to the preferred shareholders.

Nonvoting specifications on preferred shares. **Nonvoting** preferred shares are customary, despite the fact that the nonvoting feature is undesirable to the investors. This feature denies the preferred shareholder the right to vote at shareholder meetings unless their dividends are in arrears. Use of restricted voting preferred shares is one method for obtaining capital without diluting the control of the common shareholders.

In summary, preferred shares are advantageous to the investor because of dividend, conversion, and asset preferences (to the extent that they are specified), but suffers from the disadvantages of nonvoting and upper dividend limits. In contrast, common shares are not constrained on dividend limits, asset limits, and voting rights (compared to preferred shares). In prosperous times for the corporation, common shares are more attractive to investors than preferred shares. Preferred shares are usually viewed as less risky than common shares because of the dividend, conversion, and asset preferences.

ACCOUNTING FOR, AND REPORTING OF, CAPITAL STOCK

Accounting for and reporting shareholders' equity is based upon a **concept of sources.** Under this concept, the owners' equity from different sources is recorded in different accounts and reported separately in the shareholders' equity section of the balance sheet. The two basic sources of shareholders' equity usually identified are:

1. **Contributed capital**—the amount invested by shareholders through the purchase of shares from the corporation. Contributed capital is comprised of two distinct components: (*a*) stated capital—par or stated amounts derived from the sale and issuance of capital stock; and (*b*) additional contributed capital—

amounts derived from the sale of shares in excess of par. This often is termed contributed surplus.

2. **Retained earnings**—the **cumulative** amount of net income earned since organization of the corporation less the cumulative amount of dividends paid by the corporation since organization.

Sale and issuance of par value capital stock

When a par value share is sold for cash and issued, three accounts are affected: (1) cash is debited, (2) an appropriately designated contributed capital account for each type of share is credited, and (3) any difference between the sale price and the par value of the share is credited to a separate additional contributed capital account entitled "contributed surplus." The par value is recorded in a separate account because it represents legal capital.

The sale and issuance of par value common and preferred share is illustrated in Exhibit 12–5. Observe in the first journal entry that the preferred and common accounts were credited for the **par value** of the shares sold, and the differences between the sale prices and the par values were credited to two contributed surplus accounts. Tye Corporation recognized **two** different sources of shareholders' equity—preferred and common shares—and each source was subdivided between the par value and the excess received over par.[5]

Capital stock sold and issued for noncash assets and/or services

Often **noncash** considerations, such as buildings, land, machinery, and regular services (e.g., attorney fees), are received in payment for shares issued. In these cases, the assets received (or expenses incurred in the case of services) should be recorded by the issuing corporation at the **market value** of the shares issued at the date of the transaction in accordance with the **cost principle.** Alternatively, if the market value of the shares issued cannot be determined, then the market value of the consideration received should be used. To illustrate, assume Tye Corporation issued 100 shares of preferred stock for legal services when the shares were selling at $12 per share. The second journal entry given in Exhibit 12–5 records this transaction.

Reporting shareholders' equity

The **reporting principle** (Exhibit 2–6) requires that the major classifications of shareholders' equity be reported separately; viz: contributed (or paid-in) capital, retained earnings, and unrealized capital (discussed later). Also, the subdivisions of each of these major classifications must be reported.

Exhibit 12–5 illustrates the typical reporting of **contributed capital** and its subdivisions. Observe the clear separation of each type of share and of par values and amounts in excess of par. Also, notice that the number of **shares** of each kind of share issued and outstanding are reported.

---

[5]Contributed surplus sometimes is called premium on capital stock or paid-in capital in excess of par.

**EXHIBIT 12–5
Sale and issuance
of par value capital
stock**

Situation of Tye Corporation:

Types of shares:
  Preferred shares, 6 %, par $10.
  Common shares, par $1.

Sale and issuance for cash:

Preferred shares, 1,000 shares @ $12.
Common shares, 30,000 shares @ $5.

Cash (1,000 × $12) + (30,000 × $5)	162,000	
Preferred shares (1,000 × par $10)........................		10,000
Common shares (30,000 × par $1).........................		30,000
Contributed surplus preferred		
[1,000 × ($12 − $10)]		2,000
Contributed surplus, common		
[30,000 × ($5 − $1)]		120,000

Sale and issuance for services:

Issued 100 preferred shares for legal services when the shares were selling at $12.

Legal expense	1,200	
Preferred shares (100 × par $10)		1,000
Contributed surplus, preferred		
[100 × ($12 − $10)]		200

Reporting on the financial statements:

Balance sheet—shareholders' equity:
Contributed capital:
  Preferred shares, 6%, par $10;

issued and outstanding, 1,100 shares	$ 11,000	
Common shares, par $1; issued		
and outstanding, 30,000 shares........................	30,000	
Contributed surplus:		
Preferred shares	2,200	
Common shares	120,000	
Total contributed capital		$163,200
Retained earnings (illustrated later)		

Income Statement:
Legal expense		$1,200

**Sale and
issuance of
nopar capital
stock**

Nopar shares do not have a specific dollar amount designated in the charter of the corporation. However, the laws of all jurisdictions specify how legal capital must be determined. There are two typical specifications, depending upon the particular jurisdiction that issued the charter, that affect the way the sale and issuance of nopar shares is recorded, viz:

1. The corporation, in its bylaws, must specify a **stated** value per share as legal capital. This stated value is a substitute for par value.
2. The corporation must record the **total** proceeds received from each sale and issuance of nopar shares as legal capital (more common approach today).

EXHIBIT 12–6 **Sale and issuance** **of nopar capital** **stock**		

Situation of Sun Corporation:

Type of shares—common stock, **nopar.**

Issued and sold—60,000 shares @ $6 per share (cash).

Sale and Issuance:

Case A—The provincial law requires that the corporation set a **stated** value per share to represent legal capital for nopar shares. The company's charter specified a stated value of $.50 per share.

Cash (60,000 × $6)......................................	360,000	
Common shares, nopar (with stated value of $.50)		
(60,000 × $.50)		30,000
Contributed surplus in excess of stated value		
60,000 × ($6.00 − $.50)		330,000

Case B—The provincial law requires that the total proceeds received be recorded as legal capital.

Cash..	360,000	
Common shares, nopar..................................		360,000

Recall that **legal** capital is credited to the capital stock account (e.g., common or preferred shares) and any excess of sale price over legal capital is credited to a separate account (e.g., Contributed Capital in Excess of Stated Value, No-par Common, or Preferred, Shares).

Exhibit 12–6 illustrates the sale and issuance of nopar capital stock.

TREASURY STOCK

Treasury stock is a corporation's own capital stock that was sold, issued, **reacquired** subsequently and still held by the corporation. Treasury stock frequently is purchased for sound business reasons, such as to obtain shares needed for employee bonus plans, to remove fractional shares that are outstanding, to settle a claim against the corporation, or to have shares on hand for use in the acquisition of other companies. Treasury stock, while held by the issuing corporation, has no voting, dividend, or other shareholder rights.[6]

When a corporation purchases its own capital stock, the assets (usually cash) of the corporation and the shareholders' equity are reduced by equal amounts. When treasury stock is sold, the opposite effects occur. Purchases of treasury stock are recorded by debiting its cost to a shareholders' equity account called Treasury Stock (by type of stock) and crediting Cash. Because the Treasury Stock account has a debit balance, it often is referred to as a **negative** (or con-

---

[6]Section 32 of the Canada Business Corporation Act (1984) states that a company shall not purchase its own shares . . . "if there are reasonable grounds for believing that (a) the corporation is, or would after the payment be, unable to pay its liabilities as they become due; or (b) the realizable value of the corporation's assets would after the payment be less than the aggregate of its liabilities and stated capital of all classes."

tra) shareholders' equity account. When treasury stock is sold, the Treasury Stock account is credited at cost and Cash is debited. Usually the purchase and sale prices of treasury stock are different, necessitating recognition of the difference in an appropriately designated **contributed capital** account in the entry to record the sale.[7]

Accounting for, and reporting of, treasury stock are illustrated in Exhibit 12–7. Observe in the first journal entry that the **Treasury Stock** account is debited for the **cost** of the treasury stock purchased ($3,600). The second journal entry credits the Treasury Stock for the **cost** of the 100 shares of treasury stock sold. A corporation is not permitted by GAAP to increase its income or retained earnings by buying or selling its own shares. Therefore, in Exhibit 12–7, upon resale of the 100 shares of treasury stock, **contributed surplus** was increased by $100, which was the difference between cost and sales price of the treasury shares sold [i.e., 100 shares × ($13 − $12)]. Observe that this difference was not recorded as a gain as would be done for the sale of an asset (such as investments in marketable securities). The basic accounting concept is that "gains or losses" on transactions involving a corporation's own shares are balance sheet **(shareholders' equity)** items and not income statement items. Therefore, the balance sheet of May Corporation, presented at the bottom of Exhibit 12–7, reports "Contributed surplus, treasury stock transactions" of $100.

The Treasury Stock account never has a credit balance, although owners' equity accounts normally carry a credit balance. The balance in the Treasury Stock account reflects a **contraction** of shareholders' equity; thus, it is a **negative** equity account. The debit balance in the Treasury Stock account represents the acquisition **cost** of the treasury stock still held at the date of the balance sheet. Observe this deduction on the balance sheet at the bottom of Exhibit 12–7.[8] That balance sheet reports the number of shares as:

Classification	Shares
*Issued	8,000
Treasury shares	− (200)
*Outstanding.......................	7,800

*Different by the number of treasury shares held.

The purchase and/or resale of treasury stock does not affect the number of shares of **unissued** (or issued) stock; however, the number of shares of **outstanding** stock is affected. The only difference between treasury stock and unissued shares is that treasury stock has been sold at least once and recorded in the accounts.

To illustrate the **resale** of treasury stock at a price **less than cost,** assume

---

[7]*CICA Handbook,* Section 3240.20, states that if the proceeds from the subsequent resale are less than the carrying amount of the treasury stock, the difference is first debited to any previously created contributed surplus and then to retained earnings to the extent necessary. In no case are these differences to appear on the income statement.

[8]For the purpose of computing earnings per share, treasury stock should not be treated as outstanding shares (*CICA Handbook,* Section 3240.23).

EXHIBIT 12–7
Accounting for, and reporting of, treasury stock

Situation of May Corporation on January 1, 19B:

MAY CORPORATION
Summarized Balance Sheet
January 1, 19B

Assets		Shareholders' Equity	
Cash	$ 30,000	Contributed capital:	
Other assets	70,000	Common shares, par $10, authorized 10,000 shares, issued 8,000 shares	$ 80,000
		Retained earnings	20,000
Total assets	$100,000	Total shareholders' equity	$100,000

Purchase of treasury stock:

On January 2, 19B, May Corporation purchased 300 of its own outstanding shares of common stock at $12 per share.

Treasury stock, common (300 shares @ $12 per share)	3,600	
Cash		3,600

(Note: This transaction reduces both assets and shareholders' equity by $3,600.)

Sale of treasury stock:

On February 15, 19B, May sold one third of the treasury stock at $13 per share.

Cash (100 shares @ $13)	1,300	
Treasury stock, common (100 shares @ cost, $12)		1,200
Contributed surplus, treasury stock transactions		100

(Note: This transaction increases both assets and shareholders' equity by $1,300.)

Reporting treasury stock:

MAY CORPORATION*
Summarized Balance Sheet
February 15, 19B

Assets		Shareholders' Equity	
Cash	$27,700	Contributed capital:	
Other assets	70,000	Common shares, par $10, authorized 10,000 shares, issued 8,000, of which 200 shares are held as treasury stock	$ 80,000
		Contributed surplus, treasury stock transactions	100
		Total contributed capital	80,100
		Retained earnings	20,000
		Total	100,100
		Less cost of treasury stock held	2,400
Total assets	$97,700	Total shareholders' equity	$ 97,700

*Reflects the additional effects of the two transactions given above.

that an additional 50 shares of the treasury stock were resold by May Corporation on April 1, 19B, at $11 per share; that is, $1 per share below cost. The resulting entry would be:

April 1, 19B:

```
Cash ....................................................................    550
Contributed surplus, treasury stock transactions.......................     50
    Treasury stock, common (50 shares)................................            600
    Sold 50 shares of treasury stock at $11 per share; cost, $12 per share.
```

Note that the difference between sale price and cost was debited to the same contributed surplus account to which the difference in the preceding journal entry (Exhibit 12–7) was credited. Retained Earnings would be debited for some or all of the amount of the difference only if there were an insufficient credit balance in the account Contributed Surplus, Treasury Stock Transactions.

Where a restriction does not exist as to how many shares may be issued by the corporations (no authorized capital), treasury stock could be immediately canceled so no balance exists in the Treasury Stock account after the shares are purchased. Only if there are restrictions on the number of shares that can be issued would there be any reason to hold treasury shares for reissue. As was mentioned earlier in this chapter, it is common today that the number of authorized shares is unlimited so no need exists to hold treasury shares for reissue.

Part B—Accounting for Dividends and Retained Earnings and Unincorporated Businesses

DIVIDENDS DEFINED

A **dividend is a distribution of cash (or other assets) or capital stock to shareholders by a corporation.** Dividends must be approved by the board of directors of the corporation (i.e., a dividend declaration) **before** they can be paid. The term **dividend,** without a qualifier, usually is understood to mean a **cash** dividend, which is the most common type. A dividend distribution of the corporation's own share is called a **stock dividend.** Dividends usually are stated in terms of dollars per share, or as a percent of par value.

The declaration and payment of a **cash dividend** reduces the assets (cash) and the shareholders' equity (retained earnings) by the total amount of the dividend. Exhibit 12–8 illustrates the declaration and payment of a cash dividend. Observe that assets and shareholders' equity **both** were reduced by the amount of the cash dividend ($12,400).

EXHIBIT 12–8
Declaration and
payment of a cash
dividend

Situation prior to cash dividend (Box Corporation):

Cash	$ 20,000	
Remaining assets...	135,000	
Liabilities	(35,000)	$120,000

Shareholders' equity:		
Preferred shares, 6%, par $20, shares outstanding, 2,000	$ 40,000	
Common shares, par $10, shares outstanding, 5,000	50,000	
Retained earnings	30,000	$120,000

Dividend declaration:

"On December 1, 19E, the board of directors of Box Corporation hereby declares an annual cash dividend of $2 per share on the common stock and 6 percent per share on the preferred stock to the shareholders on date of record, December 10, 19E, payable on December 30, 19E."

Journal entries:*

December 1, 19E:

Retained earnings (or Dividends declared which is closed to Retained earnings)...........................	12,400	
Dividends payable (a current liability)		12,400

    Declaration of a cash dividend:
      Preferred shares (2,000 × par $20 × rate 6%) = $ 2,400.
      Common shares (5,000 shares × $2)   =   10,000.

December 30, 19E:

Dividends payable.......................................	12,400	
Cash		12,400

    Payment of dividend liability.

Effects of the cash dividend on the balance sheet:

Cash	$ 7,600	
Remaining assets...	135,000	
Liabilities	(35,000)	$107,600

Shareholders' equity:		
Preferred shares.......................................	$ 40,000	
Common shares.......................................	50,000	
Retained earnings	17,600	$107,600

*These two entries could be combined into one journal entry on the date of payment, as a debit to Retained Earnings and a credit to Cash of $12,400 because they were in the same accounting year.

DIVIDENDS FROM THE PERSPECTIVES OF THE INVESTOR AND THE ISSUER

An **investor** pays cash (and perhaps incurs some debt) to acquire shares as an investment. The incentive for buying the shares is to earn a future economic return on the investment, usually in future cash inflows. The investor's future cash inflows from the share investment are expected to come from two sources: (1) periodic cash inflows in the form of dividends on the shares and (2) a cash inflow at the time the shares are sold. The investor anticipates that the sum of the present values of these two cash inflows will be greater than the original investment in the shares. Cash dividends are considered by the investor as revenue, that is, the return on the investment. The other cash inflow, a return **of** the investment (from sale of the shares), usually results in a **realized gain or loss,** depending on whether the investor sells the shares above or below their acquisition price. The amounts and frequency of dividends paid by a corporation have an effect on the market price of the shares.

The primary objective of the issuing corporation is to earn income on the resources provided by the shareholders and creditors. The ability to attract and retain resources from present and potential shareholders (and creditors), in the long run, depends in good measure upon the income record of the company. The earnings of a corporation may be retained in the business for corporate expansion or paid to the shareholders as dividends. One of the significant decisions faced by the board of directors of a corporation is how much of the earnings should be retained and how much should be distributed to the shareholders as dividends each year.

Exhibit 12–8 demonstrated that a cash dividend reduces both assets (cash) and shareholders' equity (retained earnings). This fact suggests that there are two fundamental requirements for the payment of a cash dividend, viz:

1. **Sufficient retained earnings**—The corporation has accumulated a sufficient amount of retained earnings to cover the amount of the dividend. The legal position in Canada is unclear as to what could happen if a dividend were declared without the existence of retained earnings. It is possible, however, for a corporation to amend formally its charter in order to change the stated capital which in turn could be used to cancel the negative retained earnings (called a deficit). As a matter of financial policy, and to meet growth objectives, corporations seldom disburse more than 40 to 60 percent of the average net income amount as dividends.

2. **Sufficient cash**—The corporation must have access to cash sufficient to pay the dividend and, in addition, adequate cash to meet the continuing operating needs of the business.

The Canada Business Corporation Act (1984), Section 40, states:

A corporation shall not declare or pay a dividend if there are reasonable grounds for believing that

(a) the corporation is, or would after the payment be, unable to pay its liabilities as they become due; or

(b) the realizable value of the corporation's assets would thereby be less than the aggregate of its liabilities and stated capital of all classes.

The mere fact that there is a large **credit** in the Retained Earnings account does not indicate sufficient cash to support a cash dividend. The cash generated in the past by earnings represented in the Retained Earnings account may have been expended to acquire inventory, purchase operational assets, and/or pay liabilities. Consequently, there is no necessary relationship between the balance of retained earnings and the balance of cash on any particular date (simply, retained earnings is not cash).

Exhibit 12–8 indicated a cash balance of $20,000 and a balance in retained earnings of $30,000. In this typical example, it appears that cash may be the constraining factor on dividends. Some companies overcome this cash constraint (at least temporarily) by borrowing cash to pay cash dividends. The balance in retained earnings is a more inflexible constraint because retained earnings cannot be borrowed.

DIVIDENDS ON PREFERRED SHARES

Recall that preferred shares provide certain rights that have precedence over the rights of common shareholders. The primary distinguishing characteristics of preferred shares are dividend preferences. The **dividend preferences** may be classified as follows:[9]

1. Current dividend preference.
2. Cumulative dividend preference.
3. Participating dividend preference.

Preferred shares may have one or a combination of these three dividend preferences. The charter and the share certificates of the corporation must state specifically the distinctive features of the preferred shares.

Current dividend preference on preferred shares

Preferred shares always carry a **current dividend preference**. This annual preference assures the **preferred shareholders** that if any **current dividends are declared, the current preferred dividend must be declared and paid before any dividends can be declared and paid on the common shares**. When the current dividend preference is met (and no other preference is operative), dividends then can be paid to the common shareholders. The current dividend preference on par value preferred shares is a specified percent of the par value of the preferred shares.

Declared dividends must be **allocated** between the preferred and common shares. First, the preferences of the preferred shares are met, then the remainder of the total dividend is allocated to the common shares. Exhibit 12–9, Case A, illustrates the allocation of the **current dividend** preference under four different assumptions concerning the **total** amount of dividends to be paid.

---

[9]A dividend preference does not mean that dividends will be paid automatically. **Dividends are paid only when formally declared** by the corporation's board of directors. Thus, the declaration of a dividend is discretionary. A typical dividend problem involves the allocation of a total amount of dividends declared between the preferred shares and common shares as illustrated in the next section.

EXHIBIT 12–9
Dividends on
preferred shares

Case A—Current dividend preference only:

Preferred shares outstanding, 6%, par $20; 2,000 shares = $40,000 par.
Common shares outstanding, par $10; 5,000 shares   =   50,000 par.

Allocation of dividends between preferred and common shares assuming
current dividend preference only:

		Amount of dividend paid to shareholders of	
Assumptions	Total dividends paid	6% preferred shares (2,000 shares @ $20 par = $40,000)*	Common shares (5,000 shares @ $10 par = $50,000)
No. 1	$ 1,000	$1,000	–0–
No. 2	2,000	2,000	–0–
No. 3	3,000	2,400	$ 600
No. 4	18,000	2,400	15,600

*Preferred dividend preference, $40,000 × .06 = $2,400; or 2,000 shares × $1.20.

Case B—Cumulative dividend preference:

Preferred and common shares outstanding—same as above. Dividends in **arrears** for the two preceding years.

Allocation of dividends between preferred and common shares assuming
cumulative preferred shares:

		Amount of dividend paid to shareholders of	
Assumptions (dividends in arrears, 2 years)	Total dividends paid	6% preferred shares (2,000 shares @ $20 par = $40,000)*	Common shares (5,000 shares @ $10 par = $50,000)
No. 1......................	$ 2,400	$2,400	–0–
No. 2......................	7,200	7,200	–0–
No. 3......................	8,000	7,200	$ 800
No. 4......................	30,000	7,200	22,800

*Current dividend preference, $40,000 × .06 = $2,400; dividends in arrears preference, $2,400 × 2 years = $4,800; and current dividend preference plus dividends in arrears = $7,200.

Cumulative
dividend
preference on
preferred shares

If preferred shares have **cumulative preference,** they are called cumulative preferred shares. This preference means that if all or a part of the specified current dividend preference (6 percent in Exhibit 12–9) is not paid in full during a given year, the unpaid amount becomes **dividends in arrears.** Thus, when the preferred shares are cumulative, the amount of any preferred dividends in arrears must be paid before any common dividends can be paid. In this situation, the preferred shares in any one year cannot receive total dividends in excess of the current year dividend preference plus all dividends in arrears. Of course, if the preferred shares are **noncumulative,** dividends never can be in arrears. Therefore, any dividends passed (i.e., not declared) are lost permanently by the preferred shareholders. Because preferred shareholders are unwilling to accept this unfavourable feature, preferred shares usually are cumulative.

The allocation of dividends between **cumulative** preferred shares and common shares is illustrated in Exhibit 12–9 Case B, under four different assumptions concerning the **total** amount of dividends to be paid. Observe that the dividends in arrears are paid first, next the current dividend preference is paid, and, finally, the remainder is paid to the commn shareholders. Participating preferred shares dividends are discussed in more detail in Supplement 12A.

STOCK DIVIDENDS

Instead of declaring and paying a cash dividend, the board of directors may vote to declare and issue a stock dividend. A stock dividend is a distribution of additional shares of a corporation's own capital stock on a pro rata basis to its shareholders at no cost. Stock dividends usually consist of common shares issued to the holders of common shares. **Pro rata basis** means that each shareholder receives additional shares equal to the percentage of shares already held by the shareholder. To illustrate, if a shareholder owns 10 percent of the outstanding shares, that shareholder would receive 10 percent of any additional shares issued as a stock dividend. Therefore, a stock dividend does not change the proportionate ownership of any shareholder; it does not involve the distribution of any assets (e.g., cash or other assets) of the corporation to the shareholder; and it does not increase the **total** shareholders' equity of the issuing corporation. To illustrate, assume King Corporation has outstanding 100,000 shares of common stock, par $5, originally sold at $8 per share. The board of directors voted to declare and issue a 10 percent common stock dividend (i.e., 10,000 shares) when the market value of the common stock was $11 per share. The entry by King Corporation to record the declaration and issue of this stock dividend would be:[10]

```
Retained earnings (10,000 shares × $11) .........................  110,000
    Common shares, par $5 (10,000 shares × $5) ................          50,000
    Contributed surplus, common shares
      (10,000 shares × $11 − $5) ..............................          60,000
    Common shares dividend of 10 percent distributed when the
    market value per share was $11.
```

Observe in the above entry that **retained earnings** was **decreased** by $110,000 and that **contributed capital** (i.e., common stock and contributed surplus) was increased by $110,000; assets and liabilities were unaffected. Therefore, the stock dividend did **not** change total shareholders' equity—it only changed some of the balances of the accounts that comprise shareholders' eq-

---

[10]Some accountants prefer to debit an account called Stock Dividends Distributed, which is closed to Retained Earnings at the end of the period. The effect is precisely the same.

uity. This process of transferring an amount from retained earnings to contributed (i.e., permanent) capital often is referred to as **capitalizing earnings** because it reduces the amount of retained earnings subject to future dividends.

After a stock dividend, each **shareholder** has the same **proportionate** ownership of the corporation as before, and no additional assets are received by the shareholders (only more shares to represent the same total value previously held). Because more shares now represent the same "value," the **market price per share should drop proportionately**.

Observe in the above illustration that the amount (for the stock dividend) transferred from Retained Earnings to Contributed Capital was the **current market value** of the shares issued as a stock dividend. Market value amount is considered appropriate when the stock dividend is "small"; that is, when it is less than 25 percent of the previously outstanding shares. In those cases where a stock dividend is "large" (i.e., more than 25 percent), some accountants believe that the amount transferred should be the total par value of the shares issued. Par value is the absolute **minimum** because shares generally cannot be issued at a discount. If nopar shares were issued by the company, the stated value per share would be the minimum that should be used. Market value is preferred by many accountants in all situations (it is the maximum) primarily because (1) it is the amount that would be credited to Contributed Capital if the shares were sold at the current market price and (2) it is the amount that would be debited to Retained Earnings for all other types of dividends.

Reasons for stock dividends

Stock dividends often serve useful purposes both from the viewpoint of the corporation and the individual shareholder. The two primary purposes of a stock dividend are:

1. **To maintain dividend consistency**—Many corporations prefer to declare dividends each year. In the case of a cash shortage, the dividend record may be maintained by issuing a stock dividend. Stock dividends tend to satisfy the demands of shareholders for continuing dividends and yet avoid the demand on cash.

2. **To capitalize retained earnings**—A stock dividend is used to transfer retained earnings to permanent capital and thus remove such earnings from cash dividend availability. When a corporation consistently retains a substantial percent of its earnings for growth, the related funds are, more or less, invested permanently in long-term assets such as plant and other property. Therefore, it is considered realistic to transfer those accumulated earnings to permanent capital. A stock dividend is a convenient approach to capitalize retained earnings. This may be the fundamental reason why stock dividends often are distributed by profitable corporations that are expanding rapidly.

STOCK SPLITS

Stock splits are **not** dividends. However, we will digress for the moment to consider **stock splits** because they (a) are similar in some respects to a stock dividend, (b) are often confused with a stock dividend, and (c) are quite different from a stock dividend as to their internal impact upon the shareholders' equity accounts of the issuing corporation. In a stock split, the total number of shares is increased by a specified amount, such as a two-for-one split. In this instance, each share held is called in, and two new shares are issued in its place. Typically, a stock split is accomplished by **reducing the par or stated value** per share of all shares so that the total par value (in dollars) of all shares is unchanged. For example, assume 1,000 shares of $20 par value stock were outstanding before a two-for-one split. This stock split would involve reducing the par value of each new share to $10 and the issuance of 2,000 shares of $10 par value stock. In contrast to a stock dividend, a stock split does **not** result in a transfer of retained earnings to contributed capital. No transfer is needed because the reduction in the par value per share compensates for the increase in the number of shares. The primary reason for a stock split is to **reduce the market price per share,** which tends to increase the market activity of the shares. Sometimes a corporation desires to **reduce** the number of shares outstanding. One way to do this is to implement a **reverse** stock split. A stock dividend requires a journal entry while **a stock split does not require a journal entry.**

In both a stock dividend and a stock split the investor (i.e., shareholder) receives more shares and does not disburse any additional assets for those additional shares.

The **comparative effects** of a stock dividend versus a stock split may be summarized as follows:

	Shareholders' equity		
	Before a share dividend or split	After a 100 percent stock dividend	After a two-for-one stock split
Contributed capital:			
Number of shares outstanding......	30,000	60,000	60,000
Par value per share................	$ 10	$ 10	$ 5
Total par value outstanding.........	300,000	600,000	300,000
Retained earnings	650,000	350,000	650,000
Total shareholders' equity	950,000	950,000	950,000

DIVIDEND DATES

The preceding discussions assumed that a dividend was paid immediately after its declaration by the board of directors. Almost always, by necessity, there is a time lag between declaration and payment. For example, a typical dividend declaration is as follows:

On November 20, 19B, the Board of Directors of XY Corporation hereby declares a $.50 per share cash dividend on the 200,000 shares of nopar common stock outstanding. The dividend will be paid to shareholders of record at December 15, 19B, on January 15, 19C.

This declaration specifies **three important dates:**

1. **Declaration date—November 20, 19B.** This is the date on which the board of directors officially approved the dividend. As soon as a public announcement of the declaration is made, legally it is irrevocable; therefore, a **dividend liability** immediately is created. Accordingly, on this date the **declaration** by XY Corporation would be recorded as follows:

   November 20, 19B:

   ```
   Retained earnings (or Dividends declared) ....   100,000
        Dividends payable .....................              100,000
   Cash dividend declared: 200,000 shares ×
        $.50 = $100,000.
   ```

   The December 31, 19B, balance sheet would report **Dividends Payable as a current liability.**

2. **Date of record—December 15, 19B.** This date follows the declaration date, usually by about one month, as specified in the declaration. It is the date on which the corporation prepares the list of individuals owning the outstanding shares based on the **shareholder records.** The dividend is payable only to those names listed on the record date. Thus, share transfers between buyers and sellers reported to the corporation before this date result in the dividend being paid to the new owner. Changes reported **after** this date result in the dividend being paid to the old owner; the new owner will receive all subsequent dividends. No journal entry would be made on this date.

3. **Date of payment—January 15, 19C.** This is the date on which the **cash** is disbursed to pay the dividend liability. It follows the date of record as specified in the dividend announcement. The entry to record the cash disbursement by XY Corporation would be as follows:

January 15, 19C:

Dividends payable   100,000
    Cash.   100,000
To pay the liability for a cash dividend declared and recorded
on November 20, 19B.

For instructional purposes, this time lag customarily is disregarded because it does not pose any substantive issues. Also, when all of the three dates fall in the same accounting period, a single entry on the date of payment may be made in practice for purely practical reasons.

SHAREHOLDER RECORDS

A corporation must maintain a record of each shareholder. The record includes at least the name and address of each shareholder, number of shares purchased of each type of stock, certificate numbers, dates acquired, and the number of shares currently owned. Such a record is known as the **shareholders' subsidiary ledger.** The Capital Stock account serves as the **control account** in the general ledger for this subsidiary ledger. Sales of shares by a shareholder to others must be reported to the corporation so that new share certificates can be issued and the shareholders' subsidiary ledger can be changed accordingly. Dividends are sent only to the names and addresses shown in the shareholders' subsidiary ledger on the date of record. Large corporations with thousands of shareholders usually pay an independent **transfer agent** to handle the transfer of shares, to issue new share certificates, and to maintain the equivalent of a shareholders' subsidiary ledger.

A particularly important record that must be maintained by all corporations is called the **minute book.** This is an official record of the actions taken at all meetings of the board of directors and of the shareholders. The independent auditor is required to inspect the minute book as a part of the audit programme. Frequently, it is introduced as evidence in lawsuits and in income tax litigation.

REPORTING RETAINED EARNINGS

The preceding chapters emphasized that the income statement reports two income amounts: (1) income before extraordinary items and (2) net income (i.e., after extraordinary items). Net income is closed to the Income Summary account, and net income is reflected on the statement of retained earnings. **Extraordinary items** are reported on the income statement. *CICA Handbook,*

Section 3480, defines **extraordinary items** as those transactions and events that meet three criteria; that is, to be classified as extraordinary, a gain or loss must be (1) not typical of the normal business activities, (2) not expected to occur regularly, and (3) not considered as recurring factors in any evaluation of ordinary operations of the enterprise. Extraordinary items are set out separately on the income statement to enable statement users to focus on the usual and frequent results; that is, income **before** extraordinary items because it is more reflective of future earnings and cash inflow than is net income (i.e., after extraordinary items). Some examples would be:

1. The discontinuance, or substantial change in, a business programme that resulted in the sale of a property or segment of the business, or the sale of a long-term investment.
2. A government expropriation of properties.
3. Acts of God such as hurricanes, floods, and similar catastrophic events.

In several prior chapters we discussed and illustrated the statement of retained earnings. Although not a required statement, it almost always is presented to conform with the **reporting principle** (Exhibit 2–6). Because retained earnings is one of two basic components of shareholders' equity, users of financial statements require sufficient disclosures to understand the causes of changes in the amount of retained earnings. A typical statement of retained earnings is shown in Exhibit 12–10.

The statement of retained earnings shown in Exhibit 12–10 reports two items that have not been discussed: (1) prior period adjustments and (2) restrictions on retained earnings.

EXHIBIT 12–10
Statement of retained earnings

FERRARI CORPORATION
Statement of Retained Earnings
For the Year Ended December 31, 19C

Retained earnings balance, January 1, 19C...................		$226,000
Prior period adjustment:		
Deduct adjustment for correction of prior accounting error (net of income tax)		10,000
Balance as restated		216,000
Net income for 19C		34,000
Total...		250,000
Deduct dividends declared in 19C:		
On preferred shares.....................................	$ 6,000	
On common shares	12,000	18,000
Retained earnings balance, December 31, 19C (see Note 5)......		$232,000

Note 5. Restrictions on retained earnings; total, $100,000.
The bonds payable indenture requires that retained earnings be restricted in accordance with an agreed schedule. The schedule amounts for 19B and 19C total $100,000.

Prior period adjustments

This category of events is defined in the *CICA Handbook*, Section 3600, as adjustments having all four of the following characteristics:

    a. Are specifically identified with and directly related to the business activities of particular prior periods.

    b. Are not attributable to economic events occurring subsequent to the date of the financial statements for such prior periods.

    c. Depends primarily on decisions or determinations by persons other than management or owners.

    d. Could not be reasonably estimated prior to such decisions or determinations.

Prior period adjustments must be reported on the statement of retained earnings, as an **adjustment of the beginning balance of retained earnings** (not on the income statement). Prior period adjustments should be recorded in specially designated gain and loss accounts, which are closed at the end of the period **directly** to the Retained Earnings account. Examples of prior period adjustments would be corrections of **accounting errors** made in a prior period, retroactive application of a change in an accounting policy, settlements of income taxes, and settlements of claims from litigation.[11] Exhibit 12–10 illustrates reporting of a prior period adjustment.[12] Observe that prior period adjustments are defined and reported quite differently than extraordinary items.

Restrictions on retained earnings

Corporations frequently have restrictions on retained earnings. Basically, such a **restriction temporarily removes the restricted amount of retained earnings from availability for dividends.** When the restriction is removed, the amount that was restricted is available for dividends and other "uses" of retained earnings. Restrictions on retained earnings may be voluntary or involuntary. For example, the restriction reported on Exhibit 12–10 is considered involuntary; it was imposed by **contract.** On occasion, the management or the board of directors may voluntarily establish a restriction on retained earnings for expansion of the business; this restriction reduces the amount of retained earnings subject to dividends. The amount of retained earnings restricted for this purpose often is called "Retained earnings appropriated for earnings invested in plant and equipment." Of course, this restriction can be removed at anytime by the board of directors.

The **reporting principle** (Exhibit 2–6) requires that restrictions on retained earnings be reported on the financial statements or in a separate note to the financial statements. The approach most widely used is by note as illustrated in Exhibit 12–10.

---

[11] The first two of these examples may seem somewhat outside the four characteristics. Errors should be rare but can happen, and the treatment of changes in accounting policy is necessary to ease the effect on current income and to improve comparability among annual reports.

[12] The tax effects of such prior period adjustments are part of procedures related to income tax allocations discussed in Chapter 10. The specific term for these tax amounts is "intraperiod tax allocations."

A practice used widely in past years, but now used infrequently, was to set up a special retained earnings account for each appropriation. Such accounts, somewhat illogically, often were called reserves. To illustrate, a journal entry to establish a "reserve" for the restriction of retained earnings by Ferrari Corporation (Exhibit 12–10) would be:

```
Retained earnings............................................   100,000
    Reserve for bonds payable ...............................              100,000
```

In preparing the statement of retained earnings, Ferrari Corporation would list the "reserve" account on the statement of retained earnings, and Note 5 (Exhibit 12–10) would be unnecessary. When the restrictions are removed, the above entry is reversed. No debit other than this reversal should be made to the reserve.

An appropriation (or restriction) of retained earnings is **not cash**. Observe in the above entries that cash was not affected; the **only effect was to remove a specific amount of retained earnings from dividend availability. To set aside cash for a special purpose, cash is credited and a **fund** account (e.g., building construction fund) is debited. Such fund accounts are assets similar to a savings account.** Thus, there is no necessary relationship between appropriations of retained earnings and cash.

ACCOUNTING AND REPORTING FOR UNINCORPORATED BUSINESSES

There are three basic forms of organization for profit-making entities: **corporations** (i.e., shares owned by a number of shareholders), **sole proprietorships** (i.e., one owner), and **partnerships** (i.e., two or more owners). The fundamentals of accounting and reporting for unincorporated businesses are the same as for a corporation except for **owners' equity** and the treatment of income tax expense. Typical account structures for the three basic forms of business organizations are outlined in Exhibit 12–11.

Accounting for sole proprietorships and partnerships is discussed and illustrated in Supplement 12B.

DEMONSTRATION CASE

(Try to resolve the requirements before proceeding to the suggested solution that follows.)

This case focuses on the organization and operations for the first year of Shelly Corporation, which was organized on January 1 19A, the date on which the charter was granted by the Canadian government. The Canada Business Corporations Act specifies that the legal capital for nopar shares is the full sale amount. The corporation was organized by 10 local entrepreneurs for the pur-

EXHIBIT 12–11
Comparative account structures among types of business entities

TYPICAL ACCOUNT STRUCTURE		
Corporation (shareholders' equity)	**Sole Proprietorship** (proprietor's equity)	**Partnership** (partners' equity)
Capital stock Contributed surplus	Doe, capital	Able, capital Baker, capital
Retained earnings	Not used	Not used
Dividends paid	Doe, drawings	Able, drawings Baker, drawings
Income summary (closed to Retained Earnings)	Income summary (closed to Doe, Capital)	Income summary (closed to Able, Capital and Baker, Capital)
Revenues, expenses, gains, and losses	Same except no income tax expense	Same except no income tax expense
Assets and liabilities	Same	Same

pose of operating a business to sell various operating supplies to hotels. The charter *authorized* the following capital stock:

Common stock, nopar value shares.
Preferred stock, 5% nopar value shares (cumulative, nonparticipating, nonconvertible, and nonvoting; liquidation value, $110).

The following summarized transactions, selected from 19A, were completed on the dates indicated:

1. Jan.   Sold a total of 7,500 shares of nopar common stock to the 10 entrepreneurs for cash at $52 per share. Credit the Nopar Common Shares account for the total sales amount.

2. Feb.   Sold 1,890 shares of preferred stock at $102 per share; cash collected in full.

3. Mar.   Purchased land for a store site and made full payment by issuing 100 shares of preferred shares. Early construction of the store is planned. Debit Land (store site). The preferred shares are selling at $102 per share.

4. Apr.   Paid $1,980 cash for organization costs. Debit an intangible asset account entitled "Organization Cost."

5. May   Issued 10 shares of preferred stock to A. B. Cain in full payment of legal services rendered in connec-

tion with organization of the corporation. Assume the preferred shares are selling regularly at $102 per share. Debit Organization Cost.

6. June   Sold 500 shares of nopar common shares for cash to C. B. Abel at $54 per share.

7. July   Purchased 100 shares of preferred shares that had been sold and issued earlier. The shareholder was moving to another state and "needed the money." Shelly Corporation paid the shareholder $104 per share.

8. Aug.   Sold 20 shares of the preferred stock at $105 per share.

9. Dec. 31   Purchased equipment at a cost of $600,000; paid cash. No depreciation expense should be recorded in 19A.

10. Dec. 31   Borrowed $20,000 cash from the City Bank on a one-year, interest-bearing note. Interest is payable at a 12 percent rate at maturity.

11. Dec. 31   Gross revenues for the year amounted to $129,300; expenses, including corporation income tax but excluding amortization of organization costs, amounted to $98,000. Assume, for simplicity, that these summarized revenue and expense transactions were paid in cash. Because the equipment and the bank loan transactions were on December 31, no related adjusting entries at the end of 19A are needed.

12. Dec. 31   Shelly Corporation decided that a "reasonable" amortization period for organization costs, starting as of January 1, 19A, would be 10 years. This intangible asset must be amortized to expense. Give the required adjusting entry for 19A.

Required:

a. Give appropriate journal entries, with a brief explanation for each of the above transactions.
b. Give appropriate closing entries at December 31, 19A.
c. Prepare a balance sheet for Shelly Corporation at December 31, 19A. Emphasize full disclosure of shareholders' equity.

Suggested solution

Requirement a. Journal entries:

1. January 19A:

    ```
    Cash..............................................  390,000
        Common stock (7,500 shares) .......................            390,000
        Sale of nopar common shares ($52 × 7,500 shares = $390,000).
    ```

2. February 19A:

    ```
    Cash..............................................  192,780
        Preferred stock, $5 (1,890 shares) ....................            192,780
        Sale of preferred shares ($102 × 1,890 shares = $192,780).
    ```

3. March 19A:

    ```
    Land (store site) .......................................  10,200
        Preferred stock, $5 ...................................            10,200
        Purchased land for future store site; paid in full by issuance
        of 100 shares of preferred stock. The market value is, $102
        × 100 shares = $10,200.
    ```

4. April 19A:

    ```
    Organization cost .......................................  1,980
        Cash..............................................            1,980
        Paid organization cost.
    ```

5. May 19A:

```
Organization cost .........................................    1,020
    Preferred stock, $5 (10 shares)...........................          1,020
Organization cost (legal services) paid by issuance of 10
shares of preferred. The implied market value is, $102 × 10
shares = $1,020.
```

6. June 19A:

```
Cash....................................................   27,000
    Common stock (500 shares) ...........................          27,000
Sold 500 shares of the nopar common stock ($54 × 500
shares = $27,000).
```

7. July 19A:

```
Preferred stock, $5 .......................................   10,200
Retained earnings.........................................      200
    Cash................................................          10,400
Purchased 100 shares of preferred stock ($104 × 100 shares
= $10,400).
```

8. August 19A:

```
Cash.....................................................    2,100
    Preferred stock, $5 ....................................           2,100
Sold 20 shares of the preferred stock at $105.
```

9. December 31, 19A:

Equipment	600,000	
Cash...		600,000
Purchased equipment.		

10. December 31, 19A:

Cash...	20,000	
Note payable		20,000
Borrowed on one-year, 12 percent, interest-bearing note.		

11. December 31, 19A:

Cash...	129,300	
Revenues..		129,300
Expenses..	98,000	
Cash...		98,000
To record summarized revenues and expenses.		

12. December 31, 19A:

Expenses	300	
Organization cost		300
Adjusting entry to amortize organization cost for one year ($1,980 + $1,020) ÷ 10 years = $300.		

Requirement b. Closing entries:

13.   December 31, 19A:

Revenues...	129,300	
Income summary....................................		129,300
Income summary..	98,300	
Expenses ($98,000 + $300)		98,300
Income summary..	31,000	
Retained earnings		31,000
($129,300 − $98,300 = $31,000).		

Requirement c:

SHELLY CORPORATION
Balance Sheet
At December 31, 19A

Assets

Current assets:		
Cash...		$ 50,800
Tangible assets:		
Land	$ 10,200	
Equipment (no depreciation assumed in the problem)............	600,000	610,200
Intangible assets:		
Organization cost (cost, $3,000 less amortization, $300)...........		2,700
Total assets..		$663,700

Liabilities

Current liabilities:		
Note payable, 12%...		$ 20,000

Shareholders' Equity

Contributed capital:		
Preferred stock, $5 nopar shares, issued 1920 shares	$195,900	
Common stock, nopar value,		
issued and outstanding 8,000 shares........................	417,000	
Retained earnings..	30,800	
Total shareholders equity....................................		643,700
Total liabilities and shareholders' equity............................		$663,700

SUMMARY OF CHAPTER

This chapter discussed accounting for and reporting of owners' equity for corporations. Sole proprietorships and partnerships are discussed in Supplement 12B. With the exception of owners' equity, the accounting and reporting basically is unaffected by the type of business organization. Accounting for owners' equity is based upon the concept of **source;** each specific source of owners' equity should be accounted for and reported separately. The two basic sources of owners' equity for a corporation are contributed capital and retained earnings. Separate accounts are maintained for each type of capital stock and contributed capital.

The earnings of a corporation that are not retained in the business for growth and expansion are distributed to the shareholders by means of dividends. Dividends are paid only when formally declared by the board of directors of the corporation. A cash dividend results in a decrease in assets (cash) and a commensurate decrease in shareholders' equity (retained earnings). In contrast, a stock dividend does not change assets, liabilities, or total shareholders' equity. A stock dividend results in a transfer of retained earnings to the permanent or contributed capital of the corporation by the amount of the stock dividend (a stock dividend affects only certain account balances within shareholders' equity). A stock split affects only the par value or stated value of the shares and the number of shares outstanding; the individual equity account balances are not changed. Frequently a corporation purchases its own shares in the marketplace. Such shares, previously sold and issued by the corporation and subsequently reacquired, are known as **treasury stock** as long as it is held by the issuing corporation. The purchase of treasury stock is viewed as a contraction of corporate capital, and the subsequent resale of the treasury stock is viewed as an expansion of corporate capital.

SUPPLEMENT 12A—PARTICIPATING DIVIDEND PREFERENCE ON PREFERRED SHARES

Preferred shares may be nonparticipating, fully participating, or partially participating. Participation relates to the dividends that can be paid on preferred shares **after** dividends in arrears and **after** the current dividend preference.

Most preferred shares are **nonparticipating.** Preferred shares that are **participating** may be either noncumulative or cumulative.

Fully participating and **noncumulative** preferred shares receive a first priority for the current dividend preference; then a matching proportionate amount is allocated to the common shares, and finally any remaining balance of the total dividend is allocated on a proportionate basis to the preferred and common shares as illustrated in Exhibit 12–12, Case A.

Fully participating and **cumulative** preferred shares receive first priority on both dividends in **arrears** and the current dividend preference. After those preferences are satisfied, a proportionate amount is allocated to the common shares; and finally, any remaining balance of total dividends to be paid is allocated on a proportionate basis to the preferred and common shares as illustrated in Exhibit 12–12, Case B.

EXHIBIT 12–12   Dividends on participating preferred shares

Situation (Box Corporation; refer to Exhibit 12–8):

Preferred stock, 6 percent, par $20; shares outstanding, 2,000 = $40,000.
Common stock, par $10, shares outstanding, 5,000 = $50,000.
Dividends in arrears for the two previous years.

Allocation of dividends between preferred and common shares assuming fully participating:

Assumptions *(dividends in arrears, two years)*	6 percent preferred stock *(total par, $40,000)*	Common Stock *(total par, $50,000)*	Total dividends paid
Case A—Prefer shares are fully participating and noncumulative (Two years in arrears). Total dividends paid, $7,200:			
Current dividend ($40,000 × .06)...................	$ 2,400		$ 2,400
Equivalent amount to common ($50,000 × .06).......		$3,000	3,000
Subtotal.....................................			$5,400
Full participation—balance allocated in ratio of par values:*			
($40,000/$90,000) × ($7,200 − $5,400).............	800		800
($50,000/$90,000) × ($7,200 − $5,400).............		1,000	1,000
Totals.....................................	$ 3,200	$4,000	$ 7,200
Case B—Preferred shares are fully participating and cumulative (two years in arrears). Total dividends paid, $16,500:			
Arrears ($2,400 × 2 years)........................	$ 4,800		$ 4,800
Current preference ($40,000 × .06)	2,400		2,400
Equivalent amount to common ($50,000 × .06).......		$3,000	3,000
Subtotal.....................................			10,200
Full participation—balance allocated in ratio of par:			
($40,000/$90,000) × ($16,500 − $10,200).............	2,800		2,800
($50,000/$90,000) × ($16,500 × $10,200).............		3,500	3,500
Totals.....................................	$10,000	$6,500	$16,500

*If no par shares are used, the participating feature would have to be explicitly specified in dollar amounts.

Partially participating preferred shares essentially are the same as fully participating, except that the participating preference above the current dividend rate is limited to a stated percent of par. For example, the corporate charter may read, "and partially participating only up to an additional two percent." Fully participating and partially participating preferred shares preferences are rare.[13]

---

[13]Textbooks for more advanced courses in accounting contain additional discussion and illustrations of the participating features and the payment of a dividend in assets other than cash, such as property and shares of other corporations being held as an investment.

SUPPLEMENT 12B—ACCOUNTING FOR OWNERS' EQUITY FOR SOLE PROPRIETORSHIPS AND PARTNERSHIPS

A sole proprietorship is an unincorporated business owned by one person. The only owner's equity accounts needed are (1) a capital account for the proprietor (for example, J. Doe, Capital; or J. Doe, Owner's Equity), and (2) a drawing (or withdrawal) account for the proprietor (for example, J. Doe, Drawings; or J. Doe, Withdrawals). The **capital account** of a sole proprietorship is used to record investments by the owner and to accumulate the periodic income or loss. Thus, the **Income Summary** account is closed to the capital account at the end of each accounting period. The **drawing account** is used to record withdrawals of cash or other assets by the owner from the business. The drawing account is closed to the capital account at the end of each accounting period; thus, the capital account cumulatively reflects all investments by the owner, plus all earnings of the entity, less all withdrawals of resources from the entity by the owner. In most respects, the accounting for a sole proprietorship is the same as for a corporation.

Exhibit 12–13 presents the recording of selected transactions for 19A and the owner's equity section of the balance sheet of Doe Retail Store to illustrate the accounting for and reporting of **owner's equity** for a sole proprietorship.[14]

There are two additional differences between accounting for corporations and sole proprietorships. A sole proprietorship, as a business entity, does not pay income taxes. Therefore, the financial statements of a sole proprietorship will not reflect income tax expense or income taxes payable. The net income of a sole proprietorship must be included on the **personal** income tax return of the owner. Also, because an employer/employee contractual relationship cannot exist with only one party involved, a "salary" to the owner is not recognized as an expense of a sole proprietorship. The salary of the owner is accounted for as a distribution of profits (i.e., a withdrawal).

Owners' equity for a partnership

The Partnership Acts of most provinces define a partnership as "an association of two or more persons to carry on, as co-owners, a business for profit." The partnership form of business is used by small businesses and professionals, such as accountants, doctors, and lawyers. A partnership is formed by two or more persons reaching mutual agreement as to the terms of the partnership. The law does not require an application for a charter as in the case of a corporation. The agreement between the partners constitutes a **partnership contract** that should be in writing. The partnership contract or agreement should specify such matters as division of periodic income, management responsibilities, transfer or sale of partnership interests, disposition of assets upon liquidation, and procedures to be followed in case of the death of a partner. If the

---

[14]Alternatively, the balance sheet may reflect only "J. Doe, capital, December 31, 19A, $156,000," with a supplemental or supporting **statement of owner's equity** that would be the same as shown in the exhibit.

**EXHIBIT 12–13
Accounting and
reporting of
owner's equity
for a sole
proprietorship**

Selected entries during 19A:

January 1, 19A:

    J. Doe started a retail store by investing $150,000 of personal savings. The journal entry for the business would be as follows:

Cash..	150,000	
J. Doe, capital		150,000
Investment by owner.		

During 19A:

    Each month during the year, Doe withdrew $1,000 cash from the business for personal living costs. Accordingly, each month the following journal entry was made:

J. Doe; drawings...	1,000	
Cash...		1,000
Withdrawal of cash by owner for personal use.		

      Note: At December 31, 19A, after the last withdrawal, the drawings account will reflect a debit balance of $12,000.

December 31, 19A:

    Usual journal entries for the year, including adjusting and closing entries for the revenue and expense accounts, resulted in an $18,000 **credit balance** in the Income Summary account (i.e., $18,000 net income). The next closing entry will be:

Income summary	18,000	
J. Doe, capital		18,000
Closing entry to transfer net income for the year to the owner's equity account.		

December 31, 19A:

    The journal entry required on this date to close the drawings account would be:

J. Doe, capital	12,000	
J. Doe, drawings.......................................		12,000
Closing entry to transfer drawings for the year to the capital account.		

Balance sheet, December 31, 19A (partial):

Owner's Equity

J. Doe, capital, January 1, 19A...........	$150,000	
Add: Net income for 19A	18,000	
Total	168,000	
Less: Withdrawals for 19A	12,000	
J. Doe, capital, December 31, 19A........		$156,000

partnership agreement does not specify on these matters, the laws of the resident province will be binding. The primary advantages of a partnership are (1) ease of formation, (2) complete control by the partners, and (3) no income taxes on the business itself. The primary disadvantage is the unlimited liability of each partner for the liabilities of the partnership unless a specific restriction of the liabilities exists through the use of a special form of a partnership called a limited partnership.

As with a sole proprietorship, accounting for a partnership follows the same underlying fundamentals of accounting as any other form of business organization, **except for those entries that directly affect owners' equity.** Accounting for partners' equity follows the same pattern as illustrated earlier for a sole proprietorship, except that separate partner capital and drawings accounts must be established for **each** partner. Investments by each partner are credited to separate capital accounts. Withdrawals of cash and other resources from the partnership by each partner are debited to the respective drawings accounts. The net income for a partnership is divided between the partners in the **profit ratio** specified in the partnership contract. The Income Summary account is closed to the respective partner capital accounts in accordance with the distribution of income. The respective drawings accounts also are closed to the partner capital accounts. Therefore, after the closing process, the capital account of each partner cumulatively reflects all investments of the individual partner, plus the partner's share of all partnership earnings, less all withdrawals by the partner.

Exhibit 12–14 presents selected 19A journal entries and partial financial statements of AB Partnership to illustrate the accounting for and reporting of the distribution of income and partners' equity.

The financial statements of a partnership follow the same format as for a corporation, except (1) the income statement includes an additional section entitled "Distribution of net income," (2) the partners' equity section of the balance sheet is detailed for each partner in conformity with the reporting principle, as illustrated in Exhibit 12–14, and (3) partnerships, as an entity do not pay income taxes (each partner must report his or her share of the partnership

EXHIBIT 12–14
Accounting for and reporting of partners' equity

Selected entries during 19A:

January 1, 19A:

AB Partnership was organized by A. Able and B. Baker on this date. Able contributed $60,000 and Baker $40,000 cash in the partnership and agreed to divide net income (and net loss) 60 percent and 40 percent, respectively. The journal entry for the business to record the investment would be:

Cash...	100,000	
A. Able, capital.......................................		60,000
B. Baker, capital		40,000
Investment to initiate a partnership.		

During 19A:

It was agreed that in lieu of salaries, Able would withdraw $1,000 and Baker $650 per month in cash. Accordingly, **each month** the following journal entry for the withdrawals was made:

A. Able, drawings	1,000	
B. Baker, drawings..	650	
Cash..		1,650
Withdrawal of cash by partners for personal use.		

EXHIBIT 12–14
(concluded)

December 31, 19A:

Assume the normal closing entries for the revenue and expense accounts resulted in a $30,000 **credit balance** in the Income Summary account (i.e., $30,000 net income). The next closing entry would be:

Income summary	30,000	
A. Able, capital		18,000
B. Baker, capital		12,000

Closing entry to transfer net income to the respective capital accounts. Net income divided as follows:

    A. Able $30,000 × .60 = $18,000
    B. Baker $30,000 × .40 = <u> 12,000</u>
        Total $30,000

December 31, 19A:

The journal entry required to close the drawings accounts would be:

A. Able, capital	12,000	
B. Baker, capital	7,800	
A. Able, drawings		12,000
B. Baker, drawings		7,800

Closing entry to transfer drawings for the year to the respective capital accounts.

After the closing entries the partners' accounts would reflect the following balances:

Income summary	–0–
A. Able, drawings	–0–
B. Baker, drawings	–0–
A. Able, capital	$66,000
B. Baker, capital	44,200

Reporting partners' distribution of net income and partners' equity:

Income statement for the year ended December 31, 19A:

Net income	$ 30,000

Distribution of net income:

A. Able (60%)	$18,000
B. Baker (40%)	<u>12,000</u>
	$30,000

Balance sheet December 31, 19A:

Partners' Equity

A. Able, capital	$66,000	
B. Baker, capital	<u>44,200</u>	
Total partners' equity		$110,200

A separate statement of partners' capital similar to the following is customarily prepared to supplement the balance sheet:

AB PARTNERSHIP
Statement of Partners' Capital
For the Year Ended December 31, 19A

	A. Able	B. Baker	Total
Investment, January 1, 19A	$60,000	$40,000	$100,000
Add: Additional investments during the year	–0–	–0–	–0–
Net income for the year	<u>18,000</u>	<u>12,000</u>	<u>30,000</u>
Totals	78,000	52,000	130,000
Less: Drawings during the year	<u>12,000</u>	<u>7,800</u>	<u>19,800</u>
Partners' equity, December 31, 19A	<u>$66,000</u>	<u>$44,200</u>	<u>$110,200</u>

profits on the individual tax return); therefore, income tax expense and income taxes payable will not be recorded, and (4) salaries paid to partners are not recorded as expense but are treated as a distribution of earnings (i.e., withdrawals).

IMPORTANT TERMS DEFINED IN THIS CHAPTER

Terms (alphabetically)	Key words in definitions of important terms used in chapter	Page reference
Authorized shares	Maximum number of shares of the corporation that can be issued as specified in the charter.	630
Charter of a corporation	The legal articles of incorporation by the government that create a corporation; specifies purpose and capital.	627
Common shares	The basic, normal, voting shares issued by a corporation; not preferred shares; residual equity.	630
Convertible preferred shares	Preferred shares that are convertible, at the option of the holder, to common shares.	632
Cumulative dividend preference	Preferred shares preference that dividends not declared for a particular year cumulate as a subsequent preference.	644
Current dividend preference	The basic dividend preference on preferred shares for a particular year.	643
Dividend dates:		
Declaration	Date dividend declared; entry for cash dividend; dividends payable.	648
Payment	Date on which a cash dividend is paid to the shareholders of record; cash is disbursed.	648
Record	Date on which the shareholders are individually identified to receive a declared dividend.	648
Dividends in arrears	Dividends on cumulative preferred shares that have not been declared in prior years.	644
Issued shares	Total shares that have been issued; shares outstanding plus treasury shares held, if any.	630
Legal or stated capital	Defined by law; usually par value or stated value; provides a "cushion" for creditors; cannot be used for dividends.	631
Minute book	An official record of the actions of the board of directors of a corporation.	649
Nopar value shares	Shares of capital stock that have nopar value specified in the corporate charter.	631
Outstanding shares	Shares that are owned by shareholders on any particular date.	630
Partnership	An unincorporated business owned by two or more persons.	652
Par value	Nominal value per share of capital stock; specified in the charter; basis for legal capital.	631
Preferred shares	Shares that have specified rights over the common shares.	630
Prior period adjustments	Amounts debited or credited directly to retained earnings resulting from a correction of prior accounting periods.	651
Restrictions on retained earnings	Temporary removal of some or all of the balance of retained earnings from dividend availability.	651
Share certificate	Evidence of the number of shares held by an investor; ownership interest.	627

Terms (alphabetically)	Key words in definitions of important terms used in chapter	Page reference
Shareholders' subsidiary ledger	A record, usually maintained by a share transfer agent, of the names, addresses, and shares owned, of all of the shareholders.	649
Share transfer agent	An individual or organization appointed by a corporation to transfer shares and maintain shareholders' records.	649
Sole proprietorship	An unincorporated business owned by only one person (one owner).	652
Stock dividends	Distribution of additional shares to current shareholders on a proportional basis at no cost; decreases retained earnings.	641
Stock splits	The total number of issued shares is increased by a specified ratio; issued at no cost; does not change proportional ownership of each shareholder; does not decrease retained earnings.	647
Treasury stock	A corporation's own shares that have been issued, then reacquired and still held by that corporation.	637
Unissued shares	Shares of a corporation that have never been issued.	638

QUESTIONS FOR DISCUSSION

Part A

1. Define a corporation and cite its primary advantages.

2. What is the charter of a corporation?

3. Briefly explain each of the following terms: (a) authorized capital stock, (b) issued capital stock, (c) unissued capital stock, and (d) outstanding capital stock.

4. Briefly distinguish between common shares and preferred shares.

5. Briefly explain the distinction between par value shares and nopar value shares.

6. What are the usual characteristics of preferred shares?

7. What are the two basic sources of shareholders' equity? Explain them briefly.

8. Owners' equity is accounted for by source. Explain what is meant by source.

9. Define treasury stock. Why do corporations acquire treasury stock?

10. How is treasury stock reported on the balance sheet? How is the "gain or loss" on treasury stock which has been sold reported on the financial statements?

Part B

11. What are the two basic requirements to support a cash dividend? What are the effects of a cash dividend on assets and shareholders' equity?

12. Distinguish between cumulative and noncumulative preferred shares.

13. Define a stock dividend. In what major respects does it differ from a cash dividend?

14. What are the primary purposes in issuing a stock dividend?

15. Identify and briefly explain the three important dates in respect to dividends.

16. Define retained earnings. What are the primary components of retained earnings at the end of each period?

17. Define prior period adjustments. How are they reported?

18. Explain what is meant by restrictions on retained earnings.

19. Using the legal rules for when a dividend can be declared as specified in the chapter, does a restriction of retained earnings hinder the payment of dividends? If not, what purpose could be served by such a reserve of retained earnings?

20. Realizable value of assets is part of one of the legal restrictions of when a company is entitled to purchase its own shares or to declare a dividend. Which accounts on a traditional balance sheet would not reflect such realizable values for purposes of these calculations? What might be done to determine their realizable values?

21. Because a small business person could incorporate a limited company or operate as a sole proprietorship, the net income reported for the same operations would be different. What constitutes the difference and why would a prospective buyer of such a business be concerned?

EXERCISES

Part A

E12–1. Fox Corporation was organized in 19A for the purpose of operating an engineering service business. The charter authorized the following capital stock: common stock, par value $5 per share, 10,000 shares. During the first year, the following selected transactions were completed:

1. Sold and issued 5,000 shares of common stock for cash at $25 cash per share.
2. Issued 500 shares of common stock for a piece of land that will be used for a facilities site; construction was started immediately. Assume the shares were selling at $27 each at the date of issuance. Debit Land.
3. Sold and issued 1,000 shares of common stock for cash at $27 cash.
4. At year-end, the Income Summary account reflected a $7,000 loss. Because a loss was incurred, no income tax expense was recorded.

Required:

a. Give the journal entry required for each of the transactions listed above.
b. Assume it is the year-end and the financial statements must be prepared. Prepare the shareholders' equity section as it should be reported on the balance sheet.

E12–2. Davis Corporation was organized in January 19A by 10 shareholders to operate an air conditioning sales and service business. The charter issued by the state authorized the following capital stock:

Common stock, $1 par value, 50,000 shares.
Preferred stock, $10 par value, 7 percent, nonparticipating, noncumulative, 20,000 shares.

During January and February 19A, the following share transactions were completed:

1. Collected $30,000 cash from each of the 10 organizers and issued 1,000 shares of common stock to each of them.
2. Sold 8,000 shares of preferred stock at $30 per share; collected the cash and immediately issued the shares.

Required:

a. Give the journal entries to record the above share transactions.
b. Assume it is the end of the annual accounting period, December 31, 19A, and net income for the year was $35,000; also assume that cash dividends declared and paid at year end amounted to $15,000. Prepare the shareholders' equity section of the balance sheet at December 31, 19A.

E12–3. Video Systems, Incorporated, was issued a charter on January 15, 19A, that authorized the following capital stock:

Common stock, nopar, 80,000 shares.
Preferred stock, 6 percent, par value $10 per share, 10,000 shares.
During 19A, the following selected transactions were completed in the order given:
1. Sold and issued 30,000 shares of the nopar common stock at $30 cash per share.
2. Sold and issued 4,000 shares of preferred stock at $21 cash per share.
3. At the end of 19A, the Income Summary account reflected a credit balance of $15,000.

Required:

a. Give the journal entry indicated for each of the above transactions.
b. Prepare the shareholders' equity section of the balance sheet at December 31, 19A.

E12–4. Garcia Corporation obtained a charter at the start of 19A that authorized 50,000 shares of nopar common stock and 5,000 shares of nopar value preferred stock. The corporation was promoted and organized by five individuals who "reserved" 51 percent of the common shares for themselves. The remaining shares were to be sold to other individuals at $50 per share on a cash basis. During 19A, the following selected transactions occurred:

1. Collected $20 per share cash from four of the organizers and received two adjoining lots of land from the fifth organizer. Issued 3,000 shares of common stock to each of the five organizers and received title to the land.
2. Sold and issued 5,000 shares of common stock to an "outsider" at $50 cash per share.
3. Sold and issued 4,000 shares of preferred stock at $15 cash per share.
4. At the end of 19A, the Income Summary account, after income taxes, reflected a credit balance of $30,000.

Required:

a. Give the journal entries indicated for each of the transactions listed above.
b. Prepare the shareholders' equity section of the balance sheet at December 31, 19A.
c. Explain the basis that you used to determine the cost of the land.

E12–5. The shareholders' equity section on the December 31, 19D, balance sheet of Rice Corporation was:

Shareholders' Equity

Contributed capital:

Preferred stock, par value $30, authorized 8,000 shares; _?_ issued, of which 500 shares are held as treasury stock	$165,000
Common stock, nopar, authorized 10,000 shares; issued and outstanding 7,000 shares	632,000
Contributed surplus	7,150
Retained earnings	40,000
Cost of treasury stock, preferred	16,000

Required:

Complete the following statements and show your computations:

a. The number of shares of preferred issued was _____.

b. The number of shares of preferred outstanding was _____.

c. The average sale price of the preferred shares when issued apparently was $_____ per share.

d. Have the treasury stock transactions (1) increased corporate resources _____; or (2) decreased resources _____? By how much? $_____.

e. How much did the treasury stock transactions increase (decrease) shareholders' equity?

f. How much did the treasury stock held cost per share? $_____.

g. Total shareholders' equity is $_____.

h. What was the average issue price of the common shares?

i. Assuming one fourth of the treasury stock is sold at $30 per share, the remaining balance in the Treasury Stock account would be $_____.

E12–6. The balance sheet (summarized) of Pope Corporation reflected the information shown below at December 31, 19B:

POPE CORPORATION
Balance Sheet
At December 31, 19B

Assets		**Liabilities**	
Cash	$100,000	Current liabilities	$ 60,000
All other assets	412,000	Long-term liabilities	80,000
			140,000
		Shareholders' Equity	
		Contributed capital:	
		Common stock, par $20, authorized 20,000 shares; outstanding 12,000 shares	240,000
		Contributed surplus	72,000
	$512,000	Retained earnings	60,000
			$512,000

During the next year, 19C, the following selected transactions affecting shareholders' equity occurred:

Feb.   1 Purchased in the open market, 500 shares of Pope's own common stock at $40 cash per share.

July 15 Sold 100 of the shares purchased on February 1, 19C, at $41 cash per share.

Sept. 1 Sold 20 more of the shares purchased on February 1, 19C, at $38 cash per share.

Dec. 15 Sold an additional 80 of the treasury shares at $35 per share.

Dec. 31 The credit balance in the Income Summary account was $31,140.

Required:

a. Give the indicated journal entries for each of the five transaction.
b. Prepare the shareholders' equity section of the balance sheet at December 31, 19C.

Part B

E12–7. The records of Stewart Supply Company reflected the following balances in the shareholders' equity accounts at December 31, 19H:

Common stock, par $5 per share, 30,000 shares outstanding.

Preferred stock, 6 percent, par $10 per share, 3,000 shares outstanding.

Retained earnings, $150,000.

On September 1, 19H, the board of directors was considering the distribution of a $42,000 cash dividend. No dividends were paid during 19F and 19G. You have been asked to determine the total and per share amounts that would be paid to the common shareholders and to the preferred shareholders under three independent assumptions (show computations):

a. The preferred shares are noncumulative and nonparticipating.
b. The preferred shares are cumulative and nonparticipating.
c. The preferred shares are cumulative and fully participating (solve this assumption only if Supplement 12A is assigned for study).
d. Give the journal entry to record dividends separately for preferred and common shares under each assumption.
e. Explain why the dividend per share of common stock was less for each assumption than for the preceding assumption.
f. What factor would cause a more favourable per share result to the common shareholders?

E12–8. Rye Corporation has the following capital stock outstanding at the end of 19B:

Preferred stock, 6 percent, par $20, outstanding shares, 6,000.

Common stock, par $5, outstanding shares, 20,000.

On October 1, 19B, the board of directors declared dividends as follows:

Preferred shares, the full cash preference amount; payable December 20, 19B.

Common shares, a 10 percent common stock dividend (i.e., one additional share for each 10 held), issuable December 20, 19B.

On December 20, 19B, the market prices were: Preferred shares, $50, and common shares, $15.

Required:

a. Give any required journal entry(s) to record the declaration and subsequent payment of the dividend on the preferred shares.

b. Give any required journal entry(s) to record the declaration and issuance of the stock dividend on the common shares.

c. Explain the comparative overall effect of each of the dividends on the assets, liabilities, and shareholders' equity of Rye Corporation.

E12–9.   On December 31, 19E, the shareholders' equity section of the balance sheet of Hye Corporation reflected the following:

> Common stock, par $10, shares authorized
>   50,000; shares outstanding 20,000 . . . . $200,000
> Contributed surplus   15,000
> Retained earnings   103,000

On February 1, 19F, the board of directors declared a 20 percent stock dividend to be issued April 30, 19F (that is, one additional share will be issued for each five shares now outstanding). The market value of the stock on February 1, 19F, was $16 per share. The market value will be capitalized.

Required:

a. Give any required journal entry(s) to record the declaration and issuance of the stock dividend.

b. For comparative purposes, prepare the shareholders' equity section of the balance sheet (1) immediately before the stock dividend and (2) immediately after the stock dividend. (Hint: Use two amount columns for this requirement.)

c. Explain the effects of this stock dividend on the assets, liabilities, and shareholders' equity.

E12–10.   The following account balances were selected from the records of Tucker Corporation at December 31, 19E, after all adjusting entries were completed:

> Common stock, par $5, authorized 200,000 shares; issued 120,000 shares, of
>   which 500 shares are held as treasury stock $600,000
> Contributed surplus   280,000
> Bond sinking fund   70,000
> Dividends declared and paid in 19E   24,000
> Retained earnings, January 1, 19E   90,000
> Correction of prior period accounting error (a debit, net of income tax)   10,000
> Treasury stock at cost (500 shares)   3,000
> Income summary for 19E (credit balance)   45,000
> Restriction on retained earnings equal to the cost of treasury stock held is required
>   by law.

Required:

Based upon the above data, prepare (a) the statement of retained earnings for 19E and (b) the shareholders' equity section of the balance sheet at December 31, 19E. (Hint: Total shareholders' equity is $978,000.)

E12–11.   The data given below were selected from the records of Stonewall Corporation at December 31, 19B.

Common stock, par $2, authorized 300,000 shares, issued 110,000 shares of which 1,000 are held as treasury stock (purchased at $8 per share)	$220,000
Preferred stock, 6%, par $10, authorized 20,000 shares, issued and outstanding 15,000 shares...	150,000
Contributed surplus	
Common stock	230,000
Preferred stock	120,000
Dividends declared and paid during 19B.....................................	24,000
Net income for 19B	64,000
Retained earnings balance, January 1, 19B	130,000
Prior period adjustment (gain, net of income tax)............................	10,000
Extraordinary loss (unusual and infrequent, net of income tax).................	22,000

Required:

a. Prepare a statement of retained earnings for the year ended December 31, 19B.
b. Prepare the shareholders' equity section of the balance sheet dated December 31, 19B. (Hint: Total shareholders' equity is $892,000.)

E12–12. On July 1, 19B, PEI Corporation had the following capital structure:

Common stock, par $2, authorized shares	100,000
Common stock, par $2, unissued shares........	80,000
Contributed surplus, $60,000.	
Retained earnings, $90,000.	
Treasury stock, none.	

Required:

a. The number of issued shares is _____ .
b. The number of outstanding shares is _____ .
c. Total shareholders' equity is $_____ .
d. Assume the board of directors declared and issued a 20 percent stock dividend (i.e., one new share for each five shares already owned) when the shares were selling at $11 per share. Give any required journal entry(s). If none is required, explain why.
e. Disregard the stock dividend in (d) above. Assume instead that the board of directors voted a six-to-five stock split (i.e., a 20 percent increase in the number of shares). The market price prior to the split was $11 per share. Give any required journal entry(s). If none is required, explain why.
f. Complete the following comparative tabulation followed by comments on the comparative effects:

Items	Before Dividend and Split	After Stock Dividend	After Stock Split
Common stock account	$	$	$
Par per share	$2	$	$
Shares outstanding	#	#	#
Contributed surplus	$60,000	$	$
Retained earnings	$90,000	$	$
Total shareholders' equity	$	$	$

PROBLEMS/CASES

Part A

PC12–1. Caine Corporation received its charter during January 19A. The charter authorized the following capital stock:

> Preferred shares, 7 percent, par $10.
> Common shares, par $2.

> During 19A, the following transactions occurred in the order given:

1. Issued a total of 60,000 shares of the common stock to the six organizers at $5 per share. Caine collected cash in full from five of the organizers, and a plot of land was received from the other organizer in full payment for the shares. The shares were issued immediately.
2. Sold 3,000 shares of the preferred stock at $22 per share. Collected the cash and issued the shares immediately (10,000 shares to each organizer).
3. Sold 2,000 shares of the common stock at $7 per share and 1,000 shares of the preferred stock at $30. Collected the cash and issued the shares immediately.
4. Total revenues for 19A, $206,000, and total expenses (including income tax), $160,000.

Required:

a. Give all of the journal entries required for the above items including closing entries.
b. Prepare the shareholders' equity section of the balance sheet at December 31, 19A.
c. What was the average issue price of the common shares?
d. Explain the basis you used to value the land in the first journal entry.

PC12–2. Yukon Corporation began operations in January 19A. The charter authorized the following capital stock:

> Preferred stock, 6 percent, $10 par.
> Common stock, nopar.
> During 19A, the following transactions occurred in the order given:

1. Issued 20,000 shares of the nopar common stock to each of the three organizers. Collected $8 cash per share from two of the organizers, and received a plot of land, with a small building thereon, in full payment for the shares of the third organizer and issued the shares immediately. Assume that 20 percent of the noncash payment received applies to the building.
2. Sold 4,000 shares of the preferred stock at $15 per share. Collected the cash and issued the shares immediately.
3. Sold 200 shares of the preferred at $16 and 1,000 shares of the nopar common at $10 per share. Collected the cash and issued the shares immediately.
4. Operating results at the end of 19A, were reflected as follows:

> Revenue accounts............................ $160,000
> Expense accounts, including income taxes...... 120,000

Required:

a. Give the journal entries indicated (including closing entries) for each of the above transactions.
b. Prepare the shareholders' equity section of the balance sheet at December 31, 19A.
c. Explain what you used to determine the cost of the land and the building in the first journal entry.

PC12–3 Dyno Company was issued a charter in January 19A, which authorized 50,000 shares of common stock. During 19A, the following selected transactions occurred in the order given:

1. Sold 10,000 shares for cash at $70 per share. Collected the cash and issued the shares immediately.
2. Acquired land to be used as a future plant site; made payment in full by issuing 500 shares. Assume a market value per share of $70.
3. At the end of 19A, the Income Summary account reflected a credit balance of $30,000.

Three independent cases are assumed as follows for comparative study purposes:

Case A—Assume the common shares were $30 par value per share. The provincial law specifies that par value is legal capital.

Case B—Assume the common shares were nopar and that the total sale price is credited to the Common Stock, Nopar account because the provincial law specifies this amount as legal capital.

Case C—Assume the common shares were nopar with a stated value, specified by the board of directors, of $10 per share.

Required:

For each independent case:

a. Give the journal entries for each of the three transactions.
b. Prepare the shareholders' equity section of the balance sheet at December 31, 19A.
c. Should total shareholders' equity be the same amount among the three independent cases? Explain why.
d. Should the noncash asset (land) be recorded at the same cost under each of the three independent cases? Explain why.

PC12–4. Mika Company obtained a charter from a province in January 19A, which authorized 100,000 shares of common stock, $1 par value. The shareholders comprised 20 local citizens. During the first year, the following selected transactions occurred in the order given:

1. Sold 80,000 shares of the common stock to the 20 shareholders at $5 per share. Collected the $400,000 cash and issued the shares.
2. During the year, one of the 20 shareholders needed cash and wanted to sell the shares back to Mika. Accordingly, the corporation purchased the investor's 5,000 shares at $5.50 cash per share.
3. Two months later, 1,000 of the shares of treasury stock (purchased in 2) were resold to another individual at $5.75 cash per share.
4. An additional 2,000 shares of the treasury stock were sold at $5.40 cash per share.

5. On December 31, 19A, the end of the first year of business, the Income Summary account reflected a credit balance of $28,550.

Required:

a. Give the indicated journal entry for each of the above items.
b. Prepare the shareholders' equity section of the balance sheet at December 31, 19A.
c. What dollar effect did the treasury stock transactions have on the assets, liabilities and shareholders' equity of Mika Corporation? Explain.

PC12–5. Doss Manufacturing Company was granted a charter that authorized the following capital stock:

Common stock, nopar, 50,000 shares. Assume the nopar shares are not assigned a stated value per share.

Preferred stock, 6 percent, nopar, 10,000 shares.

During the first year, 19A, the following selected transactions occurred in the order given:

1. Sold 20,000 shares of the nopar common stock at $30 cash per share and 3,000 shares of the preferred stock at $22 cash per share. Collected cash and issued the shares immediately.
2. Issued 1,000 shares of preferred stock as full payment for a plot of land to be used as a future plant site. Assume the shares were selling at $22.
3. Purchased 300 shares of the nopar common stock sold earlier; paid cash, $26 per share.
4. Sold all of the treasury stock (common) purchased in 3 above. The sale price was $28 per share.
5. Purchased 200 shares of the company's own preferred stock at $24 cash per share.
6. At December 31, 19A, the Income Summary account reflected a credit balance of $21,200.

Required:

a. Give the journal entries indicated for each of the above transactions.
b. Prepare the shareholders' equity section of the balance sheet at December 31, 19A, end of the annual accounting period.

Part B

PC12–6. Brown Equipment Company had the following shares outstanding and retained earnings at December 31, 19E:

Common stock, $10 par, outstanding 20,000 shares	$200,000
Preferred stock, 6%, $20 par, outstanding 5,000 shares	100,000
Retained earnings	240,000

The board of directors is considering the distribution of a cash dividend to the two groups of shareholders. No dividends were declared during 19C or 19D. Three independent case situations are assumed:

Case A—The preferred shares are noncumulative and nonparticipating; the total amount of dividends is $36,000.

Case B—The preferred shares are cumulative and nonparticipating; the total amount of dividends is $18,000.

Case C—Same as Case B, except the amount is $58,000.

Required:

a. Compute the amount of dividends, in total and per share, that would be payable to each class of shareholders for each case. Show computations.

b. Give the journal entry to record the cash dividends declared and paid in 19E for Case C only. Assume for simplicity that the declaration and payment occurred simultaneously on December 31, 19E.

c. Give the required journal entry assuming, instead of a cash dividend, the declaration and issuance of a 10 percent common stock dividend on the outstanding common shares. Assume the market value per share of common was $22.

d. Complete the following comparative schedule including explanation of the comparative differences.

Item	Amount of Dollar Increase (Decrease)	
	Cash Dividend—Case C	Stock Dividend
Assets	$	$
Liabilities	$	$
Shareholders' equity	$	$

PC12–7. KAT Manufacturing Company has outstanding 50,000 shares of $5 par value common stock and 15,000 shares of $10 par value preferred stock (6 percent). On December 1, 19B, the board of directors voted a 6 percent cash dividend on the preferred shares and a 10 percent common stock dividend on the common shares (i.e., for each 10 shares of common held 1 additional share of common is to be issued as a stock dividend). At the date of declaration, the common shares were selling at $32 and the preferred at $20 per share. The dividends are to be paid, or issued on February 15, 19C. The annual accounting period ends December 31.

Required:

a. Give any journal entry(s) required to record the declaration and payment of the cash dividend.

b. Give any journal entry(s) required to record the declaration and issuance of the stock dividend.

c. Explain the comparative effects of the two dividends on the assets, liabilities, and shareholders' equity (1) through December 31, 19B, (2) on February 15, 19C, and (3) the overall effects from December 1, 19B, through February 15, 19C. A schedule similar to the following might be helpful:

Item	Comparative Effects Explained	
	Cash Dividend on Preferred	Stock Dividend on Common
1. Through December 31, 19B: Assets		
etc.		

PC12–8. The accounts of AFC Corporation reflected the following balances on January 1, 19C:

Preferred stock, 5%, $50 par value, cumulative, authorized 10,000 shares, issued and outstanding 2,000 shares	$100,000
Common stock, $10 par value, authorized 100,000 shares, outstanding 20,000 shares	200,000
Contributed surplus, preferred	5,000
Contributed surplus, common	10,000
Retained earnings	200,000
Total shareholders' equity	$515,000

The transactions during 19C relating to the shareholders' equity are listed below in order:

1. Purchased 200 shares of preferred treasury stock at $120 per share.
2. The board of directors declared and paid a cash dividend to the preferred shareholders only. No dividends were declared during 19A or 19B. The dividend was sufficient to pay the arrears plus the dividend for the current year.
3. The board of directors declared a 1-for-10 (i.e., 10 percent) common stock dividend on the outstanding common shares. Market value of $15 per share is to be capitalized.
4. Net income for the year was $50,000.

Required:

a. Give the journal entry for each of the above transactions, including the closing entries. Show computations.
b. Prepare a statement of retained earnings for 19B and the shareholders' equity section of the balance sheet at December 31 19C. (Hint: Total shareholders' equity is $527,500.)
c. Explain the comparative effects on assets and shareholders' equity of the (1) cash dividend and (2) the stock dividend.

PC12–9. (Review)   At December 31, 19E, the records of Reedy Corporation provided the following selected and incomplete data:

Common stock, par $5 (no changes during 19E):
  Shares authorized, 500,000.
  Shares issued ? issue price $12 per share; cash collected in full, $1,800,000.
  Shares held as treasury stock, 2,000 shares—cost $15 per share.
Net income for 19E, $176,000.
Dividends declared and paid during 19E, $74,000.
Bond sinking fund balance, $20,000.
Prior period adjustment—correction of 19B accounting error, $14,000 (a credit, net of income tax).
Retained earnings balance, January 1, 19E, $180,000.
The treasury stock was acquired after the stock dividend was issued.
Extraordinary gain (net of income tax), $16,000.

Required:

a.   Complete the following tabulation:
      Shares authorized _____
      Shares issued _____
      Shares outstanding _____
b.   The balance in the Contributed Surplus account appears to be $ _____.
c.   EPS on net income is $ _____.
d.   Dividend paid per share of common stock is $ _____.
e.   The bond sinking fund should be reported on the balance sheet under the classification _____.
f.   Net income before extraordinary items was $ _____.
g.   The prior period adjustment should be reported on the _____ as an addition ___ or a deduction _____.
h.   Treasury stock should be reported on the balance sheet under the major caption _____ in the amount of $ _____.
i.   The amount of retained earnings available for dividends on January 1, 19E, was $_____.
j.   Assume the board of directors voted a 100 percent stock split (the number of shares will double). After the stock split, the par value per share will be $ _____ and the number of outstanding shares will be _____.
k.   Assuming the stock split given in (j) above, give any journal entry that should be made. If none explain why.
l.   Disregard the stock split (assumed in [j] and [k] above). Assume instead that a 10 percent stock dividend (i.e., one share for each 10 shares already held) was declared and issued when the market price of the common stock was $6. Give any journal entry that should be made.

PC12–10. Walker Company is in the process of completing its year-end accounting, including the preparation of the annual financial statements, at December 31, 19E. The shareholders' equity accounts reflected the following balances at the end of the year, 19E:

Common stock, par $10, shares outstanding 50,000	$500,000
Contributed surplus	50,000
Retained earnings, January 1, 19E (credit)	300,000
Cash dividends declared and paid during 19E (debit)	30,000
Income summary account for 19E (credit balance; after tax)	60,000

The following selected transactions occurred near the end of 19E; they are not included in the above amounts:

1. During 19D, Walker Company was sued for $35,000, and it was clear that the suit would be lost. Therefore, in 19D, Walker should have debited a loss and credited a liability for this amount. This journal entry was not made, and the accounting error was found in 19E. (Hint: Credit Liability for Damages.) Disregard any income tax effects.
2. The board of directors voted a voluntary restriction on retained earnings of $100,000. It is to be designated as "Earnings appropriated for plant expansion" and effective for the 19E financial statements.

Required:

a. Give the appropriate journal entries for the events listed immediately above. If no entry is given, explain why.
b. Prepare a statement of retained earnings for 19E and the shareholders' equity section of the balance sheet at December 31, 19E. (Hint: The ending balance of shareholders' equity is $845,000.)

PC12–11. Rye Company has completed all of the annual information processing at December 31, 19D, except for preparation of the financial statements. The following account balances were reflected at that date:

RYE COMPANY
Adjusted Trial Balance
December 31, 19D

	Debit	Credit
Cash	$ 57,000	
Accounts receivable (net)	58,000	
Merchandise inventory, December 31, 19D	120,000	
Long-term investment in Company Y	20,000	
Bond sinking fund	40,000	
Land	20,000	
Buildings and equipment (net)	738,000	
Other assets	29,200	
Accounts payable		$ 86,000
Income tax payable		18,000
Bonds payable, 7%, payable December 31		100,000
Preferred stock, par $10, authorized 50,000 shares		100,000
Common stock, par $5, authorized 200,000 shares		660,000
Contributed surplus, preferred		6,100
Contributed surplus, common		19,900
Treasury stock, preferred, 10 shares at cost	1,100	
Retained earnings, January 1, 19D		163,300
19D net income		40,000
19D cash dividends on preferred	26,000	
19D common stock dividends distributed (10,000 shares)	70,000	
19D, discovered an accounting error made in 19A in recording a purchase of land (the correction required a net credit to land of $14,000)	14,000	
	$1,193,300	$1,193,300

Note: Retained earnings is restricted in an amount equal to the bond sinking fund per the provisions of the bond indenture.

Required:

Prepare a statement of retained earnings for 19D and a classified balance sheet at December 31, 19D. (Hint: Total shareholders' equity is $878,200.)

PC12–12. This case is based upon the financial statements of Consolidated Bathurst presented in Special Supplement B immediately preceding the Index. Use the 1984 data to respond to the following questions:

1. Complete the following tabulation about the capital stock for 1984:

Shares	Number of Shares				Par Value per Share
	Authorized	Issued	Treasury	Outstanding	
Common					
Preferred					

2. How much did retained earnings change during 1984? $_____. Explain what caused this change.
3. Give the amount of the 1984 ending balances in the following accounts and show proof of the total:

   a. Preferred stock.............................. $_____
   b. Common stock............................. _____
   c. Contributed surplus .... _____
   d. Treasury stock .... _____
   e. Foreign currency translation adjustments ...... _____
   f. Retained earnings .... _____
   Proof:

4. Briefly explain the "foreign current translation adjustments" of ($25,044) thousand.
5. What position did the Independent Chartered Accountant take in respect to the "currency adjustments"?
6. Complete the following tabulation:

Common Share Information	1984	1983
Dividends paid per share		
Average shares outstanding (millions)		
Issued to employees		—

PC12–13.   (Review)   The bookkeeper for Careless Company prepared the following balance sheet:

CARELESS COMPANY
Balance Sheet
For the Year 19W

Assets

Current assets	$ 45,000
Fixed assets (net of depreciation reserves, $70,000)	125,000
Other assets	50,000
Total debits	$220,000

Liabilities

Current liabilities	$ 32,000
Other debts	25,000

Capital

Stock, par $10, authorized 10,000 shares	60,000
Stock premium	30,000
Earned surplus	58,000
Treasury stock (500 shares)	(10,000)
Reserve for treasury stock (required by law)	10,000
Correction of prior year error (a credit, net)	7,000
Cash dividends paid during 19W	(12,000)
Net profit for 19W	20,000
Total credits	$220,000

Required:

a.   List all of the deficiencies you can identify in the above statement. Assume the amounts given are correct.

b.   Prepare a statement of retained earnings for 19W.

c.   Recast the above balance sheet in good form; focus especially on shareholders' equity.

PC12–14.   (Based on Supplement 12B)   Assume for each of the three independent cases below that the annual accounting period ends on December 31, 19W, and that the Income Summary account at that date reflected a debit balance of $30,000 (i.e., a loss).

Case A—Assume that the company is a **sole proprietorship** owned by Proprietor A. Prior to the closing entries, the capital account reflected a credit balance of $70,000 and the drawings account a balance of $6,000.

Case B—Assume that the company is a **partnership** owned by Partner A and Partner B. Prior to the closing entries, the owners' equity accounts reflected the following balances: A, Capital, $50,000; B, Capital, $45,000; A, Drawings, $7,000; and B, Drawings, $6,000. Profits and losses are divided equally.

Case C—Assume that the company is a **corporation.** Prior to the closing entries, the shareholders' equity accounts showed the following: Capital Stock, par $20, authorized 20,000 shares, outstanding 4,000 shares; Contributed Surplus, $2,000; and Retained Earnings, $40,000.

Required:

a.   Give all of the closing entries indicated at December 31, 19W, for each of the separate cases.

b.   Show how the owners' equity section of the balance sheet would appear at December 31, 19W, for each case.

PC12–15. Independent Grape Growers (IGG) is a partnership of grape growers in Canada. IGG is currently divided into 125 partnership units. The partnership was formed in January 1984, at which time units were allocated at a unit cost of $10,000 each to the various partners based on their projected grape harvest.

In February 1984, the partnership signed a 10-year building lease, bought equipment and supplies, and hired its first employees. Your employer, CA, was auditor for its first fiscal period ended June 30, 1984. There were no sales or sales-related expenses in this period. No depreciation was recorded because, according to management, the assets had not yet been used for productive purposes. No significant accounting policies had been adopted for the 1984 fiscal period.

Your employer, CA, has been reappointed auditor for the year ended June 30, 1985. He has also been engaged to develop an accounting system, to select suitable financial accounting policies, and to offer any other advice he feels would benefit IGG and its partners.

You have been asked to prepare a report for CA on the special engagement. Your report should identify and analyze the important issues and provide recommendations.

In August 1985, you visited IGG's offices and obtained the information in the Exhibit.

Required:

Prepare the report requested by CA.

**EXHIBIT
Information on
IGG**

1. The partners deliver their grapes to IGG where they are graded. Based on the grading, the decision is made as to which grapes will be sold fresh and which will be processed into grape juice, frozen concentrated juice, grape jelly, wine, or other products. IGG sells the fresh grapes to other wineries and to grocery chains. The harvest and fresh grape sales occur in late summer but IGG sells its processed items throughout the year.

2. Partners are credited with 80 percent of the market value of their harvest when they deliver it to IGG. Actual cash disbursement of this amount is to be made in installments of one-third each on the following December 31, March 31, and June 30.

    The partners are to receive a cash payment on September 30 for their share of IGG's income for the previous fiscal year. For purposes of the computation of this payment, IGG's partners want to use the annual financial statement income figure. However, they would like accounting policies that give consideration to the cyclical nature of their activities and cash flows as well as those of IGG. They do not want to make any withdrawals that will reduce the capital that is needed to maintain the business.

3. Partnership units can be sold only with the approval of the other partners. The value of partnership units is determined based on the June 30 financial statement results. New partners are admitted on this date.

4. Seventy percent of the partners are privately owned limited companies. The remainder are individuals.

EXHIBIT
(concluded)

5. Managers are entitled to bonuses totaling 15 percent of the operating income of the partnership. Bonuses are allocated to individual managers through a point system based on their past experience and performance.

6. IGG borrows funds when inventories and receivables are high, during the autumn and winter period. The bank requires unaudited quarterly financial statements and audited annual financial statements. IGG's loan was at its highest level of $12.5 million in early January, 1985. The current interest rate is 13 percent per annum. The loan is secured by inventories, receivables, and the guarantees of the partners.

7. IGG operates from a building that houses the facilities for processing, warehousing, wine storage and administration.

8. The employees are not unionized. Because of the seasonal nature of the processing activity, extensive use is made of temporary employees.

9. There are three physically separate departments: juice, jelly, and wine. Raisins, pie fillings and other products are processed in the jelly department. Much of the processing is mechanized. Each department has separate storage facilities in the warehouse.

10. IGG's wines will be aged for no more than two years before sale to government liquor stores. Specialized processing equipment is used in winemaking.

11. A portion of sales of nonwine products is made on long-term contracts to grocery chains. For these contracts, cash is usually not received until 120 days after delivery. Other customers pay in cash or within 30 days. IGG's managers project a steady increase in the number of noncontract customers over the next five years.

12. The market for jams and jellies was weak at June 30, 1985. Customers were offering to buy at $4 per kilogram, but IGG would not sell below its estimated cost of $6 per kilogram. In August, 1985, the offering price had dropped to $3.50 per kilogram.

13. Extracts from the audited financial statements of IGG at June 30, 1985, are as follows:

A. Packaging material, jars, boxes and similar products on hand ... $ 186,230
B. Inventories:
    Wine (1,500,000 bottle equivalent)............................ $2,000,000
    Jams and jellies (100,000 kilograms) 600,000
    Raisins (800,000 kilograms)................................. 1,120,000
    Pie fillings (200,000 kilograms) 410,000
    Juice (800,000 litres) 400,000
    Sugar (100,000 kilograms) 70,000
C. Prepaid lease .... $ 10,000
D. Unearned revenue. Deposit on sale of 150,000 kilograms of raisins @ $1.00 per kilogram, to be delivered in November, 1985.. $ 25,000
E. Bonus payable to managers..................................... $ 210,000
F. Forgivable loan of $800,000 from the provincial government on September 1, 1984, for establishing IGG and creating 10 permanent jobs. Provided certain conditions are met, one fifth

EXHIBIT
(concluded)

of the loan principal is forgiven on September 1 of each year
from 1985 to 1989. Interest at 10 percent per annum is payable
on September 1 each year .... $ 800,000

G. Balance due to partners for grape harvest $7,462,000

H. Interest and storage charges related to wine inventory currently $ 317,600
on hand ....

I. Cost of printing discount coupons for IGG brand juice (mailed
to households in June and July 1985) .... $ 12,000

(CICA Adapted)

13

Measuring and Reporting Long-Term Investments

PURPOSE OF THIS CHAPTER[1]

One corporation may invest in another corporation by acquiring either **debt securities** (e.g., bonds) or **equity securities** (e.g., capital stock) of the other corporation. The objective of an investment in another corporation often is to earn a return on idle cash, or to obtain influence or control over the other corporation.

In Chapter 8, short-term investments (a current asset) were defined as those that meet two tests: (1) **ready marketability** and (2) **management intention** to convert them to cash in the short run. Those not meeting these two tests are classified as long-term investments (a noncurrent asset).

The purpose of this chapter is to discuss measuring and reporting of long-term investments, except for those situations in which **consolidated statements** must be prepared. Consolidated statements are discussed in Chapter 14. To accomplish this purpose, the chapter is subdivided into two parts:

Part A—Long-term investments in equity securities (shares)

Part B—Long-term investments in debt securities (bonds)

---

[1]We suggest that you review the discussion of short-term investments in Chapter 8 prior to studying this chapter.

Part A—Long-Term Investments in Equity Securities (Shares)

A company may invest in the equity securities (either common or preferred shares) of one or more corporations for various reasons such as to use idle cash, to exercise influence or control over the other company, to attain growth through sales of new products and new services, to gain access to new markets and new sources of supply, or to attain other economic purposes. Basically, one entity may acquire capital stock of a corporation by purchasing outstanding shares from other shareholders for cash (or other assets); or if the investor is a corporation, by exchanging some of its own capital stock for outstanding capital stock of the other corporation.

When one company purchases **outstanding** shares of another company, the transaction is between the acquiring company and the **shareholders** of the other company (not the other company itself). Thus, the transaction affects the acquiring entity only. The accounting of the other company is unaffected.

The purchasing entity (i.e., the **investor**) may acquire **some or all** of either the preferred or the common shares **outstanding** of the other company (often called the **investee**). If the purpose of the investment is to gain influence or control, the investor typically will acquire **common shares** because they are the voting shares. The number of outstanding shares of a corporation acquired by another entity usually depends upon the investment objectives of the investing company (i.e., the acquiring company). For measuring and reporting purposes, **three different levels of ownership** are recognized. Each of these levels calls for different measuring and reporting methods. The three levels usually are related to the percentage of voting shares owned by the investing company in relation to the total number of such shares that are outstanding.

MEASURING LONG-TERM INVESTMENTS IN VOTING COMMON SHARES

Accounting for long-term investments in voting common shares involves measuring the investment amount that should be reported on the balance sheet and the periodic investment revenue that should be reported on the income statement. In accordance with the cost principle, long-term investments in the voting shares of another company are measured and recorded, at the dates of acquisition of the shares, as the total consideration given to acquire them. This total includes the market price, plus all commissions and other buying costs. Subsequent to acquisition, measurement of the investment amount and the investment revenue depends upon the relationship between the investor and the investee company. The relevant characteristic of the relationship is the extent to which the investing company can exercise **significant influence or control over the operating and financial policies** of the other company. Significant influence and control are related to the number of voting shares owned of the investee company in proportion to the total number of such shares outstanding.

For measuring and reporting long-term investments in the voting shares of another company, *CICA Handbook,* Section 3050, distinguishes between the two terms, **significant influence** and **control,** essentially as:

1. **Significant influence**—the ability of the investing company to have an important impact on the operating and financing policies of another company in which it owns voting shares. Significant influence may be indicated by *(a)* membership on the board of directors of the other company, *(b)* participation in the policy-making processes, *(c)* material transactions between the two companies, *(d)* interchange of management personnel, or *(e)* provision of technical information. In the absence of a clearcut distinction based upon these factors, **significant influence is presumed** if the investing company owns at least 20 percent but not more than 50 percent of the outstanding voting shares of the other company.

2. **Control**—the ability of the investing company to determine the operating and financing policies of another company in which it owns shares of the voting stock. For all practical purposes, **control is assumed** when the investing company owns more than 50 percent of the outstanding voting shares of the other company.

The three levels of ownership that relate to the measuring and reporting of long-term investments in voting capital stock are as follows:

	Level of ownership	*Measuring and reporting approach*
1.	Neither significant influence nor control	Cost method
2.	Significant influence but not control	Equity method
3.	Control	Consolidated statement method

Each of these approaches is outlined in Exhibit 13–1. The first two are discussed in this chapter, and the third is discussed in Chapter 14.

COST METHOD—NO SIGNIFICANT INFLUENCE

The **cost method** of accounting must be used when the investment by one entity in the **voting** shares of a corporation does not give the former the ability to exercise significant influence or control. Under the cost method of accounting, the investment is measured at the acquisition date in the accounts at cost in accordance with the cost principle. Subsequent to acquisition, the investment amount is measured at the current **lower of cost or market** (LCM), and this amount is reported on the balance sheet under "Investments and funds." Cash dividends declared by the investee corporation are reported by the investing entity as "Revenue from investments" in the period declared. The cost

EXHIBIT 13–1   Measuring and reporting long-term investments in voting shares of another company

Status of ownership	Method	Measurement at date of acquisition	Measurement after date of acquisition	
			Investment	*Revenue*
1. **Investor can exercise no significant influence or control.** Presumed if investor owns less than 20 percent of the outstanding voting shares of the investee company.	Cost method	Investor records the investment at cost. Cost is the total outlay made to acquire the shares.	Investor reports the investment on the balance sheet at LCM.	Investor recognizes revenue each period when dividends are declared by the investee company. A realized gain or loss is recognized when the investment is sold.
2. **Investor can exercise significant influence, but not control,** over the operating and financing policies of the investee company. Presumed if the investor owns at least 20 percent but not more than 50 percent of the outstanding voting shares of the investee company.	Equity method	Same as above.	Investor measures and reports the investment at cost **plus** the investor's share of the earnings (or less the losses) and **minus** the dividends received from (i.e., declared by) the other company. (Dividends received are not considered revenue. To recognize dividends as revenue, rather than as a reduction in the investment, would involve double counting.)	Investor recognizes as revenue each period the investor's proportionate share of the earnings (or losses) reported each period by the investee company.
3. **Investor can exercise control** over the operating and financing policies of the investee company. Control is presumed if the investor owns more than 50 percent of the outstanding voting shares of the investee company.	Consolidated financial statement method	Same as above.	Consolidated financial statements required each period. Discussed in Chapter 14.	

method is essentially the same as the accounting and reporting previously discussed and illustrated for short-term investments in Chapter 8.

CICA Handbook, Section 3050, requires that long-term investments accounted for under the cost method be valued at LCM after acquisition. Thus, at the end of each accounting period, the long-term investments, accounted for under the cost method, must be received as to whether or not a permanent impairment of value has occurred. If so, then a write-down in the carrying value of the investment is required. Obvious indicators of a permanent decline in value would be the bankruptcy of the investee, an agreement by the investor to sell at a loss, a prolonged period where the market value of the security is less than the carrying value, and severe or continued losses. The question of whether or not the market is compared to the carrying value by individual security or by portfolio is not explicitly dealt with in the Canadian pronouncement. Implicitly, however, the pronouncement discusses specific investments so a security by security comparison would be warranted. If a company had a long-term portfolio of securities, professional judgment could suggest the use of the portfolio approach. Comparison of the market value for the portfolio to the cost of the portfolio would permit the offsetting of a decline in the value of one security against the rise in another. Care is necessary here because a nontemporary decline in the value of a single security in a portfolio is a permanent event that may represent a permanent loss in the value of the portfolio. For illustrations and problems, the individual security approach will be used.

When long-term securities are sold, the difference between the sale price and carrying value is recorded and reported as a **realized** gain or loss. It should be noted that if the investment had been written down to market because of a permanent decline in value, it should not be increased if for some reason the market later increased. Any gain subsequently realized is recognized only when the investment is sold.

Application of the cost method is illustrated in Exhibit 13–2. The journal entry to record the acquisition of a long-term investment is in accordance with the **cost principle.** Observe that on November 30, 19A, dividend revenue was recorded on the date that cash dividends were **declared.**

In Exhibit 13–2, the investments are valued at LCM on December 31, 19A, the end of the accounting period. Observe that LCM is applied individually to each investment. For illustration purposes the decline is assumed to be permanent for the Cox preferred shares. The investment was written down to LCM, from cost ($20,000) to market ($18,000), and a loss of $2,000 was recorded.

On June 15, 19B, 300 shares of Cox stock were sold. The journal entry to record the sale removes the shares sold from the investment account at the carrying value. The difference between the original carrying value of shares ($10,800) and the sale price ($12,300) is recorded as a **realized** gain of $1,500.

Exhibit 13–2 presents the reporting effects of the cost method on the income statement and the balance sheet. The income statement is affected by dividend revenue and gains or losses on the investments.

The journal entries given in Exhibit 13–2 reflect application of the cost prin-

EXHIBIT 13–2
Cost method of measuring and reporting long-term investments in equity securities

Situation:

Able Corporation purchased the following long-term investments on February 1, 19A:

Baker Corporation common stock (nopar), 1,000 shares at $12 per share (represents 10 percent of the outstanding shares).

Cox Corporation, 5 percent preferred stock (par $20), nonvoting, 500 shares at $40 per share (represents 10 percent of the outstanding shares).

February 1, 19A, to record the acquisition:

Long-term investments......................................	32,000	
Cash		32,000

Computations:
Baker common stock, 1,000 shares × $12 = $12,000
Cox preferred stock, 500 shares × $40 = 20,000
Total acquisition cost......... $32,000

November 30, 19A, cash dividends declared (payable in January 19B) as follows: Baker common stock, $1 per share; Cox preferred stock, 5 percent of par.

Dividends receivable.......................................	1,500	
Revenue from investments		1,500

Computations:
Baker common stock, 1,000 shares × $1   = $1,000
Cox preferred stock, 500 shares × $20 × 5% =   500
Total dividends................... $1,500

December 31, 19A, end of the accounting period, quoted market prices: Baker common share, $13; Cox preferred share, $36.

Loss on long-term investments...............................	2,000	
Long-term investment—Cox...............................		2,000

Computations:

	Shares	Market Dec. 31, 19A	Acquisition cost	Market Dec. 31, 19A
Baker common stock..................	1,000	$13	$12,000	$13,000
Cox preferred stock..................	500	36	20,000	18,000
			$32,000	$31,000

LCM: $20,000 − $18,000 = $2,000 (on Cox assuming loss is permanent).

January 15, 19B, received cash for the dividends of Baker and Cox Corporations (declared on November 30, 19A).

Cash	1,500	
Dividends receivable.....................................		1,500

June 15, 19B, sold 300 shares of the Cox preferred stock at $41.

Cash (300 shares × $41)......................................	12,300	
Long-term investments (300 × $36)		10,800
Gain on sale of investment		1,500

November 30, 19B, cash dividends declared (payable December 30, 19B) as follows: Baker common stock, $.90 per share; Cox preferred stock, 5 percent of par.

Dividends receivable.......................................	1,100	
Revenue from investments		1,100

Computations:
Baker common stock, 1,000 shares × $.90   = $ 900
Cox preferred stock, 200 shares × $20 × 5% =   200
Total dividends................... $1,100

EXHIBIT 13–2
(concluded)

December 30, 19B, received cash for the dividends of Baker and Cox Corporations (declared on November 30, 19B).

Cash	1,100	
Dividends receivable		1,100

December 31, 19B, end of the accounting period, quoted market prices: Baker common share, $11; Cox preferred share, $43.

Loss on long-term investment	1,000	
Long-term investment—Baker		1,000

Computations:

	Shares	Market Dec. 31, 19B	Carrying	Market Dec. 31, 19B
Baker common shares	1,000	$11	$12,000	$11,000
Cox preferred shares	200	43	7,200	8,600
			$19,200	$19,600

LCM: $12,000 − $11,000 = $1,000. Reduction in Baker assuming the decline is permanent.

December 31, 19A, and 19B, reporting on the **income statement** and **balance sheet** (partial):

	19A	19B
Income statement:		
Revenue from investments.................................	$ 1,500	$ 1,100
Loss from long-term investments...........................	(2,000)	(1,000)
Gain on sale of investment		1,500
Balance sheet:		
Current assets:		
Dividends receivable	1,500	
Investments and funds:		
Investments in equity securities*	$30,000	$18,200
*Include a note to disclose breakdown.		

ciple at the date of acquisition and application of LCM subsequent to that time. The investment is carried continuously at LCM, and dividend revenue is recognized from the investment **only** in periods in which dividends are declared.

The fact that Able Corporation purchased 10 percent of the outstanding voting common shares of Baker Corporation and 10 percent of the outstanding preferred shares of Cox Corporation had absolutely no effect on the accounting and reporting by either Baker or Cox Corporations.

EQUITY METHOD—SIGNIFICANT INFLUENCE EXISTS (BUT NOT CONTROL)

When significant influence can be exercised over the dividend policies of an investee corporation, the dividend revenue from the investee corporation can be obtained, almost at will, by the investor company. The equity method prevents the investor company from manipulating its income by affecting the dividend policy of the investee company. Under the equity method, each year the investor company recognizes its proportionate part of the net income (or net loss) of the investee corporation as investment revenue rather than awaiting the declaration of dividends. No cash is received at the time investment revenue is recorded under the equity method; the offsetting debit is to the investment account (an asset increase). Thus, under the equity method, both the **investment account** and **investment revenue account** of the investor company reflect the investor's proportionate share of the income (and losses) of the investee corporation. When dividends are received (i.e., declared), Dividends Receivable or Cash is debited, and the investment account is credited.[2] Thus, dividends declared reduce the investment account balance; they are **not** credited to Revenue from Investments. The revenue was already recognized by the investor in the prior period in which the investee corporation earned the income.

Application of the equity method is illustrated in Exhibit 13–3.[3] The illustration is based on the assumption that Crown Corporation (the investor company) purchased from other investors 3,000 shares of the outstanding common stock of Davis Corporation (the investee company) at a cash price of $120 per share. At the date of purchase, Davis Corporation had 10,000 nopar common shares outstanding. The equity method must be used because Crown Corporation purchased 30 percent of the outstanding voting shares of Davis Corporation. The first journal entry in Exhibit 13–3 illustrates how the investment would be recorded by Crown Corporation.

After the acquisition date, each year when the investee corporation reports income (or loss), the investor company records its percentage share (i.e., equity) of the investment revenue. The second entry by Crown Corporation (the investor company) given in Exhibit 13–3 recognizes its proportionate share of the net income of Davis Corporation.

In Exhibit 13–3, the proportionate share of the net income of Davis Corporation was recorded by Crown Corporation as revenue and as an **increase** in the investment account. When a dividend is received, it is necessary to avoid double-counting the income from the investee company; therefore, the dividend from the investee company is recorded as a debit to Cash and as a **credit**

---

[2]When a cash dividend is declared in one year and paid in the following year, the dividend is recognized by the investor when declared by debiting Dividends Receivable (a current asset) instead of Cash. Subsequently, when the cash is received, the Cash account is debited and Dividends Receivable is credited. In contrast, dividends declared and paid in the same year may be recorded by the investor on payment date as a debit to Cash and credit to the Investment account.

[3]This example assumes that the investment was purchased at "book value." The accounting and reporting procedures for other situations are more complex because they involve asset write-ups and write-downs and, perhaps, the recognition of "goodwill." This chapter presents the fundamentals devoid of this complexity. Most advanced accounting courses devote considerable attention to these complexities.

Because the revenue from such investments is the net of revenue and expenses of the investee and net of certain expenses of the investor, the term investment income rather than investment revenue might be more descriptive.

EXHIBIT 13–3
Equity method of measuring and reporting long-term investments in equity securities

Situation:
  Crown Corporation (the investor company) purchased 3,000 shares of the outstanding common stock of Davis Corporation (the investee company) on January 15, 19E, at a cash cost of $120 per share. At date of purchase, Davis Corporation had outstanding 10,000 nopar shares of common stock.

Analysis:
  The equity method must be used by Crown Corporation because it now owns between 20 and 50 percent of the outstanding voting shares of the investee company.

January 15, 19E, to record the acquisition:

Investment in common shares, Davis Corporation (3,000 shares)	360,000	
Cash		360,000

Purchased 3,000 shares (30 percent) of the common stock of Davis Corporation at $120 per share.

December 31, 19E, end of the accounting period, Davis Corporation reported net income of $50,000. On this date, Crown Corporation recognized its proportionate share as follows:

Investment in common shares, Davis Corporation	15,000	
Revenue from investments		15,000

To record the proportionate share of 19E income reported by Davis Corporation ($50,000 × 30% = $15,000). The credit often is called Equity in Earnings of Partially Owned Company or income from investments.

December 31, 19E, Davis Corporation declared and paid immediately a $10,000 cash dividend, of which 30 percent (i.e., $3,000) was received by the investor, Crown Corporation. Crown Corporation recorded its share of the dividend as follows:

Cash	3,000	
Investment in common shares, Davis Corporation		3,000

To record the receipt of a cash dividend from Davis Corporation ($10,000 × 30% = $3,000).

to the investment account. This entry reflects the fact that a dividend represents the conversion of a part of the investment account balance to cash.

To recapitulate, under the equity method, the balance in the investment account initially starts at cost. Subsequently, the account balance is increased by the proportionate share of the earnings (or decreased by losses) of the investee company and decreased by the proportionate share of the dividends declared by the investee company. The investment and revenue accounts on the books of the investor company, Crown Corporation, are illustrated in Exhibit 13–3. The financial statements for Crown also are illustrated in Exhibit 13–3.

LCM is not used with long-term investments accounted for under the equity method because under the equity method, investments, after acquisition are accounted for and reported at equity, not cost.

Information in respect to the method of measuring the investment and the related investment revenue is important for interpretation and use of financial statements. The financial statements must disclose the method used. In addi-

EXHIBIT 13–3
(concluded)

December 31, 19E, the investment and income accounts of Crown Corporation for the year 19E would be as follows (based upon the above entries):

Investment in Common Shares, Davis Corporation

1/15/E	Purchased 3,000 shares	360,000	12/31/E	Proportionate share of dividends of Davis Corporation	3,000
12/31/E	Proportionate share of 19E income of Davis Corporation	15,000			

(debit balance, $372,000)

Revenue from Investments

		12/31/E	Revenue from Davis Corporation 15,000

December 31, 19E, reporting by Crown Corporation (investor) on the income statement and balance sheet (partial):

Income Statement
For the Year Ended December 31, 19E

Revenue from investments . . . . $ 15,000

Balance Sheet
At December 31, 19E

Investments and funds:
  Investment in common shares, Davis Corporation,
    equity basis (cost, $360,000; market, $369,000)* $372,000
    *Market is measured as the number of shares owned multiplied by the actual market price per share on the balance sheet date.

tion, regardless of whether the cost or the equity method is used, the original cost, current market value, and carrying value of the investment should be disclosed; this disclosure was illustrated in Exhibits 13–2 and 13–3.

The cost and equity methods to measure the effects of long-term investments represent a compromise on the part of the accounting profession. Many accountants believe that all marketable securities should be measured and reported at their **market values** at each balance sheet date. Under this approach, which is not currently acceptable, both dividends received and changes in the market value of the shares since the last period would be reported as revenue (or loss) on the income statement. Accountants who support this approach believe that it meets most closely the objective of reporting the **economic consequences** of holding an investment in marketable securities. The **cost method** measures only the dividends received by the investor as revenue, but dividends may have absolutely no relationship to the earnings of the investee company for the period. The cost method does not indicate to the investor or statement user the earnings pattern of the investee company. The **equity method** tends to overcome this deficiency; however, it does not reflect the economic impact on the investor of market changes in the investment shares held. The effect of such market changes is significant to the investor. After consideration of these and other factors, the accounting profession, for the present time, has accepted the three different measurement approaches for long-term investments in shares that are outlined in Exhibit 13–1.

Part B—Long-Term Investments in Debt Securities (Bonds)

In Chapter 11 we discussed measuring and reporting of bonds as long-term liabilities of the issuing corporation. This part of the chapter discusses bonds of another company held as a **long-term investment.** Bonds offer significantly different investment risks and returns than does capital stock. Bonds provide a stated rate of interest (which determines the dollar amount of interest that will be received on each interest date) and a specified maturity value (which will be received in cash at maturity date). For example, assume that Smith Company issued $100,000, 10 percent, 20-year bonds. At the specified maturity date, the investors in the bonds (i.e., the bondholders) will receive exactly $100,000 cash for the principal amount of the bonds. The 10 percent stated interest specified on the face of the bonds is received in cash each year (usually 5 percent semiannually, which is $5,000) regardless of the market price of the bonds or the earnings of the issuing company. If Smith Company experienced a net loss, the board of directors might elect not to pay dividends to the shareholders, but in such a situation Smith has a legal obligation to continue to pay interest to bondholders. In contrast, owners of Smith Company shares might receive very large increases in dividend payments if the company were highly profitable, but bondholders would continue to receive the interest rate stated in the bond indenture. The owner (i.e., the investor) of one or more of these bonds has no right to vote in the annual shareholders' meeting as would be the case if some of the common shares of Smith Company were owned.

Similar to capital stock, bonds can be bought and sold in the regular security markets. The market price of bonds fluctuates **inversely** with changes in the **market rate** of interest because the **stated rate** of interest, paid on the face amount of the bonds, remains constant over the life of the bonds (see Chapter 11).

MEASURING AND REPORTING BOND INVESTMENTS

Investors may buy bonds at their date of issuance or at subsequent dates during the life of the bonds. Regardless of the timing of the bonds' acquisition, at the end of each accounting period the investor must measure the (1) cost, adjusted for the cumulative amount of discount or premium that has been amortized (reported on the balance sheet) and (2) interest revenue earned (reported on the income statement). An understanding of the measurement approaches used is helpful in interpreting and using financial statements.

At the date of of acquisition, a bond investment is measured, recorded, and reported in accordance with the **cost principle.** The purchase cost, including all incidental acquisition costs (such as transfer fees and broker commissions), is debited to an investment account such as "Long-Term Investment, Bonds of Beta Corporation." The amount recorded under the cost principle is the **current cash equivalent amount;** and it may be the same as the maturity amount (if acquired at par), less than the maturity amount (if acquired at a discount), or more than the maturity amount (if acquired at a premium).[4] The premium or discount on a bond investment usually is not recorded in a separate account as is done for bonds payable (Chapter 11); rather, the investment account reflects the current book or carrying amount. However, the bond investment account can be debited at par and a separate discount or premium account can be used with precisely the same results.

On each date subsequent to acquisition, a bond investment is measured as the acquisition cost plus any amortized **discount** or minus any amortized **premium.** If the bond investment was acquired at par (maturity value) the carrying value amount remains constant over the life of the investment because there is no premium or discount to be amortized. In this situation, revenue earned from the investment each period is measured as the amount of cash interest collected (or accrued).

When a bond investment is purchased at a discount or premium, measurement of the carrying value of the investment after date of acquisition necessitates adjustment of the investment account balance from acquisition cost to maturity amount each period over the life of the investment. This adjustment is the periodic amortization of the discount or premium. The periodic amortization is made as a debit or credit to the investment account, depending on whether there was a discount or premium at acquisition, so that the investment account at the end of each period reflects the **then current carrying amount.**

When a bond investment is acquired at a discount or premium, the revenue from interest each period is measured as the cash interest collected (or accrued) plus or minus the periodic amortization of discount or premium. As was illustrated in Chapter 11 for bonds payable, bond discount or premium may be amortized by using either the straight-line or effective-interest method. The former is simpler, whereas the latter conceptually is preferable. In the paragraphs to follow, we will assume straight-line amortization; effective-interest amortization is explained at the end of this part.

In contrast to long-term investments, discount or premium is not amortized on bonds held as a **short-term** investment because the bonds will be converted to cash (i.e., sold) within the coming year (or the operating cycle if longer) instead of being held to maturity.

---

[4]Fees, commissions, and other incidental costs decrease the discount, or increase the premium; therefore, they are amortized over the remaining period to maturity. Alternatively, such costs sometimes are recorded separately and amortized on the same basis as the discount or premium.

The concepts of the carrying value of a $1,000 bond investment and amortization of a discount or premium may be portrayed graphically in the following manner:

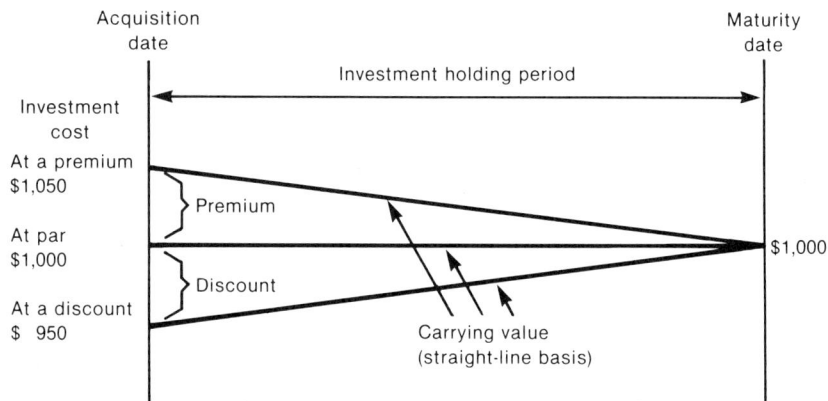

When effective-interest amortization of a discount or premium is used, the carrying value lines will be curved instead of straight.

After the date of acquisition, interest revenue must be accrued (by means of an adjusting entry) for periods between the last date on which interest revenue was collected and the end of the accounting period. The procedure for accruing interest expense and interest revenue was discussed and illustrated in several prior chapters.

One of the complications created by bond premiums and discounts on long-term investments in bonds comes about because of the treatment of these differences for income tax purposes. Ordinary minor discounts and premiums would be treated as capital gains and losses for income tax purposes in the period when the bonds mature or are sold. Thus the amortization of premiums or discounts for accounting purposes would not be included in computing taxable income. To account for this difference in timing, two income tax allocation adjustments (Chapter 10) are necessary: (1) one half of the amortization in each period is treated as a permanent difference in the deferred tax calculation and (2) one half is treated as a timing difference. The permanent difference represents the half of the capital gain or loss that is not taxed. Treatment of substantial discounts and various accounting options for recording interest revenue for taxation purposes are left to advanced courses. See Exhibit 13–5 for an illustration of the journal entries for deferred taxes on the bond discount amortization.

ACCOUNTING FOR BONDS ILLUSTRATED

To illustrate accounting and reporting for a long-term investment, we will assume that on July 1, 19E, Roth Company purchased $10,000, 8 percent, 10-year bonds in the open market. The bonds were issued originally on July 1,

19A, and mature on June 30, 19J. The 8 percent interest is paid each June 30.[5] Roth Company's annual accounting period ends December 31. The sequence of journal entries made by Roth Company during 19E are illustrated under three different purchase cost assumptions as follows:

	Assumptions	*Exhibits*
1.	Bond investment purchased at par (100)	13–4
2.	Bond investment purchased at a discount (98)	13–5
3.	Bond investment purchased at a premium (102)	13–6

BONDS PURCHASED AT PAR

When bond investors accept a rate of return (i.e., interest) on a bond investment that is the **same** as the stated rate of interest on the bonds, the bonds will sell at par (i.e., at 100). Bonds that sell at par will not have a premium or discount. Exhibit 13–4 illustrates the recording and reporting of an **investment** in bonds purchased at par.

BONDS PURCHASED AT A DISCOUNT

When bond investors demand a rate of interest that is higher than the **stated rate,** bonds will sell in the market at a **discount.** When a bond investment is purchased at a discount, the investor receives back in cash the periodic interest payments stated on the bond plus the maturity value, which is a greater amount than the initial cash invested. A discount increases the interest revenue earned on a bond investment. To illustrate, assume that on July 1, 19E, Roth Company purchased a $10,000, 8 percent bond issued by Baker Company for $9,800 cash. The bond will mature in five years (in 19J). Interest of $10,000 × .08 = $800 will be collected annually.

Although $800 cash is collected each year, the annual revenue **earned** from the investment is $840; the additional $40 is due to amortization of the discount. Analysis of the interest revenue, assuming straight-line amortization, is as follows:

Cash inflows from the investment:		
Annual interest collected, July 1, 19E, through		
June 30, 19J ($10,000 × .08 × 5 years)	$ 4,000	
Collection of bond at maturity date, June 30, 19J	10,000	$14,000
Cash outflow for the investment:		
July 1, 19E—purchase of bond.		9,800
Difference—net increase in cash (the		
total interest earned)		$ 4,200

Revenue from investment per year: $4,200 ÷ 5 years = $840 (assuming straight-line amortization).

---

[5]Bonds usually pay interest semiannually. Annual interest is used in this illustration to reduce the number of repetitive entries. The concepts are applied the same way in either case.

EXHIBIT 13–4
Bonds purchased at par

Situation:

　　On July 1, 19E, Roth Company purchased $10,000, 8 percent, 10-year bonds of Ellsworth Company for cash, $10,000 (i.e., at par). The bonds were issued originally on July 1, 19A, and mature June 30, 19J. Interest is paid each June 30. Roth's accounting period ends December 31.

July 1, 19E, to record purchase of bond investment at par (100):

Long-term investment, bonds of Ellsworth Company............	10,000	
Cash..		10,000

Purchased at par, $10,000 maturity value, 8 percent bonds of Ellsworth Company. (Note: Because the bonds were purchased on an interest date, there was no accrued interest.)

December 31, 19E, adjusting entry at end of the accounting period (and each year through maturity date):

Bond interest receivable	400	
Revenue from investments*.............................		400

Adjusting entry to accrue six months' interest revenue on Ellsworth Company bonds ($10,000 × .08 × 6/12 = $400).

　　*Alternate titles are Interest Revenue and, sometimes, Interest Income.

June 30, 19F, to record annual interest (and each year until maturity):[a]

Cash ($10,000 × .08)	800	
Bond interest receivable (from December 31 entry)		400
Revenue from investments................................		400

Receipt of annual interest payment on the Ellsworth Company bonds.

June 30, 19J, maturity date of the bonds; to record cash received for face (maturity) amount of the bond investment:[b]

Cash..	10,000	
Long-term investment, bonds of Ellsworth Company........		10,000

Retirement of bonds at maturity date (assumes last interest receipt already recorded).

December 31, 19E, Roth Company's **income statement** and **balance sheet** (partial):

Income statement for the year ended December 31, 19E:

Revenue from investments.................................	$　400

Balance sheet at December 31, 19E:

Current assets:	
Bond interest receivable	$　400
Investments and funds:	
Investments in bonds, at cost (market, $10,125).............	10,000

　　Notes:　*a.*　This entry presumes that there was no reversal on January 1, 19F, of the prior adjusting entry. A reversing entry is optional because it serves only to facilitate the subsequent entry (see Chapter 5).

　　　　　　b.　Because the bond investment was purchased at par, there was no premium or discount to be amortized.

Exhibit 13–5 illustrates the recording and reporting of a bond investment purchased at a discount.

When a bond is purchased, it is recorded at its current cash equivalent amount in accordance with the cost principle. Therefore, when a bond investment is purchased at a discount, the investment account balance at the purchase date will be less than par or maturity value. Through **amortization** of the discount, the balance of the investment account must be **increased** each period so that the carrying value will be the same as the par amount on maturity date. Amortization of the discount each period over the **remaining life** of the bond

EXHIBIT 13–5
Bonds purchased at a discount

Situation:
Exactly the situation given in Exhibit 13–4, except that on July 1, 19E, Roth Company purchased $10,000 of bonds of Baker Company for $9,800 (i.e., at 98), rather than at par.

July 1, 19E, to record purchase of bond investment at a discount (98):

Long-term investment, bonds of Baker Company (at cost)......	9,800	
Cash		9,800

Purchased $10,000 maturity value, 8 percent bonds of the Baker Company at 98.

Note: This entry records the investment at its cost; that is, net of any discount or premium. Some accountants prefer to record it at **gross** as follows with the same end result:

Long-term investment	10,000	
Discount on long-term investment		200
Cash..		9,800

December 31, 19E, end of accounting year; to record adjusting entry for interest revenue and amortization of discount on bond investment (and each year until maturity):

Bond interest receivable ($10,000 × .08 × 6/12)	400	
Long-term investment, bonds of Baker Company (amortization: $40 × 6/12).................................	20	
Revenue from investments		420

Adjusting entry to (1) accrue interest revenue for six months and (2) amortize discount on the bond investment for six months (July 1 to December 31); $200 ÷ 5 years = $40 amortization per year.*

June 30, 19F, to record cash interest received and to amortize discount on bond investment (and each year until maturity):

Cash ($10,000 × .08)......................................	800	
Long-term investment, bonds of Baker Company (amortization: $40 × 6/12).................................	20	
Bond interest receivable (from December 31 entry).........		400
Revenue from investments		420

Receipt of annual interest on Baker Company bonds and amortization of discount for six months (January 1 to June 30).

---

*Income tax expense	4	
Deferred income taxes...		4

(1/2 × 20 × .40) Adjustment to record the deferred income taxes on the bond discount amortization assuming a 40 percent tax rate.

This entry could be made each time the interest is accrued or in practice when the deferred income taxes are calculated.

**EXHIBIT 13–5
(concluded)**

June 30, 19J, maturity date; to record cash maturity amount received:

Cash 10,000
    Long-term investment, bonds of Baker Company   10,000
    Retirement of bonds at maturity (assumes last interest receipt
    already recorded).†

December 31, 19E, long-term investment account for 19E–19J:

Long-Term Investment, Bonds of Baker Company

July 1, 19E At acquisition	9,800	June 30, 19J Retirement	10,000
Yearly amortizations by:			
Dec. 31, 19E	20		
31, 19F	40		
31, 19G	40		
31, 19H	40		
31, 19I	40		
June 30, 19J	20		
	10,000		10,000

December 31, 19E, **income statement** and **balance sheet** for year 19E (partial)

Income statement for the year ended December 31, 19E:

Revenue from investments................................... $ 420

Balance Sheet at December 31, 19E:

Current assets:
  Bond interest receivable .... $ 400

Investments and funds:
  Investment in bonds, at amortized cost (market, $10,125) 9,820
Long-term liabilities:
  Deferred income taxes (see * footnote) .... $ 4

†Deferred income taxes 40
  Income taxes payable   40
  (1/2 × 200 × .40 = $40) Adjustment to record the liability for the income tax on the capital gain when the bond matures assuming an income tax rate of 40 percent.

  In practice this entry would be included with the remainder of the deferred income tax items.

also **increases** the amount of interest revenue earned. The amount of discount amortized each period is debited to the investment account and credited to Interest Revenue. The effects of this periodic amortization, over the life of the investment, are (1) to reflect in the investment account the current carrying amount of the bond at the end of each accounting period, and (2) to increase interest revenue earned each year by the amount of the amortization.

To illustrate these effects, in Exhibit 13–5, Roth Company each year must amortize a part of the discount ($10,000 − $9,800 = $200), so that the total discount ($200) will be amortized over the remaining life of the bond investment. Assuming straight-line amortization, the amount of discount amortized each full year will be $200 ÷ 5 years = $40 per year (as illustrated in Exhibit 13–5).

The increase in the balance of the long-term investment account from cost at date of purchase to par value at maturity date which results from the amortization of the bond discount is reflected in the investment ledger account in Roth's accounts shown in Exhibit 13–5.[6] Also shown in Exhibit 13–5 is 19E financial statement information for Roth Company.

BONDS PURCHASED AT A PREMIUM

When bond investors are willing to invest at a rate of interest that is **less** than the **stated rate** of interest on bonds, the bonds will sell at a **premium.** When bonds are purchased at a premium, the investment account is debited for an amount greater than the par or maturity value of the bonds. Therefore, the premium must be **amortized** over the **remaining life** of the bonds as a **decrease** in the balance of the investment account so that the investment account balance will be the par value on maturity date. The amortization parallels the procedure illustrated above for a discount, except that each period the investment account is credited and the premium amortization **decreases** interest revenue.

To illustrate the accounting and reporting where there is a premium, assume that in the preceding example, Roth Company purchased Garden Company bonds on July 1, 19E, for $10,200 cash. The bonds have an 8 percent interest rate and mature in five years from that date, on June 30, 19J. The cash outflow and inflows for this investment, assuming straight-line amortization, may be analyzed to illustrate the effect of the premium on interest revenue as follows:

Cash inflows from the investment:		
Annual interest collected, July 1, 19E, through		
June 30, 19J ($10,000 × .08 × 5 years)	$ 4,000	
June 30, 19E, collection of bond at maturity.	10,000	$14,000
Cash outflow for the investment:		
July 1, 19J—purchase of bond		10,200
Difference—net increase in cash (the total		
interest revenue earned)		$ 3,800

Revenue from investment, per year: $3,800 ÷ 5 years = $760.

Exhibit 13–6 presents the journal entries and financial statements for the investor, Roth Company.

---

[6]Observe that the amortization of discount or premium on bond investments conceptually is the same as the amortization discussed and illustrated in Chapter 11 in the issuer's accounts. Here, we simply are looking at the other side of the transaction. A minor procedural difference may be noted. In Chapter 11, premium or discount was recorded in a separate account; in this chapter, the **net amount** (i.e., the cost) was recorded in the investment account. Either procedure can be used in either situation with the same results. Common practice follows the procedures illustrated in the respective chapters. Tax allocations entries are, however, different because of the various income tax rules associated with the premiums and discount of the issuer.

EXHIBIT 13–6
Bonds purchased at
a premium

Situation:

Exactly the same situation given in Exhibit 13–4, except that on July 1, 19E, Roth Company purchased $10,000 of bonds of Garden Company for $10,200 (i.e., at 102), rather than at par.

July 1, 19E, to record purchase of bond investment at a premium (102):

Long-term investment, bonds of Garden Company (at cost)	10,200	
Cash		10,200
Purchased $10,000 maturity value, 8 percent bonds of Garden Company at 102.		

December 31, 19E, end of accounting year; to record adjusting entry for interest revenue and amortization of premium on bond investment (and each year until maturity):

Bond interest receivable ($10,000 × .08 × 6/12)	400	
Long-term investment, bonds of Garden Company (amortization: $40 × 6/12)		20
Revenue from investments		380
Adjusting entry to (1) accrue interest revenue for six months and (2) amortize premium on the investment for six months (July 1 to December 31); $200 ÷ 5 years = $40 amortization per year.		

June 30, 19F, to record cash interest received and to amortize premium on bond investment (and each year until maturity):

Cash ($10,000 × .08)	800	
Bond interest receivable (per December 31 entry)		400
Long-term investment, bonds of Garden Company (amortization: $40 × 6/12)		20
Revenue from investments		380
Receipt of annual interest revenue on Garden Company bonds and amortization of premium for six months (January 1 to June 30).		

June 30, 19J, maturity date; to record cash maturity amount received:

Cash	10,000	
Long-term investment, bonds of Garden Company		10,000
Retirement of bonds at maturity (assuming the last interest receipt has been recorded).		

December 31, 19E, **income statement** and **balance sheet** for year 19E (partial):

Income statement for year ended December 31, 19E:

Revenue from investments.	$	380

Balance sheet at December 31, 19E:

Current assets:		
Bond interest receivable	$	400
Investments and funds:		
Investment in bonds, at amortized cost (market, $10,225)		10,180

BONDS PURCHASED BETWEEN INTEREST DATES

Investors usually purchase bond investments between the interest dates specified on the bonds. In these situations, the investor must pay the amount of **interest accrued** since the last interest date in addition to the purchase price of the bond. The bond market operates in this fashion because the seller of the bond is entitled to interest from the last interest date to the date of the sale transaction; but on the next interest payment date, the new owner will receive interest for the full period between interest dates, regardless of the purchase date. To illustrate, assume Hays Company purchased a $1,000 bond, 12 percent interest, payable 6 percent each March 31 and September 30. The bond was purchased on June 1, 19F, at 100 plus any accrued interest. The purchase of this bond investment would be recorded by Hays Company as follows:

June 1, 19F:

Long-term investment, 12 percent bond   1,000
Revenue from investments ($1,000 × .12 × 2/12)*   20
    Cash [$1,000 + ($1,000 × .12 × 2/12)]   1,020

Purchase of a $1,000, 12 percent bond as a long-term investment at
100 plus accrued interest for two months, March 31, 19F (last
interest date) to June 1, 19F (date of purchase).

  *Alternatively, an account, Bond Interest Receivable, could have been debited on June 1 for $20
and then credited for that amount on September 30. The net effect would have been the same.
When the end of the accounting period falls between the purchase date and the next interest date,
such a procedure may be less complex.

In the journal entry recorded on June 1, 19F, the long-term investment account was debited for the cost of the investment, which **excludes** the accrued interest. The $20 accrued interest was paid in cash by the purchaser; however, it will be returned to the purchaser at the next interest date, September 30, 19F. At that time, the purchaser will receive the full amount of cash interest for six months, although the purchaser has owned the bond for only four months (i.e., June 1 to September 30, 19F).

The journal entry to record the first interest collection after the purchase would be:

September 30, 19F:

Cash   60
    Revenue from investments   60

After these two entries are posted, the Revenue from Investments account on the books of Hays Company will reflect $40 interest earned for the four months since the purchase as follows:

Revenue from Investments

6/1/19F	20	9/30/19F	60

(balance, $1,000 \times .12 \times 4/12 = \$40$ credit)

SALE OF A BOND INVESTMENT

When bonds are acquired as a long-term investment, they are accounted for with the expectation that they will be held to maturity. This expectation is the basis for amortizing any premium or discount over the period from the date of purchase to the maturity date. Nevertheless, a long-term bond investment may be sold prior to the maturity date. When an investor sells bonds prior to maturity, the difference between the sale price and the balance in the investment account (i.e., the book or carrying value) is recorded as a "Gain (or Loss) on the Sale of Investments."

To illustrate, assume Carson Corporation has two $1,000, 12 percent bonds of Drake Company that are being held as a long-term investment. Each bond was purchased at 104; therefore, the long-term investment account was debited for $2,080. Because of amortization of bond premium to January 1, 19F, the investment account balance is $2,040. On that date one of the bonds was sold at 100. The entry by Carson Company to record the sale would be as follows:

Cash...	1,000	
Loss on sale of investments	20	
Long-term investment, Drake Company bonds		1,020
Sale of long-term investment.		

EFFECTIVE-INTEREST AMORTIZATION ON BOND INVESTMENTS

Effective-interest amortization of the discount or premium on a bond investment is similar to the procedures discussed for bonds payable in Chapter 11. This method of amortization is superior conceptually because it is based on the **effective-interest rate;** therefore, (1) interest revenue is measured correctly each period for income statement purposes, and (2) the carrying amount of the investment is measured correctly for balance sheet purposes at the end of each accounting period. Each interest revenue collection (in cash) is assumed to be part principal and part interest. To illustrate the effective-interest method, assume that on January 1, 19A, Farmer Company purchased a five-year, $10,000, 8 percent bond of Research Corporation as a long-term investment. The purchase price, based on a 12 percent effective-interest rate, was 85.58. Therefore, the cash paid was $8,558 (a $1,442 discount). The bonds carried a stated rate of interest of 8 percent per year, payable each December 31. The acquisition was recorded by Farmer Company as follows:[7]

January 1, 19A:

Long-term investment, Research Corporation bonds		
(maturity amount, $10,000)..	8,558	
Cash...		8,558
Purchase of long-term investment.		

Farmer Company decided to use effective-interest amortization of the discount rather than straight line. The journal entries for a bond investment are the same regardless of the amortization method used, except for some of the **amounts** in the periodic interest entries.

Computation of effective-interest amortization is shown in Exhibit 13–7. Observe that the effective rate of interest of 12 percent, rather than the stated rate of 8 percent, is used to compute the interest revenue amounts.

The first amount column in Exhibit 13–7 reflects the cash inflow each period for interest (at the stated rate). The second column shows the interest revenue amount to be reported on the income statement each period (i.e., the effective

EXHIBIT 13–7
Schedule of effective-interest amortization

Date	Cash interest received each interest date	Interest revenue (based on beginning balance of investment)	Amortization (increase investment)*	Net investment
1/1/19A (acquisition)				8,558
12/31/19A	800	8,558 × .12 = 1,027	227	8,785
12/31/19B	800	8,785 × .12 = 1,054	254	9,039
12/31/19C	800	9,039 × .12 = 1,085	285	9,324
12/31/19D	800	9,324 × .12 = 1,119	319	9,643
12/31/19E	800	9,643 × .12 = 1,157	357	10,000
Totals	4,000	5,442	1,442	

Note: This example is identical to the illustration of the issuer's situation shown in Exhibit 11–8. Computation of the sale price of the bonds at an effective rate of 12 percent is shown in footnote 7.
*Adjusts the net investment balance to the maturity amount.

---

[7]Given the effective rate of 12 percent, the price of the bonds can be determined from a bond table or computed as follows:

$$\$10,000 \times p_{n = 5, i = 12\%} = \$10,000 \times .5674 \text{ (Table 10–2)} \quad \$5,674$$
$$\$800 \times P_{n = 5, i = 12\%} = \quad \$800 \times 3.6048 \text{ (Table 10–4)} = \quad \underline{2,884}$$
$$\text{Bond price } (PV \text{ of future cash flows}) \quad \underline{\$8,558}$$

rate on the net investment). The third column shows the amount of the discount that is amortized (which is the difference between the interest revenue earned and the amount of cash received). The last column shows the carrying value of the investment (i.e., the unamortized principal) that will be reported on the balance sheet at the end of each period under "Investments and funds." The entry for interest revenue each period can be taken directly from the schedule (Exhibit 13–7):

	Year 1	Year 2	Etc.
Cash	800	800	
Long-term investment..................................	227	254	
Revenue from investments	1,027	1,054	

Conceptually, the effective-interest method derives the true interest revenue earned during each period and the correct carrying value of the investment at the end of each period. The straight-line approach provides only approximations of these amounts. Straight-line amortization often is used because it is simple to apply and the different amounts of premium or discount amortized each period are not material. If the difference is not material, the departure from the conceptually superior method is justified by the exception (i.e., materiality) principle of accounting.

DEMONSTRATION CASE

(Try to resolve the requirements before proceeding to the suggested solution that follows.)

Howell Equipment Corporation has been in operation for 18 years. The company sells a major line of farm equipment. In recent years its service department has expanded significantly. Both sales and service operations have been quite profitable. At the beginning of 19S, the company had considerable excess cash. At that time, the management decided to invest in some securities of two of the manufacturers that supply most of the equipment purchased by Howell for resale. The annual accounting period ends on December 31.

This case focuses on the two long-term investments purchased in 19S. One investment was in equity securities, and the other in debt securities. The transactions follow:

19S

a. Jan. 1 Purchased 2,000 common shares of Dear Company at $40 per share. This was 1 percent of the shares outstanding.

b. Aug. 1 Purchased $100,000, 9 percent bonds payable of the Massey Company at 102, plus any accrued interest. The bonds pay semiannual interest each May 31 and November 30. The bonds mature on May 31, 19X (i.e., five years from June 1, 19S). Brokerage fees amounted to $900.

c. Nov. 30 Received semiannual interest on Massey Company bonds. Use straight-line amortization.

d. Dec. 28 Received $4,000 cash dividend on the Dear Company shares.

e. Dec. 31 Adjusting entry for accrued interest on the Massey Company bonds.

f. Dec. 31 The current market price of the Dear shares is $39 and 103 for the Massey bonds.

g. Dec. 31 Closed Revenue from Investments to Income Summary.

Required:

a. Give the journal entry for each of the above transactions.

b. Show how the two investments, the accrued interest receivable and the related revenue, would be reported on the balance sheet and income statement at December 31, 19S.

Suggested solution

Requirement a.

a. January 1, 19S:

Long-term investment, 2,000 common shares of Dear Company	80,000	
Cash......................................		80,000
Purchased 2,000 shares Dear Company common at $40 per share.		

b. August 1, 19S:

Long-term investment, bonds of Massey Company	102,900	
Revenue from investments ($100,000 × .09 × 2/12)	1,500	
Cash....................................		104,400
Purchased $100,000 bonds of the Massey Company.		

Computations:
Cost ($100,000 × 1.02) + $900 = $102,900
Accrued interest for 2 months
$100,000 × .09 × 2/12   =   1,500
Total cash paid......... $104,400

c.   November 30, 19S:

Cash   4,500
   Long-term investment, bonds of Massey
      Company   200
   Revenue from investments   4,300
Computations:
  Semiannual interest: $100,000 × .045 = $4,500
  Amortization of premium:
  $2,900 ÷ 58 months = $50*
    per month; $50 × 4 months   =   200
       Revenue from investments $4,300

*August 1, 19S, to May 31, 19X = 58 months remaining life.

d.   December 28, 19S:

Cash   4,000
   Revenue from investments   4,000
Received dividend on Dear Company common
shares.

e.   December 31, 19S:

Interest receivable   750
   Long-term investment, bonds of Massey Company   50
   Revenue from investments   700
Adjusting entry for accrued interest and premium
amortization for one month on Massey Company
bonds.
Computations:
  Accrued interest receivable:
    $100,000 × .09 × 1/12   = $750
  Amortization of premium:
    $50 × 1 month   =   50
      Revenue from investments . $700

f. December 31, 19S:

> Loss on long-term equity investment............. 2,000
>   Long-term investment – Dear Company
>   common 2,000
> To record LCM on Dear shares:
>   2,000 shares × ($40 − $39) = $2,000.

g. December 31, 19S:

> Revenue from investments...................... 7,500
>   Income summary 7,500
> Closing entry: ($4,300 − $1,500 + $4,000 + $700
> = $7,500).

Requirement b.

HOWELL EQUIPMENT CORPORATION
Balance Sheet (partial)
At December 31, 19S

Current assets:
  Interest receivable .... $ 750
Investments and funds:
  2,000 shares of Dear Company, at LCM
    (cost, $80,000)................................ $ 78,000*
  Bonds of Massey Company, at amortized cost
    ($100,000 maturity value; market, $103,000)...... 102,650†   180,650
    *Cost of equity securities.................   80,000

  Less: Write-down to reduce long-term
    equity investment to LCM.............   2,000
  Equity investment at LCM.............. $ 78,000

  †Cost of debt securities................. $102,900
  Less: Amortization of premium
    ($200 + $50).........................   250
  Debt investment at amortized cost $102,650

HOWELL EQUIPMENT CORPORATION
Income Statement (partial)
For the Year Ending December 31, 19S

Revenue from investments .... $ 7,500
Loss on write-down of long-term
  investment to market .... $(2,000)

SUMMARY OF CHAPTER

This chapter discussed the measuring and reporting of two types of long-term investments: the capital stock (equity securities) and the bonds (debt securities) of another company. An entity (investor) may acquire a part or all of the outstanding capital stock of a corporation by **purchase** of its shares or, if the investor is a corporation, by **exchange** of its own shares for shares in the other company. The measuring and reporting of long-term investments in shares of capital stock of another company are determined by the percent of shares owned in relation to the total number of shares outstanding.

If the ownership level of **voting** shares is less than 20 percent, or if the ownership is of nonvoting shares, the **cost method** must be used. Under this method, the investment amount reported by the investor company is the lower of cost or market, and investment revenue is recognized on the basis of dividends declared by the investee corporation.

If the ownership is at least 20 percent but not more than 50 percent, the **equity method** must be used. Under this method, the investment is recorded at cost by the investor company at date of acquisition. Each period thereafter, the investment amount is increased (or decreased) by the proportionate interest in the income (or loss) reported by the investee corporation and decreased by the proportionate share of the dividends declared by the investee corporation. Each period, the investor company recognizes as revenue its proportionate share of the income (or loss) reported by the investee company.

When there is a controlling interest—that is, more than 50 percent ownership of the outstanding vote shares is held by the investor—the financial statements of the affiliated companies (investor and investee) are **consolidated.** This subject is discussed in Chapter 14.

An entity may purchase the bonds (i.e., debt securities) of another entity as a long-term investment. In contrast to capital stock, bonds are a liability of the issuing company; therefore, bonds (1) have a specified maturity date and maturity amount, (2) require the payment of a stated rate of interest at regular specified interest dates, and (3) do not convey voting privileges. At the date of purchase, a long-term investment in bonds is recorded at cost, which may be at par, at a discount, or at a premium. When purchased at a premium or a discount, amortization of such premium or discount over the **remaining life** of the bonds is required. The periodic amortization adjusts (1) the investment amount to a carrying value which is reported on the balance sheet and (2) the interest revenue which is reported on the income statement.

IMPORTANT TERMS DEFINED IN THIS CHAPTER

Terms (alphabetically)	Key words in definitions of important terms used in chapter	Page reference
Control	The ability of an investor to determine the operating and financing policies of another company (the investee).	688
Cost method	Method used by investor if less than 20 percent of the voting shares of the investee company is owned by the investor.	688

Terms (alphabetically)	Key words in definitions of important terms used in chapter	Page reference
Discount	A bond that is purchased for less than par value is purchased at a discount; the difference between cost and par of a bond.	699
Effective interest	The real or true rate of interest; also called the market rate of interest.	706
Equity method	Method used by investor if 20–50 percent of the voting shares of the investee company is owned by the investor.	692
Premium	A bond that is purchased for more than par value is purchased at a premium; the difference between cost and par of a bond.	703
Significant influence	The ability of an investor to have an important impact on the operating and financing policies of another company (the investee).	688
Stated interest rate	The annual rate of cash interest specified in the bond contract.	696

QUESTIONS FOR DISCUSSION

Part A

1. Explain the difference between a short-term investment and a long-term investment.

2. Match the following:

   Measurement method
   _____ Cost method.
   _____ Equity method.
   _____ Consolidation.

   Level of ownership of the voting capital stock
   a. More than 50 percent ownership.
   b. Less than 20 percent ownership.
   c. At least 20 percent but not more than 50 percent.

3. Explain the application of the cost principle to the purchase of shares of capital stock in another company.

4. Under the cost method, when and how is revenue measured by the investor company?

5. Under the equity method, why is revenue measured on a proportionate basis by the investor company when income is reported by the other company, rather than when dividends are declared?

6. Under the equity method, dividends received from the investee company are not recorded as revenue. To record dividends as revenue would involve double counting. Explain.

7. Match the following items that relate to the long-term investment amount reported on the balance sheet of the investor company:

   Measurement method
   _____ Cost method.
   _____ Equity method.

   Explanation of balance in the investment account
   a. LCM.
   b. Original cost plus proportionate part of the income of the investee, less proportionate part of the dividends declared by investee.

8.   Why might the lower of cost or market rule in accounting for long-term investments require that the decline of market below cost to be permanent (nontemporary) to justify a write-down to market when for temporary investments such a requirement is not required?

9.   What income statement classifications could be used to disclose the gain or loss from the sale or write-down of a long-term investment? Why?

10. The equity method of valuing investments is neither cost nor market. How can such an exceptional valuation be justified when no other asset seems to use such a hybrid approach?

11. How would you justify the portfolio approach to the application of lower of cost or market to long-term investments over the individual security approach?

Part B

12. Explain the difference between an equity security and a debt security.

13. Explain why interest revenue must be accrued on a long-term investment in bonds but not on a long-term investment in capital stock.

14. Under what conditions will a bond sell at (a) par, (b) a discount, and (c) a premium?

15. Distinguish between a long-term investment in bonds and a long-term investment in the capital stock of another company.

16. Why is it necessary to amortize premium or discount that arises from the purchase of a long-term bond investment above or below par? Over what period should the premium or discount be amortized?

17. When a bond investment is purchased between interest dates, the purchaser must pay accrued interest plus the purchase price of the bond. Explain why the accrued interest must be paid.

EXERCISES

Part A

E13–1.   Company P purchased a certain number of the outstanding voting shares of Company S at $15 per share as a long-term investment. Company S had outstanding 10,000 shares of nopar value. On a separate sheet complete the following matrix relating to the measurement and reporting by Company P after acquisition of the shares of Company S.

Questions	Method of Measurement	
	Cost Method	Equity Method
a. What is the applicable level of ownership by Company P of Company S to apply the method?	Percent	Percent

For (b), (e), (f), and (g) that follow, assume:
    Number of shares acquired of Company S
    Net income reported by Company S in the first year
    Dividends declared by Company S in the first year
    Market price at end of first year, Company S shares, $13.50
	1,000
	$40,000
	$10,000
		3,000
		$40,000
		$10,000

b. At acquisition, the investment account on the books of Company P should be debited at what amount?	$	$
c. On what basis should Company P recognize revenue earned on the shares of Company S? Explanation required.		
d. After acquisition date, on what basis should Company P change the balance of investment account in respect to the shares of Company S owned (other than for disposal of the investment)? Explanation required.		
e. What would be the balance in the investment account on the books of Company P at the end of the first year?	$	$
f. What amount of revenue from the investment in Company S should Company P report at the end of the first year?	$	$
g. What amount of loss should Company P report at the end of the first year?	$	$

E13–2. During 19B, Adams Company acquired some of the 60,000 shares of the common stock, par $10, of Cox Corporation as a long-term investment. The accounting period for both companies ends December 31. The following transactions occurred:

19B
July   2   Purchased 6,000 shares of Cox common at $20 per share.
Dec. 31   Received a copy of the 19B annual financial statement of Cox Corporation that reflected net income of $40,000.
       31   Cox Corporation declared and paid a cash dividend of $.50 per share.
       31   Market price of Cox shares was $19 per share.

Required:

a. What accounting method should Adams Company use? Why?
b. Give the required journal entries by Adams Company for each transaction. If no entry is required, explain why.
c. Show how the long-term investment and the related revenue (loss) should be reported on the 19B financial statements of Adams Company.

E13–3. Black Company acquired some of the 40,000 shares of outstanding common (nopar) of Noe Corporation during 19E as a long-term investment. The annual accounting period for both companies ends December 31. The following transactions occurred during 19E:

19E
Jan. 10   Purchased 16,000 shares of Noe at $30 per share.
Dec. 31   Received the 19E financial statement of Noe Corporation which reported net income of $70,000.
    31   Noe Corporation declared and paid a cash dividend of $1.25 per share.
    31   Market price of Noe shares was $28 per share.

Required:

a.   What method of accounting should Black Company use? Why?
b.   Give the journal entries by Black Company for each of the above transactions. State if no entry is required and explain why.
c.   Show how the long-term investment and the related revenue (loss) should be reported on the 19E financial statements of Black Company.

E13–4. During 19H, Ross Company purchased some of the 100,000 shares of common stock, par $10, of Salt Marine, Inc., as a long-term investment. The annual accounting period for each company ends December 31. The following transactions occurred during 19H.

19H

Jan. 7   Purchased 15,000 shares of Salt common at $15 per share.
Dec. 31   Received the 19H financial statement of Salt Marine, which reported net income of $70,000.
    31   Salt declared and paid a cash dividend of $1.10 per share.
    31   Market price of Salt shares was $17.50 per share.

Required:

a.   What method of accounting should Ross Company use? Why?
b.   Give the journal entries for Ross Company for each of the above transactions. State if no entry is required and explain why.
c.   Show how the long-term investment and the related revenue (Loss) should be reported on the 19H financial statements of Ross Company.

E13–5. You are to use the same situation for Ross Company and the data given in Exercise 13–4, **except** for the January 7, 19H, transaction. Assume it was as follows:

19H
Jan. 7   Purchased 30,000 shares of Salt at $15 per share.

(The data for December 31 are unchanged.)

Required:

a.   What method of accounting should Ross Company use? Why?
b.   Give the journal entries for Ross Company for each transaction (refer also to transactions given in Exercise 13–4). State if no entry is required and explain why.
c.   Show how the long-term investment and the related revenue should be reported on the 19H financial statements of Ross Company.

Part B

E13–6. On July 1, 19A, AB Company purchased at par a $10,000, 9 percent, 20-year bond of CD Corporation as a long-term investment. The annual bond interest is payable each year on June 30. The accounting period for AB Company ends December 31. At the date of purchase, the bond had five years remaining before maturity.

Required:

Give the journal entries on the books of AB Company for the following transactions:

a. July 1, 19A, for acquisition.
b. December 31, 19A, adjusting entry at the end of the accounting period.
c. June 30, 19B, collection of first interest.
d. Maturity date of the bond, June 30, 19F.

E13–7. On April 1, 19A, Nash Company purchased at par eight, $1,000, 9 percent, 10-year bonds of HI Corporation as a long-term investment. The bond interest is payable semi-annually each March 31 and September 30. The accounting period for Nash Company ends on December 31. At the date of purchase, the bonds had six years remaining to maturity.

Required:

Give the journal entry for each of the following dates in the accounts of Nash Company in respect to the long-term investment: April 1, 19A; September 30, 19A; December 31, 19A; March 31, 19B; and the maturity date.

E13–8. On February 1, 19A, H Company purchased at par a $15,000, 10 percent, 20-year bond of Lam Corporation as a long-term investment. The bond interest is payable semi-annually each January 31, and July 31. The accounting period for H Company ends December 31. At the date of purchase, the bonds had four years remaining to maturity.

Required:

Give all journal entries required in the accounts of H Company for the period February 1, 19A, through January 31, 19B, and on the maturity date.

E13–9. On July 1, 19B, Ray Company purchased three different bonds as long-term investments. Data with respect to the three bonds and the purchase prices were:

Bond designation	Par of bond	Annual interest	Payable semiannually	Remaining years to maturity	Market purchase price*
A......	$1,000	10%	Dec. 31 and	5	$1,000
B......	1,000	9	June 30	5	970
C......	1,000	12	each year	5	1,020

*These amounts do not include any accrued interest.

Required:

a. Give the journal entries to record separately the purchase of each bond.
b. Give the journal entries to record separately collection of interest on the first interest date after purchase. Use straight-line amortization of any discount or premium.
c. Give the journal entries to record separately the maturity of each bond.

E13–10. On May 1, 19B, Delta Company purchased $9,000 maturity value bonds of Opel Corporation at 96.25 (plus any accrued interest) as a long-term investment. The bond interest rate is 12 percent per annum payable 6 percent each April 30 and October 31. The bonds mature in four years from May 1, 19B.

Required:

a. Give the journal entries for Delta Company on May 1, 19B; October 31, 19B; and December 31, 19B (adjusting entry for accrued interest). Use straight-line amortization and round all amounts to the nearest dollar.

b. Show how this long-term investment and the related revenue should be shown on the December 31, 19B, annual financial statements of Delta Company. (Hint: Include the investment, interest receivable, and any revenue.)

E13–11. On May 1, 19B, Kent Company purchased $10,000, 8 percent bonds of Cook Corporation, at 106 (plus any accrued interest) as a long-term investment. The bonds pay interest each April 30 and October 31. The bonds mature in five years on April 30, 19G.

Required:

a. Give the journal entries for Kent Company on May 1, 19B; October 31, 19B; and December 31, 19B (adjusting entry for accrued interest). Use straight-line amortization and round to the nearest dollar.

b. Show how this long-term investment should be shown on the December 31, 19B, annual financial statements of Kent Company.

E13–12. On March 1, 19B, Star Corporation purchased $6,000, 10 percent bonds of TU Corporation as a long-term investment. The bonds pay interest each June 30 and December 31. The bonds mature in 10 years on December 31, 19K. The purchase price was $6,236, plus any accrued interest.

Required:

a. Give the journal entry by Star Corporation to record the purchase on March 1, 19B.

b. Give the journal entry to record the interest received on June 30 and December 31, 19B. Use straight-line amortization.

c. What was the amount of interest revenue in 19B? At what amount should the bond investment be reported on the balance sheet at December 31, 19B?

E13–13. On January 1, 19A, Cotton Company purchased, as a long-term investment, a $3,000 bond of Devons Company for $2,922 (plus any accrued interest). The bond has a stated interest rate of 7 percent, payable each January 1. The bond matures in three years on December 31, 19C. Cotton Company uses effective-interest amortization. As a consequence, the amortization table given below was developed.

Date	Cash inflow	Interest revenue	Investment change	Investment balance
January 1, 19A				$2,922
End year 19A	$210	$234	$24	2,946
End year 19B	210	236	26	2,972
End year 19C	210	238	28	3,000

Required:

Respond to the following questions:

a. How much was the discount or premium?

b. What was the total cash outflow and the total cash inflow over the life of this investment? What does the difference represent? Explain.

c. How much interest revenue should be recognized on the income statement each year and in total?

d. What amounts should be reported on the balance sheet each year? For the last year give the amounts just prior to collection of the maturity amount.

e. What was the effective rate of interest per year? Show computations.

f. Show how the four different amounts that are listed on the line 19B were computed.

g. Show how the price of the bond of $2,922 was computed.

E13–14.   On January 1, 19A, Indian Company purchased, as a long-term investment, a $10,000 par value, 12 percent bond issued by Jackson Corporation. The bond pays interest each year on December 31 and has five years' remaining life to maturity from January 1, 19A. The accounting period for Indian Corporation ends December 31.

The bond was purchased to yield a 10 percent effective rate of interest; therefore, the price of the bond was computed as follows:

$$\$10,000 \times p_{n=5;\ i=10\%}\ (.6209) = \$\ 6,209$$
$$\$1,200 \times P_{n=5;i=10\%}\ (3.7908) = \underline{\ \ 4,549}$$
$$\text{Sales price} \ldots\ldots\ldots\ldots \underline{\$10,758}$$

Required:

a. Give the journal entry for Indian Company to record the purchase of the bond on January 1, 19A.

b. Prepare a schedule of effective-interest amortization similar to Exhibit 13–7.

c. Give the journal entries for the collection of interest on the bond investment during 19A and 19B.

d. Complete the following schedule (show computations):

	December 31	
	19A	19B
Income statement:		
Revenue from bond investment.....	$_____	$_____
Balance sheet:		
Bond interest receivable............	_____	_____
Long-term investment, bond of		
Jackson Corporation	_____	_____

PROBLEMS/CASES

Part A

PC13–1.   During January 19A, Seven Company purchased 10,000 shares of the 100,000 outstanding common shares (nopar value) of Eight Corporation at $40 per share. This block of shares was purchased as a long-term investment. Assume the accounting period for each company ends December 31.

Subsequent to acquisition, the following data were available:

	19A	19B
Income reported by Eight Corporation at December 31	$60,000	$70,000
Cash dividends declared and paid by Eight Corporation during the year	20,000	30,000
Market price per share of Eight common stock on December 31................................	37	38

Required:

a. What accounting method should be used by Seven Company? Why?

b. Give the journal entries required in the accounts of Seven Company for each year (use parallel columns) for the following (if none, explain why):
   (1) Acquisition of Eight Corporation stock.
   (2) Net income reported by Eight Corporation.
   (3) Dividends received from Eight Corporation.
   (4) Market value effects at year-end.

c. Show how the following amounts should be reported on the financial statements for Seven Company for each year:
   (1) Long-term investment.
   (2) Loss.
   (3) Revenues.

PC13–2. During January 19A, Doe Corporation purchased the shares listed below as a long-term investment:

		Number of shares		
Corporation	*Stock*	*Out-standing*	*Purchased*	*Cost per share*
M......	Common (nonpar)	80,000	12,000	$10
P......	Preferred, nonvoting (par $10)	10,000	4,000	15

Assume the accounting period of each company ends on December 31. Subsequent to acquisition, the following data were available:

	19A	19B
Net income reported at December 31:		
Corporation M..........................	$20,000	$22,000
Corporation P...........................	30,000	31,000
Dividends declared and paid per share during the year:		
Corporation M common stock	$ 1.00	$ 1.10
Corporation P preferred stock	.20	.20
Market value per share at December 31:		
Corporation M common stock	8.00	9.00
Corporation P common stock..............	16.00	15.00

Required:

a. What accounting method should be used by Doe for the M common stock? P preferred stock? Why?

b. Give the journal entries for Doe Corporation for each year in parallel columns (if none, state why) for each of the following:
   (1) Purchase of the investments.
   (2) Income reported by Corporations M and P.

(3) Dividends received from Corporations M and P.

(4) Market value effects at year-end.

c. For each year, show how the following amounts should be reported on the financial statements for 19A:

(1) Long-term investment.

(2) Revenue (loss).

PC13–3. Company S had outstanding 20,000 shares of common stock, par value $10 per share. On January 1, 19B, Company P purchased some of these shares at $20 per share. At the end of 19B, Company S reported the following: income, $40,000; and cash dividends declared and paid during the year, $10,000. The market value of Company S shares at the end of 19B was $15 per share.

Required:

a. For each case given below (in the tabulation), identify the method of accounting that should be used by Company P. Explain why.

b. Give the journal entries required of Company P at the dates indicated below for each of the two independent cases. If no entry is required, so indicate and explain. Use the following format:

Tabulation of items	*Case A—2,000 shares purchased*	*Case B—8,000 shares purchased*
1. Entry to record the acquisition at January 1, 19B.	_____	_____
2. Entry to recognize the income reported by Company S for 19B.	_____	_____
3. Entry to recognize the dividends declared and paid by Company S for 19B.	_____	_____
4. Entry to recognize market value effect at end of 19B.	_____	_____

c. Complete the following schedule to show the separate amounts that should be reported on the 19B financial statements of Company P.

	Dollar amounts	
	Case A	*Case B*
Balance sheet:		
Investments and funds	_____	_____
Income statement:		
Revenue (loss) from investments	_____	_____

d. Explain why assets and revenues are different between the two cases.

PC13–4. Fortner Company purchased, as a long-term investment, some of the 100,000 shares of the outstanding common stock of Towns Corporation. The annual accounting period for each company ends December 31. The following transactions occurred during 19E.

19E

Jan. 10 Purchased common shares of Towns at $11 per share as follows:

Case A—10,000 shares.

Case B—30,000 shares.

Dec. 31   Received the 19E financial statements of Towns Corporation; the reported net income was $70,000.

    31   Received a cash dividend of $.30 per share from Towns Corporation.

    31   Market price of Towns shares, $8 per share.

Required:

a.   For each case, what accounting method should be used by Fortner? Explain why.

b.   Give the journal entries for Fortner Company for each case for the above transactions. State if no entry is required and explain why. (Hint: You can save time by using parallel columns for Case A and Case B.)

c.   Give the amounts for each case that should be reported on the 19E financial statements of Fortner Corporation. Use the following format:

	Case A	Case B
Balance sheet (partial):		
Investments and funds:		
Investment in common shares, Towns Corporation	_____	_____
Income statement (partial):		
Revenue (Loss) from investments	_____	_____

PC13–5.   Sub Corporation had outstanding 200,000 shares of nopar common. On January 10, 19B, Par Company purchased a block of these shares in the open market at $20 per share. At the end of 19B, Sub Corporation reported net income of $200,000 and cash dividends of $.30 per share. At December 31, 19B, the Sub stock was selling at $19.50 per share. This problem involves two separate cases:

Case A—Par Company purchased 30,000 shares of Sub common.

Case B—Par Company purchased 60,000 shares of Sub common.

Required:

a.   For each case, what accounting method should be used by Par Company? Explain why.

b.   For each case, give, in parallel columns, the journal entries of Par Company for each of the following (if no entry is required, explain why):

    (1)   Acquisition

    (2)   Revenue recognition.

    (3)   Dividends received.

    (4)   Market value effects.

c.   For each case, show how the following should be reported on the 19B financial statements of Par Company:

    (1)   Long-term investments.

    (2)   Market effects.

    (3)   Revenue.

d.   Explain why the amounts reported (in Requirement [c]) are different between the two cases.

PC13–6.   On January 1, 19B, Emerson Company purchased 40 percent of the outstanding common shares of Reed Corporation at a total cost of $780,000. On December 31, 19B, the investment in Reed Corporation was reported by Emerson as $950,000 but Emerson did not purchase any additional Reed shares. Emerson Company received $120,000 in cash dividends from Reed. The dividends were declared and paid during 19B. Emerson used the equity method to account for its investment in Reed. The market price of Reed shares increased during 19B.

Required:

a. Explain why the investment account balance increased from $780,000 to $950,000 during 19B.
b. What amount of revenue from the Reed investment was reported by Emerson during 19B?
c. If Emerson used the cost method, what amount of revenue from the Reed investment should have been reported in 19B?
d. If Emerson used the cost method, what amount should be reported as the investment in Reed Corporation on the December 31, 19B, Emerson Company balance sheet?

Part B

PC13–7. On January 1, 19B, Ace Company purchased $60,000, 10 percent bonds of Bye Company as a long-term investment, at 100 (plus any accrued interest). Interest is payable annually on December 31. The bonds have six years to maturity from December 31, 19A. The annual accounting period for Ace Company ends December 31. In addition, on January 2, 19B, Ace Company purchased in the market 5 percent of the 10,000 shares of outstanding common stock of Bye Company at $30 per share.

Required:

a. Give the journal entry by Ace Company to record the purchase of the bonds on January 1, 19B.
b. Give the journal entry to record the purchase of the common shares on January 2, 19B.
c. Give the journal entry assuming a cash dividend of $2.50 per share was declared and received on the Bye shares on December 28, 19B.
d. Give the journal entry for the receipt of the interest on the Bye bonds on December 31, 19B.
e. Show how the long-term investments and the related revenue should be reported on the 19B annual financial statements of Ace Company. Market price of Bye shares was $31 at the end of 19B.

PC13–8. On May 1, 19B, Sun Company purchased $30,000, 8 percent bonds of Taylor Company, as a long-term investment. The interest is payable each April 30 and October 31. The bonds have four years to maturity from May 1, 19B. The bonds were purchased at 96 (plus any accrued interest). In addition, brokerage fees of $240 were paid by Sun Company.

Required:

a. Give the 19B journal entries of Sun Company on the following dates:

May 1 Purchase.
Oct. 31 First interest date. Use straight-line amortization.
Dec. 31 Adjusting entry for accrued interest at the end of the annual accounting period.

b. Show how the investment, interest receivable, and related revenue should be reported on the 19B annual financial statements of Sun Company.

c. Give the journal entry at the maturity date of the bonds.

PC13–9. On June 1, 19B, Fry Company purchased $30,000, 12 percent bonds of Gray Company, as a long-term investment. The interest is payable each April 30 and October 31. The bonds have five years to maturity from the issue date, May 1, 19B. The bonds were purchased at 103 (plus any accrued interest). In addition, Fry Company paid brokerage fees of $280. The annual accounting period for Fry Company ends December 31.

Required:

a. Give the journal entries for Fry Company on the following dates:

    June 1   Purchase plus any accrued interest.
    Oct. 31   First interest date. Use straight-line amortization.
    Dec. 31   Adjusting entry for accrued interest.

b. Show how the investment, interest receivable, and related revenue should be reported on the 19B annual financial statements of Fry Company.

c. Give the journal entry at the maturity date of the bonds, April 30, 19G.

PC13–10. During 19A, Akers Company purchased the following bonds of Pounds Corporation as a long-term investment:

	Series A	Series B	Series C	Series D
Maturity amount	$10,000	$10,000	$10,000	$10,000
Date purchased............	7/1/19A	7/1/19A	7/1/19A	9/1/19A
Interest per annum	8%	7%	9%	9%
Interest dates, annual......	June 30	June 30	June 30	June 30
Maturity date	6/30/19F	6/30/19F	6/30/19F	6/30/19F
Purchase price*............	100	95	106	100

          *Plus any accrued interest.

Required:

a. Give the journal entries to record separately the purchase of the long-term investments.

b. Give the adjusting entries of Akers Company for December 31, 19A, assuming this is the end of the accounting period. Give a separate journal entry for each series. Use straight-line amortization.

c. Give the journal entry of Akers Company for each separate series that should be made on June 30, 19B, for collection of the first interest payment.

d. Complete the following schedule to show the amounts that should be reported on the 19A financial statements (show each series separately):

        Income statement (19A):
          Revenue from investments .... $_____

        Balance sheet (at December 31, 19A):
          Long-term investment, bonds of Pounds Corporation $_____

PC13–11. On January 1, 19A, Evans Corporation purchased, as a long-term investment, a bond of Fable Corporation. The following schedule was prepared based on the investment (table captions have been omitted intentionally):

January 1, 19A				$10,339
End year 19A	$800	$724	$76	10,263
End year 19B	800	718	82	10,181
End year 19C	800	713	87	10,094
End year 19D	800	706	94	10,000

Required:

Respond to the following questions in respect to the investment by Evans Corporation:

a. What was the maturity amount of the bond?
b. What was the acquisition price of the investment?
c. Give the journal entry that Evans Corporation should make at acquisition date.
d. Was the bond acquired at a premium or discount? How much?
e. What was the stated rate of interest per year? Show computations.
f. What method of amortization apparently will be used? Explain.
g. What was the effective rate of interest?
h. What were the total cash inflow and total cash outflow on the investment? What does the difference represent? Explain.
i. How much interest revenue should be reported each period on the income statement? How does this amount relate to the difference in *(h)*?
j. What amount will be reported on the balance sheet at the end of each year? (Show the amount for year 19D just prior to collection of the maturity amount.)
k. How were the amounts in each of the four columns of the above schedule computed? Use year 19B to demonstrate the computations.
l. Why is the method of amortization being used conceptually preferable?

PC13–12. On January 1, 19A, Austin Corporation purchased $50,000, 9 percent bonds of Hamilton Company to yield an effective rate of 10 percent. The bonds pay the interest on June 30 and December 31 and will mature on December 31, 19C.

This long-term investment was recorded by Austin Corporation as follows:

January 1, 19A:

Long-term investment, Hamilton Company bonds.................	48,730	
Cash		48,730

Computations:
Principal—$50,000 × $p_{n=6;i=5\%}$ (.7462) = $37,310
Interest—$2,250 × $P_{n=6;i=5\%}$ (5.0757) = 11,420
Bond price $48,730

Required:

a. What were the stated and effective rates of interest?
b. What was the amount of the discount or premium? What would be the amount of discount or premium amortization each interest period assuming straight-line amortization?
c. Prepare a schedule of effective-interest amortization similar to Exhibit 13–7.
d. Give the journal entries to record interest (including amortization) on June 30 and December 31, 19A, assuming (1) straight-line and (2) effective-interest amortization.
e. Explain when it is appropriate to use each method of amortization.

PC13–13. Your client, ABC Ltd., owns 15 percent of the shares of Y Co. Ltd. The 1985 pretax net income of ABC Ltd. is $1,000,000 and its shareholders' equity is $3,000,000.

The investment in Y Co. Ltd. is carried on the balance sheet of ABC Ltd. (as of December 31, 1985) at $250,000, which represents original cost. Y Co. Ltd. has incurred significant losses in the past few years. A current appraisal by a qualified business evaluator indicates that the current market value of 100 percent of the issued and outstanding shares of Y Co. Ltd. is $1,000,000. You are also aware that an investor who held 20 percent of the shares of Y Co. Ltd. recently sold those shares for $180,000.

Your client, ABC Ltd., insists that the shares be shown at their original cost of $250,000 but is willing to expand note disclosure.

Required:

In the situations above:

a. Outline, with reasons, possible deviations (if any) from generally accepted accounting principles. State your assumptions.
b. Outline the minimum note disclosure which you consider adequate in the circumstances. What additional disclosure would be desirable?   (CICA Adapted)

PC13–14. The following questions concern the 1984 financial statement of Consolidated-Bathurst Inc. presented in Supplement B at end of book.

a. How does C–B value its long-term investments?
b. What justification would likely be given for the valuation of Sceptic Resources Limited?
c. What is the smallest percentage ownership held by C–B for investments classified as Equity investments?
d. What was the percentage of revenue earned (called Equity earnings) based on year-end values for the equity investments held by C–B?
e. Assuming all revenue classified as income from investments and short-term deposits was from the portfolio investments, what percentage did C–B earn of the year-end 1984: (a) carrying value, (b) market value?

14

Consolidated Statements—Measuring and Reporting

PURPOSE OF THIS CHAPTER

The preceding chapter discussed long-term investments in equity securities when one company owns 50 percent or less of the outstanding voting shares of another corporation. This chapter discusses those situations in which there is a controlling interest evidenced by ownership of more than 50 percent of the outstanding voting shares of another corporation. Prior to studying this chapter you should review Chapter 13.

Basically, when a company has a controlling interest in another company, the financial statements for each company often will be combined into a single set of financial statements by an accounting process called **consolidation.** Those persons who do not plan to study accounting beyond the introductory level need a general background in order to understand and evaluate the economic and accounting implications of business combinations. In most business courses, financial statements are encountered in various situations, and most of them will be consolidated statements. Outside the classroom, you frequently will encounter consolidated statements. For those persons who plan to study accounting further, this background will help you understand the broad issues, measurement approaches, and underlying concepts of consolidated statements. This chapter has as its primary objective the presentation of the basic issues associated with consolidated financial statements.

This chapter discusses the preparation, interpretation, and use of consolidated financial statements. Measuring approaches and reporting on a consolidated basis are accorded primary attention. The important differences that result between two alternative approaches for accounting for a combination (pooling of interests and a combination by purchase) are identified and discussed.

To accomplish the broad purpose of this chapter, two parts and two supplements are presented:

Part A—Acquiring a controlling interest

Part B—Reporting consolidated operations after acquisition

Supplement 14A—Consolidation procedures—100 percent ownership

Supplement 14B—Consolidation procedures—less than 100 percent ownership

Part A—Acquiring a Controlling Interest

CRITERIA FOR CONSOLIDATED FINANCIAL STATEMENTS

When an investor company owns more than 50 percent of the outstanding voting shares of another corporation, a **parent** and **subsidiary** relationship is said to exist. The investing corporation is known as the parent company, and the other corporation is called a subsidiary. Both corporations continue as **separate legal entities.** Each company has its own accounting system, and each prepares its own financial statements. However, because of their special relationship, they are viewed as a **single economic entity** for financial measuring and reporting purposes. Because the parent and subsidiary are viewed as a single economic entity, the parent company (but not the subsidiary) is required to prepare **consolidated financial statements.** The individual financial statements of the parent and each of its subsidiaries are combined by the parent company into one overall or consolidated set of financial statements, as if there were only one entity. The four statements—balance sheet, income statement, statement of retained earnings, and statement of changes in financial position—are consolidated by the parent company.

There are a number of operating, economic, and legal advantages to the parent-subsidiary relationship. As a consequence, most large corporations, and many medium-sized corporations, have a controlling interest in one or more other corporations.

Consolidated financial statements are prepared in situations in which two basic elements are present. The two basic elements are control and accounting compatibility.

Control is presumed to exist when more than 50 percent of the outstanding voting shares of an entity is owned by one investor. The nonvoting shares are not included in the determination of control because it does not provide the investor with any ability to control the policies of the subsidiary. In special circumstances, effective control may not exist, even though more than 50 percent of the voting shares is owned. This situation may exist when the subsidiary is located in a foreign country where **governmental restrictions** prevent the parent company from exercising meaningful control regardless of the number of voting shares owned by the parent company. In circumstances where control is lacking, consolidated statements are inappropriate. Another situation where control can be seriously impaired would be where the subsidiary (50 percent or more owned) has severe financial difficulties. In both these situations, the cost method discussed in Chapter 13 would be used.

Accounting compatibility means that the operations of the affiliated companies are related so that one complements the other. For example, the operations of an automobile manufacturer (such as General Motors) would be compatible with the operations of a company that manufactures spark plugs. On the other hand, a manufacturing company and a bank or insurance company lack compatibility and should not be consolidated because of the specific accounting rules used by the bank or insurance company. The equity method would be appropriate.

Consolidated statements are not prepared when one company owns more than 50 percent of the voting shares of another company, but the company lacks either (a) meaningful control or (b) accounting compatibility with the other company. In such situations, the investment in the subsidiary is reported as a long-term investment on the balance sheet of the parent as "Investment in unconsolidated subsidiary." The investment is accounted for under the **equity method** as discussed in Chapter 13 and is not consolidated.

Consolidated statements affect only the **reporting** by the parent company of the financial results of the parent and its subsidiaries. The accounting for each subsidiary company is unaffected. The fact that a parent company owns a controlling interest has no affect on the accounting and reporting by a subsidiary. At the end of the accounting period, the subsidiary prepares its own financial statements. Similarly, the parent company carries out the accounting for its own operations in the normal manner and prepares its own financial statements at the end of each period.

When consolidation is appropriate, the financial statements of the parent and the subsidiaries, prepared in the normal manner, are combined by the parent company on an **item-by-item basis** to develop the parent's consolidated financial statements. Thus, the consolidated statement concept does not affect the recording of transactions by the parent and the subsidiaries but affects only the **reporting phase** of the combined entity represented by the parent company and its subsidiaries.

METHODS OF ACQUIRING A CONTROLLING INTEREST

One corporation may acquire a controlling interest in another corporation either (a) by creating a new corporation and **retaining** more than 50 percent of the voting shares of the new entity or (b) by **acquiring** more than 50 percent of the outstanding voting shares of an existing corporation. Both approaches of acquiring a controlling interest are used. A parent company may acquire the voting capital stock of a subsidiary in either of the two ways that follow:[1]

1. **Exchanging shares of parent company voting shares for more than 50 percent of the outstanding voting capital stock of the subsidiary (owned by the shareholders of the subsidiary)**—If certain additional criteria are met, this type of acquisition is called a **pooling of interests.** In this situation, the shareholders of the subsidiary give up their subsidiary shares and become shareholders only of the parent company.

---

[1]There is a basic distinction between a pure combination by pooling of interest and a pure purchase. However, a controlling interest may be acquired in part by a share exchange and in part by a cash purchase. In these "nonpure" situations, a rigid list of criteria must be met to qualify as a pooling of interest (see footnote 2); otherwise, the combination must be accounted for as a combination by purchase.

EXHIBIT 14–1
Illustrative data for
consolidation

COMPANY P and COMPANY S
Separate Balance Sheets
January 1, 19A, Immediately before Combination

	Company P		Company S	
Assets				
Cash		$205,000		$ 35,000
Accounts receivable (net)*		15,000		30,000
Receivable from Company S		10,000		
Inventories.....................................		170,000		70,000
Plant and equipment (net)*		100,000		45,000
Total assets		$500,000		$180,000
Liabilities and Shareholders' Equity				
Liabilities:				
Accounts payable............................		$ 60,000		$ 20,000
Payable to Company P				10,000
Shareholders' equity:				
Common shares, Company P (par $6)	$300,000			
Common shares, Company S (par $10)			$100,000	
Retained earnings	140,000	440,000	50,000	150,000
Total liabilities and shareholders' equity		$500,000		$180,000

*Accounts receivable, less the allowance for doubtful accounts; and plant and equipment, less accumulated depreciation. The net amounts are used to simplify the example. The end results will be the same as they would have been had the separate contra accounts been used.

2. **Purchasing by the parent, using cash, other assets, or debt, of more than 50 percent of the outstanding voting shares from the shareholders of the subsidiary**—This is known as a **combination by purchase.** In this situation, the shareholders of the subsidiary sell more than 50 percent of their voting shares and subsequently they are not shareholders of either the parent or the subsidiary.

The pooling and purchase methods have significantly different impacts on the consolidated income statement and balance sheet. The next few paragraphs discuss these major impacts and the problems of measuring and reporting on the consolidated financial statements of the parent company.

Throughout the chapter we will use a continuing example to illustrate the measuring approaches involved with consolidated financial statements. We will use data for Company P (the parent) and Company S (the acquired subsidiary) shown in Exhibit 14–1.

POOLING OF INTERESTS METHOD

In the rare circumstance where it is not possible for an acquirer to be identified in a business combination, a pooling of interest accounting approach is deemed appropriate. Such an approach would see the carrying values of the original companies recorded on the combined financial statements. Income of each entity for the entire accounting period would be disclosed on the combined income statement regardless of when during the current period the combination occurred.

Even though such combinations are now rare in Canada,[2] the pooling approach is of both historical and theoretical interest because of its extensive use during the 1960s. Because of this the approach will be illustrated.

To illustrate the consolidation process, we will combine the two separate balance sheets shown in Exhibit 14–2 into a single **consolidated balance sheet.** Basically, the process of consolidation by the parent company involves combining the balances in each account on the financial statements of the parent and subsidiary companies to produce consolidated financial statements that appear as if there were a **single entity.** Thus, when the parent company consolidates the balance sheets shown in Exhibit 14–2, the consolidated balance sheet will report a cash balance of $240,000 (i.e., $205,000 + $35,000). During the consolidation process, some accounts are **eliminated** (or adjusted) to avoid including amounts that would not be reported if only a single entity existed. For example, the balance sheet of Company P shows a receivable from Company S of $10,000, and the balance sheet of Company S shows a payable to Company P of $10,000. During consolidation, these accounts must be eliminated (which means that they will not be reported on the consolidated balance sheet). The consolidated balance sheet is prepared as if a single entity existed, and it would not be proper to report an amount that the entity owed to itself.

Two items must be eliminated when the balance sheets shown in Exhibit 14–2 are consolidated on the pooling of interests method:

> a. The debit balance in the investment account of $150,000 shown in the accounts of Company P will be replaced on the consolidated balance sheet with the assets (less the liabilities) of Company S; therefore, to prevent double counting, the investment account must be eliminated (dropped out). The credit balance in the common shares account of $100,000 shown in the accounts of Company S is owned by Company P; therefore, it is an intercompany item that must be eliminated. Finally, the difference between the balances in the investment account and the common shares account of Company S ($150,000 − $100,000 = $50,000) must be eliminated from the account on Company P's books, Contributed surplus. This elimination is necessary because it is an intercompany amount (refer to the acquisition entry). These three eliminations of intercompany

---

[2]*CICA Handbook*, Section 1580, suggests that a pooling is a situation in which no party to the combination can be identified as an acquirer in the exchange of voting shares. Such combinations are considered rare even when voting shares are exchanged. If one group of prior shareholders holds more than 50 percent interest in the combined company, that group would normally be the acquirer. Other factors such as the composition of the board of directors, or active participation in management may signify the acquirer.

EXHIBIT 14–2
Balance sheets immediately after combination (pooling of interests method)

COMPANY P and COMPANY S
Separate Balance Sheets (pooling of interests method)
January 2, 19A, Immediately after Combination

	Company P	Company S
Assets		
Cash	$205,000	$ 35,000
Accounts receivable (net)........................	15,000	30,000
Receivable from Company S	10,000	
Inventories......................................	170,000	70,000
Investment in Company S (100%)	150,000*	
Plant and equipment (net).......................	100,000	45,000
Total assets	$650,000	$180,000
Liabilities and Shareholders' Equity		
Accounts payable..............................	$ 60,000	$ 20,000
Payable to Company P...........................		10,000
Common share, Company P......................	360,000*	
Common share, Company S......................		100,000
Contributed surplus	90,000*	
Retained earnings, Company P	140,000	
Retained earnings, Company S		50,000
Total liabilities and shareholders' equity	$650,000	$180,000

*Amounts changed from precombination balance sheets given in Exhibit 14–1.

items must be made by Company P to avoid double counting; they can be summarized as follows:[3]

	Eliminations	
	Consolidated assets	Consolidated shareholders' equity
Investment account—decrease	− $150,000	
Common stock, Company S—decrease		− $100,000
Contributed surplus—decrease (for the difference)..............................		− 50,000

b. The accounts of Company P show a receivable of $10,000 from Company S, and the accounts of Company S show this as a payable to Company P. This amount is called an **intercompany debt.** When the two balance sheets are combined into a single consolidated balance sheet, this intercompany debt must be eliminated because there is no external debt or receivable for

---

[3]This tabulation also can be viewed in the debit/credit format as follows:

Common stock, Company S	100,000	
Contributed surplus	50,000	
Investment in Company S......................................		150,000

the combined entity. Thus, the following elimination must be made when the two balance sheets are combined:

	Eliminations	
	Consolidated assets	*Consolidated liabilities*
Receivable from Company S—decrease	−$10,000	
Payable to Company P—decrease		−$10,000

The balance sheets of Company P and Company S are shown separately in Exhibit 14–3 and in the last column are combined (aggregated) on a line-by-line basis, after deducting the "Eliminations," to develop the "Consolidated balance sheet." In an external consolidated financial statement, only the last column—the "Consolidated balance sheet" (and not the "Separate balance sheets")—would be reported by the parent company.

In the "Consolidated balance sheet" by the pooling of interests method, as shown in the last column of Exhibit 14–3, the following measurement procedures are evident: (1) the amounts on each line for the consolidated assets, liabilities, and shareholders' equity are the **combined book values** of the parent and the subsidiary as were reflected on the separate balance sheets; (2) the intercompany amounts for investment, subsidiary common stock, a part of

EXHIBIT 14–3
Preparation of consolidated balance sheet (pooling of interests method)

COMPANY P and Its Subsidiary, COMPANY S (100 percent owned) Consolidated Balance Sheet (pooling of interests method) At January 2, 19A, Immediately after Combination				
	Separate balance sheets			*Consolidated balance sheet*
	Company P*	*Company S**	*Eliminations**	
Assets				
Cash.	$205,000	$ 35,000		$240,000
Accounts receivable (net)	15,000	30,000		45,000
Receivable from Company S	10,000		(b) − 10,000	–0–
Inventories	170,000	70,000		240,000
Investment in Company S	150,000		(a) − 150,000	–0–
Plant and equipment (net)	100,000	45,000		145,000
Total assets.	$650,000	$180,000		$670,000
Liabilities				
Accounts payable	$ 60,000	$ 20,000		$ 80,000
Payable to Company P		10,000	(b) − 10,000	–0–
Shareholders' Equity				
Common stock, Company P	360,000			360,000
Common stock, Company S.		100,000	(a) − 100,000	–0–
Contributed surplus	90,000		(a) − 50,000	40,000
Retained earnings, Company P. . . .	140,000			190,000
Retained earnings, Company S. . . .		50,000		
Total liabilities and shareholders' equity.	$650,000	$180,000		$670,000

*Included for instructional purposes only. A worksheet usually is used to derive the consolidated amounts. See Supplements 14A and 14B.

contributed surplus, and the intercompany debt are eliminated; and (3) the **consolidated** retained earnings amount is the sum of the two separate retained earnings amounts ($140,000 + $50,000 = $190,000).[4]

The balance reflected in the capital stock account of Company S is eliminated because it is an intercompany item (all of the capital stock is owned by Company P). Retained earnings balance of Company S is not eliminated because it is not an intercompany item; the old shareholders of Company P plus the new shareholders of Company P (the former Company S shareholders) have dividend claims on the **total** of retained earnings for the combined unit.

PURCHASE METHOD

The preceding discussion considered the consolidation process for a pooling of interests (an exchange of shares). In contrast, when a corporation pays cash to acquire the shares of another corporation, a **purchase** transaction takes place.[5] As was the case in previous chapters, the purchase of assets must be recorded in conformity with the **cost principle.** Thus, on the acquisition date, the investment account on the books of the parent company must be measured at cost, which is the **market value of the shares at date of purchase** (i.e., the cash or cash equivalent paid).

To illustrate a combination by **purchase,** we will use the balance sheets of Companies P and S as given in Exhibit 14–1. Assume that on January 2, 19A, Company P **purchased** 100 percent of the 10,000 outstanding voting shares of Company S, from Company S's shareholders, at $16.50 per share (i.e., for $165,000) and paid cash. On this date, Company P would make the following journal entry in its accounts:

January 2, 19A:

Investment in shares of Company S (10,000 shares, 100 percent)...	165,000	
Cash...		165,000
Acquisition by purchase.		

Note that Company P paid $165,000 cash for 100 percent of the owners' equity of Company S, although the **total book value** of the shareholders' equity of Company S that was purchased was only $150,000. Thus, Company P paid $15,000 more than "book value." In consolidating the two balance sheets, this $15,000 difference must be taken into account as explained below.

---

[4]The pooling of interests method also requires that all comparative statements presented for prior years must be restated as if consolidated statements had been prepared.

[5]Refer to footnote 2. The purchase method should be used where an acquirer can be identified even if shares rather than cash are exchanged.

This purchase by Company P will have no effect on the accounting and reporting by the subsidiary Company S because the shares were sold (and cash was received) by the shareholders of Company S (and not by Company S itself).

After the above journal entry is posted to the accounts of Company P, the two separate balance sheets then would be changed as shown in the first two columns of Exhibit 14–4. You should compare these two columns with Exhibit 14–1 and observe that for *(a)* Company P cash decreased by $165,000 and the investment increased by the same amount and *(b)* Company S accounts are unchanged.

The consolidated balance sheet under the **purchase method** is shown in Exhibit 14–4. The two separate balance sheets for Companies P and S (given in Exhibit 14–4) were combined immediately after acquisition to develop the consolidated balance sheet of Company P. The consolidation process for a purchase is similar to consolidation for a pooling of interests (as illustrated in Exhibit 14–3). There are two intercompany items that require eliminations similar to those illustrated for the pooling of interests method; however, one differs significantly. The two eliminations are:

EXHIBIT 14–4
Preparation of a consolidated balance sheet (purchase method)

COMPANY P and Its Subsidiary, COMPANY S (100 percent owned)
Consolidated Balance Sheet (purchase method)
At January 2, 19A, Immediately after Acquisition

| | Separate balance sheets | | | |
	Company P*	Company S*	Eliminations*	Consolidated balance sheet
Assets				
Cash	$ 40,000	$ 35,000		$ 75,000
Accounts receivable (net)	15,000	30,000		45,000
Receivable from Company S	10,000		*(b)* – 10,000	–0–
Inventories	170,000	70,000		240,000
Investment in Company S	165,000		*(a)* – 165,000	–0–
Plant and equipment (net)	100,000	45,000	*(a)* + 5,000	150,000
Goodwill†			*(a)* + 10,000	10,000
Total assets	$500,000	$180,000		$520,000
Liabilities				
Accounts payable	$ 60,000	$ 20,000		$ 80,000
Payable to Company P		10,000	*(b)* – 10,000	–0–
Shareholders' Equity				
Common stock, Company P	300,000			300,000
Common stock, Company S		100,000	*(a)* – 100,000	–0–
Retained earnings, Company P	140,000			140,000
Retained earnings, Company S		50,000	*(a)* – 50,000	–0–
Total liabilities and shareholders' equity	$500,000	$180,000		$520,000

*Included for instructional purposes only. A worksheet usually is used to derive the consolidated amounts. See Supplements 14A and 14B.

†A title preferred by some accountants is "Excess of purchase price over the current value of the net assets of the subsidiary" rather than "Goodwill." However, the length of this term causes the shorter term to be used extensively.

a. The investment account debit balance of $165,000, in the accounts of Company P, is at **market value** (i.e., at acquisition cost). It is eliminated against the shareholders' equity of the subsidiary, which is at **book value.** Company P paid $15,000 more than book value (i.e., $165,000 − $150,000) to acquire Company S for two reasons: (1) Company P determined that the plant and equipment owned by Company S had a market value of $50,000 at acquisition (compared with the book value of $45,000 reported by Company S), and (2) Company S had developed a good reputation with its customers which increased the overall value of Company S. The difference between the cost and the book value of the investment may be analyzed as follows:

Purchase price for 100% interest in Company S.......		$165,000
Net assets purchased, valued at market:		
Book value, $180,000 + market value increment		
of plant and equipment, $5,000 = ...	$185,000	
Less liabilities assumed..........................	30,000	
Total market value purchased................		155,000
Goodwill purchased.............................		$ 10,000

Company P paid $165,000 cash for Company S, which had net assets (total assets minus liabilities) with a **market** value of $155,000; therefore, the goodwill of Company S cost $10,000. **Goodwill** is the amount that Company P actually paid for the good reputation, customer appeal, and general acceptance of the business that Company S had developed over the years. All successful companies enjoy a measure of goodwill. Its "value" is never known except when a business is purchased, as it was in this instance.

To eliminate the investment account on the books of Company P and the owner's equity accounts on the books of Company S, the following five steps must be completed:

1. Increase the plant and equipment of Company S from the book value of $45,000 to market value of $50,000; the increase is $5,000.
2. Recognize the $10,000 goodwill purchased as an asset.
3. Eliminate the investment account balance of $165,000.
4. Eliminate the Company S common stock balance of $100,000.
5. Eliminate the Company S retained earnings balance of $50,000.

These five steps are implemented as follows:[6]

---

[6]This tabulation also can be viewed in the debit-credit format as follows (see supplements):

Plant and equipment..	5,000	
Goodwill..	10,000	
Common stock, Company S...................................	100,000	
Retained earnings, Company S	50,000	
Investment, Company S...................................		165,000

	Eliminations	
	Consolidated assets	*Consolidated shareholders' equity*
Plant and equipment—increase	+$ 5,000	
Goodwill—increase	+ 10,000	
Investment—decrease.	− 165,000	
Common stock Company S—decrease.		− $100,000
Retained earnings, Company S—decrease		− 50,000

    b.   The intercompany debt must be eliminated, viz:

	Eliminations	
	Consolidated assets	*Consolidated liabilities*
Receivable from Company S—decrease	− $10,000	
Payable to Company P—decrease		− $10,000

In contrast to the pooling of interests method, when the purchase method is used, the balance of Retained Earnings of the subsidiary at acquisition is eliminated. This elimination is made because the retained earnings of the subsidiary was in effect paid out to the former shareholders of Company S when they were reimbursed in cash for the market value of their shares (they are no longer shareholders of either company).

The accounts of Company S are not affected by a purchase because the transaction was between the parent company and the former shareholders of the subsidiary (and not the subsidiary itself).

The two "separate balance sheets" are shown in Exhibit 14–4 and, using the eliminations, are combined on a line-by-line basis to develop the "Consolidated balance sheet" of Company P shown in the last column. In an external consolidated financial statement of Company P, only the "Consolidated balance sheet" shown in the last column (and not the "Separate balance sheets") would be reported.

To reemphasize the measurements for consolidation purposes when the purchased method is used, the **market values** at date of acquisition of the subsidiary's assets are added on an item-by-item basis to the **book values** of the parent, Company P.

COMPARISON OF THE EFFECTS ON THE BALANCE SHEET OF POOLING VERSUS PURCHASE METHODS

To gain some insight into the differences in measurement of balance sheet amounts that arise when the pooling of interests method is used versus the purchase method, we can compare several of the consolidated amounts shown in Exhibits 14–3 and 14–4 as follows:

| | Acquisition method | | |
	Pooling method	Purchase method	Difference
1. Cash	$240,000	$ 75,000	$(165,000)
2. Plant and equipment (net).............	145,000	150,000	5,000 *
3. Goodwill.............................		10,000	10,000 *
4. Common stock Company P............	360,000	300,000	(60,000)
5. Contributed surplus	40,000		(40,000)
6. Retained earnings Company P	190,000	140,000	(50,000)*

*These three amounts reflect the basic differences between the two methods (see footnote 7).

The $165,000 difference in cash was the purchase price of the subsidiary (under the pooling method, only shares were exchanged). The $100,000 difference in the amount of common stock is due to the effect of issuing shares under pooling of interests rather than paying cash when the purchase method is elected.[7] The plant and equipment amount is higher when the purchase method is used than when pooling of interests is used, because the former requires application of the cost principle so that **market value** at date of acquisition rather than book value must be recognized for the assets of the subsidiary. Goodwill usually arises in a purchase but does not in a pooling of interests. These higher amounts for assets under the purchase method, of course, mean higher expenses will be reported on the income statements in the future periods; that is, depreciation expense and amortization expense for goodwill will be higher. Finally, under the pooling of interests method, the reported retained earnings amount is higher because the amount of retained earnings of the subsidiary must be added to that of the parent as shown in Exhibit 14–3.

Thus, when one compares the basic differences between the pooling of interests and purchase methods, three items usually stand out on the consolidated balance sheet, viz:

1. Operational assets almost always are higher in valuation under the purchase method because they are valued at market rather than at the subsidiary's book values.
2. Goodwill almost always is recorded under the purchase method but never is recorded under the pooling of interests method.
3. Retained earnings is lower under the purchase method because under this method only the parent company's retained earnings is reflected, while under the pooling of interests method

---

[7]In the example of the purchase method, the subsidiary shares were purchased by Company P for cash without borrowing or selling unissued shares. Had Company P borrowed the $165,000, the cash position would have been unaffected; however, there would have been an increase in debt by the same amount.

Alternatively, Company P could have sold the 10,000 shares of its common stock for $165,000 cash and then purchased the 10,000 shares of Company S with that cash. In this scenario, the cash position and the contributed capital accounts would have been the same under both methods.

consolidated retained earnings always is the sum of the parent and subsidiary retained earnings.

Part B will discuss and illustrate other significant effects that are reflected on the consolidated income statement of the parent company.

Part B—Reporting Consolidated Operations after Acquisition

The preceding discussions focused on the impact of the pooling of interests method and the purchase method on the consolidated balance sheet immediately after acquisition. The impact of the two methods on the income statement, for accounting periods following the date of acquisition, also is significant. Exhibit 14–5 presents the consolidated income statement and balance sheet for Company P and its subsidiary, Company S, after one year of opera-

EXHIBIT 14–5
Consolidated financial statements under the pooling and purchase methods one year after acquisition

COMPANY P and Its Subsidiary, COMPANY S (100% Owned)
Consolidated Financial Statements
Pooling and Purchase Methods Compared
At December 31, 19A, One Year after Acquisition

	Consolidated statements	
	Pooling method	*Purchase method*
Income statement (for the year ended December 31, 19A):		
Sales revenue	$ 510,000	$ 510,000
Expenses:		
Cost of goods sold	(279,000)	(279,000)
Expenses (not detailed)	(156,500)	(156,500)
Depreciation expense	(14,500)	(15,000)
Amortization expense (goodwill)		(500)
Income tax expense	(26,000)	(26,000)
Net income (carried to retained earnings)	$ 34,000	$ 33,000
Balance sheet (at December 31, 19A):		
Assets		
Cash	$ 271,500	$ 106,500
Accounts receivable (net)	46,000	46,000
Inventories	250,000	250,000
Plant and equipment (net)	130,500	135,000
Goodwill		9,500
Total assets	$ 698,000	$ 547,000
Liabilities		
Accounts payable	$ 74,000	$ 74,000
Shareholders' Equity		
Common stock	400,000*	300,000
Retained earnings	190,000	140,000
Add: Net income (from above)	34,000	33,000
Total liabilities and shareholders' equity	$ 698,000	$ 547,000

*Includes contributed surplus, $40,000.

tions (i.e., for the accounting year ended December 31, 19A). The underlying data and consolidation procedures used to derive these two financial statements are shown in Supplement 14A, Exhibits 14–9 and 14–10.

The objective in Part B is to provide an overview of the impact of the pooling of interests and purchase methods on reporting consolidated results after acquisition.

THE IMPACT OF THE POOLING AND PURCHASE METHODS ONE YEAR AFTER ACQUISITION

Recall that at the date of acquisition, the plant and equipment shown on the balance sheet of Company S had a market value of $5,000 in excess of book value. These assets are being depreciated over a remaining life of 10 years by Company S. Also, the acquisition of Company S resulted in the recognition of $10,000 goodwill when the purchase method was used. This goodwill will be amortized over the next 20 years.[8]

A comparison of the impact of the pooling method and the purchase method on the consolidated statements of Company P after one year of operations is shown in Exhibit 14–6.

The comparison in Exhibit 14–6 shows that 11 amounts were different between the two consolidation methods. Net income was $1,000 less under the purchase method because **additional** depreciation expense and amortization expense (goodwill) must be recognized in consolidation when the assets of the

EXHIBIT 14–6
Comparison of pooling of interests and purchase methods one year after acquisition

	Acquisition approach		
	Pooling method	Purchase method	Difference
Income statement:			
1. Depreciation expense.............................	$14,500	$15,000	$ 500*
2. Amortization expense (goodwill)		500	500*
3. Net income..	34,000	33,000	$ 1,000*
Balance sheet:			
4. Cash...	271,500	106,500	$165,000
5. Plant and equipment (net)	130,500	135,000	(4,500)
6. Goodwill...		9,500	(9,500)
7. Total...	698,000	547,000	$151,000
8. Common stock	360,000	300,000	$ 60,000
9. Contributed surplus.................................	40,000		40,000
10. Retained earnings...................................	224,000	173,000	51,000
11. Total...	698,000	547,000	$151,000

*Basic differences on the income statement.

[8]*CICA Handbook,* Section 1580.58, states that goodwill that is not permanently impaired should be amortized using the straight-line method over its estimated life but not to exceed 40 years.

subsidiary are recognized at their acquisition market values. The causes of the $1,000 difference are:

		Items	Difference
a.	Depreciation expense on pooling of interests method (on parent and subsidiary assets at book value)	$14,500	
	Add depreciation on the increased asset amount of the subsidiary (to market value from book value, $5,000 ÷ 10 years)	500	$ 500
	Depreciation expense on purchase method (on parent assets at book value and subsidiary assets at market value).	$15,000	
b.	Amortization expense on the intangible asset, goodwill, of $10,000, which is to be amortized over the next 20 years ($10,000 ÷ 20 years)		500
	(There is no goodwill recognized under pooling of interests.)		
	Total of the differences		$1,000

The additional expenses that must be recognized on the consolidated income statement in future periods cause less net income to be reported when the purchase method is used. Businesses usually do not like this unfavourable impact of the purchase method.

The $151,000 difference in the balance sheet totals shown in Exhibit 14–6 is caused by the different way in which the shares were acquired (shares exchanged versus cash payment) and the accounting measurements implicit in each of the two methods. These differences may be explained as follows:

Cash—The $165,000 difference reflects the cash price paid for the shares of the subsidiary purchased under the purchase method as opposed to the exchange of shares under pooling of interests (see footnote 7).

Plant and equipment (net)—This difference reflects the effects of including the plant and equipment of the subsidiary at book value under the pooling of interests method compared with including them at **acquisition** market value under the purchase method. The $4,500 difference in plant and equipment may be explained as follows:

Difference between market value and book value of subsidiary assets at date of acquisition.	$5,000
Deduct depreciation on the difference for one year ($5,000 ÷ 10 years)	500
Difference: Operational assets (higher under purchase method)	$4,500

Goodwill—Goodwill often is recognized under the purchase method (and amortized over 40 years or less); it is not recognized under pooling of interests.

Common stock—The common shares of Company P are greater by $60,000 under a pooling of interests because of the issuance of shares in exchange for the shares of Company S. Note that this amount is the same as it was at acquisition.

Contributed surplus—This amount arises only under pooling of interests as a result of the exchange of shares. In consolidation, a part or all of it is eliminated.

Retained earnings—Retained earnings is $51,000 more under the pooling of interests method than under the purchase method. This difference is due to two factors, viz:

Amount of retained earnings eliminated:		
Under pooling of interests method..................	$ –0–	
Under purchase method	50,000	$50,000
Amount of consolidated net income:		
Under pooling of interests method..................	34,000	
Under purchase method	33,000	1,000
Difference: Retained earnings (higher under pooling of interests method)		$51,000

The preceding discussion of the pooling of interests and purchase methods should make clear why pooling of interests usually would be preferred by the acquiring company, and also why the accounting profession established specific criteria for limiting its use. The pooling of interests method usually is preferred because it (1) requires little or no disbursement of cash, other assets, or the creation of debt; (2) results in a higher net income reported on the consolidated income statement than does the purchase method; (3) reports higher retained earnings; and (4) is susceptible to manipulation, which was evidenced by numerous abuses prior to the issuance of *CICA Handbook,* Section 1580. The pooling of interests method usually is preferred by acquiring companies because of the "favourable" reporting impacts cited above. However, in the opinion of many persons, the opportunities for manipulation of net income are significant deficiencies of the pooling of interests method. Three fairly common manipulative practices of the past were:

1. **Instant earnings**—To illustrate, assume Company P acquired Company S through a pooling of interests. At acquisition date, Company S owned three separate plants, each of which had a relatively low book value of $100,000 and a high market value of $600,000. Following the pooling of interests method, the $100,000 book value of each plant was reported on the subsequent consolidated balance sheet as an asset. Assume that during the next year one of the plants was sold for the $600,000 market value. The result was a gain on the sale of operational assets of $500,000 (disregarding income taxes), which then was reported on the income statement. This came to be referred to, in a derogatory way, as making "instant earnings." The reported gain would significantly increase **net income** and EPS and often caused the price of the shares of Company P to rise. At the higher share prices, shares were sold to the public and/or used for another round of mergers following the same pattern. Many persons believe that there was no economic gain because the cost of the plant, to the acquiring company, was the market value of the shares given in exchange (and that it should have been recorded at this amount), that is, $600,000.

Under this view (i.e., it would be the purchase method) no gain would be reported when the plant was sold for $600,000.

2. **Escalating EPS**—This term refers to what was a common practice of seeking out smaller successful companies, usually near year-end, to acquire through a pooling of interests, so that their earnings could be **added** to those of the parent. Thus, by the simple expedient of year-end pooling acquisitions, at no cash cost, the acquiring company could escalate net income and EPS reported on a consolidated basis by the parent company. Many of the year-end acquisitions for this purpose were consummated **after** the end of the year but before publication of the financial statements, in which case they were allowed for inclusion in the consolidated statements of the past year. This action became a favourite way to "doctor" net income and EPS at year-end.

3. **Tricky mixes**—This situation represented the ultimate in misleading and illogical accounting. It was referred to as "part-purchase, part-pooling of interests accounting." A corporation, in acquiring another company by pooling, often found a number of shareholders of the other company who would not accept shares in exchange; they wanted cash immediately. For example, it often worked out that, say, two thirds of the shares of the subsidiary would be acquired by exchange of shares and the remaining third would be purchased for cash. In order to derive some of the "reporting benefits" of pooling of interests accounting, two thirds of the acquisition would be accounted for on that basis and one third on the purchase basis—thus part-purchase, part-pooling accounting. This mixture of accounting approaches not only was theoretically untenable but also was misleading and not subject to any rational explanation; it was stopped by *CICA Handbook*, Section 1580.

The "merger movement" in the 1960s came under considerable criticism because pooling of interests accounting often was used in situations that were, in substance, purchases. In response to extensive criticism, the accounting professions in both Canada and the United States restricted the application of pooling to rare combinations for both conceptual and practical reasons. The conceptual argument against the pooling of interests method is that it ignores the market values on which the parties traded shares and substitutes, in violation of the cost principle, the book values carried in the accounts of the seller (i.e., the subsidiary). The practical argument against the pooling of interests method is that it leads to abuses of the kinds cited above.

The primary arguments in favour of the pooling of interests method of reporting are (1) it avoids the problems of measuring the market value of the different assets of the subsidiary at acquisition date; (2) it avoids the necessity of recognizing goodwill, then having to amortize it as an expense in future periods; and (3) the exchange of shares is not a purchase/sale transaction but, rather, is a joining of common interests and risks. Eventually pooling may be eliminated altogether as a method of accounting for business.

DEMONSTRATION CASE

This case is based on selected parts of the Consolidated-Bathurst financial statements given in Special Supplement B immediately preceding the Index. Refer to Special Supplement B and respond to the following questions:

a.   What was the amount of the short-term investments reported on the 1984 balance sheet? How were the short-term investments valued on the balance sheet?

b.   What was the amount of the long-term investments reported on the 1984 balance sheet? How were the long-term investments valued on the balance sheet?

c.   What amount of minority interest is reported on the 1984 balance sheet? Explain what this amount represents and the reason for its particular classification on the balance sheet (See Appendix B).

d.   Explain how the 1984 income statement reflects revenue from consolidated subsidiaries.

e.   Determine the amount, if any, of intercompany debt (obligations between affiliated companies) reported on the 1984 balance sheet.

f.   Did Consolidated–Bathurst have any acquisitions of subsidiary companies during 1984?

Suggested solution

a.   The short-term investment amount cannot be determined because it is aggregated with cash. The account would be valued at the lower of cost or market.

b.   The long-term investment amount is $173,665,000 for 1984. The long-term investments are valued at cost less write-downs to market for any permanent declines in value. Some investments are recorded on the equity basis.

c.   At the end of 1984, the "Minority interest" in subsidiaries was $32,903,000. This item means that the parent company, although it owned a controlling interest in the voting shares of one or more of the subsidiaries, did not own 100 percent. This amount represents the portion of the shareholders' equity of the subsidiary identified with the minority shareholders.

d.   Revenue from consolidated subsidiaries is not reported separately because it is added to the revenues of the parent.

e.   There is no intercompany debt reported on the consolidated balance sheet because intercompany debt must be eliminated during the consolidation process.

> *f.* No debts to or from affiliated unconsolidated companies is shown. No acquisitions are obvious from the financial statements.

SUMMARY OF CHAPTER

This chapter discussed the use of consolidated financial statements that must be prepared in most situations when one corporation owns more than 50 percent of the outstanding voting shares of another corporation. The concept of consolidated statements is based upon the view that a parent company and its subsidiaries constitute one economic entity. Therefore, the separate income statements, balance sheets, and statements of changes in financial position should be combined each period on an item-by item basis as a single set of financial statements for the parent company.

Ownership of a controlling interest (i.e., more than 50 percent of the outstanding voting shares) of another corporation may be accounted for and reported as either a pooling of interests or combination by purchase. The measurement of amounts reported on the consolidated financial statements of the parent company is influenced to a significant degree by these two quite different accounting methods.

In a combination by purchase, the parent company usually pays cash and/or incurs debt for the voting shares of the subsidiary. In these circumstances, a purchase/sale transaction has been completed, and the acquisition is accounted for in conformance with the cost principle. Therefore, to prepare consolidated statements under the purchase method, the assets of the subsidiary must be measured at their acquisition market values when combined with the statements of the parent company (i.e., at book value).

Consolidation under the pooling of interests method versus the purchase method causes significant differences on the consolidated financial statements. The pooling of interests method in the past led to many abuses.

A large percentage of published financial statements of corporations are consolidated statements. It is important, therefore, that statement users understand the basic concept of consolidated statements and the measurement distinctions between the pooling method and the purchase method in reporting the results of business combinations.

The differences between the pooling of interests and purchase methods in measuring and reporting the results of business combinations may be generalized, as shown in Exhibit 14–7. The acquisition of a controlling interest **does not** affect the accounting and reporting of the subsidiary companies (the subsidiary companies do not prepare consolidated statements).

EXHIBIT 14-7
Differences between the pooling of interests and purchase methods summarized

Item	Pooling of Interests	Purchase
1. Measuring and recording at date of acquisition by the parent company.	Acquisition is accomplished by exchanging shares. A purchase/sale transaction is not assumed; therefore, the cost principle **is not** applied. The investment account is debited for the **book value** of the subsidiary shares acquired.	Acquisition usually is accomplished by purchasing the shares with cash and/or debt. A purchase/sale transaction is assumed; therefore, the cost principle is applied. On acquisition date the investment account is debited for the **market value** of the resources acquired.
2. Goodwill.	Goodwill is not recognized by the parent company.	Goodwill is recognized by the parent company to the extent that the purchase price exceeds the sum of acquisition market values of the assets (less the liabilities) of the subsidiary.
3. Method of aggregating or combining by the parent company to derive the consolidated balance sheet.	Assets and liabilities (less any eliminations) of the subsidiary are added, at **book value,** to the book values of the parent.	Assets and liabilities (less any eliminations) of the subsidiary are added, at their acquisition **market values,** to the book values of the assets and liabilities of the parent.
4. Method of aggregating or combining by the parent company to derive the consolidated income statement.	Revenues and expenses as reported by each company, less any eliminations, are aggregated.	Revenues as reported, less any eliminations, are aggregated. Expenses, plus additional depreciation and amortization of goodwill, less any eliminations are aggregated.
5. Eliminations.	Eliminate all intercompany debts, revenues, and expenses. Eliminate investment account on parent's books and owners' equity of the subsidiary, excluding retained earnings.	Eliminate all intercompany debts, revenues, and expenses. Eliminate the investment account on parent's books and common stock and retained earnings of the subsidiary.
6. Usual comparative effects on the consolidated financial statements.	Expenses—lower Net income—higher EPS—higher Assets—higher cash Noncash assets—lower Liabilities—same Capital stock—higher Retained earnings—higher	Expenses—higher Net income—lower EPS—lower Assets—lower cash Noncash assets—higher Liabilities—same Capital stock—lower Retained earnings—lower

SUPPLEMENT 14A—CONSOLIDATION PROCEDURES—100 PERCENT OWNERSHIP

This supplement discusses in more depth the measurement procedures used in preparing consolidated financial statements. To accomplish this objective, we use a **consolidation worksheet** because, through it, the underlying concepts and measurement procedures come into sharp focus. The worksheet should be viewed as a learning device and not something only to be mastered mechanically. At the outset we remind you that the worksheet and the entries made on it are **supplemental** to the ledger accounts of the parent company. **The worksheet entries are not recorded in the accounts under any circumstances because the worksheet is an analytical device only.** We will consider the various topics in the same order they were presented in the body of the chapter. The example for Company P and its subsidiary, Company S, given in Exhibit 14–1, will be continued for all of the illustrations in this supplement.

The consolidated balance sheets for Company P and its subsidiary, Company S, immediately after acquisition, were shown under the pooling of interests method in Exhibit 14–3 and under the purchase method in Exhibit 14–4. Those exhibits indicated in the first three columns the worksheet procedures essential to development of the statements. There is no need to repeat those discussions.

Developing consolidated statements for periods subsequent to acquisition

At the end of each accounting period after acquisition, a consolidated balance sheet, income statement, and statement of changes in financial position must be prepared by the parent company. We will discuss consolidation procedures for both a consolidated balance sheet and a consolidated income statement for accounting periods subsequent to acquisition. We will illustrate a single worksheet that will meet this dual need.

To illustrate the consolidation worksheet, we will continue the situation involving the acquisition of Company S shares by Company P. Recall that on January 2, 19A, Company P acquired 100 percent of the outstanding shares of Company S. To adapt the example, we will assume that it is now December 31, 19A, and after operating for a year, each company has just prepared its separate income statement and balance sheet as shown in Exhibit 14–8. Two sets of financial statements are shown for Company P; the first is based on the assumption that Company S was acquired through an exchange of shares, and the second is based on the assumption that Company S shares were acquired with cash.

At the end of 19A, the following data relating to intercompany eliminations were available to Company P:

  a. The Investment in Company S balance of $165,000 was the same as at date of acquisition; the balance of Retained Earnings of Company S at acquisition was $50,000.

EXHIBIT 14–8
Illustrative data for consolidated financial statements subsequent to acquisition (100 percent ownership)

COMPANY P AND COMPANY S
Separate Financial Statements for 19A (unclassified)

	At December 31, 19A		
	Company P		
	Exchange of shares	*Purchase with cash*	*Company S*
Revenue statement (for 19A):			
Sales revenue	$ 400,000	$ 400,000	$110,000
Revenue from investments			
(dividend from Company S).	10,000	10,000	
Cost of goods sold	(220,000)	(220,000)	(59,000)
Expenses (not detailed)	(130,000)	(130,000)	(26,500)
Depreciation expense	(10,000)	(10,000)	(4,500)
Income tax expense.	(20,000)	(20,000)	(6,000)
Net income	$ 30,000	$ 30,000	$ 14,000
Balance sheet (at December 31, 19A):			
Cash	$ 226,000	$ 61,000	$ 45,500
Accounts receivable (net).	18,000	18,000	28,000
Receivable from Company S.	6,000	6,000	
Inventories	185,000	185,000	65,000
Investment in Company S			
(by purchase, at cost).	150,000*	165,000*	
Plant and equipment (net)	90,000	90,000	40,500
	$ 675,000	$ 525,000	$179,000
Accounts payable	$ 55,000	$ 55,000	$ 19,000
Payable to Company P.			6,000
Common stock, par $10.	360,000	300,000	100,000
Contributed surplus	90,000		
Beginning retained earnings*	140,000	140,000	50,000
Dividends declared and paid during 19A			(10,000)
Net income for 19A (per above).	30,000	30,000	14,000
	$ 675,000	$ 525,000	$179,000

*Balance at date of acquisition.

b. At date of purchase, January 2, 19A, the plant and equipment of Company S had an acquisition market value of $5,000 above book value and goodwill purchased amounted to $10,000.

c. Intercompany debt owed by Company S to Company P was $6,000 at the end of 19A.

d. The plant and equipment owned by Company S had a 10-year remaining life from January 1, 19A, for depreciation purposes. The company uses straight-line depreciation.

e. Goodwill is to be amortized from January 1, 19A, over 20 years on a straight-line basis.

f. During December 19A, Company S declared and paid a $10,000 cash dividend to Company P. Accordingly, each company made the following journal entry in its accounts:

```
┌─────────────────────────────────────────────────────────────────────┐
│            Company P                          Company S               │
│  Cash ............  10,000      Dividends declared                    │
│    Revenue from                   and paid.......  10,000             │
│      investments           10,000   Cash ........           10,000    │
└─────────────────────────────────────────────────────────────────────┘
```

A consolidated income statement and balance sheet must be developed at the end of 19A. These statements were shown in Exhibit 14–5, assuming (1) pooling of interests method and (2) purchase method. A consolidation worksheet for the purchase method will be discussed and illustrated.

Purchase method—income statement and balance sheet. Under the purchase method, a few eliminations are necessary because the acquisition market values for the subsidiary must be recognized when the consolidation is by purchase. The intercompany eliminations on Exhibit 14–9 are identified at the bottom of the worksheet; however, we will elaborate on them as follows:

a. Eliminate the investment account, reported on the parent's balance sheet, against the owners' equity accounts, reflected on the balance sheet of the subsidiary. This eliminating entry will be the same as at date of acquisition for each succeeding period because it is based upon the values recognized at the date of acquisition. The $15,000 difference between the purchase price and the book value must be allocated to the assets (including goodwill as shown in the analysis of the purchase transaction given earlier in the chapter).

The **worksheet** entry is as follows (illustrated in a journal entry format):

```
┌─────────────────────────────────────────────────────────────────────┐
│                                                                       │
│   Common stock, Company S..................    100,000                │
│   Retained earnings, Company S..............     50,000               │
│   Plant and equipment ......................      5,000               │
│   Goodwill..................................     10,000               │
│       Investment in Company S ..............              165,000      │
│                                                                       │
└─────────────────────────────────────────────────────────────────────┘
```

b. Eliminate the intercompany debt of $6,000 with the following entry on the worksheet:

```
┌─────────────────────────────────────────────────────────────────────┐
│                                                                       │
│   Payable to Company P .........................    6,000             │
│       Receivable from Company S ................             6,000     │
│                                                                       │
└─────────────────────────────────────────────────────────────────────┘
```

**EXHIBIT 14–9
Consolidation
worksheet
(purchase method;
100 percent
ownership)**

**COMPANY P and Its Subsidiary, COMPANY S
Consolidation Worksheet (by purchase) for the Balance Sheet
and Income Statement
December 31, 19A (100 percent ownership)**

Items	Statements Company P	Statements Company S	Intercompany Eliminations Debit	Intercompany Eliminations Credit	Consolidated Balances
Income statement:					
Sales revenue	400,000	110,000			510,000
Revenue from investments	10,000		(e) 10,000		
Cost of goods sold	(220,000)	(59,000)			(279,000)
Expenses (not detailed)	(130,000)	(26,500)			(156,500)
Depreciation expense	(10,000)	(4,500)	(c) 500		(15,000)
Amortization expense (goodwill)			(d) 500		(500)
Income tax expense	(20,000)	(6,000)			(26,000)
Net income (carried down)	30,000	14,000			33,000
Balance sheet:					
Cash	61,000	45,500			106,500
Accounts receivable (net)	18,000	28,000			46,000
Receivable from Company S	6,000			(b) 6,000	
Inventories	185,000	65,000			250,000
Investment in Company S (at cost)	165,000			(a) 165,000	
Plant and equipment (net)	90,000	40,500	(a) 5,000	(c) 500	135,000
Goodwill			(a) 10,000	(d) 500	9,500
	525,000	179,000			547,000
Accounts payable	55,000	19,000			74,000
Payable to Company P		6,000	(b) 6,000		
Common stock, Company P	300,000				300,000
Common stock, Company S		100,000	(a) 100,000		
Beginning retained earnings, Company P	140,000				140,000
Beginning retained earnings, Company S		50,000	(a) 50,000		
Dividends declared and paid during 19A		(10,000)		(e) 10,000	
Net income, 19A (from above; not added across)	30,000*	14,000*			33,000*
	525,000	179,000	182,000	182,000	547,000

*Carried down from above.

Explanation of eliminations:
  (a) To eliminate the investment account against the subsidiary shareholders' equity and to allocate the difference between purchase price and book value purchased to the appropriate accounts.
  (b) To eliminate the intercompany debt.
  (c) To record additional depreciation for one year on the increase resulting from the acquisition.
  (d) To record amortization for one year on the goodwill recognized.
  (e) To eliminate intercompany revenue and dividends (paid by the subsidiary to the parent).

c. Because the plant and equipment amount for Company S was increased to acquisition market value by $5,000, for consolidation purposes we must record additional depreciation on the $5,000 increment. The depreciation reflected on the statements of Company S does not include this $5,000 increase to market value. Accordingly, the worksheet entry must be:

```
Depreciation expense (Company S)..................    500
    Plant and equipment (Company S)
      (or accumulated depreciation).................           500
    $5,000 ÷ 10 years = $500.
```

d. Goodwill is an intangible asset (see Chapter 9) that must be amortized over a realistic period not longer than 40 years. Company P decided to use a 20-year life. Because $10,000 goodwill was recognized in entry (a) above, for consolidated statement purposes it must be amortized on the worksheet. Therefore, the worksheet entry to accomplish this effect is:

```
Amortization expense (goodwill)....................    500
    Goodwill.......................................           500
    $10,000 ÷ 20 years = $500.
```

e. During the year, Company S declared and paid dividends amounting to $10,000. Because Company P owned 100 percent of the outstanding shares, all of the dividends were paid to Company P. This is an intercompany item that must be eliminated. The Revenue from Investments account of Company P must be debited on the worksheet and the Dividends Declared and Paid account of the subsidiary credited for $10,000. Observe that separate lines are set up on the worksheet for dividends and net income. This procedure simply is for convenience and clarity. The worksheet entry to accomplish these eliminations is:

```
Revenue from investments.....................    10,000
    Dividends declared and paid (retained
      earnings, Company S).....................           10,000
```

All of the intercompany eliminations have been entered on the worksheet. The consolidated balances are determined by accumulating each line horizontally to derive the balances in the last column. The consolidated balances taken directly from the last column of the worksheet are classified in the normal manner in preparing the consolidated income statement and balance sheet.

SUPPLEMENT 14B—CONSOLIDATION PROCEDURES—LESS THAN 100 PERCENT OWNERSHIP

When the parent company owns a controlling interest that is less than 100 percent, the consolidation procedures are identical, except that certain consolidation worksheet eliminations must be based upon the **proportionate** ownership level. When there is less than 100 percent ownership, there will be a group of shareholders of the subsidiary company known as the **minority shareholders.** Their interest in the subsidiary is unaffected by the parent's interest; therefore, the minority shareholders' interest must be accorded appropriate measurement and reporting recognition. Less than 100 percent ownership causes a new kind of owners' equity on the consolidated statements referred to as the **minority interest.** It includes the minority shareholders' proportionate share of both the earnings and the contributed surplus of the subsidiary.

To illustrate the measurement of amounts for consolidated statements for a controlling interest of less than 100 percent, we will adapt the data for Company P and Company S given in Exhibit 14–1. Assume that on January 2, 19A, Company P purchased 80 percent of the 10,000 shares of outstanding capital stock of Company S for $132,000 cash.[9] At acquisition date, Company P recorded the purchase of the 8,000 shares of capital stock as follows:

January 2, 19A:

Investment, shares of Company S (80 percent ownership)	132,000	
Cash...		132,000
Acquisition of 8,000 shares (80 percent) of the capital stock of Company S at $16.50 per share.		

On the date of acquisition, the owners' equity accounts of Company S reflected the following amounts: Capital Stock, $100,000; and Retained Earnings, $50,000 (total owners' equity was $150,000). Company P paid $132,000 cash for 80 percent of the owners' equity of Company S. The book value of the investment was $120,000 ($150,000 × .80). Thus, Company P paid $12,000 more than

---

[9]Since P has obviously acquired S, the purchase method will be used.

the book value of Company S. Of this amount, $4,000 (i.e., $5,000 × 80 percent) was for the greater market value of the plant and equipment. The remaining amount, $8,000, was for **goodwill**. The analysis of the purchase transaction, at date of acquisition, follows:[10]

Purchase price for 80% interest in Company S	$132,000
Net assets purchased, valued at market:	
Book value, $150,000 + market value increment of	
plant and equipment, $5,000 × .80 =...............	124,000
Goodwill purchased	$ 8,000

Assume it is December 31, 19A, and both companies have completed one year's operations as affiliated companies. Each company has prepared the separate 19A financial statements as shown in Exhibit 14–10.

EXHIBIT 14–10
Illustrative data for consolidation (less than 100 percent ownership)

COMPANY P and COMPANY S
Separate Financial Statements for 19A

	Company P	Company S
Income statement (for 19A):		
Sales revenue	$ 400,000	$110,000
Revenue from investments (dividends		
from Company S)	8,000	
Cost of goods sold	(220,000)	(59,000)
Expenses (not detailed)	(130,000)	(26,500)
Depreciation expense	(10,000)	(4,500)
Income tax expense....................	(20,000)	(6,000)
Net income	$ 28,000	$ 14,000
Balance sheet (at December 31, 19A):		
Cash.................................	$ 92,000	$ 45,500
Accounts receivable (net)...............	18,000	28,000
Receivable from Company S.............	6,000	
Inventories	185,000	65,000
Investment in Company S (80%, at cost)	132,000	
Plant and equipment	90,000	40,500
	$ 523,000	$179,000
Accounts payable	$ 55,000	$ 19,000
Payable to Company P..................		6,000
Common stock, par $10................	300,000	100,000
Beginning retained earnings............	140,000	50,000
Dividends declared and paid during 19A		(10,000)
Net income for 19A (from above)	28,000	14,000
	$ 523,000	$179,000

[10]Some accountants believe that the plant and equipment difference should be 100 percent (i.e., $5,000) rather than 80 percent (i.e., $4,000). In Canada, *CICA Handbook,* Section 1580, requires the use of the lower amount.

Additional data developed by Company P for the consolidation worksheet:

a. Investment account balance of $132,000 to be eliminated against 80 percent of shareholders' equity of subsidiary.

b. Plant and equipment of Company S to be increased by $4,000 to market value (i.e., the increment attributable to ownership by Company P). Goodwill will be recognized, $8,000 (see analysis of purchase transaction above).

c. Company S owed Company P $6,000 on December 31, 19A.

d. The plant and equipment is being depreciated on a straight-line basis over a remaining life of 10 years by Company S (no residual value).

e. Goodwill will be amortized over 20 years.

f. Company S declared and paid $10,000 cash dividends on December 15, 19A.

The consolidation worksheet, under the purchase method, is shown in Exhibit 14–11. It is the same as the worksheet shown in Exhibit 14–9 for 100 percent ownership, except for elimination entries (a), (c), (d), and (e). These intercompany eliminations differ only as to **the amounts. They have been reduced to the 80 percent ownership level.**

On the worksheet, the minority interest (20 percent) is designated with an "M." In the income statement portion of the worksheet, 20 percent of the **subsidiary** net income (i.e., $2,800) is coded "M" and the remainder ($30,400) is identified with the parent. On the worksheet, these income amounts are carried down to the retained earnings section of the balance sheet. The 20 percent of subsidiary shareholders' equity was not eliminated; therefore, it is carried across as minority interest and coded "M." Aside from these adaptations, the Consolidated Balances column is completed as previously explained.

The consolidated income statement and balance sheet, based on the data in the Consolidated Balances column of the worksheet, are shown in Exhibit 14–12. The **minority interest** share of net income is identified separately on the income statement. The minority interest share of shareholders' equity is shown as a special caption between liabilities and shareholders' equity.

EXHIBIT 14–11
Consolidation
worksheet
(purchase method;
less than 100
percent ownership)

COMPANY P and Its Subsidiary, COMPANY S
Consolidation Worksheet (by purchase) for the Balance Sheet and Income Statement
December 31, 19A (80 percent ownership)

Items	Statements		Intercompany Eliminations		Consolidated Balances
	Company P	Company S	Debit	Credit	
Income statement:					
Sales revenue	400,000	110,000			510,000
Revenue from investments	8,000		(e) 8,000		
Cost of goods sold	(220,000)	(59,000)			(279,000)
Expenses (not detailed)	(130,000)	(26,500)			(156,500)
Depreciation expense	(10,000)	(4,500)	(c) 400		(14,900)
Amortization expense					
(goodwill)			(d) 400		(400)
Income tax expense	(20,000)	(6,000)			(26,000)
Net income	28,000	14,000			33,200
Carried down:					
Minority interest					
($14,000 × 20%)					2,800M*
Parent interest					
income					30,400
Balance sheet:					
Cash	92,000	45,500			137,500
Accounts receivable (net)	18,000	28,000			46,000
Receivable from Company S	6,000			(b) 6,000	
Inventories	185,000	65,000			250,000
Investment in Company S					
(at cost)	132,000			(a) 132,000	
Plant and equipment (net)	90,000	40,500	(a) 4,000	(c) 400	134,100
Goodwill			(a) 8,000	(d) 400	7,600
	523,000	179,000			575,200
Accounts payable	55,000	19,000			74,000
Payable to Company P		6,000	(b) 6,000		
Common stock,					
Company P	300,000				300,000
Common stock,					
Company S		100,000	(a) 80,000		20,000M
Beginning retained earnings,					
Company P	140,000				140,000
Beginning retained earnings,					
Company S		50,000	(a) 40,000		10,000M
Dividends declared and paid					
during 19A		(10,000)		(e) 8,000	(2,000)M
Net income, 19A					2,800M
(from above; not added					
across)	28,000	14,000			30,400
	523,000	179,000	146,800	146,800	575,200

M—Minority interest.
*The minority interest in the earnings of the subsidiary is unaffected by the consolidation procedures of the parent company. Thus, the minority interest in the earnings is $14,000 × 20% = $2,800. This amount is subtracted from consolidated income to derive the amount of consolidated income identifiable with the controlling interest. The two separate amounts then are carried down to the balance sheet section.
Explanation of eliminations:
(a) To eliminate the investment account against 80 percent of the owners' equity of the subsidiary and to allocate the difference between purchase price and book value to the appropriate accounts.
(b) To eliminate the intercompany debt.
(c) To record depreciation from one year on the asset increase resulting from the acquisition.
(d) To amortize goodwill recognized (one year).
(e) To eliminate intercompany revenue arising from dividends declared and paid by the subsidiary.

EXHIBIT 14–12
Consolidated
financial statements
(with minority
interest)

COMPANY P and Its Subsidiary, COMPANY S
Consolidated Income Statement (purchase method)
For the Year Ended December 31, 19A

Sales revenue		$510,000
Cost of goods sold		279,000
Gross margin		231,000
Less:		
Expenses (not detailed)	$156,500	
Depreciation expense	14,900	
Amortization expense (goodwill)	400	
Income tax expense	26,000	197,800
Consolidated net income		33,200
Less: Minority interest in net income		2,800
Controlling interest in net income		$ 30,400

EPS of common stock ($30,400 ÷ 30,000 shares) = 1.013

COMPANY P and Its Subsidiary, COMPANY S
Consolidated Balance Sheet (purchase method)
At December 31, 19A

Assets

Current assets:		
Cash	$137,500	
Accounts receivable (net)	46,000	
Inventories	250,000	$433,500
Tangible operational assets:		
Plant and equipment (net)		134,100
Intangible operational assets:		
Goodwill (or excess of cost over market value of assets of subsidiary)		7,600
Total assets		$575,200

Liabilities

Current liabilities:		
Accounts payable		$ 74,000
Minority interest		30,800*

Shareholders' Equity

Contributed capital:		
Common stock, par $10, 30,000 shares outstanding	$300,000	
Retained earnings	170,400	
Total		470,400
Total liabilities and shareholders' equity		$575,200

*$20,000 + $10,000 + $2,800 − $2,000.

IMPORTANT TERMS DEFINED IN THIS CHAPTER

Terms (alphabetically)	Key words in definitions of important terms used in chapter	Page reference
Accounting compatibility	The operations of affiliated companies complement each other.	729
Consolidation	The accounting process of combining financial statements from related companies into a single set of financial statements.	730
Control	Presumed to exist when more than 50 percent of the voting shares of an entity is owned by one investor.	729

Terms (alphabetically)	Key words in definitions of important terms used in chapter	Page reference
Goodwill	The amount that was paid for the good reputation and customer appeal of an acquired company.	737
Minority interest	The proportionate share of both the earnings and the contributed capital of the subsidiary that is not "owned" by the parent.	753
Parent company	The company that has a significant investment in a subsidiary company.	729
Pooling of interests	An acquisition that is completed by exchanging company shares for another company's voting capital stock and no acquirer can be identified.	730
Purchase	An acquisition which is completed by purchasing subsidiary company voting capital stock for cash.	731
Subsidiary	The company that is owned by a parent company as evidenced by 50 percent or more of the voting capital stock.	729

QUESTIONS FOR DISCUSSION

Part A

1. Explain what is meant by a parent-subsidiary relationship.

2. Explain the basic concept underlying consolidated statements.

3. What two basic elements must be present before consolidated statements are appropriate?

4. The concept of consolidated statements relates only to reporting as opposed to preparing and posting journal entries in the accounts. Explain.

5. Explain briefly what is meant by pooling of interests.

6. Explain briefly what is meant by combination by purchase.

7. When one corporation invests in another corporation, the investor corporation debits a long-term investment account. In the case of a pooling of interests, describe how to determine the amount that is debited to the investment account.

8. Explain what is meant by intercompany eliminations in consolidation procedures.

9. Explain why the investment account must be eliminated against shareholders' equity when consolidated statements are prepared.

10. Explain why the "book values" of the parent and subsidiary are aggregated on consolidated statements when there is a pooling of interests, but acquisition market values of the subsidiary assets are used when the combination is by purchase.

11. Why is goodwill not recognized in a pooling of interests? Why is it recognized in a combination by purchase?

Part B

12. Explain why additional depreciation expense usually must be recognized on consolidation when the combination was by purchase.

13. Explain what is meant by goodwill when the combination was by purchase.

14. Explain why pooling of interests was much more popular in the merger movement than combination by purchase.

15. Explain the basis for each of the following statements:
    a. Pooling of interests, given the same situation basically, reports a higher net income than does combination by purchase.
    b. The cash position, other things being equal, usually is better when the combination is by pooling of interests than when the combination is by purchase.
    c. Pooling of interests, other things being equal, reports a higher amount of retained earnings than does combination by purchase.

16. What reason might have been used to justify the 40-year maximum life over which goodwill can be amortized?

17. If a corner store has established an excellent reputation in a community, it would likely have above-ordinary income and therefore goodwill.

    Using the analogy of purchase and pooling, explain the apparent general rule as to when goodwill can be recognized?

18. Why might the accounting profession restrict the recognition of goodwill on the financial statements only to certain situations?

EXERCISES

Part A

E14–1. On January 2, 19A, Company P acquired all of the outstanding voting shares of Company S by exchanging, on a share-for-share basis, its own unissued shares for the shares of Company S. Immediately after the acquisition of Company S, the separate balance sheets showed the following: (next page)

	Balances, January 2, 19A, immediately after acquisition	
	Company P	Company S
Cash..	$ 38,000	$12,000
Receivable from Company S	7,000	
Inventory	35,000	18,000
Investment in Company S (100%)	60,000	
Operational assets (net of accumulated depreciation)......	80,000	50,000
Total...	$220,000	$80,000
Liabilities	$ 25,000	$13,000
Payable to Company P		7,000
Common stock (Company P, par $5)		
(Company S, par $5)	140,000	40,000
Contributed surplus.....................................	20,000	
Retained earnings..	35,000	20,000
Total...	$220,000	$80,000

Required:

a. Is this a pooling of interests or a combination by purchase? Explain why.
b. Give the journal entry that was made by Company P to record the acquisition.
c. Prepare a consolidated balance sheet immediately after the acquisition assuming it used pooling.
d. Were the assets of the subsidiary added to those of the parent, in the consolidated balance sheet, at book value or at market value? Explain why.
e. What were the balances in the accounts of Company P immediately prior to the acquisition for (1) investment and (2) common shares? Were any other account balances for either Company P or Company S changed by the acquisition? Explain.

E14–2. On January 1, 19A, Company P acquired 100 percent of the outstanding common shares of Company S. At date of acquisition, the balance sheet of Company S reflected the following book values (summarized):

Total assets (market value, $220,000)*......	$180,000
Total liabilities	30,000
Shareholders' equity:	
Common stock, par $10	100,000
Retained earnings....................	50,000

*One half subject to depreciation; 10-year remaining life and no residual value.

Two separate and independent cases are given below that indicate how Company P acquired 100 percent of the outstanding shares of Company S, viz:

Case A—Exchanged two shares of its own common stock (par $1) for each share of Company S.
Case B—Paid $20 per share of Company S.

Required:

For each case, answer the following:

a. Would this have been a combination by pooling of interests or by purchase traditionally? Explain.

    b. Give the journal entry that Company P should make to record the acquisition. If none, explain why.

    c. Give the journal entry in the accounts of Company S to record the acquisition. If none, explain why.

    d. Analyze the transaction to determine the amount of goodwill purchased. If no goodwill was purchased, explain why.

    e. In preparing a consolidated balance sheet, should the subsidiary assets be included at book value or market value? Explain.

E14–3. On January 2, 19A, Company P purchased 100 percent of the outstanding voting shares of Company S in the open market for $70,000 cash. On that date (prior to the acquisition) the separate balance sheets (summarized) of the two companies reported the following book values:

	Prior to acquisition	
	Company P	*Company S*
Cash	$ 80,000	$18,000
Receivable from Company P......		2,000
Operational assets (net)	80,000	60,000
Total	$160,000	$80,000
Liabilities	$ 28,000	$20,000
Payable to Company S...........	2,000	
Common shares:		
Company P, nopar	100,000	
Company S, par $10		50,000
Retained earnings	30,000	10,000
Total	$160,000	$80,000

It was determined on date of acquisition that the market value of the operational assets of Company S was $66,000.

Required:

    a. Would this have been a combination by pooling of interests or by purchase? Explain why.

    b. Give the journal entry that should be made by Company P at date of acquisition. If none is required, explain why.

    c. Give the journal entry that should be made by Company S at date of acquisition. If none is required, explain why.

    d. Analyze the acquisition to determine the amount of goodwill purchased.

    e. Should the assets of Company S be included on the consolidated balance sheet at book value or market value? Explain.

    f. Prepare a consolidated balance sheet immediately after acquisition.

E14–4. On January 4, 19A, Company P acquired all of the outstanding shares of Company S for $10 cash per share. At the date of acquisition, the balance sheet of Company S reflected the following:

Common stock, par $5	$50,000
Retained earnings	30,000

Immediately after the acquisition, the balance sheets reflected the following:

	Balances, Jan. 4, 19A, immediately after acquisition	
	Company P	*Company S*
Cash	$ 13,000	$17,000
Receivable from Company P..................		3,000
Investment in Company S (100%), at cost......	100,000	
Operational assets (net)	122,000	70,000*
Total	$235,000	$90,000
Liabilities	$ 22,000	$10,000
Payable to Company S	3,000	
Common stock, par $5	150,000	50,000
Retained earnings	60,000	30,000
Total	$235,000	$90,000

*Determined by Company P to have a market value of $78,000 at date of acquisition.

Required:

a. Was this a combination by pooling of interests or by purchase according to today's rules? Explain why.

b. Give the journal entry that should be made by Company P to record the acquisition.

c. Analyze the acquisition to determine the amount of goodwill purchased.

d. Should the assets of Company S be included on the consolidated balance sheet at book value or market value? Explain.

e. Prepare a consolidated balance sheet immediately after acquisition.

Part B

E14–5. On January 1, 19A, Company P acquired all of the outstanding voting shares of Company S by exchanging one of its own shares for each share of Company S. At the date of the exchange, the balance sheet of Company S showed the following:

Common stock, par $10	$40,000
Retained earnings	10,000

One year after acquisition the two companies prepared their separate financial statements as shown on the following worksheet:

COMPANY P and Its Subsidiary, COMPANY S (100 percent owned)
Consolidated Balance Sheet and Income Statement
December 31, 19A

Items	Company P	Company S	Eliminations	Consolidated Statements
	Separate Statements			
Income statement (for 19A):				
Sales revenue	96,000	42,000		
Revenue from investments	4,000			
Cost of goods sold	(60,000)	(25,000)		
Expenses (not detailed)	(17,000)	(10,000)		
Net income	23,000	7,000		
Balance sheet (at December 31, 19A):				
Cash	21,000	19,000		
Receivable from Company P		2,000		
Investment in Company S (100%)	50,000			
Operational assets (net)	59,000	47,000		
Total	130,000	68,000		
Liabilities	17,000	15,000		
Payable to Company S	2,000			
Common stock, Company P (par $10)	50,000			
Contributed surplus	10,000			
Common stock, Company S (par $10)		40,000		
Beginning retained earnings, Company P	28,000			
Beginning retained earnings, Company S		10,000		
Dividend declared and paid, 19A:				
Company S		(4,000)		
Net income, 19A (from above)	23,000	7,000		
Total	130,000	68,000		

Required:

a. Give the journal entry that was made by Company P to record the pooling of interests on January 1, 19A.

b. Complete the Eliminations column in the above worksheet, then combine the two sets of statements in the last column to develop the consolidated income statement and balance sheet. (Hint: Eliminate Revenue from Investments against Dividends Declared and Paid because this represents an intercompany transaction. The consolidated net income is $26,000.)

E14–6. (Analytical) On January 1, 19A, Company P purchased all of the outstanding voting shares of Company S at $2.50 per share. At the date the balance sheet of Company S reflected the following:

Common stock, par $1 ..... $20,000
Retained earnings.......... 10,000

One year after acquisition each company prepared its own separate financial statements and Company P set up the following consolidation worksheet (partially completed):

Items	Separate Statements		Intercompany Eliminations		Consoli-dated Balances
	Company P	Company S	Debit	Credit	
Income statement (for 19A):					
Sales revenue	99,000	59,000			
Revenue from investments	6,000		(e) 6,000		
Expenses (not detailed)	(71,000)	(40,400)			
Depreciation expense	(9,000)	(3,600)	(c) 1,200		
Amortization expense (goodwill)			(d) 400		
Net income	25,000	15,000			
Balance sheet (at December 31, 19A):					
Cash	16,000	6,000			
Receivable from Co. P		4,000		(b) 4,000	
Investment in Co. S	50,000			(a) 50,000	
Operational assets (net)	90,000	40,000*	(a) 12,000	(c) 1,200	140,800
Goodwill (amortize over 20 years)			(a) 8,000	(d) 400	
Totals	156,000	50,000			170,400
Liabilities	15,000	11,000			
Payable to Co. S	4,000		(b) 4,000		
Common stock, Co. P	80,000				
Common stock, Co. S		20,000	(a) 20,000		
Beginning retained earnings, Co. P	32,000				
Beginning retained earnings, Co. S		10,000	(a) 10,000		
Dividends declared and paid, Co. S, 19A.		(6,000)		(e) 6,000	
Net income, 19A (per above)	25,000†	15,000†			32,400†
Totals	156,000	50,000	61,600	61,600	

*Market value of the operational assets at acquisition was $12,000 above book value and their remaining useful life was 10 years.
†Carried down.

Required:

a. Give the journal entry made by Company P on January 1, 19A, to record the purchase of Company S shares.
b. Show how the $8,000 of goodwill was computed.
c. Complete the last column of the worksheet (Note that under "Eliminations" debit/credit instead of +/− were used).
d. Give a brief explanation of eliminations *(c)*, *(d)*, and *(e)*.

PROBLEMS/CASES

Part A

PC14–1. During January 19A, Company P acquired all of the outstanding voting shares of Company S by exchanging one share of its own unissued voting common stock for two shares of Company S. Immediately prior to the acquisition, the separate balance sheets of the two companies reflected the following:

	Balances immediately prior to acquisition	
	Company P	Company S
Cash	$200,000	$ 32,000
Receivable from Company P...............		3,000
Inventory................................	75,000	5,000
Operational assets (net of accumulated		
depreciation)...........................	75,000	80,000
Total	$350,000	$120,000
Liabilities...............................	$ 57,000	$ 30,000
Payable to Company S....................	3,000	
Common stock, Company P (par $4)	180,000	
Common stock, Company S (par $5)		50,000
Retained earnings	110,000	40,000
Total	$350,000	$120,000

Additional data:

At the date of acquisition, Company S stock was quoted on the market at $16 per share; there was no established market for Company P shares.

The operational assets of Company S were appraised independently at the date of acquisition at $130,000.

Required:

a. Traditionally, would this transaction have been recorded as a purchase or a pooling of interests? Explain why.
b. What account balances would be changed by the exchange of shares on each of the above balance sheets? List each account and amount.
c. Give the journal entry that should be made by each company to record the exchange assuming a pooling of interest; if no entry is required, explain why.
d. How much goodwill should be recognized assuming pooling? Why?
e. Prepare a consolidated balance sheet immediately after the acquisition.
f. Did you use any market values in solving the above requirements? Explain why.

PC14–2. Assume the same facts given in PC14–1 except that instead of an exchange of shares, Company P purchased from the shareholders 100 percent of the outstanding voting shares of Company S at a cash price of $160,000.

Required:

a. Traditionally, would this transaction have been recorded as a purchase or a pooling of interests? Explain why.
b. What account balances would be changed by the purchase of the shares on each of the balance sheets? List each account and amount.
c. Give the journal entry that should be made by each company to record the exchange assuming a purchase; if no entry is required, explain why.
d. How much goodwill should be recognized assuming a purchase? Why?
e. Prepare a consolidated balance sheet immediately after acquisition.
f. Did you use any market values in solving the above requirements? Explain why.

PC14–3.   On January 1, 19A, the separate balance sheets of two corporations showed the following:

	Balances, Jan. 1, 19A	
	Company P	Company S
Cash	$ 21,000	$ 9,000
Receivable from Company P......		4,000
Operational assets (net)	99,000	32,000
Total	$120,000	$45,000
Accounts payable................	$ 16,000	$10,000
Payable to Company S	4,000	
Common stock, par $20	60,000	20,000
Retained earnings	40,000	15,000
Total	$120,000	$45,000

On January 3, 19A, Company P acquired all of the outstanding voting shares of Company S by exchanging one share of its own for two shares of Company S.

Required:

a.   Traditionally, would this transaction have been recorded as a combination by pooling of interests or by purchase? Explain why.

b.   Company P made the following journal entry on its books, at the date of acquisition, to record the investment:

January 3, 19A:

Investment in Co. S	35,000	
Common stock............................		10,000
Contributed surplus		25,000

Explain the basis for each of the three amounts in this entry.

c.   Should any goodwill be recognized on the consolidated balance sheet assuming a pooling? Explain why.

d.   Prepare a consolidated balance sheet immediately after the acquisition.

PC14–4.   On January 2, 19A, Company P acquired all of the outstanding shares of Company S by exchanging its own shares for the shares of Company S. One share of Company P was exchanged for two shares of Company S. Company P shares were trading at the time at $14 per share. Immediately after the acquisition was recorded by Company P, the balance sheets reflected the following:

	Balances, Jan. 2, 19A, immediately after acquisition	
	Company P	Company S
Cash	$ 38,000	$26,000
Receivable from Company S	6,000	
Inventory	30,000	10,000
Investment in Company S (100%)	70,000	
Operational assets (net)	90,000	50,000
Other assets.........................	6,000	4,000
Total	$240,000	$90,000
Liabilities	$ 16,000	$14,000
Payable to Company P		6,000
Common shares, par $5	125,000	50,000
Contributed surplus	45,000	
Retained earnings	54,000	20,000
Total	$240,000	$90,000

Required:

a. Was this a combination by pooling of interests or by purchase? Explain why.
b. Give the journal entry that was made by Company P to record the acquisition on January 2, 19A. Explain the basis for each amount included in the entry.
c. Should the assets of Company S be included on the consolidated balance sheet at book value or market value? Explain.
d. Will any goodwill be recognized on the consolidated balance sheet? Explain why.
e. Prepare a consolidated balance sheet immediately after acquisition.

PC14–5. On January 5, 19A, Company P purchased all of the outstanding shares of Company S for $100,000 cash. Immediately after the acquisition the separate balance sheets of the two companies reflected the following:

	Jan. 5, 19A, immediately after acquisition	
	Company P	Company S
Cash	$ 22,000	$ 9,000
Accounts receivable (net)..............	14,000	6,000
Receivable from Company S	4,000	
Inventory	50,000	25,000
Investment in Company S (at cost)	100,000	
Operational assets (net)	153,000	67,000
Other assets.........................	7,000	3,000
Total	$350,000	$110,000
Accounts payable.....................	$ 20,000	$ 16,000
Payable to Company P		4,000
Bonds payable.......................	90,000	
Common stock, par $5	180,000	60,000
Contributed surplus	8,000	
Retained earnings	52,000	30,000
Total	$350,000	$110,000

The operational assets of Company S were estimated to have a market value at date of acquisition of $71,000.

Required:

a. Was this a combination by pooling of interests or by purchase? Explain why.
b. Give the journal entry that Company P should make at the date of acquisition.
c. Analyze the acquisition to determine the amount of goodwill purchased.
d. Should the assets of Company S be included on the consolidated balance sheet at book value or market value? Explain.
e. Prepare a consolidated balance sheet immediately after acquisition.

PC14–6. On January 4, 19A, Company P purchased 100 percent of the outstanding common shares of Company S for $240,000 cash. Immediately after the acquisition, the separate balance sheets for the two companies were prepared as shown in the worksheet below.

COMPANY P and Its Subsidiary, COMPANY S
Consolidated Balance Sheet
January 4, 19A, Immediately after Acquisition

	Separate balance sheets			Consolidated balance sheet
	Company P	Company S	Eliminations	
Assets				
Cash..............................	$ 80,000	$ 40,000		
Accounts receivable (net)..............	26,000	19,000		
Receivable from Company P...........		8,000		
Inventories.........................	170,000	80,000		
Long-term investment, bonds, Z Company..........................	15,000			
Long-term investment, Company S.....	240,000			
Land..............................	12,000	3,000		
Plant and equipment (net).............	157,000	130,000		
Goodwill...........................				
Total assets.........................	$700,000	$280,000		
Liabilities				
Accounts payable....................	$ 22,000	$ 40,000		
Payable to Company S	8,000			
Bonds payable, 5%...................	100,000	30,000		
Shareholders' Equity				
Common stock, Company P...........	500,000			
Common stock, Company S (par $10)...		150,000		
Retained earnings, Company P.........	70,000			
Retained earnings, Company S.........		60,000		
Total liabilities and shareholders' equity	$700,000	$280,000		

It was determined at the date of acquisition that on the basis of a comparison of market value and book value, the assets as reflected on the books of Company S should be adjusted as follows: (a) inventories should be reduced by $3,000, (b) plant and equipment should be increased to $148,000, and (c) land should be increased by $2,000.

Required:

a. Was this a combination by pooling of interests or by purchase? Explain why.
b. Give the journal entry that was made on the books of Company P to record the acquisition.
c. Analyze the acquisition transaction to determine the amount of goodwill purchased. Use data from the worksheet if needed.

d. At what amount will the assets of Company S be included on the consolidated balance sheet? Explain.

e. Complete the "Eliminations" column in the worksheet and then extend the amounts for the consolidated balance sheet.

Part B

PC14–7. (Analytical) On January 1, 19A, Company P acquired 100 percent of the outstanding shares of Company S for $106,000 cash. At the date of acquisition the balance sheet of Company S reflected the following:

Total assets (including operational assets*)	115,000
Total liabilities.	25,000
Common stock, par $10	60,000
Retained earnings	30,000

*Book value, $42,000; market value, $48,000 (20-year remaining life).

One year after acquisition the two companies prepared their December 31, 19A, financial statements. Company P developed the following consolidation worksheet (partially completed):

COMPANY P AND ITS SUBSIDIARY, COMPANY S
Consolidation Worksheet
Income Statement and Balance Sheet, December 31, 19A (100% ownership)

Items	Separate Statements		Eliminations		Consoli-dated balances
	Company P	Company S	Debit	Credit	
Income statement:					
Sales revenue	80,000	47,000			
Revenue from investments	4,000		(e) 4,000		
Cost of goods sold	(45,000)	(25,000)			
Expenses (not detailed)	(15,000)	(10,000)			
Depreciation expense	(4,000)	(2,000)	(c) 300		
Amortization of goodwill			(d) 500		
Net income	20,000	10,000			
Balance sheet:					
Cash	15,000	10,000			
Accounts receivable (net)	19,000	9,000			
Receivable from Co. P		1,000		(b) 1,000	
Inventories	70,000	50,000			
Investment in Co. S (100%)	106,000			(a) 106,000	
Plant and equipment (net)	80,000	40,000	(a) 6,000	(c) 300	
Goodwill			(a) 10,000	(d) 500	
	290,000	110,000			
Accounts payable	26,000	14,000			
Payable to Co. S	1,000		(b) 1,000		
Common stock, Co. P	200,000				
Common stock, Co. S		60,000	(a) 60,000		
Beginning retained earnings, Co. P	50,000				
Beginning retained earnings, Co. S		30,000	(a) 30,000		
Dividends declared and paid during 19A, Co. P	(7,000)				
Dividends declared and paid during 19A, Co. S		(4,000)		(e) 4,000	
Net income (from above)	20,000	10,000			
	290,000	110,000	111,800	111,800	308,200

Required:

a. Was this a purchase or pooling? Explain.
b. Give the journal entry made by each company to record the acquisition.
c. Complete the last column of the worksheet to develop the consolidated income statement and balance sheet.
d. How much goodwill was recognized? How was it computed?
e. Briefly explain each of the eliminations shown on the worksheet. Note that debit and credit rather than plus and minus were used in the Eliminations columns.

PC14–8. (Analytical) This problem presents the income statement and the balance sheet on a consolidated basis for Company P and its subsidiary, Company S, one year after acquisition, under two different assumptions: Case A–pooling of interests, and Case B—

purchase. The two different assumptions are used so that we can compare and analyze the differences between the pooling and purchase methods.

On January 2, 19A, Company P acquired all of the outstanding common shares of Company S. At that date the shareholders' equity of Company S showed the following: common stock, par $10, $50,000; and retained earnings, $20,000. The journal entry made by Company P to record the acquisition under each case was as follows:

Case A—Pooling of interests method:

Investment in Co. S (5,000 shares, 100%)	70,000	
Common stock, par $8.......................................		40,000
Contributed surplus		30,000

Case B—Purchase method:

Investment in Co. S (5,000 shares, 100%)	80,000	
Cash..		80,000

On January 2, 19A, the acquisition by purchase (Case B) was analyzed to determine the goodwill as follows:

Purchase price paid for 100% interest in Company S......	$80,000
Net assets purchased, valued at market:	
Book value of net assets ($50,000 + $20,000 =	
$70,000 + increase of $2,000 in operational	
assets to market value)............................	72,000
Goodwill purchased	$ 8,000

For consolidated statement purposes the operational assets are being depreciated over 10 years' remaining life and the goodwill will be amortized over 20 years.

One year after acquisition, the two companies prepared separate income statements and balance sheets (December 31, 19A). These separate statements have been consolidated under each case as reflected below:

Required:

a. Prepare a schedule of amounts that shows what items are different between each statement for Case A, compared with Case B.

b. Explain the reasons why net income is different under pooling of interests versus purchase. Use amounts from the two statements in your explanation and tell why they are different.

c. Explain why the cash balance is different between the two cases.

d. What was the balance in the account "Investment in Company S" in each case prior to its elimination? Explain.

e. Explain why the operational asset (net) amounts are different between the two cases.

f. Why is there a difference in goodwill between the two cases? Provide computations.

g. How much was eliminated for intercompany debt? Why was it eliminated?

h. What amount of "Common stock, Company S," was eliminated? Why was it eliminated?

i. Why was only $20,000 of the $30,000 of contributed surplus eliminated?

j. Explain why the account "Contributed surplus in excess of par, $10,000," was not eliminated.

k. Explain why "Beginning retained earnings, Company S, $20,000," is shown under Case A (pooling) but not under Case B (purchase).

COMPANY P and Its Subsidiary, COMPANY S (100% owned)
Consolidated Income Statement and Balance Sheet
December 31, 19A

	Consolidated statements December 31, 19A	
	Pooling method (Case A)	Purchase method (Case B)
Income statement (for the year ended December 31, 19A):		
Sales revenue	$ 236,000	$ 236,000
Revenue from investments ($4,000, eliminated)		
Cost of goods sold	(112,000)	(112,000)
Expenses (not detailed to simplify)	(75,500)	(75,500)
Depreciation expense	(12,500)	(12,700)
Amortization expense (goodwill)		(400)
Net income	$ 36,000	$ 35,400
Balance sheet (at December 31, 19A):		
Assets		
Cash	$ 128,000	$ 48,000
Accounts receivable (net)	53,000	53,000
Receivable from Company S ($5,000, eliminated)		
Inventory	37,000	37,000
Investment in Company S (eliminated)		
Operational assets (net)	125,000	126,800
Goodwill		7,600
Total	$ 343,000	$ 272,400
Liabilities		
Current liabilities	$ 30,000	$ 30,000
Payable to Company P (eliminated)		
Bonds payable	50,000	50,000
Shareholders' Equity		
Common stock, Company P	140,000	100,000
Common stock, Company S (eliminated)		
Contributed surplus in excess of par	10,000	10,000
Contributed surplus ($20,000, eliminated)	10,000	
Beginning retained earnings, Company P	47,000	47,000
Beginning retained earnings, Company S	20,000	
Dividends declared and paid in 19A (eliminated)		
Net income, 19A (from income statement above)	36,000	35,400
Total	$ 343,000	$ 272,400

PC14–9. (Based on Supplement 14A) On January 1, 19A, Company P purchased 100 percent of the outstanding capital stock of Company S for $98,000 cash. At that date the shareholders' equity section of the balance sheet of Company S reflected the following:

Capital stock, $10 par, 5,000 shares outstanding	$50,000
Retained earnings	30,000
	$80,000

At the date of acquisition, it was determined that the market values of certain assets of Company S, in comparison with the book values of those assets as reflected on the balance sheet of Company S, should be reflected by *(a)* decreasing inventories by $2,000 and *(b)* increasing equipment by $8,000.

It is now one year after acquisition, December 31, 19A, and each company has prepared the following separate financial statements (summarized):

	Company P	Company S
Balance sheet (at December 31, 19A):		
Cash	$ 52,000	$ 30,000
Accounts receivable (net)	31,000	10,000
Receivable from Company P		3,000
Inventories.	60,000	70,000
Investment in Company S (at cost)	98,000	
Equipment	80,000	20,000
Other assets.	9,000	17,000
	$ 330,000	$ 150,000
Accounts payable.	$ 42,000	$ 30,000
Payable to Company S	3,000	
Bonds payable, 10%	70,000	30,000
Capital stock, $10 par	140,000	50,000
Beginning retained earnings	50,000	30,000
Dividends declared and paid during 19A	(10,000)	(5,000)
Net income, 19A (from income statement)	35,000	15,000
	$ 330,000	$ 150,000
Income statement (for 19A):		
Sales revenue	$ 360,000	$ 140,000
Revenue from investments	5,000	
Cost of goods sold.	(220,000)	(80,000)
Expenses (not detailed).	(106,000)	(44,000)
Depreciation expense	(4,000)	(1,000)
Net income	$ 35,000	$ 15,000

Additional data during 19A:

1. Near the end of 19A, Company S declared and paid a cash dividend amounting to $5,000.
2. The equipment is being depreciated on the basis of a 20-year remaining life (no residual value).
3. Goodwill is to be amortized over a 40-year period.

Required:

a. Give the journal entry that Company P should make to record the acquisition of the capital stock of Company S on January 1, 19A.
b. Analyze the acquisition of the shares to determine the purchased goodwill.
c. Prepare a consolidation worksheet (purchase method) for the year 19A as a basis for the 19A income statement and balance sheet. (Hint: Consolidated net income is $44,300.)
d. Prepare a consolidated income statement and balance sheet based on the data provided by the consolidation worksheet.

PC14–10. (Based on Supplement 14B) On January 1, 19A, Company P purchased 90 percent of the outstanding voting shares of Company S for $100,000 cash. At the date of acquisition, the shareholders' equity accounts of Company S reflected the following: Capital Stock (par $10), $60,000; Contributed Surplus in Excess of Par, $10,000; and Retained

Earnings, $20,000. At that date it was determined that the book value of the operational assets was $10,000 less than their market value.

It is now December 31, 19A, and each company has prepared the following separate financial statements (summarized):

	Company P	Company S
Balance sheet (at December 31, 19A):		
Cash	$ 23,000	$ 11,000
Accounts receivable (net)	57,000	13,000
Receivable from Company P		7,000
Inventories	110,000	24,000
Investment in Company S (at cost; 90% owned)	100,000	
Operational assets (net)	120,000	50,000
Other assets	6,000	5,000
	$ 416,000	$ 110,000
Accounts payable	$ 30,000	$ 8,000
Payable to Company S	7,000	
Bonds payable, 9%	80,000	10,000
Capital stock, $10 par	200,000	60,000
Contributed surplus	4,000	10,000
Beginning retained earnings	80,000	20,000
Dividends declared and paid, 19A	(15,000)	(8,000)
Net income (from income statement)	30,000	10,000
	$ 416,000	$ 110,000
Income statement (for 19A):		
Sales revenue	$ 195,000	$ 75,000
Revenue from investments	7,200	
Cost of goods sold	(115,000)	(43,000)
Expenses (not detailed)	(52,200)	(19,500)
Depreciation expense	(5,000)	(2,500)
	$ 30,000	$ 10,000

Required:

a. Give the journal entry that Company P should make to record the acquisition of the shares of Company S.

b. Analyze the shares purchase to determine the amount of goodwill purchased.

c. Prepare a consolidation worksheet (purchase method) for a balance sheet and income statement for 19A. Assume the operational assets of Company S have a 10-year remaining life and that any goodwill will be amortized over 20 years. (Hint: Consolidated net income is $31,400).

d. Prepare an income statement and balance sheet for 19A based upon the data provided by the consolidation worksheet.

e. What is the minority interest claim to earnings and shareholders' equity at December 31, 19A?

PC14–11. In early September 1984, your firm's audit client, D Ltd. (D), acquired in separate transactions, an 80 percent interest in N Ltd. (N) and a 40 percent interest in K Ltd. (K). Prior to the acquisitions, both N and K were audited by other public accounting firms. D's bank and shareholders have requested that the audited consolidated financial statements of D for the year ended August 31, 1985 be available by the end of October. Your firm has been appointed the auditor of N but not of K.

All three companies are federally incorporated Canadian companies and have August 31 year-ends. They all manufacture small applicances but they do not compete with each other.

You are in charge of the audits of D and N. The partner has just received the preliminary consolidated financial statements attached (Exhibits I and II) from the controller of D. He has given you the statements and requested that you provide him with a memorandum discussing the important financial accounting issues of D and its subsidiary and investee companies. The partner has requested that the memorandum also deal with any other issues which should also be brought to attention of D's management.

D acquired the 80 percent interest in N for $4,000,000 paid as follows:

1. $2,000,000 in cash.
2. 160,000 common shares of D recorded in the books of D at $2,000,000.

D acquired its 40 percent interest in K at a cost of $2,100,000 paid as follows:

1. $100,000 in cash.
2. 160,000 common shares of D recorded in the books of D at $2,000,000.

During the course of the audits of D and N the following information was obtained:

1. The book value of 80% of N's net assets at the date of acquisition was $2,280,000. D's management provided the following acquisition data:

Price paid in excess of the book value of the shares, at the date of acquisition	$1,720,000
Comprised of:	
The excess of the current value of land over the book value.	$ 800,000
The excess of the current value of plant and equipment over the book value	700,000
Adjustment for the 20 percent minority interest's share of the excess of the current value of land, plant and equipment over the book value	(300,000)
Goodwill of N written off.	(48,000)
Deferred research and development expenditures written off	(72,000)
Pension liability not recorded (unfunded past service cost).	(200,000)
Unallocated excess	840,000
	$1,720,000

2. The price paid by D for its investment in K was 10 percent lower than 40 percent of the fair market value of K's net assets.
3. Five years ago, D purchased 100,000 shares of X Ltd. (X), being an 18 percent interest, at a cost of $780,000 and 50,000 shares of Y Ltd. (Y), being a 20 percent interest, at a cost of $200,000. On February 19, 1985, X declared a common stock dividend. At that date the additional shares to be received by D had a market value of $56,000. By the date of receipt of the shares in June 1985, the market value had dropped to $42,000.
4. The 20 percent minority shareholder in N owns a retail store which makes 30 percent of its purchases from N. On August 1, 1985, this shareholder leased equipment to N on a 10-year lease at $3,000 per month, with an option to renew for 5 years at $1,000 per month. At the end of the 10 years, N can purchase the asset for $40,000, or, at the end of the 15 years N can purchase the asset for $1.

5. During August 1985, K sold goods to D as follows:

Cost to K.................	$100,000
Normal selling price	125,000
Price paid by D	120,000

D had not sold these goods as of August 31, 1985.
N also sold goods to D in August 1985 and D had not sold them by August 31, 1985.

Cost to N...............	$ 60,000
Normal selling price	75,000
Price paid by D	85,000

6. For the year ended August 31, 1985, D's sales were $8,423,300 and N's sales were $6,144,500.

Required:

Prepare the memorandum requested by the partner.

EXHIBIT I
D LTD.
Preliminary Consolidated Balance Sheet
At August 31, 1985

Assets			Liabilities and Shareholders' Equity		
Current assets:			Current liabilities:		
Cash.....................	$	17,600	Bank loan payable		$ 3,000,000
Receivables................		2,211,400	Accounts payable and		
Inventories:			accrued liabilities		4,475,500
Finished goods at			Provision for warranty		505,500
standard cost..........		3,487,700			7,981,000
Raw materials at FIFO.....		1,062,300	Deferred income taxes........		285,000
Work in process		480,000	Long-term debt of N Ltd.		
Prepaid expenses		16,000	in U.S. dollars.............		1,000,000
		7,275,000	Minority interest in		
Investment at K Ltd.,			N Ltd.....................		568,000
at equity		2,155,000	Shareholders' equity:		
Investments in other			Capital:		
companies, at cost		980,000	1,320,000 common		
Plant and equipment.........		14,988,500	shares		5,000,000
Less accumulated			10,000 preferred;		
depreciation..............		9,373,500	10%, convertible to		
		5,615,000	eight common		
Land		675,000	shares per $100		
		6,290,000	stated value		1,000,000
		$16,700,000	Retained earnings............		866,000
					$16,700,000

D LTD.
Preliminary Consolidated Retained Earnings
For the Year Ended August 31, 1985

Balance, September 1, 1984	$ 618,000
Add net income	448,000
	1,066,000
Deduct dividends on preferred shares	200,000
Balance, August 31, 1985	$ 866,000

D LTD.
Preliminary Consolidated Income Statement
For the Year Ended August 31, 1985

Revenue	$14,567,800
Cost of goods sold	14,324,800
Gross profit	243,000
Selling and administrative expenses	1,345,000
	(1,102,000)
Income of K Ltd.	200,000
Loss before income taxes	(902,000)
Income tax recovery on loss	450,000
Loss before extraordinary item	(452,000)
Extraordinary gain on disposal of investments, less income taxes of $300,000 thereon	900,000
Net income	$ 448,000

D LTD.
Preliminary Consolidated Statement of Changes in
Financial Position
For the Year Ended August 31, 1985

Sources:	
From operations:	
Net income	$ 448,000
Add (deduct):	
Extraordinary item	(900,000)
Depreciation	1,317,300
Income of K Ltd.	(200,000)
	665,300
Dividend from K Ltd.	80,000
Issue of shares	4,000,000
Sale of investments	1,900,000
Other, net	165,000
Total sources of funds	$ 6,810,300
Uses:	
Acquisition of common shares of K Ltd. plus advance to K Ltd.	$ 2,450,000
Purchase of N Ltd.	4,000,000
Purchase of building and equipment	420,000
Increase in receivables	355,300
Decrease in working capital, excluding receivables	(415,000)
Total uses of funds	$ 6,810,300

EXHIBIT II
N LTD.
Preliminary Balance Sheet
At August 31, 1985

Assets		Liabilities and Shareholders' Equity	
Current assets:		Current liabilities:	
Cash	$ 10,000	Accounts payable and	
Receivables	900,000	accrued liabilities	$1,220,000
Inventory, at standard		Income taxes recoverable	(18,500)
cost:		Provision for warranty	5,500
Finished goods..........	360,000		1,207,000
Prepaid expenses...........	5,000		
	1,275,000	Deferred income taxes	125,000
		Long-term debt of	
Fixed assets, at cost:		$1,000,000 U.S. due in	
Building, machinery and		10 equal yearly install-	
equipment	7,638,000	ments of $100,000 U.S.	
Less accumulated		commencing February	
depreciation..............	4,331,000	1986.......................	1,000,000
	3,307,000	Shareholders' equity:	
Land	450,000	Common shares.............	1,000,000
	3,757,000	Retained earnings	1,840,000
Goodwill.....................	60,000		2,840,000
Deferred research and			
development $150,000			
less $10,000 annual			
amortization to date	80,000		
	$5,172,000		$5,172,000

N LTD.
Preliminary Retained Earnings Statement
For the Year Ended August 31, 1985

Balance, September 1, 1984	$1,850,000
Add net income...	36,500
	1,886,500
Less dividends..	46,500
Balance, August 31, 1985	$1,840,000

PC14–12. The following questions relate to the 1984 results of Consolidated-Bathurst Inc. as presented in the financial statements in Special Supplement B.

   a. What were the principles of consolidation used by C–B Inc.?
   b. List the subsidiaries of C–B that were consolidated.
   c. How much of the 1984 income went to the minority interest shareholders? What percentage was this amount of the 1984 balance sheet value for minority interest?
   d. How much sales revenue was eliminated as a result of consolidation?

C·H·A·P·T·E·R

15

The Statement of Changes in Financial Position

PURPOSE OF THIS CHAPTER

Four basic statements must be presented for external reporting purposes; they are the (1) income statement, (2) balance sheet, (3) statement of retained earnings, and (4) statement of changes in financial position. The prior chapters did not discuss or illustrate the preparation or use of the statement of changes in financial position (abbreviated SCFP).[1] The purpose of this chapter is to present the concepts of the SCFP, illustrate how the SCFP is developed, and emphasize its importance to external financial statement users. Also, this chapter discusses two alternative concepts of the SCFP—the cash basis and the working capital basis.

This chapter is subdivided as follows:

Part A—Purpose and concept of the SCFP, cash basis

Part B—Purpose and concept of the SCFP, working capital basis

Supplement 15A—T-account preparation of the SCFP

---

[1]Recent changes to the *CICA Handbook*, Section 1540, have proposed new titles for the SCFP such as cash flow statement, statement of operating, financing, and investing activities, and statement of changes in cash resources. The traditional title given here is also retained to satisfy statutory requirements where necessary. For consistency SCFP will be used in this chapter.

Part A—Purpose and Concept of the SCFP, Cash Basis

ACCRUAL BASIS REPORTING VERSUS CASH BASIS REPORTING

The income statement reports the entity's operating performance (revenues and expenses) for a period of time, and the balance sheet reports the financial position (assets, liabilities, and owners' equity) at a specific date. Both the income statement and the balance sheet are developed on the **accrual basis;** that is, the financial effects of transactions are measured and recorded in the accounting system when the various transactions occur rather than when the cash inflows and outflows resulting from those transactions occur. As a result, these two financial statements **do not report the timing, amounts,** and **causes** of the cash inflows and cash outflows during the reporting period. Therefore, they do not report the causes of the changes in the **liquidity** of the entity.

The accrual basis is used for most reporting purposes because it provides meaningful measurements of revenues, expenses, assets, and liabilities. For example, a sale transaction on credit should be recognized when the sale transaction was completed rather than the later date when the cash collection occurs because the revenue is earned when the completed transaction takes place. Similarly, an expense on credit should be recognized when the expense transaction was incurred rather than later when the cash is paid because the benefit associated with the expense is received when the completed expense transaction occurs. These two examples indicate why the income statement must be based on the accrual basis (i.e., transactions are recorded when their initial economic effects occur). For the same basic reason the balance sheet must report assets, liabilities, and owners' equity on the accrual basis.

In addition to the accrual basis income statement and balance sheet, decision makers need information on the sources and uses of cash. The SCFP, cash basis, reports only cash inflow and cash outflow transactions (including direct exchanges discussed later). Therefore, the SCFP is strictly a cash basis report. For example, instead of reporting income on the accrual basis (as reported on the income statement), the SCFP reports income for the period on the cash basis (on the SCFP this amount may be called Net cash inflow from normal operations).

HOW THE SCFP, CASH BASIS, HELPS DECISION MAKERS

Although statement users need to know the accrual basis results reported on the income statement and balance sheet, they also need financial information on the **timing, amounts,** and **causes** of the cash inflows and cash outflows of the entity during the accounting period. Fundamentally, knowledge about the **liquidity** (i.e., cash inflows and outflows) of an entity is very important to statement users because ultimately the success of an entity is measured by the cumulative amount of net cash inflow that it provides. Investors (creditors and owners) are interested in the net cash inflow of an entity because it provides their cash returns (e.g., dividends or interest, and cash received upon disposition of their shares or maturity of the debt). Also, the very existence of an entity depends upon cash flows; sufficient cash must be received and be available monthly (even daily) to pay for such items as salaries, rent, interest and principal on debt, assets purchased, and cash dividends. The first symptom of an impending economic problem is a shortage of cash. It is no wonder, then, that financial statement users need current and understandable data about the timing, sources, and uses of cash by the entity during the period covered by the financial statements. The **statement of changes in financial position, cash basis,** is designed to provide cash flow (i.e., liquidity) information for the statement users.[2] The SCFP supplements, but does not replace, the income statement and balance sheet because the SCFP provides information that is not provided by the other two statements.[3]

As a complement to the income statement and balance sheet, the SCFP (cash basis) is designed to provide information that is particularly useful to external users of the financial statements in answering questions such as:

1. How much cash was provided by the **normal operations** of the entity?
2. What were the primary sources of cash from such activities as borrowing, issuance of capital stock, and sale of operational assets?
3. How much cash was derived from **nonrecurring** transactions?
4. How much cash was used to pay long-term debts?
5. How much cash was used to acquire operational assets?
6. Why were large borrowings necessary? What uses were made of the cash borrowed?
7. What are the causes of any persistent liquidity problems of the entity?
8. Does a critical cash flow problem appear imminent?
9. What was the financial effect of noncash exchanges (such as the settlement of a debt by issuing company shares)?
10. Does the company have idle cash? How does the company "use" its idle cash?
11. What is the potential ability of the company to generate cash in the long term?

The SCFP, cash basis, serves a very useful and significant purpose because it can assist external users of the financial statements in answering the above questions.

---

[2]FASB, *Statement of Financial Accounting Concepts No. 1,* "Objectives of Financial Reporting by Business Enterprises" (Stamford, Conn., November 1978), states: "Since investors' and creditors' cash flows are related to enterprise cash flows, financial reporting should provide information to help investors, creditors, and others assess the amounts, timing, and uncertainty of prospective net cash inflows to the related enterprise."

[3]*CICA Handbook,* Section 1540.02, states specifically that the SCFP is intended to complement the other statements and should provide information different from other statements.

CONCEPT OF THE SCFP

The income statement and the SCFP often are called **change statements** because they "explain" the reasons why the **ending balance sheet** amounts for the accounting period are different from the **beginning balance sheet** amounts of that same period. As change statements, the income statement, the statement of retained earnings, and the SCFP are "dated" For the year ended December 31, 19A. In contrast, the balance sheet is dated as At December 31, 19A, because it is a **position** statement rather than a change statement.

The income statement "explains" the **changes** between the beginning and ending balance sheet amounts **caused by accrual basis** revenues, expenses, and extraordinary gains and losses. There are numerous **changes** in the beginning and ending balance sheet amounts (e.g., the purchase of an operational asset) that are not reported on the accrual basis income statement. In contrast to the income statement, the SCFP, cash basis, reports the **cash effects of all changes** between the beginning and ending balance sheets, including those

EXHIBIT 15–1
Statement of changes in financial position, cash basis (designed for instructional purposes only)

BROWNLEE SERVICE CORPORATION
Statement of Changes in Financial Position, Cash Basis
For the Year Ended December 31, 19B

Sources (inflows) of cash:

1.	Net cash inflow from normal operations (based on the income statement; computed below)...	$64,000*	
2.	Cash sale of noncash assets (such as machinery and investments)....	6,000	
3.	Cash borrowing (such as on notes and bonds payable).............	30,000	
4.	Cash sale and issuance of Brownlee capital stock..................	20,000	
	Total cash inflow during 19B		$120,000

Uses (outflows) of cash:

1.	Cash purchase of noncash assets (such as machinery and investments)	35,000	
2.	Cash payment on debts (such as notes and bonds payable)..........	50,000	
3.	Cash dividends declared and paid during 19B (such as on common or preferred shares)	10,000	
4.	Cash purchase of treasury stock	15,000	
	Total cash outflow during 19B		110,000
Net increase in cash during 19B.......................................			**$ 10,000**

*Income Statement Converted to Cash Basis
For the Year Ended December 31, 19B

Items	Accrual basis	Explanation of restatements to cash basis	Cash basis
Service revenues............	$127,000	Service not collected, $3,000	$124,000
Expenses			
Salary expense	38,000	Salaries payable, $2,000.................	36,000
Depreciation expense	18,000	A noncash expense, $18,000.............	–0–
Utilities	5,000	Paid in full............................	5,000
Remaining expenses.......	9,000	19C expense paid in advance, $3,000......	12,000
Income tax expense	8,000	Income tax payable, $1,000..............	7,000
Total expenses	78,000		60,000
Net income...............	$ 49,000	Net cash inflow from normal operations ...	$ 64,000

Proof based on net income:
Net income (accrual), $49,000 − $3,000 + $2,000 + $18,000 − $3,000 + $1,000 = $64,000 (cash inflow from normal operations).

reported on the income statement. Exhibit 15–1 presents a SCFP, cash basis, for Brownlee Service Corporation (designed for instructional purposes). Observe the two major captions "Sources (inflows) of cash" (four inflows are illustrated) and "Uses (outflows) of cash" (four outflows are illustrated). This SCFP indicates that the net increase in cash was $10,000 during the year. Most important, the SCFP reports how Brownlee Service Corporation obtained cash and specifically how that cash was used. This information is not reported on the accrual basis income statement and balance sheet. To illustrate another use of the SCFP, cash basis, assume you are interested in purchasing all of the outstanding capital stock of Brownlee Service Corporation. As a rational investor, you should be vitally concerned about the sources and uses of cash by that company during the last few years. The cash flow information should assist you in assessing the **future** cash flow problems and any advantages that you could expect as the owner.

Exhibit 15–2 presents an overview of the relationships between the beginning balance sheet, the SCFP, and the ending balance sheet. The SCFP given in Exhibit 15–1 is presented again in Exhibit 15–2 in a tabular format **between** the beginning and ending balance sheets (for instructional purposes only). Observe how the SCFP "explains" the changes in each balance sheet item in terms of the actual cash inflows and cash outflows and the **causes** of each of those changes.

FUNDS DEFINED

In business, the terms **funds, cash,** and **working capital** frequently are used interchangeably; however, clarity and precision are essential when they are used in accounting, especially with respect to the SCFP. **Cash** was defined in Chapter 8 as currency, balances on deposit in chequing accounts, and negotiable instruments that a bank will accept for immediate deposit in a chequing account. **Working capital** was defined in Chapter 2 as the **difference** between total current assets and total current liabilities.

With respect to the SCFP, "funds" **may be measured as either:**[4]

1. **Cash and cash equivalents**—Cash and cash equivalents include cash as defined above and cash equivalents which are temporary investments in the form of liquid marketable securities (Chapter 8) less short-term borrowings, such as bank loans payable on demand (Chapter 10).

2. **Working capital**—Working capital is always defined as current assets minus current liabilities. Current assets include cash, short-term investments, short-term receivables, inventory, and

---

[4]The word *funds* also is used in other ways by accountants. It has been used to refer to assets, usually cash, set aside for a specific future use, such as a building fund or a bond sinking fund; and in governmental accounting, it has an entirely different meaning. This wide range of inconsistent usage of the term suggests the desirability of using more descriptive terms, such as **cash** and **working capital,** and clearly defining the term in the financial statements.

EXHIBIT 15–2 Relationship between the SCFP (cash basis) and the balance sheet (SCFP data is from Exhibit 15–1)

Balance Sheet
At December 31, 19A

Cash...........	$ 20,000
Noncash assets.........	140,000
Total.........	$160,000
Liabilities...........	$ 50,000
Owners' equity:	
Common stock.........	100,000
Treasury stock.........	
Retained earnings......	10,000
Total.........	$160,000
Net increase in cash; to check (first line above).........	

Statement of Changes in Financial Position
For the Year Ended December 31, 19B

Sources of Cash		Uses of Cash	
Causes	*Amount*	*Causes*	*Amount*
Disposal (sold).....	$ 6,000	Purchase..........	$ 35,000
Borrowing.........	30,000	Payment.........	50,000
Issuance (sold).....	20,000	Purchase.........	15,000
Operations.........	10,000	Dividends.........	10,000
Operations.........	64,000	Total uses.........	110,000
Total sources......	120,000		
....	$120,000	....	10,000
			$120,000

Balance Sheet
At December 31, 19B

	Cash.........	$ 30,000
	Noncash assets	169,000
	Total........	$199,000
=	Liabilities.........	$ 30,000
	Owners' equity:	
=	Common stock......	120,000
=	Treasury stock......	(15,000)
=	Retained earnings	64,000
	Total.........	$199,000

A change statement that explains the causes of the changes in the balance sheet accounts—assets, liabilities, and owners' equity. (Assumptions: Funds measured as cash and no direct exchanges.)

prepaid expenses. The current liabilities are short-term debts that are expected to be paid out of the current assets.

In contrast to cash, which can be touched, counted, and used to purchase goods and services, to pay debts, and to invest, working capital is an **abstract concept because it is the arithmetical difference between the sum of the several current assets and the sum of the several current liabilities.** It is impossible to use the difference called working capital to deposit, pay debts, invest, and so on (also, it cannot be touched). Generally accepted accounting principles permit the SCFP to be prepared on either a cash or working capital basis and require that the SCFP disclose whether funds are measured as cash or as working capital. However, the trend is presently toward cash and cash equivalents as the basis for the statement. Working capital is still used because of legal provisions requiring its use. The discussions in Part A of this chapter assume the cash basis SCFP. The SCFP, working capital basis, is discussed in Part B.

ALL-RESOURCES CONCEPT OF THE SCFP

The SCFP must be based on the **all-resources concept** which means that it must report all of the **financing and investing activities** of the entity, not just those that cause an inflow or outflow of **funds** (i.e., cash or working capital). **Financing activities** are those transactions that cause a change in the size and composition of the debt or owners' equity of the business. For example, the issue or replacement of debt other than debt related to operations or short-term borrowings would be financing. Also included would be share issue or redemptions, cash dividends, and debt or share conversions. In contrast, **investing activities** are those transactions that affect the assets (replace or acquire) but are not normal operating transactions of the business that would be included in the income statement. Some common examples are fixed asset purchases or sales and the acquisition of long-term investments. Transactions that do not cause an inflow or outflow of funds are called **direct exchanges** because they involve the exchanges of **nonfund** assets, liabilities, or capital stock. An example of a direct exchange would be the purchase of an operational asset with full payment made by transferring land owned by the purchaser. This transaction would not cause a cash outflow; nevertheless, this direct exchange must be reported on the SCFP because there was, in effect, a simultaneous **source** of funds (for the sale of the land) and **use** of funds (for the purchase of the operational asset). Two additional examples of direct exchanges follow.

Case A

AB Company acquired a $6,000 machine by issuing 100 shares of its own common stock, par $50 per share. The shares were selling regularly at $60 per share; therefore, the company recorded the transaction in the accounts as follows:

Machine (100 shares × $60)...	6,000	
Common stock, par $50 (100 shares × $50).....................		5,000
Contributed surplus (100 shares × $10).......................		1,000

The above journal entry does not reflect a debit or credit to any "fund" account because neither cash nor working capital was affected. However, the transaction involved both a financing activity (the issuance of the shares) and an investing activity (the acquisition of the machine). Consequently, the all-resources concept holds that there was an implied (though not explicit) and concurrent inflow and outflow of funds. In contrast, instead of the direct exchange, assume that the company sold the common stock for $6,000 cash and immediately purchased the machine with the $6,000 received from the sale. Under this assumption, the sale of the common stock was a financing activity and the debit to Cash of $6,000 reflected a source (inflow) of funds. On the other side, the purchase of the machine was an investing activity and the credit to Cash of $6,000 reflected a use (outflow) of funds. In order to report all of the financing and investing activities, the all-resources concept requires that direct exchanges be reported on the SCFP because there is no economic difference between a direct exchange and an actual concurrent inflow and outflow of funds. Therefore, in Case A the direct exchange of the common shares for the machine must be reported on the SCFP "as if" **two separate transactions** occurred concurrently. That is, in this example, the SCFP must report (1) a **source** of cash for the financing and (2) a **use** of cash for the investment in the machine. AB Company would report the following on the SCFP:

> **Sources of cash:**
>   Sale and issuance of common shares (Note A)...... $6,000
> **Uses of cash:**
>   Purchase of machine (Note A)   6,000
> Note A: This was a direct exchange. A machine was acquired at a cost of $6,000; payment was made by issuing 100 shares of common stock, par $50 per share, that had a market value of $6,000.

Case B

AB Company owed a $30,000 note payable that was paid off in full by issuing 500 of its own common shares, par $50, with a $60 market value per share. The company would record the direct exchange as follows:

Note payable	30,000	
Common stock, par $50 (500 shares × $50)....................		25,000
Contributed surplus (500 shares × $10)......................		5,000

In the above journal entry, no fund accounts (cash or working capital) were debited or credited (i.e., there was no inflow or outflow of funds), nevertheless, the SCFP would report the $30,000 as if it were (1) a source of funds and (2) a use of funds in a manner similar to the example in Case A. Both sides of the transaction are part of the financing activities of the business.

CASH BASIS CONCEPT OF THE SCFP

The SCFP, cash basis, defines, measures, and reports the sources and uses of funds in terms of cash. For SCFP purposes, any short-term investments held almost always are added to cash because such investments are very near to cash and can be converted to cash easily at any time. Fundamentally, cash is used as the measure of funds because investors, creditors, and other external statement users view current cash flows as relevant information that can help them **project the ability of the company to generate favourable net cash inflows in the future.** In addition, a basic objective of the SCFP is to report on the liquidity of the entity, and cash is the most liquid of all assets. Cash represents the funds that circulate through a business on a daily basis. A company deals in terms of cash, and it is generated and used continuously.

In contrast to working capital, cash is accounted for separately (in the Cash account), and it can be physically counted. Cash inflows and outflows are understood and communicated easily (via the SCFP). Compared with cash, working capital is an elusive concept to many persons, particularly because the measurement of working capital includes **all** of the individual current assets with an offset which includes **all** of the current liabilities. The difference, which is called working capital, is only an amount—not a specific asset. The SCFP, cash basis, reports all of the **sources of cash** and cash equivalents, all of the **uses of cash** and its equivalents, and the **difference** between the total inflows and total outflows of the period. The **net increase or decrease in cash during the period** reported on the SCFP is the same amount as the change in Cash account balance between the two consecutive balance sheets (see Exhibit 15–2) or the change in the total of cash, short-term liquid investments less short-term borrowings.

Preparation of the SCFP, cash basis, involves identification of (a) all cash inflows including the net cash inflow from operations (i.e., from the income statement); (b) all cash investing; and (c) all cash financing. Calculation of the net cash flow from normal operations requires that the accrual basis income statement be converted to a cash basis.

PREPARING THE SCFP, CASH BASIS

Detailed knowledge of the technical procedures used to prepare a SCFP is not essential to be able to use it. However, as with the income statement and balance sheet, a general understanding of the procedures used to prepare the SCFP often is helpful in interpreting and using it more effectively.

Preparation of a SCFP, cash basis, requires identification and measurement of the amount of cash inflows from each source and the amount cash outflows for each use. The primary **sources of cash** are (a) normal operations, (b) long-term borrowing, (c) issuance of capital stock, and (d) sale of company assets. The primary **uses of cash** are (a) purchase of operational assets, (b) purchase of investments, (c) payment of long-term debt, and (d) payment of cash dividends.

Measurement of the net cash inflow (or net outflow) from **normal operations** involves a careful analysis to **convert** the income statement from the accrual basis to the cash basis. This conversion involves conversion of each revenue and each expense from the accrual basis to the cash basis.

Care should be taken to use revenues, expenses, gains, and losses that exclude extraordinary items in order to determine net cash flow from normal operations. The actual cash flow from extraordinary items should be disclosed in the operating, investing, or financing sections of the statement depending on their specific nature. For example, the extraordinary loss from the settlement of litigation could be a separate line after cash flow from normal operations. On the other hand, the proceeds from the sale of a certain part of the fixed assets or the long-term investments could be shown as an extraordinary item in the investing section of the statement.

The SCFP, cash basis, can be prepared by using one of the following three analytical approaches:[5]

1. **Direct analysis**—This approach can be used efficiently only when the situation is very simple as illustrated in Exhibit 15–1. It involves careful analysis of the income statement, the beginning and ending balance sheets, and selected transactions for the current period. It has no built-in accuracy checks except that the **net increase (decrease) in cash** must agree with the net change in the Cash account appropriately adjusted for changes in short-term investments and short-term borrowings during the period.

2. **Worksheet analysis**—This approach is widely used, especially in practical and complex situations, because it is very efficient and provides some built-in checks of accuracy. The worksheet approach is wholly consistent with the SCFP concept of "explaining" the changes between the beginning and ending balance sheet. For these reasons it is illustrated in Exhibit 15–4.

3. **T-account analysis**—This approach is similar to the worksheet approach except that a separate **T-account** is set up for each

---

[5]The discussions of the worksheet and T-account analytical approaches that follow can be omitted without significantly impinging upon the remaining discussions.

item for analysis purposes. It often is used for instructional purposes because students are familiar with T-account analyses of various sorts. The T-account approach is illustrated in Supplement 15A.

ILLUSTRATIVE CASE

Throughout the remainder of this chapter, the F Company case will be used as a basis for discussion and illustration. Assume it is December 31, 19B, the end of the annual accounting period, and that F Company has completed all of the year-end procedures, including the preparation of the income statement and the balance sheet. The remaining requirement is preparation of a SCFP for 19B.

Comparative balance sheets for the current and past year and the income statement for the current year are shown in Exhibit 15–3. The prior balance sheet, at December 31, 19A, is needed for analytical purposes regardless of the analysis approach used.

WORKSHEET ANALYSIS FOR PREPARING THE SCFP, CASH BASIS

Preparing a SCFP, cash basis, involves four procedural steps that are illustrated for F Company in Exhibits 15–4 (worksheet analysis), 15–5 (conversion of income statement from accrual to cash basis), and 15–6 (the formal SCFP). Preparing the SCFP requires data from the current income statement and the comparative balance sheets (Exhibit 15–3), and selected data about certain transactions. The preparation procedures, using either the worksheet or the T-account analysis, require an **analysis of all of the noncash balance sheet accounts**. The **net increase or decrease** in each of these noncash accounts, between the two consecutive balance sheets, must be analyzed to identify the cash inflows and cash outflows during the period. The results of this analysis are used to (1) identify and measure the amount of each cash source and each cash use and (2) determine the causes of the cash inflows and outflows (including all direct exchanges). Recall that these are the two purposes of the SCFP.

Four relatively simple procedural steps are involved in preparing the SCFP, cash basis; they are (1) data collection, (2) set up a worksheet, (3) complete the worksheet, and (4) prepare the formal SCFP.

Step 1—**Data collection.** Obtain the current income statement and comparative balance sheets (see Exhibit 15–3).

Step 2—**Set up a worksheet** with five-column headings as shown in Exhibit 15–4. In Part A—analysis of balance sheet accounts—list each balance sheet account and its balance as reported on the comparative balance sheets. In Part B—SCFP outlined—set up the two major captions on the

EXHIBIT 15–3
Comparative balance sheets and income statement, F Company

F COMPANY
Balance Sheets
At December 31, 19B, and 19A

	December 31, 19B		December 31, 19A[a]	
Assets				
Current assets:				
Cash....................................	$41,300		$31,000	
Accounts receivable (net)[b].....................	25,000		20,000	
Inventory (periodic)...........................	20,000	$ 86,300	24,000	$ 75,000
Long-term investments:				
Common shares of X Corporation		1,000		6,000
Operational assets:[b]				
Equipment (net)[c]...........................	59,000			
Patent (cost, $3,400 − amort., $200)	3,200	62,200		60,000
Total assets......................................		$149,500		$141,000
Liabilities				
Current liabilities:				
Accounts payable	$22,000		$20,000	
Income tax payable	500		1,000	
Short-term note payable (nontrade)..............	10,000	$ 32,500	14,000	$ 35,000
Long-term liabilities:				
Long-term note payable	10,000			
Bonds payable................................	32,000	42,000		40,000
Shareholders' Equity				
Shareholders' equity:				
Common shares, par $10	60,000		50,000	
Contributed surplus...........................	6,000		5,000	
Treasury stock (at cost).......................	(3,000)			
Retained earnings[d]	12,000	75,000	11,000	66,000
Total liabilities and shareholders' equity...........		$149,500		$141,000

[a]The ending balance sheet for the past period is the beginning balance sheet for the current period.

[b]In analyzing and reporting changes in financial position, accounts receivable and operational assets usually are shown **net** of the contra accounts as a matter of convenience.

[c]A machine that cost $5,000 was acquired on January 1, 19B, and payment in full was made by exchanging $5,000 of the investment in the common shares of X Corporation (the carrying value of these shares was the same as their current market value).

[d]Dividends declared and paid during 19B amounted to $7,000.

F COMPANY
Income Statement
For the Year Ended December 31, 19B

Sales revenue...		$100,000
Cost of goods sold		60,000
Gross margin		40,000
Less expenses:		
Expenses (not detailed)	$23,800	
Depreciation expense..	6,000	
Amortization expense (patent).................................	200	
Income tax expense	2,000	32,000
Net income...		$ 8,000

EXHIBIT 15–4
Worksheet to develop SCFP, cash basis (F Company for the year ended December 31, 19B)

Part A—Analysis of balance sheet accounts:

Items	Balances Dec. 31, 19A	Analysis of Interim Entries* Debit	Analysis of Interim Entries* Credit	Ending Balances Dec. 31, 19B
Debits				
Cash account less short-term note payable	31,000	(✓) 10,300		41,300
	(14,000)	(j) 4,000		(10,000)
Noncash accounts:				
Accounts receivable (net)	20,000	(d) 5,000		25,000
Inventory	24,000		(e) 4,000	20,000
LT investment, X Corp. shares†	6,000		(f-1) 5,000	1,000
Equipment (net)	60,000	(f-2) 5,000	(b) 6,000	59,000
Patent (net)		(g) 3,400	(c) 200	3,200
Total	127,000			139,500
Credits				
Accounts payable	20,000		(h) 2,000	22,000
Income tax payable	1,000	(i) 500		500
Long-term note payable			(k) 10,000	10,000
Bonds payable	40,000	(l) 8,000		32,000
Capital stock, par $10	50,000		(m) 10,000	60,000
Contributed surplus	5,000		(m) 1,000	6,000
Treasury stock		(n) 3,000		(3,000)
Retained earnings	11,000	(o) 7,000	(a) 8,000	12,000
Total	127,000	46,200	46,200	139,500

SCFP: "Sources of cash and cash equivalents" and "Use of cash and cash equivalents." The sources of cash will be represented by **debits** in this special account and the uses of cash by **credits.** Provide for two "source" subcaptions, "From normal operations" and "Financing." **"From normal operations"** is the section on the worksheet where net income (accrual basis) is converted to **net cash inflow from normal operations"** (also see Exhibit 15–1). All other **sources** of cash are identified under the subcaption **"Financing."** Step 3 (complete the worksheet) is discussed below, and Step 4 (prepare the formal SCFP) is discussed later in this chapter.

The SCFP worksheet, cash basis (Exhibit 15–4), is designed to reflect all of the accounts reported on the comparative balance sheets in the upper portion (Part A) including the current year's **beginning** balances (i.e., the ending balances from the prior period) and the **ending balances** (i.e., the ending balances for the current period). The prior year's balances are entered in the first amount column, and the current year's balances are entered in the last (fourth) amount column. The accounts making up cash and its equivalents can be conveniently grouped together at the start of the worksheet. Two inner amount columns are used for the debits and credits of the **analytical entries. The amounts entered in the two inner amount columns represent only the analyt-**

EXHIBIT 15–4
(concluded)

Part B—SCFP outlined:

Items	Income and Additions		Income Deductions	
Sources of cash:				
Normal operations:				
Net income	(a)	8,000		
Depreciation expense	(b)	6,000		
Amortization of patent	(c)	200		
Accounts receivable increase			(d)	5,000
Inventory decrease	(e)	4,000		
Accounts payable increase	(h)	2,000		
Income tax payable decrease			(i)	500
	Sources		**Uses**	
Investing				
Exchange of investment for equipment	(f-1)	5,000		
Financing				
Long-term note payable	(k)	10,000		
Issue of common stock	(m)	11,000		
Uses of cash:				
Financing:				
Payment of bonds payable			(l)	8,000
Purchase of treasury stock			(n)	3,000
Payment of cash dividend			(o)	7,000
Investing:				
Purchase of equipment			(f-2)	5,000
Purchase of patent			(g)	3,400
Net increase in cash and its equivalents				
((√) 10,300 + (j) 4,000)				14,300
		46,200		46,200

Net cash inflow from normal operations, $14,700; see Exhibits 15–5 and 15–6.

*These entries are keyed for ready reference to the text discussion; see Exhibit 15–7.
†Equipment was acquired in exchange for common shares of X Corporation, which were being held as a long-term investment.

ical entries and must account fully for the difference on each line between the beginning (first column) and ending balances (last column).

The bottom portion of the worksheet represents the SCFP; therefore, it is set up with the following side captions (leaving sufficient space under each caption to complete the analytical entries):

> **Sources of cash:**
> From normal operations
> Financing
> **Uses of cash:**
> Investing
> **Net increase (decrease) in cash and cash equivalents**

Step 3—**Complete the worksheet.** The "Analysis of Interim Entries" provides for the worksheet analysis (in summary fashion) of all changes during the period in each **noncash** account entered on the worksheet. These

EXHIBIT 15–5
Conversion of
accrual net income
from normal
operations to net
cash inflow from
normal operations

Income from normal operations	
(as reported on the income statement; accrual basis)	$ 8,000
Add (deduct) adjustments to convert to cash basis:	
Accounts receivable increase	(5,000)
Depreciation expense...	6,000
Amortization expense	200
*Merchandise inventory decrease....................................	4,000
*Accounts payable increase	2,000
*Income tax payable decrease	(500)
Net cash inflow from normal operations during the period	$14,700

*These two items may be combined as a conversion of cost of goods sold on the accrual basis to a cash basis as follows:

CGS—accrual basis (Exhibit 15–3)	$60,000
Inventory change—decrease (Exhibit 15–3)	(4,000)
Purchases—accrual basis	56,000
Accounts payable change—increase (Exhibit 15–3)	(2,000)
CGS—Cash basis	$54,000
Adjustment (add) for conversion of CGS to	
cash basis ($60,000 − $54,000) = ...	$ 6,000

changes are analyzed to determine those that (1) generated (increased) cash, (2) used (decreased) cash, and (3) those that did not affect cash. The analytical entries are entered directly on the worksheet in the normal debit-credit fashion; however, **instead of entering amounts in the Cash account, the debits to cash are entered in Part B, "Sources of cash" and the credits are entered as "Uses of cash."**

The final step in completing the worksheet is to record the **analytical entries** on the worksheet. The analytical entries are based upon data provided by the two balance sheets, the income statement, and other accounting records. The analytical entries on the worksheet for F Company (Exhibit 15–4) are entered as explained in Exhibit 15–7.[6]

After the analytical entries are made on the worksheet, a careful check should be made to ascertain whether the change between the beginning and ending balances on each line (i.e., each balance sheet account) is accounted for fully. This check indicates that the worksheet analysis is complete. At this point, the change in the Cash account during the period (as indicated on the first line), less (or plus) the change in the short-term note payable, can be entered at the bottom of the worksheet and the debit and credit columns in the bottom portion of the worksheet may be summed to test for equality. This provides a partial check on the accuracy of the results.

Completion of the worksheet involves conversion of **accrual** net income to net cash inflow from the normal operations of the entity.

Net cash inflow from normal operations reflects the net cash effect of all of the revenue and expense transactions. Accrual revenues, accrual expenses, and

---

[6]This same procedure, including the same analytical entries, is used in the T-account approach (presented in Supplement 15A, Exhibit 15–11).

EXHIBIT 15–6
Statement of
changes in financial
position, cash
basis, F Company

F COMPANY
Statement of Changes in Financial Position, Cash Basis
For the Year Ended December 31, 19B[a]

Operating activities:		
Income before extraordinary items...............................	$ 8,000	
Add (deduct) adjustments to convert to cash basis:		
Accounts receivable increase	(5,000)	
Depreciation expense..	6,000	
Amortization expense (patent)	200	
Merchandise inventory decrease................................	4,000	
Accounts payable increase	2,000	
Income tax payable decrease	(500)	
Net cash from normal operations............................		$14,700[b]
Financing:		
Issue of long-term notes...	10,000	
Issue of common shares	11,000	
Payment on bonds payable	(8,000)	
Purchase of treasury stock	(3,000)	
Payment of cash dividends	(7,000)	
Total cash from financing...................................		3,000
Investing:		
Exchange of investment for equipment (Note A).....................	5,000	
Purchase of equipment (Note A)	(5,000)	
Purchase of patent	(3,400)	
Total cash used for investing................................		(3,400)
Net increase in cash and cash equivalents............................		$14,300[c]

Note A: Equipment was acquired in exchange for common shares of X Corporation, which were being held as a long-term investment.

[a]Source of data, Exhibit 15–4.

[b]Some persons prefer to set the computations above this line to separate revenues from expenses, which has two distinct advantages: (1) separate computing and reporting of the cash inflows from revenues and the cash outflows for expenses and (2) no implication that depreciation and amortization expenses are sources of cash. To illustrate:

Revenues	$100,000	
Add (deduct) adjustments to convert to cash basis:		
Accounts receivable increase	(5,000)	
Cash generated from, revenues		$95,000
Expenses ($60,000 + $32,000).........................	92,000	
Add (deduct) adjustments to convert to cash basis:		
Depreciation expense	(6,000)	
Amortization expense...........................	(200)	
Merchandise inventory decrease	(4,000)	
Accounts payable increase	(2,000)	
Income tax payable decrease	500	
Cash disbursed for expenses....................		80,300
Net cash inflow from operations......................		$14,700

[c]Algebraically this amount is ($41,300 − $31,000) − ($10,000 − $14,000)

accrual income must be converted to a **strictly current cash basis** for reporting on the SCFP, cash basis. Cash inflow from normal operations sometimes is referred to as "Net cash generated from normal operations." **Noncash revenues** must be excluded from this amount because they do not cause cash to increase during the period. The reporting principle **requires** that the conversion adjustments of accrual income to cash inflow or outflow from operations (shown in detail on the SCFP as reflected in Exhibit 15–6).

EXHIBIT 15–7
Analytical worksheet entries, with explanations (refer to Exhibit 15–4)

Code	Data source	Analytical entry with explanation		
(a)	Income statement (Exhibit 15–3)	Sources of cash (income) .... 8,000 Retained earnings...................... 8,000		

This analytical entry (1) in Part A of the worksheet partially accounts for the $1,000 net credit increase in retained earnings and (2) in Part B reflects income as a source of cash. Because net income of $8,000 is an accrual basis amount, additions and subtractions must be made in subsequent analytical entries to convert it to a strictly current cash basis (see entries [b], [c], [d], [e], [h], and [i]).

| (b) | Income statement (Exhibit 15–3) | Sources of cash (income addition) .... 6,000 Equipment (or accumulated depreciation) .... 6,000 | | |

This analytical entry (1) in Part A accounts for the $6,000 credit increase in the equipment account and (2) in Part B adds the $6,000 to income because depreciation is a noncash expense that was deducted to derive accrual income.

| (c) | Income statement (Exhibit 15–3) | Sources of cash (income addition) .... 200 Patent (or Accumulated amortization) 200 | | |

This analytical entry accomplishes the same effects as entry (b) except that it relates to an intangible asset account.

| (d) | Balance sheet (Exhibit 15–3) | Accounts receivable (trade) .... 5,000 Sources of cash (income deduction)...... 5,000 | | |

This analytical entry (1) in Part A accounts for the $5,000 net debit increase in accounts receivable and (2) in Part B deducts the $5,000 from accrual income because credit sales were more than cash sales by this amount; it represents noncash sales for the period.

| (e) | Balance sheet (Exhibit 15–3) | Sources of cash (income addition) .... 4,000 Merchandise inventory .... 4,000 | | |

This analytical entry (1) in Part A, accounts for the net credit decrease in inventory and (2) in Part B adds the $4,000 to income because that amount of goods was withdrawn from inventory in excess of purchases. Thus, it represents a noncash expense (cost of goods sold) for this period which was deducted to derive accrual net income.

| (f) | Balance sheet (Exhibit 15–3 and related data about the direct exchange) | (f-1) Sources of cash (direct exchange) ...... 5,000 LT investment, shares of X Corp. 5,000 (f-2) Machine............................ 5,000 Uses of cash (direct exchange)..... 5,000 | | |

This was a direct exchange; therefore two entries were required. Analytical entry (f-1) reflects the investing activity; the debit recognizes the implied "as if" source of cash and the credit accounts for the net credit decrease in the investment account. Analytical entry (f-2) reflects the investing activity; the credit recognizes the implied use of cash and the debit accounts for the increase in the asset account. This $5,000 debit increase and the $6,000 credit decrease for depreciation expense (entry [b]) account fully for the $1,000 net credit decrease in the equipment account.

EXHIBIT 15–7
(continued)

Code	Data source	Analytical entry with explanation		
(g)	Balance sheet (Exhibit 15–3 and related data)	Patent	3,400	
		Uses of cash (purchase of patent)........		3,400

This analytical entry (1) in Part A accounts for a $3,400 debit increase in the patent account (which was its cost) and (2) in Part B recognizes a use of cash. This $3,400 debt increase and the $200 credit decrease for amortization (entry [c]) account fully for the net credit increase of $3,200 in the patent account.

Code	Data source	Analytical entry with explanation		
(h)	Balance sheet (Exhibit 15–3)	Sources of cash (income addition)	2,000	
		Accounts payable		2,000

This analytical entry (1) in Part A accounts for the $2,000 credit increase in accounts payable and (2) in Part B adds the $2,000 to income because the accrual expenses deducted to derive income amounted to $2,000 more than the cash currently paid; thus, this amount is recognized as a noncash expense for the period.

Code	Data source	Analytical entry with explanation		
(i)	Balance sheet (Exhibit 15–3)	Income tax payable	500	
		Sources of cash (income deduction)......		500

This analytical entry (1) in Part A accounts for the net debit increase in income tax payable and (2) in Part B deducts $500 from income because income tax expense deducted to derive accrual income was $500 less than the cash currently paid for income taxes; thus, this amount represented an additional cash expense for the current period.

Code	Data source	Analytical entry with explanation		
(j)	Balance sheet (Exhibit 15–3)	ST note payable (nontrade)	4,000	
		Uses of cash (payment of debt).........		4,000

This analytical entry (1) in Part A accounts for the net debit decrease in note payable and (2) in Part B reflects a use of cash to pay debt. The net effect is no change in the total of cash and its equivalents but it will be used as part of the calculation of the net changes in cash and its equivalents for the year. (See Exhibits 15–4 and 15–6.)

Code	Data source	Analytical entry with explanation		
(k)	Balance sheet (Exhibit 15–3)	Sources of cash (LT note)..................	10,000	
		LT note payable		10,000

This analytical entry (1) in Part A accounts for the $10,000 net credit increase in LT note payable and (2) in Part B reflects a source of cash.

Code	Data source	Analytical entry with explanation		
(l)	Balance sheet (Exhibit 15–3)	Bonds payable............................	8,000	
		Uses of cash (payment on bonds)		8,000

This analytical entry (1) in Part A accounts for the $8,000 net debit decrease in bonds payable and (2) in Part B reflects a use of cash to pay debt.

Code	Data source	Analytical entry with explanation		
(m)	Balance sheet (Exhibit 15–3)	Sources of cash (issued capital stock)	11,000	
		Common stock, par $10		10,000
		Contributed surplus..................		1,000

This analytical entry (1) in Part A accounts for the credit increases in the two capital stock accounts and (2) in Part B reflects a cash source.

EXHIBIT 15–7
(concluded)

Code	Data source	Analytical entry with explanation		
(n)	Balance sheet (Exhibit 15–3)	Treasury stock.............................	3,000	
		Uses of cash (purchase of treasury stock)...............................		3,000
		This analytical entry (1) in Part A accounts for the debit increase in the treasury stock account and (2) in Part B reflects a use of cash.		
(o)	Statement of retained earnings	Retained earnings.........................	7,000	
		Uses of cash..........................		7,000
		This analytical entry for cash dividends declared and paid during 19B, (1) in Part A accounts for a $7,000 debit decrease in retained earnings and (2) in Part B reflects a use of cash. When this $7,000 debit decrease is combined with the $8,000 credit increase (entry [a]) the net credit increase in the retained earnings account is fully accounted for. Note: A cash dividend declared in 19A and paid in 19B would not decrease cash until 19B. However, the declaration would decrease working capital in 19A (because of the credit to dividends payable) but would have no effect on working capital in 19B.		

Normal operations (i.e., as illustrated by the income statement) usually are the primary single source of cash for all businesses over the long term. Income reflects the effect of operations for the period on the **accrual basis.** As goods and services are sold during the period, there is an inflow of cash from **revenues** (i.e., from customers); however, the cash inflow from the revenues is affected by credit sales of the current and prior periods. To illustrate, assume a company sold goods during Year 1 amounting to $100,000, of which $5,000 remained uncollected at year-end. In this case, the cash inflow would be $95,000 (i.e., $100,000, minus the $5,000 in accounts receivable). Now, if sales for Year 2 totaled $120,000 and if accounts receivable decreased by $5,000, cash inflow during the period would be $125,000 (i.e., $120,000 plus the collection of $5,000 for credit sales that were reported in Year 1).

During an accounting period, **expenses** are incurred that cause a cash outflow; however, the cash outflow for expenses is affected by the amount of expenses incurred on credit in the current and prior periods. To illustrate, assume a company incurred expenses during Year 1 of $92,000, of which $2,000 was unpaid at year-end. In this case, the cash outflow would be $90,000 (i.e., $92,000, minus the $2,000 increase in accounts payable). Now, if expenses for Year 2 totaled $95,000 and at the same time accounts payable decreased by $2,000, cash outflow during the current period would be $97,000 (i.e., $95,000 plus the payment of $2,000 for expenses that were reported in Year 1).

Depreciation expense and amortization expense (e.g., patents) are **noncash expenses** of the current period that are deducted on the income statement to derive accrual income. Therefore, to measure cash flow from the income statement, such expenses must be added to the amount of accrual income. To illustrate, assume Company T sold goods for $100,000 cash, paid cash for all current expenses of $86,000, and reported depreciation expense of $6,000. Accrual income reported on the income statement would be $100,000 − $86,000 − $6,000 = $8,000. However, the cash inflow from the income statement (i.e., from operations) would be $14,000 (i.e., accrual income, $8,000 plus depreciation expense, $6,000).

Cost of goods sold is an expense; however, the cash outflow for this expense must be calculated by analyzing the changes in two related accounts—merchandise inventory and accounts payable (for purhases of merchandise). To convert accrual income to cash inflow from operations, a decrease in inventory during the period must be added to income because cash payments for purchases of inventory precede the sale or use of inventory. Similarly, an increase in inventory must be subtracted from income because a cash payment has been made for inventory that is not reflected in cost of goods sold. Relatedly, a decrease in accounts payable during the period must be subtracted from income because cash payments for accounts payable were more than the amount of purchases. Similarly, an increase in accounts payable must be added to income to convert it to the cash basis.[7]

Therefore, the amount of net cash inflow (or outflow) usually will be different from accrual income because of the effect of noncash revenues and noncash expenses.

To illustrate the income additions and deductions for the period to derive cash inflow (or cash outflow) from normal operations, refer to F Company. The income statement shown in Exhibit 15–3 reported income of $8,000. On the basis of an analysis of each revenue and each expense, income was converted to net cash inflow from normal operations as illustrated in Exhibit 15–5.

Observe in Exhibit 15–5 that net cash inflow from normal operations (i.e., $14,700) was $6,700 more than accrual income (i.e., $8,000). In some cases, net cash inflow from normal operations will be less than accrual income.

The analytical entries follow the pattern of the regular journal entries and must be made to account for all of the net increases and net decreases in each

---

[7]The adjustments to convert accrual income to cash flow from operations are quite varied. Although careful analysis is required, the following tabulation may be useful for checking purposes:

	Plus and minus adjustments to convert income to net cash flow from operations	
Item	When item increases	When item decreases
Accounts receivable (trade)	−	+
Accounts payable (trade)	+	−
Accrued liability and unearned revenue	+	−
Prepaid asset and accrued revenue	−	+
Inventory	−	+
Depreciation, depletion, and amortization	+	
Amortization of discount on bonds payable	+	
Amortization of premium on bonds payable	−	
Amortization of discount on bond investment	−	
Amortization of premium on bond investment	+	

account in Part A of the worksheet. The offsetting debits and credits to **Cash** are recorded in Part B of the worksheet.

When changes in each account in Part A of the worksheet are accounted for, the analysis is complete and Part B of the worksheet will reflect **each source and use of cash** during the period. One check of accuracy is indicated in Exhibit 15–4; that is, the balancing amount in Part B of the worksheet (i.e., $14,300) must agree with the net change in the Cash account less (or plus) the changes in short-term borrowings during the period.

> Step 4—**Prepare the formal SCFP.**   All of the information needed to prepare the formal SCFP is reflected in Part B of the worksheet. The SCFP, cash basis, for F Company (Exhibit 15–6) was prepared directly from Exhibit 15–4. Some variations in terminology and classifications may be observed in actual practice.

For study purposes, the analytical entries entered on the worksheet (Exhibit 15–4) are repeated and explained in more detail in Exhibit 15–7.

ANALYSIS OF DISPOSAL OF AN ASSET

The illustration of F Company does not include transactions involving the disposal of nonfund assets, such as the sale of an operational asset (e.g., equipment). Because of such disposals, net income (accrual basis) often includes a gain or loss on disposal. The total cash inflow from such should be reported on the SCFP, as "Investing." This requires that the gain or loss on the disposal be removed from the "Net income amount" as one of the conversion adjustments. To illustrate, assume that F Company sold an operational asset (say, equipment) that had a book (carrying) value of $2,000 for $3,000 cash. The conversion adjustment would deduct the $1,000 gain from net income and the $3,000 cash inflow would be reported under "Investing." If the $1,000 gain is not subtracted from net income, the gain would be "double counted" as a source of cash from (1) normal operations and (2) from investing. The **analytical entry** on the worksheet would be:

Sources of cash, Investing	3,000	
Equipment (net)		2,000
Sources of cash (income deduction)		1,000

Part B—Purpose and Concept of the SCFP, Working Capital Basis

CONCEPT OF WORKING CAPITAL

The only difference between the SCFP prepared on a working capital basis and one prepared on a cash basis is the way in which "funds" are **measured.** This part of the chapter discusses the sources and uses of funds in terms of **working capital** instead of cash and its equivalent. Compared with cash, working capital is a much broader, and a significantly different, concept of funds because it involves an arithmetical difference—**total current assets minus total current liabilities.** Thus, working capital is an abstraction because it does not represent a single asset, or group of similar assets; rather, it includes total current assets and an offset—total current liabilities. It cannot be counted, handled, or used to settle receivables and payables. Because of its abstract nature, working capital often is not fully understood by statement users. Although working capital is used widely as the SCFP measurement basis, a growing use of the cash basis is clearly evident.[8]

To understand and interpret properly the SCFP prepared on the working capital basis, one should understand clearly the concept of working capital as a measurement of funds. As a basis for discussion, observe in Exhibit 15–3, for F Company, that the comparative balance sheets reported working capital which may be tabulated as follows:

	December 31		Working capital increase (decrease)
	19B	19A	19A to 19B
Current assets:			
Cash................................	$41,300	$31,000	$10,300
Accounts receivable	25,000	20,000	5,000
Inventory	20,000	24,000	(4,000)
Total current assets................	86,300	75,000	
Current liabilities:			
Accounts payable	22,000	20,000	(2,000)
Income tax payable.....................	500	1,000	500
Short-term note payable (nontrade)......	10,000	14,000	4,000
Total current liabilities	32,500	35,000	
Working capital (at year-end)	$53,800	$40,000	$13,800

Examination of the working capital tabulation given above reveals two fundamental relationships that relate directly to the SCFP, working capital basis:

1. Increases in current assets and/or decreases in current liabilities **increase working capital,** and decreases in current assets and/or increases in current liabilities **decrease working capital.**
2. A transaction that affects **only** working capital accounts during

---

[8]Refer to footnote 2.

EXHIBIT 15–8
Worksheet to
develop the SCFP,
working capital
basis (F Company
for the year ended
December 31, 19B)

Part A—Analysis of the noncurrent balance sheet accounts:

Items	Balances Dec. 31, 19A	Analysis of Interim Entries† Debit	Analysis of Interim Entries† Credit	Ending Balances Dec. 31, 19B
Debits				
Working capital	40,000	(√) 13,800		53,800
Noncurrent accounts:				
LT investment, X Corp. shares	6,000		(f-1) 5,000	1,000
Equipment (net)	60,000	(f-2) 5,000	(b) 6,000	59,000
Patent (net)		(g) 3,400	(c) 200	3,200
Total	106,000			117,000
Credits				
LT note payable (nontrade)			(k) 10,000	10,000
Bonds payable	40,000	(l) 8,000		32,000
Common stock, par $10	50,000		(m) 10,000	60,000
Contributed surplus	5,000		(m) 1,000	6,000
Treasury stock		(n) 3,000		(3,000)
Retained earnings	11,000	(o) 7,000	(a) 8,000	12,000
Total	106,000	40,200	40,200	117,000

Part B—SCFP outlined:

Items	Income and Additions	Income Deductions	
			Net working capital inflow from normal operations, $14,200; see Exhibit 15–9.
Sources of working capital:			
From normal operations:			
Net income before extraordinary items			
Depreciation expense			
Amortization expense	(a) 8,000		
	(b) 6,000		
	(c) 200		

	Sources	Uses	
From other sources:			
Exchange of investment for equipment*	(f-1) 5,000		
LT note payable	(k) 10,000		
Sold and issued common stock	(m) 11,000		
Uses of working capital:			
Purchase of equipment with investment*		(f-2) 5,000	
Purchased patent		(g) 3,400	
Payment on bonds payable		(l) 8,000	
Purchased treasury stock		(n) 3,000	
Declared and paid a cash dividend		(o) 7,000	
Increase in working capital (line 1)		(√) 13,800	
	40,200	40,200	

*Equipment acquired in exchange for common shares of X Corporation, which were being held as a long-term investment.

†These entries are keyed for ready references to the text discussions (see Exhibit 15–7). The analytical entries for working capital do not include all of the analytical entries that were required for the cash basis; therefore, some of the code letters are not reflected here.

a given period does **not** change the amount of working capital for that period; therefore, the amount of working capital during a given period is changed only by transactions that affect one or more **noncurrent** (i.e., nonworking capital) accounts—noncurrent assets, noncurrent liabilities, and owners' equity accounts. This relationship may be demonstrated by using the basic accounting model (A = L + OE), assuming CA = current assets, NA = noncurrent assets, CL = current liabilities, NL = noncurrent liabilities, and OE = owners' equity:

a. CA + NA = CL + NL + OE; transposing
   Working capital   Noncurrent accounts

b. CA − CL = NL + OE − NA

Therefore, **changes in the noncurrent accounts** (i.e., NL, OE, NA) **represent sources and uses of working capital.** From this analysis we can develop the following summary of the effects of increases and decreases in the noncurrent accounts on the **uses and sources of working capital:**

Noncurrent (nonworking capital) accounts	Working capital Sources	Uses
Noncurrent assets—increase		x
—decrease	x	
Noncurrent liabilities—increase	x	
—decrease		x
Owner's equity—increase	x	
—decrease		x

Thus, an analysis of the **noncurrent** balance sheet accounts is used to develop a SCFP on the working capital basis (see Exhibits 15–8 and 15–9).

SOURCES OF WORKING CAPITAL

Transactions that **increase** working capital represent sources of working capital. Transactions of this type involve a debit to either a current asset or current liability account and a credit to one or more **nonworking capital accounts.** The four primary sources of working capital are:

1. **Current operations**—Income reflects the net results of operations. It is composed of **total revenues less total expenses** (accrual basis). As goods and services are sold during the period, there is an inflow of cash and/or accounts receivable (both working capital items). Also, during the period, as expenses are incurred, usually there is a decrease in working capital because of cash payments and/or the incurrence of current liabilities (both working capital items). Therefore, a reported income usually results in an increase (source) of working capital. In the case of a loss, working capital usually will decrease.

EXHIBIT 15–9
Statement of
changes in financial
position, working
capital basis, F
Company

F COMPANY
Statement of Changes in Financial Position, Working Capital Basis
For the Year Ended December 31, 19B

Part A—Sources and uses of working capital during the period:

Sources of working capital:
  From normal operations:
    Income before extraordinary items .... $ 8,000
      Add (deduct) to convert to working capital basis:
        Depreciation expense 6,000
        Amortization expense (patent) 200
          Total working capital generated from normal
            operations $14,200
  From other sources:
    Borrowed on long-term note 10,000
    Sale of unissued common shares 11,000
    Disposal of long-term investment (Note A) 5,000
      Total working capital generated from other sources 26,000
      Total working capital generated during the period 40,200

Uses of working capital:
  Cash dividend on common shares declared and paid during 19B 7,000
  Payment on bonds payable 8,000
  Purchase of patent 3,400
  Purchase of treasury stock 3,000
  Acquisition of equipment (Note A) 5,000
    Total working capital used during the period 26,400
Net increase in working capital during the period $13,800*

Part B—Changes in working capital during the period:

Working capital accounts	Balances December 31		Working capital increase (decrease)
	19B	19A	
Current assets:			
Cash.	$41,300	$31,000	$10,300
Accounts receivable (net)	25,000	20,000	5,000
Merchandise inventory	20,000	24,000	(4,000)
Total current assets	86,300	75,000	
Current liabilities:			
Accounts payable	22,000	20,000	(2,000)
Income tax payable	500	1,000	500
Note payable, short term (nontrade)	10,000	14,000	4,000
Total current liabilities.	32,500	35,000	
Working capital.	$53,800	$40,000	$13,800*

    Note A: Equipment was acquired in exchange for common shares of X Corporation, which were being held as a long-term investment.
      Part A—source of data, Exhibit 15–8.
      Part B—source of data, Exhibit 15–3.
      *These two amounts must agree.

The increase in working capital from operations usually is somewhat more than the amount of income for the period. This result is due to the fact that the income statement usually includes some expenses that do not involve the use of working capital during the period, such as depreciation and depletion of tangible assets and amortization of intangible assets. For example, the income statement for F Company (Exhibit 15–3) shows that there was an inflow of working capital of $100,000 from sales revenue during the year. It also shows that there were outflows of working capital for cost of goods sold, $60,000; expenses, $23,800; and income tax, $2,000 (resulting in a net working capital inflow of $14,200). In this computation, no deductions were made for depreciation expense of $6,000 and amortization expense of $200 because these two items were **nonworking capital** expenses. This latter point is evident if we recall the two expense entries:

Depreciation expense...	6,000	
Accumulated depreciation		6,000
Amortization expense	200	
Patent...		200

The journal entries neither increased nor decreased working capital because no working capital account was debited or credited; however, income was decreased. The **working capital increase from normal operations,** therefore, would be computed and reported as follows:*

Income before extraordinary items	$ 8,000
Add (deduct) to convert to working capital basis:	
Depreciation expense	6,000
Amortization expense.............................	200
Net working capital from normal operations	$14,200

    *See Exhibits 15–8 and 15–9.

This example illustrates that the conversion of income (accrual basis) to a working capital basis involves less computations than the conversion to net cash flow from normal operations.

    2. **Sale of capital stock for cash or short-term receivables**—A sale of capital stock is a source of working capital because cash or a short-term receivable flows in for the sale price of the shares.

    3. **Sale of noncurrent assets**—When a long-term investment, an operational asset, or an "other noncurrent asset" is sold, working capital is increased by the total amount of the cash and/or short-term receivable that results from its disposition (the increase is not the amount of the disposal gain or loss).

    4. **Long-term borrowing**—When a loan is obtained on a long-term basis, working capital (cash) is increased by the proceeds of the loan. In contrast, when a short-term loan is obtained, working capital is not increased because a working capital account (Cash) is increased and another working capital account (a current liability) is increased by the same amount. Because the two changes offset each other, working capital (current assets minus current liabilities) does not change. To illustrate, assume F Company borrowed $5,000 cash

on a 90-day loan near the end of 19B. The working capital effect would be as follows:

	Before short-term loan	Effect of short-term loan	After short-term loan
Current assets.........	$ 86,300	+$5,000	$ 91,300
Current liabilities	(32,500)	(+ 5,000)	(37,500)
Working capital	$ 53,800	–0–*	$ 53,800

*Effect on working capital = (+$5,000) − (+$5,000) = 0.

USES OF WORKING CAPITAL

Transactions that **decrease** working capital represent uses of working capital. Transactions of this type involve a credit to a working capital account and a debit to a **nonworking capital account.** The three primary uses of working capital are:

1. **Purchase operational assets and other noncurrent assets for cash or short-term debt**—Transactions of this type usually require a payment of cash and, sometimes, the creation of a short-term debt. To the extent that cash is paid or short-term debt is incurred, working capital is reduced.
2. **Declare cash dividends**—This transaction causes the creation of a current liability; therefore, working capital is reduced (used) by that amount. However, the subsequent cash payment of the dividend already declared does not reduce working capital.[9]
3. **Pay a long-term liability**—Payments on long-term notes, bonds, and other long-term obligations involve an outflow of cash; therefore, they represent uses of working capital. In contrast, the payment of a **current liability does not change working capital** for the same reason explained above in respect to borrowing (source) on a short-term debt basis; that is, the two working capital effects offset one another.

To summarize, (1) working capital is not increased or decreased by any transaction that involves **only** debits and credits to working capital accounts, and (2) working capital is increased or decreased by each transaction that involves debits and/or credits to working capital accounts and **also** debits and/or credits to non-working capital accounts.

---

[9]When a dividend is declared, working capital is reduced by the amount of the dividend even though payment in cash is in a later period. In this situation, the dividend payable is recorded as a current liability on declaration date. The cash payment in the later period does not affect working capital at that time because equal debits and credits to working capital accounts will be made. This distinction is important only when declaration and payment dates fall in different accounting periods. The declaration and payment of a cash dividend in the same year reduces both cash and working capital for that year.

SCFP FORMAT FOR SCFP, WORKING CAPITAL BASIS

The SCFP, working capital basis, for F Company is shown in Exhibit 15–9. The **standard format** for the SCFP, working capital basis, includes two distinct parts (in contrast to the SCFP, cash basis, which needs only the first part):

Part A—Sources and uses of working capital
Part B—Changes in the working capital during the period

Part A reports the operations, the financing activities (sources of working capital) and the investing activities (uses of working capital) during the period. Part A is the basic report because Part B simply lists each current asset and current liability, the resulting increases and decreases, and the net change in working capital during the period.[10] The format in Part A of the statement follows the cash basis format, except that it relates only to the sources and uses of **working capital.**

PREPARING THE SCFP, WORKING CAPITAL BASIS

Preparing the SCFP, working capital basis, essentially follows the cash basis approach discussed in Part A of this chapter. The four consecutive steps to prepare the SCFP worksheet are:

Step 1—**Collect data.** Obtain the current income statement and comparative balance sheets (see Exhibit 15–3).

Step 2—**Set up the worksheet format** as shown in Exhibit 15–8. In Part A of the worksheet, list each noncurrent (i.e., nonworking capital) account and its balances as reported on the comparative balance sheets. Use the first line for the working capital amounts (these are "balancing" amounts). Observe in Exhibit 15–8 how the accounts, beginning balances and ending balances are entered on the worksheet.

Step 3—**Complete the worksheet.** The analytical entries are entered only on the worksheet; they follow the pattern of regular journal entries and must account for all of the net increases and decreases in the noncurrent accounts, in Part A of the worksheet. The offsetting debits and credits that represent increases and decreases of working capital are recorded in Part B of the worksheet (debits = Sources and also credits = Uses).

Step 4—**Prepare the formal SCFP.** Part B of the worksheet completed in Step 3 provides all of the data needed to complete the "Sources and Uses" part

---

[10]Part B is copied directly from the related comparative balance sheets. For this reason, some accountants consider Part B to be redundant. The two parts of the SCFP, working capital basis, are not called "Part A and Part B" in actual practice; this designation is used here only for instructional convenience.

of the formal SCFP. The second part of the SCFP is copied directly from the comparative balance sheets. Exhibit 15–9 presents the formal SCFP, working capital basis. If desired, the formal statement in Exhibit 15–9 could be classified using the categories of Operations, Financing and Investing as was done for the cash basis statement presented in Exhibit 15–6.

The detailed discussions and illustrations provided in Part A of the chapter for the cash basis apply exactly the same for the working capital basis with two exceptions: (1) the working capital analysis is limited to only the nonworking capital asset, liability, and owners' equity accounts (therefore there are fewer analytical entries); and (2) the term **working capital** is used instead of **cash.**

Preparation of the SCFP, working capital basis, for F Company is illustrated in Exhibits 15–8 and 15–9. The analytical entry codes used in Exhibit 15–4 (cash basis) also were used in Exhibit 15–8 (working capital basis) to facilitate study and comparison. You should reread the explanations in Exhibit 15–7 for entries (a), (b), (c), (f), (g), (k), (l), (m), (n), and (o) (i.e., the working capital analytical entries).

The T-account analysis for preparation of the SCFP is illustrated in Supplement 15A.

DEMONSTRATION CASE

The 1982 statement of changes in Consolidated financial position of a real Manufacturing Company and Subsidiaries was taken from the annual report:

	(Thousands of Dollars)		
Years Ended December 31	**1982**	1981	1980
Cash Provided by Operations:			
Net earnings	**$20,637**	$30,074	$23,255
Noncash items included in net earnings:			
Depreciation	**18,353**	15,432	13,826
Deferred income taxes	**521**	655	985
Other	**298**	591	476
	39,809	46,752	38,542
Increase (decrease) in cash caused by certain working capital items:			
Trade accounts receivable	**2,474**	(16,812)	(5,404)
Inventories	**(1,582)**	(15,933)	(1,300)
Prepaid expenses and other current assets	**306**	(13)	2,031
Accounts payable	**(52)**	8,183	3,839
Other current liabilities	**5,980**	3,297	2,266
Effect of exchange rate changes	**(181)**	(477)	
Net Cash Flow from Operations	**46,754**	24,997	39,974
Financing Activities:			
Issuance of long-term debt	**2,500**	27,000	
Payment of long-term debt	**(1,104)**	(3,785)	(2,222)
Increase in current notes payable to banks	**2,622**	1,799	6,313
Payments from Employee Stock Ownership Trust	**703**	1,267	1,289
Common Stock issued in connection with acquisition of a business		2,278	
Proceeds from the exercise of stock options	**24**	487	217
Other—net	**592**	(427)	591
	5,337	28,619	6,188
Net Cash Provided from All Sources	**52,091**	53,616	46,162
Cash Used For:			
Purchase of property, plant and equipment, net	**23,206**	29,001	24,885
Net noncurrent assets of businesses acquired	**5,724**	6,690	
Acquisition of minority interests		2,840	
Cash dividends to shareholders	**14,048**	12,551	11,004
	42,978	51,082	35,889
Net Increase in Cash and Marketable Securities	**9,113**	2,534	10,273
Cash and Marketable Securities at Beginning of Year	**15,505**	12,971	2,698
Cash and Marketable Securities at End of Year	**$24,618**	$15,505	$12,971

Note the form is somewhat different than the current requirements because it was issued before the new pronouncement.

Required:

a. What period does this statement cover? How does Manufacturing define "funds"?
b. Explain why (1) depreciation and (2) deferred income taxes are added to net earnings to determine cash inflow from operations.
c. Explain why (1) accounts receivable was added to and (2) inventories was deducted from net earnings to calculate cash inflow based on operations.
d. What was the amount of net cash flow from the income statement?
e. Explain why (1) the issuance of long-term debt was added and (2) the payment of long-term debt was deducted to determine net cash provided from all sources.
f. Assume the 1982 income statement and balance sheet are available. Explain how you could verify the overall accuracy of the SCFP.

Suggested solution

a. Period covered by the SCFP, **Year ended December 31** for each year (1980, 1981, and 1982). The SCFP uses the term **cash;** however, the last three lines indicate that the cash definition includes **cash and short-term marketable securities.** Note that short-term borrowings should be included in current disclosures.
b. On the SCFP, net earnings, **accrual** basis (i.e., $20,637), must be converted to the cash basis by making certain adjustments. **Depreciation** is added to convert net earnings to the cash basis because (1) it is a noncash expense and (2) was deducted to compute net earnings. **Deferred income taxes** is the accumulated amount of the non-cash expenses charged against revenue; the related part of income tax expense is added to convert net earnings to the cash basis because (1) it is a noncash expense and (2) was deducted to compute net earnings.
c. During 1982, **accounts receivable decreased** by $2,474, which increased cash inflow (compared to accrual revenue); therefore, that amount was added to net earnings to convert it to the cash basis. **Inventories increased** during 1982 by $1,582, which caused cash of this amount to be paid (when purchased or when the related accounts payable is paid); therefore, this amount must be deducted from net earnings to convert it to the cash basis.
d. Net cash inflow from operations (i.e., the income statement) was $46,754.
e. Long-term debt of $2,500 was added because it is a source of cash borrowing. In contrast, long-term debt of $1,104 was deducted because this was the total payment on debts.
f. Overall accuracy of the SCFP can be verified by referring to the beginning and ending balances of the two "cash equivalent" accounts, viz:

	Beginning balance	Ending balance	Net increase
Cash	$	$	$
Short-term marketable securities			
Total	$15,505	$24,618	$ 9,113*

Check figure for the SCFP.

SUMMARY OF CHAPTER

The annual financial statements of publicly held companies must include, as a minimum, a balance sheet, income statement, statement of retained earnings, and statement of changes in financial position. The purpose of a SCFP is to provide investors, creditors, and other external statement users information not provided by the other two statements that will help them project the future cash flows of the entity. To accomplish this purpose, the SCFP reports on the **liquidity** of the company in terms of the **sources and uses of funds;** it also reports the **causes** of the inflows and outflows of funds. The SCFP may be prepared using **either** (1) cash or (2) working capital as the measure of funds. When prepared on a cash basis, the sources and uses of funds are measured in terms of a specific asset, cash. When prepared on a working capital basis, the sources and uses of funds are measured in abstract terms because working capital is the difference between the total current assets and total current liabilities.

The primary source of funds during the period is normal operations (i.e., the amount of funds based on the income statement). Other common sources of funds are borrowing, sale of operational assets, and the sale and issuance of capital stock. Typical uses of funds are payment on debt, purchase of operational assets, long-term investments, and payment of cash dividends.

The question of whether the cash and its equivalents basis or the working capital basis of the SCFP better serves the typical external user of financial statements has been the subject of considerable controversy. Exhibit 15–10 provides a summary of some of the issues.

SUPPLEMENT 15A—T-ACCOUNT ANALYSIS TO DEVELOP THE SCFP

Parts A and B of the chapter indicated that the SCFP, on either the cash or working capital basis, can be prepared using the (1) T-account analysis or (2) worksheet analysis. The T-account analysis traditionally has been used for instructional purposes, while the worksheet analysis is used almost exclusively in practice and in situations characterized by complexity and large amounts of data. The worksheet analysis is viewed by many persons as a more sophisticated and more efficient approach than the T-account analysis.

This supplement presents two T-account analyses—one illustrating the cash basis and the other the working capital basis. The illustrative case used in this chapter (F Company) also is used in this supplement. The T-account analysis presented in this supplement closely parallels the worksheet analysis in all respects except format. Each account is analyzed in a straightforward Debit = Credit manner, and the **analytical entries are identical** to those used in the worksheet approach. The worksheet has the distinct advantage of being designed so that the bottom portion may suffice for the formal SCFP in many problem and examination situations (see Exhibit 15–4).

T-account analysis for the SCFP, cash basis

The T-account analysis to develop the SCFP, cash basis, is started by setting up separate T-accounts for each **noncash** account reported on the comparative balance sheets and then entering in each account the net change (NC) in the account balance from the beginning and ending balance sheets (this is equivalent to Part A of the worksheet). Also, two T-accounts are set up to account

EXHIBIT 15–10   SCFP—Cash and working capital bases compared

Comparative Criteria	Evaluation		Comments
	Cash Basis	Working Capital Basis	
Choice of reporting entity	Low	High	Most companies to date have elected to use working capital basis.
Relevance in projecting future cash flows by users	High	Low	Cash basis focuses only on cash sources and uses; working capital basis merges current assets and current liabilities into a difference. Working capital basis not accorded much attention in recent statements of "concepts" and "objectives."
Measurement basis	Specific	Abstract	Because it is a broad measure, working capital basis tends to obscure the primary concern of users—cash flows.
Reports liquidity	Short term Long term	Long term	Working capital focuses primarily on the long-term assets and liabilities.
Complexity in preparing SCFP	Low	Low	Both methods involve use of either a worksheet or T-account format during preparation.
Extent of preparation analyses	More	Less	Because there are more noncash accounts than nonworking capital accounts, the cash basis requires somewhat more analysis.
Understandability of SCFP	High	Low	External users (other than security analysts) tend to have problems with the abstract concept of working capital; most people understand cash.
Objectivity (and not subject to manipulation)	High	Low	Cash is easy to define, identify, and classify; it **excludes** all estimates, such as bad debt expense, depreciation, estimates of current assets (such as certain prepayments) and current liabilities (such as current portions of deferred tax, warranties, lease liabilities, pension liabilities, and accruals). Working capital often **includes** a number of these estimates; also, working capital is plagued with subjectivity in classification of many items (such as marketable securities).
Redundancies	None	High	The current asset and current liability sections on the comparative balance sheets are repeated item by item on the SCFP, working capital basis. There are no such redundancies on the cash basis statement.
Information content related to the kind of "funds" that circulate throughout a business entity	High	Low	It has been said that a properly prepared and detailed cash flow SCFP "bares the financial soul of a company." Working capital is said to combine too many diverse items and thereby not reveal many critical financing and investing activities. Potential failure of an entity almost always is first revealed in the cash flows.

for sources and uses of cash. These T-accounts are labeled "From normal operations" and "From other." In these two accounts, Debits = Sources and Credits = Uses (this is equivalent to Part B of the worksheet). Next, the **analytical entries** are entered in the T-accounts; these entries are **identical** to those that would be entered on the worksheet analysis (Exhibit 15–4). Thus, the T-account analysis is identical to the worksheet analysis except for format. The T-account format for F Company is illustrated in Exhibit 15–11.

EXHIBIT 15–11
SCFP, cash basis;
T-account analysis

F COMPANY
T-Account Approach to Develop Sources and Uses of Cash
Noncash Balance Sheet Accounts

Accounts Receivable (net)		Inventory		LT Investment—Shares X Corporation	
NC 5,000			NC 4,000		NC 5,000
(d) 5,000			(e) 4,000		(f-1) 5,000

Equipment (net)		Patent (net)		Accounts Payable	
	NC 1,000	NC 3,200			NC 2,000
(f-2)Pur.5,000	(b) 6,000	(g) Pur.3,400	(c)Amort. 200		(h) 2,000

Income Tax Payable		ST Note Payable (nontrade)		LT Note Payable	
NC 500		NC 4,000			NC 10,000
(i) 500		(j) 4,000			(k) 10,000

Bonds Payable		Common Stock, Par $10		Contributed Surplus	
NC 8,000			NC 10,000		NC 1,000
(l) 8,000			(m) 10,000		(m) 1,000

Treasury Stock (cost)		Retained Earnings	
NC 3,000			NC 1,000
(n) 3,000		(o) Div. 7,000	(a) NI 8,000

NC = Net change from 19A to 19B.

EXHIBIT 15–11
(concluded)

Sources and Uses of Cash
From Normal Operations

	Sources			Uses	
	Income Plus Additions			*Income Reductions*	
(a)	Net income	8,000	(d)	Accounts receivable increase	5,000
(b)	Depreciation expense	6,000	(i)	Income tax payable decrease	500
(c)	Amortization of patent	200			
(e)	Inventory decrease	4,000			
(h)	Accounts payable increase	2,000			

From Other

	Sources			Uses	
(f-1)	Exchange of investment for equipment	5,000	(f-2)	Purchase of equipment with investment	5,000
(k)	LT note payable	10,000	(g)	Purchased patent	3,400
(m)	Sold and issued common shares	11,000	(l)	Payment on bonds payable	8,000
			(n)	Purchased treasury stock	3,000
			(o)	Paid cash dividend	7,000
				Check: Change in Cash account ($41,300 − $31,000) and (j) short-term note ($10,000 − $14,000)	10,300 / 4,000
	Totals	46,200			46,200

T-account analysis for the SCFP, working capital basis

The T-account analysis is started by setting up separate T-accounts for each **nonworking capital** account reported on the comparative balance sheets and entering the net change (NC) in each account balance (this is equivalent to Part A of the worksheet). Also, two T-accounts are set up for sources and uses of working capital "From operations" and "From other" (this is equivalent to Part B on the worksheet). Next, the **analytical** entries are entered in the T-accounts; these analytical entries are identical to those entered on the worksheet (see Exhibit 15–8). The T-account format is illustrated in Exhibit 15–12.

EXHIBIT 15–12
SCFP, working
capital basis; T-
account analysis

F COMPANY
T-Account Approach to Develop Sources and Uses of Working Capital
Nonworking Capital Balance Sheet Accounts*

LT Investment—Share X Corporation			Equipment (net)			Patent (net)		
	NC	5,000		NC	1,000	NC	3,200	
(f-1)		5,000	(f-2)Pur.5,000	(b)	6,000	(g) Pur. 3,400	(c)Amort. 200	

LT Note Payable			Bonds Payable			Common Stock, Par $10		
	NC	10,000	NC	8,000			NC	10,000
	(k)	10,000	(l)	8,000			(m)	10,000

Contributed Surplus			Treasury Stock			Retained Earnings		
	NC	1,000	NC	3,000			NC	1,000
	(m)	1,000	(n)	3,000		(o) Div. 7,000	(a) NI 8,000	

NC = Net change from 19A to 19B

Sources and Uses of Working Capital*
From Normal Operations

Sources		Uses	
Income Plus Additions		*Income Reductions*	
(a) Net income	8,000		
(b) Depreciation expense	6,000		
(c) Amortization of patent	200		

From Other

Sources		Uses	
(f-1) Exchange of invest. for equip.	5,000	(f-2) Purchase of equipment with investment	5,000
(k) LT note payable	10,000	(g) Purchased patent	3,400
(m) Sold and issued common shares	11,000	(l) Payment on bonds payable	8,000
		(n) Purchased treasury stock	3,000
		(o) Declared cash dividend	7,000
		Check: Change (increase) in working capital ($53,800 − $40,000)	13,800
Totals	40,200		40,200

*Analytical entry codes used are the same as in Exhibit 15–4 (cash basis) to facilitate comparison and study. Not all of the analytical entries for cash are used in working capital analysis.

IMPORTANT TERMS DEFINED IN THIS CHAPTER

Terms *(alphabetically)*	*Key words in definitions of* *important terms used in chapter*	*Page* *reference*
All-resources concept	SCFP must report **all** sources and uses of funds; this includes direct nonfund exchanges (direct swaps).	786
Analytical entries, SCFP	Entries used on a SCFP worksheet to reconcile the nonfund accounts and to develop the SCFP.	792
Cash and its equivalents	Cash plus temporary liquid investments less short-term borrowings.	784
Change statements	Statements that explain why balance sheet accounts change during a period; Income Statement and SCFP.	783
Direct exchanges, SCFP	Transactions that involve the exchange of only nonfund assets, liabilities, or capital stock; direct swaps.	786
Financing activities	Transactions and activities that cause a change in the size and composition of debt and owners' equity during the period.	786
Funds	A broad financial term; for the SCFP it means either (a) cash or (b) working capital.	784
Investing activities	Transactions and activities that cause a change in the fixed assets during the period.	786
Noncash expenses	Expenses reported on the income statement that did not require cash payments during the period; e.g., depreciation.	798
Noncash revenues	Revenues of a period reported on the income statement that did not cause funds to increase during that period.	795
SCFP, cash basis	SCFP that reports sources and uses of funds in terms of cash, or cash equivalents.	788
SCFP, working capital basis	SCFP that reports sources and uses of funds in terms of working capital.	807
Sources of cash	Activities and transactions that cause a cash inflow into a company; from operations, borrowing, etc.	789
Sources of working capital	Transactions that cause working capital to increase; debits to working capital accounts.	803
T-account approach, SCFP	Used to develop the SCFP; an organized approach used for instructional purposes; uses T-accounts.	789
Uses of cash	Transactions that increase cash; from normal operations, borrowing, issuing capital stock, etc.	789
Uses of working capital	Transactions that decrease working capital; credits to working capital accounts.	806
Working capital	Current assets minus current liabilities; one way to measure funds on the SCFP.	784
Worksheet approach, SCFP	Used to develop the SCFP; an organized and systematic approach; analyzes the nonfund accounts; used for either cash or working capital.	790

QUESTIONS FOR DISCUSSION

Part A

1. What are the basic statements that are required to be included in the annual financial statements? Fundamentally, what does each report?

2. What are the primary sources and uses of funds in a business?

3. What is the essential difference between a SCFP prepared on (a) a cash basis and (b) a working capital basis?

4. Company X acquired a tract of land in exchange for a $10,000 bond payable. How does this transaction relate to the SCFP all-resources concept?

5. What is a direct exchange? How does a direct exchange affect the SCFP?

6. Why is the SCFP called a change statement?

7. Explain what is meant by each of the following terms. Give two examples of each.
    a. Nonfund asset accounts.
    b. Nonfund liability accounts.

8. Explain why income (i.e., from normal operations) often is the primary source of funds in a business in the long term.

9. In developing "sources of funds, from operations (cash or working capital)," on the SCFP, explain why depreciation, amortization of intangible assets, and depletion are added back to net income.

10. What is the basic reason why the SCFP, cash basis, is particularly relevant to the average external statement user?

11. Explain why the SCFP, cash basis, requires the conversion of net income to another amount.

12. Assume you are completing a SCFP, cash basis, and have the data listed below. On a separate sheet, complete the blanks to the right.

Income (accrual basis).................		$10,000
Increase in accounts receivable..........	$1,400	_____
Depreciation expense..................	1,500	_____
Amortization of patent	200	_____
Decrease in merchandise inventory......	2,200	_____
Decrease in accounts payable	1,000	_____
Net cash inflow from normal operations for the period		$_____

13. Total sales revenue for 19B amounted to $300,000, of which one third was on credit. The balances in accounts receivable at year's end were 19B $15,000; and 19A, $23,000. The cash inflow from sales revenue during 19B was $_____.

14. Total expenses for 19B amounted to $200,000, of which $10,000 was depreciation expense and $30,000 was on credit (accounts payable). The balances in accounts payable at year's end were 19A, $16,000; and 19B, $12,000. The cash outflow for expenses during 19B was $_____.

15. Assume that you are preparing a SCFP, cash basis, and have the data listed below. On a separate sheet, complete the blanks to the right.

Income (accrual basis)		$20,000
Decrease in accounts receivable.	$2,000	_____
Decrease in accounts payable.	3,000	_____
Depreciation expense.	8,000	_____
Gain on sale of operational asset (cash sale price, $3,000, book value, $2,000)	1,000	_____
Net cash inflow from normal operations.		$_____

16. Company X is preparing the SCFP, cash basis, for 19B. During the year, the company acquired a tract of land and paid in full by issuing 1,000 shares of its own capital stock, par $10 per share (market value $15 per share). Show how this transaction should be reported on the SCFP. Explain. Would this transaction be reported in the same manner on the SCFP, working capital basis? Why?

Part B

17. Complete the following tabulation:

	Working capital	
Transactions	Source	Use
a. Collected on account receivable, $150.	$_____	$_____
b. Sold land for $4,000, one half collected in cash and the balance on one-year note; gain, $500.	_____	_____
c. Paid a bond payable, $1,000	_____	_____
d. Sold and issued common shares, $2,500 cash.	_____	_____
e. Paid short-term note payable, $1,300	_____	_____

18. Complete the following tabulation:

Income, $32,000 (accrual basis).	$_____
Depreciation expense, $5,000	_____
Inventory increase, $10,000 (paid cash)	_____
Working capital from normal operations	$_____

19. Company T reported working capital at year-end of 19A, $90,000; and 19B, $75,000. During 19B, the company (a) paid a $5,000 short-term note and (b) paid a $15,000 long-term note. Disregarding interest, how much did each of these transactions change working capital during 19B? Explain.

20. Company S purchased a machine that cost $30,000; payment was made as follows: cash, $10,000; short-term note payable, $4,000; and long-term note payable, $16,000. How much did working capital change? Explain. How much did cash change?

21. What are the two basic parts of a SCFP, working capital basis? Why is the second part considered by some people to be redundant?

22. As a statement user interested in the statement of changes in financial position, would you prefer the (a) cash basis or (b) working capital basis? Explain.

EXERCISES

Part A

E15–1. Below is listed a number of transactions of Rye Company during 19B. Enter a letter to the right which indicates whether the transaction usually is a source or use of funds measured as cash. Use S for source, U for use, and N for none of these. Assume cash unless otherwise stated.

Transactions	Effect on funds measured on cash basis
a. Income (accrual basis)	S
b. Write-off of a bad debt (allowance method)	
c. Purchased an operational asset	S
d. Depletion expense (on gravel pit)	S
e. Declared a cash dividend (cash to be paid later)	U
f. Depreciation expense	S
g. Collection on a long-term note.......................	S
h. Issued a stock dividend	Nothing
i. Sold a long-term investment.........................	
j. Borrowed cash on a long-term note	S
k. Sold an operational asset at a loss....................	
l. Amortization of discount on bonds payable............	S
m. Purchased treasury stock...........................	U
n. Payment on bonds payable..........................	U
o. A stock split	
p. Extraordinary gain.................................	
q. Amortization of premium on bond investment	
r. Purchased a long-term investment	
s. Exchange of unissued shares for operational asset	
t. Exchange of land for equipment	nothing
u. Sale of treasury stock	S
v. Payment of debt by issuance of company shares	nothing S
w. Net loss	U
x. Amortization of patent.............................	Nothing
y. Bad debt expense recorded...........................	S
z. Declared and paid a property dividend................	U
zz. Paid the dividend declared in (e) above..............	U

E15–2. Tower Corporation has just completed its 19A income statement and balance sheet. The SCFP, cash basis, must be prepared. The following 19A data have been extracted from the income statement, balance sheet, and other company records:

[handwritten: subtracted to get net income so you add it back.]

S a. Depreciation expense, $9,000.

U b. Purchased treasury stock, $4,000 (cash).

S c. Sold a long-term investment at book value, $6,000 (cash).

U d. Declared and paid a $7,000 cash dividend during 19A.

S e. Recorded but unpaid salaries on December 31, 19A, $1,000.

S f. Income, accrual basis, $25,000.

S g. Borrowed $10,000 on an interest-bearing note (15 percent interest). *[handwritten: Already in Income]*

U h. Recorded but uncollected service revenue on December 31, 19A, $3,000. *[handwritten: Already in Income but haven't collected]*

S i. Sold 200 shares of its own common stock, par $1, for $5 per share (cash).

U j. Paid a $16,000 note payable.

U k. Purchased operational assets, $30,000 (cash).

Required:

a. Prepare the 19A SCFP, cash basis, for Tower Corporation.
b. Reconcile the 19A income (accrual basis) of $25,000 with the "net increase (decrease) in cash during 19A."
c. Explain why "net cash inflow from normal operations" is different from "income, accrual basis." Use amounts to support your explanation.

E15–3. The 19D income statement of Coffey Company is summarized below. Additional 19D data taken from the 19C and 19D balance sheets are as follows:

a. Decrease in accounts receivable (for services rendered) during 19D, $14,000.
b. Purchased a small service machine, $6,000 (cash).
c. Increase in salaries payable during 19D, $8,000.
d. Decrease in service revenue collected in advance, during 19D, $5,000.
e. Decrease in income tax payable during 19D, $7,000.

Income Statement, 19D

Items	Accrual Basis	Cash Basis	
		Explanation	Amount
Service revenues	$ 60,000		
Expenses:			
Salaries	51,000		
Depreciation	11,000		
Depletion	200		
Utilities (cash)	4,000		
Remaining expenses (cash)	3,800		
Income tax	–0–		
Total expenses	70,000		
Net income (loss)	$(10,000)		

Required:

a. Complete the above income statement schedule to determine the "net cash inflow (outflow) from normal operations."
b. Because there is a net loss for 19D would you expect the net cash flow from normal operations to be negative (i.e., an outflow)? Explain why.
c. Present a proof of your answer to Requirement (a) by starting with the $10,000 loss.

E15–4. Stonewall Company has completed its income statement and balance sheet at December 31, 19B. The following data were taken from a worksheet (or T-account) analysis completed as a basis for the SCFP:

Net income (Revenues, $156,000 − Expenses, $128,000) $28,000
Depreciation expense.   4,000
Purchase of operational assets for cash.   220,000
Sale of long-term investment (sold at book value for cash,
   $6,000).   6,000
Inventory increase during the period   3,000
Declared and paid cash dividends during 19B   8,000
Borrowed on short-term note   20,000
Accounts payable decrease.   2,000
Payment of long-term note   30,000
Acquired land for future use; issued capital stock
   in payment.   24,000

Required:

Prepare the SCFP, cash basis, properly classified. Use the direct analysis approach.

E15–5. The accounting department of Teddy Company assembled the following unclassified SCFP data at December 31, 19B, end of the accounting period, as a basis for preparing a SCFP, cash basis:

	Cash*	
Transactions	Sources	Uses
Net income (Revenues, $204,000 − Expenses, $169,000)	$35,000	
Depreciation expense.	7,000	
Purchase of operational assets for cash		$42,000
Wages payable increase.	5,000	
Inventory decrease	5,000	
Accounts payable decrease.		8,000
Declared and paid a cash dividend on common shares during 19B.		20,000
Amortization of patent	1,000	
Payment on short-term note payable (nontrade).		40,000
Sale of common shares for cash	17,000	
Sale of operational assets for cash (sold at book
value, $9,000	9,000	
Accounts receivable increase		6,000
Long-term borrowing during the period.	50,000	
Purchase of long-term investment, shares of X Co. (paid cash)		30,000

   *Including income additions and deductions.

Required:

a. Use the above data to prepare a SCFP, cash basis, properly classified. Use the direct analysis approach.
b. Answer the following questions:
   (1) What adjustment item(s) related to revenues, and what effect did the item(s) have on cash flow?
   (2) What two adjustment items affected cost of goods sold (cash basis)? What cash flow effects did they have?
   (3) What was the amount of the increase or decrease in cash as reported on the balance sheet?
   (4) What was the effect of the increase in wages payable on cash flow for 19B?
   (5) Would the declaration and issuance of a stock dividend be reported on the SCFP, cash basis? Explain.

E15–6. The following actual statement was taken from the annual financial statements of Lazy Corporation:

LAZY CORPORATION
Funds Statement
Year, December 31, 19B

Funds generated:

Sales and service revenue	$85,000	
Depreciation	6,000	
Accounts receivable decrease	700	
Merchandise decrease	3,000	
Sale of unissued stock	15,000	
Total		$109,700

Funds applied:

Cost of sales	48,000	
Expenses (including depreciation and income tax)	20,000	
Accounts payable decrease	1,000	
Income tax payable decrease	300	
Payment on long-term mortgage	25,000	
Acquisition of operational asset	9,000	
Dividends (cash) declared and paid during 19B	7,000	
Total		110,300
Decrease in funds		$ (600)

Required:

a. Is this a cash and its equivalents basis or a working capital basis statement? Give the reason for your conclusion.

b. Did Lazy give adequate attention to the communication of financial information to shareholders?

c. What was the amount of net income (or loss) reported for 19B?

d. Recast the above statement in good form (and preferred terminology).

e. Did operations generate more or less cash than net income? Explain what caused the difference.

E15–7. The SCFP must be based on the all-resources concept. During 19B, West Corporation completed the two transactions given below on which they have asked your assistance:

1. A large machine was acquired that had a list price of $25,000. West was short of cash; therefore, it paid for the machine in full by giving a $10,000, 15 percent, interest-bearing note due at the end of two years and 200 shares of its capital stock, par $50 (market value $60).

2. A small machine was acquired (list price $9,995), and full payment was made by transferring a tract of land that had a market value of $9,500 (surprisingly, this was also its book value).

Required:

For each machine show what should be reported on the SCFP, cash basis, under (a) sources of cash and (b) uses of cash. Briefly, explain the basis for your responses.

E15–8. Brown Company prepared the tabulation given below at December 31, 19E. Provide an appropriate amount for each blank. Use parentheses for deductions and enter a zero if no adjustment is required.

	Sources of cash	SCFP, cash basis
	From normal operations:	
	Net income (accrual basis)........................	$150,000
	Add (deduct) adjustments to convert to cash basis:	
	Depreciation expense, $2,000.....................	_____
	Increase in trade accounts receivable, $6,000	_____
	Decrease in inventory, $11,000..................	_____
	Amortization of patent, $1,000..................	*doesn't change 1000*
	Decrease in rent revenue receivable, $1,500	*increase in cash 1500*
	Increase in prepaid insurance, $4,000............	*decrease 4000*
	Decrease in trade accounts payable, $7,000	*decrease 7000*
	Decrease in income tax payable, $2,500...........	*decrease 2500*
	Gain on sale of operational asset, $2,000	
	(sold for cash, $8,000)......................	*increase 8000*
	Net cash generated from normal operations.........	$ _____

E15–9. Situation (a)—Ransom Corporation reported net income of $100,000. To compute cash generated from normal operations, the corporation added the recorded depreciation expense ($20,000, on the straight-line basis) to net income deriving a cash basis amount of $120,000 because "depreciation is one of the largest sources of cash in our company." Assume the company could have used accelerated depreciation instead of straight-line depreciation and reported $30,000 depreciation expense. Would this change increase the cash inflow (disregarding any income tax considerations)? Explain and illustrate your response.

Situation (b) Ransom Corporation sold a machine (an operational asset) for $28,000 cash.

At date of sale the accounting records reflected the following:

Machine No. 12 (cost)	$30,000
Accumulated depreciation (Machine No. 12)......	10,000

At year-end the income statement (summarized) reported the following:

Revenues (all cash)	$ 900,000
Expenses (all cash except depreciation expense	
of $60,000)	(796,000)
Gain on sale of operational asset	8,000
Net income	$ 112,000

Explain and illustrate how the disposal (sale) of the machine and depreciation expense should be reflected on the SCFP, cash basis.

Part B

E15–10. Below is a tabulation that gives information relating to both cash and working capital for Ross Company.

Transactions	(a) Cash basis	(b) Working capital basis
Net income reported (accrual basis).......................	$17,000	$17,000
Depreciation expense, $2,700.............................	_____	_____
Increase in wages payable, $500.........................	_____	_____
Decrease in trade accounts receivable, $6,800..............	_____	_____
Increase in merchandise inventory, $9,300.................	_____	_____
Amortization of patents, $300............................	_____	_____
Increase in bonds payable, $10,000	_____	_____
Decrease in trade accounts payable, $7,400.................	_____	_____
Sale of unissued common shares, $5,000	_____	_____
Total cash generated from operations................	$_____	
Total working capital generated from operations......		$20,000

Required:

a. Provide appropriate amounts for each of the blanks in the above tabulation; if none, enter a zero.
b. Briefly compare the total of cash with the total of working capital and explain why they are different.
c. Which result do you think would be of most use to statement users? Why?

E15–11. The following "Funds Statement" was taken from the annual financial statements of Fisher Corporation:

FISHER CORPORATION
Funds Statement
December 31, 19B

Funds generated:

Net profit (plus $10,000 depreciation)	$18,000
Common stock	9,000
Long-term debt..........................	10,000
Total...............................	$37,000

Funds applied:

Equipment	$15,000
Dividend...............................	8,000
Debt...................................	12,000
Change	2,000
Total................................	$37,000

Working capital:

	19B	Change
Cash.....................	$ 3,200	$ 6,500
Receivables.............................	7,500	5,000*
Inventory	30,000	13,500*
Payables (trade).........................	(4,800)	2,500*
Notes...................................	(12,000)	7,500*
Total...............................	$23,900	$ 2,000*

*Increase.

Required:

a. What was the amount of 19B income?
b. Is this a working capital or cash basis statement? Explain the basis for your response.
c. Did working capital increase or did it decrease? By how much?
d. Did "operations" generate more or less working capital than income? Explain why.

e. Explain why the amount of the change in working capital was different than income.

f. Assess the soundness of the cash dividend.

g. Can you spot any potential future problems for Fisher Corporation? Explain why.

h. Did Fisher Corporation give adequate attention to communication of financial information to shareholders? Explain the basis for your response.

i. Was the dividend paid or only declared? Explain.

j. Compare and explain the amounts of change in working capital versus cash.

k. Was the equipment purchased on credit? Explain.

l. Recast the above statement in good form consistent with your comments in Requirement (h).

E15–12. The following statment has just been prepared by Slow Company:

SLOW COMPANY
Statement of Changes in Financial Position, Working Capital Basis
For the Year Ended December 31, 19B

Sources of working capital:

From operations:		
Net income	$ 2,000	
Add expenses not requiring working capital:		
Depreciation expense	4,000	
Patent amortization expense	1,000	
Total working capital generated by operations		$ 7,000
From other sources:		
Sale of unissued shares	10,000	
Long-term loan	33,000	
Sale of land (at cost)	5,000	
Total working capital from other sources		48,000
Total working capital generated during the period		55,000

Uses of working capital:

Acquisition of machinery	22,000	
Payment of mortgage	20,000	
Cash dividend declared and paid	12,000	
Total working capital applied during the period		54,000
Net increase in working capital during the period		$ 1,000

Changes in working capital accounts:

	Balances at December 31		Working capital increase (decrease)
	19B	19A	
Current assets:			
Cash	$ 1,000	$ 9,000	$ (8,000)
Accounts receivable	31,000	24,000	7,000
Inventory	38,000	21,000	17,000
Total current assets	70,000	54,000	
Current liabilities:			
Accounts payable	18,000	15,000	(3,000)
Short-term notes payable	22,000	10,000	(12,000)
Total current liabilities	40,000	25,000	
Working capital	$30,000	$29,000	$ 1,000

Required:

a. Was there an increase or decrease in working capital? How much? What were the primary source and the major use of working capital?

b. Explain how working capital of $55,000 was generated when income was only $2,000.

c. Explain the fact that while working capital increased $1,000 cash decreased $8,000.

d. How much cash was generated and how much was used? How much cash was generated by normal operations?

e. What current asset increased the most? What current liability increased the most? How were these two changes related to cash?

f. Assess the soundness of the cash dividend.

g. Can you identify a potential problem in respect to liabilities? Explain.

h. Evaluate the cash and working capital positions at the end of 19B.

E15–13. Busby Company has completed the income statement and the comparative balance sheet at year-end, December 31, 19B. A statement of changes in financial position must be developed. The following data are available:

	Balances at Dec. 31	
	19A	19B
From balance sheet:		
Current assets		
Cash	$ 8,000	$15,000
Accounts receivable (net)	17,000	12,000
Inventory	15,000	18,000
Current liabilities:		
Accounts payable	10,000	12,000
Notes payable, short term	18,000	13,000
From income statement:		
Net income		20,000
Depreciation expense		6,000
From other records:		
Purchase of long-term investment		15,000
Payment of long-term note		5,000
Sale of unissued capital stock		10,000
Declaration and payment of cash dividend during 19B		8,000
Purchased land for future plant site, issued		
capital stock as payment in full		25,000

Required:

Prepare a SCFP, working capital basis. (Hint: Unless instructed otherwise, try a direct analysis [instead of a worksheet or T-account analysis].)

E15–14. Cullen Company has never prepared a SCFP. At the end of 19B, the company bookkeeper assembled the data given below (which have been determined to be correct) for such a statement:

	Balances at Dec. 31	
	19A	*19B*
From the balance sheet:		
Current assets:		
Cash	$ 15,000	$ 20,000
Accounts receivable (net).....................................	24,000	17,000
Merchandise inventory..	30,000	27,000
Current liabilities:		
Accounts payable...	(19,000)	(15,000)
Notes payable, short term	(10,000)	(12,000)
Working capital	$ 40,000	$ 37,000

	Balances at Dec. 31
	19B
From the income statement and other sources:	
Net income	$ 21,000
Depreciation expense	4,500
Amortization of patent..	500
Purchase of operational assets	(6,000)
Sale of operational assets (at book value) for cash....................	2,000
Payment of long-term note payable...............................	(40,000)
Issuance of bonds payable for cash...............................	30,000
Sale and issuance of common shares for cash	10,000
Declaration and payment of a cash dividend on common shares	
during 19B..	(25,000)
Difference...	$ (3,000)

Required:

Use the above data to prepare a SCFP, working capital basis, for 19B. Because the information is simplified, unless instructed otherwise, you may use a direct analysis (instead of a worksheet or T-account analysis).

E15–15. Lakeland Company is developing its annual financial statements at December 31, 19B. The income statement and balance sheet have been completed, and the SCFP, working capital basis, is to be developed. The income statement and comparative balance sheets are summarized below:

	19A	19B
Balance sheet at December 31:		
Cash	$12,800	$10,800
Accounts receivable (net)	9,000	10,500
Merchandise inventory	6,600	5,000
Operational assets (net)	40,000	43,000
Patent	3,000	2,700
	$71,400	$72,000
Accounts payable	$11,000	$ 9,000
Income tax payable	400	500
Notes payable, long term	10,000	5,000
Capital stock (nopar)	42,000	45,000
Retained earnings	8,000	12,500
	$71,400	$72,000

Income statement for 19B:	
Sales revenue	$60,000
Cost of goods sold	35,000
Gross margin	25,000
Expenses (including depreciation, $4,000, and patent amortization, $300)	18,000
Net income	$ 7,000

Additional data for 19B:
Purchased operational assets for cash, $7,000.
Paid $5,000 on long-term note payable.
Sold and issued capital stock for $3,000 cash.
Declared and paid a $2,500 cash dividend on capital stock during 19B.

Required:

a. Based upon the above data, prepare a worksheet or T-account analysis to develop the SCFP, working capital basis. (This part of the exercise is optimal.)
b. Prepare the formal SCFP, working capital basis.

PROBLEMS/CASES

Part A

PC15–1.   Below is a list of 19B transactions that involve sources and uses of funds. Some of the transactions relate only to sources and uses of cash; others relate to sources and uses of both cash and working capital. You are to analyze each transaction and enter its 19B dollar effect in the spaces to the right. Assume cash transactions unless stated otherwise.

	Cash and its equivalents		Working capital	
Transactions during 19B	*Sources*	*Uses*	*Sources*	*Uses*
a. Sold a short-term investment for cash, $500.	$_____	$_____	$_____	$_____
b. Sold an operational asset and received a short-term note, $600.	_____	_____	_____	_____
c. Prepaid a one-year insurance premium, $200.	_____	_____	_____	_____
d. Purchased a small machine (an operational asset) and gave a short-term note, $150.	_____	_____	_____	_____

e. Sold a patent for $700 cash (book value, $500; gain, $200).

f. Purchased land, $9,900 cash.

g. Sold a long-term investment, $9,000; collected cash, $1,000, short-term note, $3,000, and long-term note, $5,000.

h. Purchased an operational asset, $9,000; paid cash, $4,000 short-term note, $3,000, and long-term note, $2,000.

i. Declared and paid a preferred stock cash dividend, $3,000 during 19B.

j. Declared a common stock cash dividend, $4,000 during 19B and payable during 19C.

PC15–2. This case emphasizes the effect on working capital of increases and decreases of the components of working capital.

a. Provide the missing amounts in the schedule of working capital effects given below.

Schedule of Working Capital Effects

Current (Working Capital) Accounts	December 31		Working Capital
	19B	19A	Increase (Decrease)
1. Cash	$?	$30,000	$(29,000)
2. Short-term investment in securities	5,000	20,000	?
3. Accounts receivable (net)	70,000	?	30,000
4. Inventory	95,000	70,000	?
5. Prepaid expense (e.g., insurance)	?	2,000	1,000
6. Accounts payable	74,000	?	(4,000)
7. Income tax payable	4,000	6,000	?
8. Revenue collected in advance (unearned)	?	1,000	(1,000)
9. Product warranty liability (estimated)	3,000	4,000	?
10. Working capital	?	?	10,000

b. This case emphasizes the difference between the SCFP, cash basis, versus the SCFP, working capital basis. Provide the appropriate dollar amounts in the blank spaces to the right on the following schedule of SCFP sources and uses. Assume cash transactions unless otherwise stated.

Schedule of SCFP Sources and Uses

Transaction	Cash and Its Equivalents Basis		Working Capital Basis	
	Sources	Uses	Sources	Uses
1. Sold and issued capital stock, $5,000 cash.	$	$	$	$
2. Declared and paid a cash dividend, $3,000.				
3. Sold a short-term investment, $2,000 cash.				
4. Borrowed on a long-term note, $8,000.				
5. Sold an operational asset, $7,500 cash.				
6. Purchased an operational asset; gave a one-year interest-bearing note, $6,000.				
7. Declared a cash dividend (payable next year), $1,500.				
8. Paid a short-term note, $2,500.				
9. Collected a short-term note, $1,800.				
10. Collected a long-term note, $7,000.				
11. An operational asset was sold at a gain on disposal of $500; it originally cost $10,000 and was 75 percent depreciated (straight line). Cash was collected for the sale price.				
12. Sales revenue during 19B amounted to $100,000; the balances in Accounts Receivable at year's end were 19A, $20,000; and 19B, $14,000.				
13. Sold and issued 1,000 shares of common stock, par $10; credited Contributed surplus in the amount of $5,500. Cash was collected for half of the issue price and the balance is due at the end of one year.				

PC15–3.   The following statement has just been prepared by Careless Corporation.

CARELESS CORPORATION
Funds Flow Statement
Year, December 31, 19E

Funds earned:

Sales and other incomes	$ 90,000
Accounts receivable decrease	4,200
Expenses (including depreciation and income tax)	(70,000)
Depreciation	2,000
Inventory increase....................................	(3,000)
Accounts payable increase	1,000
Prepaid insurance increase	(100)
Income tax payable decrease	(100)
Capital stock..	5,000
Total funds earned	29,000

Funds spent:

Equipment..	(7,000)
Bonds payable	(30,000)
Dividends declared and paid	(2,000)
Total funds spent	$ 10,000

Required:

a. Is the above statement based on a working capital or on a cash basis? How did you determine the basis on which the statement was prepared?

b. List the format and terminology deficiencies on the statement.

c. Recast the above statement using preferred format and terminology.

PC15–4. The income statement of Josey Corporation is given below. Provide the appropriate cash flow amounts for the blanks given to the right. Use parentheses to indicate cash deductions and enter a zero for no change. Prove the results starting with accrual net income of $40,000.

JOSEY CORPORATION
Income Statement for the Year Ended December 31, 19C
Accrual Basis

		Cash flow
Sales revenue (one third on credit; accounts receivable year's end—19A, $11,000; 19B, $15,000)	$300,000	$ _____
Cost of goods sold (one fourth on credit; accounts payable year's end—19A, $9,000; 19B, $8,000 (net); inventory at year's end—19A, $50,000; 19B, $45,000)	180,000	_____
Gross margin on sales	120,000	
Expenses:		
Salaries and wages (including accrued wages payable at year's end—19A, $500; 19B, $300) $44,000		
Depreciation expense. 8,000		_____
Rent expense (no accruals). 6,000		_____
Bad debt expense 300		_____
Remaining expenses (no accruals) 11,700		_____
Income tax expense (income tax payable at year's end—19A, $2,000; 19B, $3,000) 10,000		_____
Total expenses.	80,000	
Net income.	$ 40,000	
Cash generated from normal operations.		$ _____
Proof of results:		
Net income (accrual basis)_____		$ 40,000
Add (deduct) adjustments to convert to cash basis:		
_____		_____
_____		_____
_____		_____
_____		_____
_____		_____
_____		_____
_____		_____
Cash generated from normal operations_____		$ _____

Note: This problem depicts two somewhat different approaches to derive cash inflow from operations; the proof of results approach above is the one usually used because it is more direct.

PC15–5.   The following statement has just been prepared by Young Corporation:

YOUNG CORPORATION
Statement of Changes in Financial Position, Cash Basis
For the Year Ended December 31, 19B

Sources of cash:
  From normal operations:

Net loss	$(10,000)	
Add (deduct) adjustments to convert to cash basis:		
Accounts receivable decrease	2,000	
Depreciation expense	3,000	
Amortization expense	300	
Inventory increase	(1,500)	
Accounts payable decrease	(1,000)	
Prepaid insurance decrease	200	
Cash generated from (used in) operations		$ (7,000)
From other sources:		
Financing:		
Sales of capital stock	10,000	
Long-term note payable	30,000	
Investing:		
Land (exchanged for machinery)	7,000	
Cash from other sources		47,000
Total cash generated during the period.....		40,000
Uses of cash:		
Investing:		
Machinery (acquired in exchange for land)..........	7,000	
Financing:		
Payment on mortgage	6,000	
Cash dividends declared and paid	12,000	
Total cash expended during the period.........		25,000
Net increase in cash during the period		$15,000

Required:

a.   Explain why the net loss was $3,000 more than the cash "used" in operations.

b.   Explain how the company showed a net increase in cash of $25,000 more than the net loss.

c.   Explain the land transaction. Why is it reported under two different captions on the above SCFP?

d.   Explain why the decrease in accounts receivable is "added" as an adjustment to the net loss.

e.   Explain why both the inventory increase and the accounts payable decrease are "deducted" as an adjustment to the net loss.

f.   Explain how the amount "Net increase in cash during the period, $15,000" can be verified independent of the SCFP computations.

PC15–6.   The following statement was prepared by Old Corporation:

OLD CORPORATION
Funds Statement
December 31, 19X

Where got:

Revenues.	$ 180,000	
Accounts receivable decrease	15,000	
Expenses (including depreciation and income tax)	(160,000)	
Depreciation	14,000	
Inventory increase.	(6,000)	
Accounts payable increase	7,000	
Income tax payable decrease	(3,000)	
Total		$ 47,000
Sale of permanent assets (at book value).		17,000
Issuance of common stock for land.		25,000
Borrowing—long-term note		40,000
Total cash received		$129,000

Where gone:

Dividends	20,000	
Payment on long-term mortgage.	80,000	
Machinery.	15,000	
Land (5,000 shares of stock)	25,000	
Funds (decrease)	(11,000)	
Total		$129,000

Required:

a.   Is this a cash basis or a working capital basis statement? Explain the reason for your answer.

b.   What was the amount of net income reported for 19X?

c.   Did cash increase or decrease? Explain. How can this amount be verified independent of the SCFP?

d.   Did the company give adequate attention to communication of financial information to the shareholders? Explain the basis for your response.

e.   Recast the above statement using preferred format and terminology.

f.   What was the amount of the difference between net income and cash generated from normal operations? Why were they different?

g.   Do you suspect any potential problems for this company? Explain the reason for your response.

PC15–7.   Hamilton Company is developing the 19B annual report. A SCFP, cash basis, is being developed. The following worksheet has been set up to develop the statement:

HAMILTON COMPANY
Worksheet to Develop Statement of Changes in Financial Position, Cash Basis
For the Year Ended December 31, 19B

Items	Ending Balance, Dec. 31, 19A	Analysis of Interim Entries		Ending Balances, Dec. 31, 19B
		Debit	Credit	
Debits				
Cash account	24,000			32,200
Noncash accounts:				
Accounts receivable (net)	26,000			30,000
Inventory	30,000			28,000
Prepaid insurance	1,200			800
Investments, long term	10,800			8,000
Operational assets (net)	30,000			39,000
Patent (net)	3,000			2,700
	125,000			140,700
CREDITS				
Accounts payable	21,000			18,000
Wages payable	3,000			2,000
Income tax payable	1,000			1,200
Note payable, long term	25,000			20,000
Capital stock par $10	60,000			70,000
Contributed surplus	1,000			3,000
Retained earnings	14,000			26,500
	125,000			140,700
Sources of cash				
Uses of cash				
Change in cash				

Additional data for 19B:

a. Revenues, $120,000; expenses, $100,000; and net income, $20,000.
b. Depreciation expense, $3,000.
c. Amortization of patent, $300.
d. Sale of long-term investment $2,800 cash, which was equal to its book value.
e. Purchased operational assets, and issued 1,000 shares of capital stock as full payment (market value, $12 per share).
f. Declared and paid cash dividend, $7,500.
g. Increase in accounts receivable balance during the period.
h. Decrease in inventory during the period.
i. Decrease in prepaid insurance balance during the period.
j. Decrease in accounts payable balance during the period.
k. Decrease in wages payable balance during the period.
l. Increase in income tax payable balance during the period.

Required:

Complete the above worksheet on a cash basis. Also, show on the worksheet "Net cash inflow from normal operations."

PC15–8. Mason Company is developing the annual financial statements at December 31, 19B. The statements are complete except for the SCFP, cash basis. The completed comparative balance sheets and income statement are summarized below:

	19A	19B
Balance sheet at December 31:		
Cash	$ 20,000	$ 31,500
Accounts receivable (net)	26,000	25,000
Merchandise inventory	40,000	38,000
Operational assets (net)	64,000	67,000
	$150,000	$161,500
Accounts payable	$ 24,000	$ 27,000
Wages payable	500	400
Notes payable, long term	35,000	30,000
Capital stock, nopar	70,000	80,000
Retained earnings	20,500	24,100
	$150,000	$161,500
Income statement for 19B:		
Sales		$ 90,000
Cost of goods sold		(52,000)
Expenses (including depreciation expense, $4,000)		(32,000)
		$ 6,000

Required:

a. Set up either a worksheet analysis or a T-account analysis to develop the SCFP, cash basis. Analytical entries should be made for the following:
   a. Net income—from income statement.
   b. Depreciation expense—from income statement.
   c. Purchased operational assets for cash, $7,000.
   d. Paid $5,000 on the long-term note payable.
   e. Sold unissued common shares for $10,000 cash.
   f. Declared and paid a $2,400 cash dividend.
   g. Accounts receivable decrease—from balance sheets.
   h. Merchandise inventory decrease—from balance sheets.
   i. Accounts payable increase—from balance sheets.
   j. Wages payable decrease—from balance sheets.
b. Based upon the analysis completed in Requirement (a), prepare the formal SCFP, cash basis.

PC15–9. Texmo Company is preparing its 19B financial statements, which include the following information:

	Comparative	
	19A	19B
Balance sheet:		
Cash	$ 40,000	$ 52,000
Inventory.................................	30,000	37,000
Accounts receivable (net)..................	20,000	17,000
Long-term investment, shares Co. A	10,000	3,000
Machinery and equipment (net)..............	80,000	75,000
	$180,000	$184,000
Accounts payable...........................	$ 15,000	$ 11,000
Income tax payable	4,000	6,000
Note payable, long term....................	20,000	10,000
Bonds payable..............................	30,000	10,000
Capital stock, par $10	100,000	110,000
Contributed surplus	8,000	11,000
Retained earnings	3,000	26,000
	$180,000	$184,000
Income statement:		
Revenue...................................		$140,000
Cost of goods sold..........................		(65,000)
Depreciation expense		(8,000)
Patent expense		(600)
Remaining operating expenses...............		(28,400)
Income tax expense........................		(9,000)
Gain on disposal of machine (net of tax)		1,000
Net income		$ 30,000

Additional data for 19B:

1. Machinery that had a book value of $10,000 was sold for $11,000 cash.
2. Long-term investment (shares of Company A), which sold for $7,000 cash, had a carrying value of $7,000.
3. Equipment was acquired and payment in full was made by issuing 1,000 shares of capital stock which had a market value of $13 share.
4. Payments on debt: long-term note, $10,000; bonds payable, $20,000.
5. Declared and paid a cash dividend, $7,000.

Required:

a. Prepare either a worksheet analysis or a T-account analysis to develop a SCFP, cash basis.

b. Prepare the formal SCFP, cash basis.

PC15–10. Sureshot Oil Company prepared the following income statement:

Income Statement
For the Year Ended December 31, 1984

			Millions
a.	Revenue from sale of crude oil and natural gas		$40
b.	Depletion of crude oil and natural gas reserves	$ 5	
c.	Depreciation of production equipment	1	
d.	Salaries and wages...............................	4	
e.	Remaining expenses	20	30
f.	Net income.......................................		$10

Additional information for 1984:

a. Accounts receivable balance at year's end: 1983, $.5; and 1984, $2.5.
b. Sureshot uses cost depletion which is based on an old and low "finding cost" incurred in 1957. It is expected that the production will cease at the end of 1990 because the remaining reserves will be uneconomical to produce. The company is involved in the risky and high cost activities of searching for new reserves.
c. Depreciation is computed using the straight-line method. The equipment is very old and inefficient.
d. Salaries and wages unpaid (in millions) at year's end: 1983, $1.5; and 1984, $.5.
e. All items on the income statement, other than items *(a)*, *(b)*, and *(c)* above, were on the cash basis (including income tax).
f. The board of directors is considering declaring and paying immediately a $5 million cash dividend which the company president opposes.

Required:

a. Prepare a SCFP, cash basis (for normal operations only). You should be able to prepare the SCFP using the direct-analysis approach.
b. Compare the income statement and the SCFP results. Which statement best indicates the ability of the company (1) to pay the dividend, (2) search for new reserves, and (3) replace the equipment? Give the primary arguments for and against the dividend. Suppose $11 million should be spent in 1984–85 for new equipment and well workover projects.

PC15–11. This case is based upon the 1984 financial statements of Consolidated-Bathurst given in Special Supplement B immediately preceding the Index. You are to use the 1984 data to respond to the following requirements:

a. What period does the SCFP cover?
b. How does the company measure "funds" on the SCFP?
c. How much did funds increase, or decrease?
d. How much cash was retained in the business? How was it apparently used?
e. Reconcile the SCFP with the balance sheet.

Part B

PC15–12. The following actual SCFP was extracted from the published annual financial statements of Laird Corporation:

LAIRD CORPORATION
Statement of Working Capital
December 31, 19B

Working capital provided:

Net income..	$14,000	
Add: Depreciation	15,000	
Patent amortization................................	1,000	
Total	30,000	
Bonds	50,000	
Common shares (for equipment)	15,000	
Total working capital provided		$95,000

Working capital applied:

Mortgage	60,000	
Equipment	15,000	
Dividends...	10,000	
Total working capital applied......................		85,000
Working capital increase..................................		$10,000

Working capital changes:

	19B	Change in working capital
Cash	$ 7,400	$(12,400)
Accounts receivable....................	9,000	6,000
Inventory............................	24,900	19,900
Accounts payable.....................	(7,000)	(4,000)
Other short-term debt.................	(1,400)	500
Total	$32,900	$ 10,000

Required:

a. Compare, and explain the significance of, the change in cash and its equivalent with the change in working capital.

b. Explain why the amount of the change in working capital was different from the amount of net income.

c. What were the largest source and use of working capital?

d. Is the working capital position sound? Explain the basis for your decision.

e. Compare the cash position with the working capital position.

f. List all of the communication deficiencies in the above format.

g. Recast the above statement to correct it for the deficiencies you listed in Requirement (f).

PC15–13. The following statement was prepared by Clay Corporation:

CLAY CORPORATION
Funds Statement
December 31, 19E

Funds provided:

Net income		$ 40,000
Adjustments:		
Depreciation	12,000	
Patent amortization	1,000	
Goodwill amortization	3,000	
Total		56,000
Other:		
Bonds payable, maturity value $100,000	98,000	
Sale of land (at cost)	25,000	
Common shares (issued for plant site)	40,000	
Total funds provided		219,000

Funds applied:

Mortgage		20,000
Plant		150,000
Plant machinery		20,000
Plant site		40,000
Dividends		6,000
Total funds applied		236,000
Decrease in working capital		$ 17,000

Working capital changes:

Current items	Balances Dec. 31, 19E	Working capital increase (decrease)
Cash	$ 6,000	$(27,000)
Accounts receivable	13,000	4,000
Inventory	52,000	12,000
Accounts payable	(8,000)	5,000
Short-term notes	(16,000)	(11,000)
Working capital	$47,000	$(17,000)

Required:

a. Compare, and explain the significance of, the change in cash and its equivalent with the change in working capital.

b. What was the primary source of working capital?

c. What was the primary use of working capital?

d. Explain the transaction involving the common shares. Did it directly affect working capital? Why is it reported on the statement?

e. Explain why working capital decreased although there was a net income for the period.

f. Assess the soundness of the declaration and payment of the cash dividend.

g. Assess the cash position compared with the working capital position.

h. Can you spot any potential problems with respect to the future? Explain.

i. List all of the format, caption, and terminology deficiencies that you can identify.

j. Prepare a formal SCFP, working capital basis, to correct the deficiencies that you identified.

PC15–14. Riverside Company is completing its 19B financial statements. The following information is provided by the just completed 19B comparative balance sheet and income statement:

	19A	19B
Balance sheet:		
Cash	$ 10,000	$ 2,000
Accounts receivable (net)	16,600	21,000
Inventory	17,000	25,000
Prepaid expenses	1,400	400
Operational assets (net)	59,000	68,000
Plant site		20,000
Long-term investment	16,000	7,000
	$120,000	$143,400
Accounts payable	$ 8,000	$ 12,000
Wages payable	1,000	1,500
ST note payable (interest, December 31)	6,000	3,000
LT note payable (interest, December 31)	10,000	4,000
Bonds payable (interest, December 31)	30,000	50,000
Capital stock, par $10	60,000	60,500
Contributed surplus	3,000	3,400
Retained earnings	2,000	9,000
	$120,000	$143,400

Income statement:	
Revenues	$135,000
Depreciation expense	(15,000)
Remaining expenses	(95,000)
Loss on sale of long-term investment	(3,000)
Net income	$ 22,000

Additional data:

1. Purchased operational asset for cash, $24,000.
2. Sold long-term investment for $6,000 cash; carrying value $9,000.
3. Sold 50 shares of capital stock at $18 cash per share.
4. Declared and paid a cash dividend of $15,000.
5. Payment on short-term note, $3,000.
6. Payment on long-term note, $6,000.
7. Acquired plant site and issued bonds, $20,000, for full purchase price (the bonds were selling at par).

Required:

a. Prepare a worksheet or T-account analysis for SCFP, working capital basis. (This part of the problem is optional.)
b. Prepare the formal SCFP, working capital basis.

PC15–15. Green Acres Company is preparing the 19B annual financial statements. The 19B comparative balance sheet and income statement reports the following information:

	19A	19B
Balance sheet:		
Cash....................................	$ 10,000	$ 1,000
Accounts receivable (net)	30,000	48,500
Inventory	20,000	21,400
Short-term investments..................	7,000	
Long-term investments..................	5,000	
Operational assets (net)	50,000	57,000
Patent (net)	4,000	3,600
Land		7,500
	$126,000	$139,000
Accounts payable.......................	$ 43,500	$ 40,000
Income tax payable	500	
Wages payable	2,000	3,000
Bonds payable.........................	15,000	10,000
Capital stock, par $1	40,000	54,000
Contributed surplus.....................		3,500
Retained earnings......................	25,000	28,500
	$126,000	$139,000
Income statement:		
Revenue		$ 80,000
Depreciation expense....................		(2,000)
Amortization expense		(400)
Remaining expenses		(73,600)
Gain on sale of long-term investment......		3,000
Net income............................		$ 7,000

Additional data for 19B:

1. Sold long-term investment that cost $5,000 for $8,000 cash.
2. Annual payment on bond principal, $5,000.
3. Sold and issued 8,000 shares of capital stock at $1.25 per share (cash).
4. Declared and paid a cash dividend of $3,500.
5. Purchased an operational asset for $9,000 cash.
6. Acquired land for future use and paid in full by issuing 6,000 shares of capital stock, market value $1.25 per share.

Required:

a. Prepare a worksheet or T-account analysis to develop the SCFP, working capital basis. (This part of the problem is optional.)
b. Prepare the formal SCFP, working capital basis.

PC15–16. All-Steel Company is preparing the annual financial statements, including a SCFP, working capital basis, at December 31, 19B. The 19B comparative balance sheet and the income statement and some additional data are summarized below:

	19B	19A
Balance sheet at December 31:		
Cash	$ 21,500	$ 15,000
Accounts receivable (net)......................	23,000	20,000
Merchandise inventory.........................	27,000	22,000
Prepaid insurance	300	600
Investments, long term (S Corp. shares)	12,000	
Operational assets (net)	220,000	134,000
Patent (net)	16,000	
	$319,800	$191,600
Accounts payable..............................	$ 18,000	$ 12,000
Note payable, short term (nontrade).............	10,000	18,000
Wages payable	800	1,000
Income tax payable	1,000	600
Note payable, long term........................	10,000	30,000
Bonds payable.................................	100,000	
Capital stock, par $10	140,000	100,000
Contributed surplus	6,000	5,000
Retained earnings	34,000	25,000
	$319,800	$191,600

Income statement for 19B:		
Sales revenue		$200,000
Cost of goods sold....................		126,000
Gross margin on sales.................		74,000
Expenses (not detailed)...............	$39,000	
Depreciation expense	14,000	
Amortization of patent................	1,000	
Income tax expense...................	7,000	61,000
Net income		$ 13,000

Additional data for 19B:

1. Purchased patent on January 1, 19B, for $17,000 cash.
2. Purchased shares of S Corporation as a long-term investment for $12,000 cash.
3. Paid $20,000 on the long-term note payable.
4. Sold and issued 4,000 shares of capital stock for $41,000 cash.
5. Declared and paid a $4,000 cash dividend.
6. Acquired a building (an operational asset) and paid in full for it by issuing $100,000 bonds payable at par to the former owner—date of transaction was December 30, 19B.

Required:

a. Based upon the above data, prepare a worksheet analysis to develop the SCFP, working capital basis. (This part of the problem is optional.)
b. Based upon the completed worksheet, prepare a formal SCFP, working capital basis.

PC15–17. Spreadsheet Company keeps its records in somewhat of an unconventional way. It finds this approach useful because it represents one way to develop forecasted financial statements using a computer spreadsheet.

The general idea is to have a balance sheet at the beginning of the period. The activities for the fiscal period are kept in the form of a SCFP on the cash and its equivalents basis. The SCFP is then used to update the balance sheet so that a balance sheet, income statement, and statement of changes in retained earnings can be prepared.

The following is the balance sheet as at December 31, 19A.

Assets

Current assets:	
Cash	$ 10,200
Accounts receivable (net).............	21,400
Inventories	18,500
Prepaid insurance	700
	50,800
Property, plant and	
equipment.......................	215,000
Accumulated depreciation............	(21,500)
Total assets	$244,300

Liabilities

Current liabilities:	
Notes payable to bank	$ 8,300
Accounts payable	9,240
Wages payable	300
Income taxes payable	460
	18,300
Long-term liabilities:	
Bonds payable at	
face value	110,000
Total liabilities	128,300

Shareholders' Equity

Capital stock, no par	100,000
Retained Earnings...................	16,000
Total shareholders' equity...........	116,000
Total liabilities and	
shareholders' equity	$244,300

The following statement presents the changes in cash and its equivalents for the year 19B.

<table>
<tr><td colspan="2">Cash from normal operations:</td></tr>
<tr><td>Net income before</td><td></td></tr>
<tr><td> extraordinary items...............</td><td>$21,000</td></tr>
<tr><td>Income tax payable increase..........</td><td>10</td></tr>
<tr><td>Accounts receivable decrease.........</td><td>1,500</td></tr>
<tr><td>Inventory increase...................</td><td>(2,000)</td></tr>
<tr><td>Depreciation expense................</td><td>22,500</td></tr>
<tr><td>Accounts payable increase ....</td><td>1,100</td></tr>
<tr><td>Wages payable decrease ....</td><td>(300)</td></tr>
<tr><td> Cash flow from normal</td><td></td></tr>
<tr><td>   operations ....</td><td>43,810</td></tr>
<tr><td colspan="2">Financing activities:</td></tr>
<tr><td>Repayment of bonds</td><td></td></tr>
<tr><td> outstanding......................</td><td>(20,000)</td></tr>
<tr><td>Dividends paid.....................</td><td>(15,000)</td></tr>
<tr><td>Issue of capital stock</td><td></td></tr>
<tr><td> to purchase equipment ....</td><td>10,000</td></tr>
<tr><td>   Total financing ....</td><td>(25,000)</td></tr>
<tr><td colspan="2">Investing activities:</td></tr>
<tr><td>Purchase of new equipment</td><td></td></tr>
<tr><td> with issue of capital</td><td></td></tr>
<tr><td> stock.............................</td><td>(10,000)</td></tr>
<tr><td>Increase in cash and</td><td></td></tr>
<tr><td> its equivalents ....</td><td>$ 8,810</td></tr>
</table>

Additional information obtained from the bank indicated that Spreadsheet repaid $3,000 of its bank loan during 19B.

Required:

a.   Prepare a balance sheet and statement of changes in retained earnings for 19B.
b.   Assuming you have access to the bank records for 19B and can obtain the following information:

Cash receipts from sales..............	$259,500
Cash payments for purchases.........	160,000
Cash payments for expenses..........	40,000
Cash payments for interest	10,100
Cash payments for income taxes	5,590

Prepare the income statement for 19B.

16

Using and Interpreting Financial Statements

PURPOSE OF THIS CHAPTER

Throughout the preceding chapters, we emphasized the rationale and conceptual basis that support the accounting process. The fundamental concepts that underlie financial accounting and reporting are summarized in Exhibit 2–6. We have emphasized the conceptual foundation of accounting for two reasons: (1) an understanding of financial accounting concepts makes your understanding of accounting procedures more complete, and (2) effective analysis and interpretation of financial statements depend on an understanding of the underlying concepts. A good understanding of accounting concepts and procedures enables a decision maker to appreciate the advantages and limitations of financial statements.

The purpose of this chapter is to discuss the evaluation and interpretation of external financial statements by decision makers and some analytical techniques that are used widely to interpret financial statements.

FINANCIAL REPORTS IN THE DECISION-MAKING PROCESS

The basic objective of financial statements is to help the users make better economic decisions. Decision makers who use financial statements constitute two broad groups. One group is the management of the business (i.e., internal decision makers) who rely on accounting data in making important management decisions. This aspect of accounting is considered in management accounting.

The second broad group that uses financial reports is referred to as "external" decision makers. This group consists primarily of investors (both present and potential owners), investment analysts, creditors, government, labour organizations, and the public at large. Financial accounting and the external financial reports discussed in the preceding chapters are oriented toward serving this diverse group of decision makers.

There are three primary types of measurements that decision makers use in making decisions:

1. **Measurement of past performance**—The decision maker needs to know how the business has performed in the past. For example, information concerning such items as income, sales volume, extraordinary items, cash and working capital flows, and return earned on the investment helps assess the success of the business and the effectiveness of the management. Such information also helps the decision maker compare one entity with others.

2. **Measurement of the present condition of a business**—The decision maker must have data on how the entity stands today in order to answer questions such as: What types of assets are owned? How much debt does the business owe, and when is it due? What is the cash position? How much of the earnings have been retained in the business? What are the EPS, return-on-investment, and debt/equity ratios? What is the inventory position? Answers to these and similar economic questions help the decision maker assess the successes and failures of the past; but, more importantly, they provide useful information in assessing the cash flow and profit potentials of the business.

3. **Prediction of the future performance of the business**—Statement users typically make decisions by selecting from among several alternative courses of action. Each course of action will cause different conditions to exist **in the future.** In decision making, one is faced with the problem of predicting the probable future results of the alternatives under consideration. All decisions are future oriented because they do not (and cannot) affect the past. However, in predicting the probable future impact of a decision, reliable measurements of what has happened in the recent past are valuable. These measurements are particularly relevant when the decision relates to a business

entity. For example, the recent sales and earnings trends of a business are good indicators of what might be reasonably expected in the future. The primary value in measuring past performance and the present condition of a business is to aid in predicting the future cash flows of the business.

Thus, decision makers must rely substantially on the past data presented in financial reports in making assessments and predictions of probable future performance. Usually, this is the most important use of financial statements by decision makers.

Some decisions are made intuitively and without much supporting data. In such cases there is no systematic attempt to collect measurable data, which makes it practically impossible to array, measure, and evaluate the advantages and disadvantages of each alternative. Numerous reasons exist for intuitive decision making. Time and cost of collecting the data may prevent a careful analysis. Sometimes the decision maker is unsophisticated and consequently does not understand the systematic approach to decision making and is not aware of all of the basic factors that should be considered in making the decision. Unsophisticated decision makers tend to oversimplify the decision-making process, disregard basic information, and quite frequently overlook the financial impacts.

In contrast, a sophisticated decision maker will make a systematic analysis of each alternative. Information regarding each alternative will be collected and evaluated. In decisions relating to a business, the financial statements usually provide critical financial data relevant to the decision. We must emphasize, however, that the financial result is only one of several important factors that should be evaluated in most decisions.

To use financial information effectively, one must understand what was measured and how it was measured. With a reasonable level of understanding of the fundamentals of the accounting process, you are able to evaluate effectively the strengths and limitations of the financial data presented in the financial reports of a business. One of the objectives of the preceding chapters was to enable you to appreciate and evaluate these aspects of accounting.

The four basic financial statements—income statement, balance sheet, statement of retained earnings, and statement of changes in financial position (SCFP)—and the related disclosure notes have evolved primarily to meet the special needs of external decision makers. Because of the varied needs of these users, special and supplementary financial data and analyses frequently are needed.

INVESTORS

Investors constitute a primary group to which external financial statements are addressed. This group includes present owners, potential owners, and investment analysts (because they advise investors). Investors include individuals, other businesses, and institutions, such as your university.

When purchasing shares of a corporation, most investors do not seek a controlling interest. Instead, they do so in the anticipation of earning a return on their investment. This return is made up of two components: (1) revenue in the form of dividends during the investment period and (2) subsequent increases in the market value of the shares over the amount invested. Thus, when considering an investment of this type, the investor is faced with the problem of predicting the future **income** and **growth** of the enterprise. Investors are interested in enterprise income because it is the "source" of future dividends. They are interested in enterprise growth because it tends to cause the market value of the shares to increase. In making these predictions, the investor should consider three types of general factors:

1. **Economy wide factors**—The overall health of the economy often will have a direct impact on the performance of an individual enterprise. The investor should consider such data as the gross national product, productivity, unemployment rate, general inflation rate, and changes in interest rate.
2. **Industry factors**—Certain events have a major impact on each company within an industry, but have only a minor impact on other companies. For example, policy changes by OPEC (the oil cartel) have a major impact on the oil industry.
3. **Individual company factors**—These factors may be either financial or nonfinancial in nature. Nonfinancial factors would include the introduction of a new product, a lawsuit, and changes in key personnel. Data pertaining to financial factors are presented in the basic financial statements. The income statement provides significant information for the investor, such as revenue from products and services, extraordinary items, income tax impacts, net income, and earnings per share. Other relationships, such as gross margin, profit margin, and expense relationships, can be computed. Similarly, the balance sheet, the statement of changes in financial position, and the notes to the financial statements provide measurements of past profit performance, funds flow, and current financial position. These data constitute an important base from which predictions of future income and growth can be made. These data are particularly valuable when compared with recent past periods as illustrated in Exhibit 16–1.

CREDITORS

Financial institutions, as well as other parties, grant long-term and short-term credit to businesses. Creditors lend money in order to earn a return; that is, interest revenue. Creditors expect to collect periodic interest during the credit period and the principal at maturity. As a consequence, in granting

EXHIBIT 16–1
Illustration of comparative financial statements

PACKARD COMPANY
Comparative Income Statements (simplified for illustration)
For the Years Ended December 31, 19B, and 19A

	Year ended Dec. 31		Increase (decrease) 19B over 19A	
	19B	19A*	Amount	Percent
Sales revenue..........................	$120,000	$100,000	$20,000	20.0
Cost of goods sold	72,600	60,000	12,600	21.0
Gross margin on sales	47,400	40,000	7,400	18.5
Operating expenses:				
Distribution expenses...................	22,630	15,000	7,630	50.9
Administrative expenses...............	11,870	13,300	(1,430)	(10.8)
Interest expense	1,500	1,700	(200)	(11.8)
Total expenses...................	36,000	30,000	6,000	20.0
Pretax income	11,400	10,000	1,400	14.0
Income taxes	2,600	2,000	600	30.0
Net income............................	$ 8,800	$ 8,000	$ 800	10.0

*Base year for computing percents.

PACKARD COMPANY
Comparative Balance Sheets (simplified for illustration)
At December 31, 19B, and 19A

	At December 31		Increase (decrease) 19B over 19A	
	19B	19A*	Amount	Percent
Assets				
Current assets:				
Cash.....................................	$ 13,000	$ 9,000	$ 4,000	44.4
Accounts receivable (net)	8,400	7,000	1,400	20.0
Merchandise inventory	54,000	60,000	(6,000)	(10.0)
Prepaid expenses	2,000	4,000	(2,000)	(50.0)
Total current assets.................	77,400	80,000	(2,600)	3.3
Investments:				
Real estate............................	8,000	8,000		
Operational assets:				
Equipment and furniture	82,500	75,000	7,500	10.0
Less accumulated depreciation	(23,250)	(15,000)	8,250	55.0
Total operational assets.............	59,250	60,000	(750)	(1.3)
Other assets	1,900	2,000	(100)	(5.0)
Total assets.............................	$146,550	$150,000	$ (3,450)	(2.3)
Liabilities				
Current liabilities:				
Accounts payable	$ 13,200	$12,000	$ 1,200	10.0
Notes payable, short term	15,000	20,000	(5,000)	(25.0)
Accrued wages payable.................	7,200	8,000	(800)	(10.0)
Total current liabilities..............	35,400	40,000	(4,600)	(11.5)
Long-term liabilities:				
Notes payable, long term	7,150	10,000	(2,850)	(28.5)
Total liabilities	42,550	50,000	(7,450)	(14.9)
Shareholders' Equity				
Common stock, par $10...................	85,000	85,000		
Retained earnings........................	19,000	15,000	4,000	26.7
Total shareholders' equity...........	104,000	100,000	4,000	4.0
Total liabilities and shareholders' equity....	$146,550	$150,000	$ (3,450)	(2.3)

*Base year for computing percents.

credit to a business, the creditor is concerned basically about items such as the following:

1. Profit potential of the business because a profitable entity is much more likely to meet its maturing obligations.
2. Ability of the business to generate cash consistently from recurring operations because it will be in a more favourable position to pay its debts.
3. Financial position (assets owned and debts owed) of the business because the assets comprise security for the debts and the debts indicate the future demand for cash at debt maturity dates.

Credit grantors almost always look to the financial reports for information. To enhance the credibility of these reports, creditors often require that the reports be audited by an independent PA. In addition to the financial statements, the disclosure notes and the "auditors' opinion" convey important information because they often provide detailed quantified facts to support the reported amounts and other nonquantified explanations such as certain future contingencies (e.g., major lawsuits pending).

ANALYSIS OF FINANCIAL STATEMENTS

Financial statements include a large volume of quantitative data supplemented by disclosure notes. The notes are intended to be particularly helpful to users in interpreting the statements; therefore, they are viewed as an integral part of the financial statements. Notes elaborate on accounting policies, major financial effects and events, and certain nonquantifiable events that may contribute to the success or failure of the firm.

In respect to the quantitative data presented in the financial statements, four techniques used widely to assist decision makers in understanding and interpreting the external financial statements are: (1) comparative statements, (2) long-term summaries, (3) graphic presentations, and (4) ratio analyses.

COMPARATIVE FINANCIAL STATEMENTS

The accounting profession requires the presentation of **comparative financial statements** covering, as a minimum, the current year and the immediately prior year.

Practically all financial statements present, side by side, the results for the current and the preceding years (similar to the statements shown in Exhibit 16–1). Analysis of comparative statements is facilitated if two additional columns are added for (1) the **amount** of change for each item and (2) the **percent** of change. These additional variance columns (amount and percent) are illustrated in Exhibit 16–1. Frequently the percent of change from the prior period is more helpful for interpretative purposes than the absolute dollar amount of change. Observe that the percents are determined independently on each line by dividing the amount of the change by the amount for the preceding year. For example, in Exhibit 16–1, the percentage on the Cash line was computed as $4,000 ÷ $9,000 = 44.4 percent. Thus, the amount from the earlier year was used as the base amount.

LONG-TERM SUMMARIES

In the interest of full disclosure, many annual reports contain 5-, 10-, and even 20-year summaries of basic data, such as sales revenue, net income, total assets, total liabilities, total owners' equity, and selected ratios (a good 10-year summary is shown in Special Supplement B preceding the Index). Data for a series of years are particularly important in interpreting the financial statements for the current period. There is considerable likelihood of misinterpretation and unwarranted conclusions when the statement user limits consideration to only the last one or two periods. The vagaries of business transactions, economic events, and accounting techniques are such that the financial reports for a single time period usually do not provide a sound basis for assessing the long-term potentials of an enterprise. Sophisticated financial analysts typically use data covering a number of periods so that significant trends may be identified and interpreted.

However, care must be exercised in interpreting long-term summaries because data for a period in the distant past may not be comparable, or even useful, because of changes in the company, industry, and environment. For example, Imperial Oil is a very different company now than it was when a gallon of gasoline sold for 50 cents.

In interpreting comparative data, the items showing significant increases and decreases should receive special attention. Care should be exercised to identify evidence of significant **turning points,** either upward or downward, in trends for important items such as net income and cash flow. The turning points often provide indication of significant future trends. Fundamental to the interpretation is the need to determine the **underlying causes** for significant changes in either direction (favourable or unfavourable).

RATIO AND PERCENTAGE ANALYSIS

Some amounts on financial statements, such as net income, are highly significant in and of themselves; however, the significance of many amounts is highlighted by their relationships to other amounts. These significant relationships can be examined through the use of an analytical tool known as **ratio** or **percentage analysis.** A ratio or percent simply expresses the proportionate relationship between two different amounts. A ratio or percent is computed by dividing one quantity by another quantity. For example, the fact that a company earned net income of $500,000 assumes greater significance when net income is compared with the shareholders' investment in the company. Assuming that shareholders' equity is $5,000,000, the relationship of earnings to shareholder investment would be $500,000 ÷ $5,000,000 = .1, or 10 percent.

Clearly, this ratio indicates a different level of performance than would be the case if shareholders' equity had been $50,000,000. Thus, ratio analysis enables decision makers to compare companies more realistically than does the income amount alone.

Fundamentally, there are two aspects of ratio analysis: (1) relationships **within one period** and (2) relationships **between periods.** In addition, ratios may be computed between amounts within one statement, such as the income statement, or between statements, such as the income statement and the balance sheet. In Exhibit 16–1, the percents of change represent a percentage analysis between periods within each statement.

There is not a particular list of ratios or percentages that can be identified as appropriate to all situations. Each analytical situation may require the calculation of several ratios. There are a number of ratios or percentages that usually are used because they are appropriate to many situations. The next paragraphs will discuss and illustrate the ratios and percentages that are used often by decision makers.

COMPONENT PERCENTAGES

Component percentages are used to express each item on a particular statement as a percentage of a single **base amount** (i.e., the denominator of the ratio). Exhibit 16–2 presents a component analysis for the 19A and 19B income statements and balance sheets for Packard Company. To compute component percentages for the income statement, the base amount is **net sales revenue.** Thus, each expense is expressed as a proportionate part of net sales revenue. On the balance sheet, the base amount is **total assets.** The percents are derived by dividing the amount on each line by total assets.

Component percentages often are useful in interpreting and evaluating the reported financial data because they reveal important proportional relationships. For example, on the income statement in Exhibit 16–2, observe that distribution expenses were 18.9 percent of sales revenue in 19B, compared with 15 percent in 19A. On the balance sheet we note that at the end of 19B, merchandise inventory was 36.8 percent of total assets, compared with 40 percent for 19A. These changes in important relationships often suggest the need for further inquiry because they tend to indicate problems and opportunities for corrective action and increased profitability.

SOME WIDELY USED RATIOS

Numerous ratios and percentages can be computed from a single set of financial statements; however, only a selected number may be useful in a given situation. Thus, a common approach is to compute certain widely used ratios and then decide which additional ratios are relevant to the particular type of decisions contemplated. Because balance sheet amounts relate to one instant in time, while income statement amounts relate to a period of time, care must be exercised in calculating ratios that use amounts from both statements. Thus,

EXHIBIT 16–2
Illustration of
component
percentages

PACKARD COMPANY
Income Statements (simplified for illustration)
For the Years Ended December 31, 19B, and 19A

| | For the year ended | | | |
| | Dec. 31, 19B | | Dec. 31, 19A | |
	Amount	Percent	Amount	Percent
Sales revenue (net)*	$120,000	100.0	$100,000	100.0
Cost of goods sold	72,600	60.5	60,000	60.0
Gross margin on sales	47,400	39.5	40,000	40.0
Operating expenses:				
Distribution expenses	22,630	18.9	15,000	15.0
Administrative expenses	11,870	9.9	13,300	13.3
Interest expense	1,500	1.2	1,700	1.7
Total expenses	36,000	30.0	30,000	30.0
Pretax income	11,400	9.5	10,000	10.0
Income taxes	2,600	2.2	2,000	2.0
Net income	$ 8,800	7.3	$ 8,000	8.0

*Base amount.

PACKARD COMPANY
Balance Sheets (simplified for illustration)
At December 31, 19B, and 19A

| | At | | | |
| | Dec. 31, 19B | | Dec. 31, 19A | |
	Amount	Percent	Amount	Percent
Assets				
Current assets:				
Cash	$ 13,000	8.9	$ 9,000	6.0
Accounts receivable (net)	8,400	5.7	7,000	4.6
Merchandise inventory	54,000	36.8	60,000	40.0
Prepaid expenses	2,000	1.4	4,000	2.7
Total current assets	77,400	52.8	80,000	53.3
Investments:				
Real estate	8,000	5.5	8,000	5.3
Operational assets:				
Equipment and furniture	82,500	56.3	75,000	50.0
Less accumulated depreciation	(23,250)	(15.9)	(15,000)	(10.0)
Total operational assets	59,250	40.4	60,000	40.0
Other assets	1,900	1.3	2,000	1.4
Total assets*	$146,550	100.0	$150,000	100.0
Liabilities				
Current liabilities:				
Accounts payable	$ 13,200	9.0	$ 12,000	8.0
Notes payable, short term	15,000	10.2	20,000	13.3
Accrued wages payable	7,200	4.9	8,000	5.3
Total current liabilities	35,400	24.1	40,000	26.6
Long-term liabilities:				
Notes payable, long term	7,150	4.9	10,000	6.7
Total liabilities	42,550	29.0	50,000	33.3
Shareholders' Equity				
Common stock, par $10	85,000	58.0	85,000	56.7
Retained earnings	19,000	13.0	15,000	10.0
Total shareholders' equity	104,000	71.0	100,000	66.7
Total liabilities and shareholders' equity*	$146,550	100.0	$150,000	100.0

*Base amount.

when an income statement amount is compared with a balance sheet amount, a balance sheet **average amount** often is used to compensate for the difference in time periods. In the examples to follow, the selected balance sheet amount usually is computed as the average of the amounts shown on the beginning and ending balance sheets. When additional information is available, such as monthly or quarterly data, an average of the additional data often is more representative.

Commonly used financial ratios can be grouped into the five categories shown in Exhibit 16–3.

EXHIBIT 16–3
Widely used accounting ratios

Ratio	Basic computation
Tests of profitability:	
1. *Return on owners' investment (ROI_o).	$\dfrac{\text{Income}}{\text{Average owners' equity}}$
2. Return on total investment (ROI_t).	$\dfrac{\text{Income} + \text{Interest expense (net of tax)}}{\text{Average total assets}}$
3. Financial leverage ($ROI_o - ROI_t$).	$\dfrac{\text{Return on}}{\text{owners' investment}} - \dfrac{\text{Return on}}{\text{total investment}}$
4. Earnings per share.	$\dfrac{\text{Income}}{\text{Average number of shares of common stock outstanding}}$
5. Profit margin.	$\dfrac{\text{Income (before extraordinary items)}}{\text{Net sales revenue}}$
Tests of liquidity:	
6. Working capital ratio.	$\dfrac{\text{Current assets}}{\text{Current liabilities}}$
7. Quick ratio.	$\dfrac{\text{Quick assets}}{\text{Current liabilities}}$
8. Receivable turnover.	$\dfrac{\text{Net credit sales}}{\text{Average net trade receivables}}$
9. Inventory turnover.	$\dfrac{\text{Cost of goods sold}}{\text{Average inventory}}$
Test of solvency and equity position:	
10. Debt/equity ratio.	$\dfrac{\text{Total liabilities}}{\text{Owners' equity}}$
Market tests:	
11. Price/earnings ratio.	$\dfrac{\text{Current market price per share}}{\text{Earnings per share}}$
12. Dividend yield ratio.	$\dfrac{\text{Dividends per share}}{\text{Market price per share}}$
Miscellaneous ratio:	
13. Book value per share.	$\dfrac{\text{Common stock equity}}{\text{Number of shares of common stock outstanding}}$

*The numbers to the left are maintained in the subsequent discussions to facilitate reference.

TESTS OF PROFITABILITY

Continuing profitability is a primary measure of the overall success of a company; it is a necessary condition for survival. Investors and creditors would prefer a **single measure** of profitability that would be meaningful in all situations. Unfortunately, no single measure can be devised to meet this comprehensive need. Tests of profitability focus on measuring the adequacy of income by comparing it with one or more primary activities or factors that are measured in the financial statements. Five different tests of profitability are explained below.

1. Return on owners' investment (ROI$_o$). This ratio is regarded as a fundamental test of profitability. It relates income to the investment that was committed by the owners to earn the income. To measure the profitability of any investment, whether for a company, a project, or for an individual investment, the amount of income must be compared to the amount invested. Investors commit their funds to an enterprise because they expect to earn a return (i.e., a profit) on those funds. Fundamentally, the return on owners' investment ratio is computed as follows:

$$\text{Return on owners' investment} = \frac{\text{Income*}}{\text{Average owners' equity\dagger}}$$

$$\text{Packard Company, 19B} = \frac{\$8,800*}{\$102,000\dagger} = 8.6\%$$

Based on Exhibit 16–2.
*Income before extraordinary items should be used.
†Average owners' equity is preferable when available; that is ($100,000 + $104,000) ÷ 2 = $102,000.

Thus, Packard Company earned 8.6 percent, after income taxes, on the investment provided by the **owners.** Return on owners' investment is a particularly useful measure of profitability from the **viewpoint of the owners** because it relates the two fundamental factors in any investment situation—the amount of the owners' investment and the return earned for the owners on that investment.

2. Return on total investment (ROI$_t$). Another view of the return on investment concept relates income to **total assets** (i.e., total investment) rather than to owners' investment only. Under this broader concept, return on total investment would be computed as follows:

$$\text{Return on total investment} = \frac{\text{Income* + Interest expense (net of tax)}}{\text{Average total assets\dagger}}$$

$$\text{Packard Company, 19B} = \frac{\$8,800* + (\$1,500 \times .77)}{\$148,275\dagger} = 6.7\%$$

Based on Exhibit 16–2.
*Income before extraordinary items should be used. This illustration assumes an average income tax rate of 23 percent.
†Average total assets should be used; that is ($150,000 + $146,550) ÷ 2 = $148,275.

**EXHIBIT 16–4
Components of
return on total
investment**

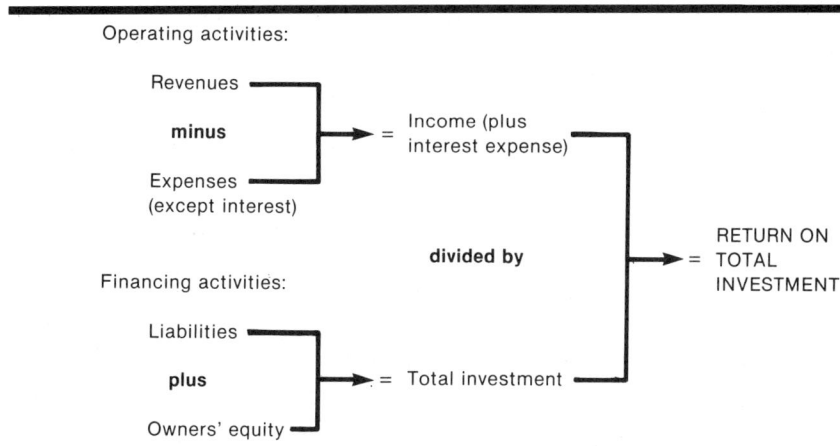

Operating activities:

Revenues

minus   = Income (plus
                                interest expense)

Expenses
(except interest)

                              divided by   RETURN ON
                                                              = TOTAL
Financing activities: INVESTMENT

Liabilities

plus   = Total investment

Owners' equity

Packard Company earned 6.7 percent on the **total resources it employed**
during the year. This concept views **investment** as the amount of resources
provided by both owners and creditors. Return is viewed as the return to both
owners and creditors. Thus, to compute return on **total** investment, interest
expense (net of income tax) must be added back to income because it is the
return on the creditors' investment and was previously deducted to derive income. The denominator represents **total** investment; therefore, interest expense must be added back to raise the numerator (income) to a **total** return
basis. Interest net of income tax is used because it represents the net cost to
the corporation of the funds provided by creditors.

Return on total investment reflects the combined effect of both the operating
and the financing activities of a company as illustrated in Exhibit 16–4 (remember that total assets always equals total liabilities plus total owners' equity).

Most analysts compute return-on-investment ratios for both total investment
and owners' equity as illustrated above. Return on total investment is viewed
as the preferable measure of **management performance** in using all of the resources available to the company. The return on owners' equity is viewed as
particularly relevant to the owners because it measures the return that has
"accrued" to them.

3. Financial leverage. Financial leverage is the advantage, or disadvantage,
which derives from earning a return on owners' investment that is different
from the return earned on total investment (i.e., $ROI_o - ROI_t$). Most companies earn a higher rate on owners' equity than on total investment and thus
enjoy positive leverage. Positive leverage occurs when the average net (aftertax) interest rate on borrowed funds is less than the company's earnings rate
on its total investment.

Financial leverage can be measured by comparing the two return-on-investment ratios as follows:

$$\text{Financial leverage} = \frac{\text{Return on}}{\text{owners' investment}} - \frac{\text{Return on}}{\text{total investment}}$$

$$\text{Packard Company, 19B} = 8.6\% - 6.7\% = 1.9\% \text{ (positive leverage)}$$

When a company can borrow funds at an aftertax (i.e., net) interest rate and invest those funds to earn a higher aftertax rate of return, the difference "accrues" to the benefit of the owners. Of course, this is the primary reason that most companies adopt a strategy of obtaining a significant amount of needed resources from creditors rather than obtaining outside resources only from the sale of their capital stock.

4. Earnings per share (EPS). This test evaluates profitability strictly from the common shareholders' point of view. Rather than being based on the dollar amount of the investment, it is based on the number of shares of common stock outstanding. It provides a measure of profitability that can be adjusted readily for the number of shares outstanding. Basically, EPS on common shares is computed as follows:

$$\text{Earnings per share} = \frac{\text{Income}}{\text{Average number of shares of common stock outstanding}}$$

$$\text{Packard Company, 19B} = \frac{\$8,800}{8,500} = \$1.04 \text{ per share}$$

EPS usually is computed on three amounts if extraordinary items are reported on the income statement: (1) income before extraordinary items (required), (2) extraordinary items (optional), and (3) net income (required). Of the three EPS amounts, the first one usually is considered the most relevant.

5. Profit margin. This percent is based on two income statement amounts. It is computed as follows:

$$\text{Profit margin} = \frac{\text{Income (before extraordinary items)}}{\text{Net sales}}$$

$$\text{Packard Company, 19B} = \frac{\$8,800}{\$120,000} = 7.3\%$$

This profitability test simply is the percent of each sales dollar, on the average, that represents profit. For Packard Company it may be interepreted as follows:

a. Income was 7.3 percent of net sales.
b. $.073 of each $1 of sales was income.

Profit margin also is reflected in the component percentages illustrated in Exhibit 16–2. Care must be exercised in analyzing the profit margin because it does not take into account the amount of resources employed (i.e., total investment) to produce the income. For example, the income statements of Company A and Company B may reflect the following:

		Company A	Company B
a.	Sales revenue	$100,000	$150,000
b.	Income	$ 5,000	$ 7,500
c.	Profit margin (b) ÷ (a)	5%	5%
d.	Total investment	$ 50,000	$125,000
e.	Return on total investment* (b) ÷ (d)	10%	6%

*Assuming no interest expense.

In this example, both companies reported the same profit margin (5 percent). Company A, however, appears to be performing much better because it is earning a 10 percent return on the total investment versus the 6 percent earned by Company B. The profit margin percents do not reflect the effect of the $50,000 total investment in Company A compared to the $125,000 total investment in Company B. The effect of the different amounts of investment in each company is reflected in the return on investment (ROI) percents. Thus, the profit margin ratio omits one of the two important factors that should be used in evaluating return on the investment.

TESTS OF LIQUIDITY

Short-term liquidity refers to a company's ability to meet its currently maturing obligations; therefore, tests of liquidity focus on the relationship between current assets and current liabilities. The ability of a company to meet its current liabilities is an important factor in evaluating short-term financial strength. For example, a company that does not have cash available to pay for purchases on a timely basis will lose its cash discounts and run the risk of discontinued credit by vendors. Recall that working capital is measured as the difference between total current assets and total current liabilities. There are two ratios that are used to measure short-term liquidity; they are the working capital (or current) ratio and the quick (or acid-test) ratio.

6. *Working capital ratio.* This ratio measures the relationship between total current assets and total current liabilities at a specific date. It is computed as follows:

$$\text{Working capital ratio} = \frac{\text{Current assets}}{\text{Current liabilities}}$$

$$\text{Packard Company, 19B} = \frac{\$77,400}{\$35,400} = 2.2 \text{ times or } 2.2 \text{ to } 1$$

The working capital ratio tends to measure the adequacy of working capital as well as liquidity. For Packard Company it can be said that at year-end current assets were 2.2 times current liabilities or, alternatively, that for each $1 of current liabilities there were $2.20 of current assets. Thus, the working capital ratio measures the cushion of working capital maintained in order to allow for the inevitable unevenness in the flow of "funds" through the working capital accounts.[1]

7. *Quick ratio.* This ratio is similar to the working capital ratio except that it is a much more stringent test of short-term liquidity. It is computed as follows:

$$\text{Quick ratio} = \frac{\text{Quick assets}}{\text{Current liabilities}}$$

$$\text{Packard Company, 19B} = \frac{\$21,400}{\$35,400} = .60 \text{ times or } .60 \text{ to } 1$$

Quick assets are assets that are readily convertible into cash at approximately their stated amounts. Quick assets include cash, short-term investments, and accounts receivable (net of the allowance for doubtful accounts). Inventories usually are omitted from quick assets because of the uncertainty of when cash will be received from the sale of inventory in the future. However, if the inventory will turn to cash very quickly, it should be included. In contrast, prepaid expenses do not "convert" to cash; rather their prepayment means that there will be no related cash outflow in the future; therefore, they are excluded from quick assets. Thus, the quick or acid-test ratio is a much more severe test of liquidity than is the working capital ratio.

8. *Receivable turnover.* Short-term liquidity is related to the specific items of working capital. Nearness to cash of some current assets is often measured in terms of **turnover.** There are two ratios, in addition to the two illustrated above, that measure nearness to cash: the receivable turnover and the inventory turnover.

Receivable turnover is computed as follows:

$$\text{Receivable turnover} = \frac{\text{Net credit sales*}}{\text{Average net trade receivables}}$$

$$\begin{array}{c}\text{Packard Company, 19B} \\ \text{(net credit sales assumed} \\ \text{to be \$77,000 for 19B)}\end{array} = \frac{\$77,000}{(\$7,000 + \$8,400) \div 2} = 10 \text{ times}$$

*When the amount of credit sales is not known, total sales may be used as a rough approximation.

---

[1]Occasionally, "working capital" is taken to mean total current assets which is confusing and unnecessary because "total current assets" is more descriptive. Sometimes the term **net working capital** is used to describe the difference between current assets and current liabilities. Throughout this book, we have followed the more general use of working capital to mean the difference between current assets and current liabilities.

This ratio is called a turnover ratio because it reflects how many times the trade receivables "turnover" (i.e., were recorded, collected, then recorded again during the period). Receivable turnover expresses the relationship of the average balance in Accounts Receivable (including Trade Notes Receivable) to the transactions that generated those receivables—credit sales. This ratio tends to measure the effectiveness of the credit-granting and collection activities of the company. A high receivable turnover ratio suggests effective collection activities. Granting credit to poor credit risks and ineffective collection efforts will cause this ratio to be low. The receivable turnover ratio often is converted to a time basis known as the average age of receivables. The computation is as follows:

$$\text{Average age of trade receivables} = \frac{\text{Days in year}}{\text{Receivable turnover}}$$

$$\text{Packard Company, 19B} = \frac{365}{10} = 36.5 \text{ average days to collect}$$

The effectiveness of credit and collection activities sometimes is judged by a "rule of thumb" that the **average days to collect** should not exceed 1½ times the credit terms. For example, if the credit terms are 2/10, n/30, the average days to collect should not exceed 45 days (i.e., not more than 15 days past due). Like all rules of thumb, this one is rough and has many exceptions. However, an increase or decrease in the receivable turnover or average days to collect, from one period to the next, would suggest changes in the implementation of credit policies and/or changes in collection efficiency. An increase in the average age of trade receivables would indicate an increasing time lag between credit sales and cash collection.

9. Inventory turnover. Inventory turnover tends to measure the liquidity (i.e., nearness to cash) of the inventory. It reflects the relationship of the inventory to the volume of goods sold during the period. The computation is as follows:

$$\text{Inventory turnover} = \frac{\text{Cost of goods sold}}{\text{Average inventory}}$$

$$\text{Packard Company, 19B} = \frac{\$72,600}{(\$60,000 + \$54,000) \div 2} = 1.3 \text{ times}$$

The inventory "turned over" 1.3 times on the average during the year because cost of goods sold was 1.3 times the average inventory level. Because profit normally is realized each time the inventory is sold (i.e., turned over), an increase in the ratio is favourable, up to a point. If the ratio is too high, sales may be lost because of items that are out of stock. The turnover ratio often is converted to a time-basis expression called the **average days' supply in inventory.** The computation would be:

$$\text{Average days' supply in inventory} = \frac{\text{Days in year}}{\text{Inventory turnover}}$$

$$\text{Packard Company, 19B} = \frac{365}{1.3}$$

$$= 281 \text{ average days' supply in inventory}$$

Turnover ratios are used extensively because they are easy to understand. Normal (or average) inventory turnover ratios vary significantly by industry classification. Companies in the food industry (grocery stores and restaurants) have high inventory turnover ratios while companies that sell expensive merchandise (jewelry stores and automobile dealers) have a much lower ratio.

TESTS OF SOLVENCY AND EQUITY POSITION

We noted above that short-term liquidity refers to the relationship between current assets and current liabilities. In contrast, **solvency** refers to the ability of a company to meet its **long-term obligations** on a continuing basis. Certain critical relationships can be identified by analyzing how a company has financed its assets and activities. The relative amount of resources provided by creditors and owners is known as a company's **equity position**. The debt/equity ratio is used to reflect the equity position of a company.

10. Debt/equity ratio. This ratio expresses the direct proportion between debt and owners' equity.[2] It is computed as follows:

$$\text{Debt/equity ratio} = \frac{\text{Total liabilities (i.e., creditors' equity)}}{\text{Owners' equity}}$$

$$\text{Packard Company, 19B} = \frac{\$42,550}{\$104,000} = .41 \text{ (or 41\%)}$$

In effect, this ratio states that for each $1 of owners' equity, there was $.41 of liabilities.

---

[2]The relationship between debt and owners' equity alternatively may be calculated with the following two ratios:

$$\text{Owners' equity to total equities} = \frac{\text{Owners' equity}}{\text{Total equities}}$$

$$\text{Packard Company, 19B} = \frac{\$104,000}{\$146,500} = 71\%$$

$$\text{Creditors' equity to total equities} = \frac{\text{Creditors' equity}}{\text{Total equities}}$$

$$\text{Packard Company, 19B} = \frac{\$42,500}{\$146,550} = 29\%$$

Debt capital is risky for a company because there are *(a)* specific maturity dates for the principal amounts and *(b)* specific interest payments that must be made. Debt obligations are enforceable by law and do not depend upon the earning of income by the company. In contrast, resources supplied by owners do not give rise to similar obligations; that is, owners' equity is not fixed as to amounts and dates of principal and dividend payments. Thus, equity capital usually is viewed as much less risky than debt capital for a company.

In the long run, the rate of return on shareholders' equity usually will be higher than interest rates paid to creditors Despite the element of risk associated with debt, it may be advantageous to the shareholders if the company derives significant amounts of resources through borrowing (because of positive financial leverage). For example, assume a company is earning 15 percent return on total investment, while its borrowing rate on debt is 7 percent (net of income tax) on the average. The difference between the earnings rate on total resources (15 percent) and the interest paid to the creditors (7 percent) "accrues" to the benefit of the shareholders.[3] In the long run, the shareholders benefit by the 15 percent earned on the resources provided by them, plus the difference between the 15 percent return and the 7 percent interest rate paid on the resources provided by the creditors. A company with a high proportion of debt is said to be **highly levered.** The debt/equity ratio indicates the balance that the management has attained between the resources provided by creditors and the resources provided by owners.

MARKET TESTS

Several ratios have been developed to measure the "market worth" of a share. Basically, these market tests attempt to relate the current market price of a share to some indicator of the gain or loss that might accrue to an investor. The tests focus on the **current market price** of the shares because that is the amount the buyer would invest. Two market test ratios quoted widely by analysts, stockbrokers, investors, and others are the price/earnings ratio and the dividend yield ratio.

11. Price/earnings ratio (P/E). This ratio measures the relationship between the current market price of the stock and its earnings per share. Assuming a current market price of $15.60 per share for Packard Company common stock in 19B and earnings per share of $1.04, the P/E ratio is computed as follows:

$$\text{Price/earnings ratio} = \frac{\text{Current market price per share}}{\text{Earnings per share}}$$

$$\text{Packard Company, 19B} = \frac{\$15.60}{\$1.04} = 15 \text{ (or 15 to 1)}$$

---

[3] Interest expense on debt is a deductible expense on the income tax return; in contrast, dividend payments to shareholders are not deductible. Thus, in addition to the lower stated rate for debt, funds obtained by means of debt tend to be less costly because of the income tax saving. The real cost of debt in the above example depends upon the income tax rate.

Thus, Packard shares were selling at 15 times the EPS. The P/E ratio frequently is referred to as the **multiple**. The P/E ratio is used widely as an indicator of the future performance of the shares. It changes with each change in the current market price per share and with each earnings report.

Sometimes the components of this ratio are inverted, giving what is referred to as the **capitalization rate**. This is said to be the rate at which the stock market apparently is capitalizing the current earnings. For example, computation of the capitalization rate on current earnings per share would be $1.04 ÷ $15.60 = 6.67 percent.

12. Dividend yield ratio. This yield ratio measures the relationship between the dividends per share paid in the past and the current market price of the shares. Assuming dividends paid by Packard Company of $.75 per share for 19B, and a current market price per share of $15.60, the ratio is computed as follows:

$$\text{Dividend yield ratio} = \frac{\text{Dividend per share}}{\text{Market price per share}}$$

$$\text{Packard Company, 19B} = \frac{\$.75}{\$15.60} = 4.81\%$$

This ratio measures the current dividend yield to the investor, based upon the dividends declared per share (which is revenue to the investor), against the cost of the investment as indicated by the current market price per share. Like the P/E ratio, it is a volatile measure because the price of a share may change materially over short periods of time, and each change in market price or dividend payment changes the ratio.

MISCELLANEOUS RATIO

13. Book value per share. The book value per share measures the owners' equity in terms of each common share outstanding. In the case of a simple capital structure, with **only** common shares outstanding, the computation of book value per share is not difficult. To illustrate, assume Day Corporation had total owners' equity of $250,000 and 10,000 outstanding common shares, par $10. The computation of book value per share would be as follows:

Book value per common share:

$$\frac{\text{Book value per}}{\text{common share}} = \frac{\text{Total owners' equity}}{\text{(applicable to common shares)}}{\text{Common shares outstanding}}$$

$$= \frac{\$250,000}{10,000 \text{ shares}} = \$25$$

Computation of book value per share is more difficult if both common and preferred shares are outstanding. In this situation, total owners' equity must be allocated between the common and preferred shares. This allocation is accomplished by assigning an amount to the preferred shares, based on its preferences, and, then, assigning the remaining amount of owners' equity to the common shares. To illustrate, assume Bye Corporation had total owners' equity of $273,000; 1,000 shares outstanding of its 5 percent preferred stock, par $20, cumulative (no dividends in arrears for past years), and liquidation value of $22 per share; and 10,000 outstanding common shares, par $10.

Allocation:

Total owners' equity		$273,000
Less equity allocated to preferred shares:		
Liquidation value (1,000 shares × $22)	$22,000	
Cumulative dividend preference for the current year		
(1,000 shares × $20 × 5%)	1,000	
Amount allocated to preferred shares		23,000
Remainder allocated to common shares		$250,000

Book value per share:
Preferred, $23,000 ÷ 1,000 shares = $23
Common, $250,000 ÷ 10,000 shares = $25

Book value per share has limited significance because it has no necessary relationship to market value. Because it is a low conservative amount (historical cost basis), some persons consider a market below book value to imply underpriced shares.

INTERPRETING RATIOS

When using ratios computed by others, it is important to remember that the computation of a particular ratio is not standardized. Neither the accounting profession nor security analysts have prescribed the manner in which a ratio must be computed (except for earnings per share). Thus, users of financial statements should compute the various ratios in accordance with their decision objectives. As a consequence, before relying on a ratio or a series of ratios, the user should be informed as to the basic computational approach used. The discussions and illustrations in this section follow the approaches commonly used.

Ratio analysis is a useful technique; however, ratios pose significant interpretative problems to the user. To evaluate a ratio, it must be compared with some **standard** that represents an optimal or desirable level. For example, the return-on-investment ratio may be compared with a long-range objective expressed in this manner. Some ratios, by their characteristics, are unfavourable if they are **either** too high or too low. For example, analysis may indicate that a working capital ratio of approximately 2:1 may be considered optimal for a given company. In this situation, a ratio of 1:1 would tend to indicate a danger of being unable to meet maturing obligations, whereas, a ratio of 3:1 may indicate that excess funds are being left idle rather than being employed prof-

EXHIBIT 16–5
Selected financial
ratios for one
corporation

	1977	1978	1979	1980	1981
Working capital ratio	1.20	.91	.74	.60	.49
Debt/equity ratio	2.03	2.45	4.88	15.67	N/A*

*In 1981, the corporation reported negative owners' equity as the result of a large net loss that produced a negative balance in retained earnings. Creditors' equity exceeded **total** equities.

itably. Furthermore, an optimal ratio for one company frequently will not be an optimal ratio for another company. Thus, comparisons of ratios among companies frequently are of questionable validity, particularly when there are important differences among the companies, such as industry and nature of operations.

Another limitation is that most ratios represent **averages** and, therefore, ratios may tend to obscure the underlying causative factors of large variations above and below the average. To illustrate, a working capital ratio of 2:1 was considered optimal in the example above. But even an optimal working capital ratio may obscure a short-term liquidity problem if the company has a very large amount of inventory and a minimal amount of cash with which to pay obligations as they mature.

Despite certain limitations, ratio analysis is a useful analytical tool. Financial ratios have been shown to be particularly effective in predicting bankruptcy. Exhibit 16–5 presents the working capital ratio and the debt/equity ratio for a large international corporation. Observe the deterioration of these ratios each year. In 1981, the independent auditor issued a qualified audit opinion and noted, "there are conditions which indicate that the company may be unable to continue as a going concern." In the spring of 1982, the corporation filed for bankruptcy. Analysts who studied the financial ratios each year probably were not surprised by the bankruptcy of this corporation.

Financial analysts often use four types of "standards" against which ratios and percents are compared:

1. **Comparison of the ratios for the current year with the historical ratios for the same company**—Particular attention is given to the **trend** of each ratio over time.

2. **Comparison of the ratios for the current year with ratios of other companies for the same year**—These comparisons include the use of ratios and percents from other similar companies and from industry averages. Industry averages are published by many trade associations, governmental agencies, and others. For example, a variety of ratios can be found in the publications of Dun & Bradstreet, Inc., Moody's *Manual of Investments,* and Standard and Poor's *Corporation Records,* and Statistics Canada.

3. **Experience of the analyst who has a subjective feel for the "right" relationships in a given situation**—These subjective

judgments of an experienced and competent observer tend to be more reliable than purely mechanical comparisons.

4. **Comparison of the ratios for the current year with planned goals and objectives expressed as ratios**—Many companies prepare comprehensive profit plans (i.e., budgets) on a continuing basis that incorporate realistic plans for the future. These plans usually incorporate planned goals for significant ratios, such as profit margin, return on investment, and EPS. These internally developed standards clearly have less inherent difficulties than any of the other comparisons; however, they seldom are available to external parties.

SUMMARY OF CHAPTER

Interpretation of amounts reported on financial statements may be enhanced by expressing certain relationships as ratios or percents. Although many ratios can be calculated, a few usually will suffice for a given decision. Having selected the relevant ratios, the analyst has the central problem of evaluating the results. This evaluation involves the task of selecting one or more realistic standards with which to compare the results. Four types of standards frequently are used: (1) historical standards, (2) external standards, (3) experience, and (4) planned standards. Experience and competence are particularly important. The interpretation of ratios often may suggest strengths and weaknesses in the operations and/or the financial position of the company that should be accorded in-depth investigation and evaluation if significant decisions are contemplated.

IMPORTANT TERMS DEFINED IN THIS CHAPTER

Terms (alphabetically)	Key words in definitions of important terms used in chapter	Page reference
Common ratios	Selected ratios that are used widely. Exhibit 16–3 presents a list of 13 commonly used accounting ratios.	855
Comparative statements	Financial statements for several years; amounts are presented side by side for comparative purposes.	851
Component percentages	A percentage that expresses each item on a particular financial statement as a percent of a single base amount.	853
Long-term summaries	Summaries of basic accounting data for many years (typically 10 years).	852
Market tests	Ratios that tend to measure the "market worth" of a share.	863
Ratio analysis	Analytical tool designed to identify significant relationships; measures proportional relationship between two financial statement amounts.	852
Tests of liquidity	Ratios that measure a company's ability to meet its currently maturing obligations.	859
Tests of solvency	Ratios that measure a company's ability to meet its long-term obligations.	862

QUESTIONS FOR DISCUSSION —————————————————————————————

1. What are the three fundamental uses of external financial statements by decision makers?

2. What are some of the primary items on financial statements about which creditors usually are concerned?

3. Explain why the notes to the financial statements are particularly important to decision makers.

4. What is the primary purpose of comparative financial statements?

5. Why are statement users especially interested in financial summaries covering several years? What is the primary limitation of long-term summaries?

6. What is ratio analysis? Why is ratio analysis useful?

7. What are component percentages? Why are component percentages useful?

8. Explain the two concepts of return on investment.

9. What is financial leverage? How is financial leverage measured?

10. Is profit margin a useful measure of profitability? Explain.

11. Compare the working capital ratio with the quick ratio.

12. What does the debt/equity ratio reflect?

13. Explain what is meant by "market tests."

14. What are the primary problems when using ratios?

15. Why is the past history of a firm as presented in the financial statements useful to persons or groups interested in the future?

16. Why is "average" owners' equity said to be preferable to period end owners' equity for computing return on owners' investment?

17. Receivable turnover uses the average of net trade receivable balances to provide a period representation of the period and balance. Would you ever want to use the period end net trade receivables rather than the average? Why?

EXERCISES

E16–1. The comparative financial statements prepared at December 31, 19B, for Doan Company reflected the following summarized data:

	19B	19A
Income statement:		
Sales revenue	$150,000*	$140,000*
Cost of goods sold	90,000	85,000
Gross margin	60,000	55,000
Operating expenses and interest expense	43,000	40,500
Pretax income.............................	17,000	14,500
Income tax.............................	5,000	4,500
Net income	$ 12,000	$ 10,000
Balance sheet:		
Cash	$ 8,000	$ 11,000
Accounts receivable (net)....................	12,000	14,000
Inventory..................................	30,000	28,000
Operational assets (net).....................	50,000	43,000
	$100,000	$ 96,000
Current liabilities (no interest)...............	$ 15,000	$ 17,000
Long-term liabilities (10% interest)	35,000	35,000
Common stock (par $10)	40,000	40,000
Retained earnings†	10,000	4,000
	$100,000	$ 96,000

*One third were credit sales.
†During 19B, cash dividends amounting to $6,000 were declared and paid.

Required:

a. Complete the following columns for each item in the above comparative financial statements:

Increase (decrease)	
19B over 19A	
Amount	Percent

b. Respond to the following questions:
  (1) Compute the percentage increases in sales revenue, net income, cash, inventory, liabilities, and owners' equity.
  (2) By what amount did working capital change?
  (3) What was the percentage change in the average income tax rate?
  (4) What was the amount of cash inflow from revenues for 19B?
  (5) By what percent did the average markup realized on goods sold change?
  (6) By how much did the book value per share change?

E16–2. Use the data given in Exercise 16–1 for Doan Company.

Required:

a. Present component percentages for 19B only.
b. Respond to the following questions for 19B:
  (1) What was the average percentage markup on sales?
  (2) What was the average income tax rate?

(3) Compute the profit margin. Was it a good or poor indicator of performance? Explain.

(4) What percent of total resources was invested in operational assets?

(5) Compute the debt/equity ratio. Does it look good or bad? Explain.

(6) What was the return on owners' investment?

(7) What was the return on total investment?

(8) Compute the financial leverage percent. Was it positive or negative? Explain.

(9) What was the book value per share of common stock?

E16–3. Use the data given in Exercise 16–1 for Doan Company. Use a separate sheet and complete the following tabulation for 19B only (assume a common stock price of $33 per share); compute the ratios that usually are included under each category:

Name and Computation of the Ratio (show computations)	Brief Explanation of the Ratio
A. **Tests of profitability:** 1. Return on owners' investment. 2. Etc.	
B. **Tests of liquidity:** 1. Working capital ratio. 2. Etc.	
C. **Tests of solvency and equity position:** 1. Debt/equity ratio. 2. Etc.	
D. **Market tests:** 1. Price/earnings ratio. 2. Etc.	
E. **Miscellaneous ratio:** 1. Book value per share.	

E16–4. Match the following by entering the appropriate letters in the blanks.

Ratio or percent		*Computation*
1. _____ Profit margin	A.	Income (before extraordinary items) ÷ Net sales.
2. _____ Inventory turnover ratio	B.	Days in year ÷ Receivable turnover.
3. _____ Average collection period	C.	Income ÷ Average owners' equity.
4. _____ Creditors' equity to total equities	D.	Income ÷ Average number of common shares outstanding.
5. _____ Dividend yield ratio	E.	Return on owners' investment − Return on total investment.
6. _____ Return on owners' investment	F.	Quick assets ÷ Current liabilities.
7. _____ Working capital ratio	G.	Current assets ÷ Current liabilities.
8. _____ Debt/equity ratio	H.	Cost of goods sold ÷ Average inventory.
9. _____ Price/earnings ratio	I.	Net credit sales ÷ Average net trade receivables.
10. _____ Financial leverage	J.	Creditors' equity (debt) ÷ Total equities.
11. _____ Receivable turnover ratio	K.	Days in year ÷ Inventory turnover.
12. _____ Average days' supply of inventory	L.	Total liabilities ÷ Owners' equity.
13. _____ Owners' equity to total equities	M.	Dividends per share ÷ Market price per share.
	N.	Owners' equity ÷ Total equities.
14. _____ Earnings per share	O.	Current market price per share ÷ Earnings per share.
15. _____ Return on total investment	P.	Owners' equity ÷ Shares outstanding.
16. _____ Quick ratio	Q.	(Income + Interest expense (net of tax)) ÷ Total assets.
17. _____ Book value per share		

E16–5. Situation A—Current assets totaled to $60,000, and the working capital ratio was 2.00. Assume the following transactions were completed: (1) purchased merchandise for $3,000 of which one third was on short-term credit; and (2) purchased a delivery truck for $8,000, paid $2,000 cash and signed a two-year interest-bearing note for the balance.

Compute the cumulative working capital ratio after each transaction.

Situation B—Sales for the year amounted to $600,000 of which one half was on credit. The average gross margin rate was 40 percent on sales. Account balances were:

	Beginning	Ending
Accounts receivable (net)	$30,000	$20,000
Inventory	20,000	16,000

Compute the turnover for the accounts receivable and inventory, the average age of the receivables and the average days' supply of inventory.

Situation C—The financial statements reported the following at year-end:

Total assets	$100,000
Total debt (10% interest)	60,000
Net income (average tax rate 20%)	12,000

Compute the financial leverage and indicate whether it was positive or negative.

E16–6. Ryan Retail Company has just prepared the comparative annual financial statements for 19B given below:

RYAN RETAIL COMPANY
Income Statement
For the Years Ended December 31, 19B, and 19A

		For the year ended	
		19B	19A
Sales revenue (one half on credit)		$100,000	$ 95,000
Cost of goods sold		48,000	46,000
Gross margin		52,000	49,000
Expenses (including $3,000 interest			
expense each year)		34,000	33,000
Pretax income		18,000	16,000
Income tax on operations (22%)		3,960	3,520
Income before extraordinary items		14,040	12,480
Extraordinary loss	$3,000		
Less income tax saved	660	2,340	
Extraordinary gain		$1,000	
Applicable income tax		220	780
Net income		$ 11,700	$ 13,260

RYAN RETAIL COMPANY
Balance Sheet
At December 31, 19B, and 19A

	19B	19A
Assets		
Cash	$ 47,200	$ 20,000
Accounts receivable (net) (terms 1/10, n/30)	35,000	30,000
Inventory	30,000	40,000
Operational assets (net)	90,000	100,000
Total assets	$202,200	$190,000
Liabilities		
Accounts payable	$ 60,000	$ 50,000
Income tax payable	1,500	1,000
Note payable, long term	25,000	25,000
Shareholders' Equity		
Capital stock, par $10	80,000	80,000
Retained earnings	35,700	34,000
Total liabilities and shareholders' equity	$202,200	$190,000

Required (round percents and ratios to two places):

a. Compute for 19B the tests of (1) profitability, (2) liquidity, (3) solvency, and (4) market. Assume the quoted price of the shares was $26.50 for 19B. Dividends declared and paid during 19B amounted to $10,000.

b. Respond to the following for 19B:
   (1) Compute the percentage changes in sales, income before extraordinary items, net income, cash, inventory, and debt.
   (2) What appears to be the pretax interest rate on the note payable?

c. Identify at least two problems facing the company that are suggested by your responses to *(a)* and *(b)*.

PROBLEMS/CASES

PC16–1. Peterson Corporation has just completed its comparative statements for the year ended December 31, 19B. At this point, certain analytical and interpretative procedures are to be undertaken. The completed statements (summarized) are as follows:

	19B	19A
Income statement:		
Sales revenue	$400,000*	$390,000*
Cost of goods sold	220,000	218,000
Gross margin	180,000	172,000
Operating expenses (including interest on bonds)	147,000	148,000
Pretax income	33,000	24,000
Income tax	9,000	7,000
Net income	$ 24,000	$ 17,000
Balance sheet:		
Cash	$ 5,400	$ 2,700
Accounts receivable (net)	44,000	30,000
Merchandise inventory	30,000	24,000
Prepaid expenses	600	500
Operational assets (net)	120,000	130,000
	$200,000	$187,200
Accounts payable	$ 19,000	$ 20,000
Income tax payable	1,000	1,200
Bonds payable (10% interest rate)	50,000	50,000
Common stock, par $10	100,000†	100,000
Retained earnings	30,000‡	16,000
	$200,000	$187,200

*Twenty-five percent were credit sales.
†The market price of a share at the end of 19B was $24.
‡During 19B, the company declared and paid a cash dividend of $10,000.

Required:

a. Complete a tabulation similar to the following (show computations, round percents and ratios to two places):

Name and Computation of the 19B Ratio	Brief Explanation of the Ratio
Tests of profitability: 1. Return on owners' investment. 2. Etc.	
Tests of liquidity: 1. Working capital ratio. 2. Etc.	
Tests of solvency and equity position: 1. Debt/equity ratio. 2. Etc.	
Market tests: 1. Price/earnings ratio. 2. Etc.	

b. Respond to the following questions for 19B:

    (1) Evaluate the financial leverage amount and explain what it means by using the computed amount(s).

    (2) Evaluate the profit margin amount and explain how a shareholder might use it.

    (3) Explain to a shareholder why the working capital ratio and the quick ratio are different. Do you observe any liquidity problems? Explain.

    (4) Assuming credit terms are 1/10, n/30, do you perceive an unfavourable situation for the company related to credit sales? Explain.

PC16–2. The following information was contained in the annual financial statements of Taterwood Company, that started business January 1, 19A (assume account balances only in Cash and Capital Stock on this date; all amounts are in thousands of dollars).

	19A	*19B*	*19C*	*19D*
Accounts receivable (net) (terms, n/30)......	$ 8	$10	$ 16	$ 22
Merchandise inventory....................	10	12	20	25
Net sales (¾ on credit)	40	60	100	120
Cost of goods sold.......................	26	36	64	80
Net income (loss)........................	(10)	6	14	10

Required (show computations and round to two decimal places):

a. Complete the tabulation given below.

b. Evaluate the results of the three related ratios (1, 2, and 3) to identify the favourable or unfavourable factors. Give your recommendations to improve Taterwood's operations.

c. Evaluate the results of the last four ratios (4, 5, 6, and 7) and identify any favourable or unfavourable factors. Give your recommendations to improve Taterwood's operations.

Items	19A	19B	19C	19D
1. Profit margin—percent.				
2. Gross margin—ratio.				
3. Expenses as a percent of sales, excluding cost of goods sold.				
4. Inventory turnover.				
5. Days' supply in inventory.				
6. Receivable turnover.				
7. Average days to collect.				

PC16–3. The 19B financial statements for Able and Baker companies are summarized below:

	Able Company	Baker Company
Balance sheet:		
Cash	$ 25,000	$ 11,000
Accounts receivable, net	30,000	17,000
Inventory...	80,000	20,000
Operational assets, net.............................	125,000	300,000
Other assets	40,000	252,000
Total assets	$300,000	$600,000
Current liabilities..................................	$ 90,000	$ 40,000
Long-term debt (10%)...............................	50,000	60,000
Capital stock, par $10..............................	120,000	400,000
Contributed surplus	10,000	60,000
Retained earnings	30,000	40,000
Total liabilities and shareholders' equity	$300,000	$600,000
Income statement:		
Sales revenue (on credit)........................... (⅓)	$600,000 (⅙)	$900,000
Cost of goods sold	(350,000)	(450,000)
Expenses (including interest and income tax)	(205,000)	(360,000)
Net income	$ 45,000	$ 90,000
Selected data from the 19A statements:		
Accounts receivable, net	$ 25,000	$ 19,000
Inventory...	70,000	24,000
Long-term debt	50,000	60,000
Other data:		
Per share price at end of 19B (offering price)..........	$ 30	$ 18
Average income tax rate	30%	30%
Dividends declared and paid in 19B..................	$ 25,800	$150,400

Able and Baker companies are in the same line of business and are direct competitors in a large metropolitan area. They have been in business approximately 10 years, and each has experienced a relatively steady growth. The two managements have essentially different viewpoints in many respects; however, Baker is considered to be the more conservative and, as the president said, "We avoid what we consider to be undue risks." Neither company is publicly held. Able Company has an annual audit by a CA but Baker Company does not.

Required:

a. Complete a schedule that reflects a ratio analysis of each company. As a minimum, compute the 13 ratios discussed in the chapter.

b. Assume a client of yours has the opportunity to purchase 10 percent of the shares in one or the other company at the per share prices given above. Your client has decided to invest in one of the companies. Based on the data given, prepare a comparative evaluation of the ratio analyses (and any other available information) and give your recommended choice with the supporting explanation.

PC16–4. The 19B financial statements for D and R companies are summarized on the next page:

	D Company	R Company
Balance sheet:		
Cash	$ 20,000	$ 40,000
Accounts receivable, net.	60,000	10,000
Inventory	120,000	30,000
Operational assets, net	500,000	150,000
Other assets.	155,000	54,000
Total	$855,000	$284,000
Current liabilities	$100,000	$ 20,000
Long-term debt (10%)	200,000	50,000
Capital stock, par $10	500,000	200,000
Contributed surplus	25,000	2,000
Retained earnings	30,000	12,000
Total	$855,000	$284,000
Income statement:		
Sales revenue (on credit)	(½) $900,000	(⅓) $300,000
Cost of goods sold	(522,000)	(180,000)
Expenses (including interest and income tax)	(288,000)	(84,000)
Net income	$ 90,000	$ 36,000
Selected data from the 19A statements:		
Accounts receivable, net.	$ 40,000	$ 14,000
Long-term debt (10% interest)	200,000	50,000
Inventory	100,000	40,000
Other data:		
Per share price at end of 19B	$ 12.75	$ 10.50
Average income tax rate	30%	20%
Dividends declared and paid in 19B	$ 40,000	$ 10,000

These two companies are in the same line of business and in the same province but in different cities. Each company has been in existence for approximately 10 years. D Company is audited by a national CA firm and R Company is audited by a local CA practitioner. Both companies received an unqualified opinion (i.e., the independent auditors found nothing wrong) on the financial statements. D Company wants to borrow $75,000 cash, and R Company needs $30,000. The loans will be for a two-year period and are needed for "working capital purposes."

Required:

a. Complete a schedule that reflects a ratio analysis of each company. As a minimum compute the ratios discussed in the chapter.
b. Assume you work in the loan department of a local bank. You have been asked to analyze the situation and recommend which loan is preferable. Based on the data given, your analysis prepared in (a), and any other information, give your choice and the supporting explanation.

PC16–5.   Refer to the financial statements of Consolidated-Bathurst, given in Special Supplement B immediately preceding the Index.

Required:

a. Compute each of the 13 accounting ratios (for 1984) listed in Exhibit 16–3. If you are unable to compute a particular ratio, explain why. Assume the current share price is $15 per share.
b. Evaluate the ratios and identify any potential problems that you think exist. Comment on any suggestions you may have for management.

PC16–6. The following information was contained in the actual financial statements of a large manufacturing company which currently is listed on a major Stock Exchange:

Balance Sheet

	December 31 (millions of dollars)	
	19B	19A
Assets		
Current assets		
Cash	$ 188.2	$ 123.2
Time deposits	120.8	248.8
Marketable securities	165.3	150.8
Accounts receivable (less allowance for doubtful accounts: 19B— $34.9 million; 19A—$16.7 million)	610.3	848.0
Inventories—at the lower of cost (substantially FIFO) or market	1,873.8	1,980.8
Prepaid insurance, taxes and other expenses	162.3	210.2
Total current assets	3,120.7	3,561.8
Total investments and other assets	1,183.5	1,396.5
Property, plant and equipment		
Land, buildings, machinery, and equipment	3,733.1	3,391.3
Less accumulated depreciation	2,097.1	1,963.9
	1,636.0	1,427.4
Special tools	712.9	595.5
Net property, plant and equipment	2,348.9	2,022.9
Total assets	$ 6,653.1	$ 6,981.2
Liabilities and Shareholders' Investment		
Current liabilities		
Accounts payable	$ 1,530.4	$ 1,725.0
Accrued expenses	807.9	698.0
Short-term debt	600.9	49.2
Payments due within one year on long-term debt	275.6	12.4
Taxes on income	16.8	1.2
Total current liabilities	3,231.6	2,485.8
Total long-term debt and other liabilities	1,559.1	1,564.1
Minority interest in consolidated subsidiaries	38.3	4.8
Preferred stock—nopar value	218.7	217.0
Common stock—par value $6.25 per share	416.9	397.7
Contributed surplus	692.2	683.1
Net earnings retained	496.3	1,628.7
Total liabilities and shareholders' investment	$ 6,653.1	$ 6,981.2

Income Statement

	Year Ended December 31 (In millions of dollars)	
	19B	19A
Net sales	$12,004.3	$13,669.8
Cost of goods sold	11,631.5	12,640.1
Depreciation of plant and equipment	180.6	154.0
Amortization of special tools	220.0	198.2
Selling and administrative expenses	598.5	572.1
Pension plans	260.6	262.3
Interest expense	215.4	128.9
	13,106.6	13,955.6
Loss before taxes on income	(1,102.3)	(285.8)
Taxes on income (credit)	(5.0)	(81.2)
Net loss	$ (1,097.3)	$ (204.6)

Required:

a. Calculate the following ratios:
    (1) Return on owners' investment.
    (2) Return on total investment.
         (For purposes of this case, assume that the interest expense reported on the income statement is net of income taxes.)
    (3) Financial leverage.
    (4) Earnings per share.
    (5) Working capital ratio.
    (6) Quick ratio.
    (7) Inventory turnover.
    (8) Debt/equity ratio.
b. Based on your analysis of the ratios that you calculated in Requirement *(a),* do you think that this company will be able to continue in existence? Explain. Would you be willing to invest in this company? Explain.

PC16–7.   Aggressive Company uses the FIFO method to cost inventory and Conservative Company uses the LIFO method. The two companies are exactly alike except for the difference in inventory costing methods. Costs of inventory items for both companies have been rising steadily in recent years and each company has increased its inventory each year. Each company has paid its tax liability in full for the current year (and all previous years), and each company uses the same accounting methods for both financial reporting and income tax reporting (assumed for discussion only). Identify which company will report the higher amount for each of the following ratios. If it is not possible, explain why.

a. Working capital ratio.
b. Quick ratio.
c. Debt/equity ratio.
d. Return on owners' investment.
e. Earnings per share.

PC16–8.   Fast Company uses the sum-of-years'-digits method to depreciate its property, plant, and equipment and Slow Company uses the straight-line method. Both companies use maximum capital cost allowance for income tax purposes. The two companies are exactly alike except for the difference in depreciation methods.

Required:

a. Identify the financial ratios discussed in this chapter that are **likely** to be affected by the difference in depreciation methods.
b. Which company will report the higher amount for each ratio that you have identified? If you cannot be certain, explain why.

PC16–9.   Nearly Broke Company requested a sizable loan from Second National Bank in order to acquire a large tract of land for future expansion. Nearly Broke reported current assets of $1,750,000 ($475,000 in cash) and current liabilities of $975,000. Second National denied the loan request for a number of reasons including the fact that the working capital ratio was below two to one. When Nearly Broke was informed of the loan denial, the comptroller of the company immediately paid $470,000 that was owed to several trade creditors. The comptroller then asked Second National to reconsider the loan application. Based on these abbreviated facts, would you recommend that Second National approve the loan request? Why?

PC16–10.   Windsor Clays Ltd., a federally incorporated company, began as a small pottery studio selling pottery made by the owners and by other local craftspeople. Gradually, other kinds of crafts and supplies were added, until the company became both a retailer of finished crafts and a supplier to the craftspeople. For example, the company sells the raw clay, the glaze materials, and the wheels and kilns used to make pottery, as well as selling finished pottery.

Over the years, the company has expanded to become a major regional supplier of craft raw materials and equipment. Although the retail business has grown, most of the company's revenue now comes from wholesale sales to craftspeople. The company now has four outlets, each of which has combined wholesale and retail operations. The company mixes most of its clay and glazes and performs other manufacturing and assembly work in a shop attached to its central warehouse.

In the past, essentially all the retail sales and a large portion of the wholesale sales were for cash. Therefore, the company has had low receivables. Recently, however, the company has tried to maintain its sales level by allowing more credit to wholesale customers.

Wholesale inventories have always been high in dollar value, and particularly for larger pieces of equipment, have been slow to turn over. Due to the nature of the craft business, it is necessary to carry a wide variety of inventory items.

Retail merchandise quantities are maintained at a high level. Most of this merchandise is held on consignment, and the remainder consists of items purchased from a few well-established craftspeople or produced in the company's shop.

Much of the wholesale inventory is imported from the United States and Japan. The company's margins have been severely squeezed because of recent currency fluctuations and because the recession has prevented recovery of cost increases. Crafts are considered a luxury good, so the company's retail sales and those to its wholesale customers have been hard hit. In spite of significant price reductions, sales volume has generally fallen.

During 1985, cash flow has been a problem. The company exceeded its credit limit and the bank expressed concern about the company's financial state and inability to determine its cash requirements. In an effort to alleviate the problem, several cost-cutting measures were implemented and advertising expenditures were increased to try to encourage sales. However, the company's position continued to deteriorate. The president then considered the following courses of action: reduction of inventory levels; the elimination of product lines; shift of emphasis from wholesale to retail sales; and further price reductions. He found that he was unable to evaluate any of these possibilities since the accounting system did not generate the necessary information.

The president was also considering entering into the industrial ceramics market. In industry, there is a wide variety of ceramic applications such as ceramic heat shields, decorative ceramic tiles, and electronic components. The president felt that this market would be less affected by the recession than the crafts market. In addition, the company's considerable expertise in glazes, kilns, and so on, could be used in the production of these industrial ceramic items. However, the president has some concerns about this diversification. The company lacks the marketing and production capabilities and there would be some initial costs to develop these capabilities. In addition, there is the problem of financing the diversification. He said, "It seems a vicious circle: the sales slump reduces cash flow and, therefore, reduces the company's ability to finance a diversification which could cure the slump!" Details of the venture are presented in Exhibit I.

EXHIBIT I
Information about the proposed industrial ceramics venture

- The starting date for the venture would be December 1, 1985.
- Anticipated annual sales volume and gross profit:

  First year: $540,000 sales and 30% gross profit.
  Subsequent years: $600,000 sales and 34% gross profit.

- Anticipated inventory levels:

  Raw materials: about equal to one month's cost of goods sold.
  Finished goods: about equal to two months' cost of goods sold

- Anticipated receivables level: about two months' sales.
- Manufacturing facilities:

  Capital cost allowance Class 3, 5%, alterations and addition to the building will cost $168,000. Capital cost allowance Class 29, 50%, equipment will cost $136,000 (or can be leased for 10 years for $25,000 per year).

- Start-up costs (prior to January 1, 1986):

Manufacturing	$23,000
Administration	7,000
Advertising	18,000
Sales force training	4,000

- Annual increases in other expenses (not included in the industrial ceramics cost of goods sold), beginning December 19, 1985.

Depreciation:	
Building (alterations and addition)	$11,200
Equipment (if purchased)	13,600
Administrative expenses:	
First year	6,000
Subsequent years	3,000
Advertising	15,000
Warehouse expenses	34,000

Due to the complexity of the company's problems, the president decided to approach a professional accountant for the first time. In September 1985, he called CA and requested a meeting. He informed CA of the company's background and the present situation. He provided CA with the quarterly financial statements, which had been prepared solely for the use of the bank. He expressed concern that these financial statements did not provide adequate information to enable him to make decisions. They are prepared by the company's bookkeeper in essentially the same summarized format as the annual statements which accompany the tax return. The quarterly statements for the last five quarters are shown in Exhibits II and III. At the conclusion of the meeting, the president requested a report which addresses the matters he raised and provides analyses and recommendations.

EXHIBIT II

WINDSOR CLAYS LTD.
Summarized Quarterly Balance Sheets
(in thousands)

	Aug. 31, 1985	May 31, 1985*	Feb. 28, 1985	Nov. 30, 1984	Aug. 31, 1984
Cash.............................	$ 43	$ 34	$ 51	$ 64	$ 86
Receivables†.........................	116	68	36	41	42
Inventories.........................	678	575	496	448	582
Warehouse land	24	24	24	24	24
Warehouse building..................	263	263	263	263	263
Equipment	92	92	92	82	82
Retail fixtures‡......................	26	26	26	26	26
Accumulated depreciation	(182)	(175)	(168)	(161)	(154)
Other assets........................	14	21	16	18	12
	$1,074	$928	$836	$805	$963
Bank loans§	$ 270	$200	$160	$140	$190
Accounts payable	281	181	126	102	246
Other liabilities†	18	21	24	59	63
11% mortgage	148	149	150	152	153
Share capital	40	40	40	40	40
Retained earnings...................	317	337	336	312	271
	$1,074	$928	$836	$805	$963

*May 31 is the company's fiscal year-end.
†Income tax amounts are included in receivables or in other liabilities.
‡All of the retail store premises are leased. The leases still have several years before renewal.
§Interest rate at August 31, 1985 was 15 percent.

EXHIBIT III

WINDSOR CLAYS LTD.
Summarized Quarterly Income Statements
(in thousands)

	Aug. 31, 1985	May 31, 1985*	Feb. 28, 1985	Nov. 30, 1984	Aug. 31, 1984
Sales: wholesale	$437	$506	$579	$592	$648
retail†	116	102	91	284	180
	553	608	670	876	828
Purchases†	457	450	443	339	539
Inventory change	(103)	(79)	(48)	134	(83)
Wages and salaries..................	92	103	109	131	116
Shop expenses......................	23	18	16	19	15
Warehouse expenses	31	32	31	34	29
Retail expenses	44	41	40	51	43
Advertising	28	16	2	6	18
Administrative expenses..............	29	32	37	43	38
Interest	14	13	12	13	11
Tax provision.......................	(42)	(19)	4	45	43
	573	607	646	815	769
Quarterly income (loss)..............	$ (20)	$ 1	$ 24	$ 61	$ 59

*May 31 is the company's fiscal year-end.
†Consignment sales are included in retail sales and the related costs of goods sold are included in purchases. The ratio of consignment sales to retail sales remains constant in each quarter.

Required:

Assume the role of CA adviser and prepare the report for the president. The report should present an assessment of the current financial position of Windsor Clays to serve as a basis for analyzing the new proposal.

(CICA Adapted)

PC16–11.   *Required:*

a. Using the data for PC16–3, prepare a spreadsheet computer program that will compute the ratios for the statements presented in Problem 16–3.

b. Load the data given in Problem 16–4 to your spreadsheet in Part a. Determine the new ratios.

C·H·A·P·T·E·R

17

Financial Reporting and Changing Prices

PURPOSE OF THIS CHAPTER

In the recent past the economy of Canada (and practically all other countries) has been affected significantly by increasing prices of most commodities and services. This fact has important, and often adverse, effects on most people because the price increases are not uniform among different goods, services, and individuals. Therefore, some groups suffer more from inflation than other groups. Also, measurements of economic events in terms of the monetary unit (dollars in Canada) become distorted. For example, from 1970 to 1984, the dollar declined in **purchasing power** (i.e., its command over real goods and services) by approximately 298 percent; that is, in 1984, it required almost $3 to purchase what $1 would have purchased in 1970.

The rapid and continuing increase in prices has caused most users of financial statements to question the dollar measurements of assets, liabilities, revenues, and expenses reported in the traditional historical cost (HC) financial statements. In periods of inflation, HC financial statements typically aggregate amounts that include dollars of different purchasing power. This aggregation of "apples and oranges" tends to produce unrealistic measurements of accounting values.

For financial accounting purposes, two distinctly different kinds of price changes usually are identified, viz:

1. **General price level changes**—These price level changes occur when the **average** level of the prices of commodities and services changes; that is, the purchasing power (i.e., the command over goods and services) of the monetary unit changes. Such changes are called **inflation** when the general price level increases (i.e., the purchasing power of the monetary unit decreases) and **deflation** when the general price level decreases (i.e., the purchasing power of the monetary unit increases). Part A discusses general price level (GPL) changes.

2. **Specific price level changes**—These price level changes occur when the price of a **specific** commodity or service changes. Such changes cause **real value changes** if the rate of specific price level change is different than the rate of general price level changes. Part B of this chapter discusses current cost (CC), which involves the reporting of real value changes.

To discuss these issues, this chapter is divided as follows:

Part A—Reporting the effects of general price level (GPL) changes

Part B—Reporting the effects of current cost (CC) changes

Part A—Reporting the Effects of General Price Level (GPL) Changes

The impact of inflation upon HC financial statements is difficult to assess by statement users, particularly when the related price change information is not reported. Accountants, economists, and persons in business and government are not in agreement as to what should be done to make the financial statements more useful under conditions of significant price changes.

First, we will consider general price level changes. Reporting the effects of general price level (GPL) changes on financial statements requires that the traditional historical cost (HC) financial statements be **restated** from the HC basis to the latest GPL dollars, usually called **constant dollars.** This restatement requires use of general price level (GPL) index numbers.[1] The resulting financial statements are known as **constant dollar** (CD) financial statements.

USING PRICE LEVEL INDEX NUMBERS

Price level index numbers may be used to restate HC financial statement amounts for price changes. A **price level index** is a statistical value that expresses the relative price level of each of a series of periods. To construct a price level index, the prices of one specific item, or a group of items, for a number of periods are expressed in relative terms as a series of index numbers. A base year is selected and assigned the base index value of 100. Subsequent changes in prices are expressed in relation to this base. Two kinds of indexes are used widely:

1. **General price level (GPL) index**—A GPL price index is computed on the basis of an **average** "market basket" of commodities and services.[2] An average index is computed by collecting the prices of each of the many items that make up the average market basket. Each period the average price of the basket is computed and then related to the base year index of 100. A GPL index is intended to measure **general inflation** (cheaper

---

[1]Throughout this chapter the descriptive term **restated** is used because the HC basis amounts simply are restated to current GPL or constant dollars. Alternatively, the term **adjusted** sometimes is used. It is less descriptive and suggests the notion of "adjusting" entries, which is based on a completely different concept.

[2]The two GPL series usually are the Gross National Expenditure Implicit Price Deflator (which is published quarterly) and the Consumer Price Index for Urban Consumers (CPI-U) which is published monthly). Both indexes are published by Statistics Canada. The CPI-U index is the more widely used index in accounting because of its ready availability.

dollars) and **general deflation** (more expensive dollars). A GPL index is used in accounting to measure the effects of general price level (GPL) changes and to restate the HC financial statements to the latest constant dollar (CD) basis. To illustrate, assume a tract of land was purchased in 1981 at a cost of $10,000 when the GPL index was 100. Assume that at the end of the current year, the land is still owned, and the GPL index is 124. The $10,000 cost of the land would be reported on a CD restated balance sheet at $10,000 × 124/100 = $12,400. The GPL increase was $2,400 (i.e., $12,400 − $10,000).

2. **Specific price level index**—A specific price level index is computed in the same manner as a GPL index except that it is related to a **single** item (or small group of homogenous items). Specific price index values often are used to estimate the current replacement cost of **specific** commodities or services. To illustrate, assume the land example given in 1 above (HC, $10,000) had a specific price index of 236.2 when acquired in 1981 and has a specific price index of 287.1 at the end of the current year. The estimated current replacement cost of the land could be computed as $10,000 × 287.1/236.2 = $12,155. This computation indicates that the specific value of the land increased by $2,155, which was less than the GPL increase of $2,400. A specific price index does **not** measure **general** inflation; rather, it measures the change in price of the specific item to which it relates. Use of specific index numbers is illustrated in Part B of this chapter.

EXHIBIT 17–1
Selected consumer price index values

	CPI-U index*	
Year	Average for the year	At year-end
1970.	41.0	41.1
1971.	42.2	43.1
1972.	44.2	45.3
1973.	47.6	49.5
1974.	52.8	55.6
1975.	58.5	60.9
1976.	62.9	64.5
1977.	67.9	70.6
1978.	73.9	76.5
1979.	80.7	84.0
1980.	88.9	93.4
1981 (Base year)	100.0	104.7
1982.	110.8	114.4
1983.	117.2	119.6
1984.	122.3	124.1

*Source: The Consumer Price Index, Statistics Canada (monthly).

The pervasiveness of **general inflation** (i.e., as measured by a GPL index) in recent years is reflected in the index values from the Consumer Price Index for Urban Consumers (CPI-U) presented in Exhibit 17–1.

Another application of a GPL index may be illustrated by indicating the effect of general inflation on the cost of attending a university. To illustrate: assume that in 1970 the average cost of attending "University" for two terms was $4,000 per student. Using the CPI-U index amounts given above, general inflation has increased the total cost as follows:

Year	CPI-U index (average)	Restatement computation	Average cost per student
1970	41.0		$ 4,000
1975	58.5	$4,000 × 58.5/41.0	5,707
1980	88.9	$4,000 × 88.9/41.0	8,673
1984	122.3	$4,000 × 122.3/41.0	11,932

THE STABLE MONETARY UNIT ASSUMPTION

One of the underlying assumptions of GAAP is the **unit-of-measure assumption** (Exhibit 2–6), which states that with many diverse items and transactions to be accounted for, it is necessary that a single unit of measure be adopted. Accounting assumes the Canadian monetary unit—the dollar—as the common denominator in the measurement process. Implicit in this assumption is that the dollar has a constant value, which is an important measurement characteristic (a "metrestick" is always one metre long!). However, during a period of inflation or deflation, the constant value assumption is not valid; the monetary unit literally becomes a "rubber" measuring unit (it stretches and contracts) as the GPL changes.

The dollar is the common denominator used for accounting measurements because it is used by the society as a measure of value. That is, the dollar will command a certain amount of real goods and services in the marketplace at a given time. Unfortunately, the dollar (or any other currency) does not maintain a stable value in terms of the real goods and services it can command.

Over time, a single dollar will command fewer goods and services in the case of inflation or, alternatively, more goods and services in the case of deflation; that is, its purchasing power changes. As a result of using the historical cost principle, transactions are recorded in the accounts and reported subsequently on the financial statements in historical cost (HC) basis dollars. Some of those dollar amounts (such as the cost of an old operational asset) remain in the accounts and are reported in the financial statements over many years. Thus, over a period of time, the accounting system accumulates and reports dollars that have different purchasing power, given inflation or deflation. Under historical cost (HC) accounting, dollars having different real values are **aggregated** on the balance sheet and **matched** on the income statement. Thus, during periods of significant inflation or deflation, the accounting amounts are apt to reflect considerable distortion from current dollars because of the effects of the changing value of the monetary unit.

To illustrate this distortion, consider a company that purchased a building for $200,000 when the general (GPL) index was 100. Assuming straight-line depreciation, no residual value, and a 40-year life, the annual depreciation would be $5,000 per year. Let's assume that the current year is Year 30 (since acquisition) and that the current general (GPL) index is 300. At the end of Year 30, the financial statements would show the following amounts, based on historical cost (HC) as recorded in the accounting system:

Balance sheet:
Operational assets:
    Building (at cost)................................. $200,000
    Accumulated depreciation ($5,000 × 30 years)......   150,000
    Carrying value................................. $50,000

Income statement:
Depreciation expense.............................. $ 5,000

All of the amounts shown above represent dollars "valued" at acquisition date (30 years earlier). Those dollars had a purchasing power equivalent of 100 (the general GPL index). With the current general (GPL) index at 300, these amounts are aggregated with other dollar amounts that have different purchasing power equivalents. On the income statement, depreciation expense, expressed in dollars with one purchasing power (index 100) is matched with revenue, which is in current dollars with another purchasing power (index 300). The current general (GPL) index of 300 means that each current dollar will command (buy) only one third (i.e., 100/300) as much **real** goods and services as when the index was 100. One could **restate** the above amounts to constant dollars for the GPL change (inflation in this case). The restatement can be accomplished by multiplying the HC amount by a CD index ratio in the following manner:

$$\text{Historical cost (HC) amount} \times \frac{\text{Current period GPL index}}{\text{Transaction date GPL index}} = \text{CD restated amount}$$

The calculations and the resulting CD restated amounts for the data given above would be as follows:

Item	HC basis	CD restatement computation	CD restated amount
Balance sheet amounts:			
Operational assets:			
Building	$200,000	× 300/100	= $600,000
Accumulated depreciation	150,000	× 300/100	= 450,000
Carrying value	$ 50,000	× 300/100	= $150,000
Income statement amount:			
Depreciation expense	$ 5,000	× 300/100	= $ 15,000

CONCEPTS UNDERLYING CD RESTATEMENT OF FINANCIAL STATEMENTS

Constant dollar (CD) restatement of financial statements does not involve the recording of journal entries; rather, it is a **supplementary reporting approach.** The traditional HC financial statements are prepared each period in accordance with GAAP. The HC statements continue as the basic periodic reports of the entity. When CD restatement is used, the HC basis financial statements simply are restated in current end-of-period dollars (i.e., in constant dollars). Thus, the CD restated financial statements continue to be cost basis statements except that all dollar amounts are in **constant dollars;** that is, dollars of constant purchasing power. The CD restatement computations are simple and straightforward; they involve the following three steps:

**EXHIBIT 17–2
Classification of
monetary and
nonmonetary items**

	Monetary	Nonmonetary
Assets		
Cash	X	
Marketable securities:		
Most common shares		X
Most bonds	X	
Accounts and notes receivable	X	
Allowance for doubtful accounts	X	
Inventories—except if valued at selling price		X
Prepaid expense:		
Claims to future services		X
Prepayments that are deposits or advance payments	X	
Long-term receivables	X	
Property, plant, and equipment		X
Accumulated depreciation		X
Patents and trademarks		X
Goodwill		X
Liabilities		
Accounts and notes payable	X	
Accrued expenses	X	
Cash dividends payable	X	
Bonds payable and other long-term debt	X	
Premium or discount on bonds payable	X	
Deferred income taxes		X†
Owners' Equity		
Preferred stock (nonmonetary if not carried at a fixed redemption price)	X	
Common stock		X
Retained earnings		
This amount usually is restated as a plug or balancing amount		X

Source: Adapted from *CICA Accounting Guidelines,* "Changes in the Purchasing Power of Money," December 1974.

†*CICA Handbook, Section 4510.47,* states that deferred income taxes should be treated as nonmonetary.

Step 1: Classify all accounts on the financial statements as either monetary or nonmonetary (defined later in the chapter). **Monetary** items are **not** restated on the CD financial statements while the **nonmonetary** items **are** restated. Exhibit 17–2 presents the classification of several accounts.

Step 2: Restate each **nonmonetary** item by multiplying its HC amount by the appropriate restatement ratio (i.e., the current period general price level (GPL) index divided by the general price level (GPL) index that existed at the date on which the transaction was recorded).

Step 3: Calculate the purchasing power gain or loss on monetary items. This gain or loss is measured as the difference between the HC amount and the CD restated amount for each monetary item. Each of these basic steps is discussed and illustrated in the remainder of this part of the chapter.

CD RESTATEMENT—ILLUSTRATIVE CASE

A simplified situation is used as the basis for discussing and illustrating the computations needed to develop CD restated financial statements.

Assume ACE Corporation was organized December 31, 19A, when the general GPL index was 120. The accounting period ends December 31, and the company prepares HC financial statements. Restatement of the HC financial statements of ACE Corporation to a CD restated basis is discussed and illustrated in the paragraphs to follow. Exhibit 17–3 presents the following data for ACE Corporation:

1. All transactions completed during 19A and 19B (summarized) and the GPL index at the date of each transaction.
2. Balance sheet at December 31, 19B (HC basis).
3. Income statement for the year ended December 31, 19B (HC basis).
4. Statement of retained earnings at December 31, 19B (HC basis).
5. Selected GPL index data.

Step 1—Identify monetary and nonmonetary items

Restatement of HC financial statements to a CD restated basis requires that a careful distinction be maintained between two distinctly different types of items on the financial statements. These two types are known as **monetary items** and **nonmonetary items.** They cause significantly different economic effects on their holder (owner) when the real value of the monetary unit (the dollar) changes (i.e., inflation or deflation occurs).

A **monetary item** is an item that by its nature or as the result of a contract is stated in a **fixed** number of dollars and the fixed number of dollars does not change in response to changes in price levels. Thus, monetary items include cash, payables, and receivables but would not include revenues or expenses. Because inflation does not affect the amount of cash or the number of dollars

EXHIBIT 17–3
Historical cost and GPL data of ACE Corporation

Summary of transactions:

Year 19A:

a. December 31, 19A: Sold and issued capital stock (nopar) for $80,000 cash (GPL index, 120).

b. December 31, 19A: Borrowed $40,000 cash from a local bank; signed a $40,000 interest-bearing note due December 31, 19C (GPL index, 120).

c. December 31, 19A: Purchased equipment for use in the business at a cash cost of $60,000 (GPL index, 120).

Year 19B:

d. March 19B: Purchased land for use in the business at a cash cost of $6,350 (GPL index, 127).

e. During 19B: Purchased merchandise (evenly throughout the year) at a cash cost of $121,500 (average GPL index for 19B, 135). Assume a perpetual inventory system (average costing), cost of goods sold, $108,000, and an ending inventory of $13,500 (i.e., total, $121,500).

f. During 19B: Sales revenue, $162,000, sold evenly throughout the year (average GPL index for 19B, 135). Assume total cash collections on sales of $129,600 and accounts receivable at year-end of $32,400 (i.e., total, $162,000).

g. During 19B: Expenses paid in cash $27,000, which included interest expense and income tax expense, but excluded depreciation expense (average GPL index for 19B, 135).

h. July 1, 19B: Declared and paid a cash dividend, $2,700 (GPL average index, 135).

i. December 31, 19B: Depreciation expense on equipment (estimated five-year life and no residual value), $60,000 ÷ 5 years = $12,000.

Balance sheet, at December 31, 19B (HC basis amounts):

Assets		Liabilities	
Cash	$ 32,050	Note payable, long term	$ 40,000
Accounts receivable (net)	32,400	**Shareholders' Equity**	
Inventory	13,500	Capital stock (nopar)	80,000
Equipment	60,000	Retained earnings	12,300
Accumulated depreciation	(12,000)		
Land	6,350		
Total	$132,300	Total	$132,300

Income statement, for the year ended December 31, 19B (HC basis amounts):

Sales revenue	$162,000
Cost of goods sold	(108,000)
Depreciation expense	(12,000)
Remaining expenses	(27,000)
Net income	$ 15,000

Statement of retained earnings, at December 31, 19B (HC basis amounts):

Beginning balance, January 1, 19B	$ –0–
Add: Net income of 19B	15,000
Deduct: Dividends of 19B	(2,700)
Ending balance, December 31, 19B	$12,300

GPL index data:

December 31, 19A	120
Average during 19A	110
January 1, 19B	120
Average during 19B	135
December 31, 19B	150

EXHIBIT 17–4   **CD restatement of financial statements, ACE Corporation, year end 19B**

Items	HC basis	CD restatement computations	CD restated basis
Balance sheet, at December 31, 19B:			
Assets			
Cash	$ 32,050	Monetary, not restated	$ 32,050
Accounts receivable (net)	32,400	Monetary, not restated	32,400
Inventory	13,500	Nonmonetary, $13,500 × 150/135	15,000
Equipment	60,000	Nonmonetary, $60,000 × 150/120	75,000
Accumulated depreciation (credit)	(12,000)	Nonmonetary, $12,000 × 150/120	(15,000)
Land	6,350	Nonmonetary, $6,350 × 150/127	7,500
Total	$ 132,300		$ 146,950
Liabilities			
Note payable, long term	$ 40,000	Monetary, not restated	$ 40,000
Shareholders' Equity			
Capital stock, nonpar	80,000	Nonmonetary, $80,000 × 150/120	100,000
Retained earnings	12,300	Nonmonetary, plug, $146,950 − $40,000 − $100,000	6,950
Total	$ 132,300		$ 146,950
Income statement, for the year ended December 31, 19B:			
Sales revenue	$ 162,000	Nonmonetary, $162,000 × 150/135	$ 180,000
Deduct:			
Cost of goods sold	(108,000)	Nonmonetary, $108,000 × 150/135	(120,000)
Depreciation expense	(12,000)	Nonmonetary, $12,000 × 150/120	(15,000)
Remaining expenses	(27,000)	Nonmonetary, $27,000 × 150/135	(30,000)
Income from normal operations	$ 15,000		15,000
Purchasing power gain (loss) on monetary items		Computed, per Exhibit 17–5	(5,050)
Income, CD restated (common dollar)		Carry to statement of retained earnings	$ 9,950
Statement of retained earnings, at December 31, 19B			
Beginning balance, January 1, 19B	$ –0–	Nonmonetary	$ –0–
Add: Income of 19B	15,000	Nonmonetary, from restated income statement	9,950
Deduct: Dividends of 19B (debit)	(2,700)	Nonmonetary, $2,700 × 150/135	(3,000)
Ending balance, December 31, 19B	$ 12,300	Proof: check per balance sheet plug amount	$ 6,950

to be paid or received for monetary items, these items are **not restated** on CD financial statements.

While monetary items are not restated on CD financial statements, the **purchasing power** of monetary items is affected by inflation. Consider what would happen if you left $1,000 in your wallet during a year in which the inflation rate was 20 percent. At the end of the year, you could buy less real goods and services with the $1,000 than you could have purchased at the beginning of the year. Your loss of purchasing power on this **asset** amounted to $200 [i.e., $1,000 − ($1,000 × 120/100)]. This $200 loss is called a purchasing power loss on monetary items.

In contrast, if you held monetary **liabilities** during a period of inflation, you would experience a purchasing power gain on monetary items because the liabilities will be paid in dollars that have less purchasing power than the dollars that were borrowed. In other words, a dollar owed through a period of inflation is still a dollar owed, although it will command fewer real goods at the end of the period.

In summary, monetary items (i.e., monetary assets and monetary liabilities) are not restated on the CD financial statements of the current period, but their existence can cause the holder (or debtor) to incur a real gain or loss during each period of inflation. A purchasing power **gain** on net monetary items is reported (on the CD financial statements) if the purchasing power gain on monetary liabilities is more than the purchasing power loss on monetary assets. Alternatively, a purchasing power **loss** is reported if the purchasing power loss on monetary assets is more than the purchasing power gain on monetary liabilities.

Observe in Exhibit 17–4 that the three monetary items (cash, accounts receivable, and note payable) are not restated in the CD financial statements. However, a purchasing power loss on monetary items of $5,050 is reported on the CD income statement (this loss is computed in Exhibit 17–5).

Nonmonetary items include all items on the financial statements except for the monetary assets and liabilities. The basic characteristic of nonmonetary items is that they have dollar amounts that are **not** fixed in the future by their nature or by contract. The value of nonmonetary items in the marketplace tend to move up and down with inflation and deflation. For example, a tract of land purchased for $6,350 (see Exhibit 17–3) when the GPL index was 127 would **tend** to increase in market value to $7,500 as a result of an increase of the GPL price index to 150 (i.e., $6,350 × 150/127 = $7,500). If this happened, the owner would not experience a real gain on this nonmonetary asset due to general inflation. The owner would not experience a real gain because, if the land that cost $6,350 could be sold for $7,500, the $7,500 would purchase (at the date of sale of the land) the same quantity of real goods and services that the $6,350 would have bought when the owner originally purchased the land. Of course, the land may have changed in "dollar value" more or less than the GPL, in which case there would have been a real value change (this situation is discussed later). Examples of nonmonetary items are inventories, investments in common shares, operational assets, patents, revenues, expenses, and the common stock accounts.[3]

---

[3]Preferred shares usually are classified as a monetary item because they usually have a fixed redeemable value. In contrast, receivables and liabilities which can be settled with goods and services (rather than cash) are classified as nonmonetary items.

EXHIBIT 17–5
Computation of the
purchasing power
gain (loss) on net
monetary items,—
ACE Corporation,
year end 19B

Items	HC basis	CD restatement computations	CD restated basis
Net monetary balances at beginning of period:			
Cash	$ 60,000		
Accounts receivable	0		
Less: Notes payable	(40,000)		
Net	20,000	$ 20,000 × 150/120	$ 25,000
Debits—increases in net monetary balances:			
Sales	162,000	162,000 × 150/135	180,000
Credits—decreases in net monetary balances:			
Purchase of land	(6,350)	6,350 × 150/127	(7,500)
Purchase of merchandise (108,000 + 13,500 − 0)	(121,500)		
Expenses except depreciation	(27,000)		
Dividends declared	(2,700)		
	(151,200)	151,200 × 150/135	(168,000)
Net monetary balances at end of period:			
Cash	32,050		
Accounts receivable	32,400		
Less: Notes payable	(40,000)		
Net			29,500*
	$ 24,450		24,450†
Purchasing power net loss			$ 5,050‡

Explanation:
    *Subtotal of restated amounts reflects net monetary items (debits in this case) that should be on hand (CD restated amount).
    †Balance reflects net monetary items (debits in this case) that are on hand. No conversion is necessary if the purchasing power gain or loss is to be stated in dollars of the end of the period.
    ‡Debits lost because of inflation (a loss of assets).

In summary, nonmonetary items are restated on the CD financial statements, and they do not cause the holder to incur a real gain or loss as a result of changes only in the GPL.

Step 2—CD
restatement of
HC financial
statements.

Now, let's return to our illustration of ACE Corporation and the three HC basis financial statements given in Exhibit 17–3. CD restatement of each HC financial statement in terms of the current GPL index of 150 is shown in Exhibit 17–4.

Restatement of the balance sheet. The ACE Corporation balance sheet reflects three monetary items: cash, accounts receivable, and the note payable. As explained above, these three **monetary items** were not restated because each has a fixed monetary amount in the future that is not affected by inflation or deflation. Therefore, the three monetary HC amounts were extended across on the balance sheet to the CD restatement column. In contrast, the four non-monetary asset amounts on the balance sheet were CD restated because their market prices are free to change as a result of changes in the general price level.

Observe in Exhibit 17–4 that 10 **nonmonetary items** are restated on the CD balance sheet and income statement. Also, observe that any real gain or loss on the **nonmonetary** items is not reported on the CD financial statements (see Part B of this chapter).

Exhibit 17–4 presents the CD restatement computation for each nonmonetary item. For example, the Land account was restated as follows:

$$\begin{array}{ccc} \text{Historical cost} & & \text{CD} \\ \text{(HC) basis} & \times \dfrac{\text{Current period GPL index}}{\text{Transaction date GPL index}} = & \text{restated} \\ \text{amount} & & \text{amount} \end{array}$$

$$\text{Land, } \$6{,}350 \ \times \ 150/127 \ = \ \$7{,}500$$

Restatement of the income statement. All items on the income statement are **nonmonetary**; therefore, each item is restated. The numerator of the GPL restatement ratio is the ending GPL index, and the denominator usually is the average GPL index for the current period because it is assumed often that price changes and business transactions occurred evenly throughout the period. Observe that depreciation expense is always restated by using the same GPL index amounts used to restate the related asset (150/120 in the illustration). The only unique feature of the income statement is inclusion of the "Purchasing power gain (loss) on monetary items." This **gain or loss** must be computed separately on the monetary assets and monetary liabilities as illustrated in step 3 (Exhibit 17–5).

Step 3—Computation of the purchasing power gain or loss on net monetary items

Computation of the purchasing power gain or loss requires restatement of each monetary asset and each monetary liability. Often this is the most tedious phase of CD restatement. Monetary items that have identical numerator indexes and identical denominator indexes can be grouped for computation purposes with the same results.

Computation of the purchasing power gain (loss) on the monetary items for ACE Corporation is illustrated in Exhibit 17–5. Observe in this exhibit that the HC amount of each monetary item (first money column) is CD restated by using the appropriate numerator and denominator indexes. The net gain or loss on monetary items simply is the difference between the **ending** actual HC basis amount and the **ending** CD restated amount (i.e., for net monetary items, $24,450 − $29,500 = $5,050 loss).

The restatement of monetary items is tedious because the beginning balance of the net monetary balance sheet accounts as well as each transaction that affects these accounts must be restated with the appropriate GPL indexes. We reemphasize that **monetary** items are restated **only** for purposes of calculating the purchasing power gain or loss on net monetary items; they are **not** restated on the balance sheet.

The total purchasing power gain (loss) on monetary items ($5,050) is the algebraic sum of the purchasing power **losses on monetary assets** and the purchasing power **gains on monetary liabilities.** In the illustration, the $5,050 is a loss during a period of inflation because the monetary assets exceeded the monetary liabilities (in the opposite case, there would have been a gain). This amount is carried to the income statement (as illustrated in Exhibit 17–4) because it can be considered to represent an economic (purchasing power) gain or loss.

In summary, CD restated financial statements are prepared by restating the **nonmonetary** HC-items on the balance sheet, income statement, and statement of retained earnings. The monetary items are included in the CD financial statements at their HC basis amounts. However, the **monetary** assets and liabilities are restated separately to compute the purchasing power gain or loss on monetary items, which is reported on the income statement. The CD restated net income is carried to the CD statement of retained earnings, and the CD restated ending balance of retained earnings is reported on the CD balance sheet.[4]

OVERVIEW OF CD EFFECTS

A comparison of the two balance sheets presented in Exhibit 17–4 shows that the CD restatement increased total assets from $132,300 to $146,950 which was an 11.1 percent increase. In contrast, the income statement reflected a decrease in reported income of $15,000 to $9,950 which was a 34 percent decrease. When there is an inflationary trend, and the relationship between monetary assets and monetary liabilities remains essentially constant, **CD restated income** usually will be lower than the cost basis amount, primarily because of higher restated assets and correspondingly higher restated depreciation expense.

Having presented the concept and related procedures to derive CD restated financial statements, let's examine them in overall perspective. The HC basis financial statements rest on the unit-of-measure assumption (Chapter 2), which holds that each transaction should be measured in those dollars that "existed" at the date of each transaction. In the case of GPL changes (i.e., inflation or deflation), the HC financial statements commingle dollars that have different amounts of purchasing power. In contrast, the concept of CD restated financial statements retains the HC amounts except that they are restated in constant dollars. That is, the HC amounts are restated for the effects of changes in the purchasing power of the monetary unit (inflation or deflation) that have oc-

---

[4]In view of CD restatement on the balance sheet of only the nonmonetary items (not the monetary items), the question always arises as to why a CD balance sheet "balances." Technically, the reason is that the monetary assets and monetary liabilities are not restated on the balance sheet, but total **owners' equity** is restated. Therefore, the residual, owners' equity (A − L = OE) **includes** a restatement amount for **both** the nonmonetary and monetary items. Inclusion of the purchasing power gain (loss) on monetary items on the income statement (and hence in retained earnings on the balance sheet) provides the mathematically necessary amount to bring the equation A − L = OE into balance on the CD restated balance sheet.

curred since each transaction was recorded. This means that all nonmonetary HC dollar amounts (but not the monetary amounts) reflected in the HC statements are restated to constant (current) dollars, each having equivalent purchasing power. The CD restated income statement reports a new type of gain or loss: purchasing power gain or loss on monetary items.

Those who advocate the concept of CD restatement contend that two sets of financial statements should be presented: (1) one set prepared on the traditional HC basis, and (2) another set prepared on the CD restated basis. The primary **arguments for** presenting CD restated financial statements are (1) during periods of significant inflation or deflation, HC basis statements contain serious measurement distortions that are not presented; (2) the CD restated amounts, including the purchasing power gain or loss on monetary items, are relevant to the users of financial statements; and (3) the HC approach essentially is retained with all amounts stated in terms of dollars of the same purchasing power. In contrast, the primary **arguments against** CD restated statements are (1) two sets of financial statements (restated and not restated) potentially can confuse statement users; (2) it is difficult to justify a particular GPL price index to use for restatement purposes; (3) statement users do not find the restated amounts to be particularly useful; and (4) GPL effects and real value changes on **nonmonetary** items are not revealed separately (discussed in Part B).

CICA Handbook, Section 4510, entitled "Reporting the Effects of Changing Prices" was issued in December 1982 to apply to large publicly held companies. Compliance was requested of such companies if they satisfied either of the following two size requirements: (1) the book value of inventories plus property, plant, and equipment before deducting accumulated depreciation, depletion, and amortization of at least $50 million, or (2) total assets before accumulated depreciation, depletion, and amortization of at least $350 million at the beginning of the current accounting year.

Because Section 4510 was issued as supplementary disclosure requirements and specifically exempted real estate, banks, trust companies, and insurance companies, not all companies have complied with the suggestions. Cost of preparation, lack of mandatory disclosure and the controversial nature of the pronouncement have all hindered its acceptance. Certainly a reduction in inflation in recent years below double digits has reduced the demand for these supplementary disclosures.

Part B—Reporting Current Cost Changes

Accounting academicians and professional accountants long have discussed the concept of reporting **current values** rather than HC basis amounts on the financial statements. The primary argument in favour of reporting current values is that statement users (investors, creditors, and others) are more interested in the "worth" of the assets at the date of the financial statements than in the HC amounts now reported under GAAP. The acceptance of current value accounting has been slow because opinions vary as to exactly what current value means and how it should be measured. Two basic implementation approaches are under consideration:

1. Report **current value** amounts in the financial statements instead of HC amounts. This view is that current value would be a substitute for, and not be supplementary information to, the traditional HC statements. A second view, which prevails currently, is that two different sets of financial statements should be presented each period: *(a)* one set on the traditional HC basis and *(b)* another set on the current value basis.

2. Report both current value and constant dollar in **combination.** In effect, under this approach, current values are restated so that both current value and GPL effects are reported.

In the discussions to follow, the **combination reporting approach** is assumed because it provides considerable information on both current value and GPL effects. This reporting approach is usually called the current cost/constant dollar (CC/CD) approach.

DEFINITION OF CURRENT VALUE IN FINANCIAL REPORTING

The term **current value,** as used in financial reporting, is a general term that encompasses three different concepts of value; that is, the:

1. **Present value** (value in use)—This value represents the present value of the expected net future cash inflow attributable to an **asset** (such as inventories, equipment, and land). This concept of the valuation of an asset was discussed briefly in Part B of Chapter 10. The expected net future cash inflows are discounted to the present at an appropriate interest rate. Conceptually, this approach is superior to HC or CD; however, it is not used widely to determine "current value" in financial statements because of uncertainty in *(a)* projecting the future net cash inflow by period, and *(b)* selecting an appropriate discount rate.

2. **Net realizable value**—The net realizable value of an asset is the expected price at which the asset could be sold in its present condition, less all disposal costs. This concept of valuing an asset was discussed in Part B of Chapter 7 in respect to inventories. This asset value is used as one possible recoverable amount.[5]

3. **Current cost (CC)**—The current cost is the cost needed at the present time to acquire the amount of service embodied in the asset being valued, technically called its service potential. Cur-

---

[5]*CICA Handbook,* Section 4510.36, specifies that current cost cannot exceed the recoverable amount of the asset. Recoverable amount can be value in use (present value) or net realizable value if the asset is to be sold.

rent cost may be current reproduction cost or current replacement cost depending on the extent of technological change. Current reproduction cost is the cash needed currently to acquire a used asset of the same age, location, and condition or a depreciated new asset. Current replacement cost is the current cash cost necessary to acquire the best available asset to perform the same function as the existing asset. Because this value is the value of a new asset the amount of the current replacement cost has to be adjusted for accumulated depreciation to the current date. Current replacement cost is used where technological change has occurred.

Estimating the CC of some assets (such as a plant, because there seldom is an established market for a one-of-a-kind plant) is a complex problem. In contrast, CC may be estimated reasonably for some assets, such as merchandise inventory, because there is an established market. Primary sources for estimating CC are current price lists, prices in established markets for used items, specific price indexes, and professional appraisals.

CONCEPTS UNDERLYING CC/CD FINANCIAL REPORTING

CC/CD financial reporting does **not** require the recording of CC/CD valuations in the accounts, although many accountants view it as a full-blown accounting and reporting method to replace the current GAAP historical cost valuation model. The discussions and illustrations that follow assume that HC basis financial statements will be reported and that CC/CD financial statements will be prepared for supplementary reporting purposes without entering the CC/CD values in the accounts.

When CC/CD financial statements are prepared, the HC amounts are converted to CC/CD amounts. Primarily, CC/CD reporting involves changes in the **non-monetary** asset and income statement amounts. For **monetary items,** the HC carrying amounts and CC/CD carrying amounts usually will be the same. Preparation of CC/CD financial statements involves the following steps:

Step 1. Calculation of the current cost of the ending inventory and cost of goods sold using specific price indexes.

Step 2. Calculation of the current cost depreciation expense and gains or losses on current period disposals of fixed assets using the current cost carrying value (current cost less accumulated depreciation based on current cost) of property, plant, and equipment (pp and e) at the beginning and end of the period.

Step 3. Calculation of the total shareholders' equity (also called net assets) on a current cost basis.

Step 4. Calculation of the general purchasing power gain or loss on net monetary items in terms of average general price levels.

Step 5. Calculation of the nominal (unadjusted) dollar and inflation adjusted dollar (real) amount of the holding gains on inventory and property, plant, and equipment.

Step 6. Calculation of the financing adjustment applied to the holding gains calculated in step 5 if the total of the monetary liabilities exceed the total monetary assets (see "Illustrative Case").

Step 7. Calculation of income after inclusion of the historical sales figures, the historical selling, administrative, and interest expenses, and the historical income tax expense. Include schedules for the remaining suggested disclosures.

Step 8. Present comparative information for the preceding year by adjusting the previous current cost and historical information using the year-end or average general price level information depending on the specific amount considered (generally balance sheet at year-end and income statement items at average).

Variations are possible in the exact form of the income presentation. However, all forms have essentially the same information either in the body of the income statement or in the supplementary information attached.

CC/CD FINANCIAL REPORTING—ILLUSTRATIVE CASE

The simplified situation of ACE Corporation used in Part A will be continued for the CC/CD illustrations and discussions in this part of the chapter. The HC financial statements were shown in Exhibit 17–3.

Step 1— Determine the current cost of the ending inventory and cost of goods sold

The first step in developing the CC/CD financial statements is to determine the current cost amount of the ending inventory and cost of goods sold. Current price lists and a record of price changes during the year are needed to develop the specific price indexes for the company. Exhibit 17–6 illustrates the application of these indexes for ACE Corporation.

Step 2— Determine the current cost depreciation expense and gains or losses on disposals of pp and e

Exhibit 17–6 illustrates the application of specific price indexes (one method of determining current cost) to equipment. Using the average current cost amounts for equipment (no additions or disposals are presented here), the current cost depreciation is then calculated. Current cost indexes for land are not available. Appraisals by real estate experts are often used as substitutes.

			CC valuation amount
EXHIBIT 17–6 Current cost/constant dollar data for ACE Corporation	Item	Current cost determination*	
	Specific indexes or values for 19B	Year-end 19B inventory prices 120 percent. Average 19B inventory prices 108 percent. Year-end equipment prices 130 percent. Professional appraisal of land $6,985. Depreciation rate per year 20 percent. Depreciation accumulated one year.	
	Ending inventory, December 31, 19B	The specific price index at year's end of the inventory, based on CC, was 120 percent of HC. $13,500 \times 1.20 =$	16,200
	Cost of goods sold	The average specific price index, based on the current cost when the goods were sold, was 108 percent of HC. $108,000 \times 1.08$	116,640
	Equipment	The specific price index at year's end of the equipment, based on estimated current cost in new condition, was 130 percent of HC. $60,000 \times 1.30 =$	78,000
	Accumulated depreciation, equipment	The equipment has a five-year useful life, no residual value, and is being depreciated on a straight-line basis. At the end of 19B, CC accumulated depreciation is one fifth of the CC amount for equipment: $78,000 \times \frac{1}{5} =$	15,600
	Depreciation expense	The CC amount for this expense is determined by applying the depreciation rate (one fifth) to the **average** CC amount for equipment during the year 19B. $\left(\dfrac{\$60,000 + \$78,000}{2}\right) \times \dfrac{1}{5} =$	13,800
	Land	Professionally appraised at year's end.	6,985
	Shareholders' equity	Increase in inventory ($16,200 − $13,500) = Increase in equipment (($78,000 − $15,600) − ($60,000 − $12,000)) = Increase in land ($6,985 − $5,350) = Historical shareholders' equity (80,000 + 12,300) = Total	$ 2,700 14,400 1,635 92,300 $111,035

Step 3— Determine the total shareholders' equity on a current cost basis

The current cost amount of the shareholders' equity can be calculated by adding the increase in inventory and the increase in pp and e to the historical amount of the shareholders' equity. Exhibit 17–6 illustrates this computation.

Step 4— Calculation of the general purchasing power gain or loss on net monetary items

In Exhibit 17–5, purchasing power gain (loss) on net monetary items is calculated in terms of year-end 19B dollars (index 150). Commonly, current cost statements apply this same methodology in terms of average of 19B dollars (index 135) (Exhibit 17–7). A careful comparison of Exhibits 17–5 and 17–7 will illustrate the differences in the restated amounts.

Step 5— Calculation of the holding gains on inventory and pp and e

The methodology for computing holding gains or losses is illustrated in Exhibit 17–8. The approach is relatively simple to apply since it makes use of a T-account.

The amounts inserted are obtained from the historical statements and the calculations made in steps 1 to 4. Unfortunately, however, the logic of these calculations is somewhat difficult to understand.

To understand the logic of the T-account calculation, a simple example is

EXHIBIT 17–7 Calculation of purchasing power gain or loss for ACE Corporation (using average dollars)

Item		Historical	General price level index adjustment	CD restated basis (average 19B dollars)
Net monetary assets—December 31, 19A:				
Cash	$60,000			
Less: Note payable	40,000	$ 20,000	135/120	$ 22,500
Increases:				
Sales		162,000	135/135	162,000
		182,000		184,500
Decreases:				
Land purchased		6,350	135/127	6,750
Purchases		121,500	135/135	121,500
Expenses		27,000	135/135	27,000
Dividends declared		2,700	135/135	2,700
		157,550		157,950
Net monetary assets—December 31, 19B			Balance	26,550
Cash	$32,050			
Accounts				
Receivable	32,400			
	64,450			
Notes payable	40,000	$ 24,450	135/150	22,005
Purchasing power loss (difference)				$ 4,545

EXHIBIT 17–8 Calculation of holding gains or losses on inventory and pp and e for ACE Corporation

Inventory

0	135/120	Inventory—Dec. 31, 19A—CC	0	Cost of goods sold—CC 116,640	135/135 =	116,640
121,500	135/135	Purchases—HC	121,500			
4,860		Calculated balance	4,860			
14,580	135/150	Inventory—Dec. 31, 19B—CC	16,200			
Holding gain—real 9,720		Holding gain—nominal	11,340			

Land

0	135/120	Balance—Dec. 31, 19A—CC	0	Disposals 0	135/ Date sold	0
6,750	135/127	Purchases—HC	6,350			
6,750		Calculated balance	6,350			
6,286	135/150	Balance—Dec. 31, 19B—CC	6,985			
Holding loss—real (464)		Holding gain—Nominal	635			

Equipment (Net of Accumulated Depreciation)

67,500	135/120	Balance—Dec. 31, 19A—CC	60,000	Depreciation expense—CC 13,800	135/135	13,800
				Disposals—Net CC 0		0
0	135/ Date purchased	Purchases—HC	0			
53,700		Calculated balance	46,200			
56,160	135/150	Balance—Dec. 31, 19A—CC	62,400			
Holding gain—real 2,460		Holding gain—nominal	16,200			

necessary. Assume that a business had one item of inventory on hand at the beginning of the year which had a current cost of $110. Next, the business bought another item for $115. It then sold the first item for $220 when the current cost of the item was $120. The one item left over had a current cost at the year-end of $130. The nominal holding gains (unadjusted) for the two inventory items is the amount by which the current cost increased while the items were held during the year. On item 1, the current cost increased from $110 to $120, or $10. On item 2, the current cost increased from $115 to $130, or $15. The total unadjusted (nominal) holding gain was $10 + $15 or $25 for the two inventory items.

The T-account will automatically compute the holding gain or loss for this simple case and all complex cases if it is used correctly. For example,

Inventory			
Balance—beg. of year CC	110		
Purchases—HC	115	Cost of goods sold—CC	120
Calculated balance	105		
Balance—end of year	130		
Difference—holding gain—nominal	25		

Exhibit 17–8 illustrates that the holding gain or loss (nominal) on land is computed in the same way as inventory. Buildings and equipment are very similar to land and inventory except depreciation expense is substituted for cost of goods sold and the balances are net of accumulated depreciation.

Real holding gains and losses represent the holding gains or losses after the effects of general inflation (general price level changes) are removed. Generally these amounts are computed in terms of average purchasing power dollars. Again the methodology to make these computations is relatively easy because it involves GPL adjusting each of the previous T-account amounts. However, the logic is difficult to understand.

Using the above inventory example, the logic is apparent. For simplicity assume the purchase of the new unit and sale of the old unit of inventory took place on July 1, 19B. The GPL adjustment would result in a cost of $135/120 \times \$110 = \$123.75$ on July 1, 19B for the unit in the beginning inventory. Therefore, general inflation resulted in a holding gain of $123.75 − $110 or $13.75. The current cost of the same item was $120 on this date. Since the specific price was only $120 there was a loss of $120 − $123.75 or $3.75 because the general price change exceeded the specific price change. The new unit was purchased for $115 on July 1 when the general index was 135. The current cost at the year-end was $130 when the general price index was 150. In terms of purchasing power on July 1, the year-end current cost was $130 \times 135/150$ or $117. The holding gain in excess of general inflation was $117 − $115 or $2. The real holding loss was the total of the two: loss of $3.75 less a gain of $2 or $1.75.

The T-account to calculate the real holding loss would look as follows:

Inventory

GPL amounts	GPL indexes	Nominal amounts			Nominal amounts		GPL indexes	GPL amounts
123.75	135/120	Balance— beg. of year CC	110		Cost of Goods Sold—CC	120.	135/135	120.
115. 118.75	135/135	Purchases Calculated balance Balance—end	115 105					
117. 1.75	135/150 Difference	of year CC Difference	130 25					
—real holding loss		—nominal holding gain						

Step 6— Calculation of financing adjustment

The financing adjustment (sometimes called gearing adjustment) represents the portion of the holding gains (losses generally ignored) attributed to the liabilities of the firm. If an amount exists, it will be shown as a reduction of the expenses on the current cost income statement or as a separate item in the supplementary disclosures statement. Generally, the gearing adjustment is stated as $0 if holding losses are present or if the average monetary assets for the year exceed the average monetary liabilities. For ACE Corporation, monetary assets exceed the monetary liabilities so the amount is required to be $0.

The general calculation of the financing adjustment, if it exists, is as follows:

Percentage = Average difference of monetary assets − monetary liabilities at beginning and end of year ÷ Average of the total of the monetary assets − monetary liabilities and current cost common shareholders' equity at the beginning and end of year

Financing adjustment = Percentage × Nominal holding gains

Notice all the amounts needed for these two calculations come from the earlier steps.

An example of this calculation assuming Ace had monetary liabilities in excess of its monetary assets would be as follows:

1. Assume net monetary liabilities at the beginning of the year of $25,000.
2. Assume net monetary liabilities at the end of the year of $27,000.
3. The average net monetary liabilities would then be ($25,000 + $27,000)/2 = $26,000.
4. Assume an average current cost shareholders' equity for the year of $110,000.
5. The percentage would be: $26,000/($26,000 + $110,000) = .19.
6. The financing adjustment = .19 × (11,340 + 16,200 + 635) = $5,353 if the holding gains for Ace were used. For specific

EXHIBIT 17–9
Current cost income statement and supplementary disclosures

ACE CORPORATION
Statement of Income on a Current
Cost Basis
For the Year Ended December 31, 19B

		Current Cost		
Historical		*19B*		*19A Restated*
$162,000	Sales.....................................	$162,000	135/AVE 19A	
	Cost of goods sold			N O P E R A T I O N S
108,000	(Exhibit 17–6)	116,640	135/AVE 19A	
54,000	Gross margin...........................	45,360		
	Expenses other than			
27,000	depreciation..........................	27,000		
	Depreciation expense			
12,000	(Exhibit 17–6)	13,800		
39,000		40,800		
	Income before			
$15,000	income taxes	$ 4,560		

Supplementary information

	19B		*19A Restated*
Holding gains—nominal dollars		135/AVE 19A	N O P E R A T I O N S
Inventory (Exhibit 17–8).................	$ 11,340		
Equipment	16,200		
Land	635		
	28,175		
Gains caused by general inflation			
(11,340 − 9,720) = 1,620			
[635 − (−464)] = 1,099			
(16,200 − 2,460) = 13,740	16,459		
Holding gains—real dollars			
Inventory (Exhibit 17–8)...............	9,720		
Equipment	2,460		
Land	(464)		
	$11,716		

Purchasing power gain (loss) on monetary items (Exhibit 17–7)....................	$ (4,545)	135/AVE 19A
Financing adjustment (step 6)............	$ 0	135/AVE 19A

Schedule of assets on a current cost basis
as at December 31, 19B

		Current Cost		
Historical 19B		*19B*		*19A Restated*
$ 13,500	Inventory (Exhibit 17–6).................	$ 16,200		0
5,350	Land	6,985		0
	Equipment (less accumulated depreciation		($60,000	
48,000	of $15,600)	62,400	150/120)	$ 75,000
			($80,000	
92,300	Common shareholders' equity	111,035	150/120)	100,000

problems, actual amounts would be substituted for the assumed ones in this example.

Step 7— Statement presentation of income and schedules for other current cost disclosures

Exhibit 17–9 provides the disclosures of the current cost information for ACE Corporation. Different arrangements of the information are possible depending on the interpretation used by the accountant preparing the statement. For example, the nominal holding gains and the financing adjustment could be placed in the body of the income statement. Alternatively, the purchasing power gain or loss could be included in the income statement. The choice depends on what the accountant or management wants to disclose.

Step 8— Determine the comparative amounts for the previous year

All current cost income items are at average dollars for the current year. If current cost amounts for the previous year were available, they would be average current costs for 19A. To express 19A amounts in the same purchasing power units as 19B, it is necessary to multiply each amount by 135/Average 19A GPL index (namely 110). For the schedule of assets, the current cost amounts are in year-end purchasing power units. Therefore, 19A amounts are multiplied by 150/120 to make them comparative to the 19B amounts.

OVERVIEW OF CC/CD EFFECTS

Now that you understand the "content" of the three different sets of financial statements—HC, CD restated, and CC/CD—it is appropriate to view them in the perspective of the needs of investors, creditors, and other users of such statements, given the expectation of continuation of the current inflationary trend.

HC financial statements often are distorted during periods of significant inflation because the measuring unit (the dollar in our case) declines in purchasing power. Large changes in purchasing power result in aggregating dollars with different values (in terms of purchasing power) in the financial statements. This "adding of apples and oranges" is not very meaningful for measuring financial results. Simply stated, **HC reporting disregards both GPL and CC effects.** On the other hand, HC reporting is quite **objective** because the HC dollars recorded are those established by transactions between two or more parties with different economic interests (i.e., the buyer is motivated to buy low while the seller is motivated to sell high, and they strike a bargain).

CD restated financial statements (in contrast to HC statements) attempt to report the effects of inflation and deflation by restating the HC amounts in terms of the current GPL (i.e., in constant dollars). CD restatement retains the HC model; however, it adds two features that the HC model does not incorporate: (1) restatement of the HC amounts to constant dollars and (2) measurement of the real purchasing power gains and losses on monetary items held during periods of inflation and deflation. Thus, it fulfills its objective to resolve one of the deficiencies of HC reporting (i.e., the changing value of the measurement unit). However, it does not report CC effects. Also, some people argue that CD restated financial statements necessitate two separate sets of financial statements (e.g., HC and CD, restated). The basic argument against the two sets of financial statements is that the decision makers would be confused by an "information overload."

CC/CD financial statements attempt to correct the two basic deficiencies of HC financial statements—the GPL and CC effects. CC/CD financial statements attempt to do this by (1) reporting all amounts at their current CC values and (2) expressing the CC values in terms of constant dollars.[6] The conceptual objective of CC/CD reporting is simple: to tell decision makers the current "worth" of each item reported. This objective is important because decision makers necessarily base their decisions on (1) the current situation and (2) their predictions about the future. For example, a person considering the purchase of a 20-year-old office building would be concerned primarily about (1) its value today and (2) its potential to generate net cash inflows during the expected holding period. The fact that it cost a certain amount 20 years earlier, or that its current HC book value is another amount, should be of little, or no, concern to the potential buyer.

Although CC/CD conceptually is an ideal financial reporting model, it has a significant implementation problem; that is, attaining objectivity and accuracy in determining the CC of each item at the end of each accounting period. This burden of attaining objective measurement of CC values is not easy to resolve. Of course, it may be relatively easy in some situations but extremely difficult in others. If it can be resolved so that CC values are reasonably accurate and believable, the CC/CD model should replace both HC and CD restated financial statements.

The Canadian current cost pronouncement, the main details of which were presented in this chapter, represents an attempt to correct the major deficiencies of HC statements caused by inflation while at the same time trying to avoid some of the more controversial areas of CC accounting. In addition, the pronouncement permits and even encourages flexibility so that practical experience in implementing these new practices can be obtained.

The *CICA Handbook* Section 4510 proposes to revise two income statement items, cost of goods sold and depreciation expense. In a period of inflation, these two items are the two income statement classifications that are most distorted. Sales and operating expenses usually are the accumulated average of the current revenues and expenses for the period. Income tax expense is stated in terms of historical amounts because the taxing authorities have not adopted current cost accounting. Therefore, these last three classifications are reasonably represented by their HC income statement amounts.

Three potentially controversial items of CC income or loss are, holding gains or losses, purchasing power gain or loss, and the financing adjustment. The *Handbook* permits flexibility by suggesting that these amounts may be reported without stating whether or not they have to be included or excluded from the determination of CC net income. The user of the financial information is free

---

[6]Previous year's comparative amounts and real holding gains and losses.

to decide which of these amounts should be used to calculate CC net income. The complex topic of capital maintenance (a topic beyond the scope of this book) constitutes the basis for the decision the users are likely to make.

The CC balance sheet disclosures are restricted to three areas: inventory, property, plant and equipment net of accumulated depreciation, and shareholders' equity in total. Inventory and pp and e represent the two asset areas most affected by inflation. The shareholders' equity also would be distorted because changes in inventory and pp and e change this total if the balance sheet is to be kept in balance. However, only the total of shareholders' equity is disclosed because the decision about the internal breakdown requires a decision about the nature of capital maintenance.

REPORTING THE EFFECTS OF CHANGING PRICES

Recent financial statements of most large companies have reported the effects of changing prices in a manner similar to the discussions and illustrations in this chapter. Special Supplement B presents an example of the supplemental disclosure required by *CICA Handbook*, Section 4510. Observe that balance sheet and income statement data are presented under the two different approaches discussed in the chapter: (1) historical cost, and (2) current cost.

The supplemental disclosure presented in these statements provides decision makers with important insights concerning how a company is affected by inflation. Analysts often calculate the accounting ratios discussed in Chapter 16 under each accounting approach. Careful review of these financial disclosures will provide insights into the effect of inflation on Consolidated-Bathurst.

IMPORTANT TERMS DEFINED IN THIS CHAPTER

Terms (alphabetically)	Key words in definitions of important terms used in chapter	Page reference
CD restatement	Restatement of financial statements to reflect general price level changes.	888
Constant dollars	Dollars with constant (or equal) purchasing power.	885
CPI-U	Consumer Price Index for Urban Consumers; a measure of general inflation.	885
Current cost	The cost of replacing an asset in its present operating condition.	898
GPL index	Any price index which measures general inflation.	885
Monetary items	Cash or the obligation to pay or receive a fixed number of dollars (Exhibit 17–2).	890
Nonmonetary items	All items which are not properly classified as monetary items (Exhibit 17–2).	890
Purchasing power gain (or loss)	The gain or loss in purchasing power that results from holding monetary items during a period of inflation (or deflation).	890
Specific price index	Similar to a general price level index except that it is related to a single item (or a small group of homogenous items).	886

QUESTIONS FOR DISCUSSION

Part A

1. Explain the difference between general price level changes and specific price level changes.

2. What is a price level index? Explain the difference between a general price level index and a specific price level index.

3. What happens to the "value" of a dollar during a period of inflation, and alternatively, during a period of deflation?

4. A tract of land was acquired for $15,000 when the GPL index was 150. Five years later the GPL index was 270. At what price would the land have to sell for the owner to keep up exactly with inflation? Explain.

5. Define monetary items and nonmonetary items. Give some examples of each. Explain why a careful distinction between monetary and nonmonetary items is essential when financial statements are restated on a CD basis.

6. At the beginning of the current period, the Land account reflected a balance of $18,000 (GPL index at acquisition date, 100), and the Note Payable account reflected no beginning balance but had an ending balance of $30,000 (GPL index at transaction date, 150). The GPL index at the end of the current period was 200. Compute the purchasing power gain (loss) on monetary items. Explain the nature of this gain or loss.

7. Items on the balance sheet may be either monetary or nonmonetary, while all items on the income statement are nonmonetary. Is this statement true or is it false? Explain why.

Part B

8. Briefly define each of the following concepts of "current value": (a) present value, (b) net realizable value, and (c) current cost (CC).

9. Are CC amounts usually entered into the journal and ledger? Explain.

10. Explain the nature and composition of the item "CC real holding gain (loss) on nonmonetary items." Contrast it with the "purchasing power gain (loss) on monetary items."

11. Contrast "GPL fictional changes" with "CC real value changes."

12. A tract of land was purchased at a cost of $10,000 when the GPL index was 100. At the end of Year 5, the GPL index was 240 and the appraised value of the land was $27,000. Prepare a diagram that exhibits the price change effects.

EXERCISES

Part A

E17–1. During 1970, a Quality Stereo set sold at $200. Assume that each year this particular set increased in price exactly the same as the changes in the GPL index. However, in 1984 it sold at $495.

Required:

a. What was the selling price in 1970, 1975, 1980, and 1984? Use the average CPI-U index values given in the chapter and round to the nearest dollar. Show computations.
b. Analyze the change in price since 1970 in 1984.

E17–2. In 1970, Norwood Company purchased a plant site for $23,100. Immediately thereafter, construction of a plant building was started. The building was completed in January 1971, at a cost of $336,000. The building is being depreciated on a straight-line basis assuming an estimated useful life of 30 years and no residual value.

Assume the GPL index in 1970 was 41.1, in 1975 it was 60.9, and at the end of 1984 it was 124.1.

Required:

a. Complete a schedule similar to the following:

	Amount to be reported assuming	
	HC basis	*CD restated*
Balance sheet at December 31, 1984:		
Operational assets:		
Land......................................		
Building...................................		
Less accumulated depreciation (14 years)......		
Income statement for 1984:		
Depreciation expense........................		

Show your computations.
b. Would the CD restatement affect income tax expense for the company? Explain. Do you think it should? Explain.

E17–3. The balance sheet for Fargo Company, prepared on the HC basis at December 31, 19F, has been completed. Supplemental statements are to be developed on a "CD restated basis." The following four items were selected from the balance sheet:

Items	*HC basis* (when acquired)	*GPL index* (when acquired or incurred)
Receivables	$69,000	115
Investment, common shares	42,000	105
Land, plant site	15,000	100
Payables......................	99,000	110

The GPL at the end of 19F was 120.

Required:

a. Indicate which items are monetary and which are nonmonetary.
b. Set up a schedule to derive the amount "CD restated basis" that should be shown on the supplementary CD balance sheet for each item. Show computations.
c. Compute the purchasing power gain (loss) on monetary items that should be reported on the CD income statement. Show computations.
d. Explain why certain items were omitted from your computation in (c).

E17–4. The items listed below were taken from the December 31, 19A, balance sheet of Environmental Systems Company (HC basis). This date is the end of the first year of operations. The GPL index at January 1, 19A, was 200, and at December 31, 19A, it was 220.

	Debits	Credits	GPL index transaction date
Cash	$ 21,000		210†
Accounts receivable (net)	45,000		210†
Investments, common shares	12,000		215
Land	15,000		205
Equipment	100,000		200
Accumulated depreciation		$ 8,000	
Accounts payable		18,000	210†
Notes payable		43,000	200
Capital stock (nopar)		110,000	200
Retained earnings*		14,000	
	$193,000	$193,000	

*Cash dividends declared and paid on December 31, 19A, amounted to $5,000.
†Average.

Required:

a. Prepare a CD restated balance sheet. Use a format similar to Exhibit 17–4 and round all amounts to the nearest dollar.
b. What was the amount of CD restated income for 19A? Explain.
c. Compute the amount of CD restated income from normal operations assuming the purchasing power gain on monetary items is $2,014. Show how this gain was computed.

E17–5. At the end of 19A (the first year of operations), Strong Company prepared the summarized HC basis income statement shown below. At January 1, 19A, the GPL index was 220; and at December 31, 19A, it was 260.

STRONG COMPANY
Income Statement
For the Year Ended December 31, 19A

	Amount	GPL index at average transaction date
Sales revenue	$ 330,000	234
Cost of goods sold	(165,000)	234
Depreciation expense*	(11,000)	
Remaining expenses	(94,000)	230
Pretax income	60,000	
Income tax expense	(18,000)	260
Net income	$ 42,000	

*The related asset was acquired when the GPL index was 220.

Required:

a. Prepare a CD restated income statement. Use a format similar to Exhibit 17–4. The monetary items and their GPL indexes at transaction dates were: receivables, $32,000 (index 234), and liabilities, $16,000 (index 220). Round all amounts to the nearest dollar.

b. Prepare a CD restated statement of retained earnings assuming cash dividends of $4,000 were declared but not paid on December 31, 19A.

E17–6. This exercise illustrates computation of the purchasing power gains and losses on two monetary items in situations that involve numerous transactions during the period. At December 31, 19D, the following summary data were taken from the ledger:

Transactions	GPL at transaction date	Cash	Payable
Beginning balance	118	$ 30,000	$18,000
Purchased land	125		+12,000
Sales revenue............	130	+150,000	
Borrowing on note........	120	+60,000	+60,000
Payment	122	−15,000	−15,000
Payment	132	−42,000	−42,000
Expenses paid	130	−90,000	
Dividends paid	132	−10,000	
Equipment purchased	120	−80,000	
Payment	125		−13,000
Ending balance		$ 3,000	$20,000

Note: GPL index numbers: January 1, 19D, 118; December 31, 19D, 132.

Required:

Compute the purchasing power gain or loss on monetary items for each account (cash and payable) separately. Round all amounts to the nearest dollar.

Part B

E17–7. On January 1, 19A, Southwest Gas Company acquired a tract of land that cost $120,000 when the GPL was 120. Payment was made in cash, $50,000, plus a $70,000, three-year, interest-bearing note. One year later the note was still outstanding, and the GPL index was 150. The specific index, related to the land, was 100 at the beginning of 19A and was 140 at the end of 19A. The land and the note will be included on the December 31, 19A, CC/CD financial statements.

Required (show computations and round to the nearest dollar):
a. The CC/CD value for the land that should be reported on the 19A CC/CD balance sheet is $_____.
b. The purchasing power gain (loss) on the monetary liability which should be reported on the 19A CC/CD statements is $_____.
c. The CC real holding gain (loss) on the nonmonetary asset that should be reported on the 19A CC/CD statements is $_____.
d. The amount of the GPL fictional change on the land was $_____.
e. Diagram the above responses in respect to the land (not the note payable).

E17–8. On January 1, 19A, Davis Company purchased a machine (an operational asset) that cost $15,000. Cash paid was $10,000 and a $5,000, three-year, interest-bearing note was given to the seller. On January 1, 19A, the GPL index was 100. At the end of 19A, the Accumulated Depreciation account reflected $1,500 (i.e., straight-line depreciation;

estimated life 10 years and no residual value). During 19A, the average GPL index was 115 and at the end of 19A the GPL index was 120. The specific price index for the machine was 110 at the beginning of 19A and 143 at the end of 19A. The machine, accumulated depreciation, and note payable will be reported on the 19A CC/CD financial statements.

Required (show computations and round to the nearest dollar):

a. Complete the following tabulation of the amounts that should be reported on the 19A financial statements:

Item	HC basis	CC/CD basis
Balance sheet:		
Machine		
Accumulated depreciation		
Note payable		
Income statement:		
Depreciation expense		

b. The purchasing power gain (loss) on monetary items that should be reported on the CC/CD statements is $_____.

c. The CC real holding gain (loss) on nonmonetary items that should be reported is $_____.

d. The amount of the GPL fictional changes for machinery was $_____.

E17–9. Rose Company purchased merchandise for resale during 19A (the first year of operations) that cost $76,000. Payment was in cash except for an $11,400 ending balance in accounts payable. The purchases, and payments on accounts payable, occurred evenly throughout the year. The average GPL index for 19A was 190 and at the end of 19A it was 200.

The ending inventory was $15,200; therefore, cost of goods sold was $60,800. Current cost of the ending inventory was $17,000 and $68,000 for cost of goods sold (the CC cost of goods sold is based on the average cost during the year). Accounts payable, inventory, and cost of goods sold will be reported on the 19A CC/CD financial statements.

Required (show computations and round to the nearest dollar):

a. Complete the following tabulation of amounts that should be reported at the end of 19A:

Item	HC basis	CC/CD basis
Balance sheet:		
Inventory		
Accounts payable		
Income statement:		
Cost of goods sold		

b. The purchasing power gain (loss) on accounts payable that should be reported in the CC/CD disclosures is $_____.

c. The CC real holding gain (loss) on the nonmonetary items that should be reported in the CC/CD disclosures is $_____.

d. The amount of the GPL fictional changes was $_____.

PROBLEMS/CASES

Part A

PC17–1. Gerald Company has prepared the annual HC basis financial statements at December 31, 19F. The company is considering the development of supplemental statements on the "CD restated basis." The following seven items were selected from the balance sheet:

Items	HC basis (when acquired)	GPL index (when acquired or incurred)
1. Cash:		
Beginning balance.......................	$ 20,000	141.5
Debits	38,800	146*
Credits................................	(44,600)	147*
2. Merchandise inventory (average cost)........	58,000	145
3. Accounts receivable, net....................	28,800	144*
4. Land (no changes during 19F)..............	12,000	100
5. Building, net (no changes during 19F)	157,500	105
6. Accounts payable	42,000	140*
7. Bonds payable (no changes during 19F)	88,000	110

At the end of 19F the price-level index was 150. Average was 145.8
*Average GPL index for these items.

Required:

a. Group the above items into two categories: monetary and nonmonetary.
b. Set up a schedule and compute the amount "CD restated basis" that should be shown on the CD balance sheet for each of the items. Show calculations. Round to the nearest $100 in the restatement.
c. Set up a schedule and compute the purchasing power gain or loss on cash items that will be shown on the CD restated income statement. Show calculations and round to the nearest $100.

PC17–2. At the end of the first year of operations, DE Company prepared the following balance sheet and income statement (HC basis):

DE COMPANY
Balance Sheet
At December 31, 19A

Assets

Cash	$ 3,330
Accounts receivable (net)............	5,650
Inventory........................	46,000
Operational assets (net)	55,000
Total	$109,980

Liabilities

Accounts payable....................	$ 3,480
Bonds payable.....................	23,000

Shareholders' Equity

Capital stock (nopar)...............	66,000
Retained earnings	17,500
Total	$109,980

Income Statement
For the Year Ended December 31, 19A

Revenues	$ 69,000
Expenses (not detailed).............	(46,000)
Depreciation expense	(5,500)
Net income	$ 17,500

Items	GPL (when acquired or incurred)
GPL at start of year—110	
Average 115	
GPL at end of year—120	
Cash (no beginning balance)	111*
Accounts receivable (balance $5,500 at beginning of year)	113*
Inventory	115
Operational assets.......................................	110
Accounts payable (no beginning balance)....................	116
Bonds payable (no beginning balance)	115
Revenues...	115*
Expenses...	115*
Depreciation expense	110
Capital stock (nopar)	110

*Average GPL index for all items in the account.

Required:

a. Restate the income statement and balance sheet; use the following headings: (1) HC Basis, (2) Restatement Computations, and (3) CD Restated Basis. Round amounts to the nearest $10.

b. Explain why net income is different between the two statements; identify amounts.

c. Why were the nonmonetary items, but not the monetary, restated on the balance sheet?

d. Does the CD income statement better match expenses with revenues? Explain.

PC17–3. After operating for one year, DO Company completed the following income statement and balance sheet:

DO COMPANY
Balance Sheet
At December 31, 19A

Assets

Cash	$ 42,300*
Accounts receivable (net)................................	29,580
Long-term investment, common shares....................	7,400
Land	11,200
Plant	154,000
Accumulated depreciation	(14,000)
Total	$230,480

Liabilities

Accounts payable......................................	$ 5,880
Bonds payable..	28,000

*Beginning balance, $58,800 (GPL index, 140); debits $57,420 (GPL index, 148) credits, $73,920 (GPL index, 145.3).

Shareholders' Equity

Capital stock (nopar).....................................	182,000
Retained earnings	14,600
Total	$230,480

Income Statement
For the Year Ended December 31, 19A

Revenues	$ 87,000
Expenses (not detailed).................................	(58,400)
Depreciation expense†	(14,000)
Net income	$ 14,600

†Depreciation is recorded on a straight-line basis; estimated life of the plant is 11 years and no residual value.

Items	GPL (when acquired or incurred)
GPL index at start of year—140	
GPL index at end of year—150	
GPL index average for 19A—145	
Cash	*above
Accounts receivable.............................	141†
Long-term investment purchased, common shares	148
Land purchased	140
Plant acquired..................................	140
Accounts payable (beginning balance $14,000)......	147†
Bonds payable (unchanged during year)...........	140
Capital stock (nopar)............................	140
Revenues	145†
Expenses	146†
Depreciation expense	140

†Average GPL for these amounts.

Required:

a. Restate the income statement and balance sheet with the following headings: (1) HC Basis, (2) Restatement Computations, and (3) CD Restated Basis. Round amounts to the nearest $10.
b. Explain why net income is different between the two statements; identify amounts.
c. Why were the nonmonetary items, but not the monetary, restated on the balance sheet?
d. Does the CD restated income statement better match expenses with revenues? Explain.

PC17–4. The transactions summarized below were completed by Sullins Company during its first year of operations. The accounting period ends December 31. The GPL index on January 1, 19A, was 100, on December 31, 19A, it was 144, and the average for the year was 120.

> January 1, 19A: Issued 10,000 shares of capital stock (nopar) for $60,000 cash and borrowed $36,000 cash on a two-year, interest-bearing note (GPL index, 100).
> February 1, 19A: Purchased equipment for use in the business, $75,000 cash (GPL index, 105).
> During 19A: Purchased merchandise on credit (evenly throughout the year), $180,000 (GPL average index, 120).

During 19A: Sales revenue (evenly throughout the year), $300,000, all cash (GPL average index, 120).

During 19A: Paid expenses (evenly throughout the year), $80,000 (GPL average index, 120); includes all expenses except depreciation expense.

During 19A: Paid accounts payable, $161,200 (GPL average index on payments, 124).

December 1, 19A: Declared and paid a cash dividend of $6,900 (GPL index, 138).

December 31, 19A: Depreciation on equipment based on estimated life of 10 years and a $5,000 residual value.

December 31, 19A: Cost of goods sold, $170,000 (GPL average index for cost of goods sold and ending inventory, 120).

The above entries resulted in the following preclosing HC account balances at December 31, 19A (the 19A adjusting entries already have been completed).

Debits

Cash	$ 72,900
Inventory	10,000
Equipment	75,000
Cost of goods sold	170,000
Expenses	80,000
Depreciation expense	7,000
Retained earnings (dividend declared and paid)	6,900
Total	$421,800

Credits

Accumulated depreciation	$ 7,000
Accounts payable	18,800
Note payable	36,000
Capital stock (nopar)	60,000
Revenues	300,000
Total	$421,800

Required:

a. Set up a format similar to Exhibit 17–4 to derive CD restated financial statements. Enter thereon the HC basis amounts for each statement.

b. Restate each item on each statement on a CD basis. Prepare a separate schedule similar to Exhibit 17–5 to compute the purchasing power gain or loss on monetary items. Round all amounts to the nearest dollar. (Hint: There was a $6,243 purchasing power loss.)

PC17–5. Small Company was organized on January 1, 19A, at which time the GPL index was 150. The accounting period ends December 31. The transactions completed during 19A were:

a. January 1, 19A: Sold and issued 10,000 shares of capital stock (par $10) for $150,000 cash (GPL index, 150).

b. January 1, 19A: Purchased merchandise on credit for resale, $60,000 (GPL index, 150).

c. February 1, 19A: Purchased equipment for use in the business; paid cash, $31,000, and gave a $46,500, interest-bearing note due December 31, 19C (GPL index, 155).

d. During 19A: Sales revenue, $180,000 (sold evenly throughout the year); one third was on credit (GPL average index, 165).

e. During February–December 19A: Purchased merchandise on credit (evenly throughout the year) for resale, $44,000 (GPL index, 165).

f. During 19A: Collected accounts receivable, $50,000 (average GPL index for collections, 170).

g. During 19A: Paid accounts payable, $84,000 (average GPL index for payments, 160).

h. During 19A: Paid expenses in cash (evenly throughout the year), $61,000 (average GPL index, 165), which included interest, income tax, and all other expenses except depreciation expense.

i. July 1, 19A: Invested $96,000 cash for common shares of X Corporation (GPL index, 160).

j. December 31, 19A: Declared and paid a dividend of $10,000 (GPL index, 180).

k. December 31, 19A: Depreciation expense on equipment, $14,000.

l. December 31, 19A: Cost of goods sold, $84,000 (average GPL index for cost of goods sold and ending inventory, 156).

The above transactions resulted in the following preclosing HC account balances (adjusting entries already have been made):

Debits

Cash.....................................	$ 38,000
Accounts receivable (net)	10,000
Inventory	20,000
Investment, common shares	96,000
Equipment	77,500
Cost of goods sold	84,000
Expenses.............................	61,000
Depreciation expense..................	14,000
Retained earnings (dividend)...........	10,000
	$410,500

Credits

Accumulated depreciation	$ 14,000
Accounts payable	20,000
Note payable	46,500
Capital stock (par $10).................	100,000
Contributed surplus...................	50,000
Revenues.............................	180,000
	$410,500

Required:

a. Set up a format similar to Exhibit 17–4 to derive CD restated financial statements. Enter thereon the historical cost basis amounts for each statement. The GPL index at December 31, 19A, was 180.

b. Restate each item on each statement on a CD basis. Prepare a separate schedule similar to Exhibit 17–5 to compute the purchasing power gain or loss on monetary items. (Hint: There was a pp loss of $319.) Round all amounts to the nearest dollar.

PC17–6. *Required:*

a. Prepare the solution for Problem 17–4 using a computer spreadsheet.

b. What is the purchasing power gain or loss and the net income if the year-end GPL index were 150?

c. Using the format prepared in Part A, prepare the solution for Problem 17–5.

d. What would be the purchasing power gain or loss and the net income if the investment in X Corporation had been purchased when the GPL index was 175?

Part B

PC17–7. The problem is based on the data given in PC17–3 (DO Company). The balance sheet and income statement (HC basis) and the GPL index numbers are not changed. Current cost (CC) information is as follows:

Item	Current cost (CC) data, December 31, 19A	
Long-term investment, common shares	Based on stock market quotation......	$ 8,500
Land	Per professional appraisal	14,000
Plant (net)	Specific index, 1.10 of carrying value.	
Expenses (not detailed)	HC average and CC average the same.	
(GPL index data given in Problem 17–3)		

Required (show computations and round all amounts to the nearest $10):

a. Set up a schedule similar to Exhibit 17–9 to develop a CC/CD balance sheet amounts and income statement at December 31, 19A. Enter the HC data and complete the CC/CD amounts through "Income from operations." The purchasing power loss on monetary items was $2,417. Show calculations clearly.

b. Compute the CC real holding gains (losses) on nonmonetary items.

PC17–8. Thu Company began operations on January 1, 19A, at which time the GPL index was 130. The 19A balance sheet and income statement, along with relevant GPL index numbers and CC information, are given below. The 19A average GPL index was 143, and it was 156 at December 31, 19A.

	HC basis	GPL index at transaction date	CC valuations (which are different from HC) at December 31, 19A
Balance sheet:			
Assets:			
Cash.........................	$ 14,300	143	
Accounts receivable	28,600	143	
Inventory (average)	57,200	143	Specific index, 165/143 of HC
Equipment	78,000	130	Specific index, 1.282 of HC
Accumulated depreciation	(7,800)	130	Specific index, 1.282 of HC
Other assets..................	19,500	130	Specific index, 160/130 of HC
Total.....................	$189,800		
Liabilities:			
Accounts payable	$ 14,300	143	
Note payable	39,000	130	
Shareholders' equity:			
Capital stock	130,000	136.84	
Retained earnings...............	6,500		
Total.....................	$189,800		
Income statement:			
Revenue	$114,400	143	
Cost of goods sold	(71,500)	143	Average specific price index, 1.0577 of HC
Depreciation expense*...........	(7,800)	143	Based on average CC of equipment during 19A
Remaining expenses	(28,600)	143	HC and CC averages are the same
Net income....................	$ 6,500		

*Straight-line depreciation, 10-year estimated life and no residual value (cost, $78,000 ÷ 10 years = $7,800).

Required:

Based on the above data, the company desires to construct CC/CD disclosures as illustrated in Exhibit 17–9.

PC17–9. (Comprehensive problem—Chapters 16 and 17) The following information was contained in the annual report of Large Oil Company.

	1981	1980	1979	1978	1977
Total revenues					
—as reported	$31,729	$27,832	$20,197	$16,350	$14,263
—constant dollars	31,729	30,719	25,307	22,793	21,407
Net income from operations					
—as reported	$ 1,922	$ 1,915	$ 1,507	$ 1.076	$ 1,032
—constant dollars	1,254	1,522	1,385	1,055	1,179
—current costs	960	1,043	977	744	909
Net income from operations per share					
—as reported	$ 6.56	$ 6.54	$ 5.12	$ 3.68	$ 3.52
—constant dollars	4.28	5.20	4.70	3.61	4.02
—current costs	3.28	3.56	3.32	2.54	3.10
Cash dividends per share					
—as reported	$ 2.60	$ 2.00	$ 1.50	$ 1.40	$ 1.30
—constant dollars	2.60	2.21	1.88	1.95	1.95
Net assets at year end					
—as reported	$10,665	$ 9,385	$8,369	$ 7,146	$ 6,475
—constant dollars	16,340	15,424	14,847	13,954	13,265
—current costs	21,273	21,444	20,413	17,810	17,143
Excess of increase in specific prices over increase due to general inflation	$ 71	$ 656	$ 965	$ 74	$ (29)
Unrealized gain from decline in purchasing power of net amounts owed	$ 490	$ 574	$ 537	$ 349	$ 279

Required:

a. Calculate the following:
 (1) Return on net assets for 1981: *(a)* as reported; *(b)* constant dollars; and *(c)* current costs (state as a percent).
 (2) Growth in revenues from 1980 to 1981: *(a)* as reported; and *(b)* constant dollars (state as a percent).
 (3) Growth in net income from operations from 1980 to 1981: *(a)* as reported; *(b)* constant dollars; and *(c)* current costs (state as a percent).
 (4) Profit margin for 1981: *(a)* as reported; *(b)* constant dollars; *(c)* current costs (state as a percent).
b. What do your calculations in Requirement *(a)* tell you about the impact of inflation on Large Oil Company?
c. By studying the data presented by Large Oil, it is possible to determine whether the constant dollar information is presented in average dollars for 1981 or year-end dollars for 1981. Did Large Oil use average dollars or year-end dollars?
d. Which amount is larger for Large Oil: total monetary assets or total monetary liabilities?

PC17–10.   Frank Smith, president of Delta Corporation, has asked that you help him understand inflation accounting. During a meeting, Mr. Smith made the following comments:

I have been told that it is possible to make money by borrowing money during a period of inflation. I plan to recommend that Delta borrow $10 million, at 18 percent interest, on January 1, 19D, and deposit the money in Delta's chequing account (which does not pay interest). One year later, we will repay the money. The average inflation rate during 19D is expected to be 12 percent, consequently Delta should have a purchasing power gain on the debt. Delta will be able to use the cash from the purchasing power gain to pay a dividend to the shareholders of the company. The only thing I don't understand is why bankers are willing to lend money during a period of inflation. If we can make money by borrowing, don't the bankers lose money by lending money?

Required:

a.   Determine the amount of the purchasing power gain that Mr. Smith *expects* Delta to earn by borrowing $10 million. Will Delta actually earn the purchasing power gain that Mr. Smith expects? Explain why. Would your answer be different if the $10 million were invested in a tract of land during the year? Why?

b.   Evaluate Mr. Smith's plan to use cash from a purchasing power gain on monetary items to pay a cash dividend to the shareholders.

c.   Prepare a response to Mr. Smith's question concerning why bankers are willing to lend money during a period of inflation.

PC17–11.   Refer to the financial statements of Consolidated-Bathurst given in Special Supplement B immediately preceding the index.

Required:

a.   By how much did current cost depreciation exceed the historical amount for 1984?

b.   Why was the income tax amount on the 1984 historical income statement the same as the current cost amount?

c.   If income taxes were computed on the current cost income and expense amounts, would the differences between the current cost and the historical amounts be considered as timing differences? Consider logically and practically.

d.   What were the real holding gains for 1984?

e.   What is "Adjustment to recognize the level of debt financing in the Corporation on specific price increases of property and plant and inventory" in the amount of $30 for 1984?

A

Overview of Income Taxes*

PURPOSES OF THIS SUPPLEMENT

Income taxes are complex and pervasive; they affect most persons and businesses. Each individual and manager should consider the income tax implications when making economic decisions. A general knowledge of income taxes enables the decision maker to (a) recognize the importance of various income tax implications, (b) know when to seek professional assistance, and (c) carry on tax planning to minimize income taxes.

The powers of governments to tax are set out in the Constitution. Various levels of governments not only assess income taxes but also customs duties, property taxes (i.e., on real property), sales taxes (i.e., on the sale of goods and services), and excise taxes (i.e., on gasoline). Because income taxes are levied by the federal government and most provinces, the total amount exceeds any other tax. As a result, tax factors significantly affect many business and personal decisions faced by the two major groups of taxpayers: corporations and individuals.

The purpose of this supplement is to present an overview of federal income taxes applicable to individuals and corporations. This overview is designed to (a) enhance your general knowledge of the primary federal income tax provisions, (b) give you a basic understanding of income tax returns, and (c) provide an overview of the relationship between accounting income (reported on the income statement) and taxable income (reported on the income tax return).[1] The discussion in this supplement is based upon current income tax information. By the time you read this supplement, certain tax provisions discussed may not be current. However, the discussion is relevant because it deals with key concepts and terminology rather than with the numerous exceptions and detailed rules. We reemphasize that our objective is to provide a broad overview of income tax provisions rather than a highly technical view. The examples given are intended to illustrate those key concepts and terminology. Parliament may change the tax

---

*Supplement prepared by E. Scott.

[1]Canada introduced a federal income tax in 1917 to help finance its participation in World War I. Since that time the Canadian *Income Tax Act* has had several major revisions, and almost continuous minor changes, in the ongoing process of attempting to define a fair and equitable revenue base. At the same time it has also been an instrument through which both fiscal and social policies have been implemented, and accordingly the concepts of "income" familiar to accounting and economics have been replaced with one that is legalistic and, in some instances, startlingly different.

rates or specific tax law which may make certain illustrations out of date but our educational objective will remain intact.

To accomplish this purpose, this supplement is subdivided as follows:

Part A—Income as a tax base

Part B—Income taxes paid by corporations

Part C—Income taxes paid by individuals

Part D—Tax planning

Part A—Income as a Tax Base

The Income Tax Act requires all taxpayers to pay taxes based on their **taxable income**—the dollar amount to which the rates are applied to determine total income taxes payable. Taxable income is determined in two major steps:

1. Determine net income (for tax purposes that is sometimes referred to as Division B income).
2. Subtract from the above a specified set of deductions (commonly called Division C deductions).

What is to be included in each of these two major items depends on the type of taxpayer. Residents and nonresidents receive different treatments and, as mentioned above, the rules for corporations are often different than those for individuals.

NET INCOME (FOR TAX PURPOSES)

Division B of the act provides in Section 3 a general formula for the determination of net income (for tax purposes), and supplements this with copious general and specific rules to be applied to each taxpayer's unique circumstances.

Exhibit A–1 gives an overview of the general formula and can be seen to have the following characteristics:

1. Positive net incomes and gains are brought in first (items *a* and *b*), with deductions and negative elements (losses) (items *c* and *d*) following in a particular sequence so that net income never falls below zero. (See "Division C Deductions" below.)
2. Capital gains and losses are generally handled separately (in *b*) from the noncapital net incomes or losses (in *a* and *d*), subject to a few specific exceptions. This is because only one half of capital gains become taxable and one half of capital losses are allowable, as explained in more detail below.
3. The noncapital net incomes or losses are further classified as to

EXHIBIT A–1
Determination of
Division B net
income for tax
purposes—per
Section 3

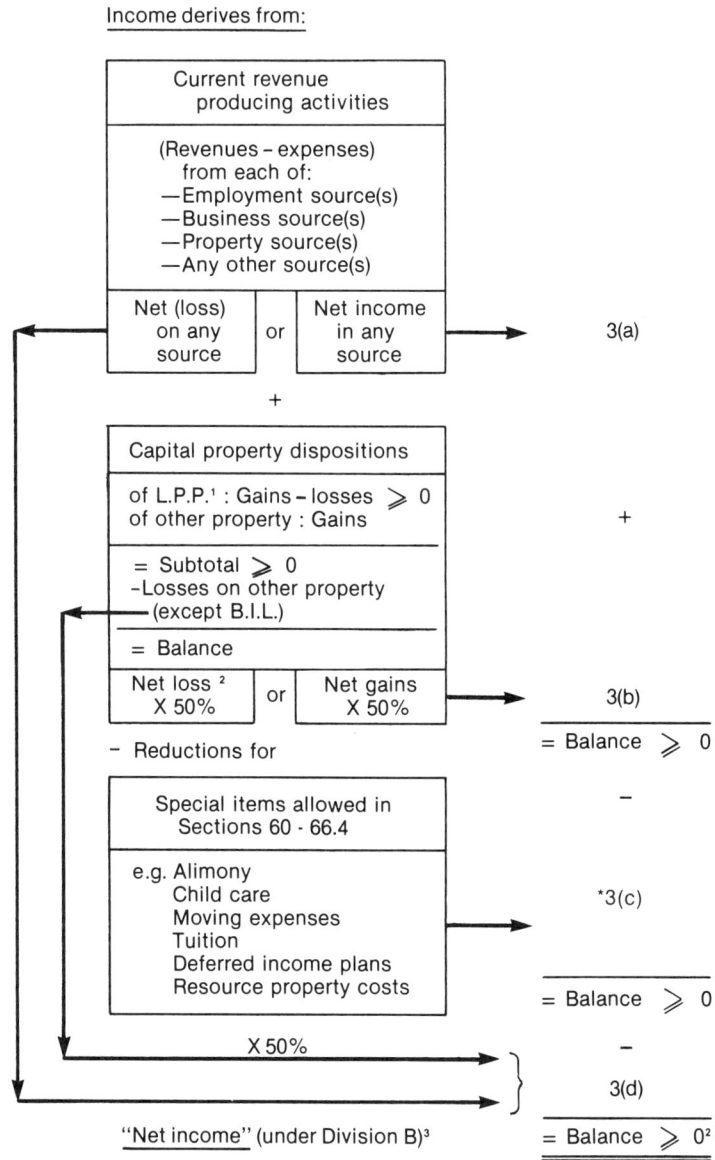

Income derives from:

Current revenue
producing activities

(Revenues – expenses)
from each of:
—Employment source(s)
—Business source(s)
—Property source(s)
—Any other source(s)

Net (loss) on any source	or	Net income in any source

→ 3(a)

+

Capital property dispositions

of L.P.P.[1] : Gains – losses $\geqslant 0$
of other property : Gains

= Subtotal $\geqslant 0$
–Losses on other property
—(except B.I.L.)

= Balance

Net loss[2] X 50%	or	Net gains X 50%

→ 3(b)

= Balance $\geqslant 0$

– Reductions for

Special items allowed in
Sections 60 - 66.4

e.g. Alimony
        Child care
        Moving expenses
        Tuition
        Deferred income plans
        Resource property costs

→ *3(c)

= Balance $\geqslant 0$

X 50%

–

3(d)

"Net income" (under Division B)[3]   = Balance $\geqslant 0^2$

Notes:
[1]If balance would have been, or is, negative (<0), the net loss may be reported in *another* taxation year as a deduction under S.3(b).

[2]If balance would have been, or is, negative (<0), the net loss may be reported in *another* taxation year as a deduction under Division C.

[3]Prior to 1986, *individuals* could deduct up to $2,000 of the "net loss × 50%" calculated under 3(b) above under a S.3(e), now repealed.

L.P.P. means listed personal property (collections or items of art, rare manuscripts, stamps, coins or jewelry).

B.I.L. means business investment loss (a capital loss arising on the disposition of shares or debt of a Canadian-controlled private corporation).

the source from which they arose—business, property, employment, and so on—to allow for differing treatments in the measurement process. (Income from business and property most closely parallels the accounting concept of net income, since these figures represent the net of revenues less allowable expenses for each source.)

4. Priority in deductions is given to a special set of items (in c) which an accountant would find hard to match with any particular income source. These exist for social reasons or because a special deductible status is bestowed on some capital expenditures not covered elsewhere.

DIVISION C DEDUCTIONS

Further deductions are permitted after the computation of net income, so that only a portion of the net income (for tax purposes) ends up in the taxable income base and is subject to the tax. The deductions allowed under Division C exist for the following reasons:

1. To allow for personal socioeconomic differences among taxpayers based on age, health, dependents, and so on.
2. To acknowledge and promote socioeconomic goals; for example, donations and investment in Canada by Canadians.
3. To minimize potential double taxation of corporate income handed on as dividends to other corporations.
4. To allow the carryover to years of positive net income the excess net losses not permitted by the net income formula in Division B.

Part B—Income Taxes Paid by Corporations

Since the corporation is singled out by the act for treatment as a separate taxpayer, and since its income is primarily from the single source **business,** we will use it as a basis for a more detailed discussion.

For corporations the taxation year is the fiscal year; accrual accounting is required subject to several special rules.

BUSINESS INCOME

A corporation's income from business is calculated as revenues minus expenses, using generally accepted accounting principles and modifying them where a special rule may alter the normal treatment. Sometimes a particular revenue may be exempted, or a particular deduction not allowed.

The general rules governing deductibility of expenses include the following:

1. Outlays must have been made to produce revenue or have a business purpose.

2. Capital outlays are not deductible unless allowed by a specific rule (see "Capital Cost Allowance" below as an example).
3. Personal and living costs are not allowable.
4. Outlays to produce exempt income are not allowed.
5. Outlays which are not reasonable in amount or nature are not deductible.
6. Some outlays are specifically allowed, limited, or prohibited as to deductibility. (This last rule is the most difficult one because of the detailed knowledge it requires.)

The result of applying these rules and related provisions regarding revenue will produce a figure analogous (but not equal) to the accountant's "Net Income before Taxes."

Special income tax rules relating to inventories parallel those used for accounting purposes, but not completely. For example, valuation may be at lower of cost or market, reasonably determined, except that LIFO is not permitted as a measure of cost.

A gratuitous deduction from income of 3 percent of the cost of beginning inventories is also permitted under tax rules. This has no parallel in ordinary accounting.

Another major area of difference between accounting and taxation business incomes arises because of the way the Income Tax Act provides for capital outlays. These give rise to various types of **property,** each with its own deduction rules. For example:

a. **Capital property**—any property owned except inventory and items placed in other special property categories—no write-off until disposition.
b. **Depreciable property**—annual write-off (as discussed in more detail below).
c. **Eligible capital property**—usually intangibles, one half of which is written off annually on a 10 percent declining balance basis. The other half is ignored for tax purposes.

Other categories, such as resource properties, receive various special treatments.

CAPITAL COST ALLOWANCE

Depreciable property is eligible for a periodic deduction familiarly described as **capital cost allowance.** Most tangible fixed assets and some intangible assets are pooled in classes prescribed in the Regulations accompanying the act. If any asset is not listed in any of the prescribed classes, it does not qualify as depreciable property. Acquisitions during the year are added to the class at their cost, and any proceeds of dispositions up to the original cost are credited to the class. Proceeds in excess of cost are treated separately as capital gains. Proceeds of disposition arise on a sale of the asset, and also may be deemed to occur in several other circumstances—for example, change of use of the asset or insurance proceeds recovered.

The annual capital cost allowance write-off is a discretionary claim and may be any amount from zero up to the maximum permitted for each class. This maximum is defined for each class by applying a specified percentage to the balance in the class at the end of the taxation year. This process continues so long as any assets of that class remain. The effect is analogous to declining balance depreciation in a group depreciation system. In early years, straight-line depreciation expense in the income statement will normally be less than capital cost allowances claimed for tax purposes. (See Exhibit A–2 for an example of capital cost allowance calculations.)

Some exceptions to the declining balance pattern do occur. A few straight-line classes exist. Several rapid write-off classes exist to create an incentive to

EXHIBIT A–2
Comparison of accounting depreciation and capital cost allowance

A. DATA—WR Limited has the following fixed assets:

Item	Land	Building	Office furniture	Auto	Delivery truck
Cost	$50,000	$400,000	$40,000	$15,000	$25,000
Useful life	n/a	30 yrs.	10 yrs.	3 yrs	6 yrs.
Salvage	n/a	$100,000	nil	$ 9,000	$ 1,000
Depreciation method	n/a		–straight line–		

B. Calculation of depreciation expense—19X1:

Building (3⅓% of $300,000)	$10,000
Office furniture (10% of $40,000)	4,000
Auto (33⅓% of $6,000)	2,000
Delivery truck (16⅔% of $24,000)	4,000
Total	$20,000

WR LIMITED
Capital Cost Allowance Schedule
For the Year Ended December 31, 19X1

	Building (Class 3) (5%)	Office equipment (Class 8) (20%)	Motor vehicles (Class 10) (30%)	Totals
Balance of undepreciated capital cost (UCC) at January 1, 19X1 (d)	$390,000	$36,000	$34,000	$460,000
Add: Acquisitions at cost (a)	—	—	—	—
Deduct: Proceeds of dispositions (b)	—	(1,000)	—	(1,000)
UCC before capital cost allowance (CCA)	$390,000	$35,000	$34,000	$459,000
CCA for 19X1 (c)	19,500	7,000	10,200	36,700
UCC December 31, 19X1	$370,500	$28,000	$23,800	$422,300

Notes: It is assumed that:
(a) There were no assets acquired during the year.
(b) The $1,000 proceeds in Class 8 represents the actual proceeds of disposition for an item that had originally cost more than $1,000.
(c) Maximum possible amounts of capital cost allowances are claimed.
(d) Starting balances are given.

businesses to invest in certain ways. For example, Class 29, allows machinery and equipment acquired for manufacturing purposes to be written off over three years in a pattern of 25 percent, 50 percent, and 25 percent.

There is one important exceptional rule for the regular declining balance classes. The capital cost allowances calculated on the net additions to a class (costs added less proceeds credited) are restricted to only one half the normal percentage. Other balances in the class are eligible for the full rate. This can sometimes produce the effect that depreciation expense on the books is greater than the tax write-off. (See Chapter 10 for the implications for deferred tax accounting.)

Since proceeds of disposal are credited to the class, a credit balance sometimes arises for the class at year-end. This credit balance is brought into income immediately as a "recapture" of capital cost allowance previously claimed, and the class continues with a zero balance.

When the proceeds of disposal for the *last* asset in the class are not large

EXHIBIT A–3

WR LIMITED
Capital Cost Allowance Schedule
For the Year Ended December 31, 19X2

	Building (Class 3) (5%)	Office equipment (Class 8) (20%)	Motor vehicles (Class 10) (30%)	Manufacturing equipment (Class 29) (irregular)	Totals
UCC, January 1 19X2..............	$370,500	$28,000	$23,800	—	$422,300
Add: Acquisitions at cost...........	—	3,000	—	$20,000	23,000
	$370,500	$31,000	$23,800	$20,000	$445,300
Deduct: Proceeds of disposition *(a)*.......	—	(1,000)	(24,000)	—	(25,000)
UCC before CCA.........	$370,500	$30,000	$ (200)	$20,000	$420,300
Recapture—100% income	—	—	200	—	200
CCA— Maximum *(b)*...........	(18,525)	(5,800)	—	$ (5,000)	$ (29,325)
UCC December 31, 19X2..............	$351,975	$24,200	nil (c)	$15,000	$391,175

Notes: It is assumed that—
(a) Proceeds of disposition in each case are less than the initial "capital cost" of the item sold.
(b) Maximum possible amounts of capital cost allowances are claimed. (See calculations below.)
(c) Some assets remain in Class 10, so it remains "open," but with a UCC of nil following the recapture which arose when proceeds credited to the class exceeded the UCC in the class during the year.

Calculations:

Class 8—Beginning balance:	20% of $28,000 =	$5,600
"Net additions"— Acquisitions	$3,000	
Less: Proceeds	1,000	
1/2 of 20% of	2,000	200
		$5,800

Class 29—A special incentive class in which CCA, is calculated by a formula. For a single asset in the class, the write-off effectively occurs over three years at 25%, 50%, and 25% of cost in each respective year. In this case—Year 1—25% of $20,000 = $5,000.

enough to eliminate the whole balance in the class, a **terminal loss** is claimed for the full amount of any remaining balance.

A number of other restrictive or special rules exist, requiring a more than casual knowledge of the system. Exhibit A–3 extends the calculation of capital cost allowances for WR Limited into 19X2, illustrating some of the special rules.

INVESTMENT INCOME—CORPORATIONS

Corporate taxpayers may also generate revenue in the form of interest and dividends; that is, income from property. For tax purposes this is called **investment income.** Net taxable capital gains by a corporation are also included with investment income.

Capital gains and losses

Capital gains, measured as the difference between **proceeds** and cost, can arise on the disposition of any capital property or depreciable property, but not on eligible capital property or resource property, which are covered by other special rules. Capital losses cannot occur for depreciable property because the capital cost allowance/terminal loss system takes care of dispositions where proceeds are less than cost.

In the Canadian system, capital gains were not taxed until 1972. Since then only one half of the capital gains are included in income for tax purposes, and one half of the losses are allowable deductions. (The other half is still ignored for tax purposes, which has the effect of taking capital gains at one half the marginal rate.) Generally, the allowable capital losses may only be deducted against the taxable capital gains. When an excess of allowable losses occurs in a year (net capital losses) they do not enter the calculation of Division B net income. Instead, the Division C deduction rules permit their deduction in other taxation years.

A great many special rules give distinctive treatments to various types of capital property (especially personal use property) and to special circumstances; for example, where deemed dispositions occurring without an actual receipt of cash may prove onerous to the taxpayer.

Because of the more favourable treatment of capital gains, the distinction between capital amounts and revenue amounts is an important one, and the source of much disagreement between taxpayers and the taxing authorities. Numerous court decisions have tended to use indicators of the taxpayer's intention as the deciding factor. The resulting case law provides some guidance, but each taxpayer's situation is still unique.

DIVISION C DEDUCTIONS—CORPORATIONS

Corporate taxpayers are generally permitted to reduce further their Division B net income (business income, investment income, and other sundry incomes and deductions) for three types of items:

1. **Dividends received from other taxable Canadian corporations**—to avoid double taxation when income already taxed in

one corporation is moved to another corporation by way of dividends.

2. **Donations to charities and governments**—to encourage corporations in their social responsibilities. Deductible charitable donations are restricted in any year to 20 percent of net income, but excess donations may be carried over and deducted in future years.

3. **Losses of other years**—to permit the taxpayer to use the excess business losses and net capital losses not deductible in other years. Specific matching and ordering rules govern the amount eligible in this category in any year.

EXHIBIT A-4
Calculation of taxable income for a corporation

A. **Normal accounting financial statements:**

WR LIMITED
Condensed Income Statement
For the Year Ended December 31, 19X1

Sales		$520,000
Cost of goods sold		365,000
Gross margin		155,000
Operating and other expenses		103,700
Net income before taxes		51,300
Current	$6,800	
Deferred	8,200	15,000
Net income		$ 36,300

B. **Additional information:**

1. Beginning inventory, at cost		$120,000
2. Included among operating and other expenses were:		
Depreciation		20,000
Donations to charities		5,000
Political contribution (federal)		1,000
Gain on disposal of shares		(3,000)
Dividends received on shares (Canadian)		(500)
3. Capital cost allowance claimed (See Exhibit A–2)		36,700

C. **Calculation of "Net Income" and "Taxable Income":**

Net income per financial statements			$ 51,300
Add Back:	Expenses not allowed for tax purposes:		
	Depreciation	$20,000	
	Donations—charities	5,000	
	—political	1,000	$26,000
			77,300
Deduct:	3% of beginning inventory	$ 3,600	
	Gain on disposal of shares		
	—50% not taxable	1,500	
	Capital cost allowance	36,700	41,800
"Net Income" for tax purposes (Division B)			35,500
Less:	Division C deductions for:		
	Canadian dividends received	$ 500	
	Donations to charities	5,000	5,500
"Taxable Income"			$30,000

The calculation of net income and taxable income of WR Limited are compared to the accounting net income in Exhibit A–4.

TAX RATES—CORPORATIONS

Revenue Canada Taxation prescribes a set of Schedules (T2–FTC) which is helpful in calculating the tax payable by a corporation. (See Exhibit A–5 for Schedule 1, page 1, which contains the major income tax calculations under Part I of the Income Tax Act).

The taxable income of corporations is subject to federal tax at the rate of 46 percent, less a 10 percent reduction for the part of the taxable income earned in a province of Canada. (This "makes room" for each of the provinces to assess their own taxes, which they do at rates up to 16 percent of taxable income earned in that province).

Income earned and taxed in another country is eligible for a "foreign tax credit," to minimize or eliminate the possibility of double taxation of the same income.

Certain corporations and/or types of income are eligible for further rate reductions or dollar tax credits, and at various times some or all corporations have been subject to a surtax. Two important kinds of rate reductions are as follows:

1. The first $200,000 of business income of Canadian-controlled private corporation receives an additional rate reduction of 21 percent, leaving a net federal rate of 15 percent on that **small business** income.
2. The manufacturing and processing profits of corporations also receive a rate reduction of 6 percent (or 5 percent if the income has already earned the small business reduction).

(Similar reductions of provincial rates exist in many provinces.)

A significant dollar reduction in the tax bill may be received through the investment tax credit. This allows taxpayers to reduce their tax liabilities in lieu of receiving grants, to encourage certain types of spending (e.g., research and development, manufacturing facilities) in designated regions of the country. Political contributions have also been singled out to earn a limited tax reduction.

Several other items may enter the calculation before the total liability is determined. For example, dividends paid out of small business income attract a (Part II) tax of 12½ percent; and Canadian dividends received (which escaped tax by virtue of the Division C deduction) may be subject to a (Part IV) tax at 25 percent which is refunded to the corporation when these dividends are distributed to its own shareholders. The result is that the effective tax rate is different for each corporation and may vary from taxation year to taxation year.

Exhibit A–5 shows part of the calculation of tax for WR Limited, on the assumption that it is a "Canadian-controlled private corporation."

EXHIBIT A–5
T2–FTC Schedule 1
Form calculation of
Part I tax for
corporations

T2-FTC Schedule 1 – 1985 and subsequent taxation years

ORIGINAL – ATTACH TO T2 CORPORATION INCOME TAX RETURN

NAME OF CORPORATION	ACCOUNT NUMBER	FISCAL YEAR END
		Day Month Year

Part I Tax on Taxable Income – All corporations

- Corporations with special rates of tax should attach a calculation of Part I Tax Payable.

Taxable Income from the front of the T2 return	$ 30,000	(A)
Tax at 46% of Amount (A)	**202** 13,800	
Tax at 5% of Taxable Income earned in the Nova Scotia offshore area	**204**	
	Sub-total	
Deduct: Small Business Deduction (see below)	6,300	
Investment Corporation Deduction (section 130)	**203** N/A	
(Taxed Capital Gains **205** _____)		
Additional Deduction – Credit Unions (section 137)	**206** N/A	
Federal Tax Abatement (section 124)	**207** 3,000	
Manufacturing and Processing Profits Deduction (see below)	N/A	
	Net amount	9,300
Add: Corporate Surtax per form T2215	**209** 4,500	N/A
	Sub-total	4,500
Deduct: Non-Business Foreign Tax Credit per T2S-TC Part II	**211** N/A	
Business Foreign Tax Credit per T2S-TC Part II	**213** N/A	
Logging Tax Credit per T2S-TC Part III	**215** N/A	
Federal Political Contribution Tax Credit	**217** 450	
(Federal Political Contributions (per receipts attached) **219** 1,000)		
Share-Purchase Tax Credit (attach slips)	**220** N/A	
Scientific Research Tax Credit	**216** N/A	
Investment Tax Credit per form T2038 (CORP.)	**221** N/A	
Employment Tax Credit per form T2208	**222** N/A	450
Part I Tax Payable – (enter on front of T2 return)		4,050

Small Business Deduction – Canadian-controlled private corporations throughout the taxation year

Income from active business carried on in Canada per T2S(7) or T2S(7)(A)	**223** 33,500	(A)
Taxable Income*	**225** 30,000	(B)
Business Limit for the year**	**227** 200,000	(C)
Small Business Deduction – 21% of the least of Amounts (A), (B) and (C)	**231** 6,300	

*To be reduced by 10/4 of the amount deducted under subsection 126(1) and two times the amount deducted under subsection 126(2).

**In the case of a corporation that is associated, that portion of the Business Limit allocated to the corporation per form T2013.

Manufacturing and Processing Profits Deduction – All corporations that have such profits

Canadian manufacturing and processing profits per T2S(27)	**233** _____	(A)	
Deduct: Least of Amounts (A), (B) and (C) per calculation of Small Business Deduction		(B)	(C)
Taxable Income			
Deduct: (i) Least of Amounts (A), (B) and (C) per calculation of Small Business Deduction			
(ii) Canadian Investment Income			
Foreign Investment Income	**449**		
Less: Net capital losses claimed on front of T2 return			
(iii) Business Foreign Tax Credit	×2		
	235		(D)
5% of the lesser of Amounts (A) and (B)			
Add: 6% of the lesser of Amounts (C) and (D)			
Manufacturing and Processing Profits Deduction	**243**		

Refundable Portion of Part I Tax – Canadian-controlled private corporations throughout the taxation year

(1) Net Canadian Investment Income or Loss per T2S(7) – – – – **247** 1,500 –
Add: Net Foreign Investment Income or Loss per T2S(7) – – – **249** 1,500 –
Deduct: Net capital losses claimed on front of T2 return – – –

1,500 – (A)

(2) Canadian Investment Income per T2S(7)* – – – – – – 1,500 –
Add: Foreign Investment Income per T2S(7)* _____ × 40%
Deduct: Non-Business Foreign Tax Credit – – – – × 4

Sub-total 1,500 –

Deduct: Net capital losses claimed on front of T2 return– – – – – –

1,500 – (B)

(3) Taxable Income – – – – – – 30,000
Deduct: Small Business Deduction 6,300 × 4 25,200 00
Non-Business Foreign
Tax Credit – – – _____ × 10/4
Business Foreign Tax Credit _____ × 2 25,200 · 4,800 – (C)

25% of least of Amounts (A), (B) and (C) – – – – – – – **257** 375 – (D)

Part I Tax Payable – – – – – – – – – – 4,050 – (E)

Refundable Portion of Part I Tax – 2/3 of the lesser of Amounts (D) and (E) – – – – – **261** 250 –
*If negative, enter nil.

Part IV Tax on Taxable Dividends Received – Private corporations and subject corporations at any time in the taxation year

Taxable Dividends subject to Part IV Tax per T2S(3) – – – – **405**

Deduct: Non-Capital and/or Farm Loss claimed for purposes of
Part IV Tax per T2S(4) – – – – – **406**
Taxable Amount – – – – – – – – –

Part IV Tax Payable – 1/4 of Taxable Amount (enter on front of T2 return) – –

Refundable Dividend Tax on Hand – Private corporations and subject corporations at the end of the taxation year

Refundable Dividend Tax on Hand at the end of the preceding taxation year **409**
Deduct: Dividend refund for the preceding taxation year – – – – **410**

Add: Refundable Portion of Part I Tax – – – – – – –
Part IV Tax Payable – – – – – – – – –

Refundable Dividend Tax on Hand at the End of the Taxation Year – – – – – **411**

Dividend Refund – Private corporations and subject corporations at the end of the taxation year

Taxable Dividends Paid in the taxation year* per T2S(3) – – – – **414** × 1/4 (F)

Refundable Dividend Tax on Hand at the end of the taxation year – – – – – – (G)

Dividend refund – Lesser of Amounts (F) and (G) – (enter on front of T2 return) – – – –

*Do not include capital gains dividends paid.

PAYMENT OF TAX—CORPORATIONS

A corporate taxpayer must pay installments each month of its current fiscal year toward its estimated tax bill. Final adjustments are made in the two or three months immediately following the end of the fiscal (taxation) year.

Part C—Income Taxes Paid by Individuals

The calculation of net income and taxable income for individuals has many similar rules to those followed by corporations, and some quite clear differences. The starting point is again the Section 3 formula to determine net income.

BUSINESS INCOME—INDIVIDUALS

Individuals with business income operate as proprietors or partners. The proprietorship or partnership is not taxed directly, but rather the income of the business (calculated using the same accrual and other rules that the corporation followed) is "flowed through" and brought into the income of the owner(s) for taxing purposes. Note that the cash drawn from the business is irrelevant, and that the business financial statements do not report the income tax expense.

The taxation year for an individual is the calendar year, so it is the income of the business for its *fiscal* period ending in any calendar year that is deemed to be the owner's business income for that calendar year. The choice of a fiscal year-end thus becomes important in determining how long the taxing of the unincorporated business income may be delayed.

INCOME FROM OTHER SOURCES—INDIVIDUALS

For individuals, income from investments is treated as a separate source, income from property, and includes such items as interest, dividends, and royalties. Whether rental income is business income or income from property depends on whether it is actively earned or passively collected by the individual. Generally, accrual rules apply to the determination of net income from property, but some exceptions exist which allow reporting on a cash basis or a mixed cash/accrual basis.

A special rule exists for dividends received from taxable Canadian corporations whereby 150 percent of the dividends received is brought into income. (This is offset in the calculation of taxes by a dividend tax credit described below.)

Investment income received during a year is reported to the taxing authority and the taxpayer by the institution making the payment on a special T5 information return. (See Exhibit A–6.)

Employment as a source of income is unique to individuals, and gets slightly different treatment. Salaries, wages, employee benefits, and fees from holding an office are included in the individual's income at their gross amount and on

**EXHIBIT A–6
Information returns**

**T5—Investment
Income:**

	Revenue Canada Taxation	Revenu Canada Impôt		**T5** Supplementary – *Supplémentaire*		STATEMENT OF INVESTMENT INCOME ÉTAT DES REVENUS DE PLACEMENTS

Dividends from Taxable Canadian Corporations
Dividendes de corporations canadiennes imposables   Rev. 84

Year	(A) Actual Amount of Eligible Dividends *Montant réel des dividendes admissibles*	(B) Taxable Amount of Eligible Dividends *Montant imposable des dividendes admissibles*	(C) Federal Dividend Tax Credit **2,040.00** *Crédit d'impôt fédéral pour dividendes*	(D) Eligible Interest from Canadian Sources *Intérêts admissibles de source canadienne*	(I) Capital Gains Dividends *Dividendes sur gains en capital*	(J) Gross Foreign Income *Revenus étrangers bruts*
Année	(E) Actual Amount of Ineligible Dividends **6,000.00** *Montant réel des dividendes non admissibles*	(F) Taxable Amount of Ineligible Dividends **9,000.00** *Montant imposable des dividendes non admissibles*	(G) Royalties from Canadian Sources *Redevances de source canadienne*	(H) Other Income from Canadian Sources **1,000.00** *Autres revenus de source canadienne*	(K) Foreign Tax Paid *Impôt étranger payé*	(L) Amount Eligible for Pension Deduction *Montant admissible à la déduction pour pensions*

RECIPIENT: SURNAME FIRST, AND FULL ADDRESS
BÉNÉFICIAIRE: NOM DE FAMILLE D'ABORD, ET ADRESSE COMPLÈTE

Social Insurance Number
Numéro d'assurance sociale
000 000 001

→ RICHARD, WILLIAM
1234 ANY STREET
SOMEWHERE, CANADA
XOX OXO

NAME AND ADDRESS OF PAYER (Must appear on each slip)
NOM ET ADRESSE DU PAYEUR (À inscrire sur chaque feuillet)

W.R. LIMITED
P.O. BOX 10,000
SOMEWHERE, CANADA
XOX OXO   • For Taxation Office
• *Pour le bureau d'Impôt*

1

	Revenue Canada Taxation	Revenu Canada Impôt		**T5** Supplementary – *Supplémentaire*		STATEMENT OF INVESTMENT INCOME ÉTAT DES REVENUS DE PLACEMENTS

Dividends from Taxable Canadian Corporations
Dividendes de corporations canadiennes imposables   Rev. 84

Year	(A) Actual Amount of Eligible Dividends **100.00** *Montant réel des dividendes admissibles*	(B) Taxable Amount of Eligible Dividends **150.00** *Montant imposable des dividendes admissibles*	(C) Federal Dividend Tax Credit **34.00** *Crédit d'impôt fédéral pour dividendes*	(D) Eligible Interest from Canadian Sources *Intérêts admissibles de source canadienne*	(I) Capital Gains Dividends *Dividendes sur gains en capital*	(J) Gross Foreign Income *Revenus étrangers bruts*
Année	(E) Actual Amount of Ineligible Dividends *Montant réel des dividendes non admissibles*	(F) Taxable Amount of Ineligible Dividends *Montant imposable des dividendes non admissibles*	(G) Royalties from Canadian Sources *Redevances de source canadienne*	(H) Other Income from Canadian Sources *Autres revenus de source canadienne*	(K) Foreign Tax Paid *Impôt étranger payé*	(L) Amount Eligible for Pension Deduction *Montant admissible à la déduction pour pensions*

RECIPIENT: SURNAME FIRST, AND FULL ADDRESS
BÉNÉFICIAIRE: NOM DE FAMILLE D'ABORD, ET ADRESSE COMPLÈTE

Social Insurance Number
Numéro d'assurance sociale
000 000 001

→ RICHARD, WILLIAM
1234 ANY STREET
SOMEWHERE, CANADA
XOX OXO

NAME AND ADDRESS OF PAYER (Must appear on each slip)
NOM ET ADRESSE DU PAYEUR (À inscrire sur chaque feuillet)

MARITIME TEL+TEL CO LTD
HALIFAX, NS
B3J 3C7

• For Recipient
Attach to your Income Tax Return
SEE INFORMATION ON REVERSE

• *Pour le bénéficiaire – Annexer à votre déclaration d'Impôt sur le revenu*
VOIR LES RENSEIGNEMENTS AU VERSO

2

---

a cash basis for the calendar year. Employers are required to report annually such amounts along with any relevant withholdings on a *T4* or *T4A* form (see Exhibit A–6).[2] All amounts received must be included unless specifically excepted, and no deductions are permitted unless they are specifically listed in Section 8 of the Income Tax Act. This list of deductions is quite short and it is often restricted to particular situations. The more common deductions allowed may be found on page 1 and the top of page 2 of the individual tax return. (See Exhibit A–7.)

---

[2]Specialized information returns also exist for amounts such as payments to nonresidents and the quasi-employment income paid to fishermen.

EXHIBIT A–6
(concluded)
T4-Employment
Income

Revenue Canada / Taxation	Revenu Canada / Impôt		**T4-1985** Supplementary - *Supplémentaire*			02-363-976 STATEMENT OF REMUNERATION PAID *ÉTAT DE LA RÉMUNÉRATION PAYÉE*				

(C) EMPLOYMENT INCOME BEFORE DEDUCTIONS	(D) EMPLOYEE'S PENSION CONTRIBUTION CANADA PLAN		(E) U.I. PREMIUM	(F) REGISTERED PENSION PLAN CONTRIBUTION	(G) INCOME TAX DEDUCTED	(H) U.I. INSURABLE EARNINGS	(I) C.P.P. PENSIONABLE EARNINGS	(J) EXEMPT
30,000 00 REVENUS D'EMPLOI AVANT RETENUES	379 80 DU CANADA COTISATION DE PENSION (EMPLOYÉ)	DU QUÉBEC	PRIME D.A.C.	1,461 60 COTISATIONS RÉGIME ENREGISTRÉ DE PENSIONS	7,153 20 IMPÔT SUR LE REVENU RETENU	GAINS ASSURABLES A.-C.	21,100 00 GAINS OUVRANT DROIT À PENSIONS - R.P.C.	X UI EXONÉRATION

BOX (C) AMOUNT ALREADY INCLUDES ANY AMOUNTS IN BOXES (K) (L) (M) (N) (O) AND (P)	(K) TAXABLE ALLOWANCES AND BENEFITS	BOARD AND LODGING	(L) RENT FREE AND LOW RENT HOUSING	(M) PERSONAL USE OF EMPLOYER'S AUTO	(N) INTEREST FREE AND LOW INTEREST LOANS	(O) OTHER TAXABLE ALLOW. AND BENEFITS
LE MONTANT DE LA CASE (C) COMPREND DÉJÀ TOUS LES MONTANTS DES CASES (K) (L) (M) (N) (O) (T) (P)	AVANTAGES IMPOSABLES	NOURRITURE ET LOGEMENT	LOGEMENT GRATUIT OU À COÛT MODIQUE	USAGE PERSONNEL DE L'AUTO DE L'EMPLOYEUR	PRÊTS SANS INTÉRÊT OU À FAIBLE INTÉRÊT	AUTRES AVANTAGES IMPOSABLES

(P) EMPLOYMENT COMMISSIONS	(Q) PENSION PLAN REGISTRATION NUMBER	(R) PAYMENTS TO DPSP	(S) CHARITABLE DONATIONS	(T) UNION DUES	(A) PROVINCE OF EMPLOYMENT	(B) SOCIAL INSURANCE NUMBER	(U) EMPLOYEE NO.
COMMISSIONS D'EMPLOI	K 76 93 N° D'ENREGISTREMENT RÉGIME DE PENSIONS	PAIEMENTS À UN RPDB	DONS DE CHARITÉ	COTISATIONS SYNDICALES	N.S. PROVINCE D'EMPLOI	000 000 001 N° D'ASSURANCE SOCIALE	N° DE L'EMPLOYÉ

→ RICHARD, WILLIAM
1234 ANY STREET
SOMEWHERE, CANADA
XOX OXO

NAME AND ADDRESS OF EMPLOYER OR PAYOR
NOM ET ADRESSE DE L'EMPLOYEUR OU DU PAYEUR

W. R. LIMITED
P. O. BOX 10,000
SOMEWHERE, CANADA
XOX OXO

TO BE RETURNED WITH T4-T4A SUMMARY
À RETOURNER AVEC LA T4-T4A SOMMAIRE

EMPLOYEE: SURNAME FIRST (in capital letters) USUAL FIRST NAME AND INITIALS AND FULL ADDRESS
EMPLOYÉ: NOM DE FAMILLE D'ABORD (en capitales) PRÉNOM USUEL ET ADRESSE COMPLÈTE

Sundry incomes from sources such as pensions, family allowances, unemployment insurance, and alimony are also normally reported on a cash basis. In many cases the payor is required to complete an annual information return similar to those used for investment income and employment income.

CAPITAL GAINS—INDIVIDUALS

Net taxable capital gains are calculated for individuals in the same way as described above for corporations, and are treated as a separate source. Once again there must be a disposition, actual or deemed, for gains and losses to be recognized.

Individuals are subject to a number of special rules not applicable to corporations. For example, beginning in 1985, individuals other than trusts are eligible for a cumulative exemption for capital gains up to a lifetime limit of $500,000 ($250,000 of net taxable capital gains). For most taxpayers this exemption will be phased in over the five years to 1990. Since the exemption is operationalized by a Division C deduction, net taxable capital gains must be calculated and included in net income for tax purposes in the usual way. Also, since the exemption is cumulative over the years, individuals realizing eligible capital gains in the year must file a return even if they have no other income and ultimately pay no tax.[3]

When an individual makes a gift, or dies, or becomes a nonresident, there is a deemed disposition of property triggering potential capital gains and

---

[3]Until the introduction of the lifetime capital gains exemption in 1985, up to $2,000 of eligible capital losses in excess of taxable capital gains (net capital losses) could be offset against other noncapital sources of income. This provision has now been canceled.

EXHIBIT A–7
T1 General form
(Pages 1 and 2—
calculation of "net
income" and
"taxable income")

| 03 | ▮✦ Revenue Canada Taxation | Revenu Canada Impôt | ▮▮▮▮ | **1985** T1 GENERAL |

Federal and Nova Scotia
Individual Income Tax Return

Identification

Complete the following

Your Social Insurance Number
`0 0 0 0 0 0 0 0 1`

Spouse's Social Insurance Number
`0 0 0 0 0 0 0 0 2`

Usual First Name and Initial Surname, Family or Last Name (Please print)
`WILLIAM   RICHARD`

Marital Status on December 31, 1985
Married 1 ☒   Widow(er) 2 ☐
Divorced 3 ☐   Separated 4 ☐
Single 5 ☐

Present Address (Please print) Number, Street and Apt. No. or P.O. No. or R.R. No.
`1234   ANY   STREET`

City
`SOMEWHERE`

Name of Spouse
`LIL`

Province or Territory
`NOVA   SCOTIA`

Postal Code
`XOX   OXO`

Your Date of Birth
Day `01` Month `04` Year `1940`

Have you filed an Income Tax Return before?   YES 1 ☐   NO 2 ☐
If "YES", please indicate for what year: 19 ☐
Name on last return: same as above ☐ or _____

Address on last return: same as above ☐ or _____

Type of work or occupation in 1985 `PRESIDENT`
Name of present employer `W. R. LIMITED`
Address of Spouse: same as mine ☐ or _____

Province or Territory of Residence on December 31, 1985 was:
`NOVA   SCOTIA`
If you were self-employed in 1985, please state province of self-employment _____

If you became or ceased to be a resident of Canada in 1985, give:
Day Month   Day Month
Date of Entry ☐☐ or Departure ☐☐

If taxpayer is deceased, Day   Month   Year
please give date of death: ☐☐

Please do not use this area

Calculation of Total Income

Income from Employment	Employment Income Before Deductions from Box (C) on all T4 slips (attach copy 2 of T4 slips) 101	`30,000 00` ⊙	
	Commissions from Box (P) on all T4 slips, included in above total 102		
	Other employment income including training allowances, tips and gratuities, etc. (please specify) 104		⊙
	Total employment earnings (add lines 101 and 104) 105	`30,000 00`	⊙
	Subtract: Employment expense deduction - If line 105 above is $2,500.00 or more, claim $500.00. If less, claim 20% of line 105. 108	`500 00`	⊙
	Other allowable expenses (please specify) 109		⊙
	Total employment expenses (add lines 108 and 109) 110 `500 00` ▷	`500 00`	
	Net employment earnings (subtract line 110 from line 105) 111	`29,500 00`	
Pension Income	Old Age Security Pension (attach copy of T4A(OAS) slip) 113		⊙
	Canada or Quebec Pension Plan benefits (attach copy 2 of T4A(P) slip) 114		⊙
	Other pensions or superannuation (attach copy 3 of T4A slips) 115		⊙
Income from Other Sources	Taxable Family Allowance payments (attach copy of TFA1 slip) 118	`375 24`	⊙
	Unemployment Insurance benefits (attach copy 2 of T4U slip) 119		⊙
	Taxable amount of dividends from taxable Canadian corporations (attach completed Schedule 4) 120	`9,150 00`	⊙
	Interest and other investment income (attach completed Schedule 4) 121	`1,000 00`	⊙
	Rental income (Schedule 7) Gross 160 Net 126		⊙
	Taxable capital gains (Allowable capital losses) - complete and attach Schedule 3 127		
	Other income (please specify) 130		⊙
Self-Employed Income	Business income Gross 162 Net 135		⊙
	Professional income Gross 164 Net 137		⊙
	Commission income Gross 166 Net 139		⊙
	Farming income Gross 168 Net 141		⊙
	Fishing income Gross 170 Net 143		⊙

Total Income (add lines 111 to 143 inclusive - please enter this amount on line 200 on page 2) 150 `40,025 24` ▷ `40,025 24`

| 03 | Please do not use this area 605 | Please do not use this area 600 |

EXHIBIT A–7
(concluded)

2 Calculation of Taxable Income

Total Income (from line 150 on page 1) 200 `40,025 24`

Canada or Quebec Pension Plan contributions			
Contributions through employment from Box (D) on all T4 slips (maximum $ 379.80)	202	`379 80`	•
Contribution payable on self-employed earnings (from page 3)	203		•
Unemployment Insurance premiums from Box (E) on all T4 slips (maximum $ 562.12)	204		•
Registered pension plan contributions (if over $ 3,500.00. See Guide "Line 207")	207	`1,461 60`	•
Registered retirement savings plan premiums (attach receipts)	208	`2,000 00`	•
Registered home ownership savings plan contributions (attach receipts)	211		
Annual union, professional or like dues (attach receipts)	212		
Tuition fees - claimable by student only (attach receipts)	213		
Child care expenses (complete and attach Schedule 5)	214		
Allowable business investment losses	217		
Indexed Security Investment Plan - allowable capital losses (attach copy of form T5 ISIP)	218		
Other deductions (please specify) *CARRYING CHARGES - INVESTMENTS*	222	`150 00`	

Deductions from Total Income

Add lines 202 to 222 inclusive 223 `3,991 40` `3,991 40`

Net Income (subtract line 223 from line 200) 224 `36,033 84`

Add: Accumulated Forward Averaging Amount Withdrawal (from form T581) 225

228 `36,033 84`

Claim for Personal Exemptions

Basic Personal Exemption	Claim $ 4,140.00	`4,140 00`
Age Exemption - If you were born in 1920 or earlier	Claim $ 2,590.00	

(If you did not receive the Old Age Security Pension, attach a letter giving reasons.)

Married Exemption - If applicable, please check ✓ box 1. or 2.
Married on or before December 31, 1985, and supported spouse in 1985
1. whose net income in that year, while married, was not over $ 510.00 1. ✓ Claim $ 3,630.00   230 `3,470 00` ⊙
2. whose net income in that year, while married, was over $ 510.00 but not over $4,140.00
   (If your marital status changed in 1985,   2. ☐   4,140 00
   please give date of change)   Subtract: spouse's net income while married
   Claim

Exemption for Dependent Children - Provide details below and claim according
to child's age and net income. **See Guide "Line 231" if child's net income exceeds limit.**
Children born in 1968 or later - Claim $ 710.00 for each child whose net income was not over $ 2,720.00
Children born in 1967 or earlier - Claim $ 1,420.00 for each child whose net income was not over $ 2,720.00
and who, if born in 1963 or earlier, was in full-time attendance at a school or university or was infirm.

Name of child (attach list if space insufficient)	Relationship to you	Date of birth of child Day Month Year	If born in 1963 or earlier state whether infirm or school attended	Net income in 1985 $	Claim
MORRIS	SON	29 02 64		2,500	1,420 00
HENRY	SON	07 01 74		—	710 00

Total claim for dependent children 231 `2,130 00` `2,130 00` ⊙

Additional Personal Exemptions from Schedule 6 attached	233		
Total Personal Exemptions (add above items)	235	`9,740 00`	`9,740 00` ⊙

Subtract line 235 from line 228 236 `26,293 84`

Other deductions from Net Income

Interest and dividend income deduction (attach completed Schedule 4)	238	`150 00`	⊙
Pension income deduction	240		⊙
Medical expenses - (attach receipts and complete Schedule 9) 241			
Subtract: 3% of "Net Income" (line 224 above)			
Allowable portion of medical expenses	242		
Charitable donations (attach receipts)	243	`2,600 00`	⊙
Gifts to Canada or a province (attach receipts)	245		⊙
Deduction for blind persons or persons confined to a bed or wheelchair			
Claim relates to: Self ☐ or dependant other than spouse (specify)	246		⊙
Education deduction (attach completed form T2202 or T2202A)	247	`400 00`	⊙
Employee stock option deduction (from T4 slip)	249		⊙
Unemployment Insurance benefit repayment payable from page 3	250		• ⊙
Deductions transferred from spouse (attach completed Schedule 2)	251		⊙
Non-capital losses of other years	252		⊙
Capital losses of other years (1972 to 1984)	253		⊙
Capital gains exemption	254		⊙

Add lines 238, 240 and lines 242 to 254 inclusive 255 `3,150 00` `3,150 00`

Subtract line 255 from line 236 256 `23,143 84`

Subtract: Forward Averaging Elective Income Deduction from form T540   257

Taxable Income (enter this amount on page 4) 260 `23,143 84`

losses. For gifts and bequests, some easing of the tax burden may be possible, depending upon the kind of property and who is the recipient.

Individuals are also more apt to encounter the special rules concerning **personal use property,** and three in particular are noteworthy:

1. Losses on personal use property are not deductible unless they arise on a special list of items called listed personal property such as coins, stamps, and works of art (but *not* antiques).
2. In measuring the gain or loss, both proceeds and capital cost are deemed to be at least $1,000 to avoid the necessity of accounting for nonmaterial items.
3. A full or partial exemption is provided on the disposition of a family home that has been used as a principal residence.

Another special rule of interest to individuals (but also applicable for corporations) allows most taxpayers to elect capital gains rather than income treatment on the sale of securities, even where the normal rules of intention would indicate the reason for investing was to produce an active trading profit rather than to obtain the usual passive income from property by the holding of the asset.

DEFERRED INCOME—INDIVIDUALS

A special set of rules exists which allows individuals to save out of income (essentially for retirement) and delay the payment of taxes on that income until it is received.[4] Registered pension plans, registered retirement savings plans, and deferred profit sharing plans are some examples of situations where limited amounts of income may be reduced currently as funds are put into the plan. Interest earned on the plan funds is untaxed while it is registered, and the ultimate tax cost is borne only when amounts are received out of the plan.

There are enough special rules in the determination of an individual's income that it may be necessary to obtain professional assistance in situations other than the most straightforward ones.

DIVISION C DEDUCTIONS—INDIVIDUALS

Individuals receive the same deductions as corporations for donations to charities and the Crown, and for excess losses carried over from other years. There is no complete deduction for Canadian dividends such as corporations receive, but rather the first $1,000 of investment income from Canadian securities may be deducted, if it is deemed **eligible.** This eligibility is lost in several special circumstances, the main one being where the investment income is not received at arm's length; that is, where some degree of relationship or control

---

[4]The whole area of retirement income planning has been under review by the government, including the taxing rules. The May 1985 budget proposals included several changes that would increase contribution limits over a five-year period, and refine eligibility requirements.

exists between the payor and the recipient. (See Exhibit A–6 where the T5 return from Mr. Richard's controlled corporation, WR Limited, reported the amounts as ineligible dividends and other income.)

It is only individuals (including trusts) that can use the Division C set of deductions that are designed to allow for some sort of equity where personal and social circumstances are different. (See Exhibit A–7, page 2, for a list of these deductions from net income.)

A set of deductions called **personal exemptions** allows a token deduction to everyone in lieu of actual personal and living expenses, and further provides additional deductions for age and the support of various types of dependents. The amounts of these deductions are changed from year to year to allow for inflation, and sometimes to reflect changing perceptions of what is considered **equitable.**

Among the other deductions available will be found categories for persons receiving pension income from private sources, an extra deduction for disabled persons, another for students paying tuition, and an opportunity for spouses who both have a positive net income to share some of their deductions in a limited way. In every case, eligibility conditions and the limitations on the amount of the deduction exist and must be observed. Supplementary information and structured **schedules** to assist calculations are provided with the tax return form.

As mentioned previously, the new lifetime capital gains exemption is received as a Division C deduction by individuals. Again, limits are provided and eligibility restrictions exist. Schedules for the detailed calculation of each year's deduction will have to be followed.

Finally, among the Division C items for individuals are two items—employee stock option deduction and the forward averaging deduction—which exists here simply to allow for the way related amounts were technically included or excluded in the Division B net income calculation.

The data in Exhibit A–7 draws on the previous information we have about Mr. William Richard. The form also shows that he is the president of WR Limited, is married with two sons (one of whom is eligible for Family Allowance). The other son is in the university, but he has insufficient income of his own to use his education deduction so he has transferred it to his father.

Mr. Richard also has contributed $2,000 to a registered retirement savings plan, $2,600 to charities, and paid $150 in carrying charges in connection with his investments.

TAX CALCULATION—INDIVIDUALS

The taxable income of individuals other than trusts are subject to a **progressive** rate structure rather than the initial flat rate faced by corporations. It is considered equitable for those with larger incomes to pay proportionately more taxes.

Individuals, like corporations, are eligible for tax credits for foreign source income, political contributions, and certain types of investment expenditures in designated regions, as well as a number of reductions in tax arising from special circumstances.[5]

A most important reduction of taxes is the federal dividend tax credit on dividends received from taxable Canadian corporations. This amounts to 34 percent of the actual dividends received (or 22⅔ percent of the taxable amount of dividends, after they have been grossed up 50 percent as described earlier). The purpose of this credit is to reduce or even eliminate the impact of the corporate taxes paid when the income was first earned by the corporation, and leave a net tax cost approximately equal to what an individual would have paid on the same business income received directly. This is referred to as the integration of corporate and personal taxes. For 1985 and 1986 taxation years, a surtax is imposed on individuals with federal tax liabilities greater than $6,000.

The provinces levy their own income taxes in addition to the federal taxes. For most provinces, the reporting is done on the same return used for filing federal taxes, and the calculation is based on the basic federal tax; that is, federal taxes before any reductions except the federal dividend tax credit and the scientific research tax credit. The province of Quebec requires the filing of a separate provincial income tax return.

Exhibit A–8 shows the forms used for the calculation of tax payable by an individual. The portion designated as Schedule 1 may be bypassed by many individuals who can use precalculated tables to determine their tax liability.

In addition to the normal taxes and reductions, the federal government has provided for a child tax credit to persons who are eligible to receive Family Allowances, whether they have income taxes to pay or not. This credit is limited by the number of eligible children (receiving Family Allowance), and also by the size of the *family* income. Details are found on the income tax return filed by individuals.

PAYMENT OF TAX—INDIVIDUALS

For many individuals, the tax will have been withheld, at source, by the payer of the income. Any balance would then be payable or refundable with the filing of the return on or before April 30 of the year following the taxation year.

Individuals (normally with large business or property income sources) whose taxes are over $1,000 and for whom tax is not withheld from at least 75 percent of their "Net Income," are required to pay installments quarterly on an estimated basis.

Both federal and provincial taxes are paid to the federal government, except for those owing to Quebec.

---

[5]Some individuals whose tax liability is significantly reduced by such credits may find themselves liable for an Alternative Minimum Tax, calculated at a flat rate on a modified form of the taxable income base.

EXHIBIT A–8
Calculation of taxes payable by an individual

A. Schedule 1—Detailed Tax Calculation:

Schedule 1 — Detailed Tax Calculation (See Guide)   *W. RICHARD   000-000-001*

Federal Income Tax — Use "1985 Rates of Federal Income Tax" at bottom.

Taxable Income from line 260 on page 2 of your return.	*23,143 84*		
On the first	*18,130 00*	tax is	*$3,212 00*
On remaining	*5,013 84*	tax at *23* % is	*1,153 18*
Total Federal Income Tax on Taxable Income			*4,365 18* ◊ *4,365 18*

Add: Tax Adjustments (please specify; see "Line 501" in Guide)   501

Total   *4,365 18*

Subtract: Federal Dividend Tax Credit — 22⅔% of Taxable amount of dividends from taxable Canadian corporations (line 120 on page 1 of your return), not to exceed "Total" above   502   *2,074 00*

Scientific Research Tax Credit (from form T2114; see "Line 503" in Guide)   503

Total of above credits   *2,074 00* ◊ *2,074 00*

Basic Federal Tax 505 *2,291 18*

Subtract: **Federal Tax Reductions:**
1. For self ($100.00 or the amount of "Basic Federal Tax", whichever is less)   *100 00*
2. For spouse — see "Line 403" in Guide   403   *100 00*

Total of above Federal Tax Reductions *(maximum $200.00)*   *200 00*

Subtract: ("Basic Federal Tax" in excess of $6,000.00) × 10%

Net Federal Tax Reductions *(if negative, enter zero)*   *200 00* ◊ *200 00*

Federal Tax *2,091 18*

Subtract: Federal Foreign Tax Credit — Make separate calculation for each foreign country   ⊙
(a) Income Tax or Profits Tax paid to a foreign country   507

(b) Net Foreign Income   508   ⊙
"Federal Tax" plus any Dividend Tax Credit and Scientific Research Tax Credit   =

Net income (line 224)†
less any capital losses of other years allowed (line 253), interest and dividend income deduction (line 238), employee stock option deduction (line 249) and capital gains exemption (line 254)
†If you filed a form T581 election, use line 9 from form T581 — if negative, enter nil.

Deduct (a) or (b) above, whichever is less

Federal Tax Payable 406 *   *2,091 18*

Federal Surtax Payable *(Complete this section if Amount (A) below is greater than $6,000.00)*
(If Tax Tables are used to determine taxes payable, Amount (A) is equal to Federal Tax from Tax Table plus $100.00.)
Total of "Basic Federal Tax" (line 505), Scientific Research Tax Credit (line 503) and Federal Forward Averaging Tax (from form T540) *minus* Federal Forward Averaging Tax Credit (from form T581)   (A)

| 1. (Amount (A)) | minus $ 6,000.00) × 2.5% | |
| 2. (Amount (A)) | minus $15,000.00) × 2.5% | |

Federal Surtax Payable 419 *

Nova Scotia Income Tax *(Applicable to residents of Nova Scotia on December 31, 1985)* — If you were not a resident of Nova Scotia on December 31, 1985 or if you had income from a business with a permanent establishment outside Nova Scotia in 1985, refer to the Guide.
Note: If your "Federal Tax" ("Basic Federal Tax" less "Federal Tax Reductions") is zero, enter zero at line 423.
Basic Nova Scotia Income Tax — 56.5% of "**Basic Federal Tax**" (line 505 above)   *1294 52*
Subtract: Provincial Foreign Tax Credit from calculation on form T2036

NOVA SCOTIA TAX PAYABLE 423 *   *1294 52*

* *Please transfer the amounts of the items indicated by an asterisk (*) to the identically numbered lines on page 4 of the return.*

1985 Rates of Federal Income Tax

Taxable Income	Tax	Taxable Income	Tax
$1,295 or less	6%	$12,950	$ 2,176 + 20% on next $ 5,180
1,295	$ 78 + 16% on next $1,295	18,130	3,212 + 23% on next 5,180
2,590	285 + 17% on next 2,590	23,310	4,403 + 25% on next 12,950
5,180	725 + 18% on next 2,590	36,260	7,641 + 30% on next 25,900
7,770	1,191 + 19% on next 5,180	62,160	15,411 + 34% on remainder

EXHIBIT A–8
(concluded)

**B. T1 General—
Page 4—Summary
of Tax and Credits:**

4 Summary of Tax and Credits There are two methods of tax calculation (see Guide).

Taxable Income from line 260 on page 2 400

Calculation of Federal Tax Payable:

Federal Tax from Tax Table	402	
Subtract: Unused portion of Spouse's Federal Tax Reduction	403	•
	405	
Federal Tax Payable - from line 405 above or from line 406 on Schedule 1	406	**2091 18**

Subtract: **Federal Political Contribution Tax Credit**   Total Contributions **409**   ⊙
from calculation on page 3   Allowable Tax Credit 410

Share-Purchase Tax Credit from form T2111	411	•
Investment Tax Credit from form T2038(IND.)	412	•
Employment Tax Credit Claimed from form T2208	413	
Total of above credits 416		◇

Federal Tax Payable Before Federal Forward Averaging Tax and Federal Surtax Payable	417	**2,091 18**
Add: **Federal Forward Averaging Tax on Elective Income** from form T540	418	
Federal Surtax Payable from line 419 on Schedule 1 (See Guide "Line 419")	419	
Net Federal Tax Payable 420		**2,091 18**

Add: **Nova Scotia Tax Payable** from Tax Table in Guide or from line 423 on Schedule 1

(If line 405 above is zero, enter zero at this line)	423	**1,294 52**
Add: Nova Scotia Forward Averaging Tax on Elective Income from form T540	426	
Net Nova Scotia Tax Payable 427	**1,294 52** ◇	**1,294 52**
Canada Pension Plan Contribution Payable on Self-Employed Earnings from page 3	432	
Unemployment Insurance Benefit Repayment Payable from page 3	433	

Total Payable 435 **3,385 70** •

— Please do not use this area —

667

683

684

Total tax deducted per information slips	440	**7153 20** • ⊙
Nova Scotia Tax Credit	448	•
Child Tax Credit (attach completed Schedule 10)	450	**N/A** •
Canada Pension Plan Overpayment	453	•
Unemployment Insurance Overpayment	454	•
Amounts paid by instalments	455	•
Forward Averaging Tax Credit (from form T581)	458	•
Refund of Investment Tax Credit (from form T2038-IND.)	459	•
Total Credits 463	**7,153 20** ◇	**7,153 20**

Subtract line 463 from line 435 and enter
the difference in applicable space below.   **3,767 50**

A difference of less than $ 1.00 is neither charged nor refunded.

Refund 464 **3767 50** •   Balance Due 465 •
IMPORTANT: The inside front cover of your   (See Guide "Line 465")
guide tells you when to expect your refund.

Refund transferred to spouse
468 •   **Amount Enclosed** ●
(See Guide "Line 468")   Please attach cheque or money order payable to
         the Receiver General. Do not mail cash.
         Payment is due not later than April 30, 1986.

467

Name and address of any individual or firm, other than the taxpayer,
who has prepared this return for compensation.

Name

Address

Telephone

I hereby certify that the information given in this return and in any
documents attached is true, correct and complete in every respect
and fully discloses my income from all sources.

Please sign here *William Richard*

Telephone   Date

Form authorized and prescribed by order of the Minister of National Revenue for purposes of Part I
and Part I.1 of the Income Tax Act, Part I of the Canada Pension Plan and Part VIII of the
Unemployment Insurance Act, 1971.

It is a serious offence to make a false return.

Privacy Act Personal Information Bank number RC-T-P20

Part D—Tax Planning

Tax planning focuses on the anticipated tax consequences of future transactions. The purpose of tax planning is to avoid the unnecessary payment of
taxes in the face of detailed and often complex tax rules. Tax planning to avoid
tax should not be confused with tax evasion. Tax evasion involves illegal activities to reduce the tax liability, and is a criminal offence.

Minimization of the tax cost can involve:

1. Ensuring that the lowest allowable *rate* of tax is levied.
2. Deferring the payment of tax to the latest permissible time to
   conserve cash resources.
3. Taking advantage of opportunities and incentives permitted by
   the law, and avoiding the traps set for tax evaders which acci-
   dentally may catch the unwary innocent taxpayer.

TAX PLANNING BY BUSINESS MANAGERS

Because income tax rates are high and the related income tax law and regulations are complex, tax planning is an important consideration in many of the
decisions made by the management of any business. To provide an overview
of tax planning we will discuss three of the major areas that affect most business entities: (1) selecting the type of business organization, (2) financing the
business, and (3) structuring transactions before they occur.

SELECTING THE TYPE OF BUSINESS ORGANIZATION

Sole proprietorships, partnerships, and corporations have different income
tax implications for owners and managers. When starting a new business or
dealing with the growth of a small business, selecting the type of business
organization poses several substantive issues, one of which is the long-term
income tax implications.

Annual earnings of proprietorships and partnerships are taxed at the increasing marginal rates of the owner(s), whether withdrawn or not. In contrast, corporate earnings are taxed at one or more of the flat rates applicable to
corporations, partly when earned and partly when distributed, and in addition
the shareholder (owner) may pay taxes on the dividends received over and
above the dividend tax credit allowed.

Whether incorporating the business will increase or decrease taxes depends
largely on the extent to which the dividend tax credit received against personal
taxes offsets or neutralizes the tax paid in the corporation. Each case is different, and depends upon what rate the corporation pays and what income other
than the business profits is being received by the owner. The salary/dividend
mix from the corporation can alter these variables, and, at some levels of income, it becomes a critical part of the decision.

Other advantages may accrue to the corporate form because of incentives
available only to corporate taxpayers, special provisions surrounding reorga-

nization and disposals or dissolution of the business, and the implications for personal estate planning by shareholders—all factors requiring expert advice.

The principal disadvantage of the corporate form, apart from those cases where the taxes are higher, is the complexity of the tax rules.

FINANCING A BUSINESS

Basically, a business obtains funds (e.g., cash) from three sources: (1) investments by owners, (2) borrowing, and (3) earnings of the business. Often when new or additional funds are needed (e.g., for operations and expansion), the management of the company must decide between equity and debt (or some combination) as the source(s) of funds. Such decisions have important income tax implications, particularly for a corporation, because interest on debt is a fully deductible expense in computing taxable income. In comparison dividends paid to shareholders (of common and preferred shares) are not deductible. To illustrate, assume ABC Co. Limited needs $500,000 cash to acquire a new productive facility. The management is considering two alternatives as follows:

1. **Alternative A.**—Borrow the needed funds at 12 percent interest; the marginal income tax for the company is 46 percent.
2. **Alternative B.**—Issue for cash, 50,000 shares of the company's cumulative 8 percent, preferred stock, at $10 par value per share.

The two financing alternatives can be analyzed as follows:

Alternative A, borrowing:

$$\$500,000 \times .12 \times (1.00 - .46) = \$32,400 \text{ after tax cost per year}$$
Net cost of funds: $32,400/$500,000 = 6.48 percent

Alternative B, issue capital stock:

$$\$500,000 \times .08 = \$40,000 \text{ after tax cost per year}$$
Net cost of funds: $40,000/$500,000 = 8.0 percent

In this case, the borrowing alternative is less costly because the interest expense is deductible from income, saving tax at the 46 percent marginal tax rate. However, a number of factors should be considered in making this decision. For instance, the company is legally required to make the fixed interest payments of $60,000 per year and to repay the $500,000 principal amount on the maturity date, regardless of whether the company earned income or incurred a loss. In contrast, by choosing to issue capital stock, these fixed payments may be avoided; dividends can be paid only if there are accumulated earnings (i.e., a positive balance in retained earnings); also, there is no payment on a maturity date for the shares issued. It may be helpful at this point to review the sections in Chapters 11 and 12 on (a) return on owner's equity, (b) return on total assets, and (c) financial leverage.

STRUCTURING AND TIMING

Business transactions often can be structured and/or timed in ways to maximize their favourable, or minimize their unfavourable, income tax consequences. It is important to realize that such structuring and timing must be accomplished prior to, and not after, the transaction has been completed. Some typical transactions that can be structured or timed for this purpose are as follows:

1. Leasing versus purchase of operating assets.
2. Installment sale of capital property.
3. Allocation of the lump-sum purchase price of depreciable versus nondepreciable assets.
4. Valuation of assets and liabilities of a purchased business.
5. Timing the purchase of depreciable assets just before year-end.
6. Recognition of investment tax credit opportunities such as choice of location and type of expenditure.
7. Choice of methods of compensation for executives (tax-free versus taxable benefits).
8. The wide range of tax incentives and tax shelters.
9. Tax-free rollovers of certain types of assets by selling at the appropriate time.
10. Triggering capital gains and losses at the right time.

TAX PLANNING FOR THE INDIVIDUAL

Individual taxpayers should also plan in order to minimize their income tax liabilities within the provisions of the tax law.

Many of the structuring and timing strategies listed above for corporations would also be considered by individuals in connection with business income. People should also be aware of additional opportunities and pitfall's that can arise in their investing and financing decisions, and in a whole group of tax provisions related to what might be called personal life events.

INVESTMENT AND FINANCING DECISIONS

Individuals should make use of the tax-free $1,000 of investment income from Canadian securities to maximize their rates of return. The choice between interest and dividends above that $1,000 level requires that the effect of the dividend tax credit must be considered in order to accurately compare yields.

Because of the lifetime capital gains exemption being phased in from 1985 to 1990, a major part of investment planning will involve the choice between investments yielding a return in the form of regular income and those yielding capital gains. Also, the timing of the realization of the gains (and/or losses) becomes very important during the phase-in years.

Individuals should always attempt to use borrowed funds for income producing rather than personal purposes to render the interest cost tax deductible. Where the personal purpose loans exist, these should be paid off first because of their higher effective after-tax cost.

Individuals have the option of reporting certain investment income on a cash or accrual basis to a limited degree. These choices may be made in ways that ease the tax burden in its amount or timing.

PERSONAL LIFE EVENTS

Several tax provisions exist which affect personal life events, including the following:

1. Retirement income planning is encouraged by the deferred income rules which allow the deduction of capital contributions and the sheltering of plan income until after retirement.
2. Splitting income among family members is sometimes possible, and helps avoid the higher marginal rates when all income is in the hands of one family member.
3. The timing and method of transferring personal and business assets to spouse or children by gift or bequest has many possibilities and requires estate planning advice.
4. Strategies that augment wealth through tax-reduced or tax-free capital gains rather than regular income should be explored.
5. Even timing marriages (and the birth of children) so that they occur close to the year-end to maximize personal exemptions has sometimes been suggested (and acted upon, other things being equal!)

SOME CAUTIONS

Individuals need to pay particular care to their reporting and payment responsibilities under the Income Tax Act, or extra costs will be incurred.

Interest penalties exist where returns are filed late, or where taxes (deductions, installment payments, or final settlements) are not remitted on time.

As well, supporting documentation for the calculation of taxable income is required to be available in the event of disagreement or tax audit. Many individuals, even in business, find this bothersome, but they should plan a document collection and filing system to avoid unnecessary tax costs.

It is evident that tax planning involves complex rules and sometimes complex strategies. Good planning will then almost always include the selection of competent professional advice.

QUESTIONS FOR DISCUSSION

1. Distinguish among the terms:
   a. Business income.
   b. Net income.
   c. Taxable income.

2. What is the taxation year for corporations? For individuals?

3. How does the Income Tax Act encourage taxpayers to pay their taxes on time? When are the payments of taxes required to be made by (a) corporations and (b) individuals?

4. In which part of the Section 3 "Net Income" formula would each of the following items appear:
   a. Wages.
   b. Rental net income.
   c. Carrying charges (allowable) on income-producing securities.
   d. Capital gain on the sale of a stamp collection.
   e. Family allowance.
   f. Capital loss on sale of Trans Canada Pipeline shares.

5. John Jones is regularly employed by Canada University at a salary of $3,000 per month. He also collected $7,500 on a consulting contract from another source. He earned $1,000 interest on deposits at his bank and received $3,000 in dividends from Lucky Strike Gold Mines Limited.

   List the information return forms that he should receive, and the basic information shown on each.

6. May income be reported on a cash basis, or must the accrual basis be used? Explain.

7. How do capital gains arise, and how are they classified by type? What is special about the taxation of capital gains?

8. Indicate which of the following business organizations is required to file a tax return: (a) sole proprietorship, (b) partnership, and (c) corporation. If no tax return is required, how is the income of the business taxed?

9. a. List six general rules governing the deductibility of expenses from business revenues to determine Net Income from business.
   b. Apply these rules to judge whether each of the following items would or would not be allowed as deductions against sales revenue:
      (1) Store supplies purchased.
      (2) Salary of $50,000 paid to a spouse for part-time work in the business.
      (3) Cost of lunch on rainy days when the owner of the business does not feel like going home.
      (4) Telephone bill for home phone on which occasional long-distance calls are made for the business.
      (5) Interest on a loan to buy a delivery van for the business.
      (6) Operating costs of the business owner's car which he uses to drive to and from work.
      (7) Fire, theft, and public liability insurance on the store and its contents.

10. How closely does the accounting for inventory under the tax rules parallel the treatment(s) allowed under generally accepted principles?

11. What do each of the following terms mean:
    a. Capital cost allowance.
    b. Undepreciated capital cost.
    c. Recapture.
    d. Terminal loss.

12. List and briefly explain three areas in which there are differences between business accounting net income and net income for tax purposes.

13. Business income earned by a corporation is taxed twice—once in the hands of the corporation, and again in the hands of shareholders when they receive dividends. How does the Canadian tax system try to alleviate this problem?

14. Explain the tax reasons why a corporation often prefers to obtain long-term funds by issuing bonds rather than shares of its capital stock.

EXERCISES

EA–1. Using Exhibit A–1 as a reference, compute net income for each of the following taxpayers:

	J. Smith	XYZ Co. Ltd.
Salary and benefits	$15,000	—
Net business income (loss)	(18,000)	$175,000
Net income from investments	3,000	28,000
Old-age pension	2,700	—
Capital gains (losses) at 50% of actual amounts:		
Listed personal property gains.......	6,000	—
Other capital property gains.........	3,000	6,000
Listed personal property losses	(2,000)	—
Business investment loss............	—	(1,000)
Other capital property losses	(9,500)	(7,000)

EA–2. Well-Stocked Co. Ltd. reported the following in its 19X3 financial statements:

	December 31	
	19X3	19X2
Balance Sheet		
Merchandise inventory, at LIFO cost in 19X3, at FIFO cost in 19X2 (Note 1)	$375,000	$300,000

Note 1: During the year the company changed its inventory valuation to LIFO from FIFO. The December 31, 19X3 inventory at FIFO cost was $325,000, and income has accordingly been increased by $50,000.

Required:

What effect(s) would this information have on reported net income for tax purposes?

EA–3. Down East Ltd. reported the following balances of undepreciated capital cost at the end of 19X1:

Building Class 3 (50%).....................	$100,000
Equipment Class 8 (20%)	20,000
Automobiles Class 10 (30%)................	10,000

During 19X2 the following transactions occurred:

Purchased equipment—Class 8.............	$ 8,000
—Class 29............	40,000
Disposed of automobile for proceeds of	3,000

Required:

Prepare the schedule calculating the capital cost allowance that may be claimed for 19X2.

EA–4.   Assume that the automobile that was sold in Exercise A–3 had originally cost $11,750 and was the only asset in class 10.

Required:

Recalculate the effect on income for tax purposes if it were sold for:
1. $3,000, as above or
2. $10,500 or
3. $12,000.

EA–5.   Generosity Limited had made the following contributions and donations during 19X6, and you have been consulted to advise as to whether or not these would be deductible for tax purposes.

1. To a Pee-Wee hockey team for uniforms that had the company's name printed on
    them. . . . . $ 800
2. To the United Appeal   5,000
3. To a resident of the city who provided a home for stray dogs   600
4. To the New Democratic Party of Canada   1,000

Required:

In each case, indicate whether the amount is deductible:
a.   In determining income.
b.   In Division C to determine taxable income.
c.   In Division E to determine taxes payable.
d.   Not at all.

EA–6.   Any Company Limited reported a net income of $250,000 and had no Division C deductions. All of the income was from nonmanufacturing business sources.

Required:

Referring to the FTC—Schedule 1 shown in Exhibit A–5, calculate the federal taxes payable if:
a.   The company was a public company.
b.   The company was a Canadian-controlled private corporation.

EA–7.   How would your answers in *(a)* and *(b)* of Exercise A–6 change if the business income arose entirely from manufacturing activities? (A descriptive rather than a calculated answer is required.)

EA–8.   Mr. E. Z. Erwin is married and has two children—a son at a university, age 18, and a 12-year-old daughter. During the summer of 19X4, the son had a temporary job and earned $2,500. Mrs. Erwin receives no income.

Mr. Erwin's 19X4 income sources were as follows:

Salary (gross)	$25,000
Less: Income tax withheld.....................	(4,500)
Canada Pension withheld................	(338)
Unemployment insurance................	(508)
Registered pension contributions	(1,162)
Net pay	$18,492
Interest on savings account...................	$ 300
Dividends received on Bell Canada shares	400
Family allowance (received by wife, but included as his income if he claims the child as a dependent)	360

He made the following donations:

His church...................................	$ 520
United Appeal	420
Federal Liberal Party.........................	100

Required:

Using the information from Exhibits A–7 and A–8 as a guide, calculate Mr. Erwin's federal income tax owing (refundable) for the 19X4 taxation year. Be sure to show clearly the calculation of: *(a)* net income, *(b)* taxable income, *(c)* federal tax payable.

PROBLEMS/CASES

PCA–1. Management of Tri-key Ltd. is contemplating the purchase of a building in which to house its expanding sales force. The company has a successful rapidly expanding business. Management is not sure whether to acquire the asset (cost $800,000, Class 3 — 5%) just before the 19X1 year-end, or just after the year-end.

Mr. Tristan, the president, is concerned that a purchase just before year-end would hurt its rate of return by increasing the asset base without giving the assets a chance to produce a return. Existing assets total $3 million and accounting net income averages $600,000 before taxes.

Mr. Keystone, the vice president of finance, acknowledges that problem, but feels that the cash flow tax savings could be significant in helping the company's already hard-pressed cash position, given that the $800,000 is going to be borrowed in 19X1 anyway.

Required:

a. Assuming an effective corporate tax rate of 50 percent, calculate the cash savings for the years 19X1 and 19X2 from the reduction of taxes associated with the extra capital cost allowances claimed if:
(1) The building were purchased in December 19X1.
(2) The building were purchased in January 19X2.
b. Calculate after-tax returns on investment for 19X1 under each of the conditions (1) and (2) in (a), *if* ROI were based on:
(1) Beginning of the year assets.
(2) Average of beginning and ending assets.
c. What would you conclude?

PCA–2. Concerns Ltd. has just completed its second year of operations, and for the first time its income statement has reported a profit.

In 19X1, a loss of $15,000 had been incurred. The 19X2 income statement showed a net income of $60,000, after taxes of $30,000 had been provided.

A review of the details of the income statement and other inquiries of management disclosed the following information:

1. Expenses included:

    Depreciation expense $240,000
    Charitable donations   10,000

2. Sundry other income included:

    Dividends on shares of a supplier
       in Toronto   2,000
    Gain on the sale of unimproved land
       used as a parking lot....................   10,000

3. Maximum capital cost allowance which
       could be claimed in 19X2 totaled   280,000

Required:

a.   Calculate for the year 19X2 the following:
     (1) Division B net income for tax purposes.
     (2) Division C deductions and taxable income.
     (3) Part I federal taxes payable, if Concerns Ltd. qualifies as a Canadian-controlled private corporation and all the income except the capital gain and dividends is business income.
b.   Should the maximum amount of capital cost allowance always be claimed by a taxpayer? For example, consider the situation if Concerns Ltd. had reported a net income *before* taxes of only $30,000 in 19X2.

PCA–3.   Mr. Hardy Cizion is the proprietor of the Newton Restaurant, and he is trying to decide whether or not he should incorporate this business.

In 19X7, last year, the restaurant produced for him a net income of $40,000, and he withdrew $20,000 of this for personal purposes.

He lives in a province where the provincial tax rate or corporate income is 10 percent, and on personal income is 50 percent of the federal tax.

Required:

Assume the $100 federal tax reduction has been canceled.

a.   Calculate the federal and provincial income taxes payable by Mr. Cizion, assuming the proprietorship business was his only source of income and his Division C deductions totaled $5,000.
b.   Assume that Newton Restaurant Limited had been incorporated. Calculate the total taxes paid by the corporation *and* Mr. Cizion personally if:
     (1) The corporation paid no dividends and he withdraw the $40,000 as salary.
     (2) The corporation paid him a salary of $20,000 and a dividend of all the remaining surplus.
     (3) The corporation paid all of its income after taxes as a dividend to Mr. Cizion.
c.   Should Mr. Cizion incorporate his restaurant business now?

B

1984 Financial Statements of Consolidated-Bathurst Inc.

Financial Section

Distribution of Revenue* (millions of dollars)

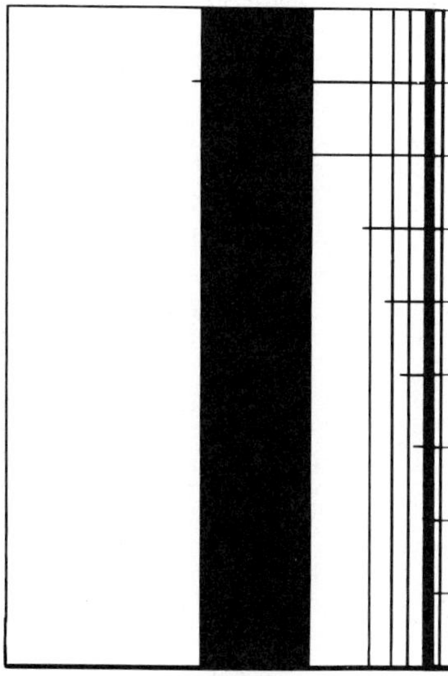

	1984	%	1983	%
Materials, supplies, etc.	**$ 725**	**44**	$ 619	44
Wages, salaries and fringe benefits	**459**	**28**	450	32
Fuel and power	**195**	**12**	159	11
Depreciation	**73**	**5**	60	4
Federal, provincial and municipal direct taxes	**45**	**3**	38	3
Interest	**67**	**4**	53	4
Dividends	**33**	**2**	29	2
Retained earnings (excluding extra-ordinary items)	**36**	**2**	3	—
	$1 633	**100**	$1 411	100

*Comprises net sales, other income and equity earnings.

Quarterly financial data

	Net sales	Net earnings	Net earnings	Dividends declared	Stock price range Low	High
	(millions of dollars)		(per common share)		(per common share)	
1983						
First quarter	$ 342	$ 9	$0.13	$0.10	$ 8⅛	$10
Second quarter	366	7	0.10	0.10	9½	11⅞
Third quarter	336	5	0.06	0.10	10⅜	12⅛
Fourth quarter	349	4	0.02	0.10	$11	$13⅜
	$1 393	$25	$0.31	$0.40		
1984						
First quarter	$ 394	$12	$0.21	$0.10	$12¾	$14½
Second quarter	439	26	0.51	0.10	13⅛	15⅛
Third quarter	390	21	0.40	0.15	12⅝	15⅞
Fourth quarter	400	—	(0.05)	0.15	$14	$16¾
	$1 623	$59	$1.07	$0.50		

Financial Review

Operating activities

As a result of improved operating earnings, cash flow from operations in 1984 amounted to $153 million, up 64% from $93 million in 1983. Operating working capital increased by $37 million in 1984, in contrast to a reduction of $31 million in 1983. Accounts receivable increased by $21 million, mainly because of higher sales of newsprint and groundwood specialties and higher selling prices for most product lines. The average number of days outstanding in accounts receivable at year-end was virtually unchanged from the level of the previous year. Inventories rose by $25 million, as higher volumes of raw materials and finished goods were required to sustain operations, particularly for the Bathurst/Bridgewater mills. They gradually increased production to reach near-capacity levels by the end of 1984. Accounts payable went up by $10 million, reflecting the higher level of business activity of the Corporation.

Dividends

The improved net earnings enabled Consolidated-Bathurst to raise its dividend on common shares from 10¢ per share to 15¢ per share in July 1984. In 1984, the Corporation paid dividends totalling $21 million on the Series A common shares and $11 million on the preferred shares. The total common dividend declared in 1984 represented a payout ratio of 36% of earnings before extraordinary items.

Investing activities

Capital expenditures were $119 million in 1984, down 32% from $175 million in 1983. Approximately $18 million was used to complete the expansion at the Bridgewater Division, the bulk of the other capital spending went to modernizing existing facilities and to reducing pollution. The Corporation also invested approximately $25 million in Sulpetro Limited and Sulbath Exploration Ltd., under the financial restructuring plan approved by Sulpetro's shareholders in the final quarter of 1984.

Financing activities

Early in 1984, Consolidated-Bathurst restructured its packaging operations in Canada under a new company called CB Pak Inc., which went public shortly thereafter. During the year, two public offerings of common shares of CB Pak, the first of which included share purchase warrants, provided the Corporation and CB Pak some $50 million of capital. New long-term debt amounted to $24 million and consisted mainly of borrowings under capital leases and of term bank loans in Europa Carton. Long-term debt repayments were $57 million and related principally to the revolving credit of Consolidated-Bathurst Pontiac and to bonds and debentures.

For 1984, the above activities resulted, after a net reduction of $33 million in long-term debt, in a net decrease in funds of $39 million which was financed by means of increased short-term borrowings and reduced cash and short-term deposits. At December 31, 1984, the capitalization of Consolidated-Bathurst consisted of $513 million in common shareholders' equity, of $103 million in preferred shares and of $587 million in debt.

The Company's debt/equity ratio at December 31, 1984, was 49/51, unchanged from the preceding year. Working capital ratio declined from 2.4 to 1.8 in 1984, chiefly as a result of the reclassification to short-term of an amount of $28 million related to the German term bank loan maturing in July 1985 and of $17 million of Consolidated-Bathurst Pontiac 11% bonds called for retraction in March 1985. The return on common shareholders' equity was 12.3% in 1984 compared with 4.7% in 1983.

Foreign currency translation

The initial foreign currency translation adjustments of $21 million recorded against shareholders' equity upon adoption of the new CICA rules on January 1, 1984, have increased to $25 million at December 31, 1984. This was a result of the continued rise of the Canadian dollar against the Deutsche mark. With respect to the deferred exchange loss on foreign debt, the strength of the U.S. dollar vis-à-vis the Canadian dollar had the effect of increasing that loss from $1.0 million at the beginning of the year to $5.6 million at December 31, 1984.

Investment tax credits

Effective January 1, 1985, the Corporation adopted the new CICA rules on investment tax credits. These credits will be accrued as a deferred credit in the balance sheet and amortized to income over a period of approximately 17 years instead of being recorded in income when realized. This new accounting policy will result in a higher tax rate on the earnings of the Corporation in 1985 compared with 1984, when $15 million of net tax credits, equivalent to $0.33 per share, were realized. The cash flow from operations will not be affected by this change. On January 1, 1985, the Corporation accrued as deferred credit approximately $32 million, representing the unrealized investment tax credits at December 31, 1984.

Sales, Property & Plant, Employees, Shareholders and Shares by Province and Country as at December 31, 1984

	Net Sales	Property & Plant - Net	Number of Employees	Number of Common Shareholders	Number of Common Shares
	(millions of dollars)				
Alberta	$ 44.4	$ 43.8	542	389	686 548
British Columbia	46.4	4.6	425	590	387 247
Manitoba	7.0	—	2	256	400 206
New Brunswick	38.8	136.5	862	399	43 674
Newfoundland	7.7	—	—	11	5 868
Nova Scotia	13.0	—	—	127	156 982
Ontario	300.4	64.8	2 267	4 418	10 671 963
Prince Edward Island	0.3	—	—	17	5 980
Quebec	239.0	525.1	6 920	5 861	24 129 298
Saskatchewan	4.6	—	—	104	43 782
Yukon & Territories	—	—	—	4	2 312
Canada	701.6	774.8	11 018	12 176	36 533 860
United Kingdom	83.9	79.2	509	618	7 646 960
United States	471.6	0.1	32	385	639 620
West Germany	302.4	67.3	2 836	648	5 160
Other Countries	63.5	—	—	81	229 179
	$1 623.0	$921.4	14 395	13 908	45 054 779

(millions of dollars)

Reporting the effects of changing prices

	Historical as reported		Adjustment		Current cost	
	1984	1983	**1984**	1983*	**1984**	1983*
Consolidated earnings for the year ended December 31, 1984						
Depreciation	$ 73	$ 60	$ 42	$ 41	$ 115	$ 101
Cost of sales	1 313	1 161	18	12	1 331	1 173
Income taxes	19	15	—	—	19	15
Earnings (loss) before extraordinary items	$ 74	$ 34	$ (60)	$ (53)	$ 14	$ (19)
Selected consolidated assets as at December 31, 1984						
Property and plant — net	$ 921	$ 911	$397	$427	$1 318	$1 338
Inventory	331	306	8	3	339	309
Common shareholders' equity	$ 513	$ 511	$405	$430	$ 918	$ 941

*Revised to reflect improved calculation techniques.

The Corporation has prepared the inflation accounting data shown above substantially in accordance with the recommendations of the Canadian Institute of Chartered Accountants (CICA) for reporting the effects of changing prices. The current replacement cost amounts for the Corporation's property and plant were determined, in most cases, by using appropriate specific indexes. This method assumes that these assets would have the same useful lives as presently used in the historical cost statements and would be replaced with similar technology although this, in fact, might not be the case. The current replacement cost of inventory and the adjustment to cost of sales were determined by using estimated specific price changes which occurred during 1984. The purpose of such accounting is to give information about the effects of both past and present inflation on the Corporation.

The effect of past inflation is measured through calculations of the current replacement cost of property and plant. The significant difference between the current replacement cost and the historical cost of these assets reflects, on the one hand, the large understatement of the net property and plant ($1 318 against $921) and, on the other hand, the increased annual cost of maintaining these assets which would result in a higher depreciation charge to earnings ($115 against $73).

The effect of present inflation on the Corporation is reflected through adjustments to the cost of goods consumed in 1984 as it was charged to cost of sales and to inventory values as they were stated on the balance sheet at year-end. These adjustments reflect several factors: the length of time the inventory has been held; the use of average cost for inventory valuation; and the rate of inflation during the year. In the pulp and paper industry, inventory — especially wood — can be in stock for a considerable period of time. The cost of that inventory when sold and as charged to cost of sales will usually be lower than the cost of replacing the inventory at that moment. In 1984, however, the current replacement cost of inventory was only marginally higher than the historical cost. The current replacement cost of the inventory as at December 31, 1984, was calculated to be $339 as against $331 in the historical accounts. The adjustment to cost of sales for 1984 was estimated to be $18.

Current cost earnings amounted to $14 in 1984 as against a loss of $19 in 1983. The total earnings adjustment in 1984 from the effects of inflation was a charge of $60 to the historical earnings. With respect to shareholders' equity, the total inflation adjustment in 1984 was an increase of $405.

Supplementary information

In addition to giving information about the direct effect of inflation on costs and on selected asset values, the CICA requires the disclosure of sufficient additional information to enable readers to make an assessment of income on a current cost basis under both an operating capability and a financial concept of capital maintenance.

The operating capability concept is concerned that sufficient capital (inventory and property and plant) is maintained in the Corporation to continue previous levels of output of goods and services. The financial concept is concerned that the current cost dollar value of inventory and property and plant does not decrease. To allow calculation of these concepts, the following information is given:

	1984	1983
i) Increase in current cost amounts of property and plant and inventory based on:		
General inflation	$58	$59
Specific prices	$69	$36
ii) Adjustment to recognize the level of debt financing in the Corporation		
On specific price increases of property and plant and inventory	$30	$15
On current cost adjustments made to earnings during the year	$26	$23
iii) General purchasing power gain on net monetary liabilities	$28	$30

Segmented information (millions of dollars)

Classes and major product lines

Sales to Customers		Inter-segment Sales		Net Sales		
1984	1983	1984	1983	1984	1983	
$ 582.6	$ 429.0	$ —	$ —	$ 582.6	$ 429.0	Newsprint and groundwood specialties
105.4	80.4	0.2	—	105.6	80.4	Bleached kraft pulp
169.0	114.2	4.3	29.4	173.3	143.6	Paperboard
35.1	31.2	—	—	35.1	31.2	Lumber
892.1	654.8	4.5	29.4	896.6	684.2	Pulp and Paper
433.6	391.9	1.1	0.8	434.7	392.7	Glass, plastic and flexible packaging containers — CB Pak
294.1	274.3	2.1	—	296.2	274.3	Containers — Europa Carton
727.7	666.2	3.2	0.8	730.9	667.0	Packaging
3.2	1.6	1.2	1.2	4.4	2.8	Oil and gas
—	70.5	(8.9)	(31.4)	(8.9)	39.1	Eliminations
$1 623.0	$1 393.1	$ —	$ —	$1 623.0	$1 393.1	Total operations

Inter-segment sales are accounted for at prices comparable to
market prices for similar products.

Geographical regions

$1 252.5	$1 113.2	$ —	$ —	$1 252.5	$1 113.2	Canada
370.5	279.9	—	—	370.5	279.9	Western Europe
$1 623.0	$1 393.1	$ —	$ —	$1 623.0	$1 393.1	Total operations

Canadian operations include export sales to the United States
of $471.6 (1983 $385.5) and to other countries
of $79.3 (1983 $80.3).

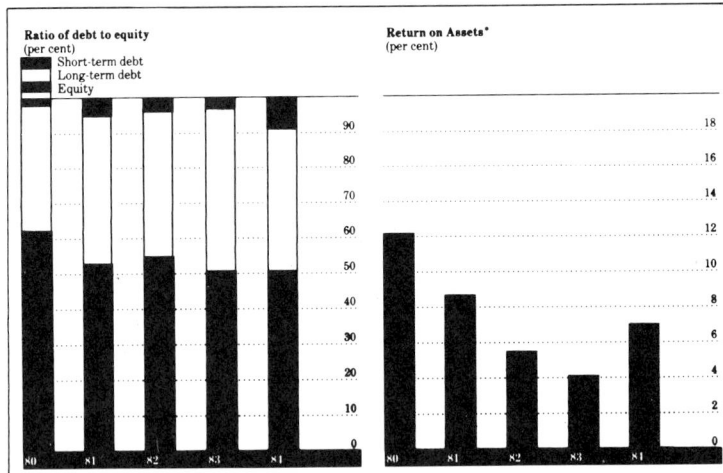

Ratio of debt to equity
(per cent)
Short-term debt
Long-term debt
Equity

Return on Assets*
(per cent)

* Return on Assets: Earnings
before extraordinary items
and after-tax interest,
divided by total assets after
accumulated depreciation.

(millions of dollars)

	Operating Earnings		Depreciation		Capital Expenditures		Identifiable Assets as at December 31	
	1984	1983	1984	1983	1984	1983	1984	1983
	$ 56.1	$ 30.0	$32.1	$22.6	$ 60.8	$130.5	$ 804.5	$ 756.5
	35.0	12.6	4.6	4.5	1.8	1.3	79.7	80.4
	20.7	7.7	6.2	5.3	9.9	4.5	126.6	114.3
	3.0	2.5	2.3	2.6	0.4	0.3	36.1	36.0
	114.8	52.8	45.2	35.0	72.9	136.6	1 046.9	987.2
	42.3	36.9	19.1	17.4	29.6	18.5	275.4	258.3
	14.8	15.9	8.0	6.2	12.0	12.5	128.9	144.5
	57.1	52.8	27.1	23.6	41.6	31.0	404.3	402.8
	2.4	1.4	0.3	0.2	4.4	7.5	128.0	148.3
	0.4	2.6	—	1.3	—	0.2	—	—
	$174.7	$109.6	$72.6	$60.1	$118.9	$175.3	$1 579.2	$1 538.3
	$199.9	$107.5	$57.8	$53.9	$ 79.2	$ 72.4	$1 208.0	$1 194.3
	(25.2)	2.1	14.8	6.2	39.7	102.9	371.2	344.0
	$174.7	$109.6	$72.6	$60.1	$118.9	$175.3	$1 579.2	$1 538.3

Unidentifiable assets amounted to $96.7 in 1984 and $114.5 in 1983.

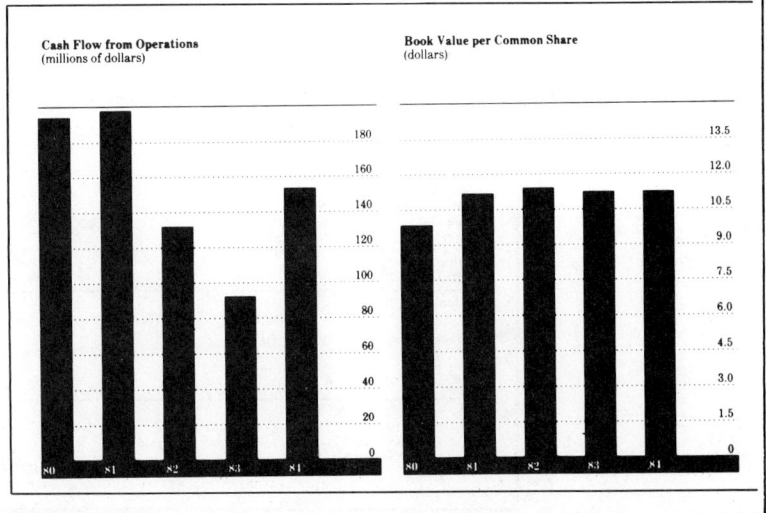

Cash Flow from Operations
(millions of dollars)

Book Value per Common Share
(dollars)

Statement of Consolidated Earnings
for the year ended December 31, 1984

		1984	1983
			(note 2)
			(thousands of dollars)
Net sales		**$1 622 984**	$1 393 065
Costs and expenses	Cost of goods sold	**1 313 221**	1 160 937
	Depreciation	**72 633**	60 060
	Administrative and selling	**62 409**	62 429
Operating earnings		**174 721**	109 639
	Interest expense — long-term	**53 124**	41 937
	— short-term	**14 103**	10 788
	Corporate administrative expense	**22 167**	24 315
	Other income (note 3)	**3 625**	10 647
Earnings before income taxes		**88 952**	43 246
	Income taxes (note 4)	**18 972**	15 357
Earnings before undernoted items		**69 980**	27 889
	Equity earnings	**6 811**	7 130
	Minority interest	**2 983**	485
Earnings before extraordinary items		**73 808**	34 534
	Extraordinary items (note 5)	**(14 907)**	(9 680)
Net earnings		**$ 58 901**	$ 24 854
Earnings per common share	Before extraordinary items	**$1.40**	$0.53
	Extraordinary items	**(0.33)**	(0.22)
	Net	**$1.07**	$0.31

Statement of Consolidated Retained Earnings
for the year ended December 31, 1984

		1984	1983
			(note 2)
			(thousands of dollars)
Retained earnings at beginning of year	As previously reported	**$328 632**	$326 469
	Reduction due to change in accounting for pre-operating expenses	**10 795**	2 318
	As restated	**317 837**	324 151
Net earnings		**58 901**	24 854
Excess cost of purchasing common shares over stated value		**(4 236)**	(2 482)
Dividends	Preferred	**(10 656)**	(10 724)
	Common	**(22 556)**	(17 962)
Retained earnings at end of year		**$339 290**	$317 837
Dividends per share	Preferred		
	1966 Series	**$1.50**	$1.50
	1978 Series	**—**	0.47
	Series A	**5.75**	5.75
	Series B	**6.88**	6.48
	Common	**$0.50**	$0.40

Statement of Consolidated Changes in Financial Position

for the year ended December 31, 1984	1984	1983
Funds provided (used)		(note 2) (thousands of dollars)
Operating activities		
Operating earnings	$174 721	$109 639
Depreciation	72 633	60 060
Interest	(67 227)	(52 725)
Current income taxes	(13 931)	(9 111)
Other items — net	(13 483)	(14 464)
Cash flow from operations	152 713	93 399
(Increase) decrease in accounts receivable	(21 178)	4 205
(Increase) decrease in inventories	(25 485)	3 846
Increase in accounts payable	10 269	10 814
Other items — net	(690)	12 243
Net (increase) decrease in operating working capital	(37 084)	31 108
	115 629	124 507
Dividends		
On common shares in cash	(21 270)	(13 767)
On preferred shares	(10 656)	(10 724)
	(31 926)	(24 491)
Investing activities		
Additions to property and plant	(118 884)	(175 309)
Grants on additions to property and plant	7 570	20 887
Increase in investments	(27 149)	(3 929)
Other items — net	3 131	(6 657)
	(135 332)	(165 008)
Financing activities		
Proceeds from public issues and secondary offerings of shares and warrants of a subsidiary	50 237	—
Issue of long-term debt	23 982	109 938
Repayments of long-term debt	(57 421)	(14 973)
Disposal of investments	2 287	3 077
Purchase of common and preferred shares	(6 488)	(20 569)
	12 597	77 473
Net (decrease) increase in funds	$(39 032)	$ 12 481
Analysis of net change in funds		
(Decrease) increase in cash and short-term deposits	$ (9 910)	$ 4 148
(Increase) decrease in short-term borrowings	(29 122)	8 333
	$(39 032)	$ 12 481

On behalf of the Board:

W.I.M. Turner, Jr.,
Director

T.O. Stangeland,
Director

Consolidated Balance Sheet
as at December 31, 1984

		1984	1983
			(note 2)
			(thousands of dollars)
	Assets		
Current assets	Cash and short-term deposits	$ 379	$ 10 289
	Accounts receivable	219 621	198 443
	Grants receivable	9 726	13 796
	Inventories (note 6)	331 309	305 752
	Prepaid expenses	4 595	5 679
		565 630	533 959
Property and plant	(note 7)	921 397	910 868
Investments	(note 8)	173 665	201 997
Other assets	(note 9)	15 221	6 019
		$1 675 913	$1 652 843

Management's Report

The consolidated financial statements have been prepared by management on the historical cost basis in accordance with Canadian generally accepted accounting principles. These statements, which necessarily include estimates and approximations, reflect information available to February 28, 1985, and have been audited by Touche Ross & Co., Chartered Accountants, whose report is included on the next page.

Management has the responsibility for the preparation and presentation of the Annual Report information; the financial information contained throughout the Annual Report conforms with that shown in the financial statements.

Management maintains an accounting system which incorporates extensive internal financial controls. The internal audit department performs independent appraisals of the effectiveness of these internal controls and reports its findings and recommendations to management and to the Audit Committee.

The Board appoints the members of the Audit Committee which is composed solely of outside directors. This Committee reviews the consolidated financial statements with management and the external auditors prior to submission to the Board for approval, as well as the recommendations of the external and internal auditors for improvements in internal controls and the actions of management to implement such recommendations.

The Board of Directors has approved this Management's Report.

T.J. Wagg,
Vice-President, Finance

Montreal, Quebec
February 28, 1985

		1984	1983
			(note 2)
			(thousands of dollars)
	Liabilities and Shareholders' Equity		
Current liabilities	Bank loans and notes payable	$ **48 739**	$ 19 617
	Accounts payable and accrued expenses	**170 577**	149 087
	Taxes payable	**24 478**	30 383
	Dividends payable	**2 509**	2 451
	Current portion of long-term debt	**62 052**	20 225
		308 355	221 763
Long-term debt	(note 10)	**476 680**	545 976
Deferred income taxes		**215 211**	216 230
Provisions	(note 11)	**26 430**	50 199
Minority interest		**32 903**	3 168
Shareholders' equity	Stated capital (note 12)		
	Preferred shares	**103 430**	104 399
	Common shares	**198 658**	193 271
	Retained earnings	**339 290**	317 837
	Foreign currency translation adjustments	**(25 044)**	—
		616 334	615 507
		$1 675 913	$1 652 843

Auditors' Report

The Shareholders,
Consolidated-Bathurst Inc.

We have examined the consolidated balance sheet
of Consolidated-Bathurst Inc. as at December 31,
1984 and the statements of consolidated earnings,
retained earnings and changes in financial position
for the year then ended. Our examination was made
in accordance with generally accepted auditing
standards, and accordingly included such tests and
other procedures as we considered necessary in the
circumstances.

In our opinion, these consolidated financial statements present fairly the financial position of the
Corporation as at December 31, 1984 and the
results of its operations and the changes in its financial position for the year then ended in accordance
with generally accepted accounting principles applied, except for the change in accounting for foreign currency translation and after giving effect to
the retroactive change in accounting for pre-
operating expenses as explained in notes 1 and 2,
respectively, to the consolidated financial statements, on a basis consistent with that of the preceding year.

Touche Ross & Co.

Chartered Accountants

Montreal, Quebec
February 28, 1985

31

Notes to Consolidated Financial Statements
December 31, 1984

1. Summary of Significant Accounting Policies

The common shares were split two for one in 1984. For comparison purposes, the number of common shares, earnings and dividends per common share relating to 1983 have been restated to reflect the stock split.

Principles of consolidation

The consolidated financial statements include the accounts of all subsidiaries. All significant inter-company items are eliminated. Acquisitions of all subsidiaries are accounted for on a purchase basis and earnings are included in the consolidated financial statements from the date of acquisition.

Foreign currency translation

Effective January 1, 1984, the Corporation adopted prospectively the recommendations of the CICA for foreign currency translation. The new rules had no material impact on the earnings of the year.

For domestic companies and integrated foreign operations, assets and liabilities are translated into Canadian dollars at exchange rates prevailing at the balance sheet date for monetary items and at exchange rates prevailing at the transaction dates for non-monetary items. Income and expenses are translated at average exchange rates prevailing during the year with the exception of depreciation which is translated at historical exchange rates. Exchange gains or losses are included in earnings except for unrealized gains or losses on translation of foreign long-term debt which are deferred and amortized over the remaining life of the related obligation. Foreign debt hedged through a forward contract is translated at the contract rate.

For self-sustaining foreign subsidiaries, all assets and liabilities are translated into Canadian dollars at the exchange rates prevailing at the balance sheet date and all income and expenses are translated at average exchange rates prevailing during the year. Foreign currency translation adjustments are deferred in the shareholders' equity section of the balance sheet.

Inventory valuation

Expenditures on wood operations are stated at average cost. Pulpwood, chips, sawlogs and wood residue at mills, and other raw materials and supplies are also stated at average cost. Work in process and finished goods inventories, the cost of which includes raw materials, direct labour and certain manufacturing overhead expenses, are stated at the lower of average cost and net realizable value. Provision is made for slow-moving and obsolete inventories.

Investments

Portfolio investments are stated at cost less write-downs for any permanent decline in value, when appropriate. Investments over which the Corporation has significant influence are accounted for by the equity method.

Property and plant, depreciation and capitalization

Mills, plants and other properties are stated at cost. On retirement or disposal of property and plant, the Corporation removes the cost of the assets and the related accumulated depreciation. Gains and losses on disposal of assets are included in earnings.

Depreciation, calculated principally on the straight-line method, is charged to operations at rates based upon the estimated useful life of each depreciable property.

Expenditures which result in material enhancement of the value of the facilities involved are capitalized. Maintenance and repair costs are expensed as incurred.

Grants relating to property and plant additions are deducted from the cost of the assets and depreciation is calculated on the net amount. Accruals are made for the appropriate portion of the estimated total of approved grants. Grants in respect of current expenses are included in earnings.

Interest is capitalized on major additions to property and plant involving the construction of new or materially improved manufacturing facilities. The interest cost is determined using the interest rate on new debt incurred by the Corporation to finance these capital expenditures.

Investments in shares of oil and gas companies are accounted for as described under Investments. Oil and gas expenditures by the Corporation are accounted for under the successful efforts method whereby geological, geophysical and carrying costs are expensed and exploratory drilling costs are capitalized as property and plant. When no reserves are discovered, exploratory costs are expensed. All development costs including dry holes are capitalized. The amortization of capitalized costs is based on proven developed reserves.

Leases

Long-term leases in which the Corporation, as a lessee, retains substantially all the benefits and risks incident to ownership are accounted for as additions to property and plant. The asset value and related obligation for such capital leases is recorded at the present value of the future minimum lease payments, using an appropriate discount rate.

Pensions

The Corporation and its Canadian subsidiaries have contributory, trusteed and funded pension plans. The current service cost portion is charged annually to earnings as funded. The German subsidiaries have non-funded pension plans; the provision and related charge to earnings is actuarially calculated in accordance with German legislation.

Income taxes

The Corporation follows the tax allocation basis in accounting for income taxes. Deferred income taxes shown in the financial statements result principally from capital cost allowance claimed for tax purposes in excess of depreciation. Investment tax credits on capital expenditures, net of deferred taxes, are accounted for as a reduction in income taxes in the year realized.

Earnings per common share

Earnings per common share are calculated after deducting dividends on preferred shares and using the weighted average number of common shares outstanding during the year. Common shares issuable as dividends on the Series B common shares are included as being outstanding from the dividend declaration dates.

(thousands of dollars)

2. Change in accounting for pre-operating expenses

In 1984, the Corporation changed its accounting policy from capitalizing pre-operating expenses related to major capital additions and amortizing them over a period of five years to recording them as a charge against income as they are incurred. As a result of this change, which has been adopted on a retroactive basis, net earnings for 1984 and 1983 have been reduced by $7 953 ($0.18 per common share) and $8 477 ($0.19 per common share), respectively, and retained earnings at January 1, 1983, have been decreased by $2 318 to give effect to the adjustments which pertain to prior years.

3. Other income

	1984	1983
Income from investments and short-term deposits	$4 120	$ 2 844
Net translation gain on long-term debt	392	—
(Loss) gain from debt retirement and disposal of property and plant	(887)	2 172
Gain on hedge of the German term bank loan	—	5 631
	$3 625	$10 647

4. Income taxes

	1984	1983
Current before tax credits	$41 211	$13 581
Less credits relating to:		
Capital expenditures	24 701	1 818
Inventories	2 579	2 652
Current	13 931	9 111
Deferred	5 041	6 246
	$18 972	$15 357

(a) As at December 31, 1984, investment tax credits on capital expenditures available to reduce future income taxes amounted to $33 986.

(b) The Corporation's effective income tax rate is determined as follows:

	1984	1983
Combined Canadian federal and provincial income tax rate	45.5%	45.7%
Increase (decrease) in the income tax rate resulting from:		
Higher effective income tax rate on earnings of foreign subsidiary	5.6	7.0
Investment tax credits	(16.8)	(2.3)
Manufacturing and processing profits deduction	(6.2)	(3.2)
Inventory allowance	(2.9)	(6.1)
Effect of tax-free dividends	(0.5)	(1.7)
Miscellaneous	(3.4)	(3.9)
Effective income tax rate	21.3%	35.5%

(c) In February 1985, the Federal Court of Canada, Trial Division, rendered judgment allowing only in part the deduction of certain interest and insurance payments of $2 024 made by the Corporation to a non-resident subsidiary for the taxation years 1971 to 1975. The resulting charge to earnings would not be significant. The Corporation is considering a further appeal on this matter.

5. Extraordinary items

	1984	1983
Write-down of investment in Sulpetro Limited, less income tax credit of $9 607 (1983 $2 685)	$(35 665)	$(9 680)
Gain resulting from public issues and secondary offerings of common shares and share purchase warrants of a subsidiary, less income taxes of $4 292	18 424	—
Gain resulting from the settlement of a fire insurance claim related to the Bridgewater mill, less income taxes of $615	2 334	—
	$(14 907)	$(9 680)

Notes to Consolidated Financial Statements   (thousands of dollars)
December 31, 1984

6. Inventories

	1984	1983
Expenditures on wood operations	$ 46 867	$ 48 458
Pulpwood, chips, sawlogs and wood residue at mills	45 724	44 296
Other raw materials and supplies	114 687	93 675
Work in process and finished goods	124 031	119 323
	$331 309	$305 752

7. Property and plant

	Gross	Accumulated depreciation	1984 Net	1983 Net
Pulp, paper, paperboard and lumber mills	$1 079 978	$383 859	$696 119	$689 319
Glass, plastic and flexible packaging container plants	263 870	130 944	132 926	122 674
Converting plants	112 060	56 909	55 151	64 863
Woodlands	22 673	15 271	7 402	7 562
Oil and gas properties	29 085	1 005	28 080	24 870
Other	2 600	881	1 719	1 580
	$1 510 266	$588 869	$921 397	$910 868

(a) Interest capitalized on major additions during 1984 was $6 559 (1983 $12 926).

(b) Pulp, paper, paperboard and lumber mills include a gross amount of $89 041 (1983 $80 515) for equipment acquired under capital lease.

(c) The following rates apply to those assets being depreciated on the straight-line method:

	Buildings	Equipment
Pulp, paper, paperboard and lumber mills	2½%	6%
Glass, plastic and flexible packaging container plants	5%	9–10%
Converting plants	2–3%	8–10%

8. Investments

	1984	1983
Portfolio:		
Sulpetro Limited		
Common shares (a) (market value $8 288; 1983 $17 375)	$ 8 288	$ 53 560
Preferred shares	25 000	500
Sceptre Resources Limited (market value $16 029; 1983 $15 994)	30 428	30 428
Canadian Pacific Limited (market value $21 023; 1983 $21 128)	13 947	13 947
German certificates of indebtedness, 8¼%, 1985 (DM 19 964) (b)	—	12 523
Other securities and loans of a non-current nature	11 141	11 294
	88 804	122 252
Equity:		
Sulbath Exploration Ltd. (c)	34 304	35 393
Diamond-Bathurst Inc. (38% owned by CB Pak Inc.)	9 309	8 231
Joint ventures		
MacMillan Bathurst Inc. (50% owned)	28 682	25 135
Libbey-St. Clair Inc. (50% owned by CB Pak Inc.)	12 566	10 986
	84 861	79 745
	$173 665	$201 997

(a) The Corporation wrote down its investment in the common shares of Sulpetro to the average stock market value in December 1984. The market value of the investment had been below book value since October 1981.

(b) The German certificates of indebtedness maturing on July 1, 1985, have been reclassified to short-term and deducted from the German term bank loan since the Corporation considers this investment a partial hedge of that loan due on the same date.

(c) Effective October 31, 1984, Sulbath Exploration Ltd., an oil and gas joint exploration company formed by Sulpetro and Consolidated-Bathurst, was restructured to acquire from Sulpetro oil and gas producing properties valued at $150 000 and to assume from Sulpetro an equivalent amount of debt. Following the restructuring, the Corporation now holds a 40% interest in Sulbath which has become an operating company.

(thousands of dollars)

9. Other assets	1984	1983
Advances to trustees under share option and purchase plans	$ 6 829	$1 639
Deferred translation loss (net) on long-term debt	5 630	—
Unamortized long-term debt expense	1 955	2 908
Deferred charges	807	1 472
	$15 221	$6 019

Of advances to trustees, $5 992 (1983 $1 470) is owing to the trustees from officers, two of whom are directors.

10. Long-term debt		1984	1983	1984	1983
		Foreign currencies		Canadian dollars	
		(thousands)			
Consolidated-Bathurst Inc.					
Sinking fund debentures					
5.85% Series A 1990	U.S. $ 5 881		6 965	$ 7 771	$ 7 489
6⅜% Series B 1991	U.S. $ 5 056		6 147	6 681	6 617
8¼% Series C 1993				7 886	9 046
9% Series F 1992	U.S. $ 16 881		16 981	22 307	18 327
17½% Series I 1988	U.S. $ 60 000		60 000	79 284	71 129
17¼% debentures, Series J, 1987				40 000	40 000
Revolving credit (a)	U.S. $100 000		100 000	132 140	123 646
Obligations under capital leases					
Bridgewater (c)	£ 35 586		34 787	54 443	69 487
Other				12 246	8 606
9¼% Swedish export credit, 1987	SEK 34 905		46 540	5 134	9 313
8½% Irish export credit, 1987	£ 287		402	439	870
Term bank loan, Canadian bank prime				—	5 000
Bathurst Paper Limited					
7½% German term bank loan, 1985 (d)	DM 50 036		72 000	28 174	19 307
8½% British export credit, 1986	£ 171		300	262	672
6% first mortgage sinking fund bonds, Series A, 1984				—	2 401
6% sinking fund debentures, Series A, 1984				—	1 879
Consolidated-Bathurst Pontiac Limited					
11% first mortgage sinking fund bonds, Series A, 1995, retractable in 1985 (e)				23 850	25 463
Revolving credit (a)	U.S. $ —		20 000	—	24 980
CB Pak Inc. and subsidiaries					
9½% sinking fund debentures, Series A, 1990				12 099	14 314
Revolving credit (a)				20 000	20 000
Other				2 441	2 891
Europa Carton AG and subsidiaries					
Term bank loans, various interest rates 1985 to 1995	DM 41 714		35 794	17 470	19 800
Reclassification of short-term borrowings (b)				66 070	67 182
Other				35	36
				538 732	568 455
Less: Current portion, at current exchange rates (historical in 1983)				62 052	22 479
				$476 680	$545 976

Notes to Consolidated Financial Statements   (thousands of dollars)
December 31, 1984

10. Long-term debt (continued)

(a) The revolving credit facilities at December 31, 1984, are summarized as follows:

	Consolidated-Bathurst Inc.	Consolidated-Bathurst Pontiac Limited	Domglas Inc.
Amount of facility	Cdn. $100 000 /U.S.	Cdn. $50 000 /U.S.	Cdn. $20 000
Outstanding borrowings at London Interbank Offered Rate (LIBOR)	U.S. $100 000	—	—
Banker's acceptance rates	—	—	$20 000
Secured by	Demand debentures, Series K	Unsecured	Demand debenture, Series B
Current revolving period ends	November 28, 1986	May 31, 1986	December 29, 1986

Under the revolving credit facilities, funds can be borrowed by way of direct advances or bankers' acceptances, repaid and re-borrowed during a two-year period, renewable annually. If not renewed, borrowings can, at the Corporation's option, either be repaid or converted to ten-year term loans at various floating interest rates.

Advances of U.S. $50 000 under the U.S. $100 000 facility of Consolidated-Bathurst Inc. have a fixed interest rate of 13.1% per annum to November 1, 1992, as a result of an interest rate swap agreement.

(b) Bank loans and notes payable of $66 070 at December 31, 1984, (1983 $67 182) were included in long-term debt as the Corporation intends to refinance these borrowings under its revolving credit facilities.

(c) Under the capital lease obligation for equipment at the Bridgewater Division, the lease payments vary until June 30, 1993, with the six-month LIBOR plus 1% and the lessor's effective tax rate in respect of the lease. Thereafter, annual lease payments will be fixed at a nominal rate based on the total cost of the leased equipment.

(d) The German term bank loan is secured by the pledge of all the shares of Europa Carton AG and by a DM 5 000 certificate of deposit. The loan, maturing on July 1, 1985, is hedged by foreign exchange contracts amounting to DM 50 000 at a rate of 1 DM = $0.5635 and by certificates of indebtedness totalling approximately DM 20 000, all of which are due on that date.

(e) Under the retraction privilege for the 11% Series A bonds, notice was given by bondholders to Consolidated-Bathurst Pontiac Limited that bonds totalling $16 507 would be retracted on March 31, 1985.

(f) Sinking fund requirements and principal payments during the next five years, based on exchange rates at December 31, 1984, are: 1985 $62 052; 1986 $30 151; 1987 $89 024; 1988 $90 717; 1989 $29 451.

11. Provisions

	1984	1983
German pensions	**$26 430**	$27 424
Potential exchange charges on German term bank loan	—	22 775
	$26 430	$50 199

As a result of the change in accounting for foreign currency translation in 1984, the potential exchange charges on the German term bank loan have been incorporated in the loan.

(thousands of dollars)

12. Stated capital

Preferred shares

(a) Authorized
— 6 000 000 preferred shares of which 1 027 169 are designated as 1966 Series
— unlimited number of second preferred shares, issuable in series

(b) Issued and outstanding

	1984		1983	
	Shares	Stated Value	Shares	Stated Value
Preferred shares — 1966 Series	819 941	$ 20 499	858 741	$ 21 468
Second preferred shares				
Series A	800 000	40 000	800 000	40 000
Series B	700 000	42 931	700 000	42 931
	2 319 941	$103 430	2 358 741	$104 399

(c) Principal features

(i) General

The shares are redeemable and are non-voting unless the Corporation fails to pay, in the aggregate, eight quarterly dividends. Subject to provisions in the Trust Deeds securing the debentures and to the provisions attaching to all preferred shares, the Corporation, at its option, may effect share redemptions on 30 days' notice at specific prices plus accrued dividends thereon. Unless the market price is in excess of the redemption price, the Corporation is obliged to make all reasonable efforts to purchase annually a certain number of shares of each series.

(ii) Cumulative dividends

1966 Series — $1.50 per share per annum, payable quarterly

Series A — $5.75 per share per annum, payable quarterly

Series B — U.S. $5.25 per share per annum, payable quarterly

(iii) Redemption

1966 Series — at $26 per share

Series A — at $52 per share, on or after April 15, 1988, and reducing by $0.40 per year to $50 per share on or after April 15, 1993

Series B — same as Series A except in U.S. dollars

(iv) Purchases for cancellation

1966 Series — 38 686 shares annually. 38 800 shares were purchased in 1984 (39 000 in 1983) at a cost of $630 ($595 in 1983)

Series A — 2% per year of the shares issued at a cost not exceeding $50 per share up to and including December 31, 1987, and thereafter, commencing January 1, 1989, 4% per year of the shares outstanding on December 31, 1988

Series B — same as Series A except in U.S. dollars

No Series A and B shares were acquired in 1984 as the shares of each series traded above $50 per share and U.S. $50 per share, respectively, throughout the year.

(v) Retraction and conversion

The Series A and Series B shares are retractable at the holder's option on April 15, 1988, at $50 per share and U.S. $50 per share, respectively, plus accrued and unpaid dividends. The Corporation may elect, by giving at least 35 days' notice prior to the retraction date, to create further series of preferred shares into which the Series A and Series B shares would be convertible at the holder's option during a conversion period commencing no later than the retraction date and ending no earlier than six months after the retraction date.

(vi) Currency election

The holders of the Series B shares may elect to receive the U.S. dollar dividend, retraction and redemption payments in the Canadian dollar equivalent thereof.

Notes to Consolidated Financial Statements   (thousands of dollars)
December 31, 1984

12. Stated capital (continued)

Common shares

(a) Authorized — unlimited number of shares

(b) Issued and outstanding

	Series A		Series B	
	Shares	Stated Value	Shares	Stated Value
Balance January 1, 1984	34 510 048	$133 048	10 448 350	$60 223
Net conversions from Series B to Series A (c)	8 370 675	36 089	(8 370 675)	(36 089)
Issued as stock dividends	—	—	92 369	1 287
Issued under the 1984 Employee Share Option Plan (d)	127 200	1 844	234 900	3 406
Issued under other plans	39 280	334	12 332	138
Purchased and cancelled	(409 700)	(1 622)	—	—
Balance December 31, 1984	42 637 503	$169 693	2 417 276	$28 965

(c) Principal features
The Series A and Series B shares are voting, inter-convertible on a share for share basis, and identical in all respects with the exception that dividends on the Series B shares are paid in the form of shares instead of cash. Dividends, other than stock dividends, are subject to restrictions under the Trust Deeds.

(d) 1984 Employee Share Option Plan
In 1984, options were granted to a number of officers and employees to purchase, until December 31, 1989, up to an aggregate of 587 000 common shares of the Corporation, at the price of $14.50 per share. As at December 31, 1984, 362 100 shares had been issued under this Plan.

(e) On August 21, 1984, the common shareholders approved the subdivision of the Corporation's common shares on a two-for-one basis, effective August 31, 1984.

13. Segmented information

The Directors have determined the classes of business of the Corporation to be pulp and paper, packaging and oil and gas. Information segmented by classes and major product lines and by geographical regions is reported on pages 26 and 27 of this report.

14. Related party transactions

Power Corporation of Canada is the major shareholder of the Corporation owning approximately 40% of the outstanding common shares. In 1984, the Corporation had transactions with certain companies in the Power Corporation group, mainly in respect of sales of newsprint and purchases of insurance services. Such transactions were made at market prices for similar products and services and the total value was not significant in relation to the total sales and purchases of the Corporation.

The Corporation had transactions with MacMillan Bathurst Inc., a joint venture company, in respect of sales of containerboard and purchases of corrugated containers. Such transactions were made at market prices and were not significant in relation to the total sales and purchases of the Corporation.

(thousands of dollars)

15. Commitments

(a) The future minimum lease payments under capital and operating leases that have initial or remaining non-cancellable lease terms in excess of one year as of December 31, 1984, are as follows:

	Capital Leases	Operating Leases
1985	$ 13 300	$ 9 900
1986	13 200	9 500
1987	13 100	9 000
1988	12 800	6 300
1989	10 200	3 800
Thereafter	33 300	4 600
	95 900	$ 43 100
Less: Imputed interest	29 211	
Present value of minimum lease payments	$66 689	

(b) At December 31, 1984, outstanding commitments for capital expenditures under purchase orders and contracts amounted to approximately $34 500.

(c) Based on actuarial estimates at December 31, 1984 and 1983, the pension plans of the Corporation and its Canadian subsidiaries were fully funded.

16. Comparative figures

Certain of the comparative figures for the consolidated financial statements have been restated to conform with the presentation adopted in 1984.

Comparative Data

		1984	1983	1982
Operations (thousands of dollars)	Net sales	$1 622 984	$1 393 065	$1 424 284
	Depreciation	72 633	60 060	54 509
	Interest — both short and long-term	67 227	52 725	61 382
	Income taxes	18 972	15 357	26 971
	Earnings before extraordinary items	73 808	31 534	51 482
	Extraordinary items — net of taxes	(14 907)	(9 680)	—
	Net earnings	$ 58 901	$ 21 854	$ 51 482
	Additions to property and plant	$ 118 884	$ 175 309	$ 242 429
	Increase in investments	27 149	3 929	35 784
	Maintenance and repair expenses	127 445	115 478	109 312
	Wages, salaries and fringe benefits	458 979	449 922	462 813
	Energy costs	195 366	158 580	142 792
	Dividends — common	22 556	17 962	35 799
	— preferred	$ 10 656	$ 10 724	$ 3 979
Per common share (dollars)	Earnings before extraordinary items	$ 1.40	$ 0.53	$ 1.06
	Net earnings	1.07	0.31	1.06
	Dividends declared	0.50	0.40	0.80
	Cash flow from operations	3.15	1.84	2.87
	Book value	$ 11.38	$ 11.37	$ 11.46
Per preferred share (dollars)	Dividends declared — 1966 Series	$ 1.50	$ 1.50	$ 1.50
	— Series A	5.75	5.75	0.72
	— Series B	$ 6.88	$ 6.48	$ 0.81
Balance sheet (thousands of dollars)	Total assets	$1 675 913	$1 652 843	$1 584 570
	Working capital	257 275	312 196	340 448
	Property and plant — gross	1 510 266	1 433 804	1 360 763
	Accumulated depreciation	588 869	522 936	515 112
	Investments	173 665	201 997	185 218
	Long-term debt	476 680	545 976	472 036
	Provision for German pensions	26 430	27 424	23 398
	Minority interest	32 903	3 168	2 824
	Stated capital — preferred	103 430	104 399	121 375
	— common	198 658	193 271	190 021
	Retained earnings	339 290	317 837	324 151
	Foreign currency translation adjustments	(25 044)	—	—
	Total shareholders' equity	$ 616 334	$ 615 507	$ 635 547
Other data	Ratio of current assets to current liabilities	1.8 to 1	2.4 to 1	2.7 to 1
	Ratio of short and long-term debt to shareholders' equity	49/51	49/51	45/55
	Return on assets — %	7.1	4.1	5.5
	Return on common shareholders' equity — %	12.3	4.7	9.2
	Shares outstanding — preferred	2 319 941	2 358 741	3 037 741
	— common	45 054 779	44 958 398	44 878 446
	Number of employees	14 395	14 156	15 168
	Number of common shareholders	13 908	13 530	14 106

1981	1980	1979	1978	1977	1976	1975	1974
$1 479 252	$1 389 433	$1 244 312	$1 078 843	$868 865	$745 193	$643 719	$689 009
44 486	42 651	38 774	36 022	32 484	28 659	26 150	25 658
43 507	29 886	26 353	26 930	26 823	22 941	18 812	18 445
65 022	78 412	57 058	36 350	10 038	9 227	20 338	34 463
101 386	122 379	98 259	59 147	21 355	18 240	32 599	47 712
10 283	–	4 589	1 568	1 361	–	–	14 608
$ 111 669	$ 122 379	$ 102 848	$ 60 715	$ 22 716	$ 18 240	$ 32 599	$ 62 320
$ 239 614	$ 143 152	$ 92 332	$ 47 475	$ 53 783	$ 56 678	$ 49 740	$ 36 992
78 664	40 483	20 414	34 039	4 695	–	–	47 637
115 013	98 334	83 294	73 038	69 889	58 267	44 467	45 861
458 224	423 067	395 386	365 745	324 995	279 653	232 204	218 340
142 082	104 899	92 393	78 059	66 357	51 705	42 459	43 220
44 501	43 964	22 254	16 540	14 591	14 543	14 471	15 108
$ 3 071	$ 3 204	$ 3 147	$ 2 057	$ 1 569	$ 1 633	$ 1 751	$ 2 198
$ 2.20	$ 2.71	$ 2.14	$ 1.30	$ 0.45	$ 0.38	$ 0.71	$ 1.19
2.43	2.71	2.24	1.34	0.49	0.38	0.71	1.57
1.00	1.00	0.50	0.38	0.33	0.33	0.33	0.38
4.35	4.26	3.43	2.63	1.48	1.12	1.49	2.38
$ 11.23	$ 9.86	$ 8.13	$ 6.40	$ 5.50	$ 5.35	$ 5.32	$ 4.95
$ 1.50	$ 1.50	$ 1.50	$ 1.50	$ 1.50	$ 1.50	$ 1.50	$ 1.50
–	–	–	–	–	–	–	–
$ –	$ –	$ –	$ –	$ –	$ –	$ –	$ –
$1 432 290	$1 136 558	$ 991 854	$ 872 944	$808 791	$742 667	$662 369	$636 632
367 860	322 891	289 633	263 141	209 233	157 860	159 084	133 045
1 170 392	968 517	851 947	784 661	769 237	730 763	678 302	634 033
474 176	445 129	416 862	392 549	375 895	363 477	339 692	317 097
152 265	114 107	73 805	52 702	30 851	26 162	26 438	26 452
430 203	278 921	231 950	228 231	245 647	178 837	157 176	129 896
23 305	19 877	15 319	12 829	11 199	7 404	6 418	4 937
2 877	2 524	2 784	2 832	5 896	5 877	6 291	6 502
41 415	44 393	45 360	46 279	26 145	27 094	28 067	31 078
185 326	178 714	165 575	165 848	89 804	89 803	88 695	88 626
318 486	264 711	192 966	120 317	150 940	144 384	142 320	125 943
–	–	–	–	–	–	–	–
$ 545 227	$ 487 818	$ 403 901	$ 332 444	$266 889	$261 281	$259 082	$245 647
2.8 to 1	2.9 to 1	2.6 to 1	2.7 to 1	2.2 to 1	1.9 to 1	2.2 to 1	1.9 to 1
47/53	37/63	37/63	42/58	53/47	50/50	43/57	42/58
8.7	12.2	11.4	8.5	4.6	4.3	6.6	9.2
19.5	26.9	26.5	20.0	8.2	7.1	13.4	21.2
1 656 608	1 775 708	1 814 408	1 851 156	1 045 808	1 083 755	1 122 684	1 243 119
44 850 114	44 963 286	44 102 724	44 763 984	43 773 204	43 772 754	43 440 204	43 401 624
15 999	16 290	17 070	17 532	17 725	17 557	17 545	19 900
14 118	14 160	14 534	13 008	11 983	12 036	11 291	11 806

Index

*This book has been set Linotron 202 in 10 and 9 point
Palatino, leaded 2 points. Chapter numbers are 12 point
Palatino Semi Bold and 36 point Palatino Bold; Chapter
titles are 18 point Palatino Bold. The size of the text page
is 30 by 48 picas.*